EDEXCEL FOR A LEVEL

PSYCHOLOGY

Includes AS level

Orders: please contact Bookpoint Ltd, 130 Milton Park, Abingdon, Oxon OX14 4SB. Telephone: (44) 01235 827720. Fax: (44) 01235 400454. Email education@bookpoint.co.uk Lines are open from 9 a.m. to 5 p.m., Monday to Saturday, with a 24-hour message answering service. You can also order through our website: www.hoddereducation.co.uk

ISBN: 978 1 4718 3538 4

First published in 2015 by

Hodder Education,

An Hachette UK Company

Carmelite House

50 Victoria Embankment

London EC4Y 0DZ

www.hoddereducation.co.uk

Impression number 10 9 8 7 6 5 4 3 2

Year 2019 2018 2017 2016 2015

Cover image © puckillustrations – Fotolia

Illustrations by Barking Dog

Typeset in India

Printed in Italy

A catalogue record for this title is available from the British Library.

EDEXCEL FOR A LEVEL BOOK 1

PSYCHOLOGY

Includes AS level

CHRISTINE BRAIN

CONTENTS

Introduction

This textbook is written for students following the Edexcel GCE 2015 AS and A level Psychology specifications. This book focuses on Year 1 of the A level and on the AS course, with Book 2 covering Year 2.

The A level course:

- All exams are at the end of the course.
- Three exam papers – covering Paper 1: four topic areas; Paper 2: two applications; Paper 3: psychological skills.
- Year 1 focuses on four topic areas – social, cognitive and biological psychology, and learning theories.
- Year 2 focuses on two applications – clinical and one from criminological, child and health psychology, as well as on psychological skills.
- 'Psychological skills' is a 'revision' paper, covering three sections: methodology in the whole course; a review of studies in psychology; issues and debates in psychology.
- Each topic area and application has some content, method, studies, a key question and a practical investigation.

The AS course:

- The AS course comprises Year 1 of the A level, with two exceptions:
  - Issues and debates, found at the end of each topic area, are not required in the AS exams.
  - Some of the 'maths' is not required for AS level (this book explains the exceptions).
- However, it is a good approach to cover the whole of Year 1.
- The AS course marks and results do not count towards the A level. They are separate examinations.

Year 1/AS – a summary

Year 1/AS covers social, cognitive, biological psychology and learning theories (topic areas).

Social psychology looks at obedience and prejudice. Methods covered are interview and questionnaire, as well as issues like sampling and ethics. The mathematical element focuses on descriptive statistics. There is one classic study, one contemporary study from a choice of three, one key question and one practical investigation. Studies, key question and practical all focus on obedience and/or prejudice.

Cognitive psychology looks at four theories of memory. Methods covered are experiments, as well as issues around doing experiments. The mathematical element includes descriptive and inferential statistics. There is one classic study, one contemporary study from a choice of three, one key question and one practical investigation. Studies, key question and practical all focus on memory.

Biological psychology looks at brain structure and functioning, evolution and hormones, largely focusing on aggression. Methods include gathering correlation data, twin and adoption studies and scanning. The mathematical element includes inferential and descriptive statistics. There is one classic study, one contemporary study from a choice of three, one key question and one practical, linking to the content.

Learning theories include classical and operant conditioning, and social learning. Methods include observation and content analysis, as well as the use of animals in experiments and related ethics. The mathematical element includes inferential and descriptive statistics. There is one classic study, one contemporary study from a choice of three, one key question and one practical, linking to the content.

Structure of each topic area

Each approach follows the same structure:

- some content in the area of focus, involving theories and studies
- methodology, to see how psychology works
- studies – one classic and one contemporary
- a key question in the area of focus
- a practical investigation to carry out in the area of focus
- issues and debates.

Issues and debates

Issues and debates allow discussion of different aspects of psychology, from how it has changed and developed over time to the ethics of dealing with both human and animal participants. In Paper 3, at the end of your course, you have to consider such issues and debates. In order to highlight such issues and debates throughout the course, they feature as part of the structure of each topic area. AS students do not need to investigate issues and debates in detail, but A level students do. You can choose to look at them throughout your course or study them at the end. In this book, issues and debates are briefly summarised in Chapter 8 and are examined in detail in Book 2. Issues and debates questions can be found in any of the three A level papers, but not in the AS papers. However, they are useful for AS students to add depth to discussion.

The exam papers

A level

Paper 1: 90 marks, two hours, covers the four foundation topic areas – social, cognitive and biological psychology, and learning theories. It is worth 35 per cent of your A level.

Paper 2: 90 marks, two hours, covers two applications – clinical psychology and a choice of one from criminological, child and health psychology. Paper 2 is part of Year 2 and is worth 35 per cent of the A level.

Paper 3: 80 marks, two hours, covers 'psychological skills'. The paper covers all the methodology in your course as Section A, a review of your classic studies and what you know about studies as Section B and an 'issues and debates' section in Section C. It is worth 30 per cent of the A level.

AS level

Paper 1: 70 marks, 1.5 hours, covers two foundation topic areas in your course – social and cognitive psychology. It is worth 50 per cent of the AS level.

Paper 2: 70 marks, 1.5 hours, covers two foundation topic areas in your course – biological psychology and learning theories. It is worth 50 per cent of the AS level.

Note: Papers 1 and 2 for the AS are completely different from those for the A level.

Types of questions

All exams have some short-answer questions and some open-response extended writing. The short-answer questions range from 1 mark (e.g. for giving the mean average of a set of data) to 4–6 marks (e.g. for describing a theory or explaining ethics in a study). Open-response extended writing questions range from 8 marks to 20 marks. 16–20-mark questions are likely to be reserved for Paper 2 and Paper 3. There are no multiple-choice sections in any of the papers.

In your specification (pp. 77–78), you will find a taxonomy. This is a list of injunctions – words that tell you what to do in an answer. Be sure to read through the taxonomy so that you know what each 'command word' requires you to do. For example:

- 'calculate': show your working
- 'analyse': examine parts of something to uncover the meaning or essential features
- 'assess': come to a conclusion after weighing up evidence
- 'compare': look at similarities and differences but not needing conclusion/judgement
- 'describe': give an account but not needing justification
- 'explain': requires points with justifications
- 'discuss': explore different views but not needing judgement/conclusion
- 'evaluate': requires you 'to come to a supported judgement of a subject's qualities and relation to its context' (p. 78)
- 'to what extent': look at information, give a balanced and reasoned argument and a judgement/conclusion.

Remember: 'assess', 'evaluate' and 'to what extent' require you to come to a judgement or conclusion.

See the specification for a full list.

Writing an answer

Your writing needs to be concise, clear and effective. Points should be made clearly, showing knowledge, and also understanding of that knowledge. It is useful to make a point and then think of an elaboration on that point, i.e. give your answer and then consider writing something else. Essays (open-response extended writing) should be written logically, with a conclusion if required (depending on the injunction). For example, if you are asked to consider something about psychology in relation to two theories, you could deal with one theory at a time, which might be logical (depending on the exact question). Always answer the question in full and tailor your answer to the question. To show your focus is on the question, refer back to it in your answer.

Assessment objectives

You will be assessed on assessment objectives (AO), which are given in full in the specification (p. 4):

- AO1 – demonstrate knowledge and understanding of scientific ideas, processes, techniques and procedures.
- AO2 – apply knowledge and understanding of scientific ideas, processes, techniques and procedures (in various contexts).
- AO3 – analyse, interpret and evaluate scientific information, ideas and evidence, including in relation to issues, to make judgements and reach conclusions and to develop and refine practical design and procedures.

The structure of this book

- Chapters 1–4 cover one of the topic areas in the order of the specification. Each of these four chapters is divided into the relevant areas, following the specification.
- Chapter 5 covers the methodology in those chapters and is presented in order of the four topic areas.
- Chapter 6 covers the maths in Year 1/AS and is presented in order of the four topic areas.
- Chapter 7 covers the practical investigations, giving an example of one for each topic area.
- Chapter 8 looks briefly at the issues and debates that relate to the four Year 1 topic areas.
- Progress check answers and the Glossary follow.

Throughout the chapters, there are features to guide you:

- *Explanation/definition* boxes provide further details on emboldened key terms in the text and can be used to build a glossary to help understanding.
- *Explore* boxes enhance your learning.
- *Individual differences* and *Developmental psychology* icons can be used to track such issues through your Year 1/AS course.
- *Method links* provide cross-references to the relevant pages in the method chapter (Chapter 5). *Maths links* provide cross-references to the relevant pages in the maths chapter (Chapter 6). *Practical links* provide cross-references to the relevant pages in the practical chapter (Chapter 7).
- *Practical* boxes help with the required practical for each topic area.
- *Progress checks* test your understanding (suggested answers are given at the back of the book).
- *Study hints* advise you on exam techniques and processes, as well as giving tips for learning.
- *Study of interest* sections bring in additional aspects for interest and can be used in discussion.
- *Test yourself* questions enable you to check what you have learned and practise writing exam-style answers.
- *You need to know about* tables are given at the start of each chapter – you can use them to check your learning after you have read the material.

Individual differences and developmental links

Individual differences and development psychology are important parts of your course.

In all the topic areas, there is focus on individual differences. In psychology, much focus is on how people are the same, such as how the brain works (biological psychology) and aspects of memory (cognitive psychology). Alongside these similarities, however, there are differences in individuals, such as intelligence and personality. Gender can also give people 'individual differences'. Even identical twins, who share 100 per cent of their genes, exhibit individual differences. In your course, you need to be aware of individual differences, alongside all the similarities. In this textbook, the 'individual differences' icon alerts you when material relates to this area of interest.

Developmental psychology follows someone's development from conception to adulthood and into older age. Areas within developmental psychology include learning theories – from our learning comes our gender behaviour and cultural norms and beliefs. Within the nature–nurture debate, you can think about developmental psychology, not only the nurture element (how we are brought up affects our development), but also our nature as issues about our biology can also affect development. For example, maturation processes (in-built processes that change us as we grow, such as puberty) affect our development. You need to be ready to discuss developmental issues in all four topic areas. In this textbook, the 'developmental psychology' icon alerts you when material relates to this area of interest.

How to use this book

In each topic area in the main chapters (Chapters 1–4), the sections follow those in the specification. However, the method, maths and practical sections are found, in topic area order, in separate chapters (Chapter 5–7). You might prefer to read topic area by topic area, which would mean reading the relevant main chapter and then reading the relevant method, maths and practical sections from Chapters 5–7.

Active learning is best

You are advised to read through each chapter without taking notes, and then go back through each section and make your own notes. Focus on terminology; making your own definitions for each term can be useful. Use headings in your notes and make your notes as clear as possible. For example, each study, theory or concept could have its own heading and summary. When carrying out your practical, keep a separate folder for your notes. Your teacher might be able to give you a proforma for keeping notes about practical investigations.

How psychology works

Throughout the Year 1/AS course (and indeed in Year 2), there is strong emphasis on how psychology works, referring to the 'study' of mind and behaviour. Chapters 5 and 6 focus on method and maths. You could read through those chapters as whole chapters, rather than splitting the method and maths into the topic areas as you come to them. That would give you a good picture of how psychology works. If you then read Chapter 7, which is about you doing psychology, this will help your understanding of the method and mathematical elements.

Studies in psychology

Each of the main chapters (Chapter 1–4) has a section on studies (one classic study and three contemporary studies). You might like to read through all the studies in those sections, to get a good picture of how studies are written up, what they entail and similar research methods, with similar evaluation points about them.

Working through the complexity

This book has a lot of detail, not only because there is a lot to learn but also because it helps to really understand the material you need to learn. Be ready to work through the complexity so that you have a good understanding. A way of doing this is to read through once, or more, for interest, without worrying about remembering it all. Then, when you go back to take notes, you will already be familiar with the material. Ebbinghaus, in the late 1800s, found that he could learn material again and again and, as he relearned the same material, each time he did better. There were 'relearning savings'. Be encouraged by this and persevere. You will get there.

About practical investigations

For each topic area, you will carry out a practical investigation to practise the skills you have learnt in the methodology and content sections. The research method is specified for each topic area and there is guidance for each practical investigation. You have a choice with regard to the specific practical investigation you undertake.

Psychology is a science, and science involves:

- putting forward a theory
- developing a hypothesis (a statement) of what might be expected from the theory
- testing the hypothesis.

Each practical investigation you carry out should come from a theory and be planned to test that theory. Check that you understand the theory that your practical is testing. This will make for a more interesting investigation and will mean that you have a better understanding of the issues.

Choices in your Year 1/AS course

You have the following choices:

- There are three contemporary studies listed for each topic area and you choose one of these. In this book, all three studies are explained for your interest.
- You have a choice of a key question in each topic area. Two are given in this book, from which you can choose one, or you can choose a different one. Whatever you chose, you might like to read the ones offered here, to help your learning of the concepts and ideas in the topic area.
- You have a choice about the focus of your practical investigations, though some of what you have to do is given in the specification. In this book, one practical investigation for each topic area is worked through in Chapter 7. However, you will have carried out your own practical investigations, so you need to use those in the exams. You might like to read through the examples in Chapter 7 to help your learning.

Year 2 of your A level course

Book 2 covers Year 2 of your course. There will be chapters on the applications, which include clinical psychology as a compulsory section and one application from criminological, child or health psychology. Book 2 will also cover psychological skills, which is 'revision' and takes you back through all the methodology you will have covered here, including the maths element. The psychological skills section will also take you back through the classic studies you covered, and issues about studies. Finally, psychological skills covers issues and debates. Your Year 1 learning will underpin a lot of Year 2 requirements, both the content and the methods.

The Edexcel website

The Edexcel website (www.edexcel.com) has a section on psychology. Use it to find out more about your course, including the specification. The specification outlines everything you need to know for your course, and this textbook follows every aspect of Year 1/AS. Use the sample assessment materials (SAMs), which include sample exam papers and mark schemes. The mark schemes will help you to see how to answer the questions and score marks. Take charge of your own learning and you will do very well.

Maintaining your interest in psychology

You will have clear reasons for studying A level or AS psychology. Remember those reasons and make sure you get what you want out of your studying. Use websites and other sources, such as books and magazines, to maintain your interest. Treat your studies separately from your interest and then, from time to time, try to bring the two together. This takes time and practice – you won't become a psychologist in your Year 1/AS course – but it is worth being patient. If you joined the course because you want to know what makes people do certain things or what makes us like we are, then you *will* find the answers by studying psychology. The material at first might not seem to answer your questions, but its relevance will become more obvious as you move through the course.

Acknowledgements

Thank you, Francesca, Susan, Julie, Caterina, Kate, Sylvia and Rowena, and all at Hodder for their hard work on this book. Thank you.

To Alex, Jenny, Jonathan, Doug, Sarah and, not least, Alastair, for being my support.

For Kevin, of course.

Photo and artwork credits

The Publishers would like to thank the following for permission to reproduce copyright material.

Page 1 (left): © Jaren Wicklund – Fotolia; page 1 (right): © Gino Santa Maria – Fotolia; page 5: © 2001 AP / Topham Picturepoint / TopFoto; page 6: © Alexandra Milgram; page 11 (top): © f11photo – Fotolia; page 11 (bottom): © Curt Teich Postcard Archives / HIP / TopFoto; page 12: © micromonkey – Fotolia; page 19: © 2006 Slater et al. Slater M, Antley A, Davison A, Swapp D, Guger C, et al. (2006) A Virtual Reprise of the Stanley Milgram Obedience Experiments. PLoS ONE 1(1): e39. doi:10.1371/journal.pone.0000039. Reproduced with permission; page 24: © Danilo Ascione – Fotolia; page 31: From the film Obedience © 1968 by Stanley Milgram; copyright renewed by Alexandra Milgram 1993, and distributed by Alexander Street Press; page 33: © Monkey Business – Fotolia; page 36: © Mike Egerton / Empics / TopFoto; page 51: © Jerry M. Burger; page 68: © Sergey Nivens – Fotolia; page 73: © Minerva Studio – Fotolia; page 74 (left): © Luftbildfotograf – Fotolia; page 74 (right): © Jenni Ogden / The Wylie Agency (UK) Ltd.; page 76: © Kike Calvo / TopFoto; page 82: © David Hartley/REX Shutterstock; page 96: © ANL/REX Shutterstock; page 101: © Alan Baddeley; page 121 (top): © Michael Flippo – Fotolia; page 121 (bottom): © terex – Fotolia; page 135: © gstockstudio – Fotolia; page 153: © ullstein bild via Getty Images; page 154: © Universal History Archive/Getty Images; page 163: © Gucio_55 – Fotolia; page 166: © World History Archive / TopFoto; page 170: © BlueSkyImages – Fotolia; page 171 (top): © Megan Lorenz – Fotolia; page 171 (bottom): © Photographee.eu – Fotolia; page 174 (left): © famveldman – Fotolia; page 174 (right): © massimhokuto – Fotolia; page 185: © nimon_t – Fotolia; page 205: © paylessimages – Fotolia; page 206: © OMIKRON/SCIENCE PHOTO LIBRARY; page 212: © PRISMA/ VWPICS /TopFoto; page 214 (top): © ullstein bild via Getty Images; page 214 (bottom): © Images Group/REX Shutterstock; page 220 (top): © SCIENCE SOURCE/SCIENCE PHOTO LIBRARY; page 220 (bottom): © 2006 Kike Calvo-V&W / TopFoto; page 226: © Jon Brenneis/Life Magazine/The LIFE Images Collection/Getty Images; page 228: © WavebreakmediaMicro – Fotolia; page 232: © Albert Bandura; page 269: © Pavel Losevsky – Fotolia; page 274: © National Pictures / TopFoto; page 290: © Monkey Business – Fotolia; page 296: © Justin Kase zninez / Alamy; page 311 (both): From the film Obedience © 1968 by Stanley Milgram; copyright renewed by Alexandra Milgram 1993, and distributed by Alexander Street Press; page 314: © FikMik – Fotolia; page 315: © Edge Hill University Department of Psychology; page 321: © Elizabeth Crews / The Image Works / TopFoto; page 333: © Petro Feketa – Fotolia; page 340: © Sergey Nivens – Fotolia; page 342: © gloszilla – Fotolia; page 344: © DR ROBERT FRIEDLAND/SCIENCE PHOTO LIBRARY; page 348: © Zephyr/Science Photo Library; page 354 (left): © jonnysek – Fotolia; page 354 (right): © Syda Productions – Fotolia; page 365: Photo by John Oates © The Open University, http://www.open.edu/openlearn/; page 385: © pfpgroup – Fotolia; page 387 (left): © bahrialtay – Fotolia; page 387 (right): © Africa Studio – Fotolia; page 398: © pergo70 – Fotolia; page 412 (left): © slp_london – Fotolia; page 412 (right): © godfather – Fotolia; page 419: © Michal Kowalski – Fotolia; page 423: © Dasha Petrenko – Fotolia; page 455: © milanmarkovic78 – Fotolia; page 463: © elnariz – Fotolia; page 471: © auremar – Fotolia; page 472: © vimax001 – Fotolia; page 473: © imagedb.com – Fotolia; page 478: © Monart Design – Fotolia; page 479: © orion_eff – Fotolia; page 481: © Ermolaev Alexandr – Fotolia.

Page 43 (right): Adapted from: Guimond *et al.* (2013) 'Diversity policy, social dominance, and intergroup relations: predicting prejudice in changing social and political contexts', *Journal of Personality and Social Psychology*, 104(6), 941–958. Reprinted with permission from APA; pages 52 and 53 (Tables 1.13 and 1.14): From Burger, J. (2009)

'Replicating Milgram: would people still obey today?' *American Psychologist*, 64(1), 1–11. Reprinted with permission from APA; page 125: From *Dementia UK: Update*, Second Edition. Reprinted with permission from Alzheimer's Society.

Every effort has been made to trace all copyright holders, but if any have been inadvertently overlooked, the Publishers will be pleased to make the necessary arrangements at the first opportunity.

Although every effort has been made to ensure that website addresses are correct at time of going to press, Hodder Education cannot be held responsible for the content of any website mentioned in this book. It is sometimes possible to find a relocated web page by typing in the address of the home page for a website in the URL window of your browser.

Chapter One: Social Psychology

Overview

This chapter is about the social approach to explaining human behaviour. It is about the effects of people, society and culture and how behaviour is guided by such effects. For example, according to social identity theory, people belong to groups ('in-groups'); rival groups become 'out-groups'. You could belong to several in-groups – for example, a gender group, an interest group, a psychology group, a family group, a race group or a work group. There are many others. Social psychology suggests that you will be prejudiced towards your in-groups and against your out-groups. 'Realistic group conflict theory' suggests that, if there is competition for scarce resources, **prejudice** can arise.

Explore

Consider the two pictures above and write a paragraph on each. Think about how you 'knew' anything about the people. An exercise like this can show us how we think about and have preconceived ideas about others. Do this task with someone else, and compare your answers to see if your ideas and beliefs about other people are similar. Maybe this is because you come from a similar background or culture?

Another example of social psychology is how people obey others, and in what circumstances. You might think that you would never give strong electric shocks to another person if put into a position to do so, but social psychology holds that it is quite likely that you would if ordered to by someone in authority. Factors affecting whether you would obey include personality or gender. Therefore, as with a lot of psychology, links are not as straightforward as they may first appear. This chapter also considers how psychology investigates issues such as **obedience** and prejudice, including use of questionnaires and interviews when researching in psychology.

Study of interest

Salvatore and Shelton (2007) studied the effect of racism on the individual. They asked 250 Princeton University undergraduates to read some fictitious CVs and fictitious employer comments. In some cases, there was blatant racism – for example, a white employer 'rejected' a well-qualified black applicant in favour of a white applicant, saying that they had too many employees from ethnic minorities. In some cases, there was ambiguous racism – for example, a white employer accepted a white applicant in favour of a better-qualified black applicant, without giving a reason. The undergraduates then carried out a task to test their cognitive (mental) abilities. It was found that the black undergraduates were more affected (when doing the task) by ambiguous racism than blatant racism; the white undergraduates were more affected by blatant racism. It was thought that black people are used to blatant racism and have strategies to cope with it, whereas white people are not used to it and have no such strategies. The study highlighted the effect of racism on cognitive abilities and the seriousness of such issues for the individual.

Explore

Use a search engine to look for and explore a study on prejudice, perhaps using the key terms 'prejudice', 'study' and 'psychology'. One example is Adorno *et al.* (1950), a study that looks at personality and fascism.

STUDY HINT

You will often see a name, '*et al.*' and a date when studies are mentioned, as with Adorno *et al.* (1950). The date is when the study was published; the name(s) identifies the researcher(s). The first name might be the main researcher or it might be that the names are in alphabetical order (as with Adorno). '*Et al.*' is short for '*et alia*', meaning 'and others' in Latin, and it is used as a short form when three or more researchers have worked on a study (in this example, the researchers are Adorno, Frenkel-Brunswik, Levinson and Sanford).

Summary of learning objectives

Content

You need to learn about theories of obedience, including **agency theory** and **social impact theory**. You also need to learn about Milgram's (1963) basic study, as well as three variations of the study, in order to consider situational factors that encourage dissent (what makes us 'not obey'). Factors that affect obedience and resistance to obedience are then covered, including personality, gender and culture, as well as features of the situation itself.

The other topic in social psychology is prejudice, including **realistic group conflict theory** (also called 'realistic conflict theory') and **social identity theory** of prejudice. You are asked to consider factors that affect prejudice, including **personality** and culture, as well as the situation itself.

Explanation

When terms are emboldened, this means they are defined in the glossary.

Individual differences and developmental psychology

In all topic areas, you need to consider two issues in psychology: individual differences and developmental psychology.

Individual differences

In social psychology, you will learn about the following links:

- Obedience is affected by personality, as well as by gender and our individual differences.
- Prejudice has explanations that link to personality, such as having a right-wing authoritarian personality (RWA).

Developmental psychology

In social psychology, you will learn about the following links:

- Obedience is affected by gender and culture, which come from environmental effects that we experience through our upbringing.
- Prejudice, similarly, is affected by our culture and we learn cultural norms as we grow up.

Methods

Chapter 5 covers the methodology you will need for Year 1 of your course (and the AS, with some exceptions). See Table 5.1 (p. 278) for a summary of which methods you need to know for this chapter. Chapter 6 covers the mathematical elements you need for your course. See Table 6.2 (p. 386) for a summary of the mathematical skills you need to know for this chapter.

Studies

The classic study you will be learning about in social psychology is Sherif *et al.* (1954/1961) 'Intergroup conflict and cooperation: The Robbers Cave Experiment'.

You will choose one contemporary study from:

- Burger (2009) 'Replicating Milgram: would people still obey today?'
- Cohrs *et al.* (2012) 'Individual differences in ideological attitudes and prejudice: evidence from peer-report data'
- Reicher and Haslam (2006) 'Rethinking the psychology of tyranny'.

Key questions

You have a choice of key questions to study. Focusing on how social psychology can help to explain or deal with a contemporary issue, suitable examples include using social psychology to reduce problem behaviour in situations such as football hooliganism or rioting, or using social psychology to explain heroism. However, you can choose any issue.

Practical investigation

Chapter 7 covers the skills you need for conducting a practical investigation, including worked-through examples. Chapter 6 covers the mathematical elements for your course, which also links to your practical investigation.

STUDY HINT

Your learning of the methodology for social psychology links closely to the practical investigation you will carry out, so you do not have to learn this twice. The practical investigation is about putting your learning of the methodology into practice.

Issues and debates

Issues and debates are in the A level course but not the AS, so if you are doing the AS, you do not need to study issues and debates, although they are interesting and will extend your understanding of psychology. The 11 issues and debates are: ethics; practical issues in research design; reductionism; comparing explanations; psychology as a science; culture and gender; nature–nurture; how psychology has developed over time; issues of social control; using psychology in society; and issues around socially sensitive research.

Chapter 8 summarises the issues and debates and how the four topic areas for your Year 1 course inform each of these. Book 2 will explain these in more detail.

STUDY HINT

Issues and debates appear in each topic area for Year 1 (and Year 2), in the same order, in the specification. For each topic area, you can use the examples against each of the issues and debates to learn how the material for that topic area illustrates that issue or debate. See Chapter 8 for more detail. Make a summary of learning objectives into a checklist, such as the one in Table 1.1. However, you could add more detail to help your learning.

Table 1.1 What you need to know for social psychology

You need to know about:	
Milgram's (1963) study of obedience	Questionnaires to gather self-report data, and social desirability/researcher bias issues
Agency theory, including agentic state, autonomous state and moral strain	Open/closed-ended questions, including ranked-data questions
Social impact theory (Latané, 1981) and dynamic social impact theory	Interviews to gather self-report data (structured, unstructured, semi-structured)
Issues of individual differences (personality), and gender and culture in obedience and dissent to authority; the role of the situation and factors that encourage dissent/disobedience	Qualitative and quantitative data and strengths and weaknesses of qualitative and quantitative data
Three of Milgram's variations: rundown office block (experiment 10), telephonic instructions (experiment 7), ordinary man gives orders (experiment 13)	BPS ethical guidelines and code of ethics and conduct (2009)
Social identity theory (Tajfel and Turner, 1979), including social categorisation, social identification, social comparison, and in-group/out-group ideas	Alternate hypotheses
Realistic group conflict theory (Sherif) and superordinate goals	Analysis of quantitative data/mathematical issues in psychology, including measures of central tendency, frequency tables and graphs, graphical presentation using a bar chart, measures of dispersion (range and standard deviation)
Issues of individual differences (personality), situation and culture in prejudice	Analysis of qualitative data, including thematic analysis
A classic study in detail: Sherif *et al.* (1954/1961), The Robbers Cave Experiment	One key question that suits what you have covered in social psychology
One contemporary study in detail from Reicher and Haslam (2006), Burger (2009), or Cohrs *et al.* (2012)	One practical investigation you have carried out to put what you have learned in social psychology into practice
Individual differences and developmental psychology and links to obedience and prejudice	
Issues and debates (not for AS)	

An introduction to social psychology

Social psychology examines human behaviour – the role of the individual's relationships with other people and groups, and how culture and society affect behaviour. This is a large field and the Year 1/AS course covers only obedience, social impact theory and prejudice.

Social psychology examines how individuals interact with one another and how people behave in groups. When people are studied as social beings, the social approach is involved. Areas of psychology, such as social psychology, have basic **assumptions** about human nature and human behaviour, such as thinking of humans as being social, interacting with others and being affected by others.

Definition

Assumptions are the underpinning beliefs and ideas that support an area of psychology, such as social psychology focusing on the 'social' aspect of humans.

The effect of interaction between individuals

Individuals interact with others and affect one another's behaviour. Agency theory suggests that people are agents for society and behave in such a way as to benefit society. People help other people, they send signals to other people by the way they look and behave and they obey certain people and not others. Helping behaviour, body language, the impact of others and issues around obedience fit within the social approach. Just the last two are included in the social psychology section of your course.

The effect of being in groups within society

The social approach assumes that people live within a culture and society and that their behaviour is affected by their experiences within society, where they are members of certain groups. For example, a child is a girl or boy, a sister or brother perhaps, a daughter or son, a friend, a school pupil, maybe a member of a club. Individuals describe themselves in these ways. Social identity theory suggests that, by identifying oneself as being a member of a group, a person can become prejudiced against members of a rival group. Groups are prejudiced against each other, members of a peer group copy one another and crowds can become unruly. Prejudice, peer-group pressure and crowd behaviour are studied within the social approach.

Explore

Try asking a few people to describe themselves briefly, in writing. They may describe themselves in terms of personality, such as generous, happy or quiet; they will probably also give their social roles. They may refer to groups they feel part of. People describe themselves according to how others see them and how they fit into their social world.

The effect of the social situation

It is not just people and groups that affect behaviour, but the social situation itself. For example, when out for an evening with friends, you might not worry about expressing your views on religion; in a business meeting in another country, you would probably not comment.

Explore

The theory of social constructionism holds that what we do and say is set within a particular society or culture and that we represent the world to ourselves through our experiences. It is claimed that there are no general laws to discover and that knowledge is relative. This goes against the idea of a scientific approach to studying human behaviour. Use the internet or some other source to research the theory of social constructionism.

Social roles

In society, people have social roles and those roles have expectations attached to them. People tend to act in accordance with their social role. Reicher and Haslam (2006) investigated the social roles of prisoner and guard and gave some evidence that people behave according to social roles. Milgram's work also involved social roles, finding that authority figures are obeyed more than 'ordinary' people – the social role determines obedience. Both these studies will be examined in depth later in this chapter.

Progress check 1.1

Explain three ways in which being 'social' influences people (this will help you to summarise what social psychology is about).

STUDY HINT

Your course covers a general overview of what 'social psychology' entails, so make some notes on this aspect.

Test yourself

Give a definition of the social approach, drawing on two of its main assumptions. **(6 marks)**

Content in social psychology

The course content for social psychology focuses on obedience and prejudice. With regard to obedience, the work of well-known researcher Milgram is examined, including his agency theory explanation of obedience. Social impact theory is also examined, looking at how others impact individuals' behaviour and how this can explain obedience. Two other studies into obedience, Meeus and Raaijmakers (1986) and Slater *et al.* (2006), add depth to the discussion. We also look at ethical issues in obedience work. With regard to prejudice, two main theories – social identity theory and realistic group conflict theory – are covered, as well as issues that affect prejudice, such as personality, situation and culture.

What is meant by obedience?

Obedience means obeying direct orders from someone in authority. This is not the same as conforming to the behaviour of others. **Conforming** is doing something which is against the individual's own inclinations, but not doing it with the intention of matching the behaviour of the majority. **Compliance** means going along with what someone says, while not necessarily agreeing with it; often compliance will be to peers rather than those in positions of authority. **Internalising** is obeying with agreement.

Compliance is, therefore, part of obedience and is referred to as such by Milgram. His research into obedience focused on issues such as why Nazi soldiers obeyed orders to perpetrate genocide on the Jewish race. He wanted to know if all people would obey in similar circumstances, or whether there was something different about those soldiers. At the time when Milgram was focusing on obedience, Adolf Eichmann was being tried in Jerusalem for crimes committed against Jews in the **Holocaust**.

Definition

The **Holocaust** was the slaughter of millions of Jews, gypsies, homosexuals and others by the Nazis during the Second World War.

Eichmann was one of the major organisers of the Holocaust. He did not appear to be evil; he was mild and ordinary looking. During his trial, he repeatedly stated that he did it because he was ordered to. This was frightening because people wondered if they would have done the same.

Explore

Investigate the Holocaust and subsequent trials of those involved. Do you think they were evil people? Or do you think they were 'just obeying orders'?

US soldiers in My Lai obeyed an order to kill women and children. Why do people obey orders like this?

Progress check 1.2

Using other sources if you wish, fill in the table below to explain the four terms:

Obedience	Conformity
Compliance	Internalisation

Theories of obedience are covered later in this chapter (pp. 19–24) as they are better understood if Milgram's work is considered first.

The study of obedience by Milgram

In 1963, Milgram carried out what is now a well-known experiment. Subsequently, he carried out variations of that study. You have to know the basic study and three specific variations.

Milgram's (1963) basic study

Milgram wanted to see if people would obey orders when the consequences were severe. In this study, he let people think that they were giving another person an electric shock to see how far they would go.

Stanley Milgram, a well-known social psychologist

Aim

The aim of this study was to test the idea that the Germans were somehow different from other people, in that they were able to carry out barbaric acts against Jews and other minority groups. Milgram wanted to see if volunteer participants would obey orders to give electric shocks to someone they thought was just another participant. He wanted to answer the question 'How far would they go?'

Procedure

Milgram advertised for participants and told them that they were taking part in an experiment on human learning. He had a helper – called a **confederate** or **accomplice** – who was the learner and would 'receive' the (fake) shocks. There was one real shock of 45 volts, which the participants received to convince them that the shock generator was real. The confederate-learner, who was middle-aged and pleasant looking, was primed. The study took place at **Yale** University and the participants took part one at a time. In the account of the study, Milgram is treated as being the experimenter, but in fact someone else took that role.

Definitions

A **confederate** is someone 'in on' a study, part of the study team, but who the participant thinks is also a participant.
Yale is a prestigious university in the USA.

Each participant arrived at the laboratory and waited in a room with the confederate. The participant was led to believe that the confederate was also a participant. They drew lots to decide who would be the learner. However, this was rigged so that the confederate was always the learner and the participant was always the teacher. Milgram reassured participants that the shocks would be painful but that there would be no permanent tissue damage.

The participant-teacher watched the confederate-learner being strapped into a chair and wired up so that the 'shocks' could be felt. Milgram then took the participant-teacher into another room where there was a long counter in front of an array of switches and an impressive-looking machine – the generator. The switches were in a row and labelled as running from 15 volts to 450 volts. Above the switches, there were comments such as 'slight shock' and 'danger'. This left the participant in no doubt that the shocks would be increasingly painful and dangerous as the voltage increased. The participant sat in front of the 15-volt switch and began the experiment, having been given instructions by Milgram. The participant was to move up one switch each time the learner gave a wrong answer.

The task required the participant to read out word pairs such as blue–box, nice–day and wild–duck. They then read out the key word and four possible pairs. For example, he might read out blue–sky, –ink, –box and –lamp. The confederate-learner had four buttons and had to press the correct one. In this example, the correct response is 'box'. An incorrect response resulted in a 15-volt 'shock'; each successive wrong answer resulted in a shock 15 volts higher – 30 volts, 45 volts and so on.

At first the learner gave correct responses, then a few wrong responses. The responses were pre-set and the same each time, with there being about three wrong answers to every one correct answer. There was no sign of protest up to 300 volts in the basic study. At 300 volts, the learner bangs on the wall and after that the learner's answers stop appearing for the participant to see. At this stage, the participant tended to look to the experimenter for guidance and was told to treat the absence of a response as no response and to go on with the shocks. If 450 volts was reached, participants were to continue with that switch. The experimenter was in the room with the participant, so the participant would think that no one was with the learner – who was now silent and could be in a bad way. It was pointless to continue with the study because the learner was not responding – no learning would take place. Would participants continue just because they were ordered to? They were, after all, free to leave.

It is worth noting that the experimenter had a script. On occasion, he prompted the participant to continue, by saying such things as 'You must continue', or 'It is absolutely essential that you continue'. These prompts are called verbal prods, and may have affected the outcome. They are shown in Table 1.2.

Table 1.2 Milgram's planned prompts to participants if they refused to continue

Order of prompt	Verbal prod
1	'Please continue'/'Please go on'
2	'The experiment requires that you continue'
3	'It is absolutely essential that you continue'
4	'You have no other choice – you must go on'
If the participant was still refusing, then the study was stopped.	

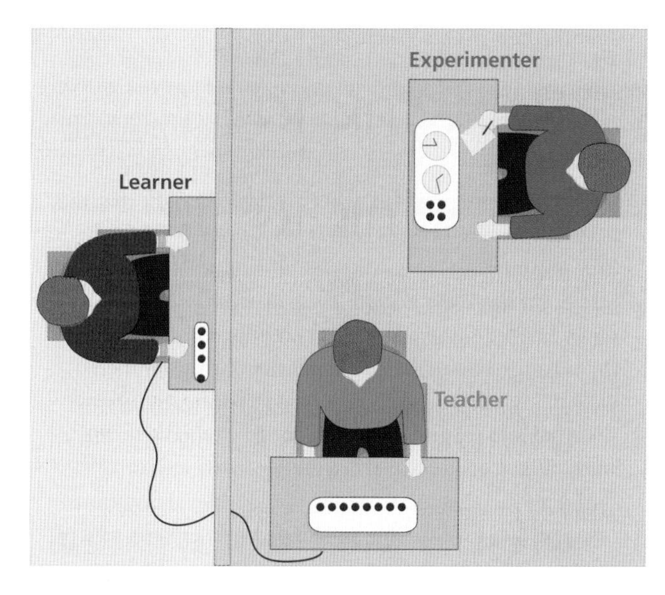

A plan of the experiment showing the teacher and experimenter in one room and the victim wired up in another room

Milgram thought the participants would refuse to go up to 450 volts. He expected to have to modify the pattern of responses and banging on the wall because participants would not agree to continue. Before carrying out the study, he asked students and colleagues what they thought; the opinion was that 2 or 3 per cent would continue to the end. When people were asked what they would do, none said they would continue to the end.

One more aspect of the study is important: at the end of the experiment, the participants were interviewed using open questions and attitude scales. Steps were taken to make sure that each participant would leave the laboratory feeling all right. For example, the victim and the participant met up, to show the victim was not hurt, and there was work to reduce any tensions that had built up from taking part.

Progress check 1.3

Decide whether the following statements are true or false:

Statement	True	False
The participants knew that the 'learner' was a confederate.		
People Milgram asked beforehand thought that there would be a lot of obedience.		
The verbal prods were pre-set and remained the same for every participant.		
Milgram's participants volunteered to take part by responding to an advert.		
There was just one actual shock, received by the participant.		

Results

The results showed that 26 of the 40 men who took part in the study (and, interestingly, 26 of the 40 women who were tested in a separate study) continued to the end. In the basic study, which used male participants, 14 participants stopped before 450 volts (see Table 1.3). Sixty-five per cent obeyed to 450 volts; 100 per cent obeyed to 300 volts.

Table 1.3 The number of participants who stopped at different voltages

Voltage	Number that stopped
Up to 300	0
300	5
315	4
330	2
345	1
360	1
375	1
Total	14 (out of 40)

Most participants thought that the experiment was real. After the study, they were asked to rate the shocks on a scale; most rated them as 14 (extremely painful). The average rating was 13.42. Many participants showed signs of nervousness, especially when 'giving' the most painful shocks. Participants were seen to sweat, tremble, stutter, groan and dig their fingernails into their flesh. Fourteen of the 40 showed nervous laughter and smiling (though after the study they made it clear that they did not think it was funny). Participants often heaved a sigh of relief when the study was ended.

Explore

Consider the results of Milgram's study. Data can be quantitative (given as numbers) or qualitative (given as quality of response) and, as such, have depth and detail. Milgram's basic study uses quantitative data, such as the voltage at which the participant stopped, or how many went to 450 volts. However, there are also qualitative data, in the form of the participants' reactions during the study.

Write a short account of how Milgram's experiment gathers both qualitative and quantitative data and consider the strengths and weaknesses of using both. Qualitative and quantitative data are explained on pp. 287-288.

Conclusions

Social influence is strong and people obey orders even when this causes them distress. It was not thought that people would obey; such obedience is surprising. Milgram summarised the features that led to obedience:

- Yale University is a prestigious institution and unlikely to allow anything unethical to occur.
- The study seemed to have a worthy cause – to learn about memory.
- The victim was not unwilling and had agreed to take part.
- The participant had volunteered and had made a commitment.
- The participant was paid and so felt an obligation.
- The learner was there by chance – he or she could have been the participant (so the participant thought).
- This was a new situation for the participant, who had no idea of what was suitable behaviour.
- It was thought that the shocks were painful, but not dangerous.
- Up to 300 volts, the learner plays the game and seems willing.

Progress check 1.4

In one paragraph, summarise Milgram's basic study. Give the aim, a short account of the procedure, a statement of the results and a few conclusion points.

Evaluation of Milgram's (1963) basic study

Strengths

- Milgram carried out a very well-controlled procedure. He had set prompts, in a set order, and had prepared the victim's responses carefully. He made every effort to make the experience of each participant the same, to avoid any bias. This lack of bias means that the conclusion – that obedience was due to a response to an authority figure – was firm. It was unlikely that other factors led to the results. This meant that cause-and-effect conclusions could be drawn.
- The controlled procedures meant that the study was replicable and so could be tested for **reliability**. The precise procedure could not be repeated for ethical reasons. However, there have been replications using the same idea, but with a different 'punishment', or with a different, more ethical, procedure. One replication was by Burger (2009) and is a study you can choose for your course (pp. 49–54). These studies have also shown that people obey those in authority, even when it goes against their own moral code.

Weaknesses

- There are ethical problems with regard to repeating the study. Milgram was aware of the ethical implications. He asked colleagues and others if they thought that the participants would obey, and it was generally thought they would not – certainly not to the level that they did. So he did not expect such levels of anxiety and stress. He debriefed the participants carefully and introduced them to his accomplice, as well as checking on their well-being. However, he described shaking, trembling, sweating and seizures, so it cannot be denied that the study was unethical. In theory, he gave the right to withdraw because participants could leave at any time (some did). However, he pressurised participants to stay by using prompts, making withdrawal from the study difficult. He deceived participants by saying that the study was about learning and by pretending that the shocks were real. He gained consent and asked for volunteers. He pointed out that they could keep their payments even if they did not continue with the study. However, the consent he obtained was not fully informed because of the deceit. More discussion about the ethics of obedience studies can be found on pp. 30–32.

STUDY HINT

When you are studying ethical issues in research, use the BPS Code of Ethics and Conduct (2009) and apply the ethical issues in the Code to Milgram's work to aid your learning, as well as to help you evaluate Milgram's work.

Explanation

The BPS Code of Ethics and Conduct (2009) emphasises the importance of 'respect', which includes getting informed consent and giving the right to withdraw. The Code also includes 'responsibility', which explains the need for a debrief. Other issues covered by the Code come under the headings 'competence' and 'integrity'.

- The basic study lacked **validity**. For example, the participants trusted that what happened at Yale University would be acceptable (they were right – the shocks were not real; though Milgram says in the study that most were convinced the experiment was 'real'). It could be argued that in a more realistic situation they would not have continued, although that is speculation.

Explanation

Psychological knowledge is really only as good as the studies that produce the knowledge. By evaluating a study, you are considering how good the knowledge is. Evaluation using two strengths and two weaknesses might not have sufficient depth in all situations, but it is a useful way to consider how good the findings of a study are and, therefore, how good the knowledge is. 'Sound' knowledge can be used for the good of society and for the good of individuals. Less sound knowledge is less useful. These are the principles behind considering strengths and weaknesses of studies (and the same can be said of theories) in this book.

STUDY HINT

Learn evaluation points, and also extend the ideas, to add more strengths or weaknesses that you see elsewhere or that you develop yourself. Remember to learn material and balance that with noting down and learning commentary.

Explore

Explore some of the ideas on the following website about Milgram and his work: www.simplypsychology.org/milgram.html. Explore Thomas Blass's research into Milgram's work, for example, on the following website: www.psychologytoday.com/articles/200203/the-man-who-shocked-the-world.

Test yourself

1. Explain Milgram's reasons for carrying out his study into obedience. **(3 marks)**
2. List four features of Milgram's (1963) procedure. **(4 marks)**
3. Discuss what was remarkable about Milgram's (1963) basic study. **(8 marks)**

Variations of Milgram's 1963 procedure

Milgram carried out variations on his original study. General issues about some of these will be explained before looking in more detail at three variations: Experiment 10 (Rundown office block), Experiment 7 (Telephonic instructions/closeness of authority) and Experiment 13 (Ordinary man giving orders). The variations use the procedure from the basic study to a large extent and so are not explained in detail again here.

Aims, procedures and results

Milgram considered what might have affected the participants in his basic study and then altered the situation to see the effect. For example, he thought that obedience might have been because the study was at Yale University, so he repeated it in an office (Experiment 10, institutional context). He wondered if having the experimenter in the room affected the level of obedience, so he carried out the study with the experimenter in touch by telephone (Experiment 7, experimenter absent). In another variation, he used two other 'teachers' (both confederates) who stopped before the 300-volt level (the level reached by all his initial participants). Milgram kept everything else constant so that he could make comparisons. The procedures and results of some of the variations (there were 19) are shown in Table 1.4.

Table 1.4 Milgram's variations on his basic study

Situation/procedure	Result
Original study	26 out of 40 participants (65 per cent) continued to the end
Two experimenters; at 110 volts, one tells the participant to stop and the other tells the participant to continue (Experiment 15)	All participants stopped
Three teachers (two were confederates); one confederate-teacher stops at 150 volts and the other at 210 volts (Experiment 17)	Only 10 per cent of participants continued to the end
Experimenter's instructions are given by tape and the participant can speak to the experimenter (who is not in the room) by phone (Experiment 7)	9 out of 40 participants (22.5 per cent) continued to the end
Moving the victim closer until the participant held the victim's hand down to receive the shock (Experiment 4)	12 of the 40 participants (30 per cent) obeyed
Held in Research Associates of Bridgeport offices, in a fairly rundown office building (Experiment 10)	19 of the 40 participants (47.5 per cent) obeyed
The participants were women (Experiment 8)	26 of the 40 (65 per cent) obeyed
Participant chooses the shock level (Experiment 11)	1 obeyed (2.5 per cent)

Conclusions

The level of obedience was highest in the basic experiment; all the variations led to a lower level. The setting had the least effect; the orders of the experimenter had the most effect. This suggests that the conclusion that obedience results from orders given by an authority figure is correct.

Telephonic instructions/closeness of authority/experimenter absent (Experiment 7)

An important part of Milgram's main study was said to be that the participants responded to an advertisement from the experimenter and it was the experimenter that they formed a relationship with, not the victim or others in the study. It was thought (e.g. Milgram, 1974) that one reason for the participants not yielding to the apparent distress of the 'victim' was that they were bound to the experimenter and trying to help a scientific study. Therefore, one set of variations varied the distance between the participant and the experimenter to see the effect on obedience. In Experiment 5, for example, the experimenter was just feet away from the participant. In Experiment 7, the one of interest here, the experimenter was away from the participants, out of sight, and gave instructions over the telephone. The experimenter gave the instructions the participants needed at the start, in the same room, but then left the laboratory and communicated only by telephone. The obedience dropped sharply when orders were given by telephone. Instead of 26 obeying the orders of the experimenter, 9 obeyed (22.5 per cent) – a significant drop.

It was concluded that, when the experimenter is not face-to-face with the participant, it is easier to not obey. Furthermore, a few participants gave lower shocks than they should have done, thinking they were not being observed. Over the phone, these participants said they were raising the shock levels, as requested, but in reality they were not, and they did not confess. It was interesting that, even though they were disobeying the orders, they found it easier to let the experimenter think they were obeying.

This suggests that the physical presence of the experimenter is a force when it comes to obedience. If someone wants obedience, they should plan to be present rather than giving orders from a distance, such as over a telephone.

Strengths

- Milgram used the same procedure in all his studies, which helps with comparisons. If everything is the same, except the one variation (such as whether the experimenter is present or giving orders over the phone), any difference in results (in this case, obedience) can be said to be caused by the one variation (the independent variable).
- When Milgram varied the physical presence of the experimenter in other variations, he found that physical presence of the person giving orders did affect obedience, which backs up his claim in Experiment 7.

Weaknesses

- This is not a natural situation. Milgram (1974) says that participants seemed to have a relationship with the experimenter in wanting to help him to find scientific evidence, so they were in the role of 'helper'. This meant they were not in an autonomous state because of the experiment itself, which means that there is a question over the validity of the results.
- Not only were the participants perhaps trying to help the experimenter, but they may not have believed there were real shocks. The experiment took place in a prestigious building and the study was clearly set up in a scientific way. Possibly participants trusted the situation and the researchers to have regard for the victim. If this was the case, and they did not believe the shocks were real, validity is under question.

Rundown office block/institutional context (Experiment 10)

Milgram moved the study to a rundown office block in order to see whether the power of the institution (Yale University in his main study) affected the results. Milgram (1974) suggests that, in experiments with animals, the location of the study will have no bearing on results; however, with human participants the setting might affect behaviour. The institutional context may have affected the obedience to commands. Milgram says that people regard Yale University with 'awe' and 'respect' (Milgram, 1974, p. 67). In the post-experiment interviews, people commented on where the study took place as well as who was running the study. Participants said they were given confidence that the study would be done with integrity and competence because of the setting. Milgram uses examples to show that location is important in real life: for example, we expose our throats to a man with a razor in a barber's shop, but would not do so elsewhere.

The study was, therefore, moved to Bridgeport, an industrial city near Yale, and all links to a university were removed. The question was whether obedience would drop if the setting were not so prestigious.

The same procedure was used, including asking for volunteers and paying them $4.50 dollars for attending. The same personnel were used and the same age and occupation details for the participants. The study was said to be conducted by Research Associates of Bridgeport. The building chosen was run down and opposite some shops. Three rooms were used. The lab was clean but without much furniture. The researchers said they were from a private firm.

There is less obedience if a study is carried out in an office block than if in a university building: Yale University (top) versus Bridgeport (bottom), location of Experiment 10

Participants appeared to have more doubts about this study. One participant made notes and asked himself a lot of questions about the legitimacy of the study and another questioned his own judgement and thought the study was 'heartless'. The participants seemed just as tense in this study as in the Yale one.

Milgram thought that if obedience dropped when the study moved to the rundown office, this might suggest that using Yale and its reputation had at least partly caused the obedience in the main study. However, the findings showed otherwise; obedience did not drop that much. Of the Bridgeport participants, 47.5 per cent obeyed to the maximum voltage level compared with 65 per cent in the original study at Yale. This was a lower level of obedience but Milgram thought it was not a significant difference.

Since there was a relatively high level of obedience in the office block, then the idea of having a legitimate setting does not seem to be backed by evidence. Milgram wondered whether it was the category of place that led to obedience. He gives as an example that people deposit money in prestigious-looking banks and 'seedy' ones, so perhaps people obey in a scientific experiment regardless of where the laboratory is. He wondered whether trying the study somewhere with no suggestion of science or a laboratory would lead to there being less obedience.

Strengths

- Using an office block added to the validity of the study in that the study took place in the real world, at least to an extent; perhaps it was seen as more real than a prestigious university. Two participants were quoted by Milgram as questioning the legitimacy of the study and competence of the researchers, so perhaps using this more naturalistic setting did add to the validity of the findings.
- The controls used – keeping the study in Bridgeport identical to the one at Yale, with just the setting moved – meant that cause-and-effect conclusions could be drawn to show that obedience in the office setting was not that much lower than obedience in the prestigious setting.

Weaknesses

- Obedience did not fall that much, so the validity might still be questioned. The study was still clearly in a laboratory, even if a 'private' one in an office block, so this might still be seen as a scientific experiment requiring co-operation from the participants, which suggests findings might lack validity. Or it could be said that obedience is more likely to take place if the setting is not natural but 'scientific'.
- By taking the study into the participants' real world, this should measure 'real' obedience, but the controls in the study, the generator and the controlled verbal prods are all likely to show participants that the task is far from real, which too questions validity.
- Nineteen participants obeyed in the office setting and 26 in the Yale setting, which Milgram claimed was not that different. However, there is still less obedience, and 47.5 per cent compared with 65 per cent is worth

pursuing. Contrary to Milgram's view, some people might think it is enough to claim that using Yale meant the findings lacked validity.

Ordinary man giving orders (Experiment 13, including 13a)

Not only did Milgram query whether the prestigious setting of Yale University led to obedience, but he also wondered whether the appearance of the experimenter led to obedience. Is a command obeyed, or is it a command only if from someone of perceived authority? A way to test this question is to retain the command but remove it from someone of perceived authority. Milgram set up a variation where an 'ordinary man' gave the orders.

The experiment is set up in the same way as the original study. The experimenter gives the instructions to the point about administering shocks but, before he can explain further, gets 'called away' and leaves the room. There is an accomplice in the room who was initially given the task of recording times and who the participant thinks is another participant, just like him and the victim. When the experimenter leaves the room, the accomplice suggests a new way of doing the study, going up the shock levels one at a time in response to the victim making a mistake. Of course, this is the usual procedure, but the participant does not know that; the participant sees this as a suggestion from an 'ordinary man' who has the role of 'writing down the times' through the draw that was done at the start. The 'ordinary man' insists throughout that the procedure to follow is to move up one step on the generator each time there is a mistake.

Milgram notes that the experimenter leaving did create an awkward atmosphere and tended to undermine the credibility of this variation. Even when the experimenter was not present, there were other features of a controlled and authority situation, such as the generator, the participant being the one to read the word pairs and administer the shocks, and so on. It was just the actual shocks to be administered that were given by the ordinary man. The basic situation had been created by authority.

Sixteen out of 20 participants broke away from the ordinary man's instructions, even though the accomplice constantly urged the participant to continue. Four of the participants (20 per cent) went to the maximum shock level.

In an experiment, it seems that people might see someone in a lab coat and lab situation as in authority, and so act on their instructions more than if it were an 'ordinary man'

Experiment 13a

When a participant refused the orders of the 'ordinary man', the accomplice then said the participant should take over the recording of the shocks given and the accomplice would do the participant role, giving the shocks. This happened to 16 participants out of the 20, and they had to watch a distressing scene where the accomplice pushed through with his scheme, despite cries from the 'victim'. The 16 participants had become bystanders. They almost all protested; some tried to disconnect the power from the generator; some tried to physically restrain the accomplice. Participants set about defending and protecting the 'victim' in the situation.

Strengths

- Keeping the procedure the same for this variation meant that comparisons could be made directly. The controls and the setup of the apparatus were the same. As in the main study, the participant thinks the victim is another participant. The experiment was done at Yale University. There is reliability in the procedure because it was used in the different variations and still mainly showed obedience, even though there were different levels of obedience in the different variations. If all is constant except the one variation, then that variation can be claimed to have caused any change in results.
- The participant saw the accomplice draw lots, just as the victim did, so the participant believed that the accomplice was another participant – an ordinary man just like himself. This helped to reduce authority in the situation as an accomplice who was already there might have been seen as part of the authority.

Weaknesses

- Milgram (1974) admitted that there was still a lot of authority in the situation, such as the scientific-looking apparatus and the obvious approval from Yale in the setting up of the experiment. Just having another apparent participant might not be enough to remove the power differential in the situation, with the actual participant seeing authority in the whole situation.
- Any experiment can be said to lack validity because of the artificial surroundings. Another issue around validity in this study is that the participant might realistically expect that a study at Yale University, for which he has been paid and which involves strong and painful shocks, would have been carefully set up and could be trusted. So the findings that the person makes their own decisions are not valid – they might have trusted the experiment and the experimenter (which of course they were right to do). The study is not then about obedience to authority, as it claims to be, but is about trust. Another validity issue is that obedience falls when an ordinary man gives orders, which supports the idea that the study was seen by the participant as obeying an authority figure. A fourth validity issue is that being told to punish someone in a lab-type setting is valid – that is, where such punishment might take place 'in the real world'.

Explore

Milgram's 1974 book called *Obedience to Authority* (now with a foreword by Philip Zimbardo, well-known in the field of issues around obedience) is worth reading. Perhaps you can get one through inter-library loan. The book explains all the variations as well as more about the main study.

Evaluation of variations of Milgram's (1963) main study

The strengths and weaknesses of Milgram's variations are similar to those of his basic procedure:

- The strong controls avoid bias and make the experience the same for all participants, so cause-and-effect conclusions can be drawn.
- Because of the clear procedures and controls, the studies are replicable and so can be tested for reliability. The findings from the studies with variations are different from each other and from the basic study, but they show obedience in similar situations and back up Milgram's conclusions.
- The studies are not ethical because they put pressure on the participants, they deceive the participants and they do not give the full right to withdraw.
- The studies lack validity because the situations are artificial.

Progress check 1.5

Using the three specific variations from your course (Experiments 7, 10 and 13), explain how situation affects obedience.

STUDY HINT

You will need to know the results of the studies listed in your course, so note down the percentage of obedience in the basic study and in the three required variations.

Milgram's variations showing situational factors that encourage dissent

How situational factors encourage dissent are examined later when issues around dissent and resistance to obedience are discussed (pp. 29–30).

Progress check 1.6

Why did Milgram carry on with the main procedure and introduce the variations?

Test yourself

1. Using Milgram's basic study and the variations, explain situational factors that reduce obedience. **(6 marks)**
2. Evaluate three of Milgram's variation studies. **(8 marks)**

Two studies of obedience, building on Milgram's work

There have been studies in other countries that have partly replicated Milgram's procedures. To an extent, they have obtained different results, although still finding a level of obedience to authority that reinforces Milgram's findings.

One such study was by Meeus and Raaijmakers (1986) into administrative obedience. Their study can be used to evaluate Milgram's work and also consider issues of culture. However, as shown in other studies, cultural issues are not thought to have affected the results (see pp. 25–26); it was more about situation, as Milgram found.

Slater *et al.* (2006) used a virtual situation when replicating Milgram's work. They wanted to look at people's obedience if the 'victim' were a virtual one.

Burger (2009) is also a replication of Milgram's work and is one of the studies that you need to know in detail, so is given in a later section (pp. 49–54).

A study into administrative obedience (Meeus and Raaijmakers, 1986)

Meeus and Raaijmakers (1986) wanted to replicate Milgram's baseline condition (his basic study) focusing on what they saw as ambiguities in the study. One such ambiguity was that some levels of shock appeared to be dangerous but the participants were told that there would be no permanent damage. Another problem they saw was that the punishment was old-fashioned: people in 1986 were unlikely to receive shocks – psychological punishment was more likely.

Aim

Meeus and Raaijmakers (1986) aimed to make the situation more real by using psychological violence. The second part of their study aimed to see if two variations would reduce obedience, as Milgram's variations did. The two variations were:

- a study with the experimenter absent
- a study with two peer-confederates present, i.e. three people administering the punishment.

General procedure

Meeus and Raaijmakers (1986) used a university researcher, the participant and someone 'applying for a job', so there were three people, as in Milgram's study. The applicant was a trained accomplice who seemingly had come to the laboratory to take a test – if he 'passed' the test, he got the job. The participant had to interrupt the applicant by making negative (stress) remarks. The applicant objected to the interruptions. The participants were told to ignore these objections, which increased as the procedure continued. Due to the stress remarks, the applicant 'failed' the test and 'did not get the job'. The dilemma here for the participant was whether scientific research should affect someone's job and career. The question was whether the participants would co-operate.

The test questions were given in four sets. The first set was undertaken by the applicant without any stress comments from the participant. This gave a **baseline measure** against which to compare the other sets. For the next three sets, there were five stress comments for each set.

STUDY HINT

When learning about studies, look for aspects of methodology to use as examples when answering questions. The study by Meeus and Raaijmakers (1986) can be used as an example of the use of a baseline measure – 'normal' achievement is measured. Achievement within the experimental conditions is compared with this, to see how it differs. This study can also be used as an example of the use of a control group. The control group did not take part in all the parts of the experiment. A control group is used as a baseline measure, so that it is clear what would have happened without the experimental intervention.

Table 1.5 Stress remarks, apparent stress levels and the number of errors made by the applicant

Set of questions	Position of stress remark	Stress level	Number of errors
Set 1	0	n/a	0
Set 2	1	29	0
	2	33	0
	3	35	0
	4	41	1
	5	45	2
Set 3	6	41	2
	7	44	3
	8	48	4
	9	51	5
	10	52	6
Set 4	11	52	7
	12	53	7
	13	58	8
	14	60	9
	15	65	10

The applicant protested at the negative remarks – for example, by saying 'But surely…' and 'My answer wasn't wrong was it?' If the participant refused to continue making stress remarks, the experimenter gave four consecutive verbal prods, just as Milgram did.

There was a **control group** in which the participants could choose when to make the negative remarks and could stop making them at any time during the test.

Results of experiment 1

- Almost all (91.7 per cent) of the participants were obedient and made all the stress remarks; the average number of stress remarks given was 14.81.
- Twenty-two of the 24 participants in the experimental group obeyed to the end.
- In the control group, no participant made the stress remarks.
- There was no real opposition from the participants in the experimental condition. Almost all had some discussion with the experimenter, but continued when ordered to do so.
- Follow-up questionnaires showed that participants did not like the experiment, so they were clearly upset by the procedure.
- Seventy-three per cent believed in the experiment, 23 per cent were not sure and 4 per cent thought it was a hoax.
- Participants were aloof with the applicant and shifted blame, acting as agents of the experimenter.
- In the experimental group, 45 per cent blamed the experimenter, 33 per cent thought they were to blame and 22 per cent blamed the applicant.
- In the control group, 41 per cent blamed the experimenter, 41 per cent thought they were to blame and 18 per cent blamed the applicant.

So in the control group, they felt that they and the experimenter were equally to blame; in the experimental group, they felt the experimenter was more to blame (though perhaps not by much). This could be evidence for the agency theory explanation of obedience, which is explored later (pp. 19–21).

The level of obedience in this study is much higher than in Milgram's study. Therefore, it seems that, when obeying orders, it is easier to administer psychological violence than physical harm.

Procedure for experiment 2

Meeus and Raaijmakers (1986) wanted to look at variations on their experiment to compare with Milgram's variations. They carried out a second study with two conditions. In one condition, the experimenter was absent from the room; in the other, there were two peers who rebelled. Milgram (1974) found 22.5 per cent obedience when the experimenter was absent and 10 per cent obedience when two peers rebelled. Meeus and Raaijmakers (1986) wanted to see if their study found a similar drop in obedience.

'Experimenter absent' meant that the experimenter ordered the stress remarks to be made and then left the room. The procedure was then the same as for experiment 1.

'Two peers rebel' meant the real participant was in a group with what he/she thought were two other participants (actually confederates) and they were all instructed together. Thereafter, the procedure was similar to experiment 1, except that after stress remark 8, both peer-confederates started protesting. The experimenter gave them the usual prods. After stress remark 10, when the applicant withdrew his consent to the experiment, the first confederate ignored all the experimenter's prods. The second confederate then did the same. The experimenter ordered the participant to continue on his own. The procedure was subsequently the same as for experiment 1.

Results of experiment 2

In both variations, obedience dropped from the baseline. A chi-squared test was carried out (see Chapter 6, pp. 412–416) and the difference in the level of obedience was found to be significant.

The results are summarised in Table 1.6, in which the stress remark number is the position of that stress remark and *N* is the number of participants.

Table 1.6 Results of the two variations

Stress remark number	Number of participants who stopped in the experimenter-absent condition (*N* = 22)	Number of participants who stopped in the two-peers-rebel condition (*N* = 19)
8	5	2
9	4	1
10	3	9
11	0	3
12	2	1
13	0	0
14	0	0
15	8	3

- In the experimenter-absent condition, 36.4 per cent were fully obedient.
- In the two-peers-rebel condition, 15.8 per cent were fully obedient.

Table 1.7 **Percentage of participants who believed in the experiment**

Belief level	Experimenter absent (%)	Two peers rebel (%)
Believed in the experiment	81	84
Had some doubts	14	16
Thought it was a hoax	5	0

Conclusions of experiments 1 and 2

The Meeus and Raaijmakers (1986) study, as in Milgram (1963/74), found that obedience dropped when variations were introduced. In all cases, obedience in Meeus and Raaijmakers' Dutch study was higher than in Milgram's USA study, in which participants thought that they were giving electric shocks to another person. It seems that administering psychological violence is easier than administering physical punishment. However, the different cultures, rather than the type of punishment, could have led to the difference in obedience.

STUDY HINT
The idea of differences in culture causing differences in obedience is not explored here because it is returned to in a later section (pp. 25–26). When you give ideas like this, however, always explore them fully to show understanding.

Meeus and Raaijmakers (1986) gave three explanations for the high levels of obedience in their studies:

- They considered the type of violence and concluded that psychological violence is different from physical violence. With psychological violence, the psychological distance is greater because the misfortune comes later and, although participants were aware that psychological harm is real, they were distanced from it and so found it easier to obey.
- They considered the legitimacy of the contract between the experimenter and the participant. In the Dutch study, the participants knew that they were going to harm the applicant and they consented to this, so the consent carried more weight. In the Milgram studies, the participants did not agree to administer harm.
- They pointed to the difference in dependency of the victim. In the Dutch study, the applicant had to continue in order to get the job so could object to the stress remarks but could not refuse to complete the test. In Milgram's study, the victim could refuse to answer because there was no gain from continuing.

Meeus and Raaijmakers (1986) concluded that levels of obedience are as high as ever 'even in the Netherlands in the 1980s'.

Evaluation of Meeus and Raaijmakers (1986)

Strengths

- The study builds on Milgram's. Their study, therefore, is all the more useful because the findings can be compared with those of Milgram.
- Due to the attention to detail, the study is replicable and can be tested for reliability. There are controls, which means that the details are clear and the study can be judged carefully. A study with good controls makes it easier to draw cause-and-effect conclusions.

Weaknesses

- The study is an experiment and is, therefore, artificial. The need for controls, such as an applicant taking a test in a laboratory, means that the findings may not be valid. The situation is not very realistic and this might have affected the results.
- Although the findings were compared with Milgram's, which is useful, there are differences between the two studies that make such comparisons difficult. One difference is that the studies were in different cultures (even though both are 'Western'); another is that the studies were 20 years apart, which could have affected obedience levels.

Definitions

Reliability is when the same results are found when a study is repeated – the results are consistent. A study that is well controlled can more easily be replicated because the controls can be implemented again, so experiments, for example, with their good controls, tend to be reliable because they are replicable and controlled. **Validity** refers to the 'reality' of results, and whether what is claimed to be measured has actually been measured. Obedience is represented in Milgram's study as a willingness to give what is thought to be electric shocks, but it can be argued that this is a representation of obedience rather than 'real' obedience. Note though that giving electric shocks in a laboratory setting is perhaps not as 'unreal' as all that. Issues of reliability and validity are useful for evaluating any study, so you need to understand them fully.

STUDY HINT

Make separate notes for the list of evaluation points that you have to cover (validity, reliability, generalisability, credibility, objectivity, subjectivity and ethics). Consider having a file with separate pages for each evaluation point. Each time you come across the issue (e.g. reliability), make a note in your file. Then, you will have a thorough account of each evaluation issue when you revise.

Progress check 1.7

Explain how Meeus and Raaijmakers' (1986) study replicated Milgram's study and give two ways in which it was different.

A comparison of the obedience studies by Milgram (1963, 1974) and Meeus and Raaijmakers (1986)

Percentage data for the three studies are shown in Table 1.8.

Table 1.8 A comparison of the results from Milgram (1963 and 1974) and Meeus and Raaijmakers (1986)

Type of study	Percentage of people obeying (Milgram 1963 and 1974)	Percentage of people obeying (Meeus and Raaijmakers 1986)
Basic study	65.0	91.7
Experimenter-absent condition	22.5	36.4
Two-peers-rebel condition	10.0	15.8

Milgram (1963) found a disturbingly high level of obedience in his basic study – 65 per cent giving a 'shock' of up to 450 volts to a victim for answering questions incorrectly or failing to answer. Meeus and Raaijmakers (1986) found an even higher level of obedience.

Milgram proposed the agency theory as an explanation for the levels of obedience (pp. 19–21). The agency theory suggests that people act as agents to those in authority and are not always in an autonomous state, meaning they are not always acting under their own judgements. Meeus and Raaijmakers (1986) accept the agency theory and explain their finding of reduced obedience when the experimenter is absent by referring to Milgram's theory. They say that with the experimenter present the participants can transfer responsibility for harm to the experimenter and act as his agents, whereas when the experimenter is absent they have to take responsibility for themselves.

Drawing cross-cultural conclusions

Meeus and Raaijmakers (1986) did not suggest that cultural differences would lead to a different level of obedience. They agreed with the agency theory explanation and did not aim to study whether Dutch participants would show a different level of obedience from American participants. They concluded that obedience was found in both the studies and was just as prevalent in the 1980s as in the 1960s. They refer to Western societies when talking about type of punishment, so they appear to think that Dutch and US cultures are similar enough to have similar obedience levels. Therefore, it is concluded that cultural differences were not responsible for the higher level of obedience in the Dutch study. Factors affecting obedience, including culture, are returned to later (pp. 25–26).

A study of obedience in a virtual setting (Slater *et al.*, 2006)

Explore

To read Slater *et al.*'s study in full, go to: www.plosone.org/article/info%3Adoi%2F10.1371%2Fjournal.pone.0000039.

Slater *et al.*'s (2006) study is called 'A virtual reprise of the Stanley Milgram obedience experiments', which shows that this is a deliberate replication but using a different procedure.

Aims

A main aim was to replicate Milgram's work in an ethical way. One aim of the study was to look at obedience in an extreme social situation – but a virtual one. A main aim was to find out if experiments in a virtual environment could be useful when studying areas where it was not possible to use direct experiments.

STUDY HINT

It is easy to think of Slater *et al.*'s (2006) study as looking at obedience but in fact that was not their main aim. Be sure to be accurate when discussing theories or studies in psychology.

Procedure

Slater *et al.* (2006) called the 'setting' for their study an **immersive virtual environment**: this was the key difference between this study and Milgram's – the setting was a virtual one. An immersive virtual environment is achieved by setting up a computer-generated display of 'virtual sensory data' so that there was a life-sized virtual reality for the participant. There were back-projected virtual screens and a floor screen, so the participant was not just looking at one computer screen. The researchers wondered how much a participant would be immersed in the situation and whether it would be enough to refuse to give electric shocks, for example. Participants had been told they could withdraw from the study. Would the participants stop because of the distress of a virtual person? There were some different conditions and the main **hypothesis** (the statement of what the researchers expected to find) was that there would be more stress if the learner (the virtual person) could be seen and heard than if the learner communicated with the participant (the teacher) using text.

The experiment was modelled on Milgram's. There was a test of learning like Milgram's and, if the learner was wrong, shocks were given. The learner gave the wrong answer on 20 out of the 32 trials and more wrong answers later in the test. The teacher was told to turn a voltage dial up one unit of voltage for each wrong answer, thus giving a 'shock'. Each 'shock' also gave an audible 'buzz'.

The experiment had two conditions. In one condition, the learner was seen and heard: the 'visible' condition. The learner protested and showed discomfort, eventually saying she had never agreed to this and wanted to stop; indeed, just before the end, her head slumped forward and she 'went quiet'. In the other condition, apart from brief introductions at the start, the learner was not seen or heard (the 'hidden' condition). In this condition, there were no protests and answers were sent by text. At the end of each trial, there was an interview, as in Milgram's study. There was also a questionnaire administered beforehand and afterwards, to measure how participants felt about their anxiety levels (physiological levels such as perspiration or trembling). Skin conductance was also measured to test for physiological arousal.

There were 34 participants: 23 in the 'visible' condition and 11 in the 'hidden' condition.

Results

Number of shocks given

All participants in the 'hidden' condition gave all 20 shocks. In the 'visible' condition, 17 gave the 20 shocks, 3 gave 19 shocks, 1 gave 18 shocks, 1 gave 16 shocks and 1 gave 9 shocks.

Thoughts of stopping, yes or no

Twelve of the 23 in the 'visible' condition said they had wanted to stop and one of the 11 in the 'hidden' condition said they had thought of stopping, all saying that this was because they felt bad about what was going on.

How much the learner was talked to

Participants in the 'visible' condition talked to the learner, such as emphasising the right answer, or making comments to her. The participants in the 'hidden' condition did not communicate with the learner.

Explanation

Slater *et al.*'s study used a chi-squared test to check the 'yes' and 'no' responses to whether the participant thought about stopping against the two conditions and against whether a participant knew about Milgram's study or not. The study also used a Wilcoxon test for another part of the results. It is useful to make notes about examples of tests being used, as you will be using these two tests (and others) in your course. Chapter 6 covers this in more details. If you are starting your studies with social psychology, you will not have come across a statistical test yet, but this will mean more later in your course.

Skin conductance measure of arousal

Skin conductance is a physiological measure rather than a self-assessment one. In both conditions, there was arousal in the participants, as might be expected. In the 'visible' condition, there was significantly higher arousal than in the 'hidden' condition.

The researchers conclude that the higher level of arousal is because of the visible presence of the learner.

Conclusions

Giving shocks to a virtual human was stressful and caused more arousal in participants who could see and hear the learner, and hear their protests, than in participants who had no communication with the learner, except for receiving their answers. The participants reacted to a virtual human as if they were real, even though they knew that the learner was not real. One result of Slater *et al.*'s study was that if the learner was more distant (in the 'hidden' condition) then obedience was greater. This links with Milgram's variation where the participant had to hold the learner's hand down to receive the shock – obedience was reduced. When the experimenter is in another room and gives orders over the phone in Milgram's study, obedience is reduced, which is again about distance. This matches the idea that in the 'visible' condition participants showed more reluctance and more said they thought of withdrawing. The researchers concluded that using an immersive virtual environment was a suitable way of replacing laboratory experiments, with improved ethics.

Two photos from Slater *et al.*'s (2006) study: the top photo shows a participant, the 'experimenter' and the virtual 'victim'; the bottom photo shows the equipment and the virtual 'victim'

Evaluation of Slater *et al.* (2006)

Strengths

- From an ethical point of view, Slater *et al.*'s study avoided the deception that Milgram had to use. The participants knew for certain that no electric shocks were given and they knew that there was no harm done to the learner.
- Much of the procedure from Milgram's work was replicated in the study, which meant that some comparisons could be made, such as the effect of distance from a 'victim'.

Weaknesses

- Though ethically there were improvements compared with Milgram's work, the participants were still put under pressure. The study was presented to them very seriously and there were a lot of different measures, including skin-resistance testing. The participants were distressed by the learner's own distress and they were given the impression that what they were doing was causing distress to 'someone' else, which has ethical implications.
- The participants complied with the study but maybe this was not obedience as such. They knew they were not giving shocks. Possibly they continued because they were putting up with their own discomfort for the sake of scientific study, which is not the same perhaps as blind obedience as studied by Milgram. They may have complied to be polite.

Progress check 1.8

What are the problems in using the virtual setting and virtual person rather than a laboratory setting and a real learner?

Theories of obedience

A main theory of obedience is **agency theory**. Another theory that links to whether people obey, because it is about how others influence the individual, is **social impact theory**. Social impact theory suggests that the strength of the impact of something on someone, the number of forces involved and whether the impact is near (immediate) or further away all affect how people behave. This theory can be applied to people obeying others in authority. This section covers both these theories.

The agency theory of obedience (Milgram 1973, 1974)

In Milgram's studies of obedience, participants who obeyed to the end tended to say that they were just doing what they were told and would not have done it otherwise. They knew that what they were doing was wrong. The participants showed **moral strain**, in that they knew that obeying the order was wrong, but they felt unable to disobey. Moral strain – when people become uncomfortable with their behaviour because they feel that it is wrong and goes against their values – comes from various sources. In Milgram's basic study:

- the participants heard the cries of the victim
- they might have feared retaliation from the victim
- they had to go against their own moral values
- there was a conflict between the needs of the victim and the needs of the authority figure
- the participants would not want to harm someone because this would go against their opinion of themselves.

Having agreed to take part, all participants in the basic study obeyed until the 'shock level' reached 300 volts. It was as if, having agreed to take part, they were in an **agentic state**. This means that they were agents of the experimenter and so obeyed his orders. The agentic state is the opposite of autonomy. **Autonomy** is being under one's own control and having the power to make one's own decisions. The participants were not simply agents of the experimenter – the grey technician's coat that the experimenter wore and the Yale University setting added to the power of the experimenter and to the role of the participants as agents.

Milgram (1973, 1974) used the idea of being in an agentic state to put forward his **agency theory**.

This is the idea that our social system leads to obedience. If people see themselves as individuals, they will respond as individuals and will be autonomous in a situation. For example, in a threatening situation, many people avoid aggression and turn away. This is likely to happen because avoiding aggression means avoiding getting hurt and aids survival. **Evolution theory** suggests that avoiding aggression is a good survival strategy.

Definition

Evolution theory is the idea of natural selection - any tendency that aids survival would lead to the gene or gene combination for that tendency being passed on.

Early humans had a better chance of survival if they lived in social groups, with leaders and followers. A tendency to have leaders and followers may also have been passed on genetically. A hierarchical social system, such as the one that Milgram's participants were used to, requires a system in which some people act as agents for those 'above' them. According to the agency theory, the agentic state is what led the participants in Milgram's basic study to obey. An agentic state involves a shift in responsibility from the person carrying out an order to the person in authority giving the order – the responsibility is 'given' to the one doing the ordering.

There is some evidence for this shift in responsibility. Gupta (1983) studied obedience in India, with a procedure modelling Milgram's. After the experiment, she asked her participants to allocate responsibility. She used both male and female participants. The males who were obedient in her study accepted 27.6 per cent of the responsibility and those who were defiant (did not obey) accepted 49.4 per cent of the responsibility. The obedient male participants gave 52 per cent responsibility to the experimenter and the defiant male participants gave 39.2 per cent to the experimenter. These findings are reported in Blass (2012), who discussed Milgram's work and the idea of an agentic state.

In an autonomous state:

- individuals see themselves as having power
- they see their actions as being voluntary.

In an agentic state:

- individuals act as agents for others
- their own consciences are not in control.

STUDY HINT

One way of learning a theory is to learn the terms, because understanding the terms (such as 'autonomous' and 'agentic' state) explains the theory. Also being able to define terms is necessary in itself. Draw up glossaries of your own, if you haven't already done so, with one 'method' glossary and one 'theory' glossary.

Milgram thought that, as well as the agentic state being a survival strategy, people learn it from their parents. In families, there are hierarchies. In schools, there are hierarchies too – it is clear who has the power, so children learn the same lesson there. In the agentic state, people do not feel responsible for their actions. They feel that they have no power, so they might well act against their own moral code, as happened in Milgram's basic study. In Milgram's variation in which the victim was nearer to the teacher, and the teacher had to hold the victim's hand on the plate to receive the 'shock', there was less obedience. This suggests that the learners felt that they had to take greater responsibility for what they were doing. In a variation in which another experimenter ordered the participants to stop, they all stopped. This reinforces the idea that they were agents of the experimenter because they obeyed and stopped when they could.

People are in an agentic state when they see the person giving an order as having legitimate authority and when they see that person as taking responsibility for them following the order.

Evaluation of the agency theory of obedience

Strengths

- The agency theory explains the different levels of obedience found in the variations to the basic study. In the basic study, the participants did not take responsibility and said that they were just doing what they were told. However, as they were made to take more responsibility because they had, for example, to hold the victim's hand down, the obedience level decreased. As they moved away from being in an agentic state, such as when in a less prestigious setting, fewer participants obeyed up to the 'shock level' of 450 volts. Evidence from the different studies reinforces the agency theory explanation of obedience.
- The theory helps to explain the issue that triggered Milgram's research into obedience – the Holocaust, where so many Jews and members of other minority groups were slaughtered. Eichmann said that he was just obeying orders; agency theory helps to explain why he (and others) would obey to such a degree.

Agency theory, which is rooted in the theory of natural selection, helps to explain seemingly inexplicable actions like the Holocaust and other atrocities, such as the My Lai massacre, which was where US soldiers obeyed an order to kill women and children in a village, when this was clearly not something soldiers should do.

Weaknesses

- There are other possible explanations for obedience, such as social power. French and Raven (1959) proposed five different kinds of power:
  - Legitimate power is held by those in certain roles; Milgram's role would have had legitimate power.
  - Reward power is held by those with certain resources; Milgram may have held reward power because he paid the participants.
  - Coercive power is held by those who can punish another; Milgram gave the participants a small shock, so they may have felt that he could punish them. However, he did say that they could keep the money whatever the outcome, so they would not have thought he could punish them by taking the money away.
  - Expert power is held by those with knowledge; the participants would see Milgram as an expert.
  - Referent power is held by those who can win people over; the participants would probably not have seen Milgram in this light.

  The obedience shown by the participants could be explained by social power theory. When another explanation is equally possible, this makes a theory less powerful as an explanation.
- Agency theory is more a description of how society works than an explanation. It suggests that the participants obeyed because they were agents of authority. However, obedience is defined as obeying authority figures, so agency theory does not explain in more detail why obedience occurs. The theory says that people are agents of others in society because that is the way society works, and natural selection means that people have evolved to obey those in 'higher' positions. There is no evidence for this, other than it is a claim that makes sense.

Test yourself

1. What is meant by the terms 'agentic state' and 'autonomous state'? **(4 marks)**
2. Explain Milgram's agency theory of obedience. **(4 marks)**
3. Evaluate the agency theory of obedience. **(8 marks)**

Progress check 1.9

Explain the idea that agency theory is more a description than an explanation so it is not useful as a theory.

The social impact theory of behaviour (Latané, 1981)

What is social impact theory?

Social impact theory can be applied to obedience but is not, as such, a theory of obedience. Social impact theory looks at the functioning of individuals in the presence of others. Latané, a main name in social impact theory, looks at attitudes and the impact of others on an individual's attitudes. Social impact theory is about how we are affected by our social environment and the variety of opinions we encounter as social beings. Social impact is 'any individual feelings, thoughts, or behaviour that is exerted by the real, implied, or imagined presence or actions of others' (Nowak *et al.*, 1990, p. 363).

Social functioning, according to social impact theory, can be partly explained by looking at the functioning of individuals; however, the functioning of individuals can be seen as affected by their social group. Individuals functioning socially may behave differently from their behaviour as individuals. It is concluded that there are probably laws about individuals functioning in a social context that laws about individual functioning cannot explain (these ideas are from Nowak *et al.* (1990), who discussed and built on social impact theory).

Studies looking at how individuals change their attitudes have found that persuasive argument can work to change an individual's beliefs. Even just knowing that others have a certain opinion can change beliefs. Usually attitudes change to be closer to those of the source of influence, such as the group's attitudes, although minority influence, when a few people change the attitudes of the majority, can happen, as may be seen in jury decision-making. Generally, according to Latané and Wolf (1981), the size and status of the group will affect when an individual's attitudes are influenced. However, the main point here is that others and 'group influence' can affect an individual's behaviour.

STUDY HINT

Social identity theory reflects the same idea as social impact theory – that people move towards their group's norms and attitudes. You should note down links between theories to aid your understanding.

One aspect of social impact (the effects of a group on individual attitudes) can be **group polarisation**. Group polarisation is the term for a group tending to have more extreme ideas and attitudes than the individuals in the group. This might be to give a group identity or to make the group seem important. This is an example of how attitudes of a group are different from the attitudes of the individuals within the group.

Linking to Milgram's work on obedience

There is a link to Milgram's work on obedience. Milgram looked at the behaviour of individuals in his experimental situation and then derived from that how people behave socially (such as people being agents to those in authority). However, in his variations he brought in the presence of others, such as his 'two peers rebel' condition, which Meeus and Raaijmakers (1986) replicated. To an extent, Milgram found that an individual's behaviour in a group was different from their behaviour when on their own, a finding supported by social impact theory. Others 'impacted' on the individual's behaviour. Perhaps the presence of others had backed the individual's attitudes and feelings of reluctance to obey, and that was the reason for reduced obedience if other 'peers rebelled'.

Milgram's studies into obedience were about behaviour, not attitudes, though he did measure the feelings and emotions of the participants when carrying out his orders (or not). This can be seen as being about attitude as the participant's distress at having to administer punishment does suggest that their attitude did not match their behaviour.

Looking for laws of behaviour

Latané claimed that it is not difficult to study group influence when considering small-group behaviour, but as the complexity of behaviour increases, studying laws of how individuals function socially becomes harder. Nowak *et al.* (1990) considered how to get to laws of such behaviour in a mathematical way. They used computer simulation, working towards developing a computer program using rules that govern how individuals react to their social environment. If predictions can be made from such a program, this could be useful for predicting the behaviour of members of society. Predictions could be made about behaviour at a group level and a system could perhaps provide rules that are more than the total of rules about individual behaviour. A society could use such rules to predict public opinion, for example.

Explanation

Nowak *et al.* call such a system 'reductive simulation', which is interesting when considering ideas around reductionism. **Reductionism** is the study of something by breaking it down into parts. For example, Milgram studied obedience by putting together a situation where people were told to obey and he looked at parts of the obedience in his variations, such as when the experimenter was out of the room. Milgram measured the parts too, such as how far up the generator a participant went, or whether participants seemed upset. It can be said that reductionism is limiting as findings are not going to 'see' the whole picture. If rules for behaviour are developed, in a mathematical way, this is likely to reduce behaviour to certain actions and situations. On the other hand, scientific study reduces the object of study into parts, to enable experiments to be carried out, so reductionism can be useful when looking for laws, such as laws of behaviour.

Issues and debates

Reductionism is one of the 11 issues and debates for the A level course. It is worth taking notes on each of the issues and debates and keeping these notes together. Start here with a section on reductionism.

Social impact theory can generate laws of behaviour by considering the effects of time and space on how individuals affect one another and also, importantly, on how the impact of others is affected by:

- the number of other people in the environment
- the immediacy of the impact
- the strength of the impact.

The strength of the message or influence is greater if there are a lot of people in agreement – change in attitude by an individual hearing that message is more likely. The strength of the message is also stronger if it is given by someone the individual sees as an expert. This suits Milgram's finding that obedience was greater if the orders were given by someone dressed in a lab coat, seeming to have authority, than if given by an 'ordinary man'. A message is also stronger if there is immediacy, such as the message being given by friends rather than a stranger.

A mathematical model

The theory is formulated as a mathematical model:

$$i = f(S/N)$$

where i is the magnitude of impact, f is a function, S is the strength of the sources (their powers of persuasion, for example), I is the immediacy of the sources (how close they are, for example, in time and space) and N is the number of sources. Sources are one or more people, or groups. So the impact of others is a function of the strength of the others, in terms of their authority perhaps, how close they are to the individual and how many there are in the group. Another issue that affects the impact is how many people are being impacted upon, not the size of the group doing the impacting but the number of people being affected. It can be the effects of others on an individual or group that makes a difference. This might account for Milgram's finding that an individual alone as the 'teacher' is more likely to show obedience than when that individual is joined by what they think of as another 'teacher'.

Evaluation of social impact theory

Strengths

- Using a mathematical formula, predictions can be made to help society in the control of its members, which can mean controlling obedience that is to the detriment of a society. As long as the factors can be measured, such as the size of social influence (the size of the group), the immediacy of the influence (how close they are) and their powers of persuasion, the likely influence on individuals can be estimated. The theory has useful predictive power.
- There is reliability in a theory that is set out so clearly, and if the same measurements about groups and individuals are put into the formula, the same predictions will emerge.
- In theory, the formula should be generalisable to different cultures as social impact theory claims that the features they highlight are present in all groups.

As a theory of obedience:

- Milgram's results showed that when the participant had what they thought was peer support, there was less obedience. Social impact theory acknowledges that the impact is affected by the number of people being influenced as much as by the number doing the influencing, so can explain this result.
- Social impact theory acknowledges strength as a feature of groups, which includes their power of persuasion, as well as how much authority they have, which suits the idea that people obey those in authority.

Weaknesses

- Social impact theory is a static theory: it does not take into account the reciprocal effects of the individual on their social environment, alongside the effects of others on the individual. The individual and the group interact – the group is not acting on a passive individual, but one who is active in the interaction.
- The impact of others involves so many different factors about the social situation, such as measuring powers of persuasion, or nearness, or even size of a group, that it does not seem that such a wealth of factors can be reduced to a mathematical formula.
- Features of the individual are not taken into account, such as that some people are more easily persuaded than others. These are likely to affect the impact of others on an individual.
- The theory discusses social influence in general rather than specifically looking at obedience or issues around group behaviour, such as social loafing. **Social loafing** is a term for people who are in a group but do not contribute to the group's decisions or actions.

As a theory of obedience:

- Social impact theory looks at social impact in general and not obedience in particular. For example, it can help to explain why the presence of others affects obedience levels, but it cannot explain why the change of setting affects obedience.
- Obedience is a behaviour by someone in response to someone else in a specific situation and is not about the influence of groups on behaviour, so only the features of obedience that involve groups are addressed.

Progress check 1.10

Consider two individuals. The first is with five friends having an enjoyable day out. The group is discussing the merits of two football teams and advocate strongly that one is better than the other. Three of the friends watch a lot of football and are very knowledgeable about the game. This individual thinks football is a waste of time but, after listening to the arguments of the friends, decides that the favoured football team may be worth watching and agrees to attend a game.

The second individual is attending a meeting at work, where training is being carried out by a group of people from a different place of work, focusing on working as a team. This individual prefers to work on their own. They are a software engineer developing computer software. They listen to the training, without taking much in. A week later they are asked to put some of the ideas into practice, but they cannot remember the ideas and they are unwilling to action them.

Explain why the first individual chose to change their attitude towards football and the second chose not to change their attitude towards team working.

Comparing social impact theory and agency theory as an explanation of obedience

Agency theory is about obedience specifically and explains that people are agents of those in authority in a society, partly because that might be a natural response since it has been an advantage to people in the past so the response has survived. People are also agents of society because of their upbringing, where they learn to obey those in authority, such as in the family or at school.

However, agency theory *describes* obedience rather than explaining it – it says that we obey those in authority because we are agents of those in authority, and 'being agents' means we obey them. This is a circular argument so possibly not useful.

Social impact theory is a good theory to apply to obedience as it incorporates various factors about obedience, such as why people might obey group orders more than orders from an individual and why their obedience might be affected if they have someone else 'on their side'.

However, social impact theory does not relate to individual factors of obedience, such as the effect of situation or personality.

On balance, social impact theory is less useful as a theory of obedience as it was not designed to explain obedience specifically, but rather to explain how people are affected by the influence of others. Agency theory arose from work on obedience, so is more focused on obedience. Both can offer an understanding of why people obey others in a society.

STUDY HINT

When asked to compare two theories, briefly describe them first. Also describe the theories' strengths and weaknesses, which should lead you to some good comparison points. Comparing means giving both similarities and differences.

Test yourself

1. Explain how social impact theory can explain some of Milgram's results. **(6 marks)**
2. Evaluate social impact theory as an explanation of obedience. **(8 marks)**

Factors affecting obedience

The factors to consider that affect obedience are the effects of the situation, the effects of personality, issues of culture and issues of gender.

The effects of the situation on obedience

Obedience occurs in many situations, including obedience to an officer

Milgram's work suggests that situation affects obedience rather than obedience being due to individual differences. One by one the participants mainly obeyed (for example, they all went up to 300 volts in his basic study), even though they were often very distressed, so it seemed that this was because of the situation (the experimental procedure) rather than differences in individuals.

In Meeus and Raaijmakers (1986), the control group did not continue to give verbal comments to the 'job applicant' because they had the choice of whether to give the remarks or not, whereas the experimental group, not given a choice, showed 91.7 per cent obedience and gave all 15 stress remarks to the job applicant. This suggests that the situation led to obedience. The participants in the experimental group had agreed to take part, were paid and thought they were helping in a study about stress and test achievement. They were told to give the stress remarks, so they did, even though they were distressed when they 'saw' the distress of the 'applicant'. It is unlikely that the control group and the experimental group were different in personality, so it is thought that the situation affected obedience.

Slater *et al.* (2006) also found obedience in a study using a procedure like Milgram's, even though the victim was 'virtual'.

Milgram varied the situation to see if it was the 'cause' of the obedience. His variations show that less pressure from authority resulted in lower obedience. As the situation changes, so does the obedience level. For example, carrying out the same procedure in a less prestigious setting led to reduced obedience. When the participant had to hold the victim's hand on a plate to receive a shock, there was less obedience – the situation had changed. When orders were given over the phone by the experimenter, obedience dropped, and when the 'experimenter' appeared as an 'ordinary man', again obedience dropped. In each case, the situation had changed so it is concluded that obedience dropped because of the changes in situation.

Meeus and Raaijmakers (1986) found that when others showed dissent (not obeying), the obedience of the participant fell. Obedience also fell when the experimenter was absent. Again this shows how changing the situation affected obedience.

Effects of situation on obedience: evaluation

- As the situation changed in Milgram's variations, so did the obedience level, even though the procedure remained the same.
- In two variations, Meeus and Raaijmakers found similar effects – changing the situation lowered obedience. The findings from this study and Milgram's work provide strong evidence for there being situational effects on obedience.
- These studies were experiments, carried out in an artificial setting, so lacked **ecological validity**. Validity is about getting results that apply in real life; ecological validity is the validity of the setting. If the situation is not natural, then perhaps the conclusions regarding the effect of situation are not sound.
- The participants might have been different in terms of personality, as there was variation in obedience, with some going to 450 volts in Milgram's basic study and others stopping earlier. Personality as a factor in obedience is discussed later (pp. 26–28).

Progress check 1.11

List three pieces of evidence that suggest obedience is due to situation.

The effects of culture on obedience

Milgram's work stimulated interest in different cultures. Researchers wanted to see whether such shocking findings would be replicated in different cultures. There is a nature–nurture theme running through psychology, and the idea of looking at culture is to see how far a behaviour (like obedience) might be due to someone's personality or due to their upbringing or the culture they are in. Milgram initially wanted to see whether people in the US would obey in a way that was similar to those in Germany during World War II. He found that his participants were more obedient than was expected, so he did not find that 'Germans are different'. His agency theory suggests that it is a feature of all societies that some are in authority and others are agents. Such explanations seem to be about 'nature' – it is in the nature of humans to obey those in authority. Though the findings suggested that it was the situation that led to the obedience (which sounds like 'nurture'), it was concluded that it was in human nature to obey in certain situations: our nature is to obey and the situation affects the level of obedience. So the question was whether such obedience would be found in all cultures when there were orders from an authority figure.

Issues and debates

Nature–nurture is one of the 'issues and debates' that you need to explore (but not for the AS course). Make some notes about how Milgram's work fits into a nature-nurture discussion. Bring in Meeus and Raaijmakers' findings too, showing obedience but in a different culture.

One way to confirm Milgram's ideas about obedience being down to situation rather than the individual is to repeat the study in different countries. To address the ethical issues of Milgram's study, Meeus and Raaijmakers (1986) use a less extreme 'punishment' (though it is still upsetting for the participants). Burger's (2009) partial replication of Milgram's study (pp. 49–54) uses the same idea as Milgram but all participants were stopped at 150 volts, so again this reduces the amount of distress. It has not been possible on ethical grounds to replicate Milgram's study completely but there have been studies in other cultures, albeit with some differences in procedures.

Slater *et al.*'s (2006) study (pp. 17–19) was set in the UK and involved similar cultural experiences to Milgram's. Burger's (2009) study was in the US, so again not different culturally. However, there are other cross-cultural studies of obedience, many of which show a higher level of obedience than Milgram's study:

- Shanab and Yahya (1977) asked children, aged 6–16, in Jordan to give 'shocks' to other children. The experimenter was female. Seventy-three per cent gave the maximum shock to same-gender peers (higher than in Milgram's basic study but lower than in Meeus and Raijmaakers'). It was concluded that children are obedient, although it was mentioned that there might be cultural differences between Jordan and the USA.
- Kilham and Mann (1974) asked first-year Australian psychology students both to order pain to be administered and to administer pain. They found there was a higher level of obedience when ordering pain than when administering it. They also found gender differences in obedience. When administering the shocks, obedience was 40 per cent for males and 16 per cent for females (28 per cent overall). When the participant gave the order to administer the shock, obedience was 68 per cent for males and

40 per cent for females (54 per cent overall). In the control group, obedience was 0 per cent. Kilham and Mann talk about a 'decade of campus unrest' and anti-war demonstrations at the time, which suggests that they felt local circumstances affected obedience levels. This could be seen as more evidence that it is the situation that gives obedience, and not just the situation in a study, but the situation at the time for the people of that place.

- Schurz (1985) carried out a study in Austria and found 80 per cent baseline obedience. Schurz asked participants to give bursts of ultrasound rather than electric shocks to a learner. The participants were told that the bursts were painful and could damage the skin.
- Mantell and Panzarella (1976) in Germany found 85 per cent obedience. They used a control group, which Milgram did not, and found that if the participants could choose the level of 'shock' to administer, none obeyed to the end. This was similar to Meeus and Raaijmakers, who also used a control group.

Blass (2012) reviewed studies done in the US and elsewhere and arrived at an average percentage of obedience in the US of 60.94 per cent and in other countries of 65.94 per cent. Despite a large variation of obedience levels in the studies, the average figures are very similar, and very similar to Milgram's result in his basic study. Blass (2012) suggests that, even if obedience had been found to differ between cultures, there were other differences such as age and gender of the participants, as well as differences in the procedures, that could have caused differences in obedience. Blass concludes that the similarity of findings in different cultures shows that people have a powerful tendency to obey authority and this may be 'one of the universals of social behaviour' (Blass, 2012, p. 203).

Issues and debates

The comment from Blass (2012) about the 'universals of social behaviour' is part of the nature-nurture debate. A behaviour that is found in all societies and appears to be universal (in this case, obedience to authority) can be said to be in our nature. Make notes about issues and debates separately, such as this one on nature, ready for Year 2 of your course.

When issues like gender are discussed to see if they affect behaviour like obedience, this is considering development, to see if girls are brought up to be more obedient perhaps, or if biologically females are more empathetic (so less likely to be obedient in Milgram's study). In fact, studies looking at obedience, as shown here, do not find gender differences in obedience as such, though there tend to be gender differences in the reaction to being part of such studies. Culture too seems not to have too strong an influence on obedience and this adds to the conclusion that obedience comes from the situation and this is a universal conclusion.

STUDY HINT

Be sure to make a note when you see the 'developmental psychology' icon so that you have these ready to revise when developmental psychology is touched upon in your course.

Effects of culture on obedience: evaluation

- If a conclusion is to be drawn about the effects of culture, then studies in different cultures need to have the same procedure, including controls, otherwise it is not possible to tell whether any differences (in this case, obedience) are down to culture or other differences in the studies.
- The obedience studies in different cultures all had differences in procedure, so we can't be sure that culture has an effect on obedience.
- Looking at the findings of other studies, which showed high levels of obedience, despite the differences in procedure, it seems likely that culture does not affect obedience.

STUDY HINT

Expect questions that ask you to compare studies and to compare theories. When preparing for such questions, look for similarities and differences to use as evaluation points. For questions about cultural differences in obedience, be ready to compare studies.

Explore

Look up studies of obedience in other cultures. Consider whether differences in obedience are due to cultural differences or to other differences between the studies.

Progress check 1.12

Explain evidence for and against cultural differences in obedience.

The effects of individual differences (personality) on obedience

Studies of obedience tend to conclude that it is the situation that gives obedience rather than individual differences (personality). Even though the situation does seem to be important, there were some participants who obeyed and some who did not (e.g. in Milgram's basic study, 35 per cent did not go to the highest shock level), so the question of whether personality is a factor in obedience is worth addressing.

Personality is about someone's unique and stable responses to specific situations. If someone reacts in a specific way to a situation and always reacts in that way, that is seen as their personality. We might say that, in some situations, everyone would react in a similar way – for example, a pressured situation might make people short-tempered. However, that might not be their personality but because of the pressure in the situation. Personality is about responding to a situation in a unique way, in a way that others might not. For example, some people are short-tempered each time they go shopping.

STUDY HINT

As your course requires you to discuss personality, with regard to both obedience and prejudice, note down a definition in your glossary of terms.

Authoritarian personality – evidence from interviews with Milgram's participants

Milgram's participants were interviewed straight after the experiments (exit interviews) and were asked questions to see if it was personality that led to the obedience/dissent. Elms (1998) discusses these ideas. Elms, who was one of Milgram's assistants, noted from the exit interviews that those in 'caring' jobs, such as teachers, showed less obedience than those in technical jobs, such as engineers. Catholics showed more obedience than those in other religious groups, and those with more years in education tended to obey less. People who had been in the armed forces longer showed more obedience, but ex-officers showed less obedience than non-officers. Occupation might be linked to personality, as people might choose an occupation that suits their personality, but the links that Elms pointed to were not strong. Also it is not certain that occupation links to personality, so there was further investigation using the interview material.

Two groups were examined, an 'obedient group' and a 'defiant group' – 20 participants in each group were chosen from the studies, with their responses used to group them. If personality was involved in obedient or dissenting behaviour, then looking at these two different groups should uncover such a link.

Definitions

Defiance is disobedience and **dissent** is not agreeing so not obeying the order. Your course uses the term 'dissent' and also 'resistance to obedience'; Elms uses 'defiant'. All of these terms are treated as sharing the same idea.

It was found that the defiant group showed more social responsibility. However, social responsibility might have a) led to obedience in that they obeyed those in authority for the sake of society, or b) led to defiance, in that they would not be responsible for another's pain. So the concept of social responsibility was not that useful as a personality trait that might lead to defiance as it seemed to be a trait that could lead to either obedience or resistance to obedience.

- The obedient group found the experimenter as 'more admirable' and the learner as 'less admirable', whereas the defiant group did not respond to the experimenter or learner in these ways. So perhaps the people seen as 'admirable' might be those that are obeyed.
- The 'defiant' group also reported receiving more punishment when they were young, and the 'obedience' group reported a more negative and distant relationship with their father. So it seemed that parenting might be a factor in whether people obey or not.
- It was found that the defiant group, when considering their military service, had never fired at 'the enemy', whereas the obedience group had 'fired at the enemy', but this was a situational issue rather than one of personality.

From the findings listed here, Milgram and Elms (1966) thought that those who were obedient fitted more into an **authoritarian personality**. Those with an authoritarian personality are said to admire rules, be distant from their fathers and be more likely to be in a military role, among other things. Cohrs *et al.* (2012), one of the 'studies in detail' for your course, looks at right-wing authoritarianism (RWA) and prejudice – this will add detail to your understanding of the authoritarian personality later (pp. 59–66).

It seems that Milgram did consider there might be a personality of obedience in some way, but it was not as straightforward as linking obedience to an authoritarian approach to life. Blass did some work on personality and obedience, and carried out a study that did link obedience to an authoritarian approach. People high in 'authoritarian submission' (giving in to authority) were more likely to obey, according to Blass. Also when Blass studied people watching film of the Milgram study, those with a high level of authoritarianism were less likely to blame those punishing the learner than those without that high level of authoritarianism. So there is some evidence that those with a so-called 'authoritarian personality' are those more likely to obey.

Internal/external locus of control

One factor that might link to whether someone resists obedience or obeys is whether they have an internal or external locus of control. This can be said to be a type of personality. The locus of control is about the reasons people give for what happens to them. Someone with an

internal locus of control thinks that they are in control of their own actions and believes that what happens is something they have caused. Someone with an **external locus of control** believes that what happens to them comes from outside their control and so if they were in a stressful situation they would feel helpless to do anything about it.

Holland (1967) looked at Milgram's ideas on obedience to see if they linked to a person's locus of control, and found no link. But Blass (1991) looked at the data Holland used again and found a link between internal locus of control and resistance to obedience. Schurz (1985) carried out a study in Austria looking at obedience (see p. 26) and found that those with an internal locus of control felt more responsible for their actions. Blass (1991) has looked at the evidence to link locus of control to obedience and the link is not clear. There is some evidence that an internal locus of control links to being more resistant to obedience.

Effects of personality on obedience: evaluation

- Milgram used many participants in his studies and found a great deal of obedience. It is unlikely that there are just personality factors at work with so many individuals obeying orders (65 per cent in the basic study).
- Elms looked at the interviews after Milgram's study to see if he could find evidence of personality at work. There was some evidence that a more authoritarian personality was more obedient.
- Those with an internal locus of control are perhaps more likely to resist obeying, though there is not strong evidence for this.
- Milgram's study did not directly control for, or focus on, personality. More research is needed to link personality to obedience.

Progress check 1.13

What evidence is there that obedience links to an authoritarian personality and what evidence is there that it is about having an internal locus of control?

The effects of gender on obedience

We have already introduced ideas about whether there are gender differences in obedience and in general it is thought that there are no differences. For example, the one study in which Milgram used female participants found 65 per cent obedience, the same as for the basic study using male participants. However, this was just one study, and the female participants seemed to show more distress, so that does suggest some differences.

Kilham and Mann (1974) did find some gender differences. When administering the shocks, obedience was 40 per cent for males and 16 per cent for the females (28 per cent overall). When the participant gave the order to someone else to administer the shock, obedience was 68 per cent for males and 40 per cent for females (54 per cent overall). This suggests that the females were less obedient than the males.

Blass (1991) carried out a **meta-analysis**, which is a study that uses findings from a number of different studies, to come up with an overall set of results. The studies used in a meta-analysis have to be very similar in procedure and focus, so that the findings can be usefully put together. Blass (1991) used nine studies and found that only Kilham and Mann (174) showed gender differences, so the general conclusion is that there are no gender differences in obedience.

STUDY HINT

Meta-analysis is a method that takes the results of many studies in one area of research and examines the results to look for overall conclusions about that area of study. Add this term to your glossary of terms. Blass (1991) is an example of a meta-analysis that can be used when discussing this method in your Year 2 work, so worth noting down in your notes on methodology. You could make a list of research methods as you come to them and note down names of researchers who have used that method.

However, Blass (2012) in a later review, reports a study in India by Gupta (1983, an unpublished study) that used seven conditions, and in six of those seven conditions she found females to be less obedient than males, so here is some evidence to support the idea that gender is a factor in obedience.

When the responses of the participants are reported, such as their emotional reactions, there do seem to be gender differences. Milgram (1974), as reported in Blass (2012), found that females reported more tension than males when taking part in the study. Shanab and Yahya (1977) also found females were more visibly anxious, and Gupta found females reported more tension than males.

The evidence presented here shows that there might be gender differences in obedience. However, the large number of studies that found no differences must be taken into account when examining the effects of gender on obedience.

Explanation

In psychology, there is often evidence for more than one viewpoint or theory, as is the case here with gender effects on obedience. Think of doing psychology as raising the questions as much as giving the answers, and when discussing issues with more than one viewpoint, weigh up the evidence and come to a tentative conclusion. Precise and definite answers are unlikely.

Effects of gender on obedience: evaluation

- The one study that Milgram carried out with female participants is probably not enough to test gender as a factor in obedience.
- Other studies have used both males and females, such as Burger (2009), and in so many studies gender differences were not found. This supports Milgram's idea that gender is not a factor in obedience.
- Blass (2012) suggests that out of 12 studies across cultures where gender is reported, ten show no gender differences and just Kilham and Mann (1974) and Gupta (1983) show some differences, with female participants being less obedient than males.
- Not all studies looked at gender when considering the emotional reaction of participants, but when such reactions are considered, females seem to show and feel more anxiety and tension.
- The studies are experiments, in artificial settings, so the findings may lack validity, which may make them less applicable to real-world settings and events.
- It could be claimed that the experiments, with strong controls over variables, especially as findings were very similar between different experiments, are reliable and give firm results.

Dissent and resistance to obedience

Although in society obedience can be helpful, such as ensuring that soldiers always obey orders in defence of their country, there are times when a society might prefer an individual to be in an autonomous state. For example, some situations in war time have led soldiers to obey 'bad' orders. One example was in the 1970s in My Lai in Vietnam, where US soldiers were ordered to kill unarmed civilians in a Vietnamese village, and did so. This was seen as a 'massacre'. Orders originally seem to have been to kill anyone running away but on the day the villagers did not run, they were herded. Nevertheless, on the day the order was to kill them, and that is what was done. Why would the soldiers have obeyed such an order? There was interest too in those who refused to obey. Why did they dissent? Some soldiers did not obey the order to kill and there was someone who landed in a helicopter and began a rescue mission. There is an account of a soldier who did carry out the order and was then seen head in hands, clearly very upset. When reading such an account, it is not as if there are 'bad soldiers' who obeyed and 'good soldiers' who did not, though those not obeying can be seen more as heroes, as they went against their training.

Explore

You can read an account of the My Lai massacre here: http://law2.umkc.edu/faculty/projects/ftrials/mylai/myl_intro.html. It is hard to get an exact account as there was natural confusion at the time, but it is clear that there were some soldiers who did not obey.

By looking at factors that affect obedience, ideas about dissent and resistance to obedience can be uncovered. For example, those who are not so led by a situation (such as the 14 who did not obey to the end in Milgram's basic study) are more likely to resist obedience and dissent. In obedience studies, there is never 100 per cent obedience when people are asked to do something against their moral code and something that distresses them, so there must be factors that lead people to disobey.

Milgram's variations point to factors that are likely to give resistance to obedience and give dissent. These include whether the authority figure is near or not (e.g. if they give orders over the telephone, then there is less obedience) and whether the individual is faced with the 'victim' or not (e.g. if they have to hold the hand on the plate to give the shock, there is less obedience). Other factors include whether someone else is around and is dissenting (e.g. with someone else dissenting, it is more likely that the individual will dissent too).

Situations where someone might be more resistant to orders from an authority figure to do something against their moral code:

- when someone can see the 'victim' (victim in same room)
- when someone has to be involved directly in the punishment (holds hand down for a shock)
- when someone is not in a setting that supports authority (in an office block)
- when the one giving the orders is remote (gives orders over the phone)
- when someone else is seen to resist (peers rebel)
- when there is confusion in the orders, perhaps someone else gives different orders (more than one experimenter, and one says 'stop').

There are situations when knowing about obedience can be useful for society. For example:

- Members of the armed forces who apparently obey orders and then subsequently have to stand trial to see if they were personally responsible for their actions – a defence can be that they were in an agentic state and gave responsibility to the one giving orders.
- People in authority, such as prison guards, may be seen by others as having overstepped the mark with regard to brutality – their defence could be that they were fulfilling their role, a role that society thinks of as a 'strong' one.
- In a trial, psychologists can use results from studies to show that some actions that go against society's moral code might still be carried out by someone under similar circumstances – the defence could be that they were in an agentic state and others would be likely to have done the same.

Explore

Using the internet or other sources, find out how Philip Zimbardo has been involved in such issues, using his understanding of the psychology of obedience, brutality and tyranny in defence of actions by an individual.

Progress check 1.14

Consider someone in authority, perhaps a police officer, and write down advice you would give to this person in order to get obedience from others. Add your reasons by relating the advice to Milgram's findings.

Progress check 1.15

Consider you are training people to be autonomous and not in an agentic state. Write down advice you would give people to help them to resist blind obedience to someone in authority and instead to follow their own moral code.

Test yourself

Discuss how far obedience can be explained by personality, culture, gender or situation. **(16 marks)**

Ethical issues arising from obedience research

One criticism of Milgram's studies is that the procedure was not ethical for participants. There are also moral issues with regard to society.

Method link: Chapter 5 covers ethical issues in research in more detail.

Ethics covers three areas: the ethics of practising psychology (being a practitioner), the ethics of carrying out studies in psychology (doing psychology) and the ethics of using findings from studies in psychology (applying psychology).

In this section, two of these areas are covered, the ethics of doing psychology and the ethics of applying psychology.

STUDY HINT

When an issue links to one of the other chapters, as in the case of methodology, maths and practical investigations, it is useful to note the general material in the topic area (Chapters 1–4) and then to turn to the link chapter (Chapters 5–8) to find out more information.

Ethical issues for participants in Milgram's studies

In the basic study, the participants showed distress – for example, sweating and shaking. Many showed signs of nervousness, including nervous laughter. Three participants had full-blown seizures, one of which was so convulsive that the experiment had to be stopped. One of the ethical guidelines, part of the ethical **principle of responsibility**, is that participants should not be distressed: the researcher must do no harm.

As part of the **principle of respect**, participants should be given the right to withdraw, which, in theory, Milgram's participants were. In practice, this was made difficult, which is against the guidelines. They should be reminded that they can withdraw, and this was not done. In fact, when they protested, verbal prods were used to encourage them to continue. Also as part of 'respect', there should have been informed consent. Participants gave consent by volunteering for the study, but they did not know what it would entail, so their consent was not informed.

Milgram deceived the participants in a number of ways. He let them think that:

- the victim was receiving real shocks
- the experiment was about memory and learning, rather than about obedience
- the victim was also a participant
- they could have been victims.

However, there were ways in which Milgram was ethical:

- He debriefed all the participants. Debriefing is part of the ethical **principle of competence**. He let them meet the victim to see that no harm had been done. As far as possible, he made sure that the participants left the situation in a reasonable frame of mind. He gave them a questionnaire to complete so that he could judge their reactions to the study. In the main, the participants said that they were pleased to have taken part.

- He gave them the right to withdraw – if they objected after the fourth verbal prompt, he ended the study. They were then able to leave.
- He observed the participants, as did others, through a mirror. If the participant became unduly distressed, as one did, then the study was terminated.
- Milgram thought beforehand that the obedience levels were not likely to be high enough for the participants to become distressed. He asked colleagues and he also asked other people. Nobody thought the participants would go as far as they did, so the ethical issues were not anticipated. By asking colleagues, Milgram was checking his own competence, so he adhered to that principle.

Explanation

The British Psychological Society's (BPS) Code of Ethics and Conduct has four main principles and within them many guidelines. The four main principles are responsibility, respect, integrity and competence. These principles are fully explained in Chapter 5 (pp. 304–314).

Progress check 1.16

Write out four ways in which Milgram's work might be said to be unethical and four ways it might be said to be ethical.

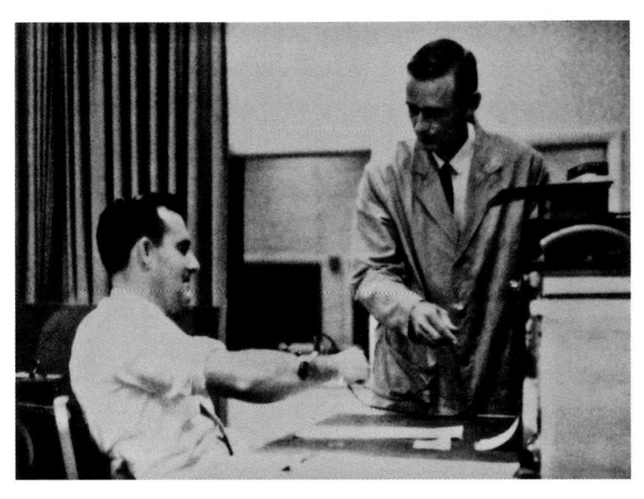

Although Milgram's participants were debriefed and given the right to withdraw, there were nevertheless serious ethical issues with his studies

Ethical issues for participants in Meeus and Raaijmakers' study

Meeus and Raaijmakers (1986) carried out a similar study to Milgram, and similar ethical issues apply:

- Meeus and Raaijmakers (1986) put their participants under stress because the participants did not like making negative remarks when a job applicant was taking a written test. They thought that the applicant might fail the test and they protested. They became distressed, which is against the principle of responsibility.
- Meeus and Raaijmakers did not give the right to withdraw until the participant had resisted their verbal prompts, which were designed to make the participant continue. This is not reminding participants of the right to withdraw, which is against the ethical principle of respect.
- The participants were deceived into thinking that the applicant was applying for a job, whereas he was an accomplice of the researchers, which is against the ethical principle of competence.

Other studies of obedience have similar problems regarding ethics. It is difficult to set up a situation in which someone has to obey an order that will 'harm' another person unless there is some deception, because researchers do not want to actually harm anyone.

STUDY HINT

When comparing studies and focusing on issues in order to make comparisons, it is useful to consider when the study was carried out. Milgram worked in the 1960s, Meeus and Raaijmakers in the 1980s and Slater *et al.* in 2006. Ethical principles have been developed over that time. Perhaps studies should only be evaluated using the ethical principles of the time.

Explore

Consider Slater *et al.*'s (2006) study (pp. 17–19) and Burger's (2009) study (pp. 49–54) and compare them with Milgram's work in terms of ethical issues. What was ethically better with these two, more modern, studies and what was still a problem?

Ethical issues of using findings from obedience studies

Not only are ethical issues important when carrying out research, but ethical issues can also arise in how the results of studies are used. They can be used 'against' a society and they can be used 'for' a society. There are ethical and moral issues in these uses.

STUDY HINT

It is useful to split these two 'sides' to ethics: ethics when doing studies in psychology and ethics when using findings from studies in psychology. When making notes, consider which 'side' you are thinking about and make your notes accordingly. There is a third 'side' that ethics relates to: being a practitioner in psychology – when you study treatments and therapies, that 'side' will be important too.

Milgram (1974, explored in De Vos, 2009) argued that it is important to carry out such studies, even though they involve deception. There is the issue of society needing to know about obedience. For example, if it is known that the Nazis obeyed orders and that anyone is likely to do the same, then maybe society could take steps to try to make sure that this cannot happen. Milgram also felt that his participants gained from the knowledge they had about themselves from the study.

It is also useful to consider issues such as whether certain societies have different obedience issues from others. So when Meeus and Raaijmakers (1986) concluded that people in the Netherlands in the 1980s were as obedient as people in the 1960s in the USA (and possibly Germany in the 1930s), then this is useful information. Meeus and Raaijmakers suggested that their study and the studies of Milgram were carried out within Western society ideas, which helps people to appreciate that there might be different levels of obedience in a different social structure.

Ideas about resistance to obedience and about dissent can be useful for society too (pp. 29–30). If those who have to follow orders may do so blindly, as research into obedience suggests, then it can be useful to highlight when resistance to obedience might be important, such as when orders go against a society's values.

Issues and debates

How psychology is used in society is an issue that you need to explore (not for the AS course, though it can be useful, such as in evaluating studies for their usefulness). Make a section in your notes on issues and debates for 'how psychology is used in society', and include how understanding obedience through studies in psychology can be used in society.

Test yourself

1 Evaluate Milgram's (1963) study in terms of its ethics. **(6 marks)**
2 Discuss the value for society of research into obedience. **(16 marks)**

Extension question:

3 Discuss why Milgram carried out his basic study of obedience and also his variations. In your answer, consider issues such as why he set up the studies in the first place and why he made the methodological decisions that he did. **(16 marks)**

Theories of prejudice

Two theories of prejudice are social identity theory (SIT) and realistic group conflict theory (RCT), also called 'realistic conflict theory'. Both theories are covered in this section. Factors affecting prejudice and discrimination include individual differences (personality), situation and culture, and these are considered later in this section.

What is meant by prejudice and discrimination?

Stereotyping means developing an idea about someone and carrying that idea forward to apply it to other similar people – for example, someone might see a woman as weak and then stereotype all women as weak. Stereotypes are common traits attributed to a large human group. Often the original idea comes from something read or heard, rather than from first-hand experience. Stereotyping leads to **prejudice** when it affects attitude – for example, not only saying that all women are weak but thinking badly (or well) of women because of this. Prejudice leads to **discrimination**, which is an act carried out because of prejudice.

Definitions

Prejudice is an attitude (usually negative); **discrimination** is an action that occurs because of prejudice.

STUDY HINT

Terms that feature in the specification, such as prejudice, must be fully understood, so keep your own glossary, perhaps adding an example to help your understanding of each term. It is useful to have one glossary for 'content' and one for 'method'.

Explore

There are often different meanings for one term so use an online dictionary, such as www.thefreedictionary.com, to explore the meaning in the context of your course.

www.understandingprejudice.org explores prejudice in many ways, including theory around prejudice and examples of prejudice. Be sure to focus on the two theories in your course when you are learning and revising theories. You will find social identity theory on this site as 'in-group favouritism'. When exploring, remember to come back to the 'basics' of what your course requires.

STUDY HINT

Keep a copy of the course specification, or find it online (www.edexcel.com/quals), and check regularly that you know what is required.

Social identity theory as an explanation of prejudice

What is social identity theory?

There are several theories of how prejudice develops. You are required to study **social identity theory**. This is a good explanation of how prejudice can come about and is helpful as an explanation of human behaviour in general.

Tajfel and Turner (1979) suggest that prejudice comes from the formation of two groups, without any other factor being present. The mere existence of two groups causes conflict. Tajfel carried out studies of minimal groups in the early 1970s in Bristol, and the studies show clearly that the creation of two groups leads to prejudicial attitudes.

Social identity theory suggests that a person has several personal 'selves' and that these 'selves' link in with group membership. Different social situations might trigger an individual to act in different ways, perhaps linked to his or her person, family or national membership. An individual also has several social identities (self-concepts).

Social identity comes from how people see themselves in relation to membership of their social groups. Belonging to a group creates in-group self-categorisation, which leads to in-group favouritism and hostility towards the out-group. To enhance self-esteem, people perceive their in-groups as better.

Definition

Social identity is an individual's self-concept.

There are three processes involved in becoming prejudiced against out-group members:

- **Social categorisation** is seeing oneself as part of a group. Any group will do, and there does not have to be conflict with other groups.
- **Social identification** is the process of moving from categorising oneself as part of the in-group to identifying with the group more overtly. An individual is likely to take on the norms and attitudes of group members.
- **Social comparison** with the out-group occurs when the individual's self-concept becomes wrapped up with the in-group. People start to see their in-group as better than the out-group, which enhances their self-esteem. To see their in-group as better, there has to be comparison with the out-group.

There are three variables that contribute to in-group favouritism. These are:

- the extent to which the individuals identify with the in-group
- the extent to which there are grounds for making comparisons with the out-group
- the relevance of the comparison group in relation to the in-group.

If an in-group is central to the individual's self-definition and it is meaningful to make comparisons with the out-group, then there is more likely to be in-group favouritism (which leads to prejudice against the out-group).

Therefore, the idea is that one group for a person is the in-group and that makes other groups out-groups. Tajfel *et al.* (1970, 1971) showed that there is in-group favouritism and that people identify with their in-group. They want to promote their in-group because it enhances their self-esteem.

First, someone categorises themselves as part of a group and then they identify with the group, such as wearing team kit. It is likely that these team members will then compare themselves to other groups and think of themselves as better, which raises the self-esteem of the group members

An example of Tajfel and Turner's theory of in-group behaviour relating to out-group prejudice is perhaps a teenager obsessed with comics – a comic geek. First, the teenager collects comics, finds a group of comic geeks on the internet and categorises themselves as part of that group. Then they pick up on group behaviour and identify with the group, such as maintaining their obsession or becoming more obsessive about collecting comics. Then there is comparison with other groups, and the comic geeks are seen as 'right' and 'knowledgeable', with non-comic collectors as outside the group. Hostility can occur towards the out-group and the comic geeks maintain their self-esteem by being in that group and by raising the status of their group.

Tajfel *et al.* (1970): the study of minimal groups

Tajfel did many studies developing and testing social identity theory. The 1970 study was outlined in another of his articles, and both are explained here as their findings help to explain one another.

Aims

Tajfel *et al.* (1970) wanted to test the idea that prejudice and discrimination can occur between groups even when there is no history between the groups and without any element of competition. Having found such prejudice and discrimination between minimal groups (groups where there is no history or competition), Tajfel *et al.* (1970) wanted to look at factors that might cause such prejudice and discrimination. In order to study discrimination as well as prejudice, it was important to have an experimental situation where actual behaviour was involved, so they aimed to generate a situation where group members had to act in relation to another group.

Procedures

Tajfel carried out two experiments – one created groups from judgements about how many dots were in a scene and the other created groups from an apparent preference for the artists Klee and Kandinsky.

Procedure for the study estimating number of dots

The participants were 64 boys aged 14–15 years from a comprehensive school in Bristol. They were tested in a laboratory in eight separate groups of eight boys. All boys were from the same form and house at school so they knew one another well. First, there was a need to establish in-group categorisation (the formation of the groups) and, second, they wanted to assess the effect of group formation on the behaviour of the boys between the two groups. The boys were taken into a lecture room and told the study was about visual judgements. Forty clusters of a varying number of dots were flashed onto a screen and the boys had to estimate the number of dots and record their estimate on a score sheet. In condition one, after they had estimated the number of dots, they were told that people constantly overestimate or underestimate the number. In condition two, they were told some people are more accurate than others. Then the judgements were 'scored' by one of the experimenters and the boys were told they could help the researchers with something else.

The boys were told that for this other task they would be put into groups according to the judgements they made about the number of dots and that this was just to make it easy to put them into groups. The boys were allocated randomly to the groups. In condition one, they were said to be 'overestimators' or 'underestimators'. In condition two, they were either better at making the judgements or worse.

The boys were told the task was about giving rewards and punishments in real money. They would have to allocate money and they would know the code number allocated to the boy receiving the reward or punishment, and the group he was in. They were shown matrices (Table 1.9). Each matrix had two rows of 14 numbers. The number given was the amount to be allocated to that person. Some numbers had minus signs, which meant that amount of money would be taken away from that person. The boys could not allocate money to themselves, but at the end they would receive the money allocated to them by the other boys. They worked through a booklet of matrices and each time were told 'these are rewards and punishments for member X of your group' or 'these are rewards and punishments for member X of the other group'.

Table 1.9 Example of the matrices in Tajfel *et al.* (1970)

-14	-12	-10											
23	19	15											

The important part of the study was that the boys had to make decisions about what rewards/punishments they would impose, and they were faced with three types of decision: 'in-group/in-group' decisions, 'in-group/out-group' decisions or 'out-group/out-group' decisions. If they allocated as much as possible to one boy, this was given a score of 14, because there were 14 decisions for each row of the matrix. If they allocated as little as possible for a boy, this was given a score of 1. For each decision, they were allocating to two boys, so a fair (equal) score would be 7 to each boy.

Results of experiment one

When decisions involved an 'in-group/out-group' decision (one boy from each group), the average score was 9 out of 14. When boys were making in-group/in-group' or 'out-group/out-group' decisions, the average score was 7.5. It seemed that decisions about boys in the same groups were fairer than decisions about boys from different groups. A large majority gave more money to their own group and showed in-group favouritism. This was found in all trials in the study, and there were eight trials involving eight boys each.

Procedure for the Klee and Kandinsky study

The second experiment involved three new groups of 16 boys each. The boys were shown 12 slides, six showing Klee paintings and six showing Kandinsky paintings. The boys had to express a preference for one of the 'foreign painters'. The paintings did not have the painter's signature so half of the boys could be randomly assigned to 'Klee' and half to 'Kandinsky'.

Explore

If you would like to see the types of paintings used in this study, type 'Klee painting' or 'Kandinsky painting' into a search engine.

Different matrices were used so the experimenters could look at factors that led to the boys making their decisions. From the first experiment, the researchers had found that forming into groups led to in-group favouritism. In this experiment, they looked at:

- maximum joint profit – what was the most the two 'boys' represented by each matrix would 'receive' from the boys?
- maximum in-group profit – what was the most the boys would give to their in-group members?
- maximum difference – what was the most difference between an in-group and out-group member, benefitting the in-group member?

As before, there were three conditions – the 'in-group/in-group' condition, the 'out-group/out-group' condition and the 'in-group/out-group' condition.

Results of the Klee and Kandinsky study

Maximum joint profit did not seem to guide the boys' choices. Maximum in-group profit and maximum difference in favour of the in-group worked against maximum joint profit. If the boys had a choice between maximum joint profit for all and maximum profit for their in-group, they acted on behalf of their own group. Even if giving more to the other group did not mean giving less to their own, they still gave more to their own.

Conclusions of the studies

- Out-group discrimination is present and is easily triggered.
- There is no need for groups to be in intense competition, which goes against what Sherif said when putting forward realistic conflict theory (see pp. 37–38).
- In these experiments, all they needed was to see themselves in an in-group/out-group situation and discrimination ensued.
- People act according to the social norms they have learnt, such as favouring the in-group.
- The boys responded to the social norms of 'groupness' and fairness and they kept a balance between the two.
- In real life, 'groupness' may over-ride fairness – for example, if the group is more important than Klee/Kandinsky or counting numbers of dots.
- Teams in schools may not be such a good idea given the side effects of discrimination that were found in these experiments.

Evaluation of Tajfel *et al.* (1970)

Strengths

- The study used controls, which means cause-and-effect conclusions can be drawn. The boys were put into groups – these were randomly assigned but made some sense to the boys. There were other controls, such as the number of matrices used and the balance of rewards and punishments to be allocated.
- The study used a fairly large number of boys and it was run more than once with the same findings, so the findings are reliable. All eight trials in the first experiment found in-group favouritism and out-group discrimination, as did the trials in the second study.

Weaknesses

- These were minimal groups. Although this was a strength, as it helped to show that discrimination can occur even from minimal groups, it is possible that the boys did not see the importance of the task because they were already a group. They may not have taken the task of rewarding and punishing seriously. This means the study lacks validity with regard to the task itself.
- The study took place in a laboratory setting, which means that the task and the setting were unnatural for the boys, so the study lacks ecological validity.

Other studies looking at in-group favouritism and out-group prejudice

Other studies have confirmed in-group favouritism and out-group prejudice. Crocker and Luhtanen (1990) showed that people who think highly of their in-group have a high collective self-esteem and show loyalty to their group. Even when a group is not performing well, there is strong group loyalty. Lalonde (1992) studied a hockey team that was performing badly. The team members knew that other teams were doing better than them, but said they were 'dirtier' in their tactics. Thus, they claimed moral superiority, which was in-group favouritism. When Lalonde watched the matches, he decided that the other teams were not 'dirtier'. Therefore, he had found in-group bias.

There are different causes of prejudice – for example, race in the USA, religion in Northern Ireland and linguistic differences in Belgium. However, Tajfel suggested that there are two features of prejudice that are the same:

- attitudes of prejudice towards an out-group
- discriminatory behaviour towards the out-group.

These are the features that Tajfel focuses on. He says that prejudice and discrimination can arise from genuine competition or can be to release emotional tensions. A vicious circle may be generated.

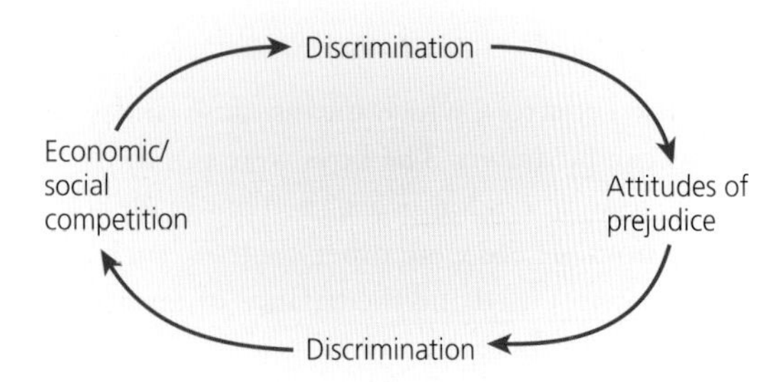

A vicious circle producing prejudice and discrimination

Children also learn such attitudes, so they may be perpetuated even without personal contact. In order to give society order, groups are classified into 'us' and 'them'. There is often competition between in-groups and out-groups and usually people act to benefit their in-group and act against their out-group. Prejudice can arise even without competition between the groups.

Football supporters are an in-group and are likely to be prejudiced against another team, which will be the out-group

Progress check 1.17

Outline the three stages in social identity theory (Tajfel and Turner, 1979) and give a real-life example to explain the three stages.

Evaluation of social identity theory as an explanation of prejudice

Strengths

- There is much evidence that shows in-group favouritism (Crocker and Luhtanen, 1990; Lalonde, 1992; Tajfel *et al.*, 1970, 1971). When there are different studies in different scenarios supporting a theory, it suggests that the theory has merit. The above studies looked at different groups, and found in-group identification and prejudice towards the out-group.

Explore

Search for more studies that find prejudice towards an out-group. Use these as examples when answering exam questions. What sorts of groups are studied? Can you find any evidence to say that there is more prejudice and discrimination in certain in-group/out-group situations than in others?

- The theory has a useful practical application. There are many in-groups in society, from football teams to racial groups. Sometimes, problems that arise can be traced back to the existence of two opposing groups, perhaps two religions in a particular country. People identify with the in-group and are prejudiced towards the out-group, sometimes to the extent of being violent against another group of people, such as when genocide occurs. When a theory can explain real-life events, it is particularly useful because it can suggest ways of solving social problems.
- Willetts and Clarke (2013) discuss problems with nursing professional identity. Nurses have many different social identities and emphasising their interrelatedness and group belongingness can help nurses to develop a professional identity. Willetts and Clarke (2013) suggest that it would be advantageous to use social identity theory to help nurses and their professional identity as this is something that nurses have struggled with, given the diversity in their profession.

Weaknesses

- Social identity theory can be seen as a part of realistic group conflict theory, another theory that attempts to explain prejudice. Rather than just the creation of two groups leading to prejudice, realistic conflict theory says that the two groups are competing in some way. For example, the hockey teams (Lalonde, 1992) were competing to win the tournament. Realistic conflict theory claims that two groups are prejudiced towards one another when there is a goal in sight or when there is the possibility of material gain.

Explanation

It is often the case that two groups live side by side in reasonable harmony until there is competition for resources. This goes against social identity theory as an explanation of prejudice.

- By focusing only on groups, no other factors are taken into account. The theory does not measure how much prejudice there is, such as whether there are some situations in which there is greater prejudice against the out-group. In practice, there are often a number of factors involved (as social impact theory suggests; see pp. 21–24). So having one theory to explain something as complex as prejudice is unlikely to be satisfactory.

Explore

Look at the situation in Nigeria (e.g. www.bbc.co.uk/news/world-africa-28019433) and see how one group has turned against another. There is some distressing material, so do this task only if you wish to. You might want to do this task after learning about realistic group conflict theory. Is the fighting in Nigeria over competition for resources, as realistic conflict theory suggests? Or is it an in-group turning against an out-group, as social identity theory suggests? Boko Haram in Nigeria opposes anything Western, such as Western education, which the government backs.

Look at the situation in Rwanda, and the fighting between the Hutu and Tutsi peoples. The fighting there is over power and resources, as well as memories of past events between the two peoples. What can you find in the situation to relate to social identity theory or realistic group conflict theory? Do you feel the two theories help to explain real-world events?

STUDY HINT

One way of illustrating weakness in a theory is to show how another theory can explain the same events as well as, or better than, the theory being evaluated. Only do this once, because putting forward an alternative theory when evaluating is a single weakness, however many alternatives you mention.

Test yourself

1. Explain how social identity theory explains prejudice. **(6 marks)**
2. Evaluate social identity theory as an explanation of prejudice. **(8 marks)**

Realistic group conflict theory as an explanation of prejudice

A theory of prejudice that was put forward by Sherif (1966), using a study he carried out and wrote about over more than one year, is realistic group conflict theory, also termed 'realistic conflict theory'.

STUDY HINT

Although the content part of each topic area comes first and the studies (a classic study and a contemporary study) come later, the separate sections are often joined. The classic study by Sherif *et al.* (1954/1961) explains realistic conflict and should be used in conjunction with the content about that theory.

What is realistic conflict theory?

The idea is that, when there is conflict between groups, there is prejudice. It is not the case that artificially created groups, which Tajfel called 'minimal groups', lead to prejudice immediately; there must be some sort of competition between groups to cause conflict. Whenever two or more groups are in competition for the same resources, conflict will occur and prejudice follows. There will be negative stereotyping against the 'other' group and discrimination can occur too. Discrimination is prejudice in action, behaviour that comes from prejudiced beliefs. Any groups competing for the same resources will tend to be in-group and out-group (with the out-group threatening the in-group for resources) so the theory does link to social identity theory, though they are seen as two separate theories.

Realistic conflict is thought to arise between two groups only when they are of equal status, but Duckitt (1994) thought that conflict and prejudice would arise even if groups are of unequal status. He thought that realistic conflict explained prejudice that arises through competition over scarce resources when groups have equal status. He thought that when groups do not have equal status, prejudice comes more from in-group and out-group behaviour, with one group dominant over the other group.

Filindra and Pearson-Merkowitz (2013) carried out an examination of data in New England to see if, when a dominant white majority perceives a threat, there is more prejudice and discrimination. They found that a perceived increase in the presence of immigrants in the community did correlate with an immigration policy with more restrictions (as measured by support for Arizona's anti-immigration policy). However, importantly, this was only the case in times of economic hardship and it was not the case at other times. This is as realistic group conflict theory would predict, as this would be about perceived competition for resources.

Explore

You can find Sherif's work on the internet: http://psychclassics.yorku.ca/Sherif/.

Scarce resources may be water and food, or they may be jobs if unemployment is high. They may be territory, financial resources, military resources or social resources (such as friends). In times of scarcity of any resource, prejudice can arise.

Prejudice is more likely if the resource is finite, such as territory. This is called 'zero-sum', where there is one winner and one loser. It may be that some resources are such that one side can 'win' some of the resource and the other lose some – conflict will then be less fierce. How long a conflict over resources lasts can depend on the scarcity of the resource. If it is a finite amount of territory, the conflict can go on for a very long time.

Progress check 1.18

Explain what is meant by 'realistic group conflict theory'.

An example of prejudice arising from realistic group conflict is in the US when a policy was introduced that led to children being transported in buses to different schools to mix the white and black populations. This was very much resisted by the white population and it seemed this was because they feared that their resources would be depleted by the black population. Their prejudice arose through what they saw as competition for scarce resources. The data for this conclusion came from the Michigan National Elections Survey.

When feelings in a group intensify and prejudice arises as the group fights for what they see as scarce resources, this can become **ethnocentrism**, which is defined as a focus on one's own in-group and hostility towards any out-group.

A real-life example of prejudice arising from competition over scarce resources

There are many reasons for the current conflict between Ukraine and Russian forces. One reason is the history over the transportation of gas through Ukraine to Europe by Russia. Russia supplies about 25 per cent of the natural gas consumed in Europe and about 80 per cent of that gas goes through Ukraine to get to Europe. In around 2005, there was a dispute over whether Ukraine was taking some of the gas going through the country, to use for themselves, and this followed an argument about the price of gas and the cost of transporting it through Ukraine. In 2006, the gas was shut off and not sent through Ukraine, who did admit to using some of it. Various agreements followed about gas transportation. Later in 2006, gas was transported again after agreements, but the recession affected Ukraine and left them with gas debts, which they disputed. Ukraine had agreed to take some gas from Russia, paying for it, but they found they did not need as much, though Russia refused to reduce the amount agreed. In 2014, there was more conflict, again about gas, the gas debt and issues around the nationalised gas company.

Russia and Ukraine, in 2015, are fighting, amidst failed ceasefire packages. It is suggested here that at least some of the conflict is about resources, in the form of gas and also territory, over which Russia exports its gas to Europe. Prejudice here seems to stem from competition over resources, although there are also territorial issues. It is rare to find conflict at national level that is explained 'simply' by reference to a shortage of resources, but realistic conflict does seem to fit some, at least, of this conflict.

How realistic conflict ideas can help to reduce prejudice

If competition for scarce resources can lead to prejudice and discrimination, it follows that if people are in the group that is defending or aiming to get these resources, they will work together to achieve their aim. They will be prejudiced against any other group trying to get the same resources. If the groups work together as one group with the shared goal of achieving the resources, and also increasing the likelihood of the resources being achieved, there will be no competition and that will reduce prejudice. To reduce prejudice, **superordinate goals** can be set up, where the goal can only be achieved by people working together. This is what Sherif *et al.* (1954/1961) did and they did find prejudice reduced. An example of how superordinate goals can reduce prejudice is when workers' unions began – people from diverse groups joined together in a common goal, such as around getting fair pay.

Progress check 1.19

How can pursuit of superordinate goals help to reduce prejudice?

Test yourself

Compare the social identity theory of prejudice with the realistic group conflict theory as explanations of prejudice. **(16 marks)**

Factors affecting prejudice (and discrimination)

One theory of prejudice is that it comes from cognition, being about stereotypes, which are stored in memory and trigger prejudice. Other theories are social ones, looking at prejudice coming from group interactions. The two theories explained in this chapter are social ones. A final focus is on personality causing prejudice. An integrative model suggests that prejudice comes from stereotypes being triggered, issues around group interaction and personality characteristics.

This section focuses mainly on prejudice with the assumption that someone who is prejudiced will act in a prejudiced way and, therefore, there will be discrimination.

There are different factors affecting prejudice when looking at both social identity theory and the theory of realistic conflict. Factors that were identified in social identity theory included being part of an in-group, identifying with that group, categorising oneself as part of the group and experiencing hostility towards an out-group to raise self-esteem by raising the esteem of the in-group. Factors identified in realistic group conflict theory included being in competition for resources, such as food and water, political power, jobs and territory. Other issues include conflict over religious beliefs, conflict over previous agreements that put pressure on groups, linking to conflict over resources and conflict over money.

Other factors that can affect prejudice include individual differences, situation and cultural issues, which we turn to now.

The effects of individual differences (personality) on prejudice and discrimination

The personality characteristics most focused on in relation to prejudice are social dominance orientation (SDO) and right-wing authoritarianism (RWA). Cohrs *et al.* (2012), one of the contemporary studies for your course, looks at the effects of individual differences on prejudice and finds that there are relationships between some aspects of personality, right-wing authoritarianism (RWA) and prejudice (pp. 59–66).

Personality dimensions and prejudice

Personality dimensions include the 'Big Five': neuroticism, extraversion, conscientiousness, openness to experience and agreeableness. There are many different theories about personality types and personality traits. This section considers the link between personality and prejudice.

STUDY HINT

Mnemonics are useful when revising - these are memory cues. A mnemonic for the Big Five personality dimensions is 'a cone' (visualise a traffic cone) - **a**greeableness, **c**onscientiousness, **o**penness to experience, **n**euroticism, **e**xtraversion.

Explore

You could try a personality test online. The test on www.outofservice.com/bigfive links to the Big Five and also offers you the chance to rate someone else, which is interesting as it suits Cohrs *et al.* (2012), who gathered both self-report data and peer-report data.

Openness to experience shows a negative relationship to prejudice – the more someone is open to experience, the less they are likely to be prejudiced against others. Agreeableness too has a negative relationship with prejudice. Conscientiousness, however, can link to right-wing authoritarianism and prejudice. Recent studies such as Cohrs *et al.* (2012) show that it is not so much that personality dimensions link directly with prejudice, but they underpin ideological attitudes, such as right-wing authoritarianism and social dominance orientation, and these ideological attitudes underpin prejudice, although in Cohrs *et al.*'s study, they show that personality dimensions *can* link directly with prejudice.

Definition

Ideological attitudes focus on social needs and wishes of a group or a society, or indeed an individual. They link to political ideas and refer to someone's outlook on how a society should be and can function.

Adorno *et al.* (1950)

Adorno *et al.* (1950) focused on personality and fascism, which involves prejudice. They used questionnaires that used a 'fascism scale' and measured people's responses to find out about a tendency to fascism. This study came after the end of the Second World War when people were trying to make sense of the horrific acts involved. The researchers uncovered what they called an authoritarian personality, which related to being prejudiced. They also interviewed some of the respondents to dig deeper about what contributed to prejudice. This use of multi-methods was a strength of their work. Adorno *et al.* described people with an authoritarian personality as being rigid in their thinking, obedient to authority, seeing the world in black and white, and adhering to social hierarchy and social rules. Already you can see that an authoritarian outlook is likely to lead to obedience, as discussed earlier in this chapter.

Adorno *et al.* thought that those with an authoritarian outlook were those likely to be prejudiced and to show discrimination, especially to low-status groups, reflecting ideas of hierarchy in a society.

Right-wing authoritarianism (RWA) and prejudice

Later studies continued to look at dimensions of personality, how such dimensions link with authoritarianism and what 'authoritarianism' is. There is a strand of authoritarianism that links to a political focus, called 'right-wing authoritarianism'. This is often looked at currently as predicting prejudice and discrimination. It has been found that right-wing authoritarianism does correlate with prejudiced attitudes (e.g. Altemeyer, 1996, and other studies).

Definition

Right-wing authoritarianism (RWA) refers to someone who has rigid thinking and likes society to have rules, which people must stick to, so that society can function. Someone with such an ideological attitude will obey the rules and obey those in authority - they will also want to punish anyone who does not obey the rules. They prefer it that everyone agrees to submit to authority rather than having to force people.

Social dominance orientation (SDO) and prejudice

Those who believe in social hierarchy are more likely than others to be prejudiced towards low-status groups and, in particular, they want their own group to dominate over other groups (this is called 'social dominance orientation') (e.g. Pratto *et al.*, 1994). Rigid thinking also correlates with prejudice. Later studies supported the findings of Adorno *et al.* (1950).

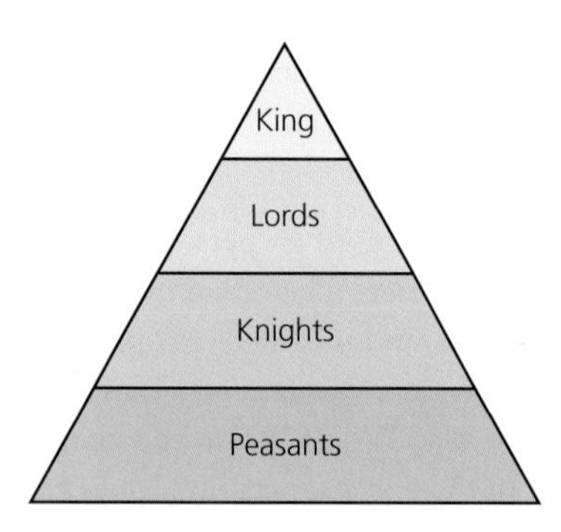

A feudal hierarchy – those with social dominance orientation (SDO) see the world in terms of hierarchy and dominance and want their own group to dominate, which links to prejudice

> **Definition**
>
> **Social dominance orientation** (SDO) refers to an ideological attitude and someone who sees society as hierarchical with themselves in a position of dominance over those of lower status. People with this ideological attitude are not egalitarian – they do not believe in equality in a society.

RWA, SDO and personality dimensions, and prejudice

Cohrs *et al.* (2012) carried out a study looking at relationships between a) right-wing authoritarianism (RWA) and social dominance orientation (SDO), which they called 'ideological attitudes', b) the Big Five personality dimensions (neuroticism, extraversion, conscientiousness, openness to experience and agreeableness), and c) prejudice (for full details of this study, see pp. 59–66). Their findings included that right-wing authoritarianism correlated with prejudice, which supports Adorno *et al.* They also found that openness to experience correlated with right-wing authoritarianism, though negatively, so the more open someone is the less they show such authoritarianism. They also discussed the findings of other studies showing links between personality dimensions, ideological attitudes and prejudice. The links do seem to be very strong, even though there are subtleties in the findings.

> **STUDY HINT**
>
> The classic and contemporary studies are in your course so that you can read about areas in more depth. You should use Cohrs *et al.* (2012) to consider how personality might affect prejudice and discrimination.

> **Progress check 1.20**
>
> Explain the idea that ideological attitudes mediate (come between) personality characteristics and prejudice.

The effects of situation on prejudice and discrimination

Both the situation and personality are involved in prejudice

Personality is often examined in relation to prejudice, as your studies in Year 1 will show you. However, social psychology also looks at how the situation can lead to prejudice. Guimond *et al.* (2003) discuss whether the power of the situation can over-ride personality when it comes to prejudice. They suggest that the way prejudice can rise and fall over time, such as a high level of prejudice in Germany during the Second World War, suggests that prejudice cannot be down to personality alone as that would not explain such variations (e.g. Brown, 1995, cited in Akrami *et al.*, 2009). Personality is seen as stable and enduring, so sudden changes in prejudice must be affected by the situation.

Akrami *et al.* (2009) suggest that personality characteristics are present in situations where there is prejudice, even if it seems they do not totally account for such prejudice. They point out that not all Germans were anti-semitic during the Second World War and not all the US soldiers attacked Iraqi prisoners at Abu Ghraib. There can be strong influence from situational factors; however, this does not mean that personality factors do not affect prejudice and discrimination.

> **Explanation**
>
> Abu Ghraib was a place where Iraqis were kept prisoner, guarded by US soldiers, and it is well-documented that there was abuse by US soldier guards. The abuse was revealed in 2003, in a report by Amnesty International.

Richard *et al.* (2003, cited in Akrami *et al.*, 2009) looked at 322 studies and concluded that both situational effects and personality effects contribute to prejudice, perhaps in equal measure. Cooper and Whitney (2009) also consider the balance of situational and personality effects on prejudice and suggest that, in examples of strong prejudice, situational factors seem strong. However, where prejudice is less strong, personality factors might account for more of the prejudice.

Changing social norms or perceived threat can led to prejudice

Situational factors affecting prejudice can link to social norms as social norms in a society tend to work against prejudice, so it will be failure in social norms or changing social norms that will lead to prejudice in a society, and these are considered situational factors. Social threat can also lead to prejudice, and is also a situational factor. Threat in fact links to personality in that right-wing authoritarianism means threat is feared and so actions that mitigate threat will be supported. Such responses, to allay fear, can be discrimination and prejudice.

Akrami *et al.* (2009) manipulated a social norm and then tested for prejudice. Their hypothesis was that a manipulated social norm would affect prejudice, and is a situational factor, but that personality factors would remain the same. This would show that situation affected prejudice. Their manipulation of the social norm was focused on sexism and they set up a situation on a university campus where there was a focus on prejudice (sexism) being reduced and against the norm – this was the experimental condition. In the control group, there was no experience of this changed norm. The experimental group, focusing on the 'no prejudice' norm, should display less prejudice than the control group if the situation (the changed norm) affected prejudice. They used an independent groups design, where half were randomly allocated to the 'changed norm' group and half to the control condition, with equal numbers of males and females in each group. This was random sampling but within a 'sex-stratified' design.

STUDY HINT

Note Akrami *et al.*'s (2009) sampling techniques as they can be useful as evidence when you are discussing sampling techniques in studies in psychology.

What was measured in Akrami *et al.* (2009) was similar to Cohrs *et al.* (2012). Scales were used to measure SDO, RWA, the Big Five and prejudice (which was about sexism – attitudes to women). The study had each participant sitting at a computer completing the scales. The difference in the 'changed norm' condition was that, as part of the sexism questionnaire, there was a comment about discrimination of women no longer being a problem. In the 'no change of norm' condition this comment was not found. They found that both situational factors (in this case, the changed norm) and personality factors (such as SDO, RWA and openness to experience, which was negatively correlated with prejudice) linked to prejudice.

Issues and debates

Akrami *et al.* (2009) comment that their results confirmed those of Pettigrew (1958). Pettigrew found that levels of prejudice might be affected by situational factors but the underlying personality traits remained. You could use past prejudice research to show similarities in psychology findings over time, which is one of the issues and debates in your course.

Some situational factors have been explored here, including changing social norms, which can affect prejudice in a society, and also level of perceived or actual threat. Situational factors include whether there is conflict, as realistic conflict theory suggests. Situational factors also relate to in-group and out-group situations, as social identity theory suggests.

One other way of looking at the effects of situation on prejudice and discrimination is to consider in what situations prejudice can occur and, importantly, how the situation can be used to reduce prejudice.

The contact hypothesis – to reduce prejudice

Allport (1954) discussed inter-group contact theory: if the situation is set up so that people in different groups have contact with one another, this can help to reduce prejudice and discrimination. This can be called the 'contact hypothesis'. This works with minority groups in that a majority group can then meet members of the minority group and find out more about them and their views, helping reduce prejudice in certain circumstances. In order for contact to work in reducing prejudice:

- there must be equal status between the people making contact – if they do not have equal status, the situation should be manipulated so that differences are minimised
- the groups should be working towards a common goal/s
- contact should be harmonious and there should be co-operation to meet the common goal
- both groups need to acknowledge the authority of the people that have brought them together
- all participants should feel comfortable in the situation
- there should be personal interaction between the people making contact, so that they can learn about one another and hear each other's views.

Additional ideas are:

- the minority group should behave in a way that does not fit the stereotype the majority group have of them
- the contact should occur often and not just in one social situation
- the minority group members should be seen as typical of their group, not atypical.

The above situational factors can help to reduce prejudice. Conversely, Table 1.10 outlines situations where prejudice might arise.

Table 1.10 **Situations where prejudice might arise between a minority and majority group (or at least will not be reduced)**

Situation not harmonious between groups	Nobody there to manage the 'listening' between groups	No equal status between the groups	Insufficient contact between groups
Not feeling comfortable in group situations	No interpersonal communication between groups	No common goal or common ground between groups	Minority group behaving 'stereotypically'

Conclusion

It seems clear that situations lead to prejudice, from changing norms, to times of threat, to the formation of in-groups and out-groups, to competition over scarce resources. These factors can be affected as well by whether the groups talk to each other or meet, whether they are of different status and whether they have common goals.

However, even when situations lead to prejudice, studies find that there are stable personality characteristics that 'go with' prejudice and discrimination. These are having a right-wing authoritarian outlook, an ideology of social dominance and conscientiousness. Characteristics that 'go away' from prejudice are agreeableness and openness to experience.

The effects of culture on prejudice and discrimination

Theories of prejudice can be 'universal' and apply to all cultures

Social identity theory, realistic conflict theory and social dominance orientation are all theories that can account for prejudice, regardless of culture. It is claimed by social identity theory that all cultures would be seen to have in-groups and out-groups and inter-group conflict is found in those countries. Realistic conflict theory too can be applied in different countries and cultures, as, according to the theory, where there is competition for resources, there is prejudice. Social dominance orientation (SDO) is the attitude that societies are hierarchical, which leads to prejudice and discrimination against those of lower status. SDO, as with social identity theory and realistic conflict theory, can be found in different cultures. These three theories look for universal laws about prejudice.

Another factor that might affect prejudice and discrimination is culture. There might be **across-culture** similarities, such as those outlined above, but there can be **between-culture** differences, as discussed below.

Definition

Across-culture means something is found in all cultures (or many cultures) and is perhaps universal, which means it is found in all human societies. It is found 'across all cultures'. This is known as **'emic'**. **Between-culture** means there are differences between cultures and so it is not universal. This is known as **'etic'**.

Ideological attitudes may differ between cultures

It might be thought that different cultural attitudes would affect levels of prejudice and discrimination, but the ideological attitudes looked at in studies, like right-wing authoritarianism and social dominance orientation, tend to be stable across cultures. Adorno *et al.* (1950) gathered data from the Americas, Cohrs *et al.* (2012) gathered data in Germany, Akrami *et al.* (2009) worked in Sweden, and Duckitt and Sibley (2010) worked in Australia. Pettigrew (1998) looked at whether factors that affect prejudice differed in different countries (Netherlands, the UK, France and West Germany) and found that there were universals with regard to what affects prejudice – more accurately, he found similarities in these four countries.

Issues and debates

It might not always be the case, but often when universal laws are claimed, this might be because the feature is in our nature. If something is different between cultures, and is not universal, that might be down to nurture because what differs between cultures is environment and effects of the environment. This argument relates to the nature-nurture debate. However, be aware that something can be found in many cultures because it is useful for a society's functioning rather than because it is innate.

Cultural norms and prejudice

Different cultures have different cultural norms (including how cultures are treated in a society) and these can affect levels of prejudice. Guimond *et al.* (2013) thought that cultures where there was multiculturalism (MC) would show less prejudice than those featuring assimilation (AS) in their culture. They looked at the pro-diversity policy of four Western countries. Multiculturalism would be pro-diversity, in that different cultures would live together, and assimilation would be less pro-diversity as the idea would be that cultures are incorporated into one country. The researchers used countries that had a low, medium or high pro-diversity policy. They found that anti-Muslim attitudes were reduced when the pro-diversity policy was high. They also found that countries had different views about multiculturalism and assimilation and that these views went along with the actual policies of the countries, regardless of individual attitudes.

STUDY HINT

Cultural norms can affect someone's beliefs and attitudes, which can be said to show that we develop under the influence of our environment, perhaps interacting with our personality. You need to be aware when developmental issues are raised, so when you see the developmental psychology icon, make notes accordingly. Or you can go back through this book to make notes about development, by looking for the icon.

Matusmoto (2007, cited in Guimond *et al.*, 2013) suggests that cultures are different because of different issues and problems they have had to (or have to) deal with, so they develop different ways of living. Countries with immigration have had political discussion about such issues, coming up with the idea either of multiculturalism, where all cultures are accepted and one is not 'right', or assimilation, where a main culture takes other cultures in and they accept the main norms.

Multiculturalism is a policy whereby many different ways of living are accepted within one country rather than one group being dominant, meaning that other beliefs and traditions are assimilated

In assimilation, the incoming culture or group must adopt the language and ways of the 'receiving' culture, the dominant group. Countries that favour assimilation are not wanting diversity and are categorised as low in pro-diversity (e.g. Meuleman and Reeskens, 2008, cited in Guimond *et al.*, 2013). Guimond *et al.* (2013) say that multiculturalism as an alternative to assimilation became popular in the 1970s, seeing acceptance of other cultures as positive. Multiculturalism supports diversity and is categorised as high in pro-diversity. Assimilation as an ideology (which means a way of seeing how society can fulfil its needs) links to prejudiced attitudes, whereas multiculturalism is more positive with regard to how groups interact with one another.

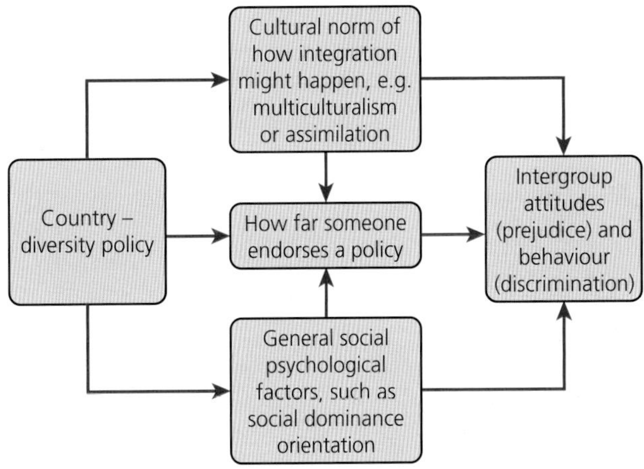

How cultural norms and attitudes, as well as individual ideology, can relate to prejudice and discrimination (adapted from Guimond *et al.*, 2013)

Guimond *et al.* (2013) make the point that studies linking policies like multiculturalism to a reduction in prejudice and stereotyping tend to take place only in one country, and what is needed is to study different countries to see how the country's diversity policy affects prejudice and discrimination in the country. Looking at prejudice and comparing countries with different diversity policies would be useful. Their hypothesis was that the stronger the pro-diversity policy in a country, the lower the prejudice. They felt that, for example, multiculturalism would show less prejudice (e.g. Verkuyten, 2005, cited in Guimond *et al.*, 2013). If different countries with different pro-diversity policies show different levels of prejudice, this does suggest that there are cultural influences when it comes to prejudice.

Personality dimensions are not likely to differ between all countries (they are said to be stable and enduring characteristics in general) and RWA and SDO have been found in different cultures, so it would be the different diversity policies and different norms that are likely to give differences in prejudice between countries.

Guimond *et al.* (2013) concluded that, although all countries to an extent are multicultural, they do not all have that policy explicitly and when the policy of a country is multiculturalism as opposed to assimilation, then there is reduced prejudice in relations between groups. The lowest level of prejudice in their study was found in Canada and the highest was found in Germany. Levels in the US and the UK were somewhere in between. Canada and the US, and to an extent the UK, according to Guimond *et al.*, have stronger norms relating to multiculturalism, and more focus on cultural diversity, than Germany. The study did not ask about personal support for either multiculturalism or assimilation; the questions were about the norms of the country, which were the cultural norms around integration. The researchers cite Becker *et al.* (2012), who looked at data from 21 cultural groups and found that there were effects of cultural norms with regard to prejudice that were over and above personal beliefs and attitudes.

Progress check 1.21

Give three pieces of evidence that suggest that cultural norms can affect prejudice.

Test yourself

Evaluate two factors that might affect prejudice.
(12 marks)

Methods in social psychology

What is required and how this book covers that requirement

In all the topic areas, there is a section on methods. In your course, you need to cover certain methods and issues around methods, and these are spread through the Year 1/AS topic areas (and there is method material in Year 2 as well). In social psychology, the research methods covered are questionnaire and interview. As has been seen, social psychology research does also use experiments, but interviews and questionnaires are the chosen research methods for this part of the course. Chapter 5 presents 'method' material for all the Year 1/AS topic areas and Chapter 6 gives 'maths' material for all the Year 1/AS topic areas. The maths material is part of the method in your course; however, having a separate chapter will help you to focus on the maths and the other method issues you need. There follows a brief list of what you need to know within social psychology. For more detail, read Chapters 5 and 6.

In social psychology, you will need to know about:

- designing and conducting questionnaires to gather self-report data, including issues around open and closed questions and ranked-scale questions

Method link: for more on designing and conducting questionnaires, go to Chapter 5 (pp. 283–294).

Practical link: in social psychology, you are asked to design and carry out a questionnaire study, which will help you put what you learn into practice. Chapter 7 explores more about practical investigations. A social psychology practical can be found on pp. 417–430.

STUDY HINT

Some of the 'maths' element in your psychology course is in GCSE Maths, so you should have already learned about it, such as measures of central tendency, graphs and measures of dispersion. Be ready to 'transfer' learning from GCSE Maths to AS and A level Psychology. However, there is full guidance throughout the course if you are not sure.

- designing and conducting interviews to gather self-report data, including issues around how structured an interview is, including knowing there are structured, semi-structured and unstructured forms of interviewing

Explore

The following link gives an account of using interviews to gather qualitative data, in a specific area of research (for your interest): www.nature.com/bdj/journal/v204/n6/full/bdj.2008.192.html. Read it and relate what is in this article to what is outlined in this section. Consider some of the strengths and weaknesses of using such a method when studying psychology.

- general issues of methodology – in this case, knowing about the alternate hypothesis
- sampling techniques, including the four sampling techniques of random, stratified, volunteer and opportunity

Method link: Chapter 5 explains more about hypotheses (pp. 318–319) and sampling and sampling techniques (pp. 299–304).

STUDY HINT

In other subjects, such as at GCSE, you have probably come across different sampling techniques, so draw on that understanding as much as you can, as that will help your learning.

- analysing quantitative data, including being able to work out measures of central tendency (mean, median, mode as appropriate) and how to draw frequency tables and graphs, and bar charts. You also need to know about measures of dispersion (the range and the standard deviation of a set of scores)

Maths link: Chapter 6 explains the maths element that you need for your course. Descriptive statistics can be found on pp. 387–396.

- analysis of qualitative data using thematic analysis
- research method issues around bias, including researcher bias, social desirability and demand characteristics
- issues of reliability, validity, generalisability, credibility and objectivity

Method link: Chapter 5 explains more about analysis of qualitative data, including using thematic analysis (pp. 290–292); issues of bias when carrying out a study (pp. 285 and 288) and issues of validity, reliability, generalisability, credibility and objectivity (p. 379).

- ethical guidelines in psychology, including the British Psychological Society's Code of Ethics and Conduct (2009), and principles of respect, responsibility, integrity and competence; also risk management issues when researching in psychology.

Method link: Chapter 5 explains more about ethical issues in psychology (pp. 304–314).

Progress check 1.22

List the three main types of interview, four sampling techniques you need to know and the four main ethical principles in the BPS Code of Ethics and Conduct.

Studies in social psychology

For each topic area, you need to cover one classic study and one contemporary study. With regard to the contemporary study, you will choose one from three named studies. This book covers all three contemporary studies so you can choose the one that you are using in your course.

For social psychology, the classic study is Sherif *et al.* (1954/1961), an experiment on prejudice using boys in a summer camp. The contemporary studies are Burger (2009), who did a replication of Milgram's study, Reicher and Haslam (2006), who did an experiment/case study to look at prisoner and guard behaviour, and Cohrs *et al.* (2012), who considered personality issues with regard to prejudice.

Classic study: Sherif *et al.* (1954/1961)

Sherif carried out research into groups, leadership and the effect of groups on attitudes and behaviour. The Robbers Cave study – so-called because it took place at a camp in Robbers Cave State Park, Oklahoma – built on his previous work and there were later records of the study too (that is why two dates are given for this study). He thought that social behaviour could not be studied by looking at individuals in isolation. He recognised that social organisation differs between cultures and affects group practices, citing, for example, that in America discussion is seen as a useful learning method but that this is not the case in India, where dependence on authority is more valued. So, he claimed that groups have to be understood as part of a social structure. The Robbers Cave study involved setting up two groups of similar participants (11-year-old boys) to find out:

- how the groups developed
- if and how conflict between the groups arose
- how to reduce any such friction.

STUDY HINT

The Robbers Cave study is an example of how the social approach focuses on interactions between people, rather than on individuals. It is also useful for answering questions about prejudice.

The conflict could be seen as prejudice; reduction of friction would be reducing prejudice. Therefore, the study has a practical application.

Three terms defined according to Sherif are:

- **small group** – individuals share a common goal that fosters interaction; individuals are affected differently by being in a group; an in-group develops with its own hierarchy and a set of norms is standardised
- **norm** – a product of group interaction that regulates the behaviour of members in terms of the expected or ideal behaviour
- **group** – a social unit with a number of individuals who are interdependent and have a set of norms and values for self-regulation; individuals have roles within the unit.

STUDY HINT

The definitions of small groups, norm and group are useful when answering questions about explanations of terms. They could be added to your glossary of terms (theory, not method).

Aims

The aims of the Robbers Cave study were to use a field experiment to produce group norms and to measure their effects on the perceptions and judgements of those involved. The plan was to use a real-life situation to lead to group norms and values. The researchers wanted to see how in-group behaviour developed to include related out-group hostility and to see how such friction could be reduced. The study looked at relationships within each group and at how the two groups related to one another. It was a study of **inter-group** relations.

The researchers aimed to trace the formation and functioning of negative and positive attitudes of members of one group towards members of another group. They examined how attitudes and behaviours developed and changed as a result of controlled alterations in conditions.

> **Definition**
> **Inter-group** means between two (or more) groups; **intra-group** means relations within a single group.

Procedure

Participants

The participants were 22 boys, aged 11 years, who did not know each other before the study. The boys were matched as far as possible and split into two groups of 11. They were all from Protestant families in Oklahoma and were screened to eliminate problems at home or other difficulties that might account for individual attitudes and behaviour. As part of the matching process, the boys were rated (including IQ) by teachers. When the boys were divided into two groups, they were reassessed and also matched for the split, including issues such as sporting ability. In order to produce 'natural' groups, participants were not informed that they were part of a study and were kept unaware of the aims of the camp. A nominal fee was charged for the camp and parents were asked not to visit, ostensibly because it might make the boys homesick.

> **STUDY HINT**
> Learning a study involves knowing evaluation points about it as well as description points. In the description of the participants, there are issues you can consider for evaluation, such as the ethical issue of deception, and the control element, such as the matching of the boys in the two groups. Think about such issues as you read a description of a study and perhaps make notes, ready for your own evaluation of the study.

Data collection

One important feature of the study was the range of data collection methods:

- ***Observation*** – a participant observer was allocated to each group for 12 hours a day.
- ***Sociometric analysis*** – issues such as friendship patterns were noted and studied.
- ***Experiment*** – e.g. the boys had to collect beans and estimate how many each boy had collected.
- ***Tape recordings*** – adjectives and phrases used to refer to their own group members and to out-group members were examined.

The participant observers were trained not to influence the boys' decision-making, but to help them once decisions had been reached. The researchers claimed that using different data-gathering methods, with similar results, meant that their results were valid.

The camp

The location was a 200-acre Boy Scouts of America camp, completely surrounded by Robbers Cave State Park. The site was isolated and keeping the two groups of boys apart at first was easy because of the layout of the site.

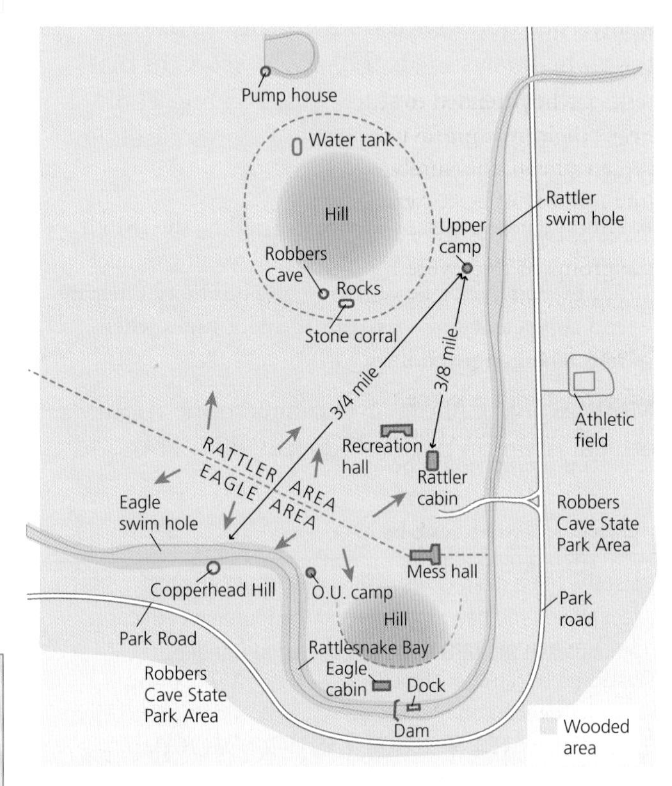

General layout of the Robbers Cave camp and respective areas of the two groups

The three stages of the study

- **Stage 1**: the two groups were formed and set up norms and hierarchies (to see how they became in-groups).
- **Stage 2**: the two groups were introduced and competition was set up in the form of a tournament (to see if this led to friction, name-calling and hostility to the out-group).
- **Stage 3**: the two groups were set goals that they needed each other to achieve (to see if **superordinate goals** led to the reduction of friction).

Definition

Superordinate goals are goals in which the resources and energies of either single group are not adequate for the attainment of the goal. To achieve the goal, two groups have to work together.

Stage 1: in-group formation

The two groups were kept apart for one week to help the formation of group norms and relations. They had to work as a group to achieve common goals that required co-operation. Data were gathered by observation, including rating of emerging relationships, sociometric measures and experimental judgements. Status positions and roles in the groups were studied. There is much detail about how hierarchies within each group developed. The measurements were thought to be both valid and reliable because different data collection methods produced similar results. For example, in the bean-collecting task, the boys tended to overestimate the number of beans their own group members had collected and underestimate the number collected by the other group (the number of beans was, in fact, the same). During Stage 1, two boys were allowed to go home from one of the groups as they were homesick – this left 11 in one group and nine in the other.

Stage 2: inter-group relations, the friction phase

After the first week, the two groups were told about one another and a tournament was set up with competitive activities. Points could be earned for the group and there were rewards. As soon as they heard about each other, the two groups became hostile. They wanted to play each other at baseball, so they effectively set up their own tournament, which was what the researchers wanted.

The aim behind the competition was to make one group frustrated because of the other group, to see if negative attitudes developed. Adjectives and phrases were recorded to see if they were derogatory and behaviour was observed as previously. The researchers introduced the 'collecting beans' experiment. The boys had to collect beans and then judge how many each boy had collected. This was to see if the boys overestimated the abilities of the in-group members and minimised the abilities of the out-group members.

STUDY HINT

Tajfel *et al.* (1970, 1971) used similar tasks to the bean task. He also found that members of the in-group talked up the abilities of their group members at the expense of the out-group members. The findings of Sherif *et al.* can be used when discussing social identity theory.

Stage 3: inter-group relations, the integration phase

The researchers wanted to achieve harmony between the two groups. First, they introduced tasks that simply brought the two groups together so they could communicate. They then introduced superordinate goals, which are outlined below.

The researchers measured the use of derogatory terms and used observation and rating of stereotyping.

Results

Stage 1: in-group formation

Near the end of Stage 1 the boys gave themselves names – the Rattlers and the Eagles. The groups developed similarly; they had been matched carefully, so this might be expected. However, there were some differences, partly because their cabins were situated in different places, which affected their decisions.

For both groups, status positions settled over the last few days of the first week and there was some stability; both groups had a recognised leader. The Rattlers discussed the existence of the other group frequently, once they knew about them. For example, they said 'they had better not be in our swimming hole'. The Eagles did not refer to the Rattlers as much, but they started to become more competitive and asked to play a game against them. It seemed that the very existence of the out-group led to hostility.

Stage 2: inter-group relations, the friction phase

As soon as the groups found out about each other, they wanted to compete at baseball, so they had naturally moved themselves on to Stage 2. The Rattlers were excited and discussed issues such as protecting their flag. The Eagles were not as keen as the Rattlers, but they made comments such as 'we will beat them'. The boy who was elected as baseball captain for the Eagles became their leader for all of Stage 2, although he was not the leader at the end of Stage 1. When the two groups first came into contact, there was some name-calling. A great deal of evidence was collected, including what the boys did and said, who they were friends with and practical issues, such as the burning of one of the flags. It was found that there were clearly negative attitudes towards the out-group members.

Stage 3: inter-group relations, the integration

During the initial contacts in this stage, hostility between the two groups remained. There were comments such as 'ladies first' and, when they watched a film together, they sat in their own groups. After seven contact activities, the need to work together was set up with situations where there were superordinate goals:

- First, the staff turned off the valve to the water supply and placed two large boulders over it. The boys were told that vandals had damaged the system in the past. The boys worked together to restore the system. When the water came through, they rejoiced in common.
- The second goal was to get a movie by chipping in to pay for it. They agreed eventually that both groups should contribute equally, even though one group had fewer members than the other group (two boys from the Eagles had earlier left the camp due to homesickness). There was co-operation between the two groups.

Table 1.11 Friendship choices of in-group and out-group members at the end of Stage 3

	Rattlers	Eagles
In-group choices of friends	63.6%	76.8%
Out-group choices of friends	36.4%	23.2%

- The third goal involved all the boys going on a trip to Cedar Lake, which required transport. As they were about to leave, the truck 'developed' a problem and they had to use the tug-of-war rope to pull it to try to get it started.

Table 1.12 Friendships compared between the end of Stage 2 and the end of Stage 3

	Rattlers	Eagles
Out-group friendship choices at end of Stage 2	6.4%	7.5%
Out-group friendship choices at end of Stage 3	36.4%	23.2%

There were other, similar situations. The result was reduced friction and increased co-operation between the groups. At the end of Stage 3, friendship choices were still found more within the in-groups but it was noticeable how friendships differed between Stage 2 and Stage 3. More out-group members were chosen as friends by the end of Stage 3, which is evidence that friction was reduced.

STUDY HINT

When writing about a study, and in particular this classic study, be sure to learn some results in the form of figures, to add depth to your knowledge and understanding of the study.

Conclusions

The hypotheses put forward at the start of the study were largely confirmed. The conclusions include the following:

- Picking matched participants ruled out home background or individual factors that would explain the attitudes and behaviour of the boys.
- Groups developed status hierarchies and group norms, although they were not stable throughout the study.
- Each group had a leadership structure by the end of the first week.
- Leader–follower relations developed as a result of having to solve problems through combined action; as group structure stabilised, an in-group formed.
- When two groups meet in competition and in frustrating situations, in-group solidarity and co-operation increases and inter-group hostility is strong.
- Because of the various means of collection, the data were considered valid.
- People tend to overestimate the abilities of their own group members and to minimise the abilities of out-group members.
- Contact between two groups is not enough to reduce hostility.
- When groups needed to work together, exchanged tools, shared responsibilities and agreed how to solve problems, friction was reduced. One example of working towards a superordinate goal was not sufficient, however; they needed to co-operate more than once.

Evaluation of Sherif *et al.* (1954/1961)

Sherif *et al.* (1954/1961) pointed out the strengths of the Robbers Cave study, but they did not point out the weaknesses.

Strengths

- There was careful planning and controls. Previous studies were used to show what was necessary – for example, the need to enable the groups to develop as naturally as possible and to brief observers not to advise when decisions were being made. The participants were matched carefully so that individual differences would not affect their attitudes and judgements. The planning and controls enabled cause-and-effect conclusions to be drawn confidently.
- The validity of the findings. The researchers used participant observers because they knew from previous research that participants' behaviour is affected when they know that they are being watched. The participants did not know that they were part of an experiment, so their behaviour was natural. Several data collection methods were used so that the findings could be compared to make sure that they were valid.

Weaknesses

- Informed consent was not obtained – the boys did not know that they were part of a study, which meant that there was deception. Parents were informed more fully, but they were asked not to visit and could not check whether the boys were happy at the camp. Debriefing is not mentioned and may not have taken place. The researchers wrote a book about the study, but some ethical issues are not considered. However, the account does not suggest that the boys were treated unethically or were unhappy.

- It might be difficult to generalise the findings beyond the type of participants used because they were so carefully selected. They were 11-year-old boys from similar family and school backgrounds, and with fairly similar abilities. It might, therefore, be hard to say that findings would be true of others – for example, girls, those in other cultures, those with 'difficult' backgrounds and those with less sporting ability. Generalising is difficult when the sample is restricted, even though the restriction was deliberate to help the study.

Progress check 1.23

Test yourself on the numbers. How many boys were in each group? For each group, what percentage of friends did they have in their own group and what percentage of friends did they have in the other group at the end of stage 3? What was the difference for each group in the percentage of out-group friends before and after the introduction of the superordinate goals?

Test yourself

1. Explain why Sherif *et al.* matched the boys when they split the groups. **(2 marks)**
2. Explain how prejudice was formed according to the Robbers Cave study. **(2 marks)**
3. Evaluate the Robbers Cave study, including focusing on validity and generalisability. **(8 marks)**

Contemporary studies

Burger (2009)

Burger (2009) carried out a study replicating Milgram's work. You will need to recall Milgram's work from earlier in this chapter, so that you can understand Burger's study sufficiently.

Background 1

Milgram's Experiment 5 was one of his variations, but is not covered in the content section of your course. Experiment 5 is called the 'new baseline' condition. Milgram had taken the study to the rundown office block and found that there was still obedience, despite the less impressive conditions than Yale, where the original study took place. He wondered what else in the situation would affect the results. He decided to introduce the idea that the 'victim' had a heart condition, and he arranged for this to be mentioned when the victim was being strapped into the chair. There was also a strict schedule for the victim to cry out, and this is the important point for Burger's variation study explained here. It was at 150 volts where the 'victim' calls out and demands to be released from the study. There were a few noises before 150 volts, but it is at 150 volts that the 'victim' uses words to protest. Burger calls this point 'the point of no return'. He emphasises that nearly all the participants at this 150 volt stage in Milgram's Experiment 5 turn to the experimenter to check whether they should continue.

Burger points out that 14 out of 40 participants stopped before 450 volts (26 went to the maximum voltage) in Milgram's experiment. One of the 14 stopped before the 150 volt stage, six stopped at 150 volts and only 7 of the 40 went beyond the 150 volts and then stopped before 450 volts. The other 26 went right up to 450 volts. The argument is that 150 volts is an important turning point in the study when it comes to obedience to authority.

Burger (2009), therefore, puts forward clear arguments as to why 150 volts was 'the point of no return'.

Background 2

One of his aims was to replicate Milgram's work in an ethical way. Burger explains that Milgram's study cannot be fully replicated because of its unethical procedures, and he cites Elms (1995, cited in Burger, 2009).

Burger felt that the 150-volt stage did not challenge ethical principles (those in 2009), though going to 450 volts would do so. As 150 volts was when nearly all the participants looked to stop the study in Experiment 5 (they all turned to the experimenter to query carrying on), that was when they should have been given the right to withdraw, according to Burger. Milgram did not give the right to withdraw, but gave verbal prods to persuade participants to continue, although of course they could stop and seven did stop at 150 volts. Burger felt that if he replicated Milgram's study, but only up to 150 volts, there was a good rationale on both ethical and other grounds, and this would address ethical issues as well as allow comparisons.

In order to address the ethical issues in replicating Milgram's work, the basic procedure that Burger used was Milgram's main procedure, but with the following differences:

- He stopped the study at 150 volts for all participants.
- He changed the procedure because he told participants at least three times that they could withdraw and still get the payment (he paid the participants just as Milgram did).
- He used a 15-volt sample shock instead of 45 volts.

- The participants were told immediately that there were no shocks and the 'learner/victim' went into the room immediately to see the participant and to show no harm had been done.
- The experimenter was a clinical psychologist with instructions to end the study if any 'excessive stress' was seen.
- The procedure was approved by the Santa Clara University review board.

Background 3

Burger (2009) examined features in the situation that caused people to obey and he thought the features were as follows:

- Being ordered to do something by a legitimate authority. We are socialised to obey legitimate authority figures. In Milgram's study, the university and the experiment suggested legitimate authority.
- The gradual increase in what was being asked (the study asked participants to move up the shock level in 15-volt increments when an answer was wrong). This is like a slippery slope and may have caused the level of obedience. Participants did not straightaway administer 450 volts. An individual wants to be seen as consistent and maybe this is why they continued.
- Not having been in the situation before could have led to a search for how to behave and the main source of information about how to behave would come from the experimenter. The experimenter acted as if nothing was wrong and was reassuring, so continuing might be because of that. Evidence for this is that, in a variation of Milgram's study, when one experimenter at 150 volts encouraged the participant to continue but another asked the participant to stop, obedience stopped too. Also in Experiment 17 when two other 'teachers' were confederates, with just the one participant teacher, 30 per cent of participants stopped as soon as the second teacher stopped (210 volts). Just 10 per cent went to the end of the study.
- Not seeing themselves as responsible may have led to the obedience. The experimenter, when asked, takes responsibility. Evidence is that in Experiment 18 when participants take a subsidiary role (as an assistant) only three out of 40 refused to take part in the study.

> **STUDY HINT**
> You can use Burger's discussion about features that may have caused the obedience as an evaluation of Milgram's claim that he found obedience to authority. Perhaps the other features of the study that Burger discusses are other ways of interpreting the results.

Aims

Burger (2009) aimed to replicate Milgram's experiment – Experiment 5 – in an ethical way. The aim was to test Milgram's findings and to make comparisons with his findings.

Hypotheses

- There would be very little difference in obedience between 1961–1962 and 2009. Situational features are likely to have remained the same.
- There would be less obedience if refusal was modelled over time by someone else before the participant engaged in the behaviour. This was about modelling norms, which it was thought could make a difference to obedience to authority.
- There would be no gender difference in the obedience of the participants. This was about gender, which Milgram found did not make a difference to obedience to authority.
- People with a strong tendency to empathise with the suffering of others will be less likely to obey the experimenter's commands than those 'low on this personality trait'. This was about personality, which it is suggested can make a difference to obedience to authority.
- People motivated to exercise control are more likely to obey the experimenter than those with low motivation to exercise control.

> **STUDY HINT**
> It is good to read the full study when you can because you get more information that way and understand the study more fully. You can find Burger's full study here: www.apa.org/pubs/journals/releases/amp-64-1-1.pdf.

Procedure

The procedure was close to Milgram's procedure.

Participants

Participants responded to an advertisement, as Milgram's did. The sample was 29 men and 41 women after screening. Their age was from 20 to 81 years. Participants were promised $50 for two sessions of 45 minutes each. People who answered the advertisement were phoned and those familiar with Milgram's work were screened out, as was anyone who had taken more than two psychology classes. Those left were then asked about their mental health and any drug dependency. Overall, around 30 per cent of those who responded to the advertisements were screened out. There was then a second screening where age, occupation, education and ethnicity were asked about and scales were administered to would-be participants, such as the Beck Anxiety Inventory, to check state of mind. Self-motivation was also checked, as well as 'empathic concerns'.

Explore

Look at Burger's (2009) study and read the discussion about the four scales used, including emphasis on their reliability and validity. This helps to show the importance of such features of studies in order to build a credible body of psychological knowledge. This is about only using measures that measure what they say they measure (valid) and are consistent over time (reliable).

A clinical psychologist used a structured interview with all prospective participants to screen out anyone who might react negatively to the study, rejecting 38.2 per cent of the 123 people left at that stage (47 people). Those excluded at this stage were paid in full and confidentiality was maintained.

STUDY HINT

It is useful to make notes of ethical issues and adherence to ethical principles as you read through a study. This will help you to evaluate and comment on the study. Then you can use the study as evidence in a discussion about, for example, right to withdraw, getting informed consent and deceit, which are issues of respect and responsibility, according to the BPS Code of Ethics and Conduct (2009).

After the screening, the remaining participants attended campus a week later to continue with the study and six more participants were then dropped from the study. Five admitted to knowing about Milgram's study and one did not come to the follow-up session. This left 70 participants.

In 2009, Jerry Burger succeeded in replicating Milgram's work, taking care over the ethics involved

Base condition

Participants were randomly put into two conditions, paying attention to gender to ensure each condition was roughly equal. Participants were given $50 to keep, whatever happened.

STUDY HINT

Notice examples of how sampling is done. In Burger's (2009) study, there is random assignment, which means all participants are available to be chosen each time and this helps to allocate to the two conditions fairly and without bias, such as regarding gender, age or other factors. However, gender was attended to separately, as Burger did want a fair number of participants of each gender. Sampling can involve an element of selectivity, even if mainly random.

While reading about Burger's (2009) study, keep Milgram's procedure in mind. This will help you to understand Burger's study and will also help with learning Milgram's study.

The experimenter was a white man in his mid-30s and the confederate was a white male in his 50s. The participant was introduced to both these people. The experimenter and the confederate were chosen to reflect those same roles in Milgram's study. The experimenter had a script that was much like Milgram's. Participants were told this study was to look at the effect of punishment on learning and they drew lots with the confederates to see who would be the teacher and who would be the learner. The participants did not know, but of course they would always be the teacher. The participants completed a consent form telling them they might be videotaped (they would be) and informing them they could end their participation at any time and still keep the money.

The apparatus was then introduced. A chair was facing a table, with an intercom box and a box with four switches on the table. The confederate was strapped into the chair with the participant watching. The experimenter talked about 'electrodes' and 'blisters', as well as mentioning the shock generator in another room.

The confederate (the learner) was told to remember 25 word pairs and it was explained that the participant/teacher would read out one of the pair and then four other words, one of which was the 'pair word' that the 'learner' had to remember. The confederate gave their answer by pressing one of the four buttons on the table. The 'learner' was told that a wrong answer would mean an electric shock. The confederate indicated that they had a 'slight heart condition' and was told by the experimenter (the participant was looking on all this time) that the shocks may be painful but were not dangerous.

STUDY HINT

Note that a lot of the base condition procedure matched Milgram's study, including Experiment 5, where the confederate pretended to have a heart condition, to which the experimenter responded in the same way as in Burger's study. It is useful to make such links to help your learning.

When this part of the base condition procedure was over, the experimenter and the participant went into another room, which was adjacent to where they left the 'learner', shutting the door on him. In this room, there was a generator built to match Milgram's, with 30 switches and volt ranges from 15 to 450 volts, in 15-volt steps. The experimenter than gave the participant a sample shock, though two declined.

The participant was given the word pairs (identical to Milgram's) and the response options. The participant was then given instructions by the experimenter. The participant had to read out the first word and the four options. A wrong answer meant saying 'wrong' and saying the voltage of shock aloud (to the confederate learner over an intercom). After a wrong answer, a 15-volt shock would be given, increasing by 15 volts for every wrong answer. The experimenter sat a little way away from the participant and told them that the 'learner' could hear through the intercom but could not speak through it. As in Milgram's study, the confederate was primed regarding the responses they should give and there were pre-recorded sounds from the 'learner'.

At the 75-volt switch, the participants heard a small 'grunt' and at each shock level after this there was another grunt, which became louder at 150 volts. The 'learner' was heard to yell that they wanted to 'get out' and they mentioned their heart condition.

Progress check 1.24

List four features of Burger's study that were the same as Milgram's.

The experimenter would end the study either when all the verbal prods had been given and the participant refused to carry on, or when the 150-volt level had been reached and the participant went to continue (but was stopped). There were four prods to encourage the participant to continue and predetermined answers, such as 'there will be no permanent tissue damage'. If the participant asked who would be responsible for harm to the learner, the experimenter took responsibility.

STUDY HINT

Note that agency theory talks about responsibility and, in Burger's study, it is seen that the experimenter takes responsibility. So perhaps this is not the participant being the agent, as such, but the participant checking overtly that it is not their responsibility, which is not quite the same thing. You could use this when discussing agency theory.

The experimenter explained immediately to the participants that the generator was not real and there were no shocks. At the same time, the confederate entered the room to show he was fine. When it was clear that the participant had understood, there was a thorough debrief in another room.

Modelled refusal condition

The 'modelled refusal condition' was the same as the base condition but with a few differences. There was another confederate this time as well as the 'learner' (who was the same man as in the base condition). The other confederate matched the participant's gender. The new confederate in the draw was always 'teacher 1' and the participant was 'teacher 2'. Both 'teachers' watched the 'learner' being strapped in and the same procedure was followed as in the base condition, until both the 'teachers' were sitting in front of the generator. Teacher 1 (the new confederate) started the experiment off and did not hesitate up to the 75-volt switch. However, after hearing the first grunt and a pause, at 90 volts the new confederate (teacher 1) turned to the experimenter and said 'I don't know about this' and did not carry on after the first verbal prod. The experimenter then asked the participant (teacher 2) to take over, on which the new confederate sat silently.

Results

Table 1.13 shows Burger's (2009) results in both the base condition and the modelled refusal condition, and also adds Milgram's Experiment 5 results.

Table 1.13 Numbers (and percentages) of participants who stopped and who continued (Burger, 2009)

Behaviour	Base condition	Modelled refusal condition	Milgram's Experiment 5
Stopped at 150 volts or sooner	12 (30%)	11 (36.7%)	7 (17.5%)
Continued (went to continue but was prevented) after 150 volts	28 (70%)	19 (63.3%)	33 (82.5%)

Table 1.14 shows the results split by gender.

Table 1.14 Numbers (and percentages) of participants who stopped and who continued, by gender (Burger, 2009)

Condition and behaviour		Men	Women
Base condition	Stopped at 150 volts or sooner	6 (33.3%)	6 (27.3%)
	Continued (went to continue) after 150 volts	12 (66.7%)	16 (72.7%)
Modelled refusal condition	Stopped at 150 volts or sooner	5 (45.5%)	6 (31.6%)
	Continued (went to continue) after 150 volts	6 (54.5%)	13 (68.4%)

Burger (2009) found that 70 per cent in the base condition went to carry on after 150 volts, compared with 82.5 per cent in Milgram's Experiment 5. This difference was not statistically significant. Also 63.3 per cent went to carry on in the modelled refusal condition, not statistically different from the base condition (70 per cent), even though a difference was expected. Burger did find though that participants in the modelled refusal condition received their first verbal prompt significantly earlier than those in the base condition, which suggests they were looking to stop earlier. However, those in the modelled refusal condition did not have the chance to hesitate until the 90-volt switch as before that a confederate had been administering the 'shocks'.

Table 1.14 shows that there is little difference in obedience between men and women, as predicted. Burger used a chi-squared test to look for significance between the figures and, though women were more reluctant to continue than men in the modelled refusal condition, the difference was not statistically significant.

STUDY HINT

Burger used the chi-squared statistical test, which you will come across in Chapter 4. Make a note of this so that when you get to that statistical test you have an example of its use.

Burger had measured personality in terms of empathic concern and desire for control. He used the participant's score and looked to see if there were differences in personality between those who stopped at 150 volts or before and those who went to carry on. He found no significant difference in either measure of personality. Those with a higher empathic concern did not differ in terms of whether they stopped at or before 150 volts or carried on. However, in the base condition, those who stopped at 150 volts or earlier had a significantly higher desire for control. This statistically significant difference in desire for control was not found in the modelled refusal condition. Age, race and education showed no difference in obedience.

Conclusions

Burger (2009) concludes that, when people ask whether the same results would be found today as Milgram found in 1963 and 1974, the answer is 'yes' if going by his partial replication. Ethically, he could not fully replicate Milgram but his partial replication found similar results. Burger suggests that the same situational factors must be around today (he was writing in 2009) as 45 years earlier. Burger also emphasises that the similarities he found were even more important because he changed various aspects of the procedure and yet still found high levels of obedience. He told participants often that they could leave the study and still keep their payment.

One issue of importance, which Burger notes, is that he did not know whether the participants in his study who were willing to go beyond 150 volts would have gone up to 450 volts, though he felt that their desire to remain consistent and their 'self-perception' would have kept them to the task.

Burger was surprised to find that participants did not take their cue from the other teacher (a confederate) who modelled refusal. If participants were taking their cue from the experimenter in the base condition, then he expected just one person refusing to mean the participant would refuse too. Burger thought this finding showed the power of the situation on obedience. Milgram showed lowered obedience when two 'peers' rebelled, but perhaps just one other 'teacher' was not enough to signal the norm in the situation. As there were no significant gender differences, that might again emphasise the power of the situation. There were some personality differences but not enough to conclude that personality affected obedience. However, the findings do suggest that it is not a lack of empathy that leads to obedience, such as Milgram found. Those with a higher desire for control did stop earlier in the base condition, though not in the modelled refusal condition, which was unusual and not easily explained. Burger concluded that there might be personality factors in obedience but he could not clearly say what these might be.

Burger noted as a criticism of the study that the screening process may have ruled out participants in a way that affected the results. For example, anyone with emotional issues was ruled out. Also Burger used all age ranges, whereas Milgram used participants under 50 years old. There were some differences, then, but there was a lot of trouble taken in the replication. Burger (2009) feels he can claim a replication of Milgram and the same results found.

Evaluation of Burger (2009)

Strengths

- Burger (2009) used Milgram's procedure to a great extent, only varying from it for ethical reasons, such as his strong screening process and repetition that participants could withdraw at any time. By using the same procedure, it was possible to claim that the study was a replication and results could legitimately be compared with those of Milgram. Being a replication, reliability could be shown. Also there was scientific credibility in the findings.
- Burger's study had strengths regarding ethics. He was careful to exclude anyone that might be affected, judged by a clinical psychologist not by himself. On three occasions, the participant was told he could withdraw. By stopping the participant at 150 volts, he made sure they did not go as far as Milgram's participants and so might not be so upset at what they had done.
- Burger obtained data about age, gender, education and ethnicity. He also used personality measures, including empathy and desire for control. So he had a lot of variables he could test to see if that affected their obedience rather than the situation, as Milgram claimed. Therefore, his conclusion that it was the situation that led to the obedience was strengthened as he had data to help him to rule out many other factors.

Weaknesses

- Burger's study was laboratory based, so the setting was artificial, which perhaps suggests there is a lack of ecological validity. It can be claimed that punishment and learning might well be studied in a restricted environment so perhaps a lab is not that far from reality, but nonetheless there are validity issues.
- As Burger acknowledged, there are issues that might lead to obedience other than the situation. These issues include the experimenter taking responsibility, and the participant not having been in the situation before so looking to the experimenter for guidance. These factors maybe still applied (though the participants did not look to the model for guidance, but they may still have been focusing on the experimenter). There are doubts about the validity of the claim that it was the situation that led to obedience because of features of the study.
- Ethics were improved in many ways; however, some might still see ethical weaknesses in the study. He did show the participants that they were willing to give what they thought were shocks to another person, which can be a distressing thing to find out about oneself. The BPS Code of Ethics and Conduct (2009) says above all that distress must not be felt, and the participants may well have been distressed. They did look to the experimenter to stop the study, even though they did continue when 'prodded' to.

Progress check 1.25

Give the number of participants who stopped at 150 volts and the number who went to go beyond 150 volts in Burger's study, for both the baseline condition and the modelled refusal condition, and in Milgram's Experiment 5.

Test yourself

1. Explain the ways in which Burger modelled his study on Milgram's (1963) study. **(6 marks)**
2. Evaluate the differences between Burger's (2009) study and Milgram's (1963) study in terms of the procedure and the findings. **(12 marks)**

Reicher and Haslam (2006)

Background

Reicher and Haslam carried out a study in conjunction with the BBC in the UK. In May 2002, four one-hour programmes showed what happened. The study involved 15 male volunteers who were either prisoners or guards in a set-up environment. Full details of the study were published in the *Psychologist* in 2006 and are summarised below.

Some background to the study is useful because it helps to link it to other areas of the social approach. The researchers point out that social psychology looks at the effects of groups and social organisation, including leadership, on the behaviour of individuals. Following the events of the Second World War, when six million Jews were exterminated, social psychologists turned their attentions to obedience and related areas, to try to understand how such horrific events could happen. These issues link to your course:

- Milgram's ideas about obedience, including the agency theory explanation, suggest that people act as agents of society and so follow orders.
- Sherif's study of group behaviour shows how realistic conflict between groups can lead to prejudice between the groups, which can explain extreme behaviours such as genocide.
- Social identity theory suggests that members of an in-group will turn against members of an out-group.

Reicher and Haslam's study tests the idea of social identification and the focus of their study is on how people come to condone tyranny or become tyrannical themselves.

This study may be seen as a replication of the Stanford prison experiment, carried out by Zimbardo and others in 1971.

STUDY HINT

This study illustrates key ideas in social psychology – for example, that interactions between people, including power in groups, are important.

However, Reicher and Haslam claim that it is more than a replication of that study. Zimbardo showed that when college students were set to control other college students who were their 'prisoners', they took on the role of guards. Brutality developed to such an extent that the study had to be stopped early. Reicher and Haslam could not replicate Zimbardo's work because his study was unethical. Since Zimbardo's research, studies into such areas have tended to be laboratory experiments, which Reicher and Haslam realised makes the findings invalid. They suggest that fieldwork is needed, so there is a need for a more ethical way to study the effects of roles, social organisation and being in groups.

Explore

Look up Zimbardo's Stanford prison experiment, written up as Haney *et al.* (1973). Also look up Philip Zimbardo. He has used the findings of Haney *et al.* (Zimbardo was part of the team) to show that, when serving soldiers are charged with committing brutal acts, social structures must be considered. This is instead of holding such soldiers completely responsible for their actions – the soldiers are acting within a social role. We look again at Zimbardo when we consider heroism later in this chapter because he later turned to the psychology of heroism. If you find material about that, note it for the key question to come (pp. 66–69).

Aims

The aim of Reicher and Haslam's study was to investigate tyranny at a group level. They defined tyranny as 'an unequal social system involving the arbitrary or oppressive use of power by one group or its agents over another'.

STUDY HINT

Reicher and Haslam's study can be used to help explain agency theory as the prisoners become agents and obey the guards' (those in authority) rules and orders.

The researchers argue that groups work against tyranny and it is only when social systems fail that tyrannical forms of social organisation come into being. One aim of the BBC prison study, *The Experiment*, was to examine the effects of group behaviour on issues such as tyranny. Because of the real-world application of such work, it is an important area for society. More precisely, the aim was to investigate the behaviour of groups that were unequal in terms of power, status and resources. Another aim was to revisit the issues raised in the Stanford prison experiment. For example, to study:

- whether participants accept their role uncritically
- whether those who have power use it without constraint
- whether those without power accept their subordination without complaint.

The aims of the researchers in summary were:

- to look at the unfolding interactions between groups of unequal power and privilege
- to see when people identify themselves as a member of a group and when they accept or challenge inter-group inequalities
- to look at social, organisational and clinical (regarding mental health issues) factors to see how they affect, and are affected by, group behaviour
- to develop ways of studying such behaviours ethically.

Procedure

To some extent, Reicher and Haslam's study is similar to a field experiment because they manipulate variables and the study is carried out in the field: it takes place in a simulated setting that is supposed to resemble real-life. However, data come from observations, video and tape recordings, analysis of conversations and measures such as psychological and physiological testing. Since so many different ways of collecting data are used, and the data are in depth, detailed and about a one-off situation, the study is more like a case study. Reicher and Haslam call it an experimental case study.

Progress check 1.26

Write a paragraph about the value of having more than one data collection method, including the reason for, and the value of, **triangulation** (taking data from different sources and comparing them).

Reicher and Haslam carried out the study but the BBC was involved in setting up the situation, providing the taped evidence and organising it into the four programmes. This was a unique collaboration. The environment had to create inequality between two groups that was real for the participants. It was a study of the behaviour of groups in dominant and subordinate positions and the developing relations between them. It rested on the ideas of social identity theory and there were manipulated variables, interventions, based on the theory. 'Prisoners' were allocated in threes to lockable cells surrounding a central area, and a lockable steel mesh separated the cells from the guards' more comfortable quarters.

STUDY HINT

When you have studied the research methods covered in the four topic areas that make up your Year 1/AS course, you will probably think that every study must fit into one research method - for example, Sherif *et al.*'s study was a field experiment. In practice, however, as in Reicher and Haslam, studies often use more than one data collection tool and can fit into more than one research method. For your course, you will usually allocate one research method to one study; however, be aware that in psychology things are not always that straightforward.

Ethics

The inter-group inequality was set up to be ethical. Details were discussed with colleagues, a university ethics committee and the BPS ethics committee. The novelty of the study was given as a reason for it taking place and various safeguards were put in place:

- Participants went through detailed screening.
- They signed a comprehensive consent form, which informed them that they may be at risk of psychological discomfort, confinement and stress.
- Two independent clinical psychologists monitored the study and could contact participants at any time. They could ask for the withdrawal of a participant from the study.
- A paramedic was on standby throughout.
- On-site security guards were ready to intervene if behaviour became dangerous.
- An independent five-person ethics committee monitored the study throughout (and at the end said that it was exemplary).

STUDY HINT

Use the detail given here when discussing ethical issues concerning human participants in psychology studies. Use the above evidence to illustrate the four ethical principles in the BPS Code of Conduct and Ethics and the guidelines within them, such as giving the right to withdraw and getting informed consent.

Although material in your course, and this book, is split into sections, in practice psychology is a 'whole' area of study, including doing psychology (such as your own practical investigations), learning about psychology (including the required theories and studies), and applying psychology in society (such as for one key question). Try to make links between the sections as often as possible, to help your knowledge and understanding.

Participants

Male participants were recruited using an advertisement in the national press and through leaflets. Those who responded were screened thoroughly, including a full weekend assessment. Well-adjusted and **pro-social** participants were selected, for both ethical and practical reasons. For example, if anti-social behaviour was found in the study, it could be claimed that this may be generalised to the whole population because the participants were not anti-social initially. Of 332 applicants screened, 27 men were chosen. Only men were used, so that there would be no issues of having males and females together in the cells and having to provide facilities for both sexes. Fifteen participants were then chosen, ensuring a spread of age, class and ethnicity. The 15 were grouped into threes that were matched as far as possible; from each 'three', one person was chosen randomly to be a guard. So there were five guards and ten prisoners.

Gathering data

Data were gathered using video and tape recordings. Tests were also carried out to investigate issues such as depression (a clinical factor), compliance with rules (an organisational factor) and right-wing authoritarianism (a social factor). Cortisol levels were measured because they link with stress and depression.

How the study was run

The evening before the study, five participants were invited to a hotel and were told that they would be guards. Their jobs were described to them. They had to:

- carry out a roll call
- allocate work duties to prisoners
- ensure the institution ran smoothly
- ensure that prisoners did all their tasks.

The guards drew up rules and punishments for the violation of the rules. They were told that they could not use physical punishments and that they had to give the prisoners basic human rights, but they were *not* told how to do their jobs. The guards were taken to the setting in a van with blacked-out windows. They had better conditions than the prisoners (e.g. better quality uniforms and more comfortable quarters).

Nine 'prisoners' arrived singly (one came later) and each was given the prison rules and a list of basic rights.

Interventions

The experimenters wanted to examine the effect of permeability on group behaviour. Permeability meant that group boundaries were drawn loosely and members could pass between the groups. To set up permeability, the researchers told the guards that they should look for guard potential among the prisoners, as there would be a promotion because the researchers thought they might have assigned the prisoners wrongly. A promotion was made on day three and after that the participants were told that there would be no more movement between the groups.

The researchers also wanted to look at the effects of **cognitive alternatives** on group behaviour. A cognitive alternative is when someone sees that there is a different way of thinking about something. A new prisoner, who had been a trade union official, was introduced on day five. The experimenters thought that he would have ideas about getting better conditions and on how to negotiate, which would give cognitive alternatives for the prisoners.

Results

There were two phases to the study. The first phase lasted until the prisoners became stronger than the guards; the second phase began with a new social organisation.

Phase 1: rejecting inequality

The guards failed to identify with one another as a group. The prisoners did not identify as a group up to day three, but after the promotion they became much more cohesive – so much so, that they became stronger than the guards and challenged them. There was a shift in power and a collapse of the prisoner–guard system. The observations showed the solidarity of the prisoners and the lack of identity within the guards; the quantitative data backed up the observational data. For example, prisoners were asked to rate their ties with other prisoners, their ties with guards and their solidarity with other prisoners.

After the promotion on day three, the prisoners started to agree norms of behaviour, but the guards did not. So the participants did not see differences in qualities between the two groups because the guards did not seem to be stronger people. Therefore, the groups did not seem to be legitimate. Cognitive alternatives emerged, such as the prisoners envisaging changing the situation and the power structure. This happened before the introduction of the additional prisoner. When the new prisoner was introduced on day five, he immediately questioned the legitimacy of the study, rather than of the groups, and suggested to his cell mates and to one of the guards that they challenge the experimenters.

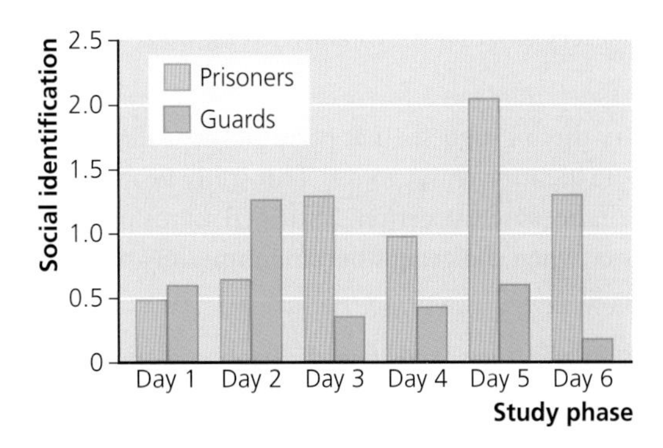

Social identification as a function of assigned group and time

At the start of the study, neither the guards nor the prisoners saw cognitive alternatives – these developed over time. Gradually, the prisoners started acting against the social inequality – for example, they started to be insubordinate during roll call. The guards remained reasonably compliant but after day three the prisoners did not. A shift in power began. Through planning and mutual support, the prisoners became progressively more dominant. No participant became very depressed but the guards, who were less depressed at the start, became more depressed than the prisoners. By late on day six, the prisoners broke out of their cells and took over the guards' quarters.

Phase 2: embracing inequality

Participants agreed to continue as a self-governing commune. All but two prisoners wanted the commune, but those who had been more rebellious towards the guards started plotting against the commune and so confidence was lost. Some participants then wanted to impose a more authoritarian system. The others agreed because they had become despondent (partly because they thought the experimenters were disappointed in them and that they had failed). To achieve the aims of the study, a strong social system that worked was seen as desirable. At day eight, the experiment was stopped because the new tyrannical system was against the ethical rules, so the study had come to a natural conclusion.

Conclusions

It was concluded that groups create social order based on shared values and norms, and the prisoners formed a group on this basis. However, when groups fail, people are inclined to accept the imposition of social order, even if this goes against their own values and norms. So tyranny arises because of group failure, not because of the development of tyrannical group behaviour. People do not accept automatically roles that are assigned to them;

other factors affect whether they identify with their social positions.

Social identity theory suggests that permeability affects how far people identify with groups. This study supports this conclusion because the prisoners formed a group after the promotion (when the groups became impermeable), rather than before.

One factor that affected social identification was the view of others, as seen by the reluctance of the guards to appear authoritarian. This was probably the effect of the study being televised because their behaviour would be seen and judged by many people. This suggests that surveillance affects behaviour. Making behaviour visible might avoid authoritarianism, which is a useful finding for society.

The researchers also found that mental state was affected by how effectively the groups performed, with a dysfunctional group leading to lower effectiveness with regard to mental health – again an important finding for society. Social support is known to help in improving mental health.

The study showed that understanding collective conflict and tyranny cannot be achieved by looking at individuals; it requires an analysis of group processes and relations between groups. Group behaviour can be anti-social or pro-social depending on the norms and values associated with the identity of the group members. Failing groups present problems for their own members and for others. It is not that group norms and values lead to anti-social behaviour, but that problems with the functioning of groups affect social organisation and mental health, and so affect society. When people cannot construct a social system for themselves, they fall back on a more authoritarian ideology.

Evaluation by the researchers

The researchers identified four problems with the study and addressed the issues.

Were the results affected by the study being televised?

The researchers accept that the participants knew their behaviour would be shown on national television and that, to an extent, this would affect their behaviour. However, they felt that the participants could not 'act' over nine days and also, as their behaviour changed in that time, it was not 'acting' but real. In any case, they argue, studies where anonymity is guaranteed are likely to be less valid. There is a way in which people think of themselves as being watched when in social roles in any case, so the study can be said to be valid because 'being watched' is a natural state in society.

Were the participants of a particular personality type?

Three prisoners had the strongest personalities of all the participants, so maybe their personalities could have caused the results. However, prisoners and guards were matched on several variables, including racism, authoritarianism and dominance. Individuals changed throughout the study, which would not be accounted for by different personalities. If people were 'rebellious', it could be asked why they deferred to the experimenters and deferred in some situations but not others.

Was the inequality real for the participants?

The evidence suggested that the situation was real for the participants. For example:

- From the start, the prisoners disliked their unequal status.
- The prisoners did not like their food being of poorer quality than the guards' food.
- The guards also engaged with their roles. They were concerned about using their power, but they accepted that they had power.
- The guards tried to ease the inequalities – for example, by offering the prisoners their leftovers.
- The guards did not gel together as a group, seemingly because they were uncomfortable with their situation, which suggests that they identified with it.

Was the study really measuring impermeability and cognitive alternatives?

The researchers admitted that there could be explanations other than their own for the changes that they found after their interventions. They felt that using different ways to collect data, including gathering both qualitative and quantitative data, helped to show both reliability and validity. However, there were problems in saying that the prisoners' group cohesion came when the groups became impermeable. It might have been that the participants distrusted the experimenters after the promotion or were uncertain about what might happen next.

General evaluation of Reicher and Haslam (2006)

Strengths

- It is a case study that used many different means of collecting data. There are both qualitative and quantitative data, so there can be **triangulation**, which means taking data from different sources and comparing them. If the data agree, then they would appear to be measuring the same thing and the findings are likely to be the same next time, which means they are reliable and the behaviour being measured is likely to be real.

- There was competence, in that different ethical committees were consulted and one was even set up especially for the study. There was informed consent and participants were warned, for example, about stress and confinement. There was no deceit – the participants knew exactly what the study involved and were told that it would be televised. There was the right to withdraw – even if the participants did not feel they could withdraw, there were people present who could ask for a participant to be withdrawn. There was a debrief after the study.

Weaknesses

- There were a number of factors at work, rather than a single manipulated variable being studied. So, although the complexity of group behaviour was being studied, it is not possible to draw firm conclusions about what causes which effect. For example, for the prisoners, strong identification with the group happened after the groups become impermeable, but it might not be the impermeability that caused the changes.
- The study was televised and the participants' behaviour was likely to be affected by such surveillance. The researchers turned this into a positive by saying that in society people are watched anyway, so the television aspect makes the study valid. However, the guards may have behaved differently had they not been constrained by what others would think of them. For example, one guard was well thought of 'in the world outside' and the researchers suggest that this might have made him reluctant to be as authoritarian as a guard might need to be. He was made artificially into a guard with another life 'outside', which was not a valid situation.

STUDY HINT

When giving strengths and weaknesses, first explain the strength or weakness fully and then give an example to illustrate it, to show your understanding. So, for example, don't just say a study is ethical; show how it is ethical.

Test yourself

1. Explain how Reicher and Haslam's (2006) study is about social identity theory and not about obedience to authority. **(8 marks)**
2. Using Reicher and Haslam's (2006) study, discuss why a study that has such complexity in its aims is always going to lack validity at least to some extent. **(8 marks)**

Cohrs *et al.* (2012)

Cohrs *et al.* (2012), like Reicher and Haslam, focused on prejudice, but they were interested in factors affecting prejudice – in particular, individual differences – rather than social identity theory.

Cohrs *et al.* (2012) consider individual differences in personality and how they can affect whether someone shows prejudice, so their study is useful when discussing individual differences in people.

Explanation

Individual differences in people are important as well as similarities between people. Psychology so often looks at 'people' with all the similarities that make us human. However, psychology also considers that individuals can be different from one another, such as in terms of personality, gender or intelligence.

STUDY HINT

When you see the 'individual differences' icon, be sure to make notes separately as you can be asked to discuss individual differences in all four topic areas.

Cohrs *et al.* (2012) wanted to see if there was a relationship between ideological attitudes, personality dimensions and prejudice. Ideological attitudes include RWA and SDO. **Right-wing authoritarianism** (RWA) is where people have rigid thinking and are conventional, thinking the world is a dangerous place and so liking authority and structure. **Social dominance orientation** (SDO) is where people see society as hierarchical and them as dominant in a society. Both are said to link to prejudice. Personality dimensions include agreeableness, conscientiousness and openness to experiences. The idea is that certain personality dimensions underpin attitudes like RWA and SDO – for example, right-wing authoritarianism goes against being open to experiences. A second focus of Cohrs *et al.*'s study is that they want to see whether **self-report data** are valid and reliable and to find this out they gather both self-report and **peer-report data** and then compare them.

Aims

Cohrs *et al.* (2012) wanted to look at relationships between ideological attitudes (right-wing authoritarianism and social dominance orientation), personality dimensions (neuroticism, extraversion, openness to experience, agreeableness and conscientiousness) and prejudice. They also wanted to use both self-report data and peer-report data so that they could compare the two, to check validity and reliability of self-report data. The researchers felt that evidence about personality and prejudice had been gathered using self-report data and this was a methodological issue that needed to be addressed. Their aims were to see whether RWA and SDO linked to personality dimensions and also to prejudice. Their other aim was to see if self-report and peer-report data agreed, to find out whether self-report data are reliable and valid.

Definitions

Self-report data are data that someone has given about themselves, such as agreeing or disagreeing with statements in a questionnaire. **Peer-report data** are data that a friend or someone who knows you gives about you, such as whether they think you would agree or disagree with certain statements in a questionnaire.

Background

'Ideological attitudes are found to be an important mediator of the influences of personality on prejudice' (Cohrs *et al.*, 2012, p. 343). 'Mediator' here means 'go between', so personality is said to affect prejudice and a personality that includes a certain sort of ideological attitude may mean more or less prejudice in that person. 'Ideological attitudes' refer to people's beliefs about the needs of their own society and what they think is required to benefit their society and culture; although 'ideology' can also be beliefs about one's own needs and requirements.

STUDY HINT

Et al. refers to the other researchers in a study. In this case, the full list of researchers is as follows: J. Christopher Cohrs, Nicole Kämpfe-Hargrace and Rainer Reimann.

Not all the information about a study can be given here. Some extra information is interesting, such as, for this study, Cohrs being based at Queen's University in Belfast and the other two researchers being at the University of Jena and University of Bielefeld, both in Germany. It is interesting to find out where a study takes place, as well as where the researchers are based, if you do have access to such information.

There are two main strands to Cohrs *et al.* (2012):

- One strand is about looking at personality in terms of the 'Big Five' dimensions (neuroticism, extraversion, openness to experience, agreeableness and conscientiousness). Ideological attitudes include right-wing authoritarianism (RWA) and social dominance orientation (SDO) and their links to prejudice.
- The other strand is about whether self-report data are reliable, valid measures or whether they show biases, such as social desirability.

STUDY HINT

You have come across RWA (right-wing authoritarianism) earlier in this chapter in the sections on the influence of personality on obedience (pp. 26–28) and the influence of personality on prejudice (pp. 39–40). Cohrs *et al.* (2012) can be used to discuss the influence of personality on prejudice, which is the focus of the study, and the ideas in this study about authoritarianism can help to explain how personality might affect obedience too.

The method section in social psychology focuses on gathering self-report data using questionnaire and interview. You can use Cohrs *et al.*'s (2012) findings about self-report data when discussing such methods. Cohrs *et al.* found that self-report data are reliable and valid in that the peer-report data that they collected reinforced the findings of the self-report data. Use such evidence in evaluation.

Strand 1: RWA, SDO, personality dimensions and prejudice

Adorno *et al.* (1950) brought into focus an important point about those with an authoritarian personality showing prejudiced attitudes, and studies have continued in this area since then. Studies have suggested that RWA and SDO are the two most important variables in an authoritarian personality. Cohrs *et al.* (2012) say that it is not that RWA and SDO are personality traits linking to prejudice (relying on evidence from, for example, Duckitt and Sibley, 2010). RWA and SDO have underlying personality traits. Generally, personality traits are seen in terms of the Big Five (neuroticism, extraversion, openness to experience, agreeableness and conscientiousness).

The dual-process model has been proposed, saying that the personality dimensions of openness to experience and agreeableness underlie someone's tendency to certain ideological attitudes, which in turn lead them to be prejudiced.

Those with a RWA personality tend to have rigid thinking and want to avoid uncertainty. They see the world as dangerous and threatening and do not want to accept rules and values other than their own. Their beliefs that the world is dangerous cause them to want social cohesion and stability, which links to conventionalism (conventional views) and submission to authority. You can see that this sort of personality is likely to link to prejudiced attitudes.

Those with SDO are 'tough-minded' (Cohrs *et al.*, 2012, p. 344) and pursue their own interests. They are not agreeable or concerned for others and tend to see a world where the strong survive. They see superiority and dominance as goals and have social-dominance attitudes. This means a hierarchical idea of how groups work and this in turn can lead to prejudice.

Studies give evidence for these ideas about RWA and SDO linking to prejudice and to openness to experience and agreeableness with regard to personality variables. Cohrs *et al.* (2012) cite Sibley and Duckitt's (2008) meta-analysis showing a negative correlation between openness to experience and RWA. This means that the more someone is open to experiences, the lower they score for right-wing authoritarianism. Sibley and Duckitt also found that SDO correlated negatively with openness to experience and that openness to experience correlated negatively with prejudice. This means that someone who is open to experiences and not rigid in their thinking (RWA) or feeling dominant over others (SDO) is less likely to be prejudiced against others. Those who were 'agreeable' in personality were less likely to be in the 'social dominance' category and those who were conscientious were more likely to be in the right-wing authoritarian category. Sibley and Duckitt also found that both RWA and SDO were linked to being prejudiced.

Cohrs *et al.* (2012) claim that personality dimensions, particularly openness to experience and agreeableness, and possibly also conscientiousness, link to prejudice. However, they link to prejudice through RWA and SDO. This means that the personality dimensions predict right-wing authoritarianism and social dominance orientation (either/or) and that those two predict prejudice.

STUDY HINT

You will learn about correlational analysis in biological psychology in Chapters 5 and 6 (p. 175). You can use Cohrs *et al.* (2012) as an example of correlational analysis. For example, Sibley and Duckitt's finding was $r = -0.36$. The minus sign shows this is a negative correlation, which means the more a score rises on one variable, the more it falls on another. The more the openness to experience score rises, the more the RWA score falls. 0.36 sounds low but was found to be significant.

Definition

A **meta-analysis** is a study that uses results from a number of other studies that have used a methodology and focus that are similar enough so that results can be compared together to come to an overall conclusion about an area of study.

STUDY HINT

You will learn about meta-analysis in Year 2. It is worth making notes about the method that studies use so that you can use these as evidence of that usage.

Strand 2: self-report data

Cohrs *et al.* (2012) were concerned because nearly all the evidence in this area of study had so far relied on self-report data, which is a potential flaw in the evidence if self-report data are found not to be reliable or valid. Common-method effects are discussed, which means if all studies use the same method and the method has flaws, then all the studies might be supporting one another because they use the same (flawed) method.

Self-report data have issues because they might be affected by social desirability. **Social desirability** means people might answer about themselves in a way that makes them look good from a social point of view. If in our culture someone is asked 'are you a racist?', they are unlikely to answer 'yes'. If they answer 'no' because they don't want to look bad from society's viewpoint, then social desirability is affecting their reply.

Social desirability might link to personality and ideological tendencies, which means that using self-report data might be problematic in this area of study and data might reflect less what someone thinks about themselves and more what they think they should say about themselves. Also people might tend to show themselves in a coherent light and that would challenge the validity of self-report data too. Another feature of self-report data is that they may reflect the aspect of oneself that someone perceives, but there might be other aspects too. Therefore, another source of data would be useful, alongside self-report data.

STUDY HINT

Social desirability is covered when self-report data are looked at so review that material to help your understanding of this study if necessary.

Definition

Social desirability in results of a study means that someone has given data that make them look good from society's point of view so this data might not be 'valid' because it might not 'really' be what they think.

To summarise issues with self-report data:

1 Social desirability might be present, the more so as it might link to ideological attitudes and personality traits so might mean data are not valid.
2 People tend to show themselves as consistent and coherent and that too affects the validity of self-report data. This tendency might also link to ideological attitude and personality traits.
3 People might focus on one aspect of themselves when giving self-report data, and other aspects may not be covered.

Another issue is that ideological attitudes (such as RWA or SDO) might not come from personality at all. They may arise because of group situations and come from social norms around group identity. If this was the case then there would be weaker associations between personality dimension, ideological attitudes and prejudice if data other than self-report were used. Self-report data might show the differences but if others are asked, the same issues around in-group and out-group might not emerge.

Alternative methods to self-report data

Cohrs *et al.* (2012) list different methods that could be used, including rating personality using independent raters (such as rating interviews about childhood experiences, hobbies and such like for RWA, SDO and personality features) and tendencies to remember statements we agree with and to forget phrases we disagree with. Using the former method (independent raters rating interviews) it was found that RWA correlated with 'being judged as defensive, prejudiced, religious, maladjusted and fraudulent' (Cohrs *et al.*, 2012, p. 345). SDO correlated with 'not agreeable, not nurturant, prejudiced, not warm, dominant, coarse and feeling superior to others' (p. 345).

As different methods show similar findings, there is some evidence that it is not just the self-report data that give the findings around RWA, SDO, personality dimensions and prejudice. However, Cohrs *et al.* (2012) suggest that what is needed is a measure other than self-report data, and they thought peer-report data would be a suitable alternative.

It is thought that people who know us can judge our ideas and opinions accurately and less social desirability would be found (McCrae and Weiss, 2007, cited in Cohrs *et al.*, 2012). Peer-report data have been found to be valid (Funder, 1995, cited in Cohrs *et al.*, 2012). For personality dimensions, peer raters tend to agree with self-raters with a high correlation value – there is a strong correlation (McCrae and Weiss, 2007, cited in Cohrs *et al.*, 2012). Cohrs *et al.* (2012) thought that peer-reports would be useful for personality dimensions and also for ideological attitudes (RWA and SDO) as well as prejudice.

Progress check 1.27

Explain why Cohrs *et al.* (2012) used peer-report data as well as self-report data.

Procedure

Cohrs *et al.* (2012) report on two studies that are related in their overall study:

- Study 1 used data from one acquaintance for each participant as well as the participant's self-report data. Participants were from Eastern Germany and opportunity sampling was used. Participants were invited to join the sample in a bid to ensure different social and educational backgrounds.

STUDY HINT

Note that Cohrs *et al.* (2012) use opportunity sampling, which is one of the sampling techniques you need to know about. Make a note that this study uses that sampling technique so you can use it as evidence in any discussion about sampling.

- Study 2 used data from two separate acquaintances for each participant as this would obtain more reliable data. One acquaintance might show bias. Participants came from the Jena Twin Registry.

Each participant had a self-report and a peer-report questionnaire (two peer-report questionnaires for Study 2). The questionnaires were coded so that they could be matched for analysis and still maintain anonymity. Participants were asked to give the peer-report questionnaire to a friend or acquaintance and to complete the self-report questionnaire themselves. Confidentiality was explained and assured and participants were asked to respond spontaneously and honestly, with peer raters to answer as best as they could, thinking about how the participant (their friend or acquaintance) would respond. Peer raters could return the questionnaire directly to the researchers or to their friend/acquaintance in an envelope to preserve confidentiality.

Participants

For Study 1, 193 participants were used because they submitted completed questionnaires and were accepted with regard to sexual orientation and being German nationals with no disability (these issues were because of questions in the questionnaire). There were 125 women and 64 men in the sample (four did not report their gender), between 18 and 67 years old. Less than half were students. The peer raters were 95 women and 97 men (one did not report gender) and most knew the participant 'very well'.

For Study 2, one twin from each pair of twins was chosen, making sure that at least one set of peer-report data was available for the twin. There were 424 participants: 103 men and 321 women, aged between 18 and 82 years old; 371 of the participants had two peer-reports available, with just one available for the other 53 participants. The peer raters were 554 women and 224 men. Of these, 215 knew the participant very well and 464 knew the participant well.

Apparatus

- To measure personality dimensions (openness to experiences, agreeableness and so on) in Study 1, a scale was used ranging from 1 (not true at all) to 7 (completely true). In Study 2, a different scale was used, ranging from 1 (reject very much) to 5 (agree very much).

STUDY HINT

Note the use of Likert-style statements to measure personality dimensions. You need to know about such means of measurement in social psychology, so you can use this study as an example. You could adapt these responses in your practical investigation, which requires a questionnaire to be carried out (see Chapter 7).

- To measure RWA, the researchers used a 12-item scale balanced with regard to wording (so that not all the items have the same response for an authoritarian reply, some statements are 'reversed'; see Chapter 5).
- To measure SDO, another scale was used, translated into German.
- In the various scales, items were removed to suit the study, but the scale mainly remained the same.
- Prejudice was measured for gay men and lesbians, foreigners and people with disabilities. Prejudice for foreigners was measured using 11 items in Study 1; for Study 2, new items were added, with seven being about discrimination of Turks (Turks are the largest non-German ethnic group in Germany).

Scale scores were obtained by averaging the completed items on each scale, though if more than 50 per cent were not answered, a score was not worked out.

Results when comparing peer and self-report data

In Study 1 for neuroticism, extraversion, agreeableness and RWA, mean scores were similar between peer and self-report data. Participants rated themselves higher in openness to experience than the peer ratings and lower in conscientiousness than the peer ratings.

In Study 2 for agreeableness and RWA, mean scores were similar between peer and self-report data. Participants rated themselves higher for neuroticism than the peer ratings and lower in extraversion, conscientiousness and prejudice itself (a general item asking about prejudice).

The differences in openness to experience, conscientiousness, SDO and prejudice were all in the same direction, in that participants presented themselves as more open, more egalitarian and less prejudiced than the peers reported. This suggests that self-report data are more open to social desirability then peer-report data.

Study results

The first research question was whether the links between RWA and SDO, personality dimensions and prejudice that had been found using self-report data were found also in peer-report data.

It was found that ideological attitudes (RWA and SDO) did correlate with prejudice, as was found by Sibley and Duckitt (2008, cited in Cohrs *et al.*, 2012).

- Openness to experience correlated negatively with RWA and prejudice. RWA did not go with being open to experience (the more right-wing authoritarian, the less open to experience someone is) but did go with being prejudiced (the more right-wing authoritarian, the more prejudiced someone is).
- Conscientiousness correlated positively with RWA (the more conscientious, the more right-wing authoritarian someone is).
- Agreeableness correlated negatively with SDO and RWA (the more agreeable someone is, the less social dominance oriented or right-wing authoritarian they are).
- SDO correlated positively with prejudice (the more social dominance orientated a person is, the more prejudiced they are). Though this was a rather weak correlation.

Peer-report correlations were in general very similar to the self-report correlations, with just a few exceptions. One exception was that in Study 1 the relationship between ideological attitudes (RWA and SDO) and prejudice tended to be smaller than was found in the self-reports. Also the correlation between agreeableness and RWA was not significant in the peer-report data. There were some other differences too, but largely the two types of data matched.

Table 1.15 shows self-report and peer-report data against the variables they measured. Response scales ranged from 1 to 7 in Study 1 and 1 to 5 in Study 2. In Study 2, the mean rating is based on the average across two peers. Table 1.15 shows a lot of similarities between the two measures, using descriptive statistics.

Table 1.15 Self-report and peer-report data against the different variables measured

	Study 1 (*N*=193)			Study 2 (*N*=424)		
		Self-report	Peer-report		Self-report	Peer-report
Variable	Number of items on scale	Mean rating	Mean score	Number of items on scale	Mean rating	Mean score
Neuroticism	12	3.60	3.56	48	2.82	2.63
Extraversion	12	4.68	4.72	48	3.35	3.42
Openness to experience	11	4.63	4.46	45	3.43	3.32
Conscientiousness	12	5.40	5.62	48	3.59	3.75
Agreeableness	12	4.86	4.95	48	3.53	3.53
Right-wing authoritarianism	11	3.65	3.70	10	2.77	2.80
Social dominance orientation	13	2.95	3.15	14	2.48	2.56
Generalised prejudice	3	2.47	2.67	3	2.09	2.23

Table 1.16 shows significant correlations for the eight variables in Study 1 and Study 2. This table gives self-report data only (Cohrs *et al.*, 2012 give peer-report data too).

The correlations shown in Table 1.16 show that there is a relationship between the two variables using the self-report data. A minus sign in front of a correlation figure means that there is a negative relationship (as one variable rises, the other falls) and no sign means a positive relationship (as one variable rises, the other rises too). For example, the table shows a positive correlation (0.50) between generalised prejudice and right-wing authoritarianism (according to self-report data), and right-wing authoritarianism correlates negatively with openness to experience (–0.43).

STUDY HINT

Table 1.16 will be clearer once you have studied correlational analysis for biological psychology and read Chapters 5 and 6, on methodology and maths. You might want to return to the table once you have a better understanding of correlations and significance.

The first research question was whether the links between RWA and SDO, personality dimensions and prejudice that had been found using self-report data were found also in peer-report data. It was seen from the results that this was the case – the two types of data matched – and also there were relationships between personality dimensions, ideological attitude and prejudice, as expected.

Table 1.16 Significant correlations with self-report data (correlations shown are significant at $p \leq 0.001$, two tailed)

	1	2	3	4	5	6	7	8
1 Neuroticism		−0.35		−0.41	−0.16			
2 Extraversion	−0.29		0.41	0.23				
3 Openness to experience						−0.43		−0.43
4 Conscientiousness						0.20		
5 Agreeableness		0.31					−0.28	−0.20
6 Right-wing authoritarianism			−0.41				0.19	0.57
7 Social dominance orientation								0.27
8 Generalised prejudice			−0.40			0.50	0.37	

There were other research questions too, which are not all explained here, but there is enough here to give evidence for their main findings.

Progress check 1.28

Other than the two correlations picked out here from the self-report data (generalised prejudice and RWA; and RWA and openness to experience), using Table 1.16, list four other variables that showed a significant correlation and state in each case whether the correlation was positive or negative.

Specific conclusions

The first research question focused not only on whether relationships would be found between personality dimensions, ideological attitudes and prejudice, as in earlier studies, but also on whether the findings using self-report data would match findings using peer-report data. The study found 'yes' to both parts of this question. The study did find relationships between the Big Five personality dimensions, ideological attitudes (RWA and SDO) and prejudice. The study also found that peer-report data largely backed self-report data, so self-report data are reliable (if a study is repeated and gets the same findings, then results are said to be reliable).

Cohrs *et al.* (2012) thought that their findings replicated the findings of others and this did suggest that the results from self-report data in other studies could be generalised to other situations, as the many studies uncovered the same relationships between personality, prejudice and ideology.

However, the researchers offer some criticisms of their own findings. They wondered whether peer-report data might have social desirability bias or bias in wanting to demonstrate consistency – both criticisms that have been levelled at self-report data. Friends may be as motivated as the individuals themselves to see their friend in a positive way and to use social desirability on their behalf. The researchers also found some differences between self-report and peer-report data, such as neuroticism and extraversion only being related in the peer-report data. So possibly using just one method does mean data tend not to be valid – there is still a question mark over using self-report data in this area of study.

Another issue the researchers discussed was that, although there was reliability in rating SDO between self-report and peer-report data, what was being measured and called SDO could have been different, which questions the validity of the data.

There were conclusions about other research questions too, but they are not all explained here as there is enough here to help in understanding the conclusions.

Overall conclusions

- The researchers concluded that their use of a multi-method design (self-report and peer-report data) meant they could look at ideological attitudes and prejudice as constructs measuring individual differences because they could check for validity between the different sources of data. For RWA and for prejudice, the agreement between self-report and peer-report data showed similarities to the Big Five dimensions.
- There was confirmation that openness to experience, conscientiousness, RWA and prejudice were related, which agrees with findings of other studies. The relationship was measured by different methods and was still similar to other studies, which reinforces the relationship and the sources of their data. Agreeableness related to SDO to an extent and SDO related to prejudice to an extent, but the relationship was not as clear as the relationship between RWA, prejudice, openness to experience and conscientiousness. The findings confirm that RWA and SDO are separate and distinct, as the dual-process model predicts.
- There was not such a clear finding that RWA and SDO (ideological attitudes) come between personality dimensions and prejudice, though this pattern was predicted by earlier research findings. This study found a direct relationship between openness to experience and agreeableness and prejudice. RWA and SDO did not feature as mediator variables between personality dimensions and prejudice, though this finding came from having both self-report and peer-report data and perhaps would not have been uncovered using just self-report data. This might be the reason that the researchers did not replicate the mediation role of RWA and SDO.
- Cohrs *et al.* (2012) reiterate McFarland's (2010) conclusion that using the dual-process model that suggests RWA and SDO mediate personality dimensions and prejudice is not enough and to look at individual differences in prejudice more variables should be considered.
- SDO did not seem to be what people saw as part of someone's personality as much as RWA did. Interestingly, the researchers suggest that other evidence suggests that RWA might link to genetic influences more than SDO (Kandler *et al.*, 2012, cited in Cohrs *et al.*, 2012).

Evaluation of Cohrs *et al.* (2012)

Strengths

- Cohrs *et al.* (2012) used two sources for their data, self-report data and peer-report data. They found that the two judgements matched well and so they concluded that self-report data has reliability. This use of multi-methods is a strength of their study as self-report data can be questioned due to social desirability issues, or bias because of a desire to be seen as coherent.

- The researchers found very similar results to other studies on the same topic. They used different measures, though their scales were all standardised. They did adjust the scales to suit their needs and their participants, but they were tried-and-tested scales. As the measures found similar results to other studies and were standardised, it would seem that there was reliability in the results, in that most of the studies found the same correlations, albeit by some different methods.

Weaknesses

- The friend or acquaintance might have shown social desirability on behalf of the participant, or aimed to make the participant seem coherent. It is possible that the peer-report data showed bias just as self-report data can do. This is a weakness because if peer-report data show the same bias as self-report data, they are likely to show a high level of agreement, so there is reliability, but the data might not be valid because of the bias.
- The researchers point out that peers can report on what their friend or acquaintance has said or done, but they cannot know their attitudes or thoughts. What the peers report on is behaviour, but prejudice is an attitude, so it might be hard to show validity in the findings of the peer-report data. However, as there was a lot of agreement between the self-report and peer-report data, this weakness may not have been borne out by the findings.

Test yourself

1 Explain Cohrs *et al.*'s (2012) results in terms of what they show about self-report data compared with peer-report data. **(8 marks)**

2 Evaluate Cohrs *et al.* (2012) in terms of how credible the findings are. **(8 marks)**

Test yourself: 'studies' section

1 Choose one of the studies from this section: Sherif *et al.* (1954/1961), Reicher and Haslam (2006), Burger (2009) or Cohrs *et al.* (2012), and answer the following questions:

- **a** Describe the procedure of the study. **(6 marks)**
- **b** Describe the results of the study (include some figures). **(4 marks)**
- **c** In terms of methodology, compare your chosen study with Milgram (1963). **(6 marks)**

2 Compare Sherif *et al.* (1954/1961) with one other study that you have covered in detail in terms of what was studied, the procedures and results/conclusions. **(16 marks)**

Key questions in social psychology

You have to study one key question in each of the topic areas for your course and apply concepts and ideas from the topic area to that issue. Concepts and ideas include research, studies and theories. The two key questions suggested for your course are covered here, but you can choose a different key question to study. In the examination, you may be asked to apply concepts and ideas to a key question that you have not come across before (called 'unseen'). Studying all the key questions will help you to learn how to apply concepts, ideas, theory and research to an unseen key question in the exam.

How can prejudice and anti-social crowd behaviour be reduced?

Describing the issue

Football hooliganism relates to crowd behaviour. For example, sports teams tend to have very loyal followers. In football, team followers can be loyal to the point of rivalry escalating into violence. Police have searched through video and other records and identified people whom they think are ring leaders of such violence. They may be banned from matches or prevented from travelling abroad to support their teams.

Rivalry between teams can spill over into violence after a match. The teams wear colours to identify them on the pitch; supporters wear the same colours, on shirts, scarves and hats. The two groups are, therefore, easily identifiable.

There is also an international dimension to football hooliganism. English fans travel abroad to support teams and there are sometimes disturbances. Examples occurred in Marseilles in 1998, in Charleroi in 2000 and in Stuttgart in 2006. Sometimes, English fans are attacked by local people or by fans of other teams, rather than causing the disturbances. However, the violence is usually reported to have come from the football supporters. The issue is what causes this sort of violence when those concerned are not violent on other occasions.

In the 1980s, English football fans tended to be the ones hitting the headlines for violence. However, more recently Russian football fans have been featured, such as in 2013 during a Russia cup game. Social psychology can help to explain why groups might fight one another.

Explore

Look up football violence in Russia to find out about recent events. For example, www.theguardian.com/football/blog/2013/nov/03/english-football-hooliganism.

Rioting behaviour is crowd behaviour where control appears to be lost and there is looting, such as of shops, as well as general violence, such as setting cars alight. One example of rioting was in Tottenham, London in 2011, when a crowd gathered and became violent. This was in response to the shooting by police of Mark Duggan. The background to the rioting was a history of distrust of the policy by the people in the area. The area of dispute over the shooting was that the police said that Mark Duggan had a gun in his hand when he was shot, but the people in the area felt very strongly that he was 'streetwise' enough to know not to have a gun when being faced by police officers. The riots ensued. Fifty-five people were arrested and 26 police officers injured, according to the *Guardian* (7 August 2011). The next night there was further looting and violence, with shops and businesses targeted in other areas of London. Buildings were set alight and shops were ransacked, with a lot of violence, arrests and people getting hurt, both rioters and police.

Crowd behaviour is something that society wishes to control because any form of violence is usually considered harmful. When crowd behaviour becomes violent, and turns into a riot, there is a cost to society, in both emotional and financial terms. When a riot is a race riot, and two or more races turn against one another, there is often a high cost to society. Social identity theory can help to explain why one racial group may turn against another.

Explore

Find out more about the 2011 riots. For example, www.theguardian.com/uk-news/2014/jan/08/mark-duggan-death-london-riots.

STUDY HINT

Be sure to phrase your key question as an actual question and not just give an explanation of an issue. What is given here describes football hooliganism and crowd rioting, which is not a key question in itself. The question is 'How can football hooliganism or crowd rioting (anti-social behaviour) be reduced?'

Application of concepts and ideas

Explaining prejudice and anti-social crowd behaviour

- With regard to football hooliganism, two groups of supporters can easily identify each other. This makes identification with an in-group stronger, which is likely to mean that prejudice against the out-group is also strong.
- Explaining the hostility involved in football hooliganism, social identity theory suggests that people identify with their in-group and think of their group as being superior because this enhances their self-esteem. There is, therefore, a need to see the members of the other group as inferior. This can lead to prejudice and violence against out-group members.
- Using social identity theory, which can apply to football hooliganism, Tajfel *et al.* (1970, 1971) found that even minimal groups discriminate in favour of their in-group and against their out-group. Football supporters are members of a group for more solid reasons than the group members in Tajfel *et al.*'s study, so they could perhaps be more prejudiced and so discriminate more. This explains the prejudiced behaviour.
- There is also the issue of 'bad' crowd behaviour, such as rioting. One explanation of this suggests that because members of a crowd cannot be identified as individuals, they are 'deindividuated'. **Deindividuation** is when individual people do not feel recognised as individuals, which means they no longer feel responsible for their own actions, which can lead to behaviour that, as individuals, would not occur. A group of football supporters can become a crowd quite quickly and rioting in a crowd can be explained using the idea of deindividuation.
- Realistic group conflict theory is another explanation for prejudice. It suggests that when teams compete, they are likely to be prejudiced against one another. Football is all about competition. The claim of social identity theory that just having two groups causes prejudice might not explain football violence – it could be just about competition. Realistic group conflict theory might also help to explain riot behaviour where there is looting of shops and stealing of goods, as this might show competition for resources in times or places of economic hardship.
- Although social impact theory has been used as a theory relating to obedience, it can be used in any situation where an individual is influenced by others and this can include being influenced by a crowd. If the influencing group is large and seen as expert (such as long-term football fans), as well as being a group the individual belongs to (e.g. they support the team too), with immediate impact (e.g. they are in the crowd), then a person's attitudes might well be affected by the group.

Reducing prejudice and anti-social crowd behaviour

- Realistic conflict theory suggests that one way of reducing prejudice is to have two groups work together towards a goal that they both aspire to. This could explain why supporters of two opposing UK teams might come together as supporters of their national team.

- Sherif *et al.* (1954/1961) found that two groups of boys who had built up rivalry and prejudice got together, and prejudice was reduced, when the boys had to work together towards a 'superordinate' goal. Crowd rioting could be calmed if the crowd had to work towards a common goal.
- However, sometimes the common goal is destructive in society and has brought the crowd together, such as dissatisfaction over a country's economic situation or, in the example of the London riots, fear and anger against the police. Perhaps Sherif *et al.*'s ideas about reducing prejudice sometimes work towards increasing prejudice by forming an 'in-group'. A common goal might be avoiding any more damage to an area the crowd lives in, so emphasising damage could be a useful tactic to help to reduce the violent behaviour.
- Avoiding deindividuation might reduce the rioting behaviour or hooliganism. This can be done by filming the action or using CCTV that the crowd members know about. If they know that they can be identified, they may not feel deindividuated and so might behave according to their own moral rules and not in an anti-social way. It could be said that one reason for the reduction of violence among English football fans is the growth of CCTV (and the heavier police presence, as well as other measures, such as seating in the stands).
- Using social impact theory as a guide to predict behaviour can be helpful for society, as steps can then be taken. Individuals are less influenced by a group, according to the theory, if there is someone else with them – if two or more people are 'being influenced'. So having others as support, even if this is minority influence and the group is the majority, can help to reduce rioting and in-group/out-group prejudice.
- Using results from obedience studies can also be useful to reduce anti-social crowd behaviour. For example, it is known that people obey someone in uniform more than 'an ordinary man', so visible police presence (in uniform) can help to encourage obedience, and obedience to authority should reduce behaviour like rioting.

How can social psychology be used to explain heroism?

Describing the issue

Heroism is a great strength in a society if the actions of a hero act to save one or more people in that society. It might be that explaining heroism and finding out factors that make someone a 'hero' can be used to encourage more individuals to act in this pro-social way. **Pro-social behaviour** is acting for members of society or for other individuals, and is the opposite of **anti-social behaviour**, which is acting in a way that is against society. **Altruism** is the term used for acts that involve risk to an individual and good to someone else, with no gain for the individual. Heroism involves an act that is voluntary and done in the absence of reward. It involves an act that has risk attached in some way, and is something that benefits others in society or individuals of a society, and often done because of a moral decision. Scott *et al.* (2011) list features of a hero as being smart, resilient, charismatic, strong, caring, inspiring, selfless and reliable, although not all these features are present in all acts of heroism (e.g. some heroes are not charismatic, as such).

Some acts of heroism are large ones, involving risking one's life, and others are smaller acts, but still heroic, such as selflessness in helping in a community. Some acts of heroism are single, brave one-off acts, such as jumping into a river to save someone. Other acts of heroism are long term, such as persistently resisting a dictator's power in a country. One-off acts can be long term too, such as donating a kidney. An heroic act is not just a brave act, it is one that there is a choice about; some acts are brave, but the person has no choice, so that is not 'heroic' as defined here (though heroic in other senses).

The issue for society is how to encourage more heroes to help society to become more pro-social and altruistic for the benefit of society's members.

What makes Superman a hero? He saves others, at risk to himself, is charismatic when in that role (but not otherwise) and is smart, caring, reliable, selfless, inspiring and strong

Application of concepts and ideas

- It might be that social identity theory can explain some acts of heroism because heroism can be about protecting members of the in-group. Self-esteem of the individual is protected by being part of an in-group according to Tajfel and Turner's social identity theory, and if someone identifies with their in-group and supports them, this might to an extent explain acts of heroism. For example, a father can save another father as they are in the 'in-group' of fathers.

- Zimbardo is a researcher who found that we are strongly influenced by our social roles. He carried out a well-known study giving participants roles as either prisoners or guards in a set-up 'prison' environment. The guards became more and more brutal towards the prisoners and it was concluded that this was because of how a guard role is seen in society. The prisoners obeyed the guards, even though it was a simulation, so they too fitted into their role. Zimbardo is also involved in the psychology of heroism and talks about social roles and how they might help to explain acts of heroism. There are stories of fathers who leave their children in the care of a stranger in order to 'jump in' and save someone they don't know. This goes against what you would expect of the 'father' role but does perhaps fit the 'rescuer' male role in society. Zimbardo sees being a hero as a mindset rather than someone 'born' to be a hero and thinks that this mindset can be taught, to encourage heroism in a society.
- Zimbardo's teaching ideas include training adolescents and part of the training informs them about Milgram's results, such as how people can be agents of society and not autonomous, and how people obey those they see as having authority. People go against their own moral code when being obedient in this way. Training people to realise that they might do this, and to think in a more autonomous way, may encourage heroic behaviour.
- It is possible that heroism is innate and from our nature but that is not the popular belief, partly because when they are asked, heroes tend to say they did nothing special and they felt anyone else would have done the same. There are nature–nurture issues in explaining heroism.
- Features in a situation that encourage dissent or resistance to obedience might encourage heroism in a society, as has been suggested when discussing encouraging autonomy of thinking rather than being in an agentic state with regard to obedience. Resistance is found when orders are not given by someone in uniform and when orders are not given by someone nearby, but someone at a distance. Dissent is found when a setting is unofficial, such as in the rundown office block variation that Milgram carried out. Heroism might be encouraged if features of authority in a situation are removed. For example, someone might be a hero if there is nobody else around in a position of authority, whereas they might not act heroically if, for example, a policeman or a nurse is around. This is not just about lack of obedience, of course, but about taking decisions and thinking in an 'autonomous' way.

Explore

There is quite a lot on the internet about the psychology of heroism. For example, have a look at this interesting article on Psychology Today: www.psychologytoday.com/blog/in-the-garden-good-and-evil/201203/moral-courage-heroism-and-heroic-rescue. Or have a look at this article by Zimbardo: http://greatergood.berkeley.edu/article/item/what_makes_a_hero.

Test yourself

Read the following passage:

There had always been unrest in the country but now the two factions had turned from legal protesting to actual fighting, so something had to be done. It had got worse since the rebel had taken over as leader – they followed her no matter what she ordered them to do. And the other side was just as bad – as soon as the violence against them had escalated, they fought back even harder. You would have thought that after so long living together in the same country they would have learned to share it – but the one group of course claimed ownership of the land, and the other group saw themselves as having an equal right to be there too.

1. Using concepts, theories and studies from the social approach, explain how the situation outlined in the paragraph above might have come about. **(8 marks)**
2. The social approach offers concepts, theories and studies that can help to explain both football hooliganism and rioting behaviour. Assess these two issues for society, considering how the social approach can offer ideas to reduce such behaviours, which seem to threaten social stability. **(16 marks)**

Practical investigation in social psychology

For each topic area in your course, you will be carrying out a practical investigation, using methodology that you have learned about in that topic area. Your practical investigation is to gather data relevant to the material covered in this social psychology section of your course, and must be ethical of course.

For social psychology, you are asked to design and conduct a questionnaire, gathering both qualitative and quantitative data, and looking for a difference in the data. You need to consider issues around constructing a questionnaire, including sampling and ethical decisions. You will need to analyse your quantitative data using measures of central tendency as appropriate, measures of dispersion too, and use bar charts, frequency graphs and tables. Chapter 6 discusses the maths element of your course, including measures of central tendency and measures of dispersion. You will also need to analyse your qualitative data, using thematic analysis. Chapter 5 discusses using a questionnaire as a research method. It is also necessary to consider strengths and weaknesses of your questionnaire and possible improvements. A practical investigation in psychology has to be written up in the form of a standard structure, called a report. However, you will not be asked to write up your practical investigations completely – just the procedure, results and discussion sections of the report.

A Likert-type scale

Tick the appropriate box in the statements below.

Key: SA = strongly agree, A = agree, DK = don't know (unsure), D = disagree, SD = strongly disagree

Statement	SA	A	DK	D	SD
I like meeting new people	☐	☐	☐	☐	☐
I enjoy finding out about others	☐	☐	☐	☐	☐
I prefer the company of people like myself	☐	☐	☐	☐	☐
I prefer to go out with my friends	☐	☐	☐	☐	☐

Questionnaires can gather quantitative data by scoring response to statements according to whether a statement is agreed with or not

A report of a study in psychology has the sections of abstract (like a summary), introduction, method (including procedure, sampling, ethics, apparatus), results, conclusions and a discussion. Burger's (2009) study is available online and shows the first page, with the title, an abstract in italics to make it stand out, and the start of the background/ introduction (www.apa.org/pubs/journals/releases/amp-64-1-1.pdf).

Method link: Chapter 5 discusses issues around using a questionnaire research method as well as issues around analysis of quantitative and qualitative data (pp. 287–288).

Maths link: Chapter 6 discusses measures of central tendency and measures of dispersion, so look there for more information (pp. 387–392).

Practical link: Chapter 7 takes you through one idea for a practical investigation, including issues around writing up a report.

Two examples suggested in the social psychology topic area of your course are:

- a questionnaire about in-group/out-group issues and prejudice
- a questionnaire to see if males or females are more obedient.

Chapter 7 focuses on working through one practical investigation for each topic area in Year 1/AS. This is partly because you will be carrying out your own practical investigation in class, so it is not that helpful to explain a practical investigation in this chapter, and partly because, if you need help with the practical investigation sections of your course, you can find all the guidance in one chapter. The first example above is chosen, which is a questionnaire about in-group/out-group issues and prejudice. This relates nicely to social identity theory, so should be interesting and relevant to your learning.

Issues and debates in social psychology

The 11 issues and debates are summarised (with links to each of the topic areas in your Year 1 course) in Chapter 8 in this book, and then in detail in Book 2.

Chapter summary

- Obedience is studied, focusing Milgram's work, including three of his variations (Experiment 7, Experiment 10 and Experiment 13).
- Two theories that can help to explain obedience are covered: agency and social impact theory.
- Factors affecting obedience are also considered, including individual differences (personality and gender), situation and culture.
- Prejudice is the other main topic, focusing on two main theories: social identity theory and realistic conflict theory.
- As with obedience, factors affecting prejudice are considered, including individual differences (personality), situation and culture.
- Issues highlighting individual differences and development in social psychology are covered.
- Methods in social psychology for your course include interviews and questionnaires, with related issues and also a focus on alternate hypotheses. Sampling is also covered, as well as the BPS Code of Ethics and Conduct (2009), although coverage is not detailed in this chapter, as Chapter 5 covers these in full.
- Methods also include analysis of qualitative and quantitative data. Analysis of qualitative data is found in more detail in Chapter 5 and analysis of quantitative data is in Chapter 6.
- Sherif *et al.* (1954/1961) is the classic study, focusing on prejudice and so suiting the prejudice area of the content for social psychology in your course.
- Three contemporary studies are explained here: Burger (2009), focusing on Milgram's work; Reicher and Haslam (2006), focusing on social identity theory; and Cohrs *et al.* (2012), focusing on individual differences and prejudice.
- Two key questions are considered relating to social psychology: 'how can prejudice and anti-social behaviour be reduced?' and 'how can social psychology be used to explain heroism?'
- A practical investigation for social psychology is explained in Chapter 7, so the practical investigation part of social psychology is only briefly mentioned in this chapter.
- The 11 issues and debates are briefly explained, along with examples from social psychology to help your learning. Chapter 8 covers all the issues and debates for your course and how they link to each topic area.

Chapter Two: Cognitive Psychology

Overview

The cognitive approach is about how information is processed in the brain. When information is taken into the brain through the eyes, ears, tongue and other senses, it is recorded, processed and then there is output. Cognitive psychology examines how this occurs. Cognitive psychology covers different aspects of information processing, including perception, language, attention, problem-solving and memory. In your course, memory is the area that is studied.

Studies of interest

Studies have shown that using a mobile phone when driving is distracting and dangerous because the individual is attending to two tasks at once. A study in *The Psychologist* (Griggs *et al.*, 2007) showed that when conversations are emotional, driving is affected to an even greater extent. The study used participants who were either frightened by spiders or not affected by them. During conversations about spiders, the phobic participants made more driving errors and had a narrower range of eye movements. This study is about cognitive psychology and how information is processed and how it affects behaviour. It is useful because it warns people not to drive when having emotionally charged conversations.

Studies have shown that paying attention to a phone while driving distracts from paying attention to driving

Dykas *et al.* (2012) asked 189 adolescents (62 per cent female) to do a ten-minute laboratory task with unfamiliar peers. Then the adolescents rated their perceptions of the interaction. After two weeks, the adolescents rated their perceptions again using the same measure. The study aimed to see if adolescents who were securely attached as young children would show different perceptions than those who were insecurely attached, based on the idea that their attachment experiences would act as schemas for their later perceptions of people they did not know. This tests the idea of memory being reconstructive, and based on schemas, a theory that is explained later in this chapter (pp. 95–99). It was found that attachment experiences did not affect the initial perceptions. However, there were differences in the later perceptions (recorded two weeks later). Those with insecure attachment history remembered the interactions more negatively in the later perceptions than those with more secure attachment history, though in both groups more hostility was recalled in the later perceptions of the interaction than in the immediate recall of the interaction. This supports the idea that memory is affected by previous experiences.

> Studies have shown that previous experiences, such as attachment type, can affect perceptions much later.

Everyday example

The NHS website discusses memory and possible causes of memory loss (accessed 2014), partly to reassure people that memory loss does not always mean the person is developing dementia. Memory loss can be caused by anxiety or depression, for example. The NHS website discusses how doctors classify memories as being immediate, short-term or long-term. Immediate memories are stored for a few seconds only. Short-term memories are stored for 15–20 seconds, like telephone numbers; about seven chunks of information can be stored at any one time in short-term memory. Long-term memories are more permanent and are reinforced repeatedly from short-term memory in order to be stored more permanently. This chapter will look at the multi-store model of memory, which puts forward the view that there is a sensory store, as well as short-term and long-term memory. This everyday example shows how findings in cognitive psychology are applied to real-life issues, such as health issues.

> Cognitive psychology can be used to inform everyday life issues, such as memory loss.

Summary of learning objectives

Content:

You have to know about:

- the **working memory** theory of memory (Baddeley and Hitch, 1974)
- the **multi-store model** of memory (Atkinson and Shiffrin, 1968)
- an explanation of long-term memory that looks at **episodic memory** (memory for episodes) and **semantic memory** (memory of meanings) (Tulving, 1972)
- the **reconstructive theory of memory** (Bartlett, 1932), including **schema theory**.

Recall of a car accident might be reconstructed according to previous schemas, such as about speeds of certain types of car or driving style of certain 'types' of driver

Individual differences and developmental psychology

In all topic areas, you need to consider two issues in psychology: individual differences and developmental psychology.

Individual differences

In cognitive psychology, you will learn about the following links:

- Reconstructive theory suggests that we remember using schemas that we have built through our learning, and our schemas are individual, so can show individual differences.
- If someone has brain damage that affects their memory, there are similarities in effects depending on where the damage is. However, there will also be individual differences in the effects of damage. Schmolck *et al.* (2002) discuss such issues, including the case study of HM, and how individual differences are important in memory, even though largely similarities are studied.
- Autobiographical memory, which is episodic memory, is by nature individual as it is about individual episodes and events in our lives. Tulving discusses the difference between episodic and semantic memory.

Developmental psychology

In cognitive psychology, you must learn about at least one of the following areas of study:

- Sebastián and Hernández-Gil (2012) look at developmental issues in memory span, showing that five year olds have a shorter memory span than 17 year olds and that the development of memory span is gradual between those ages. This is a choice of study, but if you choose this one, it will help with discussion of developmental psychology.
- Dyslexia affects children's memory span and working memory, which can affect their learning. This is in the field of development as it is about children developing and what affects them. This topic area can be used as a key question in your course.
- The impact of Alzheimer's on older people and the effects on their memory is within the field of development as it is about development into old age. This topic area can be used as a key question in your course.

Methods

Chapter 5 covers the methodology you will need for Year 1 of your course (and the AS, with some exceptions). See Table 5.1 (page 278) for a summary of which methods you need to know for this chapter. Chapter 6 covers the mathematical elements you need for your course. See Table 6.2 (page 386) for a summary of the mathematical skills you need to know for this chapter.

Henry Molaison, known as HM to protect his identity before his death. Brain damage affected his memory, enabling psychologists to see which parts of the brain had which function with regard to memory

Studies

The classic study you will be learning about in cognitive psychology is Baddeley (1966b) 'Working memory model: the influence of acoustic and semantic similarity on long-term memory for word sequences'. (Baddeley did another 1966 study, so the one in your course is referenced as '1966b'.)

You will chose one contemporary study from:

- Schmolck *et al.* (2002) 'Semantic knowledge in patient HM and other patients with bilateral medial and lateral temporal lobe lesions'
- Steyvers and Hemmer (2012) 'Reconstruction from memory in naturalistic environments'
- Sebastián and Hernández-Gil (2012) 'Developmental pattern of digit span in Spanish population'.

Key questions

You have to be able to describe one key question and explain it using concepts and theories that you have learned from cognitive psychology. You can use any key question, but two key questions are given in the specification and are explained later in this chapter. These are:

- How can psychologists' understanding of memory help dementia patients?
- How can knowledge of working memory be used to inform the treatment of dementia?

STUDY HINT

It may seem as if the separate sections in your course within each topic area (content, method, studies, key question, practical investigation and issues and debates) are not connected. However, the key questions suggested here link to the four models of memory you will be covering in cognitive psychology. Note also that material links between sections. For example, an everyday example was given at the start of this chapter showing how the NHS uses a model of memory to explain how memory works to help people to see if they have dementia or not.

Practical investigation

Chapter 7 covers the skills you need for conducting a practical investigation, including worked-through examples. Chapter 6 covers the mathematical elements for your course, which also links to your practical investigation.

Issues and debates

Issues and debates are in the A level course but not the AS, so if you are doing the AS, you do not need to study issues and debates, although they are interesting and will extend your understanding of psychology. The 11 issues and debates are: ethics; practical issues in research design; reductionism; comparing explanations; psychology as a science; culture and gender; nature–nurture; how psychology has developed over time; issues of social control; using psychology in society; and issues around socially sensitive research.

Chapter 8 summarises the issues and debates and how the four topic areas for your Year 1 course inform each of these. Book 2 will explain these in more detail.

STUDY HINT

Issues and debates appear in each topic area for Year 1 (and Year 2), in the same order, in the specification. For each topic area, you can use the examples against each of the issues and debates to learn how the material for that topic area illustrates that issue or debate. See Chapter 8 for more detail.

Make a summary of learning objectives into a checklist, such as the one in Table 2.1. However, you could add more detail to help your learning.

Table 2.1 What you need to know for cognitive psychology

You need to know about	
The working memory model	Analysis of quantitative data - measures of central tendency and measures of dispersion
The multi-store model	Bar chart, histogram, frequency tables
The 'episodic/semantic' explanation of long-term memory	The Mann-Whitney U and Wilcoxon tests
The reconstructive model of memory	Probability and levels of significance with regard to statistical testing, and one-tailed and two-tailed issues
Field and laboratory experiments; experimental and null hypothesis, directional and non-directional hypotheses	Type I and Type II errors
Variables - independent and dependent variables; operationalisation of variables	Normal and skewed distribution
Situational and participant variables	Case studies of brain-damaged patients, including the study of HM and the use of qualitative data
Confounding and extraneous variables	Baddeley's (1966b) classic study
Experimental/research designs - repeated measures, independent groups, matched pairs	One contemporary study from Schmolck *et al.* (2002), Steyvers and Hemmer (2012) and Sebastián and Hernández-Gil (2012)
Issues of counterbalancing, randomisation and order effects	One key question which can be explained using concepts, theories and/or research from cognitive psychology as explained in your course
Experimenter effects, demand characteristics and control issues	One practical investigation (an experiment) focusing on material covered in cognitive psychology in your course
Evaluation issues, including reliability, validity and objectivity	Individual differences and developmental psychology and links to memory issues
Issues and debates (not for AS)	

An introduction to cognitive psychology

Humans and chimpanzees have 98 per cent of their genes in common, which makes them very similar. However, there are obvious differences, so the small number of different genes must be important.

An important difference between humans and other animals is language ability. It is not only humans that use language – other animals (e.g. dolphins and bonobo chimps) use language in some form. Many experimental studies of chimpanzees have been made. Some can use grammar and create new sentences, as well as name objects, which is impressive. However, they cannot speak. Keyboards or signs are used to 'talk'. The ability to talk makes humans different – the structure of the brain and larynx are linked to speaking and language use. Chimpanzees and other apes can use tools as humans do and can solve problems. However, the human brain allows us to be better at solving these.

Using tools, solving problems, using language and speaking are all skills that have contributed to human society and interaction. All are areas studied within cognitive psychology. Humans rely on remembering things and on being able to take information into the brain via the senses – sight, hearing, touch, taste and smell.

Memory, forgetting, problem-solving, perception, language and thought are all studied within the cognitive approach. The overall focus is on how humans deal with information, from taking it into the brain via the senses, through processing, to producing the required output.

Chimpanzees can use language but not as comprehensively as humans can

STUDY HINT
At the start of any chapter, there will be terms that you are likely not to have come across. Terms are set out in bold and are defined in a glossary of terms. These news terms and ideas may not be explained immediately. This can be off-putting but rest assured that the ideas will be fully explained and you will have the chance to practise the ideas too.

Ideas underpinning cognitive psychology

Key ideas underpinning cognitive psychology include the focus on information processing and the idea that the brain might process information in a similar way to a computer.

STUDY HINT
It is useful to get an overview of what cognitive psychology is about as only a small part of cognitive psychology is covered in your course. For example, language is part of the cognitive approach but you study only memory. You can be asked questions about cognitive psychology in general and should learn about such general issues.

Information processing

Cognitive psychology assumes that information is processed in the brain (called **information processing**). Processing is considered to be **linear** – that is, information flows 'through' the brain in a way that seems logical.

Definition
Linear refers to a single straight line.

Information is taken in by the senses before being processed. It is thought that, when being remembered, information is **encoded** in the brain (translated into a manageable form). It is then **stored**. When remembered, it is **retrieved** from storage. This is a linear, logical process. In studies within cognitive psychology, information is mapped at each stage. The assumption that information is processed follows scientific theory. In a scientific experiment, materials are assembled (information flows into the brain), something happens (processing) and the result is recorded (there is an output). The cognitive approach uses scientific methods such as laboratory experiments. The idea of a flow of information being tracked and tested at different stages would appeal to those working within this approach.

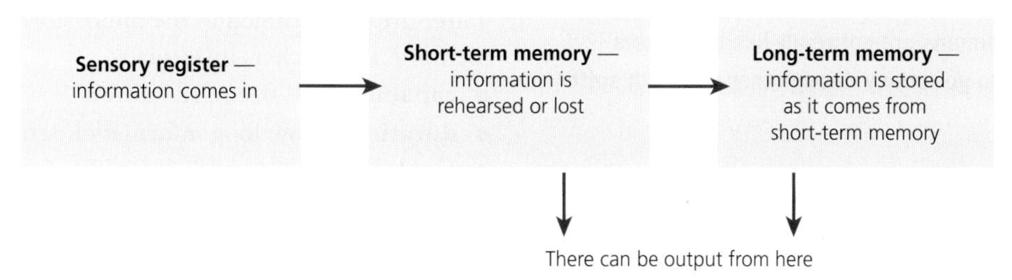

A summary of the multi-store model of memory to show the idea of information processing

An example of a theory using information processing is the multi-store model (see diagram above; also 'Content' section below).

STUDY HINT
An issue and debate in your course considers psychology and science. You can use ideas like information processing, the multi-store model of memory and learning by using experiments to discuss how psychology follows scientific principles.

Brains work like computers

A computer has input, processing and output. It receives input via a keyboard or a voice-recognition device. Unlike a computer, the human brain receives information from the senses. Input into a computer is more limited, whereas the human brain receives masses of information all the time. The computer 'perceives' all the input, whereas the human brain only perceives or pays attention to a small part of the information.

Once data have been input, the computer processes the data. The human brain processes the information it perceives, so in this way the two are similar. The computer uses memory and can solve problems. However, there are differences – the computer does not make mistakes, whereas the human brain does. The computer will do the same processing repeatedly, whereas a human brain might not repeat the same sequences for various reasons (e.g. interference from the environment).

Once the processing is complete, there is output. The computer produces output in the form of a printout or a screen display. A human being produces output using language or the written word. There are similarities between the two, but humans also use body language, emotions and other signals, so their output is more complex.

A sick computer – humans are not really like computers because humans can get poorly, though they can both suffer from viruses

Cognitive psychology treats the brain as if it were a computer, albeit more complex (the **computer analogy**). Using ideas from a computer to explain human processing is useful because the brain is not yet well understood. It is also useful to clarify how the brain processes information.

Explore

Use the internet or another source to investigate the computer analogy. Find out more about how the human brain works with regard to perception, problem-solving, language or thought. Look up the Necker cube, an illusion that helps to emphasise how the brain makes sense of what is seen.

Progress check 2.1

Explain, using examples, what cognitive psychology is about in general.

Content in cognitive psychology

You will need to know:

- the working memory model of memory (Baddeley and Hitch, 1974)
- the multi-store model of memory (Atkinson and Shiffrin, 1968), including short- and long-term memory, and ideas about information processing, encoding, storage and retrieval, capacity and duration
- episodic and semantic memory as explanations of long-term memory (Tulving, 1972)
- reconstructive memory (Bartlett, 1932), including schema theory.

We start with the multi-store model because the working memory model and the idea of episodic and semantic memory build on this model. Reconstructive memory is considered last. The theories are evaluated by identifying strengths and weaknesses.

The multi-store model of memory

The multi-store model here is based on Atkinson and Shiffrin (1968), but the basics of the other models from the same era are the same.

On page 77, you will find a diagram of the multi-store model, given as an example of information processing.

Capacity, duration and mode of representation

Three areas are studied in the multi-store model of memory. Researchers investigate:

- **capacity** – the size of the store
- **duration** – how long information remains in the store
- **mode of representation** (mode of storage) – the form in which information is encoded or stored.

Encoding, storage and retrieval

Researchers investigate:

- **encoding** – how memories are encoded, which means how they are registered as memories, such as by sound or smell
- **storage** – how memories are stored, which means how they remain as memories after they have been registered
- **retrieval** – how we retrieve memories when the output is needed, which means finding and accessing stored memories.

The concept of retrieval is important. We may have memories but, if we cannot access them, perhaps they are not true memories.

STUDY HINT

Learn the six terms (capacity, duration, mode of representation, encoding, storage and retrieval) as you will need to be able to use these ideas. You could start a cognitive psychology (memory) glossary to help your learning of this area.

Encoding	Storage	Retrieval
• This is registering information as a memory • Can be in different form/mode – visual, acoustic (sound), tactile (touch), semantic (meaning)	• This is keeping memories after encoding • Can be in sensory memory, short-term memory or long-term memory. Links to neuroscience – there is actual storage in the brain	• This is accessing memories from storage • Can be recognition or recall. Can be reconstructive (not an exact match with what was encoded and stored). Lack of retrieval = forgetting

How memory is about information processing and information flow

Explore

Look up encoding, storage and retrieval in more detail on the internet. For example, www.human-memory.net/index.html. Reading about memory in different sources is useful and helps you to become very familiar with terms.

Progress check 2.2

Fill in the gaps in the following paragraph using the terms given below.

Information is ________________, which is the early part of the process and then it is ________________, such as in short-term and long-term memory. When a memory is needed, there is ________________ and without that there would be forgetting. The ________________ of a store is its size and the ________________ is how long memory lasts in that store. Finally, there is focus on the ________________, which is the form in which the information is stored.

Terms: mode of representation; capacity; stored; duration; encoded; retrieval

The three main stores

The central idea of the multi-store model is that there are three stores of memory, which involve a flow of information. The model focuses clearly on information processing.

Sensory register

First, there is the **sensory register**, which can be called **sensory memory** and is where the information comes into the brain from the senses and is held for a short time. The information is in the store in the same format as it is received – for example, what is heard is stored as sound. This format is the **mode of representation**, the way the information is represented in the brain, in this case, in the sensory register.

All the information from the senses goes into the sensory register – that is, from touch, taste, sound, smell and sight – but only a small amount is attended to. The rest is not registered. The information lasts in the sensory register for up to two seconds (see diagram on page 80). Perception can be thought of as seeing something *as* something; in the sensory register, there is no attempt to perceive information *as* something, merely to receive it. It is information from the senses but not perception as such. From the sensory register, information that has been attended to passes to the short-term store. Any information not attended to is lost.

Definition

When information is in the same form as it is received, it is said to be **modality specific.**

Capacity, duration and mode of representation with regard to the sensory register:

- Capacity is unlimited in one sense as all information arrives at the sensory register. However, a great deal is not attended to and is lost, so capacity in that way is very limited.
- Duration is up to two seconds.
- Mode of representation is modality specific (information is in the same form as it is received, e.g. information from the eyes is visually received in the sensory register).

Short-term store

The second store is the **short-term store** (STS), often called **short-term memory** (STM). Short-term memory stores information in auditory form – by sound. Information can stay in short-term memory for up to 30 seconds. From experiments, it seems that short-term memory can hold between five and nine items or chunks. If information is rehearsed in short-term memory, it passes into the **long-term store** (LTS) or **long-term memory** (LTM). Any information that is not rehearsed is lost from the short-term store. Rehearsal is done in an acoustic form – for example, repeating it to yourself.

Capacity, duration and mode of representation with regard to the short-term store:

- Capacity is limited to 5–9 chunks or items of information.
- Duration is up to 30 seconds.
- Mode of representation is auditory.

STUDY HINT

Baddeley (1966b), which you will learn about later, shows how STM uses acoustic coding (**acoustic** and auditory mean sound) and LTM is more semantic (semantic is meaning), though can involve acoustic coding too. These findings fit with what is said here about the short-term store in the multi-store model of memory.

Displacement as a theory of forgetting

The theory that displacement causes forgetting can be understood by reference to the multi-store model of memory. As we have seen, the idea is that there is a short-term store where information is held for a short time (up to 30 seconds). It is either rehearsed, and goes into the long-term store, or is lost. The theory of displacement as a reason for forgetting is that the rehearsal loop in the short-term store has a limited capacity – perhaps nine items or fewer.

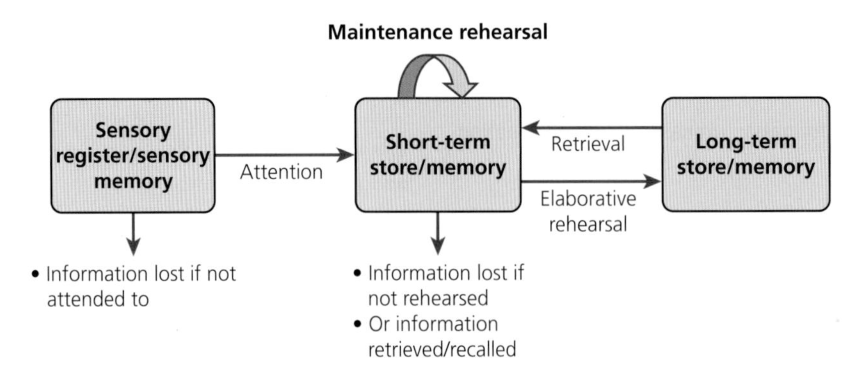

The multi-store model

Long-term store

The third store is long-term memory. Information can stay (potentially) in long-term memory forever. Information is held largely in **semantic** form, which means it is held according to meaning. It can also be visually or acoustically stored. An infinite amount of information can be stored in long-term memory. You will learn more about LTM when you read about Tulving's ideas about episodic and semantic memory and Baddeley's (1966b) classic study.

Capacity, duration and mode of representation with regard to the long-term store:

- Capacity is potentially unlimited.
- Duration is potentially unlimited.
- Mode of representation is semantic (relies on meaning) but can also be visual or acoustic.

Progress check 2.3

The following questions relate to the three stores - sensory memory, STM and LTM.

1. Which of the three stores has an unlimited capacity?
2. Which of the three stores is modality specific?
3. Which of the three stores lasts up to about 30 seconds?
4. Which of the three stores uses a mainly semantic mode?

Evidence for displacement as a theory of forgetting

The idea of primacy and recency effects comes from the multi-store model of memory:

- The **primacy effect** is that information learned first is well remembered, probably because it has gone to the long-term store through the rehearsal loop.
- The **recency effect** is that information that is learned last is well remembered, probably because it is still in the rehearsal loop and so available for immediate recall.
- Information from the middle is not well recalled. This is probably because it did not go from the rehearsal loop into the long-term store, but was displaced by new material in the loop and was lost, i.e. forgotten. This is evidence for the idea of displacement in the short-term store.

STUDY HINT

The idea of primacy and recency effects is explored further on page 82.

Waugh and Norman (1965) tested this idea. They read a list of letters to participants. After hearing the list, the participants were told one of the letters and they had to try to remember the subsequent letter. For example, if the list was 'B P S T J F A O N' and the researchers called out 'T', the participants had to say 'J'. They found that displacement did seem to occur. Although Glanzer *et al.* (1967) thought that displacement was a factor in forgetting, they also thought that decay caused forgetting. This is because there is a time delay in experiments – the longer the time before recall, the greater the forgetting. This forgetting could not be displacement alone because displacement would cause the same degree of forgetting, whatever the time delay between learning and recall. Therefore, displacement alone does not explain forgetting.

> **STUDY HINT**
> Trace decay as a theory of forgetting is explained later when looking at the working memory model (pp. 84–85). The multi-store model and the working memory model go together. The trace decay, displacement and interference explanations of forgetting also go with both the models and are explained in this textbook to help to expand your understanding. In your notes you could separate the multi-store and working memory models of memory from the three ideas about forgetting (trace decay, displacement and interference) but it is useful to also see how they fit together. Note that the forgetting theories are not directly required in your course but they can be helpful when discussing models of memory.

Evaluation of the displacement theory of forgetting

Strengths

- The theory fits with the multi-store model of memory and the working memory model. Both these models suggest a loop where information is rehearsed before going to the long-term store. If there is a loop with limited capacity (the multi-store model suggests up to nine items), then it makes sense to say that new material displaces material already in the loop. This theory of forgetting supports two models of memory that are themselves supported by a great deal of evidence. This, in turn, is support for this theory of forgetting.
- The theory is tested by experiments that are well controlled and, therefore, yield information about cause and effect. The experiments are replicable and can be tested for reliability. Therefore, displacement is tested scientifically.

Weaknesses

- The theory is difficult to operationalise. What is taken to be displacement could be interference. The information in the rehearsal loop could be written over, which is displacement. However, it could be that the incoming new information interferes with the information being rehearsed. This would be interference, rather than displacement. Interference theory is explained below (pp. 81–82 and p. 102).
- It is tested using artificial tasks, such as lists of letters. This means that what is being tested may not be valid because it is not a real-life task.

Interference theory of forgetting

The theory that interference causes forgetting differs from the theory of displacement in that it says that an item gets in the way of another item, rather than displacing it. Peterson and Peterson's (1959) study investigated interference in the short-term store – this idea is explored further in Chapter 7 (pp. 431–442). The interference theory of forgetting also focuses on the long-term store.

There are two types of interference:

- **Proactive interference** is when something learned earlier interferes with current learning.
- **Retroactive interference** is when something learned later gets in the way of something learned previously.

> **STUDY HINT**
> Think of 'pro' as 'before' (what was learned before gets in the way); think of 'retro' as 'back' (what is learned now gets in the way; interferes going backwards).

Evidence for the interference theory of forgetting

When testing interference, participants are given one set of pairs to learn, followed by a second set. The first word of each pair in each set is the same. For example, one set could include table–chair and the other set could include table–stool. Participants become confused between the two lists. It is said that this is caused by interference.

Jenkins and Dallenbach (1924) carried out an experiment to test the idea that interference causes forgetting. They thought that what is learned later will interfere with what people have already learned. Participants were given ten nonsense syllables to learn (for example, BOH or INJ). Some participants slept after the learning and others carried on with their everyday routines. Those who stayed awake did not remember as much as those who slept –there was more forgetting. The researchers claimed that this was because sleeping had not caused interference, whereas the day's activities had and that interference had caused forgetting.

STUDY HINT

When evaluating a theory, research evidence can be used to support or refute it. Therefore, Jenkins and Dallenbach's study can be used as a strength of the interference theory of forgetting because its findings are consistent with the theory.

Evaluation of the interference theory of forgetting

Strengths

- There is much evidence to support the theory. Different lists of words are used with participants and what they learn first does interfere with what they learn second. Jenkins and Dallenbach (1924) give evidence for this idea.
- The evidence comes from experiments, which are controlled and so yield cause-and-effect conclusions. This scientific approach to study is rated highly because firm conclusions can be drawn. It also means that studies are replicable and can be tested for reliability.

Weaknesses

- The theory describes a feature of forgetting in memory experiments, where similar tasks make remembering difficult, and it is thought that this is because of interference. However, it does not explain *how* this happens. The problem is separating the idea of interference from displacement or trace decay. It is difficult to show that displacement causes the loss of recall from the short-term store and not that the memory trace has simply decayed or that interference from a new set of information (rather than displacement by that new information) has caused the memory loss.
- The studies tend to use word lists and artificial tasks. In real life, it is not usual to do only one thing at once and many tasks are carried out quickly. It is not likely, therefore, that interference accounts for all forgetting, so the conclusions may not be valid. Solso (1995) says that the tasks carried out to test interference theory (e.g. learning nonsense syllables) would not occur in real life. One of the contemporary studies that you could choose to study in cognitive psychology is Steyvers and Hemmer (2012), which gives a good account of how studies need to be 'naturalistic' for findings to be useful.
- The effect of interference disappears when participants are given cues. Therefore, it seems that the memory trace was present but could not be retrieved. This goes against the idea of interference as an explanation for forgetting.

Evaluation of the multi-store model of memory

There has been a great deal of experimental work based on the multi-store model of memory. Baddeley (1966b) is an example of experiments that focus on STM and LTM. From these studies, strengths and weaknesses of the model can be found.

Strengths

- The experiments that provide support for the model are reliable because they have been repeated often and, being well controlled, are replicable. The experimental research method is scientific and so a sound body of knowledge can be built up. For example, Glanzer and Cunitz (1966) carried out a study using word lists. They found that the first words in a list were recalled well, as were the last words, but that the middle words were not remembered well. They claimed that the primacy effect was because those words had been rehearsed and so were in long-term memory and accessible. The recency effect was because those words were still in consciousness in short-term memory, so were recalled easily. The middle words were neither well-rehearsed and in long-term memory, nor in consciousness in short-term memory. Therefore, these words were the most easily forgotten.
- There is evidence from case studies that give physiological support. For example, the case study of Clive Wearing (Blakemore, 1988) showed that there is an area of the brain (the hippocampus) which, if damaged, prevents new memories from being laid down. It appears that the hippocampus holds the short-term memory because a person with a damaged hippocampus can no longer build long-term memories. If there is no rehearsal, no new long-term memories, and a particular area of the brain is damaged, this suggests that when undamaged, this area of the brain fulfils that purpose.

Sir Colin Blakemore worked with Clive Wearing and wrote up a case study about his damage to the hippocampus and his related short-term memory issues

Weaknesses

- Although case studies like Clive Wearing have suggested an area of the brain for short-term memory, another case study (Shallice and Warrington, 1970) showed that a victim of a motorbike accident was able to add long-term memories even though his short-term memory was damaged. This goes against the multi-store model. Another study (Schmolck *et al.*, 2002, one of the contemporary studies for this topic area) gives more detailed findings when looking at how brain damage affects memory. The study of Henry Molaison (HM) and others suggests that how memory works is actually very complex when it comes to showing where STM and LTM might be in the brain and how they might work. This complexity goes against the simplicity of the multi-store model.
- It is hard to say what capacity means. Craik and Lockhart (1972) ask whether it is limited processing capacity or limited storage capacity. Short-term memory tends to take limited capacity as limited storage and that capacity is five to nine items. However, if words rather than letters are used in a span test, 20 items can be recalled. This shows that capacity needs to be defined more rigorously.
- Experiments used to test the multi-store model tend to employ artificial tasks – for example, testing short-term memory using letters or digits. The findings may not be valid because, in real life, processing is rarely as isolated as these tasks suggest. Steyvers and Hemmer (2012), which is detailed later as one of the contemporary studies, focuses on how memory experiments lack ecological validity and gives useful evidence to show that experiments do not yield valid data.

Explore

Using the internet or some other source, see what you can find out about Clive Wearing. Then find out what you can about KF, one of the other case studies mentioned when evaluating the multi-store model of memory. For example, http://ai.ato.ms/MITECS/Entry/baddeley.html has some interesting information.

Practical

You can test the multi-store model yourself by doing a study along the lines of the one done by Glanzer and Cunitz in 1966. Write out about 25 words, making sure that they do not lead from one to the other with meaning (e.g. not 'white' and then 'house') so that there are no cues for learning and recall. You then need some willing participants, perhaps friends, or work in a group in your class, or ask family members. Provide the participant with a pen and paper and, in quiet conditions, and separately, ask each participant to learn the list of words, giving them about a minute to do so. Then, take the list away, and ask them to write down what they can recall on a piece of paper. They can use free recall, which means recalling the words in any order. Thank the participant, show them the list and explain what you were testing. The aim is to see if they recall more of the first words in the list and more of the last words, with fewer words in the middle, such as the first seven words, the last five words and hardly any of the eight in the middle.

The explanation is that the first words are in LTM and have been well-rehearsed. The last words are still in STM ready for recall when you stop the task and let them write the words down. The middle words are not well-rehearsed into LTM and no longer in STM so they are 'lost'. Of course some middle words will be recalled. Perhaps you have a word that everyone recalls, such as 'chocolate'. This will help you to see why controls are so important in an experiment. Hopefully, you enjoy this experience and it helps with learning the method for the cognitive psychology section of your course. Remember the most important thing is to be ethical and, if participants are reluctant in any way, you must let them withdraw from the study.

Progress check 2.4

Here are some questions about the practical testing the multi-store model:

1. How is it known that the first words in the list would be in LTM?
2. How is it known that the last words in the list would be in STM?
3. Explain one possible factor that might affect the results other than word position.
4. Why are there about 25 words in the list?

Test yourself

1. Explain the differences between the three stores in the multi-store model. **(6 marks)**
2. Using evidence, evaluate the multi-store model as an explanation of how we remember. **(12 marks)**

Working memory (Baddeley and Hitch, 1974)

This modern model of memory is probably the most dominant model today. Referring back to the multi-store model will help you to understand the **working memory model**. The multi-store model suggests that there is a short-term store and a long-term store. The working memory model focuses on the short-term store and on providing more information about short-term remembering.

General ideas about working memory and the model

The idea of working memory is that there is a system in the short term that is there to maintain and store information and this system underlies all thinking, not just focusing on memory. The idea is a system that has limited capacity to bridge between perception, long-term memory and action. Perception is getting the information in, long-term memory is storing the information and 'action' is the output. Working memory is seen as a system between perception and long-term memory.

Such a system has to have some storage, for the information, so that it can get into long-term memory. This is taking short-term memory and splitting it into different areas. Such a system also needs something as a control to sort information into such storage areas. Working memory is concerned with reasoning, understanding and learning – with thinking.

Baddeley in 2003 wrote a review about working memory and discusses the starting point of ideas about a short-term and a long-term memory. Baddeley (2003) mentions Hebb, in 1949, suggesting that short-term memory is based on some sort of electrical activity that is short-lived and long-term memory based on neuronal growth. This is interesting because this is about neuroscience – Hebb was considering the brain itself when he proposed this distinction. In your course, cognitive psychology is studied separately from biological psychology but it is worth remembering that the two are not as separate as it might seem. As Baddeley points out, it took more than ten years for evidence for Hebb's ideas, but that evidence did come, and it is thought that short-term memory is indeed short-lived unless rehearsed into long-term memory.

More research was done into STM as a separate system from LTM and what developed was a model of memory that has temporary sensory registers (Baddeley, 2003) flowing into a limited capacity short-term store. You can recognise the multi-store model here, though there are additional registers. This is the basis of the working memory model, which looks at the temporary registers. Baddeley and Hitch (1974) proposed that short-term memory has three components and is not just one system, as suggested by the multi-store model.

The trace-decay theory of forgetting, linking to the biology of the brain

The trace-decay theory of forgetting is best understood by recalling the multi-store model of memory in which there is a short-term store and a long-term store. Trace decay is a theory of forgetting that applies to both the short-term store and the long-term store.

The main point is that memories have a physical trace. Over time, this trace deteriorates until finally it is lost. It is thought that memories are stored in the brain, which means a structural change must occur. This is called an **engram**. Engrams are thought to be subject to neurological decay. As an engram decays, the memory disappears and forgetting occurs. One way of renewing the trace is to repeat and rehearse information, which reinstates the engram. The working memory model includes rehearsal in its explanation. It is thought that when something is first learned the trace is fragile, but after further learning the engram becomes more solid and is less likely to be destroyed. The change from a cognitive process to an engram is a neurochemical one. In the biological approach, you will study how neurochemicals work.

> **Explore**
> In 1949, Hebb set out the idea of an engram and what a memory is. Penfield (1891–1976) tried to help patients with epilepsy and during surgery identified places where memories are stored, which is evidence for the existence of engrams. Look up Hebb and Penfield and find their contribution to the trace-decay theory.

Evidence for the trace-decay theory of forgetting

Reitman (1974) and McKenna and Glendon (1985) carried out studies into trace decay. In one study, focusing on the short-term store, male students were shown a list of five words for two seconds and then had to listen for a faint tone over headphones. The tone was given after 15 seconds. The participants had to then try to recall the words. Word recall fell by 24 per cent in the 15-second period before recall, when recall rate was compared with no 15-second gap.

The passage of time led to forgetting. This suggested that forgetting came about because of the decay of the trace. Listening for the tone prevented rehearsal and stopped new information from being thought about. Therefore, there was no rehearsal of the current material to renew the trace and no displacement by new material, so the trace in the short-term store must have decayed.

In a study focusing on the long-term store, shop and office workers volunteered to take part in a task to learn how to resuscitate someone (restart the heart). Their performance was measured up to three years later. After three years, recall of the technique was poor. The conclusions were that such skills need renewing to be remembered and that the memory trace in the long-term store had decayed. Since memory worsens over time, it is time that causes the trace to decay.

Evaluation of the trace-decay theory

Strengths

- Physiological evidence supports the idea that there is a physical trace in the brain. This does not, however, prove that such a trace will decay. Hebb put forward the idea of an engram; Penfield provided evidence when he probed the brains of epileptic patients who were awake and found areas of the brain that held particular memories.
- Another strength is the theory's focus on the physical aspects of memory. People with Alzheimer's disease seem to lose memories, rather than not being able to retrieve them. This seems to be a physical process. Therefore, the theory helps to explain forgetting in real-life situations, which suggests that it may be valid.

Weaknesses

- In studies of memory loss in the short-term store, it is difficult to know whether new information has been attended to. Therefore, it is difficult to test only the trace-decay theory, without any suggestion that displacement could have caused the forgetting. So in the short-term store, it is difficult to test whether the trace has decayed or whether the memory cannot be retrieved for some other reason.
- Although there is evidence that memories in the long-term store become inaccessible, there are some memories that are resistant to being forgotten and can be recalled after a long time. Flashbulb memories are those that are remembered clearly. Therefore, some memories seem to retain the trace. Bahrick and Hall (1991) do not agree that forgetting is caused by decay of the trace. They found that people can remember algebra that they learned at school and after practice can improve their algebraic skills. Therefore, the traces could not have been lost.

Models of memory v. biological understanding

The multi-store model of memory is a suggestion for how memory might be processed in the brain, from a sensory store to long-term memory, using rehearsal to move information from a short-term store into a long-term store. Working memory then splits the short-term store into different components. These are models of memory – they provide an idea of how processing works and that idea can be tested.

However, a model does not necessarily fit 'reality' perfectly. To know about processing of information into memory, biological understanding is needed. Hebb made suggestions about biological elements in the process. Studies of people with brain damage can also help as their biological issues can be scanned and their abilities and difficulties can be studied. Then the assumption is made that any damage in the brain causes any difficulties in processing. More about case studies of brain damaged patients can be found in Chapter 5. Models tend to be proposed and then tested experimentally, and support for models can then be built (or the model changed). However, it is not until there is 'hard' evidence, in the form of biological evidence perhaps, that a model can become a tried-and-tested theory. Cognitive psychology got into its stride in the 1960s and scanning techniques have developed a lot since then, as well as learning about the brain, so gradually evidence for models in cognitive psychology is being built.

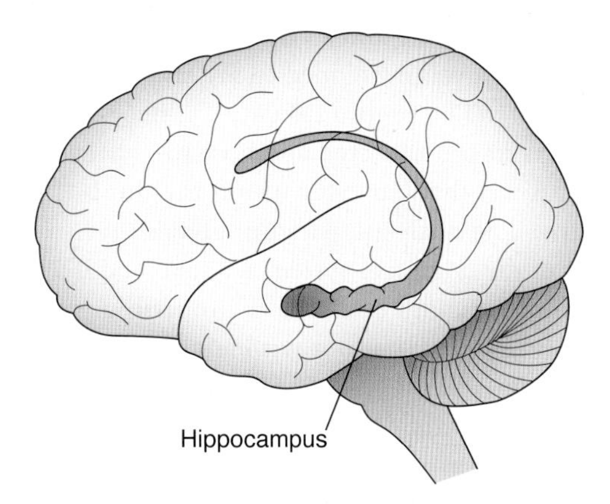

The hippocampus has been widely suggested to link to short-term memory

Progress check 2.5

Why is it important to have biological evidence from the brain for the working memory model when aiming to build a body of scientific knowledge?

Baddeley and Hitch's (1974) working memory model

Baddeley and Hitch's (1974) original model of memory, the three-component model of working memory, has the following components:

- a central executive, which supervises the system and controls the flow of information
- a phonological loop, which holds sound information
- a visuospatial sketchpad, which deals with visual and **spatial information**.

Definition

Spatial information is about where things are situated in physical space. Doing a jigsaw and reading a map require spatial awareness.

The original model has separate phonological and visuospatial systems because, according to Baddeley, if participants in an experiment are asked to do two tasks simultaneously that involve sound, they cannot do it. Similarly, people find it difficult to do two visual tasks at the same time. However, they can carry out simultaneously a visual task and a task involving sound. Therefore, the model was developed to say that the two systems are separate. The central executive is necessary to explain how tasks are allocated and how the systems are controlled. A test that Baddeley uses is the **dual-task paradigm**. The dual-task paradigm holds that different parts of the cognitive system are involved if a task seems to interfere with one type of processing (such as processing using sound) but not with another type of processing (such as using vision). The phonological loop is split into two parts, the articulatory loop and the primary acoustic store, to cater for the idea that there is voicing of information when rehearsing in short-term memory (articulatory loop) and also acoustic information (primary acoustic store), and the two are different.

Explore

Listen to Alan Baddeley talking about the dual-task paradigm: http://gocognitive.net/interviews/dual-task-interference.

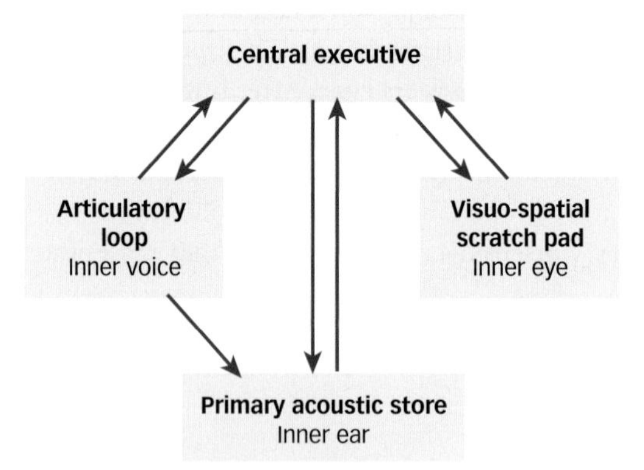

The working memory model

Explanation

A dual-task paradigm is where an experiment is done using two different tasks. The two tasks might be similar, such as having letters that sound alike, to find out whether that similarity affects recall. Or the two tasks might be different (e.g. one set of letters sound alike, the other set does not) – this would be a control condition. Performance can also be compared with single-task conditions.

The phonological loop

The phonological loop deals with auditory information:

- The short-term phonological store, or primary acoustic store, holds auditory memory traces. These decay rapidly, after a few seconds. Thus forgetting in the phonological store is by trace decay, which means the memory trace fades and decays.
- The articulatory rehearsal part, or articulatory loop, revives memory traces by rehearsing them. This is like subvocal speech (talking without vocalising).

Sound information goes directly into the primary acoustic store. This has been called the 'inner ear' and remembers sounds in their order. The articulatory system has been called the 'inner voice' because information is repeated to maintain the trace. Information in the phonological loop is assumed to last for about two seconds before it decays. Word lists and other items are stored as sound. The articulatory system is such that rehearsal refreshes memories but as there are more items, it gets to the point where memory of the first item in the phonological store fades before it can be rehearsed.

Compare the multi-store model with the working memory model. The multi-store model maintains that information in the short-term store is mainly auditory and is held as sound and suggests that information in the short-term store does not last long. So, the working memory model is an expansion of the multi-store model and they support each other.

Evidence for the phonological store comes from studies that use sets of numbers, letters or words to see how many can be rehearsed and recalled, and also to see which characteristics affect recall. For example, letters that sound alike when voiced (e.g. V, B, G, T, P, C), according to Baddeley (2003), are not recalled as well as letters that do not sound alike (e.g. W, X, K, R, Y).

Practical

To test the working memory model, make a list of 15 letters that sound alike and 15 that do not. Test participants to see if they recall fewer of the 'sound alike' words.

In STM the sound affects rehearsal and meaning does not, whereas when testing LTM it becomes clear that the meaning affects recall more than sound does. This is evidence for short-term and long-term memory being separate stores. The way to test LTM using similar studies as for STM is to leave the learning and recall for longer so that LTM is being tested. It seems that phonological similarity makes recall difficult and those that have that difficulty could learn to switch to visual or meaning cues. According to Baddeley (2003), this is an area for study.

Issues and debates

Note that the idea of instruction to help someone with difficulties with STM, when the difficulties are with the phonological loop, is an application of psychology to help others and to help society. One of the issues and debates considers how psychology can be used in this way, so this example is worth noting down.

There is neurophysiological evidence (biological evidence) for the phonological loop also having an articulatory system, in that it is the left temporoparietal area that has lesions if someone has phonological STM defects.

Function of the phonological loop

The function of the phonological loop seems to be about learning language. Function refers to what it is for. Support for this comes from evidence that an individual with a phonological loop deficit cannot learn new vocabulary even though their LTM is 'normal' verbally. Also it seems that phonological loop capacity predicts the learning of a second language.

Progress check 2.6

A study was carried out using two lists of 15 words. One list had words of three letters that sounded alike (e.g. can, man, bad, ran, sad, ham) and one list had words of three letters that did not sound alike (e.g. ben, wam, moo, sea, hug, mit). One set of participants had the first list to read through for ten seconds and another set of participants had the second list to read through for ten seconds. After a gap of a few seconds, they recalled as many words as they could from the list.

1. Was this experiment about STM or LTM, and why?
2. Which of the lists would you expect to show better recall and why (using the working memory model in your explanation)?

The visuospatial sketchpad

The visuospatial sketchpad:

- holds the information we see
- is used to manipulate spatial information, such as shapes, colours and the position of objects
- is limited in capacity to around three or four objects.

Anything to do with spatial awareness, such as finding your way through a building or doing a jigsaw, uses the visuospatial sketchpad. The visuospatial sketchpad could be called the 'inner eye'. The pad is divided into visual, spatial and perhaps kinaesthetic (movement) parts. It is thought that the pad is in the right hemisphere of the brain. As visual information tends to last longer in a scene, there would not be much need to retain a lot of the visual information in STM.

Explore

'Change blindness' is when objects in a scene can change colour or move, but this goes unnoticed. This can be explained because of the limited capacity of the visuospatial sketchpad. If the sketchpad holds about four objects, other objects can change at that time without being noticed. Explore the idea of change blindness. For example: www.youtube.com/watch?v=Qb-gT6vDrmU. However, this is also about selective attention and other areas in cognitive psychology, so it is best not to get too side-tracked in this interesting area.

> **Explore**
> Biological psychology discusses brain **lateralisation** – the idea that the brain is in two halves. It is thought that, in general, males are better at visuospatial tasks and females are better at language tasks. The centre for language is in the left hemisphere; visuospatial tasks are focused in the right hemisphere. It is thought that females tend to use both sides of the brain fairly equally, whereas males are right-brain dominant. You could explore these issues.

Neurological evidence suggests that there is a visual and a spatial memory. If a visual span is disrupted, there are different issues than if a spatial span is disrupted. Blocks can have numbers on or colours and that would be a visual sequence if those were being tested. Or they can be patterned in some way, and that is a spatial sequence, if the pattern is to be recalled. To test visual span, blocks can be laid out with numbers on them and the experimenter can tap one block in turn. The participant tries to recall the sequence of the blocks as they are tapped (e.g. the block with 1 on it, then the block with 8 on it, block with 7 on it, and so on). This continues until the sequence is not recalled in the correct order. To test spatial span, there would be a pattern of blocks to recall – they see the pattern, it is removed, and then they have to draw out the pattern. As the number of blocks in the pattern rises, so recall falls. If there is spatial activity while the visual span is being tested, that affects the visual span; if there is visual activity while the spatial span is being tested, that affects the spatial span. This suggests there are two parts to the visuospatial sketchpad.

Function of the visuospatial sketchpad

The function of the visuospatial sketchpad seems to link to non-verbal intelligence. The sketchpad might have a role in finding out about how objects appear and adding that sort of meaning to objects. It might also help in understanding objects.

The visuospatial sketchpad is divided into two parts:

- The visual cache stores information about form and colour.
- The 'inner scribe' deals with retrieval and rehearsal.

There is biological evidence for this split, from patients with neglect (damage). In two types of patients with right hemisphere damage, there was visuospatial neglect (difficulties). One type of patient has normal visual memory (such as describing a scene) so rehearsal and retrieval are fine, but damaged visual attention, so perhaps a damaged cache; the other type has normal visual attention but problems with visual memory.

The central executive

The central executive puts information from different sources into one episode. It also co-ordinates other parts of working memory. It moves between tasks, operates retrieval strategies and controls selective attention. It is a supervisory system that controls cognitive processes. Using the idea of information processing, the model suggests that there must be a system to control the flow and the processing. The central executive was at first called the supervisory activating system (SAS) and it was thought to intervene if control was required. Some attention is automatic, for example, and needs no control. Schemas are built such that attention can be automatic. This can be seen if you drive somewhere and don't recall doing it when you arrive. So not all information processing requires a supervisory activating system. Other examples of attention that are not supervised include how we mirror someone's body language without realising it. When a central executive (SAS) is needed, as this is in STM, the system will be limited in capacity and will decline rapidly.

The central executive needs to be able to pick what needs to be attended to, switch attention and connect working memory to LTM as those are the elements missing from the proposed stores – there is no mechanism for them to do these things.

> **STUDY HINT**
> Often in this textbook material goes beyond what is required, to help your understanding of what you do need to know. The episodic buffer of the working memory model was proposed after the 1974 Baddeley and Hitch model, which is the one in your course. So you might want to make notes only on their model. However, going beyond the required model (such as studying the episodic buffer) is useful as it can help in evaluation.

The episodic buffer

There are issues with the central executive being all about attention. For example, thinking about memory span in STM, it was found that using chunks helped memory span, but chunks use meaning and there must be some facility to access information from LTM about such meaning. Also there had to be a way for the phonological loop and the articulatory system to interact. These issues led Baddeley to introduce, in 2000, a fourth aspect of the working memory model: the episodic buffer.

The buffer provides time sequencing for visual, spatial and verbal information – for example, the chronological order of words or the sequence of pictures in a film. The episodic buffer might also bring in information from the long-term store. The episodic buffer has limited capacity, as do all aspects of the working memory model. The central executive controls the attention of the episodic buffer and the episodic buffer is perhaps the storage space for the central executive.

Working memory located in the brain

As we have seen, biological evidence has been used to support the model. Baddeley used such evidence to suggest where the working memory stores (and central executive) might be in the brain. Evidence comes from patients with lesions (damage to the brain) and also scanning of patients without damage.

> **STUDY HINT**
> Scanning techniques are part of the research method element of biological psychology and are used in cognitive psychology too. This section helps to show how cognitive psychology is linked to neuroscience (biology of the brain) as more techniques for studying the brain are developed.

The phonological loop does appear to involve the left temporoparietal area of the brain. Broca's area is suggested as being involved in the rehearsal side of the phonological loop. Broca's area was put forward some time ago as the area for speech. If Broca's area is damaged, someone might know the words they want to say but cannot say them, which supports the idea that Broca's area is involved in working memory. Visuospatial memory seems to be in the right hemisphere – more than one study comes to that conclusion, so the conclusion seems firm. Verbal working memory seems to be in the left hemisphere, linking to

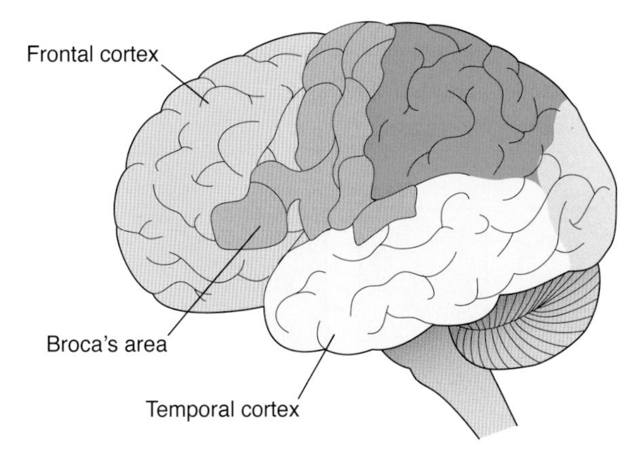

Broca's area is linked to speech and to the rehearsal side of the phonological loop

the right inferior parietal cortex, among other areas. The central executive seems to link to the frontal lobes, again taking evidence from neuroimaging (scanning) and lesion studies (brain damage). For your course, you do not have to know the brain areas in a great deal of detail, but it is useful to have some knowledge to help you understand the biological evidence for the models.

> **Explore**
> Explore Broca's area to see what you can find out and what evidence there seems to be that it is an area for speech and might be used for rehearsal.

Difference in approach regarding the working memory model

The difference between the working memory model and other models, such as the multi-store, is that the model was not first put forward and then tested to see if it worked. Instead, the working memory model started from biological ideas about how the brain might function, as well as from the multi-store model. It then continued to evolve according to evidence from the brain. As the working memory model was found to have deficits, according to the evidence, it was changed to suit. It could be argued that it is not 'just' a model but is using the neurophysiological evidence and building a model based on that evidence. It is a model that is developing, and there are many questions still being asked and answered about how STM can be explained.

> **Progress check 2.7**
> What were the reasons for proposing a central executive in the working memory model? In other words, why were the temporary stores (phonological loop and visuospatial sketchpad) not sufficient as an explanation of short-term memory?

Evidence for the working memory model

Evidence for the phonological loop is that lists of words that sound similar are more difficult to remember than lists in which the words sound different. It is claimed that whether the words have similar meaning or not has little effect compared with whether they sound alike.

If participants are asked to learn a list of words, and at the same time to say something aloud, they find the learning difficult. This is said to be because they are already using the phonological loop, so cannot do both tasks simultaneously. The articulatory loop is being used to say something aloud and is not available for repetition of the words being learnt.

Evidence for the two parts of the visuospatial sketchpad – the visual cache and the 'inner scribe' – is that when two spatial tasks are carried out they are found to be more difficult than when undertaking one visual task and one spatial task There is also neurophysiological evidence. Scans show that tasks involving visual objects activate an area in the left hemisphere and tasks involving spatial information activate areas in the right hemisphere.

Practical

You could design a study to test this idea. Half the participants could have a list of words that sound alike to learn and recall; the other half could have a list of words that do not sound similar. If the participants find it hard to learn the words that sound alike, this could be evidence for the existence of a phonological loop.

Evidence for an episodic buffer is that people with amnesia who could not lay down new memories in the long-term store could recall stories in the short-term store that contained a lot of information. This information was more than could be retained in the phonological loop.

Explore

You will study scanning techniques in the biological approach. Research these techniques using the internet or some other source.

Evaluation of the working memory model

Strengths

- The model expands on the multi-store model, giving more information and refining it. Studies showed, for example, that some dual tasks were more difficult than others, which needed an explanation. The working memory model explains such features of the memory system, introducing the ideas of an 'inner ear', an 'inner voice' and an 'inner eye'.
- The amount of research it has generated and is still generating is a strength. Studies have led to refinements of the model. Research has not only been experimental; there is neurophysiological evidence for the model from brain scans. The model has been expanded, but still helps to explain the data.

Weaknesses

- The model has been added to as new findings have been made. This means that the model itself was inadequate and was not a valid explanation of memory. The episodic buffer, which draws information from long-term memory, was an addition to the model and needs further explanation.
- The experiments tend to be artificial tasks, such as learning word lists and remembering stories. Such tasks depend heavily on either visual or sound information. In real life, tasks tend to involve many of the senses. It could, therefore, be said that the findings lack validity.

Test yourself

1 Describe the working memory model of memory. **(6 marks)**

2 Explain two reasons for accepting the working memory model and two reasons for rejecting it as a model of memory. **(8 marks)**

Episodic and semantic memory as an explanation of long-term memory (Tulving, 1972)

Just as the working memory model elaborates on the idea of STM in the multi-store model, so the idea of there being episodic and semantic memory elaborated on the LTM part of the multi-store model. Tulving points out that there are a great many categories of memory. Sensory memory, short-term memory, long-term memory, working memory, auditory memory (split into articulatory – speech, and acoustic – sound), visual memory, spatial memory and semantic memory have all been used to explain how memory works. However, short-term and long-term memory seem to be a lasting division and other 'types' of memory tend to be within those two (with sensory memory as the starting point, linking to how we attend to information as it enters the 'system').

STUDY HINT

A diagram is provided here showing the different categories of memory considered in the multi-store and working memory models. However, drawing up your own will help your understanding and revision.

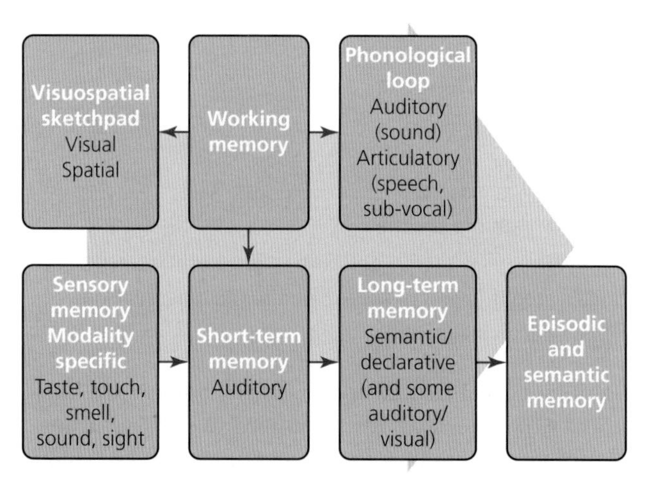

Different categories of memory considered in the multi-store and working memory models

Practical

This diagram offers a lot of ideas for doing practicals to test the various ideas. Some of the ideas are suggested in this chapter and some are suggested in Chapter 5, when the method section for cognitive psychology is explored further. You need to do one experiment in cognitive psychology, which should come from the models of memory that you are studying (though reconstructive memory, a model that is to come in this chapter, can also be tested experimentally).

Tulving focuses on semantic memory, which has not been considered much yet in this chapter but is an important feature of memory. He asks what semantic memory is and points out that it is not perhaps as easily understood as visual memory or auditory memory. We know what sight and sound are better than we understand 'semantic' memory. What is called 'semantic' memory here is better referred to as declarative memory as that saves confusion between this early use of 'semantic', as used when discussing the multi-store model earlier in this chapter, and the use of 'semantic' as opposed to 'episodic', which is discussed in this section.

Issues and debates

One debate that you will look at in your course is how far psychology is a science. Cognitive psychology offers a lot of evidence for psychology being a science. You have looked at some neurophysiology in this chapter, such as the role of the left temporoparietal area of the brain in memory, and neuroimaging has been mentioned as a method (scanning), which is a scientific approach to uncovering knowledge. Many experiments have been outlined in this chapter so far, again a scientific method. You can use cognitive psychology as an example of how psychology is scientific in its approach and its aims to build a body of knowledge that is reliable, objective and credible.

Tulving proposes two parts to what semantic/declarative memory has been understood to be, which is 'meaning', and he splits semantic/declarative memory up into semantic and episodic memory, calling these two stores. This is not a theory of memory, as such, more an exploration of memory for meaning and a suggestion that it can be seen as having two strands or stores.

Episodic v. semantic memory

Semantic and **episodic memory** differ in the nature of the information stored and in the way one is **autobiographical** (memories about the individual) and one is cognitive (meaning we give to things). Also there are differences in how retrieval takes place and in how interference might affect them.

Episodic memory receives and stores information that is about dates, times, events – things that relate to the individual. Episodes in someone's live can be encoded using visual material, sound, spatial material, smells, and so on. There is perhaps a connection to meanings but episodic memories are perceptually encoded. There might be strong links to semantic memory because encoding might use meanings of things, but episodic memories are separate from semantic ones in many ways. They are autobiographical. Episodic memories involve an element of the individual; they are about the individual's journey and are encoded and stored with personal information. Learning a list of paired words sounds like a semantic memory task if the meaning of the words is involved; however, learning the actual list is an episode for the participant, who might recall how they set about doing the learning and can store the memory of learning the list, along with time and place of learning.

Definition

Autobiographical means episodes from your life, and these come from experiences you have had. There can be meanings involved in an episode but the episodes are what make up memories of your life. Memories can be about people, events, times, and places that relate to you. **Episodic memory** is memory for episodes/events that have happened to us. **Semantic memory** is memory for meanings, such as meanings of words and symbols.

Semantic memory is needed for language as words have meanings and meanings must be encoded, stored and retrieved for there to be language use. Not just language itself, but symbols also include mathematic symbols, as well as understanding of the relationship between words and between symbols, which is part of the semantic store. Learning language can be part of the episodic memory as someone encodes, stores and retrieves their experiences of learning language, but the language learned is in semantic memory. Semantic memories have a cognitive, or thinking, element and are about objects and concepts, unrelated to the individual.

Separating semantic and episodic memories

Many tasks involve both semantic and episodic issues so it is not easy to test the two separately. Learning anything will give rise to episodes in one's life that are stored. Tulving gives a list of ideas of information stored in episodic memory and that will help to explain what episodic memory is. He mentioned himself seeing a flash of light followed by a sound, having an appointment with a student the following day and remembering some words from a list he had to remember in a study earlier. These are his autobiographical events. His own semantic memories include that summers are quite hot in Kathmandu and that the month following June is July. Episodic memories are unique to the individual and semantic memories are more general, including concepts and relationships between them.

Practical

Although the practical investigation you will do in cognitive psychology must be an experiment, qualitative data can be useful in studying issues like episodic and semantic memory. Ask someone to write as much as possible about 'their day' or do that for yourself about your 'day'. Then analyse the data into memories of episodes and things that happened to them (or to you) and analyse what appears to be semantic information. You will probably find it difficult to separate the two, but there should be some differences that help in understanding the difference.

Progress check 2.8

Decide whether the following 'memories' are episodic or semantic.

1 Recall of my first visit to a new dentist.
2 Recall of the King of England at the time of Oliver Cromwell.
3 Recall of the French word for 'house'.
4 Recall of what I did yesterday afternoon.
5 Recall of how to form the present tense in Latin of a verb ending with 'are'.

The encoding and storage of episodic and semantic memories

What is often considered in memory is capacity, duration and mode of representation. The capacity of LTM is considered to be potentially unlimited and that is the case for both episodic and semantic memories. They can potentially last forever too. The mode of representation is interesting. Studies previously suggested that LTM tends to use semantic representation, which means we store things according to meaning, though there is some visual and some auditory encoding and storage. Episodic and semantic memories are both within the overall umbrella of 'semantic'. Tulving splits what was called 'semantic' into these two separate stores.

Tulving says that episodic memory is stored and encoded according to how it is experienced, which means encoding and storing what is perceived about the memory as well as issues of time and space (where and when the episode took place, for example). People can recall any episodes equally well no matter what their type. It does not seem, for example, that birthdays are recalled any better than a line drawing of something unfamiliar that has been seen on an occasion. This is taken as evidence that there is no hierarchy of episodic memories; they are stored as they arrive. Episodic memories are stored with their time and place and so someone can be asked 'when did that happen?' or 'where were you when that happened?'. Though the answers might not refer to dates or times, it might be that the person remembers something happened 'just before I went into hospital' or 'after I moved house'. Semantic memories are not usually stored with temporal and spatial information, though some might be. The semantic memory system does not seem to be organised according to the time and place of when the memories were encoded.

STUDY HINT

If you choose to study criminological psychology in your Year 2, you will look at the unreliability of eyewitness testimony. One solution is careful interviewing. This can include asking a witness to remember from the point of view of the time the episode took place or their situation at the time. This strategy for improving recall links well to what Tulving says about episodic memories and how they are encoded and stored.

The retrieval of episodic and semantic memories

Retrieval of an episodic memory is only possible if it has been encoded and stored. Semantic memories, however, can help people to work out things they don't actually know before doing the working out. For example, if someone knows a rule, they can work something out. If you know that spelling tends to be 'i before e except after c' you might spell a word you did not previously know how to spell. So there can be retrieval in semantic memory that does not rely on stored information, just on stored rules. Also retrieval from semantic memory does not change the actual memory (though it might then mean storing a new memory). Retrieval from episodic memory, however, changes the memory that is stored, as a new episode that links to it is encoded and stored. So retrieval of semantic and of episodic memory is different.

STUDY HINT

Steyvers and Hemmer (2012) look at how, in real-life, episodic memory uses prior knowledge, which is semantic memory, so the two are perhaps not able to be studied separately while maintaining validity. It is useful to use evidence from across your course to get a better picture of an area of study.

Progress check 2.9

What are two differences between semantic and episodic memory when it comes to retrieval?

Evidence for episodic and semantic memory

Experiments looking at episodic memory require recall of a personal episode set in time and place, and among other episodic memories. The recall is either correct or incorrect. It is not about what is remembered but about whether recall of a specific event is right or wrong. This raises questions about whether qualitative data would be useful to shed light on episodic memory. Processing of information is taken to be input (from the senses), storage and output. In semantic memory, the input is often not known; it is not known when someone learned something. In episodic memory, the input can be known in an experiment because the experimenter can 'input' an event themselves.

Experiments on semantic memory tend to look at retrieval processes. Input and storage cannot be studied directly; they have to be inferred from what is recalled. Also in experiments looking at semantic memory what is recorded tends to come from **free recall** and so 'right' and 'wrong' is not what is measured. Free recall refers to when someone learns something – e.g. list of words – and then is asked to recall them but not in order. Sometimes answers are 'right' or 'wrong' in studies looking at semantic memory, such as when one word triggers another and the participant makes a mistake.

A study on semantic memory used lists of words with some in categories and some presented randomly. This type of study has been repeated by different researchers. Bower *et al.* (1969) used four lists of 28 words and presented them to participants one at a time. This was a test of LTM. After the lists had been presented, participants wrote down as many words as they could remember, using free recall (any order). One set of participants had the words in categories and the other had them presented randomly. Out of 112 words, those who had the categories recalled 73 words and those who had the 'random' words recalled on average 21. This suggests that meaning is involved in recall, and presumably in encoding and storage, and is evidence for there being a semantic memory.

Case studies of those with brain damage suggest that it is the prefrontal lobes, particularly in the left hemisphere, that are important in laying down episodic memories, though some studies suggest this is semantic memory that is affected, or perhaps both. Damage to the prefrontal lobes in the left hemisphere leads to laying down memories but in a confused way. It has been suggested that the prefrontal lobe is where the central executive is found, linking to working memory, and it is interesting to find some corroborating evidence for that in the fact that cognitive neuroscience findings suggest confusion when there is damage to the prefrontal areas. Generally it is thought that the medial temporal lobe, including the hippocampus, and the prefrontal lobes, are involved in STM but that memories then go to the neocortex for storage so LTM (episodic and semantic) should be 'in' the neocortex. This can account for why those with amnesia have their long-term memory intact.

STUDY HINT

The classic study for this part of your course is Baddeley (1966b) and more is said there about the medial temporal lobe and hippocampus (pp. 101–109). Be sure to link sections together in your notes, even though they are presented separately in this textbook.

Explore

Use the internet to explore more about episodic and semantic memory – for example, www.human-memory.net/types_episodic.html. Tulving's (1972) paper is available online too so you can explore more by reading that: http://alumni.media.mit.edu/~jorkin/generals/papers/Tulving_memory.pdf.

Dickerson and Eichenbaum (2010) write about links between episodic memory and the medial temporal lobe and the hippocampus. This shows that in 2010 episodic memory is still accepted as a category, even though it was proposed by Tulving back in 1972. The MTL (medial temporal lobe) and particularly the hippocampus (which is part of the MTL) has a role in organisation in memory and in encoding memories. Dickerson and Eichenbaum support the claims of case studies of brain-damaged patients, as outlined in the previous section. You can see that there is growing evidence from cognitive neuroscience about how information is processed in the brain.

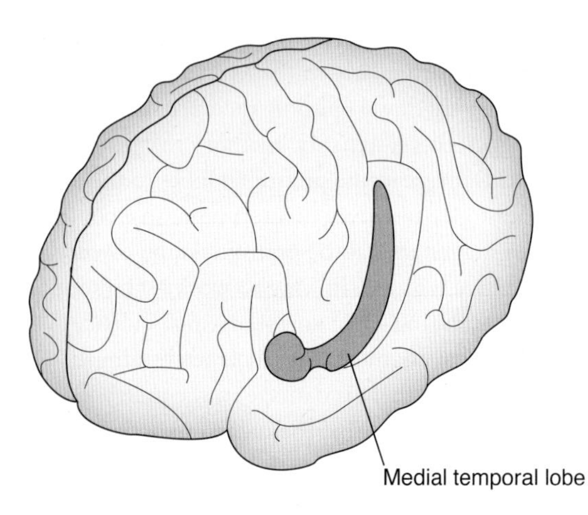

The medial temporal lobe is implicated in STM and the laying down of new memories

> **Explore**
> Have a look at the review by Dickerson and Eichenbaum (2010) as they explore aspects of episodic memory linked to brain structure and functioning: www.ncbi.nlm.nih.gov/pmc/articles/PMC2882963/. They also talk about the working memory model.

Issues and debates

One issue in your course is how psychology has developed over time. When you come across information that shows how psychology has progressed, or indeed stayed the same, make a note so that you have examples and information ready for each issue and debate.

Procedural memory

Although Tulving (1972) did not discuss procedural memory, it is a category of memory that has been used to explain memories in LTM that are about doing things, such as knowing how to ride a bike or play the piano. We seem to just be able to do these things once we have learned them, and 'recall' is instant. Procedural memory is described here to add to your understanding of LTM, but it is not directly part of your course.

There is evidence for there being a procedural memory from case studies of patients with damage to their brain. HM could not lay down new semantic or episodic memories after surgery for epilepsy but he was able to learn to play tennis, so his procedural memory seemed to be unaffected. It is assumed that the brain area for procedural memory was not that area damaged by the surgery but that the damaged area did affect the encoding of both semantic and episodic memories. The surgery affected the medial temporal lobe, which contains the hippocampus, and those areas are thought to be related to STM. You can read more about HM in the contemporary study by Schmolck *et al.* (2002) (pp. 113–119). Blakemore studied Clive Wearing, who had amnesia due to a virus which damaged the hippocampus. Clive Wearing is an accomplished musician and could play the piano in spite of not being able to lay down new memories. The research method of using case studies of patients with damage to the brain is explored in Chapter 5.

Evaluation of Tulving's (1972) ideas about episodic and semantic memory

Strengths

- There is neurophysiological evidence to support Tulving's ideas about there being two categories of 'semantic' memory in LTM. Episodic memories seem to be those that are affected when there is brain damage to areas such as the medial temporal lobe, or the prefrontal lobes, especially in the left hemisphere. Some of the evidence is rather old, such as case studies of patients with damage to those areas, although the patients continued to have such difficulties so the conclusions were supported over time. Dickerson and Eichenbaum (2010) review what is known about episodic memory and neurophysiological evidence and conclude that there is evidence for there being episodic memory.
- Tulving gives a lot of detail about the two stores and their differences and includes evidence, such as how retrieval is different for them both and how semantic memories can be 'created' through using other semantic memories, whereas episodic memories have to be encoded and stored individually. His argument is persuasive, thorough and evidenced.

Weaknesses

- Tulving explains the difference between the two stores, episodic and semantic, by drawing on examples of everyday use of memory. This helps to explain the differences between episodic and semantic but it seems as if this is about labelling only, rather than an actual difference. If we say memory for events, including time and place of the events, is 'episodic' and memory for meaning, including rules about things, is 'semantic', then this is descriptive rather than explanatory.
- It has been suggested that the medial temporal lobe (including the hippocampus) is used for both semantic and episodic memories and that means there is not

so much evidence for their being separate stores (e.g. Squire and Zola, 1998). Alongside this, it is clear, and indeed Tulving mentions this, that the two stores rely on one another; they are not perhaps as separate as might be thought.

Test yourself

Assess Tulving's (1972) ideas about episodic and semantic memory. **(16 marks)**

Reconstructive memory (Bartlett, 1932)

Your course suggests one more model of memory – **reconstructive memory**. One of the contemporary studies in your course (Steyvers and Hemmer, 2012) considers reconstructive memory (pp. 119–124). The multi-store model, together with the working memory model and the ideas of episodic and semantic memory in LTM, all work with the idea of memory being about separate stores and brain function working in separate stores, some temporary, some long term, and so on. Bartlett's ideas about memory are different as they are about memory being a reconstruction from previous knowledge and memories, which he calls schemas. The reconstructive model of memory highlights how recall is affected by previous experiences. Tulving, when talking about episodic and semantic memory, starts by asking what exactly is meant by memory, and Bartlett asks the same question. Steyvers and Hemmer (2012) discuss episodic memory and semantic memory alongside the use of schemas (previous experiences), so there are links between Tulving's ideas and Bartlett's.

Definitions

Reconstructive memory is the theory that memories are not exact copies of what is encoded and stored, but are affected by prior experience and prior knowledge in the form of schemas. **Schemas** are (cognitive) plans/scripts that are built up using experiences about everyday life and that affect the processing of information.

Study to explain the use of schema

Bransford and Johnson (1972) used the following passage to demonstrate how we use schemas and scripts when processing information. After reading the passage, turn to the end of this chapter (page 128) for the 'script/schema' – this will help you to see the point of the study and give you the findings (the 'answer' is given elsewhere, otherwise the effect would be spoiled).

'The procedure is actually quite simple. First you arrange things into different groups. Of course, one pile may be sufficient depending on how much there is to do. If you have to go somewhere else due to lack of facilities that is the next step, otherwise you are pretty well set. It is important not to overdo things. That is, it is better to do too few things at once than too many. In the short run this may not seem important but complications can easily arise. A mistake can be expensive as well. At first the whole procedure will seem complicated. Soon, however, it will become just another facet of life. It is difficult to foresee any end to the necessity for this task in the immediate future, but then one never can tell, After the procedure is completed one arranges the materials into different groups again. Then they can be put into their appropriate places. Eventually they will be used once more and the whole cycle will then have to be repeated. However, that is part of life.'

(From Bransford, J.D. and Johnson, M.K. (1972) 'Contextual prerequisites for understanding: Some investigations of comprehension and recall', *Journal of Verbal Learning and Verbal Behavior*, 11, 717–726)

Bartlett's idea that memory is reconstructive

Bartlett (1932) maintained that memory is not like a tape recorder. This idea has been taken up by other researchers – for example, Elizabeth Loftus agrees with Bartlett. Steyvers and Hemmer (2012) explain that Loftus and Mackworth's (1978) study shows that people looked more at items in a scene that were unexpected than at expected items. Loftus and Mackworth (1978) suggest that having prior knowledge and schemas about scenes can free up cognitive processing capacity, which can then be allocated to what is inconsistent. Elizabeth Loftus is a well-known researcher in the field of memory and uses ideas such as schemas to explain why eyewitness memory might be unreliable. If you study criminological psychology in your Year 2, you will study Loftus and Palmer's (1974) classic study, looking at how words used to ask about memory can affect recall.

Explore

Look up the idea of unreliability of eyewitness recall (and ear-witness recall if you like). You can read more about this key question for society, which focuses on the concern that if eyewitnesses to a crime are unreliable, this could result in innocent people being found guilty.

The idea is that a memory is not perfectly formed, perfectly encoded and then perfectly retrieved. The multi-store model suggests that memories are retrieved after more than 30 seconds only if they are in the long-term store, and that only happens if the material is attended to and rehearsed. Tulving shows how episodic memories are autobiographical and are stories about ourselves and it is unlikely that such memories will be perfectly coded, stored and retrieved. Baddeley (1966b) showed that when material is acoustically similar (similar sound) or semantically similar (similar meaning) recall is affected differently. You can see that it is unlikely that a memory that is retrieved is exactly what was originally perceived. Bartlett's view starts from this idea.

Bartlett thought that the past and current experiences of individuals would affect their memory for events. There would be input, which would be the perception of an event. Then, there would be processing. This would include the perception and also the interpretation. Interpretation would involve previous experiences and schemata/schemas.

Schemata are ideas and scripts about the world – for example, you might have an 'attending a lesson' script or a 'going to the cinema' script. These scripts or schemata give you expectations and rules about what to do. You know, for example, that before you go in to watch a film you have to buy a ticket and you also expect to watch advertisements.

Explanation

Schemata is the plural of schema. 'Schemas' can also be used as the plural.

Memory of an event involves information from specific traces encoded at the time of the event and ideas that a person has from knowledge, expectations, beliefs and attitudes. Remembering involves retrieving knowledge that has been altered to fit with knowledge that the person already has.

Evidence for memory being reconstructive

Bartlett thought about memory being reconstructive as when engaged in a game of Chinese whispers. In this game, someone invents a short story and whispers it to the next person, who whispers it to the next, and so on. The story becomes changed along the way, often for it to make more sense to the person telling it. The final retelling can be completely different from the original.

Explore

Try Chinese whispers with some friends and see how far the final story has changed after being passed around. You could look for features in the changes that match Bartlett's features, explained later, such as *confabulation* and *rationalisation*. Then explore ideas about memory being reconstructive. http://mechanism.ucsd.edu/teaching/philpsych.w03/memory4class.pdf has a useful PowerPoint presentation about reconstructive memory, including the *War of the Ghosts* story and some ideas about how it reduces when recalled over time, and ideas about the unreliability of eyewitness testimony as a key question for society.

Bartlett's book called *Remembering*, written back in 1932, includes in Chapter V an account of his *War of the Ghosts* study. His study used the idea of Chinese whispers. He starts by describing what he calls 'the method of repeated reproduction' (p. 64). His aim was to look at the sorts of changes that people make to material as they recall it after time has passed.

He used a Native American folk story, the *War of the Ghosts*. This story was unfamiliar to the participants and came from a different culture, so it did not fit in well with their existing schemata. Each participant read through the story twice at their normal reading rate. They were then asked to recall the story, starting with the first recall 15 minutes after hearing the story. The intervals between recall, after the first recall at 15 minutes, varied because the participant was asked to do the recall when there was the chance. There were several recalls – soon after the telling, some time later and after a year.

STUDY HINT

Bartlett's *War of the Ghosts* study can be found on the internet: http://mechanism.ucsd.edu/teaching/philpsych.w03/memory4class.pdf.

Frederick Bartlett is a well-known researcher in the field of memory, proposing the idea that memory is not like a tape recorder but reconstructed using prior knowledge

The results showed that changes that began in the first reproduction became more pronounced over time. The story gradually becomes more concise and more coherent. Bartlett found that there was also elaboration on the story. When there are fairly fixed repetitions over time then the story becomes rather fixed and does not change as much. One participant recalled the study two and a half years after having first read it and it was much shorter with only the 'bare outline' remaining (p. 75). There was **rationalisation** as the participant recalled the story, trying to work out what made sense, such as saying, 'There was something about a canoe but I cannot fit it in' (p. 75). There was also conformity with common ideas such as that people die at sunset (when the story has the person dying as the 'sun rose').

The story became shorter and shorter – after about six recall sessions, it was reduced from 330 words to 180. Participants altered the story. Bartlett found that people rationalised the parts that made no sense and filled in their memories so that they were recalling what was, to them, a sensible story.

Definitions

Confabulation means making up bits to fill in a memory so that it makes sense. **Rationalisation** means making something make sense.

This means that they reconstructed their memories of the story. Bartlett concluded that memory is reconstructive, rather than reproductive (which means more faithfully reproducing the memory that was encoded). Loftus has taken this idea and used it to show that eyewitness testimony is unreliable. She claims that eyewitnesses reconstruct their memories of an event so it makes sense. She showed how leading questions, such as using a particular verb, can manipulate memory. For example, if people are asked about two cars 'smashing' into each other, they 'remember' the cars going at a faster speed than if they are asked about two cars 'hitting' each other. The verbs 'smash' and 'hit' lead to different memories of the same event because they mean different things to people (Loftus and Palmer, 1974).

STUDY HINT

You will come across the Loftus and Palmer (1974) study again if you choose the criminological application in Year 2 of your course.

Features of reconstructive memory

Bartlett used the errors he found in his *War of the Ghosts* study as there were successive recalls to list some features of reconstructive memory. Some parts of the study were missed out, some parts were changed and other things were added and new to the story. There was rationalisation when participants made things make sense to them to fit their own schemas, and this might mean missing things out. There was **confabulation**, when bits were added so they made more sense. Confabulation draws on previous experiences and episodes in an individual's life so that what is being 'recalled' (more accurately, 'reconstructed') makes more sense.

Summary of findings from Bartlett's *War of the Ghosts* study

To summarise, the main issues using the method of repeated reproduction are as follows:

- There is inaccuracy in reproduction.
- There is persistence in reproductions for each individual, after the first version.
- The style of the story and rhythm are rarely reproduced.
- When reproduction is frequent, details quickly become stereotyped and after that there is little change.
- With less frequent reproduction, details are missed out, there is simplification of events and items are transformed into something more familiar.
- When remembering is from a long way back (recall is some time after reading – long-term remembering), there can be elaboration with invention and importation of ideas; it is not all about shortening the story.
- With long-term remembering, the general setting remains and people remember detail that stood out for them. This shows that memory is constructed and there is inference.
- Detail stands out if it fits in with what people are interested in or tend towards. Also that detail comes earlier in the reproductions as time passes.

Practical

Make up a short story that is hard to make sense of and read it to a few participants you have asked to help you. The story should have some specific features, people and objects, even if the story is not clear. Ask the participants to write the story down after a little while (decide how long) and ask them if you can keep the results. Then make up a story with a clear structure, involving features, people or objects (the same number as in the first story; use controls such as length of story). Ask other participants, after you have read it to them, to write the story down (after the same time period). Again, ask if you can keep the results. Analyse the two sets of results to see if there is less reconstruction (made-up events) and less confabulation (elaborating on features of the story) in the story with the clear structure than in the less clear story. You could also count how many of the features, people and objects were mentioned in the recall for all the participants and see if more of these were recalled in the 'clear' condition. This is the sort of study you can do for your practical investigation.

Wynn and Logie (1998) evaluation of Bartlett's claims about memory being reconstructive

Background

Wynn and Logie (1998) discuss Bartlett's *War of the Ghosts* study. This shows how psychology builds over time – a study in 1998 was carried out to test a 1932 study. Wynn and Logie point out that the story was reduced in the recalling but there was still a lot of detail given. There was rationalising as well as importation and invention. The recall was not an accurate reproduction of the story. It was concluded by Bartlett that memory is not 'photographic' but 'reconstructed'. There is recall of past events affected by past experiences. Wynn and Logie point out that the recalls for different participants were not at regular intervals or even at the same interval for each participant – they were done on an opportunity basis. Therefore, the study lacked controls. Wynn and Logie summarise Bartlett's findings as showing:

- omission of detail (particularly when it was detail the participant did not fully understand)
- rationalisations (to make the story more logical to the participant)
- transformations of order (putting parts of the story in a different order).

The main gist of the story was preserved and Wynn and Logie point out that other studies have found the same (e.g. Vincent and Brewer, 1993, cited in Wynn and Logie, 1998).

Procedure and aim(s)

Wynn and Logie (1998) wanted to test Bartlett's findings because they thought that having a story that had little meaning for the participants might have affected the findings. Therefore, their aim was to look at Bartlett's findings and his method of repeated recall but this time using a real-life situation. Their study also looked at trace decay and interference as explanations of errors in recall, but here their study is considered in order to evaluate Bartlett's reconstructive memory model.

The real-life event they chose was first-year psychology students recalling places and events they came across in their first week at university. The participants did not know they would be asked about what happened in their first week, which is more like what would happen in real-life recall.

STUDY HINT

Note that Steyvers and Hemmer (2012) (pp. 119–124) also challenge the idea that memory experiments can be ecologically valid. Where studies consider the same issues, make notes accordingly to help you to make links for your learning and revision.

The first description of events and places in the student's first week were taken after two weeks, and then at two months, four months and six months, with the intervals being fixed. Wynn and Logie felt that their study had the control and structure of an experiment but without the criticisms about validity of the task.

Participants were given sheets with instructions and response sheets, at both the first description and the subsequent descriptions. Two-hundred participants received the sheets for the first recall and 128 were returned. The 63 participants who went on with the study (40 female and 23 male, average age 18 years) had given a suitable description at the first recall. For each recall, participants were asked, using a noticeboard, to attend that recall – they did not know they would be asked back each time. Some participants recalled just once, in May. Some recalled twice, in March and May. Others recalled three times, in January, March and May. All had the initial recall in November (the description two weeks after they started). There was, therefore, a four recall condition (19 participants returned the sheet), a three recall condition (16 participants returned the sheet) and a two recall condition (20 participants returned the sheet).

Results

The aim was to look at how the delays in recall/description affected what was described. The recalls at two, four and six months were always compared with the initial recall at two weeks.

Table 2.2 shows the mean number of words in reports over time.

Table 2.2 Mean number of words in reports over time

Condition (number of participants)	November	January	March	May
Four recall (19)	97.58	87.74	89.00	88.21
Three recall (16)	76.50	-	60.12	60.56
Two recall (20)	74.20	-	-	69.75
Mean number (55)	82.76	87.74	74.56	72.84

The three recall group and the four recall group showed a significant difference in words recalled ($p \leq 0.05$) over time. There was some difference in recall over time with regard to number of words used in descriptions and some difference depending on the number of repetitions. Even though within each group there did not seem to be significant differences in words used, between the groups there were significant differences. In general, it was concluded that there were small differences (but significant ones) between the three groups in the number of words used when looking at the first description (after two weeks) and the first recall session.

There did not seem to be differences in the type of words that were used by different participants in the different recalls. There seemed to be a decrease in the proportion of objects recalled at the six-month recall, but up to this time there did not seem much difference in the type of detail recalled. The proportion of adjectives also changed at the six-month interval, but the introduction of new items did not increase over time. Wynn and Logie concluded that over a period of six months there is little reduction in the amount of information (accurate or inaccurate) that is there to be recalled.

One issue with Wynn and Logie's study is that they could not easily measure omission of detail as they did not start with the same detail. This made comparison with Bartlett's findings about omission of detail difficult.

Conclusions

The differences found by Wynn and Logie compared to Bartlett's findings were put down to the fact that, although the students were new to the events and locations in their first week, they were not new to the schemas and experiences. Bartlett's participants were new to the schemas in the *War of the Ghosts* story. Wynn and Logie concluded that in real life there is less reproduction in memory than proposed by Bartlett in 1932. Wynn and Logie (1998) concluded that people's memories for 'distinctive' events are resistant to change over time, no matter how many times the memory is recalled (p. 17).

Evaluation of the reconstructive theory of memory

Strengths

- A strength is the evidence for the theory, first from Bartlett and his *War of the Ghosts* study and from Loftus, who has carried out many studies on the unreliability of eyewitness testimony. Backing up the evidence is the idea of Chinese whispers, which many people have found works – people change the story to make both more sense and different sense.
- The theory can be tested by experimental method because the independent variable can be operationalised and measured. A story can have features that can be counted each time the story is recalled and the changes recorded. So, up to a point, the theory can be tested scientifically. It can be reduced into an IV and a DV and other variables can be controlled, which means reliability can be achieved.
- The theory can be usefully applied to key questions for society. The reliance of a prosecution on eyewitness memory is shown to need questioning by studies showing that memories are reconstructed and, therefore, perhaps just one version of events.

Weaknesses

- The *War of the Ghosts* story involves an unusual story that does not make sense to the participants. Therefore, it could be argued that they will alter it so it makes sense because they are being asked to retell the story. There could be demand characteristics, where the participant guesses what is intended. Therefore, the results of the study might not be reliable.
- It does not explain *how* memory is reconstructive. It takes one part of memory and describes what happens, rather than explaining it. The theory holds that memory is an active process, which is a useful contribution to the debate. However, it does not explain what that activity is, other than saying that schemata are used. Tulving explains that there is both episodic and semantic memory and reconstructive theory refers to episodic memory – for example, events that we have witnessed – so that goes some way to explaining more about the way memory is reconstructed. However, that too perhaps is more descriptive than explanatory.
- The evidence from Bartlett's and Loftus's work comes from experiments and the tasks are artificial, as is the situation where the tasks are carried out. The results from such studies might not have validity and might not be applicable to everyday life. (Though hearing stories [Bartlett, 1932] and viewing scenes [Loftus's work] might be said to represent real life to an extent, as is argued by Steyvers and Hemmer, 2012).

STUDY HINT

When presenting a strength or weakness to evaluate a theory or study, you should discuss the strength or weakness as it is likely that there is more than one viewpoint to consider, as in the final weakness suggested here.

Test yourself

1. Describe two theories of memory. **(8 marks)**
2. Compare two theories of memory. **(8 marks)**
3. Assess one theory of memory. **(8 marks)**
4. Evaluate why people forget. **(12 marks)**
5. To what extent does one theory explain memory best? Give reasons for your answer. **(12 marks)**

Methods in cognitive psychology

What is required and how this book covers that requirement

In all the topic areas, there is a section on methods. In your course, you need to cover certain methods and issues around methods, and these are spread through the Year 1/AS topic areas (there is method material in Year 2 as well). In cognitive psychology, the research methods are experiment (field and laboratory) and case studies of brain-damaged patients. Chapter 5 presents 'method' material for all the Year 1/AS topic areas and Chapter 6 gives 'maths' material for all the Year 1/AS topic areas. Therefore, there is only a brief outline in this chapter of what you need to know within cognitive psychology. For more detail, read the 'cognitive psychology' sections in Chapters 5 and 6.

STUDY HINT

Some of the 'maths' element in your psychology course is in GCSE Maths, so you should have already learned about it, such as measures of central tendency, graphs and measures of dispersion. Be ready to 'transfer' learning from GCSE Maths to AS and A level Psychology. However, there is full guidance throughout the course if you are not sure.

In cognitive psychology, you will need to know about:

- designing and conducting experiments, including field and laboratory experiments

Method link: more detail about designing and conducting experiments can be found in Chapter 5 on pp. 316–326.

Practical link: in your study of cognitive psychology you are asked to design and carry out an experiment, and that will help you put what you learn into practice. Chapter 7 explores more about practical investigations covering all four Year 1/AS topic areas, including an experiment relating to cognitive psychology (pp. 431–442).

- issues with variables when carrying out experiments in psychology, including the independent and dependent variable, operationalisation of variables and other issues around variables, including extraneous and confounding variables, situational and participant variables

Method link: Chapter 5 explains more about the independent and dependent variables and operationalising of them, as well as other variables involved in experiments (pp. 318–320).

- building on the idea of an alternative hypothesis in a study to consider experimental hypotheses and null hypotheses; in relation to that, how they can be directional or non-directional with issues of one- and two-tailed with regard to inferential testing

Method link: Chapter 5 explains more about hypotheses (pp. 318–319).

- experimental/research designs: matched pairs, independent groups, and repeated measures

Method link: Chapter 5 explains more about experimental/research designs (pp. 321–323).

- issues with bias in results when doing experiments, including counterbalancing and randomisation to counter order effects; also experimenter effects, demand characteristics and control issues

Method link: Chapter 5 explains more about issues of bias when carrying out a study, including issues of experimenter bias, control issues and demand characteristics (pp. 320–321). Chapter 5 also explains more about order effects and how to control for them (pp. 322–323).

- evaluation issues when doing research in psychology, including objectivity, reliability and validity

Method link: Chapter 5 explains more about issues of validity, reliability and objectivity (pp. 324–325).

- analysing quantitative data, including being able to work out measures of central tendency (mean, median, mode as appropriate) and how to draw frequency tables and graphs, including bar charts and histograms; measures of dispersion (the range and the standard deviation of a set of scores) and percentages

Maths link: Chapter 6 explains the maths element that you need for your course, and you will learn more there, including about descriptive statistics, measures of central tendency, measures of dispersion and graphs (pp. 387–396).

- decision-making and interpretation of inferential statistics; for cognitive psychology, this involves two non-parametric tests of difference, the Mann-Whitney U and Wilcoxon tests; also issues around probability and levels of significance ($p \leq 0.10$, $p \leq 0.05$, $p \leq 0.01$); observed and critical values and critical value tables (not for the AS); Type I and Type II errors and issues of normal and skewed distribution

Maths link: Chapter 6 explains the maths element that you need for your course, and you will learn more there (pp. 400–406 for issues around inferential statistics).

- case studies on brain-damaged patients, including Henry Molaison (HM) and the use of qualitative data in such cases.

Method link: Chapter 5 explains more about issues when the method involves case studies of patients with brain damage (pp. 336–339).

> **Explore**
> Levine *et al.* (2002) conducted a study into traumatic brain injury (TBI) and used some of the methods that you need for cognitive psychology. You can take a look at this study here: http://jnnp.bmj.com/content/73/2/173.full.

Studies in cognitive psychology

Cognitive psychology involves a lot of experiments and studies looking at how the brain processes information. For your course, the focus is on memory processing. As with the other topic areas, you are asked to cover one classic study and one from a choice of three contemporary studies, all looking at various aspects of how we remember. The classic study is by Baddeley in 1966 (called '1966b' because he did another study in that year). The three contemporary studies are:

- Sebastián and Hernández-Gil (2012) 'Developmental pattern of digit span in Spanish population'
- Schmolck *et al.* (2002) 'Semantic knowledge in patient HM and other patients with bilateral medial and lateral temporal lobe lesions'
- Steyvers and Hemmer (2012) 'Reconstruction from memory in naturalistic environments'.

The classic study is explained first and then the three contemporary studies are presented in the same order as the theories of memory to which they relate: Sebastián and Hernández-Gil (2012) carried out a study that looked at memory span, within working memory and linked to short-term memory; Schmolck *et al.* (2002) looked at how damage to specific brain areas linked to specific memory impairments, including semantic issues, and so the study links well to long-term memory and also to semantic and episodic memory; Steyvers and Hemmer (2012) looked at the reconstructive theory of memory. It is best to read the studies after knowing about the models of memory because there is an assumption about what has been covered. For example, Baddeley (1966b) looks at STM and LTM (short-term and long-term memory), an interference task is used and rehearsal is discussed. You will be familiar with these terms if you have already read about the multi-store model and working memory model.

You have to know about just one of the contemporary studies. All three are given here for your interest and because they are all useful in your learning about cognitive psychology. Each study is presented in the form of the aim(s), background, procedure, results and conclusions before considering strengths and weaknesses.

> **STUDY HINT**
> There are methodology issues in these studies as well as content issues, so they link to Chapter 5 (method) and Chapter 6 (mathematics) as well.
>
> Studies are presented in the form of aim(s), background, procedure, results and conclusion(s) because this means the overall study is explained from what the researcher(s) want to know to what they found. When you describe a study, use the aim(s), procedure, results and conclusion(s), but you can also bring in some background if you have time.

Studies in this textbook are summarised, but it is useful to also look at the full studies. Where studies are available online, links are provided. Full studies start with an **abstract**, which is a brief summary of the whole study. This gives you an idea of what was done in the study and what was found.

> **Definition**
> An **abstract** is a short summary of the aim(s), procedure, results and conclusion(s) of a study. An abstract can help when doing research as you have an idea of what a study is about without having to read it all.

Classic study: Baddeley (1966b)

Alan Baddeley is a well-known figure in the study of memory

Previous studies in short-term memory have shown that when words are acoustically similar (sound alike), recall of the words is affected more than when words are semantically similar (similar meaning). The aim of this study is to see if long-term memory is affected if there is acoustic similarity more than if there is semantic similarity.

The question is, is memory the same in this way in LTM as in STM?

Aim(s)

The aim of the study was to see if LTM was like STM or, more specifically, if in LTM acoustic similarity of words would lead to more memory impairment than would semantic similarity of words. Studies of STM show that acoustic similarity of words leads to worse recall than semantic similarity of words. The question was whether this would be the case in LTM. This is about whether STM and LTM have the same coding systems.

Background

Short-term memory (STM) lasts a matter of seconds, whereas long-term memory (LTM) lasts potentially forever. There has been the tendency for the two to be studied separately, but as interference has been found to cause forgetting in both STM and LTM this has raised questions about whether they are as separate as was first thought. To explain what interference is, it is worth showing how it works. Interference can be shown by getting someone to learn something like a list of words, then getting them to do something to prevent them rehearsing the words to learn them (like counting backwards in threes from a high number), and then seeing what they recall. Or interference can be learning some words and the interference task 'learning some other words' before trying to recall the first words. Interference affects recall in both STM and LTM. If a study wants to look at short-term memory (STM) then the learning and recall have to be within around 30 seconds, and a study looking at LTM needs to go beyond 30 seconds to make sure what was learned has 'gone into' long-term memory. You will know this from your study of the multi-store model (pp. 78–83). Interference theory was described on pp. 81–82, but there is an explanation here too to reinforce your learning.

> **STUDY HINT**
> In cognitive psychology, you will find that, because four memory theories are required and the studies link to those theories, there is repetition of material. This will be helpful when learning; be sure to make links as often as you can. Drawing diagrams will help your understanding.

Studies of interference in LTM have looked at both retroactive interference (RI), which is when something you have just learned interferes with something you had learned previously, and proactive interference (PI), which is where something you learned previously interferes with something you are learning now. An example might help. If you know the French words for a few nouns and you are learning the Spanish words for the same nouns, you may find that your learning of Spanish means you forget the French – that is retroactive interference. If you find that you knowledge of the French words makes you forget the new Spanish words, that is proactive interference. This background material is useful for understanding Baddeley's (1966b) study.

A previous study by Baddeley and a colleague, also in 1966, (Baddeley and Dale, 1966) was an experiment in LTM to see if there was retroactive interference. Participants learned two lists, List A and List B. Then they learned List A' and List C, and then they were tested on Lists A and B. You need to know that List A and List A' were adjectives with similar meaning; the other lists all had adjectives that were not similar. There was a control group who learned Lists A and B (as in the experimental condition) and then List D (matching A' but not with similar adjectives) and List C. There was more forgetting in the experimental group who first had List A and then List A' (they were in the 'similar' condition) than in the control group (the dissimilar condition). The later list (A') affected their learning of the earlier list (A) – this was retroactive interference. This is evidence that in LTM meaning is involved because lists of similar meanings showed more forgetting than in a control group where lists were all dissimilar.

> **STUDY HINT**
> The laboratory experiment as a research method is explained in detail in Chapter 5. Baddeley and Dale (1966) carried out a laboratory experiment using an experimental and a control group. You can use this study as an example of such methodological issues, so they are worth noting. Also the term 'condition' is explained. You may have already covered 'method' in cognitive psychology so you will know about such issues and, if not, then you will be doing so soon.

An interesting point about Baddeley and Dale's (1966) study is that when the study was repeated, this time keeping the learning and recall in short-term memory rather than in long-term memory (so keeping the time of the learning and recall short, within 30 seconds), the retroactive interference effect was not found. Pairs of adjectives that had similar meaning were not forgotten more than when pairs were learned and recalled but without having similar meaning.

Baddeley (1966b) explained that researchers had taken what had been found in LTM and tried to see if it was the same in STM, as Baddeley and Dale (1966) did. However, interestingly, what had not been done was to take what had been found in STM and see if it was also the case in LTM. This was the other way around. Baddeley (1966b) thought this was worth doing and hence his aim of seeing whether LTM was like STM and using methods that were traditionally used to test STM.

Baddeley (1966b) needed a method used in STM studies. Baddeley (1966), in a different study in the same year looking at STM, found that acoustic similarity (when words sound alike) did lead to lower recall (72.5 per cent lower). He also found that words similar in meaning (semantic similarity) did not lead to much lower recall (6.3 per cent lower). So it was found in STM that acoustic similarity affected recall but semantic similarity did not. This might be because in STM rehearsal tends to mean sounding out words (even if not aloud – this can be 'subvocal') (see pp. 79–80 for an explanation of the role of rehearsal in memory). According to the multi-store model, words that sound alike might become confused. Having the same meaning did not affect recall – well, hardly at all.

Explanation

There are three studies here that Baddeley carried out in 1966: 1) Baddeley and Dale did a study with two parts - a long-term memory experiment in 1966 found that the meaning of words affected recall, whereas the repeat experiment showed that in short-term memory meaning of words did not affect recall; 2) Baddeley also did a study on short-term memory and found that, when words sound alike, recall is affected but words that had similar meaning did not affect recall; 3) Your classic study, Baddeley (1966b), explained here.

Progress check 2.10

The background here gives findings from studies as evidence that short-term memory uses acoustic representation, whereas long-term memory (mainly) uses semantic representation. Describe that evidence.

There is more than one experiment in this overall study and they are separated for clarity.

Experiment I

Procedure

Baddeley used different lists in this experiment. List A had ten words that sounded similar. List B had ten words matched with List A but not sounding similar. List C had ten adjectives that had a similar meaning. List D had ten adjectives matched with List C but not having the same meaning.

- **List A**: man, cab, can, cad, cap, mad, max, mat, cat, map (acoustically similar words)
- **List B**: pit, few, cow, pen, sup, bar, day, not, rig, bun (words matched with List A but do not sound similar)
- **List C**: great, large, big, huge, broad, long, tall, fat, wide, high (adjectives with similar meaning, semantically similar)
- **List D**: good, huge, hot, safe, thin, deep, strong, foul, old, late (adjectives matched with List C but not semantically similar)

Part One (called the 'learning' part in this account) of the experiment used an independent groups design, which means different participants did each of the four conditions (List A, List B, List C and List D were the four conditions). The words were presented using a tape recorder and at three-second intervals in the order given above. The participants had 40 seconds to recall the words in the right order. This was done for all four lists and each participant did four **trials**, i.e. they learned and recalled the list four times.

Practical

The list above gives the nouns and adjectives that Baddeley (1966b) used. You could consider doing a similar experiment for your practical investigation, using these words. Chapter 7 gives more detail about just this suggestion.

Definition

In studies, **trials** are individual tests. If a participant does one trial in a study, they just do what is asked once. In Baddeley (1966b), the participants did four trials in their condition (e.g. they learned and recalled List A four times).

In Part Two (called the 're-test' part and also the 'forgetting' part), after the learning, the participants spent 20 minutes doing a different task and then were tested again, being asked to write down as many of their words in order (the list they had been allocated to) as they could. This was the re-test. They did not know about the re-test. The words themselves were in sight on cards throughout the experiment so it was not about the words themselves but their order. There were four different cards, in fact, with the words on for each list (not in the relevant order) so when a new set of participants were tested they could have a different card, to vary the order – as a control. The words participants could see throughout this second part of the experiment were the ones they had in their list, but not in the order they had. At the start of the study, a hearing test made sure the recorded words could be heard; three participants in Condition A did not do the test because of hearing issues. There were 18 participants in Condition A, 17 in Condition B, 20 in Condition C and 20 in Condition D. They were young servicemen and were tested in groups of around 20.

Scores on the four lists were compared, so at this stage the design was independent groups because different people did each list. When scores on a list were compared with the re-test scores, this was a repeated measures design, because the two scores being compared were done by the same participant (their original scores on the list they did and their re-test score).

> **STUDY HINT**
> Baddeley (1966b) used both an independent groups design and a repeated measures design. These terms are explained in Chapter 5. It means that answering a question about 'which design Baddeley (1966b) used' is not straightforward. Be ready to explain your answer.

Results

The score recorded was the number of words reproduced in the right position in the list of ten words. Analysis of the results was done using the Mann-Whitney U test (the independent groups design part) and the Wilcoxon test (the repeated measures part).

> **STUDY HINT**
> You will be learning about the Mann-Whitney U test and the Wilcoxon test in cognitive psychology and Baddeley's study can be used as an example of their use. Also the statistical significance of the results is given, e.g. $p<0.05$ one-tail. It is useful to see such terms used in practice, as that can help with understanding. Make notes when you come across methodology terms that you need to learn.

Graphs of the results are presented though they are not exact with regard to the actual mean percentage of words correct as Baddeley presented his findings in graphs only. Reading from the graphs gives these scores to within a small amount of error.

Acoustically similar words

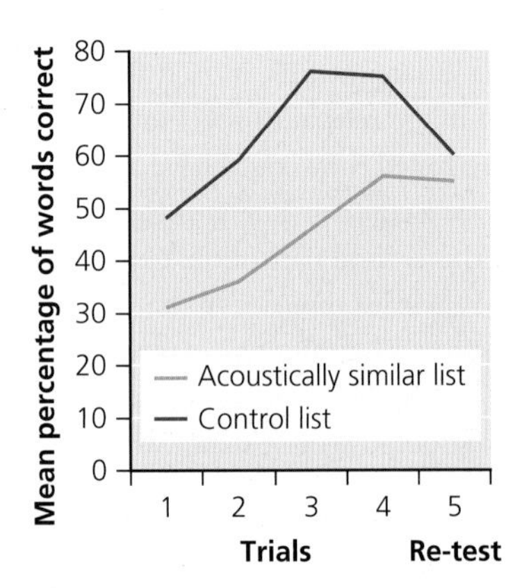

Experiment I: acoustic similarity – the learning (all four trials) and the re-test scores for the acoustically similar list and control

It can be seen that with acoustic similarity the control list was better recalled with regard to the order of the words (though Baddeley states that there was no difference in the number of words retained). By trial 4, there was less difference between the two groups. But there was more forgetting in the control condition (this is the re-test score compared with the earlier trials) than in the 'acoustically similar' condition (where recall at trial 4 is not that much different from re-test recall, which was called 'forgetting'). Baddeley reports this difference in forgetting as being significant at $p<0.05$.

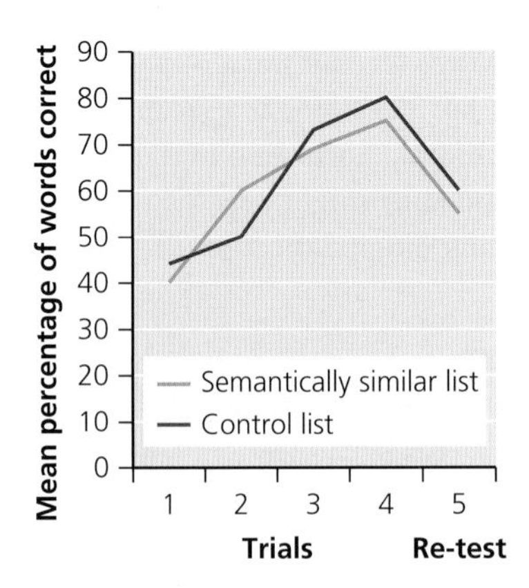

Experiment I: semantic similarity – the learning (all four trials) and the re-test scores for the semantically similar list and control

Semantically similar words

The graph shows that there was no significant differences between the semantically similar list and the control list and both showed a similar amount of forgetting (forgetting is the difference between the re-test score after the 20-minute task and the earlier score at trial 4).

Conclusions

The results showed that it was the acoustic similarity that led to less recall of the order of the words, not semantic similarity. However, it was the acoustic similarity list that showed no forgetting (which was measured using trial 4 score against the re-test score), whereas the other three lists showed forgetting.

> **Progress check 2.11**
> In Experiment I, there were two parts/scores tested. One part of Experiment I used the scores in the four trials, where recall was immediate, and interest was in how scores in different conditions compared. There were four conditions – a test where there was acoustic similarity and a control, and a test where there was semantic similarity and a control. The other part of Experiment I tested the 'forgetting' – the score at trial 4 compared with the score at re-test after 20 minutes.
>
> Briefly explain, using the results, what the two conclusions were about these two parts of Experiment I.

Explaining the results

The re-test was in LTM (20 minutes had passed) and yet semantic similarity did not have an effect (the results for the semantically similar list was the same as for the control list). It was previously found that LTM showed an effect when words were semantically similar, so Baddeley thought this was 'puzzling'. Another puzzling feature of the results (Baddeley calls this a 'paradox') was that it was in the lists where there was good performance that there was most forgetting. The 'low performance' condition, which was when words were acoustically similar, led to less forgetting.

This is a complicated part of the study, but it is important for understanding Experiment II. This is about whether STM or LTM was involved in Experiment I. Clearly after the 20 minutes task, LTM is involved. In the learning tasks (the four trials with immediate recall), there is STM as there is no interference task and there is immediate recall. But as there are four trials, this takes time and the lists are the same, so there could be some LTM in that learning part. Baddeley agrees with this idea and suggests that the four trials might not represent just LTM (as the task is done four times, meaning LTM is likely to be involved) but might also use STM; whereas the re-test score is only going to involve LTM. The acoustically similar list uses STM, as shown by the difficulties there (STM is said to use acoustic coding). The other three lists might also use STM in the four trials, as has been suggested here, but not in the re-test (which is using LTM) and that could account for the forgetting. The acoustically similar list was causing problems for STM so there was less forgetting as those participants did not use STM in the same way the first time (the acoustic coding meant using STM was not straightforward as it would be for the control and semantically similar list) so it was not missed in the re-test and there was less forgetting.

STUDY HINT

It is probably worth taking a break before going on to Experiment II. This study takes a bit of understanding because it can be hard to explain what is happening while keeping the issues clear. Make your own notes as these will help you to clarify the different aspects of the study.

Experiment II

Aim and background

Experiment II was carried out to block the use of STM in the semantically similar and control conditions, so that they matched the acoustic similarity condition (having difficulties with STM). Then it could be seen whether blocking the use of STM meant the semantically similar list was also not well recalled in the learning phase (the four trials) and in the re-test whether the semantically similar list showed less forgetting, as did the acoustically similar list in Experiment I.

In order to remove any STM influence that was found in Experiment I, an interference task was used to prevent rehearsal of words from STM into LTM. If interference is there to prevent rehearsal, it has been found (Peterson and Peterson, 1959) that there is a 'rapid decay of material in STM' (p. 305). If interference removes the STM effect for the three lists other than the one with acoustic similarity (in the learning phase, which is the four trials), then the words with semantic similarity would show a lower learning score than previously but less forgetting too. Remember, forgetting was the re-test score compared with the learning phase (the score at trial 4). The score on the acoustically similar list should not be affected by using interference to prevent rehearsal (it was thought that for that list there was less STM involved in the learning – the four trials).

Procedure

The acoustically similar list (List A) and the semantically similar list (List C) from Experiment I were used in Experiment II, so there was an acoustically similar condition and a semantically similar condition (no control condition lists this time). Within these two main conditions, there were three conditions (one group of participants in each condition) called X, Y and Z.

Explanation

If you read Baddeley's (1966b) study, you will see he uses the term 'subjects' and not 'participants'. 'Participants' is preferred now, as it is more respectful and does not sound as if experiments are 'done on' people.

In Part One, for both the acoustically similar condition and the semantically similar condition, Condition X kept learning the same as in Experiment I. Condition Y kept learning the same as in Experiment I except for a task between each presentation of the list and each test. Condition Z was the same as Condition Y but the interference task was this time between the test and the next presentation – this was a control in case of practice effects (so that there were two interference tasks), but it was Condition Y, the interference task between the learning and first recall in all four trials, that was the condition of interest as that is the one that blocks STM. The interference task was the same as the one done during the 20-minute break in Experiment I. The task presented eight numbers at one-second intervals and then the participants had to write the numbers down in the order they appeared. They had eight seconds to do this. The interference tasks in Conditions Y and Z used six trials of the eight numbers and eight seconds to write them down.

- Condition X: one set of participants has List A, acoustically similar words, and one set of participants has List C, semantically similar adjectives. In both cases, there is *immediate* recall in Part One and then a 20-minute gap and recall (the re-test).

- Condition Y: one set of participants has List A, acoustically similar words, and one set of participants has List C, semantically similar adjectives. In both cases, there is recall in Part One *but with an interference task between the learning and the recall.* And then a 20-minute gap and recall (the re-test).
- Condition Z: one set of participants has List A, acoustically similar words, and one set of participants has List C, semantically similar adjectives. In both cases, there is *immediate* recall in Part One *but with an interference task between the recall and the next trial/learning.* And then a 20-minute gap and recall (the re-test).

In Part Two, the re-test is kept the same for all three groups.

Participants

Housewives from the universities' 'subjects panel' were used this time and they were tested in groups of about 20, as with Experiment I. Six participants failed the hearing test this time. Table 2.3 gives the numbers of participants in each of the three conditions and in the acoustically similar section and the semantically similar section.

Table 2.3 Number of participants in each condition for Experiment II

	Acoustically similar condition	Semantically similar condition
Condition X	20	17
Condition Y	25	26
Condition Z	23	20

Results

The score that was recorded was the same as in Experiment I, as was the method of analysis.

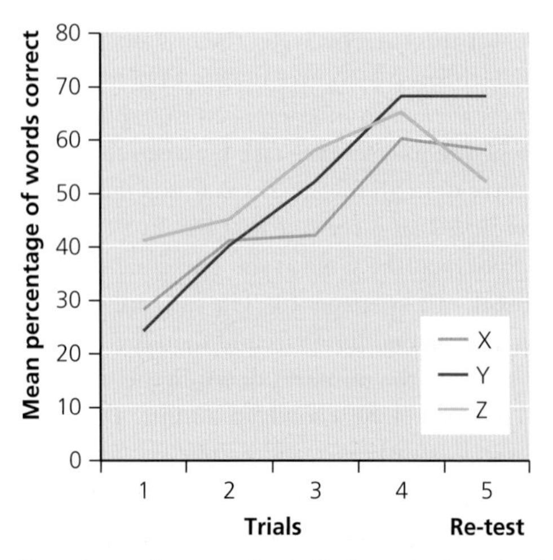

Experiment II: acoustic similarity – the learning (all four trials) and the re-test scores for the acoustically similar list

Acoustically similar words

In Condition Z, which was with the interference between each presentation of the words/recall, in the learning phase, there was more recall than in the other two conditions in trial 1 but not in the other trials ($p<0.02$). Conditions X and Y had no forgetting. Condition Z had significant forgetting at re-test ($p<0.01$). Other than that, there were no significant differences between the conditions.

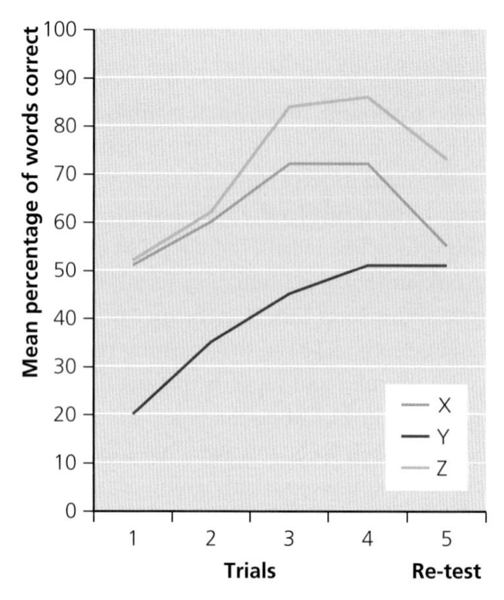

Experiment II: semantic similarity – the learning (all four trials) and the re-test scores for the semantically similar list

Semantically similar words

Learning was reduced in the condition when there was interference between the learning and the recall (Condition Y) so reduced by having the STM control. The difference between Condition X (no interference, matched Experiment I) and Condition Y (with interference between presenting the words and recalling the order) was significant ($p<0.001$). The semantically similar condition without interference showed significant forgetting at re-test (as in Experiment I). Condition Z was not significantly different from Condition X, there was a lot of forgetting in Conditions X and Z. Condition Y (the one with interference between learning and recall) is the one without forgetting.

Conclusions

Experiment II showed that the way testing was done in Experiment I did affect the learning phase, as was thought at the end of Experiment I. In Experiment I, the learning phase used both STM and LTM and the re-test used LTM and this affected the findings. It was concluded that the way the study was done could not answer the research question about the importance of acoustic or semantic factors in LTM because STM was not 'blocked', as Experiment II showed. This led to Experiment III where visual presentation was used to prevent mishearing problems and this time control groups were included.

Progress check 2.12

Here are statements about the results of Experiments I and II in Baddeley (1966b). Tick the statements that are true about the results and cross the ones that are false.

Statement about Baddeley's (1966b) results	Tick or cross
The semantic similarity condition when use of STM was blocked (Condition Y) had similar recall as in the acoustic condition in Experiment I.	
The semantic similarity condition when use of STM was blocked (Condition Y) had different recall to the acoustic condition in Experiment I.	
The semantic similarity condition when use of STM was blocked (Condition Y) shows little forgetting (recall at re-test 20 minutes later is not different).	
The semantic similarity condition without STM blocked showed significant forgetting (recall at re-test 20 minutes later is different).	
The acoustic similarity condition without interference (same in Experiment I and Experiment II) shows slower learning and recall when recall is immediate, but no forgetting (recall at re-test 20 minutes later is not different).	

Experiment III

Aim

Experiment III tested the original research question about the role of acoustic and semantic factors in LTM, this time with the STM factor properly controlled for.

Procedure

The four Experiment I lists were used (Lists A, B, C and D). Different participants did each list. In all four lists (conditions), Condition Y of Experiment II was used, where there was a task between presentation of the list and recall for each trial. This was to block the effect of STM. The words were presented visually by slide projector and were visible for three seconds. The intervening task was the same as in Experiment II (reading out eight numbers, which were then written down, and this was done six times). After the four trials, there was a 15-minute task. The words were visible throughout (not in the order).

Participants

These were males and females from the universities' 'subject panel'. List A had 15 participants, List B had 20, List C had 16 and List D had 21. List A was the acoustically similar list, List B was its control, List C was the semantically similar list and List D was its control.

Results

The scores were derived and analysed as in Experiments I and II.

Acoustically similar words

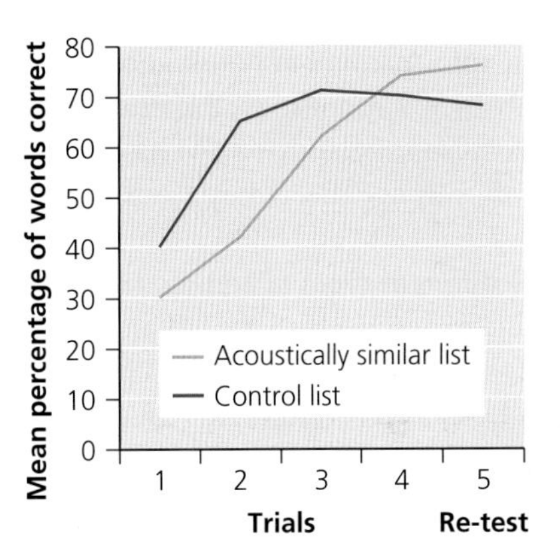

Experiment III: acoustic similarity – the results (learning and re-test) for the acoustically similar list and its control (List A and List B)

Neither group shows forgetting between trial 4 and the recall. The re-test score is not significantly different for either condition.

Semantically similar words

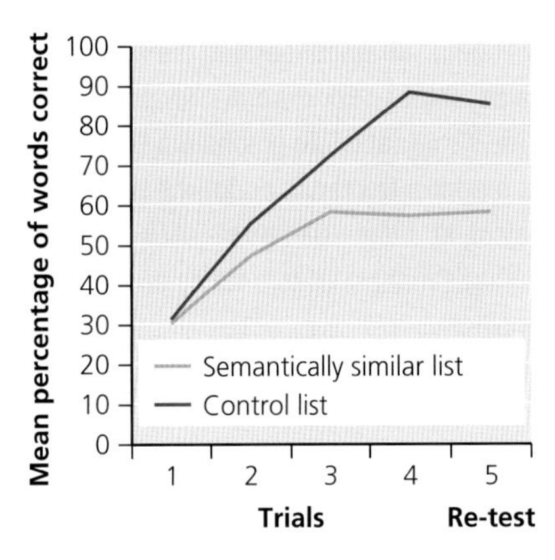

Experiment III: semantic similarity – the results (learning and re-test) for the semantically similar list and its control (List C and List D)

The semantically similar list does show that learning was harder than in the control condition and trial 4 shows significantly higher learning scores on List D (the control) than on List C (the semantically similar words) ($p<0.005$). For neither list was there significant forgetting at recall.

Conclusions

Experiment III shows that semantic similarity did affect learning and also shows that learning is retained in all groups for the 15 minutes before re-test. LTM might be based on meaning of words or on sound of words; both showed successful recall in LTM. When STM is blocked, it was hard to learn the semantically similar words so it seems that learning such words is helped by STM. STM was fine with semantic information but not so good on acoustic information (which was not so well learned in Experiment I) and that seems to suggest that STM has acoustic coding. LTM, however, was not affected by acoustic similarity and this shows that LTM and STM are indeed affected differently by different types of coding. It has also been shown by these experiments that LTM and STM do work together and not separately. Blocking STM affects learning and recall and also affects re-test after 15 minutes, which is about LTM. Material that is difficult in STM is not necessarily difficult in LTM.

Overall conclusion

Overall, the conclusion is that LTM is different from STM, which was the question Baddeley (1966b) set out to answer. The aim of this study was to see if long-term memory is affected if there is acoustic similarity more than if there is semantic similarity, and this was found not to be the case.

STUDY HINT

This is a long and complex study and a lot of detail has been given here. That is because there are issues in this study that will help you when learning the method section for cognitive psychology. For example, levels of statistical probability are shown and line graphs are used. This study is complex, so read it a few times and it will become clearer. You are studying at a high level now - stick with it and you will get there. Perhaps make your own notes as you go and use diagrams to clarify.

Explore

Using the internet or some other source, find out more about Peterson and Peterson's (1959) interference task in STM to investigate these issues more. Relate your research in this area to the multi-store model of memory and what is said about interference as a form of forgetting earlier in this chapter (pp. 81-82).

Evaluation of Baddeley's (1966b) study on long-term memory

Strengths

- Baddeley's (1966b) study uses experimental conditions and control conditions, as well as other controls, so any findings are likely to show cause and effect, as extraneous variables are well controlled. Controls include timing how long a stimulus is visible for and having the same interference tasks for Experiment II and Experiment III.
- Baddeley built on the findings of others, which adds to a body of knowledge and uses a scientific approach to psychology. He took the results from his other studies (and studies of others) and explored issues more, such as using the idea that STM uses acoustic coding to test if LTM similarly used acoustic coding. When findings from one study link well to those of other studies, this adds strength to results and an element of reliability.
- A third strength is the reliability of his work, which can be shown because he repeated some of the conditions and could show similar results (such as the similarity in findings both times participants used List A, the acoustically similar list). To be accepted, results have to be reliable – it is not helpful to rely on findings that cannot be repeated. Baddeley's findings were repeated.

Weaknesses

- Baddeley used stimulus materials that were not naturalistic and so there was a lack of ecological validity in the situation he was testing. Steyvers and Hemmer (2012) explain how, when they used pictures of scenes to look at reconstructive memory, they had different results from other studies that had not had such realism. Baddeley (1966b) used lists of words that sound alike and lists of adjectives with similar meaning, and these are not things we remember in everyday life very often. So their findings might lack validity.
- The experiments reduced memory to recall of the order of a list of ten words, with various conditions involved, so this is reductionist. An holistic study of memory might involve more qualitative case study data of how someone with memory difficulties experiences their life. Reductionism can be a strength in that findings can be reliable and a scientific body of knowledge can be built; however, it can also be a weakness if it means that findings do not represent everyday life.
- Baddeley's findings rely on there being an LTM and STM split that is accepted and his studies are set up with those two separate stores in mind. Other theories, such as the idea that memory is about the level of processing rather than down to the use of different stores, go against the multi-store and working memory models.

The levels of processing framework for memory would suggest that semantic processing leads to better recall because processing is at a deeper level than processing of sound. This is a different explanation for findings about semantic and acoustic processing.

Progress check 2.13

1. In Baddeley's (1966b) study, Experiment III, which was learned best in the four trials: acoustically similar words or semantically similar words?
2. In Baddeley's (1966b) study, Experiment III, was there forgetting (which is measured using trial 4 recall and re-test after 15 minutes recall)?

Test yourself

1. Explain experimental features of Baddeley's (1966b) study. **(8 marks)**
2. Evaluate Baddeley's (1966b) study with regards to how it helps us to know about how memory works. **(12 marks)**

STUDY HINT

When asked to evaluate, you can describe as well, in order to outline what you are evaluating. The marks are not all going to specific evaluation points; some are for describing points that you evaluate. Also, evaluation can include strengths and weaknesses but also issues such as how applicable the findings are to society

Contemporary studies

Sebastián and Hernández-Gil (2012)

The researchers used Spanish participants, which has some relevance for the findings, and the study was about how digit span (memory span using numbers/digits) develops from children to adolescence and looked at older people as well. Their study tests part of Baddeley's working memory model, the phonological loop.

Aim(s)

The researchers wanted to study the developmental pattern of working memory over time, including changes from ageing or neurodegenerative diseases under the umbrella term 'dementia'. Their aim was to analyse the developmental pattern of the phonological loop in children aged 5–17 years old. This involved looking at the age at which the **digit span** stopped increasing in adulthood/adolescence. They also wanted to look at the decline of digit span in older people, including those with two types of dementia: Alzheimer's and fronto-temporal dementia. They did this by using findings from their previous study in 2010.

Another aim was to see if Anglo-Saxon data (data using the English language), which found 15 years to be the age at which the digit span stops developing further, were replicated, or whether digit span would be higher for Spanish speakers. The researchers felt that word length might affect the digit span and Spanish word length is different from Anglo-Saxon word length.

Definition

Digit span refers to memory span and capacity of short-term memory without rehearsal. Digits are numbers. Digit span can be tested by reading a sequence of numbers to someone. If they get that right – say, a sequence of three numbers – then the next sequence they read would have four digits in it, and so on, until they get a sequence wrong. That is then their digit span.

STUDY HINT

You may need to refresh your memory of the working memory model of memory before reading this study, so that terms like 'phonological loop' are familiar to you. Be sure to make connections between the models of memory and the studies, to help your learning. Also studies within a theory can be used as evidence for or against that theory, so make a note of this sort of information.

Background

The development of short-term memory over time has been studied and it appears that young children have a different capacity than adults. Also older people might have a lower capacity and studying those with fronto-temporal dementia or Alzheimer's has shown that short-term memory is impaired. This study looks at digit span, the capacity of short-term memory and, in particular, the capacity in working memory of storing auditory information. Sebastián and Hernández-Gil (2012) mention, first, Atkinson and Shiffrin's (1968) model of memory as separating short-term and long-term memory and then Baddeley and Hitch's (1974) working memory model, which splits short-term memory up into temporary stores. These two models of memory are the background for the study. Sebastián and Hernández-Gil (2012) focus on the phonological loop in working memory. They focus on the two parts of the phonological loop, which are the phonological store, which retains verbal information, and subvocal rehearsal, which uses strategies like chunking to help to extend the temporary memory store.

Short-term memory is explained in the study using the working memory model. The short-term memory store (the phonological store) is used to store items, with the subvocal rehearsal used to remember the correct order of items. A digit span method requires a sequence of numbers to be remembered, as well as their order, so is an ideal method to use to study these two parts of working memory. Short-term memory seems to improve from the age of six to adulthood, according to Diamond (2006, cited in Sebastián and Hernández-Gil, 2012). Three-to-four year olds use the phonological loop, so it is present in very young children. Subvocal rehearsal, however, does not start until about seven or eight years, and young children quickly forget from the phonological loop, which decays quickly. Hitch (2006, cited in Sebastián and Hernández-Gil, 2012) found that the phonological loop always decays quickly and it is the use of subvocal rehearsal that increases the digit span with age. Possibly the development of the central executive function over this time helps in the development of the subvocal rehearsal.

An interesting aim in the study is to consider differences in data between Anglo-Saxon studies and Spanish studies. Gathercole and Alloway (2008, cited in Sebastián and Hernández-Gil, 2012) found that digit span does increase with age up to 15 years old. Sebastián and Hernández-Gil (2012) wondered whether doing a study using the Spanish language would affect this finding.

STUDY HINT

When discussing the key question of how psychological understanding can help with dyslexia, the idea of digit span rising up to the age of 15 is given, with this study cited. This shows how studies of memory in cognitive psychology and the models of memory are connected, as are the contemporary studies and key questions in your course. Use these connections to understand the material better.

Procedure

There were two parts to the study.

The first part gathered **primary data** and used 5–17 year olds from the Spanish population. There were 570 volunteers from various schools in Madrid. They were all born in Spain. None of the participants had repeated a school year, and none had difficulties such as in reading or writing or in hearing. This was to control for education and cognitive differences.

The second part of the study used data from the researchers' previous study in 2010 (Sebastián and Hernández-Gil, 2010) where data were gathered about digit span of elderly people without impairment, those with Alzheimer's and those with fronto-temporal dementia. Thus the second part of the study used **secondary data**. The second part used 25 healthy older people as a control group, 25 with Alzheimer's disease and nine with fronto-temporal dementia.

Definitions

Primary data are gathered by the researchers in an actual study at the time and for the purpose of testing one or more hypotheses. **Secondary data** are gathered for a previous study, possibly for a different purpose and already existing when used in a new study.

The first part was the main part of the study and the hypothesis was that there is a difference in digit span which increases with age, from 5–17 years old. The independent variable was the age of the participant and the dependent variable was the digit span. The digit span was measured by reading aloud sequences of digits (numbers) one per second. Each time a participant got the sequence right (the right digits in the right order), another digit was added to increase the span and the participant tried again. The digit span measure was the number of digits in the sequence where they recalled at least two of the three sequences correctly (right digits, right order). The starting point was three sequences of three digits. Instructions required participants to listen carefully and recall the digits in the same order that they were presented in. Participants were tested individually and in their break time.

Progress check 2.14

Explain which participants were used in this study in both parts.

Results

The first part used five age groups: 5 years, 6–8 years, 9–11 years, 12–14 years and 15–17 years. Analysis was also done using 13 year groups to see whether digit span increased by year group or by age group. The results showed clearly that digit span increased with age, as shown in Table 2.4.

Table 2.4 The average digit span in each group

Course (age)	Digit span	Developmental period
Preschool (5 years)	3.76	3.76 (5 years)
Primary school (6 years)	4.16	
Primary school (7 years)	4.26	4.34 (6-8 years)
Primary school (8 years)	4.63	
Primary school (9 years)	5.00	
Primary school (10 years)	5.13	5.13 (9-11 years)
Primary school (11 years)	5.28	
Secondary school (12 years)	5.30	
Secondary school (13 years)	5.89	5.46 (12-14 years)
Secondary school (14 years)	5.51	
Secondary school (15 years)	5.82	
Secondary school (16 years)	5.75	5.83 (15-17 years)
Secondary school (17 years)	5.91	

The preschool children aged five years had a very low digit span and showed a significant difference from the other age groups. From 6–8 years old, the children had a very similar digit span. The increase in one digit, from four to five, occurred at nine years old and rose to 11 years old. Older children aged 12–14 years had a similar digit span to one another but differed from the age groups 'above' them. A similar digit span was found for 15–17 year olds.

The researchers compared their data to data from the Wechsler Intelligence Scale for Children IV (WISC-IV), which is an intelligence test for children (they used data for Spanish children). Data from the WISC-IV showed digit span increased with age, but the digit span was higher each time than the findings of their study.

Progress check 2.15

Explain the results of the first part of the study, which looked at digit span and age of children and young people.

The second part compared the results of this study with another study from 2010. The participants were healthy older people, people with Alzheimer's dementia and people with fronto-temporal dementia. The digit span task was the same as in the first part. Table 2.5 gives the results for the second part of the study.

Table 2.5 The average digit span in each group

Group	Gender	Mean digit span
Alzheimer's dementia	7m / 18f	4.20
Fronto-temporal dementia	5m / 4f	4.22
Healthy older people (control)	6m / 19f	4.44

The performance of the elderly participants was compared with the youngest in the first part of the study and showed a higher digit span than both the five year olds (at a significance level of $p=0.0001$, two tailed) and the six year olds (at a significance level of $p=0.03$, two tailed). The performance of the elderly participants did not differ from the other year groups ($p>0.05$).

STUDY HINT

When checking for significance, Sebastián and Hernández-Gil (2012 and 2010) used a two-tailed assumption, which means that they did not assume that the elderly participants would have a lower or a higher digit span than the younger participants. Also you can see they used different levels of significance and rejected the null hypothesis (they accepted a difference, in that the elderly people had a significantly higher digit span than the five and six year olds). When the **level of significance** was greater than 5 per cent ($p>0.05$), the researchers accepted the null hypothesis and said there was no difference in the digit span in the elderly participants as compared with the other age groups. You can use the studies to learn about the methodology and make notes accordingly.

However, when the digit span of the youngest participants was compared with the participants with dementia, it was found that those with Alzheimer's dementia had a higher digit span than 5 year olds but not significantly different from the other year groups, whereas those with fronto-temporal dementia had a similar digit span to the youngest groups.

Conclusion

A main conclusion is that digit span increases with age from 5–17 years old. This contrasts with Anglo-Saxon data (such as from Gathercole and Alloway, 2008) where it was found that digit span increased to 15 years old and then reached an adult level. The adult span is about seven digits (which is in line with the multi-store model of memory and conclusions in that model about memory span in short-term memory without rehearsal).

The Spanish study figures were about one digit below the Anglo-Saxon data, and Sebastián and Hernández-Gil (2012) were interested to see why that might be the case. They highlighted the idea of differences in word length (how long it takes to say the word, not just the length) between Spanish and English as the reason. They mention Baddeley *et al.*'s (1975) study showing that memory span is affected by lists using long words compared to lists using short words. The idea of word length affecting recall is linked to the idea of using subvocal rehearsal (see the working memory model to help to explain this). The longer it takes to 'say' the digit word to oneself (subvocal rehearsal), the more the trace would decay and also the easier it is to lose information while rehearsing the digits.

Issues and debates

Note that Baddeley's work is mentioned in Sebastián and Hernández-Gil's (2012) study, showing how studies build on one another with regard to findings and a body of knowledge is built. You can use this sort of information when discussing how psychology has developed over time.

Practical

One idea for a practical investigation in cognitive psychology is to test the idea that word length affects memory span. Use a list of long words and a list of short words, with the usual controls (such as words being of similar frequency in the English language and there being the same number of words). You could choose an independent groups design (different people in the two conditions) and see if those with words longer in length recall fewer words than those with short words. This builds on Baddeley *et al.* (1975).

Spanish digit words are longer than English digit words, and take longer to say. The researchers point out that subvocal rehearsal does not start until seven years old and so there should be less difference between the English and Spanish digit spans by children below seven than from seven years onwards – that is, if their idea about the effect of word length (digit word length) is right. They did find that in the English studies the digit span for ages 5–6 years old was around four, which matches the Spanish study and supports the idea that word length (and how long it takes to say the word) is what makes a difference in the later ages. This is very interesting and backs up the claims that from the age of 7, though for both Spanish and English studies digit span increases with age, the digit span is about one digit lower than when English is used because of the effect of word length.

STUDY HINT

You can use material from anywhere in the course to help your learning. The contemporary study by Sebastián and Hernández-Gil (2012) draws on ideas from the multi-store model and can help to clarify issues in the content for cognitive psychology. Likewise, if you choose to look at working memory and dementia as a key question, you can use evidence from Sebastián and Hernández-Gil (2012 and 2010) when applying concepts, theories and research to the issue.

Spanish words for numbers one to ten:
uno (oo-noh), dos (dohs), tres, cuatro (quat-roh), cinco (sin-co), seis (say-ees), siete (see-eh-tay), ocho (oh-cho), nueve (noo-ev-ay), diez (dee-ez)

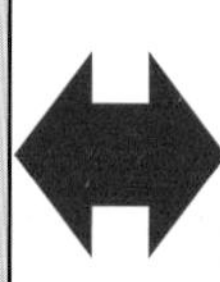

English words for numbers one to ten:
one, two, three, four, five, six, seven, eight, nine, ten
There are more sounds in the Spanish words so they take longer to say.

Spanish words for numbers one to ten compared with English words for numbers one to ten

Another conclusion is that digit span increases with age, which matches WISC-IV data showing the same development pattern. When using data from the Wechsler Adult Intelligence Scale III (WAIS-III), digit span from 16–19 years is 6.47 on average, which is higher than the digit span at 15 years of age (6.10) according to the WISC-IV. This suggests that there is an increase in years after 17, which would be interesting to study.

A conclusion around older people showed that the digit span of the healthy older people was similar to that of a seven year old, which does show an age effect in that there is decline in digit span with age (though it is not clear at what age that decline starts). The digit span of those with Alzheimer's and fronto-temporal dementia is not that much different from that of the healthy older people and similar to a six year old's digit span, so dementia did not seem to affect digit span in itself. The capacity of the phonological loop seems to be affected by age but not by dementia.

Progress check 2.16

Outline two conclusions from Sebastián and Hernández-Gil's (2012) study.

Evaluation of Sebastián and Hernández-Gil (2012)

Strengths

- One strength is the reliability because the researchers can compare their data with WISC-IV data in the Spanish population and also with other studies, albeit using English. The findings from their data, the English data and the WISC-IV data all show a very similar pattern in development, with digit span increasing up to around 17 years of age. This means results are likely to be reliable.
- Another strength is the careful controls used in the study. The digit span task is a standard one and the same procedure was used in the 2012 study as in the 2010 study. The digits are presented one per second and there are three trials. The task is carried out in the break for all participants. They use Spanish children and the Spanish language, which is a form of control too, as shown by their analysis of the findings.
- Finally, they analyse not only for actual age using school years, but also for age group so that they have individual digit span scores for each year and age group, which means they have more information from which to draw conclusions. For example, they can show not only the average digit span for 6–8 year olds, but also that 6, 7 and 8 year olds differed, which is a useful finding in itself.

Weaknesses

- The task is artificial, as we do not generally recall lists of digits, so there might be a lack of validity. However, the test looks at the use of the phonological loop and perhaps recall of sequences of digits is a valid test for that purpose. The setting is reasonably valid as it is in their schools and in break time. So, although experiments lack validity because of the controls and artificiality of the tasks, this one can claim perhaps some validity.

- Another weakness is shown in the conclusion, but by discussing it perhaps the researchers then deal with it as a weakness. This is the variable that is not controlled, which is that the digits are subvocalised by Spanish speakers. The researchers are persuasive in their argument that the word length has affected the digit span and their evidence is that the English-speaking participants had on average a span one digit higher. The weakness is that the study was done using Spanish speakers only but at least the weakness is recognised and explained.
- Although the study shows that digit span increases with age up to 17, there is the suggestion using WAIS-III data that it might increase up to 19 years of age and the use of older people shows a decrease with age. The weakness is that the study does not show at what age the decrease might start. However, perhaps this is less of a weakness and more a requirement for further study.
- It is assumed that digit span is affected by subvocalising and that is why under the age of seven the digit span is lower, as it is from the age of seven that subvocal rehearsal starts. This is an assumption rather than something the study showed. The study states the digit span, and perhaps is low on explanation.

Test yourself

1. Explain how digit span was tested in Sebastián and Hernández-Gil's (2012) study. **(4 marks)**
2. Evaluate Sebastián and Hernández-Gil's (2012) study with regards to how it gives evidence for the working memory model. **(8 marks)**

Schmolck *et al.* (2002)

Schmolck *et al.* (2002) studied damage to the medial temporal lobe (MTL) and anterolateral temporal cortex to see what the effects of such damage was on semantic memory and semantic knowledge.

Aim(s)

Schmolck *et al.* (2002) wanted to look at the relationship between performance on semantic knowledge tests and the extent of lateral temporal cortex damage to find out if the lateral temporal cortex was involved in semantic memory, and to what extent. Another aim was to look specifically at HM's performance to see what was different from the performance of the other patients, if indeed it was different.

Background

Studies have shown that having medial temporal lobe (MTL) **lesions** causes lasting memory impairment, which affects acquisition of new information as well as recalling material just learned (e.g. Scoville and Milner, 1957, cited in Schmolck *et al.*, 2002). However, information from long ago can be unaffected, such as grammar rules and definitions of words, as well as knowledge of places that were experienced some time ago. The damage to the MTL being talked about is **bilateral**, which means both sides of the brain. HM showed stable performance on intelligence tests (Kensinger *et al.*, 2001, cited in Schmolck *et al.*, 2002). Another patient with amnesia (EP) recalled the neighbourhood he grew up in (Teng and Squire, 1999, cited in Schmolck *et al.*, 2002). These findings show that the MTL is required for new knowledge to be acquired but not for material that has been in memory a long time.

> **Definitions**
>
> **Lesions** are where the brain is damaged. This can be through accident or disease, or it may be done deliberately in surgery. Brain damage can be called **bilateral** if both hemispheres have damage. For example, the MTL+ damage talked about here is bilateral – the MTL+ in both hemispheres is damaged.

However, though long-term knowledge seems to be intact for patients with MTL damage, HM and EP, and other patients with MTL damage, had difficulty with features of sentences (e.g. Schmolck *et al.*, 2001, cited in Schmolck *et al.*, 2002). This finding has not really been explained, though it is thought that, as the patients studied did have MTL damage and also had some damage to the lateral temporal cortex (including HM), it could be that difficulty with sentence ambiguity was a result of lateral temporal cortex damage, not MTL damage. One issue with studying patients with brain damage is that their damage is rarely confined to one structure in the brain. HM's difficulties with a sentence structure task were different from the difficulties the others experienced and it was thought that some of HM's difficulties were not related to the damage to his brain. It seems to be the case anyway that MTL damage affects some memory attributes but not others; some difficulties in semantic processing might come from lateral temporal cortex damage, and HM's difficulties might not only be due to his damage. Long-term memories are not affected by MTL or lateral temporal cortex damage.

Procedure

The procedure consisted of giving semantic knowledge tests to patients with medial temporal lobe lesions, who also had some damage to the lateral temporal cortex (some with more damage than others). These patients were said to have MTL+ damage. They also used patients with damage to the hippocampal formation only. The hippocampal formation is within the MTL, so this means they looked at patients with just hippocampal formation damage and not other MTL damage. They also tested HM and compared his performance with the performance of the others.

STUDY HINT
Don't be put off by the use of biological expressions such as 'lesions' and 'medial temporal lobe'. It helps to learn the names of the structures (such as MTL) and practise them. When reading through a study that uses complex terms for the first time, it is useful to ignore the actual 'labels' and get the idea of the study. As you use the terms more, such as in an essay, you will find that they become more familiar. I can say this from personal experience!

Participants

- Three patients had herpes simplex encephalitis, which had led to amnesia (EP, GP and GT). These three had large MTL damage and various amounts of damage to the anterolateral temporal cortex (MTL+).
- HM had a bilateral MTL re-section, which means surgery for epilepsy which left him with MTL damage.
- Two patients had amnesia with damage limited to the hippocampal formation (HF).
- Eight people had no damage, acting as controls (CON). These were eight healthy men who were volunteers. They were matched in terms of age and education to the patients. The average age was 74 years.

There were 14 participants in total: EP, GP, GT, HM, two HF and eight CON (this is how they are referred to in the study). MRI scanning was used to see what lesions each patient had (this included just one of the HF patients and all the patients with MTL and anterolateral temporal cortex damage).

STUDY HINT
Biological psychology includes studying various types of scanning. This study uses MRI scanning, so you can use it as an example. Make a note of this link between biological and cognitive psychology.

The full study explains for each participant what damage they have and what had happened to them. Damage to the brain is measured quantitatively by measuring segments of the temporal lobe in a prescribed way so that comparisons can be made. The researchers need to have full information on the damage to the brain because they want to look at this damage in detail and then look at the memory impairment for each patient. They want to compare memory impairment with the damage to see which part of the brain seems to be linked to which impairment. Without this detail, they wouldn't be able to make this comparison. Table 2.6 summarises some of the damage so you can see which brain structures are being studied and to help your understanding of the results.

STUDY HINT
Each patient is studied in detail, both the damage to the brain and their scores on the tests. They are case studies – this relates to the requirement for you to learn about the research method called 'case studies of brain-damaged patients'. Make notes about the case studies used here so you can use them when discussing the research method.

Table 2.6 Brain damage for each of the patients in this study

Patient	How damage occurred leading to amnesia	Some features regarding the damage to the brain
EP (male)	Herpes simplex encephalitis, 1992	Medial temporal lobe damage. All of the amygdala, all of the hippocampal region, all of the entorhinal cortex and perirhinal cortex, much of the parahippocampal cortex. The lateral temporal cortex was reduced in volume – both hemispheres.
GP (male)	Herpes simplex encephalitis, 1987	Medial temporal lobe damage mainly. Also the left and right temporal lobes, all of the amygdala, all of the hippocampal region, all of the entorhinal cortex and perirhinal cortex, much of the parahippocampal cortex. There is other damage, such as to the fusiform gyrus and the inferior temporal gyrus.
GT (male)	Herpes simplex encephalitis, 1990	Most of the temporal lobes, both hemispheres – left and right temporal lobes, all of the amygdala, all of the hippocampal region, all of the entorhinal cortex and perirhinal cortex, much of the parahippocampal cortex. Fusiform gyrus damage and other damage too.
HM (male)	Brain damaged because of epilepsy, surgery took place to 'cause' the damage	Medial temporal lobe bilateral damage mainly. Some of the hippocampal region is spared, as is the fusiform gyrus, but there is some other damage.
AB (HF patient, male)	Cardiac arrest, 1976	Could not have an MRI because of a pacemaker. A CT scan was used. Some loss of volume in the supra ventricular parts of the frontal and parietal lobes and the medial occipital lobes. The MTL was hard to study in detail using a CT scan. The temporal lobe was normal and the damage seems limited. There is damage to the hippocampal formation (HF).
LJ (HF patient, female)	Developed amnesia in 1988 and memory has remained stable since then	Hippocampal formation damage bilaterally. Hippocampal region is reduced by 46 per cent in area compared to 'normal'.

Progress check 2.17

Using Table 2.6, summarise the damage to the three MTL+ patients.

The tests used to assess semantic knowledge

The tests used were based on line drawings of 24 animals and 24 objects or their names. There were, therefore, 48 items. These were further split into eight categories: six domestic land animals, six foreign land animals, six water creatures, six birds, six electrical household items, six non-electrical household items, six vehicles and six musical instruments.

The tests are explained in Table 2.7.

Table 2.7 **The tests used in Schmolck *et al.* to test semantic memory**

Test	Explanation
1 Pointing to picture in response to a name (score is % of answers correct)	The name of each of the 48 items was given to the participants and they were asked to identify the picture that matched the name, from the six pictures in the category.
2 Pointing to picture in response to description (score is % of answers correct)	The verbal description (without physical attributes) of each of the 48 items was given to the participants and they were asked to identify the picture that matched the verbal description, from the six pictures in the category.
3 Naming in response to a picture (score is % of answers correct)	They were shown a picture of each of the 48 items and asked to name it.
4 Naming in response to a description (score is % of answers correct)	They were given a verbal description of each of the 48 items and asked to name it.
5 Semantic features (score is % of answers correct)	Participants were asked eight 'yes or no' questions about 24 of the items.
6 Category fluency (score is number of examples given)	They were asked to name examples from each of the eight categories, as many as they could – they were given one minute to respond.
7 Category sorting (score is % of answers correct)	Participants had to sort pictures of all 48 items into two categories, which were 'living' or 'man made'. Then they sorted each of those 24 sets into two narrower categories, which were land animals or household items, and then narrower categories again (e.g. fierce and non-fierce items).
8 Definitions to name*	They were given the name of the 24 items that were least common and had to define them – they had one minute for each definition.
9 Definitions to picture*	Similar to 'definitions to name' but this time they were shown a picture and asked to define it.

* Tape-recorded sessions were transcribed. Then, for each definition, the number of right and wrong statements was recorded to give a score. A quality score was given as well to show how good the definitions were (e.g. a score of 1 meant definitions were vague and not understandable). For this part of the analysis, there were 14 raters used to test for reliability. The raters had the definitions and tried to identify the item being defined. The researchers also looked for grammatical errors in this part and errors in sentence structure.

Other tests that had been used before to test semantic knowledge in dementia patients were also used. Tests included one using line drawings where 30 were real objects and 30 were non-objects. Participants had to say whether the line drawing represented a real object or not. Another test asked participants to colour in line drawings of objects using the required colour pen. In the test HM did (he only did one), the Pyramids and Palms test, there are 52 cards with each having a 'target picture and two test pictures' (Schmolck *et al.*, 2001, p. 525). The participants have to give the best match from the two test pictures to the target picture. The study gives the example of a saddle and two test pictures, a horse and a goat.

Results

Results compared the controls with the patients with hippocampal formation damage (HF) and the patients with MTL+ damage. The results are presented clearly in graphical form and the percentages given here are readings off the graphs so are not absolutely accurate but indicative of the results, enough to use the figures with confidence. Scores are mean percentages of getting the tasks right. Where exact scores are given in the study, they are indicated here with an ✲.

Object is named, point to picture

When participants were given the name of an object and had to point to the picture, the controls got the answers right, as did those with hippocampal formation damage. HM got about 98 per cent right with regard to the living objects and all the non-living objects right. Those with MTL+ damage found the task harder, getting a mean of around 85 per cent right for the living objects and about 90 per cent for the non-living objects.

Object is described, point to picture

When participants were given the description of an object and had to point to the picture, the controls again got the answers right, as did those with hippocampal formation damage. Again HM got the living objects right about 97 per cent of the time and all the non-living objects right. There were very similar results for those with MTL+ damage as when pointing to a named object, with about 85 per cent right for the living objects and 90 per cent right for the non-living objects.

Shown picture, asked to name it

When participants were shown a picture and asked to name it, it was again the MTL+ patients who had difficulty. The controls, HF patients and HM had very similar findings as those in the two conditions described above. The MTL+ patients had about 75 per cent right for living objects in this condition and 78 per cent for non-living objects, lower than in the two conditions above.

Given verbal description, asked to name it

It was in the condition where participants were given a verbal description of an object and had to name it that the MTL+ patients did worse when compared to the controls and HF patients. Compared with the controls and HF patients, who got nearly all of the tasks right, the MTL+ patients achieved about 50 per cent for the living objects and about 62 per cent for the non-living objects. HM did not do quite so well on this condition either, though again better than the MTL+ patients. He achieved *66.7 per cent for the living objects and 90 per cent for the non-living objects.

STUDY HINT

Keep checking back if you cannot remember what the initials stand for. HM is Henry Molaison, HF refers to two patients with hippocampal formation damage, and MTL+ refers to three patients with damage to the medial temporal lobe and lateral temporal cortex.

Yes/no question about 24 items

When it came to the yes/no questions about 24 of the items, the controls did not do quite as well as the HF patients, but still achieved well on the tasks, getting *91 per cent for the living objects and *92.8 per cent for the non-living objects. HF patients achieved about 98 per cent on both the living and the non-living objects. HM achieved *85.4 per cent for the living objects and *95.8 per cent for the non-living objects. The MTL+ patients again did worse than the other groups, with 76 per cent for the living objects and 85.8 per cent for the non-living objects.

Table 2.8 Mean percentage of answers right when shown a picture or given a verbal description and asked to name, and summary of the five conditions (*Figures given in the study so are exact)

Condition	Living objects	Non-living objects
Shown a picture, asked to name	Controls 100% HF patients 100% HM 97% MTL+ patients 75%	Controls 100% HF patients 100% HM 100% MTL+ patients 78%
Given verbal description, asked to name	Controls 100% HF patients 100% HM *66.7% MTL+ patients 50%	Controls 98% HF patients 100% HM 90% MTL+ patients 62%

Summary of results for the five conditions:

- MTL+ patients consistently did worse in all the five tasks presented here. MTL+ patients were mildly impaired but significantly differently impaired compared with the others ($p<0.005$).
- HM did better than MTL+ patients but less well than the HF patients and controls.
- Controls could do the tasks and HF patients could do the tasks, getting more or less 100 per cent in each condition.
- In the semantic tests overall, controls scored *98.9 per cent, HF patients scored *100 per cent and MTL+ patients scored *78.1 per cent.
- Where there was not 100 per cent correct scoring, the living things gave more errors than the non-living things.

Progress check 2.18

Explain the results in Schmolck *et al.* (2002), giving some of the figures.

Other results

The results for the other tests showed the same sort of pattern. The HF patients and the controls showed good performance. Patients in the MTL+ group and HM too made errors. Impairment was there whether the semantic test was about words or pictures. There was one interesting difference between HM and the MTL+ patients, where HM's performance was worse, and that was in errors in defining objects. Errors in grammar and form were shown in HM's performance and not in the performance of the other participants.

Ranking for the 18 tests

The study gives rankings on all of the 18 tests for all of the 14 participants. The graph shows the mean rank for each of the participants and the controls over the 18 tests.

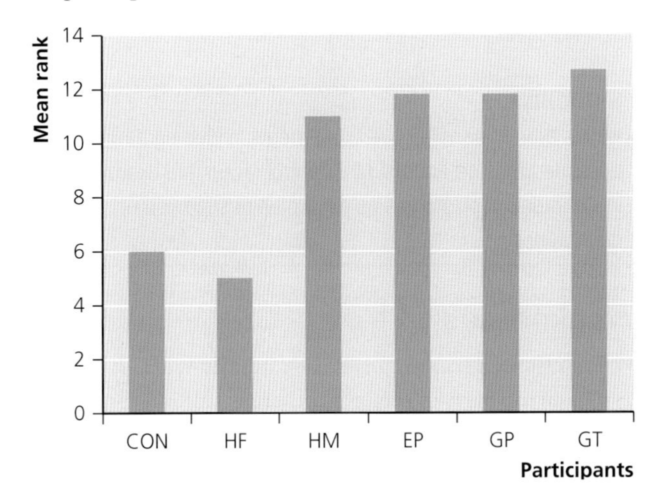

The mean rank for the participants on the 18 tests; EP, GP and GT are the patients with MTL+ damage; HF are the two patients with hippocampal formation damage; CON are the eight healthy controls

The controls and HF patients were not that different in rank over the 18 tests and showed the best performance. HM does slightly better than the MTL+ patients, who do less well than HF and the controls. The two HF patients did slightly better than the controls, but they were younger and/or better educated according to the study.

For the four patients with the highest ranks (HM and the three MTL+ patients) there was a direct relationship between their scores on the 18 tests and damage to the lateral temporal cortex. HM had less damage to the lateral temporal cortex and GT had the most.

For HM and the MTL+ patients, it was interesting to note that items that they had been able to name spontaneously before the study were the ones that they did better on. This suggests that when they could not name an item spontaneously they would have difficulty with that item on the semantic tests. It was thought that less semantic knowledge might be available for that item. Naming an object is related to semantic knowledge about that object.

Conclusions

The patients with hippocampal formation damage did as well as controls throughout. The three MTL+ patients (who had other damage too, such as to the lateral temporal cortex) had mild difficulties on most of the tests. HM had borderline scores showing some impairment a lot of the time and was particularly impaired on some of the tests. There was a relationship between how well a participant did and damage to the lateral temporal cortex, particularly for HM and the three MTL+ patients. The conclusion was that semantic knowledge and memory was linked to the lateral temporal cortex and not to hippocampal function.

Schmolck *et al.* (2000) found that people with HF lesions were not impaired, whereas those with MTL+ damage were impaired – their findings back up the findings of this study.

The study concluded that having impaired semantic knowledge is linked to damage in the anterolateral temporal cortex and not to the MTL (medial temporal lobe), which hippocampal function is within. One piece of evidence is that people with semantic dementia have a relatively intact MTL (e.g. Garrard *et al.*, 1997, cited in Schmolck *et al.*, 2002).

There is also a strong relationship between the scale of the semantic dementia and the degree of problems with the anterolateral temporal lobe, which is evidence for the anterolateral temporal lobe being implicated in semantic dementia (e.g. Mummery *et al.*, 2000, cited in Schmolck *et al.*, 2002).

There is a lot more detail in the study. For example, recognition is not as good if there is damage to the perirhinal cortex and patients with semantic dementia are fine with regard to recognition memory, even though they have problems with semantic knowledge. So recognition memory seems to be different from semantic memory.

Much evidence cited here uses MRI scanning to measure the damage to the brain and there is some use of functional neuroimaging (fMRI is a form of neuroimaging). Functional neuroimaging can look at activity in certain brain areas and measures blood flow in the brain when certain activities are taking place. fMRI can show how areas in the brain are linked during certain activities. The functioning neuroimaging in this study showed that when making semantic judgements about words or pictures looking at the temporal lobe, areas activated were the left middle temporal gyrus and the left fusiform gyrus (Vandernberghe *et al.*, 1996, cited in Schmolck *et al.*, 2002). There seems to be quite a lot of evidence for temporal lobe activity in tasks that involve semantic processing.

More evidence is that impaired naming (called 'dysnomia') relates to damage alongside the medial temporal lobe. HM performed well with medial temporal lobe damage and those with the left anterior temporal area missing have problems with naming, and that area also gives difficulty with semantic knowledge. These two pieces of evidence add to the claims in this study that it is the anterolateral temporal cortex that is used and not specifically the MTL.

The overall conclusion is that semantic knowledge difficulties are due to damage to the anterolateral temporal cortex, which is alongside the medial temporal lobe.

There were also conclusions specifically about HM. HM matched controls in performance in most of the tests and Kensinger *et al.* (2001, cited in Schmolck *et al.*, 2002) found no problems with knowledge of words or production of word forms. However, HM did not do as well as the controls when he named items from descriptions or when he had to generate examples in the categories. He found it hard to provide definitions when shown a picture of an object or when an object was named. HM had problems with fluency and this was thought to be caused by slowing in the brain rather than brain damage itself. It was also concluded that, as he did have some damage alongside the MTL, his difficulties may come from that, even though that damage was limited. HM had speech that was in a single tone and also made grammatical errors – there was evidence for this from other studies (Milner *et al.*, 1968, cited in Schmolck *et al.*, 2002). These issues were unique to HM and so were thought to come from something other than the damage from surgery. For example, HM had seizures when he was young and was from a low socioeconomic background, with interrupted schooling.

Progress check 2.19

Explain two conclusions that were drawn by Schmolck *et al.* (2002) in their study.

Evaluation of Schmolck *et al.* (2002)

Strengths

- There is a great deal of evidence for the conclusions of this study, with many studies pointing to the lateral temporal cortex being involved in semantic knowledge rather than the medial temporal lobe. When there is a lot of evidence from different studies using careful controls and experimental procedures, this adds strength to findings.
- The study uses a scientific method. It uses MRI scanning and CT scanning to measure the damage to the brain and the location of the damage in a reasonably exact manner, which adds strength to the findings. They then use controlled tests to find out about semantic ability. This means they can draw cause-and-effect conclusions about which brain area is drawn on for semantic knowledge; because variables are controlled and careful measuring has taken place, conclusions are reliable and credible.
- A third strength is the use of a healthy control group. These are people who have no damage to the brain and so there is a baseline measure of 'normal' functioning when it comes to using semantic knowledge. As the control group achieved more or less 100 per cent success in the tests, this strengthens the claim that the tests measured 'normal' functioning.

Explanation

There is scientific **credibility** if findings are seen to use the scientific method, such as careful controls and careful drawing of conclusions from data that have come from well-explained methods of measurement.

STUDY HINT

Issues around carrying out experiments, including having a baseline measure and using a control group, are examined in Chapter 5. Use studies as examples of such use of methodology.

Weaknesses

- Even though scanning is done carefully with set ways of measuring parts of the brain, there is still interpretation required when analysing the scans, and parts of the brain are hard to separate and measure. Scanning is not as exact as it might seem because someone has to carry out the interpretation. Weaknesses of scanning are considered in Chapter 5.
- Another weakness might be the low number of participants, which might signal problems with generalisability. Only eight healthy controls were used, not that many, although there is no reason to think their performance would not represent 'normal' functioning. There were just three patients with MTL+ damage and two HF patients, and HM was an individual. It could be argued that these are rather low numbers on which to base firm conclusions. Evidence from other studies does add weight to the findings, however; but bear in mind that studies often use the same patients (e.g. HM has been widely studied).

STUDY HINT

Just because a study has low numbers does not mean the results are not generalisable to the rest of the population of interest. However, if there are low numbers, you should raise the idea that the sample might have some differences from the 'normal' population and so generalisation could possibly be questioned. When discussing weaknesses, use words such as 'in doubt' and 'possibly' rather than saying 'there are low numbers so the results are not generalisable'. There is more to it that just the numbers involved, as this study shows.

- A third weakness is the possible lack of validity. Scanning of the brain takes a reductionist approach by looking at the brain as having separate functions. Looking at the MTL and the nearby lateral temporal cortex separates brain functioning into parts. Also using semantic tests is separating 'normal' functioning into small areas, such as naming pictures. The measures in this study can be said not to capture 'normal' functioning. However, the control group could do the tests, so they appeared to measure something we can usually do; and the scanning did find lesions in the brains of the patients, so it seems reasonable to say that what the patients could not do was down to the lesions. It is just that validity can be questioned as the 'whole' picture is not seen by such methods.

Progress check 2.20

Briefly discuss the idea that a small number of participants is likely to lead to low generalisability, but in Schmolck *et al.* (2002) that might not be the case.

Test yourself

1. Explain experimental features in Schmolck *et al.*'s (2012) study. **(6 marks)**
2. Evaluate Schmolck *et al.*'s (2012) study with regards to the evidence for it being the lateral temporal cortex that links to semantic knowledge and not the MTL. **(8 marks)**

Steyvers and Hemmer (2012)

Steyvers and Hemmer's (2012) chapter in *The Psychology of Learning and Motivation* is about reconstruction and memory. The main point they make is that memory studies tend not to be in someone's natural environment and use artificial tasks, whereas in real life there is an environment and cues around when recall is taking place. Wynn and Logie (1998) made a similar point when they used real-life recall of events and locations rather than the unusual *War of the Ghosts* folk tale used by Bartlett. In their chapter, Steyvers and Hemmer (2012) focus on ecological validity and they explain their studies – those are used here as this 'study' of reconstructive memory. The main study they use is Hemmer and Steyvers (2009c).

STUDY HINT

Ecological validity is an important issue when evaluating a study – in particular, a laboratory experiment. The 'ecology' of the study is the whole setting, not just the external environment. You can use the arguments in Steyvers and Hemmer (2012) when discussing the ecological validity of any study.

You can also relate Steyvers and Hemmer's (2012) chapter to Bartlett's theory that memory is about reconstruction, explained earlier in this chapter (pp. 95–99).

Steyvers and Hemmer (2012) discuss studies that claim memory is reconstructive and not like a tape recorder. They are critical of such studies being artificial in what they test. Our memory helps us and semantic memory (prior knowledge) is drawn on to smooth out issues when recalling episodes (using episodic memory). Usually prior knowledge will improve our memory, but studies that look at episodic memory are often artificial enough to remove the usefulness of prior knowledge. The focus of the study is on ecological validity, which means studies must represent real life for them to be useful. Steyvers and Hemmer (2012) say that if prior knowledge and real-life ways of remembering are not tested in a study, memory is not being tested at all. Steyvers and Hemmer (2012) discuss their study (Hemmer and Steyvers, 2009c), which aims to make sure that stimuli in their memory study represent real-life (are ecologically valid) and enable prior knowledge to be used.

Aim(s)

The aim of the studies was to make sure that the setting when looking at episodic memory is naturalistic. The researchers felt that studies that showed memory to be reconstructed did not include situations where participants could draw on prior knowledge so in previous studies there have not been ecologically valid findings. The aim of their work was to carry out studies looking at the reconstructive nature of memory but making the study look at real-life recall, which meant enabling use of prior knowledge.

Episodic memories relate to events and incidents that are recalled, such as asked about in studies about reconstructive memory (e.g. what people remember they saw in an office or how they recalled the *War of the Ghosts* story they had heard). Semantic memory is what can be drawn on in recall (such as knowing that offices have books or that people 'fall down' at sunset in literature traditionally). If semantic memory is not available, as can happen in other studies (such as taking books out of an office scene, so that knowing offices have books is not helpful but in a way a 'trick'), then Steyvers and Hemmer say this is not testing 'real-life' memory. Their aim is to test episodic and semantic memory realistically.

STUDY HINT

You learned about semantic and episodic memory earlier in this chapter when we considered Tulving's ideas on how long-term memory is split into different parts. Draw on all elements of your course whenever you can and make notes about the links.

Background

Bartlett (1932) showed that cultural norms and also our expectations affect our recall of past events. Not only are events recalled using episodic memory, but also using our experiences and general knowledge, which we draw on when recalling something. Steyvers and Hemmer (2012) explain, for example, that if you are recalling office items you might recall books because you expect them in an office. We do not actually recall everything we say we recall; we use inferences to help our recall. Studies tend to ask people to recall items and look at what the participant gets wrong. Brewer and Treyens (1981, cited in Steyvers and Hemmer, 2012) showed that if books are removed from an office people then recall seeing books. They expect to see books and recall them because they 'should' be there. This suggests that prior knowledge (such as expecting books) negatively affects memory, in that our memory for books (in this example) is wrong.

Steyvers and Hemmer suggest turning this idea around and seeing this example of false memory not so much as an error but showing one of the functions of memory. Memory uses our expectations positively, to help recall. This suggests that studies that look at what we get wrong are artificial. Memory uses what we expect, and that is helpful. It is not that putting in what we expect to see when it is not there is wrong – often doing that makes our recall better. Studies that look at false memories have not looked at memory in a natural environment.

Studies have shown that knowing about a situation helps recall (e.g. Huttenlocher *et al.*, 1991, cited in Steyvers and Hemmer, 2012). People use their knowledge of situations to improve recall because they use it to fill in an imperfect picture that they have. Older adults can be helped by knowing about a setting (Castel, 2005, cited in Steyvers and Hemmer, 2012). For example, older adults do as well at recalling prices for grocery items as younger adults, though those with impairment to their semantic memory are not good at recalling such prices, which suggests that semantic memory is what is used in such recall and that people with amnesia might be helped if they can call on prior knowledge. If recall is in a situation where people have 'pre-experimental' knowledge, they recall more than if they have to recall something like abstract shapes (Hemmer and Steyvers, 2009a, 2009b, cited in Steyvers and Hemmer, 2012).

STUDY HINT

The information cited by Steyvers and Hemmer (2012) that having prior knowledge of situations can help those with amnesia is an example of applying psychological understanding in society. You can use this in a key question about helping people with memory difficulties.

The choice of stimulus is important in laboratory studies. Random words and nonsense syllables might not represent real-life memory sufficiently. Steyvers and Hemmer (2012) want to emphasise the need for **ecological validity** in memory studies so that findings relate to real life. If studies of memory have ecological validity then they are likely to mean that someone can draw on prior knowledge in recall, which is more representative of real-life recall. Studies would have findings that are more representative of real life and so be more generalisable, and the findings would have more value in uncovering how memory works. So, for example, Steyvers and Hemmer (2012) argue that if someone is to be asked about recall within an office setting, then there should be books in the stimulus materials. If prior knowledge 'cleans up' memory then it has a role and needs to be in studies of memory. The clearer the stimulus, the less learning on prior knowledge there is. So studies that have clear stimulus materials need to worry less about having a situation where the participant would have prior knowledge. Prior knowledge links more with episodic memory the less there is familiarity with the stimulus materials.

Explanation

Ecological validity is a special type of validity. Someone's ecology is their 'niche', not just the external environment but the habitat - it is the study of people in their environment, taking all its aspects. Validity is when a measure is about real-life behaviour or issues. Ecological validity is found when real-life environments are studied and findings of studies relate to real-life environments. External validity is very similar but not quite the same. Findings can have external validity because they can be said to be true of the outside world and generalisable beyond the sample and study.

Progress check 2.21

Why is it important that memory studies have ecological validity?

Procedure and results

Phase one – testing for prior knowledge

Steyvers and Hemmer wanted to make sure that participants in a memory study could draw on prior knowledge, so they had to be sure that happened. Prior knowledge is of course unique to each individual so it is hard for researchers to be sure participants can access prior knowledge in a study. What they did was ask participants what they would expect to see in a scene of a hotel room, or office, or urban scene, or kitchen or dining scene.

We use prior knowledge about hotel rooms or offices to name objects we expect to find in them and our prior knowledge generally helps episodic memory to be more accurate

This phase of the study used five scenes (dining room, hotel room, kitchen, town scene and office). There were five different images of each scene, so 25 images. To assess prior knowledge, participants were asked to name objects they would expect to see in a scene type (e.g. an office or a kitchen), not showing the participants the scenes (the verbal cue condition).

Then the researchers used another group of participants and showed them the scenes visually, asking them to 'say what they saw' (the visual scene condition). This would show what people actually see in the scenes, to measure against their prior knowledge of such scenes.

Results of phase one

- It was found that objects that are central and important in a scene are named more frequently. For example, in the town scene, a car was central and salient (important) and was named by 20 out of 22 people. This was from the 'visual scene' condition.
- From the verbal cue condition, there was less agreement as there was no scene to see. Objects that would have a high likelihood of being in the scene were named often, such as 20 out of 22 naming a computer in an office.
- For the visual scene condition and the verbal cue condition in response to a town scene (urban scene), the top three objects named were the same – car, building, people.
- The results of this phase showed people have strong prior expectations and in this study it was seen that prior knowledge fits with the natural environment. Largely what people expect to find in a scene is what is in the scene and prior knowledge does not let them down.

Phase two – testing to see how prior knowledge interacts with episodic memory for naturalistic scenes

Ten scenes from the 25 in phase one were used in phase two – two from each of the five main scenes (two kitchen scenes, two office scenes, two hotel room scenes, two dining scenes and two urban scenes).

The images were chosen using those that had the highest responses in the visual phase above.

The scenes were shown for either two seconds or ten seconds. It was thought that the shorter time would mean more reliance on prior knowledge as if someone has quite a long time they can encode memories using episodic memory and might not need prior knowledge. With the longer time, objects that are not consistent with a scene will not be recalled using prior knowledge but will come from episodic memory (someone has to remember them specially as they are not in the schema for that scene). In the shorter time period, there would be more need for 'cleaning up' the episodic memory, as not everything could be encoded ready for recall.

Using this procedure, the researchers could see how much prior knowledge was used in recall of the ten scenes.

The researchers were interested in which objects were recalled and also if and when there were errors. Errors come from prior knowledge, such as 'recalling' a computer in an office even if there wasn't one. The researchers knew what prior knowledge for each scene was likely (since they had tested this in the verbal cue condition). They knew what people actually saw in the scene (from the visual cue condition). What they did in this phase was to see what people recalled – both their correct recall and errors they made.

Free recall was used, which means participants could recall in any order. Also participants could stop recalling when they wanted to. The scene was shown for the required number of seconds and then recall asked for, then the next scene, and so on.

Results of phase two

The researchers found that for high prior probability objects (those that were expected in the scene) the error rate was 9 per cent. There was an 18 per cent error rate for low prior probability objects (those in the scene but not expected so much).

These error rates are low, so this showed that people did recall well and did use prior knowledge successfully. What they expected was there and the more expected objects showed a lower error rate. More errors were made if the objects in the scene were not as expected, but this was low.

Participants seeing the ten scenes for two seconds recalled on average 7.75 items and for the ten seconds condition they recalled on average 10.05 items. So there was better recall for longer looking time. Participants seemed to stop recalling when they felt they were making errors. It appears that participants monitor themselves for accuracy in free recall studies.

The results explained which objects were 'recalled' that were not in the scene, and what the recall probability of that object was (such as recalling books that were not there, as Brewer and Treyens, 1981, reported, cited in Steyvers and Hemmer, 2012). Importantly, as this was a free recall task using scenes that were 'everyday' events, there were few items 'recalled' but not in the scene. However, tablecloth was frequently recalled in one dining scene, though not in another dining scene, so there were 'wrong' objects. This issue about the tablecloth (and other such objects) led to an error rate of 19 per cent when reporting objects 'recalled' but not in the scene. Brewer and Treyens (1981, cited in Steyvers and Hemmer, 2012) found a 30 per cent false recall probability, much higher than the results reported here. It is claimed that this lower rate is because the task is 'real' and prior knowledge can successfully be used, unlike Brewer and Treyens's (1981) artificial study.

Progress check 2.22

Explain how the results reported in Steyvers and Hemmer (2012) were different from those in Brewer and Treyens (1981).

Conclusions

The conclusions were that if memory studies are artificial and involve issues that seem to be 'tricking' participants' memory, such as taking something out of a scene and seeing how much participants 'recall' it, then there will be a high error rate. This is because people use their prior knowledge, which usually works to 'clean up' memory, and if that prior knowledge is in some way 'tricked' then faulty recall will be the result. Steyvers and Hemmer (2012) suggest that 'tricking' memory and then finding errors is not a useful finding. Much better to measure real-life recall, which measures episodic memory and allows the person to do what they would naturally do, which is to draw on semantic memory – their prior knowledge. When people can draw on prior knowledge and stimuli in a real-life memory study, then there are fewer errors, as shown by the results.

Extending the discussion and the study

Steyvers and Hemmer (2012) write a whole chapter about how naturalistic stimuli should be used in memory studies to get ecologically valid findings. After presenting the above study, its findings and its conclusion, they then consider another feature of memory studies relevant to their ideas. This is that some studies show expected objects are better recalled; others show the opposite – that unexpected objects are better recalled.

Recall is guided by prior knowledge so expected objects are better recalled

They point to a disagreement in findings of studies. Studies can show that objects that are consistent are better remembered (such as Brewer and Treyens, 1981). The more an object fits into a scene (fits a schema and prior knowledge) the more it is recalled or recognised. Brewers and Treyens (1981, cited in Steyvers and Hemmer, 2012) found 90 per cent of participants recalled a typewriter (at the time that was a high expectation in an office) and a skull (not expected in an office) was recalled by 50 per cent of participants. What Brewer and Treyens (1981) pointed out was that the typewriter could have been recalled from episodic memory (having seen the scene) or from prior knowledge, and they could not tell which.

Recall is guided by a novelty effect, so unexpected objects are better recalled

However, others such as Pezdek *et al.* (1989, cited in Steyvers and Hemmer, 2012) suggest that novel objects are better recalled because they are not expected in the scene. Pezdek *et al.* (1989) had two scenes with 16 items in them, half being consistent with the scene and half not consistent. Pezdek *et al.* (1989) found people recalled the items that stood out more and were inconsistent with the scene.

Practical

There is a lot of material in Steyvers and Hemmer (2012) that you could use to create your own experiment. Find some scenes like theirs - you might have some photos of your own you can use or take some photos in your school or college (with permission) of the dining room, a classroom and an office. You can have three conditions. One condition involves a group of participants noting down what would be in such scenes (e.g. a classroom) when they are simply asked verbally. One condition involves another group of participants saying what they see in the scenes. The final group of participants looks at the scenes for two seconds and then free recall what they can remember. There are a number of different hypotheses you can test, based on Hemmer and Steyers (2009c). For example, you can see if prior expectations (the first condition) give a similar list of objects to the ones actually seen in the scene (the second condition), or you can see what percentage errors there are in the participants doing the free recall and see if those errors represent unexpected objects.

Hemmer and Steyvers (2009c) looked at the 25 images they used to see which objects were consistent. For example, they could see which objects were in all five kitchen scenes – these objects would be highly consistent with kitchen scenes. For example, all the kitchen scenes had a stove, which was given a score of 5 (high consistency). In one kitchen scene only, there was a wooden sailboat, so that had a score of 1 (low consistency). The wooden sailboat is a novel object and no participants in the verbal condition thought there would be a sailboat in a kitchen scene (unsurprisingly, which is the point, it was not in their prior knowledge).

The graph below shows that high consistency and low consistency both give better recall, whereas middle consistency gives poor recall.

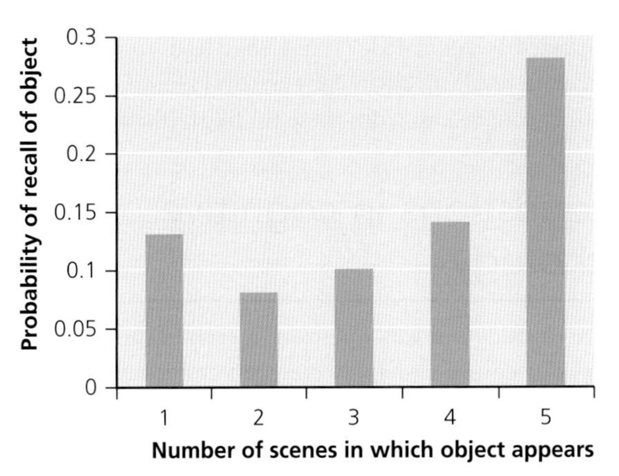

The probability of recall of an object depending on how many scenes (1–5) it appears in

The graph shows that the researchers found both a novelty effect and a consistency effect. They put this finding down to the naturalistic focus of their study, in that there was ecological validity. In real-life recall, people probably recall both highly consistent objects and novel ones. Prior knowledge can be used in both these situations. When objects are consistent, prior knowledge is useful and, when objects are novel, prior knowledge allows a scene to be scanned quickly and the gist of the scene to be understood, which can help to highlight that a novel object is 'different', and so will be recalled.

Overall conclusions

Steyvers and Hemmer (2012) found that in free recall having seen naturalistic stimuli (the images) there are not many errors in that objects not in the scene are 'recalled'. When there are such errors, these are likely to be for objects with low prior expectation for that scene. Prior knowledge leads to more accurate recall. Episodic memory is enhanced by using semantic memory, in the form of prior knowledge or schemas. Another finding was that objects with high consistency in a scene are better recalled than middle consistency but that objects with low consistency (novel objects) are also better recalled. In recall, there is a high contribution from prior knowledge so studies that do not allow for such help are not naturalistic and not measuring memory in a 'realistic' way.

Evaluation of ecological validity

Steyvers and Hemmer (2012) point out that other researchers do not agree with focusing on ecological validity in memory studies. For example, Banaji and Crowder (1989, cited in Steyvers and Hemmer, 2012) suggest that high generalisability is a better aim than high ecological validity. Experiments need to have good generalisability. Banaji and Crowder suggest that high ecological validity and high generalisability would be best, though that is unlikely. This is because if findings are to be generalisable they must have a sample that is representative of the target population and they must be the result of careful controls and scientific procedures. However, if there had to be a choice, then low ecological validity and high generalisability is better than the reverse. Steyvers and Hemmer (2012) feel that a study can be both scientific in its procedures and sampling and have good ecological validity, as they felt their studies had shown.

Steyvers and Hemmer do note that they used lab settings and what was seen was image rather than reality. So they realise they have, to an extent, not achieved ecological validity. They realised they wanted experimental findings with care in measurements and controls used; however, they felt they could achieve at least a measure of ecological validity.

> **STUDY HINT**
> You can use this discussion of ecological validity, generalisability and scientific procedures when discussing such issues in other parts of your course. Make notes accordingly so that you can use studies as evidence for such issues.

Evaluation of Steyvers and Hemmer (2012)

Strengths

- Steyvers and Hemmer (2012) focus not only on episodic long-term memory but on semantic memory as well. In memory studies, 'episodes' and 'events' are tested, such as memory for a film just shown or for a list of words. They argue that in real life memory involves schemas, expectations, prior knowledge – semantic memory. Therefore, their work incorporates prior knowledge and so can claim ecological validity. They claim to be studying real-life memory more than other lab-based studies have done.
- While using real-life scenes and so aiming for ecological validity, they also use controls and laboratory settings, so that there is scientific credibility in their findings. They use different participants for their three conditions, and use the same pictures of scenes throughout. They check the prior knowledge for their scenes instead of assuming it, so there are strong controls, meaning they can check for reliability.
- They draw on the work of others strongly, and in that way are building a body of knowledge. They take theory and findings from other studies (such as Brewer and Treyens, 1981) and not only show how their results go against such studies, but also incorporate ideas about where their findings match such studies and why there are differences. This uses scientific method nicely – taking a theory, deriving hypotheses, getting data and then amending the theory accordingly.

Weaknesses

- Steyvers and Hemmer (2012) report Neisser's view that memory studies must in fact move outside the laboratory to be useful, as focus should be more on questions, such as why someone cannot recall what they had for breakfast. This underlines their acceptance that a weakness of their work is that it is laboratory based and, therefore, there is a question over its ecological validity.
- Although a main claim is that they succeed in getting some ecological validity with regard to their data, the researchers themselves admit that showing people scenes and asking them about scenes is only moving towards such validity. In real situations, people have sounds and smells, and emotional involvement in scenes, which means their stimuli are not as ecologically valid as they might want. So not only is the lab situation not valid but the task is not valid either. Having said that, it is accepted that their stimuli move towards validity, which is all that they claimed, because they wanted to stick to a scientific focus.
- The researchers do not discuss the participants in detail, so there might be generalisability issues. They use what they call 'real-life scenes' and it is assumed that these are scenes familiar to the participants. It would be interesting to extend the study to look at cultural and gender issues with regard to prior expectations. It is worth emphasising that prior knowledge might help recall in episodic memory as long as participants have that prior knowledge, so cultural and possibly gender issues, as well as individual differences, might have to be controlled for. This is not necessarily a weakness as they presumably did control such issues, but it is a weakness in their findings if individual differences are not emphasised as they might affect generalisability. In the culture they studied, 'seeing' objects was clearly something done and related to prior expectations; perhaps in another culture other senses are equally important.

> **Progress check 2.23**
> There are two separate weaknesses here with regard to validity. At first, it might seem like one weakness - it is important to be clear about points. Explain the difference between the two weaknesses with regard to validity of Steyvers and Hemmer's (2012) study.

> **Test yourself**
> 1. Explain Steyvers and Hemmer's (2012) point that their study looked at memory in a natural environment and so had ecological validity compared to other memory studies that they said use 'artificial' tasks. **(6 marks)**
> 2. Steyvers and Hemmer (2012) found that if objects were expected in a scene, the error rate in recall was just 9 per cent, whereas there was an 18 per cent error rate for objects in the scene that were not expected as much. Prior knowledge leads to more accurate recall. Evaluate Steyvers and Hemmer's (2012) conclusions from these findings. **(8 marks)**

Key questions in cognitive psychology

You have to study one key question in each of the topic areas for your course and apply concepts and ideas from the topic area to that issue. Concepts and ideas include research, studies and theories. The two key questions suggested for your course are covered here, but you can choose a different key question to study. In the examination, you may be asked to apply concepts and ideas to a key question that you have not come across before (called 'unseen'). Studying all the key questions will help you to learn how to apply concepts, ideas, theory and research to an unseen key question in the exam.

How can psychologists' understanding of memory help patients with dementia?

Describing the issue

This is a key question for society because the number of people diagnosed as having dementia has been increasing for some time. The Alzheimer's Society estimates that there will be 850,000 people with dementia in the UK in 2015 and this is set to rise to 1 million by 2025 and over 2 million by 2051. Another organisation, Dementia Concern, has similar figures. One in three people over 65 will die from dementia, so this is clearly an issue of relevance to society. Dementia, according to the Alzheimer's Society, costs £23 billion each year, and is expected to rise to £27 billion in 2018. People with dementia can be patients in NHS hospitals and can need nursing care in other institutions. They may manage at home but need support, or they may need help in the community.

A campaign in 2014 highlighted this issue, featuring a person with dementia who was managing well but whose life could be improved if others would be more understanding and helpful. People in the community are asked to be 'dementia friends' and to advertise themselves as such. For example, a hairdresser who understands dementia can give a better experience than one who does not. This campaign is part of a government strategy to offer help to those with dementia – it includes dementia hubs, where people can be referred if dementia is suspected, and a focus on dementia care in acute hospitals. A response by the government to dementia is to ask for support in the community and a more caring attitude in response to this 'disease' that leaves the individual feeling vulnerable and lacking in confidence.

Alzheimer's is a well-known form of dementia, and there are other forms too, such as vascular dementia and fronto-temporal dementia. Dementia refers to problems in the brain that cause information processing difficulties, including memory problems and problems with everyday functioning. All types of dementia are progressive (meaning more damage will occur) and they are all about brain functioning so the more that is known about information processing such as memory, the more people with dementia can be understood and helped. The key question here is: how can psychologists help using their understanding of how memory works?

Explore

Visit the Alzheimer's Society website (www.alzheimers.org.uk). It has a lot of information not just about Alzheimer's but other forms of dementia too.

Progress check 2.24

Explain why it is helpful to society to find ways to help those with dementia.

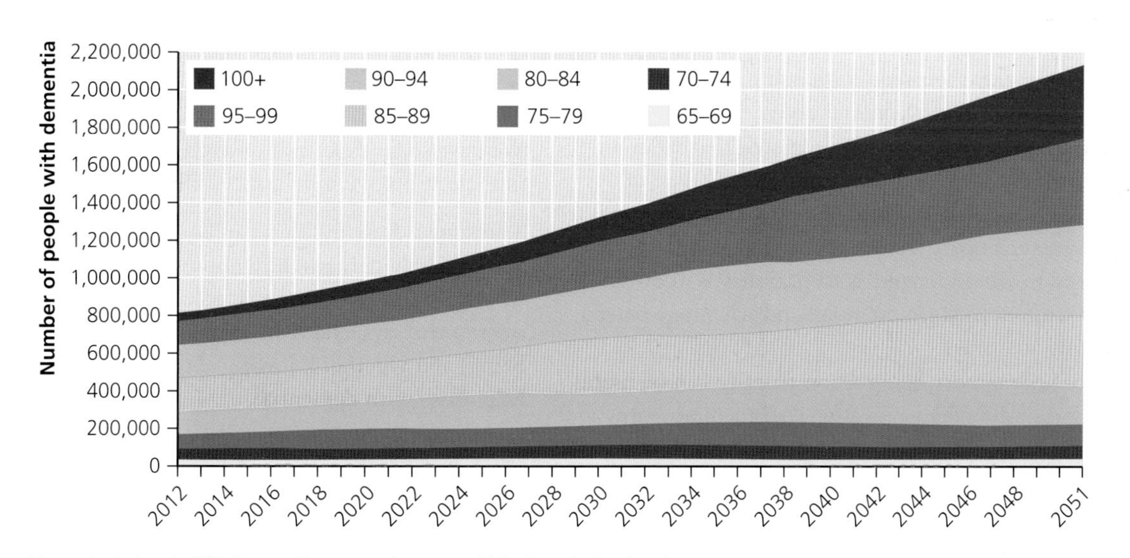

Expected rise in UK dementia cases (source: Alzheimer's Society)

Application of concepts and ideas

- Although dementia is about memory loss, it is not that people with dementia lose all their memory; they may have areas that are fully functioning. They may retain skills or facts from the past, for example. Episodic memory can be affected. Decline in episodic memory starts from the 'now' and moves later into the 'past' so people can often remember events that happened a long time ago better than what has just happened. Episodic memory has been discussed when the reproductive memory model was explained and also when Tulving's ideas about episodic and semantic memory were explored. It was shown that episodic memory does seem to be separate from semantic memory and the way dementia affects episodic memory seems to back up this account of memory. It can be helpful to understand that someone with dementia might 'live in the past' and to be with that person at that time in their past (go with their memories and do not contradict them).
- Short-term memory can be affected and someone with dementia might 'forget' what they have just been told, not because they have 'forgotten' but because the memory was not encoded, therefore, not stored and so cannot be recalled. A way to help would be to be very specific when asking questions rather than asking more general questions, to try to cue memories if possible. For example, rather than asking 'Have you had visitors today?', ask 'Has Jean, your daughter, been to visit you?' Using pictures and colour can help with encoding memories and retrieving them, as well as in everyday living. Someone might respond to a photo of a family member more than to their name, for example. Writing things down for someone with dementia can take the place of their short-term memory – for example, noting what colour tray their food for lunch is on, to act as a reminder, or labelling keys and doors.
- Working memory theory has suggested that different tasks done at the same time using the same type of processing can be very difficult, so a way of helping is to avoid any such tasks. If someone with dementia is trying to attend to what someone is saying, they will do so better without background noise and when one person is talking at a time.
- The idea of memory being reconstructive can be useful in understanding dementia as well. If memories are reconstructed using prior experiences and schemas, then someone with dementia who seems to be saying something that does not make sense might be using mixed schemas and muddled episodic memories, so listen carefully, ask limited questions, but try to follow the thought processes of the individual.
- Steyvers and Hemmer (2012) cite evidence that people with amnesia can be helped by having prior knowledge of what they are trying to recall. Those with prior knowledge draw on it when recalling and, if there is damage to semantic memory, the effect of having prior knowledge is missing. If that prior knowledge can be displayed or explained, it might help someone with a poor semantic memory.

How can knowledge of working memory be used to inform the treatment of dyslexia?

Describing the issue

Dyslexia is a difficulty with reading and speech, including issues with manipulating sound. Dyslexia can come from specific brain damage. Features include problems with auditory short-term memory and phonological awareness. Processing speed can also be affected. Language skills can be affected as well as naming of objects. Cognitive subtypes of dyslexia are visual, auditory and attentional. Features include having problems with distinguishing left and right when given directions, being distracted by background sounds and producing mirror writing and reversal of letters. Children may find it hard to produce rhyming words and to count syllables in words. There can be poor spelling and bits missed from words, as well as problems in reading aloud and summarising a story. Verbal memory is a difficulty, which is about remembering a sequence of words for a time. Dyslexia does seem to run in families, which suggests that the cause is genetic, and genes are being identified that relate to dyslexia. MRI scanning also helps and suggests that the occipito-temporal cortex is involved. Focusing on phonological skills (identifying and processing sounds) can help children with dyslexia, as can practising reading and focusing on developing vocabulary. Dyslexia is a disability and is recognised in the Equality Act 2010.

We have so far described dyslexia and shown its importance in society, but we have not described the issue for society.

The issue is how dyslexia can be 'treated' (or more appropriately perhaps, how those with dyslexia can be helped – it is interesting that using terms like 'treatment' suggest that dyslexia is an illness rather than a state of being) and whether knowing about working memory can help those with dementia.

Explore

The NHS Choices website (www.nhs.uk) has information about dyslexia which might be of interest. Also look up the British Dyslexia Association if you want to know more.

Application of concepts and ideas

- There are difficulties other than memory, such as with communication, reading and concentration, but this section focuses on memory difficulties and, in particular, how understanding of working memory can help those with dyslexia.
- Short-term memory is implicated in dyslexia, such as difficulty in remembering facts, dates, and so on, and in encoding them in long-term memory.
- There is also said to be poor working memory in that children and adults with dyslexia find it hard to carry out more than one task at a time, which seems to mean that they have difficulty with the different temporary stores in working memory.
- Those with dyslexia can have problems in breaking words up into sounds. Working memory has a visuospatial sketchpad which is for visual and spatial information, and a phonological loop, which is for speech (the articulatory system) and sound (the phonological part). If children and adults with dyslexia have problems with sounds of words, this suggests that it is the phonological loop where there are difficulties. For example, problems with sounds are shown by difficulties in transposing sounds of letters, such as moving from 'slow black' to 'blow slack'. When working memory is used to help children with dyslexia, it is the general idea of limited processing capacity in short-term memory that is looked at, rather than specific parts of the working memory model.
- A review by Holmes (2012) is helpful in showing how understanding working memory can help in understanding (and working with) dyslexia. She discusses how working memory is involved in so much of what is processed in reading, understanding text and carrying out complex instructions, and so any limitation in working memory can have important effects. Problems can be in holding information in short-term memory, such as when doing calculations, or problems in keeping place when reading. The idea of working memory can explain a lot of the difficulties experienced by someone with dyslexia, which in itself is helpful and also can help with overcoming difficulties.
- Dyslexia does not only affect reading and writing but it can affect educational attainment in general, as so much learning depends on being able to follow instructions and hold information while doing tasks. There can also be a loss of attention if working memory capacity is low, as focusing on a task is difficult. So in schools children with dyslexia can not only be low achievers but can also lack attention. It is clear that any helpful strategies would help the child to learn, and this is advantageous not only to individual children but to society, as an educated and trained population is what is aimed for.
- Holmes (2012) uses the idea of the limited capacity of working memory increasing as a child gets older up to the age of about 15, when it reaches its maximum. One of the contemporary studies you could choose for the cognitive psychology element of your course is Sebastián and Hernández-Gil (2012), who conclude that children of about five or six years old have a digit span of about four items, rising to the highest digit span at the age of 17. Though digit span is not all that working memory is, this is additional evidence that memory capacity might develop with age and helps to show that children with dyslexia might have particular difficulties in learning if their working memory is affected.
- In order to help children with dyslexia, focus is on training their working memory. Practising working memory tasks seems to work and computer programs can be used for this purpose. Dunning *et al.* (2012) showed that verbal working memory was improved in children who did such training. It is interesting that such training appears to affect the brain areas and change neural activity where working memory is thought to take place (Westerberg and Klingberg, 2007, cited in Holmes, 2009). Such improvements in working memory are found in studies, though Holmes (2009) questions whether there are effects in the children's real world – this has yet to be shown.
- Another focus for helping children with dyslexia is on adapting teaching to take into account working memory deficits and to focus on tasks that lean less on short-term memory. If tasks are broken down into small steps so there is less reliance on short-term memory and if instructions are kept short and reinforced by writing them down or restating them, this can help. Also having an environment that encourages children to ask if they have forgotten what they were supposed to be doing can help, according to Galloway and Atherton (2008, cited in Holmes, 2009).

Explore

Explore more by reading Holmes's review, which has been used to put forward ideas for this key question for society: www.mrc-cbu.cam.ac.uk/wp-content/uploads/2013/09/Working-memory-and-learning-diffculties.pdf.

Progress check 2.25

Give two ways in which knowledge of working memory has helped to inform the treatment of dyslexia.

Test yourself

1 Read the following passage:
Aaron has difficulty in school. He is disruptive and does not seem able to pay attention to what he is meant to be doing in class. He finds it difficult to write cohesively, tending to miss letters out of words and miss words from sentences. He finds reading equally problematic and finds it hard to follow his place in a passage of reading, as well as to sound out separate letters. His teachers think he is dyslexic and wonder what they can do to help him. Using concepts, theories and studies from the cognitive approach and understanding of working memory, explain how Aaron might be helped. **(8 marks)**

2 The cognitive approach offers four ideas or models of how memory works. Choosing any key question for society, assess how at least one of these models can be used when discussing it, either to help with the key question, to explain the key question, or to both explain and help. **(16 marks)**

Practical investigation in cognitive psychology

For each topic area in your course, you will be carrying out a practical investigation, using methodology that you have learned about in that topic area. Your practical investigation is to gather data relevant to the material covered in this cognitive psychology section of your course, and must be ethical of course.

For cognitive psychology, you are asked to design and conduct a laboratory experiment to gather quantitative data and include both descriptive and inferential statistics to analyse your data.

Method link: Chapter 5 discusses issues around using experimental research methods as well as issues around analysis of quantitative data (page 315–336).

Maths link: Chapter 6 discusses measures of central tendency and measures of dispersion, as well as inferential statistical testing (page 387–416).

Practical link: Chapter 7 takes you through one idea for a practical investigation, including issues around writing up a report.

Two examples suggested in the cognitive psychology topic area of your course are:

- a dual-task experiment to investigate components of working memory
- an experiment to look at acoustic similarity of words and the effect on short-term memory.

As Baddeley (1966b) looks at the acoustic and semantic similarity of words in STM, using his work as a basis for an experiment would help your learning of the models of memory, as well as your learning of methodological issues in carrying out a laboratory experiment. However, in this chapter, other ideas have been suggested, such as a study similar to Bartlett's *War of the Ghosts* story, or whether a list of words that is categorised is learned better than the same words presented in random order (a study looking at LTM). You have studied four models of memory and could choose a practical investigation that looks at any of the areas you have covered. Chapter 7 gives a worked practical investigation if you would like to read through it. However, you will be doing your practical investigations throughout your course and you should focus on one that you have carried out in cognitive psychology for this part of your course.

Issues and debates in cognitive psychology

The 11 issues and debates are summarised (with links to each of the topic areas in your Year 1 course) in Chapter 8 in this book, and then in detail in Book 2.

Study to explain the use of schema: answer (from page 95)

The passage was about doing the laundry.

Read the passage again and it will be a lot clearer. One third of the participants in the study knew that the passage was about doing the laundry and then read the passage, with it making good sense. One third read the passage as you did and then were told the script, then read it again and could make sense of it the second time. One third of participants read the passage without knowing the script and could not make sense of it. The conclusion was that we do make sense of information using prior knowledge, which can be called 'schemas'.

Chapter summary

- Four models of memory are covered: the multi-store model; the working memory model; episodic and semantic memory; and reconstruction as a theory of memory.
- Issues highlighting individual differences and development in cognitive psychology are covered.
- Field and laboratory experiments are research methods studied as well as case studies of brain-damaged patients. Issues around carrying out experiments are covered. Method issues are briefly outlined and examined in detail in Chapter 5.
- With regard to analysis of quantitative data, both descriptive and inferential statistics are required in this part of your course. These are mentioned briefly in this chapter and explained in detail in Chapter 6 (pp. 387–416).
- The classic study in cognitive psychology is Baddeley (1966b) and it is explained here in detail, including looking at strengths and weaknesses. The way Baddeley (1966b) relates to the models of memory in your course and other aspects of the course, such as the experimental method, is highlighted.
- You need to learn about one contemporary study in cognitive psychology, and the three named in your course are explained here: Sebastián and Hernández-Gil (2012), Schmolck *et al.* (2002) and Steyvers and Hemmer (2012). The way those studies relate to other aspects of cognitive psychology in your course is also explained.
- As with other topic areas in Year 1, you cover a key question in cognitive psychology and two are explained here.
- You need to carry out one practical investigation in cognitive psychology, which must be an experiment. This section is briefly outlined for you in this chapter, but in Chapter 7 a practical investigation in cognitive psychology is explained in more detail.

Chapter Three: Biological Psychology

Overview

Biological psychology is the third topic area, although you will cover some 'biology' in Chapter 2. Cognitive psychology looks to neuroscience to help to explain information processing. In cognitive psychology, you look at case studies of brain-damaged people, where, for example, the lateral temporal cortex is found to be important in memory. Brain structure and brain functioning are just some of what you will look at when considering biology in psychology. Not all areas of psychology look at biological processes behind behaviour, emotions or thinking. There are different areas of interest in psychology, including counselling, psychoanalysis, how people interact in groups and the study of human relationships, where our 'biology' might not be considered much. However, many areas do consider the working of the brain, or how hormones affect behaviour, or what evolution theory tells us about genes. Biological psychology and neuroscience have a very important place in psychology.

One definition of psychology is that it is the scientific study of the brain and behaviour. The brain can be explained according to its biological functioning; behaviour can also be explained in terms of biological and chemical actions and interactions. People act according to their inherited characteristics, an explanation that draws on biological understanding. The biological approach in psychology tends to focus on the effect of genes (including their role in hormone production) on behaviour and on the effect of the nervous system (brain, spinal cord and nerves).

In your course, you will look at the influence of genes when you touch on evolution theory and when you consider twin and adoption studies. You will also look at the nervous system, in particular the central nervous system and the working of the brain. You will consider how drugs work, as an illustration of how messages are sent in the brain, and you will consider a theory that is very different from biological psychology – the psychodynamic approach – as an alternative to biological psychology when explaining aggression. In your course, aggression is chosen as a way of focusing on brain structure, brain functioning, neurotransmitter functioning and the role of hormones.

Studies of interest

On 15 November 2007, *The Times* covered a story about research which suggests that implants into the brain could restore speech to those who can no longer speak because of paralysis. A man who was paralysed after a car accident and who was completely aware but not able to speak had received such implants. Communicating through eye movements, the researchers asked him to think of vowel sounds (such as 'oh', 'ee' and 'oo') so they could examine the patterns of activity. If the separate sounds could be identified, then the researchers could translate the patterns into speech. The electrodes in the implants take readings from the neurons that generate movement in the mouth and tongue during speech. The man was able to use the system, and research in the area is continuing. Philip Kennedy (involved in this case) founded Neural Signals in 1987 and the company continues to study the brain machine interface (BMI). Baranauskas wrote an article in *Frontiers in Systems Neuroscience* (April 2014), which reviews this technology if you would like to find out more (http://journal.frontiersin.org/article/10.3389/fnsys.2014.00068/full).

Ingram (2014) looked at how children seem to show more physical aggression than adults and how aggression seems to be an evolutionary trait. He suggests that adults do not show the same amount of physical aggression because of socialising factors, limiting their display of aggression. He puts forward three pieces of evidence to show that aggression becomes more indirect in adults. He says that physical aggression decreases from child to adult just as indirect aggression rises from child to adult, which seems to suggest an evolutionary mechanism for moving from physical to indirect aggression. He says that the same individuals who show physical aggression as children show indirect aggression as adults, suggesting that aggression is an evolved trait and differs between individuals (linking to individual and genetic differences). His third piece of evidence is that adults who are socially dominant show more indirect aggression (social dominance orientation is explained in Chapter 1, and refers to people who believe they are 'higher' in society).

Ingram's study is called 'From hitting to tattling to gossip: an evolutionary rationale for the development of indirect aggression'. As the title suggests, Ingram thought that people move from physical aggression (hitting) to tattling, to gossip, and that gossip can be indirect aggression. He gives an evolutionary explanation of how socialisation seems to control physical aggression but that aggressive tendencies can leak out as indirect aggression, including gossiping. In biological psychology, you will look at the idea of evolution as well as biological explanations of aggression.

Everyday example

Cancer has more than one cause; studying it can help to show how biology, the environment and social issues come together. All cancers involve damage to DNA and this damage promotes cell division. In leukaemia, a type of cancer, almost every white blood cell carries an unusually small chromosome 22. The bone marrow produces damaged cells, which reproduce more quickly than undamaged cells. Research suggests that, in leukaemia, chromosome 22 is smaller because part of it has broken off and transferred to chromosome 9. This transfer leads to production of a new protein, leading to abnormal cell division.

Another example is a cancer caused by a virus that damages the genes controlling cell growth. People can be born with a genetic structure that makes them vulnerable to developing cancer, but requires something to trigger it. Some factors can damage the natural system, such as smoking and other lifestyle decisions. Academic disciplines such as biology, psychology and sociology can work together in explaining problems such as disease. This is why your course looks at biology and why there is a focus on genes and the brain.

Summary of learning objectives

Content

You need to know about:

- the central nervous system (CNS) and neurotransmitters, including how the neuron is structured and the role of the neuron
- the effect of recreational drugs on the transmission process between neurons
- the structure of the brain and function of different structures, especially linked to aggression (such as the prefrontal cortex and limbic system)
- evolution and the idea of natural selection
- Freud's psychodynamic explanation of aggression as an alternative to biological explanations of aggression
- the role of hormones like testosterone to explain human behaviour (such as aggression)
- individual differences, such as differences in brain structure and functioning and how personality gives differences in individuals, taking Freud's view of personality
- developmental issues in evolution theory, how we develop using a genetic blueprint, development of a personality (Freud) and how hormones affect development.

Individual differences and developmental psychology

In all topic areas, you need to consider two issues in psychology: individual differences and developmental psychology.

Individual differences

In biological psychology, you will learn about the following links:

- There are more similarities than differences in brain structure and functioning.
- Personality gives differences in individuals, taking Freud's view of the personality.

Developmental psychology

In biological psychology, you will learn about the following links:

- Evolution theory and how we develop using a genetic blueprint.
- Freud's theory, showing development of a personality.
- Hormones are part of development too.

Methods

Chapter 5 covers the methodology you will need for Year 1 of your course (and the AS, with some exceptions). See Table 5.1 (page 278) for a summary of which methods you need to know for this chapter. Chapter 6 covers the mathematical elements you need for your course. See Table 6.2 (page 386) for a summary of the mathematical skills you need to know for this chapter.

Studies

The classic study you will be learning about in biological psychology is Raine *et al.* (1997) 'Brain abnormalities in murderers indicated by positron emission tomography'.

You will choose one contemporary study from:

- Li *et al.* (2013) 'Abnormal function of the posterior cingulate cortex in heroin addicted users during resting-state and drug-cue stimulation task'
- Brendgen *et al.* (2005) 'Examining genetic and environmental effects on social aggression: a study of 6-year-old twins'
- Van den Oever *et al.* (2008) 'Prefrontal cortex plasticity mechanisms in drug seeking and relapse'.

Key questions

You have to describe one key question and explain it using concepts and theories that you have learned from biological psychology. You can choose any key question, but two are suggested in the specification and are described later in this chapter, as follows:

- How effective is drug therapy for treating addictions?
- What are the implications for society if aggression is found to be caused by nature not nurture?

Practical investigation

Chapter 7 covers the skills you need for conducting a practical investigation, including worked-through examples. Chapter 6 covers the mathematical elements for your course, which also links to your practical investigation.

Issues and debates

Issues and debates are in the A level course but not the AS, so if you are doing the AS, you do not need to study issues and debates, although they are interesting and will extend your understanding of psychology. The 11 issues and debates are: ethics; practical issues in research design; reductionism; comparing explanations; psychology as a science; culture and gender; nature–nurture; how psychology has developed over time; issues of social control; using psychology in society; and issues around socially sensitive research.

Chapter 8 summarises the issues and debates and how the four topic areas for your Year 1 course inform each of these. Book 2 will explain these in more detail.

STUDY HINT

Issues and debates appear in each topic area for Year 1 (and Year 2), in the same order, in the specification. For each topic area, you can use the examples against each of the issues and debates to learn how the material for that topic area illustrates that issue or debate. See Chapter 8 for more detail.

Make a summary of learning objectives into a checklist, such as the one in Table 3.1. However, you could add more detail to help your learning.

Table 3.1 What you need to know for biological psychology

You need to know about:	
Central nervous system, and synaptic transmission, structure and role of the neuron, neurotransmitters	Hypotheses (alternate, null and experimental)
Recreational drugs and effects on synaptic transmission	The use of control groups and randomisation to groups compared with correlation design (no allocation to groups)
Structure of the brain and brain functioning, including a focus on aggression and which structures are implicated	Sampling
Evolution and the theory of natural selection and how this explains behaviour such as aggression	CAT, PET and fMRI scanning and use of brain scanning to investigate human behaviour like aggression
Freud's psychodynamic explanation of aggression to contrast with biological explanations; personality (id, ego, superego), catharsis, role of the unconscious	One twin study to show how that research method is helpful (e.g. link to nature-nurture and to genes)
Role of hormones to explain human behaviour such as aggression (e.g. testosterone)	One adoption study to show how that research method is used
How individual differences are shown in this material, including Freud's ideas about personality and how brain damage can (or might not) lead to differences in individuals	Raine *et al.* (1997) as the classic study
Developmental psychology shown in Freud's ideas of development (e.g. id, ego, superego and the role of the unconscious) and also shown in the theory of natural selection	One contemporary study from Li *et al.* (2013), Brendgen *et al.* (2005) and van den Oever *et al.* (2008)
Correlation design, including positive and negative correlations and what 'strength' means regarding correlations	One key question of relevance to today's society (as it applies to concepts you cover in biological psychology) (note, so can include Freud)
Levels of significance and levels of measurement (nominal, ordinal, interval/ratio)	One practical study that yields correlation data focusing on aggression or attitudes to drug usage
Spearman's rank correlation coefficient and scatter diagrams	Use descriptive statistics to analyse the results (including a scatter diagram)
Critical and observed values	Carry out a Spearman's test on your data and use related issues like level of significance and the significance of the result
Co-variables against the idea of cause and effect and IV/DV	Research question/hypothesis; research method; sampling; ethics; data collection tools; data analysis, results, discussion (and write an abstract)
Issues and debates (not for AS)	

An introduction to biological psychology

Biological psychology focuses mainly on genes and characteristics that have been inherited, and how the brain works. Other aspects of biology, such as how the body works, are less involved in psychology, although issues such as phantom limb pain and body dysmorphism are part of the biological approach, but they are not covered in your course.

> **Explore**
> Look up body dysmorphism and phantom limb pain to broaden your understanding of the biological approach.

Biological psychology examines in detail the structure and function of the brain and how drugs affect transmission, and so on. In your course, you focus on just some of the material and how it relates to aggression.

> **STUDY HINT**
> You should study the biological psychology part of your course as a whole rather than the methodology, content, studies, key issues and practical as separate sections. First, read the chapter as a whole, taking in some of the information but without taking notes or working hard to learn the terms. After reading the whole chapter, you can start learning in earnest. This advice applies for all topic areas.

Ideas underpinning biological psychology

In this part of your course, you will learn about how our biological self (brain and body) affects our behaviour, specifically focusing on aggression. This section outlines the assumptions that underpin biological psychology to give you a wider view beyond the course material.

Psychology is about people and includes aspects of how the brain works, as well as how social and environmental influences affect our behaviour. The biological approach looks at chemical activity in the brain, including how neurotransmitters act at synapses to enable messages to be transmitted. Another way that messages are transmitted is by hormones. The biological approach includes an evolutionary perspective, which examines how characteristics are inherited via genes. The function of the various parts of the brain is also touched on.

> **STUDY HINT**
> You are likely to have covered some of this material in other subjects, such as GCSE Science. Recall your earlier learning to help you in this topic area.

Functioning of neurotransmitters

One way that messages are passed within the brain is by neurotransmitters, which are chemicals that pass from neuron to neuron. Between neurons there are gaps, called synapses. If the receptors of one neuron are set to receive the neurotransmitters of another, then the message continues (explained in more detail on pp. 136–144).

Hormonal transmission

Another way that messages are passed is through hormones. These send messages more slowly that neurotransmitters and are used for different purposes. This process is explained in more detail later (pp. 162–165). Hormones have a large part to play in our development as either male or female – for example, androgens are 'male' hormones and oestrogen is 'female'. Hormones can also underpin aggressive behaviour, which is the focus in your course.

Genetic influences

Biological psychology also looks at how genes are passed on from parents to children and how they govern behaviour as well as physical characteristics. Children receive half their genes from their fathers and half from their mothers. The human genome has recently been decoded, which means that all the genes have been identified. However, this does not mean that the function of each gene is known because it is often the combination or the position of genes that leads to certain characteristics, rather than one particular gene. Twin and adoption studies can help to uncover what in our behaviour is down to our genes and our 'nature' and what might be due to environmental influences, our 'nurture'.

> **Progress check 3.1**
> Why does biological psychology look at the study of twins to help to find out about the role of genes in our behaviour and our characteristics?

Parts of the brain and their functions

The brain has many parts. For example:

- the limbic system is linked to aggression and was examined by Raine *et al.* (1997) (pp. 176–184)
- the medial temporal lobe and lateral temporal cortex are thought to be where short-term memory occurs, and where it moves memories into long-term memory.

In summary, the four aspects of biological psychology are:

- neuronal transmission
- the role of genes
- the role of hormones
- brain structure and functioning.

Test yourself

1. Describe what is meant by biological psychology, giving at least three features of this topic area in your answer. **(6 marks)**
2. Describe what is meant by 'hormones' and 'genes'. **(4 marks)**

Content in biological psychology

In your course, biological psychology covers how messages are sent in the brain using neurotransmitters and synaptic transmission, as well as how recreational drugs work in the brain, which we will cover first. Then the focus is on structures in the brain and their purpose with regard to aggression. The role of natural selection, including relating to aggression, is covered, as well as hormones in relation to aggression. Finally, we look at Freud's psychodynamic explanation of aggression as an alternative explanation to biological theories. Much of the content, although not all, relates directly to aggression because that helps to focus on specific areas of the brain and human functioning.

As in other topic areas, you need to look for links to individual differences and to developmental psychology. Individual differences can be seen where damage to the brain causes specific issues for an individual. Personality is about individual differences, and Freud's theory of personality is covered in the biological psychology topic area, even though it is offered as an alternative to biological ideas and fits outside biological psychology normally.

The idea of evolution and how those most suited to survive *will* survive is about development, as are other issues, such as the role of hormones. Hormones are released according to a genetic blueprint for each individual, for example, and hormones guide our individual development.

Aggression in humans can come from brain functioning, perhaps hormones, or from frustration

The role of the central nervous system and neurotransmitters in human behaviour

The nervous system has two main parts: the **central nervous system** and the **peripheral nervous system**. The central nervous system (CNS) consists of the brain and spinal cord. The brain is within the skull and the spinal cord is within the vertebrae. In the embryo, a tube separates into the brain and the spinal cord and there are then further subdivisions. The brain areas that are important for your course are shown in Table 3.2.

Other parts of the brain include:

- the thalamus – near the base; passes on information from the senses
- the cortex – the most recent development of the brain for humans, which stores information and is involved in problem-solving and decision-making.

STUDY HINT

It is very difficult to represent parts of the brain in two-dimensional drawings because the brain has two hemispheres and parts are found inside the two hemispheres. The drawings, however, should help you to visualise what is being talked about when different parts of the brain are discussed. Try to paint a picture of the brain in your head with the various parts in it, to get a three-dimensional picture, to help your memory.

Progress check 3.2

Name three parts of the brain and state what each part is for.

STUDY HINT

When asked to name something, you should just give the name, rather than a description. When asked to state something, you can be brief and to the point, without giving a description or an explanation. You should know what each injunction in your examination means (an injunction is the word telling you what to do in a question, such as 'state' or 'explain'). In the specification for your course, you will find a 'taxonomy', which is a list of words telling you what to do in the exam and what they are asking for. Get to know the words on this list and what they mean before sitting the examination.

Definition

The **central nervous system** is made up of the brain and the spinal column.

Table 3.2 Some important parts of the brain for your course

Brain part	Function	Topic area related to
Striatum	Important role in controlling movements and in motivation.	Biological psychology (e.g. effects of recreational drugs, pp. 141–144)
Hippocampus (part of the limbic system)	Short-term memories are passed into long-term memory via the hippocampus. It is part of the limbic system and is located in the medial temporal lobe.	Cognitive psychology (case studies of patients with brain damage, e.g. Schmolck *et al.*, 2002, pp. 113–119) Biological psychology (Raine *et al.*, 1997, pp. 176–184)
Ventricles	Concerned with the production of cerebrospinal fluid; central nervous system includes spinal column and ventricles link. Schizophrenia has been said to link to enlarged ventricles. The fluid helps to cushion the brain from blows and can provide nutrients. High pressure can block ventricles and give rise to the condition hydrocephalus (water on the brain).	Clinical psychology in Year 2 Also links to learning theories as Little Albert was said to be a child who years died from hydrocephalus at the age of six (p. 262)
Amygdala (part of the limbic system)	Emotions and aggression. There is a right and left amygdala (as in other structures too, such as the hippocampus, because the brain has two sides). The left amygdala might link to a reward system and both positive and negative emotions, whereas the right might be more about negatives, like fear and sadness.	Biological psychology (e.g. Raine *et al.*, 1997, pp. 176–184)
Hypothalamus (part of the limbic system)	Regulating eating and drinking and motivated behaviours.	Biological psychology (e.g. Raine *et al.*, 1997, pp. 176–184)
Medial temporal lobe (MTL)	Includes hippocampus and has a large role in memory.	Cognitive psychology (e.g. Schmolck *et al.*, 2002, pp. 113–119) and biological psychology (e.g. Raine *et al.*, 1997, pp. 176–184)
Cerebellum	Stores memory/learning of practical skills.	Cognitive psychology and biological psychology
Corpus callosum	This is the 'bridge' between the two hemispheres and transmits messages between the two halves.	Biological psychology (e.g. Raine *et al.*, 1997, pp. 176–184)
Limbic system	This is about emotions and memories. The limbic system likes to the side of the thalamus and includes hypothalamus, hippocampus and amygdala.	Biological psychology – in particular, aggression (pp. 147–148) Cognitive psychology and memory

There are too many parts to explain them all in your sample of biological psychology. The limbic system, including the hypothalamus, the hippocampus and amygdala, is pictured on page 147 to illustrate how the brain is made up of different structures. In your course, you are looking at a small sample of such structures.

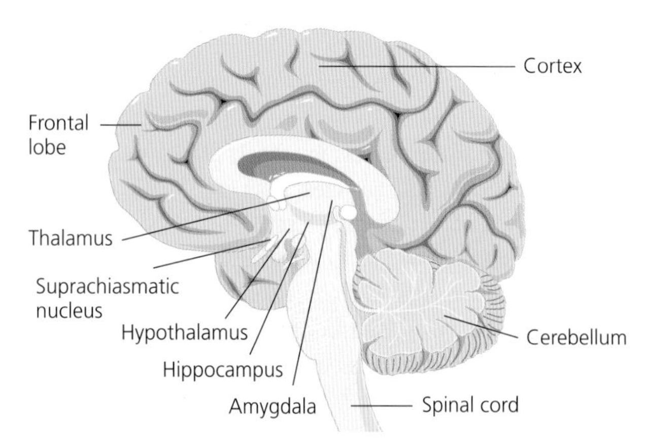

Parts of the brain and the spinal cord, which make up the central nervous system (CNS)

Explore

Using the internet or some other source, look up split-brain studies. These studies look at the behaviour of patients whose corpus callosum has been split, often to help with epilepsy. Start by looking up the work of Sperry. This work shows how the two halves of the brain work together. For example, in cognitive psychology, Schmolck *et al.* (2002) discussed the effects of bilateral brain damage – 'bilateral' refers to brain damage to a particular structure (the medial temporal lobe in this case) on both sides of the brain.

Neurotransmitters

In your course, you need to know about the role of neurotransmitters in the central nervous system/brain. With regard to the central nervous system and neurotransmitters, you need to know the **structure** (how a neuron is made up) and role of the neuron, the **function** of neurotransmitters (what they are for) and how synaptic transmission works.

Definitions

In psychology, you will find terms like 'structure' and 'function'. **Structure** is how something is set up. For example, 'structure' of a neuron is what forms the neuron. **Function** is what something is for. For example, 'function' of neurotransmitters refers to what they do and the role they play.

STUDY HINT

All terms in your course are important. It can be tempting to think that terms like 'structure' and 'function' are obvious. However, these are as important as more complex terms as they form part of your learning and understanding. An exam question may ask about the function of something like neurotransmitters or the prefrontal cortex, so you need to know what 'function' means. Add terms like this to your glossary.

Definitions

Neurotransmitters (e.g. dopamine and noradrenaline) are chemical messengers that act between the neurons in the brain. This allows the brain to process thoughts and memories. Neurotransmitters are released into the synaptic gap and taken up by the receptors of dendrites of another neuron, to send a message. Or they can inhibit a message – they can be left in the gap, not taken up, but re-used.

Some neurotransmitters and their function in the brain

- *GABA* (Gamma-aminobutyric acid) is an inhibitor in the brain, which means it blocks messages rather than taking a message on. It is there to calm nerves that are firing and to give relaxation. Having low levels of GABA can lead to anxiety. Low levels are also linked to epilepsy, so GABA can be given to help reduce epilepsy. GABA, as with other neurotransmitters, has other roles too, such as helping with control over the motor system (movement). $C_4H_9NO_2$ is the chemical notation for GABA.
- *Norepinephrine* (also known as noradrenaline) affects our attention and is involved in the fight-or-flight response, which prepares us for action. People with ADHD (attention deficit hyperactivity disorder) can be prescribed noradrenaline to help. $C_8H_{11}NO_3$ is the chemical notation for noradrenaline.
- *Acetylcholine* is linked to memory and thinking, as well as learning. Damage to the areas of the brain that produce acetylcholine has been associated with Alzheimer's disease. $C_7H_{16}NO_2^+$ is the chemical notation for acetylcholine.
- *Dopamine* is associated with pleasure feelings. These feelings may be wanted, so dopamine is linked to addiction, as the individual carries out actions to get those feelings. Dopamine in this way can be linked to drug addiction. $C_8H_{11}NO_2$ is the chemical notation for dopamine.
- *Glutamate* is a neurotransmitter associated with memory and learning (cognitive functioning) and is common in the brain. It is also associated with brain development. Having too much glutamate is harmful and can lead to stroke or can kill. $C_5H_9NO_4$ is the chemical notation for glutamate.
- *Serotonin* is the neurotransmitter for happiness and good mood. With melatonin (which is a hormone – hormones are explained later in this section), it regulates the sleep–wake cycle (melatonin for sleep, serotonin for wakefulness). Low levels of serotonin link to depression and anxiety and selective serotonin reuptake inhibitors (SSRIs) are prescribed for mental disorders like depression. Light levels also affect serotonin levels, as does exercise. $C_{10}H_{12}N_2O$ is the chemical notation for serotonin.

STUDY HINT

You may not need to remember all the neurotransmitters here, their function and their chemical notation. However, you need to have an idea about some of them, so that you can use them as examples. They will help your understanding of biological psychology, cognitive psychology and clinical psychology. If you study health psychology, which looks at drug misuse, your learning about neurotransmitter functioning will be helpful. It would be worth making some notes about three or four of these neurotransmitters.

Progress check 3.3

Name three neurotransmitters and state what they do in the brain.

GABA	Norepinephrine	Acetylcholine	Dopamine	Glutamate	Serotonin
• Inhibitor of messages • Calming	• Gives attention • Prepares for flight/fight	• Memory • Learning	• Pleasure feelings • Addiction	• Cognitive functioning • Dangerous if too much	• Happiness and good mood • Low levels give depression

Neurotransmitters and their function

Structure and function of the neuron

The nervous system consists of neurons and glia. A lot of what is covered in biological psychology for your course is about the science of the nervous system, which is called **neuroscience**. The actual biology is not explained in 'biological' detail, but covered just enough for you to understand the working of the brain and how it relates to human behaviour, thinking and emotions.

> **STUDY HINT**
> It is hard to explain the structure and function of the neuron without using terms that are at first unfamiliar. However, read through the material once and then read back, checking that you know the meaning of all the terms. It is worth drawing up the diagram of a neuron and labelling it for yourself, to help your learning.

Glial cells

Glial cells carry out repairs, act as insulators and remove waste products from the brain; research is still going on into the role of glia. Glia surrounds neurons and protects them as well as supplying nutrients. They also remove dead neurons. Until the twenty-first century, glia was not seen as having much of a role in neuronal transmission; glial cells were seen as supporting neurons. However, research now suggests that glial cells do have a role in transmitting messages (e.g. Wolosker *et al.*, 2008). For example, glial cells in the hippocampus seem to have a role in releasing gliatransmitters, which have a role in synaptic transmission, and they also seem to have role in clearing neurotransmitters away in the synaptic gap. What happens in the synaptic gap is explained later in this section (pp. 139–141). Glial cells can also wrap around nerve fibres to form a myelin sheath, which can help repair (such as when there is damage to the spinal column) and can also help in conducting messages. Neurons have a myelin sheath around the axon, demonstrating the role of such a protective layer (see page 139).

> **STUDY HINT**
> You do not need to know a lot about glial cells, but they are all around neurons and have some role to play. There is a lot more to the role of glial cells than explained here. It is worth knowing a little about the role of glia as it helps to visualise synaptic processing and how neurons interact to pass messages in the brain.

> **Definition**
> **Glial cells** surround neurons, protect them and have some other functions, such as being involved in giving a myelin sheath to protect the axon.

> **Explore**
> Look more at the role of glia if it interests you. For example: www.ncbi.nlm.nih.gov/books/NBK10869/.

Issues and debates

In the 1800s, glia was seen as purely glue around neurons. In the 1900s gradually interest rose in the role of glia. In the 2000s, glia is well researched. This shows how focus changes over time. To an extent this is biological focus – however, it is of interest in psychology. Neuroscience is a term that covers the science of the nervous system, and this has changed over time and is developing. Cognitive psychology and biological psychology draw close together under 'neuroscience'. You will have seen that, when discussing the brain, cognitive processing has been mentioned frequently.

> **Definition**
> **Neuroscience** is a term used for the scientific study of the nervous system and draws together not only biology and psychology, but also chemistry, computer science, engineering and other **disciplines**, such as physics, philosophy and genetics. A discipline is a field of study. Biological psychology in your course is very much neuroscience; there are also elements of neuroscience in cognitive psychology in your course.

> **STUDY HINT**
> A lot of the understanding of neurons and glial cells comes from experiments with animals. For example, Wolosker *et al.* (2008) used animal studies. When you learn about experiments using animals in learning theories (Chapter 4), think back to this section, as there will be examples of animal studies for you to use. Also you can use criticisms of using animals and then generalising to humans as evaluation of the studies.

> **Progress check 3.4**
> Give two functions of glial cells.

The structure of a neuron

Neurons are cells that receive and transmit messages, passing messages from cell to cell. There are motor neurons, which receive messages from the central nervous system (the brain and spinal column) to generate movements. There are sensory neurons, which transmit messages about senses, such as sight and sound, from the sense organ to the brain and spinal column. There are inter-neurons, which take message from neuron to neuron.

At one end, a neuron has **dendrites**, which are finger-like structures surrounding a cell body, and form a structure that is tree-like. From the cell body, there is also long extension coming from the **axon hillock**. This long extension is called an **axon** and can be up to a metre long in humans. The axon ends at an **axon terminal**. The axon is where the electrical signal from the **cell body** travels. The axon terminal has more than one 'branch' and at the end of each 'branch' is a **terminal button**.

The axon is protected by the **myelin sheath** (made up of Schwann cells in the peripheral nervous system and oligodendroglial cells in the central nervous system), which surrounds it to form an insulation layer. To speed up the message there are places in the myelin sheath where it thins, called **nodes of Ranvier**.

Explanation

Neurons are made up of a **cell body** sending an electrical signal down an **axon**, which is protected by a **myelin sheath**. The myelin sheath has breaks in it, where the axon is not protected, and these breaks are called the **'nodes of Ranvier'**. The electrical signal arrives at the **axon terminal** and the signal triggers the release of **neurotransmitters** into the **synaptic gap**. The synaptic gap separates the **terminal buttons** of one neuron from the **dendrites** of another neuron. If the dendrites have **receptors** that 'match' the chemical composition of the released neurotransmitter, the signal continues with the neurotransmitter sending a message to the cell body of the other neuron, which triggers an electrical impulse called the **action potential** down the axon of that neuron and so on.

Progress check 3.5

Explain the terms synaptic gap, receptors and neurotransmitters.

To make things a little complicated, not all neurons have dendrites or axons, but the basic neuron is shown in the diagram below.

How the electrical message arises in the cell body

How is the electrical signal from the cell body, travelling down the axon of the neuron, generated? Briefly, it is about the voltage of ions around and in the cell body. Ions such as sodium, potassium, chlorine and calcium arise in certain quantities/voltages outside the cell body and inside the cell body. When the voltages outside and inside differ sufficiently, there is a reaction, and that causes an **action potential**, or electrical charge, in the cell body. This action potential travels into the axon via the axon hillock, protected by the myelin sheath but speeded up by the nodes of Ranvier. It is this action potential that releases the neurotransmitter stored at the terminal of the axon.

The myelin sheath is wrapped around the axon in a spiral. There are breaks in the myelin sheath, so a small part of the axon is exposed – these are the nodes of Ranvier. The electrical signal can jump from node to node and that speeds up the action potential. Having a myelin sheath makes the message pass more quickly due to the conductance of the sheath.

The role/function of the neuron

The neuron's role is to pass messages between neurons using neurotransmitters to enable behaviour, thinking and emotions to be transmitted and to enable the working of the brain. The electrical impulses travelling down the axon trigger the release of neurotransmitters from the terminal at the end of the axon. The neurotransmitters are then released into the synaptic gap, to be picked up by receptors on the dendrites of another neuron or to be taken up again for re-use. This process in the synaptic gap is called 'synaptic transmission' (see below).

The role/function of neurotransmitters

The role of neurotransmitters is to carry messages from one neuron to another – though 'carrying messages' can also be 'blocking them', as you will see. If the neurotransmitter released from the terminal of an axon is not taken up by the dendrites of an adjacent neuron, the message stops, so although a neurotransmitter only carries a message and does not block it, it has a role in the message being blocked. This transmission and blocking is explained next.

Synaptic transmission

The axon terminal of one neuron reaches out to the dendrites of another neuron. Between the terminal and the dendrites there is a gap called a **synapse**. The synaptic gap or synaptic cleft sits between two neurons. On one side, at the dendrites, there are receptors of a certain shape prepared to receive the neurotransmitter from the other neuron. If the neurotransmitter fits the receptor, the message is passed on; if it does not, the message is blocked. **Receptors** can be thought of as locks – if a certain chemical (neurotransmitter) fits like a key in the lock then the message is received and continues along that neuron to another neuron and so on. The chemical make-up of some neurotransmitters is given earlier in this section (page 137) and shows differences between the neurotransmitters. These differences help to explain how different receptors and their neurotransmitters might match.

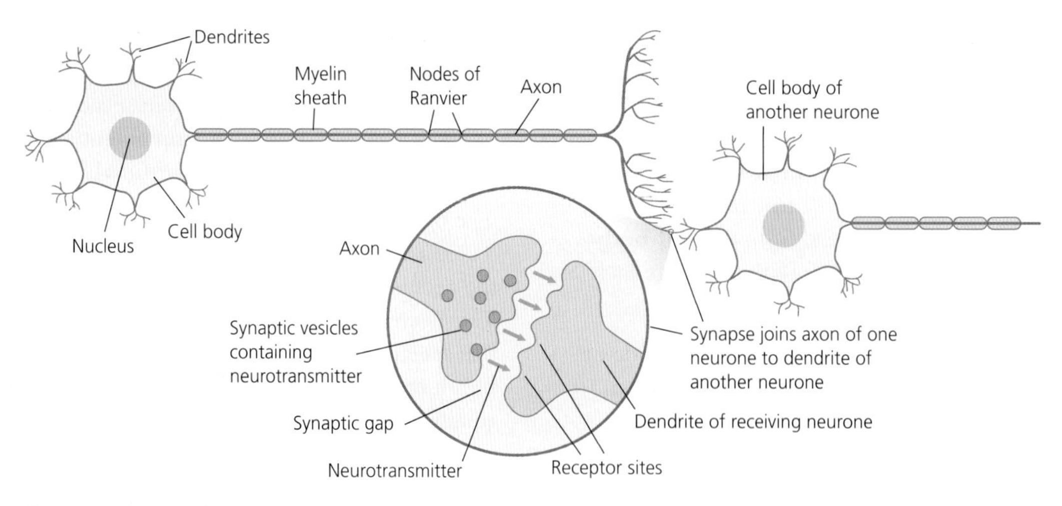

How synapses work

The simple way of sending messages between neurons is to see neurotransmitters as leaving the terminal of one axon, fitting the receptors at the dendrites of another neuron and taking the message on so that an action potential is generated in the cell body of that other neuron.

Reuptake

The neurotransmitter that is not used by the receptors is taken up again to be reused – this is called **reuptake**. Reuptake regulates the amount of neurotransmitter in the synapse, which regulates how much message there is (when the neurotransmitter is no longer in the gap, the message will stop) and also recycles the neurotransmitter so it has a useful function. Transport proteins pick up the neurotransmitter. Transporter proteins for GABA, norepinephrine, dopamine and serotonin (and for other neurotransmitters) are very similar. The transporters enable the neurotransmitter to be absorbed into the presynaptic neuron. The **presynaptic neuron** is the one with the action potential travelling down the axon to trigger the release of the neurotransmitters; the **postsynaptic neuron** is the one receiving the neurotransmitter at the receptors of the dendrites. A reuptake inhibitor stops this absorbing and means the neurotransmitter will be left in the gap for the message to continue for longer.

Definitions

A **presynaptic neuron** is the one sending the message and releasing the neurotransmitters and a **postsynaptic neuron** is the one receiving the message. **Reuptake** is when the neurotransmitter is absorbed back into the presynaptic neuron.

An example – SSRIs

Manufactured drugs mimic natural neurotransmitters; they more or less fit certain receptors (though not perfectly), are received like neurotransmitters and the message from them 'works'. Some drugs block the message. These 'blocking' drugs 'fit' and fill the receptor, so the natural neurotransmitter cannot pass the message on because the receptor is not available. An example of prescribed drugs that affect synaptic transmission is selective serotonin reuptake inhibitors (SSRIs), which are prescribed for depression and enhance serotonin levels in the brain. Serotonin is a neurotransmitter that improves mood. The drugs work by blocking the reuptake of serotonin; this leaves more serotonin at the synapse to be taken up again by the receptors of other neurons, so improving mood.

Four SSRIs prescribed in the UK for depression (and their brand names):

- Fluoxetine (Prozac)
- Paroxetine (Seroxat)
- Citalopram (Cipramil)
- Fluvoxamine (Faverin).

Explore

YouTube has video clips on the various aspects of neuronal transmission. For example: www.youtube.com/watch?v=LkJN4X6wysM. Another site explaining the whole process is www.cerebromente.org.br/n12/fundamentos/neurotransmissores/neurotransmitters2.html.

You could also find out more about neurotransmitters, such as the possible role of dopamine in schizophrenia and any links to Parkinson's disease. You could research how drugs work, either so-called recreational drugs (e.g. cocaine) or antipsychotic drugs (e.g. chlorpromazine).

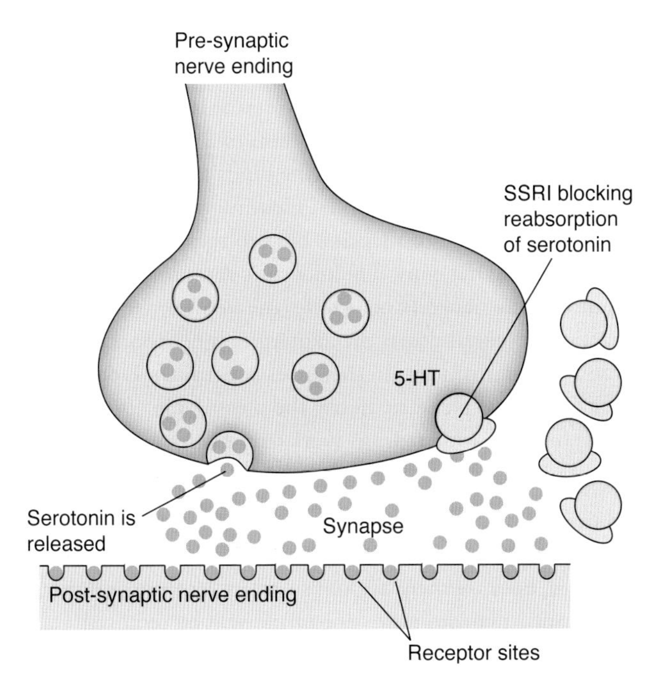

How SSRIs work at the synapse – an example of synaptic transmission and how blocking reuptake leaves more serotonin in the synapse

Progress check 3.6

How does reuptake work?

Evaluation of neurotransmitters and transmission at the synapse

Strengths of the synaptic transmission argument

- PET scanning was used by Jovanovic (2008) to look at the serotonin system of women. She used women because low serotonin levels are linked to depression more in women than in men. One part of her study looked at women with PMDD (pre-menstrual dysphoric disorder) to see if they showed differences in their serotonin system when compared with a control group. Scanning was done for each group both before and after ovulation. Those without PMDD did show differences in the synaptic receptors, which suggests that synaptic receptors have a role in pre-menstrual dysphoric disorder, a condition that links to low mood and depression. This is evidence that synaptic transmission, involving neurotransmitters (serotonin), relates to mood, including depression.
- Though some studies are done using animals, human brain scanning has increasingly been used in research – the strength of this approach is that humans are used, producing actual brain activity and brain structures at work. The method has scientific credibility. Reliability can be demonstrated, for example, as more than one person can analyse the scans to check the results.

Weaknesses of the synaptic transmission argument

- Allen and Stevens (1994) found that synaptic transmission regarding hippocampal neurons was very unreliable, with less than half the neurotransmitters arriving from the presynaptic neuron being picked up by the postsynaptic neuron. Some of this failure was due to issues with the release mechanisms in low capacity synapses. This might not be evidence that synaptic transmission is not involved in messaging in the brain; it might just mean that it is not as straightforward as it might seem. However, this is perhaps evidence that there are many factors at work in synaptic transmission. Giving a process a name implies it works steadily and regularly all the time, which does not seem to be the case.
- Much of the evidence about synaptic transmission has come from studies with animals where **lesions** can be made (damaging parts of the brain to see what effects this has). It is hard to see that finding out how the brains of animals work can be generalised completely to human brains, as human brains, involving as they do consciousness and more emotional functioning, are different.

Test yourself

1. Using a diagram in your answer, explain the structure of the neuron in the brain. **(6 marks)**
2. Using a diagram in your answer, explain how synaptic transmission takes place. **(8 marks)**
3. Evaluate the process of synaptic transmission as a means of passing messages in the brain. **(12 marks)**

The effect of recreational drugs on the transmission process in the central nervous system

Drugs are chemicals that have an effect on humans. Recreational drugs include cocaine, heroin, cannabis, ecstasy and others. Cannabis comes next in popularity after alcohol, caffeine and nicotine. They are called 'recreational' because they are taken for pleasure. They have an effect on the central nervous system and are called 'psychoactive' because of that. They are not always used as recreational drugs. For example, cannabis can be taken for medical purposes (medical cannabis or medical marijuana). It can be helpful in reducing sickness associated with chemotherapy, for example, as well as for multiple sclerosis. Most of such drugs are illegal – it is against the law in the UK to take them or to be found in possession of them.

There are so called 'legal highs', which refer to drugs that are taken for recreational purposes but are legal for other purposes and not yet illegal according to the Misuse of Drugs Act 1971. Legal highs that are popular are cannabinoids, which mimic the effects of cannabis, cathinones, which mimic the effects of ecstasy, and phenethylamines, which include stimulants and hallucinogens.

This section provides an example of neurotransmitter functioning and synaptic transmission and will help you to learn about what happens at the synapse. You will learn more about how recreational drugs work if you choose health psychology in Year 2, which looks at heroin, alcohol and nicotine as three 'recreational' drugs.

Mode of action of drugs at the synapse

Some drugs do not have a specific mode of action. For example, alcohol has many effects. One of the effects of alcohol is briefly discussed when looking at brain structure and functioning and aggression, and it is seen that alcohol affects the connection between the amygdala and the prefrontal cortex (Gorka *et al.*, 2013; p. 149 of this book).

Mainly, however, drugs do have a specific mode of action at the synapse, which means they act in a specific way. You have already seen how SSRIs can work to block serotonin reuptake and leave more in the synapse. That is the mode of action of SSRIs.

Nicotine

An important feature of the brain is that we seem to have what is called a **reward pathway** or **pleasure centre**, which means that we and animals work to receive rewards because of the pleasure we get in the reward pathway. One such reward pathway is the mesolimbic pathway – this includes the ventral tegmental area in the midbrain. It includes dopaminergic, GABAergic and glutamatergic neurons. Nicotine works on the reward pathway to give pleasure. This leads to addiction because the organism will act in order to stimulate the reward pathway.

Definitions

The **reward pathway** in the brain, or the **pleasure centre**, is where pleasure seems to be so desired that someone or an animal will continue to behave in such a manner that the pleasure is received, even when starving or thirsty. The desire for the pleasure over-rides other drives. Olds and Milner (1954) carried out a study on rats and found the pleasure centre in the septum area of the brain. Olds and Milner (1954) is the classic study in health psychology in Year 2.

Nicotine directly affects the dopamine receptors in the area of the brain that is the reward pathway. Dopamine is the neurotransmitter that relates to rewards and to feeling pleasure. Nicotine mimics the actions of acetylcholine, a natural neurotransmitter. Nicotine binds to a certain type of acetylcholine receptor, called nicotinic receptors. When either acetylcholine or nicotine bind to these receptors, the same thing happens. The nicotinic receptors cause an impulse in the neuron and 'excite' the neuron, which gives an action potential down the axon of that neuron, releasing more neurotransmitter (in this case, dopamine). Dopamine gives feelings of pleasure, hence the pleasurable effects of taking nicotine (other drugs work in the same way).

However, this binding over time affects the receptors and causes a decrease in dopamine receptors. There is also a change in the shape of the cell. When nicotine is not there, because there are not so many receptors on the postsynaptic neuron, more dopamine will be required to stimulate the postsynaptic neuron to a 'normal' level. This is called **desensitisation**, when more of a substance is required to achieve the same response/stimulation. This leads to **addiction** because nicotine is needed just to maintain what was normal functioning before the receptors and cell started to change by the binding of the nicotine at the receptors.

There are genetic factors at work as well because some people may have the allele that means they have fewer dopamine receptors. For an explanation of genes and alleles, see later in this section (pp. 150–153).

Definitions

Desensitisation refers to when more of a substance is needed to get the same feeling; this is because of changes at the synapse. There is a loss of response to a drug so more is needed to maintain the 'normal' response. This is also called tolerance. **Addiction** refers to the reward system in the brain giving such good feelings that the individual 'must' have that reward and so continues with the drug. An addictive drug is rewarding or the drug is needed for normal functioning.

Cocaine

Cocaine also works on the reward pathway and dopamine receptors, but does it in a different way from nicotine. Cocaine draws on the idea that there is reuptake by the presynaptic neuron of neurotransmitter left in the synaptic gap. Cocaine blocks the binding site on the reuptake receptor and stops the reuptake of dopamine back into the presynaptic neuron. This blocking of reuptake means excess dopamine in the synapse. It is this excess of dopamine that leads to over-stimulation at the postsynaptic receptors. This time there is not a 'foreign' substance to bind to the dopamine receptors but there is more dopamine than usual. The same feeling is achieved as with nicotine (euphoria) as this is the reward pathway at work. As with nicotine, the effect of over-stimulating the dopamine receptors of the postsynaptic neuron is that they become damaged and they become fewer, with the same consequence of desensitisation and addiction. Cocaine acts on the receptors in the reward pathway within seconds.

Amphetamines, like cocaine, block reuptake of dopamine so leave more dopamine in the synapse. Dopamine is the 'feel good' neurotransmitter.

It is interesting to note that Ritalin, which is prescribed for children with ADHD (attention deficit hyperactivity disorder), acts in the same way as cocaine on the receptors of the presynaptic neuron, leaving an excess of dopamine in the synapse in the reward pathway. However, Ritalin does take longer to have an effect – an hour rather than seconds.

Cannabis and cannabinoids

Cannabis and cannabinoids act by binding on to cannabinoid receptors. One type of cannabinoid receptor (CB1) is found in many regions in the brain; the other type is only found in the immune system. There are many cannabinoid receptors in the hippocampus and taking cannabis can affect memory function. Cannabis binds to the cannabinoid receptors, effectively blocking them; this means there is less activity in the neurons in the hippocampus. Cannabis gives less neuron activity. This means that making memories can be affected by taking cannabis.

However, in the reward system more dopamine is released, as happens with other drugs. It is this excess dopamine in the reward system that gives the 'high'. It seems strange that cannabis blocks activity and yet there is excess dopamine in the reward system. The explanation is that dopaminergic neurons do not have cannabinoid (CB1) receptors. The dopaminergic neurons are inhibited by GABAergic neurons, which do have CB1 receptors (for cannabis). The cannabis removes the inhibition from the GABAergic neurons, so the dopamine neurons can be activated and will release more dopamine. Cannabis taking will affect the CB1 receptors (doing damage), which will affect blood flow and reduce oxygen to the brain. This will affect the cannabis user, such as reducing attention and giving memory loss.

Explore

Explore more about the link between cannabis and dopamine. The following article raises some of the issues: http://news.sciencemag.org/brain-behavior/2014/07/hardcore-pot-smoking-could-damage-brains-pleasure-center.

Explore more about the legalisation of cannabis for medical purposes, e.g. explore the situation in countries. The following *Guardian* article is about the call to legalise cannabis in the UK for medical purposes: www.theguardian.com/society/2014/aug/13/cannabis-norman-baker-liberalised-drugs-laws-health.

Table 3.3 Recreational drugs and their biological functioning

Drug	Effects at the synapse
Nicotine	Releases more neurotransmitter in response to an impulse and increases number of impulses, thus there is more dopamine in the reward system
Cocaine	Blocks reuptake so there is more neurotransmitter (dopamine) in the synapse
Cannabis	Binds to CB1 receptors (cannabinoid receptors) and blocks activity; can also affect GABAergic neurons and stop them from inhibiting dopamine production in the reward system, thus there is excess dopamine there

STUDY HINT

You need to know enough about recreational drugs to be able to explain the effect on the transmission process in the brain. Relate the information about how a drug works to what is explained about synaptic transmission and neurotransmitter functioning earlier in this chapter. Be ready to talk about at least two recreational drugs.

Progress check 3.7

Using one recreational drug as an example, explain how synaptic transmission occurs in the central nervous system.

Evaluation of the effects of recreational drugs on the transmission process in the central nervous system

Strengths of the arguments about their effects on transmission

- There is a lot of evidence that points in the same direction: from Olds and Milner (1954), who found a pleasure centre in the brain, to Straiker and Mackie (2005), who used cultured hippocampal neurons from mice to study the effects of cannabis. Straiker *et al.* (2012) used cultured hippocampal neurons from mice with the human CB1 receptor. The studies are detailed and thorough with careful controls that give scientific credibility. Many studies link recreational drugs with creating excess dopamine to give a 'high' and the fact that study findings support one another suggests the findings are reliable.

- There is credibility in suggesting that recreational drugs, first, create more dopamine in the reward system and so give pleasure and, second, have a desensitising effect so there is addiction and tolerance. This credibility comes from observation of those who take recreational drugs, who at first experience great pleasure from the drug but who then (in general) become addicted and find they need more to experience the same effects. External information backs up the study of internal processes, suggesting reliability and perhaps some validity.

STUDY HINT

Remember when evaluating issues in psychology to make your point clearly. When giving strengths, you shouldn't just say that findings are reliable or valid, or that animal studies are not generalisable – you have to show understanding and explain why they are reliable/valid/not generalisable.

Weaknesses of the arguments about their effects on transmission

- The brain is very complex in its working – this chapter only touches on the biology involved. For example, there is more than one reward pathway in the reward system and more than one brain region involved, so having one explanation for the mode of action of a recreational drug seems rather simplistic. Cannabis, for example, limits activity in the hippocampus and other areas, although it stimulates dopamine in the synapse in the reward system. It is too simple to say cannabis inhibits or excites – you need to specify what area of the brain is being discussed. Neurotransmitter functioning (including chemicals like cannabis) is complex.
- It is hard to study the mode of action of recreational drugs at the synapse. Brain scanning has helped, but scans still cannot get to the level of synaptic transmission. For example, information about cannabis has focused on GABAergic and glutamatergic transmission because those are the two transmitters that are more easily studied using electrophysiological techniques (Pertwee, 2014, in a book called *Handbook of Cannabis* – you only have to start reading the book to see the enormous complexity of studying these areas).
- Animal studies are used, where lesioning and ablations can be carried out (if ethical procedures are followed) but there might be differences in the functioning of animal brains that mean the findings do not suit humans. A weakness is the difficulty in studying this area.

Test yourself

1 Explain the mode of action of two recreational drugs at the synapse in the brain. **(6 marks)**

2 Evaluate what is known about the effect of recreational drugs on the transmission process in the brain. **(12 marks)**

The structure of the brain

There are many different brain areas, too many to explain in biological psychology for your course. To make your studies manageable, we concentrate here on structures that relate to aggression, together with some others of note.

The four lobes

The brain is made up of four lobes: the temporal lobe, the parietal lobe, the occipital lobe and the prefrontal lobe. The four lobes of the brain are shown below. Raine *et al.* (1997) considered all four lobes when they looked for differences in brain structure between 41 people pleading not guilty by reason of insanity to murder and 41 controls (pp. 176–184). Schmolck *et al.* (2002), who studied people with brain damage and how such damage might link to their memory problems, looked at the medial temporal lobe. Damage to the prefrontal lobe has been linked to aggression. For example, Phineas Gage, after an unfortunate accident, suffered damage to the prefrontal lobe, which seemed to affect his temperament. Gage's story is referred to when discussing Raine *et al.* (1997), the classic study for biological psychology in your course.

Lateralisation

The brain is in two halves, called hemispheres, which is called **lateralisation**. Some structures are the same across the two hemispheres, such as the lobes – these are bilateral. 'Bilateral' means two sides; 'unilateral' means one side.

The corpus callosum

The corpus callosum is the section that joins the two hemispheres. Any messages that travel between the two hemispheres pass through the corpus callosum. If this structure is split, then the individual cannot link messages between the two hemispheres.

Sperry, working in the 1960s, is a well-known researcher in the area of splitting the corpus callosum. Of course researchers would not do this to people; it would not be ethical. However, for medical reasons, to help with epilepsy, some people underwent a procedure to split the corpus callosum. Because splitting the corpus callosum affects functioning, this procedure was a last resort only for very severe epilepsy.

An example of difficulties caused by the two hemispheres not communicating with one another is vision. The left eye sends messages to the right brain and the right eye sends messages to the left brain. Someone with a split corpus callosum would have a message from the left eye going to the right side of the brain, and the right eye would send information to the left side of the brain. However, there would then be no communication between the two sides of the brain. Usually speech is in the left side of the brain. Someone would be able to say what they saw in the right eye, as that message goes to the left side of the brain, but what they saw in the left eye would not be named. Usually we see objects with both eyes so there would be no problem as the message would come from both eyes. So studies have been done whereby each eye has one thing to 'see', by holding a card up or similar means, to prevent the other eye from seeing the same thing. This is just one example of issues found in someone with a 'split brain' and it illustrates the importance of the corpus callosum.

Progress check 3.8

What is the role of the corpus callosum in the brain?

Methodological issues in assuming brain damage tells us brain function

There is an important methodological issue to consider when looking at studies of brain structure and linked brain functioning: when researchers find a natural example of brain damage or an example of brain damage occurring from medical intervention or accident, they study any problems with functioning in that person – they then assume that any problems relate to the damage and conclude that the damaged part of the brain has the function that is missing.

For example, if someone with a split corpus callosum cannot join messages from one eye with messages from the other eye (assuming the eyes see different things), this is taken as evidence that the corpus callosum is where messages from each eye merge or cross. However, it may be that there is other damage that has caused the problem in functioning. In fact, as you will have seen in your study of case studies of patients with brain damage, there does seem to be a lot of evidence for the methodological assumption that having damage to an area and having an impairment means the impairment links to the damage. However, it is possible that how we study the brain is not sophisticated or precise enough to draw such the conclusions.

Progress check 3.9

What is the reason for using people with brain damage to study brain functioning?

Brain structure and aggression

The prefrontal cortex

The prefrontal cortex is involved in aggression, as Raine *et al.* (1997) and others have discovered. Methods used to find out which parts of the brain are associated with aggression include case studies of patients with brain damage and various neuroimaging techniques, including PET, MRI and fMRI scanning.

The **cortex** of the brain is the outer layer. Structures below this outer layer are part of the **sub-cortex**. There are various parts to the prefrontal cortex, including (but not only) the orbitofrontal cortex, lateral prefrontal cortex and ventromedial cortex. The brain is very complex – what is given in this chapter is only a small part of how the brain functions and what structures are involved.

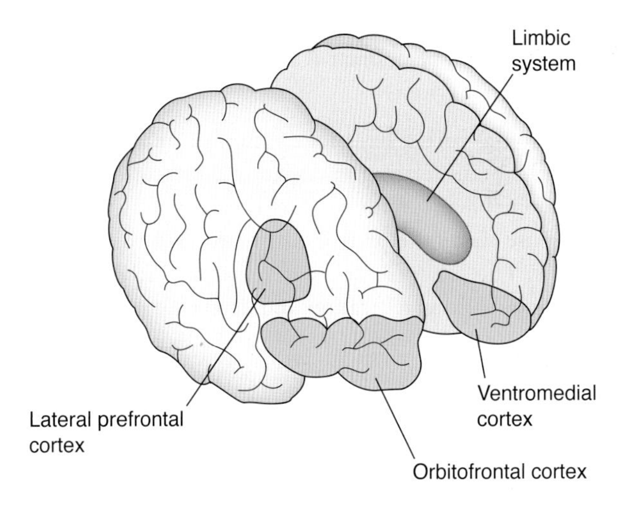

The prefrontal cortex is in both hemispheres and has different parts

Definitions

Cortices is the plural of cortex. The **cortex** is the outside layer of the brain and features of the brain; below that layer is the **sub-cortex**.

STUDY HINT

A story using terms can help. Imagine three people having a discussion. Orbitofrontal, though nearly broke, is talking about spending his last savings on a 'Round the World' ticket as he wants to travel for a year. Lateral prefrontal wants him to put that thought to one side as she thinks he should work to build up his savings for the future. Ventromedial is the mediator in their argument. Ventromedial suggests Orbitofrontal works for six months before going round the world, so that he can afford the ticket and still have some savings This is just an example to show how you can help your learning.

Prefrontal cortex role in emotions

As an example to show that a brain region relates not just to one behaviour or emotion, it is worth noting that the prefrontal cortex is also implicated in depression. Depression links to the orbitofrontal, ventromedial and lateral prefrontal cortices. The lower the activity in the prefrontal cortex, the more likely there will be depression. Therefore, the prefrontal cortex relates to emotions. It is reasonable then to fit aggression into the picture of the prefrontal cortex, though possibly the prefrontal cortex is more about regulating emotions and so aggression comes from lack of regulation, rather than aggression itself coming from the prefrontal cortex. Aggression might be defined as the lack of regulation or control over behaviour.

The prefrontal cortex has a lot of connections with parts of the brain relating to dopamine, serotonin and norepinephrine, which relate to emotions, so it makes sense to say the prefrontal cortex has a role in emotions. The orbitofrontal cortex is linked to our accepting delayed gratification and deferring rewards. The ventromedial cortex is linked to the experience of emotions and the lateral prefrontal cortex is involved in making choices in behaviour by letting us see the options. These features can be summarised as helping us to regulate our behaviour. The prefrontal cortex in the left hemisphere seems to be involved in positive emotions and the right hemisphere in negative emotions, so not only do different parts of a brain structure have different functions, but the two halves also are important. Not only are the parts of the brain complex but they interact with one another, of course, which adds to the complexity. For example, it is thought that the left side of the prefrontal cortex has a role in regulating negative emotions from the amygdala in the limbic system. The limbic system, and in particular the amygdala, is implicated in aggression, as you will see.

Explore

Explore the idea that having control, such as deferring rewards and making choices from options, might be a survival trait. Perhaps humans with those attributes survived to pass on their genes, whereas those without did not pass on their genes. It can be claimed that the functions of the prefrontal cortex have evolved. Having control over emotions and withdrawing rather than fighting might have been a useful attribute.

Prefrontal cortex role in aggression

Bechara and van der Linden (2005) reviewed studies that looked at the prefrontal cortex and confirmed that the area seems to regulate behaviour and defer rewards, so it is about planning. Bechara and van der Linden link decision-making with the ventromedial cortex. Damage to the prefrontal cortex means someone might focus on the present and not be able to plan long term, and this would tend to mean wanting immediate rewards too. This is not saying that the prefrontal cortex is 'for' aggression, but it is saying that the prefrontal cortex is about regulating behaviour and emotions, and damage there can mean someone is not able to control aggressive reactions. The prefrontal cortex has links to the amygdala that are inhibitory (messages from there are inhibited) and damage to the prefrontal cortex can mean not inhibiting such messages. The amygdala is linked to violent behaviour. Another region of the prefrontal cortex is the dorsolateral region, which has been found to link to inhibition and impulse control (Perach-Barzilay *et al.*, 2012).

Explore

You can find the study by Perach-Barzilay *et al.* (2012) online: http://sans.haifa.ac.il/publications/TMS&Aggression_Article.pdf. The study discusses the role of the prefrontal cortex in aggression as well as the role of neuroimaging in uncovering brain functioning.

Progress check 3.10

Give two pieces of evidence that show that the prefrontal cortex is involved in aggression.

Evidence that the prefrontal cortex regulates emotions and behaviour

Raine *et al.* (1998) carried out a study to see if violence that came from emotion was different from violence that was planned. The study used controls (as in Raine *et al.*, 1997) and PET scanning. Raine *et al.* (1998) found that people who had shown emotional impulsive violence (offenders) differed in their prefrontal cortex compared with those who had shown planned 'predatory' violence (also offenders). They found that there was lower left and right prefrontal functioning in the emotional impulsive offenders and other differences too in sub-cortical functioning. The planned predatory offenders had normal prefrontal functioning compared with the controls, though they had high right sub-cortical functioning, so there were some differences with controls. The researchers concluded that the offenders who had shown emotional impulsive aggression had not been able to regulate their behaviour because of low prefrontal cortex functioning, which fits with the explanation about prefrontal cortex functioning.

Study of interest

There are links between alcohol and aggression and one review of studies in that area links the idea of recreational drug use with aggression in humans. The brain areas linked to are the amygdala and the prefrontal cortex. Heinz *et al.* (2011) reviewed studies that looked at alcohol and aggression and suggest that findings include how environment, such as early life stress, are important, as well as genetic variations in genes that relate to serotonin transmission, specifically relating to serotinergic and GABAergic neurotransmission. These environmental stress and genetic predispositions increase activity in the amygdala and lower activity in the prefrontal cortex. These two effects on activity in the brain link with alcohol use and also with impulsive aggression. Also as alcohol is drunk more, this can affect executive control more (in the prefrontal cortex), leading to more aggressive tendencies. Note how Heinz *et al.* (2011) link nurture (early life stressors) and nature (genetic issues related to serotonin transmission) in their review. This is an example of a more holistic overview than reductionist studies like Raine *et al.* (1997) offer.

The limbic system

The limbic system includes the hippocampus, amygdala and hypothalamus. The hippocampus was considered in cognitive psychology in your course because it relates to memory. The hypothalamus regulates eating and the day–night cycle (among other functions). The amygdala relates to emotional responses to stimuli in the environment.

The limbic system has a role in self-preservation. The structures in the limbic system control our temperature, for example, and the fight-or-flight response, which is our arousal in the face of danger. What is controlled is in response to emotions rather than thinking, the limbic system being linked to our autonomic systems which responds 'automatically' to danger rather than in a planned way.

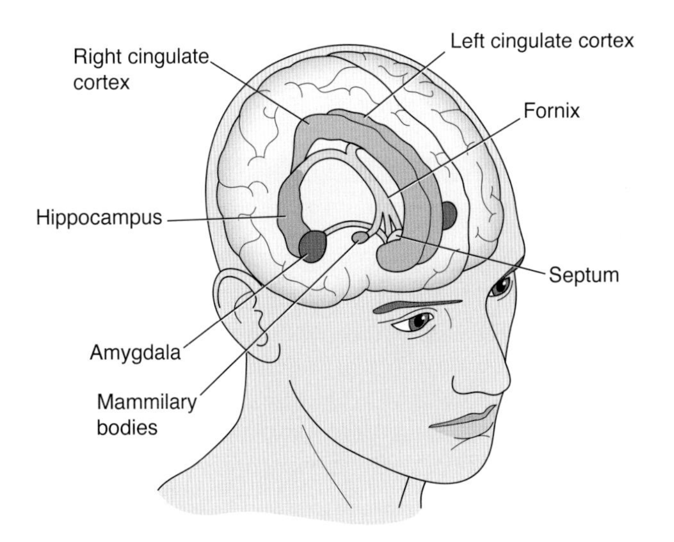

The limbic system links to aggression

Hypothalamus

The hypothalamus has a balancing role, called 'homeostasis'. This is about putting the body back into balance, like a thermostat regulating temperature. The hypothalamus regulates our hunger and thirst as well as our response to pain, anger, aggression and sexual satisfaction. It regulates the autonomic part of the nervous system too, which means regulating our blood pressure, pulse, breathing and arousal levels (fight or flight). The hypothalamus detects the levels of leptin in the body and leptin is released if we overeat, sensing the levels of fat in our bodies. By using levels of leptin, the hypothalamus controls our appetite. Lots of information goes to and from the hypothalamus.

Progress check 3.11

Outline the role of the hypothalamus.

Hippocampus

The hippocampus has an important role in taking short-term memories and converting them into long-term memories, as you will have read in Chapter 2. If someone cannot successfully build new long-term memories, they are effectively trapped in the present.

Amygdala

There are two amygdalae: the left and right amygdalae. In animal studies, if the amygdala is stimulated using an electric current, the animal shows aggression – this is taken as evidence that an aggressive response is one role of the amygdala. If the amygdala is removed, the animal becomes passive and unresponsive, the opposite of aggressive. Without an amygdala, an animal does not respond to fear either, so the amygdala is taken to have a role in arousal, aggression and the 'fight' response. The amygdala is the centre for identifying threat and its role is self-preservation.

Study of interest

Swantje *et al.* (2012) in Germany carried out MRI scanning of 20 healthy volunteers, who were all women and all right-handed. For each, the amygdala was measured by outlining the structure carefully using the brain scan and taking measurements. The Life History of Aggression Assessment was used to get an 'aggression' score for each participant. Tests were done to make sure the participants did not have psychiatric disorders and so on. The results showed that all the volunteers had a lifetime aggression score in the normal range. Those with a higher aggression score scored 16 to 18 per cent lower on amygdala volume. There was a significant negative correlation in that the more lifetime aggression, the smaller the amygdala volume. They concluded that volume of the amygdala can predict the personality trait of aggression in 'normal' people.

This study was chosen for a number of reasons: it gives up-to-date evidence of a link between the amygdala and aggression; it uses correlational analysis, which links well with the method section of biological psychology in your course; it uses scanning to find a measurement of the amygdala, again relating to the method section in this topic area; the people used are 'normal', which balances out other studies in this section where people either have damage to the brain or are offenders, or where animal studies are used; by using all women there was some control over gender, though the findings should perhaps only be generalised to women, and they were all right-handed, so another control.

Progress check 3.12

Which study found a strong negative correlation between people's self-report of their lifetime aggression and the volume of their amygdala?

Other parts of the limbic system

The cingulate gyrus is mentioned in studies that look at aggression and brain structure and functioning. It has a role in focusing attention on events that are emotional for the individual, and links the thalamus and hippocampus. It lies above the corpus callosum. The prefrontal lobe is also closely linked to the limbic system but not part of it.

The limbic system and aggression – studies using animals

1 Andy and Velamati (1978) carried out a study using cats. When they stimulated the hypothalamus and basal ganglia (part of the limbic system) of cats, the animals had aggressive seizures. Aggression was measured in a cat by the amount of hissing and growling as the cat freely walked around. Blocking catecholamine increased aggression; the opposite limited aggression. Epinephrine, norepinephrine and dopamine are catecholamines. Recall information about blocking such neurotransmitters in an earlier section of this chapter (p. 140).

2 Downer (1961) did studies with monkeys. The monkeys had one amygdala removed and the optic nerve cut. The monkey could have visual signals that went to an intact amygdala and visual signals that went to the **ablated** (removed) amygdala. If the monkeys had visual input that connected to the intact amygdala, they reacted in their normal way to the presence of humans, which was to be aggressive. If their visual input had no amygdala to reach, then the monkeys were much calmer and placid – behaviour that was not like their usual reactions. This is evidence for the amygdala being involved in an aggressive response to perceived threat.

Definitions

Lesions are cuts made in the brain either deliberately (e.g. in animals for the purpose of study) or accidentally. **Ablations** are similar to lesions but involve removing a structure.

STUDY HINT

The ethics of using animals in studies are discussed in Chapter 5 in the method section relating to learning theories. For the purposes of learning, results from using animals have been presented in this chapter, and hopefully you can accept this situation. The fact that they are used here does not mean the idea is supported. It is best if you make your own mind up after studying the ethics and arguments about using animals in this way. In academic study, however, such studies are used. In an examination, you can discuss in an academic way such usage, but you should avoid bringing in your own opinions, however hard that might be.

3 Hermans *et al.* (1993) showed that electrical stimulation of the hypothalamus gives aggression.

4 Delville *et al.* (1997) showed that the hypothalamus has receptors that interact with serotonin and vasopressin and determine aggression levels.

Progress check 3.13

Give two pieces of evidence from animal studies that link the limbic system with aggression.

Relationship between brain structure, neurotransmitter functioning and hormones as messengers in the brain

Note that in this section the focus is on brain structure and functioning and it is not directly on how functioning occurs such as by means of neurotransmitters at the synapse or by hormones. However, the information given earlier about neurotransmitter functioning is involved, as is mentioned in Delville *et al.*'s 1997 study. Serotonin is a neurotransmitter. Low levels of serotonin are related to aggression. Brain structure and function is linked, of course, to neurotransmitters as they send messages around the brain between the structures to enable and affect functioning. Vasopressin is a hormone and has many roles. One role for vasopressin is that it is released in the hypothalamus and is involved in aggression as well as temperature regulation. Hormones too are involved in messages in the brain. It can help to look at hormones, neurotransmitters and brain structures separately but, of course, they are all interrelated.

Issues and debates

One of the issues and debates in your course is reductionism and you will look at reductionism when you consider how far psychology is a science, an area of study in learning theories (Chapter 4). Studying the structures of the brain is reductionist - for example, the prefrontal cortex is just one structure and is subdivided into other structures to narrow the focus for the ease of research. Brain scanning covers the whole brain, but researchers narrow their focus to a small area so that they can manage the amount of information from a scan. When looking at brain structure and functioning, there is sometimes focus on neurotransmitter functioning or hormonal transmission, which again is reducing brain functioning to parts. Reductionism is a strength in scientific study as it enables controls, careful measurement and cause-and-effect conclusions. However, it misses an holistic view and reducing human behaviour like aggression to one brain structure like the amygdala is likely to reduce the complexity, perhaps to the extent that the knowledge gained is not useful.

Using animal studies to learn about human aggression

Blanchard and Blanchard (2003) suggest that it is reasonable to link conclusions about aggressive behaviour in animals to aggression in humans. They point out that humans, like animals, protect their territory and have competition for resources, including status and territory. They show that animals, like humans, challenge for resources and then, given higher status, turn to controlling those resources. Blanchard and Blanchard discuss evidence linking the endocrine system and aggression, not the limbic system; however, their points apply to all studies using animals and wanting to draw conclusions that relate to human behaviour.

STUDY HINT

You can use the animal studies given in this chapter when discussing issues around animal use, such as generalisability to humans.

Study of interest

Gorka *et al.* (2013) looked at the role of alcohol in judging emotions, which links to aggression. The researchers knew from other studies that the amygdala has a controlling effect on reaction to incoming stimuli and studies have also shown that alcohol acts on the amygdala, which is how alcohol seems to affect someone's reactions to social stimuli. It is also known that the amygdala 'communicates' with the prefrontal cortex and that the prefrontal cortex has a planning and controlling role.

Gorka *et al.* (2013) used fMRI scanning and had a group drinking alcohol and another group not doing so, but using a **placebo**, so the participants did not know which group they were in. Gorka *et al.* wanted to look at the links between the amygdala and the prefrontal cortex with and without alcohol. The links were to be examined in the presence of emotion-producing stimuli, which means they looked at happy, angry or fearful faces. The study used a double-blind technique, randomised controlled trials and a between-subjects design. Double-blind means that neither the participants nor the actual experimenters knew which people were in the 'alcohol' group and which were in the placebo (no alcohol) group. Randomised controlled trials means that the individuals were randomly put into either an alcohol or placebo group. Between-subjects design means that the design was independent groups - different people were in the two conditions. This means each participant either had the alcohol or the placebo.

Twelve heavy social drinkers were the participants. fMRI scanning was used while the individual was looking at the faces. The focus from the scans was to look at connections between the amygdala and the prefrontal cortex. They found that when looking at fearful or angry faces the 'alcohol' group showed less activity than the placebo group between the amygdala and the right orbitofrontal cortex. While looking at happy faces, there was reduced activity between the amygdala and the left orbitofrontal cortex. They concluded that alcohol affected the connection between the amygdala and prefrontal cortex.

This study was chosen for a number of reasons: it uses fMRI scanning so can be used as an example for the use of that method; it uses interesting experimental techniques, such as double-blind and an independent groups design as well as randomised control; it links the amygdala and the prefrontal cortex to aggression loosely in suggesting that alcohol affects functioning between the two and the study finds different processing for those under the influence of alcohol, including different processing for angry and fearful faces compared with happy ones; the study looks at effects of alcohol (and you need to look at the effects of drugs on the synapse); the study is useful because it gives evidence for an earlier claim that the left brain is more for positive emotions and the right brain for negative ones (p. 146).

Definition

A **placebo** is something that does not contain the substance of interest, but it is not possible for the participant to tell whether it is a placebo or the real thing. This is used in studies as a control. The participants (and often the experimenter) does not know whether they are in the placebo group or the experimental group.

Evaluation of the claim that there are brain structures that relate to aggression

Strengths

- There is a lot of evidence from both animal and human studies that certain areas of the brain link to aggression, such as the prefrontal cortex and the limbic system, perhaps in particular the amygdala. Animal studies show that electrical stimulation of the hypothalamus gives an aggression response (e.g. Andy and Velamati, 1978). Studies of humans show, for example, that there is a negative correlation between the volume of the amygdala and self-reported lifetime aggression (Swantje *et al.*, 2012).
- With the advent of scanning, such as PET and fMRI scanning, which has more precision than earlier scanning techniques, more can be measured and studied. Brain structures can be isolated and measured either measuring glucose functioning, as with PET scanning (e.g. Raine *et al.*, 1997), or measuring actual volume, as with MRI scanning (e.g. Swantje *et al.*, 2012). Measurements are reliable and can be done by more than one person – this gives scientific credibility.

Weaknesses

- Animal studies might have findings that cannot be generalised to humans because of differences between humans and animals. Animals do not have the same prefrontal cortex as humans – it is smaller, for example. There are other differences, including the role of consciousness and planning (which the prefrontal cortex is involved in).
- Scanning is said to be reliable; however, validity is in question because the scan has to take place while someone is processing information in some way, and this processing is likely to be an artificial task. People do not function normally in brain scanners. For example, Gorka *et al.* (2013) asked people to look at happy, angry or fearful faces and tested their prefrontal cortex to amygdala connectivity under the influence of alcohol. This might not represent everyday functioning, such as how we make judgements and react to faces.

Test yourself

1. Explain two brain areas according to how they might be linked to aggression. **(8 marks)**
2. Evaluate the claim that it is brain structure that gives aggression in someone. **(12 marks)**

The role of genes in human behaviour

In your course, there are three theories you need to cover: the role of hormones, the role of evolution and Freud's psychodynamic theory as it relates to aggression, as an alternative to biological explanations of behaviour.

The role of hormones continues nicely from the role of neurotransmitters and the role of different brain structures in aggression. However, before looking at hormones in detail, it is worth considering what gives rise to hormones in the body, which is our genotype. Therefore, genes are explained first, followed by evolution theory, before looking at the role of hormones. The psychodynamic ideas are given last as they are not biological – they are given as a contrasting theory to biological explanations.

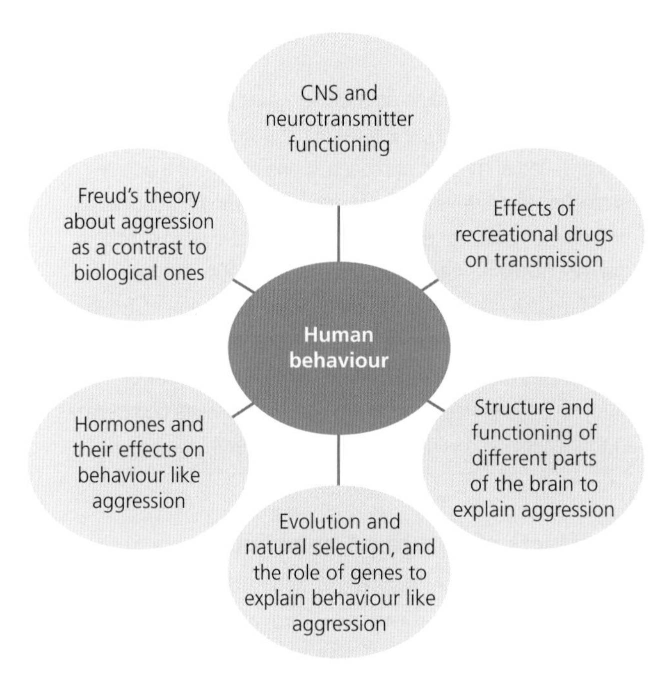

What is required in this section and how it relates to human behaviour, specifically aggression

Explaining the term 'gene'

A **gene** contains a set of instructions and is a carrier of information. Each individual human has a **genotype**, which is the genetic constitution. Each person also has a **phenotype**, which is what the individual becomes when their genes interact with each other and with the environment. Genes are inherited – 50 per cent from each of our biological parents.

Definitions

Our **genotype** is what our genes will dictate in us and our **phenotype** is what we become when our genes interact, both with one another and with our environment and experiences.

A gene consists of a long strand of DNA (deoxyribonucleic acid). A chromosome is a double chain of DNA. One of the functions of DNA is to control gene activity.

Genes contain bases (chemicals) called guanine (G), cytosine (C), adenine (A) and thymine (T) arranged along the gene. The coding sequence (three-letter combinations of G, C, A or T, each coding for an amino acid) contains the instructions as to what that gene will produce.

The sequence is copied to produce an RNA (ribonucleic acid) molecule. RNA then organises the synthesis of proteins that act according to the genetic instructions. Transfer RNA (tRNA) transports amino acids to the ribosomes of the cell and messenger RNA (mRNA) acts as a model to form proteins. The proteins dictate how the organism develops.

The **genome** is the term for all the genes in a cell. It is thought that the human genome has just under three billion base pairs and around 20,000 to 25,000 genes. The genetic message contains millions of combinations of base pairs in DNA carried on chromosomes. Humans have 23 pairs of chromosomes in each cell (apart from egg and sperm cells). Genes can be physically linked so that if one gene is inherited the other gene is also inherited.

Some genes always lead to certain characteristics; these are called **dominant genes**. To produce a characteristic, dominant genes need to be on only one of a pair of chromosomes. Some genes need more than one copy to produce a characteristic; these are called **recessive genes**. Recessive genes have to be on both chromosomes of a pair for the characteristic to occur. If a recessive gene is present on only one of the pair of chromosomes, the characteristic will not appear in that particular organism. However, they can be passed on, so the characteristic might appear in a future generation. Characteristics can be aspects of appearance (e.g. eye colour), personality (e.g. shyness) or behaviour (e.g. aggression). Genes do not control all human characteristics because the environment also has a part to play.

Definitions

Each person's **genome** is all the genes in a cell, and **genes** are the messengers, carrying a set of instructions. Each gene is a double strand of DNA, and this controls gene activity. A gene sequence is copied to produce RNA molecules and RNA organises proteins, which carry out the gene's instructions. **Dominant genes** will always lead to their characteristic(s) and **recessive genes** need more than one copy so will not always lead to their characteristic(s) (they have to be on both chromosomes for the characteristic to occur). Genes can link and some characteristics come from a combination of genes – if one gene is inherited, in some cases this means that other genes are inherited too.

Examples of the effects of genes on humans

- Human chromosome 4 has a marker known as G8. It is not yet known what G8 contributes, but the gene for Huntington's disease lies close to it. If a parent and child both have Huntington's disease, then in 98 per cent of cases they both have the same form of G8 marker. This suggests that the gene for Huntington's disease travels with the G8 marker.
- Some diseases and characteristics are sex-linked in that they are controlled by the sex genes. This is why some diseases/characteristics are more common in one particular sex. For example, most colour-blind people are men.

- If one parent contributes two copies of chromosome 21, then the child has three copies and the consequence is Down's syndrome.

> **Explore**
> Use the internet or another source to look up the story of the decoding of the human genome, which was carried out in 2003. Consider the claims of Dr Craig Venter, who stated in September 2007 that he had decoded the 'real' human genome. Think about why understanding the human genome is important. For example, look up chromosome 19 to find out what diseases are associated with it. Look up Huntington's disease to see why understanding genetics is important, but be aware that you are a student of psychology and must stick to ethical guidelines, including taking care when spreading information about what you learn.

- Cancer involves damage to the DNA and the damage occurs as the cells divide. For example, in one form of leukaemia, almost every white blood cell carries an unusually small chromosome 22. The bone marrow produces damaged cells that reproduce more quickly than other cells and the disease spreads. It appears that chromosome 22 is smaller because part has broken off and transferred to chromosome 9. This transfer leads to a new abnormal protein being produced that speeds up cell division. However, there may be other factors involved when cancer develops, such as environmental triggers.

Environmental triggers on genes

Sometimes genes do not influence physical characteristics unless the 'right' environmental conditions occur. One example is phenylketonuria (PKU). You might be aware that all babies born in the UK have a blood sample taken from their heels immediately after birth. This is to test for PKU, a disease that leads to brain damage. If a child's diet is carefully controlled, the damage from PKU can be averted (i.e. the effect of the gene can be avoided). This example shows us that in this condition a controlled environment can prevent development of what genes have in store for us.

The nature–nurture debate

The genotype is the genetic constitution of an individual; the phenotype is the result of interaction between inherited characteristics and the environment. Psychologists are interested in separating nature (inherited characteristics) from nurture (experiences) because they want to find causes for behaviour.

> **Explore**
> When people are studied as a whole – their biological make-up, their experiences and the effects of the society they live in – this is called an holistic approach. If one aspect of a person is studied, this is a reductionist approach. When psychologists and scientists look at a person's genetic make-up in isolation, they are taking a reductionist approach because they are ignoring such aspects as the effect of the environment. Explore these issues and draw up a table showing the strengths and weaknesses of both a reductionist and an holistic way of studying people. Reductionism is one of the issues and debates in your course and is also studied in Chapter 4.

The effects of nature on behaviour

The phrase 'effects of nature on behaviour' means the influence of genes and other biological structures. To discuss someone's nature, it would be necessary to consider the effects of neurotransmitter functioning, brain structure, genetic make-up and other related issues. The biological approach provides much information about the way 'nature' influences behaviour.

The effects of nurture on behaviour

The phrase 'effects of nurture on behaviour' means the effects of everything other than biological aspects – style of upbringing, experience of schooling, peer-group influences, position in the family (e.g. middle child), social and cultural influences, and other similar issues. For example, children who watch a lot of violent television may be more likely to behave aggressively (see Bandura's work in Chapter 4); children who have not made secure attachments with their main caregivers may find it harder to form secure relationships when older (you will cover Bowlby's work in Year 2 if you study child psychology).

Interaction of nature and nurture

Some areas in psychology (e.g. personality, depression and alcoholism) are often studied by looking at 'nature'. Some areas (e.g. criminal behaviour and phobias) are studied by looking at 'nurture'. In fact, many areas in psychology, including depression, alcoholism, criminal behaviour and phobias, are studied by looking at how nature and nurture interact to produce such behaviour.

For example, stress arises when people think that they do not have the resources to cope. Stress involves a biological reaction that gets the body ready for 'flight or fight' (see earlier how the hypothalamus was said to be involved in that reaction) and then something in the environment triggers that biological reaction. Aspects of both nature and nurture are needed to explain stress.

STUDY HINT

As well as an understanding of the meaning of 'nature' and 'nurture', you need to have some examples so that you can discuss the nature-nurture debate. If you are studying for the AS examination you don't need to learn about the issues and debates (nature-nurture is one of the issues and debates), but it is useful to have some understanding so you can use it in evaluation and also when learning about twin studies.

Progress check 3.14

Explain the nature-nurture debate using the concept of genes.

Evolution theory and natural selection

Genes guide a lot of our characteristics and how we are. We are a collection of genes, 50 per cent from our mother and 50 per cent from our father, which make up our genotype. It is interesting to ask how humans come to have the genome that they have. The theory that is widely accepted is that human genes have developed through evolution, through the mechanism of survival of the fittest, as have the genes of all other organisms. The way genes are passed on is through reproduction. Each of us inherits our genes from our parents and the characteristics that come from our genes are also inherited.

STUDY HINT

You will have come across the ideas of evolution and survival of the fittest in other areas of study, such as GCSE Science. It is worth drawing on that understanding for this section of biological psychology.

Evolution

Evolution is how inherited characteristics in organisms (including humans) change from generation to generation. The process is at the organism level, and is also at other levels, such as in the DNA of an organism. Not only do some changes in inherited characteristics lead to differentiation between species, so the species evolves in a positive way, but they can also lead to extinction of species, which evolves in a negative way.

Definition

Evolution refers to how inherited characteristics in organisms evolve, i.e. how they change from generation to generation. Explanations for evolution are the theories of survival of the fittest and natural selection, genetic mutation and genetic drift.

Darwin is the name most connected with evolution. He put forward the idea that evolution takes place through **natural selection**.

Charles Darwin, whose name is linked to the idea of survival of the fittest to explain evolution; in 1842, he began to write *On the Origin of Species*, explaining his ideas

Before Darwin, others had noted that there was evolution of species and different ideas were proposed to explain evolution. One theory was that a species could degenerate into a different species (through problems occurring in reproduction). Another theory suggested that during reproduction there could be modifications in the organism, leading in the end to a new species. In a different theory, Lamarck thought that parents either used or did not use certain characteristics and those that were used (and useful in the environment) were those passed on to offspring – this was called 'Lamarckism'. Others thought that species were not related and so there was no evolution. These ideas did not have enough evidence to be backed by the whole scientific community.

It was around this time that Darwin considered the idea that in an environment there would be a large population of an organism and not all would survive. Importantly, he noted that not all would survive to the stage of reproduction. It was this focus on what would lead to survival so that there could be reproduction that started the idea of natural selection, which led to Darwin's explanation of evolution as 'survival of the fittest' (though the full idea developed later, it took some time and other evidence to develop). Others were working on similar ideas and in 1858 (Darwin started writing about his theory in 1838) Wallace sent Darwin the same idea as Darwin himself was working on, and they presented the same idea separately at around this time.

Definition

Natural selection refers to how some characteristics are inherited because they aid survival of an organism so that there can be reproduction and passing on of genes, whereas some characteristics do not aid survival in the environment so there is no reproduction of those genes.

Natural selection/survival of the fittest

Natural selection refers to the way some characteristics might aid survival over other characteristics which do not help survival. The important points Darwin took into account are that organisms have more offspring than are required, some characteristics aid survival, and characteristics are inherited. He put this together to suggest that those characteristics that aided the survival of the organism so that that organism reproduced their genes are bound to be the characteristics for survival, by definition. Any characteristic that did not help survival would die out because that organism with that characteristic would not survive to reproduce. If the organism did not reproduce its genes, those genes would die out.

This means that we are the best that we could be in terms of how we have evolved, as all our inherited characteristics will be those that helped our ancestors to survive and reproduce. Unhelpful inherited characteristics would not be passed on through reproduction. That is why the idea is called **survival of the fittest**. This is 'survival of the fittest genes' – 'fittest' means 'most suitable' in this phrase. For example, Darwin considered finches and their different shaped beaks which would suit different environments. Those with the 'suitable' beak shape in a certain environment would feed, survive and reproduce, thus passing on the genes for the suitable beak shape.

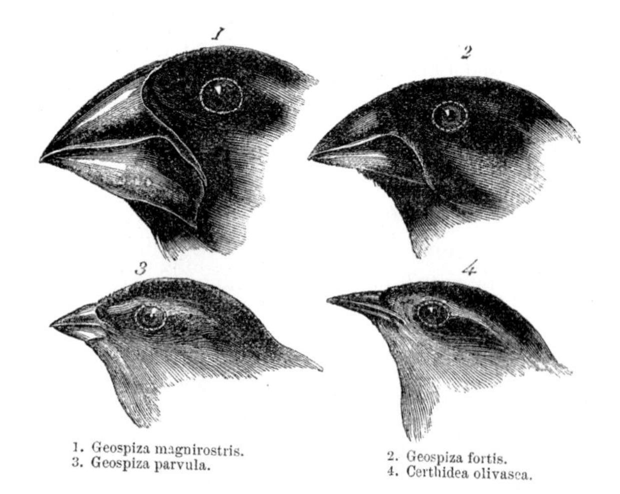

Darwin considered finches and their different shaped beaks which would suit different environments. Those with the 'suitable' beak shape in a certain environment would feed, survive and reproduce, thus passing on genes for the suitable beak shape

Survival of the fittest is one explanation for how organisms adapt. Only inherited characteristics that help with survival so that reproduction can take place are passed on in genes because it is only through reproduction that genes are passed on. There can also be **genetic mutations** that can change genes in a species (or lead to a new species) as well as random chance in genes that are passed on, which is called **genetic drift**.

Definition

Survival of the fittest refers to how organisms that suit their environment will survive long enough to reproduce so their genes will continue, whereas organisms not suited to their environment will not survive so their genes will not continue.

Progress check 3.15

Name three mechanisms that affect evolution of the human species.

Natural selection only works if there is sufficient **variation** in the species for certain genes to lead to characteristics that help the organism to survive and other genes that give characteristics not useful for survival. This process will not work if there is very little variation in the species. Variation comes from mutations. Having said that, in spite of mutations and other features of reproduction such as genetic drift, species have many genes in common, with only a small amount of variation. That small amount is what leads to natural selection and evolution of the species, including producing new species. Humans and chimpanzees only differ in about 5 per cent of their genes (though it is a bit more complicated because it depends on which genes are shared), but they are, as we know, considerably different. Those small differences in genes can make a big difference to the organism.

Definition

Variation in the case of natural selection means differences between the genes of organisms in a species.

Progress check 3.16

Why would natural selection not occur without variation within a species?

Genetic mutation

Definition

Genetic mutation refers to a permanent change in the gene sequence, which can come, for example, from a virus or damage due to radiation.

Genetic mutation can affect the organism visibly, can occur with no obvious effect or can prevent a gene from functioning properly. A mutation can occur in a protein, for example, which can be harmful to an organism. It is not just about a mutation that has a visible effect. In an organism, mutations might not be beneficial and so there is a DNA repair mechanism, though DNA repair can go wrong, which can lead to a mutation. Mutation itself can involve large new sections of DNA, and these mutations can be advantageous. Mutations can come from external sources such as carcinogens (which cause cancer). There are many different causes of mutations. Thinking about evolution, it will be the mutations that are advantageous to the organism that will change the gene pool, in that those that are of benefit increase the chances of reproduction and so the mutated gene would then be inherited. This type of mutation can lead to a new species being produced, if it is different enough from the original, and that is how different species emerge.

Evolution rests to an extent on the idea of genetic mutation. Survival of the fittest is affected by genetic mutation as not only will those with the original genes survive if their characteristics suit the environment, but also those with advantageous mutations will survive too, as they will have 'fit' (suitable) characteristics. It could be that the original genes aid survival as a survival of the fittest explanation suggests. Alongside that, genetic mutations might develop other 'fit' characteristics that lead to survival too, through the 'survival of the fittest' mechanism.

Genetic drift

Definition

Genetic drift refers to the way that, when an organism inherits 50 per cent of the genes from the father and 50 per cent from the mother, there are chance factors involved in which genes are inherited. Genes can 'drift' out of the gene pool in this way.

Genetic drift refers to the way that not 100 per cent of genes are passed on through reproduction in the case of each organism – each male and female human passes on 50 per cent of their genes. Therefore, there is an element of chance in which genes are passed on to an offspring, and that element of chance might mean that some genes are lost. If genes are lost, this reduces genetic variation. It reduces the genes that are available to be inherited. This seems to be a minor process in evolution compared with genetic mutations and natural selection (Fisher, e.g. 1930). However, Kimura (1968) thought that genetic drift had a more important role to play, with many genetic changes being due to genetic drift.

Explore

Fisher worked on analysis of variance and statistical tests as well as working on Darwin's theory of evolution. You could research his contribution to these different areas in science as it makes interesting reading.

Progress check 3.17

Explain the difference between genetic mutation and genetic drift as mechanisms for evolution.

Heritable traits

Not all characteristics or traits are heritable (able to be inherited). Eye colour is inherited, temperament is likely to be inherited, many other characteristics are inherited; however, many other traits in humans are not inherited – they come from interaction with the environment. Many characteristics that we have come from an underlying genetic tendency combined with experiences in the environment. For example, someone might have a genetic height from their parents (for example, both parents are tall and the child has inherited 'tall' genes); however, their final height/size can be affected by their environment (for example, nutrition might affect growth).

Kin selection

Darwin's theory of natural selection works at the level of one individual's genes being passed on if that individual survives to reproduce. This idea has been criticised because animals have been observed using altruistic behaviour. For example, animals can save their group by calling out to warn them of danger, even though by calling out they risk their own life. This seemed to be contrary to the idea of natural selection – that one animal would not live to reproduce and pass on its genes. However, the others in the group would survive – at least they are more likely to survive – if they have an animal 'on watch'.

It is claimed that this is not going against the idea of natural selection. The animals that are being saved in the example here are likely to be related to the animal 'on watch', on the principle that offspring will be those nearby. This means that the genes of the animal drawing attention to itself by giving the warning are in fact being saved, because at least some of that animal's genes will be passed on through the offspring that are saved. This is the **kin selection** theory. **Direct fitness** in natural selection is the idea that an individual's genes are passed on when that individual survives in an environment long enough to reproduce their genes. **Inclusive fitness** is the idea that genes can survive when relatives survive and reproduce too. This idea came from Hamilton (1963). Natural selection, given this interpretation, is about the genes that adapt to an environment surviving through reproduction rather than any individual. Looked at in this way, features that might be seen as disadvantageous (e.g. animals with bright colouring might attract predators) can be seen as advantageous to the gene (bright colouring also attracts a mate). The closer the animal is to those around it in terms of genes (the closer the kinship), the more beneficial it is for that animal to use self-sacrificing behaviour. That is, the more beneficial it is to the animal's genes.

Definitions

Kin selection is the idea that it is not necessarily that the individual organism most suited to the environment survives to reproduce its genes. Kin selection emphasises that the genes survive and the gene is driving the behaviour (being suitable for the environment and so surviving to reproduce). This explains altruism - acting in a way that is risky to the individual in order to save others. The 'others' that are saved are likely to be relatives in many animal situations, and relatives share genes, so altruistic acts can be disadvantageous to the individual but will benefit the gene. **Direct fitness** is when a gene gives a characteristic that benefits survival of the individual so they live to reproduce and pass on that gene. **Inclusive fitness** involves direct fitness and also how a gene, with a characteristic that seems to be disadvantageous to the individual but can help relatives of that individual, will also survive to be passed on.

Examples of organism altruism include vampire bats sharing blood, and ground squirrels, prairie dogs and meerkats giving warning calls.

Group selection

Group selection holds that behaviour that protects a group benefits the individuals in the group. The individuals in a group might survive when they might not survive as individuals because a group can help with protection from predators and protecting resources. This is still direct fitness, because it is the individual that benefits and the individual's genes that predispose that individual to be a 'social' being and live in a group, although the idea of 'group' is specific and not just about any 'group' behaviour, as is explained below.

Definition

Group selection refers to how social beings are benefitted in that they are more protected in terms of safety, food and shelter, and so individuals that are predisposed by their genes to live in groups are likely to survive and pass on their genes.

Wilson is a proponent of group selection. The idea is that a group can help with care of offspring, there can be adults of different generations in a society, and there can be division of labour within a group. In a group, there can be individuals who cannot do some of the necessary work, but as a group all the necessary work is covered by the group members as a whole. Clearly there are a lot of 'survival' benefits in group selection. It is not like kin selection, in that the group will not always share genes (though some will); it is the success of living in a group that leads to survival of the genes that give such group co-operation behaviour. Wilson gives the example of species like ants and bees. In such species, there might be a queen, soldiers and workers. This type of group living is called 'eusocial' (Batra, 1966) and is a special type of group living because it has these specific roles that benefit individuals and that individuals cannot fulfil alone.

Definition

Eusocial refers to groups that function as a whole, with different roles and abilities, such that the individuals could not perform all the required roles alone.

It is interesting that organisms exhibiting eusocial behaviour can come to be unable to reproduce as that is not their role in the colony (such as worker bees). That role survives, however, so the genes for that behaviour are being passed on. This seems to go against the theory of natural selection, and it means that those in the colony that do reproduce must carry the genes for all the different behaviours in that colony that are carried out by organisms that cannot themselves reproduce.

Problems with group selection theory

There are problems with group selection theory if it is taken out of the context of 'eusocial colonies' and applied to all animal group living. Herd of deer seem to be a group but are just a lot of deer living together. They are not co-operating as a 'group' doing different roles, for example, so not a group in the sense of group selection theory. Kin selection theory shows that groups benefit genes because a 'warning' from one animal can seem to be self-destructive from a gene point of view, but if that warning saves family members then the gene can survive. However, this is a 'family' group and so a special group. Eusocial groups are special groups and it is that type of group where group selection theory works as an explanation of evolution. The point is that the survival of just any 'group' behaviour cannot be explained using group selection theory. It is not that the evolution of humans as social animals can be explained using group selection theory. Human social behaviour is better explained using the idea that an individual who searches out a group to live with has better survival opportunities and so that individual's genes will survive. Some say (e.g. Pinker, 2014) that it is important to separate 'group behaviour' from group selection theory.

Group selection theory can suggest that those who live in social groups, like humans, are better off in groups and individuals must support the group, such as fitting into an appropriate social role (which can be seen as an appropriate social class perhaps), or living in a hierarchy (which can mean having less power in the group). This goes against the idea that everyone in a society is equal. This is the sort of discussion that is being held about group selection theory and how it has been over-generalised to apply to all group behaviour. It is the biological explanation, however, that is under discussion, as much as moral arguments.

> **Explore**
>
> Richard Dawkins and Edward Wilson, two extremely important people in the area of evolution and natural selection, have publicly argued about details around Darwin's theory, kin selection and group selection. See this *Guardian* article about their disagreement: www.theguardian.com/science/2012/jun/24/battle-of-the-professors.
>
> This is another link about kin selection, natural selection and group selection theories: http://edge.org/conversation/the-false-allure-of-group-selection.

Evaluation of the theory of natural selection

Strengths

- The theory of natural selection has stood the test of time and many studies have observed animal and human behaviour, and the behaviour of other organisms. The evidence supports the idea that genes are passed down through reproduction and those inherited features in an organism that do not aid survival up to reproduction age do not survive. Darwin's own evidence from his voyage on the *Beagle*, such as the different finches he found on different islands, is still used as evidence. Kettlewell in the 1950s found evidence that moths that fitted the environment and were not conspicuous lived to reproduce; non-fitting moths did not. This was about bird predation. The birds would eat more of the moths they could see. Kettlewell set about capturing moths and found 27.5 per cent of those he caught were dark-coloured moths in industrial woods, which were blackened by soot and industrial waste. Just 13 per cent of moths he found in the 'industrial' woods were light coloured. In contrast, 14.6 per cent of the moths he caught in non-industrial woods were light-coloured compared with 4.7 per cent dark-coloured moths. He took this as evidence for the theory of natural selection. In the non-industrial woods, light colour would be camouflage; in the industrial woods, dark colour would be camouflage.
- Darwin's theory is a good example of the use of scientific method in many ways. The theory reduces behaviour to the genes that guide it, and so the focus can be on the individual's genotype. Behaviours and characteristics that are inherited (but not learned behaviour) can be observed and a behaviour that enhances survival is said to have evolved because of that. Darwin had to carefully observe what inherited characteristics fitted the environment and then could conclude that it was because the behaviour or characteristic suited the environment that it survived. This seems to be good scientific method and the idea has credibility. Reducing to observable features means observations can be careful and supported by evidence (e.g. pictures).

Weaknesses

- A weakness with using reductionism to focus on specific aspects of behaviour is that the whole situation is not taken into account. Darwin looked at inherited behaviour and characteristics in terms of genetic transmission. Behaviour can be learned from observation – for example, animals learn from their parents. Behaviour can be learned by association as well, such as learning that something hot is to be avoided when the heat causes pain on the first encounter. Darwin was looking at inherited behaviours and explained how they might have evolved; however, he did not consider all behaviour. Kin selection theory, for example, had to be put forward to explain behaviour that seemed to be inherited but put the animal at risk (such as a warning call). Darwin's theory had to be expanded to suit such apparent contradictions. However, you could argue that he didn't claim his theory accounted for all behaviour – he was putting forward a theory to be worked on.
- A related weakness is that Darwin looked to confirm his theory, not to falsify it. The idea here is that only falsifying a theory can lead to proof. We can see the sun rise every morning and have a theory that the sun always rises every morning; however, one instance where it did not rise would disprove our theory. We can note as many instances when it rises in the morning as we like, we cannot prove the theory 'the sun always rises each morning'. We can only disprove such a theory by finding one piece of contradictory evidence. Falsification is meant to be good science. We should look to falsify a theory. Darwin, however, could find

ideas to falsify his theory, such as an animal giving an alarm call to save other animals at its own expense. He focused though on evidence that confirmed his theory.

STUDY HINT
You will find more information about psychology and science, including reductionism and falsification, when you study the learning theories section of your course, and in particular the focus on psychology as science.

- There are those who believe in creationism. Creationism holds that humans and the earth, together with all organisms and plants, are created and did not evolve into what they are through the mechanisms of natural selection. The idea of humans and the earth being created fits with Christianity and other religions. The idea is that God created the universe and different religions have different explanations about how this happened, though they agree on the basic idea that the earth was created by a God. Though there could be an argument that the theory of natural selection has scientifically gathered evidence and creationism does not have such evidence, another view is that science is not to be revered as the best way of understanding everything; beliefs are important too. This 'weakness' of the theory of natural selection is not only offered here as an evaluation point, it is included so you can consider your own beliefs if they go against Darwin's explanation – you would not be alone in sticking to your beliefs.

STUDY HINT
When studying issues in psychology, you need to be able to explain the content you are asked to cover and to discuss the content. However, you do not have to adopt the content if it goes against your own beliefs.

Progress check 3.18

Explain one strength and one weakness of Darwin's theory of natural selection.

Evolution, natural selection and aggression in humans

Aggression as well as its opposite, living together peacefully, are both human traits. According to the theory of natural selection, traits that humans (as individuals) have evolved over generations would be useful for survival. Humans have emotions and it is, therefore, assumed that emotions are useful for survival. Humans with the emotions that we have would have survived and passed on genes through reproduction. For example, caring for offspring enhances their chances of survival so having a 'maternal instinct' might be something we have inherited through natural selection. Living together peacefully in groups might increase the likelihood of survival (of the genes) because together people could fight off predators and live longer to reproduce more. These are the explanations that are offered by the theory of natural selection for human behaviours that might be genetically driven.

Explore

If you study child psychology in Year 2, you will look at issues such as attachments between a mother and child, so you can consider the issue of whether this is thought to be an instinct. In fact, studies tend to suggest it might not be, though not harming a child might be different from 'naturally' attaching to your own baby. This is an interesting area to research - you might want to explore further.

STUDY HINT
You can link this to what you have learned about regions of the brain, specifically the amygdala and other features of the limbic system, where it is thought emotions are found. Evolution is about genes and if our emotions come from natural selection (i.e. they aided survival and so we have evolved with those emotions), then the structures in the brain that link to those emotions would have been passed on.

Aggression might be something that led to survival in certain environments, such as aggression against threat in order to protect offspring. In this way, aggression can be explained using the theory of natural selection. Aggression might aid survival (of the genes) if a male is aggressive to protect a female (mate) or their child. It is interesting that in both these examples (protecting offspring or protecting mate) this is not aggression for the sake of it, but aggression that would aid survival of the genes. Even though this would not be planned by the individual to aid survival of the genes, it makes sense from a natural selection explanation to show how such behaviour would have benefitted the genes, which would then survive and be passed on to offspring.

Infidelity, jealousy and aggression

Aggression towards another person threatening a male–female pair makes sense in terms of evolution. If someone is jealous of another male talking to 'their' female, for example, that jealousy, which can take the form of aggression, makes sense in terms of natural selection. The male needs to reproduce to pass on their genes so another male competing for a female's attention would threaten that situation and it makes sense that an evolved response to such a threat is aggression. The male who aggressively defended 'his' female would have been the one who reproduced and whose genes survived. Jealousy and resulting aggression can be seen as a survival trait. A male can guard the female to protect them or can defend them. Both these strategies can lead to aggressive behaviour.

Buss and Shackleton (1997) gathered evidence to see what men do in response to feeling threatened in a relationship, to see if the evidence is there for the idea of natural selection. The researchers found men tended to give in to the female, giving her everything she wanted (debasement), and they were threatening to any other males around (intersexual threats). Both these strategies would aid survival of the male's genes. They also looked at women and how they maintained their own male–female relationships. For women, too, it is helpful for survival of their genes if they maintain a relationship to reproduce genes. However, they use different strategies according to Buss and Shackleton (1997). Women tend to threaten to leave the man if he is unfaithful and also to use verbal threats, such as saying 'he is taken'. For women it is a bit different as they know their baby is carrying on their genes, whereas a man needs to ensure any offspring is his. This, of course, is not really explaining at the level of decision-making by an individual, but explaining current inherited behaviour in humans that can be explained using the theory of natural selection and drawing on how humans might have behaved in the past. Dobash and Dobash (1984) found when studying violence against women that it often came from partner jealousy. Sexual jealousy was found to lead to aggression. These studies give evidence to the theory of natural selection and linking aggression as a trait that helps survival of genes.

Limited resources

Historically, one reason for aggression might be to fight over limited resources, such as food and shelter. Those who successfully defended food and shelter would survive longer and reproduce, so any such behaviour can be inherited as genes leading to such aggression would survive. Lorenz (1966) wrote about aggression being an evolved trait, particularly in males, to fight over limited resources.

Being seen as stronger

Humans who were aggressive and so seen as stronger in a social group would be the ones more likely to survive. If they are 'higher' in the group or not attacked because they are seen as stronger, that puts them in a good position with regard to passing on those genes.

STUDY HINT

Later, you will read about Freud's explanation for aggression, which links to the idea of aggression coming from a death instinct and using energy to protect the self from that death instinct. Aggression must be displaced (such as using aggression to protect the self) so that the individual is not taken over by the death instinct. The life instinct is about reproduction as well as staying alive – you can see that there is an element of natural selection and evolution in Freud's ideas. You can use this as evidence to show that Freud's views, despite many differences from biological explanations, have similarities too.

If asked to discuss the theory of natural selection to explain human aggression, you can use the theory itself to explain such behaviour. However, use examples that focus on aggression.

Evaluation of the 'evolution' explanation of aggression

Strengths

- The strengths of the theory of natural selection apply to a discussion about how the theory can explain aggression in humans. Therefore, one strength is the amount of evidence to support the theory, such as Kettlewell's study on moths.
- The scientific method is used in research looking at the theory. Darwin took careful observations and observed visible behaviour, which could be confirmed by others. There is scientific credibility in the idea of evolution. In fact, it is very widely accepted and an important theory, as Dawkins says in an interview published by the *National Geographic* magazine to commemorate 200 years since Darwin's birth. Dawkins says, 'Darwin devoted himself to making his theory clear, to listing all the evidence and spending decades of his life gathering the evidence so no one could doubt it.'

Explore

The interview with Richard Dawkins published in the National Geographic can be found here: http://natgeotv.com/uk/dawkins-darwin-evolution/dawkins-interview-darwin.

Weaknesses

- An aggressive individual might protect their offspring and, therefore, protect their genes, as the theory of natural selection would predict. However, by being aggressive, they might put themselves at risk. They might attract aggression in others. By using energy in aggressive behaviour, they might not use resources successfully and might not survive. Aggression can be seen as counter-productive in evolution terms as well as in a positive light regarding survival of the fittest (the most suited to the environment). Kin selection theory can answer this weakness to an extent as aggression on the part of one parent might save that parent's genes in their offspring. However, there is still the argument that behaviour that draws attention from predators puts the organism at risk of not surviving.
- If one theory explains behaviour, it can be used as a criticism of a different theory explaining the same behaviour. For example, the frustration-aggression theory, which suggests that aggression in humans comes from frustration from environmental influences, is an alternative to the theory of natural selection. Dollard *et al.*'s frustration-aggression theory (1939) suggests that if there is frustration and aggression cannot be displayed in a situation, that aggression can be displaced onto someone or something else. For example, if someone is frustrated at work but cannot show this because they are afraid of losing their job, they might take their frustration out on someone else by being aggressive to them. Evidence is found in conflicts between people where those being aggressive in the conflict are the ones with fewer of the resources, which frustrates them. This theory can, therefore, explain seemingly inexplicable aggression, such as why someone in the street turns on a stranger. The theory of natural selection does not have that flexibility.

Progress check 3.19

Explain how aggression from jealousy can be accounted for by the theory of natural selection.

Test yourself

To what extent can the role of natural selection explain human aggression? **(12 marks)**

The role of hormones in human behaviour

A final biological theory considers how hormones affect human behaviour.

What hormones are

Hormones are the chemical messengers of the body. They differ from neurotransmitters, which are also chemical messengers, in that hormones take time to relay messages and they work over time. Hormones have different roles in the body. They affect metabolism, which is the way the body converts food into energy, and they affect mood. They have a role in reproduction and sexual function. They also have an important role in growth and development. It only takes a very small amount of hormone to make a difference. Hormones travel via the circulatory system of the body, via the bloodstream. They can travel to parts of the body that are distant from one another, quite different from neuronal transmission at the synapse, where the synaptic gap is tiny.

The endocrine system makes hormones. The thyroid, adrenal, thymus and pituitary glands make up the endocrine system, which also includes the pancreas and hypothalamus. Hormones come from men's testes and women's ovaries as well. Hormones regulate physiology and behaviour, such as breathing and temperature, tissue function, metabolic rate, reproduction, stress and growth and development, as well as sleep and mood.

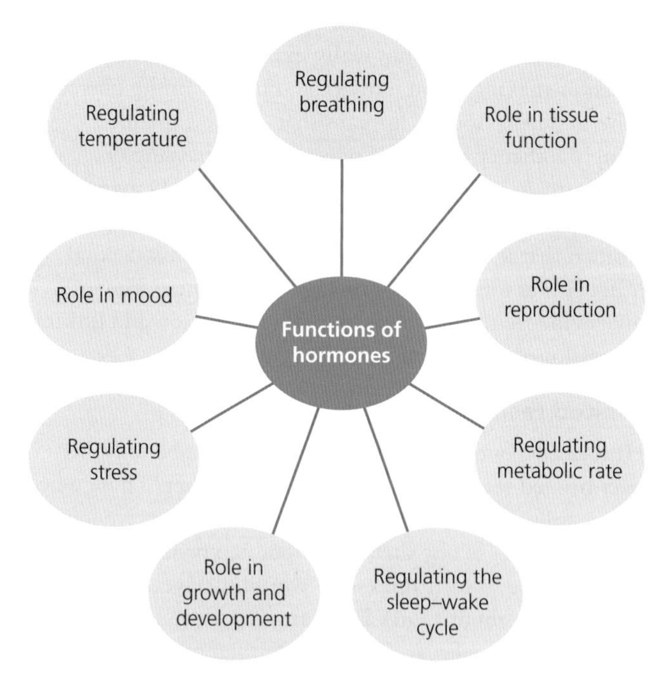

Functions of hormones in the human body

Progress check 3.20

List five functions of hormones in the human body.

Specific glands and their hormones

The pituitary gland is found in the brain and is very important for the production of hormones. For example, it produces the growth hormone. It also produces adrenocorticotropic, which produces cortisol. Cortisol is needed to combat stress and maintain a healthy blood pressure. The pituitary gland produces the antidiuretic hormone known as vasopressin, which regulates water balance in the body. There is also thyroid-stimulating hormone produced in the pituitary gland, which helps to regulate the body's metabolism. The hypothalamus links to the pituitary gland in producing hormones that help body regulation too. The thymus produces hormones linked to puberty. The pineal gland produces melatonin, which links to sleep. The testes produce testosterone, which has a role in maintaining the sex drive and producing sperm. The ovaries produce oestrogen and progesterone, which relate to women's menstrual cycle and the development of breasts. The thyroid controls the metabolism, and the adrenal glands relate to heart functioning and distributing stored fat. The parathyroid relates to good bone development, and the pancreas promotes healthy levels of blood sugar.

STUDY HINT

Vasopressin is mentioned in Chapter 5 when Brunnlieb *et al.*'s (2013) study using fMRI scanning is outlined. It is useful to make links as much as you can in your course, as that will help you to get a good overview of psychology and help your learning.

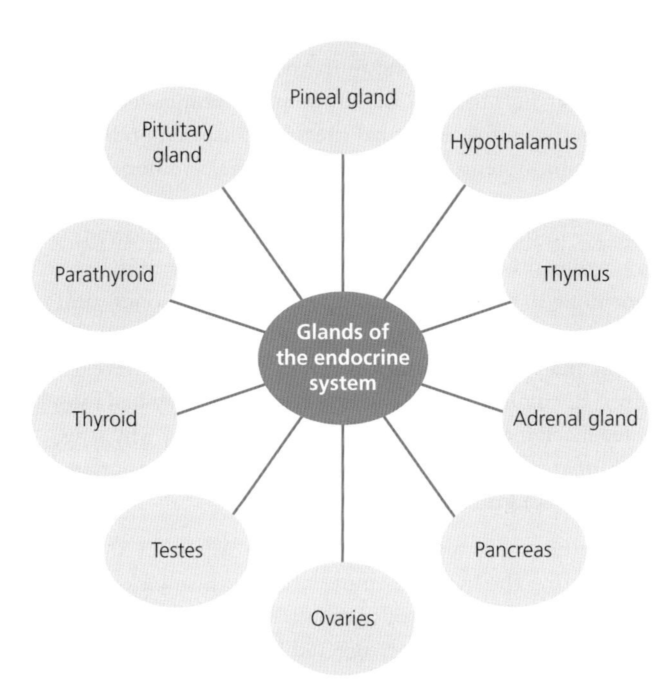

Glands of the endocrine system, where hormones are produced

How hormones work

Hormones work by binding to receptor proteins in target cells and changing cell function. The cells respond in a particular way to the hormones. Hormone secretion can be triggered by other hormones or by activity and the neuronal level.

Behaviour is affected by hormones based on when they are released, how they are received at the cell level and the receptors reached, and also how concentrated they are, which refers to their levels. The environment can affect the release of hormones too, such as in a stress situation or depending on the light in the environment, so not only is the environment and behaviour affected by hormones in the body, but hormones in the body are affected by the environment and behaviour.

Progress check 3.21

Briefly explain how hormones work.

Hormones as medication

Hormones can be used as medication, such as the use of oestrogens and progestogens as a contraceptive or in hormone replacement therapy (HRT) to prevent menopausal symptoms. Insulin is used by diabetics and steroid creams can be used for skin disorders. Thyroxin is used for people with thyroid conditions to help regulate the body, and steroids are hormones used for autoimmune disorders, as well as other problems. Glucocorticoids can help to reduce inflammation.

Neurotransmitter v. hormonal messaging:

- Hormones take messages over a larger distance and over a longer period of time.
- Hormones can travel anywhere in the circulatory system, whereas neurotransmitters are restricted to their appropriate neurons.
- Neurotransmitter signals travel very quickly, in milliseconds, whereas hormones travel more slowly and can be measured in seconds, minutes or even hours.
- Neurotransmitter signalling is all or nothing; hormone messages can vary in intensity depending on the amount of hormone.

The role of hormones in human behaviour

Hormones have many different roles. For example, they can regulate the sleep–wake cycle and they can regulate someone's metabolism, which can affect their eating habits. Hormones affect people at around puberty, and hormones affect mood both during the menstrual cycle and around the menopause. Hormones can be implicated in diabetes, which in turn can affect behaviour. Hormones help to regulate stress, and stress affects our behaviour. The sex drive is regulated by hormones and hormones affect body regulation mechanisms such as temperature. It is clear that hormones affect our behaviour either directly (such as sleeping) or more indirectly (such as affecting our mood, which affects our behaviour).

The role of hormones in aggression in humans

Many studies have looked at the role of hormones in aggression, using both human participants and animal participants. Studies using animal participants tend to generalise the findings to humans.

Dabbs *et al.* (1987), using humans

Dabbs *et al.* (1987) measured levels of testosterone in the saliva of 89 male prisoners involved in violent and non-violent crime and found that the level of testosterone was higher in those who had been involved in violent crime. Ten out of the 11 prisoners who had committed violent crime had high levels of testosterone. Those with the low levels of testosterone had a 9 out of 11 chance of committing the non-violent crime. Those with high levels of testosterone were rated by their peers as being tough. These findings suggest that a high level of the hormone testosterone links to aggressive behaviour in humans.

Explore

James Dabbs has done a lot of work in the area of aggression, dominance and the links with testosterone, and it is worth exploring his work more. He moved away from saying that testosterone gives aggression, and focused more on testosterone linking to dominance, which then might link to aggression. He found, for example, that aggressive males and females were more likely to have high-status jobs. He also found that males with more testosterone had less friendly smiles.

Barzman *et al.* (2013), using human children

Barzman *et al.* (2013) carried out a study looking at children in a psychiatric hospital. They recruited 17 boys in the hospital aged 7–9 years old. The researchers aimed to see if they would find hormones in saliva (they were interested in testosterone, dehydroepiandrosterone [DHEA], and cortisol) related to aggressive behaviour. When the children were admitted, they carried out two rating scales measuring aggression, one of which was the Brief Rating of Aggression by Children and Adolescents (BRACHA). Within the first 24 hours after admission, saliva samples were taken three times, once just after the boys woke up, once 30 minutes later and once again between 3.45 and 7.45pm. Twice a day, nurses recorded aggression (recording what they could see) using a scale.

The findings showed that the amount of cortisol in the saliva taken 30 minutes after waking up correlated with the number of aggressive incidents recorded by the nurses. That amount also related more to boys who were aggressive than to non-aggressive boys in the sample. There were also declines in the cortisol levels over the day in the aggressive boys. The levels of DHEA and testosterone after waking up correlated with the amount of aggression in the first aggressive incident noted that day. The rating on the aggression scales on admission gave a much higher aggression score of those boys noted as aggressive using the incidents than for boys called 'not aggressive'. The researchers concluded that it was feasible to use saliva to test for levels of the hormones, considering this is a non-invasive procedure and a way of getting hormone levels without taking blood. They concluded that the ratings of aggression using BRACHA were useful for future studies. They also concluded that there are links between salivary hormones and aggressive behaviour in children in psychiatric hospitals.

Progress check 3.22

Use two studies using humans to briefly conclude about the role of hormones in aggression.

Animal studies using rats

Adelson (2004) reported that rats showing activity in the aggression systems in their brain also showed a hormonal stress response. Rats have similar neurology to humans and the researchers thought that by demonstrating a feedback loop between the hormonal stress response and brain aggression systems, this might help humans to understand aggression responses. The rats had their aggression control centres in the brain electrically stimulated and showed a hormonal stress response, measured by levels of the hormone in the blood. Raising the stress hormones went with raised stimulation of the aggression centre in the brain and lowered stimulation went with a lower level of stress hormone. The researchers concluded they had found a feedback loop. In humans, this could explain why stress in humans can lead to aggression and why aggression in humans can lead to stress.

In another study with rats, reported in Adelson (2004), stimulating the hypothalamus, which is the attack centre in rats, led to a release of corticosterone, a stress hormone. The stress hormone was triggered *just* by stimulating the attack centre – there was no fighting. Even the threat of aggression triggered the hormone. These studies support one another. Another study, working on the same hypothesis, removed the rat's adrenal gland so stress hormone would not be released and then injected the corticosterone into the rat. The immediate effect was the attack response that was given by stimulating the hypothalamus. This is yet more evidence for the feedback loop between stress hormone and the brain's attack centre. It is known that a stress hormone will prepare the animal for the fight-or-flight reaction; from these studies, it was also concluded that the stress hormone lowers the reluctance for aggression by stimulating an attack response in the brain.

Chang *et al.* (2012), using fish

Chang *et al.* (2012) carried out a study looking at fish behaviour using the mangrove rivulus fish. They focused on aggression, which was measured by how the fish reacted to its mirror image in terms of an aggressive display, as well as exploring behaviour, which was measured by how ready the fish was to approach a new shelter. They measured boldness, measured by readiness to emerge from their shelter, and learning, by looking at the likelihood of the fish entering the correct reservoir in a maze. The aim was to look at these four behaviours and link them to hormones. The researchers wanted to see if these behaviours linked to cortisol and testosterone. They used other studies that suggested a link between aggression and the endocrine system and hormones to set up their own hypotheses. They also used findings of, for example, Dahlbom *et al.* (2011), who found that aggressive individuals tend to put themselves in more risky situations. Chang *et al.* (2012) explain that aggressiveness positively relates to reproductive success and that boldness has a positive effect on reproductive success but a negative effect on survival, and exploration has a positive effect on survival (Smith and Blumstein, 2008, cited in Chang *et al.*, 2012).

Chang *et al.* (2012) found that aggression, exploring and boldness all correlated with amount of testosterone before the behaviours. Aggression and boldness also correlated with amount of cortisol before the behaviours. Exploratory behaviour did not correlate with amount of cortisol before the behaviours. Aggressiveness and boldness showed a strong correlation. There was a weaker correlation between exploratory behaviour,and boldness and aggression. Learning did not correlate with the other behaviours or with cortisol or testosterone. It was concluded that cortisol and testosterone linked to the behavioural traits of aggression, boldness and exploring.

Chang *et al.* (2012) studied aggression, exploration and boldness in fish

STUDY HINT

Note that behaviours such as aggression, exploration and boldness might be survival instincts and might be arrived at through natural selection. The fish in Chang *et al.*'s study who displayed such behaviour may have survived because they found new shelters where others did not, or because they attacked predators and survived, being bold, where others did not. You can link the different theories about aggression – they are not necessarily separate.

Progress check 3.23

Use two studies using animals to briefly conclude about the role of hormones in aggression.

Evaluation

Against generalisation from animal studies to humans

Sluyter *et al.* (2003, cited in Trainor, 2009) say that, although mice and humans share more than 90 per cent of their genes, there are sufficient differences between them to suggest that findings about aggression in mice cannot be generalised to humans. Trainor (2009) explains that mice are in artificial situations when the link between aggression and hormones is studied and also their social behaviour is not the same as human social behaviour. Male mice are rarely aggressive to female mice, for example, which is not the case with male humans, who can be aggressive to female humans.

For generalisation from animal studies to humans

Trainor (2009), however, gives some evidence that studies using animals can be generalised to humans. The hypothalamus and limbic systems in humans and rodents are similar enough for generalisations to be made. For example, the attack centre is found in the hypothalamus and aggression links to that area and the limbic system in humans too. Also as there are similar systems that link to aggression in mammals and non-mammals, it seems that there might be a genetic cause underlying such aggression. As there are shared genes, conclusions from studies with rats can be used to discuss aggression in humans.

Progress check 3.24

Give a brief summary of the issues to consider when using animal studies to discuss human behaviour, including the 'for' and 'against' arguments of using animals.

Further evidence about the link between hormones and aggression

A review by Montoya *et al.* (2011) gives information about hormones and aggression and their relationship. Montoya *et al.* (2011) show how the testosterone(T)/cortisol(CRT) balance (the T and CRT ratio) predicts both impulsive and instrumental aggression (e.g. van Honk *et al.*, 2010, cited in Montoya *et al.*, 2011). Impulsive aggression is unplanned aggression driven by emotions. Instrumental aggression is premeditated and occurs with a lack of emotions. Both relate to the hormones testosterone and cortisol. Dabbs *et al.* (1991, cited in Montoya *et al.*, 2011) found in a study of 113 offenders that there was a relationship between testosterone, cortisol and aggression. However, Dabbs *et al.* found that aggression linked with testosterone only when there were low levels of cortisol. This led Dabbs *et al.* to think that cortisol is released in response to the environment and it is that response or that link which gives the high testosterone. Cortisol is linked with social withdrawal not with aggression, according to Dabbs *et al.* (1991).

Montoya *et al.* (2011) also discuss the neurotransmitter serotonin (5-Hydroxytryptamine, also called 5-HT). They cite van Honk *et al.* (2010), who found that low levels of serotonin (5-HT) seem to link to impulsive behaviour. Montoya *et al.* (2011) summarise by saying that high testosterone, low levels of cortisol and low levels of 5-HT would tend to find impulsive aggression. This explanation includes both hormones and neurotransmitters.

Montoya *et al.* (2011) looked for studies that showed low 5-HT levels and high testosterone levels linked with aggression and only found it in Kuepper *et al.* (2010), and interestingly this relationship was in males and not females. Hermans *et al.* (2008, cited in Montoya *et al.*, 2011) found that a high T/CRT ratio was correlated with activity in the amygdala-hypothalamus-PAG (PAG stands for periaqueductal grey) in response to threat. This is evidence that the aggression centre is in the limbic system, specifically the amygdala and hypothalamus. Marsh *et al.* (2008, cited in Montoya *et al.*, 2011) also found low connectivity between the amygdala and prefrontal cortex when there is aggression, supporting the suggestion earlier in this section about 'where' aggression is in the brain.

STUDY HINT

There is a lot of evidence presented in this section, and there are so many other studies you could study to find evidence. Note, however, that evidence points to a hormone-aggression link in humans. Make sure you have some evidence for your conclusions to offer in evaluation of the claim, and make sure you have enough information to describe the link in detail.

Serotonin–aggression hypothesis

Duke *et al.* (2013) carried out a **meta-analysis** to look at the serotonin–aggression hypothesis. This is about the role of serotonin, a neurotransmitter, in aggression, and is included here briefly to give more information in response to Montoya *et al.*'s (2011) review, which highlights not only hormone influence in aggression, but also serotonin.

Definition

A **meta-analysis** is a study that uses data from other studies and pools that data to find an overall conclusion about an issue.

Duke *et al.* (2013) say that the inverse relationship between serotonin and aggression (i.e. the lower the serotonin levels, the more the aggression) is well known. Serotonin is a neurotransmitter that links to good mood and 'happiness', so it makes sense that low levels will link to aggressive responses. However, Duke *et al.*'s (2013) review finds that this link is not upheld when studies are examined together. This meta-analysis shows that there are not always definite conclusions and often the body of knowledge being built up by studies can be questioned. Studying the brain is not easy, as the complexity makes it hard to study specific aspects like hormone or neurotransmitter functioning at specific sites.

Duke *et al.* (2013) examined 175 samples and around 6,500 participants and found a small inverse relationship between serotonin and aggression (as well as anger and hostility). The resulting correlation was –0.12. This is a very small correlation, but it does show a relationship, suggesting that at least to that extent the serotonin–aggression hypothesis might be correct. Duke *et al.* (2013) looked at four methods that had been used to study the hypothesis and concluded there were differences in the strength of the correlation using the different methods. They found that low serotonin was linked with higher aggression to a small extent, but there were issues with methods and study findings that led them to caution against drawing overall conclusions of an inverse relationship between serotonin and aggression. They suggested that researchers should take care not to use selective reporting, which means not to report findings that support the hypothesis without including caveats, such as about their methods. Duke *et al.* (2013) also said that contradictory findings must be reported. The reliability and validity of the measures used in studies to gather data about serotonin and aggression levels must be emphasised, and there must be an examination of environmental and personality factors that might relate to the serotonin–aggression link, as well as the complexity of how serotonin affects brain functioning.

Duke *et al.*'s (2013) meta-analysis is useful when considering evaluation of a study. They highlight issues of validity and reliability, issues of careful measurement of the variables under examination and dangers of reductionism in looking closely at some aspects of functioning without other possible variables (such as environment and personality).

Evaluation of the role of hormones in aggression

Strengths

- Studies tend to use careful controls even when they look for correlation evidence, such as Barzman *et al.* (2013). Studies using animals can use even stronger controls, such as Chang *et al.* (2012). The methods are scientific and so there is scientific credibility in the conclusions. Also the findings support one another, as there is a consistent finding about cortisol linking to aggression, for example; therefore there is reliability.
- Both human and animal studies find a link between cortisol and testosterone and aggression. There are so many studies, using different methods and measures, that have found this link so this gives scientific credibility and reliability to the findings. Chang *et al.* (2012) found links between testosterone and aggression/boldness in fish and between cortisol and aggression/boldness. Adelson (2004) reported that studies found a link between stress hormone and the aggression centre in the brain of rats. Dabbs *et al.* (1987) found that high testosterone levels linked with prisoners who had committed violent crime and lower testosterone levels with those who had committed non-violent crime. Barzman *et al.* (2013) found that the level of cortisol on waking correlated with the number of aggressive behaviours recorded during the day, and that the levels of testosterone on waking correlated with the amount of aggression in the first recorded incident of the day for that child. These findings support one another, suggesting reliability.

Weaknesses

- In humans, the data tend to be correlation data, which means cause-and-effect conclusions cannot be drawn because what is found is a relationship. Links are found between levels of cortisol and aggression. Cortisol is a stress hormone so it is said that stress and aggression relate to one other (e.g. Barzman *et al.*, 2013). What is not known is whether there is another variable causing both the stress and the aggression. Also what is not known is whether stress gives aggression or aggression gives stress.
- The explanation about hormones and aggression in humans, when it is investigated further, tends to bring in links to neurotransmitter functioning and brain structure and function too (e.g. Montoya *et al.*, 2011). The way theories of human aggression are separated into neurotransmitter functioning, brain structure and regions and hormones, as well as ideas about natural selection, means that the study of human aggression is done in a reductionist way. However, Montoya *et al.* (2011) show that the complexity of human behaviour means that the researcher must be willing to look beyond purely hormonal explanations and draw in other variables, to take a more holistic view.
- Many studies use animals and it is not easy to generalise these findings to humans. Issues include differences in motivation and planning between humans and animals. Studies suggest that hormones and aggression link; however, the environment can lead to the release of hormones (such as a stressor in the environment) and to aggression, and studies of animals are likely to be in an unnatural environment. Using animal experiments and generalising the findings to humans might not be a helpful thing to do.

Test yourself

1. Explain the role of hormones in human behaviour such as aggression. **(8 marks)**
2. Evaluate the role of hormones in aggression. **(12 marks)**

Test yourself

Discuss biological psychology in terms of how biology affects an individual's behaviour. In your answer, include at least two strengths and two weaknesses of the biological explanation you have offered. **(12 marks)**

The psychodynamic explanation of aggression

This section is about Freud's psychodynamic theory, focusing on how the theory explains aggression, as well as on some basics of the theory, to help with understanding how it explains aggression.

> **STUDY HINT**
>
> Freud's psychodynamic theory is not a biological explanation. It is presented in biological psychology in your course as a contrast to biological explanations for human behaviour and aggression. There is a separate approach called the 'psychodynamic approach', which stands alone. It does fit within developmental psychology, however, and does focus on individual differences. Therefore, it is a useful example of developmental psychology and individual differences, an explanation for aggression in its own right and a contrast to the biological explanations offered in this chapter.

You need to know about the three parts of the personality according to Freud's theory: the id, ego and superego. You also need to know about the importance of the unconscious in his ideas and about how catharsis links to aggression. The rest of the material here gives some background information and adds detail to help your understanding.

Personality	Parts of the mind	Aggression
• Id • Ego • Superego	• Conscious • Preconscious • Unconscious	• Life instinct • Death instinct • Catharsis

The psychodynamic element of your course

Background to the psychodynamic approach

Freud made some basic assumptions about human nature that have to be appreciated in order to understand his theory. In this section, just a small part of this theory is considered, but some background is required before giving more detail. His ideas are still used today in the field of counselling and there is still research into psychodynamic ideas. Freud has been accused of having 'rather fantastic ideas' and some have said they were drug-induced. Freud used cocaine, which almost certainly did him physical harm. However, as his theory was developed over his lifetime, it is probably not true to say that his use of drugs led to his unusual theory and ideas.

A brief background to Freud

Freud was a medical doctor. He saw people in hospitals with severe mental health problems getting either very little treatment or no treatment at all. We would consider the treatment to be barbaric – for example, trying to shake the madness out of them or giving them cold baths.

He was an ambitious man who wanted to develop a theory applicable to all people. He had what he thought of as interesting dreams and could remember that as a child he had strong feelings for his mother, the relevance of which becomes clear once you study his ideas. His world was upper-middle class, mixing with people in Viennese 'high' society. He married, had children and lived a comfortable existence. However, he was also Jewish at a time of persecution of Jews. He experienced hatred, his books were burned and he eventually left his home country of Austria.

He seems to have been a compassionate man, who believed in his own ideas. These changed throughout his life as he continued to develop his theory. His training as a medical doctor made him scientific in his approach and, although he has been criticised strongly for being unscientific, he did make an effort to be scientific in his studies. For example, Little Hans was a small boy whose development was relayed by the boy's father to Freud over quite a long time. When studying Little Hans, Freud says that he tried hard to consider only data that came directly from Little Hans and to discount interpretations by Little Hans's father. The story of Little Hans provided evidence for some of Freud's ideas. The Little Hans case study was published in 1909 and Freud's theory was developed around the turn of the twentieth century.

> **Explore**
>
> You can find out more about the Little Hans study here: www.simplypsychology.org/little-hans.html.

Sigmund Freud

Explore

In developing his theory and treating patients with neuroses, Freud studied individuals in detail. This type of approach to developing a theory is called **idiographic**. When scientists look for general laws, it is called a **nomothetic** approach to developing a theory. Freud, though working in an idiographic way, claimed to have found a general theory for all mankind and claimed to be working in a nomothetic way. Exploring the issues of idiographic and nomothetic approaches is a useful way of evaluating Freud's work.

Key assumptions underlying Freud's theory

The first key assumption is that the first five years of life are the most important time for forming a personality. Unsolved problems that arose in those years would affect development.

The second key assumption is that development occurs through stages that all children pass through. According to Freud, in the first five years, there are three important psychosexual stages. If all is well and the child resolves any issues that arise within those stages, then the child will develop a stable personality and be able to form good adult relationships. If, however, there are problems in one or more of those stages, then the adult will not have a stable personality and will have problems to resolve.

A third key assumption is the importance of the unconscious. For Freud, the unconscious part of the mind is the largest and the most powerful – and almost inaccessible.

A fourth key assumption is that everyone has an amount of energy that does not decrease or increase and that some of that energy is **libido**, which is sexual energy. This assumption is what leads to Freud's theory being called 'psychosexual'. It is a theory of the mind and a theory of instinctive energy and innate (inborn) drives. He thought that the basic drives of hunger, thirst and need for shelter were catered for in the Viennese society he moved in, so he focused on the sexual drive. His theory also includes the death instinct, which is important when discussing Freud's ideas about aggression.

Explore

The Freud Museum website (www.freud.org.uk) has lots of information, including some original letters. There are Freud museums in London and Vienna. The one in Vienna is in the house where he lived.

Progress check 3.25

Describe two of Freud's underpinning ideas.

An insight into psychoanalysis: Freud's 'talking cure'

Freud focused on adult patients with neuroses and looked for problems in their early lives to explain these. **Neuroses** are mental health problems in individuals who are aware that they have difficulties and are capable of having insight into these problems to help themselves get better. At first, Freud thought of neuroses as neural problems (problems to do with the nerves) rather than mental ones. Examples of neuroses are phobias and some types of depression. It could be said that most people have some neurosis, such as a tendency to be over anxious, which prevents their normal functioning. **Psychoses** are mental health problems in individuals where they are not aware of their problems and do not have the insight to help themselves to get better because of the nature of the problems. A psychosis is a break from reality. An example of a psychosis is schizophrenia, though someone with schizophrenia might not always be having a 'psychotic episode'. Psychosis is a label for this break with reality rather than a label that goes with a specific mental health disorder.

Definitions

Neuroses are issues where someone knows they have them and neuroses are simply normal functioning moved down the line from normal. **Psychoses** are different – they are problems that the individual cannot deal with and is not totally aware of so there is little or no insight there for someone to help themselves. There is a break from reality, which is very different from neurosis.

Freud's 'cure' needed patients who could gain insight into their problems, so he treated only neuroses. One particular neurosis that Freud thought interesting was hysteria. Hysterical symptoms are physical symptoms that have no physical cause (although Freud thought there was a physical cause to do with the nerves). An example is Anna O, whose case helped the development of Freud's theory. Anna O had some difficulties in speaking and listening and some minor paralyses, with no apparent physical cause. Freud thought that the symptoms were hysterical and that the problems came from the unconscious. Some desire in the person's unconscious was solved or granted by such hysterical symptoms. For example, if someone cannot see but there seems to be no physical reason for the blindness, perhaps there is something that he or she does not want to see.

Explore

Look up the case of Bertha von Pappenheim (Anna O), who was a patient of Breuer (a colleague of Freud). She had typical symptoms of hysteria and when she talked about forgotten memories she seemed to get better. Anna O said that Breuer and Freud's therapy was a 'talking cure'.

Repressed memories may cause neuroses

In the case of Anna O, Freud suggested that **repressed** memories were causing problems. For example, after remembering seeing a dog lick a glass, she had no problem drinking from a glass, whereas she had been unable to do so before recovering the memory.

So Freud had the idea of repressed memories being inaccessible, but still guiding behaviour. He thought that if such memories were made conscious, then they would no longer guide behaviour inappropriately. From this idea, Freud built the therapy of **psychoanalysis**. The aim of psychoanalysis is to make unconscious thoughts conscious, thus releasing the thoughts and the energy that the individual was using to keep those thoughts unconscious. With that energy released, the individual can progress.

Explanation

The idea of energy being important is the 'dynamic' part of psychodynamic; the 'psycho' part is because it is a theory of the mind.

Definitions

Repression is, according to Freud, one of many defence mechanisms whereby material is in the unconscious and not accessible to conscious thought. This protects the individual from traumatic memories and defends the ego, maintaining rational thought. **Psychoanalysis** is the name for Freud's therapy, and involves uncovering unconscious thoughts and desires, including repressed material, bringing them into the conscious so that they can be dealt with.

The role of the unconscious

Freud thought that the mind was made up of three parts:

- The **conscious mind** holds the thoughts, ideas, emotions and other aspects of thinking of which the individual is aware. The conscious is perceptual awareness, awareness of things around.
- The **preconscious mind** holds thoughts and ideas that can be accessed and are ready to be known about, but are not actually conscious at that time. The preconscious holds our memories and these are accessible, not repressed, though they are not in our conscious minds at that moment.
- The **unconscious mind** is the main part. It is where all thoughts originate, with some becoming conscious and some being allowed into the preconscious. We do not repress thoughts into the unconscious in a considered way; repression happens on an unconscious level. Freud claimed that what is in the unconscious mind uses up our energy, it is not passive and it affects us.

It is common to use an iceberg analogy – the conscious mind is the part of the iceberg above the surface, the preconscious is a small part just below the surface and the unconscious is the remainder of the iceberg, below the surface, largely inaccessible, yet very important for the individual. Thoughts in the unconscious mind are active and trying to find a means of expression. According to Freud, the unconscious can only be accessed through research methods, such as free association, slips of the tongue, dream analysis and symbol analysis.

Definitions

The **conscious mind** has the thoughts and ideas that we are aware of. We can manipulate those thoughts and make decisions using them. The **preconscious mind** has the thoughts that we can be aware of and we can access, but currently are not being accessed so not in the conscious mind. The **unconscious mind** is not knowable in any easy way – it holds many thoughts, emotions and desires that we do not know about. It can guide our thinking and emotions nonetheless and the 'cure' is to get those thoughts into our conscious mind.

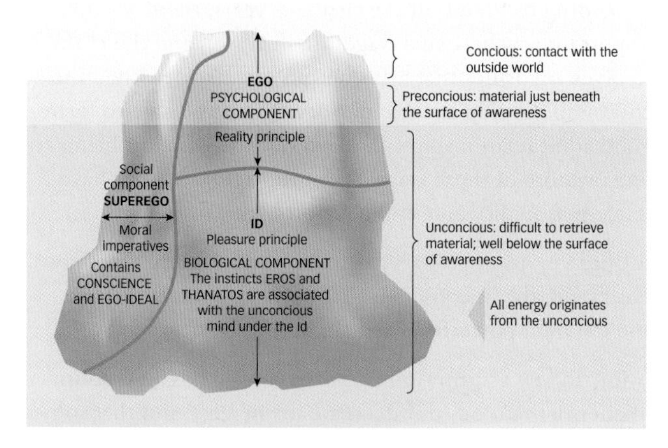

Freud's model of personality structure

Progress check 3.26

Explain the difference between the conscious, preconscious and unconscious parts of the mind in psychodynamic theory.

Life and death instincts

For repression to take place, energy must be used to keep thoughts unconscious. According to Freud, the energy that we possess is focused into a life instinct (**eros**), which is an instinct for both self-preservation and sexual energy.

His idea was that urges and wishes from the life instinct in the unconscious lead to arousal, and that one of our drives is to reduce arousal. One way to reduce arousal is death, and Freud put forward the idea of the death instinct, which he called **thanatos**. Thanatos provides energy for the ego to inhibit the sexual instinct; eros provides the energy to inhibit the instinct that leads to death. With aggression, the death instinct is channelled into something more productive – for example, sport.

Definitions

Eros is our instinct for life and self-preservation; **thanatos** is our drive to reduce arousal, to reduce 'life', so is a death instinct.

The three parts of the personality

According to Freud, there are three parts to the personality:

- The **id** is the part of the personality we are born with. It is the demanding part (id is 'it' in Latin, i.e. not yet a rational person). The infant is all 'I want' and demands to be satisfied. The id is in the unconscious in that the demands are not conscious – a baby knows what it wants, but unconsciously. The id works on the pleasure principle.
- The **ego** is the rational part of the personality. It works on reality principles, and tries to obtain for the id what the id wants. Ego is Latin for 'I' and the ego is the part of the personality that works out how to satisfy the person. The ego develops from the age of about 18 months.
- The **superego** develops during the phallic stage, at around four years of age. The superego (Latin for 'above I') works on the morality principle. The superego is made up of the conscience, given to individuals by their parents and by society indicating what is right and wrong, and the **ego ideal**. The ego ideal is the idea people have of what they should be like, again given by parents and society. The superego is the 'you can't have' part of the personality.

The ego has to pacify the id and the superego and find a balance between their conflicting demands. If two conflicting things are desired, the id also makes conflicting demands. The ego has to find a course of action that maintains a balance. The ego might do this by repressing memories or using other defence mechanisms.

The id wants satisfaction

The ego juggles demands

Superego = conscience

The id, ego and superego

Definitions

The **id** is one of the three parts of the personality according to Freud. It is all that an individual wants, their desires and needs. The **superego** is almost the opposite in that it holds our 'shoulds' and 'oughts' and is what we should be like, as well as holding our conscience, given by society and others. The **ego** is in the middle, so to speak, and balances the demands of the id with the demands of the superego, to make rational decisions.

Progress check 3.27

In the table below, note down which part of the personality is being described for each situation given.

Situation	Part of the personality according to Freud
We want to move to a bigger house to show off to friends.	
We always stop at traffic lights when they are red and even when just turning red.	
We want to go to a party that will go on into the early hours but our parents are worried and don't want us to go. We decide to go but to leave to go home at eleven o'clock.	

Freud and aggression

Freud's theory often focuses on aggression. For example, he sees aggression in the jealousy a boy will feel towards his father for getting in the way of the boy's feelings towards his mother. He sees aggression when analysing ideas from free association, which is where someone will talk freely about whatever thoughts are in their head at the time. Little Hans, one of Freud's case studies, focused on a young boy who showed aggression (including towards his father) when issues around his mother and his feelings for his mother were discussed.

For Freud, the main drives are the libido, the sex drive and self-preservation. The ego, to preserve the self and respond to these drives, while balancing the superego's demands too, represses thoughts that are unacceptable into the unconscious. Those thoughts can leak out in dreams, defence mechanisms such as displacement, or free association, which is why Freud used dream analysis and free association to uncover unconscious desires and make them conscious. Displacement is when someone focuses thoughts onto one person when they 'belong' to someone else, as this can help to release the thoughts in a way that is safe for the ego without upsetting the superego (the conscience). So drives can be pushed out of the way by using defence mechanisms (not literally but unconsciously) but are still there to affect someone.

Someone might shout at a colleague over the phone when their anger is in fact about someone else – this is displacement in psychodynamic terms

> **STUDY HINT**
> When explaining Freud's ideas, such as about the role of the unconscious, be sure to write carefully because it is easy to say that 'we' repress our desires, whereas in fact 'we' don't do that consciously. It is better to say 'desires are repressed' so that there is no implication that it is done consciously and deliberately. This may not seem important, but you need to explain the theory accurately and if you add in some 'decision', such as to use defence mechanisms that is not there in reality, then the sentence would not be accurate.

Aggression in Freud's theory is also a drive, though he came to this conclusion later in the development of his theory (in the 1920s). Aggression links to the death instinct. Aggression is the outlet for the death instinct and is what preserves life because, without it, someone would have a strong death instinct with no outlet and would, therefore, affect the person's behaviour and thinking. The life instinct (eros) opposes the death instinct in everyone and this life instinct is supported by aggression, which can help to release the drive towards death in everyone (thanatos). These drives are unconscious and Freud thought they related to the drive to go back to before being born (the death instinct) as well as the strong drive to go forward in life (the life instinct). These instincts are linked in Freud's theory to our biology and they are biological drives, going back to cells in our bodies rather than being conscious drives. Some psychodynamic theorists that came after Freud (e.g. Jones, 1957) suggest that there is no need to go beyond the forces of aggression and the sexual drive to look at underpinning drives like eros and thanatos. Others stick to Freud's ideas about the underlying drives (e.g. Klein, 1948).

Freud thought that frustration – both about not getting something that leads to pleasure or not being able to avoid something that leads to pain – is what leads to aggression. This idea is developed by Dollard *et al.* as the frustration–aggression hypothesis. The frustration–aggression hypothesis, however, is more about learning and response than about internal drives and mechanisms. Freud was interested in the emotions and ideas behind aggressive behaviour. In these terms, aggression is not just the outward behaviour but is within the individual as well.

Aggression is linked in Freud's theory to the superego. The superego is the conscience of the child, formed from the parents' demands about what should and should not be done and thought in a society. The child (unconsciously) feels aggression towards the parents as they prevent things that will give the child pleasure (demands from the id) and aggression is, for Freud, caught up in the superego. The child loves the parents and so cannot direct the aggression at them so it is taken into the child's superego and how strong the superego is depends on the amount of aggression within it. The aggressive part of any desire turns into guilt as it is caught up in the superego. The death instinct is not visible in any way, and it becomes visible only when there is an outward manifestation in the form of aggression.

Fromm (1973), another psychoanalyst, discusses two types of aggression: benign and destructive aggression. He saw one type of aggression as a response to the environment and a natural response too, so it was benign for the person. The individual might show aggression in response to threat, but the aggression would pass when the threat disappeared. However, he also saw another type of aggression, destructive aggression, that was there for someone to achieve their own goals and was not benign.

> **Explore**
> In social psychology, you may have looked at how right-wing authoritarian views are linked with being prejudiced, as one of the contemporary studies in social psychology discusses this issue (Cohrs *et al.*, 2012). Right-wing authoritarianism is characterised by having strong views about right and wrong, and a lack of tolerance, hence the link to prejudice. These ideas are linked to psychodynamic ideas, in that the idea of a strong superego can explain why someone strongly obeys rules and wants things to be 'right' (in cultural terms). If you study Bowlby's work in child psychology in Year 2, you will again look at psychodynamic views. Explore these issues more if they interest you. The psychodynamic approach is very detailed and what is given here covers just some of the theory.

Aggression can be to protect young and when the threat is gone so is the aggression – this is natural aggression

Aggression can be for gain, which is not benign – this is destructive aggression

Progress check 3.28

Explain two ideas in the psychodynamic theory of aggression.

Catharsis

One other feature of Freud's theory is catharsis. Freud thought that when something that is unconscious is brought into the conscious mind (which is of course a very hard thing to do, and is the aim of psychoanalysis) then the thoughts or memories bring emotions with them and so the emotions (including aggression) are released. He called this release 'catharsis' and the word 'cathartic' is used today to mean something is cleansed from the mind. When repressed ideas are brought into the conscious mind, the feelings are released, and that releases the energy that was being used up, hence the person is 'freed' from those emotions and thoughts. This is the basis of psychoanalysis, where the aim is to release unconscious thoughts and desires, so that the energy is released and the person can move on.

Catharsis has been said to be a way of venting aggression. This may be by watching aggression on television or by watching other people being aggressive. Watching aggression can release feelings of aggression. Well, this is the theory. Another idea is that doing sport that is aggressive or having other 'permitted' ways of releasing aggression can be cathartic. Catharsis might be releasing actual stress in a physical sense, such as dealing with the fight response when an arousal reaction in the body has been triggered. Catharsis can also mean releasing emotions such as anger rather than physical stress. Freud's theory focuses on emotions, thoughts and anger and, for him, aggression can be internal.

However, studies tend to show that watching aggression makes someone feel more aggressive, as Bandura and others have shown (Chapter 4, pp. 232–243). There is disagreement whether expressing aggression in sport or, in fact, watching aggression or aggressive sport is cathartic or whether it builds more aggression. Freud thought that releasing pent up feelings was cathartic, but there are studies that have not backed up this claim. There is some evidence for Freud's ideas, but it is not conclusive. Verona and Sullivan (2008) shed some light on this (see 'Study of interest' box).

Study of interest

Verona and Sullivan (2008) carried out a laboratory experiment to see how participants would react to a frustrating situation, which was achieved by a confederate in the study behaving in a way calculated to frustrate the participant. The idea was to see if acting in an aggressive way (pressing a 'shock' button) would lead to reduction of aggression (measured by heart rate) compared to a control situation where someone responded in a non-aggressive way (pressing a non-shock button). They also wanted to see if reducing the aggression predicted later aggressive behaviour.

Verona and Sullivan (2008) explain that Buss (1961) took the psychodynamic view of aggression and proposed the hydraulic model of aggression. This model holds that someone builds up aggression due to experiences and then behaves aggressively, thus releasing the build-up. Schafer (1970, cited in Verona and Sullivan, 2008) went on to say that using this model, and linking in the idea of catharsis, would mean that later aggression is also reduced (the tension has gone). This idea of later aggression also being reduced is seen as saying the aggression drive is reduced as well as the aggression.

Hokanson (1974) and others, according to Verona and Sullivan (2008) found physiological evidence for aggression reduction, which is evidence for catharsis.

Behaving in an aggressive way reduced tension in the individual as measured by physiological measures. However, Hokanson (1974) did not find that subsequent aggression was reduced. Reduction in tension after behaving aggressively in fact seemed to increase the likelihood of later aggression, which goes against Freud's idea of catharsis, at least in the longer term.

Verona and Sullivan (2008) go on to cite later work on catharsis. They explain how Bushman *et al.* (1999) carried out an experiment into catharsis, spurred on by the popular idea that doing sport or watching aggression on television is cathartic. They gave half their participants an article explaining that hitting an inanimate article was cathartic and had another group of participants who did not read the article. They then gave both groups negative feedback on an essay. Those who read the 'pro-catharsis' essay were more likely to hit out at a punch bag after the negative feedback than the other group. Therefore, it seems that reading about hitting a punch bag was not cathartic and in fact led to more aggression. This supports Bandura and others who see the media as being modelled on by others (see Chapter 4).

Bushman found that people who believe that acting aggressively is cathartic act more aggressively. Therefore, there is some evidence that behaving aggressively reduces tension and is cathartic, which supports Freud's ideas, and some evidence that at least reading about aggression makes people more aggressive. Also when tension is reduced and aggressive behaviour acts in a cathartic way for someone, there is evidence that aggression will then follow – the reduction is not long-lasting, which is not how the psychodynamic theory explains tension reduction.

Verona and Sullivan's study (2008) found that participants who reacted in an aggressive way to the frustration that was caused for them in the study (by pressing the 'shock' button) did have a reduced heart rate and those who did not react that way (by pressing the 'non-shock' button) did not have a reduced heart rate. This seems to support the idea of aggressive behaviour being cathartic, thus supporting the psychodynamic view. However, when there was a blast of hot air delivered during the study, in the condition where aggression had been exhibited with the resulting decrease in heart rate, the participants were in fact more aggressive in their response to the hot air. Their tension may have been reduced by their pressing the 'shock' button but their aggressive drive was not reduced, it was increased. Reducing tension at first did not lead to reduced tension and no aggression throughout. There was more later aggression if the heart rate had reduced in fact.

Progress check 3.29

Give two pieces of evidence that support the view that either playing sport or watching aggression is cathartic and one piece of evidence that does not support that view.

Freud's ideas and neuroscience

Freud's ideas might seem a long way from the neuroscience covered earlier in this chapter. However, there is a recent idea that the two might be linked. Taking the biological view first, the limbic system was seen as where emotions were 'housed', with aggression being one of those emotions. The amygdala, for example, when damaged in animals, seemed to lead to passive responses, and it is thought that the amygdala links to aggression. The prefrontal cortex, however, was seen as the place where planning and decision-making takes place. Studies looked at links between the limbic system (which includes the amygdala) and the prefrontal cortex. With regard to the psychodynamic approach, there is a theory that the limbic system, which is about emotions in the conscious mind, and the prefrontal cortex, where decision-making takes place, is the analytical part of the conscious mind.

There is a branch of psychoanalysis called 'neuro-psychoanalysis', which links the different hemispheres to the different ideas in psychodynamic theory. Emotional aspects of the mind are linked to the right hemisphere and the limbic system and analytic verbal processing is linked to the left hemisphere. The unconscious is within the brain stem, the deepest part of the mind, and also in the pons and cerebellum. The cerebellum in biological terms is where well-learned skills are, such as playing the piano. The superego could be the left frontal lobe and the id could be the part of the brain that is deep and not known for specific control functions.

Study of interest

Divino and Moore (2010) discuss how new understanding in neurobiology needs to be incorporated into psychodynamic training, not just regarding training therapists but also the way of teaching to take into account the effects of possible trauma from the material being taught. In fact their ideas could be of interest in all areas of training. For example, if students are faced with material that might be received as traumatic, the students can be trained to keep their prefrontal lobes active and self-regulating systems working, so that unconscious thoughts in their brains are not triggered by the material. Learning is conscious, left hemisphere and verbal, for example, and those areas are focused on. Learning requires some level of activation in the right hemisphere, midbrain and limbic system and this is non-conscious and non-verbal (e.g. Ogden *et al.*, 2006, cited in Divino and Moore, 2010). Knowing about such learning can be important when teaching. Learning from watching a video can be at this non-conscious, non-verbal level.

Divino and Moore (2010) explain some of the neurobiology that informs the psychodynamic approach. They mention how experience will change the brain throughout our life time so we are all unique, due to plasticity of the brain. They point out that the right hemisphere is functional at birth and, until about three years old, emotions will dominate over verbal reasoning, which takes place in the left hemisphere. This early right hemisphere functioning involves procedural memories (how to do things) and non-conscious memories that do not move into the conscious as the left hemisphere comes to be used around the age of three years. Childhood attachments predict later relationships, and early problems with attachment can mean unresolved trauma for the adult. The right hemisphere, brain stem and limbic system are involved in survival, and early trauma can lead to these being overdeveloped, which can mean a strong fear response that picks up on negative feelings more than in others. Perry (1993) showed that internal imagery activates the same brain systems as sensory input (cited in Divino and Moore, 2010). Divino and Moore (2010) discuss using some of these ideas in training and explain that these ideas need to be used in psychotherapy. For example, non-verbal communication between a therapist and a client can be useful in accessing the right hemisphere dominated experiences of early childhood, which are not available to verbal expression.

The ideas from Divino and Moore's (2010) study should help you to see how neurobiology might be beginning to link to psychodynamic ideas. This is a new area of study and not one that we can explore fully here. However, it is important to realise that there is perhaps some evidence for Freud's ideas and also that the psychodynamic approach and biology are perhaps not as far apart as they initially seem.

However, not everyone would agree with the account given in this chapter about how neurobiological evidence for the psychodynamic approach is emerging. In such a new area, there are sure to be sceptics.

Progress check 3.30

Give two pieces of neurobiological evidence that might support the psychodynamic view and make the links to psychodynamic theory.

Evaluation of Freud's theory and the psychodynamic approach to aggression

Strengths

- Freud's ideas about treating mental health problems provided solutions that at the time were unavailable. Psychoanalysis addressed neuroses, such as hysteria, whereas previously treatments were, what we would consider now, barbaric. So people were helped who would otherwise not have been helped.
- Freud generated his theory from in-depth case studies in which he looked at many aspects of a person's background and mental state. His theory was built from valid data and it focused on the dreams and problems of each individual.

Weaknesses

- Freud's approach does not use scientific method. Data are qualitative and personal, so an overall theory should not be generated from such individual data. The findings are not seen as generalisable.
- The concepts are not measurable and so cannot be rigorously tested. For example, the unconscious is unreachable by normal means, and the id, ego and superego cannot be measured. There is a lack of scientific credibility.
- The case studies (such as Anna O and Little Hans) had to involve some element of interpretation of symbols in dreams or of free association data. There is, therefore, subjectivity, whereas science requires objectivity.
- Freud worked in middle-class Vienna, mostly with women, so the sample is limited to this group. It is difficult to then generalise to the whole population, although Freud did so. The sample is biased, which makes generalisation difficult.
- Freud looked only at development up to puberty and adolescence and focused on psychosexual aspects, so his work was limited. However, this weakness only shows that his theory cannot be proved correct – it doesn't show that the theory is wrong. Later, others within the approach looked at development over the whole lifespan. Erikson developed the 'eight stages of man' and looked at different stages, including old age. He also focused on social development rather than sexual development.

Freud focused on development from childhood to adolescence, whereas later researchers considered development over a lifespan, from birth to old age

Comparing psychodynamic ideas about aggression with biological ones

The inclusion of psychodynamic explanations for aggression is to help to evaluate biological ones so you need to be able to compare the two explanations.

Focus on internal structures and features

- The psychodynamic approach focuses on internal aggression in the form of unconscious thoughts and desires generating frustration, and therefore aggression. Biological psychology also focuses on internal mechanisms, such as brain structure and functioning. For example, the amygdala is an internal structure.
- However, biological psychology looks at physical structures in the brain and actual brain functioning, whereas the psychodynamic approach considers a model rather than 'reality' in claiming that a lot of our mind is not accessible, and that our conscious mind is comparatively small and even then not knowable in a physical way.

Biological evidence for the psychodynamic approach

- Recently, since brain scanning has become more widely available, some researchers believe that biological psychology is beginning to meet up with the psychodynamic approach. For example, the limbic system (which includes the amygdala) is 'for' emotions and not rational thinking, which matches with the psychodynamic idea that emotions and feelings such as desires are in the unconscious and not in our rational mind.
- Another piece of evidence that is biological and fits psychodynamic theory is that up to about the age of three a child is thought not to have developed their thinking capacity, and to focus on the right-brain features of thinking, which involve emotions more than rational thought. This could be evidence that a young child is all 'id' and the ego starts to develop at the toddler stage, with the superego not far behind.

Soundness of data used to draw conclusions

- The psychodynamic approach found its evidence in Freud's case studies of people who had mental health issues and needed or wanted treatment. Case studies are about unique individuals and it is hard to generalise from such data, though that is what Freud did. His theory is hard to replicate as it rests on case study evidence and validity is questioned, as the theory requires interpretation from the analyst/researcher, so perhaps the theory lacks scientific credibility.
- Biological psychology, however, draws on scientific data from scientific methods. Methods tend to be experimental and more recently involve brain scanning, as well as studies of animals. Such studies can involve careful controls. Biological psychology tends to have more scientific credibility than the psychodynamic approach.

Conclusions about aggression

- The psychodynamic approach suggests that displays of aggression release tension and desires and thoughts from the unconscious and releasing them frees the person from such ideas holding them back. The basic idea is that aggression, such as in sport, is cathartic.
- This is very similar to the biological explanation in that the 'release of tension' can be seen as release at a biological level, perhaps releasing stress so that the alarm reaction can settle back to a resting state using the parasympathetic part of the nervous system.
- However, the psychodynamic approach discusses the role of the unconscious and drives in aggression, whereas biological psychology looks for the actual structure in the body that is involved. It could be said that psychodynamic ideas are about the emotional part of us and biological psychology is about our physical side.

Catharsis is the idea that playing sport can release tension and avoid aggression, though not everyone agrees with this

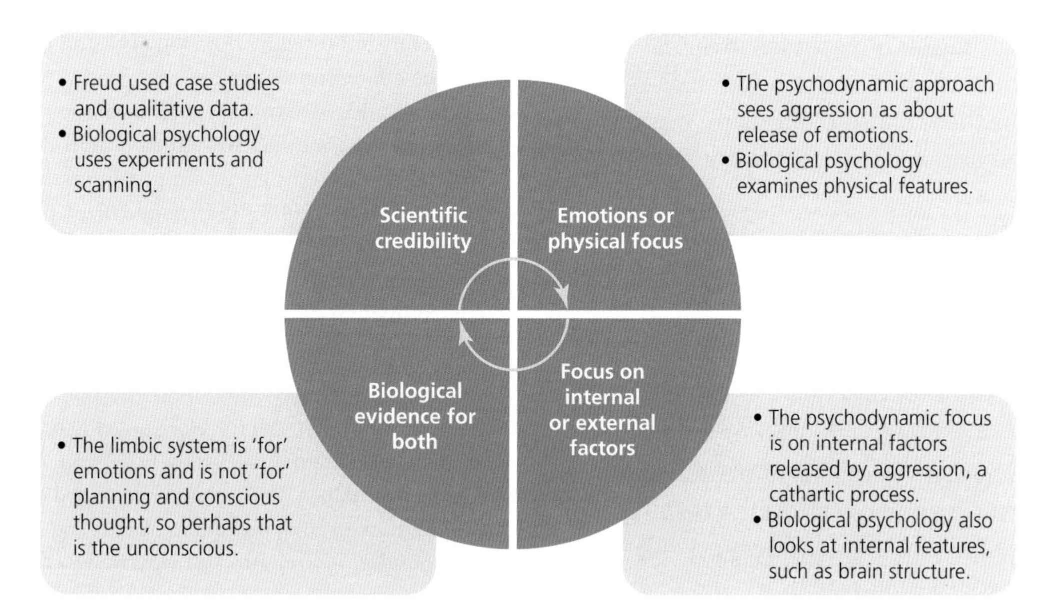

Similarities and differences between the psychodynamic view of aggression and biological psychology's views of aggression

Test yourself

1 Explain Freud's theory of personality. **(8 marks)**
2 To what extent does catharsis work? **(6 marks)**
3 Compare Freud's psychodynamic ideas about aggression with biological explanations for aggression. **(18 marks)**

Methods in biological psychology

What is required and how this book covers that requirement

In biological psychology, you need to know about the following:

- correlation research including positive and negative correlations

Practical link: a piece of correlation research is worked through as the biological psychology practical in Chapter 7.

- strength of correlations (strong or weak)

Maths link: Chapter 6 (pp. 406–411) explains issues around the strength of correlations.

- alternate, experimental and null hypotheses

Method link: Chapter 5 (p. 339) explains issues about hypotheses, which are also covered in cognitive psychology in your course.

- the use of co-variables in correlations compared with: a) variables in experimental methods (IV/DV) b) other variables, c) cause-and-effect conclusions from experiments d) sampling, e) control groups, f) randomisation to groups

Method link: correlations are discussed in Chapter 5 (pp. 339–341). Experiments are also discussed in Chapter 5 (pp. 315–326) when the method required for cognitive psychology is covered. Issues with experiments and correlations are discussed when the method required for biological psychology is covered (pp. 339–341).

- analysis of correlations, including a Spearman's test and related issues around inferential testing (statistical significance, critical and observed values)

Maths link: Chapter 6 explains how to use the Spearman's test for correlation data and works through the test (pp. 409–411). Chapter 7 also works through a Spearman's test.

Maths and method link: To find out more about inferential testing and related issues required in biological psychology read the relevant sections in Chapter 5, about the method (pp. 339–341), and Chapter 6, about the mathematics you need (pp. 406–411).

- levels of measurement (A level only): nominal data (categories, e.g. yes/no), ordinal data (ranked, e.g. attractiveness on a scale of 0–5), interval/ratio data (real numbers, e.g. temperature or number or words recalled)

Method link: Chapter 5 discusses levels of measurement and what they are (pp. 328–336), including how they relate to choosing a statistical test and more about statistical theory.

- scatter diagrams

Maths link: Chapter 6 discusses graphs, including scatter diagrams (pp. 408–409), to help when learning about correlations.

- reasons for choosing a Spearman's test

Method link: Chapter 5 explains more about why certain tests are chosen (pp. 330–331).

Maths link: Chapter 6 explains more about inferential testing and how to do the tests, as well as looking at statistical significance (pp. 409–411).

- brain scanning (PET, CAT, fMRI)

Method link: brain scanning is explained in Chapter 5, which looks at the method for your course, including the use of brain scanning to look at human behaviour (pp. 341–352).

- the use of brain scanning to look at human behaviour
- one twin study

Method link: you need to know one twin study so that you can discuss the use of twin studies as a method in biological psychology. Chapter 5 explains Lacourse *et al.* (2014) in some detail (pp. 352–359).

- one adoption study.

Method link: you need to know one adoption study so you can discuss the use of adoption studies as a method in biological psychology. Chapter 5 explains Leve *et al.* (2010) in some detail (pp. 359–364).

Issues and debates

The nature-nurture debate is about whether characteristics of humans, including their behaviour, come from genes and someone's biology or from environmental influences. Twin studies and adoption studies can help to unpick what comes from genes and what comes from environment. If you are studying the AS, you do not need to study the issues and debates part of the Year 1 course; however, as you are covering twin studies and adoption studies, you will need to be able to link to the nature-nurture debate in psychology.

Studies in biological psychology

In biological psychology, you have to cover one classic study and one from a choice of three contemporary studies. The classic study is Raine *et al.* (1997) 'Brain abnormalities in murderers indicated by positron emission tomography'. The three contemporary studies are:

- Li *et al.* (2013) 'Abnormal function of the posterior cingulate cortex in heroin addicted users during resting-state and drug-cue stimulation task'
- Van den Oever (2008) 'Prefrontal cortex plasticity mechanisms in drug seeking and relapse'
- Brendgen *et al.* (2005) 'Examining genetic and environmental effects on social aggression: a study of 6-year-old twins'.

Remember you have to know about just one of the contemporary studies. All three are given here for your interest and because they are all useful in your learning about biological psychology. Each study is presented in the form of the aim(s), background, procedure, results and conclusions before considering strengths and weaknesses of the study.

STUDY HINT

Note that there are methodology issues in these studies as well as content issues, so they link to Chapter 5 (method) and Chapter 6 (mathematics) as well.

Classic study: Raine *et al.* (1997)

This classic study looked at people charged with murder and pleading not guilty by reason of insanity to see if there were brain differences that might link to their aggression. Raine *et al.* (1997) used PET scanning to look for differences in brain functioning between murderers who pleaded not guilty by reason of insanity (NGRI) and a control group. This study is useful not only as a study looking at brain structure and functioning in relation to aggression, which suits the content required in this topic area, but also because it is an example of brain scanning, a method you need to know about.

STUDY HINT

Et al. refers to the other researchers in a study. In this case, the full list of researchers is as follows: Adrian Raine, Monte Buchsbaum and Lori LaCasse.

Explore

You can find out more about Adrian Raine here: https://crim.sas.upenn.edu/people/faculty/adrian-raine. Explore more about him as a researcher, to provide background when understanding the classic study, and also to see what sorts of things are researched in his area of study.

Aims

The study aimed to show that the brains of murderers who pleaded not guilty by reason of insanity were different from the brains of non-murderers. Raine *et al.* investigated whether brain dysfunction predisposed people to violent behaviour. Their specific hypotheses were that individuals who showed serious violence would have dysfunction in specific areas of the brain but not in other specific areas.

- The areas they thought would show dysfunction were: 'the prefrontal cortex, angular gyrus, amygdala, hippocampus, thalamus and the corpus callosum' (p. 496).
- The areas they thought would not show dysfunction were: 'caudate, putamen, globus pallidus, midbrain or cerebellum' (p. 496).

Their aim was to use PET scanning so that they could study localised areas in the brain to check for dysfunction in those areas. They used a matched control group so that they could compare those areas in violent individuals with those areas in matched non-violent individuals.

Background

Raine *et al.* (1997) start from the idea that some brain damage or dysfunction may lead people to exhibit violent behaviour. In Chapter 5, the case of Phineas Gage is given, whereby damage to his prefrontal lobe seemed to change his character and behaviour. The researchers note, however, that isolating specific parts of the brain to see what links to violent behaviour had not been possible.

- Raine *et al.* (1997) suggest that damage to the prefrontal cortex is thought to give aggression (e.g. Damasio *et al.*, 1990, cited in Raine *et al.*, 1997).
- There might be 'abnormalities in hemispheric asymmetries of function' (suggested by Raine *et al.*, 1990a, cited in Raine *et al.*, 1997). This means that the way the two hemispheres work together might be abnormal. Structures in the brain tend to be across the two hemispheres and there can be different functioning in the different sides of the brain. Bilateral functioning means working across both hemispheres; unilateral refers to one hemisphere.
- There might be issues with the corpus callosum, which links the two hemispheres (e.g. Yeudall, 1977, cited in Raine *et al.*, 1997).
- There could be dysfunction in the left angular gyrus, another area of the brain.
- Animal studies have suggested that the limbic system (such as the amygdala and hippocampus) affect whether there is aggressive behaviour or not (e.g. Bear, 1991, cited in Raine *et al.*, 1997).
- The thalamus might be linked to aggression, as suggested by the study of cats (Mirsky and Siegel, 1994, cited in Raine *et al.*, 1997).
- Frontal brain regions and the temporal cortex are thought to link to violent behaviour (e.g. Goyer *et al.*, 1994, cited in Raine *et al.*, 1997).

Raine *et al.* (1997) point out that the findings of animal studies might not be related to the idea that violent offenders have brain dysfunction in the areas found in animals linked to aggression. Another limitation of brain scanning studies is that they tend to have small samples of violent people, found in hospitals. However, they have given a lot of evidence to show that brain structures and functioning seem to be important in studying causes for aggression in humans. Their main focus in this 1997 study was to use brain scanning to investigate those areas further to find more evidence about brain structure and function and aggression in humans.

STUDY HINT

In the learning theories topic area, you will learn about the use of animals in experiments and how findings tend to be applied to human functioning. You could use Raine *et al.*'s (1997) comments in the introduction as an illustration of how results from animal studies are used to inform the investigation of human functioning but are treated with caution. This would be a useful evaluation point when thinking about the use of animals in experiments in psychology.

Use the information given in the content section of this chapter to familiarise yourself with the different parts of the brain mentioned in the study, so you can visualise them while reading.

Raine *et al.* (1997) listed the regions and studied them both in murderers pleading not guilty by reason of insanity (NGRI) and in a control group. A preliminary study of 22 such murderers and 22 'normal' participants gave some support for prefrontal dysfunction in the murderers (Raine *et al.*, 1994, cited in Raine *et al.*, 1997). The 1997 study used 41 participants and 41 controls, so the sample size was large compared with previous studies. Indeed they say that it is the largest sample in a study looking at violent offenders and assessing brain functioning.

STUDY HINT

In this background information, three evaluation points for this study have been raised by the researchers. They mention that animal study findings might not be generalisable to human behaviour and they suggest that studies of patients in hospital might use samples that are too small (and possibly unique individuals) to generalise successfully to all violent behaviour. These are two criticisms of previous research. They then give a strength of their study, which is that it involves the largest sample they know about in a study using scanning to look at the brains of violent offenders. Make notes about evaluation points as you can use them in discussion.

Raine *et al.* (1997) take what is known about brain functioning to suggest that brain dysfunction in 'the prefrontal cortex, angular gyrus, amygdala, hippocampus, thalamus and the corpus callosum' (p. 496) will be found in 'seriously violent individuals' (p. 496) and that there will be no dysfunction in the 'caudate, putamen, globus pallidus, midbrain or cerebellum' (p. 496), a list they get from looking at brain functioning in other psychiatric conditions but not linked to violence. You do not need to learn all these different brain areas but keep them in mind for the results of this study, which refer to these areas.

Progress check 3.31

Give three brain areas where Raine *et al.* (1997) thought there might be dysfunction in violent individuals.

Procedure

The study used 41 murderers pleading not guilty by reason of insanity (NGRI) and 41 controls. The main participants (average age 34.3 years) were 39 men and two women who had been charged with either murder or manslaughter (labelled murderers in this study). All had been referred to the University of California Irvine Imaging Center to obtain evidence relating to a 'not guilty by reason of insanity' defence, to gather evidence that they could not understand the jury process (incompetence to stand trial) or, if already found guilty, to look for information of diminished capacity.

Sample

The group consisted of 23 people with a history of brain damage, six people with schizophrenia, three people with a history of substance abuse, two with an affective disorder, two with epilepsy, three were diagnosed as hyperactive or with a learning disability and two had paranoid personality disorder. None was on medication when the scanning took place. The control group matched each murderer with a normal participant of the same sex and age, and who was similar in other ways, e.g. there were six with schizophrenia. None of the control group was on medication. The group (average age 31.7 years) consisted of 39 males and two females, mean age 31.7 years. Raine *et al.* made sure that the control participants were not on medication and did not have a history of mental illness, except for the six with schizophrenia, who were chosen for matching reasons. They all consented to the study and the University of California Human Subjects Committee approved the study.

This study could be called a matched pairs design – there is a clear attempt at matching individuals. However, the researchers could not match the variables in the same people – for example, they could not match handedness, head injury and ethnicity in the same individuals, just overall. Therefore, it can be argued that this is an independent groups design. The independent variable is whether or not the participant is a murderer; the dependent variable is the measures of brain activity as found by PET scanning.

PET scanning procedure

The procedure of the study was as follows:

- Each participant carried out a practice test on the continuous performance task that would be used – this practice test was carried out ten minutes before the fluorodeoxyglucose (FDG) tracer was injected.
- Thirty seconds before the tracer was injected, the continuous performance task was started so that the brain activity was being recorded before the tracer was injected.
- The participant carried on with the continuous performance task and target recognition was recorded. The continuous performance task chosen was one that had been shown to give an increase in glucose metabolic rates in the frontal lobes, so would help to highlight brain areas of interest.
- After 32 minutes for the FDG uptake to occur, the participant was taken for a PET scan of the head and images of slices of the brain were produced.

Brain regions were identified by:

- the cortical peel technique – slices were examined and glucose values for each region of interest were compared with those of other areas in a slice; three prefrontal values were found, those for the superior frontal gyrus, the middle frontal gyrus and the inferior frontal gyrus; they also recorded measures in the bilateral temporal, parietal and occipital areas
- a box technique – $2mm^2$ pixels (using boxes of 3x3 pixels) of brain area were examined and linked scan results to the suggested areas for violence.

STUDY HINT

The above information is useful when describing the use of PET scans, so it is worth learning it as an example.

Look back at Table 3.2, which shows some areas of the brain, including the hippocampus, cerebellum, amygdala, thalamus and corpus callosum, to help your understanding of Raine *et al.*'s study.

Progress check 3.32

Explain the procedure of Raine *et al.* (1997) with regard to the scanning.

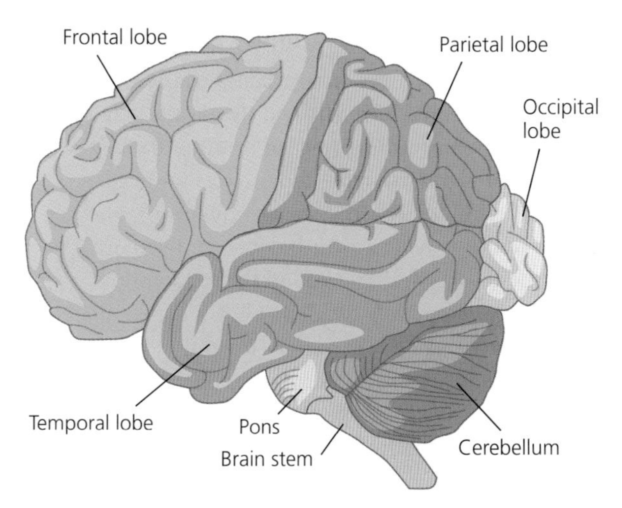

The four lobes of the cerebral cortex

Results

In the tasks that were carried out before the PET scans, there were no differences in performance between the two groups.

Raine *et al.* presented the results for the cortical and sub-cortical regions of the brain separately. The cortical regions are the lobes of the cerebral cortex (see diagram above); the sub-cortical regions are the other regions of interest.

Results for the cortical regions

- **Prefrontal lobe** – the murderers had lower glucose metabolism relative to the controls in some of the prefrontal areas. The murderers had specifically lower glucose metabolism for the left and right medial superior frontal cortex, the left anterior medial cortex, the right orbitofrontal cortex and the lateral middle frontal gyri of both the left and the right hemispheres. This shows that specific brain areas in the prefrontal lobe showed different activation in the murderers compared with the controls.
- **Parietal lobe** – the murderers had lower glucose metabolism than the controls, particularly in the left angular gyrus and bilateral superior parietal regions.
- **Temporal lobe** – there were no significant differences between the murderers and control group with regard to lateral temporal lobe glucose metabolism.
- **Occipital lobe** – the murderers had higher glucose metabolism than the controls.

Results for the sub-cortical regions

- **Corpus callosum** – the murderers had lower glucose metabolism in the corpus callosum than the control group.
- **Amygdala** – the murderers had reduced activity in the left amygdala and greater activity in the right amygdala than the controls.
- **Medial temporal lobe, including the hippocampus** – the murderers had reduced left activity and greater right activity than the controls.
- **Thalamus** – the murderers had greater right thalamic activity than the controls.

The following graph shows the difference in relative glucose for the controls and the murderers in the thalamus. Difference in the right thalamus is clear from the graph. Left and right indicates the two hemispheres.

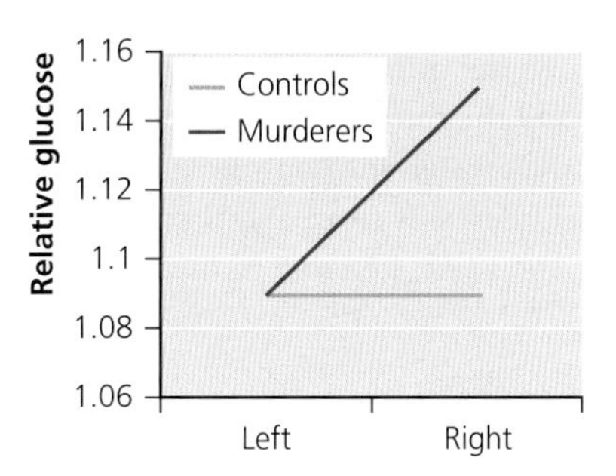

Difference in relative glucose for the controls and the murderers in the thalamus

The following graph shows the difference in relative glucose for the controls and the murderers in the amygdala. Differences between the controls and the murderers are not so clear, though there is more variation in the controls between left and right compared with the murderers. Left and right indicates the two hemispheres.

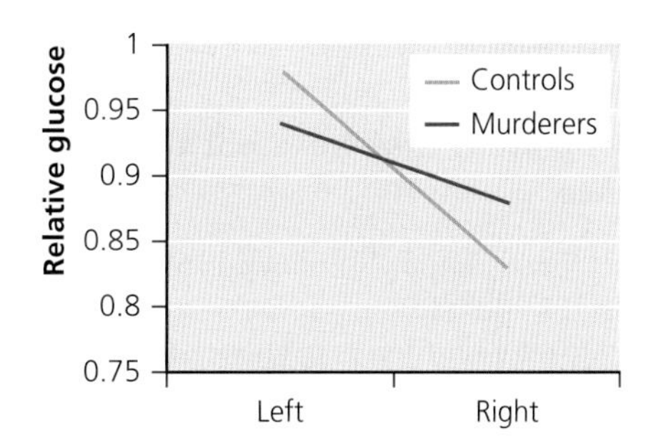

Difference in relative glucose for the controls and the murderers in the amygdala

The following graph shows the difference in relative glucose for the controls and the murderers in the medial temporal lobe/hippocampus. Differences between the controls and the murderers are clear. Left and right indicates the two hemispheres.

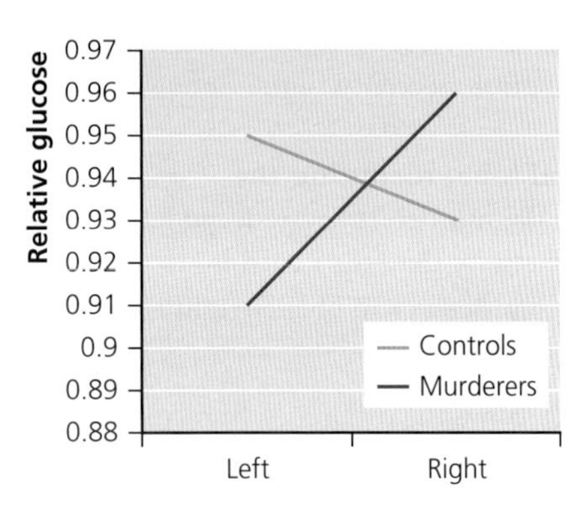

Difference in relative glucose for the controls and the murderers in the medial temporal lobe/hippocampus

The following graph shows the difference in relative glucose for the controls and the murderers in the corpus callosum. The differences between the controls and the reduced glucose in the murderers is clear, and there are few differences between left and right. Left and right indicates the two hemispheres.

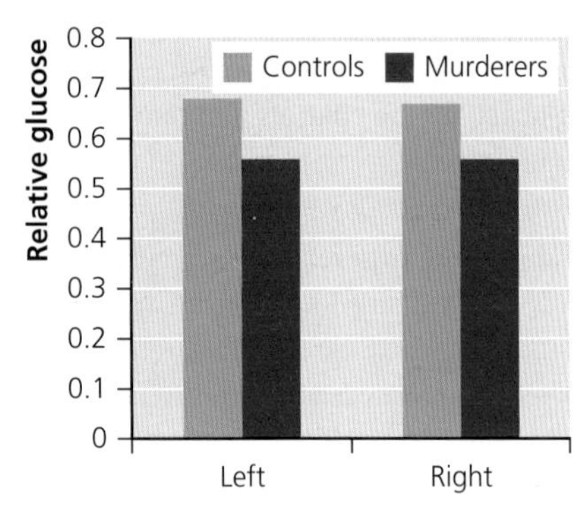

Difference in relative glucose for the controls and the murderers in the corpus callosum

Results for the brain areas that were not thought to link with violence

- The caudate, putamen, globus pallidus and midbrain all showed no significant differences.
- There was a trend for the murderers to show slightly higher glucose metabolic activity in the cerebellum compared with controls.

Progress check 3.33

Explain three parts of the brain that were affected in the study and how they were affected.

How the groups did on the continuous performance task

- The two groups did not differ in how well they did on the task.

The effects of handedness, injury and ethnicity

Raine *et al.* also looked at other variables where the groups differed and that could have affected the results. They had not managed to match the groups in terms of handedness (left-handed or right-handed), injury (relevant head injuries) and ethnicity together, which questions whether the design was matched pairs or independent groups. On checking these variables, they found the following:

- Six murderers were left-handed. They were compared with the right-handed murderers and only some slight differences were found. It was concluded that handedness would not have affected the results. The differences were that the left-handed murderers tend to show higher medial prefrontal activity and to show less abnormal amygdala symmetry.
- Fourteen of the murderers were non-white. They were compared with white murderers and no significant differences were found. This suggests that ethnicity did not affect the findings.
- Twenty-three murderers had a history of head injury. They differed from the other murderers on only one measure – lower activity in the corpus callosum. This may affect the findings of differences in the corpus callosum.

Conclusions

It was concluded that murderers pleading not guilty by reason of insanity have:

- reduced glucose metabolism in the bilateral prefrontal cortex, the posterior parietal cortex and the corpus callosum
- abnormal activity with regard to symmetry in the two hemispheres in the amygdala, thalamus and medial temporal gyrus, including the hippocampus, with the left hemisphere having lower activity than the right in the medial temporal gyrus, including the hippocampus and in the thalamus.

These findings support the idea that violence has biological causes and give ideas about specific issues that might link to violent behaviour.

The researchers looked at how the biological deficits that they found translate into violence, with the following conclusions:

- Prefrontal deficits can result in impulsivity and loss of self-control, as well as emotionality and an inability to modify behaviour. This inability to modify can result in aggression.
- Limbic deficits show the amygdala is associated with aggressive behaviour, in both animals and humans. The amygdala (part of the limbic system), hippocampus and prefrontal cortex govern the expression of emotion and the thalamus relays information. The hippocampus is

thought to modulate aggression (in cats) and there is other evidence linking the limbic system to aggression, emotion and control. The hippocampus, amygdala and thalamus feature in learning, memory and attention and abnormalities in their functioning might result in failure to learn from experience or failure in classically conditioning emotional responses. In animals, the destruction of the amygdala gives lack of fear. These conclusions show how these areas of the brain might be linked to aggressive behaviour.

- The posterior parietal cortex seems to be linked to cognitive functioning, in relation to forming abstract concepts and in relation to input from the senses. For example, reductions in glucose metabolism in the left angular gyrus have been correlated with reduced verbal ability. Cognitive dysfunction could mean educational and occupational failure, which may lead to crime and violence.
- A dysfunction in the corpus callosum may explain hemisphere differences because the corpus callosum links the two hemispheres. The right hemisphere has been said to generate negative effects in humans and in the murderers may be less regulated by the left hemisphere. Studies of rats reinforce this idea. Sperry (1974, cited in Raine *et al.*, 1997) studied patients with split brain (the corpus callosum is split) and found inappropriate emotional expression and difficulty in grasping long-term implications of a situation. This further reinforces the idea that the corpus callosum needs both sides for decision-making and someone with less left hemisphere regulation might be more prone to violence (such as reacting with less long-term planning).
- Socially inappropriate behaviour found in violent individuals might come from the posterial parietal cortex, amygdala and medial temporal lobe, including the hippocampus, and there seem to be differences in glucose activity in these areas in murderers. These areas link to recognition systems. Misunderstanding social situations might lead to violent behaviour, for example.

Findings show that neural processes underlying violence are complex and that there is no single mechanism in the brain that causes violence. 'Violent behaviour probably involves disruption of a network of multiple interacting brain mechanisms that predispose to violence in the presence of other social, environmental and psychological predispositions' (p. 503).

There were brain areas that appear to be relevant to violent behaviour that were not measured in the study, such as the hypothalamus, so the findings are not thought to be a complete account of brain mechanisms and aggression. The researchers felt that they could conclude that, overall, murderers pleading not guilty by reason of insanity seem to have different brain functioning from controls. They also felt that the brain structures they measured and the findings of the study did show that certain brain areas linked to aggression, especially as the brain areas were chosen from the findings of other studies in the first place. The findings show that murderers pleading not guilty by reason of insanity have statistically significant differences in glucose metabolism in certain brain areas compared to a control group (p. 505). The conclusion is that reduced activity in the prefrontal, parietal and callosal areas in the brain, as well as some abnormal asymmetry between left and right hemispheres in the amygdala, thalamus and medial temporal lobe, including the hippocampus, may lead to violence in this group of people.

Progress check 3.34

Give two conclusions from Raine *et al.* (1997).

Evaluation (by the researchers): factors that might have affected the conclusions

The researchers looked at some extraneous factors that may have affected their results and concluded that they were controlled for sufficiently:

- Forty-one is a reasonably good sample size for PET scanning. The sample size is a lot larger than found in other studies using neuroimaging and looking at violent behaviour.
- The strengths of the effects were large enough to draw fairly firm conclusions.
- All but one of the areas that they thought would be important gave significant results, so the findings of earlier studies are supported.
- Areas that they thought would not be important (because of earlier research) were not important.
- The groups were well matched; areas that were not matched (e.g. handedness) were tested, so comparisons between the two groups could be drawn fairly. Age, gender, schizophrenia, handedness, ethnicity and history of head injury were all ruled out as confounding variables (variables that might have caused the results). There was just one trend to note and that is that murderers with a history of head injury had reduced glucose metabolism in the corpus callosum. This may have been because the head injury damaged the corpus callosum.
- All the participants could do the tasks, so there did not seem to be differences in attention, although IQ was not measured. However, low IQ should have given higher cerebral glucose metabolism. The murderers had lower glucose metabolism, so reduced IQ does not seem to account for the differences.

Evaluation (by the researchers): consideration of the strengths and limitations of their conclusions

Strengths

- This is the largest sample ever imaged in this way for this reason.
- The control group includes some good matching.
- The study looks at many brain areas associated with violence rather than just one.

Weaknesses

- The images produced by PET scanning at the time of the study are not particularly clear and the measuring had limitations.
- Findings only apply to one group of murderers pleading not guilty by reason of insanity, not to all violence.
- The findings do not say that violence is just biological; social, psychological, cultural and situational factors are all likely to play a part in violence.
- The study does not give the causes of the brain dysfunctions, such as genes or the environment.
- The findings cannot be generalised to all murderers.
- The control group did not include non-violent criminals so it was not possible to link the brain differences with violence.

Evaluation by Bufkin and Luttrell (2005)

Bufkin and Luttrell (2005) carried out an analysis of 17 studies that used neuroimaging (brain scanning) to look at brain structure and functioning linked to aggression in offenders, one of which was Raine *et al.* (1997). Their article was published in *Trauma, Violence and Abuse*, a journal that speaks for itself perhaps.

Explore

You can access Bufkin and Luttrell's article online using this link: http://acdlaonline.com/zoomdocs/presentations/neuroimagingaggession(1).pdf. You will find a lot of useful information in it relating to brain scanning and in relation to brain structure and functioning linked to aggression.

Bufkin and Luttrell (2005), like Raine *et al.* (1997), were interested in which brain areas might be dysfunctional in violent people. They considered studies that used PET scanning, MRI and fMRI, as well as other neuroimaging techniques to look at brain dysfunction in violent offenders. They summarised the findings of such studies and it is interesting to see how far their findings agree with those of Raine *et al.* (1997).

Bufkin and Luttrell (2005) emphasised the link between faulty regulation of emotions and aggressive/violent behaviour. They claimed that emotion is governed by the prefrontal cortex, the anterior cingulate cortex and the posterior right hemisphere. Also involved are the amygdala, hippocampus and thalamus. Bufkin and Luttrell focused on the prefrontal cortex, the anterior cingulate cortex and the amygdala. They say that the prefrontal cortex has been shown to be about governing behaviour. Bufkin and Luttrell say that Phineas Gage was irresponsible after his injury and 'lacked respect for social conventions' (p. 177). Gage had damage to two parts of the prefrontal cortex: the ventromedial and orbitofrontal regions. Studies of other people also show that damage in such areas can lead to not focusing on future consequences of one's actions. Raine *et al.* also thought that such damage might lead to these consequences.

STUDY HINT

You will be using Bufkin and Luttrell to evaluate Raine *et al.* (1997) so you do not have to learn all about their review. Aim to learn about what they say that supports Raine *et al.*'s study.

Bufkin and Luttrell (2005) consider the amygdala to be an important brain area in aggression, as did Raine *et al.* (1997). The amygdala seems to be about getting emotional material from our environment and might link to someone's ability to control negative emotion. According to scanning studies, the left amygdala is activated when there is a perceived threat, such as seeing fear in someone's face. fMRI scanning showed that if participants were asked to maintain a negative emotion there was more activation in the amygdala than in participants maintaining a passive view of unpleasant pictures (Davidson, Putnam *et al.*, 2000, cited in Bufkin and Luttrell, 2005). Using cues from the environment about threat is useful for people regulating their own responses, and the amygdala has a role in receiving this information. Other parts of the limbic system are also involved in integrating information from a social context into one's own perceptions.

STUDY HINT

Note the use of fMRI scanning in studies used in Bufkin and Luttrell's argument about the amygdala being an area that reacts to emotion. You can use this as an example of fMRI scanning when discussing that method of brain scanning. Look for ways in which you can use information in the different areas of your course.

If there is dysfunction in the prefrontal areas or the amygdala, then this can lead to impulsivity and aggression in the individual. They may not be regulating their responses as someone else might. Such people might misinterpret, for example, the facial expressions of others. Also those with prefrontal dysfunction, in the form of decreased activity, might have more problems in suppressing negative emotions, again possibly leading to more aggression.

Table 3.4 A sample of the 17 studies reviewed by Bufkin and Luttrell (2005)

Study	Participants	Scanning method	Results
Volkow *et al.* (1995)	Eight violent psychiatric patients and eight controls	PET	Violent patients had left and right prefrontal cortex, left frontal cortex and left and right temporal medial cortex reduced functioning.
Goyer *et al.* (1994)	17 personality disorder patients and 43 controls	PET	Orbitofrontal and anterior-medial frontal cortices reduced functioning was linked to self-reported aggression.
Raine *et al.* (1997)	41 murderers pleading NGRI and 41 matched controls	PET	Lateral prefrontal cortex, medial prefrontal cortex and posterial parietal cortex all showed reduced activity (in the murderers). Also reduced activity (in the murderers) in the corpus callosum, left amygdala, thalamus and medial temporal lobes.
Tonkonogy (1991)	23 patients with organic mental disorders, of which 14 were violent and 9 non-violent	MRI	Only 1 of the 14 violent patients had damage to the orbitofrontal cortex area. Violent patients were more likely to have damage in the anterior-inferior temporal lobe, in particular the amygdalo-hippocampal region.
Sakuta and Fukushima (1998)	69 criminals, of which 52 were murderers and 17 not murderers	MRI	The murderers were more likely to have structural abnormalities and those were more likely in the temporal lobes.

Issues and debates

Studies show, using brain scanning, that there are links between certain brain areas and aggressive behaviour. However, social and psychological influences in aggression are also found. Indeed information from the environment can be what leads to violence, perhaps if the brain is not filtering such information in a 'normal' way. The brain of someone who displays violence may not be regulating emotions as normal; however, what stimulates the emotions comes from their environment. Thus explaining aggressive behaviour seems to have a strong nature element, but there are nurture aspects too in the triggers. This is an example of the nature-nurture debate.

Bufkin and Luttrell (2005) present a lot of information that gives evidence for there being neurological aspects relating to violence in individuals. The evidence from studies tends to point to similar brain areas, adding to the weight of the evidence. The brain areas link to those found in Raine *et al.* (1997), strengthening their findings.

Progress check 3.35

From Table 3.4, give two pieces of evidence that show that aggression and violent behaviour can come from our biology.

Overall evaluation of Raine *et al.* (1997)

Strengths

- PET scanning was used and such scans can be interpreted objectively by more than one researcher. Therefore, the results tend to be reliable. PET scanning is a scientific method because there is objectivity and replicability and the procedures are controlled.
- A large group was involved. The researchers pointed out that this was the largest sample that had been used in a PET scan study (up to 1997). There were sufficient people in each group for conclusions to have been fairly firm and generalisation might have been possible to other murderers pleading not guilty by reason of insanity.

Weaknesses

- The results can only be generalised to murderers pleading not guilty by reason of insanity because that was the specific group studied. The findings cannot be said to be true of all violent offenders, even though it was violence that was being studied.
- The reasons for the brain dysfunctions cannot be explained by the study. The findings describe the differences but do not *explain* them. It could be that such differences were present from birth and are biologically given. However, it could also be that such differences came about from environmental influences and that, although they are biological differences, they are not caused biologically. This is an example of the nature–nurture debate and how it is difficult to separate the two when looking for causes of behaviour.

STUDY HINT

If you go on to study criminological psychology in Year 2, you can use the review by Bufkin and Luttrell (2005) not only as evidence for there being a neurological aspect to violent behaviour, but also because they discuss possible ways of 'treating' such behaviour.

Test yourself

1 Explain experimental features of Raine *et al.* (1997). **(4 marks)**
2 Evaluate Raine *et al.* (1997) in terms of the method used (brain scanning) and in terms of how the findings are supported by other studies. **(12 marks)**

Contemporary studies

Li *et al.* (2013)

Li *et al.* (2013) focus on one specific area of the brain, the posterior cingulate cortex, and connections made between it and other brain regions. They look at heroin use to see if changes related to craving for the drug give changes in the connections with the posterior cingulate cortex.

Aim(s)

The aim was to measure brain changes in chronic heroin users against healthy controls to look at the effects of such heroin use. In particular, the area of the posterior cingulate cortex was focused on because previous studies have suggested that is an area of interest in heroin use. Li *et al.* (2013) wanted to look at changes in functional connectivity of the posterior cingulate cortex when a cue-induced task was carried out and fMRI scanning was used to look at brain functioning. The researchers felt that this study would shed light on heroin addiction and how it affects the brain.

Functioning connectivity means brain areas that connect and share functions – this is about looking at the connections between two (or more) brain areas. A cue-induced task means having cues around that link to heroin for the user, as such cues have been shown to produce physiological changes in the brain linked to heroin use. fMRI scanning, which you will study in this topic area, involves taking pictures of the functioning brain.

STUDY HINT

There are a lot of different brain regions mentioned in this study, and other features of studies too, such as using cue-induced tasks and measuring functional connectivity. This is probably going to make this study hard to read and understand at first. To begin with, read through without stopping to get an idea of what happened in the study. Then you can go back to understand it in more detail. The terms will become more familiar the more you use them.

Background

Reward, motivation, working memory and neurotransmitter inhibition are reasons for heroin users to continue with drug usage. Brain areas connected with craving when heroin users are confronted with drug-related cues are the dorsolateral prefrontal cortex, orbitofrontal cortex, posterior cingulate cortex and insula. Li *et al.* (2013) focus on the posterior cingulate cortex because they say it has not had much attention in relation to this area of study. Greicius *et al.* (2003, cited in Li *et al.*, 2013) link the posterior cingulate cortex with episodic memories and this area is related to mental processing in the resting state (when someone is not actively doing cognitive tasks). You look at episodic memory in cognitive psychology in your course (pp. 90–95). Wang *et al.* (2010, cited in Li *et al.*, 2013) showed that heroin users showed a decrease in functional connectivity between different brain areas (the ventral anterior cingulate cortex and the posterior cingulate cortex) compared with healthy controls. The findings of these and other studies mentioned in Li *et al.* (2013) come from neuroimaging (brain scanning). Another finding was that cue-induced craving showed greater activity in the posterior cingulate cortex in heroin users compared with healthy controls (e.g. Wang *et al.*, 2011, cited in Li *et al.*, 2013).

The fMRI scan shows the level of blood oxygen signals across different brain regions and that is what this study is measuring. The first scan for an individual is in resting state, which means the individual is not doing any special tasks. It is necessary to start with a resting-state measure so that the experimental measure (when there is a cue-induced task happening) can be compared with the resting state. Changes in functioning in the brain in the experimental condition can highlight the area of the brain that is functioning in both the resting state and the experimental condition. Li *et al.* (2013) wanted to look at differences in heroin users and healthy controls. Therefore, they wanted to see the activation in the posterior cingulate cortex in the heroin users when the cue-induced task took place and take measurements of the functioning (the experimental condition). Then they could look at the relevant areas (highlighted by the experimental condition) in a resting state for both sets of participants and compare those areas between the two groups. The researchers wanted to see if there had been changes in brain functioning in the heroin-user group that were not found in the healthy controls. This was to look for evidence of damage in the brain because of the use of heroin.

Procedure

There were 14 male participants, all chronic heroin users (chronic means long-time, habitual users). Their age range was 25–47 years and they were all right-handed. They were in China in a Drug Rehabilitation Centre. The participants were all in the detoxification stage. They had to have no psychiatric illness or history of head trauma, and any other issues such as claustrophobia as they would have to lie in an MRI scanner for about 40 minutes.

Fifteen healthy controls were matched to the participants. They had no drug dependence (other than nicotine). The Ethics Committee of the hospital in which the study was run oversaw the study and all participants gave written informed consent.

The study used two fMRI scans, one in the resting state and one in the cue-related task state. Resting state meant focusing on the centre of a screen to relax, moving as little as possible – this state lasted five minutes. This scan was done first. The cue-related task (the experimental task) was done by each participant, the 'heroin user' group and the control group, one at a time, in the scanner. There was a 490-second exposure for them to watch involving 48 pictures. There were 24 'heroin' pictures and 24 neutral pictures. The pictures were shown individually for two seconds and the 'resting state' screen was then shown before the next picture – this took place 48 times. Craving was assessed before the cue-related task and afterwards.

Scoring took place using the scans of the brain and volume difference in the brain regions were calculated between the two groups.

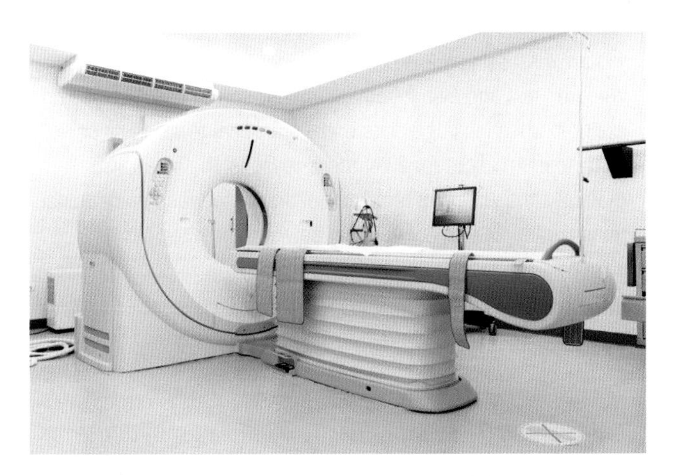

An fMRI scanner, such as used in Li *et al.* (2013)

A lot of other details are given in the study relating to the scanning procedures and the analysis. Analysis was also carried out on differences between the groups, such as using a Wilcoxon rank sum test to see if there were differences between the two groups in nicotine dependence.

A main analysis was to look for differences in brain connections between the heroin users and controls, and a measure of whether connectivity correlated with length of heroin use was also undertaken, using age and education as variables.

Progress check 3.36

What was the main purpose of Li *et al.* (2013)?

Results

- It was found that level of education, nicotine usage and age did not vary between the heroin-user group and the controls.
- The scanning showed that areas activated during the cue-related task for the heroin-user group compared with the controls were the bilateral posterior cingulate cortex, anterior cingulate cortex, caudate, putamen, precuneus and thalamus. The differences in areas activated were found to be significant at $p \leq 0.001$. The posterior cingulate cortex was circled on the scans as that was the main area of focus. Drawing in this circle picked up mostly the heroin users, as would be expected. There were clear differences in the cue-related task scans between the two groups.
- In resting state, and again looking at the circle around the posterior cingulate cortex, it was found that stronger connectivity was found between the posterior cingulate cortex and the bilateral insula and the posterior cingulate cortex and the bilateral dorsal striatum in the chronic heroin users compared with the controls. Other areas that showed connections with the posterior cingulate cortex were also picked out in the heroin users in a resting state. In the controls, there was no brain region that showed more significant connectivity with the posterior cingulate cortex. There were clear differences in resting state between the two groups.
- The connectivity between the posterior cingulate cortex and the bilateral insula and the posterior cingulate cortex (PCC) and the bilateral dorsal striatum, which were the differences in resting state between the heroin-user group and the controls, correlated with the duration of heroin use ($r = 0.60$, $p \leq 0.05$ for the PCC and insula and $r = 0.58$, $p \leq 0.05$ for the PCC and striatum).

STUDY HINT

The correlation results are given, with the levels of significance, to help you to link aspects of the method you learn about in biological psychology with the content and studies.

Summarising the results it was found that:

1. The healthy controls and the heroin users did match well, including their use of nicotine, so conclusions were fairly drawn using the controls against the heroin users.
2. There were clear differences in activity in the scans done during the cue-related task with heroin users having activity and links (connectivity) between areas and the posterior cingulate cortex and the controls not having the links to the same extent, if at all.

3 There were clear differences in the same areas that were highlighted using the cue-related task when the resting-state scans were compared. The controls did not show the connectivity around the posterior cingulate cortex that was found in the heroin users.
4 There was a correlation between the activity in the areas of interest (the posterior cingulate cortex connecting with the bilateral insula and the posterior cingulate cortex connecting with the bilateral dorsal striatum) and the length of time for heroin use.

Conclusions

The posterior cingulate cortex (PCC) was more active when the heroin users did the cue-related tasks. This shows that cues do trigger habituated reactions. The PCC is an area that relates to rewards, so it is not surprising that this area is activated when cues are shown as they would be strongly associated with heroin use. The findings, and the findings of other studies, suggest that the posterior cingulate cortex is likely to have an important role in the limbic system, an area believed to be linked to reward and cravings.

STUDY HINT

The idea of association of rewards with cues fits with classical and operant conditioning, two theories that are presented in Chapter 4 on learning theories. You can use your learning about conditioning to help in understanding this study and its findings. However, learning theories do not focus on the biology involved in conditioning, whereas in biological psychology that is precisely the area of interest.

The dorsolateral striatum was also involved when the cue-dependent task was taking place. This region of the brain seems to relate to compulsive drug-seeking behaviour and it is suggested that this region is important in dopamine-regulated neural circuits. You can link this idea to what is said about the effects of recreational drugs on transmission in the brain earlier in this chapter (pp. 141–144).

The conclusion does seem to be that connectivity has changed in the heroin-user group, and that the connections that were found link to areas for dependency and reward in the brain. There seemed to be an abnormal level of connection between the areas listed here in the addicts compared with the controls.

Another reason for concluding that the changes in links in the brain come from heroin use is that the longer the heroin use, the stronger the functional connectivity between the brain areas mentioned. This suggests that the addict's brain changes over time in response to heroin use.

Overall, Li *et al.* (2013) show that there are changes in the brain that come from long-term heroin use and those changes are where connections are made between areas that are for rewards and addiction, including involving dopamine. The researchers mention that their study had a small sample size, which they saw as a problem when drawing conclusions about all heroin users. Another issue is that they only used males because males were available – that too might limit the generalisability of the findings. Also all of the participants, heroin users and healthy controls were smokers, which again might limit the generalisability of the findings, though the researchers did check that there were no differences between the heroin users and controls in their nicotine ingestion.

Progress check 3.37

Explain two conclusions of Li *et al.* (2013).

STUDY HINT

This study uses fMRI scanning, so you can use it as an example when discussing that method. The study looks at brain functioning and brain structures, so you can use it as an example when discussing that content area. It uses an experimental design with a control group, so is useful when you are discussing the experimental method. The study uses a Wilcoxon test and also a correlation test, so you can use it as an example when looking at inferential statistical tests. It is a useful study to learn about for all of those reasons. The study also examines the effects of recreational drugs, not quite on neuronal transmission, but on connectivity between brain regions.

Evaluation of Li *et al.* (2013)

Strengths

- Using an fMRI scan is non-invasive, so it is ethical, and easy to perform, so it is convenient for both the researchers and the participants. The researchers checked that none of the participants suffered from claustrophobia (as each person was in the scanner for around 40 minutes), so ethically the experience should have been acceptable.
- The researchers took a lot of trouble when measuring what they were looking for in the scanning, though not all the detail is reported in this account of their study. They were careful to look at other issues that might affect the change in scan data from the resting state to the cue-related task condition, for example.

Weaknesses

- Scanning when cue-related processing was taking place is likely to have involved a lot of other thought too, so even with care taken to isolate certain variables that might affect the functioning they were looking at, there may have been confounding variables. The healthy controls would have had the same conditions; however, there might well be individual differences between individuals that affected the conclusions as cognitive processing is hard to isolate to just one task.

- The researchers did say they felt their sample was rather small to generalise from and they also felt that having just males limited the generalisability of their study. However, as other studies had pinpointed the same areas of interest, relating them to addiction and the reward system, there was some justification in generalising the results to say heroin does cause brain damage (which is basically what the study claims, though of course it is a lot more specific than that).

Test yourself

1. Explain the procedure of Li *et al.*'s (2013) study. **(8 marks)**
2. Evaluate Li *et al.*'s (2013) study in terms of its generalisability and validity. **(10 marks)**

Brendgen *et al.* (2005)

Brendgen *et al.* (2005) used six-year old twins to look at social and physical aggression and nature–nurture implications.

STUDY HINT

At the start of this chapter, Ingram's (2014) study was briefly explained as a study of interest (p. 131). Ingram looked at how physical aggression moves to social aggression as a child develops into adolescence. Ingram's study links with Brendgen *et al.*'s study.

Aim(s)

One aim was to study the relative contribution to social aggression compared with physical aggression of genes and two types of environment (shared and non-shared). Brendgen *et al.* (2005) also wanted to study what might lead to the positive correlation that is found between social and physical aggression.

Background

The study starts from the view that aggression in children is seen as a risk factor in later development, in terms of not only being perpetrators of crimes, but also being victims. Therefore, understanding the cause(s) of a child's aggression has importance for society. Brendgen *et al.* (2005) suggest that physical aggression has had a lot of focus but that there are other forms of aggression, such as more subtle forms, like spreading rumours (e.g. Willoughby *et al.*, 2001, cited in Brendgen *et al.*, 2005). Sometimes this more subtle aggression is called 'indirect' aggression, sometimes 'relational aggression' and sometimes 'social aggression'. Brendgen *et al.* (2005) explain that indirect aggression is covert (not done openly), whereas relational aggression can be covert, like spreading a rumour, or overt, like threatening to withdraw friendship. Social aggression involves overt and covert behaviour and also non-verbal aggression (e.g. pulling faces at someone). Brendgen *et al.* (2005) use the term 'social aggression' because they cover covert and overt behaviour. It appears that social aggression and physical aggression are separate types of aggression (Vaillancourt *et al.*, 2003, cited in Brendgen *et al.*, 2005).

There is interest in what causes social and physical aggression. However, a difficulty is that genes and the environment as causes are hard to look at if only one child in each family is studied. Brendgen *et al.* (2005) give the example of aggression in a child and consider environmental factors by looking at parental aggressive behaviour. The difficulty is that the child shares genes with their parents as well as environment, so the two cannot be separated for study. The use of twin designs can help to overcome this problem (Plomin, 1974, cited in Brendgen *et al.*, 2005).

Brendgen *et al.* (2005) talk about phenotypic similarity. Our genotype is what we are in the way of genes. Our phenotype is what we are when our genes and environment combine as we develop. The idea of phenotype similarity needs to be explained. Identical twins (monozygotic, MZ twins) share 100 per cent of their genes and tend to share their environment, though they might have different peer interactions and other differences in their environment. Therefore, they are likely to have differences in their phenotypes. Non-identical twins of the same gender (dizygotic, DZ twins) share 50 per cent of their genes and tend to share their environment, though they too might have different peers and different environments. They too are likely to have different phenotypes, though it can be argued that the phenotypes of MZ twins are likely to be more similar (with each other) than the phenotypes of DZ twins. This is the assumption Brendgen *et al.* (2005) make.

The study of phenotype difference between identical twins and non-identical twins who share the same gender can separate genetic factors, environmental influences from parents (shared environment) and environmental influences from others, such as peers (non-shared environments). Brendgen *et al.* (2005) use the idea of studying differences in phenotype between MZ and DZ (same gender) twins to look at the contribution of genes and the environment on social and physical aggression. They also want to look at what might cause the positive correlation between social and physical aggression.

Studies show that about 50 per cent of physical aggression might be down to genes (studies vary and find that between 40 and 80 per cent is down to genes, with an average finding around 50 per cent). The other 50 per cent seems to be down to non-shared environment (environment outside the family). Brendgen *et al.* (2005) say that no study has looked at social aggression to find the relative percentages relating to whether social aggression comes from genes, shared or non-shared environment. They suggest that social aggression and physical aggression might come from the same source and it is just the behaviour (physical or social) that differs. Dettling *et al.* (1999, cited in Brendgen *et al.*, 2005) found that in 3–8-year-old children measures of cortisol rise from the morning to the afternoon and these levels are linked to both social and physical aggression rising. Others suggest there are different causes behind physical and social aggression, with social aggression involving more imitation of others and learning by reinforcement and rewards than physical aggression (Grotpeter and Crick, 1996, cited in Brendgen *et al.*, 2005). There might be more peer influence in social aggression and physical aggression might have more of a genetic cause than social aggression. (You will learn more about social learning and the role of imitation, and about how we learn by a pattern of reinforcements and rewards, when you study learning theories in Chapter 4.) Therefore, there is evidence that social and physical aggression might come from the same cause or might come from different causes.

Another idea is that very young children tend to exhibit physical aggression because they do not have other tools available to them. Up to school age, they are learning, and both their verbal skills and their social skills are improving. Physical and verbal aggression are more noticeable, whereas social aggression can be less obvious and carry less chance of retribution, so social aggression comes to be preferred (Bjoerkqvist *et al.*, 1992, cited in Brendgen *et al.*, 2005). This should mean that high levels of physical aggression become high levels of social aggression. Indeed it is found that physical aggression reduces through early childhood into middle childhood.

The research questions were:

- Compared with physical aggression, how far is social aggression down to genes, shared or non-shared environment?
- How far can the link in an individual between social and physical aggression be explained by genes, shared or non-shared environment?
- How far can the link in an individual between social and physical aggression be explained by physical aggression being taken over by social aggression from early to middle childhood?

Progress check 3.38

State two of Brendgen *et al.*'s (2005) research questions.

Procedure

The methods used to get the information about social and physical aggression were teacher and peer ratings. Other studies have shown that such data have reliability and both construct and predictive validity (e.g. Willoughby *et al.*, 2001, cited in Brendgen *et al.*, 2005). One difficulty though is that teacher and peer ratings do not show good correspondence to one another. They may both show good reliability and validity with regard to measuring the child, but they only have a low or medium correspondence with one another. Brendgen *et al.* (2005) wanted to see whether the teacher and peer ratings would give the same pattern of results with regard to their research questions.

STUDY HINT

You need to know about reliability in studies: if a study is done again (replicated) and the same results are found, then those results are reliable. Of course, results can be found over and over again and still not measure what has been claimed, which is where validity comes in.

Validity means that the results of a study are about real-life behaviour or issues, rather than, for example, unnatural laboratory behaviour. You also need to know about construct validity. Construct validity refers to whether what is being measured is what is claimed to be measured.

In Brendgen *et al.*'s (2005) study, did teacher and peer ratings capture someone's social and physical aggression as it was claimed? Predictive validity refers to whether, for example, if a score is done twice, the score would be the same. This means that the first score predicts the second score because they are both measuring the same thing. In this case, it would be that a child's social and physical aggression scores are really measuring their social and physical aggression levels, and if that is the case, then later scores will come up with the same results for these two types of aggression for that child.

The participants came from the Quebec Newborn Twin Study. Twin studies often use such secondary data as it would be hard for individual researchers to find sufficient twins and to collect the data. The data are already gathered, and it is sensible (and perhaps ethical) to use it. The twins in the Quebec Newborn Twin Study were from the Montreal area of Canada and were recruited from birth from November 1995 to July 1998. There were 322 twin pairs. 237 twin pairs were same sex and physical resemblance was used to allocate them to the category of identical or non-identical twins. For

123 twin pairs, DNA was obtained and the results compared with the decision based on physical resemblance, with 94 per cent agreement, which is seen as good enough.

A comparison was made between the twins and single children with regard to parental education, yearly income, age of parents when the twins were born and marital status, and it was thought that the twins were not different in these aspects.

Brendgen *et al.* (2005) used the data that were gathered at the age of six (data were gathered from birth at fairly regular intervals). At this stage of the study, there were 234 twin pairs: 44 were identical and males; 50 were identical and females; 41 were non-identical and males; 32 were non-identical and females; 67 were non-identical and mixed gender.

Written consent was obtained from the parents of all the children in the classroom and the research questions and questionnaires were approved by the Institutional Review Board. As the twins were sometimes but not always in the same classrooms, 409 classrooms were involved in the main twin study (from which the data for Brendgen *et al.*'s study came). Peer data were collected from sociometric data, which means finding out who is friends with whom.

- The teachers completed behaviour questionnaires for the twin(s) in their class. The teachers rated the child's social and physical aggression using standardised scales. For example, with regard to social aggression, they rated to what extent the child 'tries to make others dislike a child' and for physical aggression they rated 'gets into fights', for example. From the scales, each child had a social aggression score and a physical aggression score. For a child, with different teachers rating that child, it was found that the scores did agree with one another – a measure of reliability.
- Peers also gave data about the twins' level of social and physical aggression. Photos of all the children in the classroom were circulated (making sure peers knew which child was which), and peers were asked to circle photographs in answer to instructions, such as 'Circle three children who best fit the behaviour': 'tells others not to play with a child' or 'hits, bites or kicks others'. From the peer data, each child received a total social aggression score and a total physical aggression score. Again there was internal consistency between the scores of an individual child from the peer ratings.

Progress check 3.39

Explain how both the peer and the teacher ratings of each child for social and physical aggression were obtained.

Results

Gender differences

According to teachers, boys were rated more physically aggressive than girls and girls more socially aggressive than boys. However, this was not borne out by the data, as no gender difference was found.

Overlap between social and physical aggression

There was overlap between social and physical aggression in both the teacher and the peer ratings, meaning a child seen as socially aggressive was seen as physically aggressive too and vice versa, though this link was what the researchers called a 'moderate' one.

Comparing boys and girls and social and physical aggression statistically

This was done using a chi-squared test. The results found a very close match between teacher ratings and peer ratings. The scores looked at teacher ratings of MZ pairs and DZ pairs and peer ratings of MZ pairs and DZ pairs. It was found that, with regard to gender, neither the overlap of social and physical aggression, nor the amount of genetic and environmental contributions differed between boys and girls. After this analysis, therefore, boys and girls data were pooled as they did not differ. Having greater numbers in the overall analysis helped the statistical power.

The role of genes and the environment

By looking at similarities or differences within identical twins and within same-sex non-identical twins, it is possible to look for genetic and environmental influences and their relative contributions.

- To find the contribution from genes: the difference between the MZ (identical twins) correlation (between the two of them) and the DZ (non-identical twins, same sex) correlation is looked at. The usual rule is to take the MZ correlation from the DZ correlation and the genetic contribution is about twice that difference. Just using any figures for the moment as an example, if a correlation between MZ twins is 0.60 on a characteristic and a correlation between DZ twins is 0.40 then the difference is 0.20 – and double that is supposed to be down to genes. In this fictitious example, that would be 40 per cent down to genes.
- To find the contribution from the shared environment: take the MZ correlation for a characteristic from twice the DZ correlation. In the fictitious example given here, that would be 0.60 from 0.80 (which is twice 0.40), which gives 0.20. So around 20 per cent of the variance is down to shared environment.

- To find the contribution from the non-shared environment: this is how far the MZ correlation is different from 1, which is 0.40 in the example being given here. So 40 per cent of the difference is down to non-shared environment in this fictitious example.

Brendgren *et al.*'s results were as follows:

- MZ correlations were nearly twice as high as same-sex DZ correlations when it came to physical aggression, and this was for both teacher and peer ratings. This means that it was nearly twice as likely that the identical twins matched in physical aggression compared with the non-identical same sex twins. This shows quite a high contribution from genetic factors for physical aggression (this is because MZ twins share 100 per cent of their genes and DZ twins share just 50 per cent, but they share their environment). There is more evidence for this focus on genes for physical aggression later in this section.
- MZ correlations and same-sex DZ correlations for social aggression were similar, again both for peer and teacher ratings. This suggests that social aggression comes more from shared environment than from genes (both DZ and MZ share an environment with each other, but they do not share the same number of genes, with DZ having 50 per cent and MZ having 100 per cent).
- For both MZ and DZ twins, the size of the correlations mentioned above is just moderate, which suggests a high contribution in the case of both 'twin types' for non-shared environment, and this is for both social and physical aggression.
- The researchers tried various modelling techniques to look at the teacher and peer ratings with regard to MZ and DZ (same-sex) twins to see how far contributions to social and physical aggression came from genes, shared environment or non-shared environment.
  - First, looking at teacher ratings: with regard to physical aggression, causes seemed to be genes and non-shared environment, with about 63 per cent down to genetics, leaving 37 per cent down to non-shared environment (no influence from shared environment). With regard to social aggression, the modelling suggested 20 per cent down to genes, 20 per cent down to shared environment and 60 per cent down to non-shared environment. These figures used the model that best fitted the data.
  - Second, looking at peer ratings: using the same process, physical aggression came out as 54 per cent down to genes and 46 per cent down to non-shared environment (no influence from shared environment). Social aggression had genetic and shared environment contributing 23 per cent each, with 54 per cent down to non-shared environment. These figures used the model that best fitted the data.
- Results looking at correlations for social and physical aggression and how they appear together:
  - For teacher ratings: there was a strong correlation between the genetic reasons for social and physical aggression (correlation = 0.79). However, there was a much lower correlation between the non-shared environmental factors leading to social and physical aggression (correlation 0.31). The researchers found that 62 per cent of genetic factors that influenced social aggression also influenced physical aggression according to teacher ratings, for example, whereas only 9 per cent of non-shared environment (e.g. friendship group unique to one of the twins) influenced the two types of aggression.
  - For peer ratings: there was a perfect correlation with regard to the same genetic factors influencing social and physical aggression (correlation = 1.00) and a non-significant weak correlation in non-shared environmental influences (correlation = 0.12).
  - These findings mean that the correlation between social and physical aggression in children might be mainly due to overlapping genes and hardly at all due to overlapping environment. If genes predict both social and physical aggression, then a child who is physically aggressive will also show (or be judged to show) social aggression.

Conclusions

One aim of the study was to look at how far genes, shared environment and non-shared environment explain the differences between social and physical aggression. Another aim was to see if differences between social and physical aggression are explained either because one type

Table 3.5 Explaining the variance for the type of aggression: teacher and peer ratings

Explaining the variance for the type of aggression	Teacher ratings		Peer ratings	
	Physical aggression	Social aggression	Physical aggression	Social aggression
Genetic	63%	20%	54%	23%
Shared environment	0%	20%	0%	23%
Non-shared environment	37%	60%	46%	54%

of aggression relates to the other or because both have the same genetic, shared environmental and/or non-shared environmental causes.

Genetic and environmental influences on social and physical aggression

The findings for six year olds were that about 50–60 per cent of differences in physical aggression was down to genes and the rest to non-shared environment – which is the environment that each twin has uniquely, not their home and parents. For social aggression, genetic effects accounted for only 20 per cent of the differences between the children, 20 per cent was said to be from shared environment, and 60 per cent was explained by non-shared environment.

Social aggression seems to be caused more by environmental factors and physical aggression more by genetic factors.

Links between social and physical aggression in the same child

Those showing physical aggression did tend to show social aggression too, and there was overlap, but this was moderate. It seemed that this link between the two types of aggression could be best explained by looking at genes and only to an extent by looking at environment. Possibly some children are predisposed by their genes to behave in an aggressive way in general (so both social and physical aggression is seen in them). With regard to the environmental factors that relate to both social and physical aggression, what might lead to social aggression is parental psychological control, such as love withdrawal. Social aggression follows a similar pattern (such as threatening friendship withdrawal). This sort of behaviour might account for environmental effects on aggression.

Moving from physical to social aggression as the child matures – the directional effect

Brendgen *et al.* (2005) found that the more physical aggression in an individual, the higher their social aggression. The two were connected. However, a high level of social aggression did not seem to predict a high level of physical aggression – the link just went one way. This is a directional effect and is found in other studies too. Children seem to express their aggression physically up to a certain age and then switch to social aggression. Possibly because they are told off for physical aggression, which is not socially acceptable, they turn to another outlet for their aggression, using less risky strategies.

The finding that both social and physical aggression share their genetic underpinnings supports this idea that physical aggression in a child can turn into social aggression as the child matures. This might also explain why social aggression is affected more by environment than physical aggression, as social aggression is driven by environmental and social factors, including what the child might imitate, such as a parent withdrawing love as a punishment. The children in Brendgen *et al.*'s study are six years old so not yet moving away from physical aggression enough for it to have disappeared, as it might as they mature.

Strengths and limitations of the study, expressed by the researchers

- An advantage is that both teacher and peer ratings are used, whereas peer ratings are not usually available for this sort of study. It was interesting that the two sets of ratings showed a lot of similarities.
- A limitation was the small sample sizes, though as 409 classrooms were studied this meant a larger size was not practical. Future studies should use larger samples and the findings need to be replicated.
- Another limitation was that just six year olds were used and generalising beyond that age is difficult. Social aggression might not develop until the age of about eight years old and physical aggression by the age of six has diminished, so this is a specific age for testing these two types of aggression. Developmental changes are occurring, which means generalisation is hard. Also other studies (e.g. Rhee and Waldman, 2002, cited in Brendgen *et al.*, 2005) have found that non-shared environmental influences rise and genetic and shared environmental influences fall with age.
- Longitudinal data are better when looking at genetic influences on behaviour as cross-sectional studies like this one just show one moment in time and developmental issues cannot be followed through.

The most important finding is that environmental influences are strong in social aggression. There are practical applications in these findings. If social aggression links to environment, such as peers and friendship groups, then that can be addressed. Also if physical aggression is reduced in the younger child then social aggression is less likely as they get older, as the two are linked.

Progress check 3.40

In the following table, note 'yes' to the statements that correctly identify conclusions of Brendgen *et al.* (2005) and 'no' to the incorrect statements.

Statement	Correct
Children who show physical aggression rarely show social aggression.	
A child who shows physical aggression when young is likely to move to social aggression as they mature.	
Social aggression can replace physical aggression because it is more subtle and less likely to be punished as less overtly disapproved of by society and parents.	
Physical aggression is mostly down to environmental factors.	
About 50 to 60 per cent of physical aggression is genetic.	
Physical aggression in a child predicts social aggression, so is best reduced as much as possible.	

Evaluation of Brendgen *et al.* (2005)

Strengths

- Both teachers and peers rated the children for social and physical aggression, which gave two ratings to compare and, as they mostly agreed, this suggests that the findings have reliability and perhaps validity.
- Using twin studies and comparing identical and non-identical twins is a good way of studying nature versus nurture and looking at the weighting of genes, shared and non-shared environment on a behaviour such as aggression. The researchers used same-sex DZ twins to match the MZ twins, which is a useful design feature, to make the twin pairs as similar as possible except for shared genes.

Weaknesses

- They were measuring ratings of physical and social aggression and ratings might not match reality. For example, perhaps a child remembers one act of physical aggression from one of their peers more than another act from a different child. There may be stereotyping, perhaps especially as twins are involved – even if they are in different classrooms, they will still perhaps be known to all teachers and children in the year group. Ratings are not direct observations, so there may not be validity.
- It is possible that the non-shared environment of twins is very different; however, it is possible that it is very similar. Twins might share friends, for example. A difficulty with twins, if trying to separate shared from non-shared environment, is that assumptions have to be made. A study that looks scientific in its approach (and the analysis in this study has many elements of being scientific, such as statistical testing) might not be as scientific as it seems.
- The twins were judged by looking at them to decide whether they were identical or not, and, although some were DNA tested to check the decision, others were not. As the DNA testing showed that the judgements seemed to be justified (around 94 per cent), this was not necessarily the case for those not DNA tested, so there might be some effect on the findings if the type of twin was not appropriately allocated.

Test yourself

1. Explain how Brendgen *et al.* (2005) carried out their study so that they could investigate how far genes and the environment explain social and physical aggression in children. **(6 marks)**
2. Evaluate Brendgen *et al.*'s (2005) study in relation to its scientific credibility. **(10 marks)**

Van den Oever *et al.* (2008)

The biology in this study is rather complicated, so an explanation is provided before giving the details of the study.

You need to know that the AMPA receptor is a receptor for glutamate and speeds up transmission at the synapse. AMPA is artificial glutamate. This is the most common receptor in the central nervous system and is found throughout the brain. The mPFC is mentioned in this study – that is the medial prefrontal cortex, which you already know something about. Glutamatergic pyramidal neurons are deep inside the medial prefrontal cortex and send out excitory messages to other areas, which are the reward circuit. You have already come across the reward circuit earlier in this chapter. High-frequency synaptic stimulation is known to cause a rapid and lasting change in AMPA receptors (Liu and Cull Candy, 2002).

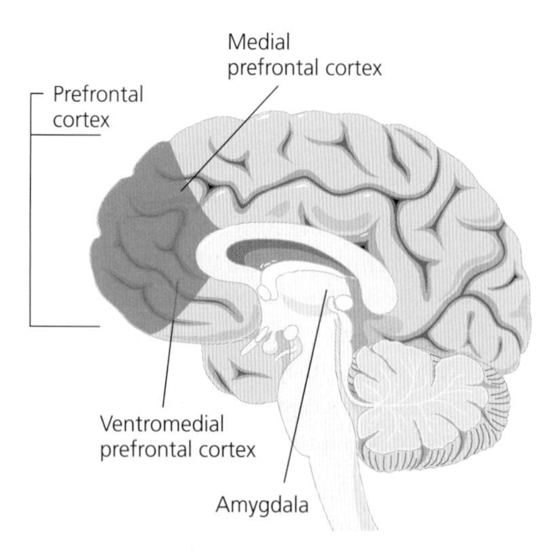

Showing the medial prefrontal cortex, the area of focus in van den Oever *et al.*'s (2008) study

Van den Oever *et al.* (2008) were interested in heroin addiction and more precisely in the cues that can lead to taking up heroin again after extinction. They wanted to see what brain changes are related to this idea that cues lead to relapse. Extinction (explained in Chapter 4) refers to when a learned association is extinguished, which means someone or an animal no longer associates a stimulus that has been paired with a response – their learning has been extinguished.

It is recognised that heroin addicts learn to pair the cues around taking heroin with the high they experience. When someone no longer takes heroin, a problem in maintaining that abstention is that cues might be around, and cues are known to give relapse. Li *et al.* (2013) looked at cue-related pictures regarding drug-taking and at brain functioning related to that. Van den Oever *et al.* had a similar focus. They carried out animal experiments to look at changes in receptors in response to re-exposure to heroin-related cues.

Aim(s)

The aim was to look at what happens at the synapse and what changes occur when rats with an extinguished heroin addiction are exposed to cues related to their heroin-taking. The researchers want to see what such re-exposure to drug-related cues does to the synaptic transmission in the brain. They focus on the medial prefrontal cortex, an area known to be associated with drug-taking.

Background

- Van den Oever *et al.* (2008) point out that what for others are neutral stimuli in an environment – but, for someone taking drugs, are drug paraphernalia – become cues associated with the drug-taking. Importantly, there is then association between the cues and the reinforcement that comes from taking drugs. You may be reading this study before you have studied conditioning in the learning theories chapter. When you get to that chapter, you will read more about how reinforcement works and how rewards associated with something directly, like taking a drug, can become associated with things, even people, around. This is a main point in this study – that cues in the environment can become associated with the reward of taking drugs.
- A second main point is that such learning by association is linked to the brain's synaptic plasticity. Plasticity means that there are actual physical changes at the synapse. The synapse can change in response to experience. Some people may think that the brain is formed and then remains as it is, fixed, with permanent links. Actually there are more or less continual changes at the synapses. You will have learned about that when looking at how transmission at the synapse is affected by recreational drugs (pp. 141–144). You will have seen that changes occur and that is where the 'danger' of taking drugs lies – it affects our brains. In the section looking at the effects of recreational drugs, this was called 'brain damage'. Heroin is a recreational drug and you can use this study when discussing how synaptic transmission is affected by recreational drugs. Van den Oever *et al.* (2008) accept that there is plasticity.
- Their aim is to see what changes at the synapse occur when cue-related relapse occurs (in rats). 'Cue-related' means relapse into heroin-taking again because of cues being in the environment that were previously linked by the organism to heroin-taking.
- The brain changes that occur during long-term drug-taking involve long-term depression (LTD) in the neurons that are related to reward learning. This involves the reward circuit. 'Depression' in this sense is literal and means that the synapse does not work as well, for reasons such as level of calcium in the postsynaptic neuron.
- Some of the changes are long-lasting and this means that long-term drug-taking can change the way the neurons work in the brain.
- Van den Oever *et al.* (2008) also note that, when an addict is faced with stimuli linked with their drug-taking, this can lead to craving and then relapse, even if someone has stopped taking drugs for a long time.
- The aim of the study is to look at the synaptic changes that occur straight after the cues are presented (cues that have been linked to the drug-taking).
- The researchers already know from their previous work that such re-exposure (to cues) affects the medial prefrontal cortex.
- Advances in ways to measure what happens at the synapse allow the researchers to measure small but important changes in the amount of protein at the synaptic membrane in the medial prefrontal cortex (mPFC) of rats. In particular, they focus on the AMPA receptor because they know it is affected by re-exposure to heroin cues. They found a 25 per cent reduction in activity in the AMPA receptors.

Progress check 3.41

Explain the aims of the van den Oever *et al.* (2008) study.

Explore

You can find out more about AMPA receptors and synaptic depression on the internet, such as on the following page of Bristol University's site: www.bristol.ac.uk/synaptic/receptors/ampar/plasticity/. By exploring more, you will find a link to the hippocampus and memory, as well as explanations that help in understanding this study.

Procedure

Male rats were used in this study. The Animal Users Care Committee of the researchers' university approved all the experiments.

> **STUDY HINT**
> In learning theories, you will look at the use of animals in laboratory experiments and you can apply your learning to this study, as well as use this study as an example of using animals in lab experiments.

The rats were trained to take heroin themselves (self-administration by nose-poking in a hole that gave heroin) in three-hour sessions over 15 days. During this stage, there were cues around that the rats would associate with the heroin reward they received. Then half the rats abstained from heroin for 21 days in their home cage. The other half of the rats underwent one-hour extinction sessions once a day over 15 days. Then they took half the 'home cage' rats and half the 'extinction group' rats and exposed them to heroin-conditioned cues for 60 minutes. The rats who were exposed to the cues were then studied for brain changes. This was done by looking at brain slices. There were also control rats who were trained to nose-poke for sucrose, not heroin.

In a separate part of the study, the researchers gave rats an injection to block activity at the synapse in a specific way, with the aim of blocking the changes that were of concern (in the medial prefrontal cortex).

Results

Results of the reintroduction to cues

The study involved rats nose-poking for heroin that was delivered intravenously when they poked. It is important for the study that there are visual cues around when they poked for the heroin. There were other holes and the 'addiction' was noted when rats developed a preference for the hole that meant they received heroin. The result of this part of the study is that the rats became addicted to heroin.

Then there was a period of abstinence from the heroin (three weeks), either in their home cage without any extinction process, or in the condition where there was extinction training in the training cage. The 'training' condition involved no heroin when they nose-poked and no heroin-linked visual cues either. The 'home cage' condition also had no heroin-linked visual cues. There were also rats not exposed to the visual cues as controls. This was the period of extinction. The result of this part of the study was that the rats were no longer addicted to heroin.

Then came the important bit, where cues were reintroduced to see what would happen. (There were rats with no cues who acted as controls.) The results were that, when cues were introduced, in both the 'home cage' (the abstinence group) and 'extinction training' conditions, rats showed relapse with regard to heroin-seeking behaviour.

It is at this stage that the researchers wanted to see what effect relapse had on the brain.

> **STUDY HINT**
> Van den Oever *et al.* (2008) used controls in their experiment using animals, so this is a useful study for understanding issues around such research methods. When looking at experiments in general, whether animal or human, the use of controls is important.

To find out the effect on the brain of the cue-induced relapse, the rats' brains were studied immediately after the reintroduction of cues showed heroin relapse. The area studied was the medial prefrontal cortex and what was looked at was a synaptic membrane. Different tests were carried out, including testing the rats with cues against the rats with no cues, and the rats who had the heroin addiction extinguished by abstinence (in the home cage) against those by extinction training. This was to look for differences in the brain possibly caused by the cues or by the differences in ways the addiction was extinguished.

They found that, out of 417 proteins identified at the synapse, there was a significant amount, six proteins ($p \leq 0.01$), that were changed after exposure to the cues. They gave details of the actual proteins and the differences, and concluded that exposure to the cues results in synaptic depression in the medial prefrontal cortex as expected. The changes were in GLuR2/3 AMPAR protein levels, as expected.

There were further investigations to see if changes in the pyramidal neurons in the medial prefrontal cortex (mPFC) were found. The researchers recorded glutamatergic synaptic transmission in the pyramidal neurons in the mPFC. Rats that were re-exposed to the heroin cues showed significant differences compared with those who were not exposed to the cues – the differences were in the AMPA/NMDA areas as expected. The control rats showed no such changes. The findings were reduced levels of synaptic GluR2/3 AMPAR subunits after exposure to the cues. It is not necessary to fully understand the changes themselves, just to see that there were changes in the synapses after the cues were introduced and the relapse occurred. The graph below shows that there is a lower ratio of AMPA/NMDA for the rats who self-administered heroin and had cues for relapse than the other three conditions, which is what was predicted. The heroin-addicted rats who did not have cues to trigger the relapse had very similar ratios of AMPA/NMDA.

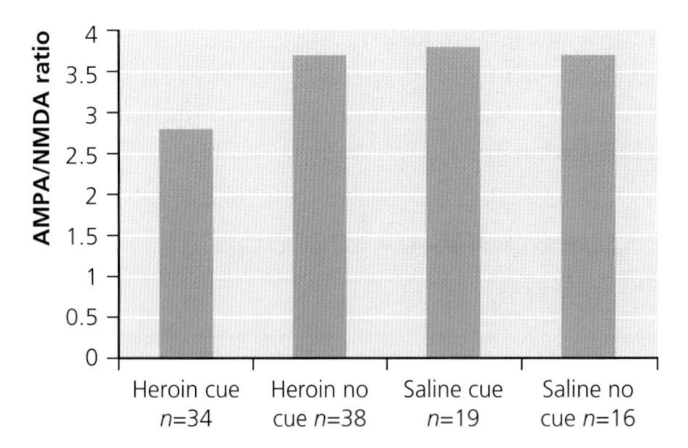

AMPA/NMDA ratio for four conditions: the rats who self-administered heroin and those who self-administered saline and for both these two conditions, with and without cues

STUDY HINT

Note that, in the results section, there is some discussion of the procedure. This is because the study is rather complex and clarity was needed. Also, some of the results are alongside the procedure as it progresses, such as the resulting heroin addiction and the resulting extinction of the addiction. The main results really are the changes in the brain when cues are reintroduced and there is relapse. If you are asked for results, be sure to focus on results, not the procedure, and vice versa.

Results of the injections to block the synaptic depression

There was work in the study to see how the depression at the synapse when cues triggered relapse might be prevented. The injections were done before the cue-induced relapse part of the study. It was found that injecting TAT-GluR2_{3Y} peptide meant that the AMPA synaptic currents that were found to be different in the 'heroin cue' rats were no longer different from the other conditions. That injection stopped the synaptic depression that occurred when the cues were re-introduced and led to relapse. TAT-GluR2_{3Y} prevents GluR2 endocytosis, which is what alters the synaptic AMPA currents in the medial prefrontal cortex after the re-exposure to cues, though it was also found that the location of the injection of TAT-GluR2_{3Y} is important. There is in fact a lot of biological detail in this study, which has been considerably reduced in this summary of the study. However, the basic findings are presented. For example, using other tests, they found that the relapse to heroin affected the ventral medial prefrontal cortex but not the dorsal medial prefrontal cortex.

The researchers also found that the injection did not work for sucrose-seeking (which was one of the controls) but just for heroin-associated stimuli. Relapse to sucrose-seeking behaviour was not related to GluR2 endocytosis. So the specific findings relate to heroin addiction and relapse.

Progress check 3.42

Explain two results of van den Oever *et al.*'s (2008) study.

Conclusions

The researchers felt that, if treatment of heroin using drugs such as injections is to be developed, then the neurobiology that relates to the cue-related relapse had to be fully understood. There were synaptic changes that arose from the cue-related relapse that were important. The researchers identified specific mechanisms for these synaptic changes and these changes were specific to heroin-seeking behaviour not just any reward-seeking behaviour.

They found that exposing someone to 'drugs of abuse' changes the ratio of AMPA and NMDA currents in glutamatergic synapses in the medial prefrontal cortex. They have done other work that shows that cocaine increases such currents and then re-exposure to cocaine reverses the AMPA/NDMA current ratios. This is all about synaptic depression (lowered activity) from re-exposure to cues for a drug after that drug habit has been extinguished.

Previous studies have found that glutamate signalling is important in cue-induced heroin-seeking and glutamate systems are important in motivation that relates to drug addiction. This study agrees with those findings.

A main finding was that acute synaptic depression of the ventral medial prefrontal cortex when there is re-exposure to heroin-seeking cues leads to a 'loss of inhibitory control over heroin-seeking' (p. 1057). The other main finding was that an injection of a substance may prevent the synaptic depression and prevent the relapse.

It is interesting to note that it is not the taking of the heroin that led to the synaptic changes but the cue-induced retrieval of memories related to heroin use. It is the cue-induced retrieval of memories and how that leads to wanting the reward, and the retrieval of the memories leading to relapse comes from decreases in AMPAR in the ventral medial prefrontal cortex.

A final comment from the researchers in their discussion is that their findings can be relevant to heroin addiction, since an injection to avoid the changes at the synapse might be a treatment for cue-induced relapse to heroin use.

Evaluation of van den Oever *et al.* (2008)

Strengths

- This study builds on other studies, and the findings agree with those from earlier studies. This suggests reliability in the findings – the studies have been replicated. The idea, for example, that AMPA receptors linked to their aim is widely accepted.
- By using animals in the experiments, there could be clear and careful controls. For example, there were rats trained to seek out sucrose to measure against the heroin-seeking behaviour. Also there were rats who learned to seek heroin and had cues in the environment and there was another group that did not have the cues. Some rats had the heroin-seeking behaviour extinguished in their home cage without intervention; others had training to extinguish the behaviour. There were other controls in the biological interventions. This all means that cause-and-effect conclusions can be drawn as any changes found in the brain can be measured against a control condition.

Weaknesses

- A difficulty is that the study used rats throughout and yet one of the conclusions was that the injections might help to prevent depression at the synapse in human heroin-takers who are re-exposed to cues, and this might prevent relapse. This means that the researcher generalised from the findings from animal studies to say the findings are true of humans. As synaptic transmission seems to be very similar in rats and humans, there is perhaps some justification in this generalisation. However, there are important differences too, such as in motivation and consciousness, so the generalising might not be justifiable.
- The study used a great deal of careful measuring of the rats' brains and this was done with very small areas of the brain, such as synaptic membranes. The controls suggest reliability in their findings; however, validity might be questioned in that the brain is very complex and it might be too hard using current methods to understand enough of what is happening. The study explains in great detail the different processes being studied, which backs the idea that brain complexity is such that even careful study using scientific methods might not be measuring what it claims to measure.

Progress check 3.43

Give two conclusions of van den Oever *et al.* (2008).

Test yourself

1. Explain the three parts of the procedure of van den Oever *et al.* (2008) – the addiction to heroin phase, the extinction phase and the cue-induced relapse phase. **(8 marks)**
2. Evaluate van den Oever *et al.* (2008) as a study claiming to lead towards treatment for humans. **(12 marks)**

Key questions in biological psychology

You have to study one key question in each of the topic areas for your course and apply concepts and ideas from the topic area to that issue. Concepts and ideas include research, studies and theories. The two key questions suggested for your course are covered here, but you can choose a different key question to study. In the examination, you may be asked to apply concepts and ideas to a key question that you have not come across before (called 'unseen'). Studying all the key questions will help you to learn how to apply concepts, ideas, theory and research to an unseen key question in the exam.

How effective is drug therapy for treating addictions?

Describing the issue

- Addiction, such as to heroin, affects the individual, not only their biology but also their living. Public Health England publishes facts and figures to show that the issue is important for society as well as for individuals. The number of opiate users in England (2013/2014) was 293,879. The number of adults successfully using drug therapy to become free of drug-taking was 29,150. The number of adults receiving treatment for alcohol in England was 114,920. These are high numbers and show that drug addiction and therapy for drug addiction is a key issue for society. If addiction is an illness, then society needs to address it just like any illness. It is cheaper for society and better for the individual if treatment is effective of course.
- The National Institute for Drug Abuse calls addiction an illness and explains that there are many features of drug addiction. These include cravings and compulsion to seek the drug. Drug-taking at the start is voluntary but, when someone is addicted, the drug-taking becomes a compulsion. The NIH (National Institutes of Health, a US body; in the UK, the equivalent body is the National Institute for Health Research) explain why

addiction is an illness, saying that the drug gives 'brain disease', which needs treating. The effects on the brain are what lead to difficulty in controlling behaviour, such as the compulsion to take the drug. All this leads to the conclusion that someone addicted to drugs is unable to stop by themselves and is suffering from an illness. It is logical then to look for a treatment.

- Treatment needs to cover all aspects of someone's life, not just the effects of the drug itself, because cues in someone's life that are associated with the drug can lead to relapse, even if therapy can extinguish the 'habit'. A National Survey on Drug Use and Health in the US found that 23.2 million people aged 12 or over in 2007 needed treatment for drug abuse.
- Public Health England have published a leaflet about the effectiveness of drug therapy for addiction. The Public Health England leaflet discusses how drug users are different, and one therapy will not suit everyone. Therapy must be tailored to the individual, which suggests that the question of whether drug therapy is effective for addiction depends on each individual. The Public Health England leaflet discusses the use of substitute drugs as treatment for drug addiction. They say that using drug therapy is the most common form of treatment for heroin and for other similar drugs. They call this 'substitute prescribing'.

To treat heroin addiction, a doctor will prescribe methadone or buprenorphine. Suboxone, Subutex, Prefibin are some brand names for buprenorphine, though Suboxone includes naxolone as well as buprenorphine. Also some buprenorphine, such as Buprenex, may not be approved for heroin addiction. These drugs will help the individual to avoid withdrawal symptoms and also not to 'reach' for the drug in the same way. This gives the individual space to get rid of their habit in terms of changing associations in their environment. The doctor will also prescribe other therapies alongside the medication.

- Treatment often involves medication alongside psychotherapy. Psychotherapy treatments include treatment clinics, focus on motivation and behavioural therapy. One important question is how effective drug therapy is. In a common-sense view, it might be thought that if drugs in the brain cause brain damage or 'brain disease' then it makes sense that other drugs can combat that.
- An article in the *New York Times* said that, in fact, most addicts either get over their addiction by themselves, by attending self-help groups, or by seeing a counsellor or therapist themselves. The article, however, also discusses the need for addicts to have both medical treatment and support, and over a long period of time. In the article, Dr Willenbring says he is particularly worried about heroin addiction because addicts are not given Suboxone as maintenance therapy. This suggests that drug therapy is not only effective but necessary. There are difficulties though, such as Alcoholics Anonymous not wanting to use medication in their 12-step programme as they see it as a crutch.

Explore

The *New York Times* article discussed above has some useful information relating to the effectiveness of drug therapy for treating addictions. Read the article here: http://well.blogs.nytimes.com/2013/02/04/effective-addiction-treatment/.

Progress check 3.44

Briefly explain why the question of how effective drug therapy is for addictions is one that affects society.

Application of concepts and ideas

- The effectiveness of drug therapy for treating addictions, such as methadone or buprenorphrine for heroin, is an important issue. To consider the effectiveness of drug therapy, buprenorphine is considered, so that the way it works in the brain, and thus its effectiveness, can be considered. Buprenorphine is an opiate and is a substitute for heroin. It is used for pain relief in medicine as well as for drug addiction. It can slow someone's breathing, which can be an important side effect. It can cause drowsiness, headache, sickness and other side effects. Clearly it has to be effective to be prescribed, otherwise side effects would not be considered acceptable.
- Buprenorphine acts as an opioid and so produces euphoria, as do other opioids, as well as slowing of breathing. This drug acts in a different way from heroin and methadone as it has less effect. Therefore, at low doses, it can be taken without the withdrawal symptoms and can aid someone in stopping taking heroin. The effects of buprenorphine do rise as the dosage rises; however, there is a ceiling effect, in that higher doses do not continue to increase the effect, so the drug is safer and will not move the person into addiction or lead to overdose. The drug has not led to respiratory problems (it depresses breathing so there is a risk, but less than for opiates) and has not shown cognitive or psychomotor (movement) problems. It does have side effects and it is not clear how the drug affects pregnancy in heroin-addicted women. Although studies have not shown that there is a problem, there is insufficient data.
- Buprenorphine can be abused as a drug, which is a disadvantage with regard to this being a substitute

for heroin; however, adding naxolone, as happens in Suboxone (a brand name), reduces the likelihood of addiction to buprenorphine.

- Methadone can be more effective for those with a high heroin addiction as it mimics heroin in the way it works at the synapse more closely; however, buprenorphine has other advantages regarding its addictive properties.
- Li *et al.* (2013) showed that cues for heroin linked to activation and connectivity between certain brain areas (limbic system and prefrontal cortex), which suggests that cues themselves affect brain functioning. Therefore, drug therapy, involving using a substitute to help with withdrawal symptoms and addiction, might not be enough if the conditioned cues around the addict are not addressed.
- Van den Oever *et al.* (2008) showed that animals who experience cues they associate with heroin addiction have changes in their brain from the experience of the cues. The changes are at the synapses and the researchers found that injections could affect those synaptic changes and prevent the synaptic depression that seemed to lead to relapse. Van den Oever *et al.* (2008) suggest that injections for heroin addicts, to prevent that synaptic depression, might help with relapse from exposure to cues. This is a different form of drug therapy from using substitute drugs, which is an interesting avenue of research.
- Other therapies, such as group therapy, can be very effective in treating drug abuse. People in groups can get support from one another, they are less isolated, and they can see others succeeding, which can help motivation. Also vicarious reinforcement, where someone is seen as rewarded and so their behaviour is imitated, can be helpful and can come from group therapy (vicarious reinforcement is explained more in Chapter 4). *Treatment Improvement Protocols* (TIP) is a book from SAMHSA (Substance Abuse and Mental Health Services Administration) and discusses group therapy and its effectiveness.

Progress check 3.45

List four terms that relate to the key question of the effectiveness of drug therapy for addiction.

What are the implications for society if aggression is found to be caused by nature not nurture?

Describing the issue

- Aggression in humans might come from their nature or their nurture. They may act aggressively from some biological cause or they may act aggressively in response to something in their environment.
- It might be said that, if a behaviour is caused by environmental factors, which is nurture, then someone can choose not to behave in that way. They can perhaps choose to avoid environments that are likely to trigger aggressive behaviour, for example, or they can choose to act differently, such as by retraining to react differently to certain cues.
- It could be said, however, that if a behaviour comes from someone's nature, there is not such an element of choice. We cannot help our biology and perhaps should not be blamed for behaviour stemming from our biology.
- Another way of looking at the issue of blame for aggression is that aggression does come from nature but that people have to learn control, so they can be blamed for not being in control rather than for the innate aggression.
- The implication is that, if we should not be blamed if aggression comes from our nature, then using imprisonment to prevent aggression might not be ethical. If imprisonment is a punishment, the question for society is whether someone should be punished for something they cannot help doing. This is a moral issue for society.
- Anxiety and depression get attention from society and are treated, whereas anger and aggression are punished. Yet it could be argued that all are linked to emotions and if one sort of emotion is treated and brings sympathy from society but another sort of emotion leads to blame, this seems unfair of society.

Explore

The Independent, on Sunday 7 December 2014, published an article about children and how aggression is nature not nurture. You can explore more using this link: www.independent.co.uk/news/education/education-news/nature-not-nurture-is-to-blame-for-aggressive-children-394842.html.

Application of concepts and ideas

- Aggression can be provoked in an animal if certain brain regions, like the hypothalamus or other limbic system areas, are electrically stimulated (e.g. Adelson, 2004, a review). This suggests that aggression comes from brain functioning, and this is our biology, our nature. The animal would not be blamed for the aggression response from the stimulation and perhaps people who exhibit aggression should not be blamed either. This study and others like it also suggest that at some level at least aggression comes from our nature and our biology rather than from the environment.
- Charles Whitman in 1966 killed many people in the US and it was discovered that he had a brain tumour pressing on his limbic system. This is an example of

aggression coming from nature and not being someone's 'fault', and it is also evidence that there is an aggression centre in the brain, in the limbic system. This evidence ties in with the studies reported by Adelson (2004).

- High testosterone and low cortisol can link to aggression, as found by van Honk *et al.* (2010, cited in Montoya *et al.*, 2011). Dabbs *et al.* (1991, cited in Montoya *et al.*, 2011) also found links between testosterone and activity in the aggression centre in the brain. Hormones, therefore, are implicated in aggression, again being our biology and in our nature.
- However, cortisol is the stress hormone and is triggered by stressors in the environment, and also when animals' brains are stimulated showing aggression in the limbic system, this can be seen as coming from the environment. Using this argument, aggression is triggered by environmental factors, which perhaps gives the individual some control over their behaviour. For example, they could avoid stressful situations.
- The theory of natural selection can help to explain aggression. For example, males might react aggressively to protect offspring or to protect their mate, both of these behaviours helping in some way to protect that male's genes. Therefore, genes in someone with this aggressive tendency survive to be passed on through reproduction. This would be a biological explanation and would be nature. From this viewpoint, society would not blame someone for the genes they inherit, and punishing someone for being aggressive would not be useful. Punishment such as imprisonment is intended to teach someone a lesson, but if aggression is in someone's nature they cannot unlearn it.
- It seems that the implications if aggression is in someone's nature are that it might be seen as needing treatment, with the individual seen as needing support, whereas if aggression comes from something someone can do something about, society might then think punishment is worthwhile. Punishment is part of operant conditioning (covered in Chapter 4). Operant conditioning holds that if someone is rewarded for a behaviour they will repeat it, and if punished they should stop that behaviour. This is about learning. If someone has learned aggression because they have been rewarded for it, such as getting their own way at school or in the family, then punishment might work to stop that learned behaviour. This is about nurture. If aggression comes from nature, then punishment cannot work, as the solution is not 'unlearning'.
- Raine *et al.* (1997) found brain differences (using PET scanning) in people charged with murder and pleading not guilty by reason of insanity (NGRI) compared with non-murderers. This is evidence that aggression comes from our nature. The idea of getting evidence that murder might come from brain differences, and that a plea of not guilty by reason of insanity can follow, supports the view that society does not hold people responsible for aggression if it is 'in their nature'.

Explore

A discussion about the causes of aggression and some implications of that can be found in the following article in *Nature*: www.nature.com/news/2008/080130/full/451512a.html. You will see that the classic study for biological psychology in your course is mentioned in this article, as well as many issues you have covered in this chapter.

Progress check 3.46

List four terms that relate to the key question of what the implications would be for society if aggression was down to nature alone.

Test yourself

1 Read the following passage:

> Endo up to the age of two was a biddable child, not really any trouble for his parents and fun to be with. At around the age of two years, he began to show much less willingness to share toys and became very aggressive if another child tried to take a toy he was playing with. He also became angry when something did not work or when he wanted something and it was not given. This was new to his parents. He would still play with them happily, ate his food, enjoyed going out on trips. They tried to reason with him to stop his aggression and they tried to reward him for non-aggressive behaviour when playing with other children, but nothing worked. His tantrums remained.

Using concepts, theories and studies from biological psychology, explain Endo's aggression and whether Endo is responsible for his aggression. **(8 marks)**

2 Biological psychology offers ideas and theories of how the brain and body works in areas related to psychology, such as synaptic transmission, hormones, evolution and brain structure and functioning. Choosing any key question for society, discuss how at least one of these ideas/theories can be used when discussing it, either to help with the key question, to explain the key question, or to both explain and help. **(16 marks)**

Practical investigation in biological psychology

For each topic area in your course, you will be carrying out a practical investigation using methodology that you have learned about in the topic area. Your practical investigation is to gather data relevant to the material covered in this biological psychology section of your course, and must be ethical of course. The practical must focus on aggression or drug use.

For biological psychology, you are asked to design and conduct a correlational study, gathering quantitative data and including both descriptive and inferential statistics to analyse your data. You need to write an abstract and a discussion section, which includes the conclusion. You need to include a research question, a hypothesis, research methods, sampling, ethical considerations, data collection tools, data analysis, results and discussion.

Method link: Chapter 5 discusses issues around using correlation design as well as issues around analysis of quantitative data (pp. 339–341). Sampling, hypotheses, ethics, data collection and data analysis are also covered in Chapter 5.

Maths link: Chapter 6 discusses measures of central tendency and measures of dispersion, as well as inferential statistical testing, including Spearman's test (pp. 406–411).

Practical link: Chapter 7 takes you through one idea for a practical investigation in biological psychology, including issues around writing up a report.

Two examples suggested in the biological psychology topic area of your course are:

- a correlation into age and attitudes to drug use
- a correlation to see if there is a relationship between height and a self-rating of aggressive tendencies.

Chapter 7 gives a worked practical investigation. However, you will be doing your practical investigations throughout your course and you should focus on one that you have carried out in biological psychology for this part of your course.

Issues and debates in biological psychology

The 11 issues and debates are summarised (with links to each of the topic areas in your Year 1 course) in Chapter 8 in this book, and then in detail in Book 2.

Chapter summary

- The main focus of the content is four areas covered in biological psychology. These are: the role of neurotransmitter functioning and the central nervous system in human behaviour, including how recreational drugs function at the synapse; brain structure and functioning, including as an explanation of human aggression; the role of evolution and natural selection; and the role of hormones.
- The content also includes Freud's psychodynamic explanation of aggression as a contrast to biological explanations of aggression.
- Issues highlighting individual differences and development in biological psychology are covered.
- Correlation research is a main focus of the method section in biological psychology. Method issues are briefly outlined in this chapter and examined in detail in Chapter 5.
- The use of experiments is touched upon as a contrast to correlation design.
- Another method studied in biological psychology is brain scanning techniques (CAT, PET, fMRI), including their use to investigate human behaviour.
- A further method is twin and adoption studies, with one study for each of these two methods.
- With regard to analysis of correlation data, Spearman's rho is required with all the issues required about inferential statistical testing. These issues are mentioned briefly in this chapter and explained in detail in Chapter 6.
- The classic study in biological psychology in your course is Raine *et al.* (1997) and it is explained here in detail, including looking at strengths and weaknesses. Raine *et al.* (1997) use PET scanning and measure parts of the brain that might affect violence, so the study links well to the content of your course.
- You need to learn about one contemporary study in biological psychology for your course from: Li *et al.* (2013), Brendgen *et al.* (2005) and van den Oever *et al.* (2008). All three studies are explained in this chapter, as well as the way they relate to other aspects of biological psychology.
- As with other topic areas in Year 1, you cover a key question in biological psychology and two are explained here.
- You need to carry out one practical investigation in biological psychology, which must be a study giving correlation data. This section is briefly outlined in this chapter, but a practical investigation in biological psychology is explained in more detail in Chapter 7.

Chapter Four: Learning Theories

Overview

Psychology is the study of the brain and behaviour, and the learning approach focuses on behaviour. In the early 1900s, there was focus on consciousness – for example, Wundt investigated how people think and remember. He studied such issues by asking people to introspect, which means thinking about their own cognitive (thinking) processes. At the same time, there was focus on the unconscious, as seen by Freud's psychodynamic approach. However, other researchers realised that neither the conscious nor the unconscious is easily measurable scientifically. Emphasis on the 'mental' became emphasis on the 'physical', which for psychology meant behaviour. These researchers focused on observable actions. In behaviourism, the focus is on measurable behaviour – for example, Pavlov showed that at least some of a dog's behaviour was the result of learned associations. You will look at Pavlov's work later in this chapter and see that learning theories are about measuring behaviour.

There are three main learning theories – two of them are collectively known as 'behaviourism'. Classical and operant conditioning make up the behaviourist approach in psychology and are about how behaviour develops. Social learning theory is the third main theory and is about observational learning and how we learn by observing others and copying their behaviour. These three theories form the major part of the content in this topic area.

Study of interest

Gholipour *et al.* (2012) looked at the effectiveness of token behaviour therapy for reducing negative symptoms in those with schizophrenia. They had one group of 15 patients with schizophrenia who had an intervention which involved exercise, one group of 15 patients with schizophrenia who had an intervention that involved token behaviour therapy (token economy) and another group of 15 patients with schizophrenia who had no intervention – they were the control group. The study was done in Iran. Token behaviour therapy involves tokens being given for desired behaviour which can be exchanged for something that is wanted, so this is reward therapy. The study found that token behaviour therapy was the most effective in reducing negative aspects of schizophrenia, and that exercise, though less effective than token behaviour therapy, was better than no intervention. Drug therapy was used alongside the interventions and in the control group so would not have led to the results being different for the token behaviour therapy group or the exercise group.

Everyday example

Learning theories can be applied to the training of animals. For example, to train a dog to bark for a biscuit, you would hold the biscuit towards the dog so that the dog is aware of it and then you would withhold the biscuit. As soon as the dog barks, you would give it the biscuit. After repeating this several times, the dog would learn that the reward follows the bark. This is an example of positive reinforcement. However, you might want to train the dog not to bark, in which case you would give the biscuit when the dog stops barking.

Summary of learning objectives

Content

The content covers:

- classical conditioning, including Pavlov's (1927) experiments explained in his 23 lectures
- operant conditioning and various features of operant conditioning
- social learning theory, including three of Bandura's experiments
- how learning theories explain how we acquire a phobia and how that phobia is maintained rather than disappearing
- treatments for phobias based on learning theories, including systematic desensitisation and one other treatment
- individual differences and developmental issues that apply to learning theories.

Individual differences and developmental psychology

In all topic areas, you need to consider two issues in psychology: individual differences and developmental psychology.

Individual differences

In learning theories, you will learn about the following links:

- People differ because of environmental differences, such as different patterns of reward giving different ways of responding to situations.
- Different behaviour observed leads to each person being different.
- Gender too can be learned and give individual differences.

Developmental psychology

In learning theories, you will learn about the following links:

- Development occurs through different patterns of rewards and punishment - that is how we learn.
- According to social learning, we develop through observing others and copying their behaviour.
- Issues like gender can shape who we are as we develop and much gender behaviour is learned.

Study of interest

Meiliyana and Fauzia (2014) carried out a study in Indonesia with one man who had a phobia of flying. They used systematic desensitisation over an eight-week period and a month later did a follow-up to see if the treatment had been successful. They developed a hierarchy of his fear, from what he was least afraid of with regard to flying to what he was most afraid of. They used imagery when carrying out the treatment, which meant that he had to picture the issue that was being focused on, such as getting on the plane. They used relaxation to pair with the phobia. They found that the therapy was successful and that relaxation, the use of imagery and some exposure to the stimuli (facing what frightened him - this occurred after the therapy and was measured by the participant phoning the researchers from the departure lounge, just before flying) worked, so he could get onto a plane again to attend a seminar, which was the aim.

Explore

You could start your study of learning theories by looking at what Mind (a charity focusing on mental health) says about phobias, their causes and treatments. There are a lot of different causes suggested, and different treatments, but your course just focuses on how someone might learn a phobia and use learning theories to overcome it. For your own interest, though, you should consider the different ideas. The Mind site is: www.mind.org.uk/information-support/types-of-mental-health-problems/phobias/causes/.

STUDY HINT

In your course, you need to learn about two treatments for phobia. You can use the two studies that have already been described to help with your learning in that area.

Methods

Chapter 5 covers the methodology you will need for Year 1 of your course (and the AS, with some exceptions). See Table 5.1 (p. 278) for a summary of which methods you need to know for this chapter. Chapter 6 covers the mathematical elements you need for your course. See Table 6.2 (p. 386) for a summary of the mathematical skills you need to know for this chapter.

Studies

The classic study you will be learning about in learning theories is Watson and Rayner (1920) 'Little Albert: conditioned emotional reactions'.

You will choose one contemporary study from:

- Becker *et al.* (2002) 'Eating behaviours and attitudes following prolonged exposure to television among ethnic Fijian adolescent girls'
- Bastian *et al.* (2011) 'Cyber-dehumanization: violent video game play diminishes our humanity'
- Capafóns *et al.* (1998) 'Systematic desensitisation in the treatment of the fear of flying'.

Key questions

You have to be able to describe one key question that can be explained using concepts and research from learning theories. Two key questions are suggested in the specification and are explained in this chapter. These are:

- Is the influence of role models and celebrities something that causes anorexia?
- Would it be a good idea for airline companies to offer treatment programmes for fear of flying?

However, you could choose a completely different key issue, relevant to today's society.

Practical investigation

Chapter 7 covers the skills you need for conducting a practical investigation, including worked-through examples. Chapter 6 covers the mathematical elements for your course, which also links to your practical investigation.

Issues and debates

Issues and debates are in the A level course but not the AS, so if you are doing the AS, you do not need to study issues and debates, although they are interesting and will extend your understanding of psychology. The 11 issues and debates are: ethics; practical issues in research design; reductionism; comparing explanations; psychology as a science; culture and gender; nature–nurture; how psychology has developed over time; issues of social control; using psychology in society; and issues around socially sensitive research.

Chapter 8 summarises the issues and debates and how the four topic areas for your Year 1 course inform each of these. Book 2 will explain these in more detail.

STUDY HINT
Issues and debates appear in each topic area for Year 1 (and Year 2), in the same order, in the specification. For each topic area, you can use the examples against each of the issues and debates to learn how the material for that topic area illustrates that issue or debate. See Chapter 8 for more detail.

STUDY HINT
Make a summary of learning objectives into a checklist, such as the one in Table 4.1. However, you could add more detail to help your learning.

Table 4.1 What you need to know for learning theories

You need to know about:	
Main features of classical conditioning, including UCS, UCR, CS, NS, CR	Structured and naturalistic observations gathering both qualitative and quantitative data
Main features of classical conditioning - extinction, spontaneous recovery and stimulus generalisation	Tallying, event and time sampling
Pavlov's (1927) experiments with salivation in dogs	Participant, non-participant, covert and overt observations
Main features of operant conditioning, including types of reinforcement and punishment (positive and negative)	Content analysis as a research method
Main features of operant conditioning - properties of reinforcement, including primary and secondary reinforcement and schedules of reinforcement	The use of animals in lab experiments and the ethics involved in using animals
Behaviour modification, including shaping	Inferential testing, including the chi-squared test. For A level only: levels of measurement, reasons for choosing the test and comparing observed and critical values
Main features of social learning theory, including observation, imitation, modelling and vicarious reinforcement	Analysis of qualitative data using thematic analysis
Social learning stages - attention, retention, reproduction and motivation (reinforcement)	A classic study in detail: Watson and Rayner (1920)
Bandura's work in 1961 and 1963 - the original Bobo doll experiments	One contemporary study in detail from: Becker *et al.* (2002), Bastian *et al.* (2011) and Capafóns *et al.* (1998)
Bandura's work in 1965, a Bobo doll experiment including vicarious reinforcement	One key question that suits what you have covered in learning theories
Learning theories and a) acquiring phobias, b) maintaining phobias	One practical investigation you have carried out to put what you have learned in learning theories into practice
Two treatments for phobias - systematic desensitisation and one other	Individual differences and developmental psychology and links to the three learning theories
Issues and debates (not for AS)	

An introduction to learning theories

This chapter is about how human behaviour is learned and, even when animal experiments are considered, there is focus on how they shed light on human behaviour. Learning theories focus on how nurture shapes individuals in terms of their environment – for example, family, peer group, social and cultural situations. For the learning theories, it is as if the individual is born 'blank', ready to be shaped into the person they become; although there is some acknowledgement of the importance of brain processing (see Pavlov, 1927), how those processes work in a physiological sense are not studied in depth. The research methods used are often scientific – for example, laboratory experiments using both animals and human participants.

STUDY HINT

Study the approach as a whole rather than the methodology, content, studies, key issues and practical separately. Read the chapter through first, taking in some of the information but without taking notes or learning the terms. Then, you can then start learning in earnest.

Key assumptions of learning theories

Out of the many approaches in psychology, learning theories focuses most on environmental influences. They include behaviourism, which, at the start of the twentieth century, developed from other aspects of psychology. By the end of the nineteenth century, when Freud was developing his psychodynamic approach (see Chapter 3, pp. 166–175), other people were moving from philosophical thinking to more psychological questions. Wundt, for example, used **introspection** to answer such questions as how we remember. Introspection involves participants thinking about their thinking or how they process information and then explaining those processes to the researcher. Wundt is credited with setting up the first laboratory for the subject. However, as introspection was the method used to collect data, they were not measured carefully and it was difficult to draw scientific conclusions.

In response to the problems in drawing conclusions from research using introspection, the behaviourists (e.g. Watson) chose to study measurable and observable behaviour. Others, such as Pavlov, who was carrying out laboratory experiments with animals to investigate physiological (biological) responses, were publishing findings about behaviour that were scientifically gathered. The theory of operant conditioning developed from Watson's work; that of classical conditioning developed from Pavlov's studies. Behaviourism comprises classical and operant conditioning. Later, Bandura developed social learning theory. Classical conditioning, operant conditioning and social learning theory are the three theories that you will study.

Explore

Try using introspection to see how you remember a list of words. Here are some words: orange, book, car, green, lorry, red, magazine, paper, blue, leaflet, train, bus. Try to learn them and at the same time think about the processing you used. This is similar to how Wundt studied psychology. Make some notes about how far you think this is a good method to use and what you think are the disadvantages. You could ask others to do the same task, tell you what was happening when they were doing it and compare their answers to your own. Are they similar? Why do you think these particular words were chosen?

Definition

Assumptions of an area of psychology are the underpinning beliefs and ideas that support this being a particular area, such as learning theories focusing on learning from our environment rather than biology or other aspects of human behaviour.

Explore

Using the internet or some other source, look up Wundt and Ebbinghaus to see how these early researchers studied psychological aspects of behaviour. Then look up Watson and Pavlov to find out about the beginnings of behaviourism, which forms the basis of the learning approach.

Focus on the environment

The learning approach holds that the environment that is experienced shapes people, by means of reinforcements, to develop in specific ways. For example, young children learn to speak a particular language by copying their parents and family. A baby babbles sounds such as 'mmm' and, in return, the parents say 'mum'; the baby, to get attention, repeats the sound and is reinforced for doing so. Such reinforcement leads to talking. Punishment can also shape behaviour. When people are punished for an action, they are less likely to repeat it – unless that punishment is the only attention they receive, in which case they may repeat the behaviour because attention itself becomes rewarding.

Focus on scientific methods

Behaviour is difficult to study and it is even more difficult to draw scientific conclusions. Therefore, specific actions are isolated and studied to find out what leads to those actions or what would stop them. A single piece of behaviour – for example, a rat pressing a lever to receive a food pellet – is studied to see when the rat presses the lever and how quickly it learns to press the lever for the reward. Such a study involves an independent variable (e.g. a red light when the rat gains the food, or a green light when it does not). All other variables are controlled. A dependent variable (e.g. how often the rat presses the lever when the red, but not the green, light is on) is then measured. Scientific principles such as these are a feature of the learning approach. Behaviourists saw that it would be difficult to build knowledge if data were not reliable, so they turned to measurable aspects of behaviour and to scientific methodology.

Learning is stimulus–response, without considering mental processes in detail

Social learning theory is slightly different as there are elements that involve mental processes, such as paying attention by observing behaviour. However, the other two learning theories – classical and operant conditioning – focus on the environment (a stimulus) and the individual (their response). Mental processes are considered, in that learning creates pathways in the brain, but the brain is treated as a 'black box' when it comes to knowing the exact processing. This is very different from the focus of cognitive psychology, which is the exploration of how we process information. Learning theories simply focus on what happens in the environment and the response from the organism, assuming a pathway in the brain for each association, but not looking in more depth, at least when the theories were first developed. As in our example above, when there is a red light, food arrives, so when the rat presses a lever when the red light is on, a reward is given. A green light means no food, so the rat presses in vain. The rat learns to press only when the red light is on. The stimulus is the red light; the response is pressing the lever. What the rat 'thinks', if that happens, is not studied.

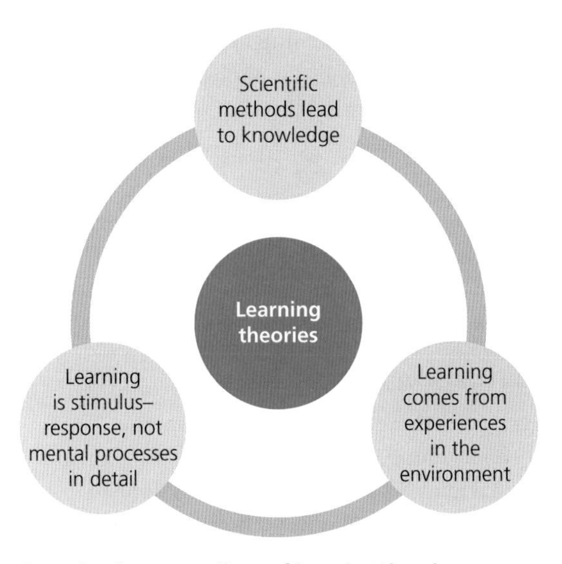

Some basic assumptions of learning theories

Progress check 4.1

Explain three features of learning theories.

Types of learning to illustrate the learning approach

The three types of learning you will study – classical conditioning, operant conditioning and social learning – are briefly outlined here to help your understanding. They are explained in detail later in this chapter.

Explanation

In 1884, Ebbinghaus, an early researcher in psychology, did many studies looking at how people remember. He found that there are what he called 'relearning savings', which means that once something has been learned once, the second time learning is better. This means that just reading through the general principles of the three learning theories will help your learning when you get to the content section of this chapter.

General principles of classical conditioning

Classical conditioning is about how a stimulus is associated with a response. It applies *only* to the conditioning of reflexes. Human reflexes include, for example, a fear response, eye blinking in response to certain stimuli, knee-jerk reactions and breathing. However, behaviour goes beyond reflex actions, so classical conditioning is limited in its application.

STUDY HINT

When asked to give ideas that underpin the learning approach, avoid giving the particular theories. Instead, consider the underlying principles – for example, the focus on experience within an environment and the desire to build a body of knowledge using scientific methods. You could, however, use the three types of learning to illustrate points about environmental influences or the scientific approach. Alternatively, you could choose a different underpinning idea, such as using animals in laboratory experiments and applying findings to humans.

Fear can be conditioned, as fear is a reflexive response. For example, a reflexive fear response to something in an individual's life (such as stress) could occur in a lift. From then on, that person might be afraid of being in a lift because the response was associated with the lift (see pp. 207–210 for more detail).

Someone can develop a phobia of lifts if they experience anxiety because of a life event that happened in a lift; the lift becomes associated with anxiety and fear is learned through classical conditioning

Explore

Use the internet or some other source to look up Pavlov's work with dogs. In the early 1900s, he started the idea of learning by association and classical conditioning. You could consider ethical issues involved with using animals in laboratory experiments, which are discussed later in this chapter.

General principles of operant conditioning

Most behaviour is voluntary, not reflexive. Operant conditioning examines voluntary behaviour and considers how rewards and punishments shape it. For example, schoolchildren may work hard for the reward of gold stars, so their behaviour (hard work) is repeated for the reward (a gold star). Other children might not work hard and be punished by being given extra homework. These are the sorts of principles involved in operant conditioning.

Explore

Use the internet or some other source to look up the work of B.F. Skinner, who, in the mid-1900s, explained the idea of operant conditioning. He used many laboratory experiments involving animals. Consider the problems of generalising from animal studies to humans – is it fair to say that what is found in animals is necessarily true of humans?

B.F. Skinner

General principles of social learning

Social learning theory, explained by Bandura from about 1960, shows how people learn by observing other people, particularly those they look up to (i.e. their role models). Not all learning is reinforced or involves reflexes. Social learning theory suggests that much of what is learnt comes from watching others and copying them.

Explore

Use the internet or some other source to look up the work of Bandura, focusing on social learning theory. You could also find out what he investigated later – for example, self-efficacy.

Test yourself

1. Explain two ways in which the learning approach differs from biological psychology. **(4 marks)**
2. Explain two ways in which the learning approach differs from cognitive psychology. **(4 marks)**
3. Give a definition of the learning theories as a topic area, drawing on two of its main assumptions. **(6 marks)**

Content in learning theories

The learning approach comprises classical conditioning, operant conditioning and social learning theories. You need to know:

- some of the main features of the three theories (classical conditioning, operant conditioning and social learning theory)
- some studies linked to the three theories, specifically Pavlov (1927), focusing on classical conditioning, and three studies Bandura was involved in (1961, 1963, 1965), focusing on social learning theory
- learning theory explanations for phobias and two treatments based on learning theory.

Classical conditioning

Classical conditioning is a theory of learning that examines how a response is associated with a stimulus to cause conditioning. It is illustrated by Pavlov's work with dogs and can be called 'Pavlovian conditioning'.

Stimulus–response learning

A **stimulus** is something that produces a response. In classical conditioning, the response is a reflex – an automatic behaviour. The stimulus is what is done to the person or animal; the response is how the person or animal responds to the stimulus. Neither classical nor operant conditioning examines what happens between the stimulus and the response – they do not consider cognitive (thinking) processes in detail; though Pavlov is very interested in such processes, he can only assume how they work using pathways created in the cerebral cortex. Classical conditioning is a stimulus–response (S–R) theory.

Explore

When considering stimulus-response learning, it is sometimes said that between the stimulus and the response there is a 'black box'. This is because learning theories do not look at what happens between the stimulus and the response, which could be cognitive processing (they may be interested in it, but do not have the means of studying that area). Use the internet or some other source to look up this idea of a 'black box'. A similar idea associated with the learning approach is that people are born a 'blank slate' ('tabula rasa' in Latin) and develop only through their learning experiences. Research the idea of a 'blank slate'.

In classical conditioning, the responses to stimuli are reflex actions – that is, they are *involuntary* responses. Examples include blinking to a puff of air, knee-jerking to a tap on the correct part of the knee, sneezing because of certain stimuli, showing a startle response (fear) to a noise, and a fight-or-flight response when there is a threat.

- The UCS is then paired (+) with a **neutral stimulus** (NS). In one of Pavlov's studies, the NS was a bell. It is called a neutral stimulus because at this stage it does not produce the response. The UCS still gives the UCR as before, which is salivation.
- After a few pairings, the NS on its own produces the response of salivation and at this stage, when the NS is producing the response on its own, it becomes a **conditioned stimulus** (CS). The response is now a **conditioned response** (CR) – it is conditioned to occur in response to the stimulus of the bell alone.

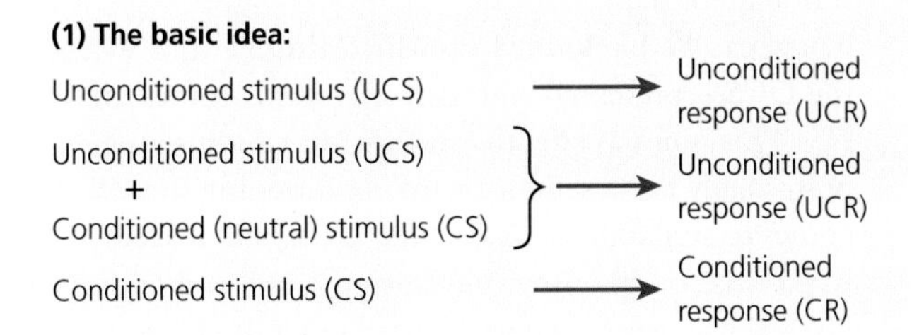

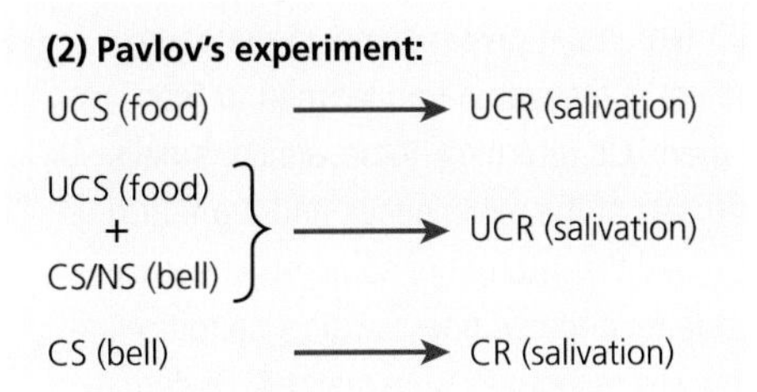

Classical conditioning

STUDY HINT

There are a lot of terms in classical conditioning, which can make it seem complicated at first. However, the actual process involved in classical conditioning is quite simple. Perhaps use the diagram first, to see the process at work, and then work on adding in the terms.

The process of classical conditioning

Classical conditioning explains how someone can be conditioned into a response from a stimulus that is not the one that would naturally produce that response. For example, if you sneeze when flowers are in the room, and your aunt's house always has flowers, you may 'learn' to sneeze whenever you see your aunt because you associate her with the flowers and the flowers lead to the response of sneezing. A diagram is a good way to explain the process of classical conditioning and the example of Pavlov's dogs will show you how the idea came about.

- The process starts with an **unconditioned stimulus** (UCS) that automatically provokes an **unconditioned response** (UCR). The stimulus and the response are called unconditioned because the response is bound to happen – for example, a dog salivating (dribbling) in response to food.

Definition

The **unconditioned stimulus** is what gives the unconditioned response naturally - it is a stimulus that gives a reflex response. The **unconditioned response** is the term for the reflex response. The **neutral stimulus** is what is going to be paired with the unconditioned stimulus and will eventually give the same response (which will then be called a 'conditioned' response). When the neutral stimulus is paired with the unconditioned stimulus, it becomes the **conditioned stimulus.** After the association has been set up, the conditioned stimulus is what gives the **conditioned response.**

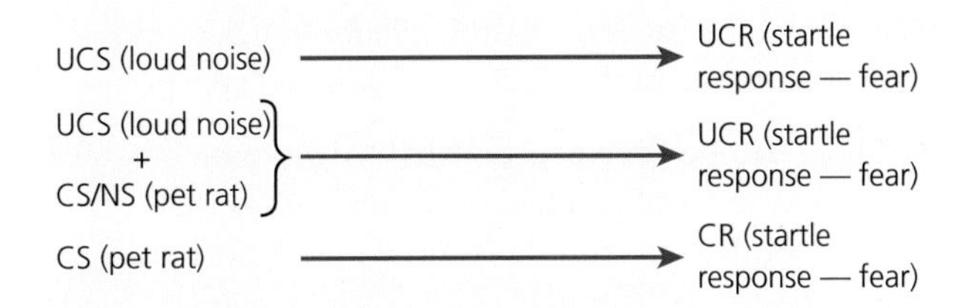

The Little Albert conditioning experiment

Some other examples of classical conditioning are explained later when phobias are considered (pp. 243–246). Another example is explained in the study of Little Albert by Watson and Rayner (1920), which is the classic study for this topic area. Little Albert's conditioning experiences are shown in the diagram above. Little Albert was a baby who learned to fear a pet white rat as part of an experiment.

Explore

Conditioning can be found in a number of situations, some of which lead to problems for the individual. For example, prisoners of war can be conditioned into fearing whatever was associated with fear in the prison camp. It has been suggested that soldiers in the war in Iraq learned to fear the smells around them. On returning home, similar smells brought back the horrors of the experiences and the fear (i.e. Gulf War syndrome). Use the internet or some other source to look up such incidents and see how classical conditioning might have been the way responses were learned. Of course, Gulf War syndrome could have a physical cause unconnected with conditioning. Consider the different explanations, including classical conditioning, and the effects on the individuals concerned.

Progress check 4.2

When Sarah visits her aunt's house, she finds herself sneezing because all the flowers in her house set off her hayfever. She then sneezes whenever she meets her aunt, even when there are no flowers around! Draw up a diagram, such as that on page 207, to show the process of Sarah moving from sneezing because of the flowers, to sneezing whenever in the presence of her aunt.

When the pairing occurs

There are some issues in classical conditioning around when the pairing of the UCS and CS should take place.

1. There can be **forward conditioning**, which is the best form of conditioning, and means that the conditioned stimulus is presented before the unconditioned stimulus. There can be overlap, which is called **delayed conditioning** (the conditioned stimulus keeps going as the unconditioned stimulus is introduced), or a break between the pairing, which is called **trace conditioning** (the conditioned stimulus can start and end before the unconditioned stimulus is introduced).

Definition

Forward conditioning is when the conditioned stimulus is presented before the unconditioned stimulus when pairing them. One type of forward conditioning is **delayed conditioning**, when the conditioned stimulus appears and continues as the unconditioned stimulus is introduced, so there is overlap. **Trace conditioning** is when the conditioned stimulus appears, stops and then the unconditioned stimulus is introduced - there is no overlap.

2. There can be **spontaneous conditioning**, which means presenting the CS and UCS at the same time – simultaneously.
3. There can be **backward conditioning**. This is when the UCS is presented and then afterwards comes the CS. This is not as effective as forward conditioning, presumably because in forward conditioning the CS comes to signal the arrival of the UCS, whereas in backward conditioning the CS signals the end of the UCS and so is less likely to elicit the UCR. Pavlov in his lectures (1927) found that it was forward conditioning that worked.

Definition

Spontaneous conditioning is when the conditioned stimulus and unconditioned stimulus are presented together. **Backward conditioning** is when the unconditioned stimulus is presented and ends and then the conditioned stimulus is presented, which is not as effective as forward conditioning.

Progress check 4.3

Explain the difference between two types of forward conditioning.

Explanations for classical conditioning

Pavlov suggested the **stimulus-substitution theory**, which means that the UCR is the same as the CR but appears in response to a different stimulus. This seems straightforward. In our earlier example, if you sneeze when there are flowers around, your sneeze when you see your aunt is the same response. So the stimulus is substituted – the aunt for the flowers – with the same response but this time called a 'conditioned' response.

However, studies have found that the CR is not always exactly the same as the UCR – it can be weaker. For example, a biological response to an electrical shock is a faster heart rate, whereas if something is paired with the shock and becomes a conditioned stimulus, then the response to that conditioned stimulus is a lowered heart rate. This is not what classical conditioning predicts and it seems that the central nervous system (see Chapter 3), when involved, can yield different responses to what is expected.

Explanation

The **stimulus-substitution theory** of how classical conditioning works says that the conditioned stimulus simply replaces the unconditioned stimulus as something that elicits the reflexive response.

There are other ideas around classical conditioning. For example, the UCS is not one 'thing' that produces the UCR – well, often it is not. Dogs will salivate to meat perhaps more than they would salivate to something less 'tasty'. A CS paired with meat might then produce more salivation in the dog than if it is paired with something less tasty. The CS can have more or less strength too. The CS conditions the dog to expect the UCS and the association can be strong or weak. Also the CS might be more or less attended to, so the pairing might be affected by the amount of attention paid to the CS. There are issues like this that affect how strong the learned association is.

Extinction, spontaneous recovery and stimulus generalisation

As well as the main principles, there are other aspects of classical conditioning:

- extinction – how does the conditioning disappear?
- spontaneous recovery – if the conditioning has disappeared, can it reappear?
- stimulus generalisation – is the response specific to one stimulus or can it 'generalise' to similar stimuli?

Extinction

Extinction occurs when the association between the UCS and the CS no longer occurs; after a few trials of separating the two stimuli, the learned response is extinguished. In one of Pavlov's examples, the bell was no longer rung when the food was presented. After a little while, the dog did not salivate to the sound of the bell alone – the association was extinguished. Extinction occurs when the UCS (the stimulus that naturally elicits the response) appears a few times without the CS and then the association is lost.

Definition

Extinction is the term used when an association using classical conditioning has been extinguished – it is no longer there.

Spontaneous recovery

After extinction, the association sometimes recurs for no apparent reason. The CS (e.g. the bell) suddenly produces the response (e.g. salivation) that was conditioned previously. The reappearance of a CR is called **spontaneous recovery**. For example, if you have a startle response (fear) to loud noises and were shopping when there was an incident nearby involving shouting and some disturbance, you might learn a fear of shopping. If you then went shopping (you might need help to achieve this) and there was no noise or disturbance, then you could unlearn the association (this is not easy to achieve if a person has a phobia but is a usual treatment for anxiety and panic attacks). This would mean that your fear response to shopping has been extinguished. However, it might suddenly reappear at a later date without the noise, which would be spontaneous recovery. After spontaneous recovery, the association does diminish very quickly.

Definition

Spontaneous recovery is when, after extinction, suddenly and without re-conditioning, an association reappears. **Stimulus generalisation** is when a stimulus similar to the specific (conditioned) one elicits the conditioned response.

Progress check 4.4

Think of other occasions when a response might be learned in this way. Consider how advertising aims to make an association between a conditioned stimulus (the product) and a response (e.g. salivation to a certain brand of chocolate or a 'sexual' response to a product). Maybe you can think of an association that you or someone else has made, such as a fear in response to a stimulus. When you have thought of one or two examples of learning by classical conditioning, draw a diagram to represent the processes.

Stimulus generalisation

The stimulus that evokes the conditioned response, such as the bell giving salivation in a dog, or the aunt leading to sneezing in the niece, or the pet rat leading to the startle response in Little Albert (see pp. 259–262), is specific. There is the specific pet rat, that tone of bell and that particular aunt who had flowers in her house.

However, it has been found that there can be **stimulus generalisation**, which means that a stimulus similar to the specific one can elicit the conditioned response. For example, there can be generalisation to different tones of bell, or other furry animals, not just the pet rat.

This is an important feature of classical conditioning. Someone who develops a fear of going into a shop after having had an anxiety attack in that shop might find it is not just that shop that brings the anxiety. The fear of the one shop is generalised to 'shopping'.

The opposite of stimulus generalisation is **discrimination**, which means that the conditioning can be focused in on a specific stimulus. A dog can be trained to associate food with just one bell tone and to salivate to just that one bell tone. This is done by using other bell tones without food and just food with the required bell tone. Little Albert could have been conditioned to 'startle' just in response to his pet rat and not other furry objects (though this was not done).

Using classical conditioning principles to treat alcoholism

One way to explain stimulus generalisation (and discrimination) is to use an example of classical conditioning principles being used to treat alcoholism. There are drugs that are 'emetic', which means they make someone feel sick. If such a drug is paired with alcoholic drink, then the alcoholic drink will make the person feel sick. Then the alcoholic drink becomes the conditioned stimulus, which leads to the sick feeling, which is the conditioned response, which is unpleasant and should stop the person wanting to drink alcohol. A problem is that it would not be good for the person to generalise the sick feeling to all drinks, as water and other drinks are necessary. So stimulus discrimination must occur. This can be done by giving water (or any other soft drink) and not the drug, so that the sick feeling discriminates to just the alcohol being 'treated'. This treatment, called 'aversive therapy', is discussed more when we look at treatments (pp. 254–255).

Progress check 4.5

Explain why it is important that the individual does not generalise the sick feeling/unpleasant feeling to all drinks. How can stimulus discrimination be ensured?

Study of interest

Kareken *et al.* (2012) carried out a study with humans. They were looking at conditioned stimuli, alcohol consumption and changes in the brain, measured using fMRI scanning. Scanning can show the brain in action. Kareken *et al.* (2012) noted that intoxication as a response from alcohol (this is a reflexive, natural response) could be associated with smells and other issues around alcohol that the senses pick up. This means that sensory information around drink becomes a conditioned stimulus associated with intoxication, which would be the conditioned response. Conditioned stimuli around the smells and so on of alcohol can also be linked to cravings and relapse as the associations between the CS and the CR. The aim was to see what areas of the brain were affected when a CS (e.g. the smell of alcohol) gave the CR (e.g. feeling of intoxication, craving or relapse). Brain areas involved were thought to include the medial prefrontal regions and reward areas of the brain (e.g. Harber *et al.*, 2006, cited in Kareken *et al.*, 2012). A difficulty in studying the area of alcohol as the UCS leading to intoxication or reward feelings as the UCR, and related conditioned stimuli experienced by individuals, is that they are indeed individuals and conditioned stimuli will vary between individuals. The study wanted to use new conditioned stimuli and study the association with intoxication using fMRI scanning.

They used 14 heavy drinkers and told them that they were testing them for reaction time under the influence of alcohol. While doing that, the researchers embedded some new stimuli (geometric shapes) into the task without highlighting the fact. The participants were told that the study was about the effect of alcohol on speed. The alcohol was administered by infusion (intravenously) and there was a condition where there was an infusion of a saline solution – the participants knew that one infusion was alcohol and one saline but did not know which was which (this was a single-blind condition).

The procedure involved the conditioned stimulus (a shape) and an asterisk presented on a screen the participants were looking at, just before there was a green arrow. The task for the participants was to enter using a keyboard the direction of the green arrow but they were to pay attention to what was on the screen (including the CS). Participants were told that the shape and asterisk hid the green arrow and that was their purpose. The experimenters knew which task went with alcohol and which with saline but the participants did not know.

What was measured by the fMRI scan was blood flow in the brain, showing activity in the brain. Participants also gave their subjective reactions to the study. For example, they could tell whether the infusion was alcohol or saline. Results went against what was predicted. The medial prefrontal cortex is usually active in response to rewards from alcohol and the conditioned stimuli associated with alcohol (e.g. smells) trigger such activity.

So new conditioned stimuli, paired with alcohol, should activate the reward areas in the medial prefrontal cortex. However, in this study there was less activity found in the medial prefrontal cortex when alcohol was the infusion than when saline was the infusion. Saline gave baseline activity and the alcohol infusion gave negative activity, a reduction in the baseline. It was thought that this had to do with the design of the study. The CS is paired with the alcohol infusion but then there might be extinction because the pairing does not last and is not revisited. During the scanning, the participant is connected to an IV (intravenous) pump but without the alcohol so the participant sees the conditioned stimulus but without the alcohol. Extinction of the association might account for the brain activity in the medial prefrontal cortex being lower than normal (the baseline situation).

Kareken *et al.*'s (2012) study shows:

- how classical conditioning works
- how classical conditioning can be used in studies to help to understand brain activity and intoxication, relapse and craving
- how issues like extinction belie classical conditioning as an apparently simply process
- that classical conditioning processes are still used in studies today, not just in the early 1900s when Pavlov first developed the ideas.

Explanation

Kareken *et al.* (2012) used a **single-blind** procedure, where the participants did not know whether an infusion they were undergoing was saline or alcohol. The experimenters knew - if they had not known either, it would have been a **double-blind** procedure.

STUDY HINT

Use studies as examples of method issues, such as fMRI scanning and single-blind procedures. Kareken *et al.* (2012) also illustrate the use of a placebo.

Issues and debates

One of the issues and debates is how psychological understanding has developed over time. Pavlov started off research into classical conditioning in the early 1900s and Kareken *et al.*'s (2012) study shows that research into classical conditioning continues. Their study links classical conditioning ideas to neuroscience, which shows how psychology uses methods like brain imaging to find information about the brain. Pavlov in his lectures (1927) discusses neurological aspects of conditioning, though not using scanning, so what was done in 2012 reflects what was done in 1927, although methods have changed.

Test yourself

1. Explain three features of classical conditioning – extinction, spontaneous recovery and stimulus generalisation. **(6 marks)**
2. Discuss classical conditioning in relation to one therapy that uses its principles. **(6 marks)**

Pavlov's (1927) experiments with dogs

In 1927, Pavlov gave a series of 23 lectures, detailing his many experiments looking at processes related to classical conditioning. The basics of the lectures relating to his experiments with dogs are explained here.

Explore

The lectures are available online and contain a great deal of information. You could explore more here: http://psychclassics.yorku.ca/Pavlov/.

Pavlov's lectures explain in detail his, and others', experiments with dogs. He sets out the idea of reflexes and links to the cerebral cortex where he feels paths are already there with regard to reflexes already present (innate) and where he feels paths are established when new associations are made. He shows how a dog will salivate when meat is put in its mouth. The dog then associates something (conditioned stimulus) with the meat in the mouth, and that conditioned stimulus then brings about the reflex of salivation. He also says that something else can be associated with that conditioned stimulus and that second conditioned stimulus will then give salivation – this is secondary conditioning. He also discusses features like extinction. He goes to some pains to explain that any other stimuli that will affect the dog will affect the conditioning process, showing its sensitivity. He also says that different dogs respond in different ways and, if a dog is not alert, conditioning may not take place or may take a lot longer. He discusses his use of scientific methods and controls and says they are necessary because of how much other stimuli can affect the dogs' responses. He also mentions the issue of generalising from dogs to humans, though feels it is possible to do that, and draws on evolution ideas to justify that claim.

Aim(s)

Pavlov wanted to study how the cerebral cortex works and to do so he started with natural associations between stimuli and reflex responses in organisms. He chose dogs as they have some higher-order thinking and yet are manageable in terms of being tested. His aim was to look at reflexes and to work out pathways in the brain. He found that a dog not able to use cerebral functioning still exhibits reflexes but would not survive. So he wanted to see what it is about cerebral functioning that leads to survival. Even meat will not cause salivation in the dog unless it is in its mouth, so how does the animal survive in the natural world? There must be a mechanism linking to reflexes in the cerebral cortex. His aim is to look at these issues.

Background

Pavlov starts his lectures by looking at the cerebral hemispheres and thinking about the complexity of human behaviour that relies on brain functioning. This was a time when not much was known about the cerebral hemispheres, except that man could not function 'normally' without them. The physiology of animals, too, had not been studied much. Pavlov also noted that the hemispheres (the brain) had not been seen to be subject matter that physiology would study, but more the field of psychology.

> **STUDY HINT**
> Pavlov's work started by considering physiology and cell functioning. Use what you learn in biological psychology when learning about Pavlov's work, such as synaptic transmission. In cognitive psychology you have learned about case studies of brain damage, and, for example, more about medial temporal lobes, similar to the areas studied by Kareken *et al.* (2012). Aim to keep reading the material for your course, rather than just reading it through once. The more you read through, the more you will see connections and the clearer the material will become.

Issues and debates

Pavlov's issue about whether psychology is a science, and he thinks it is not, relates to one of the issues and debates in your course – the issue of psychology as a science. You could refer to Pavlov's claim in 1927 that it is not a science, and you could argue that developments since have led to it being a science, perhaps, including Pavlov's own work.

Pavlov comments that perhaps psychology is not a science at all, and it is interesting to know that that was a view at the time. Pavlov cites James as saying that psychology is a 'hope of science' (cited in Pavlov, 1929) and Wundt before the First World War opposed the creation of a Chair of Psychology and separately a Chair of Physiology (because he said they were hard to separate), which Pavlov uses as evidence that Wundt did not see psychology as a separate science at that time. Therefore, Pavlov felt that physiology could proceed to study the hemispheres, without leaving that research to psychology, and that is what Pavlov did – he branched into studying the hemispheres from a physiological viewpoint.

Ivan Pavlov

Reflex and the nervous system

Pavlov points out that it was Descartes who put forward the view that reflexes worked using a stimulus (something setting off behaviour) followed by an automatic response, which was a reflex. It was suggested that responses like fear and anger (and Pavlov included playfulness) were reflexes in the cerebral cortex – they were what Pavlov called 'determined', which means the physiological responses in the brain were bound to occur in response to certain stimuli.

Evolution theory

In Lecture I, Pavlov points out that the focus on evolution and the idea of survival of the fittest emphasised the animal side of humans, and a jump was made to the idea that studying animals would yield findings that could be said to be true of humans. This was an important consideration for someone who wanted to study the physiology of the brain, as this could be done using animals and still relate to humans. Animals (including humans) have reflexes that help their survival and are immediate and automatic, such as an instinct for food when hungry, or an instinct to drink water. These instincts are not going to change or waver, as they would not be a useful survival trait if they did. So the physiology behind them must be stable and automatic. Pavlov presents a long argument about the difference between reflexes and instincts – it is the reflex that is the focus in his main study.

Thorndike's Puzzle Box (1898)

Pavlov mentions Thorndike's use of a box with an animal inside it having to solve the puzzle of how to get out, showing that higher-order thinking of animals was being studied at the time. Thorndike's work is explained later in this chapter (pp. 217–218), when operant conditioning is considered. Thorndike's work was of interest to Pavlov because it was experimental and there were careful controls so that cause-and-effect conclusions could be drawn.

STUDY HINT

Using animals in experiments is part of the method section in your course. You can use Thorndike and Pavlov as examples of researchers using animals in laboratory experiments. You will also be considering the ethics of using animals in laboratory experiments (see Chapter 5 for detailed discussion). You might think that animals should never be used in experiments, and you would not be alone in thinking that, but such experiments are used and are part of your learning. Hopefully, you can move past what you might see as cruelty to animals to understand what was discovered from the experiments.

Use of objective methods for research

Pavlov says that he was unaware of Thorndike's work when he himself realised that looking at issues such as secretion from glands in dogs (salivation) subjectively, wondering what was causing it, would not build a body of knowledge. Pavlov says that he needed to study this phenomenon objectively. So he started to record everything that was happening around the animal at the time of the secretion/salivation. The lectures in 1927 were 25 years after drawing these conclusions and summarised 25 years of work. Pavlov had 100 or more collaborators so not all the findings come from him. He points out that in America work was going on too (e.g. Thorndike's work); however, this focused on external behaviour and was in the field of psychology, whereas Pavlov in Russia, and his collaborators, were using a physiological approach to look at internal factors.

The freedom reflex

One of Pavlov's early experiments was to hold the dog steady in one position using loops round its legs and to feed the dog. The dog responded after a time in what the researchers found to be a puzzling way, being very fractious and behaving oddly. After a time, the researchers realised that it had problems in standing for that length of time and it was not related to the food regime. They thought they had found a freedom reflex. This helps you to see the sorts of issues they were studying. Pavlov and his collaborators, through their experiments, realised that dogs would have such reflexes even with damage to their cerebral cortex, but they would not survive. So they realised that some higher-order thinking was necessary for survival, not simple basic reflexes like the freedom reflex or the reflex to eat.

The salivation reflex

Pavlov had started his work by noticing that dogs salivated at surprising times, such as when there was no food. This is what started him off on using objective experimental work in the area of study. Dogs salivate because that helps them if food is bad and needs to be 'carried away' and 'dissipated' in the mouth – salivation is a survival reflex. The researchers noticed that the dog salivated even if food was too far away to be eaten – the smell or sight of the food, for example, led to salivation. They soon realised that even the sight of the person who brought the food led to salivation, or the sound of his footsteps (Pavlov, 1927).

Reflexes alone are not enough for survival

Reflexes work to an extent to help the organism to survive but they are not enough. In the wild, animals have to avoid becoming prey as well as having to, perhaps, prey on other animals. Reflexes are of interest but mechanisms of learning are also important. Other thinking, other than reflexive behaviour, takes place in the cerebral hemispheres, according to Pavlov, and he comes to this conclusion because dogs without access to their cerebral hemispheres do not survive even though some reflex behaviour remains.

Experiments are artificial

In Lecture II, Pavlov discusses the artificiality of experiments and agrees that they involve isolation from real-life stimuli. However, he argues that, without this isolation of variables, study of the complexity of the cerebral cortex is not possible. He seems willing to sacrifice validity for the sake of reliability, objectivity and scientific credibility.

STUDY HINT

You can use Pavlov's argument that some reality has to be sacrificed in favour of objectivity and scientific credibility when discussing such issues in experiments and psychology studies using other methods too.

Issues and debates

One issue that is in your list of issues and debates is reductionism. Reductionism is doing research by reducing something to its parts in order to study it. Pavlov wants to study the physiology of the brain, which he sees as complex, and so he reduces the complexity by reducing what stimulates the brain to a single stimulus so he can measure the corresponding response. You can use Pavlov's study when discussing reductionism in psychology.

Progress check 4.6

Explain three background issues that Pavlov put forward about his work.

Procedure

Pavlov used dogs in his experiments. He chose the reflex that is salivation to food and the salivation reflex that is there to reject 'bad' food from the mouth. He felt these were measurable reflexes and also relatively calm ones, for the purpose of study. Salivation is measurable as the drops can be counted or the quantity can be seen in a glass tube and measured that way. Pavlov and his colleagues set about sorting out apparatus that measured saliva, as well as isolating variables that the dog would have as stimuli, such as the experimenter himself. The experimenter's blinks of the eye, movements, sweating – all were stimuli for the dog. They eventually built a special chamber/room for the dog, so that even hearing footsteps outside the room was not possible. This was to isolate all variables so that study of the cerebral cortex and reflex behaviour was possible.

In Lecture II, the dog heard a metronome and salivated to the metronome. Pavlov had paired the metronome with the food (giving food with the metronome sound a few times) and could then get the dog to salivate and lick its lips when it heard the metronome beat, without food. Later in the lectures, Pavlov explains that usually the pairing in a conditioning task has to take place about 20 times, but there is variation depending on the strength of the conditioned stimulus. He also put meat into the dog's mouth to check the salivation reflex.

Pavlov then discusses the nature of the link between the metronome and the salivation reflex compared with the meat in the mouth and the salivation reflex. He argues that the meat in the mouth is a ready-made, inborn link and the metronome beat is different – the link goes through higher-order paths in the cortex, making new paths. So he calls the salivation to the metronome a conditioned response and the salivation to the meat in the mouth an unconditioned response. He discusses the idea that the conditioned stimulus must come before the unconditioned stimulus (i.e. forward conditioning).

A procedure to show that the conditioned stimulus must come before the unconditioned stimulus was carried out. An electric buzzer, made louder over time and 5–10 seconds after the unconditioned stimulus (meat), did not achieve salivation, but an electric buzzer appearing with meat once, but before the meat, did give salivation.

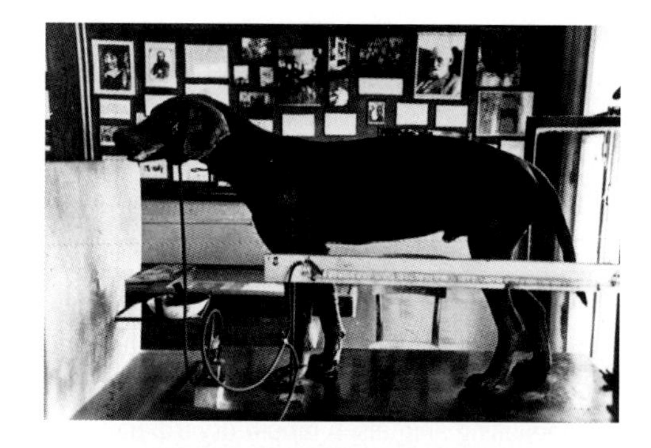

The upper picture shows one of Pavlov's dogs in the testing chamber and the lower picture shows the experimenter's section of the chamber

Results

In the metronome study, salivation started after 9 seconds and, by 45 seconds 11 drops had been collected (Pavlov, Lecture II, 1927). Pavlov also explains that he tested the dog's salivation to meat, the natural reflex, by putting meat into its mouth and found, as expected, immediate salivation, so this tested the reflex itself. An electric buzzer sounded after the meat did not give salivation, but an electric buzzer before the meat and paired just once did give salivation. Pavlov also found that the dog had to be alert and no other stimuli present to distract or affect the acquired learning, for conditioning to take place. Pavlov also found that there could be secondary conditioning when the first conditioned stimulus (such as the metronome), which gives the conditioned response (the salivation), is paired with another neutral stimulus (for example, a buzzer). Then the buzzer can become a conditioned stimulus and give the conditioned response (salivation).

Conclusions

From the metronome study, Pavlov concludes that it is 'signalisation' in the brain that links the metronome to food and thus gives the reflex response of salivation. With regard to the finding that meat has to be in the dog's mouth before salivation occurs, he explains that the reflex occurs in response to the food in the mouth, so the dog in a natural environment would have to seek out the meat – reflex responses would not keep the dog alive. Signalisation is needed for an organism to survive (such as the learned association between the metronome and meat), as well as natural inborn reflexive responses (such as salivation to the meat). Pavlov found that he could repeat his conditioning experiments with dogs and get the same findings; however, he did find that any external stimuli present could disrupt the conditioning process. He also found in one experiment that the same experiment done on two different dogs produced the opposite effects. Conditioning was found to be sensitive to many extraneous variables (factors external to the experiment) and to individual differences. He also concludes that, as there is no possibility of looking at the cerebral cortex's functioning, there is a complexity about the 'paths' that develop through conditioning that it is hard to study. (The more recent study using conditioning by Kareken *et al.*, 2012 [pp. 210–211] was able to use fMRI scanning, showing the differences in research methods from the early 1900s to the twenty-first century.)

Progress check 4.7

Describe two procedures Pavlov used and two results from his studies.

Evaluation of Pavlov's (1927) studies with dogs

Strengths

- Pavlov used carefully controlled experiments with the environment of the dogs controlled completely, except for the variables being tested. He found that any stimuli would produce conditioned responses so he had to control for all stimuli other than the stimulus being studied. His results are, therefore, objective and scientifically credible, which was his aim.
- Pavlov and his team repeated many classical conditioning experiments on dogs and so his results can be taken to be reliable. He continually found that conditioned stimuli would produce conditioned responses, using a buzzer, the metronome and other stimuli. When a study is repeated and the same results found, there can be reliability in the data.

Weaknesses

- At the time he was working, Pavlov was unable to measure brain activity in any direct way and had to assume what was happening in the cerebral cortex from his experiments. He felt he had shown inbuilt pathways that led from unconditioned stimulus to unconditioned response and he felt he showed new associations, which would be new pathways, between conditioned stimuli and conditioned responses. However, he could not study the exact mechanisms as we can today, such as using fMRI scanning.
- Ideas about evolution led Pavlov to think he could generalise from findings using dogs to say that the same processes are true of humans. This seems in a way to be a justifiable claim as humans do have reflexes (including salivation) as dogs do. However, there are differences between humans and dogs and, as Pavlov was studying higher brain processing in dogs, it might be assumed that humans would have different higher-order processing, so maybe generalising Pavlov's findings to humans is not as easy as that. Having said that, classical conditioning is used in the treatment of alcoholism, so perhaps the processes of classical conditioning do apply to humans.
- Pavlov discussed the possible lack of validity in his work, as he recognised that he took the naturalness out of the situation. The dog was in a chamber and no other stimuli were present (except for the stimuli being tested), which means 'real-life' behaviour is not being looked at, so data are not valid. However, Pavlov argued that, as stimuli in the environment are so complex and his studies are actually focusing on such stimuli, he must isolate them for study, and they are 'natural' stimuli so there is some validity. For example, the salivation of the dogs is valid – it is salivation. His work can be said to lack validity but perhaps the findings are applicable to real-life situations.

STUDY HINT

In the second weakness provided here, a criticism of Pavlov's work is offered but then some argument has been put forward that perhaps the weakness does not hold. Be sure when discussing a weakness to present it as a weakness and then you can add some critical argument, as is done here, to add depth to your discussion.

Test yourself

1 Explain the principles of classical conditioning. **(8 marks)**
2 Evaluate Pavlov's work with dogs. **(12 marks)**

Operant conditioning

Operant conditioning differs from classical conditioning because it considers the learning of *voluntary*, rather than involuntary, behaviour. The idea is that when people behave in a particular way and are rewarded for that behaviour, then they will repeat it; if they are punished for it, they will stop the behaviour. Operant conditioning also differs from classical conditioning because the consequences come after the response, whereas in classical conditioning the stimulus comes before the response.

Reinforcement and punishment

Reinforcement

Reinforcement is the central feature of operant conditioning. The theory identifies two types of reinforcement, both of which encourage repetition of the desired behaviour:

- **Positive reinforcement** is when something desired (a reward) is given in response to a behaviour – for example, if children tidy their rooms as asked and are given additional pocket money as a reward. They have been reinforced to tidy their rooms because they want to receive the additional pocket money.
- **Negative reinforcement** is when something undesired is taken away in response to a behaviour – for example, if people do not like the loud music in one restaurant, they will go to a quieter restaurant instead. They have been reinforced to go to the other restaurant because they want to avoid the loud music.

Punishment

Punishment is different from reinforcement because it is discouraging behaviour, not encouraging it. Negative reinforcement encourages behaviour to avoid something unpleasant. **Punishment** means doing something unpleasant to stop the behaviour. For example, a child who is behaving badly in a shop (perhaps shouting at a parent) might be punished by not being allowed to play with his or her friend as arranged previously.

- **Positive punishment** is when something undesired is given as a punishment for bad or unwanted behaviour. If a child is told off for misbehaving, such as running off in a shop, then that is an example of positive punishment. The child is given a 'telling off'. Another example is if someone is speeding while driving a car, they are given a speeding ticket.
- **Negative punishment** is the removal of something nice as punishment. This is to stop the child or adult behaving badly or to reduce the bad behaviour. Taking away the fun time with a friend is negative punishment. Negative punishment works best if it is consistent and applied at the time; otherwise the effect is not felt in conjunction with the bad behaviour. Something reinforcing might have happened in between.

Definitions

Reinforcement is when a behaviour has pleasant consequences of reward and so is likely to be done again. Reinforcement is in response to wanted behaviour.

Negative reinforcement is when the reward is removal of something unpleasant and **positive reinforcement** is when the reward is given.

Punishment is when a behaviour has unpleasant consequences and so is likely to stop. Punishment is in response to unwanted behaviour. **Negative punishment** is when something pleasant is taken away to stop or reduce the unwanted behaviour. **Positive punishment** is when something unpleasant is given to stop or reduce the unwanted behaviour.

An issue here is that punishment does not help to achieve the desired behaviour; it only stops undesired behaviour. Therefore, it is not usually recommended. If it is the only attention someone gets, then punishment can be rewarding, which is another reason why it is not usually used in therapy or when wanting to change someone's behaviour.

Contingency and contiguity

Operant conditioning depends on **contingency**, which means what is going to affect the organism – the reinforcer or the punishment – has to relate sufficiently to the behaviour so that there is a clear link between them. It must be clear that the behaviour and reward or punishment depend on one another. If a rat presses a lever when the red light is on, the reward of a food pellet has to be linked by the rat to the pressing of the lever. There is also **contiguity**, which means that there must not be a time lapse between the reward or punishment and the behaviour. If there is too long a period of time between the behaviour and the reward or punishment, the learning might not occur.

Definition

Contingency means that the behaviour and the consequences (reward or punishment) must be dependent on one another - the link must be clear. **Contiguity** means that the timing between the behaviour and the consequences must not be too long, so that they relate to one another.

Table 4.2 **Positive reinforcement, negative reinforcement and punishment**

Feature of operant conditioning	How behaviour is elicited
Positive reinforcement	A reward of something good is given because of the behaviour. The behaviour is repeated.
Negative reinforcement	The reward of the removal of something unpleasant is given because of the behaviour. The behaviour is repeated.
Positive punishment	Something unpleasant happens because of the behaviour. The behaviour is not repeated.
Negative punishment	Something pleasant is taken away because of the behaviour. The behaviour is not repeated.

Progress check 4.8

1 For each of the following four examples of behaviour, decide whether it is an example of positive reinforcement, negative reinforcement, positive punishment or positive reinforcement.
   a John continues with his driving lessons because the instructor says he is doing very well and will soon pass his test.
   b Jenny stops going to her driving lessons because she does not like how the instructor criticises her.
   c Jean's driving instructor shouts at her for going through a red light so she does not do it again.
   d Janet does not pass her test because she does not park correctly so on the next test she parks correctly.

2 Identify with regard to these two scenarios whether each is punishment or negative reinforcement (and if punishment, whether positive or negative punishment):
   a A child stops shouting at her mother because she is made to stay in her room after shouting like that.
   b A family once sat down on a bench to have a picnic but moved to another bench further away because of a noisy train track nearby; when they arrive for a picnic on another day, they go to the second bench straightaway.

Punishment versus negative reinforcement

It was suggested above that a child could be punished for shouting at a parent by not being allowed to play with a friend. Perhaps on another occasion, the child behaves well in order to avoid being prevented from playing with his or her friend. In this example, the child's behaviour was negatively reinforced – the child behaved well in order to avoid something that he or she did not like. So, if the child behaves well, that is through negative reinforcement; if the child stops behaving badly, that is through punishment. The difference is whether or not the punishment is given. If it is given, that is punishment. If it is avoided by behaving differently, that is negative reinforcement.

How operant conditioning is studied

Skinner is a key researcher linked with developing the theory of operant conditioning (e.g. Skinner, 1935). He used animals so that he could isolate measurable behaviour and reinforce it in various ways to investigate the effect(s). For example, he developed various ways of reinforcing rats using food pellets, which, because the rats were hungry, rewarded them. His apparatus included levers and coloured lights. He could vary the conditions so that, for example, food was only released if the rat pulled the lever when a red light was on and not when a green light was on. The rats quickly learnt to press the lever when the red light was on.

Thorndike (e.g. 1911) also carried out experiments to examine operant conditioning principles. He used a puzzle box with a single exit that could only be opened by a system of levers. A cat was placed in the box and food was placed just outside the box. The cat moved around in the box, trying to get out because of the food. When moving about, the cat accidentally pressed levers and gradually learned by trial and error how to open the box. Then the cat could get the food, which was the reward. This sort of learning, in which the solution is hit upon, and a reward is given so that the behaviour is repeated, is called 'trial-and-error' learning. Thorndike stated that this was the **law of effect** – if the effect of the learning (to get out of the box) is good (obtains food) then the behaviour is learned and repeated. Learning takes place because of what happens after the action.

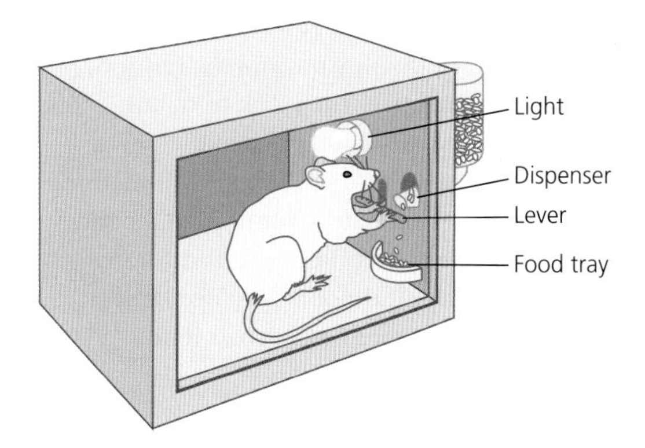

A drawing of a Skinner box showing a typical experiment using a rat, a light and a lever with food as a reward

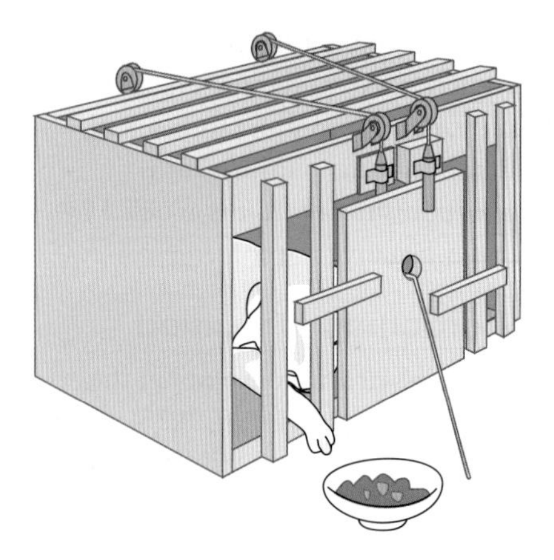

A drawing of the type of box used by Thorndike

Skinner's studies using rats and other animals and Thorndike's work with cats are examples of positive reinforcement because the animals are carrying out the behaviour to obtain a reward. Another study about rewards and reinforcement (Skinner, 1948) is covered later in this section.

Primary and secondary reinforcement

- **Primary reinforcement** – the reward is a basic need (e.g. food, drink, warmth, pleasure and shelter). For example, when a pigeon pecks at a disk to obtain a food pellet, the food is a primary reinforcement.
- **Secondary reinforcement** – the reward is something that can satisfy a basic need but is not in itself a basic need. For example, when a child is given additional pocket money that in itself is not a basic need but it could be used to buy a basic need, such as food.

Definition

Primary reinforcement is when the reward is a basic need like food and water. **Secondary reinforcement** is when the reward is something that is not a basic need but leads to a basic need, such as money (to buy food).

Progress check 4.9

For the following examples, choose whether they are primary or secondary reinforcement:

1. A bird pecks on a bird table and receives food.
2. A prisoner is given tokens for good behaviour, which they can then spend in a prison shop.
3. A dog 'sits' and gets a food treat.
4. A worker works overtime for extra pay.

Primary reinforcers are clearly going to be rewards as they fit basic needs and secondary reinforcers become reinforcing because they are linked in the organism's mind to primary reinforcement. For example, if gold was the currency not pounds sterling, you would want to be rewarded with gold, so ten pound notes would not be reinforcing.

Schedules of reinforcement

This section is about how many behaviours should get the reward (ratio of number of behaviours before the consequences happen) or in what time period when the behaviours are being executed the reward should be given (interval or time period before the consequences happen). Continuous reinforcement is when each behaviour gets the consequence – for example, every peck the rat makes when the red light is on receives the reward of a food pellet. This is not strictly a schedule as it always happens – every time and every peck.

There are four schedules of reinforcement:

- Interval – fixed: a fixed interval schedule means that, regarding the time of the reward (or punishment), there is a fixed time, such as every five minutes. This reward schedule results in more behaviours as the time for the reward increases.
- Interval – variable: a variable interval schedule means that, regarding the time of the reward (or punishment), there is a variable time, such as one in two minutes, one in five minutes, one in three minutes, varying the time the reward (or punishment) is received. This schedule means that behaviours are reasonably steady as it is not known when the consequences (e.g. a reward) will happen.
- Ratio – fixed: fixed ratio means that, regarding the number of behaviours, the reward or punishment is at a set number. For example, for every five pecks at a button a reward (or punishment) is given. This schedule means that there will be a high number of responses up to the consequences being given but that there might be a period of not many responses once that reward has been given.
- Ratio – variable: variable ratio means that a reward or punishment is given rather randomly with regard to the number of behaviours, such as after three, then after seven

then after two. This schedule is probably the most efficient as it is not known when the consequences will arrive – they could be at any time, so behaviour can be continuous.

Human examples of the various schedules

- A fixed interval schedule of reinforcement would be getting a cup of tea at work after every two hours worked if a good job was done. There would be no surprise so the reward is good but perhaps not as exciting as a surprise reward. It might be that, just before the two hours, 'good' work would be produced and made visible, whereas for the rest of the time work would not be as good.
- A variable interval schedule of reinforcement would be getting applause from an audience for running well in a race but not being sure at what time period in the race the applause would occur. You would know you would get applause through the race for running well, but would not know when, so you would run well most of the time, ready for the applause.

Progress check 4.10

For the following scenarios, decide which schedule of reinforcement is being used.

1. A teacher gives out a gold star to pupils for every two pieces of writing they do well, up to eight good pieces of writing during the day.
2. A teacher gives out two gold stars to pupils every day, provided they do eight good pieces of work, but they do not know at what time they are going to receive their gold stars.
3. A teacher gives out a gold star every two hours in class to each child who has done good work.
4. A teacher gives out two gold stars to pupils every day provided they have done eight good pieces of work, but they do not know how many pieces they have to do to get one gold star.

- A fixed ratio schedule would be getting paid piece work, so for every 100 parts made a payment would be made. You could put a part together at any time and could have rests as long as you produced 100, so that you got paid. Or you could work really hard to build up as many lots of 100 as possible, so get paid more.
- A variable ratio schedule would be gambling using a slot machine. The machine would be expected to pay out over time but the person would not know when the reward would be given. The individual is likely to play steadily and not want to stop as they never know when they will get a reward. Even getting a reward will not slow the behaviour as another reward could be immediate.

Shaping behaviour – behaviour modification

One important aspect of operant conditioning is that the complete desired behaviour may not be exhibited immediately so that it can be reinforced. The outcome (the desired behaviour) might have to be shaped by reinforcing steps towards that behaviour. This is behaviour modification as it is not just rewarding one behaviour, such as doing a gymnastic vault, it is modifying behaviour from the start (e.g. running up to the vault) to the end (the actual vault from the running to the landing). A nicely executed vault would not happen by itself to be rewarded and thus maintained.

Shaping is when behaviour is arrived at by:

- rewarding moves towards the desired behaviour
- then, waiting for an action that is nearer to the desired behaviour
- finally, waiting for the actual behaviour before offering the reinforcement.

For example, for an advertisement, a squirrel was taught to conquer an assault course. The whole course could not be achieved in one attempt. It was necessary to reward each part of the course until the squirrel had learnt the whole course, i.e. shaping was used. Similarly, teaching a pigeon to roll a ball towards small pins (as in tenpin bowling) can be achieved by shaping. At first the pigeon is rewarded for pecking near to the ground; the reinforcement is then withheld until the pecking is near the ball. Subsequently, the reward (food) is not given until the ball is hit. Then the ball has to be hit in the right direction before food is given, and so on, until the ball hits the pins.

Definition

Shaping is a term for using operant conditioning in the form of rewards and punishments to form a complex behaviour that would not occur as a whole naturally so could not be reinforced itself. A lot of behaviour is complex and would be achieved using shaping, reinforcing small parts of the behaviour and gradually asking for more before a reward is given.

Explore

Thorndike explained the law of effect and also put forward other laws. Use the internet or some other source to investigate Thorndike's research into operant conditioning.

A pigeon in an operant conditioning study in which the pigeon learns to peck an object to obtain food

> **Explore**
> Use the internet to find out how the principles of operant conditioning are used by some zoos and similar institutions to teach behaviour. Training at *Sea World*, for example, uses such principles.

Training orcas at Sea World

The superstitious pigeon (Skinner, 1948)

Skinner carried out many studies of the processes involved in operant conditioning and used laboratory experiments with animals for this purpose. One study using pigeons is useful for showing aspects of operant conditioning as well as showing how operant conditioning is studied. This study is not given in as much detail as those in the 'studies' section of your course, but is here to help your understanding of operant conditioning. You can also use this study as an example of using animals in laboratory experiments.

Aims and background

Skinner (1948) was interested in how reinforcement led to behaviour in animals. For this study, he wanted to see if *any* reinforcing situation would yield a response, even if that situation was not reinforced *deliberately*. He knew that a particular behaviour could be chosen and reinforced deliberately by giving a reward when the behaviour happened, so that it would be repeated. However, he wondered if any behaviour that occurred and was reinforced (though not deliberately by a researcher) would be repeated. At the end of this study, he called such behaviour 'superstitious' because the connection had not been planned.

Procedure

The experiment was run with eight pigeons. Two observers noted the pigeons' behaviour, which was also recorded photographically (100 photos in 10 seconds).

Each pigeon was starved to 75 per cent of its usual 'well-fed' weight. For a few minutes each day, it was put into a cage into which a food hopper could be swung so that the pigeon could eat from it. The hopper was held in place for five seconds and was then swung out, so that the pigeon could no longer eat. This happened at regular intervals during the day (a fixed interval reinforcement schedule). The food was the reinforcement. The hopper was swung in with no attention being paid to what the pigeon was doing. This was to ensure that the pigeon was not rewarded for a specific behaviour, such as pecking in a certain spot or hopping from side-to-side. The idea was to offer the food but without any particular behaviour being rewarded deliberately.

Results

In six of the eight trials, the observers agreed about which behaviour had been reinforced:

- One bird turned anticlockwise, making two or three turns between reinforcements.
- One pushed its head into the upper corners of the cage.
- One showed a head-tossing response.
- Two showed a pendulum motion with their bodies.
- One made incomplete pecking movements towards the floor.

In the other two trials, conditioning processes were not clearly marked.

It seemed that the bird executed a response when the hopper appeared to give a reward of food. The bird then carried out that response as if it were causing the reward (hopper) to appear. If the hopper reappeared within a period that was too short for extinction (behaviour stopped) to have taken place, then the behaviour was conditioned and strengthened further. The birds rapidly repeated the response while awaiting the return of the hopper. Photographs showed that the shorter the interval (time) between reinforcements, the more marked the conditioning; longer intervals resulted in the birds carrying out other responses in different parts of the cage. The sooner a second reinforcement appeared, the more likely it was that the second response would be the same as the first and the stronger the association was. Fifteen seconds was an effective time interval for this study, but Skinner concluded that this would depend on the strength of the drive and the species being studied.

The study was then extended. A one-minute interval produced different responses. At first there was a lot of energy, but the bird settled gradually on a particular well-defined part of the response – for example, a sharp movement of the head was exaggerated until the bird started turning. This involved taking steps until the stepping response became another main feature. The stepping response made an electrical contact that produced a sound that could be recorded. When the hopper no longer appeared, the bird continued to do the side hopping. Extinction was only found after a 10–15-minute interval. When the hopper reappeared after this interval, there was gradual reconditioning. However, the previous response was replaced with a new response, suggesting that retention of learning is brief.

Conclusions

The bird behaved as if there was a connection between the behaviour and the response but there was no such causal link. This resembles superstitious behaviour, such as good luck rituals in humans.

Explanation

If you took a four-leafed clover (which is considered lucky because it is rare) into an exam and passed, you might think carrying the leaf had the consequences of the reward of passing the exam and might take it with you into your next exam. This is superstitious behaviour because the leaf would not have led to the reward.

Evaluation of Skinner (1948)

Strengths

- There is inter-observer reliability because there were two observers who agreed about the observed behaviour. For example, both agreed that one bird turned anticlockwise for two or three turns and that another bird made pecking movements towards the floor. Reliability is important in a scientific study because the findings are then more secure and, if the study is repeated, the same results are likely to be found.
- There were controls, such as the timing of the introduction of the hopper into the cage using a clock, so that there was no likelihood that a particular behaviour was reinforced deliberately. Other controls were that the cage was the same size in each experiment and the birds were starved systematically. Experiments need good controls so that cause-and-effect conclusions can be drawn.

Weaknesses

- The study used animals and it might not be credible to draw conclusions about humans by relying on data from pigeons. Humans have motivation and think about their behaviour; it is assumed that pigeons do not think in the same way.
- It studies one particular aspect of behaviour separated from normal behaviour. It is possible that there is some validity in the conclusion that pigeons learn to link a certain action with a reward. However, this is short-lived learning – the behaviour was changed or lost quickly. Real behaviour, outside laboratory conditions, is likely to be more complex and last longer, so the study lacks validity.

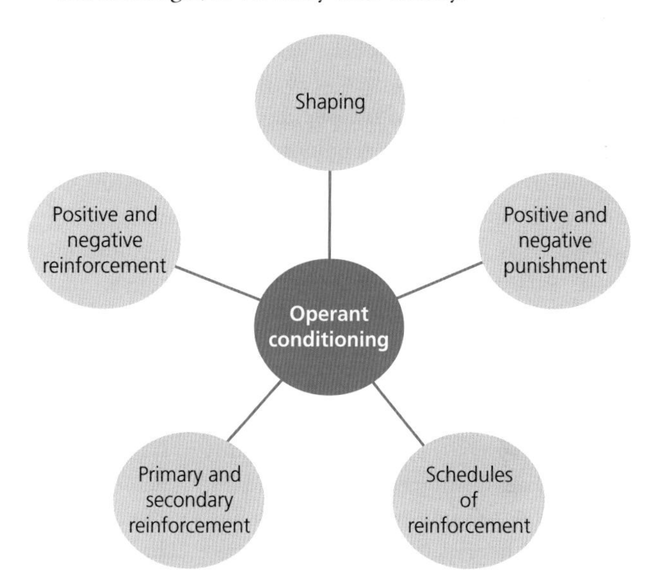

The main features of operant conditioning

Progress check 4.11

Explain what was 'superstitious' about the pigeons' behaviour in Skinner's (1948) study.

Test yourself

1. In relation to operant conditioning, explain the terms: positive reinforcement, negative reinforcement, positive punishment, negative punishment, variable ratio as a schedule of reinforcement and shaping. **(12 marks)**
2. Discuss operant conditioning as a way of explaining human behaviour. **(16 marks)**

Behaviourism

Behaviourism is an approach to understanding human behaviour and largely involves classical and operant conditioning as they both consider that, to understand behaviour, it is important to use scientific methods, isolate variables that are measurable and focus on behaviour rather than mental processes. Pavlov wanted to know about brain functioning and processes that mediated the stimulus and the response; however, they were not scientifically testable at the time and, because he used scientific methods to study behaviour without looking at information processing, his work has been put under the 'behaviourist' umbrella. In the late 1800s, it was introspection that was used to try to look at human information processing and that was seen as so unscientific and unable to be tested that the behaviourist school of thought proposed excluding mental processes and focusing on observable behaviour. Skinner, Thorndike and Watson also worked in the behaviourist field.

Classical and operant conditioning are different, studied by different researchers. Pavlov looked at classical conditioning, as well as Watson and Rayner. Thorndike looked at the law of effect, and Skinner built understanding of operant conditioning. Watson was also involved in studies of animal behaviour in their natural setting. However, both classical and operant conditioning can be seen as 'behaviourism' and they do have common aspects, such as using scientific methods and using animals to study behaviour, generalising the findings to humans.

Vaughan *et al.*'s (2014) study of operant v. classical conditioning in cows

In 2014, Vaughan *et al.* carried out a study in Canada with a practical application. The study used both operant and classical conditioning with animals and is a useful example to see how theories can be used in practice. The aim was to see if cows could be trained with regard to urination so that barns could be kept cleaner.

Aim(s)

The researchers wanted to find more out about the urination and defecation (elimination) habits of cows. They knew that electric cow trainers (giving a shock to get the cows to step backwards to keep their stalls clean) were used to keep cows from urinating and defecating in their stalls but that with these trainers came increased health risks for the cows. The aim of this study was to see if there was a better way of keeping the cows clean and managing the situation. Vaughan *et al.* (2014) explain that Whistance *et al.* (2009) had not managed to use shaping to get cows to urinate in a particular place and that was the area they wanted to focus on. They used calves that were younger than Whistance *et al.*'s (2009) cows and they focused only on urination, not defecation. Their question was: could they train the cows to urinate in a particular place?

Vaughan *et al.* (2014) used both classical and operant conditioning. One aim was to see if classical conditioning (pairing a particular place with diuretic-induced urination) would lead to the cows' associating urination with that particular place. The other aim was to see if operant conditioning using rewards would mean urination in one place only. The focus was on urination in a particular stall receiving a positive reward that would lead to learning.

Background

This study has a practical application as it is about dairy cows and the issues around cleaning up after them. A reduced amount of cleaning up would help both infection control and work involved. It would also help the environment as urine and faeces mix and that can harm the environment (such as the release of ammonia when they mix). Also the health of the cows can be harmed by not being in clean conditions, such as developing mastitis (e.g. Reneau *et al.*, 2005, cited in Vaughan *et al.*, 2014). Bergsten and Pettersson (1992, cited in Vaughan *et al.*, 2014) discussed using electric cow trainers, which used an electric shock to get the cow to step backwards to urinate or defecate, away from their stall, to keep their stalls clean. However, the use of the trainers has been linked with health problems, such as mastitis and injuries to the hock, and poor cleanliness. Whistance *et al.* (2009, cited in Vaughan *et al.*, 2014) discussed cows having an apparent lack of control over elimination, though Bailey *et al.* (1886) suggested cows have a good memory. Therefore, Whistance *et al.* (2009) and Vaughan *et al.*, (2014) suggest cows may be able to learn when and where to eliminate. This is where operant conditioning comes in. Whistance *et al.* used food as a reward before and after elimination, and it worked in that the cows learned to come for the reward both before and after elimination. However, the cows did not learn to urinate and defecate in a specific area, so that part did not work.

Procedure

Vaughan *et al.* (2014) used young calves as they could be more easily handled, and just looked at urination as it could be induced using a diuretic, which would mean a lot of urination so trials could be moved through quickly.

Vaughan *et al.* (2014) used both classical and operant conditioning to see if either (or both) would lead to an association or learning between place and urination. The study took place at the UBC Dairy and Education Research Centre in Canada and was subject to ethical scrutiny (meeting the requirements for the Canadian Council for Animal Care). Twenty-four calves were used in treatment and control conditions (12 in each). The calves were in group housing with nine calves in each pen. They were taken out of the pen on their own and into the experimental area where training took place. The experimental area was an identical pen to the one they were in, with apparatus added.

Experiment 1 – classical conditioning

The calves were led through the experimental stall to get them used to it before training. The training consisted of the calf being injected with a diuretic while in the stall and then their urination was recorded by observers. There was a control group of calves injected with saline but, apart from that, they were subjected to the same procedures. This was to ensure that the experimental group produced urine and so were more classically conditioned – the control group would produce urine normally anyway, but it would not be so much and so conditioning would not take place in the same intense way. The training period was from days 3–7 and the test period from days 8–15. During the test period, the calves were simply taken into the stall and held for ten minutes, without the injection, and their urination was recorded.

The process was:

Unconditioned stimulus (UCS) – diuretic → Unconditioned response (UCR) – urination

UCS + Neutral stimulus (NS) → Unconditioned response (UCR) – urination

Diuretic (UCS) + Stall (NS)

Stall (CS when conditioned, no longer NS) → Conditioned response (CR) – urination

STUDY HINT

Whenever you read about a method in a study, make links to what you have learned. This study uses an experimental method with careful controls to make sure that cause-and-effect conclusions can be drawn. For example, there is a control condition where calves have all the same experiences, except the experimental group have the diuretic and the control group do not. The diuretic is the unconditioned stimulus and part of the training; using saline would not have the same effect.

Experiment 2 – operant conditioning

In this experiment, using operant conditioning, the calves' milk allowance was cut and remained low during the experiments. Also access to the milk feeder was blocked an hour before the experiment started. This was all done to make milk a better reward. For three days before the experiment, three times a day, the calves were walked through the stall without stopping and led either right, when they received milk and heard the sound of a bell (reward), or left, where they had time out but no milk or bell (punishment).

There were six pairs of calves in the operant condition and six pairs in a control condition. The pairs were matched, one operant and one control calf. Where the 'operant' calf received either reward or punishment depending on whether the calf urinated or not, the yoked (control) calf received the same whether it urinated or not.

On a training day, the calf in the operant condition was guided into the stall for each experimental day and given a diuretic to help with the urination. When the calf urinated, a bell sounded and the calf was led to the right to receive milk. The calf had the milk and, when finished, was taken back into the stall. This pattern of urination and reward took place three times each day during this period of the study.

On a test day, which followed a training day, the calf was led into the stall and if it urinated within 15 minutes, the bell sounded and the calf was led out to get the milk. If the calf did not urinate in that time, it was let into another part of the pen to have 'time out'. If a calf urinated within the 15 minutes, the next day was a test day; if it did not, the next day was a training day.

The sessions went on for 17 days, though on the first day the yoked calf was not with the 'operant' calf – that just took place after the first day. The yoked calf always did what the 'operant' calf did, except for the diuretic and the waiting for urination.

Progress check 4.12

Explain how Experiment 1 of Vaughan *et al.* (2014) is an example of classical conditioning, using terms such as UCS and UCR.

Results

Table 4.3 gives the results of Experiment 1, showing the urination on training and test days for both conditions to see if there is more on test days (in the right place) for the treatment condition, which would show classical conditioning had taken place. Scores are number of urinations in the period of time.

Table 4.3 Results of Experiment 1: number of urinations on training and test days in both conditions

Treatment condition			Control condition		
Calf	Training day	Test day	Calf	Training day	Test day
44	8	1	43	4	9
46	13	9	45	4	8
48	8	6	47	5	5
50	11	6	49	2	1
52	11	2	51	9	-
56	8	2	53	3	7
Mean	9.8	4.3	Mean	4.5	6.0

There was no significant difference between the treatment and control conditions in Experiment 1, the one using classical conditioning. The training day urinations suggest that the diuretic worked but the association with the stall did not work.

For Experiment 2, however, operant calves did urinate more frequently on test days than their matched control calves ($p \leq 0.02$), with five of the six operant cows urinating more frequently than their matched control cows. The different 'operant' cows did show differences in their learning, however, with some learning more quickly than others.

Conclusions

The researchers concluded that young cows could learn to associate a stall with urination using a reward system. However, using classical conditioning did not work and no association was formed. With regard to classical conditioning, the researchers felt there may have been too long a delay between giving the diuretic and urination, so holding the calf in the stall all that time might not have given the required association. The researchers comment that they did not run the experiment for long enough to see if there was an extinction response or spontaneous recovery, but it would have been interesting to see if anything like that did occur. Overall, regarding the classical conditioning, they felt that had not worked.

The operant conditioning, however, did seem to work and also there were individual differences in the different cows, some learning more quickly than others, which was interesting. They felt that individual differences may relate to age, ability, physical issues, temperament or motivation. They felt they had a lot of other issues they could investigate in other studies and that operant conditioning was a possibility in helping when it comes to keeping cows clean in their stalls.

Explore

Use the internet to search for examples of operant conditioning to train animals and pick out issues such as the schedule of reinforcement and whether positive or negative reinforcement, or positive or negative punishment is used. The following example is about training lions: http://entertainment.howstuffworks.com/arts/circus-arts/lion-taming3.htm.

Progress check 4.13

Explain Experiment 2 in the Vaughan *et al.* (2014) study in terms of operant conditioning.

Evaluation of Vaughan *et al.* (2014)

Strengths

- They used an experimental method and made sure, as far as they could, that they had careful controls, largely by using control 'cows' that experienced everything that the 'experimental' cow experienced except for the main condition (such as being injected with diuretic in the classical conditioning experiment and being rewarded in the operant conditioning experiment for elimination). This meant that conclusions that were drawn were scientifically credible and cause could be related to effect.
- There was validity in the situation they used up to a point, as these were real calves in stalls where they were kept and the experimental stall(s) were the same as those they were used to. This was a study looking at natural issues with a real-life application, so there is some validity.
- The study was done for practical reasons to see if either classical or operant conditioning would work to train cows to keep their stall clean, which is good for the environment, infection and workload of farm workers. The results are generalised to cows but there is no attempt to generalise to humans – this is an animal study for animals. One could say that humans benefit from dairy cattle in many ways, but it can also be said that this study is for the cows, so generalisation is fair and possible. However, the researchers did comment that there were individual differences between cows, which might affect generalisability.

Weaknesses

- Although there is some validity in the study, the experimental stall was artificially set up and the diuretic that was used was something artificial introduced for

the purposes of study (as was the saline in the classical conditioning experiment). The experimenters would not normally be there and being led to and fro from their own stall to an experimental stall was not normal for the calves. There would be some artificiality and that might have led to stress, which may have affected the findings. In fact, the researchers tried to test for such effects and, testing their results, concluded that they felt they had allowed for such artificiality; nonetheless, the validity of the findings can be questioned.
- The researchers mention that in the operant condition, where it was concluded that the results were useful and operant conditioning might work to train the cows, the individual cows did show differences in how well they learned. If that is the case, and not many cows were used, perhaps generalising the findings to say they are true of all cows is not a fair thing to do. This would affect the conclusion that operant conditioning would help to train cows.

Test yourself

Explain the differences between classical and operant conditioning, giving four terms that apply to each, to show the differences. **(6 marks)**

Using animals to study operant and classical conditioning

In the method section for this topic area, you will look at using animals in laboratory experiments and the ethics involved. Vaughan *et al.* (2014) used calves in their study and adhered to the ethical code (they in fact did not continue to use one calf because of its distress). Pavlov used dogs; Skinner used pigeons and rats. These are all examples you can use when discussing the use of animals in laboratory experiments. Chapter 5 examines these issues in detail. However, we now briefly look at the issues of using animals in laboratory experiments, as this can be useful when evaluating classical and operant conditioning theories, or any other theories that use animals in studies.

Reasons for behaviourists to use animals in experiments include the following:

- Animals are fairly easy to handle.
- In ethical terms, experiments can be carried out on animals that cannot be carried out on humans.
- Animals can learn something new, which it is fairly certain they have not experienced before, so learning is testable.
- Laboratory studies mean strict controls.
- Objectivity can be achieved.
- Measurable stimuli and responses can be isolated from other experiences.
- Experiments are fairly easy to repeat and quite cheap (e.g. more animals can be obtained).
- Darwin's ideas about evolution suggested that animals could be studied and the findings applied to humans.

Problems with using animals in experiments include the following:

- There are brain differences between humans and animals, so generalisation is difficult.
- Ethically, the rights of animals must be acknowledged.
- It is not certain that animal learning is the same as human learning.
- There could be factors involved other than the stimulus–response situation set up by the experimenter.
- Animals do not have the same emotional responses as humans, which might affect generalisation of the findings to humans.
- Animals are different from each other and respond differently to different stimuli.
- Laboratory experimenters are not natural, so the findings are not valid.

Progress check 4.14

State two reasons for using animals to study human behaviour and two reasons against such use.

Evaluation of operant and classical conditioning theories as explanations of human behaviour

Strengths

- In both operant and classical conditioning, objective measures and careful controls are used when researching the concepts. Both theories are studied scientifically. Some behaviour is isolated and a way of measuring it is devised. The behaviour is then tested and, because of the controls, scientific conclusions can be drawn. For example, Skinner (operant conditioning):
  - isolated animals in a cage, to control all variables other than the independent variable
  - varied the independent variable in such a way that the differences being introduced were clear
  - measured the dependent variable carefully.

  In this way, cause-and-effect conclusions could be drawn.
- Both types of conditioning can be used in therapy and so have real-life applications to society. Therefore, they are useful theories.

Weaknesses

- Both operant and classical conditioning mainly involve animals. The differences between humans and animals make it difficult to draw conclusions from animal studies and generalise the results to humans. For example, cats may learn to get out of a puzzle box by trial and error and, once rewarded, they may repeat the behaviour to get more rewards. However, humans would be likely to use problem-solving techniques together with previous experience to work out how to open the box, which is not trial-and-error learning. Therefore, generalising findings from animal studies to say they apply to humans may not be useful.

- Both operant and classical conditioning theories – partly because the studies use animals and partly because the studies are experiments – lack validity. Studies isolate behaviour to investigate it scientifically, which means reducing such behaviour to a small part of 'normal' activities, so the results are not true to life. The situation is not valid because laboratories are used; the concepts might not be valid if they apply just to small parts of overall behaviour.

Test yourself

Evaluate classical and operant conditioning as explanations of human behaviour. **(8 marks)**

Social learning theory

The third main type of learning is social learning. Social learning theory (SLT) explains that learning can occur by observation, imitation, modelling and vicarious reinforcement.

Observation, imitation and modelling

Social learning theory was developed by Bandura, three of whose studies are explained in the next section. It seemed clear that not all behaviour was conditioned because some behaviour appeared without conditioning. So, alongside (not replacing) operant conditioning, social learning theory suggests that people learn by observing others. This is **observational learning** – people watch what others do and copy their actions, thus learning new behaviours. Some animals (e.g. monkeys) have been found to use observational learning as well. One of Bandura's ideas about social learning is that learning goes two ways – it is not, as operant conditioning suggests, that the environment acts on the individual and learning takes place (such as behaviour – consequences). Learning involves the individual affecting the environment as well, such as there being cognitive processes involved in whether someone learns or not. This idea of learning being two-way, with the environment and the individual interacting, is called **reciprocal determinism**.

Albert Bandura in the 1960s did a lot of experiments on observational learning and is the main name linked to social learning theory

Definition

Observational learning means watching someone rather than doing something oneself. **Reciprocal determinism** is the idea that not only does the environment act on the individual to 'cause' learning, but also the individual acts on their environment, such as by attending to a modelled behaviour, retaining it, reproducing it and being motivated to reproduce it.

Explore

Use the internet or some other source to look up Mineka's work with monkeys, where observational learning can be found. This will help to illustrate the principles of social learning theory. One of her studies, with Michael Cook, can be found here: http://homepage.psy.utexas.edu/HomePage/Class/Psy394Q/Research%20Methods/Assigned%20readings/Experimental%20Research%20Paradigms/Cook%20&%20Mineka.pdf. Their work uses animals to see if observational learning takes place and whether a fear can be learned by watching fear in others. This idea is also found in Olsson *et al.* (2007), which is explained later in this section.

Observation
- Watching someone rather than doing something oneself

Modelling
- Displaying behaviour

Imitation
- Copying the behaviour of others

Vicarious reinforcement
- Copying the behaviour of others because you see them rewarded for it

Main terms in social learning theory

The steps in observational learning are as follows:

- First, the behaviour is modelled by a role model, though **modelling** means more than this. A **role model** may be a parent, a friend, someone in a peer group, a media personality or any person who is significant in some way. A role model tends to have some importance for the observer.
- The observer **identifies** with the role model.
- The behaviour is observed and noted.
- The behaviour is **imitated** and so it is learned. Whether it is repeated again depends on reinforcements and rewards.

Definition

Modelling means displaying behaviour and also the process of being the model. A **role model** is someone significant/important to an individual, such as a friend, a parent or someone they look up to, perhaps an athlete. The individual will **identify** with the role model in some way, which means they can connect them to themselves and see something in them that is a link. **Imitation** means copying the behaviour of others.

Modelling can occur using a live model – someone is actually doing the behaviour. It can occur using verbal instruction, where someone is talked through the behaviour. It can also occur through symbols, such as on television, even using cartoon figures or actual symbols such as representing happiness through certain behaviour or objects.

Not all behaviour is imitated:

- It depends on the model.
- It depends on the consequences of the observed behaviour. If the model's behaviour is seen to be punished, then it might not be imitated; if it is seen to be rewarded, it is more likely to be imitated (this is vicarious reinforcement – see later).
- Reinforcement is motivational and people are more likely to imitate behaviour if they are motivated to do so, possibly because of the likelihood of rewards.
- 'Modelling' entails the role model being identified with and involved, as well as meaning the role model 'demonstrating' the behaviour.

Social learning theory, therefore, accepts an element of thinking in the processes of learning, which was not considered in either classical or operant conditioning theories.

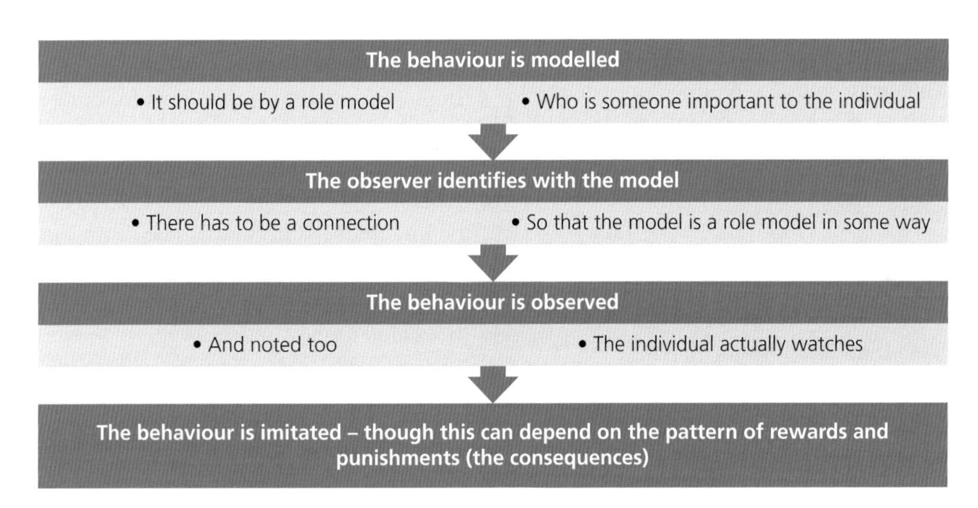

The steps in social learning

Cognitive processes in observational learning

There are cognitive elements involved in observational learning. When observing, the learner has to pay attention to the important, not the incidental, parts of the action, and has to record the information in memory, which younger children may find more difficult than older children. Motivation is also important as the consequences of the action for the role model are involved in deciding whether or not to carry out the behaviour. The child must also have the physical ability to carry out the action. Therefore, the issues that govern whether a modelled behaviour is imitated are that:

- it is observed
- it is attended to
- it is stored in memory
- it is rewarded in such a way that there is motivation to reproduce the action.

Behaviour that is learned through observation may not be exhibited until some time after the learning has taken place.

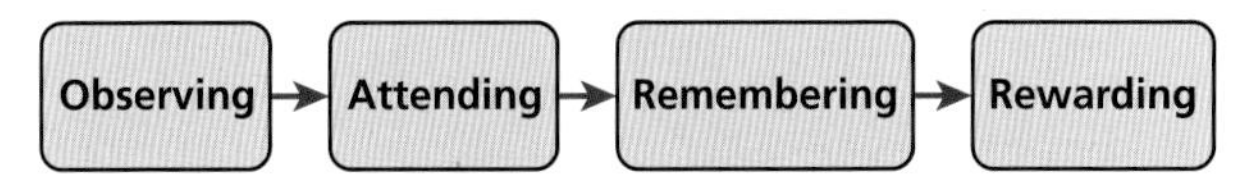

The steps of observational learning focusing on cognitive processes

Social learning stages

You can see there are various stages in social learning and various factors involved. Stages cover both the learning side of the theory and the cognitive side of the theory.

Attention

With the behaviour being modelled, first, there is attention. The individual must notice the behaviour and pay attention to it. You can link this to the multi-store model of memory in cognitive psychology, where information is coming into the brain but only some of it is attended to in the sensory register, and then what is attended to goes into the short-term store. Behaviour that is modelled must be attended to for learning to take place. Factors affecting whether someone attends to the behaviour of others can depend on how distinctive it is and how relevant it is for that individual.

Retention

The multi-store model of memory showed how memories are lost (forgotten) if they are not rehearsed and in that way stored in long-term memory. Episodic memories are memories of events and experiences in long-term memory and behaviour that is modelled would fall into that category. What is attended to must be retained in memory. This is 'retention'. Factors affecting retention include using visual imagery perhaps, or coding the behaviour so that it has meaning.

Reproduction

Once the modelled behaviour is in memory, the behaviour can then be imitated. However, it will only be reproduced under certain circumstances. These circumstances depend on the consequences of reproducing the behaviour, which give the motivation for doing so. Reproduction is the stage where the modelled behaviour is carried out.

Motivation

Reproduction takes place because of motivation and that depends on the reinforcement for reproducing the behaviour. This is linked to operant conditioning. Rewards motivate behaviour. Behaviour that is rewarded is more likely to be shown, as Thorndike's law of effect predicted. The idea of vicarious learning can link to motivation – if someone is seen to be rewarded for their behaviour then the observer might be more motivated to imitate their behaviour than if they were punished for their behaviour. Punishment would demotivate someone.

STUDY HINT

There are a lot of terms in social learning theory. You could use mnemonics to help you to remember them. ARRM stands for attention, retention, reproduction and motivation. Make up a sentence, such as 'A Real Role Model', to help you in your learning. Or you could use colours to add visual imagery, such as Amber, Red, Red, Maroon. If you use colours, use coloured ink when writing about each. Adding meaning to what you are learning helps recall.

Progress check 4.15

List the four stages in social learning that relate to cognitive processes.

Results of studies showing the most likely occasions when behaviour is imitated

Bandura carried out studies to investigate when children are likely to imitate behaviour. Here are some of his findings:

- Aggressive male models are imitated more than aggressive females. This may show relevance – aggression is seen as more appropriate in males in US society, where Bandura worked.
- Boys are more likely than girls to imitate an aggressive male model. This shows relevance – male models are more relevant to boys.
- Role models that show consistency are more likely to be imitated. If a person says one thing and does another (inconsistency), this is confusing. Actions are imitated more than words.
- Boys tend to show physical aggression when they imitate aggression and girls tend to be more aggressive verbally.

You have to learn about three of Bandura's studies for your course in this topic area and the evidence for the claims made here will be found in those studies.

Children learn through the mechanisms of observational learning

Vicarious learning

Vicarious reinforcement is a term used to explain that reinforcement can occur through others being reinforced. Vicarious reinforcement is connected with observational learning – social learning theory explains that learning takes place through direct reinforcement *and* indirect (vicarious) reinforcement. It examines how imitation is affected by perceived reinforcements and punishments. Examples include:

- vicarious reinforcement – a person works hard because a colleague has been rewarded for hard work
- vicarious punishment – someone does not park in a particular place because he or she has seen someone get a parking ticket there
- vicarious extinction – people stop doing something because they have seen that people are not rewarded for doing it.

There are four aspects to vicarious reinforcement, as shown in the following diagram:

Modelling effect	Eliciting effect	Disinhibiting effect	Inhibitory effect
• Someone does something they have seen and would not have done otherwise	• Someone watches a behaviour and copies it but does it a bit differently	• Behaviour is done that someone would not have thought OK but has seen it done without negative consequences and now thinks it is OK	• Someone sees a role model punished for a behaviour and so they don't do it

Features of vicarious learning

Important factors in vicarious learning

Models are more likely to be imitated:

- if they are similar to the observers; however, similarity is in the mind of the observer, e.g. a girl might imitate a celebrity whom she thinks she is similar to, even though others would not recognise the similarity
- if they are perceived by the observers as important or prestigious
- if the behaviour is observable – the more observable the behaviour, the more likely it is to be imitated.

Definition

Vicarious reinforcement means copying the behaviour of others because of seeing them rewarded for it.

Progress check 4.16

Match the following situations with the most likely person to imitate that behaviour. Allocate numbers to show which match.

Situation	Number	Person observing	Number
A father holding his hand up to be heard when at a family meal		A teenage boy who likes technology	
A teenage boy playing a video game in a shop		Formula One fan	
A bank advert using a racing driver		A young mother	
A mother taking cupcakes to a school function		The father's young son	

Evaluation of social learning theory as an explanation of human behaviour

Evaluating a theory is useful when applying the theory to a situation. For example, social learning theory is used to explain why violence on television seems to be imitated. In order to evaluate this, it is necessary to be able to evaluate the theory as an explanation of human behaviour. Note that you will learn more about social learning theory when studying Bandura's work, so come back to the evaluation after that perhaps.

Strengths

- There is a great deal of experimental evidence to support social learning. Much of this is the work of Bandura, but others have also found that behaviour is observed and then imitated. It is not difficult to set up a situation in which a distinctive behaviour is modelled and then to see if it is imitated, as it often is. This has been found in studies with children and with some animal species. Mineka's work showing how monkeys use observational learning is briefly explained below, as is another study, by Olsson *et al.* (2007), who have shown observational learning in humans.
- The theory is useful in explaining human behaviour and can be applied as a therapy. For example, obsessive compulsive disorder is sometimes treated by using operant conditioning principles and shaping. One piece of obsessive behaviour is chosen

and the patient is rewarded for not carrying out that behaviour. Observational learning can be used alongside the system of rewards. Someone the patient trusts can carry out the desired behaviour and the patient can see that the consequences are not unpleasant. For example, people with obsessive compulsive disorder may not be able to touch things without afterwards washing their hands many times. Someone trusted can keep touching an object without hand washing so that it can be seen that there are no bad consequences.

Weaknesses

- Behaviour might not be exhibited immediately. Therefore, it is difficult to test for observational learning. Experiments show only specific behaviours at a specific time, so the results are limited and there might be a lack of validity in the findings.
- Some experiments are carried out on animals. Therefore, there are the usual issues involved in claiming that behaviour shown by animals is also true of humans, given the differences between them. However, the animals used are often monkeys and chimpanzees, which are close to humans in evolutionary terms, so the evidence from animals could be quite strong.

Study of interest

In their 1990 study, Cook and Mineka report on three experiments with monkeys looking at learning. Just one is reported here as it shows observational learning of fear using monkeys and is an example of observational learning and learning from others. Their study starts with the knowledge from other studies that fears are not indiscriminate but are specific, such as having a fear of snakes, but not of flowers (e.g. Mineka, 1985). The stimuli that give fear are called 'fear-relevant' and snakes, for monkeys, are 'fear-relevant'.

Monkeys, in an experimental situation, looked at a video of a model monkey reacting to different 'snakes' – a real snake, a huge toy snake, a big toy snake and a small snake, as well as other things like blocks (neutral). One model monkey was lab reared and had already been conditioned to have a fear of snakes in a previous study. The other model was a monkey who was reared in the wild. The two models (separately) were in what was called the 'circus' as it housed the model monkey in the middle of a 'circus ring' with glass compartments surrounding it. The model monkey could be allowed to see into the compartments and what the monkey was watching was captured on the video for the participant/watching monkey. The model monkeys were videoed and the participant monkeys (one at a time) watched the video of the other monkey. The question was if the model monkey showed fear of an object, would the participant monkey observe that fear and learn fear by observational learning?

In the video, the model monkeys showed fear of the live snake and the huge toy snake but not of other stimuli. The fear of the model monkeys was rated according to whether the model monkey climbed over the box to get food which was arranged beyond the box. The researchers reasoned that if the model monkey was afraid, it would not climb over the box to get the food. The researchers observing the participant monkey sat behind a one-way mirror to record the data, which were the reactions of the watching monkey (the participant monkey) after some sessions of watching the videos to let learning take place. There was more than one observer and between observers there was an 88 per cent agreement in their ratings, so reliability was claimed. It was found that the observer monkeys (the participants) did learn a fear of the real snake and 'snake-like' objects from observing the model monkeys show fear of snakes.

Humans show observational learning and the amygdala is activated (Olsson *et al.*, 2007)

A study is outlined here that demonstrates observational learning in humans and also links to parts of the brain activated when fear is learned through observing others. The biological element to this study means it will be useful when studying biological psychology in Chapter 3.

Background

Olsson *et al.* (2007) looked at brain functioning in acquisition of a fear. Classical conditioning can explain fears, as you will see when studying Watson and Rayner's (1920) work with Little Albert, and it is the amygdala that is involved (a lot of studies have suggested this, such as Kapp *et al.*, 1992, cited in Olsson *et al.*, 2007). You will have looked at this area of the brain when studying biological psychology (page 000). Olsson *et al.* (2007) note that fears can be acquired through observation alone and wonder what parts of the brain are active. They found that people who watched someone being fearful in a situation they themselves would then encounter showed activity in the amygdala, as they also did when being afraid in the situation themselves. This confirms that it is the amygdala that is involved in fears and that classically conditioned fear, fear acquired through social observation (with no direct experience of the situation), and fear that comes from empathy all rely on the same brain functioning.

Procedure

This study used fMRI scanning to find out which areas of the brain were involved in 'being fearful'. The participants were 11 right-handed males. (Interestingly, during selection, one participant was not used because he expressed doubt that the shocks were real, which might reflect the number of people in the US who know about Milgram's work.) A movie was created of someone looking at blue and at yellow squares on a screen and receiving a small uncomfortable shock when one colour appeared (CS+) but not when the other was shown (CS–). The person in the movie was the model. Skin conductance assessed the learning.

Skin conductance measures resistance in the skin, and can gather information about sweating and such responses that characterise activation of a reaction in the person. There were two stages in the study, both involving a functional scan (fMRI). They were told to watch the movie carefully (it lasted just over three minutes) as it showed them the procedure they were going to go through, including the shocks. One scan took place when they were watching the movie of the person watching the coloured squares on a screen, and one when they were watching the screen and coloured squares themselves, this time expecting to receive the shocks. The first time was observation of the other person getting the shocks; the second time was when they were doing the experiment themselves. They did not in fact receive any shocks. The second part, when they believed they would be getting the shocks, used the same colours for getting shocks (CS+) or not getting shocks (CS–), so the participants knew in their session which colour was going to be the one linked to shocks. Then they were debriefed and the study was explained to them. They were also asked if they believed the instructions.

Results

The scans were studied both at the CS+ time (when the coloured squares were those when a shock would be received, either by the model or by the participant) and at the CS– time (when the colour was such that no shock was given).

Using the skin conductance measures, it was found that in the movie, watching the model, the participants did react to the colour that would give the shock and showed less reaction to the colour which would not get the shock. This confirms that there is a physiological response (the skin conductance measure shows that) when watching someone else getting a shock. This shows observational learning taking part and someone else's emotional distress being 'felt'.

Using the fMRI results and looking at blood flow, it was seen that it was the amygdala that was activated, both left and right hemisphere (bilateral). The scan results were very similar for the observational session and the session where the participant thought they were going to receive the shocks.

Conclusion

The conclusion was that observational learning without any stimuli has the same reaction in the brain as more direct learning where a stimulus is anticipated.

Explore

You can look at Olsson *et al.*'s (2007) study more closely using the following link: www.ncbi.nlm.nih.gov/pmc/articles/PMC2555428/.

STUDY HINT

In this book, there are some studies added (such as Olsson *et al.* and Cook and Mineka's work). Keep an eye on the specification (which you can access from the Edexcel website) and make notes on what is useful additional information, such as this, and what is specifically named in your specification. Use a symbol to note which is which and what you are focusing on, or use a clear diagram to help you.

Bandura's studies – social learning and aggression

Albert Bandura did a lot of work in the 1960s that focused on social learning theory and how we learn by observation. Social learning theory came from his findings. He went on to study different areas, such as self-efficacy, but your course asks you to know about his work in the 1960s focusing on social learning. He worked with colleagues, and three of his studies are explained in this section. Use the studies and their findings when discussing social learning theory. Bandura focused on observational learning of aggression and this links well with your learning of biological psychology in Chapter 3, where you learn about biological underpinning of aggression as well as Freud's ideas about aggression. In this chapter, you learn about how aggression can be learned through social learning. These links can be useful for your learning.

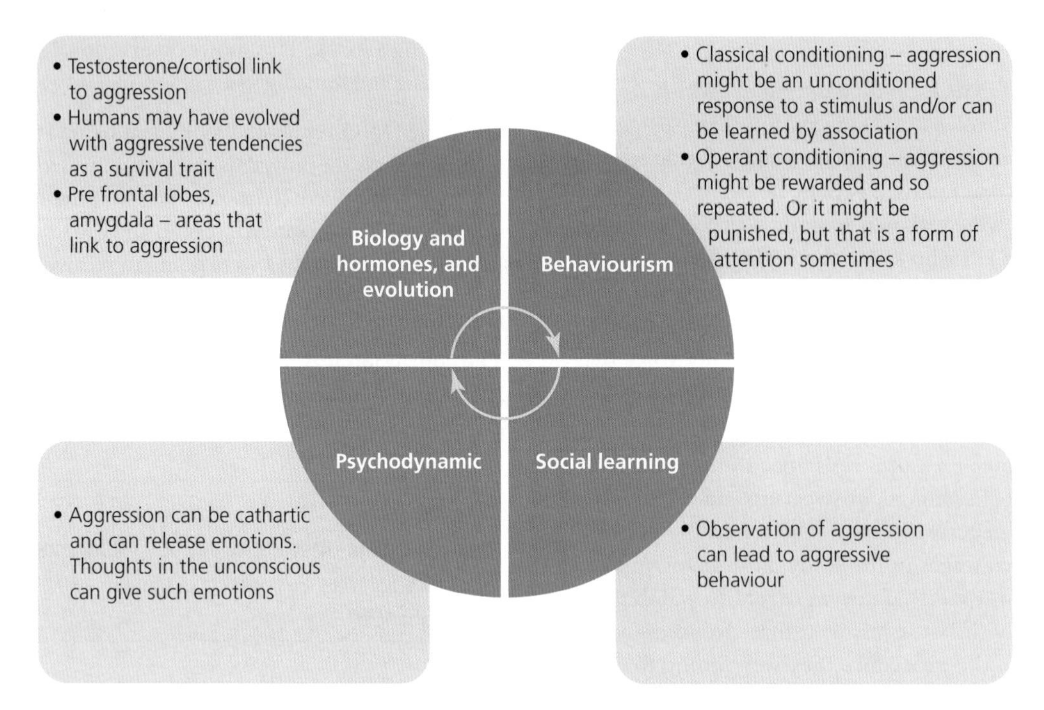

Explanations for aggression from the different approaches covered in Chapters 3 and 4

The three studies you need to learn about are:

- Bandura, Ross and Ross (1961), who looked at whether children would copy aggression they saw; they also looked at their copying of non-aggressive behaviour and gender differences in such behaviour
- Bandura, Ross and Ross (1963), who looked at modelling of aggression considering real-life, film and cartoon models
- Bandura (1965), who built on previous studies and this time also looked at vicarious learning (e.g. model rewarded and model punished).

Learning about all three studies will cover a lot of the issues that have been explained in this section on social learning theory. The studies are in the 'Bobo doll' series of studies. A Bobo doll is a large doll more than 1.5 metres tall that is rounded at the bottom and so rocks on its base. It can be punched and will come back to its original position.

STUDY HINT

You need to be able to talk about each of these studies separately and accurately. In order to remember them, you could think of 1961 being aggression v. non-aggression (type of aggression), 1963 being real-life v. film aggression (filmed aggression) and 1965 being about whether aggression is rewarded (vicarious reinforcement).

Bandura's studies in the 1960s used a Bobo doll, a toy which can be hit and will bounce back, having a rounded base

Bandura, Ross and Ross (1961) 'Transmission of aggression through imitation of aggressive models'

One reason for this study being prescribed for your course is that it is an experiment with clear controls and procedures, so it is useful as an example for methodological issues. It provides evidence for observational learning and social learning theory and is straightforward to learn and remember.

Aims

The study had several aims, reflected by the number of hypotheses. The general aim was to see whether children would imitate behaviour, not at the time they see it, but later, even if it was not rewarded. The hypotheses were:

- Participants exposed to an aggressive model would later reproduce aggressive acts similar to those modelled.
- Those exposed to non-aggressive models and those who had no modelled behaviour (a control group) would not produce aggressive acts.
- Observation of non-aggressive behaviour would inhibit subsequent behaviour. Therefore, control group participants (who saw no modelled behaviour) would show more aggression than the group that saw non-aggressive behaviour.
- Participants are more likely to copy same-sex models than opposite-sex models. This is based on the idea that parents tend to reinforce sex-appropriate behaviour.
- Aggression is more a masculine behaviour, so boys will be more aggressive than girls, particularly when the model is aggressive.

Background

Bandura and Huston (1961) had found that children imitate a model's behaviour in the presence of that model and there were other studies that had shown observational learning. Bandura wanted to see if behaviour would be displayed, after observing it, when the model was absent. He thought that children who watched aggressive actions would display them with the model then absent and that those who watched non-aggression would display less, and indeed less than a control group who watched no aggression at all. Non-aggression should be copied as well as aggression, so those who saw non-aggression should be less aggressive than 'normal'. 'Normal' would be indicated by the control group, giving a baseline measure. He thought that those who watched aggression would display acts that were like the ones they saw (this is after the watching, with the model no longer present). Bandura also thought from previous studies (he cites Fauls and Smith, 1956) that boys would tend to imitate a male model and girls a female model (this comes from the idea that children tend to imitate their same-sex parent and also that behaviour that is 'suitable' for the gender of the child tends to be rewarded in a culture). Bandura, working with colleagues, set about testing these ideas in this study.

Procedure

The participants were 36 boys and 36 girls, aged from 37 to 69 months, who were enrolled in the Stanford University Nursery School. There was also a male role model, a female role model and a female experimenter. There were eight experimental groups, each with six participants, and a control group of 24 participants. Half the participants in the experimental group had an aggressive model, half had a non-aggressive model. The groups were subdivided into an equal number of boys and girls in each group and further subdivided so that half had a model of the same sex and half had a model of the opposite sex.

Before the study, participants in the experimental and control groups were matched for their original levels of aggression. They were rated on five-part scales covering:

- physical aggression
- verbal aggression
- aggression towards objects
- aggressive inhibition.

They were rated by an experimenter and a nursery-school teacher, both of whom knew the children well. The two judges achieved a high level of **inter-rater reliability**. Participants were then grouped into threes according to the aggression ratings and were allocated randomly to the control group, a group that watched an aggressive model or a group that watched the non-aggressive model.

Definition

Inter-rater reliability means that more than one person rates the behaviour (what is of interest) and their ratings are compared. If there is agreement between the ratings, then there is said to be reliability. It is as if the study was done again with the same results being found.

STUDY HINT

So far in this study you have read about the use of a control group, the use of hypotheses and the use of inter-rater reliability. Check that you fully understand these terms. This study can be used when describing these terms.

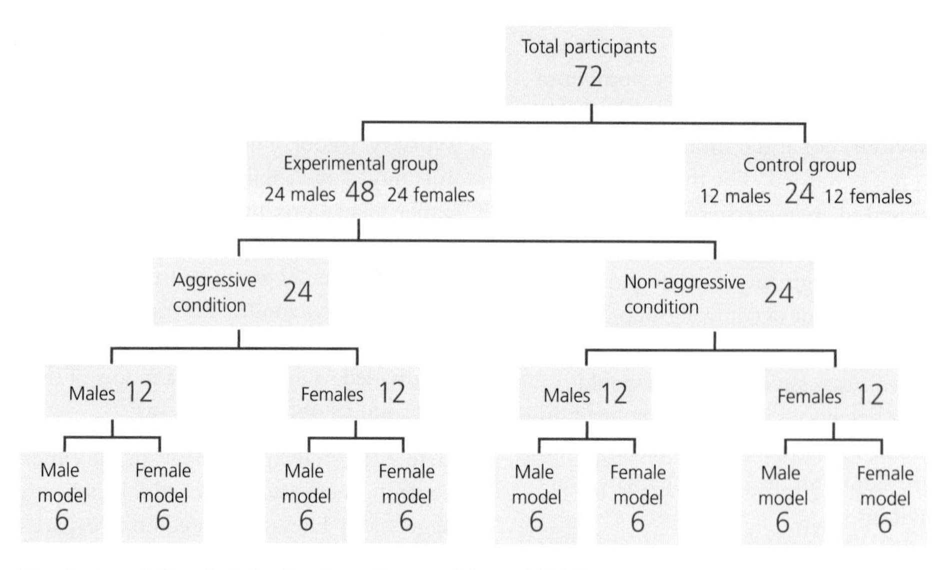

The design of the study by Bandura, Ross and Ross (1961)

Participants were taken individually into one corner of a room and were seated at a table with materials to occupy them. A model then went to another corner of the room where there was a mallet, a toy set and a Bobo doll. The children did not have access to a mallet, a Bobo doll or a toy set – they had different play materials. In the non-aggressive condition, the model played with the toy set and was subdued. In the aggressive condition, after a minute of playing quietly, the model acted aggressively towards the Bobo doll. The aggressive acts were carefully modelled so that, if they were repeated later, this could be observed clearly. For example, the doll was laid on its side and the model sat on it and punched it. In another aggressive act, the model struck the doll on the head with the mallet. There was also verbal aggression, such as the model saying 'sock him on the nose…' and verbal comments that were not aggressive. The control group underwent the same procedures with regard to play, but there was no model present.

The participants were then taken to a different area and were shown some attractive toys that they started to play with. They were then told that the toys were not for them, they were special, and they were not allowed to play with them anymore. This made the children frustrated. This was to make sure that their emotional levels were similar before the next phase.

Each child was then taken to another room where there were many sorts of play materials. The toys included a Bobo doll similar, but not identical, to the one they had seen, a mallet and the toy set, together with other toys. Some of these were toys with which the child could be aggressive, such as a toy gun and a ball with a face on it hanging from the ceiling; some were 'non-aggressive' toys.

There were two judges who watched through a one-way mirror and recorded each child's play behaviour. One of the judges did not know the child or to which condition they had been allocated. By having more than one judge, inter-observer reliability could be tested.

Results

Three types of imitation were measured:

- imitation of verbal aggression
- imitation of physical aggression
- imitation of non-aggressive verbal responses.

In the 'aggressive' condition, there was much verbal and physical aggression that resembled that of the model. In the 'non-aggressive' condition and in the control group, very little aggressive behaviour was found; around 70 per cent of these participants had a zero score for aggression. About one-third of those in the 'aggressive' condition also imitated the model's non-aggressive responses; no one in the other two conditions made such remarks.

Table 4.4 Mean aggression score for experimental and control group participants

		Experimental group				
		Aggressive condition		Non-aggressive condition		
		Female model	Male model	Female model	Male model	Control group
Physical aggression	Girls	5.5	7.2	2.5	0.0	1.2
	Boys	12.4	25.8	0.2	1.5	2.0
Verbal aggression	Girls	13.7	2.0	0.3	0.0	0.7
	Boys	4.3	12.7	1.1	0.0	1.7
Mallet aggression	Girls	17.2	18.7	0.5	0.5	13.1
	Boys	15.5	28.8	18.7	6.7	13.5
Non-imitative aggression	Girls	21.3	8.4	7.2	1.4	6.1
	Boys	16.2	36.7	26.1	22.3	24.6
Gun play	Girls	1.8	4.5	2.6	2.3	3.7
	Boys	7.3	15.9	8.9	16.7	14.3

STUDY HINT

When a table of results has a lot of data in it, try picking out two cells so that you can start to see patterns. For example, the boys in the control group showed quite a bit of gun play (14.3 acts), even though they saw no aggression.

There are a great many results that can be picked out from this table. Some ideas follow and you can probably pick out some results yourself.

- The mallet was used aggressively on objects other than the Bobo doll to a greater extent by those in the 'aggressive' and control conditions than by those in the 'non-aggressive' group. Perhaps modelling subdued non-aggressive behaviour leads to less aggression.
- This was particularly true for girls. Girls who observed a non-aggressive model performed a mean number of 0.5 mallet aggressive responses compared with 18.0 for girls in the 'aggressive' condition and 13.1 for girls in the control condition.
- In the non-aggressive group male model, boys produced more imitative physical aggression than girls but they did not differ with regard to verbal aggression.
- Male participants showed more physical and verbal aggression, more non-imitative aggression and more aggressive gun play when exposed to the aggressive model than girls did.
- Girls exposed to the female aggressive model performed more verbal imitative aggression and more non-imitative aggression than boys, although there were only small numbers in the groups from which to draw conclusions.
- In general, it seemed that a male model had more influence on behaviour than a female model.
- Apart from mallet aggression, there were no significant differences between the 'non-aggressive' group and the control group. However, this was because exposure to the female model in both the 'aggressive' and the 'non-aggressive' conditions did not differ from the controls.
- This masked the finding that, regarding the male model, there were large differences between the 'non-aggressive' group and the control group. Comparing controls and the 'non-aggressive' group regarding the male model, participants were less aggressive in all measures than the control group (except gun play).
- An interesting finding regarding social learning theory in general was that girls spent more time than boys playing with a tea set ($p \leq 0.001$) and colouring books ($p \leq 0.001$) and boys spent more time in exploratory play with guns ($p \leq 0.01$).
- No sex differences were found with regard to farm animals, cars or other toys.
- It was also interesting that those who were in the 'non-aggressive' condition spent more time sitting quietly and not playing.

Progress check 4.17

Using Table 4.4, insert the correct aggression scores in the following table.

Group	Aggression score	Group	Aggression score
Aggression condition, physical aggression, boys, male model		Aggression condition, mallet aggression, girls, female model	
Aggression condition, physical aggression, girls, male model		Aggression condition, physical aggression, girls, female model	
Non-aggression condition, non-imitative aggression, boys, male model		Non-aggression condition, non-imitative aggression, girls, male model	
Control condition, gun play, boys		Control condition, gun play, girls	

Conclusions

The study shows that not all behaviour is shaped by reward or punishment, as Skinner (1953, cited in Bandura *et al.*, 1961) suggested. In order for all behaviour to be shaped in this way, it has to be produced first, and observational learning can explain how it is produced. Some behaviour is learned through observation and observed behaviour can later be reproduced. The researchers also concluded that, as aggression by the male model was imitated most, it might be that male aggression is culturally accepted and expected, so both girls and boys imitated the male model exhibiting aggression more. Whereas with verbal aggression, there is no gender link so for verbal aggression there was a gender focus, in that girls imitated the female model more with regard to verbal aggression (13.7 for the female model compared with 2.0 for the male model) and boys the male model (4.3 for the female model compared with 12.7 for the male model). This brings in the idea of cultural effects (e.g. how behaviour is sex-typed) on what is imitated as well as gender effects.

One theory of aggression (e.g. Freud, 1946, and Mowrer, 1950, cited in Bandura *et al.*, 1961) is that of identification. It is thought that someone identifies with the person being aggressive and so imitates their behaviour (as if 'being them') and thus displays aggression. Bandura's theory of observational learning (social learning theory) agrees with these other two theorists. In this study, however, Bandura, Ross and Ross found that aggression was imitated even though the adult watched was not known to the child (was 'neutral') and this suggests that behaviour is not simply a result of identification, but can be 'pure' observational learning.

An overall conclusion was that observing aggressive behaviour may weaken social inhibitions, particularly if the behaviour is performed by adults and observed by children, as children observing the aggression were more aggressive overall than the control group who watched no aggression (though they were perhaps surprisingly aggressive if measured by gun play, perhaps that was an effect of culture too and thinking that they 'ought' to play with guns that way).

This study is important because it did not involve reinforcement of the modelled behaviour and yet the behaviour was later imitated. The male model appeared to be imitated more than the female model. This might have been due to sex typing – boys imitated physical aggression more than girls but did not differ with regard to verbal aggression. Maybe what is imitated depends on social norms and values.

Explore

To explore more about this study, you can read the full article here: http://psychclassics.yorku.ca/Bandura/bobo.htm.

Evaluation of Bandura, Ross and Ross (1961)

Strengths

- The study was a carefully set up and controlled laboratory experiment. For example, care was taken to get the children into a similar emotional state before the observation and to set up measurable acts that could be recorded. This means that cause-and-effect conclusions could be drawn because the variables were isolated and operationalised, with controls.
- There was reliability of the measurement of the dependent variable. Two judges were used and their observations were checked for reliability. One judge did not know to which condition the child had been allocated – a 'blind' procedure was used to avoid bias when recording the play behaviour. Therefore, the results were reliable.

Weaknesses

- The study lacked validity. It could be claimed that the setting was realistic as the rooms were set up to be like the nursery rooms with which the children were familiar. However, the situation was not valid because the adult either deliberately punched and kicked the Bobo doll or was deliberately subdued. In either case, this was not a natural situation – all the more so because the doll and other materials were placed in the room where the children were observed. They may have thought that they were supposed to act towards the doll in the same way that the model had acted.

- The study can be criticised on ethical grounds. The researchers do not explain in any detail how permission was obtained for the study, though it might be assumed that the university had an ethical committee who oversaw the study. However, even if this were the case, the children observed an adult being aggressive and then copied that behaviour. For some children, there was modelling of both verbal and physical aggression. Parents were not mentioned in the study, so they may not have given permission.
- Perhaps there is an issue with generalising the results to say they are true of all people or even all children. The children were all from a university nursery, which perhaps means they are a biased sample (not all children will go to nursery, for example). The study was done in the US, which perhaps limits the generalisability. Bandura, Ross and Ross (1961) conclude that there might be cultural issues in what is observed, so a study set within one culture might not have findings that are generalisable to other cultures. Although the findings that children learn by imitation do seem generalisable (since this study, other studies have been done in different cultures), it cannot be certain from this study.

Progress check 4.18

Explain three conclusions that Bandura, Ross and Ross (1961) drew from their study.

Bandura, Ross and Ross (1963) 'Imitation of film-mediated aggressive models'

This 1963 study compared the copying of aggression using a real-life human model, the human model filmed and a cartoon 'model'. This study was different in its focus from the 1961 study, but they were both building a body of knowledge around social learning and aggression.

Explore

Bandura, Ross and Ross's 1963 study is summarised in a YouTube video, which you might like to watch: www.youtube.com/watch?v=jAZigUL9-38.

Background

Bandura, Ross and Ross (1963) start the study off by talking about the effects of watching film violence. Subsequently, the findings of the 'Bobo doll' studies (referring to the 1961 and 1963 studies) are taken to apply to TV violence and video game violence and their influence on aggression. Bandura, Ross and Ross (1963) talk about the idea that watching violence on film can be cathartic and can reduce the aggressive drive in people. This links to Freud's view that aggressive behaviour can be cathartic (see Chapter 3, p. 171).

Bandura, Ross and Ross (1963) cite an incident in San Francisco in 1961 where boys seemed to have re-enacted a fight seen on the TV and a boy was seriously hurt. The researchers suggest that studying the influence of film violence on children is worthwhile and necessary given these sorts of incidents. The 1961 study explained above showed that children will copy aggression that models display. The 1963 study explained here was to see if aggression seen on film will lead to imitation of the behaviour.

Bandura, Ross and Ross (1963) say that aggressive models can be human models live, human models filmed and cartoon models on film – there are grades of how life-like the aggression is on film. They thought that the further away from reality, the less the imitation. This was because observational learning suggests that relevant models are copied and cartoon figures are not that relevant to the observer. The researchers also think that those who have had negative feedback from being aggressive are less likely to imitate aggression than those who have found behaving aggressively rewarding. This is because finding something rewarding is likely to mean doing it again because the feeling of being rewarded is itself rewarding. Those who had a negative experience when having been aggressive are likely to feel anxiety if seeing aggression. The researchers felt that those who displayed anxiety about aggression would imitate aggression less than others. Also as aggression is seen as inappropriate for females and they would have a negative feeling towards it, so it would be expected that boys would imitate aggression more than girls. Also if adults are seen displaying aggression (e.g. on film), this might lead to a feeling that it is fine to do that (it reduces inhibitions about behaving aggressively) and this reinforces the idea that those who watch aggression show more aggression when frustrated than those who were also made to be frustrated but had not seen models behaving aggressively.

Aim(s)

The researchers wanted to build on previous studies, including their own in 1961, and they wanted to see if aggression seen on film would be imitated, as it had been when live models were seen to use aggression (in the 1961 study). They thought that boys would show more imitative aggression than girls. Another aim came from the idea that, when made frustrated, those who had watched aggression would show aggression more than those who had not watched aggression. Those more anxious about aggression would show less imitative aggression.

Procedure

Participants were 48 boys and 48 girls at Stanford University Nursery School, as in their 1961 study, although more participants were used this time. The children were aged from three years to nearly six years old. As in the 1961 study, the models were a male and a female, and there was one female experimenter.

> **STUDY HINT**
> To help you separate the 1961and 1963 studies, remember that the 1963 study used film and cartoon models and the 1961 study used non-aggression, aggression and a control. Another way to differentiate the two is to remember that the 1961 study had 36 boys and 36 girls and the 1963 study had 48 boys and 48 girls.

There were three experimental groups with 24 children in each and one control group, also made up of 24 children. The 'real-life aggression' group watched a human model being aggressive and the 'filmed aggression' group watched the same model but this time filmed being aggressive. A third group watched a cartoon character being aggressive. As in the 1961 study, the groups were divided into boys and girls and also different gender models so that some children watched a same-sex model and some did not. After watching the aggression (or not, in the case of the control group), the children went somewhere else and the amount of aggression in their behaviour was noted.

As in the 1961 study, the children were rated for aggression by those in the nursery, and the children in the groups were matched for aggression (so that, for example, the control group was made up of similar children to the experimental groups with regard to gender and aggression). In fact, the data for the 'real-life' aggression condition and the data for the control group condition were used from the 1961 study. In this 1963 study, just the filmed aggressive model condition and the cartoon aggression condition were carried out and data gathered.

The procedure for the 'real-life' condition was the same as the 1961 study (see above), so is not explained here. Participants in the human film aggression condition were in a darkened room and worked on potato prints while the film was running about six feet away from them. The models in the film were the same as in the 'real-life' condition. The cartoon model condition was a bit different as the TV was turned on rather casually by the experimenter for the cartoon condition, whereas in the film condition there was a projector and a screen. However, largely, the conditions were kept the same except for the independent variable (IV), which was the way the children observed the aggression (real-life model, filmed model, cartoon character). The cartoon showed the female model dressed as a black cat and she behaved as a cartoon cat would. There was artificial grass, flowers and things to make the scene look artificial. There was also cartoon music at the end.

> **STUDY HINT**
> You might notice that, in studies, participants are sometimes referred to as 'subjects', whereas in this book, they are always referred to as 'participants'. This is because it is now thought that people who are part of the study are 'participating' rather than being 'subjected' to something, so it is more ethical to acknowledge their participation.

As in the 1961 study, aggressive behaviour was measured in a different room and the children were made mildly aggressive before they went into the room to play. The play materials in the room were the same as the 1961 study and again the behaviour was recorded by observers behind a one-way mirror. For each participant, the observation lasted 20 minutes and observations took place at five-second intervals. Therefore, each participant had 240 responses recorded. There was a high level of agreement between the two observers.

Responses recorded were: imitative aggression (exhibiting aggressive acts that the model had shown), partially imitative acts (the main components of the model's actions but not exactly the same), mallet aggression (striking an object – not the Bobo doll as that would be imitative – with the mallet aggressively), non-imitative aggression (doing something aggressive towards the doll but not the same as the model) and aggressive gun play. Behaviour units (every five seconds) were noted for non-aggressive behaviour, such as sitting quietly.

> **STUDY HINT**
> In your course, you need to know about time sampling and event sampling. Time sampling is used in Bandura's Bobo doll studies, so you can use these as examples. Make links where possible so that one piece of learning (such as this study) helps other areas of learning.

> **Progress check 4.19**
> Explain four 'aggression' behaviours that were recorded in Bandura, Ross and Ross (1963).

Results

Table 4.5 Mean aggression scores

Response category	Experimental groups					Control group
	Real-life aggression		Human film aggression		Cartoon film aggression	
	Female model	Male model	Female model	Male model		
Total aggression:						
Girls	65.8	57.3	87.0	79.5	80.9	36.4
Boys	76.8	131.8	114.5	85.0	117.2	72.2
Imitative aggression:						
Girls	19.2	9.2	10.0	8.0	7.8	1.8
Boys	18.4	38.4	34.3	13.3	16.2	3.9
Mallet aggression:						
Girls	17.2	18.7	49.2	19.5	36.8	13.1
Boys	15.5	28.8	20.5	16.3	12.5	13.5
Non-imitative aggression:						
Girls	27.6	24.9	24.0	34.3	27.5	17.8
Boys	35.5	48.6	46.8	31.8	71.8	40.4
Aggressive gun play:						
Girls	1.8	4.5	3.8	17.6	8.8	3.7
Boys	7.3	15.9	12.8	23.7	16.6	14.3

For both the 1961 and 1963 studies, 'mean aggression' is the mean of the score when a behaviour is recorded every five seconds over a 20-minute period: 240 acts for each child. Table 4.5 shows clearly the three conditions of the study and the control group, the type of aggression that was recorded and the differences by gender.

Table 4.6 Mean total aggression scores for the three conditions and the control group

Mean total real-life aggression	Mean total human film aggression	Mean total cartoon aggression	Mean total control group aggression
83	92	99	54

Table 4.6 shows that the control group's aggression (mean average) is nearly half that of the 'cartoon' aggression and a lot lower than the 'real-life' and 'film' aggression as well.

Bandura, Ross and Ross (1963) take this to mean that exposing the participant to models displaying aggression increases the likelihood that there will be aggression displayed later, when not in the presence of the model.

- The researchers used a Wilcoxon test (Chapter 6, pp. 402–404) and found that all three 'aggression' groups differed significantly from the control group, though those watching the 'real-life' model and those watching the 'human film' model did not differ from one another significantly.
- They also found that those who observed the real-life and those who observed the human film conditions, against those in the control group, showed a lot more imitative physical and verbal aggression.

STUDY HINT

Bandura, Ross and Ross (1963) used a Wilcoxon test, so you may assume that it is a repeated measures design. However, this is not the case - because the researchers measured children's aggression and matched aggression across groups, they called this a matched pairs design (even though different participants were in the different conditions). Therefore, Wilcoxon is the right test. Check this sort of detail as it helps you to learn about other areas in the course, such as the inferential tests. Also you can use studies like this as examples when discussing method issues like experimental design. Designs are discussed in Chapter 5.

- Bandura, Ross and Ross (1963) provide some qualitative data as well because they show clips of the children imitating the model, to show how alike the imitative acts were.
- Overall, they concluded that it was the human film model that led to more aggression in relation to the control group – this was more aggression in total, more imitative aggression and more aggressive gun play.

STUDY HINT

Both the human film condition and the cartoon condition gave a lot of aggression (both overall and in specific areas of aggression), so it is a small step to then say that children watching violence on TV are likely to exhibit such violence/aggression later, which is how Bandura's work tends to be interpreted and applied. This is useful information for a key question (see pp. 272-275).

- The gender of the model affected the aggression displayed, according to the gender of the child too. Participants exposed to the male model rather than the female model showed more aggressive gun play ($p \leq 0.001$).

Progress check 4.20

What does it mean when a result is followed by ($p \leq 0.001$)?

Conclusions

Bandura and his colleagues (1963) concluded that observing filmed aggression will lead to aggressive acts in children. Those watching either the filmed human model or the cartoon model showed a lot more aggression than the control group. The idea that watching aggression can be cathartic (see Freud's explanation, Chapter 3, page 171) is not borne out by these findings. The children watched aggression and then showed aggression; watching it did not decrease aggression. The idea that watching violence is cathartic assumes that it reduces aggression, so Bandura, Ross and Ross (1963) reject the theory that watching violence is cathartic.

It was not just that watching aggression led to aggression, but the acts watched were imitated, so the type of aggression and actual acts were observed and reproduced. The researchers suggest that social behaviour might well come from 'pictorial' media, perhaps in particular TV.

The children showing aggression were not deviant in any way, and yet still copied the aggression they watched. Eighty-eight per cent of those watching the real-life model and the human film model and 79 per cent of those watching the cartoon model showed some imitative aggression.

The researchers claim reliability for their findings as there was more than one observer and there was inter-observer reliability. They say this does not mean there is validity, but it does show consistency. There is the importance of other cues in the environment, which may not have been present in this study, but would be in a more real-life situation, such as parental disapproval and some aspect of negative reinforcement (not doing the aggression in order to avoid being disapproved of). There might be some vicarious learning too as the model exhibiting the aggression was not punished. The model might not have been directly rewarded either but, if the behaviour seemed acceptable to the child (since, for example, they were allowed to see the aggression), they may have imitated the behaviour because they thought it was fine to do so. In his 1965 study, which follows, Bandura looked at the influence on the display of imitative aggression of the model being punished or rewarded.

Evaluation of Bandura, Ross and Ross (1963)

Strengths

- The use of two observers, and checking that the two observers agreed in their scoring using the agreed categories, gives reliability to the findings. As some results were from Bandura, Ross and Ross (1961), where they also had inter-observer reliability, it is thought that the results are consistent.
- A related strength is the experimental method is used and the three conditions (real-life model, filmed human model, cartoon model) are the same in all ways except for the independent variable. A control condition also helps, which was kept the same except for the independent variable. This gives the results scientific credibility and cause-and-effect conclusions can be claimed: the researchers claim that it is because of the modelled aggression that the children in those conditions display more aggression than the children in the control group.
- Another strength, which draws on the reliability and scientific credibility of the study, is that the results have a practical application. Bandura, Ross and Ross (1963) claim that their findings suggest that violence on TV is likely to be modelled by those watching.

Weaknesses

- A possible weakness is validity. The children were in an artificial setting when their behaviour was being observed. There were no other cues to check their behaviour, as Bandura, Ross and Ross themselves observe. There were no parents to use negative reinforcement to prevent the aggression and the models seemed to get no punishment for their behaviour so the children might not see it as wrong. This might then not be 'real-life' aggression at all, but modelled aggression that the children thought they ought to display.
- Another possible weakness is generalisability. As with the 1961 study, the children were from a university nursery in the US and, as such, a specific sample. Perhaps it is not right to generalise from this sample and say that all children watching aggression will behave in the same way. Having said that, there seems to be no evidence to say that all children would not use observational learning in such situations.

Progress check 4.21

Explain how a study with reliability is likely to show a lack of validity.

Bandura (1965) 'Influence of models' reinforcement contingencies on the acquisition of imitative responses'

Background

Bandura (1965) cites an important part of imitative learning when he explains how Miller and Dollard (1941) suggest that imitative learning only takes place if the person copying the behaviour is motivated to copy that behaviour by being rewarded for matching the rewarded behaviour. So it is not as simple as just seeing behaviour and then imitating it. Whether behaviour is copied or not depends on whether the model is rewarded and whether the person imitating the behaviour is rewarded for doing so. However, this would mean someone had to imitate the behaviour, be rewarded for it and then learn the behaviour, which means doing the behaviour before learning it. Bandura discusses this further, suggesting that if a model is rewarded for an observed behaviour, the observer can in a way reward themselves by doing the behaviour and empathically receives the reward the model received. This is higher-order vicarious conditioning. For the observer, there can be direct reward for themselves and vicarious reward. Bandura (1965) points out that, in the 1961 and 1963 studies, there was no reward to the models for their aggressive behaviour and the children did not get rewarded either, and yet there was still observational learning and imitative behaviour.

A proposal is that the acquiring of the behaviours comes from observational learning. The performance of the learned behaviours (such as the imitative aggression in the Bobo doll studies) might depend on whether the model receives rewards or punishments.

Bandura wanted to see if reinforcement was linked to learning (the acquisition of behaviour) or to performance (carrying out the behaviour), and that was the focus of his 1965 study explained here.

Aim(s)

The 1965 study involved children watching a filmed model showing new physical and verbal aggression ('new' meaning they had not seen the behaviour before). In one condition, the model was rewarded, in another they were punished and in a third condition there were no consequences for the model. The children were tested for imitative behaviour after watching the model and all children were offered rewards for reproducing the behaviour of the model they had watched. The aim was to see if the consequences to the model (reinforced, punished or no consequences) would affect whether the children performed imitative acts. Bandura thought that the rewarded model would produce more matching responses by the children, then the no consequences group, and the least imitation would be shown by the group who had watched the model being punished. Another aim was to see if the boys would be more aggressive than the girls, as was found in the 1961 and 1963 studies. Another aim was to see if the boys showed not just more aggression than the girls but more imitative aggression. Finally, an important aim was to see whether, if a direct reward was introduced, the differences found from rewarding or punishing the model (or no consequence) would be wiped out. The direct reward, it was thought, would overrule the effect of whether the model was rewarded or punished.

Procedure

Participants were 33 boys and 33 girls at the university nursery (see the 1961 and 1963 studies for more about this), aged from three and a half years old to nearly six years old. They were randomly assigned to one of the three conditions (model rewarded, model punished, no consequences for the model), so there were 11 boys and 11 girls in each condition. There were two adults as the models and one female experimenter, as in the earlier studies.

> **STUDY HINT**
> This is the third Bandura study you need to know about, and it is important to separate the three. 1961 is about the type of aggression modelled and gender; 1963 is about how they observed the aggression: film, real life or cartoon; 1965 is about whether the model's aggression is rewarded, punished or no consequences. Find a way of separating out these three different independent variables - for example, '1961 Type, 1963 Film, 1965 Reward or Punishment'. Or perhaps use a diagram such as the one on page 243.

The children watched TV as they did in the cartoon condition in the 1963 study. Again there was a Bobo doll in the study, this time adult-sized, and in the film. The four aggressive responses to the Bobo doll were new ones (not the same as in the other two studies). The acts still involved a mallet and verbal aggression (such as 'sockeroo... stay down'), as well as kicking. The acts might have been previously learned (such as using a mallet) but the sequence was new and was carried out twice. It was at the end that the reward, punishment or no consequences part was introduced. In the 'model rewarded' condition, another adult came into the room (on the film) with sweets and soft drinks and told the model he was a 'strong champion' with 'superb aggressive performance'. The model consumed the treats, clearly enjoying them. In the 'model punished' condition, the other person came in (on the film) and shook a finger at the model, calling the model a 'big bully'. The other adult hit the model with a rolled-up newspaper. In the 'no consequences' condition, there was no added reinforcement at the end of the film.

Immediately after watching television, the children were taken into a different room and were watched playing. The observation lasted ten minutes with a behaviour recorded every five seconds. Again there were two observers and it was shown that there was inter-observer reliability.

There was another part added to this study. After the ten minutes, the children were brought fruit juices and booklets of sticker pictures. The children had the juice and then were told that they would get a sticker picture and more juice for every verbally aggressive or physically aggressive act they reproduced. The children were then asked to 'show me what Rocky did' or 'tell me what he said' and if there was an imitative response (i.e. if the child did what they saw being done in the film they watched), the child was rewarded straight away. This was the positive incentive condition.

Results

The results showed that, with a positive incentive, the number of imitative responses was higher in all condition (model rewarded, model punished, no consequences) and higher for both boys and girls. When there was no incentive, the highest aggression was shown by boys – this was both in the 'model rewarded' condition and in the 'no consequences' condition. With no incentive, for the boys, the lowest mean imitative acts were in the 'model punished' condition. In all three conditions in the 'no incentive' condition (which was before the juice and stickers were introduced), the boys showed most imitative acts. The girls showed very low imitative acts when the model was punished (in the 'no incentive' condition) but a higher mean imitative acts in the 'rewarded' and 'no consequences' conditions. For both boys and girls, it was when the model was punished, in the no incentive condition, that the imitative acts were lowest. This does suggest that there is vicarious learning in the sense of learning not to do things that someone else is punished for. In the incentive condition (when stickers were available for imitative responses), the girls were not that far from the boys in mean number of imitative acts in all three conditions (though they showed fewer such acts in all conditions).

The introduction of direct rewards for imitative acts did take away the difference in the 'model punished' condition.

It was noticeable that, even when rewarded for doing the actions they observed, the children did not do them all. They might not have noticed the whole sequence of actions, and might just have displayed the acts they remembered. It is likely that acts that are distinct are imitated more. Also the complexity of the sequence of events may affect observational learning and it might also depend on the acts that had been previously seen – perhaps the more that were already known, the more the sequence was observed, recalled and reproduced.

STUDY HINT

You can see here the link to the 'stages' of social learning explained earlier in this section on social learning theory. Here is the idea of having to attend to what is happening, remember it, be motivated to reproduce it and so on (ARRM: Attention, Retention, Reproduction, Motivation, pp. 227–228).

Conclusions

Bandura concluded that there were many variables involved in whether learning by observation is acquired or performed. Variables included whether the model is rewarded, whether there are no consequences or whether they are punished (in which case, there are fewer imitative acts). There is also a strong effect according to whether the person is motivated to imitate what they have seen through being rewarded. In fact, this direct reward over-rides the impact of whether a model is rewarded, punished or there are no consequences. Other variables might include whether the observer has seen the modelled acts before and whether the observer has a cultural history that includes such acts. To observe, retain and reproduce what has been seen, especially if it is a complex sequence of behaviours, includes many variables both in the situation and in the observer. Having looked at the pattern of rewards and punishments for a model being observed, Bandura concluded that behaviour does not have to be rewarded or punished to be imitated. The 'no consequences' condition was imitated as the 'reward' condition was (though the 'punished' condition did show less imitative behaviour).

The gender differences before the incentive was introduced, compared with the lower number of gender differences in the 'incentive' condition, suggests that perhaps the girls were reluctant do show the observed behaviour. However, when incentivised to do so, they performed the imitative acts nearly as much as the boys.

Bandura (1965) does show the effect of vicarious reinforcement on whether observed behaviour is imitated in that the punished behaviour was much less imitated (this is if there is no incentive – no direct reward).

Explore

If you would like to learn more about Bandura (1965), you can find the full study, as well as some of Bandura's other articles, here: www.uky.edu/~eushe2/Bandura/BanduraPubs.html.

Evaluation of Bandura (1965)

Strengths

- As for the 1961 and 1963 studies, a strength is the controlled experiment. Controls mean cause-and-effect conclusions can be drawn. Although the variables that Bandura points to, such as what the children have already seen or cultural norms with regard to the modelled behaviour, were not controlled for. As a general strength, it can be said that there is scientific credibility because of the controls. Indeed, as it is Bandura himself who points to the variables that were not controlled for but might have affected the results, this confirms his careful analysis of the results and how he aims for scientific credibility.
- Another strength, as with the 1961 and 1963 studies, is the reliability not only because of the controls and standardised procedures, but because there were two observers and inter-observer reliability was found.

Weaknesses

- A weakness is, as Bandura points out, the question over validity. There were variables that were not controlled for, such as which of the acts had been previously observed, and individual differences in each child coming from their previous experiences, and perhaps their temperament too. The imitation of the aggressive acts seemed quite clear; however, the 'real-life' aspect of the study was not so clear and, even with good reliability, if there is no validity (if a study is not measuring what it claims to measure) then results are not useful.
- Another weakness is, as with the 1961 and 1963 studies, the possible lack of generalisability from the sample to the target population. Bandura seems to see the target population as all children, whereas his sample comes from a specific group of children in the US in Stanford University's nursery. Possibly there are differences in his sample, such as particular bias from their culture or the children being used to nursery, that leads them not to represent the target population.

STUDY HINT

Get used to using the terms. In the second weakness here, terms include 'sample', 'generalisability' and 'target population'. Sampling is discussed in the social psychology topic area for your course (pp. 229–304) and Chapter 5 enlarges upon all the method issues. If you are not sure about the terms, refresh your memory to help your learning.

STUDY HINT

The strengths and weaknesses for Bandura's three studies are more or less the same because the experiments had similar procedures. However, when discussing strengths or weaknesses (when evaluating), aim to refer to the actual study. Avoid general points, such as 'this was a lab experiment so it lacked validity' – you could add 'which means that real-life behaviour was not studied'. This general point, which might apply to all lab experiments, does not show understanding, and marks are awarded for knowledge with understanding, not 'just' knowledge.

Bandura, Ross and Ross (1961)

- Watched aggression, non-aggression, control group
- Girls were verbally aggressive; boys were more physically aggressive

Bandura, Ross and Ross (1963)

- Real-life, human filmed aggression, cartoon aggression, control group
- The filmed aggression and cartoon aggression led to much more aggression than in the control group

Bandura (1965)

- Model rewarded, model punished, no consequences
- Model rewarded gives more aggression than if model punished, but direct reward for the participant wipes out that difference

Bandura and colleagues' 1961, 1963 and 1965 studies

Test yourself

1. Explain four features of the experiment that are the same for all three Bandura studies explained for your course. **(8 marks)**
2. Using studies you have covered in your course, evaluate the role of social learning theory in explaining the argument that watching violence on television is likely to lead to aggressive behaviour. **(16 marks)**

How learning theories explain the acquisition and maintenance of phobias

You will need to be clear about what a **phobia** is and what a fear is, even though the two terms are often used interchangeably. A fear can be sensible, such as a fear of heights to stop you leaning over too far, and a fear of closed spaces to stop you being shut in. A phobia is more than a fear because it is irrational. Fears can be limiting and can stop you doing things you would like to do, but they tend to be rational. Phobias are fears that limit you and are irrational. This section first explains more about phobias, for your interest, and then considers how phobias might be acquired and maintained. The following section then considers some treatments for phobias that draw on learning theories.

What are phobias?

Phobias are irrational fears and are life-limiting. Anyone with a phobia, when they get near to their phobic situation or object, will experience strong anxiety. Symptoms may include fast breathing, feeling sick, dry mouth, fast heart rate and chest pain, among others. Phobias tend to mean people avoid certain situations.

Types of phobia

Phobias tend to focus on fears that would have been rational at some time in human existence, such as spiders and snakes perhaps, or heights or enclosed spaces. A lot of psychological research has gone into the way phobias tend to be about such issues and not about equally dangerous things like guns, which are more 'socially' given. You do not need to know more for this topic area.

> **Explore**
>
> If you would like to know more about phobias, then you can research online. One site you could start with is Mind: www.mind.org.uk/information-support/types-of-mental-health-problems/phobias. This site is also a useful source of information on mental health disorders.

There are simple phobias, such as:

- phobias of animals, e.g. dogs, insects, snakes, spiders
- phobias of situations, e.g. flying, going to the dentist
- phobias of the environment, e.g. dark, enclosed spaces, open spaces, water.

There are more complex phobias, such as:

- social anxiety disorder, when someone feels others are judging them and so they avoid social situations and become very withdrawn
- agoraphobia, which is the fear of open spaces or, perhaps more commonly, fear of going outside one's own home. This fear is clearly limiting as someone becomes imprisoned in their own home. Agoraphobia is really a fear of not being somewhere safe and, since people tend to see their own home as safe, they are often 'stuck inside' their home. They fear going on a bus or public transport, anywhere that is crowded and/or threatening.

Acquiring a phobia

Phobias can be acquired through the principles of classical conditioning, operant conditioning or modelling.

Classical conditioning

Learning theories can account for how a phobia is acquired. Classical conditioning has already been explained, including some mention of Watson and Rayner's (1920) study of Little Albert, who was conditioned, using classical conditioning principles, to fear his pet white rat. This study is the classic study for this topic area and is given in detail on pp. 259–262. If it is possible to use classical conditioning to bring about a phobia, then this is one way that phobias can be acquired.

Something that yields a fear or startle response naturally, such as a loud bang, is the unconditioned stimulus. That stimulus is paired with a neutral stimulus, such as the white rat. After a few pairings, an association is learned and the white rat (in this case) will give the fear response. A fear has been conditioned.

A phobia to dogs might be acquired through classical conditioning as follows:

UCS – dog bite → UCR – fear (went with pain)

UCS – dog bite + NS – any dog → UCR – fear

CS – any dog → CR – fear

> **Progress check 4.22**
>
> What do the following mean in relation to classical conditioning: UCS, UCR, NS, CS, CR? Look back at page 207 if you cannot remember.

Operant conditioning

Someone might acquire a phobia through a pattern of rewards and punishments, but classical conditioning is a better explanation because it would underpin an operant conditioning explanation. For example, if someone is bitten by a dog, that might be positive punishment (getting something unpleasant for stroking the dog). This would stop that person from stroking the dog in future and they may develop a phobia of dogs. However, the phobia would link to fear of being punished and that is best explained through classical conditioning (see above). Nonetheless, there is an element of operant conditioning here, in the punishment that led to the phobia being developed. Another operant conditioning explanation for avoiding dogs would be negative reinforcement. To remove the possibility of getting bitten, the person avoids being in the presence of dogs. Not being able to be with dogs could be interpreted as a phobia.

Social learning

Bandura explained in his three studies (1961, 1963 and 1965) that children learned to imitate behaviour that they watched. This was without any consequences for the model (such as the model being rewarded for the behaviour) or for them (such as their being rewarded for the imitative behaviour). The children did imitate the behaviour for the reward, admittedly, but they also showed imitative aggression without being rewarded (in the 1961 and 1963 studies). This suggests that, if a role model shows fear in a certain situation or when faced with a certain object, then someone watching can learn that fear or phobia. Mineka showed that monkeys watching other monkeys show fear of snakes themselves then showed fear of snakes, so acquiring phobias through observation of others modelling fear is not just about humans but can be found in some animals as well. Leib *et al.* (2000) found that children of parents with social phobia were likely to have social phobia as well. There is evidence that phobias can be acquired through the processes explained by classical conditioning, operant conditioning and social learning theory.

Maintenance of a phobia

Learning theories can also help to show why a phobia would be maintained once learned.

Classical conditioning

Classical conditioning shows how a phobia might be learned. However, classical conditioning tends not to last long so the association would have to be paired often (such as a dog keeps biting), but that tends not to happen. Watson and Rayner (1920) confirm that classical conditioning does not last long. So classical conditioning is probably not responsible for the maintenance of a phobia normally. Of course if the individual kept getting a dog bite, the fear can be maintained and this would be explained using classical conditioning principles. This can happen, for example, if a panic attack or something similar was experienced while shopping, then the thought of shopping could lead to further anxiety (possibly as strong as a panic attack). This renewal of the association between shopping and anxiety would maintain the phobia.

STUDY HINT

This part of your course asks you to learn about 'how learning theories explain the acquisition and maintenance of phobias'. Acquiring, or learning, a phobia is one thing; after the learning, maintaining the phobia is different. Practise picking out such differences by breaking phrases down as this can help in an examination. For example, 'evaluate in terms of strengths and weaknesses' clearly means offer both, but this sort of detail can be missed under exam pressure. Get used to analysing carefully what is required in a course and in an examination.

Phobias are fears that prevent someone living their life and they are fears that bring out a strong anxiety reaction in someone. A fear is normal in the sense that we need to fear things that threaten us, such as being afraid of being high up as we might fall. Phobias tend to focus on something we are afraid of but where the fear is irrational. Nevertheless, a phobia does represent an association between a stimulus (something that makes us afraid) and a response (the fear). This clearly shows classical conditioning at work, so classical conditioning is a useful explanation for phobias. Classical conditioning explains how we associate a response to a stimulus. Also with a phobia we tend to generalise one extreme fear situation (perhaps being stuck in a lift) to all similar situations (all lifts). Classical conditioning neatly explains such processes and how phobias are acquired.

There is another type of learning not mentioned so far, which is one-trial learning. This means that the association can be so strong (one trial is enough) that the learning is very hard to undo. This can happen, for example, if you eat bad food somewhere – say, bad chicken. You will feel ill from the food and associate feeling ill with chicken – this might not wear off if the learning is very strong (which means the association is very strong: you felt bad enough to never want to eat chicken again). You might know that next time the chicken will be fine, but you just cannot eat it. One-trial learning might mean that a phobia, once acquired, may be maintained.

Operant conditioning

Behaviour that is rewarded is done again (this is the law of effect). Behaviour that is punished is not repeated. Once a phobia is learned, it can be maintained through operant conditioning. If someone gets very anxious, again using the example of going shopping, then they may choose not to go shopping to avoid the anxiety, which is negative reinforcement. This in fact is what often happens and the issue is that the person does not find out that they can control their anxiety, manage to shop, and then get out of their phobic reaction to shopping. Operant conditioning maintains the phobia through negative reinforcement. If shopping keeps bringing anxiety symptoms, and maybe even panic attack, that is positive punishment (something bad is received) and so the behaviour might be maintained for that reason too (the behaviour being not going shopping).

Social learning theory

If someone else is modelling the phobia, social learning would explain how a phobia is maintained. For example, if a mother has social phobia, perhaps the child will use their mother as a role model and develop social phobia. If the mother's social phobia is maintained by operant conditioning (avoiding a bad situation, which is in a way a reward), then the child might model on the mother, and her own phobia of being with people might be maintained in that way.

Evaluation of how learning theories explain the acquisition and maintenance of phobias

Strengths

- Classical conditioning has been said to account for the acquisition of phobias and a strength of classical conditioning is that it has been developed as a theory using experiments with careful controls, and experiments where the findings have been replicated. This makes the evidence for classical conditioning strong (such as Watson and Rayner, 1920, which is a carefully planned study).
- Operant conditioning has been said to explain how phobias are maintained once learned, and operant conditioning too has a lot of evidence for its principles, including Skinner (1948), explained earlier. Experiments into the principles of operant conditioning show careful planning and controls. Social learning theory too, such as Bandura's work, which is explained in good detail in this chapter. The findings of experiments are reliable as there have been many studies with the same results.

Weaknesses

- A difficulty with the use of experiments, though they give strong evidence for learning theories and their explanations of human behaviour (including phobias), is that when they are used in classical or operant conditioning, so often they use animals rather than human participants. Although animals do have similar brain structures as humans, they are not the same. They are not the same in respect of anxiety and fear and how in humans these can arise from cognition (thinking) and problem-solving, which is less likely in animals. If there are differences between humans and animals, perhaps we cannot generalise results from animal experiments to humans.
- Learning theories rely on experiments to show evidence for them, and experiments, with their careful controls, are likely to lack validity. Phobias arise in real life, taking into account all the surroundings and situations a person is in. A person may be anxious because of their life situation and that can generalise to where they are when they have a panic attack, perhaps feeling overwhelmed with all they have to do. Animals are not likely to share these sorts of worries and thoughts.

Test yourself

Explain how classical conditioning can show how a phobia might be acquired and operant conditioning can show how a phobia can be maintained. **(8 marks)**

Treatments/therapies for phobias based on learning theories

You need to know two treatments or therapies that use the principles of either classical conditioning, operant conditioning or social learning theory. You need to know about systematic desensitisation (classical conditioning principles) and one other. Three treatments/therapies are explained here to help you choose. If you study all three therapies given in this section, that will help you to understand how the two types of conditioning work and you will be able to use them as examples. If you wish, you could choose a different therapy.

Systematic desensitisation

Systematic desensitisation is based on the principles of classical conditioning. Classical conditioning theory indicates how a stimulus and an involuntary response are associated. One such response is a phobia, which is a fear response thought to be acquired through classical conditioning processes. A phobia is not just any fear:

- It is a fear that prevents normal functioning in life.
- It is irrational, and the phobic person needs treatment to help overcome the fear.

Explore

Find out more about phobias and how they are an anxiety disorder, not 'just' a fear. For example: www.nhs.uk/Conditions/phobias/Pages/Introduction.aspx.

One way of overcoming a phobia is to use systematic desensitisation (SD), which was developed by Wolpe, a South African psychiatrist (1958). It is sometimes called graduated exposure therapy or counter conditioning (Watson, 1924).

Systematic desensitisation involves a step-by-step approach (systematic) to get the person used to the phobic object or situation (desensitised). The idea is that the phobia has been learned through classical conditioning, so it can be unlearned in the same way. Instead of the fear response to the phobic object or situation, a relaxed response is required. People are taught to relax their muscles (not easy to learn) and they are then introduced gradually to the object or situation. People might also be taught to imagine happy scenarios, meditate, and maybe to try and change their thinking about the phobic object; these ideas focus on reducing the anxiety and replacing it with a relaxed response. To check for relaxation, pulse rate or breathing rate can be used, as biofeedback. Biofeedback is a useful technique for the individual to learn to control their own physiological responses. A measure is taken, that the individual knows about, and they can learn to control what is being measured, such as pulse rate and breathing rate.

The gradual introduction involves a hierarchy – from a slight introduction (e.g. a photograph), through to a little more exposure (e.g. a film) and so on, through to the real object or situation. Individuals undergoing therapy set up the hierarchy for themselves, so that it is meaningful for them. If people relax at each stage, then they should be relaxed with the object present. Systematic desensitisation is also used to treat anxiety disorders other than phobias. The diagrams below show how a phobia of going out shopping can be explained using classical conditioning principles and the result of a systematic desensitisation process to overcome the phobia.

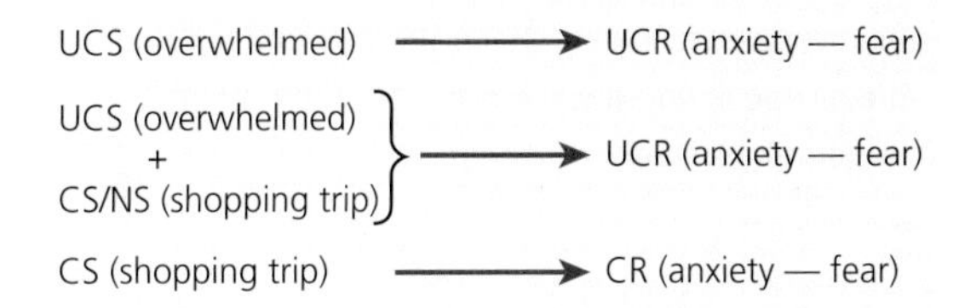

How a phobia of going out shopping is explained using classical conditioning principles

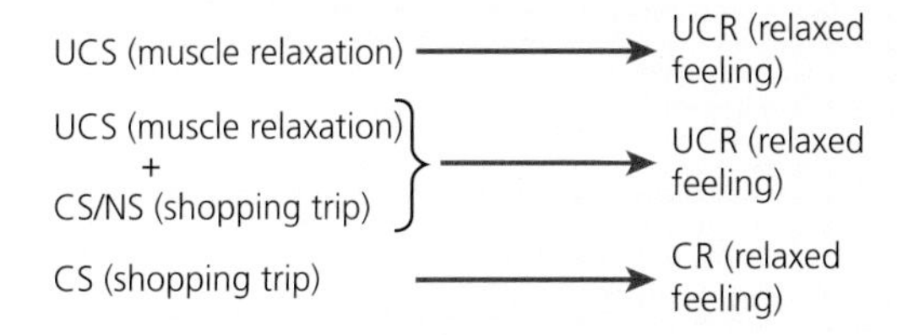

The final stage of systematic desensitisation to overcome a 'shopping' phobia

A fear of going out (e.g. to go shopping) can be limiting and can be diagnosed as a phobia. Having agreed to systematic desensitisation, sufferers learn to relax. While relaxing, the idea of going out a short distance is introduced, then going a little further, going with someone on a bus, and so on, until they manage eventually to go shopping alone, which is the goal.

Social learning can also be used to help with systematic desensitisation. A model can be used to demonstrate the required behaviour or to show relaxation in the face of the feared object. This has been called participant modelling (Bernstein, 1977).

Explore

The specific example of fear of going out shopping is given here as a phobia. However, if someone has agoraphobia, which means fear of going out at all, then systematic desensitisation has been found to be less effective, perhaps because the phobia is so general. It is not easy to test the effectiveness of systematic desensitisation. Research this area using the internet or some other source.

Some issues with systematic desensitisation

- Although the therapy can be shown to work using classical conditioning principles, there are also operant conditioning principles at work. People with phobias avoid the phobic object or situation. The phobic object or situation is unpleasant; the individual avoids it through negative reinforcement. Systematic desensitisation could work because the object or situation is no longer unpleasant, and so no longer needs to be avoided. This is an alternative explanation of why systematic desensitisation works. However, it does not explain the phobia as thoroughly as classical conditioning because it does not explain why the phobic object or situation became unpleasant in the first place.
- Although systematic desensitisation is usually thought to be a therapy based on the learning approach and learning theory, an element of the cognitive approach is involved when the relaxation is being taught. For example, to relax, the individual is taught to think differently about the phobic object. Systematic desensitisation has sometimes been referred to as a cognitive behavioural therapy because of this element. However, as the concept is based firmly on classical conditioning principles, it is considered in your course as a therapy based on behaviourism and learning theory.

Studies to look at the effectiveness of systematic desensitisation

Toozandehjani (2011) used three conditions in a study to look at the effectiveness of two therapies on social phobia. He used systematic desensitisation, assertiveness training, the two combined, and a control group. He used 32 people aged between 18 and 22 years old to test the effectiveness of the different therapies on social phobia disorder. The participants/patients were allocated to the groups randomly. Toozandehjani used interview and self-report data to ask people about the effectiveness of the therapy they had received and he returned to ask again three months later.

It was found that the separate treatments worked, as did the combined treatments, though in all three cases the effects did not last the three months. The effects were only there during the treatment. The combined treatments (systematic desensitisation and assertive training) were more effective than the individual treatments.

Inglesias and Inglesias (2013) used hypnosis-aided systematic desensitisation (HASD) on someone with driving phobia but who had not had an accident. They focused in fact on someone with a phobia for driving on a specific interstate road (in the US), which is similar to having a phobia of driving on the motorway. This is a case study of a real situation in private practice, not a study as such, but the case is written up and published in the *American Journal of Clinical Hypnosis*. After six office sessions, there followed 12 live sessions where what had been covered in the office sessions was put into practice. The person was able to drive on the interstate and after 12 months had no reoccurring of symptoms. This was taken to show effectiveness of the treatment.

STUDY HINT

Toozandehjani (2011) allocated people to groups randomly and used a control group. These issues arise in cognitive psychology in your course where you look at the experimental method. Toozandehjani gathered self-report data using interviewing, and you looked at self-report data and interviewing in the social psychology part of your course. Use studies like this to illustrate the use of such methods as this helps to show understanding.

Evaluation of systematic desensitisation as a therapy

Strengths

- Compared with other therapies that deal with phobias (e.g. flooding), systematic desensitisation is a fairly ethical procedure because it involves a gradual exposure to phobic objects or situations and individuals are involved fully in their therapy. Flooding is about someone facing their fear directly, which is much more stressful (see below).
- Systematic desensitisation has a clear rationale based on classical conditioning principles. Therefore, it can be explained to people, which can give them confidence that the therapy will work. This does not make the therapy more successful, but if it is more likely to be accepted, then that is more successful. If the explanation for the phobia follows the same principles as the therapy, then this makes sense.
- The therapy has been shown to work. For example, a study in Spain, which is one of the contemporary choices in this section, Capafóns *et al.* (1998), found the fear of flying was reduced by a programme of systematic desensitisation. See pp. 268–272 for more on this study.

Weaknesses

- There are other factors besides classical conditioning involved – for example, operant conditioning principles and cognitive processing, as well as elements of social learning. This does not make the therapy less successful, but does question the reasoning behind it.
- Although systematic desensitisation is useful for phobias and anxiety disorders, it is not useful for other mental health issues, such as psychoses. The individual needs to be able to learn to relax and has to be involved in the whole process; not everyone can do this.

STUDY HINT

When evaluating treatments or therapies, often a question is about effectiveness. Use strengths and weaknesses to discuss effectiveness: evidence that a therapy works would show its effectiveness and a weakness about the theory behind it might affect its effectiveness.

Progress check 4.23

As well as classical conditioning, what are the other three theories/areas in psychology that seem to be involved in systematic desensitisation as a treatment for phobias?

Flooding (exposure therapy)

Flooding is an example of exposure therapy and, as mentioned above, might be seen as less ethical than systematic desensitisation. Flooding has classical conditioning principles and, as with systematic desensitisation, the idea is to replace the fear response with a different response (non-fear). The principle is biological, in that someone can only experience an alarm reaction for a certain length of time and then it would have to subside. The alarm reaction is a biological reaction giving the organism (animal or person) energy to fight or flee from a situation. Blood sugar is made available, other activities in the body cease (such as digestion), the body is on 'high alert'. As the energy is used up and no more is available, the body will calm. This is the parasympathetic part of the nervous system bringing the calm, with the alarm reaction being the action of the sympathetic part of the nervous system. This might seem a long way from learning theories. However, fear is an autonomic reaction, and body reflexes are the unconditioned responses in classical conditioning.

Flooding works on the principle that someone can only be at 'alarm' stage for so long. If they are exposed to the feared object or situation, then the fear response will be triggered, which is the alarm reaction in the body. That will then subside. So the person will learn by association that a calmer response links to the previously feared object or situation. That calmer response has been forced, whereas in systematic desensitisation it is brought about by the individual as they relax. This is really the main difference between systematic desensitisation and flooding – in systematic desensitisation, the person has the power to relax and they control the hierarchy and the exposure, whereas in flooding they do not have the control. The feared situation or object is there for them to endure until the fear reaction subsides and they become calm. This treatment can work with post-traumatic stress disorder (PTSD) where someone calls up their memories and sticks with them until the overwhelming physical responses have calmed, though generally for flooding the stimuli are 'in vivo', which means 'live'.

Phobias are irrational thoughts, not fears as such, and flooding is a treatment for phobias. One useful element of flooding is that it can demonstrate that the phobia is irrational because, after 'flooding', the person can see that they have calmed down and the 'worst' did not happen.

Study looking at the effectiveness of flooding

Mott *et al.* (2013) looked at the effectiveness of flooding for post-traumatic stress disorder (PTSD), which involves considerable anxiety and fear; therefore, findings of studies about PTSD can perhaps show the effectiveness of flooding for anxiety and fear that manifests as a phobia. Mott *et al.* (2013) discuss how it might be thought that focusing on the trauma that had been experienced could refresh the trauma, and so flooding might not only be ineffective but actually harmful. Foa *et al.* (2002, cited in Mott *et al.*, 2013) show that flooding is indeed effective for individuals with PTSD, even though there might be some effects of bringing back the trauma at first. There is a drop-out rate of 20.5 per cent to exposure therapy (flooding), according to Mott *et al.* (2013), but they point out this is about the same as for other treatments for PTSD (e.g. Newman *et al.*, 2011, cited in Mott *et al.*, 2013). 'Other treatments' include CBT with EMDR (see later in this section).

Mott *et al.*'s study used 20 veterans and an exposure therapy which used group therapy rather than the more usual individual therapy. What was interesting about this study was that they asked the participants/patients how they felt about the therapy afterwards, using questionnaire data. The results were that there was considerable satisfaction with the group-based exposure therapy. The study gathered both qualitative and quantitative self-report data. The participants were highly satisfied and found the therapy helpful and acceptable: 85 per cent felt they had experienced reduction in their symptoms. The participants/patients felt that commitment to the group had helped them to stay with the programme, and just 5 per cent dropped out, although this is likely to be less about the effectiveness of exposure therapy itself. The veterans thought that hearing others relive the experience gave a normalising effect (made the feelings seem normal), which they felt was the most helpful part of the therapy, alongside the comments of the other veterans about their own exposures (their feelings about the trauma, to relive them, which was the 'exposure' part).

Studies looking at the effectiveness of systematic desensitisation over flooding

Studies have shown that systematic desensitisation is more effective than flooding.

In 1969, Willis and Edwards tested 50 female participants who showed a fear of mice and used three conditions. They used systematic desensitisation, implosion therapy (flooding) and a control group. They found that systematic desensitisation was more successful than implosion therapy in reducing the fear of mice and that two therapists using systematic desensitisation produced similar effects from the therapy. Implosion therapy was no more effective than no therapy, as experienced by the control group. They found that the effects of systematic desensitisation were still present after about seven weeks.

In 1971, Mealiea and Nawas tested the effectiveness of systematic desensitisation as opposed to implosion therapy too and also found that systematic desensitisation was better. They studied people with a snake phobia and found that implosion therapy was no better than no therapy (measured using a control group), but systematic desensitisation was successful and the effect lasted at least a month, which was when the follow-up took place.

However, as is often the case in psychology, there are studies that show the opposite, and see flooding as more effective. In 1971, Boulougouris, Mark and Marset gave 16 people, each with a phobia, half implosion therapy and half systematic desensitisation (a cross-over design – six sessions of each) and found that not only was flooding better but the effects lasted over 12 months.

These studies are rather old now, because current studies tend to compare different therapies, such as CBT and EMDR (see later in this section), as well as hypnosis-based systematic desensitisation or assertiveness training.

Issues and debates

Note how, in the 1960s and 1970s, there were studies comparing flooding and systematic desensitisation and how both those treatments are still used, but the comparisons between treatments tend to bring in more complex treatments, such as CBT with systematic desensitisation. One of the issues and debates you will look at in the A level course is the history of psychology, and you can use these studies to evaluate the various treatments presented in this section to discuss how psychological research both stays the same in many ways (such as methods of collecting data) and changes in its focus.

Evaluation of flooding as a treatment for phobia

Strengths

- Flooding can be stressful, if not traumatic, but it is quick because the alarm reaction cannot be maintained for long. For some people with a very strong phobia, it can be more successful for them to endure this quick, though very frightening, experience, perhaps because they are not successful in maintaining relaxation so systematic desensitisation does not work for them.
- Wolpe (1973) provided evidence for flooding being successful as he took a girl who was scared of cars on a drive until she calmed down and it is said that this procedure did work, even though she was extremely upset at the start. When there is evidence for a treatment working, that helps to show its effectiveness.
- It rests on strong theory, and classical conditioning principles as well as biological knowledge are both used to explain the treatment and how and why it works. Cars might be associated with something that gave fear at some stage. Then immersing in a car ride and getting over the phobic response should replace that response with a response of being calm. The underpinning theory is clear and well evidenced.

Weaknesses

- The treatment can be frightening and perhaps not ethical. Systematic desensitisation with its focus on gradual exposure to the feared object seems less distressing.
- Classical conditioning involves extinction and a phobia can be extinguished using flooding because the association would no longer be made between the phobic object or situation and the fear response. However, there can be spontaneous recovery. This can happen with systematic desensitisation but is less likely as the process would be over time and with a stronger disconnection between the phobic object or situation and the fear, as the relaxation is stronger than simply 'non-fear'. This suggests that the treatment might be short-lived, which is a weakness.
- If flooding starts to use imagination rather than the 'live' situation or object, it becomes similar to systematic desensitisation. This is perhaps not a weakness but it does show that there might be more to it than simply immersing someone in their fear. The idea of using imagined situations might be better from an ethical viewpoint though. So in order to help with the ethics of the treatment, it starts to turn into another treatment, which is a weakness in the original treatment.

Progress check 4.24

Which of the following statements relates to flooding and which to systematic desensitisation (SD)?

Statement about a treatment for phobia	Flooding	SD
The individual is immersed into their feared situation or object.		
The individual learns muscle relaxation.		
It is about not being able to maintain the fear over the short period.		

Cognitive behavioural therapy

Cognitive behaviour therapy (CBT), in its treatment for phobias, draws on behavioural principles and so it is included here. The principles involved are the same as in flooding and systematic desensitisation, in that the fear response is focused on to remove it and change it to a different emotion.

There is a cognitive element in CBT as well as a behavioural element, though when it comes to treating phobias it is the behavioural element that is helpful as well as some cognitive input. The basic idea with cognitive behavioural therapy is that we have thoughts, feelings and actions, and that for all these there are consequences. A thought (such as 'last time I went shopping I felt really bad') gives a feeling (such as anxiety) and behaviour (such as not going shopping), which leads to consequences (such as not going shopping so not finding out that it was not so bad).

The aim of CBT is to break this cycle. It can be broken at the thought, the feeling or the behaviour.

- Someone can change their thinking (such as about going shopping) and focus on the good parts (such as getting something they really want). Then their behaviour might be to go shopping and, as long as there was no panic attack or bad feelings, they would start to lose their fear.
- Changing one's emotions is hard without changing thinking (it might mean taking medication, for example) so that is not really focused on as much.
- Changing behaviour can work, such as just going shopping without changing the thinking, and as long as there was no panic attack or similar, the consequences might be that the fear goes.

In practice, what happens is to look at thoughts, feelings and behaviour together. When focusing on a phobia, someone can:

- look at their thoughts and try to think 'what is the worst that can happen?' – this means focusing on what a panic attack is and reassuring themselves that it is not dangerous
- monitor their feelings to see if they can keep their anxiety down to a manageable level for them, such as six out of ten
- try some behaviour that works towards getting rid of the phobia while not being too threatening, so the anxiety stays about six out of ten.

Gradually, this would work, with behaviour going closer to the required behaviour and anxiety being maintained just at the manageable level.

This is not the same as systematic desensitisation as it is not about a hierarchy of fears as such, and it is not about learning to relax, but the principles are similar.

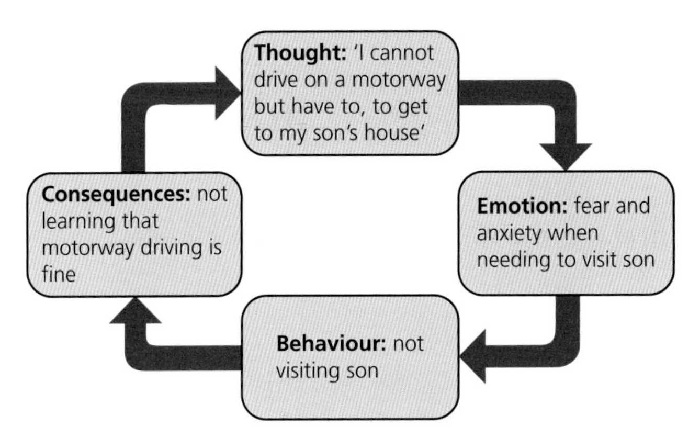

An example of how a phobia can be formed (applying CBT concepts – the vicious cycle)

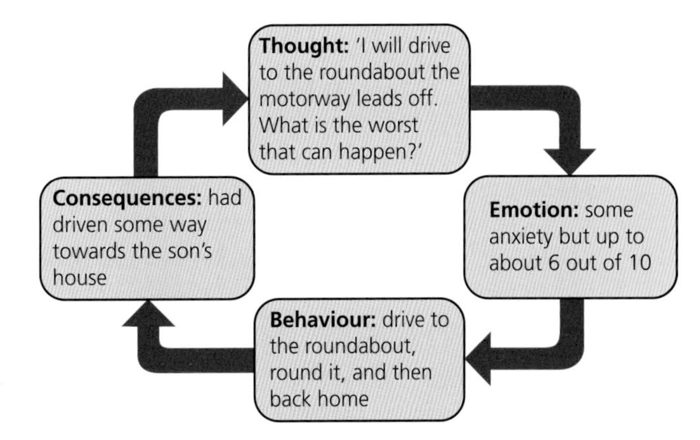

An example of how a phobia can be unlearned using CBT concepts

The diagram above shows how the required behaviour (driving to the son's house) can be shaped by keeping the anxiety as manageable as possible (otherwise try another day or don't go quite as far) and doing at least some of the required behaviour, step by step.

Fitting learning theory to CBT and reduction of phobias

Classical conditioning

If the phobia comes from an association, then replacing the fear response with a more acceptable response (even six out of ten for anxiety, but hopefully less over time) will work. CBT has the fear response monitored so that it is manageable. This is not the same as relaxation but the person would get it down to a relaxed state over time.

Operant conditioning

The original behaviour, avoiding the phobic object or situation to avoid the emotional reaction of fear, is negatively reinforced. The individual is avoiding what is negative, which is successful. In fact, fears can be dealt with that way. Some fears are not a problem because the individual avoids the situation, such as not going anywhere where there are snakes. However, a phobia is different from a fear because it limits someone's life, and then it has to be dealt with, such as someone who cannot leave their house.

CBT uses rewards, such as holding the anxiety to a manageable level and doing at least something towards the required behaviour. The reward is that behaviour, which is an achievement. This is using positive reinforcement. The client would get reward from the counsellor and hopefully friends and family for having got so far, and the reward should help move to the next step. There is positive reward and also shaping.

Social learning

There might be an element of social learning if the counsellor acts as a role model and goes through the behaviour to be attempted and the maintaining of anxiety at a manageable level, but this is not usually formally modelled, so observational learning is not usually involved. This can happen though, and a counsellor might accompany someone on a short trip if they are afraid of going out.

Cognitive element

There is a cognitive element to this therapy, as the individual can use their thinking to help. The idea of thinking 'what is the worst that can happen?' is to help to rationalise the phobia, which can be helpful. This links to flooding, where someone will realise that they are OK even if immersed in their fear situation.

Linking CBT with classical and operant conditioning

CBT does not look at the past and how a phobia has been acquired or maintained; it focuses on the present, with the aim of getting rid of the phobia. Though it might be argued that, if the explanation for the phobia is conditioning in some way (classical and/or operant), then this is what has led to the treatment. For example, the idea of maintaining the anxiety response as far as possible fits with the idea of biofeedback and how flooding works, but CBT does it in a more gradual way and with the client in control. There is the idea of systematically desensitising too, though again done in a different way. The shaping that is done is the 'systematic' part and the desensitising is about keeping anxiety at a manageable level (until it has gone).

Study looking at the effectiveness of CBT with SD measured against CBT with EMDR

Triscari *et al.* (2011) looked at different therapies for a phobia of flying to consider their effectiveness. Triscari *et al.* (2011) suggest that between 10 and 25 per cent of people have a flying phobia and this can seriously limit their lives, and so treating the phobia is of interest to society as well as to the individuals. There are many therapies that can be used for a flying phobia, and the researchers here list them as: systematic desensitisation, flooding, exposure in simulators, relaxation, traditional psychotherapy, coping self-talk, cognitive preparation and others. One therapy used eye movement desensitisation and reprocessing (EMDR), which is a comparatively new therapy and only briefly outlined here. The idea is that someone's fears and distressing thoughts, such as from past learning, are trapped inside their brains to be remembered and relived. A therapist can ask them to recall their experiences and related emotions and focus on the rapid eye movements involved in the recall. They can then redirect the eye movements to a light, an object or movement, and the negative thoughts from before are replaced with more positive ones. The thoughts can be reprocessed without the negative thinking that went with them.

Triscari *et al.* (2011) aimed to look at the effectiveness of CBT with systematic desensitisation (CBT-SD) compared with CBT with EMDR (CBT-EMDR). They claim that the effectiveness of CBT is already shown.

They used 57 participants in the study, all volunteering because they wanted to get help with their phobia of flying. Thirty-four were in the CBT-SD group and 23 were in the CBT-EMDR group. The whole group underwent educational training about anxiety and fears, some CBT to look at issues around thinking connected to emotions and behaviour, training about relaxation and information about flying and safety. Then the EMDR group had the EMDR therapy and the other group did not. The whole group then worked together, such as building up to going on a flight. Only the EMDR was different.

Measures of their anxiety and fears were taken before and after the treatment. Results showed that the two groups were not different before the treatment. The two treatments (CBT-SD and CBT-EMDR) both were seen to be effective, with little or no difference between them. Thirty-one (93.9 per cent) participants/patients flew at the end of the CBT-SD treatment (one seems to have dropped out) and 21 (91 per cent) flew after the CBT-EMDR treatment. This study suggests strongly that both treatments were effective and successful.

Evaluation of CBT as a therapy for phobias

Strengths

- CBT does not look into the past; it focuses on the present and, importantly, the future for the individual. This gives it a positive element. It involves action as well as talk, which is also positive. The therapy tends to be finite (often a course of six weeks) and there is action planning and monitoring of progress. Someone wants to get over a phobia and CBT helps in that this gives the therapy a practical and positive focus, which can be seen as a strength.

- CBT gives the person with the phobia the power to decide what behaviour to try and how much anxiety they feel they can 'stick with', so this is an ethical therapy, as is systematic desensitisation. The individual is in charge. This is in contrast to flooding, where the therapy is 'done to' them. Ethically, it is a strength if a therapy gives power to the client and not to the therapist.

Issues and debates

One issue you will cover in your course is the issue of social control. Therapies are a good way of showing how psychology can lead to social control in some way, such as control over an individual, as tends to happen in flooding. Use examples like this to help you to learn and discuss the issues and debates.

STUDY HINT

If you are taking the A level course, you will come across therapies again, such as in clinical psychology. You can use your learning in other areas of your course to back up your learning here, such as considering CBT as a treatment for depression, if depression is a mental health issue you choose to study in clinical psychology.

- CBT is evidence-based, which means there is evidence for its effectiveness. The UK's National Institute for Clinical Excellence (NICE) recommends CBT because there is evidence that it is effective. This is a strength. Hofmann *et al.* (2013) reviewed different meta-analyses and found evidence for effectiveness of CBT for anxiety disorders (which include phobias) as well as other disorders, such as anger control problems, general stress and bulimia. The evidence came from studies where there was an intervention using CBT and a control group, so the evidence is seen as strong. The evidence showed that CBT was better than other treatments and, in general, it is said to be at least as good as medication. Westbrook *et al.* (2007) discuss the effectiveness of CBT and find a lot of evidence to support its effectiveness.

Weaknesses

- CBT is a practical therapy in the sense of the client focusing on solving particular issues for them, such as a fear limiting their life opportunities. Not all problems are practical ones – some cannot be 'solved' and emotion focusing is better.
- A similar issue is that the individual has to be able to focus on issues, do homework and stick with anxiety to help to overcome it, for example. This means CBT is limited to practical problems in people that have the ability at that time to work on their issues.
- Sometimes medication is considered to be needed alongside CBT (NICE guidelines, 2004), so that someone is in a position to benefit from CBT. Grazebook and Garland (2005) support the idea that CBT is effective but they agree that it might not work for everyone and that therapy must suit the individual.
- CBT has been used together with systematic desensitisation. Triscari *et al.* (2011) used CBT with systematic desensitisation and also with eye movement desensitisation reprocessing (EMDR). CBT is used with mindfulness (which involves being mindful of the moment and focusing on the here and now, including techniques like meditation). It is not exactly a weakness of CBT to say it is used with other treatments but this does suggest that CBT works well with other treatments (Triscari *et al.*, 2011) so perhaps is not wholly effective on its own. Leung and Cottler (2009, cited in Hoffmann *et al.*, 2013) suggested that CBT seemed to be more effective when paired with other brief therapies than with drug treatments, though it was more effective than the other brief therapies mentioned. This piece of evidence looked at CBT as used in substance abuse, so that might be different from when it is used for phobias. Mitte (2005) showed that CBT, together with applied relaxation, worked for phobias (those without agoraphobia) and that the two together were more effective than just one of them. Even alone, though, each treatment was more effective than drug therapy. There seems to be some idea that CBT with another treatment can be more effective, but the evidence is not that strong and findings consistently show the effectiveness of CBT.

Explore

To explore more about Hoffmann *et al.* (2013), the meta-analysis that discusses the effectiveness of CBT, see the full article here: www.ncbi.nlm.nih.gov/pmc/articles/PMC3584580/.

Progress check 4.25

Write out a vicious cycle for someone who has agoraphobia.

Test yourself

Explain two differences and two similarities between systematic desensitisation and one other therapy for phobias. **(6 marks)**

Other treatments and therapies based on learning theory principles (not for phobias)

Other treatments are included here as this is Year 1 of your course and in Year 2 you will come across other treatments and therapies that draw on learning theory principles. It is useful to explain them here, ready for Year 2, so that you can make links between treatments and therapies and their underlying theories.

Aversion therapy

Aversion therapy is another therapy based on classical conditioning principles. It is used for addictions – for example, addiction to alcohol. Other areas in which aversion therapy is used include using nasty-tasting substances on the fingernails to discourage nail-biting and using electric shocks to discourage certain types of behaviour. It would not be used for phobias but is included here because it can help to show how classical conditioning principles are used in society and thus look at the applications of learning theories.

Aversion therapy uses the principles of classical conditioning. The therapy replaces the pleasure response with an aversion response (e.g. pain or something unpleasant). Using the example of alcoholism, in order to be free from the addiction, the pleasure response given by alcohol has to be replaced by an aversion response. In treating alcoholism, a prescribed emetic drug (that makes people feel, or be, sick) is paired with the alcohol. After a few trials, alcohol will make the person feel sick even in the absence of the drug.

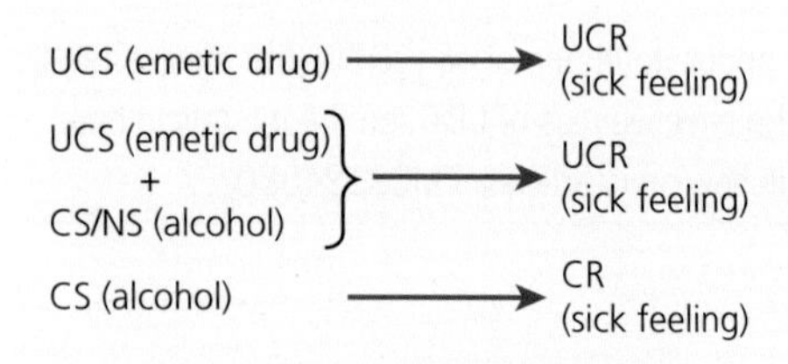

Aversion therapy used to treat alcoholism

It is important that during the therapy people drink soft drinks, so that they are not conditioned to feel sick in response to all drinks. Aversion therapy features in some films, including *One Flew Over the Cuckoo's Nest* and *Clockwork Orange*.

STUDY HINT

Sometimes, to treat alcoholism, a drug is prescribed that people are told will make them ill, so they don't drink because they fear being ill. However, this treatment does not use classical conditioning principles because the alcohol is not paired with an involuntary action (feeling sick), but with a cognitive thought. It is important to note that classical conditioning involves only involuntary actions. Always check that the behaviour being conditioned is involuntary.

Explore

Use this website or some other source to find out more about aversion therapy: www.minddisorders.com/A-Br/Aversion-therapy.html.

Explore

An important aspect of psychology is how studies and knowledge change over time and how social issues are addressed at different times in history. For example, homosexuality used to be considered a mental illness and at one time it was also illegal. Use the internet or some other source to investigate this issue, partly to help in understanding aversion therapy and partly to see how things have changed.

Study using aversion therapy to treat cocaine addiction

Frawley and Smith (1990) used aversion therapy to treat cocaine addiction, with some success. They used 20 patients, 11 being treated for cocaine addiction and 9 being treated for cocaine and alcohol addiction. They used chemical aversion therapy to condition the patients to an aversion to the sight, sound and taste of a cocaine substitute. They followed the patients up after six months (95 per cent of them) and found 56 per cent abstinence in the cocaine-only group and 70 per cent abstinence in the cocaine and alcohol group. Ninety per cent were followed up again at 18 months and 38 per cent of the cocaine-only group had remained abstinent (with 75 per cent showing abstinence at the time of the follow-up); 50 per cent of the alcohol and cocaine group had remained abstinent, with 80 per cent showing abstinence at the time of the follow-up. They asked others in the patients' lives about the abstinence and found a 90 per cent agreement, so there was validity in the findings.

Electrical aversion therapy

There are different stimuli used in aversion therapy and electric shock has been said to be the best in the sense that it is controllable and without side effects. Using chemicals as stimuli can give side effects. Electrical aversion gives uncomfortable shocks but safe ones. Taking drugs like antabuse can cause people to become ill. Disulfiram (another drug used) affects neurotransmitter processing in the brain and means that, when alcohol is consumed, there is an unpleasant reaction. (Neurotransmitter processing is explained in Chapter 3.) Electrical aversion therapy does not seem to last long, though; it is reported that people revert to their normal behaviour if there is no follow-up programme (alcoholrehab.com, accessed October 2014). A problem with using shock is that it is seen as punishment and not considered ethical as a treatment. In 2009, it was reported that in China children with an 'internet addiction' were treated with electrical aversion therapy. It appeared that, although parents may have agreed to the treatment, children did not, and this is considered unethical.

> **Explore**
> You can access a media report about the use of electrical aversion therapy in China in 2009 here: www.chinahush.com/2009/05/14/cure-your-childrens-internet-addiction-with-electric-shocks-aversion-therapy.

Although aversion therapy uses classical conditioning principles, there is an element of operant conditioning at work. If a child is given an uncomfortable electric shock for what is seen as 'bad' behaviour, such as an 'addiction' to the internet, they are likely to see this as punishment. To avoid the punishment, they stop the 'bad' behaviour, which is an example of negative reinforcement (see page 216 to explain positive and negative reinforcement, as well as positive and negative punishment).

Strengths of electrical aversion therapy

- Electrical aversion therapy is relatively easy to administer, has no side effects, is uncomfortable but not too painful and is relatively quick. So there are strengths to its use.
- It is better than chemical aversion therapy (pairing a 'bad' behaviour with a drug that gives an unpleasant response) in terms of ethics, though both treatments are perhaps ethically dubious.

Weaknesses of electrical aversion therapy

- The effectiveness of electrical aversion therapy is in doubt and, even with follow-up programmes, pre-therapy behaviour can return. Perhaps just as classical conditioning seems not to last (e.g. Watson and Rayner, 1920, had to 'recondition' Little Albert), so using classical conditioning in therapy perhaps does not lead to lasting results.
- Ethically, the treatment is questionable, perhaps especially when informed consent is not given – or, in the case of the children in China, apparently no permission is given from the children.
- Covert sensitisation (Cautela and Kearney, 1986) is considered better. Covert sensitisation uses the same principles, but the person imagines the unpleasant consequences and also imagines the relief at 'being cured'. This of course is more ethical and preferred.

Evaluation of aversion therapy

Strengths

- In some situations, aversion therapy has been shown to be successful. Follow-up studies have shown that it achieved better abstinence rates (people stopped the undesired behaviour) than other treatments (e.g. Smith and Frawley, 1990). Smith and Frawley used 200 patients undergoing aversion therapy for alcohol use (misuse). They found 71.3 per cent abstinence after 12 months (though the people they studied did have other treatment as well, such as family therapy, counselling and education). In spite of criticisms on ethical grounds, aversion therapy has been claimed to work well. Seligman (1966) said that 50 per cent of gay men who received the therapy did not continue homosexual practices (remember this therapy for homosexuality is not now considered appropriate).
- It rests on a clear theoretical explanation of how the behaviour being treated came about. A therapy that has a clear rationale is likely to be more acceptable to people – bearing in mind that today such therapy is neither part of a punishment nor a legal requirement.

Weaknesses

- As Seligman later reported, most of the men studied when he reported that the therapy was successful were bisexual. When homosexual (not bisexual) males were studied, the treatment was much less successful. Other studies have suggested a 99.5 per cent failure rate and at least one gay man has died.
- There are ethical issues involved in using aversion therapy because those administering the therapy have power over the patient. Patients may be asked to give permission for the therapy to take place, but they may not feel that they have the power to decline. As was seen when the therapy was used for homosexuality, society decides which behaviours are acceptable and which ought to be changed.

Token economy programmes

Token economy programmes are based on operant conditioning principles. Operant conditioning theory has led to the development of ways to help people change their learning by using rewards as reinforcements. You may have watched television programmes in which families with disruptive children are helped to enable the family to function better. The advice is usually to reward good behaviour and to ignore unwanted behaviour – perhaps, if a young child is involved, by using a 'naughty step', where the child has to stay while being ignored for a set amount of time, rather than being punished. One method of shaping behaviour, based on operant conditioning, is the token economy programme (TEP).

Token economy programmes can be used in prisons, mental health units and schools. The aim is to obtain the desired behaviour through a system of rewards:

- The tokens act as rewards and can be used to purchase something that is desired – this is the 'token' part of the therapy.
- People are 'paid' in tokens as a reward for acting in a desired way – this is the 'economy' part of the therapy.
- It is a 'programme' because there has to be a plan – the people involved have to be clear about what is to be rewarded and by how much each time.

Rewards have to be given consistently by all the staff involved. People involved in the programme have to understand what they have to do to gain the rewards and how they can exchange them. Token economy programmes are used in schools when other reinforcements (classroom rewards and teacher attention) have not worked. For example, they can be used for children with attention deficit disorder. The tokens can be chips or stars, for example, or points. Poker chips have been suggested as rewards for children who behave in a desirable way, and the chips can then be exchanged for something the child wants (Christophersen and VanSkoyoc, 2006).

These are the steps in using a token economy programme:

1. Identify the behaviour that has to be changed. A few behaviours are selected to be changed. The behaviours must be outlined clearly and everyone involved in the programme must understand them. If possible, they should be positive – asking people to 'remain quiet at meal times' is better than asking them 'not to shout at meal times'. It is the positive behaviour that is desired, rather than just the absence of the negative behaviour. The behaviour must also be observable, so that everyone is clear when it occurs and what is to be rewarded.
2. Select the tokens and decide what they can be exchanged for. Actual plastic tokens can be useful, but points can be used. Decide how to give them out if they are tokens, and where they should be kept. If they are points, decide how to record them clearly.
3. Make sure that the tokens or points 'buy' significant rewards. It is important that the rewards have meaning for the individual concerned and that they are worthwhile. Individuals could maybe help to make a list of what they would like. If what the tokens or points buy is not rewarding enough, there will be no motivation to perform the behaviour.
4. Set goals that are achievable. The individuals involved need to know what they have to do to earn the tokens or points. The goals should be achievable, but not necessarily easy. They can be adjusted as the behaviour improves. Knowing what is to be rewarded is not difficult if it is a particular behaviour, but if it is a percentage improvement in something, then this must be clear to everyone.
5. Explain the whole programme to the individuals concerned. The programme must be clear to the individuals so that they know what the tokens are for and can repeat the behaviour to gain more tokens. If they are not clear what the desired behaviour or goal is, then the programme is not likely to work.
6. Feed back on progress. Individuals need feedback on their progress and, if they are not doing the correct thing to earn the token, they need guidance. There can be some element of punishment, such as **response cost** – tokens are either withheld or taken away for undesirable behaviour. It is recommended that this only happens after a few weeks of the programme. Response cost can also be used if part of a goal has not been met, rather than just if undesirable behaviour is shown.
7. Provide the reward. At some stage, there must be a time for the tokens or points to be exchanged for rewards. If no tokens have been earned, there should be no fuss about the individual not getting a token; the person should just be informed that a token has not been achieved. No critical comments should be made.
8. Reviewing the programme. As people make progress, goals can be reviewed. People might also be given more tokens or the tokens could be exchanged more often. There should be praise to go with the programme. If there is no further progress, an earlier goal can be returned to.

Explore

Barkley (1990) has discussed the use of token economy programmes in schools. Investigate the work of Barkley to find out more about such programmes.

Evaluation of the token economy programme

Strengths

- The token economy programme has been seen to work – and quickly. O'Leary and O'Leary (1976) point out that such programmes work in schools. The powerful incentives produce the desired behaviour, possibly because the recognition is immediate and tokens may be given at the time of the desired behaviour.
- The programme can be adjusted to suit each individual. The rewards the tokens buy can be personal and the goals can be set individually. This is a therapy that can be focused clearly; it is not a group therapy. If necessary, each individual can be rewarded differently. Therefore, the programme is likely to be more successful because it can address specific difficulties.

Weaknesses

- The system is time consuming. In schools, formal token programmes are used by only about 30 per cent of teachers. The system requires an investment of time, which is difficult when staff are busy. If staff do not all focus on the programme, then it is likely to fail.
- The programme is targeted at a certain situation. Once outside that situation, the individual may not exhibit the shaped behaviour. Therefore, the programme might have limited application. For example, in a prison setting, the person may behave as desired but that behaviour may not be exhibited in the outside world.

Progress check 4.26

Allocate each of the four statements below to a therapy.

Statement	Therapy
Rewarding required behaviour with something that can be exchanged for something desired	
Exchanging an unpleasant feeling for the pleasant feeling that a drug gives, to help to prevent use of the drug	
Immersing someone 'in' their fear so that their reaction, which cannot last, recedes and they think they have overcome the fear	
Gradually facing a fear bit-by-bit while remaining relaxed, to replace the fear response with a relaxation response	

Test yourself

1 List five therapies that use learning theory principles. **(5 marks)**
2 With reference to two therapies, discuss their effectiveness. **(8 marks)**

Methods in learning theories

What is required and how this book covers that requirement

In all the topic areas, there is a section on methods. In your course, you need to cover certain methods and issues around methods, and these are spread through the Year 1/AS topic areas (and there is method material in Year 2 as well). In learning theories, the chosen method is observation, including gathering both qualitative and quantitative data using observation. Chapter 5 presents 'method' material for all the Year 1/AS topic areas and Chapter 6 gives 'maths' material for all the Year 1/AS topic areas. Therefore, there is only a brief outline in this chapter of what you need to know within learning theories. For more detail, read the 'learning theories' sections in Chapters 5 and 6.

In learning theories, you will need to know about:

- observations, including the different types – overt, covert, participant, non-participant, structured, naturalistic

Method link: Chapter 5 looks at observations in the section on learning theories (pp. 364–370).

- use of qualitative and quantitative data

Method link: Chapter 5 looks at qualitative and quantitative data (pp. 287–288).

STUDY HINT
Social psychology (Chapter 1) considers the use of qualitative and quantitative data so use your learning there when considering both types of data used in observations.

- time and event sampling as well as the use of tallying

Method link: Chapter 5 looks at how observations are done, including tallying and time and event sampling (pp. 365–366).

- content analysis as a way of gathering data in psychology

STUDY HINT
If you are doing the full A level and choose health psychology as one of your options in Year 2, you will carry out a content analysis so will learn more about it then. Remember that you are learning Year 1 and then Year 2 but there will be examinations after you have studied Year 2 too, so you will be able to build on your learning.

- the use of animals in laboratory experiments, where results of the experiments are related to humans, including practical and ethical issues
- the use of independent and dependent variables, controls and manipulation of variables in laboratory experiments with animals

Method link: there is more on using animals in research in Chapter 5 (pp. 372–379). Chapter 5 also has more information about using experiments in psychology when looking at material in cognitive psychology (pp. 315–326) because such material can relate to using animals in experiments.

- the ethical issues involved in using animals in laboratory experiments

Method link: Chapter 5 has more information about the ethics of using animals in experiments in psychology (pp. 372–376).

- the chi-squared test to analyse quantitative data, including issues around using inferential statistics: levels of measurement; reasons for choosing the chi-squared test; comparing observed and critical values to judge significance

Maths link: Chapter 6 has more information on the chi-squared test (pp. 412–416).

- using thematic analysis to analyse qualitative data, by sorting data into themes and categories

Method link: Chapter 5 has more information on the analysis of qualitative data using thematic analysis (pp. 290–292), which is also a method covered in social psychology.

- the scientific status of psychology, which is one of the issues and debates in your course. For the AS, you need to be able to discuss how far psychology is a science, if at all, including:
  - replicability and reliability
  - validity (internal, predictive and ecological validity)
  - reductionism
  - falsification
  - empiricism
  - hypothesis testing
  - controls.

Method link: issues about psychology and science are part of the method section of the learning theories part of your course and are discussed in Chapter 5 (pp. 379–383).

STUDY HINT

Reductionism and psychology as a science are two of the issues and debates for your course so make a note that the material you learn for the psychology and science part of this topic area can be used when discussing those two issues and debates, and vice versa. Even if you are an AS student (so you do not *need* to learn about the issues and debates), it would be worth learning the material because the issues and debates are interwoven into the course and you can make good use of them in discussion.

Progress check 4.27

Define four of the terms in the list you need to learn for the section about the scientific status of psychology. (You might need to look these terms up if you have not come across them yet in your course.)

STUDY HINT

Remember to check the answers of the progress checks (at the back of this book) as they can be useful in explaining issues further. If you read about an issue (e.g. validity) in a few different ways, including using the internet perhaps, then it is more likely that one of those 'ways' will suit you and your understanding will improve.

Test yourself

1. What is the difference between a naturalistic observation and a structured observation? **(3 marks)**
2. Evaluate how far psychology is a science, giving reasons for and reasons against the claim. **(12 marks)**

Studies in learning theories

For each topic area of your course, you need to cover one classic study and one contemporary study. With regard to the contemporary study, you will choose one from three named studies. This book covers all three contemporary studies so you can choose the one that you have used or are using in your course.

In learning theories, the classic study is Watson and Rayner (1920), which is about an 11-month-old child who is conditioned to fear a pet rat using classical conditioning principles. The contemporary studies are Becker *et al.* (2002), who looked at eating behaviours and attitudes in

Fiji after exposure to television, Bastian *et al.* (2011), who considered the effect of violent video games on those playing them, and Capafóns *et al.* (1998), who considered the use of systematic desensitisation to help fear of flying.

The four studies all look at learning theories, with Watson and Rayner (1920) showing the successful use of classical conditioning to instil a phobia and Capafóns *et al.* (1998) showing how systematic desensitisation works as a therapy for phobias. Becker *et al.* (2002) and Bastian *et al.* (2011) consider the influence of media on behaviour, which includes using social learning theory as an explanation. For an example of a study using operant conditioning, see Skinner (1948), explained earlier (pp. 220–221).

Classic study: Watson and Rayner (1920)

Watson and Rayner (1920) carried out a study using classical conditioning principles to see if they could cause a human baby to develop a fear that he did not have previously. This was to test whether classical conditioning worked with humans. This study is important because not many studies of classical conditioning using humans have been carried out.

Background

Watson and Rayner (1920) set out to gather experimental evidence for classical conditioning in humans. They needed a reflex action that occurred in response to a stimulus and some other behaviour to condition to cause that reaction. In infancy, there are some instinctive emotional reactions, such as fear, rage and love. The researchers felt that there must be some way in which the range of emotional reactions becomes increased because humans have emotional reactions to many stimuli. They thought that these early reactions were increased through associations developed by classical conditioning. They also thought that a child's early experiences in the home were like being in a laboratory where such conditioning takes place. This led them to find a baby whom they could condition to have an emotional response to something new.

Aims

The researchers aimed to find out:

- whether they could condition fear of an animal by simultaneously presenting the animal and striking a steel bar to make a loud noise to frighten the child
- whether the fear would be transferred to other animals and objects
- the effect of time on the conditioned response.

Procedure and results

The procedure and results of this study are given in one section because this is an experiment where reactions are built according to different stimuli, so it is clearer to explain the study and results as the study progresses.

Watson and Rayner (1920) chose Albert B as the participant for their study. He had been reared from birth in a hospital environment because his mother was a wet nurse (she breastfed children other than her own) in a home for invalid children.

Albert was not the child's real name; a pseudonym was used for confidentiality reasons. The child was healthy from birth and was well developed, stolid and unemotional, so they thought they could do him 'relatively little harm' by carrying out their experiments. This background is important because it may affect what you think about the ethics of the study. It also affects the conclusions because it is important that he was relatively fearless. This was an experiment, not a case study, because they did not gather in-depth information about Albert. It was a single-case experiment because there was only one participant. It was well controlled, there was careful manipulation of the independent variable (IV) (though it changed through the study) and careful measurement and recording of the dependent variable (DV).

Watson and Rayner (1920) tested Albert for fear reactions when he was about nine months old. They introduced a white rat, a rabbit, cotton wool and other stimuli and filmed his reactions. He showed no fear whatsoever. The mother and hospital attendants witnessed some of these events. The researchers also banged a hammer against a suspended steel bar to make a loud noise. They found a fear response – the baby's lips puckered and trembled and he had a sudden crying fit. This was the first time he had cried in the laboratory where the tests took place.

Establishing a conditioned emotional response

The researchers did consider whether what they wanted to do was ethical but they decided that Albert would in any case have worrying situations once he went to nursery. They waited until he was 11 months old and checked again that he had no fear. The procedure and results at 11 months and 3 days are shown in Table 4.7.

Table 4.7 Little Albert: procedure and results at 11 months and 3 days

Procedure	Resulting response
A white rat (real) was presented to Albert.	He reached for it with his left hand.
As his left hand touched the rat, the bar was struck behind his head.	He jumped and fell forward but did not cry.
Just as his right hand touched the rat, the bar was struck again.	Albert jumped violently, fell forward and started to whimper.

The researchers waited for one week before continuing the experiment. The rat was then presented suddenly to Albert, without a sound. He reached out tentatively, but did not touch the rat. He was then given blocks, which he played with without a problem. They concluded that there had been some effect from the conditioning.

The experiment continued as summarised in Table 4.8. The conclusion was that the conditioning had been successful.

Table 4.8 Little Albert: procedure and results at 11 months and 10 days

Stimulus	Response
Rat + sound	Albert started to fall over immediately; he did not cry
Rat + sound	Fell to the right; he did not cry
Rat + sound	Fell to the right; he did not cry
Rat alone	Puckered face, whimpered and withdrew his body to the left
Rat + sound	Fell to the right and began to whimper
Rat + sound	Stared and cried; did not fall
Rat alone	Albert started to cry immediately, turned and started to crawl away

Transfer of fear to other objects

The researchers then continued with the study to see if there was a transfer to other objects. The results at 11 months and 15 days are shown in Table 4.9.

Table 4.9 Little Albert: procedure and results at 11 months and 15 days

Stimulus	Response
Blocks alone	Played well
Rat alone	Whimpered, turned away
Blocks	Played and smiled
Rat alone	Leaned to the left, fell and crawled away
Blocks	Smiling and happy

They concluded that the conditioning of rat with fear had lasted for five days. The experiment was continued, using different stimuli (Table 4.10).

Table 4.10 Little Albert: use of different stimuli at 11 months and 15 days

Stimulus	Response
Rabbit alone	Immediate negative responses; leaned away, whimpered, burst into tears
Blocks	Played well and energetically
Dog alone	Not as violent a reaction as to the rabbit; tried to crawl away but only cried when dog approached his head
Blocks	Played well
Fur coat	Withdrew to left side and began to fret; began to cry when coat brought nearer
Cotton wool was presented wrapped in paper with some cotton wool showing	Not the same negativity, but played with the paper; withdrew his hand from the wool itself
Hair	Negative response but OK with hair of two observers
Santa mask	Negative behaviour

At 11 months and 20 days, when the researchers introduced the rat alone, Little Albert's response was less marked than previously. The researchers decided that the association had weakened so they renewed it (Table 4.11).

Table 4.11 Little Albert: renewal of association at 11 months and 20 days

Stimulus	Response
Rat + sound	Violent reaction
Rat alone	Fell to left side and strong reaction
Rat alone	Fell over to left and crawled away; no crying and gurgled happily
Rabbit alone	Leaned to left and whimpered a little
Blocks	Played well

The researchers then tried to condition the fear to the dog and the rabbit (Table 4.12).

Table 4.12 Little Albert at 11 months and 20 days: rabbit and dog were the stimuli

Stimulus	Response
Rabbit alone	Whimpered and leaned over
Rabbit + sound	Violent fear reaction
Rabbit alone	Whimpered and leaned over
Rabbit alone	Whimpered, but wanted to reach out to the rabbit as well
Dog alone	Whimpered and held hands away from dog
Dog + sound	Violent negative reaction
Blocks	Played well

Fear could, therefore, be transferred to other objects.

The experiment was then moved from the dark room where the previous studies had taken place to a lecture room in the presence of four people. This was to study the effect of different surroundings (Table 4.13).

Table 4.13 Little Albert at 11 months and 20 days: the effects of a different setting

Procedure	Resulting response
Rat alone	No fear reaction but hands held away
Rabbit alone	Slight fear reaction; turned away a little
Dog alone	Turned away and cried
Rat alone	Slight negative reaction
Rat + sound	Jumped but did not cry
Rat alone, moved near	Began whimpering as rat brought near
Blocks	Played well
Rat alone	Withdrawal and whimpering
Blocks	Played well
Rabbit alone	Pronounced reaction
Dog alone	Did not cry until the dog barked

It was concluded that there were transfers to different stimuli and to a different situation.

The effect of time on conditioning

The final part of the experiment took place when Little Albert was aged 1 year and 21 days (Table 4.14).

Table 4.14 Little Albert at 1 year and 21 days: the effect of passage of time on conditioning

Stimulus	Response
Santa Claus mask	Negative
Fur coat	Negative
Blocks	Played
Rat	Negative
Blocks	Played
Rabbit	Somewhat negative
Dog	Cried

The researchers concluded that conditioned emotional reactions lasted longer than one month, though became a little weaker. On that day, when he was 1 year and 21 days old, Albert was taken from the hospital, as had been going to happen in any case. The researchers could not, therefore, remove the conditioned emotional responses. They felt that the responses would last for a lifetime.

The results of Watson and Rayner's (1920) study on Little Albert are detailed in Tables 4.7 to 4.14. To summarise briefly, each time the blocks were given to Albert, he played with them happily and each time the rat was presented, after it had been paired with the noise, there was a negative response. Little Albert's fear of a white rat and other similar animals and objects can be explained using classical conditioning principles (see diagram below).

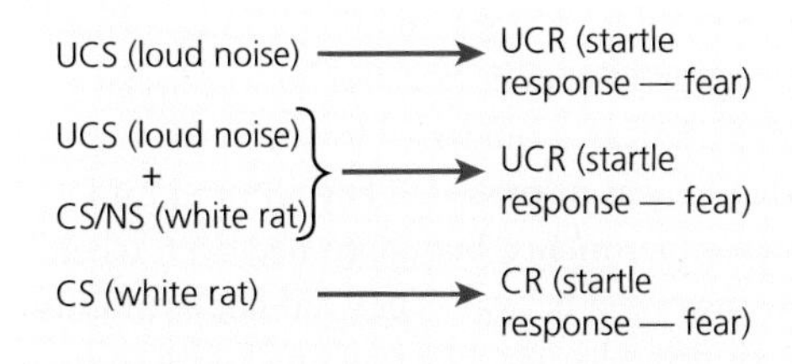

Explanation of Little Albert's fear using the principles of classical conditioning

When objects similar to the white rat, such as cotton wool, a rabbit and a Santa Claus mask, were presented, Albert responded negatively. Therefore, there was a conditioned emotional response, as the researchers had thought there would be. It was generalised to other similar objects and animals and, albeit somewhat reduced, it lasted over time. Note that, during the experiment, the researchers had to reintroduce the pairing of the unconditioned and conditioned stimulus.

Conclusions

A conditioned emotional response can occur in humans after only a few pairings of stimuli, but the pairings might have to be repeated. The conditioned response can be transferred to other similar objects. Albert was removed from the study, so there was no means of seeing if the responses could be extinguished.

> **Progress check 4.28**
>
> Explain three ethical issues with the Watson and Rayner (1920) study.

Evaluation of Watson and Rayner (1920)

Strengths

- The Little Albert study was carefully documented; witnesses helped to record the data and there were strict controls. Albert's reactions were recorded carefully, the setting(s) were controlled and only one variable was changed at a time. If it could have been repeated ethically, it would have been replicable and could, therefore, have been tested for reliability.

- The study is evidence that classical conditioning occurs in humans. Pavlov had shown that it exists in dogs, but it might have been difficult to generalise the results to humans had Watson and Rayner (1920) not carried out this study.

Weaknesses

- The study is not ethical. The researchers made sure that Albert was not easily frightened and they thought that the experiment was acceptable because he would have frightening experiences at nursery. However, there is little doubt that he was distressed. They allowed him to rest between experiments, but continued even when they saw how distressed he was. They did not extinguish the fears, so it is possible that they remained with him. However, one month later, his fear responses had started to weaken, so it is possible that they disappeared when the unconditioned and conditioned stimuli were no longer paired. (Note that there is now some information about what happened to Little Albert, but the issue about his conditioning is not known – see below).
- The study may not be valid. The setting and tasks were artificial. It could be argued that a noise from a hammer and steel bar could represent a real-life noise and that playing with white fur and animals is natural. However, the setting was not natural and Albert was in a laboratory situation, which may have made him initially fearful.

> **STUDY HINT**
> You might learn best by learning trigger words, such as 'lack of consent', 'doing harm' and 'not competent'. This can help learning. However, it is important to explain points thoroughly. For example, it is not that the researchers lacked competence fully, but there was an element of competence missing.

An addition to the Little Albert story

After the study was done, a long time afterwards in fact, Albert's real identity was discovered by a journalist. Little Albert was Douglas Merritte. It was never considered very satisfactory that Little Albert was not de-conditioned and Watson was said to have been dismissed from the university around the time of the study because of having had an affair with Rayner, so many wondered what had happened to the boy in the study. A team of scholars led by Hall Beck tracked down the people working at the hospital at the time of Watson and Rayner's (1920) study and narrowed the field, eventually finding that Douglas Merritte and his mother (who was a wet nurse at the hospital at the time) fitted the situation best. The researchers were sad to find that Douglas Merritte had died at the age of six from hydrocephalus (water on the brain) and they were never able to confirm whether he still had the fear of white furry objects that he had been conditioned to have.

There is a bit more to the story, according to other reports (Cosh, 2012). The APA published Beck's findings about Little Albert being Douglas Merritte, but it is hard to verify the following addition to the story by Cosh (2012); it is interesting nonetheless. Little Albert had been said by Watson to be healthy. However, hydrocephalus got Beck wondering. It was said that the child had meningitis three years before his death and that explained the hydrocephalus, but photos of Little Albert did seem to show that he lacked attention and focus. The question was raised whether he was a child who was not well. Records seemed to show, for example, that he never walked. Possibly the findings of Watson and Rayner (1920) came from a child who was unwell and not 'the norm', and so the findings might not be generalisable to all children.

> **STUDY HINT**
> If there is an addition to a study after the study has been published, then it should not be included as part of the study, though it can provide interesting additional information.

> **Explore**
> Use the internet to find out more about Little Albert/Douglas Merritte. A good source is: www.apa.org/monitor/2010/01/little-albert.aspx.

Contemporary studies

Becker *et al.* (2002)

Becker *et al.* (2002) aimed to see if television affected eating disorders – they wanted to know whether the introduction of television in a culture might lead to more attention paid to dieting, more self-induced vomiting behaviour and focus on media models. They chose a place in Fiji where television was being introduced in 1995 and they thought that, three years later, in 1998, they could see if there were differences in eating behaviour.

Aims

As television was about to be introduced into the Fijian culture, it was a good time to study the effects of television on eating disorders. There had been no previous media influence. If measures of eating disorders are taken before the introduction of television and then afterwards, there can be some measure of whether media impacts on behaviour to the extent that eating behaviour is affected. The study's aim is to consider the impact of media on eating behaviour (specifically television). Research questions included whether exposure to Western television triggered disordered eating behaviour when traditionally in Fiji appetites were healthy. Another question was whether disordered eating went with body dissatisfaction in Fiji, as was found in the West. Also they wondered whether any shift in eating behaviour would go with a shift in cultural values too, around diet.

Background

Becker *et al.* (2002) explain that eating disorders are more common in industrialised countries than in developing societies. This suggests a role for culture, as it is culture that is different in these societies so culture might be a 'cause' of eating disorders.

Issues and debates

The idea of nature-nurture can be found here. If a behaviour or characteristic differs between people, then it is likely that culture has a role in the cause of that behaviour or characteristic. If it was down to human nature, it would be found across all cultures.

STUDY HINT

Use Becker *et al.* (2002) if you are using as your key question issues around anorexia as explained by learning theories.

A difficulty in studying cultural effects on eating disorders is that often studies are done in an environment where there is exposure to Western images, so finding a culture that is 'media-free' is not easy. This means that cultures of the different societies are not different in terms of media, which spoils studies. When television is to be introduced, as it was in Fiji, this is a good time to study the effects of television on eating behaviour, as in the aim of this study. In Fiji at that time, eating disorders were rare and the girls studied were 'media-naive' (p. 509). Becker *et al.* (2002) say that there was only one reported case of anorexia by the mid-1990s and there was no cultural 'pressure to be thin' (p. 509).

Procedure

There were two samples of Fijian girls used: first, in 1995, within a few weeks of television being introduced and then again in 1998, after three years of television in the area. Both quantitative and qualitative data were gathered. Qualitative data came from narratives – stories about feelings and behaviours around the introduction of television. The population for the study was Fijian adolescent girls, in forms 5–7 at the time the data were collected, in two secondary schools in one area of Fiji. Written informed consent was given both by the participants and by a parent or guardian. There were 63 participants in 1995 and 65 in 1998. All participants spoke fluent English. In 1995, the average age of the girls was 17.3 years and in 1998 it was 16.9 years.

The data were collected by questionnaire about eating behaviours. Although the questionnaire did not need to be translated, any cultural issues that might not be understood in the questionnaire were explained verbally to the participants. The questionnaire was EAT-26 and a score of 20 was considered high. There were also questions about use of television in the household and viewing of television, and weight and height were measured. There was also a semi-structured interview, used with the participants who reported bingeing or purging on the questionnaire.

Explore

EAT-26 has been used since 1982 (and, before that, EAT-40 in 1979) to measure attitudes to eating. You can find out more using the link: www.eat-26.com.

In 1998, there were additional questions about body image and dieting, as well as questions about differences in the girls' attitudes to eating and how they saw their parents' views. Some of the questions that were asked in the 1998 survey are as follows:

- Have you ever tried to change how much you eat in order to change your weight?
- Do your parents or family ever say that you should eat more?
- How important is it that you weigh what you would like to weigh?
- Do you ever think that you should eat less?

The qualitative narrative data were collected using open-ended questions in semi-structured interviews using 30 girls chosen from the original sample because they showed disordered eating attitudes and behaviours and television viewing habits. Questions asked what they thought about their weight as well as questions like 'what do you think of American TV?'.

STUDY HINT

Becker *et al.* (2002) use both questionnaires and interviews, gathering both qualitative and quantitative data. They gather self-report data and use open-ended as well as closed questions. In social psychology, you look at these methodological issues and you can use this study as an example to show understanding. You can also use this study as an example of the use of thematic analysis to analyse qualitative data and an example of using the chi-squared test.

Results

The qualitative data were audio-taped and then transcribed with thematic analysis following the transcribing. The quantitative data were analysed in various ways, including using a chi-squared test to look for significance in the data.

The mean BMI (body mass index) was 24.5 in 1995 and 24.9 in 1998, showing similarities in the two samples. As this was an independent groups design, similarity in the two samples is important when drawing conclusions about differences before and after television was introduced. Television exposure after 1995 and over the three years to 1998 was similar between the groups as well. The important point was that it was the 1995 television viewing habits (which were limited as television had just been introduced at that time) and the 1998 television viewing habits (which were more, as there had been three years of television by then) that gave the independent variable; other variables were checked for differences and found to have remained sufficiently the same. As this was a naturally occurring independent variable (television was being introduced anyway, not by the researchers), this is a naturalistic experiment. Of the 1995 sample, 41.3 per cent said their household had a television, compared with 70.8 per cent in 1998, which confirmed that television viewing was likely to be different between the two samples. A chi-squared test was done, with a significance level of $p \leq 0.001$. The test was between the two sets of girls (1995 and 1998) and whether there was a television in the household or not.

There were differences between the two samples in the dependent variable measures, which included scores on the EAT-26 questionnaire. In 1995, 12.7 per cent had a score more than 20 and in 1998 that rose to 29.2 per cent (more than double). In the 1998 sample, EAT-26 scores that were higher than 20 were associated with dieting and self-induced purging (making oneself sick). None of the participants said they used self-induced vomiting to control weight in 1995, compared with 11.3 per cent in 1998.

There was not enough difference in television viewing habits to show a link with the dieting behaviour; however, there was an association between television ownership and disordered eating. Girls in a household with a television were three times as likely to have an EAT-26 score over 20.

It was found that girls who thought they should eat less used self-induced vomiting more (21.4 per cent) than those who did not think they should eat less (2.7 per cent). By 1998, 69 per cent said they had dieted at some time. This question was not asked in 1995 as it was not thought that dieting was part of the culture. In 1998, 74 per cent felt too big or too fat compared with Fijian norms about eating and body weight.

The qualitative data showed admiration for characters and a desire to be like them with regard to clothing, hairstyle and body reshaping. This links to social learning theory's idea that there is imitation of role models on television. From the interview data, 83 per cent said they felt television had influenced their friends or themselves with regard to their body weight and body image. Forty per cent linked losing weight or a desire to lose weight to future career prospects or being more useful at home, seemingly linking losing weight to being useful and successful. All the interviewed participants thought that television affected traditions in their culture.

Conclusions

An EAT-26 score of over 20 and self-induced vomiting were two measures that showed differences between 1995 (just as television was being introduced) and 1998 (three years after television had been introduced). There was also an increase in households owning television sets. Narrative data (the qualitative data) showed changing attitudes around diet and weight loss as well as body image in the period of the study (1995 compared with 1998). The qualitative data linked such changes to television watching, such as identifying with role models. There were also data showing that cultural values about dieting and weight were changing between the girls and the older generations.

Studies have linked media exposure (such as the fashion industry) with disordered eating (e.g. Heinberg and Thompson, 1992, cited in Becker *et al.*, 2002). Some studies found only vulnerable people were affected by media exposure (e.g. Hamilton and Waller, 1993, cited in Becker *et al.*, 2002). Other studies showed that media exposure did not link with disordered eating (Becker *et al.*, 2002). It was noticeable that in the main these studies did not include qualitative data and it was in the qualitative data that Becker *et al.* (2002) found evidence of imitation of role models on television. Other studies were also carried out in environments where media were already in evidence and they tended to look at the impact on individuals. Becker *et al.* (2002) focused on a peer group and also on a place where television was just being introduced. Becker *et al.* (2002) felt that other studies had been inconclusive for these reasons, whereas their own study enabled stronger conclusions to be drawn. They concluded that television had affected eating habits and attitudes in Fiji after it was introduced. The study shows that prolonged exposure to television affects peer behaviour around eating attitudes and behaviour.

Becker *et al.* (2002) identified some limitations in their study:

- They did not diagnose eating disorders – they used self-report data, though induced vomiting is what they called a 'worrying sign' (p. 512).
- Characteristics of bulimia nervosa were not found in the 1995 sample (e.g. use of diuretics) and this did not increase in the 1998 sample either. The BMI of both samples was also similar – there did not seem to be individuals of a low weight in either sample. There was no increase in bingeing either.
- The study used an independent groups design and there may have been differences in the samples that accounted for the differences in eating behaviour, as well as other differences around television ownership. However, the samples were the same age, the same gender, drawn from the same schools, so perhaps the samples were matched enough.
- It is not easy to generalise from the specific Fijian population to say the findings are true of other cultures. In Fiji, as healthy eating is encouraged, perhaps television showing different body shapes affected the Fijian girls more.

Progress check 4.29

Give four figures from the results of Becker *et al.*'s (2002) study.

Evaluation of Becker *et al.* (2002)

Strengths

- The use of qualitative data through interviewing helped to add detail and depth to the quantitative data and it was in the qualitative data that there was the confirmation that the girls felt they did imitate television role models. The quantitative data did not uncover attitudes like this.
- The questionnaire (EAT-26) was kept the same for both samples (there were some differences but there were the same questions as well, so comparisons could be made). This meant that a score of over 20 in 1995 compared with a score of over 20 in 1998. The measure remained similar enough for careful comparisons to be made.

Weaknesses

- Using a specific culture with cultural attitudes about healthy eating and against dieting and being thin helped the study to control the variable that the girls might have had different attitudes to begin with. However, it may limit generalisability. Having specific cultural attitudes means that the findings may be culturally specific and not generalisable to all cultures.
- The samples in 1995 and in 1998 were different. There were attempts to use a matched sample, but the actual sample was independent groups and there might have been differences between the two samples that led to the differences in the results. However, the researchers did control for gender, age and schooling, at least to an extent, which helps the idea that conclusions can be drawn about differences between the two samples and that conclusions were not down to participant variables.

Bastian *et al.* (2011)

Bastian *et al.* (2011) use two studies to look at how playing violent video games not only makes someone lose sight of their own humanity, but also lowers how we see the humanity of others (opponents in the game).

Aim(s)

The main aim is to see what people think of themselves when they have been violent in a video game, and whether they see themselves in terms of their humanity. The question is whether they perceive themselves as lacking in humanity and also how they see their opponent in terms of humanity too. They also considered whether playing against an avatar rather than another player would affect the player's perception of humanity. In Study 1 (how the player sees themselves in terms of humanity and how they see the other player), the game *Mortal Kombat* was used. In Study 2 (how the players sees themselves in terms of humanity if they are playing against an avatar), the game *Call of Duty* was used.

Background

Mortal Kombat is a video game that encourages players to 'finish him' when they win the game. This is telling them to use violent behaviour in the game and it has been shown that violent video games affect aggressive behaviour (e.g. Anderson and Bushman, 2001, cited in Bastian *et al.*, 2011). Dill *et al.* (2008, cited in Bastian *et al.*, 2011) showed that those that play violent video games are more likely to say that real-life aggression is OK. Busman and Anderson (2009, cited in Bastian *et al.*, 2011) suggest that playing violent video games numbs people 'to the pain and suffering of others' (p. 486). Bastian *et al.* (2011) cite other studies, too, that show that playing violent video games affects the player in terms of their aggression and what they think about violence and aggression. They also show that when playing video games the individual does identify with their behaviour; it is not that the video game is 'unreal' to them. Anderson *et al.* (2010, cited in Bastian *et al.*, 2011) show that players do engage with video content.

Bastian *et al.* (2011) are interested in the dehumanising effect of playing violent video games. Studies show that there are consequences in playing such video games related to how we see ourselves and others. The researchers here say 'dehumanisation oils the wheels of aggression and violence against others' (p. 486). The questions they asked concerned whether violence against a virtual opponent affected someone's views of their own humanity or the humanity of the opponent. They wondered whether people see themselves as aggressive if they act violently in the game and whether, when someone observes their own behaviour, this affected their perception of themselves.

The two games used were *Mortal Kombat* (Study 1) and *Call of Duty* (Study 2) and in both studies there was a non-violent video game as a control (*Top Spin Tennis*).

- Hypothesis 1: The players of the violent video game would see themselves as less human than would those playing the non-violent game.
- Hypothesis 2: People would see opponents as less human when they were receiving the violence in the video game as opposed to opponents in the non-violent game.
- Hypothesis 3: When there were co-players playing with the participant, the co-players would not be seen as less human, not being the target of violence.

Progress check 4.30

In the first hypothesis, give the independent and the dependent variable.

Procedure: Study 1

The researchers thought that playing a violent video game would lead to perceptions of both the player and the opponent as less human (this is 'dehumanising'). In *Mortal Kombat*, someone fights against an opponent having selected a character. The researchers measured humanity and thought that the players of the violent video game would see themselves as less human and also see the opponent as less human than those playing a similar but non-violent game. The researchers thought there were two ways of talking about lack of humanity. One way is to liken someone to a machine (cold, lacking emotions...); the other way is to liken someone to animals (immature, irrational...). They thought both these ideas about lacking humanity would be found in the players of the violent games, as opposed to the players of the non-violent games.

The participants were 106 students: 74 female and 32 male. They were randomly assigned to two conditions (playing the violent game or the non-violent game). The participants used an Xbox controller and headphones to play the game. Participants were instructed not to interact with one another. They either played two-player *Mortal Kombat* (52 of them) or *Top Spin Tennis* for 15 minutes (54 of them).

Then participants completed a questionnaire and indicated how much they enjoyed the game (from 1 to 7, 7 being 'very enjoyable'). They were also asked how frustrating the game was, again using a scale of 1 to 7, with 7 being 'very frustrating'. Participants also rated themselves using a scale to assess, in the first part of the scale, their 'human nature' – items such as 'I was responsive and warm' or 'I felt like I was mechanical' were put forward and the participants rated themselves on a 1 to 7 scale. Part two of the scale assessed their 'human uniqueness' with items like 'I felt I lacked self-restraint'. The participants used such statements to rate themselves and then used similar items to rate the other person. The scores from 'human nature' and 'human uniqueness' were put together to find a score for their perception of self and a score for perception of the other in terms of their humanity.

Results: Study 1

The results showed that participants found both games frustrating (mean 3.27 for the violent game, *Mortal Kombat*, and mean 3.04 for the non-violent game, *Top Spin Tennis*). *Mortal Kombat* was said to be more enjoyable, but the difference was small (mean 4.86 for the violent game and mean 4.35 for the non-violent game). *Mortal Kombat* was quite a bit more exciting (mean 4.52 for *Mortal Kombat* and mean 3.46 for *Top Spin Tennis*).

Self-humanity ratings were lower when playing *Mortal Kombat* (mean 3.74 for the violent game and mean 4.35 for the non-violent game). Humanity ratings of the other were also lower when playing *Mortal Kombat* (mean 4.43 for the violent game and mean 4.93 for the non-violent game). The researchers controlled for gender and found the results still remained significant (in that humanity ratings were lower with regard to both self and other in the violent game). As they also controlled for how frustrating, exciting and enjoyable the game was, the researchers thought that those features were similar enough between the two games to suggest that these features did not affect the findings.

Conclusions: Study 1

The conclusion was that playing the violent video game led to a lower perception of the player's own humanity and a lower perception of the humanity of the other player too.

Procedure: Study 2

Bastian *et al.* (2011) thought it might be being in combat with another person that led to their findings, rather than it being the violence in the game that made the player give a lower view of their own and the other's humanity. They thought that if the players were against a computer-generated avatar, rather than an avatar controlled by the other player, this might help to see if it was the violence in the game that led to the lowered perceptions of humanity. The researchers also felt that simply feeling bad about having 'done' the violence in the game may have led to the lowered perceptions of own humanity and the humanity of the opponent, rather than the violence in the game itself. Perhaps they just felt less optimistic after the game and in a lower mood. Bastian *et al.* (2011) also felt that the characters in *Mortal Kombat* are non-human, which might be an issue as the players might then see themselves as non-human. Therefore, the researchers set up Study 2.

They used a co-player with the participant, so two players played together against a computer avatar. It was thought that in this scenario players would still see themselves as less human after playing a violent game. However, they thought that how the participant would see the co-player was less clear – they may not see them as less human as they were not targets of violence. For Study 2, the participants played *Call of Duty* rather than *Mortal Kombat* because this game uses soldiers killing the enemy in time of war. The game uses 'human' figures and the player is the one that does the shooting (the player only has the gun view, which is why the co-player would not be seen as being violent in the game).

In Study 2, 38 students (28 female, 10 male) were again randomly assigned to two conditions. The two conditions were either to play *Call of Duty* (20 participants) or a non-violent game, which again was *Top Spin Tennis* (18 participants). In both games, the participants played as a team of two against computer-programmed avatars.

Participants were asked how frustrating, enjoyable and exciting the game was, as in Study 1. The same questionnaire and questions were used as Study 1. In Study 2, as well as all the other measures, participants were asked to rate their mood and to complete a self-esteem questionnaire.

Results: Study 2

Participants found both games equally enjoyable (mean 2.70 for the violent game and mean 3.56 for the non-violent game). Both games were also equally exciting (mean 3.05 for the violent game and mean 3.44 for the non-violent game). *Call of Duty* was seen as more frustrating than *Top Spin Tennis* (mean 5.00 for the violent game and mean 3.83 for the non-violent game). Self-esteem was similar between the two conditions (mean 3.37 for the violent game and mean 3.48 for the non-violent condition), and positive mood (mean 2.30 for the violent game and mean 2.50 for the non-violent game) and negative mood (mean 1.84 for the violent game and mean 1.66 for the non-violent game) were also very similar between the two conditions.

Ratings of self for humanity were different between the two conditions (mean 3.82 for the violent game and mean 4.48 for the non-violent game). This means participants rated themselves as less human in the violent condition (playing *Call of Duty*) than in the non-violent condition (playing *Top Spin Tennis*). This time though, unlike Study 1, there was no difference in the rating of the 'other' with regard to humanity (mean 4.89 for the violent game and mean 4.86 for the non-violent game). The 'other' in Study 2 was their co-player, unlike Study 1, where the 'other' was the player they were playing against.

Conclusions: overall

Playing a violent video game seems to lower someone's perceptions of their own humanity – this finding was the same in both studies. Changes in mood or self-esteem did not seem to account for the results (they were the same for the non-violent condition too). Playing a violent video game makes us feel less human. Study 1 showed that people saw the humanity of the person they played against as lower as well, but in Study 2, when the 'other' was their co-player, they did not 'lower' their humanity. This might be because the co-player did not engage in violence themselves – they did not have the view behind the gun so did not look as if they were the 'first shooter'. However, they might be seen as being part of the violence, you would think. In Study 1, the other player was being violent in a more direct way and was the target for the violence being perpetrated by the participant. The researchers suggest that the co-player was supporting the goals of the 'self' participant so might not be seen in the same 'dehumanised' light.

Self-perception theory holds that people draw conclusions about themselves from observing their own behaviour. It seems that people are 'dehumanised by their own brutality' (p. 489), and see themselves as less human when they observe their own behaviour (such as shooting 'others' in a video game). If we hurt others, then we see them as less human too. Perhaps seeing others as dehumanised facilitates being aggressive towards them.

Another possible interpretation of the results is that being a victim of violence leads to seeing oneself as less human. This interpretation is suggested by Bastian *et al.* (2011). Also they do not claim to show that real-life violence means people see themselves as less human; the study concludes only about playing violent video games. Bastian *et al.* (2011) point out that conclusions about playing such games are valid in themselves as people do spend a long time playing such games and it is important to see that they are dehumanising for the individual. The researchers also think that there may have been demand characteristics in that the participants had just played a violent video game and may have thought that they should, therefore, rate themselves as less human. However, they point out that people did not feel bad about themselves after playing, even though they rated themselves as less human. The researchers also asked whether participants had suspected links between violent video games and dehumanisation and the participants said they had not had these suspicions. Therefore, the researchers felt that their findings were not due to demand characteristics.

Evaluation of Bastian *et al.* (2011)

Strengths

- By carrying out two studies, and having a main hypothesis the same in the two studies, reliability was shown in the results. There was a different video game in Study 2 and there were some differences in questions asked, such as about mood and self-esteem; however, the main questions were the same as in Study 1, and the main finding – that people see themselves as less human if they play a violent video game – was present in both studies. This shows reliability in that finding.
- The researchers took some precautions to avoid demand characteristics, such as asking the participants if they had suspected a link between dehumanisation and playing violent video games, which the participants said they had not. The researchers also thought their questions were subtle enough for the aim not to be transparent, which would help to avoid demand characteristics.
- The researchers tested for the effects of gender, mood, level of self-esteem, amount of enjoyment in the games, amount of frustration in the games and the excitement of playing the games. They found that none of these variables explained the differences in the means between the important variables – the main one being whether someone played a violent video game or a non-violent one. By looking for effects from other variables, the researchers helped to make the link between their independent variable (the two types of video game) and the dependent variable (their own measure of their humanity).
- It is tempting to say that there is a weakness in the validity of the findings – however, the researchers emphasise that their aim was to study the dehumanising effect of playing violent video games and they did not intend to generalise to violence in real life having a dehumanising effect. As their study used the playing of video games and their conclusions were about playing video games, validity can be claimed.

Weaknesses

- In spite of attempts at validity, such as playing real games and having either a co-player or an opponent, the study did take place in artificial conditions with students participating as part of their course. There was artificiality, then, and this might have affected the responses of the participants.
- The conclusions about the individual showing a lower perception of their own humanity in both studies but showing a lower perception of the 'other' if they were their opponent but not if they were their co-player could have been affected by the change in the violent game. The change in game meant there were differences between Study 1 and Study 2, such as change in 'position' of the participant in that they were 'behind the gun' in Study 2 but playing as a non-human avatar in Study 1. Differences in the studies might have affected this second conclusion about the perception of the 'other'. Indeed differences in the studies may have affected the first conclusion about lower perception of their own humanity but, as the same result was found in both studies, this first conclusion did seem firmer.
- There may have been ethical issues with this study because the students had to participate in studies as part of their course, so they may not have felt they could withdraw, and they may have felt distressed after the study. The study did show that their perception of their own humanity was lowered after the playing of the violent video game so those in that condition may have been unduly distressed. This is not clear from the report on the study, but is a possible weakness.

Progress check 4.31

In Bastian *et al.* (2011), there are two studies. In both studies, the two important measures are the self-perception of being human and the perception of 'the other' with regard to being human. Study 1 and Study 2 have different 'others'. Explain for each study which is 'the other'.

Capafóns *et al.* (1998)

Aim(s)

The aim was to see if systematic desensitisation is a successful therapy for fear of flying. Capafóns *et al.* (1998) wanted to draw conclusions about the success of systematic desensitisation with this specific phobia and to see if they could find out what might lead to the greatest success. They felt that, in 1998 (when their study was written up), systematic desensitisation might be seen as a rather old therapy and they wanted to show that it is still a good choice for the treatment of fear of flying.

Background

Capafóns *et al.* (1998) say in their report that they think systematic desensitisation works for fear of flying for various reasons. One reason is that people travel in aeroplanes many times and still have the fear, so flooding has not worked for them. Systematic desensitisation includes an element of control over the situation and that might be what is added to the 'flooding' idea and what makes systematic desensitisation a better choice. A second reason is that systematic desensitisation is practical because it can involve imagining the feared situation, and the 'live' situation (which is not easy to create in this phobia) is not necessary. A third reason is the need for self-control, which means less dependence on the therapist, which is likely to help in the success of the therapy. Their fourth reason is that systematic desensitisation is not as stressful as flooding as the patient can go at their own speed. This means the therapy is likely to be continued.

STUDY HINT

Capafóns *et al.* (1998) give four reasons for preferring systematic desensitisation. You can use these four reasons as criticisms of other therapies, like flooding, or as strengths of systematic desensitisation. You can use this study as evidence too. Where possible, make use of material like this when discussing issues in psychology.

Someone with a fear of flying might manage to fly on a plane; however, this does not seem to stop the phobia, which suggests flooding in this case does not help

Procedure

The procedure of the study consists of the therapy itself. There were three phases: one for the relaxation and imagination training, one focusing on developing the hierarchy and then the final phase of applying the systematic desensitisation therapy.

Participants

There were 20 patients, and 21 patients waiting for the therapy acted as a control group. There was random assignment to the waiting group or the therapy group, though the two groups were balanced in terms of age, gender, strength of the fear and physical measures. The treatment group had 8 males and 12 females (mean age: about 30 years) and the control group had 9 males and 12 females (mean age: about 35 years). Patients were found by advertising to offer the treatment free of charge, so they were volunteers who responded to the adverts, a self-selected sample.

Progress check 4.32

What is the reason for using random assignment when a study involves a therapy group and a waiting control group?

Explanation

When looking at the effectiveness of a therapy, it is difficult to get a control group in order to measure what the person would be like without the therapy. Ethically, holding back a therapy is not possible. However, those waiting for the therapy will receive it, so it is seen as ethical to use them as a control group. This is what Capafóns *et al.* (1998) did. The control group can show that the mere passage of time (without therapy) can affect a phobia, and this helps to show that it is the therapy in the treatment group that works and not merely the passage of time.

Measures

The researchers measured the success of the therapy by using self-report scales and clinical interviewing. They also recorded some physical variables. Measures were:

- an interview to find out about the fear of flying for each person, including their life history
- a fear of flying scale that measured level of anxiety in different flying situations
- two scales measuring a person's catastrophic thoughts (how much they thought a catastrophe would happen) and how much they thought they would have a physical reaction to flying
- a video of a trip on a plane, beginning with packing a case and ending with touchdown at the destination
- physical measures of heart rate, muscular tension and skin temperature.

The dependent variable also needed to be measured – that is, the level of the fear of flying. Effective treatment would mean a lowering or disappearance of the phobia. Measures included:

- answers to three questions: a) how afraid of flying would you say you were? (not at all, a little, very, extremely); b) do you travel by plane when there is no alternative? (various answers to find the level); c) while flying have

you ever had the following symptoms or feelings? (list of answers such as sweating and loss of control)
- fear scales measuring fear during a flight, fear of what goes before the flight and fear about flying when not actually involved in flying
- scales to measure catastrophic thoughts and anxiety
- physical measures of heart rate, palm temperature and muscular tension.

After the treatment, measures were taken after two flights and the first flight was within seven days of the treatment. The physical measures were taken while the patient was watching the video (this was called 'simulation') at the take-off point in the video – this was before the actual flight.

The treatment

All participants were interviewed by the researchers at the start but the other measures were thereafter self-report measures using the scales outlined above. After the interview, the video of someone else taking a flight was shown to the person and physical measures were taken in the university department. The participant (individually) watched the video on a TV screen. There was a practice situation before the video and the 'resting' physical measures were taken then, before the video was shown, and the corresponding physical measures were taken (heart rate, palm temperature and muscle tension). Then there was another interview scheduled either to explain moving on to the treatment or for the next assessment session (for the waiting control group).

The treatment took place in the university and there were two one-hour sessions a week for a patient (between 12 and 15 sessions altogether, finishing the treatment in eight weeks). The treatment involved training in relaxation, imagination and breathing techniques and some 'live' (in vivo) elements as well. There was also a technique of 'stop thinking' and brief relaxation taught, to help in the actual phobic situation.

Results

Results were presented in separate sections because a lot of measures were taken.

- Before and after measures for the control group showed that just the passing of time (the control group did not have the treatment) did not lead to significant changes in the phobia. The before and after measures were the self-report scales, the interview data and the physical measures (anxiety responses).
- Before and after measures for the treatment group showed that 'significant changes took place' (p. 14). There were changes showing improvement in the phobia from the self-report data and the interview data. The physical measures also showed significant improvement. Skin surface temperature and fear without involvement did not show differences between before and after the treatment, but all the other measures did show differences.

Table 4.15 **Results for the treatment group before and after the treatment, giving the mean average as the 'score' – all significantly different (at least $p \leq 0.05$) unless specified**

Measure	Before the treatment	After the treatment
Fear during the flight	25.60	13.25
Fear of preliminaries	21.50	10.15
Fear without involvement (*not significantly different*)	2.40	1.40
Catastrophic thoughts	10.30	5.00
Subjective physiological anxiety	22.60	14.35
Fear level	2.40	1.25
Avoidance behaviour	2.95	1.25
Disagreeable responses	19.00	8.70
Heart rate	1.04	0.99
Temperature (*not significantly different*)	0.99	1.01
Muscular tension	1.34	1.02

- The control group and the treatment group matched well before the treatment.
- The control group and the treatment group showed significant differences after the treatment (palm temperature and fear without involvement were the two measures that showed no significant differences).

Table 4.16 **Results for the control group and the treatment group after the treatment, giving the mean average as the 'score' – all significantly different (at least $p \leq 0.05$) unless specified**

Measure (after the treatment)	Control group	Treatment group
Fear during the flight	25.81	13.25
Fear of preliminaries	21.05	10.15
Fear without involvement (*not significantly different*)	2.24	1.40
Catastrophic thoughts	9.67	5.00
Subjective physiological anxiety	21.90	14.35
Fear level	2.71	1.25
Avoidance behaviour	3.33	1.25
Disagreeable responses	19.90	8.70
Heart rate	1.31	0.99
Temperature (*not significantly different*)	1.01	1.01
Muscular tension	1.31	1.02

- Only one control patient showed similar scores to the treatment group after they had the treatment and two treatment patients maintained scores similar to the control group. These findings added to the conclusion that the treatment had worked well in this phobia.
- Just 10 per cent of the patients with a fear of flying did not show significant changes with regard to their fear after treatment.
- In about 5 per cent of patients, the fear may subside over time (without treatment).

Conclusions

It was clear that the treatment group showed significant improvement in their fear compared with a control group, where such improvement was not found. The two groups did not differ enough before the treatment to think that differences between the groups caused the differences in post-treatment scores. The researchers thought that the passage of time did not help with the phobia (except in one patient) and there was a failure in the treatment for two patients, so the treatment does not work for everyone all of the time.

Capafóns *et al.* (1998) considered aspects of the treatment they thought may have contributed to its success:

- The training in breathing and relaxation was thorough, and practising at home was encouraged.
- The hierarchy was sloped for each individual carefully, with a minimum difference in intensity for each element so that the slope was gradual – and also carefully making sure there was no repetition and the slope kept rising. Each patient had between 25 and 33 elements in the hierarchy.
- Imagination situations were used first and 'real' ones only introduced later, so the move towards 'real' situations was measured and gradual rather than being premature. This meant there were few failures when the real situations were encountered, which would mean the patients saw themselves as more in control and successful.
- The introduction of 'stop–think' and the brief relaxation later in the therapy, to help in real situations, seemed positive.

Progress check 4.33

List four features of systematic desensitisation that might make it successful or contribute to its success (using Capafóns *et al.*'s findings).

Evaluation of Capafóns *et al.* (1998)

Strengths

- Capafóns *et al.* (1998) used a control group that was carefully matched with the treatment group with regards to gender, age, strength of fear and physical measures like heart rate (before treatment). This meant they had a baseline measure for the phobia that they could use when seeing if the treatment had been effective. They could also control for any improvement in the phobia that arose from the simple passage of time. Their study had experimental features that gave it scientific credibility.
- The researchers used a great many measures to see if the phobia had reduced, including interview, self-report measures using scales, and physiological/physical measures like heart rate and muscle tension. They could check all these measures, rather than one measure, and this gives the results credibility too.
- They did not try to generalise the findings beyond showing that systematic desensitisation was successful for a fear of flying and their results were found using people with a fear of flying, so there is validity in the results. The interviews discussed fear of flying with each patient/participant and the researchers made sure that each participant did have such a fear.

Weaknesses

- The results cannot easily be generalised to other fears, which is why the researchers only claim that systematic desensitisation is successful for a phobia of flying. It is tempting to think that the results are likely to be true of other phobias, as the treatment was not different from the 'standard' use of systematic desensitisation. It would have been useful to have included participants with other phobias or to have carried out another study within their main study, focusing on people with a different phobia to see if systematic desensitisation worked for those as well. The researchers admit this and it is a strength that they do not try to generalise beyond the target population; however, having such limited generalisability can still be seen as a weakness. The sample was self-selected, which may also affect the generalisability, though the treatment sample was matched to the control sample so perhaps the sampling did not affect the results.
- Their results also have limited application, which links to the generalisability point above. Ten per cent of the patients (2 out of 20) did not have a reduction in their phobia and 5 per cent of the control group reached the same level of reduction as those in the treatment group (apart from that 10 per cent). These issues about the results do limit the application of the findings. The researchers can only claim that systematic desensitisation helps with a phobia of flying; they cannot claim that it works with other phobias.
- Two measures – fear that needs no involvement in flying and palm temperature – did not show an improvement. This suggests that one of the physical measures did not represent the experience of phobia, which is perhaps

a weakness. Also one of the fear measures did not represent the 'phobia' either. This suggests that the measures were not appropriate, and that is something that could be examined in more detail.

Progress check 4.34

Using the evaluation terms 'validity', 'generalisability' and 'credibility', would you say that Capafóns *et al.*'s (1998) study has value or not?

Test yourself

1 Explain the results of the contemporary study you have covered in the learning theories topic area. **(6 marks)**
2 Compare the procedure of the classic study you covered in learning theories and the contemporary study you chose in the same topic area. **(12 marks)**

Key questions in learning theories

You have to study one key question in each of the topic areas for your course and apply concepts and ideas from the topic area to that issue. Concepts and ideas include research, studies and theories. The two key questions suggested for your course are covered here, but you can choose a different key question to study. In the examination, you may be asked to apply concepts and ideas to a key question that you have not come across before (called 'unseen'). Studying all the key questions will help you to learn how to apply concepts, ideas, theory and research to an unseen key question in the exam.

Would it be a good idea for airline companies to offer treatment programmes for fear of flying?

The issue of therapies for fear of flying relates to classical and operant conditioning and social learning theory.

Describing the issue

Fear of flying is quite common. A *Guardian* article from 28 December 2014 talks about it being a 'spectre that haunts modern life', which suggests that it is something that needs to be addressed. The article suggests that 30 per cent of people flying find air travel challenging, though not all find it terrifying. The article's author talks about the 'pace of contemporary life', which suggests that being able to travel by plane is something people expect to be able to do. Therefore, a phobia of flying, which means someone being unable to fly and thus limiting their life, is an important issue for society. The article discusses Virgin's 'Flying Without Fear' course (www.flyingwithoutfear.co.uk), which focuses on giving information to show that air travel is safe. The course also uses relaxation techniques. EasyJet has a website (www.fearlessflyer.easyjet.com) focusing on the nervous flyer. EasyJet says one in six people has a fear of flying. Another website (www.airsafe.com) says that research in 1980 showed that 18.1 per cent of adults in the US were afraid to fly, and another poll in 1999 found that 50 per cent of the adults who flew on commercial airlines were sometimes afraid. Airlines do address fear of flying and there are other companies offering therapy for fear of flying too. British Airways have a 'flying with confidence' course, and other companies acknowledge the issues. Clearly, the figures about, and the interest in, fear of flying show that it is an issue of sufficient interest to society to warrant investigation and investment. As the airlines are responsible for their passengers, can it be argued that they should be the ones providing the support?

Explaining the issue

- Fears can be acquired through classical conditioning. If someone is feeling stressed at an airport because of all that they have had to do before leaving for a trip, then they can learn to associate their very anxious feelings with flying (or perhaps just the airport).
- Fears can be learned through a pattern of reinforcements, though perhaps it is less likely than the classical conditioning explanation when it comes to flying. Someone might be rewarded for being fearful, such as a child being cuddled by a parent when flying or being about to fly, because of their fear. The child might learn to be fearful for the reward.
- Fears can be learned through social learning. Someone that an individual looks up to might be afraid of flying, so the fear is imitated. Another way that a fear of flying might be learned through social learning is if someone is observed being afraid of flying and is somehow rewarded. Perhaps someone does not want to go somewhere and has to go by plane – if they show fear, they do not have to travel. Someone watching that behaviour might learn that fear.
- These explanations do not link to the airline, however, and do not perhaps suggest that the airline should offer treatment programmes. Having said that, the airline is responsible for getting their passengers to their chosen destination up to a point, and so has a responsibility perhaps to ensure the passengers can board the plan and get to the destination.
- Treatment can include systematic desensitisation, which means facing your fear gradually, working through a

hierarchy of the fear and relaxing throughout. Someone might at first just look at a picture of a plane, and then watch one taking off (on DVD), then they can go to an airport and watch planes taking off, before, in the end, going on a flight. All the time they use relaxation (which is taught) so that their fear response is replaced by a relaxation response.

- Capafóns *et al.* (1998) showed that systematic desensitisation is successful in treating fear of flying with, over a number of measures, finding that the treatment group (compared with a control group not having the treatment) did have reduced fear.
- The programme works using classical conditioning principles. A fear response might have been associated with flying for some reason. This is classical conditioning, as Pavlov explained it. The conditioning works, in this example, by linking the stimulus (flying) with the response (fear). Then there is an association between the stimulus (flying) with another stressful stimulus (e.g. sorting work out before going on holiday). Flying becomes stressful, giving an anxiety response.
- Classical conditioning principles are used to replace relaxation with the anxiety. It would help, too, to try to decrease any anxiety that comes before going on holiday, such as sorting a work situation so that going on holiday is less stressful.
- Meiliyana and Fauzia (2014) carried out a study on one man (a single case study) and used systematic desensitisation to help with his fear of flying (aerophobia). They carried out the programme for eight weeks, using two meetings for each level of the hierarchy, with anxiety and relaxation exercises throughout. There was reduction in anxiety levels after the treatment. However, one participant perhaps does not give sufficient evidence to generalise the findings to others.
- Triscari *et al.* (2011) compared different therapies, which included systematic desensitisation with CBT as opposed to eye movement desensitisation and reprogramming. They found both therapies were effective, showing significant improvement in reducing fear. This shows that systematic desensitisation is effective, as are other methods (and it is with CBT in this example). This study shows that therapy can help the fear.
- As airlines are aware of people's fear of flying, there is perhaps a responsibility to help in overcoming this fear. One way of helping would be to make a simulator available for systematic desensitisation as that would help to make the stimuli realistic while working through the hierarchy. Relaxation must be maintained and the easier it is to access the stimuli in the hierarchy, the more the situation could be practised to help the association.

Explore

Use some of the websites given in the description of the key question above to look at airlines' programmes to help with fear of flying. They tend not to use a full form of systematic desensitisation, instead using a programme of education as well as relaxation.

Progress check 4.35

Give two pieces of evidence that show that airlines could rely on systematic desensitisation as a treatment for fear of flying, to help passengers.

The influence of role models on anorexia

It has been claimed that anorexia could be caused by cultural images, such as 'size-zero' models.

Describing the issue

Anorexia is an eating disorder characterised by being extremely underweight (about 15 per cent lower than it should be) and refusing to eat properly, if at all. Sufferers tend to see themselves as fat even when they are painfully thin. Anorexia usually starts in the teenage years. Girls stop menstruating because their bodies 'shut down'. Boys also suffer from anorexia, but less so than girls, although the rate of anorexia in boys is rising. Around 10 to 15 per cent of those wanting treatment for anorexia or bulimia (another eating disorder) are male. The Anorexia Nervosa and Associated Disorders website (www.ANAD.org) gives statistics. They say that only one in ten people with anorexia receive treatment and only 35 per cent of those getting treatment receive it at a specialist facility. Eating disorders have the highest death rate of any mental disorder. In the American Journal of Psychiatry in 2009, it was claimed by Crow *et al.* that 4 per cent of people with anorexia die; 95 per cent of people with an eating disorder are aged between 12 and 29 years; and 91 per cent of women on a university campus had attempted to control their weight by dieting.

Anorexia is less common outside the Western world. In Britain, it is thought that up to 1 per cent of girls in school and university are anorexic but exact figures are hard to obtain. It is common in some professions, such as models and ballet dancers. Anorexia is self-induced by not eating or by doing too much exercise or by a combination of these behaviours. There are side effects, such as losing interest in socialising, tiredness, feeling cold and stomach pains. Anorexia can last for years. Without treatment, sufferers become ill and may die.

Explore

There is a lot of information about eating disorders on the internet. For example, the National Association of Anorexia Nervosa and Related Disorders (ANAD) contains statistics: www.anad.org/get-information/about-eating-disorders/eating-disorders-statistics/.

Another site focuses on younger people with anorexia nervosa: www.youngminds.org.uk/for_children_young_people/whats_worrying_you/anorexia?gclid=CjwKEAjwk_OhBRD06abu3qSoxlwSJACt7sZ7F0v4eE7Sk5vWtwzKalFh9XPjK4Cgb_ghfMu59la46hoCyrfw_wcB.

Explaining the issue

- Social learning theory suggests that people imitate role models; celebrities and people with prestige are likely to be imitated, although the National Association of Anorexia Nervosa and Associated Disorders state that only about 5 per cent of women in the US match the size shown in advertising as the ideal.
- People who are perceived as similar are also imitated. Therefore, girls are likely to imitate female role models, rather than male role models.
- As the trend in the 2000s is for 'size-zero' catwalk models, it is not surprising, given the principles of social learning theory, that wanting to be thin is commonplace in young people; anorexia can follow that desire. That trend is continuing.

Explore

A *Daily Mail* article in 2010 showed that the trend for size-zero role models has not changed over time. There were concerns before the year 2000 and they continue. Explore more at: www.dailymail.co.uk/health/article-1249683/Teenage-girls-starving-bodies-essential-nutrients-warns-food-watchdog.html.

- Anorexia can also be explained by operant conditioning because of the rewards for being thin and the negative reinforcement against being fat. If peers tease fat children, then to avoid being teased, they will stop eating in order to be thin. If peers are envious of thin children, they will do what they can to become thin, including not eating.
- It could be said that the current focus on an 'obesity crisis' will lead to an increased desire to be thin in order to avoid the criticism of being obese. This would be an example of negative reinforcement.

If thin models and celebrities act as role models, it is likely to lead to girls under-eating

- There are, however, alternative explanations for anorexia. For example, the psychodynamic explanation is that it prevents a girl, who may want to remain a child because of fixation at an early developmental stage, from growing up.
- Cross-cultural differences in levels of anorexia tend to support the explanation for anorexia given by the learning approach because different types of behaviour and social norms are likely to be modelled in different countries. Therefore, if in another culture, there is less emphasis on being thin, then fewer people will try to be thin.

Progress check 4.36

Complete the following table with the figures from this section.

Statement	%
Percentage of people getting treatment for anorexia who receive it in a specialist facility	
Percentage of those with an eating disorder between 12 and 29 years old	
Percentage of those waiting for treatment for anorexia or bulimia that are male	

Test yourself

1 Describe one key question that can be explained using learning theories. (**6 marks**)
2 Explain one key question using concepts, studies and/or research from learning theories. (**8 marks**)

Practical investigation in learning theories

For each topic area in your course, you will be carrying out a practical investigation, using methodology that you have learned about in that topic area. Your practical investigation is to gather data relevant to the material covered in the learning theories section of your course, and must be ethical of course.

Method link: Chapter 5 discusses issues around using observation as a research method as well as issues around analysis of quantitative and qualitative data (pp. 364–370).

Maths link: Chapter 6 discusses graphs and tables, as well as the chi-squared test (pp. 412–416).

Practical link: Chapter 7 takes you through one idea for a practical investigation, including issues around writing up results using qualitative and quantitative data (pp. 454–466).

Issues and debates in learning theories

The 11 issues and debates are summarised (with links to each of the topic areas in your Year 1 course) in Chapter 8 in this book, and then in detail in Book 2.

Chapter summary

- This chapter explains three learning theories - classical conditioning, operant conditioning and social learning theory.
- The chapter covers the work of Pavlov (classical conditioning), Skinner (operant conditioning) and Bandura (social learning theory), including Pavlov's account of his work (1927), Skinner's study about superstition in pigeons (1948) and three studies involving Bandura, looking at how children imitate role models (1961, 1963, 1965).
- The acquisition and maintenance of phobias is explained using learning theories.
- Three therapies that can help with phobias and use learning theory principles are covered (systematic desensitisation, flooding and CBT).
- Two therapies that draw on learning theory principles are covered to help with discussion of this topic area (aversion therapy and token economy).
- Issues highlighting individual differences and development in learning theories are covered.
- Methods in this topic area are observation and content analysis, with focus also on using animals in laboratory experiments, and the ethical issues involved in doing this. There is also focus on psychology as a science as well as on analysis, both of quantitative data (e.g. using the chi-squared test) and qualitative data and use of thematic analysis. This material is covered in detail in Chapters 5 and 6.
- The classic study is Watson and Rayner (1920), the study of Little Albert, and the three contemporary studies covered are Becker *et al.* (2002), Bastian *et al.* (2011) and Capafóns *et al.* (1998).
- The chosen key questions are whether it would be a good idea for airline companies to offer treatment programmes for fear of flying and also how anorexia nervosa can be explained using learning theory principles.
- The practical investigation is to carry out an observation gathering both qualitative and quantitative data and using a chi-squared test to analyse the data. This is covered in detail in Chapter 7.

Chapter Five: Methodology

In your course, for each topic area (social psychology, cognitive psychology, biological psychology and learning theories), there is a method section. In the chapters that focus on each topic area, you will find a brief account of the methodology you have to cover in that topic area. However, Chapter 5 explains the methodology that you need in more detail. Chapter 6 focuses on the mathematical element of your course.

How this chapter is set out

This chapter starts with the methodology required in social psychology, then cognitive psychology, followed by biological psychology and, finally, learning theories.

There is repetition between the topic areas in Year 1 of your course (and the AS) when it comes to methodology. Where there is repetition, links are provided to where the material is first covered in this chapter.

Table 5.1 gives a list of what you need to know for all four topic areas. Note there is some repetition – for example, about controls and analysis of qualitative data, as well as issues around doing experiments. Analysis of quantitative data, focusing on descriptive and inferential statistics, has been left out of this list and will be covered in Chapter 6, which provides the mathematical elements for your Year 1 (and AS) course. However, this chapter does explain issues around both descriptive and inferential testing, in readiness for Chapter 6.

An introduction to methodology in your course

Methodology is the study of how research is carried out and is about how science works. In your course, methodology is part of every topic area: social psychology (Chapter 1), cognitive psychology (Chapter 2), biological psychology (Chapter 3) and learning theories (Chapter 4). Each chapter briefly outlined the methodology to be covered in that topic area. This chapter goes into more detail about all these aspects of methodology, using the order of the topic areas as presented in this book.

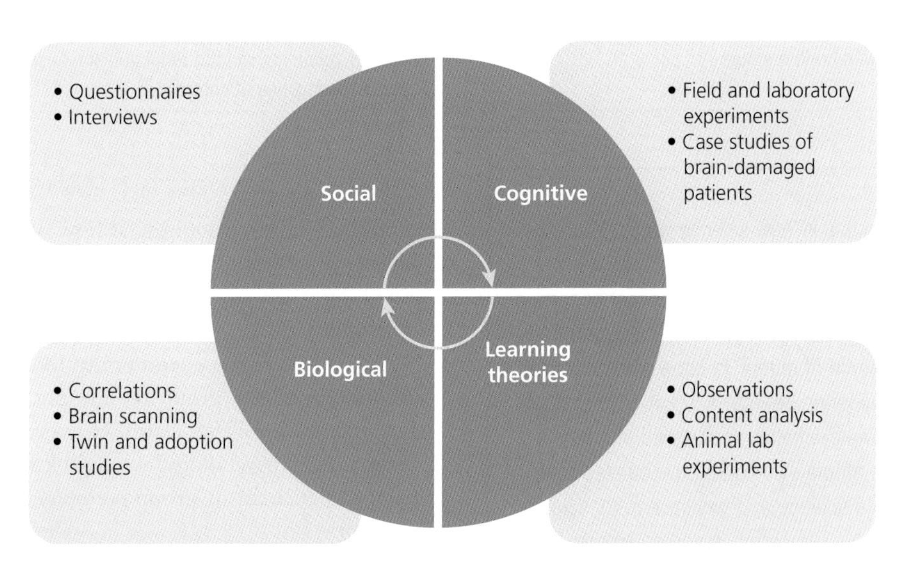

An overview of the research methods covered in Year 1, linked to the topic areas

Table 5.1 What you need to know regarding methods (excluding the maths)

You need to know about:	
Social psychology	**Biological psychology**
Designing and conducting questionnaires	Designing and conducting correlational research
Designing and conducting interviews	Co-variables in correlations compared with IV and DV in experiments
Researcher effects in questionnaires and interviews	Positive, negative correlations and scatter diagrams
Types of interview – structured, unstructured, semi-structured	Issues in using correlations, comparing cause-and-effect analysis, other variables
Open and closed questions (including ranked scale closed questions), qualitative and quantitative data	Experiments to contrast with correlations – control groups, randomising to groups and sampling
Alternate hypotheses	Alternative, experimental and null hypotheses
Four sampling techniques (random, stratified, volunteer, opportunity)	Levels of measurement
BPS Code of Ethics and Conduct (2009) and risk management	Brain scanning – fMRI, CAT, PET
Cognitive psychology	Brain scanning to investigate human behaviour
Designing and conducting experiments, field and laboratory	One twin study and one adoption study
Variables (1) situational, participant, extraneous, confounding	**Learning theories**
Variables (2) IV, DV, operationalisation	Observation as a research method in psychology
Experimental/research designs: repeated measures, independent groups, matched pairs	Qualitative and quantitative data, tallying, event sampling and time sampling
Experimental and null hypotheses	Participant, non-participant, overt and covert observations
Directional (one-tailed) and non-directional (two-tailed) hypotheses and tests	Content analysis as a research method
Counterbalancing, randomising and order effects	Using animals in lab experiments to get data related to humans
Objectivity, reliability and validity	Ethics of using animals in lab experiments
Experimenter effects, demand characteristics and control issues	Analysis of qualitative data using thematic analysis
Analysis of qualitative data – thematic analysis	Scientific study of psychology
Case studies of patients with brain damage	Replicability, reliability, validity, reductionism, falsification, empiricism, hypothesis testing, use of controls

STUDY HINT

A main focus of your course is 'how science works'. You may not feel that methodology is why you chose to study psychology, but if you want to know why people act in certain ways, or how you make decisions when with others, you need to learn about the research of others. To know whether study findings are worth considering, you need to know about their methodology – for example, whether they asked enough people, or whether something else could have caused their findings. Psychology is a science and you have to be scientific when studying it. In each examination, some questions will focus on how science works.

Why study research methods?

Methodology involves looking at how psychology is studied. If you do not know how information has been obtained, how can you know how useful or accurate it is? For example:

- If you are told that we tend not to like people who are not part of our 'group', you might wonder where the evidence is for that claim. However, if you have studied social psychology, you will know that there is a lot of evidence for in-group preference and out-group hostility.
- If you wonder why you tend to obey people in authority and yet your friend does not, you might wonder about

individual differences in obedience. If you have studied social psychology, you will know more about such individual differences and, importantly, how strong the evidence is for the claim that individual differences exist in obedience.

As you have chosen to study psychology, you will be interested in how evidence is gathered – both 'how do they do that?' and 'how do they know that?'

Study of interest

Greenwald and Pettigrew (2014) in the US reviewed findings of studies over the last ten years and found that it is not so much hostility to an out-group that leads to prejudice as it is favouritism towards an in-group. This is a matter of focus, as there is still out-group hostility. It seems to be the case that people prefer those similar to them more than they want to harm people that are different. Greenwald and Pettigrew found that it is not so much that people prefer people who look like them or are similar in age, status or gender. People prefer those who attended the same school or live in the same area. Out-groups are formed of people that are not identified with. If an employer interviews someone who went to the same school or has similar interests, for example, they might dismiss another candidate, not because of discriminating against them directly, but because of in-group favouritism. These conclusions come from a review of studies in the area.

The researchers had difficulties though in using results from the many different studies that looked at in-group and out-group behaviour. For example, they needed studies that found out about both in-group favouritism and out-group hostility in order to pursue their study of these in prejudicial behaviour and not many studies did that. Greenwald and Pettigrew mention that perhaps it is easier ethically to study in-group favouritism, which is another issue when using the findings of many studies to draw conclusions about behaviour. What is interesting is that the two researchers need to discuss the issues around methodology in order to explain their conclusions. This study shows that we cannot simply accept findings of a study or review, but we must look carefully at how conclusions are drawn, to see if they are 'acceptable' conclusions or not.

Hopefully the discussion so far has helped you to see that studying methodology is as interesting as looking at what studies find out. Without understanding methodology in psychology, it is not only hard to judge the value of the findings of studies, but it is also hard to carry out research ourselves, as researchers.

Why evaluate research methods?

When studying psychology, you need to evaluate how secure the information is that you are reading or finding out.

Definition

Evaluation means weighing up different points of view and coming to a conclusion.

In this textbook, **evaluation** points are often presented in the form of strengths and weaknesses; occasionally advantages and disadvantages are given. If what you discover goes against common sense, then it is unlikely to be true. However, you need evidence in order to argue whether it is true or untrue. For example, you might want to claim that no one would obey someone in authority and give electric shocks to a person they have just met. However, psychologists claim that we obey authority figures even when they tell us to do something that we think is unacceptable. Milgram (1963) did an experiment that used good methodology and showed just that. Psychological investigations into obedience have suggested that, in 1968, when US soldiers in My Lai, Vietnam, shot and killed civilian women and children because they were told to, they just did what many of us are likely to do – obeyed orders. Such claims need to be substantiated by strong evidence, which is why all studies and theories are evaluated.

STUDY HINT

This methodology chapter introduces and defines new terms. You should read this section carefully and make notes so that you can build on your learning about methodology.

Method issues can be evaluated according to their **validity**, **reliability**, **generalisability**, credibility, objectivity and subjectivity. Valid findings are those that are 'real life', where what is being measured is what is claimed to be measured. Reliable findings are those where, if a study is done again, the same results are found. Study results are generalisable if the sampling is such that the findings can be said to be true of the wider population that the sample is taken from. Credible findings are those that adhere to common sense and fit with what we think we already know. Objectivity is about not bringing in personal opinions or affecting results in any way that might make them 'subjective'.

Progress check 5.1

Write a paragraph about why methodology is important in psychology. Include three reasons.

Definitions

Generalisability is when a sample in a study represents the chosen population, so that any findings can be said to be true of that population and not just true of that sample. **Reliability** is when results are found again after a study has been repeated. Findings must be reliable for them to be accepted into a body of knowledge in psychology. **Validity** is when a study is done in a setting or a set of circumstances that means that the findings are about 'real life' and are about what they claim to be about. A laboratory experiment is generally in a very controlled setting, which might make the findings not valid.

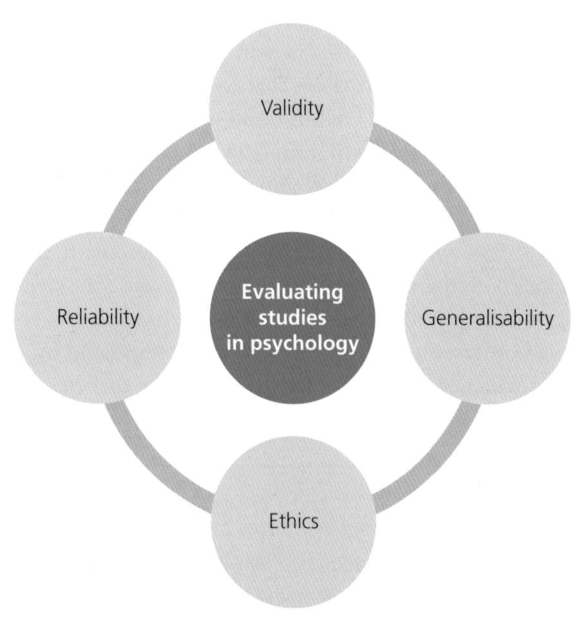

Issues to use when evaluating studies

Progress check 5.2

Using the terms 'valid', 'reliable' and 'generalisable', complete the following paragraph:

Study findings are ________________ if they represent real life in some way and the data are not artificial. Study findings are ________________ if they are such that, when a study is done again, the same results are found. Study findings are ________________ if the sample is representative enough of the population of interest so that findings can be said to apply to that whole population.

Report-writing in psychology

This chapter discusses how psychology is done, which is focusing on methodology, the study of method. Your course covers a lot of studies, including those with a case study focus (e.g. Schmolck *et al.*, 2002, one of the contemporary studies in cognitive psychology), experiments (e.g. the classic study in cognitive psychology, Baddeley, 1966b), and questionnaires (e.g. Cohrs *et al.*, 2012, one of the contemporary studies in social psychology). These research methods and others are the subject matter in this chapter.

Studies in this textbook are summarised as there would be no room for each study to be reproduced in full and, in any case, studies are copyrighted and permission has to be granted for them to be used in the same format as they are written. You may, however, have looked at some full studies – some are easily available online.

Explanation

When a study is written up, no matter what research method is used or what is investigated, the write-up is in the format of a **report**, which has a set structure. The structure is title, abstract, introduction, method (participants, materials, procedure, design), results, discussion (conclusions), references, appendices. For your practical investigations in your course, you will write up some of your own study each time. This is so that you understand how to write up the various parts of a report.

A study is written up in a **report** with a formal structure. Studies start with what is called an **abstract**, which is a brief summary of the whole study and a useful start to reading a study. This is because you then already have an idea of what has been done and what was found.

Title | Abstract | Introduction | Method | Results | Discussion | References | Appendices

The format of a report in psychology

Explanation

A full study has the **abstract** first, which is a very short summary of the aim(s), procedure, results and conclusion(s) so that the reader knows the overview before reading the study. An abstract can also help when doing research as you then have an idea of what is in a study without having to read the whole report.

The structure of a report can vary a little because different academic journals, where studies are published, have some different requirements but the format is very similar for all reports in psychology. Chapter 7 includes more information about what each part of a report needs to contain because it covers the practical investigations you need to do for your course, and it is in the practical investigations that you will be writing up parts of a report.

Academic journals

When a study has been carried out, it is usual for the researchers to want it to be published in an academic journal for other researchers to read about it and perhaps use the findings to build a body of knowledge. Other researchers can replicate the study or take a part of it to test. There are many academic journals, and the researchers will choose the one that best suits their area of work. Some academic journals are listed in Table 5.2. Academic journals present new studies and also give comment on existing work. Some journal articles review the work of others, and some present new studies. In psychology, there are a great many academic journals globally, numbering more than 90.

Table 5.2 Some academic journals in psychology

Academic journals	
Behavioural and Brain Sciences	*Evolutionary Psychology*
British Journal of Psychology	*The International Journal of Aviation Psychology*
British Journal of Clinical Psychology	*Journal of Applied Social Psychology*
Cerebral Cortex	*Personality and Individual Differences*
Developmental Psychology	*Psychology of Music*
Ecological Psychology	*Work and Stress*

Progress check 5.3

Match the journals with their likely area of interest:

Journal	Area of interest
A *Psychology of Music*	1 Effects of community service on adolescent development
B *Personality and Individual Differences*	2 Relationship and communication in music therapy
C *Child Psychology*	3 Adaptive and maladaptive thinking after loss
D *British Journal of Clinical Psychology*	4 Why people use Facebook

Peer reviewing

Before a study is accepted by the editors of a journal, it will be sent to others in the area of work for them to read and 'pass' it as suitable for publication. These are peers of the researchers, people working in the same area of study at the same time. This is called **peer reviewing**. Peer reviewing is necessary as it means that anyone using the study can rely on it having scientific credibility.

Definition

Peer reviewing is the process whereby peers of researchers, people who know the area of study, check a study before it is published, to make sure there is scientific credibility. The reviewers look at validity, reliability, generalisability and other issues, such as the analysis of the data, to make sure that a study is suitable for publication.

STUDY HINT

You need to know about the peer reviewing process for the full A level, so it is worth making a note about it here. It is a way of ensuring that studies that are published are done in a way that makes them scientifically credible. You can use the existence of peer reviewing when discussing the issue and debate about psychology and science.

Progress check 5.4

Which of the following definitions best describes peer reviewing?

1. Peer reviewing is about checking with other researchers before writing up a study.
2. Peer reviewing involves a publisher sending out a study report to check for scientific credibility before publishing the study.
3. Peer reviewing involves researchers helping one another when analysing results of a study.

Methods in social psychology

In your Year 1 study of psychology, there are method issues in the social psychology section that are unique to that topic area and also method issues that appear again. This chapter is written to be readable in sequence, so where method issues appear again, you are signposted to where the issue was previously explained, to avoid repetition. Therefore, the social psychology method section explains all the method issues required, whereas the cognitive psychology section might refer you back to previously discussed issues.

At the start of a study is the research question, which is what the researcher wants to find out about. The research question gives the aim/s of the study. This section starts with aims and hypotheses and then looks at the main methods for social psychology: questionnaires and interviews.

Aims and hypotheses

Studies are planned with an **aim**, or aims, in mind – for example, in social psychology, aims can be 'to find out attitudes to prejudice' or 'to look at why we obey those in authority'. The aim of a study should be summed up in a general statement without detail of what is to be measured or examined in order to find the answers.

Definition

The **aim** of a study is what the research question is - what the researcher wants to find out.

From some aims, a researcher needs to generate one or more **hypotheses**. For example, you could ask people about their attitudes to prejudice (the aim) but you would find out more if you decided what you were looking for in more detail (the hypothesis) – to try to find out if 'older people (50–60 year olds) say they dislike younger people more than younger people (20–30 year olds) say they dislike older people'. The hypothesis would be: older people (50–60 year olds) say they dislike younger people more than younger people (20–30 year olds) say they dislike older people.

In this example, the aim might be to see if older people are more prejudiced than young people. The hypothesis must have **operationalised** variables. So age has to be measurable, and 'older' and 'younger' have to be. Prejudice is defined too as 'who is said to be disliked by the participants' – which is measurable because we can ask participants. Variables that are not operationalised (made measurable) can be used in a study, because some studies gather more qualitative data in the form of narrative, for example (see page 287). A study where variables are not operationalised would have an aim but not a hypothesis.

Definitions

An **hypothesis** is a statement that is set out in such a way that it is testable, what is to be measured is operationalised, and how it is to be measured is operationalised too.

Operationalisation of a variable means making it measurable in practice. For example, 'prejudice' can be measured by asking someone to rate their liking of a group. 'Older' people can be operationalised as being 50-60 years old. 'Younger' people can be operationalised as being 20-30 years old.

For another study, you could decide what aspect of prejudice to measure. For example, you could measure discrimination in employment (you could investigate the race of employees or applicants) or prejudice at a personal level (you could ask who people like to have living next door to them). Possible hypotheses are: 'there are more white people than black people in well-paid jobs' (over a particular salary) and 'there are more people who prefer those of the same race to live nearby than those who do not mind who lives nearby'.

A hypothesis about obedience might be: 'When told to queue in a bank, more older people (45+) than younger people (under 45) obey'.

The hypothesis in a study is the statement of the predicted result and should involve testable elements. Questionnaires and interviews require **alternative hypotheses**; they are alternatives to the **null hypothesis**, which is tested using statistics.

Experiments are specific and have hypotheses that are alternatives to the null hypothesis. In an experiment, the alternative hypothesis is called the **experimental hypothesis**. More about experimental and null hypotheses is discussed in the cognitive psychology section of this chapter (page 318).

Definitions

The **alternative hypothesis** is the hypothesis that states what will happen in a given situation. The **null hypothesis** is the hypothesis that states that something that is predicted in an alternative hypothesis will not happen, and changes that are found as a result of a study are down to chance and not to the prediction. In an experiment, the alternative hypothesis is called the **experimental hypothesis**.

Progress check 5.5

One of the following statements is the aim of a study; the other is the hypothesis. Choose which is which and then make notes about what 'aim' and 'hypothesis' mean in a study:

1. The researchers wanted to know whether there were gender differences in verbal tasks.
2. Girls describe more features in a picture than boys describe.

The questionnaire research method

In social psychology, the two **research methods** covered are questionnaires and interviews. First, we will look at questionnaires. Questionnaires are data collection tools. There are many other data collection tools, such as using videos, photos from cameras, drawings, essays, conversations or newspaper articles. A questionnaire is a research method in its own right. Questionnaires usually ask people to give responses about themselves and/or their ideas – this is **self-report data**.

Strengths of self-report data include the following:

- The individual is answering about themselves, so the data are direct and not likely to be affected by **subjectivity** of a researcher. Subjectivity can come from the researcher's views or the way the questions are asked; it is a form of bias. There is an **objectivity** about the data. Though the replies are subjective (being from the individual about the individual), this is being subjective in a good way as it is more likely to mean the data are valid (e.g. because data reflect the meanings of the participant).
- Self-report data are likely to be **valid** because the person concerned is giving the data themselves. This links to the strength above.

Definitions

Objectivity is found when results are not affected by the researcher or by preconceived ideas. The opposite is **subjectivity**, which is when data are affected by individuals. For example, a researcher can analyse qualitative data with their own views in mind, which is not being objective, and is likely to affect the data. In general, subjectivity is not good, unless someone wants a person's own opinions.

Weaknesses of self-report data include the following:

- People can be biased when reporting on their own feelings, views, attitudes, behaviour and other such issues. An example of such bias is **social desirability**, which is explained later in this section (page 288). People might answer how they think they 'should' answer, which won't uncover their own meanings. A multi-modal approach is usually preferred, which means using ways other than 'self-report' alone, as that avoids bias. Cohrs *et al.* (2012) tested whether **peer-report data** are different from self-report data. They found peers rated people for prejudice in a similar way to how the person rated themselves, so self-report data seem reasonably reliable, which is a strength.
- People might be in different moods or have different ideas about their behaviour on one day compared with another day. So, to that extent, data are valid for the day the questions were asked, but might not be true for every day and all situations.

Definitions

Research method is the term for a main method such as questionnaire, interview, experiment, case study. 'Method' can be used for different parts of methodology, so in this book 'research method' is used for the overall method used. **Self-report data** are gathered mainly by interview and questionnaire and self-report data represent what someone says about themselves. **Peer-report data** are where someone who knows the participant (a peer) answers questions about the participant.

Explanation

Be aware that experiments can use questionnaires to gather data - whether something is a questionnaire or an experiment is about the controls and how the research is set up, not just whether a questionnaire is used. See later in this chapter when experiments are discussed (pp. 317-326).

Explore

Use the internet to find three questionnaires about different issues. Note three similarities and three differences between them. Consider the construction of each questionnaire, what the aim is and how well it succeeds. www.surveymonkey.com enables the construction of questionnaires – you could look at that site for examples and templates.

STUDY HINT

This section looks at questionnaires, and you have probably come across the use of questionnaires in other subjects or at GCSE. When you can, use your previous learning.

Planning questionnaires

Questionnaires involve asking people items about a topic of interest, which seems quite a simple thing to do. However, questionnaires have to be designed carefully. They ask for **personal data**, such as age, gender and background, and have other questions/items relevant to the topic. Ethically, questionnaires must only ever ask what the researcher really needs to know. Questionnaires also gather the **data** needed to answer the questions posed in the aim and hypothesis. Items in a questionnaire can take different formats and there is no right or wrong way of writing a questionnaire. Four formats for the topic of 'finding out about yourself and your friends' are given below.

Definitions

An **item** on a questionnaire is often a question but can be a statement asking for a response. For example, if a questionnaire includes 'explain your sleep patterns', this isn't technically a question, so is called an 'item'. **Data** are the numbers or writing, photos or conversations, gathered or recorded in a study. 'Data' is plural, just as 'media' is plural. Scores on a test are data and essays written by children can be data. All psychology studies involve collecting data. **Personal data** involve information about someone that is personal to them, such as their age, occupation, gender, characteristics.

A Likert-type/ranked scale item

Tick the appropriate box in the statements below.

Key: SA = strongly agree, A = agree, DK = don't know (unsure), D = disagree, SD = strongly disagree

Statement	SA	A	DK	D	SD
I like meeting new people	❑	❑	❑	❑	❑
I enjoy finding out about others	❑	❑	❑	❑	❑
I prefer the company of people like myself	❑	❑	❑	❑	❑
I prefer to go out with my friends	❑	❑	❑	❑	❑

A rating scale item

Rate yourself on the following scales by putting a mark in the appropriate place on the line:

Happy	0 ______________________	10	Sad
Generous	0 ______________________	10	Mean
Friendly	0 ______________________	10	Unfriendly

Identifying characteristics

Circle those characteristics that you think apply to your best friend.

Mean Caring Unkind

Kind Spiteful Only child Slow

Thoughtful Intelligent Sporty Fussy

Sweet Untidy Gentle Pretty

Handsome Neat

An open question

How do you think that you are perceived by others?

____

____

____

Progress check 5.6

Write out one example for each of the questions/item types given above. For example, you could focus on a questionnaire to find out about eating habits of pupils in a school.

Some general points about questionnaires include the following:

- You can use any question/item format that you like, depending on your aim.
- More straightforward questions usually come first, followed by more in-depth questions.
- Questions gathering personal data are best placed at the end, so that they do not take up the time of the **respondent**, who might get bored too quickly.
- For ethical and practical reasons, questionnaires should not be very long – you do not want the respondent to give up halfway through. Two sides of A4 are often enough; longer than four sides is probably too long, although there are exceptions.
- A **pilot** survey is usually carried out, perhaps using friends and family as the respondents. This tests questions for clarity and allows the person conducting the survey to make sure that the required information will be gathered.
- Data from a questionnaire are analysed and the analysis, taking perhaps two questions and their responses, can then fit into one of the participant **designs** explained in the cognitive psychology section of this chapter. For example, if data from the same person are used as two scores (perhaps their score being an agent to authority in one situation and their score in a different situation, looking for a difference in their obedience in the two situations) then that would be a **repeated measures design**, so called because the same person responds to two conditions. If data from different participants are compared to look for a difference, such as the male scores on one question and the female scores on another question, the scores come from different people, and this is called an **independent groups design**. When you read more about research designs in the cognitive psychology section in this chapter (pp. 321–333), remember to relate your learning back to other research methods, including questionnaires.

Questions should be set so that the respondent will read them carefully and respond accurately. If, for a particular respondent, the answer to the first four questions is likely to be 'no', the respondent might continue to answer 'no'. For example, when asking about gender and driving, if the first four questions were whether females drive bigger cars better, whether females pass their tests sooner, whether females are better drivers and whether females are good at parking, a respondent might want to answer 'no' to each one and a pattern might be formed. It would be better to change at least one of the questions – for example, ask whether males are better at parking. A response set, or **response bias**, is the tendency to stick to one response throughout and the way questions are asked can lead to a response bias. Questions should be set up in order to obtain a range of responses.

In general, negatives in questions should be avoided – for example, asking whether a person is *not* a racist or whether females do *not* drive bigger cars better than males. In a face-to-face situation when carrying out a questionnaire, care should be taken to ask questions impartially. This is to avoid any bias, either from the tone in which the questions are asked or from other bias from the researcher, such as facial expression.

Definitions

A **response bias** is when someone starts off answering 'no' to a few questions (or 'yes' to a few questions – this is called an acquiescence response bias) on a questionnaire and then continues with the same response, giving a pattern of responses. Such responses may be due to the response bias, not what the person would have said in response to the item. **Respondent** is the term for the person answering the items on a questionnaire – the person responding. A **pilot** is a practice run, which is used, for example, to test the clarity of the wording of items in a questionnaire. A pilot can lead to more reliability if issues are dealt with – for example, rewording an item if it might be interpreted differently by different people.

Closed-ended and open-ended questions

Questionnaires involve **closed-ended questions** (or **closed questions**) in which the response choices are limited – for example, **dichotomies** (e.g. yes/no answers).

> ### Definition
> **Dichotomy** means division into two parts.

In the examples on page 284, the Likert-type scale, the rating scale and 'identifying characteristics' show closed-ended questions. There are also **open-ended** questions (or **open questions**), such as 'How do you think others see you?' Open-ended questions allow the respondent to state their attitudes and opinions. Both types of question have strengths and weaknesses, so questionnaires usually include both.

> ### Definitions
> **Closed-ended (closed)** questions are where there is a specific answer and no possibility of extending the answer.
> **Open-ended (open)** questions are where the respondent can answer freely, without the responses being constrained.

Strengths and weaknesses of closed-ended questions

- One strength is that all respondents give standard answers (e.g. 'yes', 'no' or 'unsure', or a rating out of 5), therefore, numbers can be generated (e.g. how many say 'yes' or 'no', or a score from adding up the ratings). Analysis is straightforward because one set of responses can be compared fairly with another set. Percentages and averages can be calculated.
- A second strength is that questions are the same for all respondents and the set of answers, and the question wording, can be used to make the sense of the question clear. If the meaning is the same for all respondents, then the questionnaire is more reliable. Questionnaires using closed-ended questions are reasonably reliable.
- One weakness of closed-ended questions is that they force a respondent to choose from a set of answers, when the respondent might not agree with any of the choices. For example, if asked whether someone is being obedient or not, even if there is an 'unsure' category, respondents have to consider obedience, and they may not see the situation in that way. If respondents cannot say what they want to say, then the answers are not accurate and are therefore not valid. Questionnaires using closed-ended questions may not be valid.
- A second weakness is that the choice answers could mean different things to different respondents. For example, 'unsure' could mean 'don't know' or 'sometimes yes and sometimes no', but would be scored the same. This would mean that the questionnaire is not producing valid data.

Strengths and weaknesses of open-ended questions

- One strength of open-ended questions is that respondents are not forced into specific answers but can say what they want to say. Questionnaires using open-ended questions tend to obtain richer, more detailed data.
- Another strength is that not only are the answers more detailed, but the questions can be interpreted by the respondents. If the question asks what respondents think about prejudice, the reply can interpret what 'prejudice' means to them. For example, some might write about the rights of immigrants; others might write about the rights of the indigenous population (those 'naturally' from that country). Questionnaires using open-ended questions are, therefore, more valid because they enable respondents to talk more about what they 'really' think.
- One weakness of open-ended questions is that they are difficult to analyse because the answers are likely to be detailed and also different from one another.
- A second weakness is the difficulty of displaying the results after they have been analysed. Because the data are qualitative, averages cannot be calculated and the data cannot be displayed in tables or graphs.
- A third weakness is that respondents often fail to complete their answers to open-ended questions, probably because such responses take longer and also because it is more difficult to think of the answer than it is to tick a forced-choice set of boxes.

> **STUDY HINT**
> Notice that when two opposing aspects of methodology are considered – for example, two types of question (closed or open) – often a strength for one is a weakness for the other.

Issues and debates

Make a list of reasons why validity might be more important than reliability in a study's findings, and a list of reasons for why you might choose reliability over validity. Link your ideas to psychology as a science – you might find that reliability is better if you are focusing on psychology as a science and validity is more important if you are thinking of studying people as a whole. File your ideas in your 'Issues and Debates' section of notes.

Test yourself

1 Explain, using examples, the differences between closed and open-ended questions. **(6 marks)**
2 Discuss problems with using a questionnaire to gather data, in terms of biases that affect either the reliability or the validity of the data. **(8 marks)**

Quantitative and qualitative data

Questionnaires tend to gather both qualitative and quantitative data, as can interviews. Some research methods gather either qualitative or quantitative data (e.g. experiments tend to focus on quantitative data) and some studies use **mixed methods**, where both qualitative and quantitative data are likely to be involved.

- **Qualitative data** involve ideas and opinions. People relate a story in answer to a question, such as why they prefer people that are similar to them.
- **Quantitative data** involve numbers (e.g. numbers of 'yes' and 'no' answers) or percentages (e.g. percentage of people saying that they would offer a job to someone from the same school over someone they did not know).
- Open-ended questions produce qualitative data; closed-ended questions produce quantitative data.

Progress check 5.7

Decide whether the following questions would produce qualitative or quantitative data.

1 Do you agree that everyone should have the same job opportunities? Yes or no?
2 Rate on a scale of 0-5 (0 = not at all; 5 = totally) how much you agree with the statement 'everyone should have the same job opportunities'.
3 What do you think about people who discriminate against others because of their race?

Definitions

Quantitative data are about quantity - numbers.
Qualitative data are about quality - detailed and free answers, such as giving ideas and opinions.

Strengths and weaknesses of qualitative data

- A strength is that they give detailed information on a subject and allow in-depth analysis. For example, a respondent might say, 'I think it is right to stop any discrimination on grounds of race *and* I want to know more', and another respondent might say, 'I think it is right to stop any discrimination on the grounds of race *but* I want to know more'. The first respondent wants to stop discrimination; the second respondent thinks it is right to stop discrimination, but perhaps only to an extent. The use of 'and' or 'but' has changed the meaning. Such in-depth analysis adds useful understanding.
- Another strength of qualitative data, which in a questionnaire comes from open-ended questions, is that there is more validity. Respondents can say what they really think about an issue.
- One weakness of qualitative data is that they are hard to analyse in order to compare responses. Answers might be so different that they are difficult to categorise, and the results can be long and hard to summarise.
- A second weakness is that they are not easy to gather because respondents might be reluctant to give an in-depth response or because the data might take a long time to gather. On questionnaires, respondents often miss out the open-ended questions – perhaps because it takes longer to write out answers than to tick boxes. Qualitative data are also gathered from other research methods. Whatever the method used, it tends to take a long time to gather such data compared with gathering quantitative data.

Strengths and weaknesses of quantitative data

- A strength is that they can be fairly quickly and easily analysed, and averages, percentages and other statistics can be calculated. The data can be represented in graphs and tables, which means that research results can be more easily and efficiently communicated to others.

STUDY HINT
When learning strengths and weaknesses, don't make your notes too short. The text here says that quantitative data can be fairly easily analysed, but if you just say 'they are easy to analyse', this is not enough to show understanding. Better to say what you mean by 'easy', e.g. averages can be calculated and put into tables, which is easier than generating themes, as is done for qualitative data.

- Another strength is reliability. The way that they are gathered is controlled sufficiently well for the test to be repeated to see if similar results are found. Quantitative data in questionnaires come from closed-ended questions, so the strengths of closed-ended questions apply. Quantitative data can also be gathered by other research methods, such as experiments, and the strength of reliability still applies.
- A further strength is that the researcher puts **controls** into place to make sure that any test can be repeated and give the same results. Control of the setting and the **tools** used are all important.

- One weakness of quantitative data is that they may not be valid because the respondents have a forced choice of answer. They may have to reply 'untruthfully'.

Explanation

The same strengths of gathering quantitative data apply in all research methods that gather quantitative data, not just questionnaires - good controls, giving reliable data.

- A second weakness of quantitative data is that respondents may be answering so quickly that they do not check their answers or simply do not bother about their answers.
- A third weakness is that respondents may be so guided by how the questions are set that they do not answer 'truthfully'. When writing their opinions in answer to open-ended questions (or talking about themselves for a case study), they are unlikely to lie – they would probably miss out the question instead. However, with quantitative data from closed-ended questions, respondents could lie or be misled:
    - One aspect of 'lying' in answer to a questionnaire is **social desirability**. Respondents might say what they think they ought to say. For example, in British culture, if asked if they are racist, with options of 'yes', 'no' and 'unsure', respondents are unlikely to say 'yes' or 'unsure', because it is not acceptable in Britain to be racist. Social desirability may also affect answers to open-ended questions and qualitative data. However, the opportunity to analyse the wording used and the detail of the answer may mean that such a tendency comes to light, whereas with quantitative data, social desirability is less likely to be detected.
    - A second aspect of 'lying' in answer to a questionnaire is **demand characteristics**. Questions that produce quantitative data and give forced-choice answers might hint at the aim of the questionnaire. Respondents might want to help the researcher, so they give the answers they think are wanted – or they might not want to help and give different answers. In either case, the responses lack validity because they are not 'true' answers. Quantitative data tend to come from controlled studies and are more likely to suffer from demand characteristics than do qualitative data. This is because, with a clear aim and hypothesis, there are more likely to be clues about what the researcher is investigating.
    - A third aspect of 'lying' in a questionnaire is when there is a response set or response bias. If questions are listed so that respondents are likely to be answering 'no' to a number of questions in a pattern, they might continue to answer 'no' out of habit. It is also possible that a respondent may have a personality trait to agree, or to disagree, all the time.

Definitions

Tools in a study refer to the means of collecting the data. A questionnaire is a tool, as is an interview schedule. **Social desirability** is the tendency to answer in a way that is socially acceptable, and this would mean data are not valid. **Demand characteristics** refer to when a participant can guess the aim(s) of a study and so works to 'help' the researcher (or works against the researcher), which means data are not valid. **Controls** are put in place in a study to make sure that only what is of interest is affecting the findings of a study, not other issues or variables. For example, if some respondents had different instructions about completing a questionnaire than other respondents, the instructions could affect their answers, so the answers cannot be compared fairly. A control would be having **standardised instructions**, when what is said to the participant about a study is the same for all participants so that the findings are not different because of different instructions. This is a control.

Summary of methodology terms so far

Stopping at this stage to review what has been covered would be a good idea, as a lot of terms and ideas have been introduced. You will find that these terms are repeated throughout this methodology chapter, so they will become more familiar. For example, qualitative and quantitative data are important in the other topic areas as well as social psychology, as are controls. The evaluation terms, such as validity and reliability, also occur throughout your course. It is worth remembering why studying methodology in psychology is important, and to make it relevant and interesting. For example, if government policy about putting up the price of alcohol comes from figures about the rising health damage being done to young people through drinking alcohol, we would want such figures to be accurate, and to come from 'good' studies and 'strong' findings.

Explore

Have a look at an area where there are official policies coming from evidence from studies. For example, www.drinkaware.co.uk. At first, you might find statements that do not seem to be evidence based (such as about alcohol causing liver damage) as a website often does not explain the evidence for the arguments. However, try to find mention of percentages or evidence. Go further and track the evidence down. This will show how important it is to consider the methodology involved in finding out information when deciding how far to accept that evidence.

You could group terms to help learning:

- terms about the research question: aims, alternative hypothesis, experimental hypothesis, null hypothesis, operationalisation
- terms about questionnaires: pilot study, Likert-style questions, ranked scales, personal data, respondent, tools, open questions, closed questions
- types of data: qualitative, quantitative
- evaluation terms: validity, reliability, objectivity, subjectivity, generalisability and credibility
- terms about bias in studies: social desirability, demand characteristics
- terms to control (or avoid) bias: controls, standardised instructions, response set.

STUDY HINT

Use index cards and put a term on one side with its explanation/description on the other side, to help with learning and revision. Work with someone else to recall the term from the explanation or to define the term given.

Progress check 5.8

Complete this passage using the following terms: valid, standardised instructions, qualitative, social desirability, respondent, quantitative, demand characteristics

A problem with a questionnaire is that the ________________ might not tell the truth. They may say what they think society wants them to say, which is called ____________________________.
They may respond to try and help the researcher by guessing the aim of the study and replying accordingly. This is called ____________________________.
If data are affected by these sorts of issues, then they are probably not ________________ data. A researcher uses ________________ ________________ as a control, to be sure all the respondents receive the same information about the study. Often a questionnaire involves gathering both in-depth, detailed ________________ data as well as using closed questions, which yield ________________ data.

Test yourself

Why is it important to know how a study is carried out, in terms of methodological decisions? **(6 marks)**

Ethical and sampling issues in research

Ethical and sampling issues are discussed in depth later in this chapter (pp. 299–314). They are both important issues when carrying out questionnaires and when carrying out interviews (as well as when using other research methods), so are dealt with together after the questionnaire and the interview research method are considered. These issues are mentioned here because questionnaires have been covered now in good detail and could not be carried out without knowing about ethics and sampling.

Issues and debates

Psychology can be defined as the scientific study of mind and behaviour. Ethical issues are always there in any study, just as ethics are important in any dealings with people. Consider why every study is going to involve being ethical and why 'ethics' is a debate in psychology. Ethical issues in psychology is one of the issues and debates in your course, so make notes to file in your 'Issues and Debates' section of notes.

Analysing questionnaires

Questionnaires gather both qualitative and quantitative data, so both need to be analysed.

Analysis of quantitative data

Analysis of a questionnaire depends on whether the questions are open-ended or closed-ended. Closed-ended questions need the answers adding up (for example, the total number of 'yes' answers compared with the total number of 'no' answers). From totals, percentages can be calculated. Chapter 6 (pp. 387–397) explores analysis of quantitative data from closed-ended questions further.

Maths link: Chapter 6 is about the mathematical skills (such as showing how to analyse quantitative data) you will need for Year 1 of your course (and the AS).

Analysis of qualitative data

As analysis of qualitative data does not have a mathematical element, so is dealt with here.

Open questions gather qualitative data and qualitative data are analysed differently from quantitative data. Since respondents present their answers to open-ended questions in different ways, analysis of such qualitative data is in the form of generating themes. For example, if participants were asked the question, 'How do you think you are perceived by others?', some responses might be:

- **Participant 1**: 'I think in general everyone likes me, but I'm not attractive.'
- **Participant 2**: 'I don't think I'm liked much, but they think I'm clever.'
- **Participant 3**: 'I'm seen as fat and jolly, so they think I'm fun.'

From these responses, the following four themes could be generated:

- being liked
- physical appearance
- being clever
- being fun.

The participants' responses are then analysed by theme:

- being liked – yes, 1; no, 1
- being clever – yes, 1; no, 0
- physical appearance – 2 (fat, unattractive)
- being fun – yes, 1

In this example, more data would be analysed and, assuming similar themes were involved, a conclusion could be that people judge how others see them in terms of physical appearance, whether they are liked or not, and using other traits like 'fun to be with' or 'clever'. With regard to physical appearance, perhaps people are insecure and think they are seen in a negative way (fat, unattractive). There is also one theme here of fat = jolly = fun, which may be found in other data too.

In general, young people like having friends around them – perhaps those with more friends are happier meeting new people

There are various different strategies for analysing qualitative data. This section looks at thematic analysis, a basic technique, as that is what you need to know about for the social psychology element of your course. For Year 2, you will look at grounded theory as well, but you don't need to know about that in Year 1 (or the AS).

> **STUDY HINT**
> At the start of Chapters 1–4, you will find a suggested checklist giving you all that you need to cover in that topic area. In Chapter 1, social psychology, the checklist mentions knowing about thematic analysis. Make your own checklist and keep it nearby as you study. Have the specification near you as well. You should know what you need to cover: realising that thematic analysis is an important part of your course will help you to learn about it, and to take notes.

Thematic analysis

Since respondents present their answers to open-ended questions in different ways, and their answers can take any direction, analysis of such qualitative data is in the form of generating themes, using **thematic analysis**. Thematic analysis requires the researcher to be very familiar with their data. The researcher uses **coding** to group the data and, from the coding, develop a limited number of themes. The themes must represent the data fairly. The analysis develops, and a researcher might go back and forth, going over the data more than once, re-coding in the light of developing themes. Instances of the themes can then be counted, turning qualitative data into quantitative data, and then calculations can be carried out (as explained in Chapter 6).

> **Definitions**
> **Thematic analysis** means the researcher identifies a limited number of themes that reflect their data, by going into great detail in studying their data to develop the themes. **Coding** refers to interpreting and grouping data somehow. For example, when there are a lot of qualitative data about a question, such as 'why do you think prejudice occurs?', coding might take the form of interpreting every idea so that ideas can then be grouped, for example by annotating an (a) against the first idea that is come across and a (b) to the next one. If at any time the coder comes across the first idea again, (a) is written alongside it, and so on.

There are phases in thematic analysis. The first phase is to become very familiar with the data, and then coding. The coding is worked through to group together the ideas and the ideas are considered to see if they are common enough to become a theme, or whether ideas have to be grouped into one theme. Themes must suit the researcher's purpose. Themes are defined and named, which will tend to happen during the process as identifying them is likely to involve summarising them/naming them.

The coding is an important phase as the coder works to identify the ideas in the data, and not to interpret the data into ideas. A researcher could have their research idea in mind and look for instances that relate to their research question, but this interpretation will bring in subjectivity. The idea is that analysis of qualitative data picks up on the meanings of the respondents and not the meanings of the researcher.

The general idea is that coding must be done without preconceptions about what will be found (e.g. not having ideas already about what people think causes prejudice). One idea it to use a coder who does not know the research question or aim(s). Another idea is to use more than one coder to see if the ideas that are identified agree with one another. A researcher can code the data themselves and also ask another researcher to do the coding separately.

Sometimes thematic analysis can be done using existing theory, and coding would follow existing ideas.

A **reflexive journal** can be used during thematic analysis. This is a record of the whole process, from starting with the raw data. In a questionnaire, data are likely to come from an open question; in an interview, there might be a full transcript. The original data are the raw data, collected before analysis. The researcher starts with coding and at that stage starts their reflexive journal. The end report, after the analysis, can include ideas from the reflexive journal, so that the reader of the report can judge the 'accuracy' of the analysed data presented in the report. A reflexive journal can log how coding is done, thoughts when doing the coding, ideas that develop about themes during the coding process, and ideas that relate to the research question, ready for the part of the analysis that links to the aims of the study.

Table 5.3 Doing thematic analysis

Stage of thematic analysis	Explanation of each stage
Gather	Gather qualitative data using a suitable data-gathering tool, such as a questionnaire or interview.
Journal	Begin a reflexive journal, which is kept throughout. This is to log the process of carrying out a thematic analysis, so that the process is transparent and can form part of the final report.
Prepare	Transcribe the data carefully, using no interpretation, and prepare the data ready for analysis. This can mean typing notes out into one document or photocopying data so that they are readily available.
Appoint	Appoint coders. The researcher can be a coder but does not have to be. Coders might not know the aims of the study, which can help (though if the study is theory-driven perhaps the theory must be known by the coder). There can be more than one coder to test for reliability.
Familiarise	The data have to become well-known and familiar to the coder(s). Decisions have to be made about where to start but if coding is faithful to the original it should not matter which data are coded first.
Ideas	Each piece of data (e.g. a statement by a respondent) has to be identified as an idea, to shorten what is said or found into something manageable. For example, when asked about what they think about prejudice, someone might say that it is natural for people to prefer their own kind. This idea can be identified as 'nature' and/or 'in-group preference'. Another person might reply saying 'we are all humans and should all be treated equally'. This idea can be identified as 'nature' again perhaps, or 'one species' or 'equality'.
Identifying themes	From the ideas, the coder will identify themes. An idea can be a theme in its own right. 'Equality' might be a theme and might appear a lot in the data, for example. In-group favouritism might be a theme (and links to a theory) and 'nature' might be a theme that takes in the idea that there is a nature explanation for in-group/out-group behaviour and also that we are all humans, as in a way these two can go together.
Naming themes	Themes are named and then the analysis can be reviewed to check where the data fit and to reconsider ideas in the light of the themes generated.
Reliability/validity check	Review the journal to look for interpretation, and to put that right so that data are valid. Any subjective interpretation from a coder goes against the validity of the data. If there is more than one coder, there can be checks to see how the themes fit together, to look for reliability.
Report of the results	Write up the report of the results. A report would include a description of the analysis process as well as issues raised by the reflexive journal.

Evaluation of thematic analysis

The 'accuracy' of the analysed data refers to reliability and validity. With regard to reliability, if there is more than one coder then comparisons between the themes derived from the data from each coder can be a check for reliability. If a study is done again and gets the same results, then the results can be said to be reliable. Using two coders in analysis is like doing the study again. With regard to validity, if there is care taken not to interpret data, particularly when noting the ideas the data give or when allocating ideas to themes, then it can be said that data are valid. Qualitative data are in depth and detailed and come directly from the respondent, so if they are not then 'interpreted' they can be said to be valid. This is about 'hearing the voice' of the participant, which means their meanings are recorded, so data have validity.

Strengths of thematic analysis

- Thematic analysis is a way of reducing a large amount of data into a manageable summary and conclusion, without losing validity of the data, if the analysis is done well.
- It encourages the researcher to derive themes from the data rather than to impose pre-selected themes. This is likely to achieve better validity.

Weaknesses of thematic analysis

- Researchers often do not explain fully how they arrived at the themes, and so a study is not easily judged for its validity.
- Another weakness is that identifying some themes at the start might be quite easy but identifying a limited number of themes that represent the data fully is much more difficult and requires time and skill from the researcher (e.g. they will know their data best). The weakness is that it is time-consuming and requires skill.
- The researcher might have themes in mind when doing the initial coding, so validity might be in doubt. The themes might come from the researcher rather than from the data, as is the intention. It is the case that sometimes a thematic analysis might be driven by theory – in which case, this is the intention. However, validity can still be questioned.

More about thematic analysis is found in Chapter 6, which considers mathematical elements of such analytic techniques, such as when themes are counted and qualitative data become quantitative data.

Maths link: Chapter 6 is about the mathematical skills (such as showing how to analyse quantitative data) you will need for Year 1 of your course (and the AS).

Progress check 5.9

Explain thematic analysis, giving the ten steps in carrying out this analysis.

Practical: checklist for planning a questionnaire

- Do the questions/items address the aim/hypothesis?
- Are the questions/items clear and unambiguous?
- Is the sample size of respondents large enough and representative?
- Are ethical issues, such as confidentiality, addressed?
- Is the questionnaire a reasonable length?
- When will the questionnaire be carried out and over what length of time?
- Has a pilot study been carried out?
- How will the questionnaire be administered (e.g. post, face-to-face)?
- Will the data be both qualitative and quantitative, and how will the data be analysed?
- Will the respondents answer on the questionnaire or on a separate grid?

STUDY HINT

During this year of your course, you will carry out four main practical investigations which you will need to learn. From the start, keep a practical notebook folder for your own practical work and keep your class practical notes, data and comments in the folder. This will make it easier to revise for the exams.

Evaluation of questionnaires

Strengths

- The same questions are asked of all participants, using a set procedure. There is little variation in how people are asked for the information, so the answers should not be affected by anything other than the opinions of the respondent.
- A questionnaire can be carried out by post, which removes any potential **researcher bias**. If the researcher does not affect the situation, then in that sense there is also validity – responses are real as they are not affected by someone else. If you use methods that do not gather valid (real-life) data, then you are not really studying people at all. Validity exists when a study is measuring what it claims to measure. Of course, if questions restrict possible answers, then in that sense they do not give valid (real-life) data.
- Another strength of questionnaires is that they can be repeated accurately because:
  - they use set procedures
  - the same questions are asked of all the participants.

  This means that they are fairly easily and cheaply **replicable** – simply by administering the questionnaire again. When a replicable study is repeated and similar data are gathered, the study is said to be reliable. To a large extent, questionnaires are reliable.

STUDY HINT

Note that research methods can be valid in one sense and not valid in another. A questionnaire is valid if the person asking the questions and the situation itself do not affect the responses; it is not valid if forced-choice questions can miss 'real' answers. These distinctions need to be made. Explaining that 'questionnaires are valid' or 'questionnaires are not valid' is not enough; expand the answer with a reason to show understanding.
Validity and reliability are issues that occur throughout your course. Make sure that you understand what they mean. Learn one or two examples, so that you can always refer to validity and reliability when discussing a study.

Definitions

Researcher bias refers to when a researcher affects the responses/data that are gathered. The gender or age of the researcher, or the way they are dressed, for example, might affect what someone says or does. An experimenter can affect findings too in a similar way – in an experiment, this would be **experimenter bias**. **Replicability** means that a study can be done again. There is enough information to repeat it fully, so that findings from a replication can be compared with the original findings to help to build a body of knowledge. Replicability is required to test reliability.

Practical link: Chapter 7 explains four practical investigations, one for each topic area (social, cognitive and biological psychology, and learning theories). The one suggested in this book for social psychology is a questionnaire – more about using the questionnaire research method can be found on pp. 417–430.

Weaknesses

- Although questionnaires have set procedures and are replicable, they have to be administered, and the way that this is done might vary, which challenges reliability. For example, on one occasion, a female student might find respondents in a local shopping centre on Saturday and ask them the questions personally. On another occasion, a male adult might find respondents at a golf club on a Tuesday lunchtime and might leave the questionnaires at the bar for completion. In these two instances, there are several differences that could affect the results. Usually, a researcher will control the way the questionnaire is administered, but differences may still arise.

Progress check 5.10

Two scenarios are described above to show how the same questionnaire could be administered differently: one in which a female student visits a shopping centre on a Saturday, asking questions personally; the other in which a male adult visits a golf club on a Tuesday lunchtime, leaving the questionnaire at the bar. List the differences between these scenarios and suggest how these differences might affect the results.

- A second weakness of questionnaires is that they usually have fixed questions that do not allow respondents to expand on their answers. Therefore, the responses might not be valid. (This point is discussed in more detail under weaknesses of closed-ended questions on page 286.)
- Another weakness is that open-ended questions are often restricted in the length of the answers allowed, so qualitative data can also be limited in a questionnaire, again raising the question of validity. If respondents are not free to say exactly what they want to say, then their answers may not be 'true' and are, therefore, not valid.

Studies using the methodology

Adorno *et al.* (1950) used a questionnaire to see if authoritarian personality linked to prejudice. They developed a 'fascism' scale (F-scale). Their findings suggested that people who were more fascist (authoritarian) were more prejudiced in their views. This suggests that prejudice relates to personality.

Cohrs *et al.* (2012) used questionnaires gathering both self-report and peer-report data to look at personality linked to prejudice, and also to consider the validity of self-report data by comparing them with peer-report data. Cohrs *et al.* (2012) is one of the contemporary studies you can choose in social psychology (pp. 59–66). Interestingly, Cohrs *et al.* in 2012 looked at right-wing authoritarianism and prejudice, just as Adorno *et al.* did in 1950, which shows that historically similar issues in psychology are still studied. However, interestingly, there were methodological issues with Adorno *et al.* in 1950 that did not appear in Cohrs *et al.* in 2012, such as how in Adorno *et al.*'s study items were all in the same direction when it comes to authoritarian personality and prejudice, which is likely to give a bias in the findings. Link this to ideas around a response set as a bias.

Issues and debates

One issue and debate for your course relates to how psychology has developed over time. Using Adorno *et al.* (1950) and Cohrs *et al.* (2012) can be useful as there are similarities in the methods and what is studied, though there are important differences too. For example, Adorno *et al.* in 1950 focused on self-report data, whereas Cohrs *et al.* in 2012 focused on the validity of self-report data.

Explore

A web version of the F-scale (www.anesi.com/fscale.htm) is available for you to try. There are some comments at the end about the questionnaire and the findings of Adorno *et al.*

Test yourself

Alice is interested in carrying out a study to look at obedience. She thinks that males are more obedient to authority than females. She could set up an experiment, but for various reasons wants to use a questionnaire. She wants to include ranked scale items as well as other items, and wants to gather both qualitative and quantitative data.

Design a questionnaire that could suit her purpose, and give reasons for your design decisions. Give enough depth, such as two sides of A4.

STUDY HINT

The practical investigation in social psychology requires you to design and carry out a questionnaire - for example, you could carry out the questionnaire suggested in the 'Test yourself' box.

Test yourself

Imagine you were reading about a study using a questionnaire looking at agency theory and obedience. The study used Likert-style items, where there were statements which the respondent agreed with on a scale of 1 (strongly disagree) to 5 (strongly agree). Each statement was written so that strong agreement meant someone identified themselves as behaving as an agent in society, and strong disagreement measured autonomy. A score of 3 had 'don't know' against it, so someone scoring 3 presumably felt they neither agreed nor disagreed. The study used a postal questionnaire and, out of 2,000 sent out, 150 were returned.

Write a page of A4 paper commenting on this study. Comment about reliability, validity, generalisability, credibility and objectivity/subjectivity.

STUDY HINT

You could develop your own mnemonic for lists of ideas, such as evaluation points when judging a study. For example, reliability, validity, generalisability, credibility, objectivity/subjectivity might be remembered as 'really very good, clear outstanding study'. Develop an idea that suits you, as that can help in examinations.

The interview research method

In social psychology, not only are questionnaires studied as a research method, but also **interviews**. Interviews have similar features and issues as questionnaires and both are surveys. Some of what you have learned when studying the use of questionnaires apply to using the interview method.

Explanation

Interviews involve asking questions, just as questionnaires do, but interviews involve a researcher carrying them out, and although there is a series of questions, these can be varied according to responses. The aim of an interview is to find out some detail from a respondent according to the aim of a study.

Planning interviews

Interviews tend to involve a personal situation, often face-to-face, although they can be over the phone or online, such as using Skype, and a series of questions. They can involve a complete set of questions (such as a questionnaire), but the difference is that the face-to-face or personal situation allows the researcher the opportunity to expand, or clarify, questions.

An interview is chosen instead of a questionnaire:

- if some questions are to be explored in more depth
- when the respondent may need reassurance
- when access is difficult.

Access refers to reaching the participants – physically reaching them and also finding them in the first place. Access can be a difficult issue – for example, if data are to be gathered from a child, from someone with mental health problems or from a business or venture. The appropriate people have to be contacted and have to agree to co-operate. Issues around access can involve ethical and practical considerations, which can restrict the data gathered.

Definition

Access is about finding the participants and getting permission from them and/or for them to take part in a study. Access covers the period from uncovering who would be suitable participants, through ethical issues, to finding a way for them to take part. Access can be more difficult for some participants than for others.

Practical

When you decide to carry out a practical, you must consider ethical issues and issues of access. Will you be able to easily find the participants/respondents that you need? Choose to focus on areas where you can access participants/respondents ethically and easily.

Explore

Use your textbooks or the internet to find some interviews or case studies. They do not have to be psychological studies – for example, they could be interviews with media personalities. In each case, consider the issue of access. How was the person reached? What were the ethical issues involved? Was it possible to ask all the required questions? What restrictions did problems with access impose on the interview findings?

The following is an interview with an entrepreneur and is a place to start perhaps – it might not have all the answers to the questions here, but you can imagine some of the difficulties concerning access: http://theteenagemillionaire.com/interview-with-an-entrepreneur-founder-of-lenstore-mitesh-patel/.

Types of interview

- A **structured interview** follows a set format. It is a questionnaire administered by an individual. There might be extra instructions for using the questionnaire, such as where and how to expand on answers. Structured interviews are useful for gathering quantitative as well as qualitative data, and results can be compared between respondents. Structured interviews can be carried out over the phone, face-to-face or over the internet. A structured interview is strongly planned and in that sense more replicable, so more likely to yield reliable data.
- An **unstructured interview** involves questions that are not in a set format and which allow the interviewer to explore the area with further questions arising from the respondent's answers. Unstructured interviews are useful when depth and detail are required and perhaps less is known about the topic in question, so that issues can be explored. Qualitative data are gathered, with corresponding richness and variety.
- A **semi-structured interview** has set questions, some of which can be explored further by the interviewer. The semi-structured interview can produce qualitative and quantitative data and can offer insight as well as data that can be compared between respondents. A semi-structured interview can have the advantages of a structured interview, in being replicable, having set questions, and the advantages of an unstructured interview, in allowing the respondent to lead and so getting more valid data.

Definitions

Unstructured interview means open for the respondent to lead the questions and the course of the interview. **Structured interview** means closed and predetermined so that a respondent has no options and does not lead the direction of the interview. **Semi-structured interview** means some fixed questions and some structure regarding what will be asked – there is room for the respondent to lead the direction of the questions.

Progress check 5.11

Decide whether the following interviews are structured, unstructured or semi-structured.

1. Simon asks ten participants the same set of questions about their attitudes to obedience, making sure he uses the same tone of voice and exactly the same wording.
2. Aisha has a list of what she wants to find out about, and has some specific questions, but she lets respondents enlarge on issues when they want to.
3. Sam is carrying out what can be called a conversational interview, because he does not have a specific hypothesis and wants to get in-depth data about feelings about work. So he goes with what each respondent is talking about, rather than asking specific questions.

Interviews gather mainly qualitative data

Interviews are usually used when in-depth and detailed information is required, so the data are qualitative and can be in the form of a story, or attitudes. There are likely to be some quantitative data, such as age, length of time in a job, or other personal data. There might also be some 'yes/no' questions, or interviewees might be asked to rate some information, but the data are mainly qualitative. The more structured an interview is, the more likely it is to include quantitative data; the less structured the interview, the more qualitative data are likely to be gathered.

STUDY HINT

See pp. 287-288 for advantages and disadvantages of using qualitative data and quantitative data. You can use those ideas to generate strengths and weaknesses of using interviews.

Issues to consider when conducting interviews

Interview schedules must be prepared in advance so that the aims and research hypotheses (if any) are addressed. During an interview, notes can be taken or the interview can be recorded. Whichever format is used, all notes must be **transcribed** in full after the interview. This is time-consuming but necessary, so that all data are available for analysis.

STUDY HINT

When a research method collects qualitative data, then ways of analysing qualitative data are used, such as thematic analysis. Be sure to use information from one research method (such as the importance for thematic analysis of transcribing data) when reading about another, because there is a lot of overlap. Methodology that applies to one research method often applies to another (such as the use of open and closed questions in both questionnaires and interviews).

Definitions

Transcribing refers to preparing the data in written form, whether from a video, a discussion or something similar. All qualitative data must be transcribed ready for analysis.

Schedule is the term for a list of questions or an idea of what is to be asked in an interview. The interview schedule can be sent to a participant, so that they are aware of what they will be asked (and what they are consenting to).

In order to carry out an interview, the participants must be involved at each stage:

- They must see the **schedule** before the interview, so that they can be ready.
- They must agree to the chosen format for recording the interview.
- They must see the full transcript (copy) of the interview afterwards and agree that it is what was said or occurred.

There are both ethical and practical issues here. Ethical issues in carrying out research in psychology are outlined on pp. 304–314. Practical issues are mainly to do with reliability, validity and objectivity.

Explore

Use Google Scholar or another search engine to find studies using interviewing, as that can help to show important issues when interviewing. For example, Keen *et al.* (2003) carried out a study looking at the effectiveness of methadone treatment and used interviewing (an 'interview administered questionnaire', so structured) as well as other measures. The interviews gathered self-report data and had a longitudinal focus (meaning the interviews were carried out three times during the programme). The interviewers were trained 'to apply standardised interviewing techniques'. This study is useful for later in your course if you study health psychology. The idea is to look at studies to see how they are carried out and to see how psychology can work in practice. You can find the Keen *et al.* study here: http://bjgp.org/content/53/491/461.full.pdf+html.

Interviewing must be objective and ethical

Issues and debates

One of the issues and debates in your course is ethical issues when carrying out research. All research must be carried out ethically, even though doing that can affect the data. Practical issues such as reliability, validity and objectivity, relate to psychology as a science, which is also a debate in psychology. For example, if findings are valid, they may not be as 'scientific', and if they are less valid, they may be more reliable, because controls help to derive scientific findings but controls restrict the 'reality' of data. Keep notes on ethical issues and 'psychology as a science' throughout your course as you come across points.

Exploratory research

Interviews, especially unstructured interviews, are useful if a research question moves into an area that is not well researched. Qualitative data are useful in **exploratory research** because depth and detail is usually required. This is because there might be an aim but not a hypothesis. The aim is likely to be broad as it is exploring an area rather than investigating a specific hypothesis. Interviews are useful tools for gathering in-depth and detailed qualitative data.

Explanation

Exploratory research is when not much is already known about an area of study and where a researcher wants to start off a research process, finding qualitative, in-depth, valid data, before perhaps choosing a more focused research question.

Relating to policy and practice

Research is often carried out with a view to affecting policy and practice. Sometimes research has academic value and is not focused so much on having an application in society, but very often research questions are there to be answered because the answers can then shed light on a key question in society and can be used to help individuals. Interviews are useful in affecting policy and practice because they are likely to yield valid data and can be used to hear the participant's voice. They tend to uncover personal meanings – for example, as in the study by Jordal *et al.* (2013), outlined on page 298.

Subjectivity and objectivity

In all research, the researcher can cause bias. The issues that can affect questionnaires, such as social desirability, demand characteristics and response bias, can also affect interviews. Researchers can also cause bias by interpreting the results using their own views and judgements: subjectivity is when the analysis of the results includes input from the person doing the analysis; objectivity is when there is no bias affecting the results, including no bias from the researcher's opinions. Scientific studies must be objective.

Issues and debates

Science is defined by how knowledge is gained and how findings are built upon, as much as by the subject matter. For example, we can be scientific in our choice of friends or scientific in our study of archaeology. Psychology is a science because of its methodology. When psychology involves studying, for example, the genes or the structure of the brain, then it is easy to show that it is a science because techniques for microbiology and brain scanning are involved. However, psychology involves areas such as prejudice and obedience. Here, science refers to the research methods used, not the subject matter. Science involves:

- objectivity - it is important not to let subjective (personal) opinions affect results
- generating hypotheses - such as in psychology about differences between male and female driving behaviour
- careful controls - to avoid bias
- measurable concepts.

Psychology involves all these factors and issues around psychology and science are covered in the Learning Theories topic area (pp. 379-383).

Explore

Consider whether a researcher could ever be entirely objective. Is it possible to record data, transcribe and analyse without your own ideas influencing the data? Consider how all data have to come through our own brains, which would entail some filtering. In cognitive psychology, you will study how memory is about processing information, such as using schemas which we have developed. Objectivity might be the ideal for research to be scientific and reliable, but is it achievable? Research on the internet to see what you can find out about such issues. The following blog raises some interesting questions: http://blogs.scientificamerican.com/the-curious-wavefunction/2013/08/13/is-psychology-a-real-science-does-it-really-matter.

Objectivity when interviewing

Interviewing involves someone carrying out the interview personally, either face-to-face, over the phone or online. Researchers must not be affected by whether or not they like, or agree with, the **interviewee**. Ways of remaining objective include:

- producing a complete transcript of the interview – this ensures that researchers cannot select what they include
- ensuring that the interviewee sees the results and agrees that they are accurately recorded
- having another researcher analyse the results.

It is important to maintain objectivity both when asking questions and when analysing results. If results are not objective, then the findings will not be useful.

Definitions

The **interviewee** is the person being interviewed and the **interviewer** is the person carrying out the interview.

Practical: checklist for carrying out an interview

- Have you decided whether to use a structured, unstructured or semi-structured interview?
- Have you decided how to record the interview (written, tape-recorded)?
- Have you drawn up the interview schedule?
- Have you included a question for each area in which you are interested?
- Have you included questions requesting necessary personal data?
- Have you included an explanation, so that the interviewee knows what is expected?
- Have you prepared the interviewee appropriately beforehand, including obtaining permission?
- Have you prepared all the materials, such as, if appropriate, a record sheet for the answers?
- Have you considered whether you will gather both qualitative and quantitative data?

After the interview, for the results:

- Have you completely transcribed the interview, with all the detail?
- Have you generated the themes and categories from the data, not from your own ideas?

Evaluation of interviews

Strengths

- The interviewer can explain questions and explore issues by asking further questions. A questionnaire is limited to the questions written down and, even when gathering qualitative data, usually there will be limited space available. When a researcher needs to be able to explain issues to a participant or to investigate further, an interview is the ideal method.
- Interviews obtain in-depth and detailed data that are likely to be valid. Interviewees talk in their own words and are not restricted. The data are 'real life' and 'true', and so are valid. For these reasons, an interview is often an important part of a **case study**.

Weaknesses

- When asking questions, interviewers might find it hard not to influence the answers. They might ask in a particular way or with a certain emphasis, such as 'You are not prejudiced, are you?' How they look or act may also affect responses – for example, interviewees might give different responses to male and female interviewers. These would be forms of researcher bias.

- The researcher might find it hard not to interpret the responses when analysing the data and forming themes. It might be difficult to maintain objectivity; subjectivity can be a problem with analysing interviews. Generating themes involves selection and the appropriate grouping of data – that choice can be subjective.

Study using the methodology

Jordal *et al.* (2013) carried out a qualitative study using semi-structured interviewing with single pregnant women or single mothers with a child under one year old in Sri Lanka. The study used 28 women with an average age of 23. The idea was to find out their feelings and attitudes, and ways of coping with single motherhood, considering how the culture in Sri Lanka was against single motherhood. The study wanted to obtain 'complex descriptions from the participants' perspective' and chose interviewing for this reason. Interviewers used different languages to suit the participants, who were recruited from different regions. The interviews were conversational in style to enable detail and depth in the data, with the participants able to reflect on their answers. The interviews were audio-recorded and data were carefully transcribed (after translation into English). Analysis followed the way thematic analysis takes place (pp. 290–292) with meaning being carefully attended to, then ideas understood before coding and finally, themes generated. You can read the full study here: www.biomedcentral.com/1472-6874/13/5.

STUDY HINT

In the Jordal *et al.* (2013) study outlined here, there is a table of results that gives an example of thematic analysis, which can be useful when understanding such analytic techniques.

Test yourself

Alice is interested in carrying out a study to look at obedience. She thinks that males are more obedient to authority than females. She has already carried out a questionnaire, but some of the answers have raised further questions. She decides to ask ten of the questionnaire respondents for permission to interview them, to check aspects of the questionnaire findings and to help with **triangulation** of findings.

Design an interview that could suit her purpose, and give reasons for your design decisions. Give enough depth, such as two sides of A4.

Explanation

Triangulation is about getting data from different sources and then comparing the data to see whether they come to the same findings, if the focus is on the same issues. Someone can use a questionnaire, followed up by an interview, and then findings from the two research methods can form part of triangulation. Triangulation can help with checking for validity because, if the same data are found using different sources, that suggests the data does represent real life, though this comment relates mainly to using questionnaires or interviews where data are self-report. Triangulation can help with reliability too because, if the same results are found using different methods, that means data are reliable.

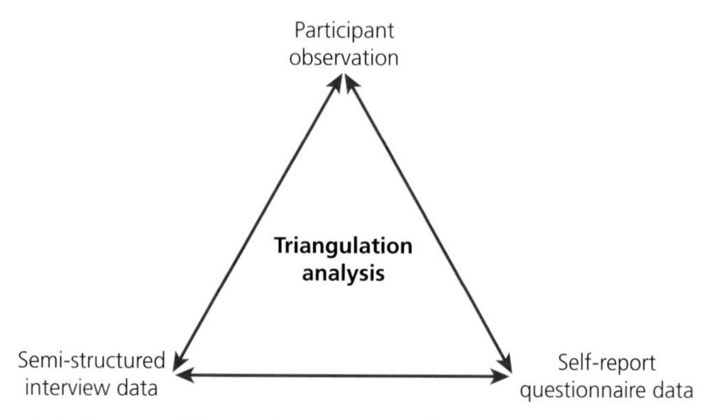

Data from participant observation, self-report questionnaires and semi-structured interviews could be triangulated to check the strength of results, such as in terms of validity and reliability

Explore

Adorno *et al.* (1950) used interviewing to follow up questionnaire findings (see details of their study on page 293). Explore the use of questionnaires and interviewing by looking more at Adorno *et al.*'s (1950) study.

Progress check 5.12

Write a short paragraph outlining the advantages of unstructured interviews as a research method compared with structured interviews.

Comparing questionnaires and interviews

In all research methods, there can be a trade-off between reliability and validity; subjectivity has to be avoided, so that knowledge is secure and can be relied upon. In general:

- Interviews tend to give data with more validity. However, they can involve subjectivity and are hard to repeat. Therefore, it is hard to test for reliability.
- Questionnaires are reliable and are less likely to involve subjectivity. However, they tend to be less valid, as any open questions may be missed out or answered only briefly.

Data can be collected from questionnaires more quickly than from interviews because questionnaires can be given to a number of people in the time it takes to interview one person in depth. However, it is not true that questionnaires are quick because:

- they take a long time to draw up
- it is more important to run a pilot study because the questions are more fixed
- they can take as long to analyse as interviews, since a lot of data are gathered.

The usefulness of interviews and questionnaires, in terms of reliability, validity and subjectivity is shown in Table 5.4.

Table 5.4 Comparing questionnaires and interviews in terms of reliability, validity and subjectivity

	Questionnaires	Interviews
Reliability	Structured questions; the same for all respondents; so replicable and likely to be reliable	Each person interviewed separately in different settings and on different occasions and perhaps by a different person; difficult to replicate and test for reliability
Validity	Set questions with forced-choice answers are likely to be less valid as may not yield 'true' data	Questions can be explained and explored, so likely to be valid and give 'real-life' and 'true' data
Subjectivity	Structured format; less open to researcher bias in the analysis; closed questions do not require interpretation; open questions are likely to give short answers, so themes are clearer	Open to bias in analysis as generating themes requires interpretation; open to subjectivity, but analysis can be objective if the steps are made clear

Test yourself

1. Explain two strengths and two weaknesses when using the interview research method to study obedience. **(4 marks)**
2. Assess by comparing (and contrasting) the use of the questionnaire research method and the interview research method to investigate the social identity theory of prejudice. **(16 marks)**

STUDY HINT

In your course, 'compare' involves giving both similarities and differences, so is treated the same as 'compare and contrast'.

STUDY HINT

An essay involves describing evidence and material that suits the title as well as presenting an argument that relates to the essay title. Avoid giving just description as the argument is very important. Be sure that throughout you are fully focusing on the exact title. Leave out material that is not relevant, even if you want to show that you know it. Remain focused throughout on the title, even referring to the title perhaps, to make the links, such as, for a 'compare' essay: 'another difference between them is...'

Sampling issues in research

You are likely to first come across sampling issues when studying the questionnaire and interview research methods, so they are used as examples here, though some examples relate to Milgram's work and he used the experimental method. Sampling issues are found in all research methods and studies, so the material here can be used in relation to other studies too.

STUDY HINT

Methodology is explained as you would come to it in your course, so sampling techniques are in with social psychology because it is the first topic area in your course. However, issues around 'doing psychology', which are methodology issues, cover all topic areas so be sure to use what you have learned (such as about sampling) in other areas when appropriate. You might want to keep your notes on methodology separate from 'content' notes (such as notes about obedience) for this reason.

When any study is carried out, it is rarely possible to include everyone who should be involved as participants. For example, the findings of a study about prejudice will potentially be applied to everyone, but it would be impossible to include everyone in the study. Even if a study is to look at a smaller group – for example, differences in obedience between male and female soldiers – there are too many to test them all. Almost always in psychology, a study involves a sample of the population of interest. The **target population** is all the people the study is about – those to whom the findings will be applied. The chosen sample must be representative of the population and, if possible, not biased. **Representative** here means including members of each type of person in that population, usually in the correct proportion. An example of bias would be having only young males and older females in the sample of a study where gender is important.

It is difficult to get a representative sample because there are problems in obtaining participants. Even if you can get access to the relevant people, you still have to choose who will be involved. There are a number of **sampling** techniques in use, none of which is ideal for getting a representative sample, although some techniques are better than others.

Definitions

The **target population** is the people the researchers want the findings to represent - the population of interest to the researcher. **Sampling** is done when not all members of a target population can be involved in a study. Sampling involves choosing participants from the target population. There are different types of sampling; in your course, you need to learn about random, stratified, opportunity and volunteer sampling. **Representative** means that the people chosen as participants represent the target population. Therefore, they need to have the characteristics of the target population, including age, gender, educational background perhaps, occupation, and other such issues.

Practical: how sampling takes place

- Define the population of interest.
- Specify the sampling frame - the people you can choose from.
- Use a sampling method to choose people from the frame.
- Decide the sample size.
- Find the sample.
- Collect the data.
- Review the sampling process to evaluate the findings.

Sample size

The sample size depends on the confidence interval and the confidence level:

- The confidence interval is how far it is thought that answers, for example, might not be reliable/valid. For example, a researcher might say that the results are true within plus or minus (±) 3 in the scoring. So a score of 10 on a questionnaire rating prejudice may have a confidence interval of ±3 – the true score being between 7 and 13.
- The confidence level is the percentage of the sample that is likely to represent the population.

Explore

Do some research using the internet or some other source to see how many participants are used in studies. Look at the number of participants used in the studies that are detailed in your course. For example, Raine *et al.* (1997) used 41 participants and had a control group of 41, so 82 in total; Sherif's Robber's Cave study used 22 boys; Watson and Rayner (1920) had just one participant; and Milgram's main study (1963) used 26 men. So if you carry out a study and don't have many participants, it is worth noting that neither did many researchers - the sample sizes vary a lot.

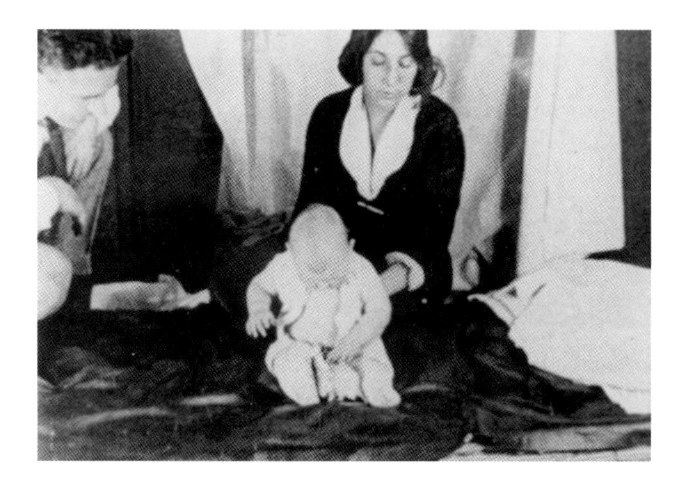

Watson and Rayner (1920) carried out a well-known study to see how a little boy might learn a phobia; only one child was used and yet the findings were widely accepted

STUDY HINT

It can seem a good evaluation of a study to say that the findings are not generalisable because the sample size is too small but, as can be seen from the classic study by Watson and Rayner in 1920, one participant can be enough. Avoid short evaluation points, such as saying the sample is too small (or saying a questionnaire is quick and easy); always explain evaluation points in full. Note that generalisability is when a sample fairly represents the target population so findings from the sample can be said to apply to the target population.

It is common for researchers to choose a confidence level of 95 per cent; and a confidence interval of ±3 is also a sensible choice. To decide on sample size, you need to know:

- the size of the sampling frame (those you are choosing from)
- the confidence interval that is chosen (e.g. ±3)
- the confidence level that is chosen (e.g. 95 per cent).

The internet has calculators for the sampling process, but there are variations in the advice – for example, about the size of the sampling frame. One example is that, with a confidence interval of ±3, a confidence level of 95 per cent and a sampling frame of 2,000 people, the sample size should be 704. You could assume, therefore, that if you have a sampling frame of 200, the sample should be around 70. In practice, when studying psychology as you are, a sample size of 20 will give you some idea of the results you would find if you asked more people.

Explore

You can use the internet to find either a confidence level or a sample size, and also to look more about how to choose a sample size. For example: www.surveysystem.com/sscalc.htm. Make up some figures for confidence levels and confidence intervals and find out what sample sizes you would need for different population sizes. It would be worth checking the different advice given by various sites.

Sampling techniques

You need to learn about random, stratified, volunteer and opportunity sampling, but there are other sampling techniques.

STUDY HINT

You may have learned about sampling and sampling techniques in another subject, such as at GCSE, and be able to apply what you learned here.

Simple random sampling

This method gives everyone an equal chance of being chosen. The main rule is that everyone in the target population is available for selection each time a participant is picked out. However, the larger target population is usually reduced to a manageable **sampling frame**. For example, to examine obedience in male and female soldiers, researchers could choose one regiment. The population that the sample is taken from is already reduced into a manageable sampling frame. Then, to get a **random sample**, the names of all the soldiers in the regiment could be put into a box and one picked out each time until the required number of participants was reached.

Another way of taking a random sample is to use random number tables or a random number generator. People are allocated numbers and whatever number occurs, that participant is chosen. Often in practice sampling is done some other way to arrive at a small enough sampling frame and then random sampling is done from that point, so there might be more than one sampling technique used.

Definitions

Sampling frame is the people available to choose a sample from, such as all sixth-formers in a school. **Random sampling** is when everyone in the sampling frame has the chance of being picked each time a participant is chosen. It is the most representative as nobody is excluded from being chosen. Lottery balls are chosen using this method.

Advantages of simple random sampling

- There is no bias in the way the participants are chosen; everyone has the opportunity to be chosen and no one is systematically excluded from the sample. Therefore, the sample is likely to be representative of the target population.
- It is clear to everyone how the sample was chosen. Each step of the process can be explained and understood. When studies are carried out scientifically, their results and conclusions are more widely recognised and can be added more easily to the body of psychological knowledge. With random sampling, any possible bias (as explained below) can be worked out mathematically and taken into account.

Disadvantages of simple random sampling

- It is difficult to ensure that everyone in the target population/sampling frame is available to be included in the sample, which may cause bias. There is a problem, for example, in getting the names of people because of the Data Protection Act (1998). Even if everyone's name were included, it would not be known if they were available to take part. For example, someone might not be available on the required day; someone might not want to take part. So even if random sampling took place, it would not mean that all those chosen would be part of the study, so there could be bias.
- Even with simple random sampling, when everyone has an equal chance of being chosen, there can be a bias in the sample. For example, if the hypothesis was to examine obedience in male and female soldiers, it is possible that a random sample would not include any female soldiers, which would not be useful.

STUDY HINT

In your practical work, you are unlikely to use random sampling, so avoid saying that your sample was 'random'. If you find yourself writing about something being random, check your use of the term. Random sampling is rarely achieved completely.

Study using the methodology

Källmén *et al.* (2014) used random sampling to study the usefulness of a scale to measure risky alcohol consumption in elderly people. The study's aim was to test the reliability and validity of the Alcohol Use Disorders Identification Test (AUDIT) using elderly people in Sweden and a comparison group (non-elderly), to see if the scale was suitable for use with the elderly. The participants were 1,459 Swedish adults aged between 79 and 80, who were sent the questionnaire by post. There was a response rate (those who returned the questionnaire) of 73.3 per cent, although this was after two reminders. The results showed that the tool (AUDIT) was more reliable and valid in the general population than in the elderly population. To find the sample of elderly people, a random sample was obtained from all people (of that age) living in Sweden. The 1,459 participants were made up of 538 males and 528 females, which suggests that random sampling does give a 'fair' and unbiased sample. The comparison was done using data collected from 663 adults in Sweden (aged 17–79) in 2009. The practical application of the findings of this study is that care should be taken in using an assessment tool that might not have been tested for a specific population.

Stratified sampling

To make sure that certain groups are represented in the sample, **stratified sampling** is used. Groups arise from the study and it is decided how many participants are needed within each group. The number of participants from each group should represent the numbers of that group in the target population. For example, if the study was about obedience in male and female soldiers, there are two main groups; within those, age could be a factor, so there might be four groups:

- young male soldiers
- young female soldiers
- older male soldiers
- older female soldiers.

These are the four strata for the stratified sampling. If there are five times as many male soldiers as female soldiers, then there should be five times as many male soldiers in the sample.

Definition

Stratified sampling is when certain groups need to be represented in a study and so sampling is done to ensure those groups are found in the sample. The proportion of the sample should match the proportions in the groups themselves.

Advantages of stratified sampling

- Each group is bound to be represented, so conclusions about differences between those groups can be drawn.
- Stratified sampling is an efficient way of ensuring that there is representation from each group. Random sampling would probably still provide some participants from each group, but the researcher cannot be sure of this and may, therefore, need a larger sample. Stratified sampling limits the numbers needed to obtain representation from each group.

Disadvantages of stratified sampling

- It is difficult to know how many of each group to choose in order to make sure that the findings are **generalisable**. It is always difficult to know how many individuals make up an appropriate sample; with stratified sampling, where the numbers in each group may be small, it is harder.
- The groups set by the study may not be the important groups. Having the groups already decided means that some people will be ruled out as participants. This could mean that the sample is not representative of the population. For example, obedience in soldiers may depend on whether or not they have a family. That grouping was not considered in the sampling, so may not be represented.

Definition

A study is **generalisable** if the findings can be said to be true of the target population.

Study using the methodology

Sorensen *et al.* (2013) carried out a study to look at whether students at university knew a victim or a perpetrator of a sexual assault. The study was part of a rape awareness and prevention programme. The idea was that not enough was known about students' previous understanding of sexual assault so an online questionnaire was used to find out. A stratified random sample of 2,400 students was used to collect the data. There was 53.5 per cent participation and the findings were that students had a lot of personal knowledge about victimisation or perpetration of sexual assault. Knowledge varied by age and ethnicity. The 2,400 sample consisted of 600 freshmen (first-year students), 600 sophomores (second-year students) 600 juniors (third-year students) and 600 seniors (fourth-year students) – this was the 'stratified' part of the sample. The sample had about 25 per cent of each of these groups and was checked regarding a gender split, which was about 50 per cent male and 50 per cent female. Blacks, Hispanics, Asians and Native Americans comprised about 40.8 per cent of the university population and 41.8 per cent of the study participants. This sort of information is to show that, although random sampling was used, it was important to check representativeness of the sample against the relevant population (in this case, university students).

Volunteer/self-selected sampling

Sometimes it is best to ask for volunteers for a study – participants select themselves by volunteering. They might answer an advertisement or respond to a letter. When the sample is a **volunteer sample**, it is self-selected. Milgram (1963) used a volunteer sample. His participants answered an advertisement.

> **Definition**
> **Volunteer sampling** is when the participants select themselves by putting themselves forward as volunteers.

Advantages of volunteer/self-selected sampling

- It is more ethical than other methods (e.g. simple random sampling) because the participants come to the researcher, rather than the researcher seeking them out.
- Volunteers are interested and are, therefore, perhaps less likely to give biased information or to go against the researcher's instructions. There is less likely to be social desirability or demand characteristics – unless they are so keen that they do what they think the researcher wants, having guessed what that is (demand characteristics). In general, it is an advantage to have volunteers, in that they are willing to be involved in the study.

Disadvantages of volunteer/self-selected sampling

- It can take a long time to get sufficient numbers of participants because the researcher has to wait for volunteers to apply. For example, one advertisement or request may not raise enough people.
- Because the participants select themselves, they might be similar in some way. For example, Milgram's participants all read the advertisement, so they read the same publication. They also had to have time to take part, which could rule out those in certain occupations. Therefore, a volunteer sample, being self-selected, is biased and is not likely to be representative of the target population.

Opportunity sampling

Opportunity sampling is not really a true method of sampling, because it means taking whoever is available. Researchers use whoever they can find to take part – they take the opportunity to involve participants. The way participants are chosen is not structured. Psychology students tend to use opportunity sampling, as the people to whom they have access are limited.

> **Definition**
> **Opportunity sampling** means using whoever is available; sometimes called grab sampling or convenience sampling.

> **STUDY HINT**
> You are likely to use an opportunity sample in your practical investigations as you will probably take who is available at the time. You can use advantages and disadvantages of this method of sampling when evaluating your practical investigation.

> **STUDY HINT**
> A sampling technique is a useful way of evaluating a study in psychology. For example, in Milgram's (1963) study, you can ask whether the sample of men used were representative of the population. However, not all such evaluation points apply to all studies – in practice, Milgram used many different sets of participants in his variations and still found a high level of obedience, so perhaps an evaluation point about his sampling technique would not be useful in this case. It is, however, worth looking at sampling issues when evaluating a study.

Advantages of opportunity sampling

- It tends to be more ethical because the researcher can judge if the participant is likely to be upset by the study or is too busy to take part. Other forms of sampling often do not give this information readily.
- The researcher has more control over who is asked, so finding participants should be quick and efficient, because access is not a problem.

Simple random sampling
Everyone in the sampling frame or population has an equal chance of being chosen for the sample

Opportunity sampling
The researcher takes whomsoever they can to take part in the study

Sampling methods

Stratified sampling
The population is divided into the required groups and the correct proportions of people are picked out for the sample

Volunteer/self-selected sampling
People are asked to volunteer for the study, either personally or via an advertisement or some such means. By volunteering, they self-select

Four sampling procedures

Disadvantages of opportunity sampling

- There is more chance of bias than with other methods. One source of bias is that researchers have more control over who is chosen and may be biased towards people who are easy to access, such as people they know. They may be biased towards choosing people like themselves, people of their own age or people who look friendly. These issues connected with researchers are likely to lead to a biased sample.
- Those who are picked are available and willing to take part in the study, so they are self-selected. This would rule out anyone not available or not willing, which again will cause bias. These issues connected with participants are likely to lead to a biased sample.

STUDY HINT

It could be said that all samples of participants are volunteer samples because they all have to agree to take part (see the section on ethics), but it is not directly a volunteer sample if they were found using another sampling technique. Similarly, there is an extent to which all samples are opportunity, as the researcher would take who they can get, but if there is another sampling technique used, then that is the main technique. Opportunity sampling is only the sampling technique to 'name' if no other technique was used.

Progress check 5.13

Why is the sampling technique important when considering the value of a study?

Test yourself

1. Outline one advantage and one disadvantage of two sampling techniques used in psychology. **(4 marks)**
2. Evaluate in terms of similarities and differences three different methods of sampling used in psychology. **(8 marks)**

Ethical issues in psychological research

You are likely to come across **ethical issues** as soon as you start studying psychology. Ethical issues are by definition featured in all studies because they are about what is done to people (or to animals). What is done must be ethical. And psychological research usually involves 'doing things' to people. Ethical issues in questionnaire and interview research are considered as that is where you are likely to first come across 'ethics' in psychology, and these are ethical issues that relate to all studies in psychology.

Ethics are issues around what is seen as right and wrong with regard to the actions of others or of societies. Psychology uses both humans and animals in studies and there are associated ethical issues. Such issues lead to published ethical principles and ethical guidelines can be drawn up to supplement the basic ethical principles.

There are ethical issues to cover the use of animals in studies in psychology; they are not just about psychology and interactions with humans. In our society, it is felt that animals have rights. However, not all animals appear to be considered equal. Some people may think, for example, that spiders cannot be treated unethically. Others would not agree, thinking that it is unethical to use any animals in research. The issue of using animals in research is found briefly in Chapter 3 (pp. 149–150) and later in this chapter in more detail (pp. 372–379).

Here, the focus is on ethical issues surrounding the use of humans as participants in psychological studies.

Definitions

Ethics refers to how psychology is done in practice, both as a practitioner and as a researcher. Ethics refer to values and beliefs, what is right and wrong when working with people in society. **Ethical issues** are those that arise from such values and beliefs, such as giving participants in research the right to withdraw from a study at any time.

Explore

Make a list of ethical issues that you think are important when dealing with human participants in psychology. Use the internet or other sources to find at least two sets of ethical principles or guidelines for using humans in psychological studies. Compare your list with the principles or guidelines you found and note the similarities. Find two studies that you think are unethical and make two lists, one giving points in favour of each study and one giving points against. In each case, do you think the study should have been carried out? Finally, make notes about how the studies could have been carried out more ethically. It should be difficult to do this if the studies are modern because all studies are supposed to follow ethical guidelines carefully. If you have chosen older studies, note how far society has changed in what is considered ethical practice.

Study using the methodology

Adams *et al.* (1996) carried out a study to investigate homophobia. There were two groups of male heterosexual participants, but one group was more homophobic than the other. They measured changes in penile circumference when the men were shown erotic stimuli of three sorts – heterosexual, male homosexual and lesbian. All men showed greater penile erection for the heterosexual images. Only the homophobic men showed penile erection for the male homosexual images. It was concluded that homophobia masks homosexual feelings of which men are either unaware or which they deny. The ethical issues of doing a study like this must be fairly obvious. Not only issues in obtaining informed consent about the study, but also ethics involved in explaining the findings of the study to the participant in a debriefing session.

Ethics is not a new focus for psychology. Ethical issues were discussed from the time that the American Psychological Association (APA) was set up in 1900. In 1959, the APA published an abbreviated code of ethics and a Canadian psychology association adopted the code in 1963.

- The APA has a set of ethical principles that covers issues such as the competence of the psychologist and issues of assessment and therapy. The most recent code was in 2010 when the 2002 code was amended. The APA advocates responsible conduct research (RCR), which covers professional activities under nine headings, including research misconduct, human participants, research involving animals and data acquisition.

Explore

The 2010 amendments of the APA ethics code can be found on the APA website: www.apa.org/ethics/code/index.aspx. It is worth exploring to learn more about the code of ethics of a different country and to think, for example, about why there are more similarities than differences between the APA code and that of the British Psychological Society (BPS).

STUDY HINT

Remember that studies should be assessed for their ethics according to the code of their time, even though there can be some discussion about changes in ethics over time.

- UNESCO (United Nations Educational, Scientific and Cultural Organisation) has a set of ethical principles for social scientists, which focus on issues such as confidentiality, responsibility and care.
- Health workers have their own ethical guidelines and psychologists working with health workers also have to obey rules. From July 2009, psychologists are governed by the Health and Care Professions Council (HCPC) (the HCPC is considered in Year 2 of your course, within clinical psychology). The HCPC has its own code of conduct and you can find out more on their own website (www.hcpc-uk.org).
- The British Psychological Society (BPS) was formed in 1901. It put forward a code of conduct in 1985 and adopted it in 1993. The most recent version of the BPS Code of Ethics and Conduct was published in 2009. Its main principles are respect, competence, responsibility and integrity. The 2009 code covers both research and practice in psychology. Some of the BPS ethical principles that affect you as students of psychology are outlined below, after the four main principles are explained.

The BPS principles

The BPS is the association that supports psychologists and regulates the profession. It is based in Leicester and its website (www.bps.org.uk) contains a great deal of information. One purpose of the BPS is to make sure that people involved in psychology, including clients and research participants, are treated ethically. Students of psychology must work within BPS ethical principles. Some of the principles are for practitioners – for example, completing an annual continuing professional development log. Others apply to research, and all researchers must follow these principles.

Principles, guidelines, researchers, psychologists – use of terms

In this section, those researching in psychology are called 'researchers' and those practising in psychology are called 'psychologists'.

The BPS Code of Ethics and Conduct (2009) is outlined below and refers to ethical 'principles'. Ethical 'guidelines' are often mentioned when discussing ethics in psychology, rather than principles. Guidelines tend to build on the principles and to supplement them.

For example, there are guidelines for Internet Mediated Research (IMR), and the guidelines supplement the main BPS Code of Ethics and Conduct, to highlight specific issues in such research. Specific issues that arise when researching online include checking the identity of the person responding, considering issues of privacy and data protection, as well as many of the issues in the code, such as getting informed consent, considering right to withdraw and the important issues of deception and debriefing.

Explore

Find the BPS 'Guidelines for ethical practice in psychological research online' to consider what special ethical issues arise in this area of research.

STUDY HINT

All practical work must follow ethical guidelines. You will be guided about this throughout your course, but you are responsible for your research. Always note in your practical folder the ethical issues that arose from the study and how they were addressed. You are likely to be asked exam questions about such issues.

The BPS four main principles

The four main principles in the BPS Code of Ethics and Conduct (2009) are respect, competence, responsibility and integrity. After discussing these, some specific ethical issues are explored, which link to the four main principles, so that you can use them when discussing studies and in your own practical investigations.

The ethical principle of respect

Respect is about a psychologist or researcher being willing to explain the ethics of any study or practice, and respecting the dignity of others, including any cultural differences, role differences and individual differences. **Individual differences** refer to how people have different identities, such as cultural, age and gender identity. Individual differences can be about language, economic status, marital status, disability, education, religion and other differences too. Respect includes avoiding any unfair practice and avoiding prejudice, and it involves respecting the opinions of others (such as clients and participants).

Definitions

Respect refers to a number of different ethical issues around treating a person as an individual and in a fair and unprejudiced way. **Individual differences** refers to how people are individual rather than 'just' being members of a society (such as part of an 'in-group') and they have different temperaments (related to their 'nature') and different experiences that make them who they are (related to their 'nurture'). Psychology can study people 'as a whole', such as questions in Chapter 1 around 'why people obey' and questions in Chapter 3 about how heroin works in the brain. The study of individual differences importantly focuses not on what is the same in people (looking at people as a whole), but what is different, which can be their memory, their personality, their self-esteem, or other factors around their age, race, gender and economic status.

Respect also includes **privacy** and **confidentiality**. Confidentiality is returned to later in this section (page 313). Privacy is about being sure that a client's or participant's data are what they want shared with others, and being sure that any information they want kept private is not shared. Confidentiality is about not identifying the participant (or client). Privacy and confidentiality come under 'respect' and it is about respecting the person's wishes and hiding their identity from others. In practice, maintaining privacy and confidentiality cannot be promised on all occasions. For example, there are issues around safeguarding children and others, and legal issues have to be exceptions when a promise of confidentiality is given (such as having to disclose illegal acts). A researcher or psychologist must be sure to explain the limits of confidentiality. This is part of giving respect.

Definitions

Privacy refers to avoiding publicising something that someone would prefer not to be known to others. Privacy refers to maintaining silence (in writing, in visual form and in speech) rather than enabling others to find out about such issues. It is about not using someone's name in a way that they would not want it used. Privacy is difficult to define because it can be **socially constructed**, which means it can differ in different cultures. For example, in one culture, people would not just walk into someone else's house, whereas in another culture that might be acceptable and not be an invasion of privacy. **Confidentiality** refers to someone's identity being kept secret, so that someone is not identifiable from information given in a study (or information given about a client by a practitioner).

Definition

Social constructionism is the theory that 'things' are 'what we think they are' rather then 'real' – they are constructed by a society. An example helps to explain. 'Gender' seems to be one thing – it is about the different behaviour and aspects of boys and girls. However, gender behaviour varies in different cultures, so it is said that gender is socially constructed rather than a 'thing'. It can be said that 'education' is socially constructed because what 'education' is differs between cultures and societies.

Another part of respect is getting **informed consent**. Consent must be obtained and must be informed, so that a person knows what they are consenting to. We return to this issue later in this section.

Definition

Informed consent in psychological research refers to getting permission from participants when 'using' them in a study, and permission must come after all possible information has been given to the participants. The consent must be 'informed' in that way.

Another part of respect is self-determination and allowing a participant or client to have power in making their own decisions. This includes the idea of having the **right to withdraw** from therapy or from a piece of research. Issues around right to withdraw are covered in more detail later in this section. Self-determination involves the client or participant having the right to make their own path through life, to make their own decisions and to be respected in that way.

Definition

Right to withdraw refers not only to allowing someone to withdraw from a study or from therapy, which is very important, but also to making sure they understand this right, at the start and throughout the process.

The ethical principle of competence

Competence is about the researcher (and practitioner) and their level of competence with regard to what they are attempting. The issue of competence is examined in more detail later in this section and is about a researcher or psychologist being aware of ethics and the ethical implications around what they are proposing to do. They must be competent to carry out any chosen therapy or research and must refer to others who do have competence, if they are in any doubt. They must watch for any impairment in their performance, taking steps to do something about any such impairment, and they must keep up to date regarding knowledge and developments in the area they are working within, in order to maintain competence in their field.

Definition

Competence is an ethical principle that holds that someone will not claim to be competent when they are not, as a researcher as a psychologist. All research and practice in psychology should be carried out within the researcher's or the psychologist's ability.

The ethical principle of responsibility

Responsibility includes being responsible to a client or participant and doing no harm. This principle is about taking care of clients or participants, such as avoiding distress. Distress is something considered later in this section. The BPS principle of responsibility includes being responsible for the actions of other professionals, such as keeping an eye out for any bad practice and not then 'looking away'. A researcher or practitioner should ask a client or participant to find out about any issues that need to be known that might affect any harm being done to the individual, and they must monitor both physical and mental health, such as when carrying out a study. The researcher must have due regard to individual differences when considering any likely harm that might come from doing their research. No compensation must be offered and there must be reassurance that any right to withdraw does not depend on any financial recompense.

Study using the methodology

Burger (2009), a study you might have looked at in social psychology, replicated Milgram's study going up to just the 150-volt stage rather than the more stressful 450 volts. Burger was careful to explain to participants about their right to withdraw and to assure them that the payment that was made at the start of the study would not be affected if they withdrew at any time. As in Milgram's work, Burger too was careful to give a thorough and immediate debrief.

Within the principle of responsibility, there is mention of researching with animals and the need to be responsible for the welfare of animals, just as with humans. Animals must be well treated, minimising any pain or suffering, including boredom or lasting harm. The BPS Guidelines for Psychologists Working with Animals are part of the Code of Ethics and Conduct. An important part of being responsible when doing research in psychology is **debriefing** after a study. Participants must be told what the study was about and told how their results will be used. They must be assessed for any harm and steps taken to put things right. Debriefing is considered later in this section on ethics.

Definition

Responsibility is an ethical principle that holds a researcher or psychologist responsible for their work. They must be sure that they do no harm and they must assess harm in a debrief after a study (or after therapy). If there is harm, they must take steps to put things right, though the main principle is 'do no harm' and allow no harm to be done to others.

The ethical principle of integrity

The final principle in the BPS code is that of integrity. **Integrity** covers honesty and accuracy in all dealings with others. Results of studies should be published with honesty and accuracy and any representations the researchers make of themselves must be honest and accurate (this relates, for example, to competence). Any conflicts in roles must be clarified (e.g. if someone acting as a therapist is also doing research) and conflicts of interest must be clearly identified and explained. There must be clear personal boundaries with regard to relationships with clients and participants. The principle of integrity includes looking for any misconduct in others and acting on any such misconduct, as well as there being no deceit. **Deception** in research can be seen as necessary by the researcher(s); however, it goes against the ethical principles. This problem is considered later in this section when considering what to do if deception is deemed necessary.

Definitions

Integrity is an ethical principle about a psychologist or researcher as an individual. They must maintain professional boundaries and look for misconduct in others. If they see such misconduct, they must act on it. They must be honest and accurate, and be clear to others about any conflicts of interest. **Deception** refers to being honest and accurate in all dealings with others; it can be a problem when doing research because if the aims of research are made clear to the participants then they may act in accordance with the aims, which will affect the findings. Deception is often 'solved' by a thorough debrief, though there is discussion about whether this is an ethical solution or not.

The BPS Code of Ethics and Conduct: four principles

Progress check 5.14

Identify two issues within each of the four ethical principles in the BPS Code of Ethics and Conduct (2009).

Five ethical guidelines relating to doing research in psychology

The above four principles (respect, responsibility, competence and integrity) underpin all research and practice in psychology. However, it is useful to consider five specific guidelines when evaluating research from an ethical viewpoint. These five guidelines are found in the principles above, and are explained more here because of their focus on carrying out research, which will be your main focus in your course. The full set of principles can be useful when you consider psychology in practice, such as when considering how learning theories contribute to therapy to help with phobias (Chapter 4).

The five guidelines chosen are:

- informed consent
- deceit
- right to withdraw
- debriefing
- competence.

Getting informed consent

All participants should consent to the study, whatever the research method and whatever the study is about. Getting informed consent is part of the ethical principle of respect. It is usually easy to ask people if they will take part, but there is more to it than that. What is the value of their consent if they do not know what is going to happen? There should be informed consent. This means that those who agree to take part must know (be informed about) what the study is about. Observations may be carried out without consent (because you don't know who you will observe – it will depend on who is there). They should be carried out in a public setting where people know that they are likely to be seen. There are special cases with regard to getting informed consent. Children are a special case and parents or guardians must give informed consent as well as the child or young person. Those who are detained for some reason require special treatment as well – for example, they may consent because they feel they have to. Students are a special case because many university psychology courses require students to take part in studies as part of their course.

Assessing the guideline 'getting informed consent'

It is often difficult to get informed consent without affecting the data. For example, in Milgram's (1963) study, if the participants had known that the electric 'shocks' were not real, then the results would not have been about obedience in the same way because the participants would have known that the consequences were not 'real'. Milgram could not get informed consent, but he did try to make his study ethical:

- He asked for volunteers, so participants knew that they were taking part in a study.
- He asked other people (who would not be the participants) before the study if they would agree to take part in such a study and they said that they would. This is **presumptive consent**.
- He asked others, including psychologists, whether they thought that the consequences for the participants would be severe, to which they said no.

Another way is to obtain consent some time before the study starts. This is **prior consent** and involves asking people beforehand to volunteer and explaining that sometimes deception will be necessary. So even if informed consent is not possible, there are other ways of making a study reasonably ethical, although Milgram's study is criticised widely as being unethical.

Milgram said the following about one of his participants:

'I observed a mature and initially poised businessman enter the laboratory smiling and confident. Within 20 minutes he was reduced to a twitching, stuttering wreck, who was rapidly approaching nervous collapse. He constantly pulled on his ear lobe, and twisted his hands. At one point he pushed his fist into his forehead and muttered "Oh God, let's stop it". And yet he continued to respond to every word of the experimenter and obeyed to the end.'

Informed consent is not as difficult to obtain for questionnaires and interviews as it is for experiments because the questions in the survey will suggest what the survey is about (e.g. prejudice). Therefore, the participant is likely to guess the purpose and so it is sensible for the participant to be fully informed for ethical reasons.

However, if it is not possible to obtain informed consent because the data could not then be gathered, a thorough debriefing can make the study more ethical. An offer could also be made to withdraw data from the study if the participant is not happy with having taken part. If this is the case, then follow-up contact should be made to ensure that there is no lasting damage. No study should be carried out if the participant leaves the study in a different state from that when the study began.

Definitions

Prior consent means that, before a study takes part, participants have agreed to whatever is going to take place, even though they are not able to give informed consent for the study itself. **Presumptive consent** means that other people are asked whether they would take part in the study, if they were the participants. They are not the participants but can show whether people would be OK with doing what was going to be asked.

Explore

Investigate different issues around informed consent, such as practices in different cultures, which must be respected. For example: www.who.int/rpc/research_ethics/Process_seeking_IF_printing.pdf.

Avoiding deception

Deception in a study can take many forms. One way of deceiving participants is when informed consent is not obtained. Participants can be deceived when they are not told what they have to do or if they are not told the truth about what they have to do. They can be deceived by not telling them what results are expected, by not telling them how the results will be used or not telling them the roles of other participants within the study.

Assessing the guideline 'avoiding deception'

In experiments in particular, it is sometimes necessary to deceive participants because otherwise their knowledge would affect the results. Milgram (1963) deceived his participants in a number of ways. He told them that the shocks that they would give were real and even gave them a small shock (45 volts) to back this up. He told them that the person they were to give shocks to was another participant, when in fact it was one of his colleagues. He did not tell them that the colleague knew about the study and had been asked to scream and shout to pretend that he was receiving shocks. The participants were deceived from the start because they had volunteered for a learning experiment, whereas the study was about obedience. You can see why Milgram's study has been criticised so strongly for not being ethical.

In questionnaires and interviews, there is often no need for deception, and questions need to be clear. However, even in surveys there is sometimes deception – for example, asking more questions than necessary in order to hide the 'real' question within the set. This is done to avoid demand characteristics (the respondent guessing the aim of the study). However, there should not be too many 'other questions' so that the respondent is not inconvenienced.

If there is deception, then thorough debriefing (below) can help to make the study more ethical. As with lack of informed consent, if participants are unhappy about having taken part, their data should be withdrawn and follow-up contact made to ensure that there are no long-term effects. Milgram contacted his participants after the 1963 study and found that most were happy to have taken part, which went some way towards making his study more ethical.

STUDY HINT

Note here how there is a short paragraph describing the ethical guideline before assessing it and discussing the issues further. Be aware in your reading of what is description and what is evaluation and comment, as questions can ask for either, and a question must be directly focused on.

Giving the right to withdraw

Throughout any study, participants should be given the right to withdraw. At the start, when they have been told all that they can be told about the study without affecting the results, participants should be asked if they want to continue. They should be asked periodically whether they are still happy to continue. At the end, they should be given the right to withdraw their data.

Assessing the guideline 'giving the right to withdraw'

Usually it is quite easy to ask participants if they are happy to continue. However, in some studies, this would affect the results. One example is in the study of obedience. To be obedient, participants have to do as they are told by someone in authority – usually the researcher. That won't work if participants can say they want to leave. Milgram, in a way, did not give the right to withdraw and, when participants seemed to want to leave, he used planned verbal comments to make them continue. Of course, they could still leave the study, as some did, so Milgram was able to say that they always had the right to withdraw. However, this right should have been more explicit.

In interviews, it is easy to give the right to withdraw both at the start and throughout, because the interviewer is interacting with one participant and talking with him or her. However, in questionnaires, it is likely that the right to withdraw will be outlined only at the start. Without anyone there to press the respondent to continue, questions can be missed out or the questionnaire not completed at all, which is equivalent to withdrawing from the study.

There should never be an occasion in any psychology study when a participant is not given the right to leave the study. Children or vulnerable people might not feel that they can leave and should be reminded that they can leave at any time.

Debriefing the participants

Participants are **briefed** at the start of a study to tell them about it – as far as is possible without affecting the data. Then they are asked to give informed consent. It is likely that fully informed consent from a full briefing will not be achieved because something has to be held back for the sake of the study. This means that a complete **debrief** should take place immediately after the study. Participants should also be told at this point that, if they wish, they can withdraw their data. Participants should not be left upset or confused. The debrief should:

- explain the study
- explain what results were expected
- explain the participant's results
- ask the participant about possible withdrawal of results
- check that the participant has no further questions and is not distressed by the study.

Assessing the guideline 'debriefing the participants'

Debrief is usually straightforward because the study is over and the participants can be told all about it. However, debriefing can be difficult in observations of people in public places because, by the time the observation is over, they will have moved on. It might be thought that, as long as they are not looked at as individuals in the observation (for example, they may be studied for their gender alone), then no real personal data are recorded and a debrief is unnecessary. If observing a crowd and keeping a record like a film of events, if individuals are identifiable, they should be found and debriefed. Observations are usually considered to be ethical if they take place in a public setting where those being observed would expect to be seen.

Definitions

The **brief** is before a study and tells the participant all about the study. The **debrief** is afterwards and is the opportunity to put right any misunderstandings, distress or other issues arising from the study. Debriefing is an ethical guideline.

STUDY HINT

'Brief' and 'debrief' have different meanings (see 'Definitions' box). Be sure to use 'debrief' and not 'brief' as these are different.

Being competent to run the study

No researcher should try to carry out a study for which they are not competent, including students and all psychologists. If in doubt, the researcher should ask the opinion of a qualified person. Competence includes:

- understanding the implications of the study
- knowing the ethical guidelines
- getting advice in any area about which the researcher does not feel confident
- being suitably qualified
- adhering to safe practice
- adhering to the Data Protection Act
- knowing where and how to store data.

Assessing the guideline 'being competent to run the study'

There is the problem of not knowing what the results of a study will be and it is hard to assess competence without knowing this. Milgram asked colleagues what they thought and he was careful to obtain advice from other qualified people. With hindsight, it is clear that Milgram's study upset his participants a great deal, but at the time nobody thought that this would be the case. It is interesting to ask whether this makes it more ethical, since it is hard to know if the researcher is competent to run the study or not.

Explore

Do some research into Milgram's views on his study. He was criticised widely for the ethics of his work but he defended himself and made some excellent points - for example, that it is our duty to study tricky areas such as obedience.

Milgram asked participants to give what they thought were very strong electric shocks to another person, and 65 per cent obeyed

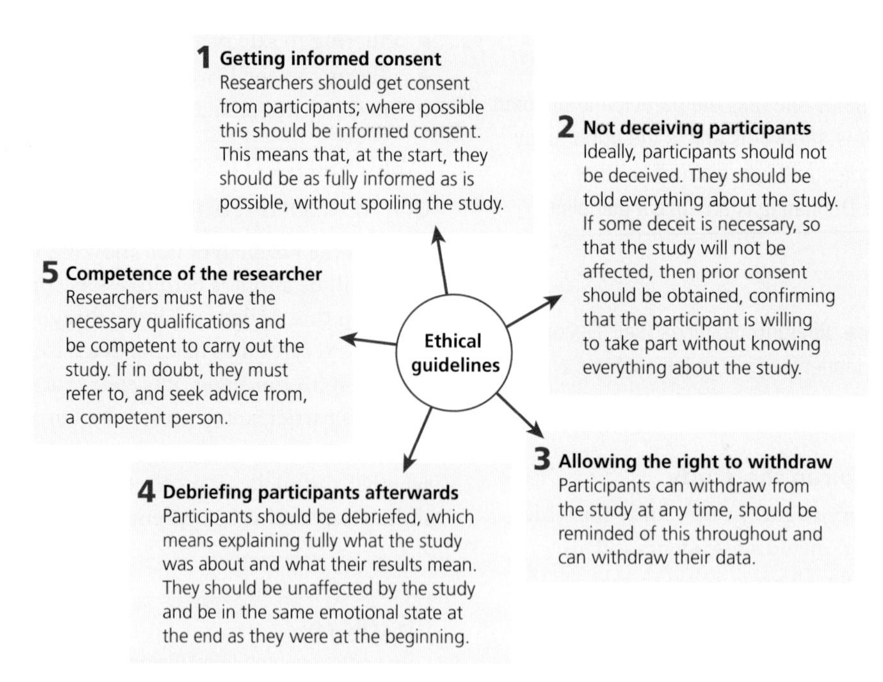

Five ethical guidelines

Risk management

One important issue when carrying out a study is to consider management of risk. It is important when weighing up whether to carry out a study and how to carry it out. There can be risk to participants, researchers and others around, and animals as participants also need to have their risk managed.

There are other risks, not just to humans and animals, but to the environment, for example. There can be political risks and risks for society. However, in studies in psychology a main risk would be to the people or animals involved.

Issues when managing risk

Risk should be managed by taking the highest threat first and considering that, before working down to the lowest level of threat. However, 'highest' is hard to measure. There can be a high risk in that there is a high probability of the risk occurring. There can be a high risk in that there is a low probability of it occurring but any consequences are severe. In practice, risk management is about balancing the features of any threat, looking at the probability of it occurring against the consequences if it does. A high probability of something happening that has severe consequences is the 'highest' threat and must be dealt with first.

There is also intangible risk, which is something that has a high probability of occurring (even 100 per cent) but the consequences are not known. This is hard to manage. This is a knowledge risk – not enough is known to assess the risk properly.

Milgram managed risk by asking both colleagues and students separately what they thought would happen in his study. None of those asked thought any participant would go to the highest voltage level of shock, but in his main study 65 per cent did just that. This shows that it is not easy to manage risk, but that it is very important to try to do so.

Process of risk management

The process is to identify the situation and the likely risk, and then to follow the risk through the procedure of the study, to find as much information about the risk as possible. The idea then is to set out how the risk is going to occur. Ideas about managing the risk can then be put forward and an analysis of the risk can take place, looking at the probability of it occurring and the severity of any consequences, if this is known. Further knowledge can then be sought, before deciding whether the risk can be managed sufficiently for the study to take place. Finally, measures that have been decided upon are put into place. At the end, an assessment can take place, which can add to the knowledge base about that risk and so help in other situations.

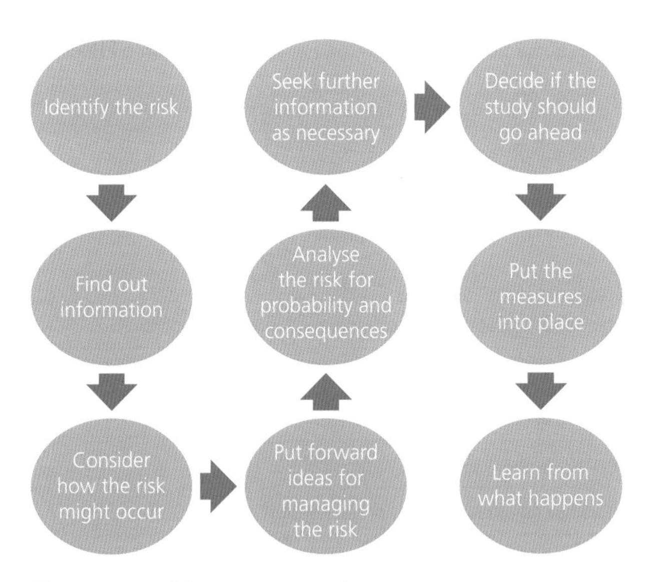

The process of risk management

Solutions to manage risk

A risk can be:

- avoided completely (avoidance)
- reduced as far as possible (mitigation)
- transferred, such as using insurance against the risk (transfer)
- accepted and budgeted for (acceptance).

In psychology studies, avoidance or mitigation are the ideal solutions as transferring a risk or budgeting for it would not fit in with other ethical principles, such as doing no harm.

Risk management in psychology in practice

The BPS is interested in managing risk to people involved with psychologists in practice, such as clinical psychologists and forensic psychologists. For example, people undergoing therapy for depression or anxiety may be at risk of self-harm, and indeed clinical psychologists work with people who are 'self-harming' too. There is the need then to manage the risk to the client/patient. This is done by using a supervisor who oversees any therapy in clinical or counselling psychology and checks the situation carefully throughout, making a referral if necessary.

Forensic psychologists have a special case with offender behaviour, such as when they are in the situation of balancing the risk to the public if behaviour has been threatening to the public, and the benefit to the offender of being released into the community. There are other issues with offenders too, when in prison, and risks have to be managed. There is a need to consider the risk to others if someone has a history of harming others and the probability versus the consequences has to be weighed up.

There is also special consideration given to safeguarding children, and it is clear that confidentiality, such as in the counselling room, only goes so far. If there is any risk detected to children at any stage (not only when a child is a client, but also when an adult reveals issues that might affect a child), then there is a duty for this risk to be passed on. Confidentiality at that stage must be broken. This means that, before a session of counselling, it has to be explained to the client that confidentiality has these limits.

Children are a particular case also because of the rights of the child, which are given in a UN charter (1989). Children have the right to participate in a study and to participate in decisions about them. However, they have a right to be protected too. Studies with children have difficulties in balancing the right to participate with the right to be protected, and there is risk here that must be managed.

BPS Code of Human Research Ethics

The BPS has a code that supplements the Code of Ethics and Conduct (2009) and discusses the principle when doing research of scientific value. Within that section, ethics are considered and management of risk features. Later in the Code of Human Research Ethics, it is stated that the risk of harm must be no greater than what they would be exposed to in their 'normal lifestyle'.

Risk has its own section in the code discussed here. Risk is defined as the potential physical or psychological harm that might be caused by a study being done, including discomfort and stress. Risk concerns someone's values and beliefs, their social status, their privacy and their relationships. The code holds as important that risk should be considered and there should be protocols to address any risk. Ethical issues must be adhered to.

The code lists situations where there is likely to be more than minimal risk, and these situations are listed in Table 5.5.

Table 5.5 Situations where there is likely to be risk in psychological research (according to the BPS Code of Human Research Ethics)

Situation	Risk
Vulnerable participants	Children under 18 are considered to be especially vulnerable, and also some adults, those lacking capacity or in an unequal relationship
Sensitive topics	Topics sensitive in their nature, such as sexuality, experience of violence, ethnicity or gender
Deception	Research involving quite a bit of deception poses a risk
Records	Research where records are accessed, such as getting genetic information or private information about people
Sensitive data	Some data are sensitive to individuals, such as employee data
Harm	Research that causes more than minimum pain, causes distress or harm
Experiences	Research that gives someone an experience like hypnosis or invasive techniques or physical exercise
Labelling	Research that leads someone to label themselves, such as having a bad memory or feeling stupid
Biological samples	Research that involves collection of biological samples, such as taking blood

The BPS Code of Human Research Ethics requires a researcher submitting research to an ethics committee to explain their protocol(s) for risk management and to use cost–benefit analysis when planning a study.

Explore

To explore more, the BPS Code of Human Research Ethics can be accessed here: www.bps.org.uk/sites/default/files/documents/code_of_human_research_ethics.pdf.

Progress check 5.15

List five different situations where there might be risk and where a risk protocol would be needed for a study to be approved by an ethics committee.

Ethical rules when using animal participants

The ethical rules for using animal participants in psychological research are explained in detail in this chapter (pp. 372–375). They are not included in this chapter because your course does not involve doing studies using animals. Ethical issues when using animals in research in psychology include requirements regarding caging and rules about the number of animals used, the use of endangered species and the use of anaesthetics. A Home Office licence is needed. When discussing ethical issues regarding the use of animals in psychological research, do not refer to the guidelines for using humans. Special rules to protect them are needed and it is these that you should discuss when considering non-human animals.

Animals are used in psychological research and guidelines must be followed to protect them

STUDY HINT

In an examination, you might be asked about ethical 'principles' or 'guidelines' and the two terms can be used interchangeably in this case. In this book, 'principles' are the overarching principles of the BPS Code of Ethics and Conduct (2009) and 'guidelines' are taken as the ideas within those principles that are applicable to research, such as 'right to withdraw' and 'informed consent'. However, this is just a way of distinguishing rather than a hard and fast rule.

Test yourself

1. Discuss, using examples from studies, the issues around giving the right to withdraw from a study and the issue of getting informed consent. **(18 marks)**
2. Assess the four ethical principles in the BPS Code of Ethics and Conduct (2009). **(16 marks)**
3. Discuss why ethical principles of research are necessary. **(10 marks)**

Methods in cognitive psychology

In cognitive psychology for your course, you need to learn about field and laboratory experiments as well as case studies of brain-damaged patients, including HM. A lot of what you will cover in cognitive psychology involves laboratory experiments, but field experiments are often used as well. Experiments looking at issues with eyewitness testimony are often field experiments because there is something more natural about doing an experiment 'in the field', which means in a natural setting. If you look at criminological psychology in Year 2, you will find out more about issues with eyewitness testimony. There are a lot of issues when carrying out experiments and you will cover those in cognitive psychology as they fit so well there. Also you will carry out an experiment as your practical investigation in cognitive psychology (pp. 431–442), which is another good reason for examining the experimental research method in this topic area.

This section covers the experimental research method, both laboratory and field, and case studies of brain-damaged patients, including HM. When looking at HM, there is a section on qualitative data since case studies can involve both qualitative and quantitative data. In Chapter 6, you can read about analysis of quantitative data, including using inferential statistics.

Lab experiments are often used in cognitive psychology to test memory

The experimental research method

One research method used in the cognitive approach is the experimental research method. Cognition means thinking and the process of thinking cannot be measured easily by using an interview or a questionnaire. If questions were asked about thinking processes, a participant is not likely to be able to answer them.

Thinking is not easy to study. Early psychologists wanted to find out how information is processed in the brain and they used experiments to find out. A recent method of studying thinking processes is to scan the working brain. In the cognitive approach, you will look at older studies, before scanning was invented. Older studies were experimental, and modern studies still use experiments. Scanning is covered in this chapter (pp. 341–352).

Experiments are used in other areas of psychology, of course, including social psychology. Milgram's studies were experiments. Experiments are used in biological psychology. In learning theories, experiments are also carried out using animals as well as human participants and in that topic area you will look at how experiments use animals (pp. 372–379). So you will come across the experimental research method in all the topic areas.

> **STUDY HINT**
> Although in your course, research methods are split into topic areas so that they make more sense and you can link them to your learning, there are methodological issues that are common between research methods so be ready to use your learning about one research method (e.g. questionnaire) when learning about another research method (e.g. experiment).

Psychology uses experiments for the same reasons that they are used in other sciences. It is important for you to know something about psychology as a science and also about how science works. The experimental research method illustrates clearly how science works.

Psychology is a science

Science involves developing theories that explain events. For example, there is the theory that the Earth moves in a set pattern around the sun. As this theory explains all current measurements and findings, it is accepted as 'true'. Through the development of theories, psychologists want to claim certain 'truths'. For example, in cognitive psychology, you will study a theory of memory that says remembering is not like a tape recorder, it is reconstructive and memories are built using schemas, which are existing templates. You will also study a theory of memory that looks at different parts of memory, under the umbrella term 'working memory'. These are tested theories that are accepted. They have been tested using scientific methods, which tried to show them to be false.

Falsifiability is an important element of scientific testing. Popper is an important name when explaining falsifiability. Popper said that there are many occasions when something is found to be true, but that there is no proof of the truth. This is because to show that the theory is not true there needs to be only one occasion when the theory is found to be false. It can never be known whether this is going to occur. For example, take the theory that 'all swans are white'. Lots of white swans can be found as evidence, but this does not prove that the theory is true. This is because it is impossible to know whether a black swan is going to be found. Once that black swan is found, it is certain that the theory that 'all swans are white' is not true. The only certainty is when something is not true.

Explore

Use the internet or other sources to read about Karl Popper's ideas about falsifiability and science.

Definition

Falsifiability is the idea that, in science, the search should be for falsification of a theory not focusing on finding data that fit the theory. We can say more certainly that a hypothesis is not always right when we find something that goes against it, but no matter how many things go with a hypothesis, that does not prove we will not find something that goes against it in the end. So we cannot really prove anything 'right' – we can only perhaps prove it 'wrong'.

STUDY HINT

In learning theories, you need to know about psychology and science so this material is useful there too.

Science uses experiments

Science involves generating **hypotheses** (predictions) from theories and testing to see whether they are false or whether the findings support the prediction. A theory is an idea about why something happens, usually based on previous theories or research. A hypothesis is a statement of what the theory predicts.

Practice memory span experiment

The 'multi-store model' of memory (pp. 78–83) has three areas of processing:

- sensory memory, which is fleeting, and if information is attended to it goes into the second store
- short-term memory, which lasts longer but still only up to about 30 seconds and which holds just a small amount of information (about seven chunks of information)
- long-term memory, which lasts potentially forever and which can hold a potentially unlimited amount of information.

All these elements have been tested using the experimental method.

You could carry out a short experiment to test the multi-store model. This experiment tests the capacity of short-term memory according to the multi-store model of memory. You need about ten willing participants, perhaps family and friends. First, prepare materials: a) Write out a series of 15 letters of the alphabet and set them out in groups of three letters, so that each group of three is a recognisable pattern, such as FBI CAB USA PHD LOL – this is List A. b) Using the same letters, present them in threes again but this time having no meaning, such as BFL CUH SAA BOI PDL – this is List B. Then carry out the study. Alternately using List A and List B, ask each participant (separately, so that the others cannot hear the letters) if you can test their memory span. Remember to adhere to ethical principles. Explain that you will show them a string of letters for about 30 seconds, which you will time. Then you will ask them to write down in order any letters they can remember. Check that the instructions have been understood, check ethics (such as giving the right to withdraw) and be sure to debrief by telling each participant what the study was about.

Many studies have been done to look at memory span, which is generally seen as spanning 5–9 items. For example, Baddeley and Logie (1999) suggested that the span of 5–9 items was found for linguistic information (but not for visual spatial information, which was more like 3–5 items – this difference relates to the working memory model, which you will study in cognitive psychology). You would expect your participants to be able to write down 5–9 letters in order when the letters are mixed up (List B) as that is the capacity of short-term memory and 30 seconds keeps the task within short-term memory. However, you should find that the participants with List A can remember them all probably. That is because they will have five chunks of information that has meaning for them, so given that memory span is from 5–9 items, having five chunks should mean all are recalled and in order.

In evaluation of your study, you could say that, perhaps, List B items have meaning for a participant, such as having PDL as their initials.

Once you have done this study using these instructions, or have done something similar in class, you will have carried out an experiment.

Explore

See what other studies you can find using the terms 'memory span' and 'short-term memory'. Focus on their use of the experimental method and consider why the experiment is so useful in cognitive psychology.

STUDY HINT

One of the contemporary studies in cognitive psychology looks at age and memory span. Sebastián and Hernández-Gil (2012) measure memory span of five year olds, right up to 17 year olds, and then compare with elderly people and two other groups. They found that from five years through to 17 years memory span improves. This shows that this chapter is not an isolated part of your course – it links closely to what you are studying in your topic areas.

Even if you do not carry out the study looking at capacity of short-term memory explained above, it is worth reading through it because it is an experiment and can be used to illustrate issues in experiments. The hypothesis is 'there is a difference in recall of 15 letters grouped in threes, and the letters that are grouped according to meaning will be recalled better (in order) than the same letters not grouped'.

When testing a hypothesis based on a theory, science uses controls to avoid bias. Everything other than what is being studied must be controlled to keep it the same throughout, so that it does not affect the study. Concepts have to be measurable and produce quantitative data (involve numbers). Therefore, mathematical analysis can be carried out. Science is objective; it is important not to let subjective (personal) opinions affect results.

If studies involve careful controls, objectivity and measurable concepts, then the results should be replicable. Replicability means that a study can be repeated exactly. A study is said to be reliable if, when repeated, the same results are found. If findings are **reliable** and support the hypothesis, then the theory is supported and a body of knowledge is built. If, however, the findings do not support the hypothesis, then the theory is either abandoned or amended (see diagram below). Then further hypotheses are generated and scientific knowledge is built up.

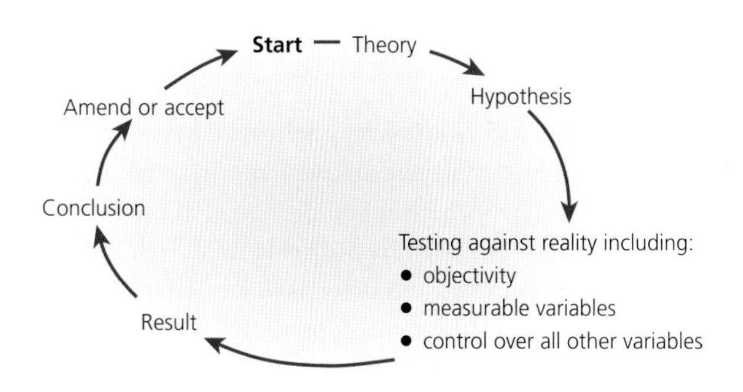

Processes involved in scientific testing

Features of experiments in psychology

STUDY HINT

Note that some terms have already been explained earlier in this chapter, such as hypotheses when discussing questionnaires. If you have already noted down a term and its meaning, check the meaning each time, as that will help you to fully understand it. The emboldened terms are also defined in the Glossary at the back of the book.

Features of experiments in psychology mirror features of experiments in science. This section probably has a lot of new ideas in it, with new terms to learn. It is worth reading this through more than once to be sure that all is understood. You will find that you need all these features of experiments when you come to doing your own practical investigation and this is a main section when studying psychology, so be ready to spend some time on this. Remember, a study is only as good as the methodology it uses, and findings from studies are usually sought in order to help people or society, so studying psychology necessarily involves studying its methodology, even if that does not seem the most interesting area.

Explore

Late in his career, psychologist Cyril Burt is widely thought to have made up his data, one piece of evidence being that his data from twins were the same even after new data were added. Use the internet or some other source to investigate Cyril Burt and the accusations made, so that you can see how important it is to study the methodology of a study, before accepting the findings.

Hypotheses

An **experimental hypothesis** is generated – this is a statement of what is expected. The experimental hypothesis is the **alternative hypothesis** (alternative to the null hypothesis). The alternative hypothesis is called an experimental hypothesis when the research method is an experiment. The **null hypothesis** states that any difference or relationship expected is due to chance – there is no relationship or difference as predicted. It is the null hypothesis that is tested when using statistical tests. For example, in the practice memory span study (page 316), the experimental hypothesis was given as 'there is a difference in recall of 15 letters grouped in threes, and the letters that are grouped according to meaning will be recalled better (in order) than the same letters not grouped'. A null hypothesis could be 'any difference between recall of the letters (in order) depending on whether the "meaningful" list or the "non-meaningful" list is used is due to chance or some other variable, not to the "meaningfulness" of the lists'.

STUDY HINT

It is useful to know how to write out an alternative/experimental hypothesis and a null hypothesis. Exam questions that involve stimulus material in the form of a study often ask for a hypothesis.

STUDY HINT

Hypotheses were discussed earlier in this chapter when questionnaires were considered as a research method (pp. 282–283). Be sure to make links when learning about methodology.

Progress check 5.16

Here are some suggested studies that you could carry out using the experimental research method. For each study, write out an experimental hypothesis and a null hypothesis.

1. To see whether an interference task in short-term memory, such as counting backwards for 15 seconds after seeing a list of letters, affects recall of those letters.
2. To see whether, after hearing a story read out, recall of that story is poorer over time, with less and less of the story being recalled correctly over a period of a few weeks.
3. To see whether a list of words in categories is better recalled than a list of the same words but randomly presented.

Directional and non-directional hypotheses

A hypothesis may or may not predict the direction that the results will take. For example, if the experimental hypothesis is 'presenting 20 words grouped into five categories leads to better recall of the words than if the same words are presented in a randomised order' then a direction is predicted – recall of words will be better if words are categorised. However, if the hypothesis is 'presenting in categories affects recall of words' then there is no direction. It is not clear whether recall of words will be better or worse if presented in categories. The first example is a **directional** (or **one-tailed**) **hypothesis**; the second example is a **non-directional** (or **two-tailed**) **hypothesis**.

Progress check 5.17

Note down whether the following hypotheses are directional or non-directional.

1. Divers remember more words when recalling words in the same situation in which they were learnt than when recalling in a different situation.
2. Counting backwards to provide interference in short-term memory affects recall of letters.
3. Recall of a story is affected by the length of time since hearing the story.

Definitions

Hypotheses can be directional or non-directional. A **directional hypothesis** states the direction that is expected. It is clear in a directional hypothesis which way the results are expected to go, such as 'more words will be recalled...' A **non-directional hypothesis** does not make this claim; the results can go either way, such as 'there is a difference in recall of words...' When you get to statistical testing, you will find you need to know if a hypothesis is one- or two-tailed: **one-tailed** is directional; **two-tailed** is non-directional.

The two main variables

Variables are whatever is likely to affect the experiment. They include:

- what is being tested
- what is being measured
- what else is likely to affect the results.

There are two important variables in any study – the **independent variable (IV)** and the **dependent variable (DV)**. The independent variable is changed or manipulated by the researcher. This is to see the effect on the dependent variable. The dependent variable is measured by the researcher. It changes as a result of manipulating the independent variable. It is common practice to use the abbreviations 'IV' and 'DV' when referring to these variables, but you need to know the full terms. Both the independent and dependent variables have to be measurable; to make them measurable is to operationalise them. An independent variable often has two conditions. A **condition** is one part of a study, and two conditions means there are two parts to a study. In the memory span practice experiment suggested earlier, one condition was that the 15 letters were set out in threes that had meaning and the other condition had the same 15 letters but set out in threes with no meaning.

STUDY HINT

Operationalisation was covered earlier when looking at method in social psychology. Be sure to link ideas to build up a full understanding of methodology in psychology.

These ideas can be better understood by using an example (see box below)

A practice blocking rehearsal experiment to explain the experimental method

Memories are said to move from short-term to long-term memory using rehearsal. Memories are in short-term memory for up to 30 seconds. Here is an example study based on the idea of rehearsal. Two participants are given a task for about 30 seconds, such as learning 20 words, One participant then has an interference task to stop them rehearsing the words. The interference task is having to count backwards aloud in threes from 357 for 30 seconds (354 is the first number they call out). The other participant does not count backwards - they have a 30-second delay. The participant without interference should be able to transfer the words into long-term memory using rehearsal and should recall more words.

The hypothesis for the practice 'interference' study is 'there is a difference in recall of 20 words depending on whether someone has to count backwards aloud for 30 seconds directly after learning the words or whether someone has a 30-second silence directly after learning the words'. There is an important reason for the hypothesis being the fuller version. The independent variable in this study could be said to be having an interference task or not. However, this is not accurate enough and does not give enough detail. The variables 'interference task or not' and 'recall' have to be operationalised because they are not measurable directly, and the experimental method requires measurable factors. Interference has to be explained – it means doing something to prevent rehearsal – but this too requires explanation. Recall also needs explaining. The fuller hypothesis includes the detail that an interference task of counting backwards for 30 seconds was compared with silence for 30 seconds. The independent variable is whether or not there is the interference task of counting backwards for 30 seconds or not, and the dependent variable is the number of words recalled from the list of 20 words.

It is usually easy to identify what is being measured in a study because that will be the scores and the data gathered (dependent variable). Once this has been identified, it is usually easy to identify the independent variable.

STUDY HINT

When you have to find the variables in a study, identify the dependent variable first.

Progress check 5.18

Explain why the example hypothesis given for the memory span experiment (page 136) is spelled out in so much detail. Consider issues around operationalisation, which were explained when discussing aims and hypotheses at the start of this chapter (page 282).

Definitions

The **dependent variable** is what is measured in a study, and in a table of results the dependent variable is represented by the numbers. The dependent variable is what is being scored and noted down, such as number of words recalled. The **independent variable** is the other main variable in a study, the one that is set up by the experimenter, such as whether there is an interference task or not. A **condition** in an experiment is part of the independent variable, which has been set up by the experimenter. For example, if half the participants have a categorised list to recall and half have the same list but randomly presented, one condition is 'categorised' and one condition is 'randomised'.

Progress check 5.19

Here are some alternative/experimental hypotheses. Identify the independent and dependent variables for each hypothesis.

1. Divers will recall more words from a list that they learnt underwater when they recall underwater than when they recall on land.
2. Students will score more marks in an examination if it is taken in the room where they learnt the material than if they take the examination in a different room.
3. There will be more letters recalled from a list of 21 letters if the letters are grouped (chunked) into recognisable sets of three letters (such as CSI) than if the letters are presented randomly.

Other variables

There are other variables that might affect the results in a study. These are **extraneous variables**. A requirement in an experiment is to control to decrease the number of extraneous variables. Extraneous variables are those that might affect the results, as well as, or instead of, the independent variable. Examples of variables that have to be controlled in an experiment are:

- **participant variables** – for example, age, gender, experience and mood of the participants
- **situational variables** – for example, temperature, noise, interruptions and light.

When extraneous variables are not controlled for and affect the results, they are called **confounding variables**.

Definitions

Situational variables are those that are connected with the situation that the study takes place in, such as a noisy environment or it being morning. **Participant variables** are those that are connected with the participant, such as their mood, or whether they are hungry, or male or female. **Extraneous variables** are those that can affect the findings of a study; situational and participant variables are extraneous variables. If an extraneous variable is not controlled in a study, and if it, therefore, affects the results, it becomes a **confounding variable**.

Controls

In any experiment, the researcher must control as many variables as possible (other than the independent variable). The aim is to show that the change in the independent variable causes the change in the dependent variable. Therefore, it is important to ensure that nothing else, including participant and situational variables, can affect the results. One aspect that is controlled is the information given to participants with standardised instructions, so that each participant has the same information. Standardised instructions are used for questionnaires and for interviews and were discussed earlier in this chapter (page 000). If controls are thorough, so that all extraneous variables are kept the same in all conditions in an experiment, then it can be said that nothing causes any change in the dependent variable except for the changes set up by the experimenter in the independent variable. Therefore, it can be claimed, as the experimental hypothesis claims, that the change in the independent variable caused the change in the dependent variable. The independent and dependent variable have a **cause-and-effect relationship** – the change in the IV caused the effect in the DV.

Progress check 5.20

In the practice memory span experiment that was suggested earlier, what were the controls that were put into place?

Explanation

When controls are put in place, only changes in the independent variable should cause any changes in the dependent variable. This means there is a **cause-and-effect relationship** between the independent and dependent variable, and that is what the hypothesis is suggesting.

Independent variable: what the experimenter changes

Dependent variable: what is measured as a result of the IV

Extraneous variables: might affect the result so should be controlled for

Participant variables: extraneous variables such as mood and state

Situational variables: extraneous variables such as time of day or place

Confounding variables: if extraneous variables do affect the findings, they are then called confounding variables

Different variables in experiments

Experimenter effects

Another aspect that needs to be controlled as far as possible is the effect of the experimenter. **Experimenter effects** come from cues or signals from an experimenter that can affect the participant's response. Cues might be tone of voice or non-verbal cues, such as gestures or facial expression. It is difficult to control such effects. The best way is to have someone else carry out the experiment, rather than the designer.

In a **double-blind technique**, the participants are not aware which group they are in or what the study is about. The study is carried out by someone other than the person who knows who is doing what. Neither the participants nor the person running the study knows precisely what is expected.

In a **single-blind technique**, the participants are not aware of what is expected or the condition they are in but the person carrying out the study is. The single-blind technique stops participants' expectations from affecting the results but does not stop experimenter effects.

The double-blind technique is the better of the two.

Experimenters must make sure that they do not affect the results

Definitions

Experimenter effects are things about the experimenter that affect the results, rather than the change in the independent variable. They are researcher effects but are called 'experimenter effects' in experiments. Issues such as gender, age, tone of voice and what the experimenter is wearing can all be experimenter effects. A **double-blind technique** stops experimenter effects because neither the participant nor the experimenter knows which group a participant is in. A **single-blind technique** is when a participant does not know what group they are in. The idea is that any bias from knowing something about the study cannot occur.

Explore

Robert Rosenthal has studied experimenter effects and their power to affect experimental results. Use the internet or another source to find out what Rosenthal says about such effects and what should be done to try to avoid them.

Experimental (participant) design

When designing a study that uses an experiment or another research method, a decision has to be made about what design to use with regard to the participants. The researcher can ask participants to partake in all the conditions of the study or in only one condition. When participants do all the conditions of the study, this is called **repeated measures design** because the 'measures' or 'conditions' are repeated (participants do all parts). When participants do only one of the conditions, this is called **independent groups** because there are different participants in the groups and they do different conditions. There is one more experimental design – **matched pairs** – which is explained below.

Suppose that a researcher hypothesises that: 'more is recalled about a story after two hours than after two days'.

In a repeated measures design, the researcher would ask participants to hear the story and recall it after two hours and then they would go back to the same participants and ask them to recall the story again in two days. This is similar to Bartlett's idea when carrying out the *War of the Ghosts* study, which looks at the reconstructive theory of memory (pp. 95–99). In the repeated measures design, the participants do both conditions (recall after two hours and recall after two days). In an independent groups design, the researcher would ask one group of participants to hear the story and recall it after two hours and a different group of participants (an independent group) to hear the story and recall it after two days.

A **matched pairs design** uses different participants, as does an independent groups design. Here, the participants are paired up, one from each group, according to what the researcher thinks are important factors – for example age, gender, social class or ethnicity. Although there are different participants doing each condition, this design is treated as if it is a repeated measures design because the researcher is trying to use participants who are as similar as possible to control the participant variables. It is difficult to match participants and make sure they are matched in all important ways. For these reasons, matched pairs designs are rare (unless perhaps using identical twins).

Progress check 5.21

Decide which participant design should be used in each of the following studies.

1. The aim is to look at the effect of gender on driving ability on a specially laid-out driving course.
2. The aim is to look at whether recall of a story involves less and less detail over time.
3. The aim is to see whether a list of words that sound alike are recalled better or worse than a list of words that do not sound alike.

Strengths and weaknesses of participant design

Repeated measures

- One strength of a repeated measures design is that the same participants do all the conditions, so participant variables (features of a participant that might affect the results) are controlled. Each participant does all the conditions, so any feature will affect both (or all) conditions and, therefore, will cancel out. For example, no matter what characteristics a participant has, if they affect the data at all, these will affect both conditions.
- Another strength is that more data can be gathered because each person does all conditions. If a different person is needed for each of two conditions, then double the number of people is needed. This could be inconvenient or costly and, possibly, less ethical.
- One weakness of a repeated measures design is that there might be **order effects**. Whichever condition participants do first might be their best performance simply because they are less tired than when undertaking the task for the next condition (**fatigue effect**). Participants might do the second task better because, having already done the first task, they know what to do (**practice effect**). An order effect will affect the results and, if not noticed, would mean drawing a wrong conclusion. With a fatigue effect, the results of the first task will be better than the results of the second task; with a practice effect, the results of the second task will be better. Either effect could mean the results are not due to manipulating the independent variable, so the study will not be useful.
- Another weakness is that there might be demand characteristics. These occur when participants' responses are affected by guessing what the study is about. They might try to please the researcher or go against what they think is predicted. Either way the results are affected. For example, when participants are asked to decide whether words rhyme or not and are then asked to decide whether characteristics of a word are true or not, they might guess that the second task is harder, and so do worse. This is not true – they should do better – but their thinking may affect the results.

Definitions

Order effects refer to when participants do more than one condition in a study and they all do the conditions in the same order. For example, if someone is learning a list of words in categories and then a list of the same words but randomised in order, order effects can occur if they all do the categorised list first (or the randomised list first). There are two order effects. The **practice effect** means that a participant might do the second condition better, having practised with the first. The **fatigue effect** means that they might do the second condition worse, having got tired doing the first condition. Either way there is resulting bias in the data.

Independent groups

- One strength of an independent groups design is that there are no order effects because different people do the different conditions. This strength of independent groups designs is a weakness of repeated measures designs.
- Another strength of an independent groups design is that it is less likely that demand characteristics will affect the results. This strength of independent groups designs is a weakness of repeated measures designs.
- One weakness is that participant variables might affect the results. For example, there might be more older people in one group than in the other, which, if age affects recall, might influence the results. This weakness of independent groups designs is a strength of repeated measures designs.
- Another weakness is that more participants are needed because different people do the different conditions. This is a weakness for a number of reasons:
  - It might be more unethical.
  - It might mean that the sample takes longer to obtain.
  - It might mean that the study either takes longer or is more difficult to carry out because the participants have to be split into groups and do the study at a different time.

STUDY HINT

Note that strengths for one design are often weaknesses for another, and vice versa. Learn them in this way to help you to remember them.

Matched pairs designs

- Matched pairs designs are similar to repeated measures designs, so participant variables should not affect the findings. *If* the important participant variables for a study have been matched, then the results should be the same as if the same participants had carried out the study.

- Another strength is that because different people are doing the different conditions, there will not be order effects.
- A weakness of matched pairs designs is that different people are used (even though matched in some ways) so there will still be participant variables that might affect the results. For example, it might be difficult to match type of education or background. Matching exactly will not occur, even if identical twins are used.
- Another weakness is that more people are needed than for a repeated measures design, with the problems that this may entail.

Counterbalancing and randomisation

When a repeated measures design is used, order effects can affect the results to such an extent that the findings are not useful. However, steps can be taken to minimise order effects.

In **counterbalancing**, the researcher alternates the conditions for each participant. For example, when there are two conditions, one participant does the first condition followed by the second condition. The next participant does the second condition followed by the first condition, and so on. Order effects can still occur but should cancel out. If the participants get tired after the first condition, then the first participant will do less well on the second condition. However, the order is reversed for the next participant.

In **randomisation**, the order in which the participants do the conditions is randomised. For example, if a study has two conditions, a coin could be tossed to see which condition is done first. This should help to cancel out order effects.

Practical

When carrying out an experiment with a repeated measures design, make sure that you use counterbalancing or randomisation when allocating conditions to participants.

Explanation

Counterbalancing is about alternating the order of the conditions that each participant does. Participant 1 can do condition one first, then condition two; Participant 2 does condition two first and then condition one. This can help with order effects. **Randomisation** can work too, where a coin is tossed (for example) to decide which condition is done first for each participant.

Progress check 5.22

How does counterbalancing help to alleviate order effects in a repeated measures design?

Two types of experiment

Two types of experiment are **laboratory experiments** and **field experiments**. The material outlined above about experiments applies, to a greater or lesser degree, to both types. It is important, however, to know the differences between them.

Laboratory experiments

Laboratory experiments take place either in a laboratory or in a controlled setting, which is unnatural for the participants and artificial. Scientific experiments take place in laboratories, and laboratory experiments in psychology are seen as the most scientific. This is because one variable (independent variable) is manipulated and other variables are kept constant or controlled so that the effects of that manipulation can be seen on what is being measured (dependent variable). A common design is to have an **experimental group** and a **control group** – the experimental group does something and the control group does not. Therefore, the control group provides a **baseline measure** – that is, what the dependent variable would be like without manipulation. The results for the experimental group are compared against the baseline measure. This is important because otherwise the 'normal' situation would not be known.

For example, consider the hypothesis 'there will be more letters recalled from a list of 21 letters if the letters are grouped (chunked) into recognisable sets of three letters (e.g. CSI, FBI, and CIA) than if the same letters are presented randomly (e.g. FIS, BIA and CIC)'. One group of participants, the experimental group, has the letters presented in groups (chunked); the other, the control group, has the letters presented randomly.

There are two groups of participants, so this is an independent groups design. If it were a repeated measures design, the participants would have to learn the same list (albeit differently presented) twice. The two conditions would have to be carried out some time apart so that the participants forgot the letters.

Explanation

A **laboratory experiment** takes place in an artificial, controlled environment that is not natural for the participants. It has careful controls, as do all experiments; the features of experiments explained above are involved in a laboratory experiment. Experiments often have a **control group** and an **experimental group**. In biological psychology, you will study Raine *et al.*'s (1997) study, which uses PET scanning to see if the brains of people pleading not guilty (to murder) by reason of insanity are in some way different. The researchers have to be able to say 'different from those not charged with murder' and to do this they use a control group, which is matched in many ways to the experimental group (the participants pleading not guilty by reason of insanity).

Definitions

A **baseline measure** is the measure of a participant before a manipulation. For example, if a researcher wants to know if an intervention changes a measure, they need to know the original measure – the baseline. In a study to see if children copy an adult's hitting behaviour, there is a baseline measure of how aggressive the children are to start with. Otherwise, if children are very aggressive after manipulation, the researchers cannot be sure that it was watching the aggressive adult that caused it. Often a baseline measure is a score and can come from a control group.

Explore

When you study learning theories, you will come across Bandura's work in the 1960s, called the Bobo doll studies. You might like to explore his work now, using the internet, to look at the controls he used, including checking that the baseline measure of aggression was similar for all the children who took part.

Field experiments

Field experiments are experiments with as many controls as possible and a manipulated independent variable, but which are carried out **in the field**, rather than in a laboratory situation. Sherif *et al.* (1954/1961) carried out a field experiment (Chapter 1) that involved boys in a natural setting: a summer camp. Other than the study being in the field rather than a laboratory, all other features of a laboratory experiment apply to field experiments.

Definition

In this context, **in the field** means in the participant's natural setting.

Strengths and weaknesses of the different types of experiment

Laboratory experiments

- Laboratory experiments are replicable, which means that they can be repeated. This is because of controls, such as standardised instructions. **Reliability** is tested by carrying out a study more than once. For there to be reliability, there must first be replicability. Reliability can be tested using statistical tests (Chapter 6).

STUDY HINT

It is often said that experiments are reliable when what is meant is that they are replicable. They are only reliable if they have been repeated and the same results have been obtained. Baddeley's studies of working memory (such as his 1966b study, which is covered in cognitive psychology) are replicated a lot and also similar studies have been carried out, so his findings about working memory are reliable. You should only say that experiments are reliable if they have been repeated and the same results found. It is safer to say that experiments are useful because they are replicable and can be tested for reliability.

- Another strength of laboratory experiments is that a cause-and-effect relationship between variables can be shown. The laboratory experiment is the only way of doing this. This is because of the controls – if only the independent variable is altered, any change in the dependent variable must be due to the change in the independent variable. There is **internal validity** if there are no confounding variables so cause and effect can be claimed.
- A third strength of laboratory experiments is their **objectivity**. There are strict controls over all variables except for the independent and dependent variables so nothing should affect the data other than the independent variable. Regarding the people running the experiment, nothing about them should affect the data because they are not interpreting data; they are measuring in a controlled way that can be repeated by others and, to a large extent, gathering quantitative data. There should be no **subjectivity** or interpretation as there can be when gathering and analysing qualitative data.
- A weakness of laboratory experiments is that the tasks that arise from manipulating the independent variable are not natural. Therefore, they might not be measuring 'real' behaviour. If the task is not natural, the results of the task lack **validity**, which means it is difficult to apply the results to the real world. This is a problem because the idea is to find out about real behaviour *not* behaviour set up by a researcher. Consider the example of investigating whether recall of a list of 21 letters is affected by whether or not they are grouped – it is not often that we need to learn in this way in real life.

(Though knowing more about memory span can have practical applications, as Sebastián and Hernández-Gil (2012) demonstrate, when they show that older people have a better memory span than children at 5–6 years, but not as good as young people at 15–17 years.)

- A second weakness is the unnatural setting. Not only are participants likely to be doing an unnatural task, they are in an unnatural environment. This means that there is no **ecological validity**. Occasionally, the laboratory experiment has valid findings because, even if the setting is not natural, the response is. This is true of some classical conditioning studies – for example, measuring salivation in dogs. When food is brought in, a dog will salivate to the same extent whatever the situation (Chapter 4). When the response is a reflex such as this, it is likely to be valid anywhere. However, Pavlov's studies are an exception; laboratory experiments are not usually ecologically valid, particularly those in the cognitive approach.

Definition

Ecological validity is connected with the setting (ecology) of the participant/experiment.

- A third weakness of laboratory experiments is that the strict control of all variables apart from the independent variable and the use of experimental and control groups mean that the experimenter will focus on the conditions of the independent variable and on which group participants are in. Everything else is equal, so the experimenter will focus on, for example, whether the participants are learning grouped (chunked) or randomised letters. That focus may be picked up by the participants. Something about the tone, gestures or facial expression of the experimenter might give them a clue about what is expected and they could react accordingly. Such cues can lead to experimenter effects. One way to avoid this is to use a double-blind technique.

STUDY HINT

Use your learning about features of experiments when considering strengths and weaknesses of experiments, such as double-blind techniques and experimenter effects.

STUDY HINT

Note how in this section about lab and field experiments, examples have been used from other topic areas in your course. For example, Bandura and Pavlov (learning theories), Raine *et al.* (biological psychology), Sherif *et al.* (social psychology) and Sebastián and Hernández-Gil (cognitive psychology). Try to bring in all your learning when you are studying methodology as there are many examples you can use from your course to help your learning.

Field experiments

- One strength of field experiments is that they take place in a more natural environment than laboratory experiments. Therefore, field experiments are more likely to have ecological validity. The results relate more closely to situations in real life than those of laboratory experiments and may, therefore, be more valid.
- Another strength is that they have most of the controls of a laboratory experiment. Cause-and-effect conclusions can often be drawn, giving **internal validity**.
- A third strength is that, as with laboratory experiments, there should be objectivity in that the independent variable should be affecting the depending variable and nothing else, given the careful controls. There should be no interpretation of data by experimenters as, usually, quantitative data are used and measures are carefully controlled.
- A weakness of field experiments is that it is harder to control the variables than it is in a laboratory because the setting is natural. Therefore, features of the setting can affect the results. So the results may not be valid (internal validity) with regard to the task; they may be caused by something other than the independent variable.
- A second weakness is that they are more difficult to replicate than laboratory experiments. The setting and circumstances are likely to have aspects that are unique even if, in general terms, the experiment can be set up again in a similar way. If a study is difficult to replicate then it is difficult to show that the results are reliable. Replication may show **predictive validity** in that a measure (for example, aggression) can be tested later (for example, to see if the score matrices show 'real' measures of aggression) and if it does, there is predictive validity.
- A third weakness is that field experiments can be affected by experimenter effects. With the setting not well controlled, it is even more difficult to make sure that participants do not react because of their expectations of the study, by deriving cues from the experimenter.

STUDY HINT

Note that strengths and weaknesses of research methods are general, rather than specific. It is better, for example, to say a research method 'gathers more valid data than another method', than to say it 'gathers valid data'. Avoid statements that are too precise.

When evaluating a study, you could use issues around its methodology, such as questioning validity if it is an experiment. However, although experiments have general strengths and weaknesses, when discussing a particular study, you should be specific.

Progress check 5.23

Explain the difference between field and laboratory experiments.

Test yourself

1 Describe two types of experiment. For each type of experiment, explain one strength and one weakness. **(12 marks)**
2 Describe the three types of participant designs. For each design, explain two strengths and two weaknesses. **(18 marks)**
3 Give three studies that are laboratory experiments. For each experiment, identify the independent and dependent variables and whether the hypothesis is directional or non-directional. **(12 marks)**
4 Discuss when each type of experiment should be used and the relative values of each type of experiment to society and/or psychology. Use examples of studies in your answer. **(12 marks)**
5 Explain the links between a particular participant design and psychology as a science. In your answer, consider aspects of control and the aim to establish cause-and-effect relationships. **(12 marks)**
6 Discuss whether experiments are more valid or more reliable and why this is important. **(12 marks)**

Analysing data from experiments

When analysing quantitative data from experiments, you will be using descriptive statistics and inferential statistics.

Descriptive statistics

Descriptive statistics include the mean, median and mode (measures of central tendency) and graphs (bar chart, histogram and frequency). You will also be covering measures of dispersion (the range and standard deviation), which also describe the data.

- The mean is the average where you add up a set of scores and then divide the result of the addition by the number of scores in the set.
- The median is the middle score in a set of scores.
- The mode is the most common score in a set of scores.

Using the mean, median and mode

If data are interval or ratio (actual scores used mathematically), then using all three measures of central tendency helps to show the pattern of the scores.

Table 5.6 Scores of five participants and how many letters they recalled in a test of memory span

Participant	Number of letters recalled in a memory span study without chunking (21 letters)	Number of letters recalled in a memory span study with chunking (21 letters)
1	6	18
2	8	12
3	6	12
4	5	15
5	9	10
Mean	6.8	11.2
Median	6	12
Mode	6	12

It can be seen that both sets of scores are normally distributed in that the mean, median and mode are very similar. A sense check of the data (which means looking closely without doing any testing) shows that when the 21 letters were chunked, the participants did do a lot better than when they did not have the chunking.

Whether a mean, median or mode can be calculated depends on the level of measurement – the type of data. Data in categories, such as 'yes/no' data (nominal data), can be counted but this is just counting the numbers in each category and so a mathematical calculation does not work and neither the median nor the mode is possible. Data that are rankings or ratings use numbers but the numbers are not 'real' numbers. Your rank of '8' for attractiveness might match my '6'. They are numbers but some mathematical calculations are not possible and only the median and mode would suit. It is when data are truly mathematical, such as measuring reaction time or temperature, or number of letters recalled, that the mean average is suitable. The median and mode would also be suitable.

Table 5.7 Measures of central tendency that can be used depending on the data

	Categories (nominal)	Ranking or rating (ordinal)	Real numbers with equal intervals between them (interval/ratio)
Mode	✔	✔	✔
Median		✔	✔
Mean			✔

- Percentages help to display data too as they make scores directly comparable (because the percentage is out of 100 in all cases, so there is comparability).

Using percentages

The advantage of using percentages is that they take into account the numbers in the sample, which might be different. For example, see the following government figures for December 2012:

- 42 per cent of marriages end in divorce in England and Wales.
- 34 per cent of marriages are expected to end in divorce by the twentieth wedding anniversary.
- 16 per cent of marriages last to the sixtieth wedding anniversary.
- Of women who married for the first time in 1976, 53 per cent were divorced by the thirtieth wedding anniversary if they married before they were 20 years old.

- Graphs help to display data. They need to be carefully labelled so that they can be interpreted without any more information.

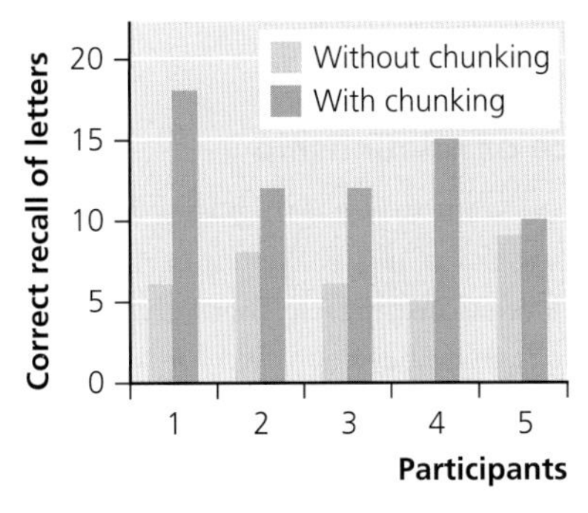

Bar graph to show scores of five participants' recall of 21 letters depending on whether chunking was used or not

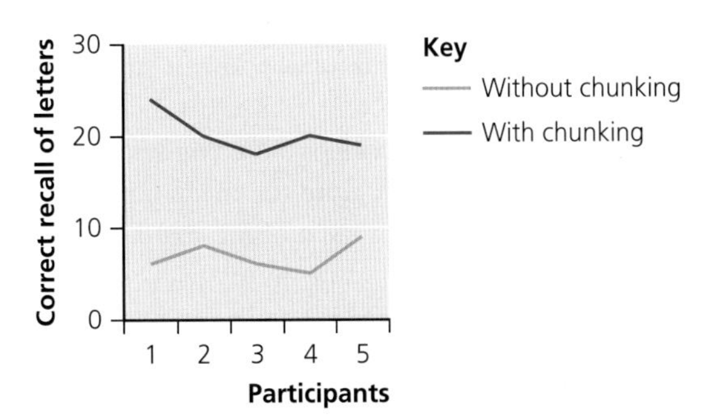

Line graph to show scores of five participants' recall of 21 letters depending on whether chunking was used or not

Using a histogram/frequency graph and frequency table

A frequency table is the number of times a score is found, rather than the score itself being displayed against each participant. The usefulness of knowing the frequency of scores is that the distribution can be seen in table form. A histogram (or frequency graph) can then be used to display the data.

Table 5.8 Frequency of scores on a memory span test using 20 participants: raw data

Memory span score	Tallying	Frequency
4	II	2
5	~~IIII~~	5
6	~~IIII~~	5
7	IIII	4
8	II	2
9	II	2

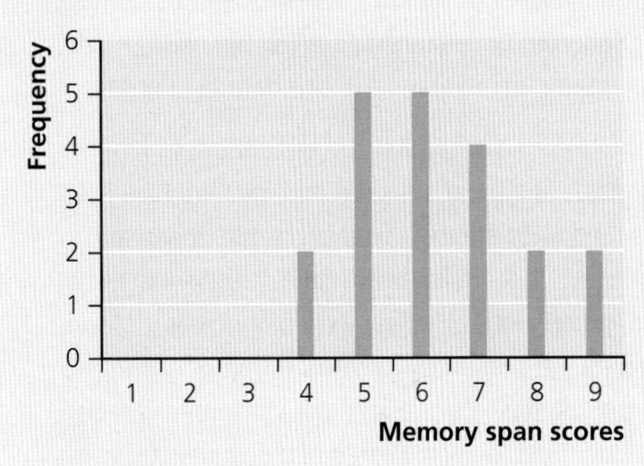

Graph to show frequency of memory span scores for 20 participants

- The range is the gap between the highest and the lowest score and is found by taking the lowest from the highest.
- The standard deviation is a score obtained by seeing how far individual scores vary from the mean, and standard deviation shows the spread of the scores. A small standard deviation shows a tightly packed group of scores and a high standard deviation shows a wide spread of scores. More about range and standard deviation is found in Chapter 6 (pp. 394–396).
- Normal and skewed distribution are mentioned in the method section of cognitive psychology. **Normal distribution** is found when results cluster around the mean, and this is shown when the mode and median are very similar to the mean. If the mean, median and mode are not similar to one another then there is **skewed distribution**. You can find out more about this in Chapter 6.

This is just a summary of the ways of analysing data – these are explained in more detail in Chapter 6.

Definitions

Normal distribution is found when results cluster nicely around the mean and around the centre point of a spread of scores. There is normal distribution when the mean, median and mode more or less match. If they do not match, then distribution is **skewed**.

Progress check 5.24

Fill in the gaps in the paragraph below using the following terms from this summary of descriptive statistics and percentages and from your own understanding: range; bar chart; mode; scatter diagram; mean; standard; raw data; line graph.

In order to analyse data, they are described, which means displaying them in useful and meaningful ways. When all the data are displayed in a table, these are the ____________. Using these data, graphs can be created, which help to display data more clearly. If two simple bars are presented, to show different scores of two groups, this is a ____________. Another graph that can be used to show scores of individuals on two different conditions is a ____________. If the design is a correlation, then a ____________ is used to show all the individual scores using both measures so that a line of best fit can be created. Graphs help to compare data and they are visual. Graphs can display percentages too, which are another way of making data comparable. When it comes to seeing the distribution of scores of sets of data, measures of central tendency are required. These are the ____________, median and ____________. If they are more or less the same, it is said that the scores are normally distributed. Another useful statistic, to show the distribution of data, is the ____________, which is the span between the highest and lowest score. A similar statistic is the ____________ deviation, which shows how the scores differ from the mean average.

Inferential statistical tests

In cognitive psychology in your Year 1 course, you will learn about statistical tests and have to carry one out in your practical investigation. Chapter 6 looks at the mathematical elements of your course, including carrying out statistical tests. The two tests you need for cognitive psychology are dealt with in Chapter 6 with regard to the calculations and what results of testing means (pp. 400–406).

As choosing and using inferential statistical testing is common to all the tests, and there are only a few differences in the issues around statistical testing between tests, to save repetition between topic areas, all four tests in your course are covered in this section.

- Descriptive statistics, as explained above briefly, describe the data and include measures of central tendency (the mode, median, mean) and measures of dispersion (the range and standard deviation). Descriptive statistics also include graphs and charts.
- Inferential statistics draw inferences about the data, rather than merely describing them. Inferential statistics involve the use of statistical tests. Your Year 1 course includes four statistical tests:
  - Mann-Whitney U (cognitive psychology)
  - Wilcoxon signed-rank test (cognitive psychology)
  - Spearman rank correlation coefficient (biological psychology)
  - chi-squared (learning theories).

Testing for difference or relationship

If two scores vary and you want to see if they vary in a pattern, such as ice cream sales rising as the temperature rises, then you look for a relationship. Alternatively, you may want to look at a difference between two (or more) sets of scores. For example, if you want to see if memory span is lower depending on whether people are 'old' or 'young', you are looking for a difference. If you want to see whether memory span increases with training, then you are looking for a relationship. Look at the measures being taken. If they are not both scores, then these data cannot test for a relationship. 'Young' and 'old' are two categories and are not scored.

Alternative and experimental hypotheses look for either *differences* between variables or for *relationships* between variables:

- The Spearman test is a test for relationships and correlations.
- The Mann-Whitney U, Wilcoxon signed-rank and chi-squared tests are tests of difference.

Progress check 5.25

Decide whether each of the following studies is testing for a difference between variables or for a relationship. If testing for a relationship, a test of correlation is required; if testing for a difference, a test of difference is required.

1. To see if the number of words generated on a topic while undergoing a scan is linked with length of time in education.
2. To see if women have more activity in a certain brain region than men, when participants carry out a language task while undergoing a PET scan.
3. To see whether men do better than women on a driving-test circuit where obstacles have to be avoided.

Choosing and using a statistical test

Inferential statistical tests examine whether the variables being studied are different or related enough to draw conclusions to that effect. This section explains why this is important and how to draw conclusions from statistical tests.

STUDY HINT

If you are an AS student, you will not need to know about choosing a statistical test but you do need to know about using a statistical test.

In order to use statistical tests, you need to know about:

- participant (experimental) design
- experimental/alternative and null hypotheses so that you know about one- or two-tailed
- levels of measurement
- which test to choose
- levels of significance
- choosing a level of significance
- what '*N*' is (or for the chi-squared test, what *df* is)
- whether a difference or a relationship is being tested for
- what 'critical value' means.

These are issues explained in this section, or reviewed if already explained elsewhere.

Experimental (research) designs

Experimental designs are explained earlier in this chapter (pp. 321–323), and can be repeated measures (the same participants for each part of a study), independent groups (different participants for each part of a study) or matched pairs (different participants for each part of a study but matching those participants on important variables).

These three experimental designs are used when *differences* between variables are tested. You need to know the design of a study in order to choose an appropriate test of difference. (If you are using a correlation then the test will be different anyway and a correlation is a design; there is no other experimental design to consider).

Alternative, experimental and null hypotheses

Hypotheses are explained in detail earlier in this chapter (page 318). A hypothesis is the statement in a study of what is expected:

- The alternative hypothesis is the statement itself; it becomes an experimental hypothesis when the research method is an experiment.
- The alternative hypothesis is the 'alternative' to the null hypothesis; the null hypothesis is important where inferential tests are concerned.
- The null hypothesis is the statement that what is predicted is *not* going to be true and any difference or relationship found is due to chance. A statistical test examines how far it is the case that the statement of what is expected will not happen. The question is: 'What is the probability of the results being due to chance?' For example, for the alternative hypothesis 'women are better at language tasks then men', the null hypothesis would be 'any difference found between men and women with regard to language tasks is due to chance and not due to the independent variable'.

Progress check 5.26

For each of the following alternative hypotheses, write out a null hypothesis.

1. There is a positive relationship in that the number of words generated on a topic while undergoing a scan increases with length of time in education.
2. There is a difference between the sexes and women have more activity in a certain brain region than men when participants carry out a language task while undergoing a PET scan.
3. There is a difference between men and women when performing on a driving test circuit where obstacles have to be avoided.

Directional (one-tailed) and non-directional (two-tailed) hypotheses

When using statistical tests, in order to judge whether or not the test result is significant, you have to know whether the hypothesis is one-tailed or two-tailed:

- **Directional (one-tailed) hypothesis** – the statement predicts not only a difference or a relationship but also the direction of the results, e.g. whether there will be a *positive* correlation or whether women will be *better* drivers.
- **Non-directional (two-tailed) hypothesis** – the statement predicts a difference or a relationship but does not give the direction of the difference or relationship, e.g. that gender affects driving or that there will be a relationship between gender and language ability.

Progress check 5.27

For each of the following three hypotheses, decide whether it is directional (one-tailed) or non-directional (two-tailed).

1. There is a positive relationship in that the number of words generated on a topic while undergoing a scan increases with length of time in education.
2. There is a difference and women have more activity in a certain brain region than men, when participants carry out a language task while undergoing a PET scan.
3. There is a difference between men and women when performing on a driving test circuit where obstacles have to be avoided.

Levels of measurement

There are three levels of measurement covered in the A level course:

- **Nominal data** are in the form of categories, simply putting data into sets. For example, categorising answers as 'yes' or 'no' is putting them into categories. There are no scores; the number of 'yes' answers and the number of 'no' answers are the data. Whether someone is male or females is nominal data. The chi-squared test is a test for nominal data in an independent groups design. In terms of detail of data, nominal data are the lowest level of measurement.
- **Ordinal data** are ranked data, such as ratings. When data are put into a hierarchy (such as rating a day for whether it is cold or hot on a scale of 1 to 10), then they are ranked and are ordinal data. In terms of detail of data, ordinal data are the 'middle' level of measurement.
- **Interval data** are data where real measurements are involved. For example, if temperature was recorded in degrees Celsius, that would be interval/ratio data, as would, for example, measurements of time, height, blood pressure and age. Interval/ratio data are scores that have equal intervals between them. For example, if you are two years older than one friend and four years older than another friend, then the numbers (number of years) have Mathematical meaning. This is important because inferential tests for interval/ratio data involve calculations because the data are mathematical. In terms of amount of information provided, interval/ratio data are the highest level of measurement.

Explanation

Interval data and **ratio data** are not exactly the same, but are treated as such for the purposes of your course.

Progress check 5.28

Decide which level of measurement applies to each of the following measures.

1. Whether a person is aggressive or not.
2. Reaction time to a stimulus shown on a screen.
3. How attractive we rate people to be.

Choosing a statistical test

There are many different statistical tests, but for A level and AS psychology you need to know only four:

- If the study is a correlation, then the test to choose is the Spearman's rank correlation coefficient test. Note that this test is for ordinal data only in reality; another test (Pearson's) is for a correlation using interval data, but in your course just Spearman's is asked for.
- If the study is an independent groups design and the data are nominal, then the test to choose is the chi-squared test.
- If the study is an independent groups design and the data are ordinal or interval/ratio, then the test to choose is the Mann-Whitney U test. Note that this test is for ordinal data only in reality; another test (unrelated t test) is for a difference, independent groups, using interval data, but in your course just Mann-Whitney U is asked for.
- If the study is a repeated measures design and the data are ordinal or interval/ratio, then the test to choose is the Wilcoxon signed-rank test. Note that this test is for ordinal data only in reality, another test (related t test) is for a difference, repeated measures or matched pairs, using interval data, but in your course just Wilcoxon is asked for.

Table 5.9 shows the four tests and what they should be used for. There are other tests, and this table is not complete, but these are the four tests you need to know.

Table 5.9 The four statistical tests you need to know for your course

Test of difference	Level of measurement	
	Nominal	Ordinal (or interval/ratio for your course)
Independent groups	Chi-squared test	Mann-Whitney U test
Repeated measures or matched pairs	*You do not need this test*	Wilcoxon signed-rank test
Test of relationship	**Ordinal (or interval/ratio for your course)**	
	Spearman's rank correlation coefficient	

STUDY HINT

Baddeley (1966b), the classic study in cognitive psychology in your course, uses both the Mann-Whitney U and the Wilcoxon test in his study. It is worth looking at his study to see why these were chosen, as this helps in understanding how to choose a statistical test. He had both a repeated measures design and independent groups and gathered interval data (numbers of words recalled in order).

Progress check 5.29

Using Table 5.9, choose the appropriate test in the following two situations. In your answer, explain your choice.

1. An experiment looking for a difference between recall of events (episodic memory) between people aged 40 and people aged 80. Scores are number of events recalled in a ten-minute free recall period, talking about their lives ten years previously.
2. A study testing to see whether the more days passed since first hearing a story will mean fewer words written when asked to recall the story.

STUDY HINT

Progress check 5.29 relates to episodic memory (1) and reconstructive memory (2). When reading about method, be sure to keep focusing on the content in the topic area too, as this will help your learning.

Levels of significance

Your interest in psychology may be because you want to learn about people, how they think and, for example, how you make your own decisions. However, you need to know that the results of the studies from which such conclusions are drawn are sound results. Therefore, it is worth learning about levels of significance. The statistical test will see if the null hypothesis, which claims that any difference or relationship is due to chance or to some other variable, not the independent variable, is true. So the test is to see if what was found was found by chance.

Calculating the odds of something being due to chance

There will be chance factors in any study. The idea is to decide what is down to chance and to be able to determine whether a difference or relationship is significant. Two examples of calculating odds are as follows:

- Imagine that a scientist found a vaccine for a life-threatening illness but also found that, although there was only a 1 in 100,000 chance of getting the illness, there was a 1 in 100 chance that the vaccine would lead to a different life-threatening illness. It is a safe bet that nobody would have the vaccine.
- Imagine that a personality test gave a 1 in 50 chance of finding the right employee for your company, but interviewing gave a 1 in 10 chance of finding the right person. You would choose the interview.

People work on such odds all the time but do not always know what they are. We cross the road regularly but may be more likely to be afraid of flying even though, according to figures, crossing the road is more dangerous. In 2013, 1,713 deaths on the roads were reported in Great Britain, with a population of around 64,000,000, which is 0.003 per cent. Deaths in the air (not just in Great Britain) were 265 out of 30,000,000 flights, which is 0.0009 per cent. What statistical tests do is calculate the odds of results being due to chance. When we know the odds of something being due to chance, we can decide whether to accept something as knowledge or not.

Accepted levels of significance in psychology

In psychology, anything that occurs due to chance in more than 1 in 20 cases is not accepted as knowledge. So, if you test 20 people to see if women gossip more than men, and more than one person goes against your hypothesis (perhaps there are several gossipy men in the sample), then this is not accepted as knowledge. Similarly, if you test 100 people and more than five people go against your hypothesis, then these are odds of more than 1 in 20, so this is also not accepted. The statistical test works out that likelihood for you. In psychology:

- results are not accepted if there is a 1 in 10 likelihood or more of the results being due to chance (this is expressed as $p \leq 0.10$ – more about that later)

- results are often accepted as statistically significant if there is a 1 in 20 likelihood or less of the results being due to chance (this is expressed as $p \leq 0.05$ – more about that later)
- results are nearly always accepted if there is a 1 in 100 likelihood or less of the results being due to chance (this is expressed as $p \leq 0.01$ – more about that later).

The example above of a vaccine for a life-threatening illness is dramatic and possible in medical research. In psychology, however, most findings are not so dramatic and some chance factors have to be accepted. There are so many difficulties in measuring the variables in psychology studies that it is accepted that a level of 1 in 100 or even 1 in 20 may be due to chance.

You will be using the phrases 'the probability that results are equal to or less than 1 in 20 due to chance' or 'the probability that results are equal to or less than 1 in 100 due to chance'. You will be accepting your results as statistically significant if you find one of those two probability levels. If you find that the results are significant at the probability that 1 in 1,000 or less are due to chance, then that will be a highly significant result. If the results are more than 1 in 20 likely to be due to chance, you would not accept them because they are not statistically significant.

Instead of using '1 in 20' or '1 in 100', it is customary to use the mathematical (decimal) equivalent. Expressed as decimals:

- 1 in 20 (5 in 100) is 0.05
- 1 in 100 is 0.01
- 1 in 1,000 is 0.001.

The correct number of zeros goes in front of the probability. For example:

- 1 in 1,000 is expressed as 0.001
- 2 in 1,000 is expressed as 0.002
- 1 in 10,000 is expressed as 0.0001
- 2 in 10,000 is expressed as 0.0002.

Suppose you have to convert a probability (e.g. 1 in 200) to a decimal:

- Find the lowest number needed by which to multiply the second figure (200) to obtain a number such as 10, 100, 1,000, 10,000. (In this example, the number to choose is 1,000 because 200 is more than 100 and less than 1,000.)
- The number needed to multiply 200 by is 5 (to get to 1,000).
- Then, multiply both numbers by 5 (1 and 200). This gives 5 in 1,000, which expressed as a decimal is 0.005).

Similarly, 2 in 200 is 10 in 1,000 (multiply both by 5), which expressed as a decimal is 0.01; 6 in 500 is 12 in 1,000 (multiply both by 2), which expressed as a decimal is 0.012.

The way of expressing 'the probability that results are equal to or less than 1 in 20 due to chance' is:

$p \leq 0.05$

where p = the probability of the results being due to chance; ≤ means less than or equal to; 0.05 means 1 in 20.

'The probability that results are equal to or less than 1 in 100 due to chance' is expressed as:

$p \leq 0.01$

When the likelihood of the results being due to chance is 1 in 1,000, the probability is $p \leq 0.001$. The values $p \leq 0.05$, $p \leq 0.01$ and $p \leq 0.001$ are examples of levels of significance. A **level of significance** is the probability that the results are due to chance. In psychology, $p \leq 0.05$ (1 in 20) is the probability at which the results are accepted as being statistically significant.

Progress check 5.30

Convert the following probabilities into decimal form:

1 1 in 200
2 1 in 50
3 1 in 10,000
4 1 in 2,000

STUDY HINT

It is worth making a note of what $p \leq 0.05$ and $p \leq 0.01$ mean because this question can be asked in the exams:

- *p* means 'probability of the results being due to chance'.
- ≤ means less than or equal to.
- 0.05 means 1 in 20.
- 0.01 means 1 in 100.

Other levels of significance that you may be asked about are: 0.10, 0.05 and 0.01; 0.025 is one mentioned in the critical value tables.

STUDY HINT

Practise using levels of significance. If something seems difficult, practice is the way forward as that makes it familiar. Think about what you have learned about semantic knowledge, semantic memories, episodic memories and reconstruction in memory. We use schemas in memory. If you create schemas, such as for levels of significance, what might have seemed difficult at first will become straightforward. Schemas are created by experiences, and practice gives such experiences.

Choosing a level of significance

Whether the researcher chooses a lenient level of significance (e.g. 1 in 20, or $p \leq 0.05$) or a stricter one (e.g. 1 in 100, or $p \leq 0.01$) depends on what is being tested. Lenient here refers to it being easier to find that 19 out of 20 do what is predicted than to find that 99 out of

100 do what is predicted. If the test has been carried out previously and found to be true, it might be reasonable to ask for 1 in 100 ($p \leq 0.01$) of the results or fewer to be due to chance. If the study is new, and it is not known what is likely, then a result of 1 in 20 ($p \leq 0.05$) being due to chance might be a good result. It also depends on how 'serious' the consequences of the study might be. If a new education programme is launched on the basis of a study that has a high likelihood of its results being due to chance, then 1 in 20 might not be acceptable. (This is a rather high likelihood: it means that out of every 20 children, 19 do whatever is predicted, which leaves quite a few children not doing what is predicted, and a large proportion across the country – 1 in 20 is 5 per cent.)

If a reading scheme is going to be rolled out across the UK, it is important that any improvement in reading shown when testing the scheme is due to the reading scheme and less to chance factors

Progress check 5.31

Explain two factors to take into account when choosing a level of significance.

Study using the methodology

Söderland *et al.* (2014) carried out a study looking at people with major depression to see if there was some link to their autobiographical episodic memory. It has been thought that a generalised version of episodes in the past is used by those with depression, rather than recall of specific details. The Autobiographical Interview was used as a research method and then the use of both semantic and episodic memory was studied. The participants were 21 people with major depressive disorder from a clinic in Toronto, and there was also a control group. It was found that semantic memories from two weeks to ten years before were not as impaired as episodic memories.

There was impairment on memory of public events, but the researchers thought that perhaps the patients with depression did not watch the news as much. Results found that, with regard to autobiographical memories, depressed people recalled fewer events than the controls, and the level of significance was p 0.004: four results in 100 were likely to be due to chance, which is a good level of significance with regard to rejection of the null hypothesis.

STUDY HINT

Söderland *et al.* (2014) had a lot of results and only a brief summary of them is given here. This study is summarised to demonstrate a level of significance in a real study, to show its purpose and meaning. However, the study is about episodic and semantic memory being different, as Tulving suggested, so the findings are useful for your study of memory within cognitive psychology. There is also a practical application, in that understanding of episodic and semantic memory can help in the study of depression and possibly its treatment. With regard to levels of significance, you will find in other studies summarised in this book that there is mention of the level of significance at which results were accepted.

The meaning of *N* and *df*

Statistical tests differ, but they all need either N or df.

N is simply the number of participants/number of scores. If there are 20 scores (from 20 people), $N = 20$. The Spearman test, the Wilcoxon test and the Mann-Whitney U test all use N. However, for the Mann-Whitney U test on an independent groups design, there are two values for N – one number of participants (N_A) in one condition and another number or participants (N_B) in the other condition. If there is the same number of participants in each condition, N_A and N_B are the same; if the number of participants in each condition is different, then N_A and N_B are different. Also for the Wilcoxon test, although N does mean the number of participants, any participants who have a 0 difference between their two scores are not counted in N (this is explained more in Chapter 6).

df stands for 'degrees of freedom'. The inferential test for the learning approach is the chi-squared test, which uses df, not N. Degrees of freedom refers to the number of values in the final calculation that are free to vary. Consider the data in Table 5.10:

- If you know that the total of a row is 20 (e.g. row 1 in Table 5.10) and there are two numbers in the row, one of which is 15, the other number must be 5 and has no freedom to vary. The first score (15) has the freedom to vary; the second score (5) does not.

- If you know that the total of a column is 20 (e.g. column 2 in Table 5.10) and there are two numbers in the column, one of which is 5, then the other number must be 15 and has no freedom to vary. The first score (5) has the freedom to vary; the second score (15) does not.

A table that has two rows and two columns has a degree of freedom of 1. This is calculated as number of rows minus 1 multiplied by number of columns minus 1, which is 1 overall:

$df = (r-1)(c-1$

STUDY HINT
The formulae for the various tests you have to carry out will be in the examination paper. The formula for *df* will be there, as will the formula for standard deviation and the four tests.

where r = number of rows and c = number of columns.

For the data in Table 5.10:

$df = (2-1) \times (2-1) = 1 \times 1 = 1$

So for a two-by-two table, *df* is always 1.

Table 5.10 A two-by-two table

	Column 1	Column 2	Total
Row 1	15	5	20
Row 2	15	15	30
Total	**30**	**20**	**50**

STUDY HINT
You might just want to learn that for a two-by-two table (two rows and two columns), *df* is always 1; for a three-by-two table (three rows and two columns or three columns and two rows), *df* is always 2. Though it is worth learning the formula so that you understand it and so that you can explain it and use it.

Whether a difference or a relationship is being tested for

The idea of testing for a difference or a relationship has been discussed earlier in this chapter (pp. 328–329).

Critical value

Once you have chosen and carried out a statistical test, you need to know about **critical value** tables and critical values. What has been explained in this section takes you through choosing an appropriate test. You have learnt about choosing a suitable level of significance, deciding whether the hypothesis is 'one-tailed' or 'two-tailed', and what *N* and *df* are. In Chapters 5 and Chapter 6, these issues are explained often more than once, to help you to become familiar with them.

Maths link: The tests are explained in Chapter 6, where the mathematics element of your course is covered.

- When you have carried out the test, you will have an 'answer' to the test. This will be a number, such as T = 2 (Wilcoxon) or U = 6 (Mann-Whitney U).
- You will then need to know what that statistic – the answer to the chosen test – means. That is where critical values come in.

Critical value tables

Each test has its own critical values tables or statistical tables. You have to find such tables in order to proceed from the 'answer'. Tables will be in your examination paper for you to use, and they are available over the internet. Table 5.11 gives a sample of one test, to illustrate what is meant by 'critical value'.

Table 5.11 Sample from a critical values table for Wilcoxon signed-rank tests

	Level of significance for a one-tailed test		
	0.05	0.025	0.1
	Level of significance for a two-tailed test		
N	0.1	0.05	0.02
5	0	-	-
6	2	0	-
7	3	2	0

Table 5.11 shows critical values for a Wilcoxon test for *N* = 5, 6 or 7. This means that the number of participants (excluding anyone with a 0 difference between their two scores in a study) is 5, 6 or 7. This is just a sample of a critical values table. You might of course have N = 10 or some other number, and this sample of a table is then not suitable.

- The reason that anyone with a 0 difference is missed out is because the test involves examining the difference between two scores for each participant. If there is 0 difference, then that participant is not included in the test. For more detail, see Chapter 7 (pp. 439–440), where a Wilcoxon test is carried out in the practical investigation for cognitive psychology.

The critical value is worked out by statisticians as the score that is needed to be reached so that we know that a certain level of significance applies. For example, using Table 5.11 for a two-tailed (non-directional) hypothesis and a level of significance of $p \leq 0.05$, if there are seven participants to be considered (*N* = 7) the critical value is 2. T must be equal to or less than 2 for the result to be accepted.

Greater than v. equal to or less than

- Each test has its own rule about whether the answer from the test has to be 'equal to or less than' the critical value or 'more than' the critical value in order for the answer to the test to be accepted.
- The Wilcoxon signed-rank test and the Mann-Whitney U test all have 'answers' that must be *equal to or smaller than* the critical value number to have the hypothesis accepted and the null rejected in that the level of significance is accepted (e.g. it is accepted that 1 in 20 results will be due to chance if $p \leq 0.05$ is chosen)
- The chi-squared test and Spearman's rank correlation coefficient has to have a result that is *equal to or more than* the critical value to be accepted.
- You need to learn this aspect of each test so that you can use the critical values tables. The information is in the front of your exam paper.

STUDY HINT

Perhaps remember that the two tests in cognitive psychology in your course have to have an observed value that is equal to or smaller than the critical value. The other two tests, in biological psychology and learning theories, have to have an observed value that is equal to or greater than the critical value. Or the two with 'W' in them have 'equal to or smaller than'.

Progress check 5.32

Two of the tests in your course need the observed value (the answer from doing the test) to be equal to or smaller than the critical value (the number in the table). Which are these two tests?

Accepting the hypothesis

In the explanation here, there has been mention of 'accepting the hypothesis'. Let's go back and remember the experimental or alternative hypothesis. For example, consider a hypothesis 'there will be a difference in the memory span depending on whether someone is 40 or 80 years old'. The null hypothesis would be 'there will be no difference in memory span depending on whether someone is 40 or 80 years old and any difference will be due to chance or some other factor'. An inferential test is done to see if the null hypothesis seems to be the case – the question is, 'are the results such that the null hypothesis can be rejected?' Doing an appropriate statistical test will test the level at which results are likely to be due to chance. The result of the statistical test, which can be seen as the **observed value**, can be tested against the **critical value**, looking at the level of significance chosen, to show how likely the result is to be due to chance at that level of significance. If the result is 'significant' then the experimental hypothesis is accepted at the stated level of significance. The following example will help your understanding.

Definitions

The **observed value** is the result of the test, the answer to your calculations. The **critical value** is the number you find when you use the critical value tables. You compare your observed value with the critical value to decide whether the experimental hypothesis is accepted at your chosen level of significance.

Carrying out the Wilcoxon signed-rank test on the data

Table 5.12 shows the scores and working out of the Wilcoxon signed-rank test for the data in the cognitive practical investigation explained in Chapter 7 (pp. 439–440).

Table 5.12 Scores and working out of the Wilcoxon signed-rank test for the data in the cognitive practical investigation

Participants' scores – once rehearsed	Participants' scores – three times rehearsed	Differences in scores between the two conditions	Ranking the differences (ignoring 0 differences)
1	3	-2	4
3	3	0	/
0	2	-2	4
2	3	-1	1
3	3	0	/
1	1	0	/
1	3	-2	4
1	3	-2	4
3	3	0	/
1	3	-2	4

- Total of ranks for differences with a plus (+) sign = 0.
- Total of ranks for differences with a minus (–) sign = 21.
- The smaller of these is the T statistic so T = 0.
- Just one more figure is required: you need to know *N*, the number of participants. However, this is not ten, even though there were ten participants. Results are used for only six participants because the other four participants' scores were the same in the two conditions. So here *N* = 6.

Use the sample critical values table for the Wilcoxon test to see that when *N* = 6, T has to be equal to or lower than the critical value. T = 0 and the critical value is 0, so it can be accepted that at $p \leq 0.025$ (25 in 1,000) the one-tailed experimental hypothesis is accepted and the null 'rejected'.

Type I and Type II errors

There is a final consideration around accepting or rejecting the null hypothesis and whether to claim that an experimental hypothesis 'works'. Type I and Type II errors concern the issue of accepting or rejecting the null hypothesis incorrectly. The statistical test will let you know whether a result is significant at a chosen level of significance, and will help you to accept or reject the null hypothesis. However, there is always the possibility that the acceptance or rejection is incorrect, and statistics can be used to assess the likelihood of the acceptance or rejection being incorrect. If the null is wrongly rejected (you said the study 'worked' and accepted the alternative/experimental hypothesis) then that is a **Type I error**. If the null is wrongly accepted (you said the study did not 'work' and rejected the alternative/experimental hypothesis), that is a **Type II error**. One way of knowing that you had made one of these errors would be if another researcher replicated a study and found different results. They might find results not significant at $p \leq 0.05$, for example, where you found they were significant, pointing to you having made a Type I error (wrongly rejecting the null hypothesis).

Definitions

A **Type I error** is made when someone optimistically accepts their alternative/experimental hypothesis and rejects the null hypothesis. A **Type II error** is made when someone accepts the null hypothesis pessimistically.

STUDY HINT

Use mnemonics in your notes to help you remember terms. For example, one way of remembering the difference between Type I and II errors is to see Type I errors as being over optimistic, rejecting the null and saying a study has 'worked': Type One and optimistic might help you to remember.

Progress check 5.33

In each of these two examples, which is a Type I error and which is a Type II error?

1. A researcher has found out, after a lot of studies replicated their experiment, that they wrongly accepted their experimental hypothesis when they should have rejected it.
2. By being cautious and choosing a strict level of significance, a researcher has wrongly accepted their null hypothesis and rejected their alternative hypothesis.

Test yourself

1. Explain what features in a study need to be known in order for an appropriate statistical test to be chosen. **(4 marks)**
2. What is the purpose of carrying out a statistical test on quantitative data? **(6 marks)**
3. Discuss the use of inferential statistical tests in psychology. **(12 marks)**

Case studies of brain-damaged patients

Cognitive psychology not only uses field or laboratory experiments. With the rise of neuroscience, studies of cognitive processing can involve brain scanning or measuring of the brain. Cognitive psychology is close to biological psychology now that more is becoming known about the brain.

In the 1960s, when cognitive psychology developed, not much was known about brain structure and functioning so researchers developed models about how processing might take place in the brain. Models included the multi-store model (Atkinson and Shiffrin, 1968) and the earlier reconstructive memory model put forward by Bartlett (1932). You will have seen from the classic study in cognitive psychology that another well-known researcher in the area of memory, Alan Baddeley, worked on memory for many years, using models and ideas about how memory might work, including the working memory model. As knowledge and understanding of the brain has increased, evidence has been found relating to these models and gradually parts of the brain are being linked to the ideas of some of the models. One of the contemporary studies in cognitive psychology for your course is Schmolck *et al.* (2002), who look in detail at some cases of brain damage, including HM. Case studies of patients with brain damage add evidence for ideas about memory and show how memory works in practice rather than just using models. In addition, if you have studied Tulving's ideas on episodic and semantic memory, you may have read about evidence for these two 'types' of memory coming from case studies of patients with brain damage (see Chapter 2, pp. 113–119), such as Henry Molaison.

Progress check 5.34

Briefly explain one study that uses evidence from case studies of patients with brain damage as evidence for their findings. You can look back at Chapter 2 (pp. 113-119), if you wish, to answer this question.

The case of Phineas Gage, 1823–1860

This idea of using evidence for how the brain works is not new. In 1848, Phineas Gage, a railroad construction worker in New Hampshire, USA, had an accident that made him very well known. A bar went through his skull and damaged his brain. His behaviour changed, and it was thought that this change was due to the brain damage. The changes included him showing more unrestrained behaviour and not being so organised. The brain damage was to his frontal lobes, so it was concluded that the frontal lobes are for problem-solving and restraining emotions like aggression.

However, as there was no baseline measure as to what he was like before the accident, it is hard to draw firm conclusions. Data tended to come from those who knew him before and after the accident. He was not able to go back to work (having been hard working) so there does seem to have been important effects of the brain damage (as we might expect). There is more to the story than this as it is reported that he in fact did get another job and did it well. It is suggested that his behaviour change was not as marked as has been reported. However, the story of Phineas Gage attracted a lot of interest in how the brain works and how damage to the brain (considerable damage) can be overcome, at least to an extent.

The case of Henry Molaison (HM)

In your course, you need to know about the case of HM as an example of using brain-damaged patients to learn more about how the brain works and, in the case of HM, about how memory works. The study of Henry Molaison uses a case study research method. So far in this chapter, you have covered questionnaires, interviews, and laboratory and field experiments. Case studies are research methods too.

Henry Molaison had surgery at the age of 26, in 1953. The surgery was to help with his epilepsy. The bilateral (on both sides) medial temporal lobe (MTL) was removed. He had amnesia after the surgery – he could not lay down new long-term memories, although he still had procedural skills (knowledge of how to do things) and could learn new skills. He could use his working memory but not to move material into his long-term memory, such as learning semantic information. He lived in the present. As it was not known whether he had problems with memories before the surgery, it was thought that it was the removal of the MTL that caused his difficulties.

As is shown in Schmolck *et al.* (2002), looking more closely at brain structures in and around the MTL it is possible that some lateral temporal cortex damage was involved in his memory problems, though there are links to the MTL. The MTL has within it the hippocampus, widely thought to relate to short-term memory and moving information from short-term to long-term memory. As neuroimaging has become more precise, areas of the brain for memory in its different forms are being discovered, including Schmolck *et al.* (2002), who claim that there are specific areas involved in semantic knowledge.

Explore

HM was widely studied and there is a lot more information about him on the internet, if you would like to learn more. For example: www.psychologytoday.com/blog/trouble-in-mind/201201/hm-the-man-no-memory and www.ncbi.nlm.nih.gov/pmc/articles/PMC2649674/.

Schmolck *et al.* (2002) used six patients with brain damage in their study and eight people as controls. They used HM as one of the patients and then two others with hippocampal formation (HF) damage and three others with medial temporal lobe damage with damage to the lateral temporal cortex. They used neuroimaging (MRI, CT and fMRI scanning) to measure the damage to the brain and tests of the semantic knowledge of the patients to see what their cognitive functioning was like. Any difficulties with cognitive functioning were attributed to the damage to the brain. That is how case studies of patients with brain damage are used in psychology.

Schmolck *et al.* (2002) found that HM had difficulty with semantic knowledge, more than the controls did and more than the HF patients did, although HM's performance in the tests was better than patients with medial temporal lobe damage together with lateral temporal cortex damage. They found that HM had particular difficulties with grammar and sentence structure, which the others did not have in the same way. The researchers concluded that HM might have had some issues not related to the damage to his brain. He had epilepsy when younger and they wondered if he had grammar and sentence difficulties before the damage.

Study using the methodology

A study by Maeshima *et al.* (2014) involved a 56-year-old man who had had a brain haemorrhage, which was treated, but which resulted in difficulties – in particular, memory problems. There was damage to the hippocampus on both sides of the brain. As has been demonstrated in other studies, areas around and including the hippocampus are related to memory problems. His immediate recall was not affected and his recent memory was somewhat impaired. A CT scan and an MRI scan highlighted the damage to his brain and a type of PET scanning showed brain functioning being affected in the left medial temporal lobe. It was concluded that the damage in the specific areas caused the difficulties with memory.

STUDY HINT

Maeshima *et al.* (2014) made use of CT, MRI and PET scanning -you can use this study as an example of their use when learning about brain scanning as a research method in biological psychology.

Maeshima *et al.* (2014) highlight the same areas of the brain as were highlighted in Schmolck *et al.* (2002), one of the contemporary studies for cognitive psychology in your course. Use the evidence from one study as reinforcement for the findings of another study.

Progress check 5.35

Explain, using HM as an example, how case studies of people with brain damage can help to study how the brain processes information and, in particular, how memory works in the brain.

Qualitative and quantitative data in case studies

The study used here to illustrate the use of case studies of patients with brain damage gathers quantitative data. There are measurements of brain areas damaged and numbers of correct answers with regard to semantic testing (Schmolck *et al.*, 2002). Quantitative data can be tested using statistical tests to see how far results are due to chance, and they can also be displayed in graphs and tables, which means data are made clear and transparent.

However, case studies also gather qualitative data. You will look at case studies in other areas in your course, such as in clinical psychology in Year 2 (but not if you are doing the AS course). Case studies are known for getting rich, in-depth and detailed data from individuals, including emotions and feelings, not just their ability to use memory, as in the case of HM when studying his amnesia. HM was studied over 55 years by a maximum of 100 people, to protect him from being the subject of too much research (though 100 researchers over 55 years does sound rather excessive perhaps). In that time, a lot of qualitative data would have been gathered. For example, researchers talked to him about episodic memories, which are about personal episodes and events in his life, and he could recall the stock market crash in 1929, which occurred well before his surgery took place. Researchers could discuss his procedural skills, which were intact, as well as his long-term memories, which seemed to be 'stuck' 11 years before his surgery. Therefore, there were qualitative data as well as quantitative data used in the case study.

Progress check 5.36

Briefly explain the value of quantitative data in the study of patients with brain damage and the value of qualitative data too.

Evaluation of the case study method, using patients with brain damage

Strengths

- When more than one patient can be found with similar damage, as in Schmolck *et al.* (2002), where three patients were found with medial temporal lobe damage and at least some damage to the lateral temporal cortex (MTL+ patients), if their performance has similarities then the case studies back one another up in their conclusions about the damage causing the difficulties in processing.
- Measurements of damage to the brain are done using neuroimaging/scanning, which has a certain amount of accuracy. Pictures are produced by the scanning and so there is visual information. Actual measurements can be made using the pictures and more than one person can take the measurements to test for reliability. It can be claimed that scanning for such damage is a reliable and scientific measure. Measurements of cognitive ability can also be said to be reliable as they take the form of carefully controlled measurements in an experimental setting. For example, Schmolck *et al.* (2002) used a control group to get a baseline score for each of the tests in their study.
- Brain scanning for damage to the brain and using experiments to test semantic knowledge and functioning are both scientific methods and have the credibility to go with that. Both research methods can look at very specific information regarding both the specific brain damage and the specific issues with semantic functioning, again giving results and conclusions credibility. By using a reductionist approach and studying variables in a controlled way in a controlled setting, a body of scientific knowledge can be built.

Weaknesses

- As seen in HM's case, although there is damage to the brain in such cases, there might be other issues in a person that cause difficulties with the processing of information. It is assumed that a) difficulties with processing and b) damage to the brain means c) the area damaged is where that processing takes place. But this might not necessarily be so as there are other variables involved in individuals.

- One issue is that damage to the brain from a virus or from surgery rarely focuses on just one brain structure. As in the case of the MTL+ patients studied by Schmolck *et al.* (2002) the damage, though similar, was not identical. As there are differences, it is hard to be sure that the damage caused the difficulties in cognitive functioning.
- Measurements of semantic knowledge and memory using tests of pointing and naming, for example, are perhaps not particularly valid as the variables are isolated for study. Then again, they are perhaps valid measurements of specific areas of semantic functioning because those areas are narrowed for study in this controlled way.
- People with damage to the brain are unique individuals with individual characteristics, and comparing them as if they are the same, on the basis of some very similar damage to the brain, might not be fair. Also, findings from individuals with brain damage might not be generalisable to the population without brain damage.
- Neuroimaging might not be sensitive enough to pick up smaller sites of damage enough to study them, such as in the case of those with mild traumatic brain injury. Neuroimaging is more successful perhaps where the brain damage is much more visible. Even then, there is the suggestion that the lack of 'fine tuning' in neuroimaging can mean damage is not picked up and so conclusions are not sound.

Test yourself

1. Explain weaknesses in using evidence from case studies of patients with brain damage when exploring how memory works. **(6 marks)**
2. Assess the value of using evidence from case studies of patients with brain damage when discussing models of memory in cognitive psychology. **(8 marks)**

Methods in biological psychology

The methods that you need to know for biological psychology are correlational research, brain scanning (CAT, PET and fMRI), one twin study and one adoption study

Correlation designs

Earlier in this chapter, when looking at methods in cognitive psychology, three participant (experimental) designs were outlined (pp. 321–323):

- matched pairs
- independent groups
- repeated measures.

Another type of design, though not an experimental one, is **correlation design**. Correlation design involves comparing data from the same participants or two sets of data. Two measures are taken from one individual and recorded. Once the two scores are obtained from enough participants, the relationship between the scores is tested. Possible relationships are:

- scoring highly on both measures
- scoring highly on one of the measures and having a low score on the other.

There are two types of correlation:

- A **positive correlation** is when one score rises as the other rises – for example, as age increases so does the time it takes to react to a stimulus.
- A **negative correlation** is when one score rises as the other falls – for example, as age rises, average driving speed falls.

The main points in a correlation are that the same person produces the two scores or there are two sets of data and that both measures have numerical data.

Important features and issues about correlation designs include the following:

- There is no independent or dependent variable. There are two variables of equal importance. For example, one variable might be length of time having therapy for aggression and the other might be the measured benefit of therapy.
- The hypothesis will not be about a difference between two conditions; it will be about a relationship between the two variables. For a discussion on studies looking for differences or relationships, see pp. 328–329 of this chapter.
- The hypothesis could be directional because it could predict a positive or negative correlation. For example, a directional hypothesis for a correlation might be that 'there is a positive relationship between length of time having therapy and the benefit of therapy'. The direction is predicted – the hypothesis mentions a positive relationship rather than 'a relationship'.
- A scatter diagram (pp. 408–409) will show whether a correlation is positive, negative or neither. Correlations involve using a lot of controls, just as experiments do, and questionnaires and interviews. Controls involve keeping all variables the same except the ones being studied; however, when looking for a relationship between two variables, that is not easy. For example, if we claim that height affects brain size, on the principle that both are about body size, then we might want to control for gender as gender has been shown to affect both height and brain size.

Height may correlate with size of brain, and a relationship might be established – though of course size of brain does not indicate difference in intelligence!

- Correlations also involve sampling, as do all research methods. Sampling in your course covers just four techniques: random, stratified, opportunity and volunteer. These are explained on pp. 299–304. Random sampling is the most representative of the target population as random sampling means everyone has the opportunity to be included in the sample, which helps to reduce bias.
- Correlations do not involve randomising to groups. The same participant is scored for both the variables (such as height and brain size or age and driving speed), so there is no need to sort out which participant goes in which group.
- Similarly, control groups are not likely to apply to correlation studies. Correlations look at relationships between variables and not cause-and-effect conclusions.

The issues of difference or relationship (pp. 328-329), directional and non-directional hypotheses (page 318) and the way a correlation works (pp. 406–411), including using a scatter diagram to display correlations, have been discussed earlier in this chapter or in Chapter 6 so are only summarised here. You will find more out about positive and negative correlations and the strength of a correlation in Chapter 6 (pp. 406–411).

Study using the methodology

Matthies *et al.* (2012) carried out a study to see whether the size and shape of a brain structure (the amygdala) related to lifetime aggression. The amygdala has been linked to aggression. Lifetime aggression was measured by asking 20 healthy female volunteers using a standard measure (Life History of Aggression Assessment) and the size (volume) of the amygdala was found by using MRI scanning of the 20 volunteers and measuring according to standard measures. The data were analysed using tests for correlations, including the Spearman's test, with data from the size of the amygdala. A p value of 0.05 was chosen. All volunteers scored within the normal range of lifetime aggression and the higher scores regarding lifetime aggression showed a 16-18 per cent reduction in size of the amygdala, which went against what was thought. One of the results using the Spearman test was −0.672, which was significant at $p \leq 0.002$. This was a negative correlation. A smaller amygdala might be a marker for higher aggression. There are issues with this study, such as the use of only females and the small numbers, but small numbers alone do not make the findings ungeneralisable.

STUDY HINT

In the brief account of Matthies *et al.* (2012), information has been chosen to help you with learning not only about correlations in psychology, but also about levels of significance and doing a Spearman's test. Use such information in your learning, to check understanding. The more you practise, the easier it will be to understand. For example, a Spearman test value of −0.672 is very high as it is close to 1, which is a perfect correlation. Note that it has a minus sign, which denotes a strong negative correlation. The level of significance is 0.002, which means it would be expected that just 2 in 1,000 would go against the experimental hypothesis.

The study also shows use of MRI scanning. MRI is used because it is brain structure (physical parts of the brain) that is being measured. If brain functioning (the brain at work) is to be measured, then fMRI would be chosen, or PET scanning. This study is also an example of the use of scanning to study human behaviour – in this case, aggression – which is the focus of biological psychology in your course. Use examples where they fit, not just for one purpose.

Progress check 5.37

State whether these examples are expected to yield a positive or a negative correlation or whether direction is not stated. (These are for fun and not necessarily from data.)

1. The older someone is, the lower their driving speed.
2. The larger the area of a certain part of the brain, the higher the scores on a measure of aggression.
3. There is a relationship between the height of a person and their brain size.

Evaluation of correlation designs

Strengths

- Initial relationships can be discovered which might not have been realised previously. Whenever there are two scaled measures and the same people are producing both sets of data, a correlation test can be carried out. Therefore, this is a flexible design, which, if an unexpected relationship is indicated, can lead to new research. A study investigating the relationship between the size of a part of the brain (measured by scanning) could be new and a relationship might be uncovered between that part of the brain and tendency to aggression. The relationship would be only partly unexpected because studies like Raine *et al.* (1997), the classic study for biological psychology, do show that size of parts of the brain can seemingly relate to aggression.
- The same people are providing both sets of data, so the data will not be affected by individual differences. To be scientific, a research method must include controls to ensure that results are not affected by participant variables. Scores for a correlation are not affected in this way.

Weaknesses

- Correlation designs only indicate a relationship. To be scientific, a research method should be strong enough, with controls and no bias, to show a cause-and-effect relationship between the independent and dependent variables. A correlation cannot show a cause-and-effect relationship. For example, length of time in therapy and benefit of therapy could be connected, but it might not be the length of time that causes the benefit. It might be that the person staying in therapy for a long time has insight, whereas a person who leaves does not have such insight. It could be that it is the ability to have insight that gives the greater benefits, not the length of time in therapy. A correlation shows a relationship but does not show that one of the variables depends on the other.
- The measures might not produce valid data. Time in therapy is a clear measure but the benefits of therapy are not easy to quantify. Some variables are more valid than others, but a correlation can use data from unnatural measures.

Analysis of correlations

Correlations are analysed using a Spearman's rank correlation coefficient, which is explained more in Chapter 6 (pp. 409–411). Ideas about choosing a test and using inferential testing have been discussed earlier in this chapter. Correlations can be displayed using a scatter diagram. Issues about using inferential tests that you need to know about are levels of measurement (A level only), critical and observed values and levels of statistical significance. All of this information was presented earlier in the cognitive psychology section as the same issues about inferential testing are needed in cognitive psychology, biological psychology and learning theories in Year 1 of your course.

Test yourself

1. Explain the difference between positive and negative correlations. **(2 marks)**
2. Explain when a researcher would use a correlation design in psychology. **(4 marks)**
3. Evaluate the use of correlations in psychology. **(16 marks)**

CAT/CT, PET and fMRI scanning techniques as research methods

Biological psychology often gets evidence from brain scanning. In fact, if you have already studied the cognitive psychology topic in your course, you may have looked at the contemporary study by Schmolck *et al.* (2002). They studied patients with damage to specific areas of the brain to find out where memory activity takes place. The study is briefly discussed earlier in this chapter (pp. 336–337). Schmolck *et al.* (2002) talk about using CT scanning and MRI scanning, as well as mentioning neuroimaging. For your course, you are asked to study CAT/CT, PET and fMRI scanning.

Introduction

There are different types of scanning, which give different types of information. Some scans are used to study biological, rather than psychological, aspects of an individual – for example, looking for diseases and tumours. Psychology is interested in scans that examine all aspects of the brain and information processing (thinking, remembering, using language, attending to information, forgetting and problem-solving), as well as some physiological aspects of the brain, such as which brain area works when certain processing takes place and which areas in the brain might relate to behaviour like aggression. The information that is needed guides the type of scan that is chosen.

In your course, you need to study CAT/CT, PET and fMRI scanning and look at the use of scanning techniques to study human behaviour such as aggression. As biological psychology in your course features aggression, that is the behaviour focused on in this section. The way scanning gives information about the processing of information in the brain is studied more in cognitive psychology.

STUDY HINT

You will have come across the use of scanning/neuroimaging when studying other areas of your course, such as in cognitive psychology. The classic study for biological psychology is Raine *et al.* (1997), which uses PET scanning to gather the data. Be sure to link up elements of your course, such as when the same research method is used to collect data in different studies, as that will help your understanding.

Explanation

CAT/CT, PET and fMRI scanning techniques are being refined constantly, so you might find more up-to-date information than is given here. However, the ideas presented are those needed for your course.

Scans used to be used solely for medical purposes. However, scans are now also used for research purposes. Much information is being gathered, although the machines are still expensive and relatively hard to access.

In studies in psychology, such as Schmolck *et al.* (2002), you will see scanning referred to as **neuroimaging**, which refers to generating images about the nervous system. Neuroimaging can be about functioning of the brain or about structure, and both are studied using neuroimaging or scanning. Scans looking at brain functioning can detect issues such as Alzheimer's and scans looking at structure can detect brain damage, for example. Neuroimaging looking at function is used to study information processing, such as parts of the brain that are used for short-term memory. The idea of neuroimaging is that, if a brain area is used, such as in processing of specific information, then that will increase the metabolic rate, which shows up on the image.

Definition

Neuroimaging means using scans to generate images either of brain functioning and the brain at work or of brain structure, such as where there is damage.

Progress check 5.38

Explain the difference between brain structure and brain functioning, when discussing how scanning techniques can focus on one or the other.

CAT/CT scanning techniques

X-ray computed tomography is known as CAT or CT scanning. In 1979, the inventors of CT scanning received the Nobel Prize in medicine, which underlines its importance. Tomography is about imaging using sections. It takes a slice or slices and produces drawings of the slice or slices. In CT scanning, an x-ray is used to get the picture; in PET scanning, it is a radioactive tracer; in MRI, magnetic imaging is used. Scans have the same underpinning ideas but use different ways to get the pictures. CAT stands for computer axial tomography and is the same as CT scanning in essence. CT is used mostly in this section. CT scanning is computed or computerised tomography. The 'axial' bit of 'CAT' is about the angle of the 'slices' (perpendicular to the area) and that no longer applies so 'CT' is the term used. X-rays do not help when structures overlap because it is not possible to see behind the overlap. CT scans do not have the overlap issue as images are in sections.

A CT scan produces pictures in slices which can be looked at individually or can be put together to give a three-dimensional view of the 'whole' area, such as a part of the body. Older CT scans involved slices, but newer ones take pictures using a helix shape, which has advantages over the old way, though the basic idea is the same. The pictures are formed and pick up how the area being scanned reacts to the x-ray being passed through it, showing how far the x-ray is blocked. Knowing how areas block the x-ray shows something about the areas, such as whether a tumour is present. In psychology, CT scanning can be used to understand damage to the brain.

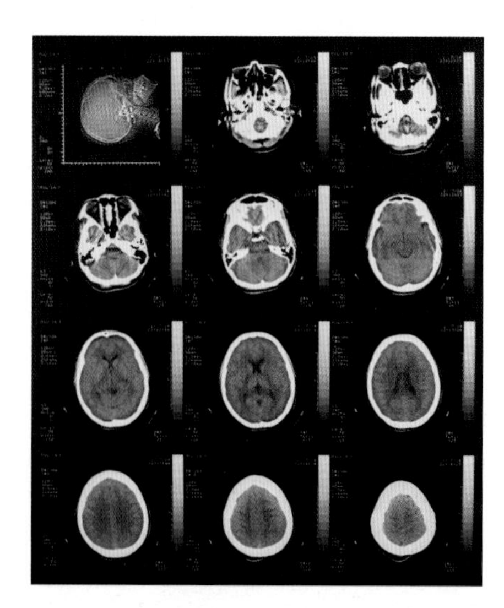

Images using a CT scan of the human brain, showing the images in 'slices' from the base of the skull to the top

The procedure of CT scanning is for someone to lie on a moving platform to be passed through the scanner or for the person to lie still and the scanner moves around them. Sometimes a dye is used for highlighting purposes. Iodine and barium are two dyes. The dye makes the picture clearer for analysis. A CT scan can take from a few minutes to around 30 minutes. As MRI scanning gives better images and PET scanning can look at brain functioning, CT scanning is not really used to look at information processing. It is used more for medical purposes and to check damage to the brain.

Review of using scanning

Betts (2009) is a review of the use of scanning in defence of people pleading not guilty by reason of insanity (NGRI) in courts. She mentions the use of CT, PET, MRI and fMRI scanning to provide neurological data to support claims of NGRI. She discusses issues with the use of such evidence. NGRI is a plea that the person has a mental defect that relates to any crime, is a reason for their actions and means they cannot understand that their act is wrong. The evidence from scanning can provide actual evidence of any defect or deficit. Betts argues that neurological evidence does not show that a mental deficit will stop someone from knowing that what they are doing is wrong and juries may be affected by scientific evidence from scanning that suggests a cause-and-effect relationship when there is not one. Some types of brain damage may show impaired understanding of actions, and the review examines different cases and types to try to show more about when scanning evidence might be useful in a trial situation.

She cites the case of Herbert Weinstein, a 64-year-old man who in 1991 strangled his wife after an argument. His defence was that a cyst had caused pressure on his prefrontal cortex, which had affected his understanding of right and wrong. There was CAT scan evidence of differences in his brain (widening sulci) that related to those with schizophrenia. After a long argument, the evidence was admitted and he was acquitted but admitted to a hospital. There is a lot of similar evidence of the use of neuroimaging in trials, some related to the amygdala and aggression. Betts summarises by saying that between 60 and 77 per cent of people using the plea NGRI are found to have a psychosis and 10 per cent have a diagnosis of psychosis that is neurologically based (e.g. Warren *et al.*, 2006, cited in Betts, 2009). Betts concludes that there is a place for evidence from neuroimaging but other evidence about a person's mental state should also be used and scanning evidence should not carry more weight when sentencing.

Explore

Look up the case of Herbert Weinstein to find out more about the use of scanning in pleas of not guilty by reason of insanity. Though sources tend to differ over his age at the time and what happened at the end of the trial (some sources say he was imprisoned and found guilty of manslaughter rather than murder), there is a great deal of interest in such cases. The following *New York Times* article could be a starting point: www.nytimes.com/2007/03/11/magazine/11Neurolaw.t.html?pagewanted=all&_r=0.

STUDY HINT

The argument presented by Betts (2009) relates to the classic study in biological psychology in your course, Raine *et al.* (1997), so there is relevance to you course not just for the use of scanning but when discussing that study too. Also this is about aggression, which relates to another part of the method section in biological psychology, knowing about the use of brain scanning to investigate human behaviour such as aggression.

Evaluation of CT scanning

Strengths

- CT scanning is less harmful than PET scans, which use a radioactive tracer, although x-rays can be damaging so are used infrequently.
- A CT scan can detect changes in physical structures to quite a good level and so it is valuable when looking for tumours, haemorrhages or calcifications, particularly as it produces a 3D image, which helps diagnosis – though this is used in medicine more than in psychology. CT scans can also be used in industry. So a strength is its wide application in general, including studying damage to the brain of individuals to help with studying the brain.
- With the modern approach of using helix formations rather than slices, different angles of an area of interest can be studied. This helps with an overall picture, again helping to look at damage to the brain in detail. Not having overlap to deal with also helps with the overall picture.
- A CT scan is not painful at all and is non-invasive, which means there is no need to 'enter' the body, although if a dye is used, that is not entirely the case.

Weaknesses

- MRI gives a clearer picture when it comes to examining causes of a headache, for example, and is more likely to be used when scanning the brain, so that fits more with the need in psychology. An MRI is also better for infection (but not as good at detecting fractures).

STUDY HINT

When explaining a strength or weakness of any method, don't just give a simple statement: if you say 'CT scanning is better than MRI scanning', that would not be accurate. Be sure to make full, accurate notes.

- CT scanning involves x-raying, which can cause damage, notably cancers. This is a known feature of CT scans so they are used sparingly. This means as a method of studying the brain for research purposes, CT scanning would not be recommended. The radiation from a CT scan is what someone is normally exposed to in the course of a year. Note, though, that CT scanning for children uses a reduced dosage and the information given in this textbook is by no means the whole picture for the use of CT scanning in medicine.

Progress check 5.39

Answer the following short questions about CT and MRI scanning:

1. Which type of scanning is the least invasive?
2. Which type of scanning uses x-rays to examine what goes on inside the body?
3. Which type of scanning gives a better picture and more detail in the brain?

PET scanning techniques

PET (positron emission tomography) can be used to study the brain. It picks up 'hot spots' in the brain, enabling researchers to find out which parts are working at a particular time. A radioactive tracer is added to a chemical (usually glucose) that the body uses and is injected into a vein in the arm. The tracer provides small, positively charged particles called positrons, which give signals that are recorded. As the glucose is used in the brain, this shows up as an area of activity. The recordings can be displayed as images, which are then interpreted. Different radioactive tracers are used depending on the information required.

A PET scan can be used to study blood flow in the brain. For example, if someone is talking during a PET scan, the areas of most blood flow in the brain will be the areas used during talking and the scan detects these areas. Cognitive

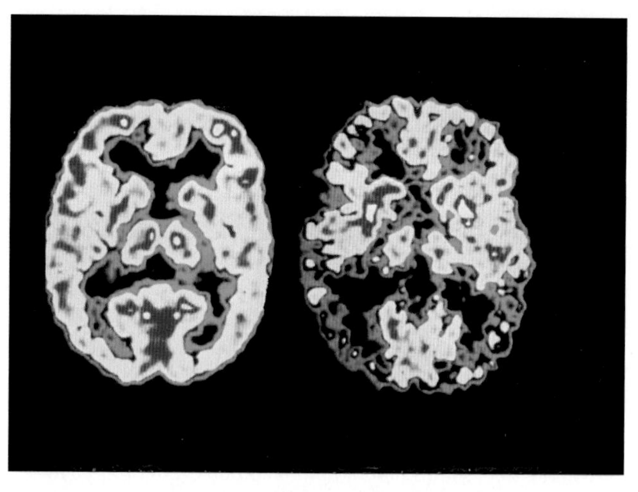

Images from a PET scan, showing activity in the brain

activity and other types of brain activity can be tracked in this way and much information has been found about the functions of different parts of the brain. Language involves a number of brain areas because the individual has to find the word, prepare to speak it and then say it. By asking someone to think of words, read words, speak words and other such tasks, researchers can find which part of the brain works for a particular language function.

- PET scanning can also show size of brain areas and they can then be measured and compared between people, which is what Raine *et al.* (1997) did in their study, to see which areas seemed larger in people charged with murder.
- PET scanning is limited to shorter tasks as the radioactive tracer does not last long.
- PET-CT scans give a 3D image by using CT scanning with PET scanning. PET-CT scanning is a modern advance on PET scanning. The ideas behind PET scanning were introduced in the mid-twentieth century, and there has been a lot of development since then, and indeed development is still continuing. The PET and CT scan is done one after the other with the patient not moving and then the areas of malfunctioning (if that is the case) can be highlighted in the body (including the brain). However, this is more often used if the area of focus is not the brain. Psychology is more likely to look at brain areas and brain functioning.
- PET-MRI scans also combine scanning of the body with scanning to see functioning so that a fuller picture can emerge. The functioning is what the body is doing biochemically. PET scanning gives the functioning. Only the head and brain are covered using a PET-MRI at the moment, as that is where the required magnetic field is possible.

Table 5.13 shows some differences between a CT scan and a PET scan.

Table 5.13 Comparison of CT and PET scans

Feature	C(A)T (computed (axial) tomography) scan	PET (positron emission tomography) scan
Cost	$1,200 to $3,200	$3,000 to $6,000, much higher than CT scanning
Time to complete the scan	Usually completed in five minutes so movement not so much of a problem	2–4 hours
Radiation exposure	Radiation dose is 2 to 10 mSv, the same dose as over about 1–3 years normally.	Moderate to high radiation
Imaging principles	X-rays	Radioactive tracers emitting positrons
Effects on the body	Painless, non-invasive, but radiation	Radiation risk same as an x-ray
Date began	Early 1970s	1976

Adapted from: www.diffen.com/difference/CT_Scan_vs_PET_Scan

Reasons for using PET scans as a research method

PET scanning is mainly carried out for medical purposes – for example, to check the damage made by a stroke or to check other nervous system problems. However, PET scans can also be used in research to map how the brain works. For example, PET scanning can be used in the study of schizophrenia to see which parts of the brain are working. The scans can then be compared with scans of the brain of a person without schizophrenia so that more can be learnt about it. Epilepsy and other conditions can also be studied by looking at blood flow in the brain.

> **STUDY HINT**
> Remember when discussing a data-gathering method, you can use examples from your course, such as Raine *et al.* (1997) for PET scanning.

Evaluation of PET scanning

Strengths

- PET scanning, as in all scanning techniques, is a reasonably non-invasive way of studying inside the brain (and body). The individual has to have the radioactive tracer injected, though, which is invasive, but the images are taken from outside the body, which is less dangerous and less distressing than surgery. Surgery for research purposes is carried out using animals, so scans using humans are more ethical for that reason. PET scanning is, therefore, a reasonably non-invasive and ethical way of researching the brain.
- As with all scanning techniques, there is validity – the scan seems to measure what it claims to measure. It is not easy to check validity when it comes to cognitive functions, such as using language. However, when speech was studied using PET scanning, it was confirmed that what was previously thought to be the area for speech (found by examining the brains of people who had speech problems when they died) was indeed the area of activity (Broca's area). So scanning seems to be a valid measure.
- PET scanning is reliable because it can be repeated and the same results found. This can be tested – for example, whenever someone speaks, the same area of the brain is used. The same areas of the brain are consistently found for different activities, which means the method is reliable.

Weaknesses

- The use of the radioactive tracer is an invasive procedure and so there are ethical implications for the individual. The researcher must follow ethical guidelines carefully. Injecting someone with a substance is not something to be done lightly. There has to be informed consent and a good reason for carrying it out. The scan itself can make some people panic because having one's head inside a tube can be a claustrophobic experience and this must be fully explained to the participant.
- Although the activity shows up quite clearly on the image, it is difficult to isolate different brain functioning precisely. For example, people can read passages of text while being scanned but they would almost certainly be using other parts of their brain as well. So although PET scanning is valid up to a point, it is hard to claim from a scan exactly which part of the brain is performing which function, and this is often the aim of the research. Consequently, the validity of any claims can be criticised.

> **STUDY HINT**
> To find out what you need to know about any topic, read your course specification carefully. Be sure to know exactly what is required. For example, with regard to scanning, you need to know about CAT, PET and fMRI scanning and also how scanning is used to investigate human behaviour such as aggression.

Progress check 5.40

Explain the idea that PET scanning has validity.

MRI scanning techniques

MRI scanning uses magnetic resonance imaging and started in the 1950s. Hospitals began to have MRI scanners between the 1980s and 1990s, not that long ago. The scanners were used for medical purposes, such as scanning to find cancers and, as they were expensive, they were not widely available for studies in psychology. In 2003, the Nobel Prize in physiology/medicine went to people working on MRI scanning, as with CT scanning, emphasising the value of the scanning revolution for diagnosis and treatment.

A strong magnetic field is passed over the body. The whole body may be inside a tube, which can be claustrophobic. The process is noisy, but not painful. MRI scans are affected by movement, so the person has to keep very still. The effect of passing the magnetic field over the chosen area, which could be just the head, is measured and images are produced, which are then interpreted. As the magnetic field passes through the body, hydrogen atoms are 'excited' and that can be detected. The time it takes for the hydrogen atoms to return to their resting state can show something about tissues in the body.

An MRI scan gives cross-sectional views of the body, like a CT scan, and can produce images from different angles. MRI scans do not show activity to the same degree as PET scans and are used to look at structure not function. This means looking at what is there, such as enabling measurement of grey matter in the brain (e.g. De Bellis *et al.*, 2001). This is not about measuring blood flow to see how the brain works (though an fMRI does that, as explained later). Before an MRI scan is carried out, a dye, called a contrast medium, is injected into the body to help show up body organs and relevant areas.

Studies using the methodology

De Bellis *et al.* (2001) used MRI scanning to see if the volume of three areas of the brain (grey matter, white matter and corpus callosum) changed with age and sex of children aged between 6 and 18 years. They found that, with increasing age, grey matter decreased; white matter and the corpus callosum increased. They also found that these changes were greater in males than in females.

Evaluation of MRI scanning

Strengths

- As with PET scanning, there is validity because what is found by the scan is then often found in reality. They are accurate in checking for abnormalities in the brain and the rest of the body.
- Compared with surgery, MRI scans are non-invasive (apart from the injected dye). As a research method, surgery involving humans is unlikely. However, it is carried out on animals. MRI scanning is, therefore, a more ethical way of studying the brain and the rest of the body, partly because it is non-invasive and partly because it means animals do not have to be used.
- MRI scanning is replicable. It can be repeated and the same results found. It is a scientific method because the resulting images can be checked by more than one person and the interpretation checked for objectivity. The images generated are evidence that the MRI scanner measures what was previously difficult to measure.
- MRI scanning is preferred over CT scanning because it is less harmful. Studies have shown that the radiation from CT scanning is harmful and can cause cancers.

Weaknesses

- MRI scans are stressful because an injection has to be given. They are also extremely noisy and can make people feel closed in. This sort of stress should not be imposed on a participant without careful consideration of ethical guidelines and issues.
- MRI scanning only measures particular things. There are, for example, clear images of soft tissue and body organs, but brain activity is not measured. This means that knowledge from such scans is limited.

Table 5.14 shows some comparison points between MRI and PET scans.

Table 5.14 Comparison of MRI and PET scans

Issue	MRI scan	PET scan
Non invasive	Yes – except for an injection of dye	Yes – except for an injection of radioactive tracer
Can study activity in the brain	No – studies tissues and looks for abnormalities, although can measure blood flow	Yes – the tracer picks up activity in the brain
Needs interpretation	Yes – from images generated by computer	Yes – from images generated by computer
Scientific method	Yes – objective technique that is the same for everyone	Yes – objective technique that is the same for everyone
Validity	Yes – measures what it claims to measure; can be fairly unspecific	Yes – measures what it claims to measure; unspecific because the brain is active in so many areas
Reliability	Yes – expensive and difficult to set up initially, but can be repeated easily	Yes – expensive and difficult to set up initially, but can be repeated easily
Generalisability	Yes – same structures found for all people; specific problems relate to individuals	Yes – same brain functions found for all people; specific problems relate to individuals
Uses magnets	Yes – strong magnetic field used to scan parts of the body	No
Uses radioactive tracer	No	Yes
Focus on biological issues	Yes	Yes

STUDY HINT

Note that you are asked to know about fMRI rather than MRI scanning, but you need to know the basic idea of MRI scanning, such as the use of the magnetic field, to understand fMRI. Remember, though, when taking notes that it is the fMRI scanning technique that you need to know about.

fMRI scanning

fMRI scanning refers to functional MRI scanning, which as the name implies builds on MRI scanning and can look at the functioning of the brain. Blood and oxygen levels are measured. The scan picks up on changes of use of brain areas depending on the task being carried out. What the fMRI relies on is that blood flow and neuronal activity are linked. So changes in blood flow highlight neuronal activity. The fMRI looks at the blood flow showing brain cell use of energy.

An MRI scan does not pick up on functions of the brain; a PET scan does, so historically MRI was not used to look at brain functioning. Then it was discovered that an MRI could be used to look at blood flow and so could be used to look at brain functioning, and that was the start of fMRI (you can see why it is called *functional* magnetic resonance imaging), which can look at brain functioning using changes in blood flow when different areas of the brain are used. Oxygenated and deoxygenated haemoglobin is looked at using magnetic resonance imaging to see which areas of the brain are active in certain conditions.

This is very similar to how a PET scan works, though a PET scan can highlight actual receptors and an fMRI cannot. Largely though, fMRI is used now in place of PET scanning. An fMRI scan, which highlights differences in brain flow to a high degree of accuracy and with sensitivity, is useful for those at risk of, or who have had, stroke. So there is medical application as well as application for understanding the brain. It is used a lot for research, however, unlike (in general) MRI and CT scanning.

Blood flow in the brain relates to consumption or flow of glucose and different structures do that differently. The amygdala, basal ganglia, cingulate cortex and thalamus relate to the flow of glucose not its consumption. There is different glucose activity in other areas, such as the lateral frontal lobe. Some of these features of the brain are mentioned here as they arise in the study by Schmolck *et al.* (2002), which used neuroimaging to measure damage in the brain of patients and then looked at which cognitive tasks they found difficult, before relating the difficulty to the damage. However, use of fMRI is not so good for people with brain damage as that affects the blood flow. fMRI is good for finding out how the brain functions by using 'normal' participants. Schmolck *et al.* (2002) used MRI and CT scanning rather than fMRI.

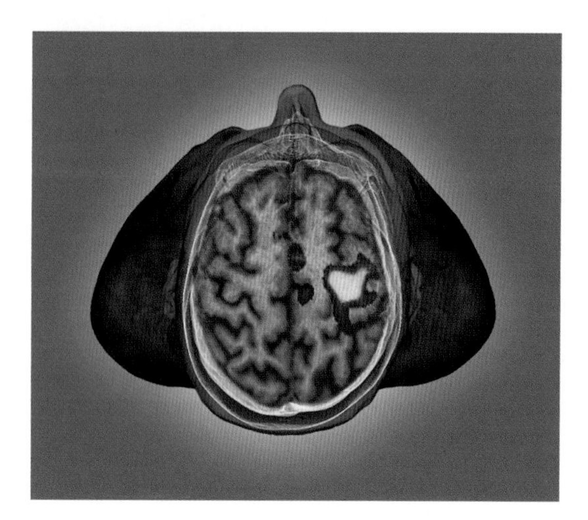

An fMRI scan of the brain

Areas in psychology that fMRI scanning has contributed to include looking at regions of the brain at work when we use language and seeing if both sides of the brain are equally used, checking memory regions, looking for the onset of Alzheimer's and looking at mental health issues like depression to see effects on brain functioning.

Study using the methodology

Dimoka (2010) used fMRI neuroimaging to look at trust and distrust. Dimoka (2010) suggests that most studies of trust and distrust use psychometric measures (tests) and the idea of this research was to use neuroimaging to see if evidence of brain function and structure linked to trust and distrust would complement evidence from psychometric testing. The study also wanted to see if there is brain functioning linking to trust and distrust that was not previously known about. The study measured trust as benevolence and credibility and distrust as the opposite (malevolence and discredibility). Previous studies link the caudate nucleus with anticipating a positive reward and this area links to dopamine receptors, which also link to a positive reward. The orbitofrontal cortex is linked to uncertainty so lower levels of orbitofrontal cortex activity are expected if there is trust. These are just two areas that were studied, to give a sense of what this study is about.

The study used 177 participants from a university in the US to carry out a standard behavioural task. Then they scanned 15 people (all right-handed; nine males, six females) using fMRI neuroimaging while the same task was carried out. The 15 participants were given $35 for taking part. The data from the behavioural study could help to give validity to the fMRI findings and also could inform the fMRI study if there were difficulties with the task, such as how long to give. The findings showed that 'trust' areas were areas relating to positive reward, predictions and uncertainty and the 'distrust' areas related to intense emotions and fear of loss. The fMRI study suggests that different brain areas are involved in trust than in distrust, which was not found in the psychometric testing studies. Dimoka (2010) found that credibility and discredibility (how far you think someone is credible) linked to the cognitive brain areas of the prefrontal cortex. However, benevolence and malevolence (whether you think someone is kind or not) linked to the emotion area of the brain (the limbic system). The findings of the behavioural study about trust and distrust did relate to the fMRI findings, giving some validity. The study points to difficulties with using fMRI scanning, including its high cost and the difficulty of analysing the data from the high amount of images.

STUDY HINT

You can use studies as evidence for a methodology's strengths or weaknesses. For example, Dimoka (2010) suggested that the fMRI part of the study was expensive and also that it took a long time to analyse the data. These are weaknesses with using fMRI in research. The study also says, however, that there seems to be validity in that what was being measured really was trust and distrust.

Progress check 5.41

In the table below, tick the correct statements about scanning techniques as research methods.

Statement	**Tick if the statement is true**
fMRI scanning uses magnetic imaging and is useful for looking at brain structure only.	
PET scanning is less expensive than CT scanning.	
MRI scans are more useful for looking at brain structure than brain functioning.	
CT scans can be used with PET scans to show a 3D image as well as brain activity.	
To an extent, fMRI scans are starting to take the place of PET scans.	
CAT stands for computed axial tomography.	
Tomography means the study of images of sections (e.g. of the body).	

Evaluation of fMRI scanning

Strengths

- One strength of fMRI, as with MRI, is that there is no danger from radiation, unlike CT scanning and, to an extent, PET scanning. From the 1990s, fMRI has been the main type of scan chosen because there is no invasion or surgery and no radiation exposure.
- Another strength of fMRI is that the detection of changes in blood flow is very precise and so even slight changes can be detected. This means that, for medical use, fMRI is very good at detecting issues around stroke. Also the sensitivity to blood flow changes makes fMRI very good for looking at brain functioning and brain structure when it comes to learning about the brain. Cognitive tasks can be carried out and the brain areas in use are identified clearly.

Weaknesses

- One weakness is that an fMRI scan cannot look at the actual receptors of neurotransmitters, whereas a PET scan can do that, so an fMRI is not suitable for everything that a PET scan can do.
- There can be problems with using fMRI scanning – for example, too much head movement can distort the imaging.
- If an fMRI is used to see where certain types of information processing take place in the brain, and the idea is to measure the brain at rest and then the brain when using that functioning, there is an issue in that the brain is never at rest. It is not easy to get a baseline measure. For example, even breathing is an activity that requires processing in the brain.
- There are risks when undergoing fMRI scanning, such as to those with pacemakers and more generally because of issues like claustrophobia. Scanning is not risk free. There can be tingling felt when magnetic fields switch during the scan, for example.

Test yourself

1. Explain what is meant by 'brain scanning' as a research method in psychology. **(6 marks)**
2. Evaluate brain scanning as a research method in psychology using examples from studies to explain your points. **(12 marks)**

The use of brain scanning techniques to investigate human behaviour such as aggression

In the biological psychology area of your course, you also need to look at the use of brain scanning techniques to investigate aggression. Some of the studies mentioned in this section have already been discussed, so are just summarised here.

Human behaviour v. cognitive processing and emotions

Before summarising studies and adding a few more that use scanning to study aggression, it is worth mentioning a possible difference between human behaviour and brain processing by humans. Human behaviour is about what people do, and that is what you are being asked about. Human cognitive processing is not behaviour as such. However, cognitive processing can link to behaviour, so there is a fine line here. For example, Dimoka (2010) (page 348) looked at how trust and mistrust 'work' in the brain, such as which areas are active in trust and which in mistrust. The study looked at cognitive processing (being trusting) and emotions (fearing someone). Neither of these are human behaviour but if trust is measured as how much someone is swayed by a salesman then what is being measured (such as their acceptance of a sale) is human behaviour. De Bellis *et al.* (2001) (page 346) is another example of the use of scanning. Their study looked at how brain structure, size and format changes with age, which is not looking at human behaviour as such, so again not relevant for this section on how brain scanning is used to study human behaviour.

STUDY HINT

Be careful to analyse any question or issue in psychology carefully. This particular section of your course asks specifically about the study of human behaviour and you can argue that brain activity, cognitive processing and emotional reactions are not human behaviour as such. This shows the importance of relating to a question or to material in a specific and focused way.

Raine *et al.* (1997) and PET scanning

One study that stands out is Raine *et al.* (1997), the classic study for the biological psychology element of your course. Raine *et al.* (1997) is explained in detail in Chapter 3 (pp. 176–184). You will see clearly that PET scanning is used to show a link between aggression – in this case, possible murder as the participants are charged with murder and pleading not guilty by reason of insanity (NGRI). PET scanning was used to give images of the participants' brains and then certain areas linked with aggression in other studies were measured to see if they differed in any significant way. If the brains of the 'murderers' were found to differ, then perhaps their aggressive behaviour comes from certain brain structures. This was in fact found, as you will have read about in Chapter 3, so Raine *et al.* (1997) use brain scanning techniques to investigate aggression, which is human behaviour.

Betts (2009): a review about people pleading not guilty by reason of insanity

Betts (2009) discussed the case of Herbert Weinstein, whose defence used CAT scanning to show he had damage to the brain that might have led to his aggression (he strangled his wife). The scan showed some damage, including widened sulci, and this evidence was used to persuade the jury that his actions were not thought through; he did not know sufficiently right from wrong. Betts (2009) cites Warren *et al.* (2006) as suggesting that 60–77 per cent of people pleading NGRI have a psychosis and 10 per cent of those have a psychosis that is neurologically based. This is evidence that aggressive behaviour might be based on someone's brain physiology and so scanning is a useful research method when investigating human behaviour such as aggression.

Matthies *et al.* (2012) and MRI scanning

Matthies *et al.* (2012) used MRI scanning to measure the volume of the amygdala in 21 female volunteer participants. Alongside that measure, they also obtained an aggression score about lifetime aggression. The two scores were tested for a relationship and a significant correlation was found. Previous studies suggest that the amygdala (in the limbic system) is the place for aggression in the brain (e.g. Reimann and Zimbardo, 2011). However, Matthies *et al.* (2012) found that there was a significant relationship in that the smaller the amygdala, the higher the aggression score, which was surprising. Nonetheless, the finding was that amygdala volume did relate to lifetime aggression score. This suggests using an MRI scan is helpful in finding out where aggression might 'be' in the brain. Matthies *et al.* (2012) was briefly explained when discussing correlation design (page 340). Scanning does seem to be useful in explaining the human behaviour of aggression and where in the brain aggression may be based.

> **STUDY HINT**
> If you need to remind yourself about where the amygdala is in the brain, have a look back at the diagram on page 000 of Chapter 3.

Reimann and Zimbardo (2011): a meta-analysis that draws on neuroimaging

Reimann and Zimbardo (2011) carried out a **meta-analysis** to look at what they called the 'neuroscience of evil'. They wanted to see what others had found out using brain scanning (and other research methods) about evil and links to brain structure and brain functioning. Zimbardo was mentioned in Chapter 1 of this book and is well-known in social psychology for his work on obedience and brutality in human behaviour. He has also looked at psychology and heroism (see Key questions section in Chapter 1, pp. 68–69). In the study outlined here, Zimbardo, with Reimann, looks at other studies. Their method is a meta-analysis, which is a way of looking at data that you will cover in Year 2 of your course. They present evidence from various scanning techniques, which they call 'neuroimaging', to show areas of the brain that link to aggressive behaviour. For example, scanning of Phineas Gage's preserved skull showed damage to the prefrontal cortex (Damasio *et al.*, 1994, cited in Reimann and Zimbardo, 2011), which is thought to relate to aggression (or more likely, when not damaged, to link to problem-solving and calming the individual, against being aggressive).

Reimann and Zimbardo (2011) cite a number of studies using neuroimaging to show that damage to the frontal lobes links with aggressive behaviour in humans. Seiver (2008, cited in Reimann and Zimbardo, 2011) pointed to the amygdala in aggression rather than the prefrontal lobes. Somatic marker theory holds that there are links between the ventromedial prefrontal cortex and areas such as the amygdala (and hypothalamus) – emotional responses (in the amygdala) are linked to cognitive responses (in the prefrontal cortex) and can account for aggressive behaviour. This is a rather complex theory to explain in this summary of Reimann and Zimbardo's (2011) meta-analysis, and it is considerably simplified here, but it shows how neuroimaging can help to uncover such links and to shed light on human behaviour, such as aggression. Reimann and Zimbardo (2011) demonstrate how brain scanning is useful in investigating human behaviour – in particular, aggression and what they called 'evil'.

> **Definition**
> A **meta-analysis** is a study that uses data from other studies and pools such data to get the bigger picture in an area of research.

Brunnlieb *et al.* (2013) and fMRI

Brunnlieb *et al.* (2013) carried out a study to see if taking vasopressin would moderate aggression – that is, calm people down. Studies using animals have already suggested that the neuropeptide argonin vasopressin (called just 'vasopressin' here) moderated aggression in rats. For this section, however, the focus is just on human behaviour and how scanning helps to shed light on human behaviour. However, the study using rats prompted Brunnlieb *et al.* (2013) to see if vasopressin would be calming in humans. Their study used healthy adults who took vasopressin nasally (though the nose). One group had vasopressin; the other had a **placebo** – a harmless substance in place of the vasopressin. This study used a **double-blind technique**, meaning neither those running the study nor the participants knew which was the 'real' group and which was the placebo group. The participants were given the drug (vasopressin, or the placebo). Then they did a competitive reaction time test which was meant to induce aggression. At the same time, fMRI scanning was done to see activity in the brain. They also completed a questionnaire after the scanning, rating themselves for aggressive behaviour.

When decision-making about punishment (part of the task) was taking place, there was increased activity in the right superior temporal sulcus, which might relate to aggression. However, no differences were found in aggressive behaviour between the vasopressin condition and the placebo group. The researchers wondered whether the dosage of vasopressin was not enough to affect human behaviour and there were other discussion points raised about the way this study did not produce the expected findings. Vasopressin was meant to help to produce less aggression and so the control group (the placebo group) should show more aggressive behaviour, but they did not. There is some evidence that the right superior temporal sulcus is implicated in decision-making about punishment so the scan does give evidence of brain functioning and this might affect human behaviour, but as the behaviour itself was not affected, the finding was inconclusive.

Explore

Vasopressin acts as a neurotransmitter in the brain (but is synthesised as a hormone) and is involved in issues such as control of daily rhythms, temperature and hormone release. It is used in medicine for control of bleeding in the brain, heart attack and when the body goes into shock. Vasopressin has also been shown to have an effect on memory, improving it – studies have shown this in specific situations, depending on how well memories have been stored, for example, and the effects do seem to relate to the hippocampus (e.g. Alescio-Lautier and Soumireu-Mourat, 1998, who studied rats). You could investigate these findings further. Note that here there is mention of neurotransmitter functioning, memory, the hippocampus and the use of animals in experiments, all of which are mentioned in the topic areas of your course.

Progress check 5.42

Give one piece of evidence to show that MRI scanning helps to explain human behaviour. Do the same for PET and fMRI. That will give you three pieces of evidence that neuroimaging helps to explain human behaviour.

STUDY HINT

Brunnlieb *et al.* (2013) did not get the findings they expected. In your practical investigations, you might find that they do not 'work'. This is not a failure; it is an interesting finding to investigate more, as Brunnlieb *et al.* (2013) concluded.

Explore

You can watch Philip Zimbardo talk about evil and discuss issues like the situation in Abu Ghraib where, according to accounts, soldiers turned to torture, by following this link: www.youtube.com/watch?v=OsFEV35tWsg. This is not so much about adding evidence from neuroscience but it will help you to see how he wanted to get evidence from the brain to link to evidence from experiments in social psychology.

Conclusion of brain scanning techniques and using them to investigate human behaviour

- Five studies (or meta-analyses or reviews) have been briefly outlined in this section to show how the use of neuroimaging has helped in the study of human aggression. PET, MRI, fMRI and neuroimaging in general have featured in these examples, to show that a range of scanning techniques are used.
- Prefrontal cortex areas seem to be featured in aggressive behaviour in that damage there can bring aggression. This area might be about problem-solving and cognition, thinking and control, rather than about the emotional side of aggression. Damage to this area prevents that control possibly. Evidence includes that from Phineas Gage's preserved skull.
- The amygdala, part of the limbic system, seems to be a part of the brain involved in aggression, focusing on the emotional side of aggression. Reimann and Zimbardo (2011) mention the amygdala and also the prefrontal cortex, giving evidence that both are involved in aggressive behaviour in humans. However, Matthies *et al.* (2012) found that a smaller amygdala gave more aggression, which goes against what the other studies suggest. It was thought that having all female participants might have led to this finding, and there were other discussion points too. This study used MRI scanning.
- Widened sulci seemed to relate to aggression, according to Matthies *et al.* (2012), and Brunnlieb *et al.* (2013) mention the right superior temporal sulcus, a similar finding perhaps, using fMRI scanning.
- What has not been discussed here is how human behaviour such as aggression can be studied using research methods other than scanning. You can find that information in Chapter 3 when you learn about the content in biological psychology for your course.

Evaluation of using brain scanning techniques to investigate human behaviour such as aggression

Strengths

- Meta-analyses are used, which draw on many different studies using different evidence and techniques, and when the results of such studies support one another, such as pointing to damage to the prefrontal cortex linking to aggressive behaviour in humans, then that suggests findings are reliable and adds scientific credibility. Reliable findings are when studies have been repeated and the same results found, and drawing on many studies has the same effect.
- There is something fairly valid about brain scanning as it does measure brain activity and that is not denied. The results are visible and measurable and it is generally accepted that brain scanning, such as fMRI, does show actual brain activity, including the sites of such activity, although whether the responses in the brain measure validly the behaviour of interest is in doubt, as the weaknesses below show.

Weaknesses

- Criticisms of scanning techniques can be used as weaknesses of using brain scanning to investigate human behaviour – for example, the criticism of fMRI that it cannot measure the brain in a resting state so has no baseline measure to set activity against (such as when someone is aggressive).
- A similar criticism is that there might be a lack of validity in that tasks intended to generate aggression in someone (such as the competitive reaction time tasks that Brunnlieb *et al.*, 2013, used) might not lead to aggression – that is an assumption. Indeed, Brunnlieb *et al.* (2013) found that the tasks did not lead to aggressive behaviour. A questionnaire measure was also used and did not show a difference in aggression between the control group and the vasopressin group either. The criticism here is that getting someone to behave aggressively in a study is not easy – it might not be ethical and tasks might not yield aggression in all individuals. There are individual differences at work, for example. Brunnlieb *et al.* (2013) used an independent groups design.

Test yourself

Evaluate the use of brain scanning techniques to investigate aggression in humans. **(12 marks)**

Twin and adoption studies as a method

The biological approach in psychology is a scientific approach in that the research methods are those used when looking for scientific truths – for example, experiments, scanning to study the brain and the use of animals in experiments, such as in van den Oever's (2008) study. However, some studies – for example twin and adoption studies – are not as scientific as might at first be thought because variables are not manipulated; twin and adoption studies look at naturally occurring events. Twin and adoption studies are research methods used in the biological approach to look mainly at the causes of characteristics that might be genetically controlled.

Influence of genes on behaviour

Twin and adoption studies are used to study the influence of **genes** on behaviour. Genes and DNA give the biological blueprint for each person's development; they interact with the environment as the person grows. Identical twins have identical genes; non-identical twins share 50 per cent of their genes. By comparing identical and non-identical twins with regard to a certain characteristic, it can be seen what influence genes have. A problem is that twins tend to share much of their environment as well as their genes, which is why adoption studies are important. Adopted children are brought up in different families and do not share their environment with their biological family. Identical twins that are reared apart, not sharing the same environment but sharing the same genes, are important as participants as that too controls the effects of environment, to an extent at least.

Explore

How much of 'you' do you think is due to inherited characteristics (50 per cent from your father, 50 per cent from your mother) and how much is due to your own character and experiences? Does it feel strange thinking of yourself as 'just' your parents' son or daughter? This is why people discuss the nature-nurture debate. Most people like to think they make their own decisions and are not slaves to their genes. Ask some of your friends what they think.

Twin and adoption studies relate to the nature–nurture debate, which is about how far a characteristic comes from nature and how far it comes from nurture:

- Nature is what we are born with and is controlled by our genes.
- Nurture is what we experience from the environment as we develop. Environment includes influence from parents, culture, interactions with others and all other experiences.

Issues and debates

Nature–nurture is one of the debates focused on in your course. Twin studies, the study of twins reared apart and the study of adopted children can be useful when examining issues of nature and nurture, so be sure to make notes about this material.

For your course, you need to understand about twin and adoption studies as research methods through learning about one twin study and one adoption study. Arguably, one of the most well-known studies of twins was done by Gottesman and Shields in 1966. It is briefly outlined here because it is a classic study and is suggested in your course. A more detailed account is given of Lacourse *et al.* (2014) because their study is about aggression, which is what biological psychology focuses on in your course. The adoption study chosen is Leve *et al.* (2010). Twin studies are considered first, along with Lacourse *et al.* (2014), followed by adoption studies, with Leve *et al.* (2010) as the example study.

Explanation

Genes refer to strings of DNA (deoxyribonucleic acids). Genes specify proteins and RNA chains which are what make us function as humans. Genes build our cells and pass traits on to our offspring. They are our blueprint for life. We have between 20,000 and 25,000 genes. They code for eye colour, blood type, height, some diseases and many other characteristics. They can also code for intelligence and natural talent. The gene is the basic instruction and it is an allele that is a variant of that gene (different in people) and that is really what is doing the coding. It is not about having the gene for a trait, as all would have that gene. It is about the **allele** (the variant) someone has of that gene. In one person, all their genes are called the **genome** and that is stored on chromosomes.

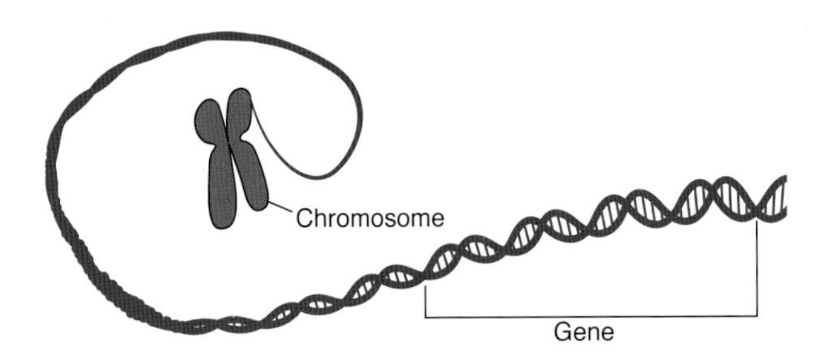

This shows the X-shaped chromosome dividing, the double helix of DNA and the gene, which is a strip of DNA

Twin studies

Identical twins are **monozygotic (MZ) twins** – they come from one fertilised egg (mono = one). There is one sperm and one egg and one product of fertilisation, so MZ twins have identical genes. Their DNA is 100 per cent the same and they are always the same sex. If a characteristic is genetic, then MZ twins should both show that characteristic. For example, if the cause of schizophrenia is totally genetic, then if one MZ twin has schizophrenia, the other must also have it. If IQ is genetic, then the IQ of one MZ twin should exactly match the IQ of the other. In practice, no characteristic connected with behaviour is shared completely by MZ twins – there is always some influence from the environment.

Some important points include:

- MZ twins do not share the same environment, even in the womb, so they tend to develop differently, despite their DNA being the same.
- From the start, there are some small physical differences between MZ twins, such as their fingerprints.
- Some characteristics that are genetic are triggered by the environment, so identical twins can become less identical over time, although of course their DNA does not change.
- **Epigenetic modification** is the term for how, over time, different environmental influences affect which genes are switched on and off. Young MZ twins have few epigenetic differences. However, 50-year-old MZ twins have over three times the epigenetic differences of young MZ twins.
- Some characteristics, such as IQ and personality, might become more alike as the twins age.

This shows the importance of both genes and the environment on development. It is useful information when discussing the nature–nurture debate because it shows that it is unlikely that any characteristic comes wholly from either nature or nurture.

Non-identical twins are **dizygotic (DZ) twins**, which means that they come from two fertilised eggs (di = two). Since they develop from different eggs, the DNA of DZ twins is only as similar as that of any siblings; it is not 100 per cent the same, as it is in identical twins. This means that if a characteristic is genetic, DZ twins would be expected to share that characteristic to an extent but not as much as MZ twins would share it.

Non-identical twins (left) and identical twins (right)

Definitions

Monozygotic twins (MZ) are identical twins and share 100 per cent of their DNA – they are from a single egg. **Dizygotic twins** (DZ) are non-identical twins and share 50 per cent of their DNA from their mother and 50 per cent from their father, like other siblings. **Epigenetic modification** is the term for how genes are switched off and on by the environment and it is not that our genes make us who we are at birth and that is fixed. So MZ twins can become more different because of epigenetic modification.

Twin studies compare MZ and DZ twins on certain characteristics to see if there are differences between the MZ twins and the characteristic and between DZ twins and the characteristic. If there are quite strong differences between MZ and DZ twins and MZ twins share the characteristic more, then that characteristic is said to have a genetic basis, at least to an extent. When both twins share a characteristic, there is said to be a **concordance rate**. Characteristics that have been studied in this way include schizophrenia, IQ, alcoholism, depression, personality and anorexia.

Definition

A **concordance rate** is an agreement rate ('concordance' means 'agreement'). When both twins have the same characteristic, that is concordance; a concordance rate for a characteristic is how much, in a study of twins, they have both got a characteristic.

Studies using the methodology

One well-known study that compares MZ and DZ twins is that by Gottesman and Shields (1966), who investigated schizophrenia. They obtained data from five studies about twins and traced whether, if one twin had schizophrenia, the other also had it, or some similar mental health problem. They looked at both MZ and DZ twins. They thought that if both MZ twins had schizophrenia or some similar mental health problem more often than both DZ twins, then this suggested a strong genetic basis for schizophrenia. When both twins share a characteristic, there is a concordance rate for that characteristic. In MZ twins, there was a concordance rate for schizophrenia and similar illnesses of between 35 and 58 per cent; in DZ twins, the rate was between 9 and 26 per cent. This means that, for MZ twins, around 42 per cent of the time when one twin has schizophrenia, the other has it or a similar illness. For DZ twins, the average figure is around 17 per cent. When only the most severe cases of schizophrenia were considered, the concordance rate for MZ twins was between 75 and 91 per cent. The study strongly suggests that there is at least some genetic basis for schizophrenia.

Explore

It is interesting to look further at twin studies and schizophrenia. For example, Boklage (1977) found that there is more to it. When the researchers looked at left- and right-handedness in MZ twins, they found that when the MZ twins were right-handed there was a concordance rate for schizophrenia of 92 per cent – in almost all cases, when one MZ twin had schizophrenia, the other did too. However, when one MZ twin was right-handed and the other was left-handed, the concordance rate for schizophrenia was 25 per cent. This suggests a genetic link, and also a genetic link with handedness. It also shows that percentages can hide facts and need to be used carefully. Explore this issue using the internet or other sources.

Evaluation of twin studies

Strengths

- Both MZ and DZ twin babies are born at the same time and share a similar environment, but MZ twins have exactly the same DNA as each other whereas DZ twins share 50 per cent of their genes. So twin studies are the main way that the influence of genes on behaviour can be studied – there is no other way of having identical DNA.
- Both MZ twins and DZ twins share their environments and are treated as twins. For the most part, people treat twins as twins, whether they are MZ or DZ twins. So although there are differences between an MZ and a DZ set of twins in terms of their shared genes, for either type of twin there should not be environmental differences between the twins themselves.

STUDY HINT

In an exam, avoid giving a strength that merely says something does what it does. It is so easy to say, for example, that twin studies are 'good because they study identical twins'. This is unlikely to score a mark. You should expand your answer to say that they are good because identical twins have DNA that is 100 per cent the same and that there are no other types of people with identical DNA. Twin studies, therefore, control for the effects of genes.

Weaknesses

- MZ twins, being of the same sex and likely to look identical, will be treated more alike than DZ twins, which means that their environments are not the same. MZ twins may share the same environment to a greater extent than DZ twins.
- Although the genetic differences between MZ and DZ twins are what make twin studies useful, there is epigenetic modification to take into account. From the moment of conception for MZ twins, there are differences – for example, some share the placenta and some do not. Many genes need an environmental switch; if environments are different, then, over time, MZ twins may become more different. So, even though MZ twins have identical DNA (100 per cent) and can be compared with DZ twins that do not have identical DNA (only 50 per cent), neither share their environment completely. Therefore, it is difficult to say that a characteristic is caused by genes just because MZ twins share it and DZ twins do not share it to the same extent. No study has found any behavioural characteristic that is 100 per cent shared by MZ twins, so environment is bound to play a part.

Progress check 5.43

Explain how looking at concordance rates with regard to a behaviour or characteristic in MZ twins and comparing it with DZ twins can give evidence for there being a genetic cause for that behaviour or characteristic.

A twin study: Lacourse *et al.* (2014)

This study was carried out in Canada using 254 MZ (identical) and 413 DZ (non-identical) twins. As with many twin studies, the twins were part of a longitudinal study and Lacourse *et al.* did not choose the sample as such. This longitudinal study was the Quebec Newborn Twin Study. Twins are such a good source of data that data are gathered from them over a long period of time; they were not just recruited for this study. The study was about physical aggression and the measure of physical aggression was the mothers' report of physical aggression at 20, 32 and 50 months old. Physical aggression is said by Lacourse *et al.* (2014) to start in infancy and increase in frequency rather quickly. This study aimed to look at how physical aggression developed over time through childhood.

Background

Lacourse *et al.* (2014) open the study by referring to Bandura, and others, and the focus on social learning theory to explain both the start and maintenance of physical aggression. Chapter 4 of this book considers social learning theory (pp. 226–231) and makes the same claims. It is interesting that Lacourse *et al.* focus on genes and their role in the development of physical aggression in childhood, as a contrast to the widely accepted social learning theory.

STUDY HINT

When explaining a behaviour such as aggression, you can use both social learning theory and genes as contrasting explanations. In your course, explanations are split into topic areas, but to explain human behaviour it is useful to cross areas and use whatever explanations fit. Note that social learning theory and genes are 'nurture' and 'nature' explanations, useful in evaluation.

Many studies (e.g. NICHD Early Child Care Research Network, 2004, cited in Lacourse *et al.*, 2014) show that physical aggression starts in infancy and gets to a peak at between two and four years old. It is generally thought that about 50 per cent of aggression comes from genes (e.g. Tuvblad *et al.*, 2011, cited in Lacourse *et al.*, 2014). The other 50 per cent is thought to be down to environment. Lacourse *et al.* point out that studies of aggression tend to focus on anger or disruptive behaviour rather than on physical aggression. When physical aggression is studied (van Beijsterveldt *et al.*, 2003, cited in Lacourse *et al.*, 2014), it has been found that genes can account for 65 per cent of individual differences over time and shared (25 per cent) and non-shared (10 per cent) environment account for the rest. The focus was on individual differences both in initial physical aggression in infancy and in the growth/path of physical aggression through childhood. However, in the scale used by van Beijsterveldt *et al.* (2003), only three items measured physical aggression; the others focused on disruptive behaviour. Also, the study started at three years old.

Lacourse *et al.* (2014) looked at issues around development of physical aggression in early childhood. They considered three possible ways that genes and environment might account for physical aggression in early childhood: A) They considered both genes and environment to be responsible for physical aggression and its development; B) Another view is that environmental influences might be limited and a single set of genetic factors might account for the development of physical aggression. In studies, it is thought that environmental influences on the development of physical aggression might be small and might affect differences between twins more than similarities between them (e.g. van Beijsterveldt *et al.*, 2003). Also environmental factors tend to have short-term effects; genes have long-term effects. C) Possibly there are new genetic and environmental influences over time, and these are 'innovation effects'. These innovation effects were thought perhaps to be due to new genetic factors, and this is 'genetic maturation'. There is stability in physical aggression from 20, 32 and 50 months, in that order, with physical aggression settling more at each measure. Lacourse *et al.* looked at whether genetic and environmental transmission (both coming from the start, in infancy) or new genetic and environmental factors 'caused' the stability in how physical aggression starts in infancy quickly and then subsides over time.

- In their model A, they would find both genetic and environmental factors throughout the 20, 32 and 50 months slope in physical aggression (the growth tails off). Model A suggests 50/50 for genes and environment as causes for early childhood physical aggression.
- In model B, they would expect to see a strong genetic link to the slope. Model B suggests stronger genetic influence than environmental.
- In model C, there would be less strong genetic factors at the start and then stronger genetic factors linked to the slope – if there is genetic innovation. Model C suggests new genetic effects and not all the genetic effects present at the start, in infancy.

Lacourse *et al.* (2014) test these three models.

Aim(s)

Their aim was to look at genetic and environmental issues underlying the development of physical aggression from infancy to when the child is school age. Lacourse *et al.* (2014) wanted to use twins to look at genetic and environmental factors to explain the change in physical aggression in individuals from infancy to 50 months. There is a quick increase in physical aggression in infancy, followed by a more gradual increase through 20 months, 32 months and 50 months. There are three possible explanations. One (Model A) is that both environment and genes cause this increase/decline. Another explanation (Model B) is that it is more from genes. A third explanation (Model C) is that there is later genetic influence (on the declining rise in aggression). The aim of the study is to test these three possibilities using twins.

Progress check 5.44

Using the background information, explain the aims of Lacourse *et al.* (2014).

STUDY HINT

Note that Lacourse *et al.* (2014) used secondary data – they did not gather data themselves, but used data from an existing longitudinal twin study. Their study is useful as an example of using secondary data, which you will learn about in the clinical psychology part of your course, and also as an example of longitudinal design, also in clinical psychology. Remember to use material when it fits into other areas.

Procedure

Lacourse *et al.* (2014) used MZ and DZ twins. They also looked at shared environment (when they are brought up together) and non-shared environment (when they are apart and possibly brought up apart). This was to get the genetic factors and environmental factors into their study. Then they measured physical aggression using reports from mothers.

The twins were born between 1995 and 1998 in Canada. All parents of twins born in those years were invited to take part in the Quebec Newborn Twin Study (Boivin *et al.*, 2013a, cited in Lacourse *et al.*, 2014). In the sample, there were 254 MZ twins and 413 DZ twins. Within the DZ twins, there were 210 that were the same-sex pairs (MZ twins are all same sex because of their 100 per cent shared genes). Information about their physical aggression was collected by the Quebec Newborn Twin Study at around 19.6 months, 31.9 months and 50.2 months. Some twin pairs did not have the physical aggression data for various reasons so Lacourse *et al.* used 588 twin pairs where there was physical aggression data for at least one of the twins at the three separate periods (20, 32 and 50 months).

Physical aggression was measured as part of a questionnaire given to mothers, with three items measuring physical aggression. The measure was how many times a child hits, bites, kicks (one item); a child fights (another item); one attacks another (the third item). The mothers answered 'never (0), sometimes (1), often (2)' for each item.

Analysis of physical aggression used a correlation statistical test (they used Pearson's, which is similar to Spearman's) to look at the relationship between the child's age and the aggression score (over time).

Analysis of genetic influences was based on MZ twins sharing 100 per cent of their genes and DZ twins sharing 50 per cent of their genes. Using the results for twins and knowing whether they are identical twins (MZ) or non-identical twins (DZ) can show information for genes and environment can also be looked at, either shared environment or non-shared. Differences between MZ and DZ twins can show the genetic contribution. Shared and non-shared environmental data were gathered from the Quebec Newborn Twin Study.

Results

Table 5.15 shows the mean physical aggression scores for the whole sample, measured by mothers rating the three items as 'never, sometimes, often' and the standard deviation. The slow steady growth in physical aggression is seen from 20 months to 50 months, as predicted by other studies, and the rate at 20 months is rather high already, showing the initial early spurt in physical aggression, also predicted.

Table 5.15 Mean physical aggression scores

	At 20 months	At 32 months	At 50 months
Mean physical aggression score (standard deviation in brackets)	1.82 (1.49)	2.19 (1.46)	2.24 (1.50)

The study measured the differences in scores between the MZ and DZ twins at each age and found that MZ twins, within the pairs, correlated at 0.68 to 0.72, and DZ twins, within the pairs, correlated at 0.32 to 0.47. This means that the MZ twin pairs were more likely to both show the same scores for physical aggression than the DZ twin pairs. The correlation figures are high and likely to show a statistical significance. Not only were the physical aggression scores related, with MZ twins being more alike with regard to physical aggression scores than DZ twins, but also the rising slow slope in physical aggression also showed MZ and DZ differences. For MZ twins, the correlation between them for the rising slope was 0.25 to 0.39 and for DZ twins it was 0.14 to 0.20. As MZ twins are found to be more similar than DZ twins both in their physical aggression scores and in the way they rise between the three age periods, this is taken as evidence that genes contribute to physical aggression.

Another analysis was carried out to look at genetic, non-shared environment and shared environment differences between the two types of twins. It was found that both genes and non-shared environment contributed to physical aggression levels. However, with regard to shared environment influences, these showed some effect at 50 months but not otherwise, and effects were marginal. Genetic factors were associated with physical aggression at all three ages (20, 32 and 50 months). New genetic factors contributed at 32 months and at 50 months.

Conclusions

The conclusion was that the early onset of physical aggression was explained by genetic factors (the transmission effect) and these declined over time. Then new genetic factors at each age contributed to physical aggression at each of the ages, and this was an innovation effect. At each age, genetic factors explained at least half of the variance in physical aggression. The remaining variance was down to non-shared environmental factors.

They found an increase in frequency of physical aggression from 20 months to 50 months, though the speed of increase did slow over time. Individual differences in physical aggression were large, however, and that should be taken into account. The measures and findings given here are averages and correlations, and they mask individual differences. Indeed, some children show high physical aggression that is stable over time and some children show no use of physical aggression (e.g. Broidy *et al.*, 2003, cited in Lacourse *et al.*, 2014). What is of interest from Lacourse *et al.* (2014) is that the influence of genetic factors is strong in physical aggression use, both at the start, giving a genetic set point, and also as the child develops, showing genetic maturation. Genetic factors always accounted for differences in physical aggression at 20 months (60 per cent of the variance), at 30 months (60 per cent of the variance) and at 50 months (50 per cent of the variance). There were new sources of genetic influences by 50 months, as well as the genetic influences from birth.

There were non-shared environmental influences but they did not relate to the stability in physical aggression over time (the slope upwards that is steady). There was also a small effect from shared environment at 50 months. As other studies tended to use measures such as disruption, and found more environmental influences and not so much genetic influence, it is possible that the development of physical aggression is more genetically controlled than disruptive behaviour and other such behaviour.

Other studies looking at individual children (not twins) show an effect from shared environment, such as more physical aggression if there is physical aggression modelled in the home (e.g. NICHD Early Child Care Research Network, 2004, cited in Lacourse *et al.*, 2014). Lacourse *et al.* did not reflect this finding. They thought perhaps the family influences could have a genetic basis and that might explain the difference in their findings, or the family 'genes' could interact in a specific way with the environment, which could account for shared environment effects in other studies that were not found in their study. If a gene was in a family that led to certain responses to a shared environment, that would show as a difference between MZ and DZ twins. This suggests that looking 'just' at genes and 'just' at environment is not suitable because the two interact.

The researchers emphasise that finding a genetic link to physical aggression both in infancy and then developmentally in early childhood does not mean an individual child is fixed in their physical aggression tendencies. They can learn how to deal with such tendencies and to use alternatives (e.g. Tremblay, 2010, cited in Lacourse *et al.*, 2014). The researchers mention the need to be aware of this tendency to physical aggression because of what they call 'feedback processes' (p. 2624). This is the idea that, if a child is aggressive, parents and peers can respond to them accordingly and the aggression can in that way be maintained and reinforced.

STUDY HINT

Lacourse *et al.* (2014) talk about a 'feedback process' that relates to the self-fulfilling prophecy and labelling – a theory about crime and anti-social behaviour that you will come across if you study criminological psychology in Year 2. It is worth making notes about such 'alternative' theories. They are useful in evaluating the study and also evaluating biological psychology views on causes of aggression.

Evaluation of Lacourse *et al.* (2014)

Strengths

- The study uses repeated measures in that the same child is measured for physical aggression at ages 20 months, 32 months and 50 months so developmental trends can be measured and compared. There are no individual differences that will affect the three measures for the same child.
- The analysis is thorough, using more than one process (the analysis is far more complex than the summary given here). The researchers themselves point to this strength in their study. The study uses a Cholesky decomposition and a latent growth curve. These are beyond the scope of what you need to know for your course, but you can learn this strength and use it in evaluation of the study.
- Another strength is the size of the sample and the access to both MZ and DZ twins with a lot of information about them. There can be some certainty that the measure of MZ or DZ is accurate (which is not always the case with twins), and even if not accurate in a few cases, the large number should take care of a few issues in the sample. The MZ twins share 100 per cent of their genes and the DZ share 50 per cent of their genes, so that measure is strongly going to show genetic influences on behaviour. If analysis is carried out by more than one means with the same results found, that helps reliability of a study.

Weaknesses

- The researchers point to a weakness in the measuring of physical aggression, with just the mother contributing the data. One mother might emphasise similarity in the family, which would lead to more emphasis on the shared environment, for example. It would be better to gather data about their physical aggression from more than one person and in more than one setting, to help validity of the measure.
- In twin studies, there is an assumption that the environment is shared if twins are brought up together and this might not be a fair assumption.
- Twins might differ from non-twins in that there is socialisation between them that might not be found in 'single' children. So generalising from a twin study like this to say that the findings are true of all children might not be fair.

STUDY HINT

When evaluating a study, you can use strengths and weaknesses of the method; however, be sure to bring the study in too, so that your evaluation is not just a general one of the method. You can use general evaluation points (such as twins perhaps not sharing their environment as much as might be thought), but relate this to the study.

STUDY HINT

Consider having a separate set of notes for these 'Study hints'. They often apply more widely than to the specific area under discussion.

Test yourself

1. Explain what is meant by the 'twin study research method'. **(6 marks)**
2. Discuss one twin study with regard to how the research method is used. **(12 marks)**

Adoption studies

Adoption studies are carried out because the environment of adopted children is not the same as that of their biological families, yet they have genes in common. For example, if the effect of genes on schizophrenia is being studied, a researcher might want to find out whether children of a parent with schizophrenia are more likely to develop schizophrenia than children without a family history of it. The problem is that children usually have both genes and the environment in common with their biological parents. If researchers study children who have a parent with schizophrenia and compare them with children without a parent with schizophrenia and choose all adopted children, then the issue of environment is controlled. Adopted children do not share their environment with their biological families. Therefore, if there are similarities with their biological families, it is likely to be because of genes not environment.

Studies using the methodology

Kety *et al.* (1994) carried out an adoptive family study in Finland and found evidence for a genetic cause of schizophrenia. Out of a sample of 155, schizophrenia was diagnosed in nine adopted children, eight of whom had biological mothers either with schizophrenia or diagnosed as having spectrum psychoses.

Studies have found more evidence of schizophrenia among adopted children whose biological mothers had schizophrenia, or a similar diagnosis, than among adopted children whose mothers did not have schizophrenia. However, the problem with such studies is that the adoptive family might be matched closely to the biological family, so the environments of the two families might not have been as different as first thought.

Adoption studies look at issues other than schizophrenia. However, it is a useful example and it is a mental health issue studied in the clinical psychology application in Year 2 of your course.

Evaluation of adoption studies

Strengths

- Adoption studies are a way of separating genes from the environment. They keep the genetic link because they compare children with their biological parents; they control for the environment because the children are in a different environment from their biological families, so similarities cannot be because of environmental or learning factors. Using children who are brought up away from their biological families removes that influence, so if the children are similar to their biological families then it is their genes that cause the similarity and not the environment. Adoption studies remove this 'environment' issue from the study. This is hard to do any other way, which is the strength of this method.
- Developmental trends can be studied because the studies can be **longitudinal**. The same child or group of children can be followed as they develop, so characteristics that come about as genes are triggered (e.g. schizophrenia) can be studied. The longitudinal approach means that the same children are studied at different times during their development, so trends can be found. Trends can then be linked to genetic influences.

Weaknesses

- It is likely that only certain types of family are accepted as adopters of children, so 'adopting families' are likely to be similar to one another. This makes the environment of an adopted child perhaps something different/unique.
- Children tend to be placed in families like their own, so their birth family and their adopted family might have similarities. This makes the 'adopting' environment similar to the 'biological' environment.

Explanation

Longitudinal studies are where the same people are studied over time to look for developmental issues and patterns. The opposite is using a cross-sectional design, where different people are studied, at one moment in time. For example, to study the development of aggression, researchers could study, at one time, a group of two year olds, a group of five year olds and a group of eight year olds to see how the groups compared with regard to aggression at each of the ages. This would be a cross-sectional design: at one moment in time, three age groups are studied. For a longitudinal design, researchers could follow a group of participants when they are two years old, again when they are five years old and again when they are eight years old. The advantage is they have the same people so individual differences are controlled for.

Progress check 5.45

Explain why adoption studies help to see which behaviours or characteristics are genetically based.

Studying MZ twins reared apart

Another form of adoption study is to look at MZ twins who have been separated at birth and brought up apart (usually adopted, but not always, so this method is called 'studying twins reared apart'). This is a way of controlling the fact that MZ twins, as well as having 100 per cent of their DNA in common, are usually brought up in a very similar environment. If MZ twins reared apart share characteristics, it can be more certainly claimed that those characteristics have a genetic basis. If the twins are reared together, their shared environment might cause the characteristics, rather than their genes.

Studies using the methodology

Bergeman *et al.* (1988) carried out a study of identical twins with non-shared environments. The study of non-shared environments can include twins reared together but who have differences in their environments, such as attending different schools. In this study, the twins had been separated all their lives, so were 'reared apart'. Therefore, because they did not share the same environment, their characteristics would come from their identical genes. Two factors covered by the study were personality traits and how impulsive the twins were. The findings were that the way in which the environment affects individuals depends on their genetic make-up as well as on the type of environment. For example, those who scored low on extraversion genetically also showed low extraversion in a highly controlled organised environment; those that scored high on extraversion showed high extraversion whatever the amount of control in their reared environment. So, interaction between genetic make-up and the environment depends on the match between them. This suggests that nature and nurture are not separate, but act on one another in all situations.

Evaluation of studying MZ twins reared apart

Strengths

- Environmental conditions are controlled. Therefore, because their environments are different, if the MZ twins are similar in a characteristic, this is likely to be due to their identical DNA. When looking for causes of behaviour, it is not easy to control for environment. The strength of studying MZ twins reared apart is that it does control for environment, as do adoption studies.
- Rearing MZ twins apart is a unique research method controlling for genetic differences. There is no other way of finding identical human DNA and having two different environments, other than carrying out an experiment, which would not be allowed for ethical reasons. Adoption studies do not have the advantage of comparing individuals who have identical genes; they compare adopted children with their biological parents, which is not the same thing.

Weaknesses

- There are not many MZ twins who have been reared apart, so there are not large numbers from which to draw conclusions. It is difficult to find them, and they or their families may not want to take part in a study.
- When it is claimed that MZ twins are reared apart, this may not be entirely true. Up to the second half of the twentieth century (and later) when an unmarried girl gave birth, the girl's mother often brought up the child as her own and the biological mother acted as the child's sister. In the case of twins, sometimes another member of the family, such as an aunt or the biological mother's grandmother, brought up one of the twins. So they were reared apart, but in the same family. They may even have gone to the same school and played together. In such cases, they would have shared much of their environment, so the purpose of using MZ twins reared apart would have been lost.
- Although in theory it should be clear whether twins are MZ or DZ, in practice it is not always the case. Sometimes twins have had to be excluded from a study because it was not clear whether they were identical (MZ) or non-identical (DZ). Mistakes can be made.

STUDY HINT

The study of twins reared apart is better seen as a twin study than an adoption study if they are not actually adopted. It is included here to show that there is such a research method. Your course asks you to cover one twin study and one adoption study so you do not need to know about the research method in great detail, just enough to understand the two studies and their use of the research method.

An adoption study: Leve *et al.* (2010)

Leve *et al.* (2010) looked at data from the Early Growth and Development Study (EGDS) in the United States, which followed 360 linked sets of birth and adoptive parents and the adopted children involved. The focus was on genes and environment, looking at issues such as how inheritable characteristics influenced the behaviour of adoptive parents towards their adopted children.

Background

Leve *et al.* (2010) show that the characteristics that a child inherits influence how parents respond to the child and how adoptive parents respond to characteristics in a child that have been inherited. For example, children with anti-social birth parents experience more negative controlling behaviour from adoptive parents than do children with less anti-social birth parents (O'Connor *et al.*, 1998, cited in Leve *et al.*, 2010).

Leve *et al.* (2010) explain that adoption is a natural experiment because children are reared in families where there is no genetic relationship, so genes are separated successfully from environment. In studies like this one, genetic influences are assumed, looking at similarities between birth parents, adoptive parents and adopted children. Environmental factors are assumed from looking at adoptive parents' behaviour and environment and the adopted child's behaviour. This all rests on there being no contact between the birth parents and the child and on the placing of the child in the adoption family not being done in a selective way (such as matching adoptive parents with birth parents). The Early Growth and Development Study (EGDS) is an adoptive study.

STUDY HINT

Leve *et al.* (2010) focus on the influence of genes and environment on a child. You can include such arguments in a discussion of the nature-nurture debate.

Aims

The EGDS aimed to look at family relationships and features in such relationships that affect genetic influences from infancy. The question was what might affect the way genes manifest themselves in an individual's behaviour from birth. This was to look at environmental influences that might 'buffer' genetic tendencies as well as genetic influences that might 'buffer' against environmental risk (Leve *et al.*, 2010, p. 307). The EGDS wanted to find areas in upbringing where intervention could take place, considering problems that might arise either from genes (that might be environmentally controlled) or from environment (that certain genes, such as resilience, might help with).

- Aim 1 of the EGDS – to look at specific environmental issues related to parenting and family processes that mediate (interact with) genetic factors on a child. The effects looked at are behaviour, school performance, the child internalising problems, the child externalising problems and their competence socially.
- Aim 2 – the same as Aim 1, but this time not about mediating between parenting and the child's genetic inheritance but about how the environment might moderate (be protective with regard to) genetic influences.
- Aim 3 – to look at the adoptive parent and adopted child to see how, when and why genes and environment interactions occur between them. The study looks at child evocative genes/environment interactions (when the child had genes that evoked a change in some family environments and not others) and child sensitive genes/environment interactions (when the child had genes that made the child sensitive to the family environments).

Procedure

The study used what they called an 'adoptive triad', which is the birth parents, the adoptive parents and the child. By studying all three, researchers could see which genetic influences and which environmental influences affected one another and possibly how.

Participants were 360 linked sets of adoptive triads (a child, their birth parents, their adoptive parents). Leve *et al.* (2010) was looking at the second phase of the study, assessing the participants in the school entry periods. The infancy and toddler assessments had taken place in other published studies within the EGDS. Further participants were being recruited to extend the study, but the focus of the current study is on the 360 linked sets and the assessment as the children entered school. Participants were recruited from 2003 to 2006, by firstly recruiting adoption agencies (33 of them in ten states) and then an agency liaison from each agency to recruit the adoptive triads. The baby had to be adopted within three months of birth for the triad to be accepted and there were other conditions too, such as no known major medical conditions.

Recruitment was by means of 'opt out', which meant if the families did not want to be involved they had to return a card (provided in the initial recruitment letter) to say so. The birth mother was recruited first and, if they agreed, then the adoptive family were approached. If the adoptive family agreed, then the birth father was recruited. Once recruited, the participants did not in general decline to take part (2 per cent of birth mothers, 17 per cent of adoptive families and 8 per cent of birth fathers declined). Drop-out was more because the individuals could not then be found. Different staff members dealt with the adoptive family and birth mother – with the birth mother and birth father also being given confidentiality. The sample included 360 adoptive parents, 360 adopted children, 359 birth mothers and 114 birth fathers. Forty-three per cent of the children were female. There was analysis of the demographics and, in general, the birth mother, birth father, adoptive mother and adoptive father pictures were similar.

Progress check 5.46

Explain why using adopted children is a useful way to study how genes and environment interact from birth and how they affect one another.

The study measured executive function (a measure that can foretell externalising problems), early literacy skills (a measure that can foretell school performance) and cortisol reactivity (linked to internalising problems).

Assessment was by means of questionnaire and interviews (in person and by telephone) for birth and adoptive parents; observation (adoptive families only); standardised testing for both sets of parents and the children; salivary cortisol collection for birth parents and adoptive children; and salivary DNA collection from all participants.

There was quite frequent assessment: for example, for birth parents, in person at 3–6 months, 18 months and 54 months and by telephone at 12, 22, 30, 36 and 42 months.

In-person assessments

For the birth parents, in-person assessments were done where convenient, usually at home, and involved interviews and questionnaires. There were intelligence testing questions and questions about anti-social personality and conduct disorder, as well as questions about functioning.

For the adoptive families, in-person assessments were done in the home, with the adoptive parents completing a questionnaire before the interview. There were also child temperament tasks, parent–child interaction tasks and standardised tests, such as about early literacy.

Telephone interviews

Telephone interviews took place between the in-person assessments to help with building rapport and to aid retention. The phone interviews were about well-being and the adopted child's daily behaviour, as well as parenting.

Salivary cortisol collection

Cortisol was collected 30 minutes after waking up and 30 minutes before sleep on three weekdays (six collections). The participants took their own samples after they had seen how to do it and posted the samples in prepaid envelopes to the research team.

Teacher and school data collection

Preschool, nursery and school teachers contributed to the study. They completed questionnaires about child behaviour and peer relations using a website. Reading performance was measured at 72 and 84 months.

DNA collection

The collection of DNA was new to the 2010 study, during one of the in-home assessments, so the research team could later look at genes associated to anti-social behaviour, depression, anxiety and attention problems.

Results

Generalisability from the sample

Leve *et al.* (2010) found that their sample was representative. They did testing to make sure this was the case. There were no significant demographic differences, for example, between birth mothers where birth fathers were recruited and birth mothers where birth fathers were not recruited. There were some differences, but very few, and with just a small effect size. They concluded that generalisation of the findings to adoptive families throughout the country (US) was possible.

Progress check 5.47

Leve *et al.* (2010) make the claim that generalisability in their study was good and that the sample represented the population. Explain this argument.

Bias from openness and selective placements

If adoption practices include selective placements, such as matching birth parent characteristics to adoptive parent characteristics, then the idea that the child inherits genes from birth parents and gets their environment from adoptive parents does not work so well. Openness can also be a problem. Openness means a lot of contact between birth and adoptive parents, which can confuse the environmental influences. The researchers used correlations to check out characteristics that might come from selective placements and found no effects. They also correlated the number of times of meeting between birth and adoptive parents (rated as 'never' to 'daily', for example) and how much they knew about one another. Again, they found no statistical significance so thought that openness was not a problem. The researchers concluded that neither selective placement nor openness had affected their findings about genes and environmental interaction and effect on adopted children.

Genes and environment interaction

With so many tests and measurements, there were a lot of findings. For example, nine-month-old infants took part in trials to see their level of attention when a task they were taking part in was neutral or when the task led to frustration. Linking attention level to frustration can indicate whether the child is likely, later in their development, to externalise problems. For example, children who do not shift attention away from a frustrating event show more aggressive behaviour at two and a half (Crockenberg *et al.*, 2008, cited in Leve *et al.*, 2010).

The researchers felt that the externalising behaviour of birth mothers could show genetic risk for externalising problems and adoptive parents' level of anxiety or depression could be an environmental issue that was associated with a child being unable to shift attention from a frustrating task or event. This environmental issue was the adoptive parents' failure to model appropriate emotions for the child. The researchers found that the adoptive mother's emotional state, but not the adoptive father's, related to a child not shifting attention from being frustrated. This was thought to be because an adoptive mother might have more involvement in the upbringing of the adopted child. For adoptive mothers showing anxiety and depression, the mean score linking birth mother's externalising behaviour to child attention to frustration was higher. The conclusion is that the genetic issue around externalising behaviour and attention remaining on frustrating tasks is affected by environment (where an adoptive mother showed anxiety or depression, there was an effect on attention remaining on frustrating tasks, but this was not the case where the adoptive mother did not show anxiety or depression). This helps to show the complexity of human interaction and also shows that environment has an effect on whether genetic tendencies manifest or not, or perhaps more accurately by how much.

Conclusions

Leve *et al.* (2010) and the EGDS study, with its focus on environment and genes and their interplay from a very young age, is the first of its kind. It is able to look at the interplay between family processes and genetic influences in a way that other studies cannot achieve because of its focus on adoption.

The goal is to develop interventions that can improve well-being both in families and for the children. Genetic factors are unique to the individual so interventions and service delivery programmes might not work for all children. Studies like Leve *et al.* (2010) can help to show the influence of specific genetic factors on specific environmental factors, and vice versa.

The main conclusion is that genetic factors in an adopted child can interact with environmental influences within the adoptive family to produce behaviour and, if such things are known about, there can be intervention to alleviate the issue. For example, it would be useful to know that for some children (those who focus on frustrating events rather than moving on, and so likely to show more aggression) an anxious or depressed adoptive mother would mean that behaviour is continued with, whereas an adoptive mother without such issues would mean less of that behaviour.

STUDY HINT

Leve *et al.* (2010) talk about generalisability. Putting such issues into a 'real' context and a 'real' study can help your learning. Also you can use these examples in discussion of issues like generalisability and its limitations and importance.

Evaluation of Leve *et al.* (2010)

Strengths

- The size of the sample and the focus on it being representative is a strength. Leve *et al.* (2010) used correlation analysis to check that the demographics of the different parts of the sample (adoptive mother, adoptive father, birth mother and birth father) were not sufficiently different demographically for generalisability to be a problem.
- The researchers gathered data using a lot of different methods, which meant they could use triangulation to check reliability of data. For example, they collected cortisol six times, which would help reliability, and they had questionnaire data before the interviews so they could cross-reference.

Weaknesses

- It would be hard to show cause-and-effect relationships between the variables as they were hard to measure exactly. For example, it was hard to measure attention to frustration and hard to relate to later aggressive behaviour. They claimed a link and had evidence from another study to back them up, but there are many variables in their study and inferences have to be made.
- Inferring genetic influence from looking at birth mother and child similarities is not the same as using DNA to show genotype. Although the researchers were intending to move the study forward by collecting DNA, they were not doing that at the time of this study and the findings from DNA evidence were not reported. The results reported in this study were limited in the way they drew conclusions about the adopted child's genetic profile.

Test yourself

1 Explain why studying children who have been adopted and reared apart from their biological family can help to study the nature–nurture debate. **(6 marks)**
2 Discuss issues involved in studies of adopted children. **(8 marks)**

Methods in learning theories

This section focuses on the observational research method, which is an important technique in psychology. The learning approach also features aspects of inferential statistics; the chi-squared test is new and is detailed here, with the mathematical element given in Chapter 6. The learning approach methodology also includes content analysis and animal research, including laboratory experiments using animals and ethical issues about their use. The scientific focus of psychology is also examined.

STUDY HINT
You have nearly covered all the key terms you need to know with regards to methodology. Using the checklists near the start of each chapter, make a list of all the terms and check that you know what they mean. This can be a daunting exercise – so work with one or two friends, taking it in turns to define the terms. Working together is a good way to learn. You could even turn the exercise into a quiz.

The observational research method

You might think that all research methods in psychology involve observing people's behaviour, which of course is right – up to a point. Scanning may involve some observing of behaviour and it is essential to look at the images produced, but this is not an observational research method. Case studies may involve observation because in-depth data are gathered. However, although they may use observations, the research method is case study. In laboratory experiments, scores may come from the observation of behaviour. For example, Bandura set up laboratory experiments to observe whether or not children copy aggressive behaviour. However, this is not an observational research method and it is important not to call this an observation. It is an experiment because there were careful controls of sampling, allocation to groups and control over the behaviour watched by the participants and over what was carried out at each stage of the study. The independent variable was carefully manipulated.

The observational research method features observation as the main way that data are gathered, without setting up an experiment or using scanning techniques, or any other research method. In an observation, behaviour is observed and recorded without necessarily controlling all aspects of the study, and an independent variable is not manipulated, at least in naturalistic observations, as it is in an experiment. There might be an independent variable such as gender, but it is likely to be naturally occurring, not manipulated. Your course asks you to learn about 'the observational research method' and both naturalistic observation and structured observation are required.

Structured observations

Observations can be structured so that the same situation is repeated with different participants and researchers observe what happens. There is manipulation of the setting and situation, which makes the observation structured. One difficulty of using a structured observation is that setting up the situation does not lead to valid results – there is artificiality. However, a **structured observation** can be set up to organise, but not destroy, natural interactions. Structured observations have the advantage of being replicable. Therefore, they can be tested for reliability.

One reason for using structured observation is that the behaviour of interest does not often occur naturally so it is hard to observe in a natural setting. For example, Ainsworth set up a structured situation where a mother and child are together, a stranger enters, and there are various points in the situation where the stranger or the mother leave, to engineer two reunions between the mother and child (see below). The reunions are what are of interest. It would not be easy perhaps to observe reunions like that in a natural setting and also no two reunions would be alike so there could not be comparison between the observations. Using a structured observation, there is a procedure that can be used in other places and other countries and comparisons can be made between findings.

What is structured is the behaviour to be observed and that can be done with any behaviour and anywhere as long as ethical issues are adhered to. Often the setting is structured as well, and observation through a one-way mirror perhaps, as that has more control than using a structured situation in a more natural setting. Control is important as then there can be replication and also cause-and-effect findings might be claimed. A structured observation is close to being an experiment, but the behaviour is less controlled even though 'set up' to an extent. When an observation is structured, there are many of the advantages (and disadvantages) of the experimental method.

STUDY HINT

Structured observations are used in child psychology, which you might study in Year 2.

Studies using the methodology

Mary Ainsworth used structured observations. She set up a situation that she called the 'strange situation' and then observed interactions between mothers and their infants to examine attachment patterns. The interactions were watched through a one-way mirror and all the data were gathered by observation. Apart from the situation, everything else was natural. The 'strange' situation involved the mother and child together 'normally' in a strange place and then a stranger entering the room. The observations were to see what the child did when the mother was both in and out of the room, with or without the stranger being present. The main focus was on how the child behaved in the two reunions, which refers to when the mother re-enters the room to be with the child.

STUDY HINT

To identify a structured observation, check to see if there is a manipulated independent variable, controls, and so on. If there are, then the study is likely to be an experiment (even if the data were gathered by observation). There can be some manipulation in a structured observation (that is the 'structure' part), but the basic behaviour of interest is going to be naturally occurring. This is how to separate an experiment (where data are so often collected by observing) from a structured observation.

An example of a structured observation is Ainsworth's use of the 'strange situation' procedure, observing mother–child interactions when a stranger is present

Definitions

Structured observations are different from **naturalistic observations**. Naturalistic observations capture real-life data in a real situation and real behaviour. Structured observations also aim to capture real-life data. However, some behaviour and situations are hard to study perhaps because of ethical issues or because they do not happen often. Such behaviour and situations can be 'set up' for the purposes of studying them, and they are 'structured' in some way.

Naturalistic observations

Many observations, in which data are collected by observation only and there is no manipulation by the researcher, are naturalistic observations. Naturalistic observations take place in the participant's natural setting. The different ways of designing a naturalistic observation are outlined here. When observations are referred to in this methodology section, they are naturalistic observations. A structured observation can take place in a natural setting when some behaviour is set up to see how people respond. If there is no element of setting up what will happen and what will be observed, then you have a naturalistic observation.

Progress check 5.48

Explain the difference between structured and naturalistic observations.

Time and event sampling, and tallying

Naturalistic observations more or less involve someone watching behaviour and making notes. However, this is not as easy as it sounds. You need to decide beforehand what is to be watched, for example. Then you decide when to make notes and how to capture the data. **Tallying** is a way of making a note about a behaviour. If you use **time sampling**, you can record behaviour for a set time, such as five minutes, then wait for a set time (perhaps two minutes) and then record for another five minutes. Another way of observing is to use **event sampling**. This means not worrying so much about time but about the event being looked at – for example, aggressive behaviour in boys. Further details on tallying and time sampling are given on page 369.

Definitions

Time sampling means, when observing, making a note of behaviour or what is being observed every so often, measured by time and over a specified period of time. For example, tallying behaviour in categories that have been agreed and doing that for five minutes followed by a break of a set period, then another five minutes. **Event sampling** involves deciding beforehand what is to be watched (such as child peer aggressive interactions, with aggressive interactions defined beforehand) and then those interactions are focused on, perhaps with what is happening just before and what is happening just after too, to get data around the event. Every time that event occurs, it is recorded as long as the observation lasts. **Tallying** refers to making a mark when observing. The observer might have a table for recording toy use against gender of child and make a mark every five minutes for one boy and one girl they are watching.

Participant or non-participant observations

- **Participant observations** – observers are part of what they are observing; they are involved in the activity, group or situation. An example of participant observation is infiltration of a group by a researcher in order to find out more about how the group works or when a researcher is already part of the group. So someone could be a member of the team and could observe, for example, team cohesion. The person collecting the data by observing might already have a role in the situation and that too is participant observation.
- **Non-participant observations** – observers are not part of what is happening. They sit away from the activity and are not involved in it. Examples of non-participant observation are when researchers are studying a childcare programme but are not part of that programme, or when they are studying team cohesion in sports psychology but are not members of the team.

Studies using the methodology

Donna Weston reports on a naturalistic observation of parents and their children from birth to around 18 months, recording patterns of communication. Five non-participant observers observed day-to-day interactions in the home weekly. They wrote up the story and scored the behaviour on a scale. (If a parent had carried out the observation and scored the behaviour, that would have been participant observation.)

Grady *et al.* (2012) looked at parents dropping children off at preschool and used naturalistic observation to gather the data. The study looked at parental behaviour, the length of time the separation between the child and parents took, and how the child interacted with peers. The aim was to see the effect of parental lingering when dropping their child off at school. The hypothesis was that the longer the parent lingered, the less the child interacted with peers after the parent had left. The researchers predicted that there would be a negative relationship between the time the parent lingered and the amount of interaction with peers after they had gone. There was also interest in what behaviour the parent exhibited while lingering, such as hugging. Another idea was that perhaps parents stayed longer if the child wanted to stay near them, so the interaction between the parent and child while the parent lingered was also of interest. The researchers also looked at father and mother behaviour to see if there were differences in mothers' behaviour and fathers' behaviour and how the child interacted with them.

Between 6.30am and 9.00am, a naturalistic observation took place with the parents and children in their natural environment, and with the study not affecting that at all. Forty-six parents and their 3–5-year-old children were observed, 12 of the parents being male. The study was done in the US. Behaviours were recorded at ten-second intervals to aim to get all the behaviour. Two young adults gathered the data with three-minute observations of each parent–child pair and the peers. The three minutes started as the preschool was entered. There was inter-rater reliability (the ratings from the two observers agreed). There were set categories for recording, such as 'parental hug', 'hover' and 'walk away'. It was found that, when parents took longer to leave, children stayed longer near them and spent less time with peers in social interaction. Children whose parents pick them up and do not leave might be indicating that there is something to fear, so children stay close. There were other findings too, but just a few of the findings are reported here to illustrate the research method.

Progress check 5.49

Using Grady *et al.* (2012), briefly outlined above, answer the following questions:

1. Is the observation used participant or non-participant?
2. Give two categories that the observers gathered data about.
3. Where is there an example of time sampling?
4. How did the researchers check for reliability?

Evaluation of non-participant observations

Strengths

- The observer has no other role to play and so can concentrate on observation and be impartial and objective.
- Recording the data is easier in non-participant observations and the observer can record more data, more efficiently. A non-participant observer might be able to make notes during the study whereas a participant observer might not be able to do that until afterwards.
- A non-participant observer should be able to carry out time sampling, event sampling and tallying more systematically than a participant observer.

Weaknesses

- The observer in non-participant observations has to be nearby and is likely to be noticeable, which would affect the situation. The observations would lack validity because what is recorded would not be 'normal'.
- Compared with participant observation, the observer may have insufficient understanding of what he/she is observing to record valid data. A participant observer would have useful background knowledge that would help in understanding the data.

Definitions

Non-participant observation is when the person getting the data by observing is not part of what is happening; they are apart from the situation. **Participant observation** means the person getting the data by observing has a role in what is happening; they are part of the situation.

Practical idea for a study using the method

Consider doing a naturalistic observation of people in a shopping centre with the aim of finding out about helping behaviour.

1 Explain how you could use event sampling.
2 Explain how you could use time sampling.
3 Explain how you could use tallying.

For this idea, ethics are not considered, but of course you would have to be sure that the observation is ethical. Observing in a public place without informed consent is not in itself unethical but respect, responsibility, competence and integrity apply (see pp. 305–311).

It would be important to identify helping behaviour that might be seen, such as someone holding a door open for another person with a lot of bags, or someone letting someone else past them. Those could be two events. Then each time you saw someone holding a door or letting someone go in front, you would make notes about that event (such as the gender of the helper and the gender of the one helped, if gender was a theme of interest). You might not have specific events in mind; you want to observe more generally. So every five minutes, for five minutes, you write down any helping behaviour you see. After a while using time sampling, you might have some categories of helping behaviour. Then you could list those categories down and use a tally mark each time that behaviour was observed. This could be done using time sampling if the place you are observing is busy, or you could note each occurrence of each category.

Evaluation of participant observations

Strengths

- The observers in participant observations do not disrupt what is happening – they are not additional people who would affect the situation. Therefore, **ecological validity** is greater because the observers do not affect the situation and make it unnatural.
- The observers in participant observations are likely to have additional information that they can offer as data. They are likely to obtain more data from the observations because they would have better access to such data. They are likely to observe things that non-participant observers would miss.
- It is not normally easy to get access when carrying out a study, but a strength of participant observation is access because participant observers are already present.

Weaknesses

- The observers may be so involved in the situation that they cannot step back sufficiently to make the observations. Non-participant observers can observe all the time; participant observers also have other roles.
- Because the observer is part of the group, participant observations are hard to replicate. Therefore, it is difficult to check for reliability.

Covert and overt observations

- In a **covert observation**, the participants do not know that the observation is taking place – it is being done secretly. The participants do not know they are being observed, although someone in the setting is likely to know because of the need to give permission and to check ethics. A covert observation can be either participant or non-participant.

- In an **overt observation**, the participants know that the observation is taking place and they are aware of all aspects of the study. An overt observation can be either participant or non-participant.

Evaluation of covert observations

Strengths

- Because the participants in covert observations are unaware of the study, the behaviour being observed is likely to be natural. Therefore, the data are valid.
- In covert observations, the observer can maintain a distance (literally if a non-participant observer; figuratively if a participant observer) from the participants and can, for example, make notes without being concerned about the effect this is having on the participants. The participants are not aware of the study and so will not be looking at what the observer is doing.

Weaknesses

- Covert observations can be unethical. Ethical guidelines:
  - ask for informed consent, which cannot be obtained in covert observations
  - do not allow for participants to be distressed, which they may be on discovering that they have been observed secretly
  - do not allow secret observations if the situation is not public (observations in a public place are permitted).
- Non-participant observers may find observation difficult because they cannot be helped by the participants to find a suitable place to watch from. It is not easy to observe behaviour secretly because, in practice:
  - the observers have to be in a suitable position to gather the necessary data
  - in a participant observation, the observer may need to do something different from the norm, thus making secrecy difficult.

Evaluation of overt observations

Strengths

- It is much more ethical than covert observation – for example, the participants can give informed consent and can be offered the right to withdraw.
- The observer can ask for help in setting up a suitable place for observation.
- Participant observers can ask for help in getting data to which they might not usually have access.

Weaknesses

- The participants may not act normally because they know they are being observed. Therefore, the data might not be valid.
- Participant observers may find it difficult to carry out their duties as the people being observed would be aware that the observers are taking on different roles. If it is a non-participant observation, then this is less of a problem.

STUDY HINT

Be ready to describe each aspect of observation (covert, overt, non-participant, participant, naturalistic and structured). You also need to be able to identify these aspects and use them, for example, in a study scenario. If you cannot describe a term fully, use an example to show understanding and perhaps contrast one aspect with another. For example, to describe overt observations, you could contrast them with covert observations, but don't spend long doing this because you need to say what the aspect is, not what it is not.

Progress check 5.50

Give one strength and one weakness of the practical on page 367 with regard to the research method and research decisions.

Inter-observer/inter-rater reliability

It could be said that observations are one-off situations that are hard to replicate because they take place at one moment in time and involve naturally occurring events. However, if there is more than one observer, their observations can be compared. The separate sets of data are recorded and then tested to see if there is a correlation between them. If there is a correlation, then it is said that the observation has **inter-observer reliability**, which is a strength.

Recording data from naturalistic observations

When observations are carried out, the data have to be recorded and how they are recorded is important. A single observer, for example, can only observe when not writing things down and can, in any case, only observe certain aspects of the situation. Two observers can do better and inter-observer reliability can be tested. However, a system for recording observations must be agreed. Much depends on whether the study needs qualitative or quantitative data, or both.

- **Qualitative data** involve attitudes or emotions; detail, rather than numbers, is important.
- **Quantitative data** are numerical; they are useful when analysing results. If quantitative data are required, tallying can be used as a way of recording.

Tallying

Tallying involves making a mark each time a behaviour (or whatever is being observed) occurs.

There needs to be an initial observation session, preferably with more than one observer, in which categories of behaviour are recorded so that all the researchers know which behaviour should be tallied. For example, if observing boys and girls in a nursery to look for gender-specific behaviour, it would first be necessary to record some gender-specific behaviour in order to list what is relevant and what is likely to be seen in that nursery. In the nursery, there might be, for example, bikes, a climbing frame, a painting corner and books; there might be a play mat with cars, a play-dough area, a large wooden train set and a soft play area. The toys and play equipment available will guide the play behaviour and researchers need to decide on their categories before gathering the data. Once they have the categories, they can draw up a table for tallying. An example is given in Table 5.16.

Time sampling

If you carry out tallying for your practical, there will be one important problem that needs addressing: you need to know when to make a tally mark. If a child plays with play dough, you make a mark. Do you then wait until the child does something else? Playing with play dough may continue for ages. One way round this is to use time sampling, which means making a tally mark every minute or other chosen interval. This provides a better picture of what the child has been doing during the observation.

Table 5.16 shows data (artificial) from two observers who watched two children each, one boy and one girl (i.e. two boys and two girls were observed). Since the observers watched different children, inter-observer reliability could not be tested. However, the observers were trained in the use of the categories by watching a video beforehand, to ensure that they would note the same behaviour.

Table 5.16 An example of the use of tallying to examine gender-specific behaviour in a nursery; a mark was made every minute for each child for ten minutes, followed by a five-minute break, over a session of two hours

Play behaviour	Boys	Girls
Playing on the climbing frame	IIII IIII	III
Playing in the book corner	III	IIII II
Painting	IIII	IIII
Playing in the Wendy house	IIII III	IIII II
Riding on bikes	IIII IIII II	IIII
Playing quietly alone	IIII	IIII IIII III
Playing with other adults	IIII IIII I	IIII III
Watching, not playing	III	IIII III
Playing with play dough	IIII	IIII IIII II

Evaluation of naturalistic observation

Strengths

- The setting is natural, so there is ecological validity. This means that:
  - the setting is real life and the data are, therefore, real
  - the study, with regard to the situation, gathers the data that it claims to gather.

  If an observation is not carried out in a natural setting, in a natural situation, you cannot be sure that natural behaviour is being observed.
- Detail can be gathered in naturalistic observation. Observation can potentially capture all the behaviour exhibited at that time (provided that there is more than one observer). Observers can record speech, actions, interactions, body language, information about the setting and emotions. Other research methods tend not to be able to gather so much detail (except case studies with observation used as a research method within the study).

Weaknesses

- The observer makes decisions about what to record and, in some cases, what categories to use and into which categories particular behaviour should be placed, to gather quantitative data. So there is an element of interpretation, which means that the study could involve subjectivity, which is not a scientific way of carrying out research. Even if a video is made and all behaviour recorded as a story afterwards (as qualitative data), there will still be selection of data.
- Data gathered by an observational research method tend to lack generalisability because an observation at that moment in time is specific. It is difficult to generalise from that specific situation to other situations, even if they are similar. Tallying gives quantitative data, but there is some interpretation involved; observations often gather qualitative data and a specific situation is involved. For these reasons, generalisation is difficult.

Progress check 5.51

Using the terms covert, overt, participant, non-participant, inter-observer reliability and naturalistic, explain the research method used in the following study. Make sure that you use each term in such a way that makes it clear that you understand it:

A study was carried out to see if girls chose different toys from boys. The study took place in a local nursery; children aged between two and four years were observed. There were two observers, both sitting to one side of the nursery, on opposite sides of the room. The nursery staff, parents and children were aware that a study was taking place and had agreed to take part.

Test yourself

1 Describe an example of an overt participant observation, a covert participant observation, an overt non-participant observation and a covert non-participant observation (you can make up the examples). **(8 marks)**
2 Explain two strengths and two weaknesses of observation as a research method in psychology. **(8 marks)**
3 Choose one research method other than observation and compare it with observation in terms of strengths and weaknesses. Include issues of validity, reliability, generalisability and credibility in your answer. **(12 marks)**

Content analysis

One way of gathering data in psychology is to use content analysis. This is a fairly straightforward and ethical way of gathering data. In this section, the content analysis research method and an example of its use are described and evaluated.

Description

A content analysis can include qualitative data if excerpts from texts are used. However, often it is about gathering quantitative data in the form of numbers of instances in certain categories. For example, it is a systematic study of use of key words or key ideas in a text. A hypothesis is generated about a topic that can be studied using texts of some sort, but can be videos or pictures. Then coding frames are generated, which means finding out what instances are to be noted or counted, such as gender, age, a certain view (e.g. prejudice). Coding frames can include more than one 'variable' to consider at the same time.

- The content that is analysed is from media sources such as magazine articles or television, or any such written or recorded information.
- The aim is to look for themes, categories or behaviours, depending on the purpose of the study.
- Behaviours or examples of the categories are then counted to see how often they appear or are mentioned – this is tallying.
- In this way, quantitative data are gathered.

You will learn more about content analysis in Year 2.

Example of a content analysis: Cumberbatch and Gauntlett (2005)

Aim

Cumberbatch and Gauntlett carried out a content analysis as part of an Ofcom-funded piece of research. Their aim was to find out more about whether smoking, alcohol and drug abuse featured in television programmes watched by 10–15 year olds, and how it was treated.

Procedure

The researchers carried out a content analysis to see how alcohol and drug abuse were depicted. The research focused on the ten programmes most watched by 10–15 year olds and the study was carried out from August to October in 2004. There were 256 programmes involved, with 70 per cent or more of them being soap operas. All were broadcast before the 9 p.m. watershed. Categories that were tallied involved scenes where alcohol, smoking and legal or illegal drugs featured. Overall, 2,099 scenes were used. Material that was counted included observed or implied alcohol, smoking or drug-related behaviour, as well as references to alcohol, smoking or drugs. Visual representations of alcohol, smoking or drugs were also recorded (such as a cigarette packet or drink in a scene).

Results

Alcohol featured more than smoking or drugs did in the most popular television programmes. Alcohol-related scenes occurred at the rate of about 12 incidences each hour. Smoking-related scenes occurred at about 3.4 incidences each hour and drug-related incidences were half that again, at 1.7 scenes each hour. Just 4 per cent of the programmes contained none of the target incidences. Both drinkers and smokers had large roles in the scenes; 37 per cent of the major characters were drinkers and 4 per cent were smokers. When considering the type of message rather than just the incidence, it was found that messages about alcohol were more or less neutral (84 per cent of the scenes), 6 per cent of the messages about alcohol were negative, 6 per cent mixed and 4 per cent positive. With smoking, 91 per cent of the messages were neutral, while 57 per cent of the drug scenes carried an anti-drugs message, with 40 per cent neutral and 3 per cent mixed. There were no scenes carrying a positive message about drugs.

Table 5.17 Results of the study of Cumberbatch and Gauntlett (2005)

Programmes containing target material	Alcohol (%)	Smoking (%)	Drugs (%)
Overt portrayal	84	33	2
Implied portrayal	4	4	6
Discussion/references/visuals	87	53	21
None of the above	7	38	79

Table 5.17 shows that there are more references to alcohol than to smoking or drugs.

Conclusions

Being a content analysis, the results *are* the conclusions because they are the reason for the content analysis being carried out – to find out about alcohol, smoking and drugs and how they are portrayed in the media. The conclusion is, therefore, the same as the results – that alcohol features quite a lot, whereas smoking is referred to less often and drugs even less. In general, the messages with regard to alcohol and smoking are fairly neutral.

Evaluation of Cumberbatch and Gauntlett (2005) use of content analysis

Strengths

- A content analysis is simply a counting of categories, so there are no ethical issues with regard to using participants.
- Many different programmes and scenes were included so that the analysis was thorough and within the limits of the study (programmes for 10–15 year olds before the watershed). There is generalisability with regard to the findings.
- There was validity, in that the programmes were real and broadcast, so the findings were about what children aged between 10 and 15 really watched.

Weaknesses

- The programmes were mainly soap operas (70 per cent or more) and so the findings should be generalised to soap operas rather than all television. Also, there was a limitation: all the programmes were shown before the 9 p.m. watershed, so findings should be generalised only to before the watershed.
- The assumption was made that children aged between 10 and 15 would imitate behaviour in their favourite programmes. Social learning theory is accepted, given this assumption. However, children may also see alcohol, smoking and/or drugs in other situations, such as at home, so it cannot be shown that there is a causal link between alcohol, smoking and/or drugs being shown in a television programme and children using such drugs. A content analysis does not show that causal link.

Practical

You could carry out a content analysis yourself. One idea is to use the pages of a newspaper. Separate out the sports pages and then another set of the same number of pages not focusing on sport. To make it manageable, you might want to choose five pages of each 'type'. Go through carefully highlighting in one colour any reference to women and in another colour any reference to men. Count the references for each 'type'. You should end up with a table of results (e.g. Table 5.18) on which a chi-squared statistical test can be carried out, which you could do for practice. It would be expected that there would be a lot more references to males in sport than to females and perhaps more references to females in other pages, depending on what you chose.

Table 5.18 Suggested table for recording references to males and females in a newspaper

	Sports pages – reference to males	Sports pages – reference to females	Total
Other pages – reference to males			
Other pages – reference to females			
Total			

Progress check 5.52

Explain one situation where a content analysis could be used to gather data in psychology.

Test yourself

1. Explain what is meant by a content analysis in psychology. **(6 marks)**
2. Compare the validity and reliability of data from content analyses with data from observations. **(16 marks)**

Use of animals in laboratory experiments, including ethics

In this section, the use of animals in laboratory experiments is considered, looking at both practical and ethical issues. Your course asks you to look at the use of animals in studies where the findings relate to humans, so this section considers the issue of drugs. In learning theories, the focus is on finding out about learning behaviour, such as Pavlov using dogs to develop the idea of classical conditioning and Skinner using rats and pigeons to look at the power of reinforcements and operant conditioning. These studies have been explained in Chapter 4, so we use the different example here of animals used to study the effects of drugs on humans. Biological psychology (Chapter 3) considered the issue of how drugs work in the brain and health psychology in your Year 2 course continues with that theme. If you choose health psychology as your application, you will be able to draw on the material in this section. This section also evaluates the use of animals in laboratory experiments and applying the findings to human behaviour, as well as the ethical issues involved.

Features of animal laboratory studies

Laboratory studies using animals are laboratory *experiments*. Ethology is a research method where animals are observed and studied in their own environment. In your course, you need to learn about using animals in laboratory experiments, not in their natural setting. Animal experiments involve observing an animal's behaviour with manipulation of an independent variable, so it is the experimental method that is being discussed (as opposed to the observational research method).

STUDY HINT
Animal experiments use the experimental research method, so what you have learned earlier in this chapter about that method will be useful here.

An animal experiment has an independent variable (IV) that is manipulated to see the effect on a dependent variable (DV). There are strong controls, such as the environment, duration of the study, biochemical factors, gender, age, type of animal and whatever variables are important for a particular study. The aim is to control all variables except the IV, so that it can be shown that a change in the IV has caused any change in the DV. This means laboratory experiments can show a cause-and-effect relationship.

Using animals instead of humans has some effect on how a laboratory experiment is run because animals have to be fed, housed, looked after and handled in ways that humans do not. Such issues have to be incorporated into the study. Studies cannot last too long and they must be suitable for the species – animals are only able to act and react in certain ways. The animal also has to have the right features, such as biochemistry or brain structure, depending on what knowledge is sought. Part of a description of animal laboratory experiments, therefore, needs to include features such as preparing appropriate housing, feeding and care routines, planning the necessary controls and how they will be put into place. On the whole, there can be more control with animals in laboratory experiments than with humans. Animal studies are scientific in that they draw hypotheses from theory, control all variables except the IV and often use scientific equipment to measure the DV.

Ethical guidelines for the use of animals in laboratory experiments

This section of your course considers ethical issues when using animals in laboratory experiments. Ethical issues relating to human participants are not related to the use of animals in studies. It might seem that an animal should have the right to withdraw and if the animal seems distressed the study should be stopped – there is an argument for that viewpoint. However, in psychology the ethics for using animals are different from the ethics for using humans and each should be used appropriately. Ethical guidelines for human participants were covered in social psychology (Chapter 5, pp. 304–315) – review this material to refresh your memory if needed.

Guidelines for Psychologists Working with Animals (2012)

The British Psychological Society (BPS) has published Guidelines for Psychologists Working with Animals (2012) based on the Animals (Scientific Procedures) Act, 1986. Where animals (protected animals only) might suffer pain, distress or harm, the study is covered by this Act and ethical issues apply. Clearly when using animals in laboratory experiments such issues are likely to found. 'Protected animals' refers to all living vertebrates other than humans. In 1993, an amendment added single invertebrate species, such as the octopus. In 2013, the Act referred to 'cephalopods' as well as living vertebrates. These amendments show how the Act has changed to keep up with what is required to protect animals when being used in studies.

The Act has various provisions aimed at protecting animals. From the start, it makes clear that the law is under the jurisdiction of the Secretary of State at the Home Office. The Act considered 'regulated procedures', which are experimental and scientific procedures to animals which might cause pain, suffering or lasting harm. Anyone carrying out a regulated procedure must hold a personal licence and the place used must be specified and must be a scientific procedure establishment. A programme of work requires a project licence. The Secretary of State grants the licences. You can see a lot of certification is required for any laboratory experimental testing with animals. There are also rules around where animals can be bred for testing purposes. The Act has a lot of detail and specifics, such as that cats and dogs can only be used if specifically bred for lab purposes and animals that have already been used and given a general anaesthetic cannot be used for any more procedures. The details are summarised here, but there is a lot more around specific regulations and certification. There are schedules in the Act, such as methods of humane killing and how animals must come from designated breeding or supplying establishments (mouse, rat, guinea pig, hamster, rabbit, dog, cat, primate).

Explore

You can find out more about the Act online, such as this link: www.legislation.gov.uk/ukpga/1986/14/pdfs/ukpga_19860014_en.pdf, or www.gov.uk/research-and-testing-using-animals, which gives information about the 3Rs.

The BPS (2012) guidance adds that any harm or distress to any animal, whether covered by the Act or not, has ethical implications that must be considered. This is about protecting animals under the Animal Welfare Act (2006). The BPS document refers to the three 'Rs' (Russell and Birch, 1959, in the BPS document): replacing, reducing and refining. The requirement is to replace the use of animals where possible, with non-sentient alternatives, reduce the number of animals used and refine procedures so that there is the least impact on animals. A general requirement is to cause the least possible distress.

The BPS guidance summarises what is required under the headings: legal requirements; replacing the use of animals; choice of species and strain; number of animals; procedures; procurement of animals; animal care; disposing of animals; animals in psychology teaching; the use of animals for therapeutic purposes; clinical assessment and treatment of animal behaviour. Under 'procedures', they have: housing conditions; reward, deprivation and aversive stimuli; aggression and predation; fieldwork (not within experiments); anaesthesia, analgesia and euthanasia. From these lists, it can be seen that a great deal is covered and some of what is required will be clear from the headings in the BPS document. Some of the principles in the BPS document relate to the study of animals in the wild, or to using animals in therapy. The ideas given in Tables 5.19 and 5.20 include only those that relate to using animals in laboratory conditions.

Explore

You can access the BPS guidelines on using animals in psychology research (2012) here: www.bps.org.uk/system/files/images/guideline_for_psychologists_working_with_animals_2012_rep55_2012_web.pdf.

Table 5.19 BPS guidelines (2012) for using animals (in laboratory experiments) with explanations

BPS heading	Explanation
Legal requirements	There are animal welfare laws and laws relating to endangered and protected species.
Replacing the use of animals	Videos can be used, such as a video of a rat's behaviour. Computer simulations can also be used. Animals should only be used if alternatives have been considered and rejected.
Choice of species	The species must be appropriate for the study and regarding ethics. Whether an animal is bred in captivity is also taken into account. The level of sentience (feelings) should be taken into account as that relates to distress.
Number of animals	The Scientific Procedures Act (1986) requires the use of the smallest number possible. Using careful experimental methods as well as statistics can help to minimise the number used.
Procedures	Procedures require a project licence and registered premises. The individual also needs a personal licence. More detail about procedures is given in Table 5.20.
Procurement of animals	Home Office Designated Breeding and Supply Establishments must be used to obtain common laboratory species and other animals must be obtained from 'high quality suppliers'.
Animal care	There is a responsibility to care for animals well when they are not being used in a study. The animal should have suitable accommodation and environment, suitable food and water, and space, all sufficient for the animal's health and well-being.
Disposing of animals	When studies are complete, it is appropriate then to use the animals for breeding or to look after them as companion animals, or to use them in further studies. There should always be appropriate care.

Table 5.20 Procedures according to the BPS guidelines (2012) for using animals (in laboratory experiments)

BPS heading: procedures	Explanation
Housing conditions	Caging must be suitable for the species. Caging affects a social species, for example. Overcrowding should be avoided. Previous social experiences of the animal must be taken into account. This is all about minimising distress.
Reward, deprivation and aversive stimuli	There can be some food deprivation, and giving free access to food is perhaps not good for animals in any case. However, deprivation can cause distress, and distress must be minimised. When a study requires deprivation, normal requirements of the animal must be taken into account, including its metabolic rate. A short period of deprivation for one animal might be long for another. When deprivation is used, alternatives should be considered first.
Anaesthetic, analgesic and euthanasia	*This section can be distressing to read.* Anaesthetic or analgesic (pain killers) should be used in an experiment if necessary, to alleviate suffering. There should be post-operative care to minimise stress. There should be frequent monitoring and, if pain is found, a consideration of humane killing should be undertaken.

Cost–benefit analysis – Bateson's decision cube

The BPS guidelines for using animals (2012) discuss how any study using animals should weigh up the costs to the animal with the benefits of doing the study. Bateson (e.g. 1986, 2011) discusses ethics and using animals in research and suggests that there are three aspects to consider. The cost to the animal must be taken into account, in terms of ethics, such as suffering and distress. The benefits of the study must be weighed against the costs, to make sure that benefits do outweigh the costs. And third, consideration should be made of how good the research is – if the findings will not have validity or reliability, or generalisibility perhaps, then that is not good research. These three axes all have to be weighed up before the research is accepted in ethical terms.

The diagram below shows a summary of Bateson's ideas about decision-making around animal studies and ethics.

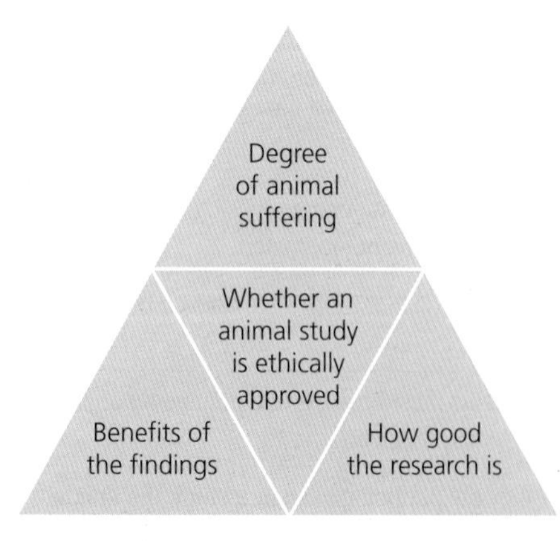

Summary of Bateson's ideas about decision-making around animal studies and ethics

Evaluation of ethics of using animals in laboratory experiments

It is hard to talk about strengths and weaknesses here because ethics is about strengths (how to use animals ethically) and weaknesses (where ethics might not be considered). A discussion of ethics will be evaluation after describing the ethical principles. Issues include pro-animal use and anti-animal use.

Pro-animal use includes:

- the argument that humans should use animals if it benefits the human species; Gray (1991) argued that we have a responsibility to our species to understand as much as we can and this is a moral responsibility
- the argument that research should take place if it is for the greater good of the greater number (Singer, 1975)
- the idea from Darwin that evolution means we have similarities with animals and generalising findings from animal studies is appropriate
- the claim that it is practical to use animals because of a shorter breeding cycle and so on, where it is not practical to use humans; there are controls in such studies too, so findings are valuable and appropriate and understanding comes through practical means – this argument links to the moral obligation argument
- the claim that there are now sufficient guidelines, rules and laws in place to protect animals from unnecessary suffering so using them is ethical and acceptable.

Anti-animal use includes:

- the animal rights argument that no animals should be used in any studies; making research more humane is not enough – there is never a justification, and cost–benefit analysis is not appropriate
- the idea of Singer (1975) that we should not carry out studies on animals that we would not do on humans;

Singer calls this 'speciesism' and says it is like racism – humans are not more important than other species

- the argument that we have a moral obligation to protect other species
- the idea that animals are different from humans, such as in having different drives and consciousness; this means findings from animal studies are not useful so it is not ethical to carry them out
- a criticism that research with animals lacks validity sufficiently (and generalisability), so they should not be carried out and it is not ethical because the findings have no value
- the argument against cost–benefit analysis on the principle that the costs to the animals might not be known at the outset; indeed, the benefits might not be certain either as the findings are yet to be uncovered.

Progress check 5.53

Give three arguments for using animals in lab experiments in ethical terms and three arguments against.

Numbers and types of animal used

Having looked at the ethics involved in using animals in laboratory experiments, what follows is about the practicalities of using them.

Figures for animals used in laboratory experiments in psychology are hard to find because the data tend to show overall animal testing numbers, not just use of animals in psychology studies. Home Office figures in the UK in 2011 showed 3.79 million tests started using scientific procedures on animals. This was 1.08 million more than in 2000 and it is reported that figures are rising. There was a reduction from 1976 to the 1990s but then an increase, which is continuing.

The pie chart below shows procedures by species in 2011 – this is all scientific procedures, not just experiments in psychology. 'Other mammals' includes dogs, cats and non-human primates.

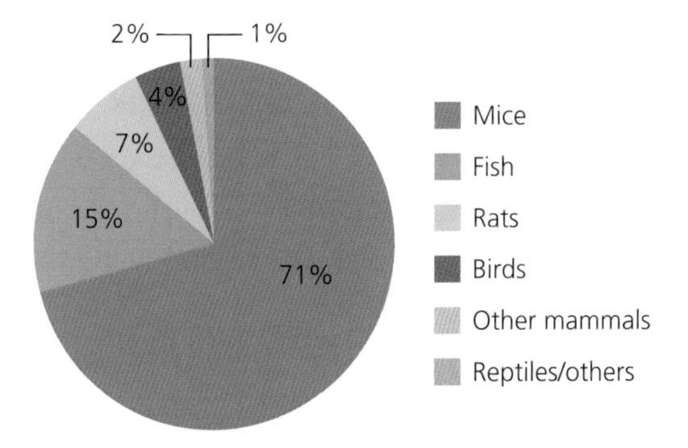

Procedures by species in 2011. Data from the Home Office paper on Statistics of Scientific Procedures on Living Animals in Great Britain (2011)

Explore

You can look at the Home Office document from which these figures come here: www.gov.uk/government/uploads/system/uploads/attachment_data/file/115853/spanimals11.pdf. More on the use of animals, including discussion, can be found using the following link: www.hsi.org/campaigns/end_animal_testing/qa/about.html. This is the site of the Humane Society International so will have a 'view' – however, that view is of interest for discussion.

STUDY HINT

When discussing issues around using animals in research, you are likely to have your own viewpoint, but try to discuss the issues in an open-minded way. You need to be able to understand all the arguments and to discuss them, but this does not mean you have to agree with them. In psychology, you are likely to find other areas that you are emotionally involved in. If possible when studying an area, maintain impartiality for the purpose of study. Of course, you do not have to remain impartial in your own beliefs.

Explore

Find out about animal experiments to get an idea of which animals are used and whether particular animals are preferred for particular studies.

Different animals are chosen for different purposes. Insects, for example, do not have a brain structure at all similar to that of humans, whereas mice and humans share many characteristics. The size of mice is useful, they are low cost and they have fast reproduction rates. Genetically modified mice can be bred to suit whatever purpose is required. Other types of animal are used in experiments, such as rhesus monkeys, as explained in one example later in this section.

Rhesus monkeys are used in research in psychology because they are genetically close to humans, as are chimpanzees. Rhesus monkeys share about 93 per cent of their genes with chimpanzees and with humans. Mice share about 90 per cent of their genes with humans. Rats have 21 pairs of chromosomes, mice have 20 and humans have 23. Recent research has found similarities, showing 280 large regions of similarities in the genome sequences. Interestingly, research shows that rats and mice are not as similar as they look with regard to genes. This was a National Institutes of Health funded project (2004). This sort of research is carried out because, when findings using animals are to be used in humans, there needs to be some understanding that there are sufficient similarities between humans and the animals to make findings applicable.

It is perhaps not so much the genes we share but those that are different that should be the focus. The differences are visible. This isn't only about our biological similarities with the animals that are studied – there is an important point about our lifestyle and **phenotype**. A **genotype** is the genes of someone, their inherited factors. The phenotype is more than the genotype – it is the observed person, with the effects of the genes. MZ twins share their genotype but their phenotype might be a little different. Parents of MZ twins, for example, can tell them apart. The animals might suit to an extent the genotype but the phenotype is different. Also human behaviour is affected by environment as well as genes, such as their social interactions and cultural habits and customs. Therefore, using animals in laboratory experiments and generalising the findings to humans, though often helpful, might not be straightforward.

Explore

Use the internet to find out how the human brain differs from the brains of other animals. For example, if you type in 'mouse and human brain picture', you can find a picture of the two compared.

STUDY HINT

You will have looked at studies that used animals in other topic areas, such as van den Oever *et al.* (2008) in biological psychology (pp. 192–196). In learning theories, many of the studies on which ideas about conditioning were built used animals. Use evidence from those studies when discussing the use of animals in laboratory experiments.

Animal experiments for research into drugs

Three examples of animal laboratory experiments are given here: two using monkeys and one using mice. This is to give you some ideas about how animals are used in laboratory experiments and for what purposes. You can use these ideas as evidence when discussing such issues.

The link between cocaine/heroin use and renal disease

Experiments have used animals to help to understand the prevalence of renal disease in heroin and cocaine users. Renal disease occurs when the kidneys fail to function properly. In laboratory experiments, mice are given either heroin or cocaine in various doses and then their renal function is tested. Animal studies have shown that renal disease is linked more to cocaine use than to heroin, which could point to the drug itself being implicated in renal disease (rather than taking any drug).

Explore

Look up some of the many other animal laboratory experiments that are used to study the effects of drugs. The ones chosen here focus on heroin and cocaine, but you could look at studies that consider other recreational drugs.

Studies other than animal experiments have also investigated the link between heroin/cocaine and renal disease. For example, it was concluded with regard to heroin (Jaffe and Kimmel, 2006) that economic conditions, behavioural practices and culture were factors more likely to relate to renal disease than heroin use itself, partly because renal disease in heroin users is not as common as it once was. If heroin caused the renal disease, then there would still be the same level of link, and there is not. Their findings support the animal experiments that found more of a link between cocaine and renal disease than heroin and renal disease. Animal studies can be used in this way to back up studies of humans.

STUDY HINT

You can use evidence from studies to illustrate the use of animal laboratory experiments in research, as well as considering the ethics of such use. Also use evidence from other studies in argument. For example, you can use the study of mice looking at a link between cocaine/heroin and renal disease and then Jaffe and Kimmel's (2006) study, to suggest that it is not useful to use animal studies and then generalise to humans because human lives have different complexities.

Strengths of studies into the link between heroin and renal disease

- The human study cited reinforces the conclusions from the animal studies, which tends to give reliability to the conclusion that it is likely that cocaine affects renal function more than heroin does. Animal studies can be used to back up human studies.

- The animal studies are evidence for a biological explanation – that taking drugs into the body affects physical aspects of the body. This is possibly the case for some drugs more than others. Controls regarding biological aspects make animal studies useful in this way.
- An advantage of using mice is that such studies would not be possible with humans because you could not inject humans with cocaine or heroin and then test their renal function in such controlled conditions.

Weaknesses of studies into the link between heroin and renal disease

- There are differences in brain structure between mice and humans, so conclusions about the effects of drugs on the brain and behaviour might not be generalisable.
- The human study shows how important it is to look at factors other than the drug-taking because it seems that, although taking heroin correlated with renal disease, there were other factors. Psychosocial factors are not studied using animals.
- The human study is evidence for the biopsychosocial model, which suggests that with complex human behaviour there are complex causes affecting such behaviour.

Looking at drugs as reinforcers

Meisch (2001) considered animal laboratory experiments into oral self-administration of drugs (taking it themselves by mouth). For example, rhesus monkeys were given the opportunity to take drugs so that researchers could see whether drugs are reinforcing. Here 'reinforcing' refers to the drug being taken as a reward, which would link to factors like addiction. Drugs used included barbiturates, opioids, stimulants and ethanol. Animal laboratory experiments showed that drugs of this kind become reinforcers if they are taken by mouth, which means that the animal will choose to take the drug as a reward, so it will get pleasure from taking the drug.

There are problems in animal experiments like this because the study has to take the taste into account (which the animal may not like). The delay before the drug starts to work also has to be considered, as it has to be clear that it is the effect of the drug that is the reinforcer rather than something else. Animal studies have shown that monkeys will choose to take in more drug solution than water, which is taken to show that they choose the drug as a reward.

STUDY HINT

Meisch's (2001) study is about the power of reward in starting and maintaining behaviour, and this is operant conditioning. The reward of the drug was enough for the monkeys to choose it over water. There is a suggestion (from other studies) that a pleasure centre in the brain links to reward and this pleasure centre seems to over-ride other needs (such as water). Perhaps there is a biological element in operant conditioning that learning theorists did not consider. Use examples from anywhere in your course where they suit an argument. Meisch's (2001) study can be used to evaluate the theory of operant conditioning.

Strengths of the study looking at drugs as reinforcers

- Monkeys share many of the genes of humans, so generalising from monkeys may be a reasonable thing to do.
- Humans can become addicted to certain drugs, which appear to be taken for their reward value, so the findings of the study of monkeys fits with known human behaviour, which gives them reliability.

Weaknesses of the study looking at drugs as reinforcers

- Rhesus monkeys are not human, so generalising from monkeys to humans might not be reasonable.
- Ethical issues about using animals might be raised, though if the guidelines for using animals are adhered to, then such experiments are generally allowed.

Testing the properties of amphetamines in reducing cocaine addiction

Czoty *et al.*, at Wake Forest University School of Medicine in California, found that amphetamines can reduce in monkeys, for up to a month, the behaviour of obtaining cocaine for reward. According to an article written by the researchers in 2008, amphetamine seems to mimic cocaine, but without leading to drug abuse. This means that cocaine addiction could be treated in the same way as nicotine and heroin addiction – by prescribing a replacement drug.

The monkey was taught to press levers to get food or an injection of cocaine as a reward. The number of times the monkey had to press the lever to receive cocaine was increased until it was too much for the monkey to keep pressing. At this stage, the cocaine was removed and the monkey was treated by injection (intravenously) with an amphetamine for 24 hours a day. A week later the monkey was offered the possibility of getting cocaine again and the researchers found a large decrease in the number of times the monkey responded. They tried different doses of amphetamine and found a moderate dose was the most effective. Cocaine use over the month was reduced by about 60 per cent.

Evaluation of the study testing the properties of amphetamines in reducing cocaine addiction

You can make the same points here as the study on cocaine as reinforcer above:

- Monkeys are not humans so it is hard to generalise, but they do share many genes with humans, so perhaps some generalisation is possible.
- Human behaviour shows that cocaine is reinforcing, which suggests the study findings can be generalised.
- There are ethical issues you could discuss, such as asking how many monkeys were used (the researchers should use a restricted number) and how the animals were cared for (a licence is required, and caging should be suitable).

Progress check 5.54

Briefly describe two studies that have used animals in laboratory experiments.

Evaluation of animal laboratory experiments

In this section, experiments are evaluated with regard to practical and ethical issues, as well as how useful they are in relating them to humans.

Practical issues

Strengths

- Animals are relatively small and usually easy to handle, which means some procedures are more feasible.
- Some animals have short gestation periods and reproductive cycles so generations and genes can be studied more easily than with humans.
- Some animals, such as mice, have a similar brain structure to humans so there is value in studying animals and relating results to humans.
- Some procedures are not suitable for humans but they can be done on animals (ethical guidelines allowing).
- There can be stronger control over the environment than for humans, which means that findings of studies are more likely to be objective.

Weaknesses

- The brains of animals are not exactly the same as those of humans, so relating the results from animals to humans may not be accurate. Furthermore, animals' genetic structure is not the same as that of humans, again making generalisation difficult.
- Human behaviour is complex, so isolating variables, especially in animals, will not address that complexity.
- There is a lack of credibility when using animals and concluding about humans because of differences in genes and brain functioning.

Ethical issues

Strengths

- Procedures can be carried out on animals that cannot be done on humans – there are ethical reasons for using animals rather than humans.
- The moral obligation argument (Gray, 1991) puts forward the view that we must do all we can to protect our own species, so using animals is one way of discovery that does not harm humans and which also benefits them.
- The knowledge found can sometimes benefit animals as well, which makes a study more ethical.
- There are strong guidelines that have to be followed when using animals in laboratory experiments, so there are safeguards that make such studies ethical, to an extent at least.

STUDY HINT

Remember to make each point very clearly when discussing strengths and weaknesses. If you are discussing an ethical issue, make sure you explain the ethics, and if discussing a practical issue, explain the practical element. For example, mentioning the numbers used can apply in a practical way (e.g. insufficient to draw firm findings) or an ethical way (e.g. using more than was necessary so going against guidelines). Saying 'the number of animals used was a problem' is not enough.

Weaknesses

- Many animals feel pain and become distressed during experiments, although there are guidelines to avoid unwanted discomfort.
- Some people believe that animals should not be treated as objects. They argue that humans are animals and there is an obligation to treat non-human animals well. This is the opposite view to pro-speciesism.

Progress check 5.55

Explain the issue with generalisability when it comes to using animals in lab experiments.

Applying findings from drug research to human behaviour

You can evaluate animal laboratory experiments used to research drugs in the same way as you would evaluate them in general, by looking at practical and ethical issues as well as issues of generalisability, validity and reliability.

Explore

Find out about the various organisations that are against using animals in experiments. There are a relatively large number of people in the UK who would like to liberate all animals from being used in this way.

Validity

The validity of using findings from animal studies to apply to humans can be argued either way. If an animal experiment is being used to test the effects of a drug, this is not a valid study because the effects of a drug on an animal will not necessarily be the same as the effects on a human being. However, neuronal transmission takes place in the same way in the brain of mammals as in humans, so it may be possible to generalise from other mammals to humans.

Generalisability

Animals are different from humans, so to claim that findings from animals are true of humans may not be safe. One example is the drug thalidomide, which was tested on rabbits and found to be safe but was far from safe when given to pregnant humans. This suggests that any drug, including recreational drugs, might have a different effect on humans than on animals. Amphetamines have been shown to have a different effect on humans than on rats.

Reliability

Animal studies tend to be reliable because of the strong controls in the experimental situation, where more can be controlled than with a study using humans. Variables that might be controlled are the type of animal, size, age, gender, environment, what the animal has eaten, how thirsty it is, its body weight and whether it is in a crowded situation. With such control and a well-documented procedure, it is possible to repeat the study and to show that the findings are reliable. Usually a study is repeated as a matter of course and findings are not published from just one study on one animal.

Test yourself

1. Evaluate the results from animals in laboratory experiments in so far as they can be applied to humans. **(12 marks)**
2. Evaluate the ethics of the use of animals in laboratory experiments. **(12 marks)**

Scientific status of psychology

This chapter on method has mainly focused on research methods that have scientific credibility. There has been a lot of 'science' in the material used as examples for the different research methods. There has been mention of qualitative data, gathered from interviews, questionnaires, case studies and observations, and it can be said that using qualitative data is less 'scientific'. There has been use of quantitative data, gathered from laboratory experiments, field experiments, questionnaires, brain scanning and content analysis, as well as in correlations.

In your course, content involves social psychology, cognitive psychology, biological psychology (with a look at the psychodynamic approach) and learning theories. Some of the material is more 'scientific' than other material. Cognitive psychology and biological psychology both look at the brain and brain processing and functioning, which is 'scientific'. Social psychology looks at theories around prejudice and obedience, but does that in a controlled way, often using experiments, so again there is an element of science. Learning theories aim to be scientific as they consider just observable behaviour mostly, precisely because it is observable and, therefore, measurable in a scientific way. A lot of the content in Year 1 of your course is 'scientific'.

This section considers the scientific status of psychology including replicability, reliability, validity, reductionism, falsification, empiricism, hypothesis testing and use of controls. Some of these issues have been covered in this chapter because they relate to the study of methods. Replicability, for example, refers to whether a study can be repeated and, if it is repeated with the same results, reliability can be claimed. Validity concerns whether findings are about real life. Hypothesis testing is about generating a statement and then testing against reality to see if that statement can be supported by evidence. Controls are used when hypothesis testing to make sure that what is being tested actually is, and no other variables are confounding the results.

Terms new to you are likely to be reductionism, falsification and empiricism, so these are explained in more detail here. The material will help you to draw conclusions about what science is and how far psychology fits the definition of science.

What is meant by science?

The hypothetico-deductive model

The word 'science' describes a procedure in which a theory is formulated and a suggestion drawn from this theory about what might happen in the world. The suggestion forms a hypothesis, which can then be tested against reality to see if it works. If it does, then more knowledge is added to the theory. If the suggestion does not work, the theory is amended, or perhaps even rejected. Through this cycle of testing a theory and amending it, scientific knowledge is built. Karl Popper called this the **hypothetico-deductive model** of reasoning. From the theory, a hypothesis is deduced. Testing against reality means gathering **empirical data** – those gathered from the senses through seeing, touching, tasting, hearing or smelling. **Empiricism** is the use of sense data to test an idea and get evidence for it.

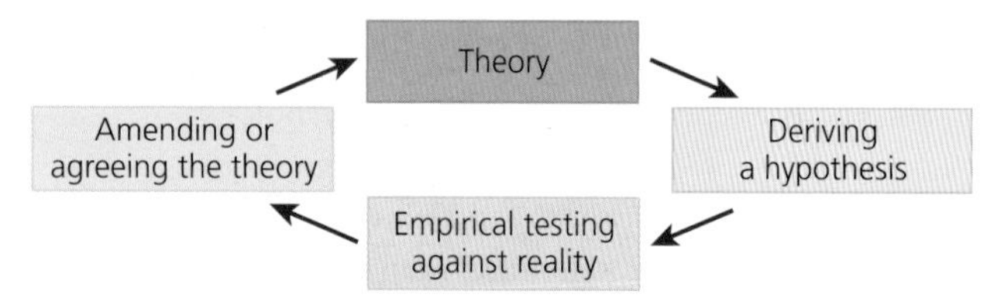

The hypothetico-deductive model

> **Explanation**
> **Empiricism** refers to getting data from the senses - touch, sight, sound, taste and smell. Such data are evidence for theories and hypotheses are generated from theories and then the statements are tested against reality (empirically) to see if the theory can be supported, amended or rejected.

Relating this idea to psychology

Psychology uses the hypothetico-deductive method a great deal, particularly for experimental research methods, questionnaires, brain scanning and methods like that. An idea is drawn from a theory, and a hypothesis put forward. The researcher makes sure that the variables in the hypothesis are measurable and then gathers data to test the hypothesis. From the findings, the researcher either concludes that they have supported the theory/idea or not and amends the theory accordingly. A case study, on the other hand, would perhaps have an aim, look at an individual in depth and consider their individual differences; it is thus unlikely to use a hypothetico-deductive method so clearly.

Generally, it would seem that psychology is a science with regard to the overall building of knowledge.

Falsification

Popper also emphasised the idea of **falsification**. His point is that nothing can be proved. A well-known example is the idea of testing the hypothesis 'all swans are white'. Someone can find a great many white swans but cannot prove all swans are white, because they cannot ever find and see all swans. However, if they find a black swan, they have disproved the hypothesis that 'all swans are white'. Science aims to falsify not to verify. If psychology is a science, it also must seek to falsify hypotheses.

Relating this idea to psychology

Relating the idea of falsification to psychology is difficult. For example, social identity theory claims that people act more favourably towards their in-group compared to any out-group member. This could be found many, many times (and has been), but if psychology is a science, just one instance where someone acted more favourably to an out-group member would be enough to disprove social identity theory. However, in psychology any general law or universal law is not 'proved' in this way, because the subject matter involves humans. There are going to be elements of chance and of individual differences to consider. In general, psychology does not try to falsify hypotheses and therefore it is not a science by this definition.

> **Explanation**
> **Falsification** is the idea that the only thing we can prove is that something is not the case - we cannot prove a positive. For example, though we know that the sun will rise every day, we cannot prove it. If one day the sun did not rise (which would of course be catastrophic for us!), then we can prove the negative - that the sun will not rise every day. Falsification is not often used in psychology. For example, many patients with brain damage have damage to areas related to the mediate temporal lobe, which contains the hippocampus, and they tend to have similar memory difficulties. So we accept the idea that this area of the brain is where short-term memory 'lives'. The best proof is that someone with damage in the same area has no problems with memory, but that may never be found. People have individual differences and there are issues with studying humans; therefore, psychology tends to rely on assuming that, if there are a lot of positive instances, then it is likely to be 'true'. This is not 'proof'.

Reductionism versus holism

Science also uses **reductionism**. To use the hypothetico-deductive method, a hypothesis must be specific and measurable. Sometimes it is hard to make a variable measurable because it is too broad and too many things affect it. For example, even the task of measuring the temperature of water is affected by air pressure; water boils at a different temperature in an aeroplane than at sea level. So measurement is reduced to one factor or feature. This is an example of reductionism.

Explanation

Holism means looking at something in its entirety, rather than breaking it down into parts, thus losing the 'whole'. By reducing elements of science to one factor, the 'whole' situation might not be studied. For example, brain scans usually study and measure one particular area of the brain rather than the working of the brain as a whole. It has been said that the whole is 'more than the sum of its parts'. **Reductionism** refers to studying things by looking at parts and not the whole. The idea is that something is just the sum of its parts and so there can be understanding by examining parts. For example, we can say the brain has many structures and specific functioning but it is not more than the total of those parts.

Relating this idea to psychology

Psychology does study the parts of human behaviour. Behaviourists study only observable behaviour, such as stimulus–response learning. For example, they look at how an association could be made between lifts and fear by transferring a fear of closed spaces to a fear of lifts. Taking a holistic approach to someone with a phobia of lifts might involve looking at their overall functioning to find out how to treat such a fear.

You could argue that case studies take a more holistic view of behaviour. For example, even though case studies of patients with brain damage narrow focus to one area of damage in the brain, which is reductionist (and testing takes place that is reductionist), there is an element of listening to the person's views and finding out in detail about their memory loss, such as in episodic memory. Experiments are likely to take a reductionist view, as both the IV and the DV have to be measured clearly. Overall, psychological research does reduce what is being measured to something measurable and testable and so, to this extent, it would fit the definition of science. Freud, however, did not look at measurable concepts – neither the id nor the unconscious are measurable (Chapter 3, pp. 166–175). There are also areas of psychology that take a holistic view.

Scientific subject matter

Sciences are areas of study where scientific methods are used. In general, there is a tendency to call certain subject matter 'scientific' because there are specific sciences such as chemistry, biology and physics. There are other sciences, including environmental science, geology and neuroscience.

Relating this idea to psychology

Psychology at A level is called a science because of its use of scientific methods, as argued above. Psychology covers subject matter that is regarded as 'scientific', such as DNA, genes, hormones, neurotransmitters, ideas of evolution, animal experiments, drugs and aspects of mental health disorders. To this extent, psychology is scientific. However, a significant proportion of the subject matter of psychology is less scientific. Theories discussed in the psychodynamic approach (in your course, given as an alternative explanation for aggression) are not measurable – for example, Freud's concept of 'the unconscious'. As much psychological material is not easily measured, it is therefore often thought of as 'not scientific'. The concepts of obedience, prejudice and learning are not easily operationalised.

STUDY HINT

Make a list of areas of psychology where the subject matter could be called 'science' and a list of areas where the subject matter is not scientific. This can help with revision and also helps in discussing psychology and science, which is required in the method for learning theories.

Progress check 5.56

Explain two of the issues around whether psychology is a science.

The paradigm

Thomas Kuhn talked about the need for a **paradigm**, or an overall theory, because hypotheses are deduced from an overall theory in order to build scientific and firm knowledge. It is hard to say what the paradigm in psychology is – it could be said to be pre-paradigmatic. The psychodynamic approach has a paradigm of its own but it is far from being accepted by everyone in psychology. Behaviourism is a paradigm as it has its own set of explanations about behaviour. The cognitive approach links with the biological approach and neuroscience, and it could be said that this is the most accepted and researched area of psychology and could thus be taken as the main paradigm. However, that would be to deny all the other areas in psychology and ideas that are well researched and contribute both to psychology and to society. In summary, it is not easy to explain psychology as one area of knowledge, which makes it hard to say it is a science.

Explore

Look up the work of Kuhn on paradigms.

Explanation

A **paradigm** is an accepted theory of how things work. Psychology has more than one theory of how things work so either has no paradigm or has many. Either way, without a single paradigm, it is hard to build one single body of knowledge, as science would tend to require.

Science and areas in psychology

The question of whether psychology is a science focuses on two aspects – scientific content and scientific methodology. The content, however, links with the methodology because it is content that is measurable, testable and subject to universal laws and therefore considered 'scientific'. Content that is less measurable or about individuals is not considered scientific. It follows that areas in psychology that use scientific methodology are thought of as more scientific than areas that do not, and have content that is more measurable and universal.

Social psychology

Social psychology uses a lot of experimentation. Milgram's work is experimental in that he controls variables as independent variables to measure a clearly operationalised dependent variable.

Explore

Consider the idea that Milgram's studies are not, in fact, straightforward laboratory experiments. The issue is that his main variable, which in his main study is setting the procedure up so that participants obey an authority figure, is not in fact an independent variable. This is because there is no other condition (such as having participants 'give' shocks without orders), as this would not be possible given the design. The careful controls and the carefully set up procedure and DV are why the studies are generally called laboratory experiments. Consider other studies you have looked at and think about the research methodology.

Sherif and Tajfel also carried out studies using experimentation. Sherif used field experiments and Tajfel worked in the laboratory. There is much evidence, therefore, to suggest that social psychology is scientific.

However, ethnographic studies – for example, looking at differences in gender roles across cultures – involve gathering qualitative data, which is almost the opposite of scientific method. This means a lot of social psychology is not regarded as scientific.

Finally, social psychology looks at concepts that are hard to make measurable, such as obedience and prejudice, as well as behaviour and gender roles. From the point of view of the content, therefore, social psychology is not a science.

Cognitive psychology

Cognitive psychology uses a lot of experimentation. Concepts such as 'memory' are studied by reducing them to parts that can be tested, such as memory for lists of words. For example, Baddeley (1966b) set up three experiments with very careful controls.

Cognitive psychology also uses case studies of brain-damaged people, where scanning and testing is done to find out how the brain damage has affected cognitive functioning. Such data are gathered scientifically. However, case studies of brain-damaged patients do use qualitative data and listen to individual patients to find out about them and about their memory issues.

Cognitive psychology looks at concepts that are hard to measure. However, as it looks at processing within the brain, there is a lot of biological information used, such as that gathered by scanning the brain to see where there is activity in certain situations. It seems, therefore, that, with regard to content, cognitive psychology is close to being scientific.

STUDY HINT

Prepare an answer to a question about how scientific each topic area in your course is. For each area, try to find evidence for and against it being scientific so that you are presenting an argument.

The psychodynamic approach

The psychodynamic approach focuses on the unconscious and the idea that a lot of what guides behaviour comes from unconscious wishes and desires. The unconscious, by definition, is not measurable or testable in a direct way. The personality is made up of the id, ego and superego, none of which is measurable. Freud gathered data about each individual to interpret what they say (and their dreams) and these data were qualitative. There is little that is scientific in the research methodology. In psychoanalysis, there has to be interpretation, which means there could be subjectivity with regard to the data, and science demands objective data from which to draw conclusions.

With regard to content, the psychodynamic approach is not scientific because the concepts are so hard to measure.

Biological psychology

Biological psychology is considered to be scientific. It uses a lot of experimentation, often on animals. For example, data are gathered by scanning the brain and studying its functions. However, case studies can be carried out non-scientifically – for example, twin studies (where MZ twins are compared with DZ twins) to investigate which characteristics derive from biology and which from the environment. Data are gathered from the twins and questionnaires or interviews may be used, with qualitative data being gathered.

With regard to content, biological psychology is scientific, as it is concerned with genes, hormones, neurotransmitters and brain functioning. Variables can be selected for study in these areas, although not always easily. In all these areas, a lot of the functioning is thought to be universal, which helps understanding not only of humans, but also of animals.

Learning theories

The learning approach specifically uses experiments to find out about learning and to separate learning into stimulus and response behaviour without focusing on thought processes that occur. Behaviour is made measurable and reduced to parts, so the methodology can be regarded as scientific. Some parts of learning theory may be considered less scientific: Bandura's work on social learning theory includes looking at cognitive elements such as motivation, for example. However, the research methods are scientific: the aim is to obtain information about general laws of behaviour through forming a hypothesis and testing it.

With regard to content, behaviour in general might be thought of as too complex and too individual to be scientifically studied. However, behaviourists have deliberately broken the content down into measurable parts in order to study it scientifically.

Table 5.21 Five areas in psychology from Year 1 and how far they might be seen as scientific

Approach	Scientific	Not scientific
Social	Experiments, objectivity, cause-and-effect conclusions	Ethnography, qualitative data, focus on the individual
Cognitive	Experiments, objectivity, scientific subject matter (brain and processing)	Processing hard to measure, some qualitative data (e.g. case studies)
Psychodynamic	Aimed at general (universal) laws	Concepts not measurable, case study method, qualitative data, focus on individual functioning, subjectivity possible (interpretation needed)
Biological	Subject matter (e.g. genes, hormones), experiments, objectivity, universal laws	Twin studies, case studies, subject matter can be hard to measure
Learning	Experiments, cause-and-effect conclusions, objectivity, measurable	Social learning theory includes cognition, such as motivation and attention

Test yourself

1 Discuss the scientific status of psychology, including reliability, validity, hypothesis testing and the use of controls. **(8 marks)**

2 Use different parts of psychology that you have studied to give evidence for both the claim that psychology is a science and the claim that it is not. **(16 marks)**

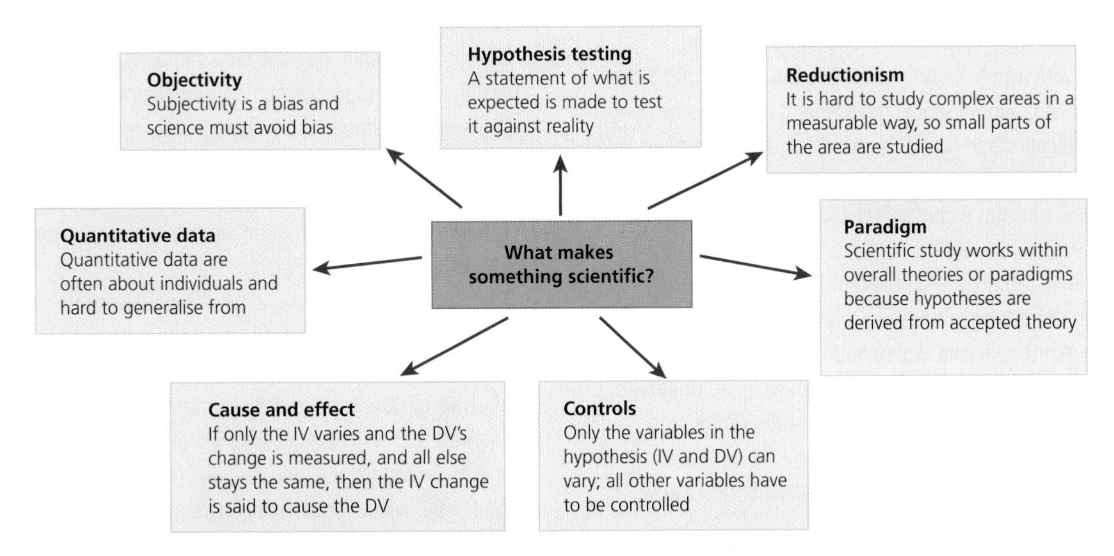

Elements of study that make something scientific

Chapter summary

Social psychology

The method you need to cover includes issues around questionnaire and interview use. This chapter focuses on the method elements but not the mathematical elements, which are found in Chapter 6.

- Types of interview covered: structured, unstructured and semi-structured. Elements around designing a questionnaire are important too. Closed (including ranked scales) and open questions are considered, as well as qualitative and quantitative data. Alternative hypotheses should also be understood.
- Researcher effects are looked at, as well as four sampling techniques.
- An important element of all research in psychology is covered in this section, and that is ethics.
- Analysis of qualitative data using thematic analysis is covered.
- Analysis of data, including measures of central tendency, measures of dispersion, bar charts and frequency tables, is covered in Chapter 6.

Cognitive psychology

The method you need to cover is experiment, field and laboratory. This chapter focuses on the method elements but not the mathematical elements, which are found in Chapter 6.

- Variables are important, including knowing about the independent and dependent variables, confounding variables, extraneous variables, situational and participant variables and operationalisation of variables.
- The experimental and null hypotheses are considered, as well as directional (one-tailed) and non-directional (two-tailed) hypotheses.
- Experimental/research designs are covered – matched pairs, repeated measures, independent groups.
- Issues with experiments, including counterbalancing, order effects and randomisation, are covered, as well as demand characteristics and control issues. Evaluation of experiments includes considering objectivity, validity and reliability.
- Analysis of data, including measures of central tendency, measures of dispersion, bar charts, histograms and frequency tables, are covered in Chapter 6.
- Issues of inferential testing are covered, including the Mann-Whitney U and Wilcoxon tests and related issues around probability and levels of significance, observed and critical values, use of critical values tables and sense checking data. Type I and Type II errors are covered, as is normal and skewed distribution. More detail is given in Chapter 6.

Biological psychology

The methods you need to cover are correlation, brain scanning and twin and adoption studies. This chapter focuses on the method elements but not the mathematical elements, which are found in Chapter 6.

- You need to know about correlations, including positive, negative and no correlation, as well as strong and weak correlations, and the use of scatter diagram. The mathematical element is covered in Chapter 6.
- Experimental method and correlation analysis are compared, including the independent and dependent variables compared with co-variables, issues of cause and effect (which experiments can show and correlations cannot) and issues of randomising to groups, which concerns experiments not correlations.
- Sampling and use of alternative, experimental and null hypotheses arise again (covered in social and cognitive psychology).
- Brain scanning is another required method (CAT, PET and fMRI), as are twin and adoption studies (one study that uses twin studies and one that uses adoption studies).
- Analysis of quantitative data includes using the Spearman's test and issues of levels of measurement, critical and observed values and levels of significance are covered, a lot of which is in cognitive psychology too. The mathematical elements are given in Chapter 6.

Learning theories

The methods you need to cover are observation and content analysis, as well as considering the scientific status of psychology. Using non-human animals in laboratory experiments together with ethical issues therein is also required. This chapter focuses on the method elements but not the mathematical elements, which are found in Chapter 6.

- Observations include qualitative and quantitative data, tallying, event sampling and time sampling, as well as types of observation (participant, non-participant, covert, overt).
- The scientific status of psychology involves consideration of replicability, reliability, validity, reductionism, falsification, empiricism, hypothesis testing and use of controls.
- The use of non-human animals in laboratory experiments and ethical issues are covered.
- The use of content analysis in psychology research is covered.
- Analysis of qualitative data using thematic analysis is required, which is already covered in social psychology.
- Analysis of quantitative data involves using the chi-squared test, with issues of levels of measurement, critical and observed values, and reasons for choosing the test – a lot of which is covered in cognitive psychology too. The mathematical elements are given in Chapter 6.

Chapter Six: Mathematical Elements

Introduction

In your AS/Year 1 A level course, for each of the topic areas, you will have to use mathematics to analyse results of studies. Psychology is a science and, as such, needs to have firm findings that can be challenged so that they can be used in, for example, policy and practice. In Chapter 5, you will have looked in detail at the scientific status of psychology (pp. 379-383) and you will have studied issues like reliability of data, validity, objectivity, credibility and generalisability. These issues link to how far findings from studies can be accepted and how firm and credible they are.

STUDY HINT

Link the ideas about how psychology is a science to any other sciences that you have studied, whether at GCSE, AS or A level. You will see that issues around controls and avoiding bias, such as getting fair results, are the same issues as those discussed when considering results in psychology. Be sure to use your learning of such issues when studying psychology.

You can take a calculator into your examination, so use one when studying this chapter to practise

The role of analysis in studies in psychology

In psychology, using a research method, data are produced. The data can take many forms, including written essays about friendship, videos of play behaviour, numbers of words recalled in a task, rankings of attractiveness, children's drawings and attendance rates at school. The data themselves are hard to sort into something that will be fairly easily understood, and so there is analysis, with the aim of displaying results in a way that suits the data and helps the reader. Table 6.1 considers types of data and some ideas about how the data might be analysed.

Table 6.1 Types of data and how they might be analysed

Types of analysis	Types of data	
	Qualitative data	**Quantitative data**
Qualitative analysis	Interpreting meaning	Qualitative data, using themes, can be turned into quantitative data
	From text, pictures, sounds	From, for example, open questions
	Examples: thematic analysis	Examples: bar graph, scatter diagram, tables
Quantitative analysis	Use content analysis or other ways to form categories (nominal level of measurement)	Use numerical data - ordinal, interval-ratio levels of measurement (categories might be used, nominal data, chi-squared test)
	And statistical testing	And statistical testing
	Such as a chi-squared	Such as Spearman's, Mann-Whitney U or Wilcoxon

Two ways in which data can be seen differently in terms of analysis are: 1) qualitative data, and 2) quantitative data.

Summary of analysis of qualitative data in your course

Qualitative data are data that are rich in detail and in the form of stories, ideas, feelings and comment. There are no mathematical calculations when analysing qualitative data but, as you will see, qualitative data can be 'turned into' quantitative data and then all the issues around analysis of quantitative data can apply. For example, if you analyse qualitative data from a questionnaire about prejudice to see how many people seem to focus on in-group preference, then you could count the number of people in that category and you would have quantitative data. Qualitative data can include comments such as 'I prefer going out with my friends as I find other people intimidating' or 'I like going to the same café because I am used to the people in the café'. There is more than just numbers in the qualitative data, which can add value – nonetheless, qualitative data can become quantitative data.

Once qualitative data are quantitative data, the same ways of analysing quantitative data will of course apply. Qualitative data can be analysed in a variety of ways, mostly focusing on clustering the data into some sort of themes. In Year 1, you will analyse qualitative data using thematic analysis, which is explained in Chapter 5 (pp. 290–292). As this chapter looks at mathematical analysis, analysis of qualitative data is not dealt with (unless it becomes quantitative in nature).

Summary of analysis of quantitative data in your course

Quantitative data are in the form of numbers, and mathematical calculations are used to analyse quantitative data. You are likely to have come across a lot of the information that follows in this section because you will have covered it in other subjects, such as GCSE Mathematics. However, reasonably full explanations are given here to help you not only with the mathematical elements of this course, but also to relate your learning to studies done in psychology.

Issues regarding the analysis of quantitative data in each topic area are summarised in Table 6.2. Chapter 5 explained in detail issues around both descriptive and inferential testing, in readiness for the mathematical element of your course, explained in this chapter.

Table 6.2 What you need to know regarding maths and analysis of quantitative data

You need to know about:	
Social psychology	**Biological psychology**
Calculating measures of central tendency – mean, median, mode	Positive and negative correlations
Frequency graphs and tables	Scatter diagrams
Bar charts	Spearman's correlation coefficient test
Measures of dispersion – range and standard deviation	Statistical significance
Cognitive psychology	Critical and observed values
Measures of central tendency – mean, median, mode	**Learning theories**
Frequency graphs, histograms and tables	Tallying
Bar charts	Chi-squared test
Measures of dispersion – range and standard deviation	Comparing observed and critical values
Percentages	Notes: • Social psychology 'maths' is repeated in cognitive psychology. • There are four inferential tests: different tests, similar issues. • Observed values, critical values and levels of significance are repeated (in cognitive, biological psychology and learning theories).
Mann-Whitney U test	
Wilcoxon signed-rank test	
Levels of significance – $p \leq 0.10$, $p \leq 0.05$, $p \leq 0.01$	
Observed and critical values, use of critical values tables (not for AS)	
Sense checking of data	
Normal and skewed distribution	

You can see that there is repetition between the topic areas. This chapter deals with the following requirements in your Year 1 course:

- measures of central tendency (mode, median, mean)
- producing frequency tables and tables in general
- graphical representation of quantitative data – bar chart, histogram, frequency graph and scatter diagram
- measures of dispersion (range and standard deviation)
- normal and skewed frequency distributions
- using inferential statistical testing and issues around doing such testing (building on Chapter 5)
- how to carry out the four named tests: Wilcoxon signed-rank test, Mann-Whitney U, Spearman rank correlation coefficient and chi-squared.

STUDY HINT

When working through this chapter, have a calculator to hand and use it to check figures. Make up some figures of your own and use them to practise what is being explained. The more you practise analysis using numbers, the easier it will be and the clearer it will become.

STUDY HINT

Check your state of mind when you hear words like 'maths' and 'statistics'. Do you shut down mentally? If so, there might be many reasons for this, such as lack of interest or fear of failure. You might be enjoying psychology but not want to do the 'maths' part. One way to overcome a 'block' in this way is to think about why this is necessary as that can help you to enjoy it. We have to know whether what is found out is worthwhile; otherwise neither policy nor practice could build on the findings. Use ideas about fear and phobias in learning theories to help, perhaps rewarding yourself for every ten minutes you spend studying what you find hard.

To help when studying something you find hard or not interesting, keep your motivation in mind. Perhaps you are studying psychology for career purposes. If not, then focus on what is motivating you to do A levels or to find out more about psychology, such as learning about people

General issues about analysing and displaying data

Some issues about analysis of data are general ones, which will occur more than once through your course, and which you are likely to have come across in studying other subjects, such as GCSE Maths. These are covered first. They are:

- measures of central tendency (mean, median, mode)
- using decimals
- normal and skewed distribution
- using tables to display data
- using graphs to display data
- measures of dispersion (range and standard deviation).

Measures of central tendency

As measures of central tendency are a main feature of analysis of quantitative data in psychology, they are explained near the start of this chapter. When you have a table of results, you should include the relevant measures of central tendency, whatever the research method used.

There are three **measures of central tendency** you need to know: the **mean**, the **median** and the **mode**. They cannot all be used for all data. When you learned about levels of measurement in Chapter 5, you will have seen that, when data are in categories (nominal data), then the measure is just 'this' or 'that', for example. You can count up the numbers in the categories, but this is not 'mathematical data' so only a mode is suitable. For ordinal data (when data are in order), you can use the median and mode. For interval data (when data are real mathematical measures), you can use the mean, median and mode.

The basics of measures of central tendency

Mode

This is the most usual score (the 'fashionable' one) in a set of scores. If there is not a single mode, then you can note more than one. If there are two, then the data set is bi-modal and there would not be normal distribution (the scores would be distributed oddly). The mode can be used for all data. The mode is an average in a way, and that is what is meant by 'central tendency'.

Median

This is the middle of a set of scores. If there is no actual middle, you work out the middle number. The median cannot be used for interval data (real mathematical measurements) because the rank scoring is not 'real' – there is no equal interval between the numbers. The median is an average in a way.

Mean

This is what tends to be known as the average of a set of scores (even though strictly the mode and median are in their own way also averages). Add the scores up and then divide by the number of scores (number of participants). The number of scores or number of participants is usually referred to as *N*. The mean can be used only for interval data (real mathematical numbers) because it involves real calculations (totalling and dividing).

Table 6.3 demonstrates how to calculate measures of central tendency.

Table 6.3 Calculating measures of central tendency; scores are memory span (number of letters recalled) and are taken to be interval data

<table>
<tr><th>Scores</th><th>Mode</th><th>Median</th><th>Mean</th><th>Ranking</th></tr>
<tr><td>6</td><td rowspan="4">See which score is repeated most. There are two scores of 6, so 6 is repeated the most.</td><td rowspan="4">See which is the middle score. It does not matter that there are two scores of 6, the median is still 6.</td><td rowspan="4">Add up the scores (6 + 8 + 6 + 3 + 7 = 30) and then divide by the number of scores (5). Mean is 6.</td><td>2.5</td></tr>
<tr><td>8</td><td>5</td></tr>
<tr><td>6</td><td>2.5</td></tr>
<tr><td>3</td><td>1</td></tr>
<tr><td>7</td><td>6</td><td>6</td><td>6</td><td>4</td></tr>
</table>

Definitions

The **mode** is the most usual in the set of scores, the score that appears most often. The **median** is the middle score - even if that is 'between' scores, it is what would be in the middle. The **mean** is found by adding up the scores and dividing by *N*. ***N*** is the number of scores (number of participants often, in psychology). The mode, median and mean are all **measures of central tendency**.

Calculating measures of central tendency

Mode

Sometimes there is no mode (no score is repeated), so it is not shown. Sometimes there are two modes (two scores are repeated the same number of times) and the data are bi-modal. With more than two modes, the numbers are multi-modal.

To find the mode, put the scores in order so it is easier to see which scores are repeated and how many times.

a scores: 5, 8, 9, 12, 15, 15, 15, 17, 21, 21, 21, 23 – you can see two modes here, 15 and 21.

b scores: 5, 5, 8, 9, 9, 12, 15, 15, 17, 20, 21, 22, 23 – you can see three modes here, 5, 9 and 15.

c scores: 4, 5, 7, 9, 11, 12, 14, 15, 17, 20, 21, 22, 23 – you can see there is no mode.

The mode is useful to show that there are scores that are repeated and so found often in a test or experiment. However, it might not represent the data set very well as the mode could be the lowest score – it is just that three people had that lowest score. The mode though does represent actual scores. The mean average is just the average of a set of scores and nobody might have actually achieved that score. The mode is at least a normal score. If a set of scores does not have normal distribution (pp. 390-392) then the mode will show the 'normal' score.

Median

There is only one difficulty when finding the median and that is if there is no middle score. In Table 6.3, there are five scores so the third score is the median. But if there were six scores, there is no middle score as such. Then you would need to add up the two scores that are around the middle score and divide them by two to get the median.

a scores: 4, 5, 7, 9, 11, 12, 14, 15, 17. There are nine scores so the middle one is the fifth, 11, which is the median score for this set of data.

b scores: 8, 9, 12, 15, 15, 15, 17, 21, 21, 23. There are ten scores so the middle one is between the fifth and sixth. The fifth score is 15 and the sixth score is 15 so, no problem, the median is 15: 15 (the fifth score) and 15 (the sixth score) = 30, divided by 2 = 15.

c scores: 4, 5, 7, 9, 11, 12, 14, 15, 17, 20. There are ten scores so the middle one is between the fifth and sixth. The fifth score is 11 and the sixth score is 12: 11 (the fifth score) and 12 (the sixth score) = 23, divided by 2 = 11.5. The median is 11.5.

The median is useful when the number of scores (*N*) is small but very hard to work out with a large set of data. It is not useful in that it does not show an outlying score; it just shows the middle of a set of scores. A median is useful as it can show where the majority of scores lie, which the mean average does not always show, if there are outliers.

Mean

There are no difficulties with a mean average. Total the scores and divide by the number of scores.

a scores: 4, 5, 7, 9, 11, 12, 14, 15, 17, 20. Use a calculator to find that added up these scores = 114. Divide by the number of scores (*N*), which is 10, so 114/10 = 11.4. The mean for this set of scores is 11.4.

However, the mean average must be used only for actual numbers that have equal intervals between them (sometimes called 'mathematical data' in this book because you can safely do mathematical calculations with them, such as calculating a mean average).

A mean average sometimes makes no sense, such as the average number of children in a family of 1.7 (using current UK statistics). Also a mean average can work out with many decimal points and that is often not helpful. Reduce it to one or two decimal places (see pp. 389-390).

Another issue with a mean average is that an outlying score can skew the data, making a mean average not very useful. For example, if scores are 5, 7, 9, 11, 12, 14, 15, 17, the mean is 11.25. If scores are 5, 7, 9, 11, 12, 14, 15, 30, the mean is 12.875. If scores are 5, 7, 9, 11, 12, 14, 15, 50, the mean is 15.375. One score changes the mean quite noticeably.

The mean is not suitable if the scores are not reasonably spread. For example, a set of scores 10, 10, 10, 10, 20, 20 would not be displayed usefully by using the mean of 13.3333.

STUDY HINT

You will use measures of central tendency in your practical investigations (see Chapter 7) and you can practise there. You will have covered measures of central tendency in your studies of maths in school, too, which should help. Be ready to do such calculations in an examination. You can take a calculator into the examination.

Mode is the most usual score in a set of scores. It works for all data.

Median is the middle score in a set of scores. It works for data other than interval data.

Mean is the average of a set of scores. It works only for interval (mathematical) data.

Measures of central tendency

Progress check 6.1

Give the mean, median and mode for the following scores: 9, 4, 7, 2, 5, 6, 8, 9, 2, 3, 2, 8.

Using decimals

Looking at the mean average has raised issues about decimal use, so that is briefly looked at here. When using numbers, decimal places are important. When using measures like a mean average in psychology, however, it is not necessary to use a lot of decimal places. Decimal places are fractions of numbers and divided numbers, which is rather specific for a figure like the mean average in psychology. Sometimes accuracy is needed, such as when using levels of significance (pp. 331-333); however, often decimal places can be kept to a minimum.

Choosing the number of decimal places

You could choose to show one or two decimal places with regard to many of the figures you will use. You might be asked to do a calculation in an examination and show one or two decimal places, or even three, so you need to know what this means.

Obtaining a decimal figure from a fraction

Decimals are a way of displaying data. If a fraction such as $\frac{3}{4}$ is found, this can be shown as a decimal figure: 3 divided by 4 is 0.75. A calculator will do this for you. 0.75 is a figure with two decimal places, which is fine for many purposes in psychology. To find a decimal figure from a fraction, take the top number and divide by the bottom number. (Do the same in fact to find a percentage, but then multiply by 100.)

Examples of use of decimal places

The mean averages given in the examples above were: 11.25, 12.875 and 15.375. Two of these are shown to three decimal places. To reduce to two decimal places, start at the end and round up or down. As 12.875 and 15.375 have a '5' at the end, you can choose whether to round up or down. By choosing to round up, 12.875 becomes 12.88 and 15.375 becomes 15.38.

Rounding up or down

To use 'rounding', start at the right-hand side of the number, the end of the number. Then decide whether to round up to the next figure (to the left) or not to round up (leave the number as it is). Do that for each number, one by one, from right to left. For example, 12.9846. The '6' at the end on the right-hand side is more than 5 (the middle number in decimals), so round up, to take that 'more' into account. Then you have 12.985. Then the '5' at the end, on the right-hand side is a middle number so choose to round up, to take it into account. You then have 12.99. The '9' at the end, on the right-hand side is a large number so round up. 12.99 becomes 13.0 because the other '9' has to be rounded up too. You will have done rounding in other subjects, so hopefully this makes sense and acts as a reminder.

Table 6.4 gives some decimal figures and changes them to one, two or three decimal places.

Table 6.4 Decimal figures to different decimal places

Decimal figure	Three decimal places	Two decimal places	One decimal place
12.9846	12.985	12.99	13.0
1.5723	1.572	1.57	1.6
15.4979	15.498	15.50	15.5
4.6273	4.627	4.63	4.6

Progress check 6.2

Put the following fractions into decimal figures using two decimal places. A bit of context is offered to give the calculations relevance.

1. 75 people out of 210 did not remember 5 ±2 – in decimal figures (75/210)
2. 4 people out of 15 wore red – in decimal figures (4/15)
3. 9 times out of 10 hitting a cone when driving a car – in decimal figures (9/10).

Normal and skewed distribution

As distribution goes with measures of central tendency, it is covered here. If the mean, median and mode are reasonably similar and focus around the middle of a set of scores (which will be the median), then there is normal distribution in the scores. Table 6.3 showed five scores that were normally distributed. The mean, median and mode were all 6.

If scores are bi-modal or multi-modal (have more than one mode), then scores will not be normally distributed.

If the mean, median and mode are not similar, then distribution will be skewed. If scores fall mainly below the mean, then that is **negative skew** and if the scores fall mainly above the mean, that is **positive skew**.

Distribution is only considered if the data are interval, what has been called 'mathematical' data, so that mathematical calculations can be carried out. Distribution is not considered for nominal or ordinal data. As a reminder, Table 6.5 illustrates the difference between nominal, ordinal and interval data.

Table 6.5 Nominal, ordinal and interval data

Level of measurement	Explanation
Nominal	Categories such as 'helping', 'not helping', 'watching'. E.g. tallies are made when observing such behaviour.
Ordinal	Ranks or ratings, such as rating on a scale of 0 to 10 for attractiveness. E.g. a score of 8 is 'attractive' and a score of '3' less attractive.
Interval	Actual scores that are mathematical in having equal intervals between them so that calculations can be done, such as the mean average. E.g. reaction times, height, age, numbers of words recalled.

Table 6.6 shows three sets of scores to demonstrate normal, positively skewed and negatively skewed distribution.

Table 6.6 Sets of scores demonstrating normal, positively skewed and negatively skewed distribution (number of words recalled out of 16 in a memory experiment)

Set of scores showing normal distribution	Set of scores showing negatively skewed distribution	Set of scores showing positively skewed distribution
2	2	2
3	3	3
5	3	4
6	3	5
6	4	6
9	5	7
9	6	8
9	6	8
11	9	12
11	11	12
13	12	12
16	13	16
Mode = 9	Mode = 3	Mode = 12
Median = 9	Median = 5.5	Median = 7.5
Mean = 8.33	Mean = 6.42	Mean = 7.92

Table 6.7 shows a frequency table for the 'normal distribution' data in Table 6.6.

Table 6.7 Frequency table for the 'normal distribution' data in Table 6.6

Score (number of words recalled in a memory experiment out of 16)	Frequency of that score occurring
0	0
1	0
2	1
3	1
4	0
5	1
6	2
7	0
8	0
9	3
10	0
11	2
12	0
13	1
14	0
15	0
16	1

The following three graphs show the frequency for the normally distributed scores, negatively distributed scores and positively distributed scores in Table 6.6.

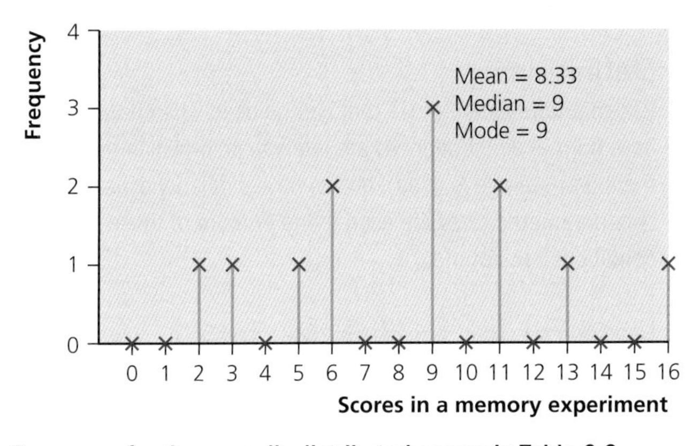

Frequency for the normally distributed scores in Table 6.6

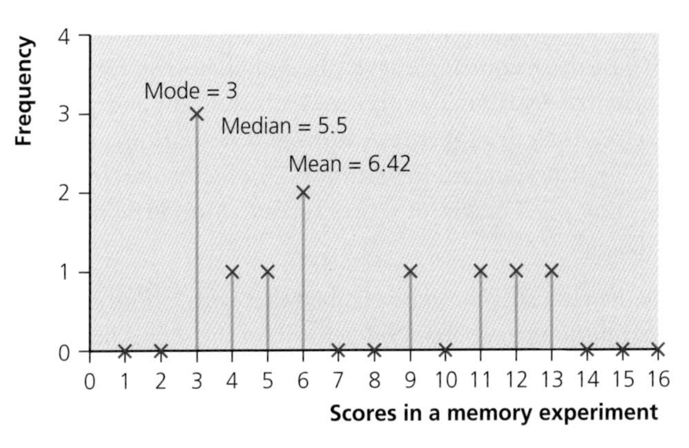

Frequency for the negatively distributed scores in Table 6.6

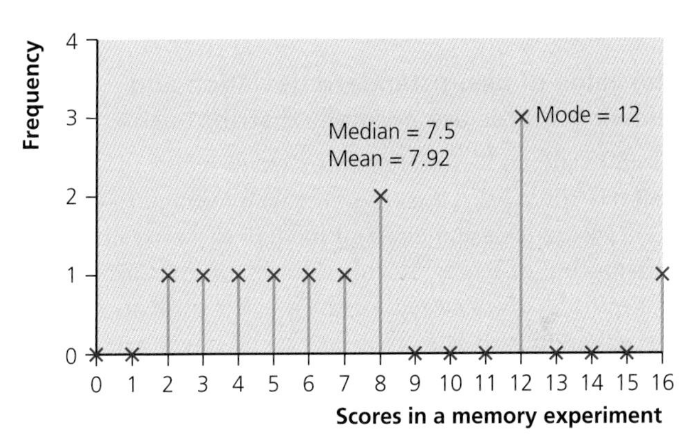

Frequency for the positively distributed scores in Table 6.6

Definitions

Normal distribution is when scores are clustered around the mean, and the mode, median and mean are very similar. **Positively skewed distribution** is when the scores are clustered above the mean, and the mode shows that. **Negatively skewed distribution** is when the scores are clustered below the mean, and the mode shows that.

Progress check 6.3

Given the following pattern of measures of central tendency, would you say the data will be normally distributed, negatively skewed or positively skewed?

1. mode 5.5, median 6.7, mean 6.8
2. mode 6, median 3, mean 3.6
3. mode 5, median 5, mean 4.8

Features of distribution linked to standard deviation – a bell curve

An important feature of normal distribution is that it has the features of what can be called a bell curve. The mean, median and mode are in the centre (more or less) of the frequency curve (the graph, above, for the normally distributed scores uses a histogram and you can see the curve there). A normal distribution curve can use the standard deviation (SD) of a set of scores to show percentages of scores spread around the mean average.

Mathematically, it can be claimed that with a normal distribution curve about 68 per cent of the scores lies within one standard deviation either side of the mean. The remaining 28 per cent lies within two standard deviations either side of the mean and 4 per cent lies outside two standard deviations. This sounds rather abstract but in fact does apply to real data.

The value of using standard deviation and knowing scores are normally distributed

As an example, it is useful to use exam scores in a test that has 100 marks. Assume the mean average to be 60 marks, with the mode and median showing normal distribution of scores. In this examination, assume it was quite easily accessed for the weaker students so there were not that many marks at the lower end, but hard for the stronger students so there were not that many marks at the higher end. Of course, these data are made up. The standard deviation for the set of scores is taken to be 8.5.

From characteristics of a normal distribution it is known that 34 per cent of the scores lie within one standard deviation below the mean – with a mean of 60 and the SD of 8.5, this is between 51.5 and 60 marks on the test. 34 per cent of scores lie above the mean within one SD, which is 60 + the SD of 8.5, which gives 68.5 marks. So 68 per cent of those sitting the examination had scores between 51.5 and 68.5 marks. Another 14 per cent are between 1SD and 2SD below the mean, which is 17 marks below the mean, giving 43 marks. Another 14 per cent are between 1SD and 2SD above the mean, which is 77 marks. So 96 per cent of those taking that examination got between 43 and 77 marks, and you can see that this is clustering quite tightly around the mean mark of 60. The other 2 per cent at the bottom got below 43 marks and the 2 per cent at the top got above 77 marks, so not many getting the higher marks. This is what the rather small standard deviation tells us. Hopefully, this helps to show the value of a) knowing the standard deviation as well as the mean, and b) knowing that the data are normally distributed.

The graph below shows a normal distribution and allocation of scores using the data explained in the example above.

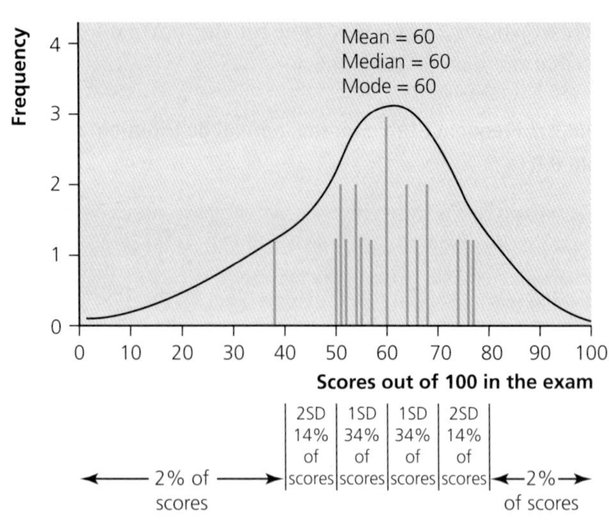

Normal distribution curve of examination scores

Why distribution matters

In your course, you are learning about four inferential tests, which you will know a lot more about if you have studied Chapter 5. The four inferential tests are referred to as 'non-parametric'. Although you do not have to know what 'parametric' means, you do need to know what 'non-parametric' means, and to explain that 'parametric' is needed.

Parametric tests rely on mathematical calculations being done, such as squaring numbers and square rooting them. This can only be done safely if data are normally distributed. A skewed distribution or an outlier that affects the mean average will distort the data sufficiently for a **non-parametric test** to be preferred. That is why you need to know about normal distribution. You choose a parametric test if there is normal distribution, interval ratio data and similarity in variance. Variance is discussed just below this section (page 395). You are only asked to use non-parametric tests because of the complications of using parametric testing, but knowing about it, in the detail given here, is very useful for your course. 'Parametric' means assuming characteristics of a number or set of data.

Definitions

Parametric tests are those that can be used when data a) have normal distribution, b) are interval/ratio (which means the mean average is used), and c) have similarity of variance. **Non-parametric** tests are used if one or more of these three conditions are not met.

Using tables to display data

When discussing measures of central tendency and frequency distribution, tables have been used (e.g. Table 6.6, pp. 390–391). Tables must be fully labelled, including a title to show exactly what the table displays. All columns and rows must be fully labelled, including totals columns and totals rows. A table must explain very clearly what the data are in the table. A table must stand alone and be understood without reading any of the explanation in the text.

Tables in this chapter tend to be fully labelled to show how this is done, though you have a choice of how to label a table. Be ready to draw up and label a table in your course, such as in your practical investigations (see Chapter 7).

Usually only quantitative data are displayed in tables but a table can include qualitative data, as in Table 6.1 when explaining how to turn qualitative data into quantitative data.

Frequency tables

You need to know how to use frequency tables (e.g. see Table 6.7). You need to decide what is to be displayed in a table and then draw up and label the table accordingly. In frequency tables, remember it is not the data themselves that are being displayed but the number of times they occur. The first column has all the possible scores and then the second column has the number of times in a set of data that each score occurs. You can have another column for tallying if you need to do that to decide the number for each score.

Frequency tables can summarise data by offering groups of scores so the table isn't too long. For example, a frequency table of the ages of 50 participants used in a study might have to list ages from 16 to 65. To make the table shorter, groups could be used, such as 16–25, 26–35, 36–45, 46–55 and 56–65 (Table 6.8).

Table 6.8 Ages of 50 participants responding to a questionnaire on prejudice

Age group of the participants	Tallying	Frequency
16-25	IIII	4
26-35	~~IIII~~ ~~IIII~~	10
36-45	~~IIII~~ ~~IIII~~ IIII	14
46-55	~~IIII~~ ~~IIII~~ II	12
56-65	~~IIII~~ ~~IIII~~	10
Total		50

Using graphs to display data

A graph is a visual display and usually two dimensional. It makes it easier to compare data. There are two axes, a vertical axis (y) and a horizontal axis (x). One way to remember which is which is to think of the horizontal axis as going 'across' the page – 'a cross' or an 'x'.

Both axes must be fully labelled as far as possible, and graphs in this chapter are carefully labelled to give examples of how to do it. Like a table, a graph must stand alone. A reader must be able to read a graph with all the information included.

Graphs can be used instead of tables to display data. Baddeley (1966b) used graphs in his study to display his data. An issue with the graphs in Baddeley's (1966b) study is that they do not clearly give the actual numbers. However, they do helpfully show patterns and trends, which the tables do not highlight as successfully.

You have to know about bar charts and histograms as well as scatter diagrams. Scatter diagrams are explained when mathematics in biological psychology is discussed (pp. 408–409). Bar charts are used when discussing mathematics in social psychology, as they are useful for displaying data from questionnaires (page 397). Histograms are useful for displaying frequency data and have already been used above in the graphs on page 000. Line graphs are not mentioned in your course but can be useful and are used in studies, so they are briefly explained in the cognitive psychology section of Chapter 5 (page 327). Table 6.9 details the types of graphs and what they are used for.

STUDY HINT

When drawing graphs, be accurate, include a title and labels, clearly show what the scores are, be simple, show trends and/or differences and show no distortion (which can happen if two graphs are to be compared but the scales are different).

Table 6.9 Types of graph and what they display

Type of graph	What is to be displayed and more about the graph
Scatter diagram	Relationship/correlation. Scores are plotted, one plot for each score, against the x and y axis. The graph on page 409 shows a scatter diagram.
Bar chart	Comparisons between categories (e.g. number of males and females in two conditions being measured). The graph on page 327 shows a bar chart. Columns showing different variables are not joined. Skewed distribution cannot be shown as data are in categories only.
Histogram	Frequency distribution. Data are quantities (such as the different age groups in Table 6.8) rather than categories. Columns may not be separated from one another (in a frequency graph though with some 0 scores, there will be separation). Histograms are used to show whether data are skewed or not (see graphs on page 391).
Line chart	Series of information. For example, showing scores for those with words that sound alike compared with scores for a control group.
Pie chart	Description of parts that make up a whole. For example, percentages of people in the age groups for Table 6.8 (percentages will give a whole, 100 per cent). An example of a pie chart can be found in Chapter 5, page 375.

Graphs are useful because they show data visually and quickly, and can help in understanding data, such as trends and differences. Being visual they can be easier to recall as well because there is a picture as well as words/numbers.

Progress check 6.4

Highlight six things that are wrong with the following table.

Scores	Tallying	
0-6	‡	2
7-13	‡‡	3
14-20	‡‡‡	
20-25	‡	2

Measures of dispersion

As measures of dispersion (range and standard deviation) are a main feature of analysis of quantitative data in psychology, they are explained in this general section. When you have a table of results, you should include the relevant measures of dispersion, whatever the research method used; and when a mean average is displayed, it is usual to show the standard deviation of the scores too, which you will have seen in studies you have been looking at. One example is Sebastián and Hernández-Gill (2012), whose study is in cognitive psychology in your course as a choice of contemporary study. They explain how digit span increases with age and present their results giving age, mean digit span and standard deviation. For example, 6 years, M=4.16, SD=0.56; 7 years, M=4.26, SD=0.54; 8 years, M=4.63, SD=0.54. This shows that, though the mean digit span is increasing as age increases (4.16 at 6 years old and 4.63 at 8 years old), the spread of scores is very similar (around 0.54 for all three age groups).

Range

The range of a set of scores is the highest to the lowest to show the spread of scores. Take the lowest score from the highest score to get the range.

a scores: 4, 5, 7, 9, 11, 12, 14, 15, 17. The range is from 4 to 17; 17 minus 4 = 13, which is the range of the scores.

b scores: 15, 18, 19, 21, 15, 36, 44, 56, 57, 68, 95. The range is from 15 to 95; 95 minus 15 = 80, so the range is 80.

c scores: 4.5, 5.9, 7, 8.6, 9, 10. The range is from 4.5 to 10; 10 minus 4.5 = 5.5, so the range is 5.5.

Standard deviation

Standard deviation refers to how far scores in a set of data vary from the mean. This can show whether a set of data are tightly clustered around the mean or spread out from the mean. This might not seem important but it does say something about the data. For example, if someone gets a 'C' grade in an exam, you get a 'B' grade and nobody gets any grade other than 'D', 'C' and 'B', that means that scores are not spread to include 'E' and 'A'. This shows that your 'B' grade was in fact rather good in the group and the 'C' grade might be good as well, if quite a high mark in that 'C' band. If, however, marks go to a top 'A' and a low 'E', then your 'B' grade does not look quite as good. Obviously, this is just an example! If you knew the standard deviation of the scores, you would know how good your score was. A high standard deviation means the spread of scores is wide; a low one means not so wide. 'High' or 'low' means in relation to the set of scores. In an example given below, the standard deviation comes out at 1.87, which is quite wide when scores are between 2 and 7, with a mean of 4.5. This example, however, has only b scores, so standard deviation is not so meaningful; b scores are used to show the calculation; more are needed to draw conclusions about the standard deviation of a set of scores.

Dealing with signs of numbers (e.g. +5 and –5)

One point about a standard deviation is that it deals with signs against numbers. Signs can pose a difficulty because a number can be the same (e.g. '5') and yet –5 and +5 are very different. In calculations, the sign needs to be taken into account and numbers are squared, which removes the sign, and then after the calculation, a square root is carried out, to take away the effect of squaring the data. The square root reverses the squaring.

Just to practise that for a moment, consider –5 as a number and square it. You get 25. Then consider +5 as a number and square it. You get 25. Then perhaps after doing calculations, you arrive at 36 (unlikely with this example, but it serves the purpose). You have squared the original numbers so to make sense of the sum at the end (36) you need to square root it, and get '6'. You will see that working out a standard deviation involves squaring numbers (multiply a number by itself to find the square) and square rooting (this can be done using a calculator). In algebra, a number squared is shown as X^2 (e.g. 5^2) and a square root is shown as $\surd$.

If two numbers are both minus numbers, two minuses = a plus. If two numbers are both plus numbers, two plus numbers = a plus. Multiplying two numbers together gets rid of the sign: two minuses = plus and two pluses = plus, so multiplying by two = plus signs.

Calculating the variance and the standard deviation

Use Table 6.10 to help in understanding this if you have not done it before.

When the idea of parametric testing was considered earlier in this chapter, variance was mentioned. Parametric testing is only possible if scores have similar variance. The variance is found before finalising the standard deviation. Calculating variance is part of calculating standard deviation and is about finding how much scores differ from the mean (how much they vary from the mean), including dealing with – and + signs.

The calculation: first, calculate the mean of a set of scores. Then find out for each score its difference from the mean, using a – or + sign accordingly. Then square each difference to get rid of the minus sign (calculating the standard deviation starts with finding the difference from the mean for each score and then squaring each difference). Add up all the squared differences (a total is shown by Σ in algebra) and you have the sum of the squared differences. The mean of the squared differences is the variance.

Work out the mean of the squared differences by dividing by the number of scores (N). Note that it is usual in psychology to use N-1 rather than N because it is a sample of the population being used not the whole population. So that practice is adhered to here and is the formula in your exam papers. Note also that N and n are interchangeable for your purposes.

The standard deviation is the square root of the variance, as this takes away the squaring that was done earlier.

Table 6.10 shows how to calculate the standard deviation (and variance) of a set of scores, given as Example 1.

Using the formula

A calculation like the standard deviation has a formula, which is given here. It might look complicated, but it is what is shown above and step-by-step you can use this formula.

Standard deviation:

$$\sqrt{\left(\frac{\Sigma(x-\bar{x})^2}{n-1}\right)}$$

$\sqrt{}$ is taking a square root at the end, which you can do using a calculator (look for the symbol shown here).

Σ is the sum of (add together to get Σ)

x is the score (six scores in this example)

$\bar{x}$ is the mean of the scores

^{2} means square the number

$n(N)$ = number of scores

The brackets mean all this has to be done first, before the square root.

The step-by-step calculation is given here (the example used is Example 1, given in Table 6.10):

Step 1: Work out for each score (gives you column 3 in Table 6.10) the difference from the mean.

Step 2: For each of the differences from the mean, square the number (gives you column 4 in Table 6.10).

Step 3: Add up the squared differences from the mean (see total of numbers in column 4 in Table 6.10).

Step 4: Divide by the number of scores minus 1 (in Table 6.10, there are six scores and 6 – 1 = 5).

Table 6.10 **Calculating the standard deviation (and variance) of a set of scores (Example 1)**

Participant	Score (x)	Difference from the mean for each score ($x-\bar{x}$)	Squared difference for each score $(x-\bar{x})^2$
1	5	5 - 4.5 = +0.5	0.5 × 0.5 = 0.25
2	3	3 - 4.5 = -1.5	1.5 × 1.5 = 2.25
3	4	4 - 4.5 = -0.5	0.5 × 0.5 = 0.25
4	7	7 - 4.5 = +2.5	2.5 × 2.5 = 6.25
5	6	6 – 4.5 = +1.5	1.5 × 1.5 = 2.25
6	2	2 – 4.5 = –2.5	2.5 × 2.5 = 6.25
n = 6	Mean $\bar{x}$ = 4.5		Total of the squared differences: $(\Sigma(x-\bar{x})^2)$ = 17.5
Standard deviation for this set of scores: Take the sum of the squared differences (17.5) and divide by the number of scores minus 1 (N – 1) (which is 5 in this example): 17.5/5 = **3.5, which is the variance.** Then square root the variance. The square root of 3.5 is the standard deviation, which is $\sqrt{3.5}$ = 1.87, **which is the standard deviation**. (Though from six scores a distribution cannot really be explained.)			

Progress check 6.5

This section has used the formula and also used an explanation to show how to work out the standard deviation (SD) of a set of scores. Hopefully, you have understood the sequences that you need to go through. Here is another set of scores for you to practise on, as it is only through practice that you will become happier with using these sorts of formulae. If you are comfortable with calculating the standard deviation, there is no need to do any practice. However, use it in your practical investigations where it is appropriate.

Table 6.11 gives some example scores for you to use to calculate the variance and the standard deviation (Example 2).

Table 6.11 Calculating the standard deviation (and variance) of a set of scores (Example 2)

Participant	Score (x)	Difference from the mean for each score ($x - \bar{x}$)	Squared difference for each score $x - \bar{x})^2$
1	10		
2	6		
3	15		
4	3		
5	20		
6	12		
N=	Mean = $\bar{x}$		Total of the squared differences ($\Sigma(x - \bar{x})^2$) =
Standard deviation for this set of scores: Take the sum of the squared differences and divide by the number of scores minus 1. This is the variance. The square root of the variance is the standard deviation.			

Step 5: Take the number in Step 3 and divide by the number in Step 4 to get Step 5. This is the variance.

Step 6: Square root the variance (the number in Step 5) and that is the standard deviation.

Progress check 6.6

Identify the following symbols in the standard deviation formula:

1 √ **2** Σ **3** N-1 **4** $\bar{x}$

Test yourself

1. Explain how measures of central tendency are chosen depending on the level of measurement/ type of data involved. **(4 marks)**
2. Explain what decisions affect which graph is chosen to display data. **(4 marks)**
3. How does the distribution of the data (skewed or normal) affect choice of statistical test? **(4 marks)**
4. Discuss why it is important to display data appropriately. **(12 marks)**

Mathematical elements in social psychology

In social psychology, the research methods focused on in your course are interview and questionnaire. Both gather quantitative data and these data require analysis. Interview data that are quantitative are analysed in a similar way as data from questionnaires and, since your practical investigation is a questionnaire, this is the analysis that is covered here.

Within the analysis of questionnaire data, percentages and bar charts are explained – two elements that you need to know about.

Questionnaire analysis

Questionnaires gather personal data (which will be in categories, such as male or female), quantitative data from closed questions and qualitative data from open questions. Chapter 5 explains more about the interview and the questionnaire research methods. This chapter deals with the mathematical element of research.

Analysing quantitative data from personal data questions

Using totals and percentages

A questionnaire gathers personal data, such as gender, age or type of upbringing. You can summarise such data neatly using percentages or just totals.

For example, if you have 200 questionnaires and 70 respondents are male and 130 female, you can simply state this feature of the questionnaires or use percentages. If using percentages, simply divide the number you have with the total number there are and multiply by 100. For example, $70/200 \times 100 = 35$ per cent. This means 35 per cent of the respondents are male and so 65 per cent are female.

Using bar charts

You can represent percentages or totals using a simple bar chart. There is one bar per item/measurement and the bar's height represents the score given. More information about using graphs to display data has been given earlier (pp. 393-394).

Using the data that 70 respondents were male out of 200 and 130 were female, a bar chart can be produced. The x axis of a graph is the horizontal one, along the bottom. The y axis is the vertical one, along the left-hand side. The bars will sit on the x axis, which is labelled 'Gender of the participants', with two bars inserted rising from the x axis, one labelled 'Males' and one labelled 'Females'. The y axis is labelled 'Number out of 200 respondents'. The title of the bar graph would be something like 'Number of males and females returning the questionnaire' (see graph below).

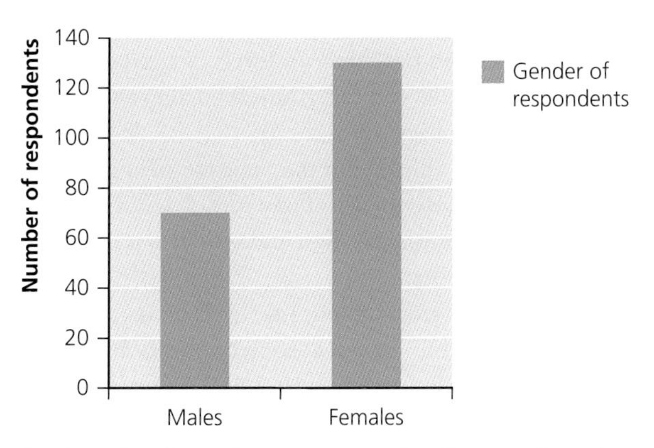

Number of males and females returning the questionnaire

Points about using a bar chart

- Always give a graph a full title.
- Always label both axes of a graph clearly, so that it tells the reader what the scores are.
- A bar chart can also be called a column chart if the bars are vertical.
- A bar chart can display the bars horizontally instead of vertically.
- The bars can be any width – it is the height that is important (if the bars are presented vertically, as is done here).

Analysing quantitative data from closed-ended questions

Example 1: using a Likert-type/ranked scale

Key: SA = strongly agree, A = agree, DK = don't know (unsure), D = disagree, SD = strongly disagree

Statement	SA	A	DK	D	SD
1* I like meeting new people.	☐	☐	☐	☐	☐
2* I enjoy finding out about others.	☐	☐	☐	☐	☐
3** I prefer the company of people like myself.	☐	☐	☐	☐	☐
4** I prefer to go out with my friends.	☐	☐	☐	☐	☐

A high score on the scale indicates 'liking new people'.

- *The scoring for statements 1 and 2 is from 5 for 'strongly agree' to 1 for 'strongly disagree'.
- **The scoring for statements 3 and 4 is from 1 for 'strongly agree' to 5 for 'strongly disagree'.

Participant 1

Statement	SA	A	DK	D	SD
1 I like meeting new people.	☑	☐	☐	☐	☐
2 I enjoy finding out about others.	☐	☑	☐	☐	☐
3 I prefer the company of people like myself.	☐	☐	☑	☐	☐
4 I prefer to go out with my friends.	☐	☐	☐	☑	☐

Participant 1 scores 16. The highest possible score is 20, so this is a high score and suggests that the participant likes new people.

Participant 2

Statement	SA	A	DK	D	SD
1 I like meeting new people.	☐	☐	☐	☑	☐
2 I enjoy finding out about others.	☐	☐	☐	☐	☑
3 I prefer the company of people like myself.	☐	☑	☐	☐	☐
4 I prefer to go out with my friends.	☐	☑	☐	☐	☐

Participant 2 scores 7. This is a low score and suggests that this participant does not like new people.

Example 2: yes/no/unsure answers

Fifty people answered a question on liking new people. The results are shown in Table 6.12.

Of those questioned, 60 per cent said they liked meeting new people, compared with 20 per cent who said they did not and 20 per cent who were unsure.

Table 6.12 Results of a question on liking new people

Answer	Number of answers	Percentage
Yes	30	60
Unsure	10	20
No	10	20
Total	**50**	**100**

Progress check 6.7

A questionnaire was carried out and 300 people took part: 100 were male and 200 were female. It was found that 60 males and 150 females showed hostility to an out-group. First, looking just at the information here, would you say that males or females showed more prejudice? Then work out the percentages of males and females who showed hostility/prejudice. Consider why it is helpful to have the percentages, rather than just making a judgement without them.

STUDY HINT

Figures can be hard to interpret. It is good to use a graph or percentages, or some way of displaying figures, so that interpretation is clearer. This is why analysis is important. Be ready to work out percentages or draw simple graphs, so that you can better interpret figures in studies.

STUDY HINT

Chapter 7 presents a practical investigation in social psychology for your course, which is a questionnaire. Data are suggested there, together with some analysis, and you can use these ideas about analysis in your own practical investigation too.

Data on a questionnaire can include ratings of agreement, such as asking whether older cars on the road are more dangerous than newer cars and ticking 'strongly agree', 'agree', 'don't know', 'disagree' or 'strongly disagree' – these are then quantitative data and scored according to the hypothesis

Analysing qualitative data from open-ended questions

Since respondents present their answers to open-ended questions in different ways, analysis of such qualitative data is in the form of generating themes, using **thematic analysis**. For example, participants were asked questions about their perception of their own levels of aggression, asking 'How far would you call yourself an aggressive person?'. Their responses were:

- **Participant 1**: 'I think I am the opposite of aggressive because I don't like conflict of any sort. I would always walk away from any aggression and would work hard to calm a situation down.'
- **Participant 2**: 'I worry about my levels of aggression. Sometimes I want to hit out at someone and, though I don't, I worry a lot that one day I will do just that. I would call myself aggressive, but under control. I don't understand myself sometimes because I don't like conflict, I just want to defend myself.'
- **Participant 3**: 'If you mean being aggressive when someone has a go at me, then yes I am aggressive, I would give back as good as I got. If you mean would I start a fight or something, then no, I would not start one.'

From these responses, the following three themes could be generated:

- not liking conflict
- wanting to hit out/back
- giving as good as I got/defending myself.

The participants' responses are then analysed by theme:

- not liking conflict – yes, 2; no, 0
- wanting to hit out/back – yes, 2; no, 0
- giving as good as I got/defending myself – yes, 2; no, 1.

Data from thematic analysis can also be direct quotes from the open questions, to illustrate the themes and the details that people tended to discuss. This chapter focuses on the mathematical element of your course. For more about analysis of qualitative data, see Chapter 5, which discusses methods in your course, including analysis of qualitative data (pp. 290–292). Here focus is on how qualitative data can be turned into quantitative data and analysed accordingly. As you can see, the data started off in qualitative form but were turned into numbers by counting how many times a theme or category was used.

Conclusions about thematic analysis generating quantitative data

More data would be analysed and, assuming similar themes were involved, a conclusion could be that people judge how others see them in terms of aggression using characteristics such as 'preferring to walk away' or 'only if provoked'. With regard to being aggressive, perhaps in general people think they should avoid conflict and should walk away, not starting a fight. However, if someone is aggressive towards them, some might feel they are entitled to defend themselves and to get aggressive themselves in order to do so. Themes can be then counted, and data will then be quantitative, so analysis can use statistical testing (see later in this chapter).

Issues with analysing qualitative data

Positives

- Using thematic analysis can help to reduce qualitative data to a manageable level to present them as results and for others to see conclusions from the study.
- Giving reasons for decisions when analysing can show evidence that others can follow, to check that there is minimal interpretation so the validity of the data is preserved.
- Two (or more) people can do the analysis separately and their findings compared to look for reliability.

Negatives

- No matter how transparent the process is, there is going to be interpretation, such as themes being chosen to represent the data. Such interpretation can have an element of subjectivity.
- Qualitative data tend to involve a snapshot of a situation at a particular moment and place, and analysis should reflect that element of reliability in the data.
- If coding to get categories that can then be counted to become quantitative data, then that coding will reduce the data in some form, a process that carries likely bias.

Comparing analysis of qualitative data with analysis of quantitative data

- **Validity**: Qualitative data are analysed into themes to retain the element of depth and detail, with a strong focus on retaining validity. Quantitative data are reduced to numbers so there is less depth and detail, so less validity.
- **Reliability**: Qualitative data involve depth and detail and are likely to be ideas at one moment in time and in one place, which suggests they may not be reliable in a scientific sense. Quantitative data gather less detail and are less personal in that sense, so might be found at another time and on another occasion. Also the way quantitative data are gathered means the study is more easily repeated, for the reasons given here (e.g. time and place affect them less).
- **Generalisability**: Qualitative data tend to focus on one person or a group and sampling is limited. A study using quantitative data is likely to be more replicable as measures are more tightly controlled, so a sample can be larger and more carefully chosen. Careful sampling means generalisability is possible, so qualitative data have less generalisability (in general) than quantitative data.
- **Scientific credibility**: Qualitative data involve depth and looking carefully at a situation, individual or group. Controls and careful measuring of variables is not often a feature of studies gathering qualitative data. A study using quantitative data is likely to have control, not only over what is being measured, but over other variables too. A carefully controlled study is more likely to have scientific credibility than a less controlled study, so quantitative data tend to have more credibility.
- **Objectivity**: Qualitative data tend to require interpretation in analysis and so there might be an element of subjectivity in analysis. Also in themselves qualitative data can require subjectivity in the sense of wanting people's own views. Quantitative data, with focus on scientific credibility, are aiming for objectivity, so there is no subjective bias.

STUDY HINT

When evaluating in psychology, you should draw on issues of reliability, generalisability, subjectivity/objectivity, validity and credibility. Work out a mnemonic for them if you have not done so already, such as 'really good students open various coursebooks'.

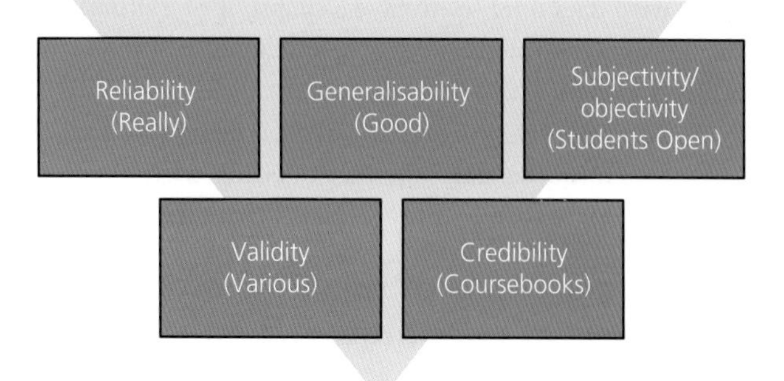

Terms used to evaluate methods with a mnemonic to help memory

Test yourself

1. Explain, using your own examples, how to use thematic analysis when analysing qualitative data. **(8 marks)**
2. Assess issues with analysing qualitative data compared with analysing quantitative data. **(12 marks)**

Mathematical elements in cognitive psychology

In cognitive psychology for your course, you need to know about the experimental research method. For the mathematical requirements, you need to know about measures of central tendency (mean, median and mode), measures of dispersion (range and standard deviation), percentages, frequency tables, bar charts, histograms and frequency charts, which are areas that have been covered earlier in this chapter. Table 6.13 shows where you can find details of these aspects, if not covered in this section.

Inferential tests

It is in cognitive psychology that we first come across the idea of inferential statistical testing. For cognitive psychology, you are asked to know about two inferential tests, the Mann-Whitney U test and the Wilcoxon signed-rank test. For biological psychology, you need to know the Spearman rank correlation coefficient and, for learning theories, you need to know the chi-squared test.

You will have learned the elements of what is required to use statistical testing in Chapter 5, but the 'whole' process is explained in this chapter. Often when the mathematical testing draws on other methodological issues, they are briefly outlined here, with more detail given in Chapter 5. If you study the main topic area chapters (Chapters 1–4) for an overview, then Chapter 5 to learn about the methodology and then Chapter 6 to learn about mathematical elements, you will find issues are repeated somewhat, which should help your learning. If you are studying Chapter 6 in isolation, then you can look up some of the method issues if you are not sure about them.

- The detail of what you need to understand about inferential tests is covered in Chapter 5 (pp. 328-336).
- You will be using a Mann-Whitney U test, a Wilcoxon signed-rank test, a chi-squared test and a Spearman's test, which are explained in this chapter.
- A summary of issues involved in inferential testing is given here.

Choosing and using an inferential test involves some careful steps/calculations but, taken one at a time, none of them is difficult. In order to choose a test and carry one out, you need to know a lot about your study first, including the level of measurement of the data, your design, whether your hypothesis is directional or not (one- or two-tailed) and whether your study involves looking for a difference or a relationship between the variables. You should also choose a level of significance. Then you can choose and run your test.

Table 6.13 Mathematical elements in cognitive psychology and where to find details in this book

Area to be covered relating to maths in cognitive psychology	Where to find details in this chapter
Measures of central tendency (mean, median, mode)	pp. 387-389
Measures of dispersion (range and standard deviation)	pp. 394-396
Graphs - bar chart, frequency graph, histogram	pp. 393-394
Percentages	p. 397
Inferential statistics	In this section, from p. 400

Issues involved in choosing and using a test

- Determine the level of measurement – nominal (categories), ordinal (ranked data) and interval/ratio (real mathematical scores). Levels of measurement are outlined above (pp. 330).
- Review the study to find the participant design. If the hypothesis is testing for a relationship, then the design is a correlation. If the hypothesis is testing for a difference, the design is either:
  - matched pairs or repeated measures (taken as one design for the purpose of inferential testing and, in your course, the test is the Wilcoxon signed-rank test); *or*
  - an independent groups design (Mann-Whitney U test for ordinal or interval/ratio data; chi-squared for nominal data).

  Designs are explained in Chapter 5 (pp. 321–323), so look there if you cannot remember this information.
- Review the alternative (experimental) hypothesis to see if it is directional (one-tailed test needed) or non-directional (two-tailed test needed). Directional means that the hypothesis states the predicted direction of results. For example, 'boys play *more* noisily and girls are *more* involved in quiet play' is directional (one-tailed). These issues are discussed in Chapter 5 (p. 318).
- Review the hypothesis to see whether a difference or a relationship is predicted. If a relationship is predicted, then a test for correlation is needed (Spearman's rank correlation coefficient). For a test of difference, use one of the other three tests. The tests of difference in your course are the Mann-Whitney U test, for looking at a difference when scores are ordinal or interval/ratio and the design is independent groups; the Wilcoxon signed-rank test, for looking at a difference when scores are ordinal or interval/ratio and the design is repeated measures or matched pairs; and the chi-squared test, when looking for a difference, and using nominal data and an independent groups design.
- Choose a level of significance. For your purposes, $p \leq 0.05$ or $p \leq 0.01$ level of significance is likely to be suitable, though sometimes other levels are used. A probability of 0.05 means a 1 in 20 (5 in 100) likelihood that the results are due to chance; 0.01 means a 1 in 100 likelihood; $p \leq 0.025$ means 25 in 1,000 likelihood that the results are due to chance. With these probability levels, the results are accepted as statistically significant. The least significant but still accepted is $p \leq 0.05$ and the most significant in the examples here is $p \leq 0.025$. In your course $p \leq 0.10$ is mentioned and that means 10 in every 100 people would go against your hypothesis, which is considered too large to be accepted in psychology. Levels of significance are explained in Chapter 5 (pp. 331–333), so look there if you cannot remember or have not learned this information.
- Write out the null hypothesis, which says that any difference or relationship predicted by the alternative (or experimental) hypothesis is due to chance and not due to the manipulation of the independent variable.
- Choose the Spearman test if the hypothesis predicts a correlation and the level of measurement of data is at least ordinal. Both scores must be on a scale that can be ranked or real scores (equal intervals between the scores).
- Choose the Mann-Whitney U test if the level of measurement of the data is ordinal or interval/ratio, if the hypothesis predicts a difference and it is an independent groups design.
- Choose the Wilcoxon signed-rank test if the level of measurement of the data is ordinal or interval/ratio, if the hypothesis predicts a difference and it is a repeated measures or matched pairs design.
- Choose a chi-squared test if the level of measurement of the data is nominal, the hypothesis predicts a difference and it is an independent groups design.
- Carry out the relevant test using the step-by-step instructions in this chapter: for the Spearman test, pp. 409-411; Mann-Whitney U test, pp. 404-406; Wilcoxon signed-rank test, pp. 403-404; chi-squared test, pp. 412-416.
- Find the relevant critical value table. There is more than one table for the Mann-Whitney U test so check that it is the correct one for your chosen level of significance. Determine whether the test must be one-tailed or two-tailed. Tables can be found in statistics textbooks and on the internet, as well as in your examination papers and your specification.
- For the Spearman test, the Wilcoxon and the Mann-Whitney U test, find N (or n), which is the number of participants. For the Mann-Whitney U test, where the participant design is independent groups, there are two N scores (because there are two groups). For the Mann-Whitney U test, use the U (U_1 or U_2) which is the smaller of the two. For the Wilcoxon test, N is not quite the number of participants; $N =$ the number of differences there are that are not 0. This makes more sense when the test is worked through.
- For the chi-squared test, find the degrees of freedom (*df*). For a two-by-two table, $df = 1$. The degrees of freedom, *df*, is the number of rows minus 1 multiplied by the number of columns minus 1. Step-by-step instructions for calculating this are given later (page 000).

- Use the tables to find the critical value for the test. This depends on *df* and/or *N*(*n*), the level of significance and whether the test is one- or two-tailed.
- Check the result of your test against the critical value. For the result to be significant and the null hypothesis (that the resulting data are due to chance) to be rejected, the Mann-Whitney U test and the Wilcoxon test require the result (*U* and *T*, respectively) to be equal to or *less* than the critical value to be significant. The chi-squared and Spearman tests requires the result (χ^2 and *rho*, respectively) to be equal to or *greater* than the critical value.
- Note whether your null hypothesis is rejected (or whether the test is significant).

STUDY HINT
Issues around choosing a statistical test are covered in Chapter 5 (pp. 330–331) and there is a table there to help you to choose, as well as giving ideas about reasons for the choices.

Progress check 6.8

With regard to the four statistical tests in your course, complete the following table:

Statistical test	Does the observed value have to be equal to, greater than or less than the critical value in the table (in order to be significant)?
Mann-Whitney U (U)	
Wilcoxon signed-rank (T)	
Spearman's rank correlation coefficient (rho)	
Chi-squared (χ^2)	

Test yourself

1 Explain what critical values tables are and how to use them to find significance. **(6 marks)**
2 Explain what information is needed in order to choose an appropriate statistical test. **(6 marks)**

Choosing a Mann-Whitney U test or Wilcoxon signed-rank test

The first two tests in your course, working in order through the specification, are the Mann-Whitney U and the Wilcoxon signed-rank test. The Spearman's test is considered in the biological psychology section of this chapter (pp. 409–411), and the chi-squared in the learning theories section (pp. 412–416).

In cognitive psychology, you are asked to carry out for your practical investigation an experiment that uses either a repeated measures (or matched pairs) or an independent groups design and generates at least ordinal data. This means you will carry out a Mann-Whitney U test or a Wilcoxon test to see if your results are statistically significant. The diagram below shows the factors affecting your choice of test.

Mann-Whitney U test
- Test of difference
- Independent groups design
- Data at last ordinal (can be interval/ratio)

Wilcoxon signed-rank test
- Test of difference
- Repeated measures/ matched pairs design
- Data at last ordinal (can be interval/ratio)

Factors affecting choice of Mann-Whitney U or Wilcoxon signed-rank test

You need to know how to use both a Mann-Whitney U test and a Wilcoxon signed-rank test for your course, even though you will only use one in your practical investigation. It is worth generating some data of your own and practising using the two tests.

Using the Wilcoxon signed-rank test

The Wilcoxon test is covered first, partly because it does not have an algebraic formula as such, and is for that reason more straightforward than the Mann-Whitney U test. However, with practice, all four tests in your course are accessible.

The procedure when carrying out a Wilcoxon signed-rank test

- For each pair of scores in a data set, calculate the difference between two scores by taking one from the other.
- Rank the differences, giving the smallest difference Rank 1.
- Note: do not rank any differences of 0 and, when adding the number of scores, do not count those with a difference of 0, and ignore the signs when ranking the difference.
- Add up the ranks for positive differences.
- Add up the ranks for negative differences.
- T is the figure that is the smallest when the ranks are totalled (may be positive or negative).
- *N* (*n*) is the number of scores left; ignore those with 0 difference.

Carrying out a Wilcoxon signed-rank test on example data

The hypothesis that is chosen for the example here is: 'There is a difference in recall in long-term memory of the order of ten words depending on whether they sound alike or have similar meaning.' The null hypothesis is: 'There is no difference in recall of the order of ten words depending on whether they sound alike or have similar meaning and any difference is due to chance or some other variable.'

This hypothesis is two-tailed because direction has not been predicted. The hypothesis does not say whether the words with similar meaning will be better recalled (in order) than the words that sound alike, or vice versa.

The level of significance chosen is $p \leq 0.05$ because this is the most lenient level accepted in psychology (0.05, which is 5 people out of 100) so the most suitable for the purpose of this example.

Table 6.14 shows scores for ten participants in our example study.

Checking for significance using sense checking

Participant 2 shows no difference between the two conditions so that one is discounted when considering whether a significant difference would be found or not.

Participants 6, 7 and 9 all do better in the 'sound alike' condition.

Participants 1, 3, 4, 5, 8, and 10 all do better in the 'similar meaning' condition.

A **sense check** seems to show that participants did better in the condition where words had similar meaning, though perhaps there is not much of a difference.

Definition

A **sense check** means looking carefully at data in a table or a graph to see if it looks as if the appropriate statistical test would show a significant difference or relationship or not. This can be called an eye-ball test. You may have come across this before when studying other sciences.

Table 6.14 Example scores for ten participants: number of words correctly recalled in order depending on whether they sound alike or have similar meaning in a long-term memory task

Participant	Number of words recalled in order that sound alike (out of ten)	Number of words recalled in order that have similar meaning (out of ten)	Difference between the two scores	Ranks for the differences, ignoring the signs and the 0 score – then put the sign back
1	6	8	-2	5 -
2	4	4	0	
3	5	7	-2	5 -
4	3	6	-3	8.5 -
5	7	9	-2	5 -
6	8	7	+1	1.5 +
7	7	5	+2	5 +
8	4	7	-3	8.5 -
9	5	3	+2	5 +
10	5	6	-1	1.5 -
Mode	5	7		Total the ranks with - sign = 33.5 Total the ranks with + sign = 11.5
Median	5	6.5		
Mean	5.4	6.2		
Range	5	6		
Standard deviation	1.58	1.81		
			T = 11.5 (this is the smallest of the two totals)	

Checking for significance using the test

Critical values tables are used to see if T = 11.5 is a significant observed value. You need to know:

- N (n) = 9 (one score was not used because the pair of scores showed no difference)
- $p \leq 0.05$
- two-tailed
- For the Wilcoxon test, the observed value must be equal to or less than the critical value

Table 6.15 shows critical values for the Wilcoxon signed-rank test. The numbers relevant to this example are in bold.

Table 6.15 Critical values for the Wilcoxon signed-rank test

	Level of significance for a one-tailed test		
	0.05	0.025	0.1
	Level of significance for a two-tailed test		
n	0.1	**0.05**	0.02
5	0	-	-
6	2	0	-
7	3	2	0
8	5	3	1
9	8	**5**	3
10	10	8	5
11	13	10	7
12	17	13	9

- To use the table:
  - Find n, which is the number of participants minus any 0 differences; in the example set, there is one 0 so the number of participants used is 9.
  - Look for the two-tailed columns.
  - Look for the chosen level of significance in the right columns.
- Using the critical values tables, it can be seen that the critical value when n=9, p is 0.05 and two-tailed is 5. T is greater than 5 so is not significant at $p \leq 0.05$.
- The null hypothesis is accepted: it is not found that there is a difference in recall of the order of words whether they sound alike or have similar meaning. Any difference is not significant.
- The sense check was not borne out by the statistical test, which is interesting, though the T value was rather low. Although three out of the nine participants had results in favour of acoustic similarity and six out of nine in favour of semantic similarity, there simply were not enough differences found.

Progress check 6.9

Using Table 6.15, find out whether the following data are statistically significant:

1. T = 13, $p \leq 0.05$, one-tailed, n = 12
2. T = 8, $p \leq 0.025$, one-tailed, n = 10
3. T = 4, $p \leq 0.05$, two-tailed, n = 8

Using the Mann-Whitney U test

As with other tests, the formula for the Mann-Whitney U test can look rather difficult but if you work through step-by-step, you will find it is not as difficult as it might look. In this chapter, it is assumed that everyone is starting from the beginning. You can read quickly through the procedures if you understand them.

Carrying out a Mann-Whitney U test

The formula may look complicated but, as with the Spearman test, a step-by-step approach can be taken.

$$U_A = N_A N_B + \frac{N_A(N_A + 1)}{2} - \Sigma R_A$$

$$U_B = N_A N_B + \frac{N_B(N_B + 1)}{2} - \Sigma R_B$$

Suppose that a group of seven females and a group of eight males are set the task of completing an eight-piece jigsaw and the time (seconds) taken to complete the jigsaw is recorded. The hypothesis is that males will be better than females at jigsaws (males are supposed to be better than females at visuospatial tasks). When following the steps, refer to Table 6.16.

Step 1: If one group is smaller, this is group A. If there are the same number of participants in the group, just call one group A. (Here, N_A = **7**; N_B = **8**)

Step 2: Rank all the scores together as if they are one set of scores from one group.

Step 3: Consider the groups separately and find the total (ΣR_A) of the ranks for group A. (Here, ΣR_A = **79**.)

Step 4: Find the total (ΣR_B) of the ranks for group B. (Here, ΣR_B = **41**.)

Table 6.16 Scores (time in seconds that it took) for males and females doing an eight-piece jigsaw (made-up scores)

Participants, N_A = 7 (Step 1)	Scores for females	Rank (from all 15 participants) (Step 2)	Participants, N_B = 8 (Step 1)	Scores for males	Rank (from all 15 participants) (Step 2)
1	123	13	1	95	8
2	89	5	2	78	2
3	140	14	3	102	10
4	97	9	4	79	3
5	110	12	5	84	4
6	150	15	6	93	7
7	104	11	7	62	1
			8	92	6
	Total rank, R_A (Step 3): 79			Total rank, R_B (Step 4): 41	

Steps 5 to 9 provide a test result (U_A) for group A:

Step 5: Multiply N_A by N_B. (Here, 7 × 8 = **56**)

Step 6: Add 1 to N_A and multiply the result by N_A. (Here, (7 + 1) × 7 = **56**.)

Step 7: Divide the answer to Step 6 by 2. (Here, 56 ÷ 2 = **28**.)

Step 8: Add together the answers to Step 5 and Step 7. (Here, 56 + 28 = **84**.)

Step 9: Subtract the answer to Step 3 from the answer to Step 8. (Here, 84 – 79 = **5**.)

This result is U_A. (Here, U_A = 5.)

Steps 10 to 15 provide a test result (U_B) for group B.

Step 10: Multiply N_A by N_B. (Here, 7 × 8 = **56**.)

Step 11: Add 1 to N_B and multiply the result by N_B. (Here, (8 + 1) × 8 = **72**.)

Step 12: Divide the answer to Step 11 by 2. (Here, 72 ÷ 2 = **36**.)

Step 13: Add together the answers to Step 10 and Step 12. (Here, 56 + 36 = **92**.)

Step 14: Subtract the answer to Step 4 from the answer to Step 13. (Here, 92 – 41 = **51**.)

This result is U_B. (Here, U_B = 51.)

The smaller of U_A and U_B becomes U and is the number to look up in statistical tables to see whether or not the result is significant. For the example given, U_A is smaller than U_B, so U = 5.

Using critical values tables for the Mann-Whitney U test

To find out if the results of a statistical test are significant, you have to look it up in a critical values table (see Table 6.17). If your number of participants is not included in Table 6.17, you will need to find a full table in a statistics book or on the internet. To be significant, the value of U has to be equal to or less than the critical values shown in Table 6.17.

Note that the table given here assumes a one-tailed test is appropriate, which means that the hypothesis being tested is directional. For a non-directional hypothesis, a two-tailed test is appropriate and a different table would be needed.

Table 6.17 Critical values of *U* for a one-tailed test, level of significance $p \leq 0.05$

N_A	N_B				
	8	9	10	11	12
7	13	15	17	19	21
8	15	18	20	23	26
9	18	21	24	27	30
10	20	24	27	30	33
11	23	27	31	34	37
12	26	30	34	38	42

Explanation

Tables of critical values can be found in statistics textbooks or using the internet. There are also critical values given in your examination papers.

Assuming that you need a one-tailed test and have calculated the U value, all you have to do is to compare the critical value from Table 6.17 for the number of participants in each group with your U result. If your own U is larger than the critical value, then the data from your study are not significant at $p \leq 0.05$ (assuming the hypothesis is one-tailed, as this one is).

In the example, the hypothesis was that males would be better at jigsaws. This is a directional hypothesis (it gives direction, because it says males will be better), so a one-tailed test is suitable. The test gave a value of $U = 5$. This is less than 13, which is the critical value when N_A is 7 and N_B is 8 (Table 6.17). Therefore, the result is statistically significant and supports the hypothesis.

Progress check 6.10

Using Table 6.17, find out whether the following data are statistically significant:

1 $U = 20$, $p \leq 0.05$, one-tailed, $N_A = 10$, $N_B = 10$
2 $U = 39$, $p \leq 0.05$, one-tailed, $N_A = 12$, $N_B = 11$

Test yourself

Explain how you find the information needed so that you can decide whether the observed value from a Mann-Whitney U test is significant or not. **(8 marks)**

Mathematical elements in biological psychology

In biological psychology in your course, you will cover correlation analysis. Chapter 5 explains more about using correlations (pp. 339–341) and this chapter focuses on the mathematical elements and analysis you need to know with regard to correlations.

Correlation analysis

Correlation data can come from different research methods, such as questionnaires or tests. Any data that involve two measured variables to be compared to see if there is a relationship can be analysed using correlation testing. The two variables must both have an actual measurement and not just be categories, and scores for both variables must be available for each participant or each variable. The idea is to see if the way something varies in a person relates to the way something else varies. This is not always about people. For example, studies are done to see if the hotter the day, the more aggression there is, measured by the number of cars hooting their horns in a busy city.

Examples of correlations

One example of a correlation is the older people get, the shorter their memory span becomes. Age is something that varies, as does memory span, and both are measured using real numbers.

STUDY HINT
Sebastián and Hernández-Gil (2012), one of the contemporary study choices in cognitive psychology, look at age and memory span and show that from 5 years old to about 17 years old memory span increases but elderly people then have a short memory span again, so it seems that as we get older (from adulthood) our memory span declines. Use material from your course, whenever you can, to make links and help learning.

STUDY HINT
You are asked to carry out a practical investigation that leads to correlation analysis in biological psychology in your course, so, although the examples here are from other areas in your course, be sure to focus on biological psychology in your practical investigation.

Another example is the more prejudiced someone is, the more they have an authoritarian personality. This example would require a prejudice score going from 'not prejudiced' to 'very prejudiced' and an authoritarian score from 'not authoritarian' to 'very authoritarian'. This shows that the variables (in this case, 'prejudiced' and 'authoritarian') have to have a sliding scale and a measurement using numbers.

A worked-through example

The example used here to show analysis of correlation data involves invented data where people have had therapy because of a desire to control their aggressive behaviour and have had a before and after measure using an aggression scale. **Before and after** measuring means that the scale is administered by the therapist at the start of the therapy sessions and again at the end (and possibly in between, but these data show benefit from the start to the end of the therapy).

Definition

Before and after studies take a measure before an intervention, then a measure afterwards, to see if the intervention has made a difference and, if so, how much of a difference.

Table 6.18 contains artificial correlation data in order to show how such data can be analysed.

Table 6.18 Correlation data (artificial) to show the relationship between months having therapy for aggression and therapeutic benefit in terms of reduced score on an aggression scale

Participant	Months having therapy	Reduction in aggression score (therapeutic benefit)	Months having therapy (ranked from low to high)	Therapeutic benefit (ranked from low to high)
1	65	35	10	9
2	34	41	4	10
3	20	15	1	1
4	24	22	2.5	3
5	24	26	2.5	5.5
6	58	28	8	7
7	52	18	7	2
8	46	26	6	5.5
9	38	23	5	4
10	63	30	9	8
	Mode = 24 Median = 42 Mean = 42.4 Range = 45	Mode = 26 Median = 26 Mean = 26.4 Range = 26		

Table 6.18 shows the ranking of time in therapy over months and therapeutic benefit measured by reduction in aggression score (out of 100). You will have learned about ranking data when learning how to find the median of a set of scores (page 388). Use the same procedure when ranking a set of scores like this. The ranks can be compared to show if there is a relationship between the two variables (months having therapy and reduction in aggression score).

Explore

A scale to measure aggression in therapy is the Buss Perry scale, which you can look at using this link: http://public.psych.iastate.edu/caa/Scales/BussPerry.pdf. There are other scales used too, such as the overt aggression scale, or the modified version. Explore such scales to see the sorts of measures used.

STUDY HINT

The correlation explained here is about therapy and aggression so not in a way about biological explanations of aggression, as if therapy works, it might be said that aggression is more learned than innate. However, perhaps even those who are 'aggressive' by nature would benefit from therapy to help to control their behaviour. So this idea of months in therapy relating to benefit in reducing aggressive behaviour is offered within biological psychology. Bear in mind though that it has stepped beyond a purely biological account of aggression.

STUDY HINT

Note that measures of central tendency (mean, median and mode) are calculated when a table of results is drawn up, even if a correlation will be used. This can help to show the distribution of scores. Take the opportunity to work out measures of central tendency when you gather data in practical investigations, as it is all good practice. The range too can be useful for a set of scores.

Sense checking data

A requirement in your course is that you are able to interpret patterns from data and carry out a sense check, which means looking carefully at the data to see patterns and then to decide whether data look as if they are 'significant'. How a sense check works to see significant differences can vary with each statistical test, and in this section sense checking to see if there is a relationship between the scores is done, because that is what will show whether there is a significant correlation or not.

Table 6.19 shows the ranks from Table 6.18 to help with sense checking the data.

Table 6.19 Ranks for each of the ten participants looking at months having therapy against reduction in aggression score

Participant	Months having therapy (ranked from low to high)	Therapeutic benefit (ranked from low to high)	Tick if ranks are within one of each other either way, which suggests a correlation
1	10	9	✓
2	4	10	
3	1	1	✓
4	2.5	3	✓
5	2.5	5.5	
6	8	7	✓
7	7	2	
8	6	5.5	✓
9	5	4	✓
10	9	8	✓

If a participant's ranks are both low, and another participant's scores are both middle, with a third one's scores being both high, then there is a pattern:

- Participant 1 is ranked 10 for months having therapy and 9 for improvement in aggression score. Both ranks are high.
- Participant 3 is ranked 1 for months having therapy and 1 for improvement in aggression score. Both the ranks are low.
- Participant 4 is ranked joint second for months having therapy and third lowest for aggression score – again, a close match.
- Seven of the ten participants have ranks that are either the same or within 1 of each other, which shows a strong relationship (see Table 6.19).
- Three participants (2, 5 and 7) have ranks that do not match, which shows that the correlation is not perfect.

STUDY HINT

By examining the data, patterns may emerge. You should familiarise yourself with drawing conclusions from the data in this way. A statistical test can be carried out, but it is useful to know beforehand what sort of result one might expect. It would be useful to do that in your practical investigation for cognitive psychology, biological psychology and learning theories before carrying out the relevant test.

The sense check for the example data used here suggests that there is indeed a relationship here between months in therapy and changes in aggression score. The higher the number of months in therapy, the more the reduction in aggression score. Note that though this is a reduction in score, it is measuring the benefit of the therapy, so the more there is of the therapy (in months), the higher the benefit (measured in reduction in score on an aggression scale).

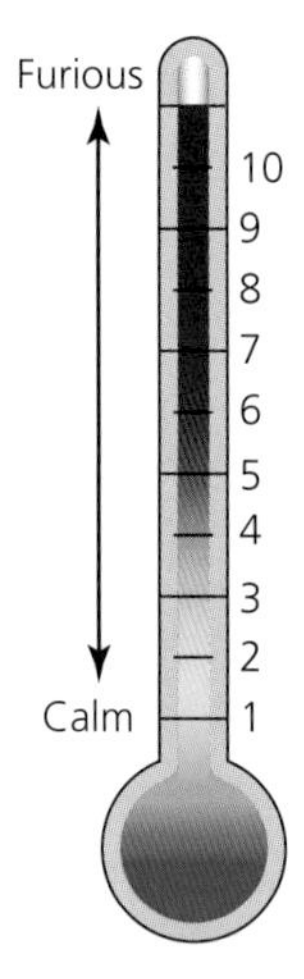

Aggression can come from biological, learned or social causes, and can be helped by techniques used in anger management

Using a scatter diagram to display the results of a correlation

Correlation data are displayed graphically by using a **scatter diagram**. A scatter diagram can be called a scatter graph or a scattergram. The two scores from each participant or variable generate a point on the graph, so in our example there are ten points. A **line of best fit** is drawn. If there is a relationship, the line of best fit is close to most of the points.

Drawing a scatter diagram displays the data in a way that suggests, using a line of best fit, whether there is a relationship between the two variables or not. A line of best fit is drawn that shows the best straight line that can be fitted with the points on the scatter diagram evenly distributed either side of the line. The line is diagonal, either from left to right rising from top to bottom, or from left to right falling from top to bottom. The line should run from left to right. If it is not clear which way the line should go (top to bottom or bottom to top), this suggests there is no relationship. If plots are 'scattered' all over the graph, then no relationship was found.

- **Positive correlation**: If the line rises from left to right on the scatter diagram, then that shows a positive relationship – as one score rises, the other rises too.
- **Negative correlation**: If the line falls from left to right on the scatter diagram, then that shows a negative relationship – as one score rises, the other falls.
- **No correlation**: If scores do not cluster well either side of the line of best fit, then the graph suggests that there is no relationship between the variables.

Correlations can be said to be 'strong' if the plots are close to the line of best fit with few outlying scores. They are 'weak' if they cluster around a line of best fit but only rather loosely. They can have 'medium' strength too.

A scatter diagram can suggest:

- whether there is a correlation or not
- whether, if there is one, a correlation is negative or positive
- how strong the correlation is.

Explanation

Scatter diagrams are used only for correlations. They can be called scattergraphs, scatterplots or scattergrams. A **line of best fit** on a scatter diagram is the line that takes in most of the plots on the graph. The line can be drawn by eye so that the points are as evenly distributed each side of the line as possible.

A scatter diagram of the data in Table 6.18 is shown below.

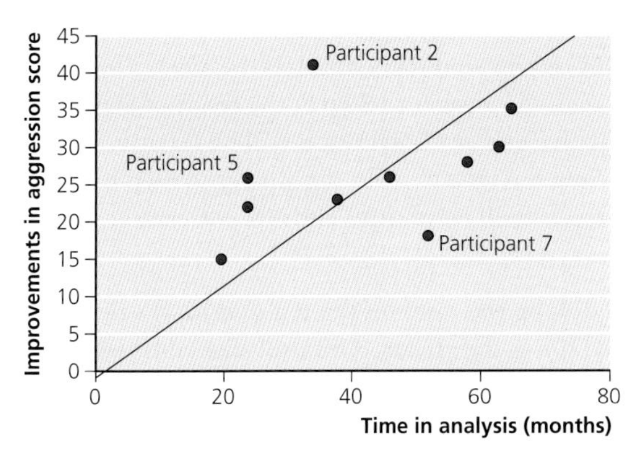

Scatter diagram to show the correlation between time having therapy and improvement in aggression score

The line of best fit, with five scores on each side, is in a positive direction. The three scores that do not fit well are clearly shown on this graph. Overall, this graph suggests that there is a positive correlation between time having therapy and improvement in aggression score.

When does the result of a test for a correlation indicate that a relationship exists?

A sense check – looking at data sets to see how they compare – is useful, but is difficult to draw firm conclusions from a sense check. Table 6.18 shows that, for seven out of ten participants, there seems to be a relationship between time spent having therapy and benefit in terms of reduced aggression. A statistical test (Spearman test) can be carried out to see if the relationship is real for the group as a whole.

First, it is important to know how to interpret the results of interpreting the Spearman test:

- If both scores rise, there is a positive correlation. A result of +1 means a perfect positive correlation. There is a perfect relationship between the two scores.
- A result of 0 means that there is no correlation. The two scores do not relate to each other.
- If one score rises and the other falls, there is a negative correlation. A result of –1 means a perfect negative correlation. There is a perfect relationship between the two scores.
- The closer a correlation is (the result of the test) to 1 (either negative or positive), the 'better' the correlation is ('1' is a perfect correlation).

For example, a test result of +0.70 or higher shows a positive relationship; a test result of –0.70 or lower shows a negative relationship. That is not to say that a result of a +0.45 does not show a relationship (see page 411), but when a result is close to 0, it would seem there is no correlation.

Carrying out a Spearman test

The diagram below shows factors affecting choice of the Spearman rank correlation coefficient.

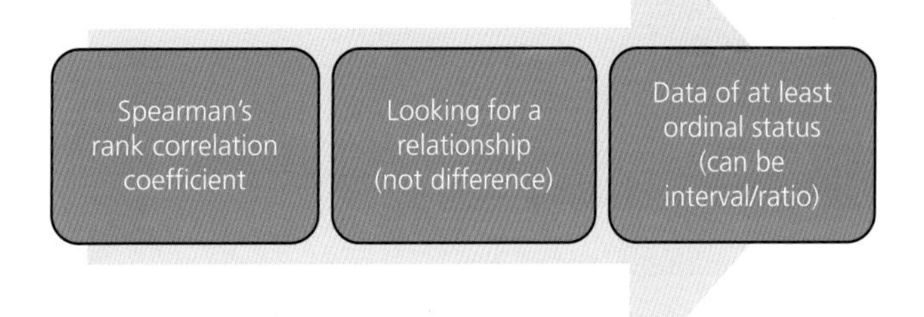

Factors affecting choice of the Spearman rank correlation coefficient

Table 6.20 Data for a Spearman test, based on Table 6.18

Participant	Months in analysis	Improvement in health score (therapeutic benefit)	Months in analysis (ranked from low to high – Step 1)	Therapeutic benefit (ranked from low to high – Step 1)	Difference between ranks (Step 2)	Differences squared (Step 3)
1	65	35	10	9	+1	1
2	34	41	4	10	-6	36
3	20	15	1	1	0	0
4	24	22	2.5	3	-0.5	0.25
5	24	26	2.5	5.5	-3	9
6	58	28	8	7	+1	1
7	52	18	7	2	+5	25
8	46	26	6	5.5	+0.5	0.25
9	38	23	5	4	+1	1
10	63	30	9	8	+1	1
	Mode = 24 Median = 42	Mode = 26 Median = 26				Total (Σ) = 74.5 (Step 4)

To rank data:

- Start with the lowest score. Give it a rank of 1.
- Allocate ranks as the scores rise.
- If there are two or more scores that are the same, allocate all those scores to the same rank by finding the middle rank. For example, if there are two scores of 20 that would be ranked 3 and 4, give them both the rank of 3.5. If there are three scores of 20 that would be ranked 3, 4 and 5, give them all a rank of 4.

> **STUDY HINT**
> You will have learned to rank data when looking at how to find the median of a set of scores (page 388). Remember to transfer your learning from one situation to another. You are likely to have carried out ranking of scores in other subjects as well as psychology.

Refer to Table 6.20. The formula for the calculation of Spearman's rank correlation coefficient (R_s) is:

$$R_s = 1 - \frac{6\Sigma d^2}{N^3 - N}$$

Note that this formula can read $N(N^2 - 1)$, which is the same as $N^3 - N$. Here $N(N^2 - 1)$ is used.

Step 1: Rank both sets of data.

Step 2: Work out the difference (d) between the ranks for each participant.

Step 3: Square (multiply by itself) the difference found in Step 2 for each participant. This gets rid of the minus signs.

Step 4: Add up the squared differences (the numbers worked out in Step 3). For the data given in Table 6.20, the total is **74.5**.

Step 5: Find N, which is the number of scores. (Here, N = **10**.)

Step 6: Multiply the sum of the squared differences (from Step 4) by 6. (Here, 74.5 × 6 = **447**)

Step 7: Square N and subtract 1. (Here, 10 × 10 – 1 = **99**)

Step 8: Multiply the answer found in Step 7 by N. (Here, 99 × 10 = **990**)

Step 9: Divide the answer to Step 6 by the answer to Step 8. (Here, 447/990 = **0.45**)

Step 10: Subtract the answer to Step 9 from 1. (Here, 1 – 0.45 = **+0.55**.) This is the result of the test. It is in Step 10 that a minus or plus sign is allocated. If the answer to Step 6 is larger than the answer to Step 8, the result of Step 10 will be negative and any correlation will be negative. If the answer to Step 6 is smaller than the answer to Step 8, the result of Step 10 will be positive and any correlation will be positive.

Step 11: Look up the result of the test in critical value tables to see if it is significant. Critical value tables for the various statistical tests, including Spearman's, can be found in a statistics textbook or using the internet, and also in your exam papers.

STUDY HINT

Critical value tables are given in your exam papers so you can use them.

Critical values tables

Table 6.21 shows part of a critical values table for Spearman's rank.

Table 6.21 Critical values for Spearman's rank, one-tailed

n	0.05	0.025	0.01	0.005
5	0.900	1.000	1.000	-
6	0.829	0.886	0.943	1.000
7	0.714	0.786	0.893	0.929
8	0.643	0.738	0.833	0.881
9	0.600	0.700	0.783	0.833
10	0.564	0.648	0.746	0.794
11	0.536	0.618	0.709	0.755
12	0.503	0.587	0.671	0.727
13	0.484	0.560	0.648	0.703
14	0.456	0.538	0.622	0.675

For $N = 10$ and 0.05 level of significance, the result has to be greater than 0.56 for it to be significant. The scores given here as an example seem to show a positive correlation from the sense check and from the scatter diagram. However, the Spearman test shows that the result of +0.55 is not quite significant.

STUDY HINT

Keep everything very clear when carrying out a statistical test. The overall calculation can look difficult, but use a step-by-step procedure so you are clear about each step and answer. Practice helps. Make up some data and carry out the Spearman's rank correlation coefficient test a few times. You will also be carrying out this test when doing your biological psychology practical investigation (Chapter 7, pp. 450–452, gives an example). Note that, using the internet, you might find some tables with different critical values, though they shouldn't differ too much.

Progress check 6.11

Imagine the following results from a Spearman's test and, using Table 6.21 (critical values, one-tailed), explain whether the observed value is significant:

1. rho = 0.40, $N = 14$, $p \leq 0.05$
2. rho = 0.85, $N = 10$, $p \leq 0.01$
3. rho = 0.23, $N = 11$, $p \leq 0.025$

Progress check 6.12

Using these three observed values (one-tailed), explain in each case whether they show a correlation or not and, if they do show a correlation, whether it is positive or negative. Also say whether you think it is a strong correlation or not.

1. +0.74, $N = 10$, $p \leq 0.025$
2. -0.48, $N = 14$, $p \leq 0.05$
3. +0.24, $N = 8$, $p \leq 0.01$

Test yourself

1. Explain what is meant by the line of best fit with regard to using a scatter diagram. **(4 marks)**
2. Discuss the use of correlational analysis in psychology. **(16 marks)**

Mathematical elements in learning theories

In the learning theories area of your course, you are asked to carry out an observation as the practical investigation and to know about analysis of observation data. You need to know about using animals in laboratory experiments too, but you are not asked to link this research method to methods of analysis, so there is no mention of that method in this chapter. In learning theories, you are asked to consider analysis of qualitative data using thematic analysis, which is explained earlier in this chapter in the social psychology section (pp. 398–399). You also need to know how to use a chi-squared test to analyse data, including observed and critical values, using critical value tables, considering levels of measurement and reasons for choosing a chi-squared test. Table 6.22 shows you where to find the mathematical elements for learning theories in this chapter.

Table 6.22 Mathematical elements in learning theories and where to find details in this book

Area to be covered relating to maths in learning theories	Where to find details in this chapter
Analysing qualitative data using themes	pp. 290–292 pp. 398–399
Levels of measurement	page 330
Knowing about observed and critical values	pp. 334–335
Reasons for choosing a test	pp. 330–331, 401
Doing a chi-squared test	In this section, pp. 412–415
Using chi-squared critical values tables	In this section, page 415

The chi-squared test

In learning theories, you need to know about the chi-squared test, which, like the Mann-Whitney U and Wilcoxon tests, is a test of difference.

Each test that you cover in your course can be used in any topic area, but they are fitted in as they are because they suit the research method in specific topic areas. The Mann-Whitney U and the Wilcoxon tests both suit experiments. The Spearman test is for a correlation. The chi-squared test fits well with doing observations, which is the research method for learning theories in your course. This does not mean that you cannot carry out an observation in social psychology – indeed you can, such as to look at helping behaviour – but in your course research methods have been divided up and put where they make most sense.

An example to explain the chi-squared test

To show how to carry out a chi-squared test, some tally data are used. A chi-squared test can test for more factors than those given here – a three-by-two table, for example. However, the most straightforward chi-squared test is when there is a **two-by-two table**, as used here.

Definition

A **two-by-two table** consists of two rows and two columns.

The columns in this example (Table 6.23) are the two sexes, boys and girls. The rows could be any of the categories but the sensible thing is to choose two categories in which boys and girls have shown different behaviour. For this example, the two rows are 'playing on the climbing frame' and 'playing in the book corner'. There are likely to be other categories (e.g. playing alone), but the chosen categories involve activity choice because the purpose of the study was to investigate children's activity choice in a nursery setting. The hypothesis for this example is that more girls will play in the book corner and more boys will play on the climbing frame. This is a rather stereotypical idea but suits the purpose for explaining the chi-squared test. The null hypothesis is that there is no difference in gender and playing on the climbing frame or in the book corner and any difference is due to chance of some other variable.

Table 6.23 A two-by-two table for a chi-squared test

Play behaviour	Boys	Girls	Total
Playing on the climbing frame	9	3	12
Playing in the book corner	3	7	10
Total	**12**	**10**	**22**

STUDY HINT

It is worth noting that, if you carry out an observation in a nursery to see if toy use varies according to gender, you might well find that there is no difference.

Note that the example of different activity choice for boys and girls links to learning as it has the underpinning idea that boys and girls learn what suitable activities are through operant conditioning and/or social learning. You will carry out a practical investigation that is an observation. Choose something that you can link to learning theories, as is done here.

For this example, 22 behaviours were recorded – 12 for boys and 10 for girls; 12 on the climbing frame and 10 playing in the book corner. For each of the 22 behaviours, it was noted whether the child playing was male or female.

Perhaps there is a gender difference in choice of climbing frame or book corner in a nursery setting

Progress check 6.13

Explain what is meant by a two-by-two table.

Carrying out the chi-squared test

The diagram below shows the factors affecting choice of the chi-squared test.

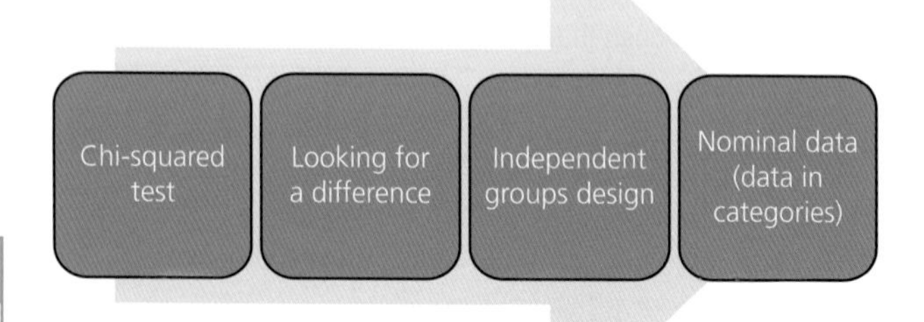

Factors affecting choice of the chi-squared test

In our example, the independent variable is gender, so there will be different people in the two conditions, so this is an independent groups design. (Chapter 5, pp. 321-323, explains designs, so refresh your memory if you need to.)

Progress check 6.14

The table below shows four examples of studies giving sufficient information for a choice of test to be made. Using the four tests for your course, allocate the right test to each box in the table. Check back to pp. 330–331 or p. 401 to see how a test is chosen if you cannot remember.

Information available regarding four studies	Appropriate statistical test out of Mann-Whitney U, Wilcoxon, Spearman's, chi-squared
Study 1: An experiment using a repeated measures design, giving interval data	
Study 2: A study looking for a relationship between two variables measured using at least ordinal data	
Study 3: An experiment using an independent groups design, giving at least ordinal data	
Study 4: An observation gathering nominal data looking for a difference using an independent groups design	

First, label the cells in the two-by-two table, as in Table 6.24.

In a chi-squared test using a two-by-two table, the expected values for the four cells (A, B, C and D) are calculated and then compared with the observed values (the observed values are in Table 6.24).

Table 6.24 Observed values (artificial) for a chi-squared test

Play behaviour	Boys	Girls	Total
Playing on the climbing frame	9 (Cell A)	3 (Cell B)	**12**
Playing in the book corner	3 (Cell C)	7 (Cell D)	**10**
Total	**12**	**10**	**22**

Carry out a sense check

The number of boys and girls observed on the two activities overall is more or less equal (12 boys and 10 girls) and the number of observations of the two activities is more or less equal (12 and 10 again), so if there were no difference in gender and choice of activity, the tallying in Cells A to D should be more or less similar. They are not similar. The climbing frame is played on by boys 75 per cent of the time ($9/12 \times 100 = 75$) and by girls 25 per cent of the time ($3/12 \times 100 = 25$). The book corner is chosen by boys 30 per cent of the time ($3/10 \times 100 = 30$) and by girls 70 per cent of the time ($7/10 \times 100 = 70$). Only the times when a child is doing each of the activities are recorded so we cannot say that the boys play on the climbing frame 75 per cent of their time, just that those two activities have that gender split as a choice of activity. The boys could do painting for more time than they are on the climbing frame or in the book corner, but that has not been measured in this observation.

The figures and percentages suggest that a difference in choice of activity between boys and girls has been found in this limited observation.

STUDY HINT

Percentages are used when carrying out this sense check. Check that you have understood how to use percentages, which are explained earlier in this chapter (page 397), as you will be expected to be able to calculate percentages in your course.

Progress check 6.15

Work out the percentages for the following figures from a study looking at holding doors open for younger and older people:

1. Older people are seen to open doors for younger people 6 times in a set of 30 observations.
2. Older people are seen to open doors for older people 24 times in a set of 30 observations.
3. Younger people are seen to open doors for younger people 15 times in a set of 22 observations.
4. Younger people are seen to open doors for older people 7 times in a set of 22 observations.

Progress check 6.16

Draw up a two-by-two table showing the scores for the study described in Progress check 6.15.

Finding the expected values

The formula for the expected value for each cell is:

$$\frac{\text{total of the row of cells} \times \text{total of the column of cells}}{\text{total of all cells}}.$$

where

total of the row of cells = total of the row of cells containing the required cell

total of the column of cells = total of the column of cells containing the required cell

Data found from Table 6.24 are:

- observed frequency for Cell A = 9
- observed frequency for Cell B = 3
- observed frequency for Cell C = 3
- observed frequency for Cell D = 7
- row total for C and D = 10
- row total for A and B = 12
- column total for A and C = 12
- column total for B and D = 10
- total observations = 22

Using cell A as an example:

Step 1: Find the total of the row containing the cell. (Here, row total = **12**)

Step 2: Find the total of the column containing the cell. (Here, column total = **12**)

Step 3: Multiply the answer to Step 1 by the answer to Step 2. (Here, 12 × 12 = **144**)

Step 4: Find the overall total of observations. (Here, overall total = **22**)

Step 5: Divide the answer to Step 3 by the answer to Step 4. (Here, 144/22 = **6.55**)

This is the expected value for the cell. (Here, the cell is A.)

Repeat Steps 1 to 5 for each cell. The results are shown in Table 6.25.

Redraw the two-by-two table, giving both the observed (*O*) and the expected (*E*) frequencies (Table 6.26).

Table 6.26 Observed (*O*) and expected (*E*) frequencies

Play behaviour	Boys	Girls	Total
Playing on the climbing frame	9 (*O*); 6.55 (*E*)	3 (*O*); 5.45 (*E*)	**12**
Playing in the book corner	3 (*O*); 5.45 (*E*)	7 (*O*); 4.55 (*E*)	**10**
Total	**12**	**10**	**22**

Carrying out another sense check on the data

While carrying out a statistical test, keep looking at the data to see what the test is doing. A chi-squared test is taking what is observed (e.g. the result of the tallying) and seeing if we would expect those scores to be there if there were no differences between the variables – this means if there were no differences in activity choice between the boys and the girls. Looking at the expected values (*E*), it can be seen that they are more or less equal, given that there are different numbers of boys and girls (12 and 10) and different numbers of observation of each activity (12 and 10). Then the observed values (which are not equal, being 9 and 3, 3 and 7) are compared with what would be expected if there were no difference (in this case, between boys' and girls' activity choice). A sense check shows that 9 is different from 6.55 (Cell A), 3 is different from 5.45 (Cell B), 3 is different from 5.45 (Cell C) and 7 is different from 4.55 (Cell D). So, to an extent, a difference is likely, though these differences are not very large, so perhaps a small difference. It would be expected that a chi-squared test will show a significant difference.

Doing the test

The formula to find the chi-squared result is:

$$\chi^2 = \Sigma \frac{(O - E)^2}{E}$$

Table 6.25 Expected values for Cells A, B, C and D

Step	Cell A	Cell B	Cell C	Cell D
Step 1: Find the total of the row containing the cell	12	12	10	10
Step 2: Find the total of the column containing the cell	12	10	12	10
Step 3: Multiply the answer to Step 1 by the answer to Step 2	12 × 12 = 144	12 × 10 = 120	10 × 12 = 120	10 × 10 = 100
Step 4: Find the overall total of observations	22	22	22	22
Step 5: Divide the answer to Step 3 by the answer to Step 4	144/22 = 6.55	120/22 = 5.45	120/22 = 5.45	100/22 = 4.55
Expected value for cell	6.55	5.45	5.45	4.55

where

χ^2 = chi-squared (the result of the test)

Σ = the sum of (note: calculate the sum after doing the rest of the calculation as the symbol is alongside the rest)

O = the observed result

E = the expected result

( ) = do this bit separately

$( )^2$ = square the answer that is found after doing the task in brackets.

Referring to Table 6.26 and using Cell A (boys) as an example:

Step 1: Subtract E from O. (Here, $9 - 6.55 =$ **2.45**.)

Step 2: Square the answer from Step 1 (multiply the answer to Step 1 by itself). (Here, $2.45 \times 2.45 =$ **6.00**.)

Step 3: Divide the answer to Step 2 by E. (Here, $6.00/6.55 =$ **0.92**.)

The results for all four cells are shown in Table 6.27.

The final step is the calculation of the value of chi-squared (χ^2). This is obtained by adding together all answers (in this case, four) for Step 3. In this example:

$\chi^2 = 0.92 + 1.10 + 1.10 + 1.32 =$ **4.44**.

This is the value of chi-squared.

Is the chi-squared test result statistically significant?

For a two-by-two study, the degree of freedom, *df*, is always 1. As you will probably choose to do a two-by-two study, the critical table value for $df = 1$ is displayed here (Table 6.28). If you carry out a study with, for example, a three-by-two table, *df* is 2, so that part of the critical values table is also shown in Table 6.28.

To find the degree of freedom, *df*:

Step 1: Subtract 1 from the number of rows. (For a two-by-two table, $2 - 1 = 1$.). Rows are horizontal in a table and columns are vertical.

Step 2: Subtract 1 from the number of columns. (For a two-by-two table, $2 - 1 = 1$.)

Step 3: Multiply the answer to Step 1 by the answer to Step 2. (For a two-by-two table, $1 \times 1 = 1$.)

The answer to Step 3 is the degree of freedom. For a two-by-two table, $df = 1$.

Table 6.28 Critical values for chi-squared when df = 1 or 2

	Level of significance, *p*, for a one-tailed test			
	0.05	0.025	0.01	0.005
	Level of significance, *p*, for a two-tailed test			
df	0.10	0.05	0.02	0.01
1	2.71	3.84	5.41	6.64
2	4.60	5.99	7.82	9.21

The example given here tested the hypothesis that activity choice is different depending on gender. This is a non-directional hypothesis because it does not predict which activities which gender will choose more of the time. The test required is a two-tailed test. If the $p \leq 0.05$ level of significance is chosen, this means that it is accepted that the probability of the results being due to chance is 1 in 20, or 5 per cent, and the null hypothesis will be rejected. At this level of significance, when *df* is 1, the critical value to be equalled or exceeded is 3.84. In the example given, the chi-squared value is 4.44. This is greater than 3.84, so the null hypothesis is rejected and the alternative hypothesis is accepted – there is a difference in activity

Table 6.27 Calculating χ^2 for the study of gender and development

	Cell A	Cell B	Cell C	Cell D
Step 1: Subtract E from O	9 - 6.55 = 2.45	3 - 5.45 = −2.45	3 - 5.45 = −2.45	7 - 4.55 = 2.45
Step 2: Square the answer from Step 1	2.45 × 2.45 = 6.00	−2.45 × −2.45 = 6.00*	−2.45 × −2.45 = 6.00*	2.45 × 2.45 = 6.00
Step 3: Divide the answer to Step 2 by E	6.00/6.55 = 0.92	6.00/5.45 = 1.10	6.00/5.45 = 1.10	6.00/4.55 = 1.32
*Squaring numbers removes the minus sign				

choice depending on gender and there are more boys on the climbing frame with more girls in the book corner. Note that before the test was carried out, it was possible to see the difference by reading the two-by-two table, using a sense check. However, the test is carried out to find whether or not the result is statistically significant.

STUDY HINT

You could use the table from Progress check 6.16 and carry out the chi-squared test on it for practice. It does not take as long as you might think and the more you practise, the better your understanding will be.

STUDY HINT

You do not need to memorise how to carry out the inferential tests because the formulae are given in the examination papers. However, it is useful to practise the step-by-step approach so that you fully understand and can use the formulae. Also, you need to know how to choose a test (A level only), when to use each of the three tests given in the specification, and how to interpret the result of the test using critical value tables (A level only). You also need to know how to use a level of significance and what is meant by the result of a test being significant (or not).

Progress check 6.17

Here are some results of chi-squared testing. Use the critical values table (Table 6.28) to see if these results are significant or not.

1. $\chi^2 = 2.5$, $p \leq 0.05$, one-tailed test, df = 1
2. $\chi^2 = 6.1$, $p \leq 0.02$, two-tailed test, df = 1
3. $\chi^2 = 4.51$, $p \leq 0.05$, two-tailed test, df = 2

Test yourself

1. Explain why inferential testing is carried out in psychology. **(8 marks)**
2. Assess strengths and weaknesses of using quantitative data in psychology. **(20 marks)**

Chapter summary

- Some general mathematical issues are covered looking at analysis of quantitative data, measures of central tendency and using decimals, normal and skewed distribution, using graphs and tables to display data, and measures of dispersion – the range and standard deviation.
- Social psychology mathematical issues include analysis of questionnaires, such as personal data and using percentages and bar charts. Social psychology also brings in analysis of qualitative data, which is covered.
- Cognitive psychology mathematical issues include inferential testing (as well as descriptive statistics, explained earlier in the chapter). In cognitive psychology, the two tests are the Mann-Whitney U test and the Wilcoxon signed-rank test. These are considered and the calculations demonstrated. Issues around choosing a test are also considered in this section.
- Biological psychology mathematical issues include inferential testing (again, as well as descriptive statistics). The focus is on doing correlations and the test is Spearman's rank correlation coefficient, which is worked through.
- Learning theories mathematical issues include inferential testing (again, as well as descriptive statistics). The focus is on doing a chi-squared test and, as with the other tests, calculations are explained.

Chapter Seven: Practical Investigations

Introduction

In your AS/Year 1 A level course, for each of the topic areas, you need to carry out one practical investigation (although you can, of course, do more as it helps with learning). In social psychology, you have to use the questionnaire research method, gathering both qualitative and quantitative data; in cognitive psychology, you have to use the laboratory experiment method; in biological psychology, you need to look at a correlation; and in learning theories, you need to do an observation that collects both qualitative and quantitative data.

The practical investigation element of each topic area is briefly outlined in each chapter and then one practical investigation for each topic area is worked through in this chapter. You will carry out your practical investigations as you work through your course, so you will be using your own. However, it might be useful to read through one worked through for you, for your interest, and also to help with this part of your course. Therefore, four practical investigations are explained here. Each of the practical investigations outlined here use the methodology that you need for your course, so reading through this chapter will also help with learning the methodology.

Social psychology – a questionnaire

Course requirements for this practical investigation

In social psychology, you are asked to carry out a practical investigation using a questionnaire, gathering both qualitative and quantitative data and looking for a difference in the data. You are not looking for a relationship, as that would be correlation analysis, which is the practical investigation in biological psychology. The topic that your questionnaire focuses on must link to what you have studied in social psychology for your course.

Check that the focus suits the course material

The questionnaire suggested in this textbook as a practical investigation tests Milgram's claims about the agentic and autonomous state and also ideas about how the authoritarian personality might underpin prejudice.

What must be done

You need to consider questionnaire construction, sampling, design and ethical issues. Data analysis must cover analysis of quantitative data using measures of central tendency and measures of dispersion, including bar charts and a frequency table. Analysis of qualitative data must use thematic analysis. You also need to consider strengths and weaknesses of your questionnaire, as well as writing up the procedure, results and a discussion of the findings. Here, a questionnaire about obedience is worked through.

Self-report data and rating scales

Self-report data are data obtained by participants reporting on their own feelings and circumstances. For example, you could report that you have a good relationship with your parents or that you have few friends. You could report that you class yourself as obedient and supportive of society, or you could say the opposite. The social psychology practical investigation reported here gathers self-report data.

Self-report data often include rating scales. The participants rate themselves on a scale of, say, 1 to 5. A Likert-type scale uses categories such as 'strongly agree', 'agree', 'don't know', 'disagree' and 'strongly disagree', which are chosen by the participants and then scored on the scale of 1 to 5. This type of scale is outlined in Chapter 5 (pp. 284–286).

Aim of this practical investigation

The aim is to see, using self-report data, if people who have an authoritarian personality are also 'agentic' in obeying an authority figure, and if those who do not have an authoritarian personality tend to be more autonomous than agentic. The aim is also to look at other related areas,

Table 7.1 What you need to know regarding practical investigations

You need to know about/how to:	
Social psychology	**Biological psychology**
Design and conduct a questionnaire on some aspect of social psychology in your course	One practical research exercise to gather data relevant to aggression or attitudes to drugs (as covered in your course)
Adhere to ethical principles in content and intention	Adhere to ethical principles in content and intention
Gather both qualitative and quantitative data to look for a difference in the data (not a correlation)	Design and conduct a correlation (study leading to a correlation)
Consider questionnaire construction, sampling decisions and ethical issues	Include inferential testing (Spearman's) and explain the significance of the result using levels of significance. Also use descriptive statistics (strength and direction of the correlation result) to explain the relationship
Collect and present analysis of quantitative data using measures of central tendency and measures of dispersion (including range and standard deviation as appropriate), bar chart and frequency table	Produce an abstract of the method and a discussion section of a report, which includes conclusions
Collect and present an analysis of qualitative data using thematic analysis	Include research question/hypothesis, research method, sampling, ethical considerations, data collection tools, data analysis, results, discussion
Consider strengths and weaknesses of your questionnaire	**Learning theories**
Write up the procedure, results and discussion section of a report	Two observations (one if gathers both qualitative and quantitative)
Cognitive psychology	Must relate to an aspect of learned behaviour
One laboratory experiment to gather data relevant to what you have studied in cognitive psychology for your course	Must gather both qualitative and quantitative data (including using note-taking, tallying and thematic analysis)
Adhere to ethical principles in content and intention	Analyse the findings to produce results, including using a chi-squared test
Gather quantitative data, including descriptive statistics as analysis and a test of difference (non-parametric)	Evaluate your study in terms of validity, reliability, generalisability and credibility
Make decisions including experimental design, sampling decisions, operationalisation, control, ethical considerations, hypothesis construction, experimenter effects and demand characteristics	Write up the results of the quantitative data, including appropriate graphs and tables
Collect, present and comment on data gathered, including measures of central tendency (mean, median, mode as appropriate), measures of dispersion (range and standard deviation as appropriate), bar graph, histogram, frequency table as appropriate, normal distribution if appropriate, and draw conclusions	Write up the results of the qualitative analysis (thematic analysis)
Use a Mann-Whitney U or Wilcoxon to test significance (as appropriate), including level of significance and critical/observed values	
Consider strengths and weaknesses of your experiment and possible improvements	
Objectivity, reliability and validity	
Write up procedure, results and discussion sections of a report	

such as whether those with a controlled upbringing see themselves as more authoritarian or whether older people see themselves as more autonomous than do younger people.

The data are self-report data so it is not so much they 'have' an authoritarian personality as that they put themselves in that category, and the same with being 'agentic' in obedience to authority.

The research questions include:

- Do people who report themselves as having an authoritarian personality tend to see themselves as agentic in that they obey authority figures?
- Do people who report themselves as less authoritarian see themselves as autonomous in their obedience?
- Do older people see themselves as autonomous more than younger people?
- Do those who report a controlled upbringing see themselves as authoritarian more than those who do not report control in their upbringing?

You would not have to analyse the questionnaire to answer all these questions, but the aim is to include data that would cover these questions.

Brief background

In order to understand the research questions, some background from social psychology is given. Milgram's agency theory states that, in general, people in society are agents of others, rather than being in charge of their own decisions. If you have not already covered this theory of obedience, look at it now (Chapter 1, pp. 19–21) because it will help you to understand the practical. People are agents of others if they obey people in authority, assuming they are not being forced to obey and that they can make a choice, and they obey even if obeying goes against their own moral code and their conscience. People are autonomous if they make their own decisions about obeying or not and follow their own moral code. It is interesting to ask people, to see if their self-report data will back up the idea that they obey people in authority because they see themselves as being agents in society, so that they see society as being the higher authority. This is likely in order to relate to an ordered society rather than anarchy. The idea is that people do not obey authority under their own autonomous decision-making – they obey to keep society functioning.

Research in prejudice considers people with an authoritarian personality, which refers to various characteristics, such as in psychodynamic terms having a strong superego (conscience) and a weaker ego (decision-maker) when faced with id demands (what the individual wants at a basic level). An authoritarian personality means obeying authority and defining it that way makes it obvious that someone who is 'authoritarian' will obey authority, and be in an agentic state. Authoritarian also means conventional and obeying social norms, so that can be measured by questionnaire. Other characteristics of the authoritarian personality include strict ideas of right and wrong, and adherence to society, such as 'I love my country'. These are characteristics that can be tested.

Progress check 7.1

Using your own practical investigation in social psychology, briefly outline the background behind your aim(s). In this chapter, the example questionnaire explained in this section is used to answer the progress checks, as a guide.

People with an authoritarian personality are likely to obey orders as agents of society, to support order in a society

Research method

The research method required is a questionnaire. You could carry out this practical investigation alone, or work in a small group so that you can pool data. For the purposes of this section, it is assumed that you are working alone. You will have carried out practical investigations while covering your course and should rely on your own work. This practical investigation is explained here to help you to see what should be learned and what can be done.

STUDY HINT

You should use your own practical investigations for each topic area as, while carrying out the practical, you will have learned a lot about the process, results and conclusions that reading about a study cannot replicate.

Design

This is a questionnaire and the focus is on the research question to see if people who obey authority do so for 'agentic' reasons rather than in an autonomous state and whether they tend to a more authoritarian personality than those who seem more autonomous. Clearly it will be different people who are compared when seeing who is agentic and who is authoritarian when obeying authority (though this will be just self-report data rather than 'fact' – they put themselves into categories that are called 'authoritarian'). The design would use the same people if comparing how authoritarian someone is who declares themselves agentic. It would be between people if comparing those who put themselves into an authoritarian category with those who do not put themselves into that category. The questionnaire is going to cover more than one research question. If you were using statistical testing, which in this practical you do not need to do, you could choose data that used an independent groups design (comparing between people) or a repeated measures design (comparing within individuals).

The design, therefore, is a questionnaire using certain types of questions, which are explained more below.

STUDY HINT

You will come across a lot of key terms in this chapter, as it is drawing on course content to test some aspect in a practical investigation, and it is also drawing on method and maths in your course. Terms are not always highlighted in this chapter as there are a lot of them and they have already been explained in earlier chapters. If you are not sure about the meaning of a term, use the glossary to remind yourself. It would not be unusual to forget the meaning of such terms, and researching will help your learning.

Sampling

Use opportunity sampling to find between 10 and 20 people (respondents) to do your questionnaire. If you are working in a small group of five, you could gather data from four people each. Even if working alone, you could ask someone to help you to gather the data. In this example practical investigation, 14 people are asked as this helps to limit the data for analysis (just to be practical) but should be enough to draw at least some conclusions. Using more people would be better. Of course you can use another method of sampling if you wish – for example, random sampling is more representative.

Progress check 7.2

There are four sampling techniques to be learned in your course. Opportunity sampling is one of them and another is random sampling. What are the other two, and why is random sampling considered to be more representative? (You can check back to Chapter 5, pp. 299–304, to help.)

Participants

You will be able to describe characteristics of the actual participants when you gather the data. This example practical investigation does not give details of the 14 participants, but the questionnaire gathers information about their gender, age range, education, employment and upbringing. As you will have gathered data, be ready to explain features of your participants, such as numbers in each gender. You do not have to ask the personal data suggested here, just ask what is relevant to your own research question(s).

Ethical issues

It is important for every practical that you address the ethical guidelines, including:

- your competence
- debriefing participants fully
- getting informed consent from your participants
- giving participants the right of withdrawal
- avoiding deception as much as possible.

Include written standardised instructions to give participants the necessary information. Standardised instructions are the same for everyone and are written so that the briefing the participants have had is recorded because it might affect the results. They include both the ethical requirements and also instructions for completing the questionnaire.

Practical

Do not proceed with your investigation until your teacher or supervisor has approved it in terms of ethics.

Risk management

Risk management is part of ethical procedures and should be considered for all studies in psychology. A questionnaire can carry risk for the respondent, such as their getting distressed by the content of the questionnaire or by thinking about their replies. There can be risk to a researcher, as in any study, as the participant might pose a threat, though this is rather unlikely. There might be risk to others around.

Risk to the participant

Filling in a questionnaire will not pose any physical risk to a participant, or should not. However, there might be risk of distressing the participant because of specific items or asking personal data. Such risk must be kept to a minimum. In this study, the items are not that personal in some ways, though asking about education level or work situation might give some distress. A debrief can help to overcome such distress and standardised instructions can, in the main, make the focus of the questionnaire clear, to mitigate risk of being upset. Some questionnaire items might give distress and, if a questionnaire is deemed to be too distressing, it should be changed. This is adhering to ethics in psychology. This particular questionnaire is considered to be reasonable, with a debrief to make sure of that.

Risk to the researcher(s)

A researcher is not at risk directly because of a questionnaire, which can be carried out anywhere they choose. It might be worth making sure that the questionnaire is used in a public place or with others around, as that would be a safety measure.

Risk to others

The questionnaire used here is unlikely to pose a risk to others. It is not interfering with others, such as when they are driving a car, which might pose a risk. The researcher must be sure to ask people when they are free to answer and when it is safe. That should minimise what is an unlikely risk for this particular study.

Drawing up the questionnaire

A list of decisions to be made when drawing up a questionnaire is given below for you to work through.

- Find participants and note the sampling method for your records.
- Write out instructions for the participants, including ethical issues.
- Plan how you will carry out the questionnaire – for example, by post, face-to-face, using just yourself as researcher or drawing in others too, leaving the questionnaire in a room, such as a library, with envelopes for return... There are various options. Here the option chosen is one researcher and each questionnaire being completed individually face-to-face with the participant.
- Decide what personal data you need (e.g. age, gender, education level, occupation).
- Decide what closed-ended questions will be asked. The questionnaire must gather quantitative data. Closed-ended questions have limited answers, such as 'yes/no' or a list of choices.
- If choosing statements that need to be ranked ('strongly agree' and so on), check that all statements for one type of person (e.g. authoritarian) do not lead to the same response (e.g. 'strongly agree') to avoid response bias.
- Decide what open-ended questions will be asked. The questionnaire must gather qualitative data. Open questions are those where the respondent can give their own opinions or write their own story.
- Construct the actual questionnaire, set out appropriately, so that data can be recorded accurately.
- Check to make sure the questionnaire gathers data that will answer the research question(s).
- You could carry out a small pilot study to test the questions, using just a few people as participants and asking them for feedback.

STUDY HINT

When working through the list and making decisions, write notes explaining why you made those decisions. Recording how you progressed through the practical investigation will help you to remember problems and how you dealt with them, in readiness for the examination.

Progress check 7.3

Explain what is meant by 'closed-ended' and 'open-ended' when applied to questions on a questionnaire.

The example questionnaire

A questionnaire about agency theory, obedience to authority and authoritarian personality

Thank you for agreeing to answer this questionnaire, which is about why we obey people in authority and what sort of people obey those in authority. Please note that you can stop taking part in the study at any time. It will take less than half an hour. Your name is not being recorded and all details are confidential. I can let you have my findings at a later date if you would be interested and I will also tell you more about the study once you have completed the questionnaire, if that is OK with you. I am writing down the answers you give and you can watch me do that – or you can write the answers in yourself. Is it OK to start?

For questions 1 to 7, please select the answer that most closely describes yourself. Only answer the parts that you are happy to answer.

(1) **Gender:**

Male ☐ Female ☐

(2) **Age group:**

18–24 ☐ 25–30 ☐ 31–39 ☐ 40–49 ☐ 50–59 ☐ 60+ ☐

(3) **Type of work:**

Mainly manual ☐
Self-employed ☐
Not working ☐
Mainly professional ☐
Clerical ☐
Other ☐

(4) **Type of upbringing:**

Very controlled ☐
Reasonably controlled ☐
Fairly free ☐
Uncontrolled ☐

(5) **Type of schooling:**

Grammar ☐
Secondary modern ☐
Comprehensive ☐
Private ☐
Mixture ☐
Specific religion ☐
Other ☐

(6) **Would you say that you are law abiding?**

Yes ☐ No ☐

(7) **Would you say that you are a leader or a follower?**

Leader ☐ Follower ☐

For questions 8 to 13, please select the answer that most represents your response to the statements below. Only answer the questions that you are happy to answer.

SA = strongly agree; A = agree; DK = unsure (don't know); D = disagree; SD = strongly disagree

Statement	SA	A	DK	D	SD
(8) I tend to do what I am told.	☐	☐	☐	☐	☐
(9) I like to make my own decisions even when that goes against authority.	☐	☐	☐	☐	☐
(10) I agree that a society needs strong rules.	☐	☐	☐	☐	☐
(11) I obey all laws, which is right as we need control.	☐	☐	☐	☐	☐
(12) We need authority figures to maintain order.	☐	☐	☐	☐	☐
(13) I stick to my own moral code, even if it means breaking the law.	☐	☐	☐	☐	☐

The following questions ask for more detail about you. Is it OK to continue?

(14) Please tell me about your parents' style when bringing you up. Of course, only give information you are happy to give. What was your upbringing like?

(15) Please give me an example of when you have not wanted to obey someone in authority.

(16) If you are a parent, please tell me about your own parenting style when bringing up your own children.

(17) What do you think about the need for obedience to those in authority in society?

Thank you very much for taking part in this questionnaire. It is generally thought that people in a society are agents of that society – they obey the rules because that is how society works best. However, most people like to think that they make their own decisions, rather than obey others. I am looking at how far we obey others and how much we make our own decisions. I am also seeing if people who prefer rules and have firm views about right and wrong are more likely to obey people in authority because they agree that social norms must be adhered to for the good of society. Are you happy that I use the information you have given me for my psychology course?

STUDY HINT
It is best to design your own schedule. You will learn a lot from making the decisions and you will enjoy the practical more if it is your own.

Progress check 7.4
Which questions in the example questionnaire are open questions?

Perhaps the type of school attended affects self-report data around obedience

Carrying out the study

You will carry out the study and gather the data, so guidance is given here. Some data are offered here, to help to illustrate the analysis of results and the discussion.

Gathering the data

Decisions have to be made about gathering the data. Some issues include:

- being on time
- dressing appropriately
- having the necessary equipment (e.g. pens and questionnaires)
- remaining objective if asking questions directly, and when giving standardised instructions, if reading them out
- not taking too much of the respondent's time
- sticking to good ethical practices, such as explaining everything to the participants before starting, frequently giving the right to withdraw, debriefing, letting the respondents know what will be done with their data and, at a later date, contacting them with the results.

Once you have planned everything, then the data can be gathered.

Some example personal data and closed questions data for 3 of the participants (scores are in brackets for the Likert-style questions):

Participant 8

Q1) Male; Q2) aged 60+; Q3) Self-employed; Q4) Very controlled; Q5) Grammar; Q6) Yes; Q7) Leader; Q8) Agree (4); Q9) Disagree (2); Q10) Agree (4); Q11) Agree (4); Q12) Agree (4); Q13) Disagree (2).

Participant 10

Q1) Female; Q2) aged 18–24; Q3) Other; Q4) Fairly free; Q5) Private; Q6) Yes; Q7) Follower; Q8) Don't know (3); Q9) Strongly agree (5); Q10) Don't know (3); Q11) Don't know (3); Q12) Agree (4); Q13) Disagree (2).

Participant 12

Q1) Male; Q2) aged 18–24; Q3) Other; Q4) Fairly free; Q5) Comprehensive; Q6) Yes; Q7) Follower; Q8) Disagree (2); Q9) Don't know (3); Q10) Disagree (2); Q11) Disagree (2); Q12) Disagree (2); Q13) Agree (4).

Displaying the quantitative data

The quantitative data can be displayed in a number of ways. Tables are useful for displaying data in good detail, as illustrated by Table 7.2. Graphs are good ways of displaying data too, to show results. The method section in social psychology in your course asks you to know about bar charts, so a bar chart would be a good idea for this practical investigation. You can also use pie charts and line graphs, as appropriate. Ways of displaying the data are used in the results section (pp. 427–428). Qualitative data can be displayed in a table too, such as Table 7.3, though that depends on how they are to be analysed. If qualitative data are turned into quantitative data, then ways of displaying quantitative data apply. If thematic analysis is to take place, then the full transcripts would be used and qualitative data would be displayed in a results section. This is illustrated in the results section below.

Table 7.2 Quantitative data from the questionnaire for three participants

Questionnaire question – closed questions (refer to questionnaire)	Participant 8	Participant 10	Participant 12
Q1 (gender)	Male	Female	Male
Q2 (age group)	60+	18–24	18–24
Q3 (type of work)	Self-employed	Other	Other
Q4 (type of upbringing)	Very controlled	Fairly free	Fairly free
Q5 (type of schooling)	Grammar	Private	Comprehensive
Q6 (law abiding or not)	Yes	Yes	Yes
Q7 (leader or follower)	Leader	Follower	Follower
Q8 (do what told)	Agree	Don't know	Disagree
Q9 (make own decisions)	Disagree	Strongly agree	Don't know
Q10 (society needs laws)	Agree	Don't know	Disagree
Q11 (I obey laws)	Agree	Don't know	Disagree
Q12 (we need authority)	Agree	Agree	Disagree
Q13 (I obey my own moral code)	Disagree	Disagree	Agree

Transcribing the qualitative data

Once the data have been collected, a **transcript** of the qualitative data has to be produced. For each of the open questions (Q14 to Q17 in the example above), type out the answers. An example table for the data is given in Table 7.3.

Table 7.3 Qualitative data from the questionnaire

Question number	Participant responses (allocated the participant number alongside their data)
14	E.g. My parents were rather free and easy and let me do more or less what I wanted (Participant 10). E.g. My father was very strict, for example, I had to be back home by 10.00pm even when I was in my twenties and living at home (Participant 8).
15	E.g. When a parking attendant has told me to park in a certain place and I would rather choose my own (Participant 10). E.g. I always obey people in authority, because I like to do what is right (Participant 8).
16	E.g. I like to let them make their own choices but sometimes I have to make the decisions, such as if they are bothering other people (Participant 10). E.g. I make sure they obey the rules, as that will be what they have to do when they are older (Participant 8).
17	E.g. I think we have to obey people in authority as we live in a democracy and having voted people in we have to accept their decisions (Participant 10). E.g. Of course we must obey those in authority, they have the power (Participant 8)

Definition

A **transcript** is a full account of the data, including, with regard to qualitative data, all the words from each respondent, so that a full analysis can take place.

Analysis of the data

Analysis of the personal data, the quantitative data and the qualitative data has to be carried out.

Analysing the personal data from the example questionnaire

- Add up the numbers, such as those of each gender, or age group, and any other information you gathered.
- Personal data are useful when looking for trends. An example of a trend would be to see whether type of upbringing (Q4, part of the personal data) relates to agency score as found from the statement scores (Q8 and Q12). The statement scoring is explained below. The other items/questions should be straightforward to summarise. Another example would be to look at whether older people (Q2, part of the personal data) would tend to have had a more controlled upbringing (Q4, part of the personal data).

Progress check 7.5

Why are personal data asked for on a questionnaire?

Analysing the quantitative data from the closed questions in the example questionnaire

- Add up numbers according to the questions asked – for example, if you used a Likert-type scale of strongly agree, agree, don't know, disagree, strongly disagree. In the example questionnaire, there are two statements that score 5 for strongly agree relating to the participant being agentic (Q8 and Q12). There are two statements that score 5 for strongly agree relating to the participant being authoritarian (Q10 and Q11). There are two statements that score 5 for strongly agree relating to the participant being autonomous (Q9 and Q13). A score of 5 for strongly agree means 4 for agree, 3 for not sure 2 for disagree and 1 for strongly disagree. In this way, you can get an 'authoritarian' score for each participant, an 'agentic' score and an 'autonomous' score. Then you can start comparing data, such as seeing if a high agentic score (max. 10, adding up Q8 and Q12) matches a high authoritarian score (max. 10, adding up Q10 and Q11).
- Note that this practical investigation is not looking at a correlation and it is not claimed that the *more* someone is authoritarian the *more* they are 'agentic', though this could be tested. Here comparisons are made, looking at *differences* between groups so a participant can be allocated a label 'agentic' or 'autonomous' (opposites according to Milgram) and then it can be seen if someone 'agentic' has had a controlled upbringing. There are many other ways of analysing the data from this example questionnaire; you can choose which data to choose to match your research aim(s).
- Present graphs and tables, as appropriate, to display your data. Aim to include one bar chart and one frequency table and chart, as those are the required ways of presenting the analysis in your course, for social psychology.
- In your table of data, be sure to include measures of central tendency (mean, median and mode) as appropriate. Also include the range of two lots of data and the standard deviation, as that is required too.
- You can test the data for reliability. For example, you would expect the Q7 answer for one participant to agree with their Q8 answer, and that is a way of checking for reliability. Reliability is found when a test is repeated and the same result found, and you can say that Q8 repeats Q7 so they should agree.
- Draw some conclusions by examining all the data. For example, separate the male and female 'obedience' scores arising from the Likert-type scale and see if there are differences. For example, do female participants have a higher autonomous than agentic score (the total of Q9 and Q13 compared with the total of Q8 and Q12), and vice versa for male participants? Does strict parenting mean a high agentic state (the total score for Q8 and Q12)? Does gender, age or job affect how autonomous someone feels? Are leaders more autonomous than followers? These are suitable questions to ask yourself. Drawing conclusions from limited data is difficult, but practise how to analyse them.

Progress check 7.6

Why is a frequency table and graph useful in results?

Using the example data from the personal data and closed questions to demonstrate analysis of quantitative data

Table 7.4 shows some example scores for three participants for Q1 to Q13.

Table 7.4 Example scores for three participants

Question number	Participant 8	Participant 10	Participant 12
1	M	F	M
2	60+	18–24	18–24
3	Self-employed	Other	Other
4	Very controlled	Fairly free	Fairly free
5	Grammar	Private	Comprehensive
6	Yes	Yes	Yes
7	Leader	Follower	Follower
8	4	3	2
9	2	5	3
10	4	3	2
11	4	3	2
12	4	4	2
13	2	2	4
Total agentic score (Q8 + Q12)	8	7	4
Total autonomous score (Q9 + Q13)	4	7	7
Total authoritarian score (Q10 + Q11)	8	6	4

Table 7.5 shows the median and modal scores, and the range for Q8 to Q13 using the example data for the three participants.

Table 7.5 Median, mode and range for Q1 to Q13 for three participants

Question	Participant 8	Participant 10	Participant 12	Median	Mode	Range
8	4	3	2	3	2,3,4	2
9	2	5	3	3	2,3,5	3
10	4	3	2	3	2,3,4	2
11	4	3	2	3	2,3,4	2
12	4	4	2	4	4	2
13	2	2	4	2	2	2

Note that, with just three scores, not much analysis is possible; the analysis here illustrates the process only.

Scoring the Likert-type answers (strongly agree...)

- Note that as the statements score '3' for don't know, this can distort the data as you might argue that 'don't know' is not midway between 'strongly agree' and 'strongly disagree' when talking about obedience.
- Note that allocating 'strongly agree' or 'agree' and so on to statements is giving a ranking and so the scores are ordinal with regard to levels of measurement. A mean average requires interval/ratio data and so a mean average cannot be calculated for the data given in Q8 to Q13 (see Chapter 6, pp. 387–389, for an explanation). A standard deviation also is not possible, as the scores are ordinal, and not 'real' mathematical scores.

Two-by-two tables

- There are other ways to analyse the data, such as looking at gender and obedience. You can see if there is a difference between males and females, according to whether they see themselves as agentic or autonomous. A two-by-two table such as Table 7.6 can be drawn up for many of the categories in the example questionnaire. Use tallying against male or female and whether their 'agentic' score is higher or their 'autonomous' score is higher.

Table 7.6 suggests a way of displaying and analysing data.

Table 7.6 A two-by-two table

	Agentic (Q8 + Q12) higher	Autonomous (Q9 + Q13) higher	Total
Males	8	12	20
Females	4	16	20
Total	12	28	40

STUDY HINT

If you have studied how to use a chi-squared test, which you cover in the learning theories part of your course, you could carry out a test on this data. Tallying means the data are nominal; male versus female means this is an independent groups design; this is looking at differences between males and females – therefore, a chi-squared test is suitable. Note though that you do not have to use inferential statistics in your social psychology practical investigation.

Frequency table and graph (histogram)

- A frequency table is possible if there are more data. Chapter 6 explains more about frequency tables and graphs (pp 391–392). A frequency table is given here as an example (Table 7.7), using the ages of the 40 made-up participants, for the purpose of illustration.

Table 7.7 Frequency of age ranges for a set of data

Age ranges	Tallying	Frequency
18-24	~~IIII~~ ~~IIII~~	10
25-30	~~IIII~~ II	7
31-40	~~IIII~~	5
41-50	IIII	4
51-60	~~IIII~~ I	6
60+	~~IIII~~ III	8

Bar chart

- Chapter 6 explains more about bar charts and graphs (page 397). A bar chart is given here with made-up data for males and their 'leader or follower' answers and then another bar chart with females and their 'leader or follower' answers, for comparison. The scales are the same, to help the comparison.

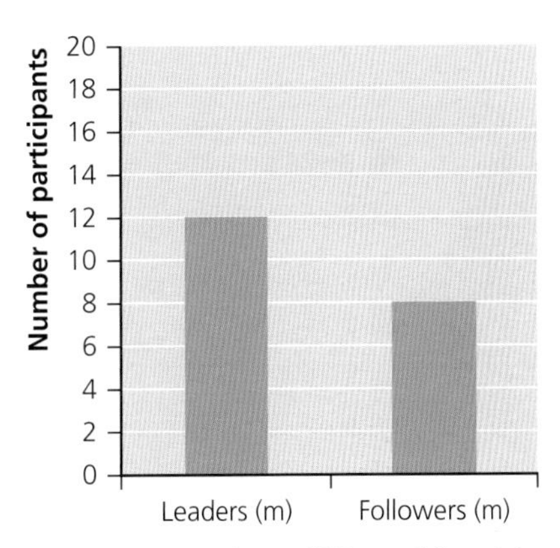

Male responses (out of 20 participants) regarding 'yes' to leader or follower

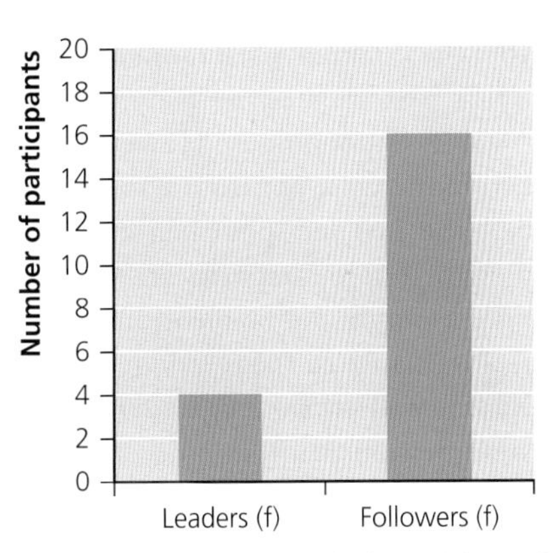

Female responses (out of 20 participants) regarding 'yes' to leader or follower

Pie chart and percentages

- You could also use a pie chart to display the ages of your sample. You would work out the percentages of people in each age group so you could generate a pie chart. One is given here as an example. Table 7.8 gives the figures and the percentages for the pie chart.

Table 7.8 Numbers of participants in the different age groups and percentages

Age range	18–24	25–30	31–40	41–50	51–60	60+
Frequency	10	7	5	4	6	8
Percentage	25	17.5	12.5	10	15	20
Calculation of percentages	$\frac{10}{40} \times 100$	$\frac{7}{40} \times 100$	$\frac{5}{40} \times 100$	$\frac{4}{40} \times 100$	$\frac{6}{40} \times 100$	$\frac{8}{40} \times 100$

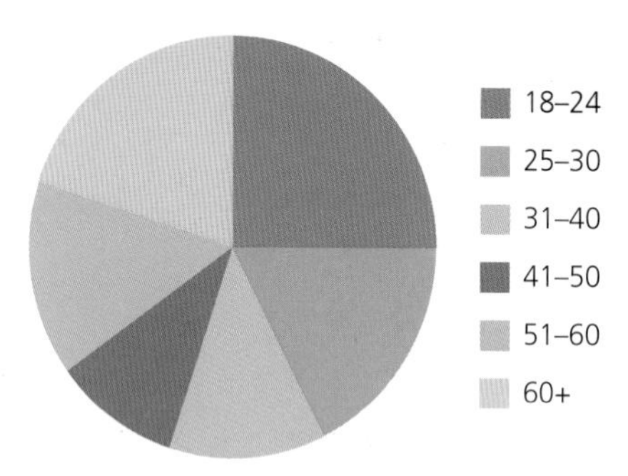

Age range of the participants

Analysing the qualitative data from the example questionnaire

- Draw up themes from the qualitative data (open questions: Q14 to Q17). Two themes are likely to be 'act as an agent' and 'be autonomous'. However, themes must come from the data, not from what you expect. Read through the data and spot categories that are mentioned often. Those categories are your themes. Other categories might not be mentioned often but might be of relevance to the respondent. These are also themes. It will not be easy to generate themes from just four questions without much space available for detail, but there should be some common ideas. Pooled data would help to show trends as you would have more participants. This is doing thematic analysis, which you need to know about for your course. Using the examples in Table 7.3, some themes might be 'free and easy' parenting as opposed to 'strict' parenting, or 'rather choose my own' as opposed to 'doing what is right'.
- Make a note of quotes that illustrate the themes so that you have evidence.
- The quotes are needed in the results section of your questionnaire, as evidence for your themes. A reader would need such evidence, not just the themes. They need to be displayed and explained too.

Progress check 7.7

What is meant by 'thematic analysis'?

Consider your findings

One aim is to see, using self-report data, if people who have an authoritarian personality are also 'agentic' in obeying an authority figure, and if those who do not have an authoritarian personality tend to be more autonomous than agentic. There are other aims too, including looking at other related areas such as whether those with a controlled upbringing are more authoritarian or whether older people are more autonomous than younger people.

You need to look carefully at the data, both qualitative and quantitative, to summarise the results in the light of the aim(s) you chose and the research questions. Write out a discussion, bringing together the background information, the research ideas and aims, and the results, so that you can show how your study supports or does not support the ideas being looked at.

Strengths and weaknesses of the example study

Strengths

- The questionnaire gathers a lot of data and answers to different questions can help to check reliability of the answers. For example, Q7 asks whether someone is a leader or a follower and Q8 asks whether they agree or not with a statement that they do as they are told. You would expect a follower to do as they are told, so you can see if these two questions are answered consistently. If so, there is reliability in the data.
- All of the participants have the same instructions and the same questions set out in the same way, so the data are comparable. Even if there is some bias in a question, all participants have the same experience and so bias would affect them all. Data are, therefore, able to be compared and contrasted. There are controls.
- There are both quantitative and qualitative data, which means that the respondents answer fixed questions giving comparable answers but also can give detail and some depth, so there is some richness in the data that can be used to expand on the limited choice closed-ended questions. This will give a richer and

more detailed picture of each respondent and gives background that can be useful in analysis. There is validity in the qualitative data that the forced choice questions can lack.

Weaknesses

- The limited choice questions restrict validity. The respondent may not, for example, fit into the 'employment' categories. In the example data, two of the respondents were students and chose 'other' because they did not feel they fitted into any of the categories. This means that the forced choice data are not offering validity. A similar example is the age group choices. The two students were 18 years old and yet they had to choose '18–24', which is relatively large age group.
- All the questions reflect the choice of the researchers, such as asking about upbringing and parenting style, to reflect an authoritarian personality or not. A respondent might not have had a strict upbringing and might not be a strict parent, but they might well have prejudiced views and an authoritarian outlook.
- Self-report data might be limited and the questionnaire only considers what people say they are like rather than reflecting their behaviour. However, Cohrs *et al.* (2012), one of the contemporary studies in social psychology, tested self-report data against peer-report data with regard to prejudiced attitudes and found a good agreement, so perhaps self-report data are relatively reliable. Also, by definition, if we are measuring someone's personality or thinking about their decision-making, self-report data are valid. Nonetheless, it must be remembered that the questionnaire gathers information about what people see themselves as being like and how they want to present themselves. There is likely to be an element of social desirability, for example.

STUDY HINT

Note that we might say that a weakness of this questionnaire is that it uses self-report data. By itself, that is not a weakness, but it is a statement that can be explained as a weakness. You need to explain issues of social desirability and how there might be bias in the data or lack of validity. Be sure to explain a strength or weakness of a study, research method or theory.

STUDY HINT

Although this chapter is about the practical investigations in your Year 1 or AS course, you can use material from the topic area when discussing your practical investigation, such as using the Cohrs *et al.* (2012) study to discuss a weakness. Be sure to link up the material from the different chapters. Chapters 5, 6 and 7 are presented separately but, for each of them, material 'belongs' in the relevant chapter. In the background to this questionnaire study, Milgram was mentioned, for example, and his theory about the agentic state, which comes from Chapter 1.

Progress check 7.8

Outline one strength and one weakness of your questionnaire. In the answers at the back of this book, the example questionnaire presented here is used to provide a suggested answer, but you should use your own questionnaire.

Possible improvements

Before carrying out a study in psychology, you would do all that you could both to build on theory and the work of others and to control the situation and study so that results are credible. That is why background information is given, to show the theory from which a hypothesis or research question is drawn. That is why a questionnaire, for example, is piloted, to make sure questions mean the same to others.

After a study has been carried out, strengths and weaknesses are discussed so that other researchers and those with power over policy and practice, for example, can see how good the study is. They can judge its validity and reliability, as well as its generalisability, objectivity and credibility. After this, there should be a focus on what could be done next. This is about progressing understanding in the field of interest, and also about improvements in the study itself. In your course, you are asked to consider studies and be ready to suggest improvements.

In this study, improvements might be:

- Gathering more qualitative data as the spaces offered to the respondents were quite limiting. One way to do this would be to use follow-up interviewing, if participants gave permission. That would add more depth and detail to the qualitative data and could also clarify the quantitative data. This would add validity and, if interviews showed the same data as the questionnaires, that might show reliability too.
- Using stratified sampling to ensure a wide range of age groups, educational background, types of work and other issues that were required. Opportunity sampling is limited as only those people around at the time are available to be in the sample. If, for example, you are in a city centre at 3.00 p.m. you would not get workers who

finish at 5.00 p.m. A better sample would mean more generalisability. Random sampling could also be chosen instead of opportunity sampling.

- Using more items that focus on a) agentic state, b) autonomous state and c) authoritarian personality, as there were only two items for each, which was just 10 as a score. This does limit the analysis and there could be a more robust way of allocating someone to these three conditions.
- Observation might be a useful research method that could gather data about obedience in everyday situations. Observing in a car park might uncover issues in obeying the parking attendant, for example. Age, gender, obedient behaviour and perhaps body language could all be scored. However, there is information here that is missed but that the questionnaire gathers, such as more about the participant's background and thinking.

STUDY HINT

Be ready to make suggestions about improving any study you are asked about. Work through issues of validity, reliability, objectivity, generalisability and credibility (and ethics), and ask yourself how good the study is regarding these issues and whether (and how) it could be improved.

Writing up the practical investigation

For the practical investigation in social psychology, you have to know how to write up the procedure, results and discussion sections of a report. Studies that have been explained in the relevant chapters will give you guidance on how to do that. You can also find full reports on the internet.

Explore

Look up Burger's (2009) study (one of the contemporary studies in social psychology) and scroll through it, noting how the report is written up: www.scu.edu/cas/psychology/faculty/upload/Replicating-Milgrampdf.pdf.

Sections of a report in psychology

A report has the following sections:

- **Abstract** – a summary of the study, so that anyone looking for a study in a particular area can quickly scan what it is about. Also it is a way of summarising the study at the start, so that the reader already has an idea before reading on.
- **Background/introduction** – can use headings and gives the reader details of past research in the area of study, so that the scene is set for the study to come. The background tends to include aims and hypotheses.
- **Method** – this is split into parts, which can vary. Sections tend to include participants, sampling technique(s) and procedure (how the study is carried out). In some studies, you will find more than one 'experiment' as part of a main study.
- **Results** – likely to include graphs and tables to display data, and results are explained in detail. It can be useful to read the discussion first, as that summarises the results and gives you an idea of what was found, before tackling the results in more detail.
- **Discussion** – links the results to the background in the introduction and links back to the aim(s) and (if relevant) hypotheses to see if what was expected was found.
- **References** – these are very important because, when someone is researching an area, they can use the references to check the facts in the report and also to explore studies in an area.

There is sufficient information in this example questionnaire to write up a report. Write up the procedure (what was done), the results (what was found) and the conclusion/discussion (a discussion about the findings, including summarising the results and discussing strengths and weaknesses of the study).

STUDY HINT

Although this part of social psychology is called the practical investigation, you need to know about it for the written examination as questions can be asked about your own practical investigation/study, just as they can be asked about the work of others.

When asked questions in an examination, if there is any link (such as 'in your own practical investigation' or 'in the study outlined in this question'), be sure to relate to that link clearly in your answer and do not answer 'more generally' as the question is asking you to 'apply' your knowledge and understanding, not just to 'show' your knowledge and understanding.

Test yourself

1 In your own practical investigation in social psychology, what were the advantages of gathering both qualitative and quantitative data? Be sure to refer to your own questionnaire in your answer and not just questionnaires in general. **(4 marks)**

2 With regard to your own practical investigation in social psychology, discuss strengths and weaknesses. Be sure to identify the focus of your questionnaire in your answer. **(12 marks)**

Cognitive psychology – a laboratory experiment

Course requirements for this practical investigation

In cognitive psychology, you have to carry out a laboratory experiment. You must choose a focus for your experiment that relates to what you have studied in cognitive psychology for your course, so be sure to focus on material that is in your course. Here a laboratory experiment looking at interference in short-term memory is worked through, but you can do a different experiment.

Check that the focus suits the course material

The influence of rehearsal on recall is part of the multi-store model of memory, as it is the way that information in short-term memory is passed into the long-term store. Working memory looks more into short-term memory and discusses the way sound is important in memory in the short-term store, looking at a phonological loop and subvocal rehearsal. It can be seen that the subject of this experiment fits the requirements well. There is a clear link between the focus of the practical investigation and the material in cognitive psychology.

What must be done

You are required to carry out a lab experiment, which will gather quantitative data. For the analysis of your practical investigation, you need to include descriptive statistics and a test of difference. You have to choose between a Mann-Whitney U test or a Wilcoxon test, depending on your experimental/research design. Carrying out one of the two statistical tests must include considerations of levels of significance and using critical and observed values.

You have to make appropriate design decisions to plan and conduct the experiment, including experimental/participant design (independent groups, repeated measures or matched pairs), sampling decisions, operationalisation of the independent and dependent variables, use of appropriate controls, ethical considerations and hypotheses. The design decisions should also consider the avoidance of demand characteristics and experimenter effects.

The data must be collected and commented on, including using measures of central tendency, measures of dispersion, bar graph, histogram/frequency graph and issues of normal distribution, as appropriate. Commenting on the study includes considering strengths and weaknesses as well as possible improvements. There is also a requirement, as with the questionnaire for social psychology, to write up the procedure, results and discussion sections of a report.

STUDY HINT

In the examination, you will be asked questions about your practical investigations. Keep a notebook, so that you have information that you can revise for each examination.

Progress check 7.9

In the table below, tick the elements you have to cover in your practical investigation in cognitive psychology and cross those you do not, so you can see what is required.

Statement about the cognitive psychology practical investigation	Tick if true	Cross if not
Write out the experimental and null hypothesis		
Give the relevant experimental design		
Give the standardised instructions		
Use a Spearman's rank correlation coefficient		
Use relevant measures of central tendency and dispersion		
Write up the background, procedure, results, discussion sections		
Consider experimenter effects and demand characteristics		
Discuss sampling decisions		

Aim of the practical

The aim is to partly replicate the study by Peterson and Peterson (1959) and to see if repetition improves recall. The aim is to look at rehearsal (repetition) in short-term memory and to see if the number of repetitions affects recall. This links to a number of areas in your course. The multi-store model sets up the idea that for information to be processed from short-term memory into long-term memory rehearsal has to take place; otherwise, in short-term memory, there is a capacity of just 5–9 items (called 7±2), which is very limited. The working memory model looks more at short-term memory, including the element of rehearsal, and puts forward the idea of a phonological loop, which includes a phonological store and a subvocal rehearsal element, the articulatory loop. This practical helps to shed light on both the multi-store and the working memory model of memory. Baddeley (1966b), which is the classic study in your course, looks at the subvocal rehearsal element of the phonological loop, so this study can relate to that study too.

Here the aim is to look at the rehearsal process in short-term memory to see if the longer that items are rehearsed, the better the recall.

Brief background

You will have studied Atkinson and Shiffrin's (1968) multi-store model of memory (Chapter 2, pp. 78–83), and covered short-term memory and rehearsal. Issues within short-term memory, such as the need for rehearsal, are also important in other models of memory and forgetting, including the working memory model and the interference explanation for forgetting. The multi-store model suggests that short-term and long-term memory have different features. Short-term memory lasts for up to 30 seconds and we remember in short-term memory by sound. Long-term memory can last a lifetime and is in different forms (e.g. pictures, sound and meaning). The model suggests that, if information is rehearsed in short-term memory, it can go into long-term memory. If it is not rehearsed, it is lost. Findings from studies such as Peterson and Peterson (1959) suggest that rehearsal leads to better recall. This backs up the model and supports the idea that rehearsed information is transferred into long-term memory and non-rehearsed information is lost.

The experiment replicated partially here is the second experiment from the Peterson and Peterson (1959) study. Some of Peterson and Peterson's (1959) results are given in Table 7.9.

Table 7.9 Proportion of items correctly recalled after two different times for repetition of items and two different times of interference (Peterson and Peterson, 1959)

Repetition time (seconds)	Proportion recalled after a time interval of 9 seconds	Proportion recalled after a time interval of 18 seconds
1	0.34	0.21
3	0.48	0.34

A greater proportion of items were recalled after 9 seconds than after 18 seconds. In each case, a greater proportion of items were recalled when there was more repetition time. The experiment shown here looks at the effect of repetition time, to see if rehearsal aids recall, just looking at rehearsal over one or three seconds. The experiment suggested here does not look at the additional part of the study which looked at recall at 9 or 18 seconds.

Explore

Berman *et al.* (2009) looked more at the issues outlined here, about short-term memory, interference and the rehearsal loop. Explore more by reading their study, which can be accessed online: www-personal.umich.edu/~rickl/pubs/berman-jonides-lewis-2009-jeplmc.pdf.

Progress check 7.10

How does rehearsal fit as an idea in both the short-term memory and working memory models? You can refer to Chapter 2 (pp. 78-83 and 86-90) to remind yourself about this area of study.

Research method and design decisions

The research method required is a laboratory experiment. You could carry out this practical alone or work in a small group so that you can pool data. You are asked to gather quantitative data and to include both descriptive and inferential statistics in analysis.

This is one idea for a practical investigation. You will be doing other practical investigations in your learning and you should use one you have done, rather than using the data here. When designing and carrying out the study, you will do a lot of learning about the issues, which means you will be able to write about these with more understanding in the examination.

Experimental and null hypothesis

The basic experimental hypothesis for this study is: 'In short-term memory the longer participants rehearse an item, the better their recall'.

- Recall is the number of three-letter nonsense syllables correctly repeated at the end of the trials (a trial is one of the series of tests). Three-letter nonsense syllables are three-letter 'words' without meaning, e.g. POK.
- Rehearsal is repeating the nonsense syllables aloud.
- 'More rehearsal' is set up (operationalised) as the number of times the nonsense syllables are repeated aloud increases – the more times participants repeat the material, the more they are said to have rehearsed it. 'More times' in this practical investigation means whether they repeat for one second (one repetition) or three seconds (three repetitions).

- So that rehearsal is limited to once or three times (the two conditions), after that rehearsal (aloud, so that it is clear it has taken place), there is a 'counting backwards' task to interfere and prevent any further rehearsal before recall.

A hypothesis is: 'In short-term memory participants correctly recall more three-letter nonsense syllables the more times they repeat the material aloud before recall'. More fully still, the hypothesis is: 'In short-term memory participants correctly recall more three-letter nonsense syllables whether they repeat the material aloud once (one second) or three times (three seconds) before recall'. The null hypothesis would be: 'There will be no difference in the recall of three-letter nonsense syllables whether the participants repeat the material aloud once or three times before recall, and any difference found is due to chance factors or some other variable'.

STUDY HINT
Here, terms are used but not explained, such as 'operationalisation'. Terms are explained in detail in Chapter 5 (if they are about methodology) or Chapter 6 (if they involve mathematical elements). If you do not remember what a term means, refer back to the relevant chapter, or look in the Glossary.

Directional or non-directional hypothesis

The hypothesis is directional because it is saying that the *more* the participants rehearse, the *better* their recall will be. Thus the direction of the results – being clear when participants will do *better* – is given. When considering statistics later in this practical investigation, it will be important to know whether to look at 'one-tailed' or 'two-tailed'; this hypothesis is directional, so 'one-tailed' will be chosen.

Independent and dependent variables

The independent variable is what is manipulated – in this experiment, how many times the participant repeats the stimulus. This is how 'more rehearsal' will be operationalised. It is difficult to measure one and three seconds. Therefore, one repeat of the nonsense syllable is taken as allowing one second and three repeats of the nonsense syllable is taken as allowing three seconds.

The dependent variable is what is measured as a result of the manipulation of the independent variable. In this case, it is the number of three-letter nonsense syllables correctly recalled.

Progress check 7.11

In a study where memory span is tested to see if letters that are chunked for meaning are better recalled (in the same order) than the same letters not chunked according to meaning, what is the independent variable and what is the dependent variable? For example, one group of participants had to recall letters from 'PHD FBI RAM PIC SUE' (chunked) and another group of participants had to recall letters from 'RMB PUF IAI HDE PSC' (not chunked).

Conditions in the experiment

There are two conditions in this experiment:

- The participant repeats the stimulus material aloud once.
- The participant repeats the stimulus material aloud three times.

Design

This is a repeated measures design because the same participants are doing the two conditions.

Progress check 7.12

What does it mean to say a study uses a repeated measures design?

Participants

Use opportunity sampling to find ten people to take part in the study. Note down features such as their age group, gender – any features that might affect the results – though for most people, gender and age should not affect the results of the study. Avoid asking anyone who has memory problems or people old enough to feel that they have memory problems.

Ethical issues

It is important for every practical that you address the ethical guidelines, including:

- your competence
- debriefing participants fully
- getting informed consent from your participants
- giving participants the right of withdrawal
- avoiding deception as much as possible.

Include written standardised instructions to give participants the necessary information. Standardised instructions are the same for everyone and are written so that the briefing the participants have had is recorded because this might affect the results.

Practical

Do not proceed with your investigation until your teacher or supervisor has approved it in terms of ethics.

Risk management

As part of ethical considerations, take into account the management of risk. In a study in psychology, there can be risk to the participants, risk to researchers and risk to others. Risk management is about avoiding risk or lowering the effects or likelihood of risk. In an experiment where participants are controlled, in the sense of the situation and setting they are in, any risk to them is particularly important. In a non-participant covert observation, it might be argued that a study poses less risk to the participants.

Risk to participants

For this study, which looks at memory, there is not much risk that the participants will leave feeling distressed, which is one risk that must be managed. Each participant does both conditions and they are not being compared to others. They should find that repeating the syllable three times is easier, and that it makes sense to them that this should be the case (when debriefed) and the finding should not threaten their self-concept as it is a study about memory rather than about individuals.

Any risk of distress can be reduced by having a thorough debrief to explain that the study is not about individuals. Also standardised instructions can let the participant know that the study is not looking at them as individuals, but at memory in general.

Risk to others

In an experiment, others are not involved or in the setting so there should be no risk to others. The researcher can make sure that the study is carried out with each participant when they are alone, so that there is no risk to others.

Risk to the researcher

It is unlikely that this study would pose a risk to a researcher in itself. It is a study about memory and does not involve apparatus that has risk. The only possible risk would be from the participant perhaps, and the researcher's safety must be considered. It is very unlikely that a participant will pose a threat; however, it might be a good idea to have someone nearby, in reach, in the event of problems for either the researcher or the participant.

Preparing the apparatus

For a laboratory experiment, **apparatus** is usually needed. In this study, the dependent variable is recall of three-letter nonsense syllables. Peterson and Peterson (1959) used nonsense syllables rather than 'real' words so that each participant had an equal chance of remembering them. This removes any advantage due to familiarity with the words. Adding meaning to words also means using other cognitive processes, rather than 'pure' short-term memory. Therefore, meaningless materials are better for carrying out such a task.

Definition

Apparatus means the materials used in a study.

Prepare ten sets of three-letter nonsense syllables. Suggested items are given below.

Decisions about the study

In this experiment, the remaining decisions are based largely on the Peterson and Peterson (1959) study. However, other decisions could be made. Here, the decisions are:

- The participants are asked to repeat the nonsense syllable aloud either once or three times. This is to represent Peterson and Peterson's (1959) measures of one second and three seconds for rehearsal.
- The time that the participants count backwards for before recalling is 18 seconds (replicating Peterson and Peterson, 1959).
- Ten three-letter nonsense syllables are prepared for the task. Eight are needed, but it could be useful to have two more to practise on.
- Participants will take part in two practice trials, to make sure they understand the instructions, followed by six actual trials. Three of the six main trials involve repeating the nonsense syllable aloud once; three involve repeating the nonsense syllable aloud three times.
- Aim to avoid demand characteristics, by not explaining the full procedure to the participants, such as explaining rehearsal and memory and how the 'once aloud' condition will be harder. As this is deception, a full debrief will be required.
- Aim to keep experimenter bias to a minimum by maintaining the same tone and pace when giving standardised instructions and the same tone and pace when giving the nonsense syllables. Also keep the experimenter constant throughout the study.
- Data are to be recorded for each participant from the six trials (not from the practice trials). Record the letters

recalled, the nonsense syllable itself and whether the recalled nonsense syllable is complete.
- Use counterbalancing so that one participant does the 'once aloud' condition first and the next participant does the 'three times aloud' condition first. This will help to control order effects.
- Ten numbers from which the participants will count backwards need to be written down, so that the same number is used for each participant as a control. Use numbers in the hundreds and ask them to count backwards in ones so that the task is not too difficult. Eight numbers are needed, but ten are prepared in case of difficulties arising.

Suggested three-letter nonsense syllables are:

BUH	VID	FOM	REL	DUS	WOV	QIY	RIH	PEB	KEC

Suggested sets of three numbers are:

475	396	259	639	502	489	326	843	740	582

Progress check 7.13

What are the two types of order effect that counterbalancing is there to take care of so that bias is reduced? You can refer to Chapter 5 (page 323) if you wish to remind yourself about order effects and counterbalancing.

Use of controls

Controls include:

- Using the same nonsense syllables in the same order for all participants, including the same ones for the 'once rehearsed' and the 'three times rehearsed' conditions. Though alternating or randomising the use of the nonsense syllables between the two conditions might be useful. This is a decision you could make.
- Giving the participants the same standardised instructions and aiming to keep situational variables the same for all participants.
- Using the same procedure for all participants, such as timing 18 seconds between rehearsal and recall for all participants in both conditions.
- Making sure as far as possible that the nonsense syllables have no meaning for any participant.

Carrying out the study

The main points about carrying out the study (having found the participants and prepared the materials) are listed below. Copy the list so that you can use it to remind you of the steps that have to be followed:

- Give out the standardised instructions (see below) and check that all is in order.
- With each participant individually, once they are happy and ethical issues are adhered to, carry out two practice trials, one using the 'once aloud' condition and the other using the 'three times aloud' condition.
- Check all is well and start the main study.
- Inform the participant that the first trials are the 'once aloud' trials. (If possible, use counterbalancing – with one participant doing the 'once aloud' condition first and with the next participant doing the 'three times aloud' condition first.)
- Inform the participant that, when you read them a number, they must count backwards in 1s from that number aloud until you tell them to stop (this can be illustrated to the participant to make this part of the study clear).
- Read one of the nonsense syllables out to the participant.
- Wait for the participant to repeat it *once*.
- Read one of the numbers to the participant.
- Wait 18 seconds while the participant counts backwards from that number.
- Ask the participant to recall the nonsense syllable.
- Note down the letters recalled, the actual nonsense syllable and whether the nonsense syllable is complete or not.
- Repeat this twice more (i.e. do three 'once aloud' trials).
- Inform the participant that the next trials are the 'three-times aloud' trials. (If counterbalancing, this would be the 'once aloud' trial.)
- Repeat the steps for the 'once aloud' trials, as given above, but this time waiting for the participant to repeat the nonsense syllable *three times* before reading out one of the numbers.
- Thank the participant and debrief him or her.

Instructions

When a participant has been chosen, find somewhere comfortable to carry out the experiment.

An example of standardised instructions for this study could be as follows:

Thank you for taking part in this study. Please note that you can stop at any time. I am looking at memory to see how we process information and I will explain what this particular study is about once you have taken part. Is that all right? This is not about you as an individual but about how we all remember. The study will take about 20 minutes. I hope that is all right.

I am going to read out three letters. You then repeat them out loud to rehearse them briefly. Then, when I ask you to, I would like you to start counting backwards in ones from a number that I will give you, such as from 487 you would then say aloud '486, 485...' and so on. Finally, I will ask you to recall the three letters I read out at the start. I would like to do this eight times altogether. The first two times are for practice. Then, I would like to do six trials, and each time I will note down what you recall of the letters. For some of the trials, I will ask you to repeat the letters once and for other trials I will ask you to repeat the letters three times.

Carry out the study

Start with the two practice trials, answer any questions and then carry out the six proper trials, recording what the participants recall each time.

Debriefing participants

Once the experiment is over, the participants have to be debriefed. This means telling them what the study is about and how their results will be used. Explain the two conditions and inform them of their results. Tell them that rehearsal is meant to aid recall and to help transfer memories into the long-term memory. Ask them if you can use their results and explain it is for your A level or AS psychology course. Debriefing should be done individually, after each participant has completed the experiment.

Recording results

You should record your results in a table. Table 7.10 could be used to show the letters recalled by each participant in each of six trials and the total number of complete nonsense syllables recalled correctly. These are the **raw scores**.

Definition

The **raw scores** are the actual scores of the participants.

Analysing the data

Use the raw scores table (Table 7.10), which is your completed table once the ten participants have been tested in both conditions. You could use the total number of letters recalled correctly by each participant for each condition, or you could use the total number of nonsense syllables recalled correctly. Work out a mode, median, mean, range and standard deviation for the data. Number of letters or nonsense syllables can be seen as interval/ratio data and so the mean and standard deviation are suitable, as are the median, mode and range. If you use the number of syllables recalled correctly, there are only three possible scores, which limits the data; if you use the letters recalled in the right order, then there might be an element of guessing. Decide which you think is best for your data.

You should also present your data in graphical form. This experiment is a repeated measures design, so you should be able to compare the scores from the two conditions.

Work out the proportion/percentage of recall for the two conditions. Then compare your results with those of Peterson and Peterson (1959). They found a proportion of 0.21 for the one-second repetition condition and 0.34 for the three-second repetition condition when they used an 18-second interference task (counting backwards).

Suggestions about presentation of data

Some possible data are shown in Table 7.11.

Table 7.10 A table for recording results

Repeat 'once aloud' condition					Repeat 'three times aloud' condition				
Participant	Trial 1	Trial 2	Trial 3	Total of correct syllables recalled	Participant	Trial 1	Trial 2	Trial 3	Total of correct syllables recalled
1					1				
2					2				
3					3				
4					4				
5					5				
6					6				
7					7				
8					8				
9					9				
10					10				

Table 7.11 Possible data

Repeat 'once aloud' condition					Repeat 'three times aloud' condition				
Participant	Trial 1	Trial 2	Trial 3	Total of correct syllables recalled	Participant	Trial 1	Trial 2	Trial 3	Total of correct syllables recalled
1	R	DUS	WV	1	1	BUH	VID	FOM	3
2	REL	DUS	WOV	3	2	BUH	VID	FOM	3
3	REM	DUH	OV	0	3	BS	VID	FOM	2
4	RM	DUS	WOV	2	4	BUH	VID	FOM	3
5	REL	DUS	WOV	3	5	BUH	VID	FOM	3
6	REP	DUS	VW	1	6	UH	VD	FOM	1
7	TL	DUS	WV	1	7	BUH	VID	FOM	3
8	REP	DUS	OV	1	8	BUH	VID	FOM	3
9	REL	DUS	WOV	3	9	BUH	VID	FOM	3
10	PEP	VUS	WOV	1	10	BUH	VID	FOM	3

Descriptive statistics

- The raw scores are the actual scores of the participants.
- The measures of central tendency are the mode, median and mean.
  - The mode is the most usual score, the one that appears most often. There can be more than one mode. If there are two, the data are bi-modal.
  - The median is the middle score. If there is an even number of scores, there will be two points in the middle. For example with ten sets of scores, the median is the average of the scores ranked 5 and 6. Here, both sets of scores have the same number at 5 and 6, so there is no problem. However, if the fifth score was 2 and the sixth score was 3, then the median would be 2.5.
  - The mean is the average. It is calculated by adding up the set of scores and dividing by the number of scores (*N*/*n*) in the set. The mean can only be used if data are 'real' mathematical measurements ('real' means that numbers are mathematical, such as having equal gaps between them), and interval/ratio data.
- The measures of dispersion are the range and the standard deviation.
  - The range is worked out by subtracting the lowest score from the highest score.
  - See Chapter 6 (pp. 394–396) for how to work out the standard deviation. The standard deviation can only be used if data are 'real' mathematical measurements, and interval/ratio data.

Levels of measurement and measures of central tendency

It is not always correct to work out the mode, median and mean for all data. It depends on the level of measurement of the data. In psychology, three levels of measurement are used:

- nominal data, which are data in categories – the mode is suitable
- ordinal data, which are data in ranks such as rating scales – the mode and median are suitable
- interval/ratio data, which are mathematical scores – all three measures of central tendency are suitable.

Explanation

For this course, **interval** and **ratio data** are taken to be the same.

One way to remember levels of measurement is to think of temperature:

- Sorting days into hot and cold days is a nominal level of measurement because the data are in categories.
- Rating days according to how cold, warm and hot they are is an ordinal level of measurement because a rating scale is used to rank the days.
- Recording the temperature in degrees Celsius is an interval/ratio level of measurement. This is a 'real' mathematical measurement, so the mean can be used.

We can take 'number of nonsense syllables recalled correctly' or 'number of letters recalled correctly' as interval/ratio data because these are numbers with equal intervals between them, not ratings.

STUDY HINT

Note that, if you are doing the AS course, levels of measurement do not have to be known for the examination.

Progress check 7.14

Which of the three measures of central tendency cannot be used unless data are interval or ratio (real mathematical measurements)? Explain why this is the case.

STUDY HINT

Use the Progress checks to learn more if you are uncertain about an area of study. They are there for that purpose, as well as to test your understanding. It is tempting to miss out such activities, but it is useful, particularly when revising, to use these sorts of aids.

Summary table

When presenting data, it is usual to give the measures of central tendency and dispersion, not the raw scores. This makes it easier to compare the scores. The results calculated from the suggested data for this experiment are summarised in Table 7.12. The data are for the number of complete nonsense syllables (out of three) recalled correctly in each condition.

Table 7.12 Summary of results

Repeat 'once aloud' condition		Repeat 'three times aloud' condition	
Statistic	**Value**	**Statistic**	**Value**
Mode	1	Mode	3
Median	1	Median	3
Mean	1.6	Mean	2.7
Range	3	Range	2
Standard deviation	1.07	Standard deviation	0.67

Graphs

You need to be able to interpret graphs. You also need to know how to produce them, and this aids understanding. Graphs have been explained in Chapter 5 (page 327) and Chapter 6 (page 393). Here are some rules about drawing graphs:

- A computer-generated graph may not help when comparing data because the computer tends to adjust the scales automatically. You would need to adjust the scales if you use a computer but this requires the necessary skills. If you do adjust this correctly, a computer-generated graph is fine. When comparing graphical data, the scales have to be the same.
- If the experimental design uses independent groups, you should not compare the data for one person directly with the data for their opposite number. At least one of the sets of data should be in rank order to make comparisons worthwhile. Or present the two sets of data on separate sets of axes, but using the same scale. (As the practical investigation uses a repeated measures design, the participant is the same for both scores so a bar chart, as shown below, can be used.)
- A simple graph is used to present the two means for comparison. Make sure that the scale is sensible.
- There may be so many raw data that it is not useful to present them graphically. However, this is done here as an illustration and because there are only ten sets of data.

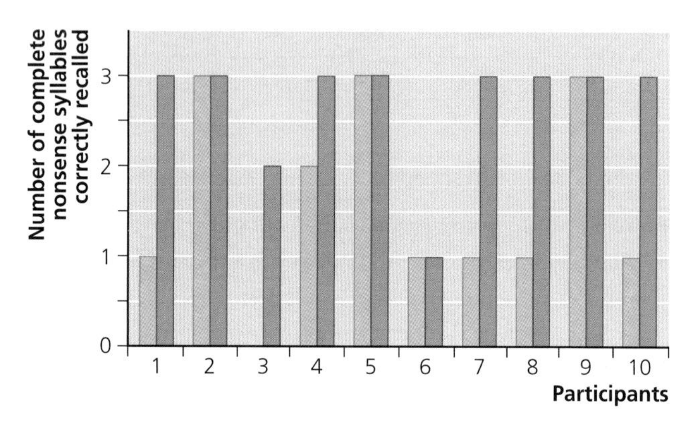

The effects of rehearsal on recall

- In a frequency graph (see below), the number of times each score is achieved is recorded. Frequency graphs are useful because they show clearly the differences between data.

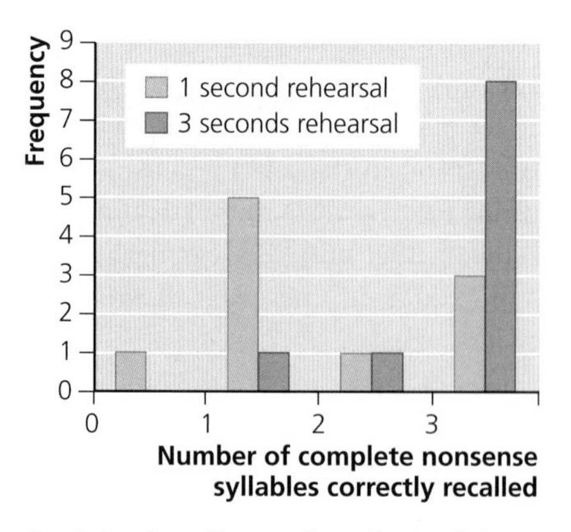

Frequency graph to show the number of complete nonsense syllables recalled correctly after one-second rehearsal and three-second rehearsal

Table 7.13 Frequency data for the two conditions

Scores	Repeat 'once aloud' condition	Repeat 'three times aloud' condition
0	1	0
1	5	1
2	1	1
3	3	8
Total	**10**	**10**

The frequency graph shows that more syllables are recalled correctly with rehearsal for three seconds than with rehearsal for one second.

Inferential statistics

Choosing a test – the Wilcoxon signed-rank test

You need to carry out a statistical test to see if your results are significant or not. The test you need is the Wilcoxon signed-rank test. More about choosing and carrying out a statistical test is explained in Chapter 5 (pp. 330–331), which focuses on method, and how to carry out the test is explained in Chapter 6 (pp. 402–404), where the mathematical element of your course is covered. The tests you need for your course are the chi-squared test, Spearman's rank correlation coefficient test, the Mann-Whitney U test and the Wilcoxon signed-rank test. All four are called 'non-parametric' because they do not need parametric conditions to be met. Parametric conditions include having normal distribution. You do not need to know about parametric tests for your course.

A Wilcoxon signed-rank test is the one for a test of difference, when the design is repeated measures and the level of measurement is at least ordinal data. This practical investigation suits those elements for choosing a test. You may have used a Mann-Whitney U test for your data as your own practical investigation might have involved using an independent groups design.

Level of significance

In order to use a statistical test to see if results are significant or not, you need to choose a level of significance. As the study here replicates part of Peterson and Peterson (1959), you should be able to choose quite a tough level of significance as the results are likely to show a difference. Here the level chosen is $p \leq 0.025$, which means 25 in 1,000 people might get the result by chance but it is expected that 975 people in 1,000 will recall more if they rehearse a nonsense syllable three times than if they rehearse once.

One-tailed or two-tailed

In order to test for significance, you also need to know whether to look at tables for one-tailed or two-tailed hypotheses. The practical investigation explained here is one-tailed in the hypothesis, as it is said that *more* nonsense syllables are recalled with *more* rehearsal (direction is stated).

Critical value tables

You will need to use critical value tables to see if the results of the Wilcoxon signed-rank test are significant (one-tailed and at $p \leq 0.025$). In an examination, the critical value tables will be provided. You can look them up using the internet too, to help you when doing the practical investigation. For example: www.uwe.ac.uk/hlss/llas/statistics-in-linguistics/Appenix1.pdf.

Carrying out the Wilcoxon signed-rank test

The Wilcoxon signed-rank test is not that difficult. The workings for this practical investigation are shown in Table 7.14.

Table 7.14 Workings for the Wilcoxon signed-rank test

Participants' scores – once rehearsed	Participants' scores – three times rehearsed	Differences in scores between the two conditions	Ranking the differences (ignoring 0 differences)
1	3	-2	4
3	3	0	/
0	2	-2	4
2	3	-1	1
3	3	0	/
1	1	0	/
1	3	-2	4
1	3	-2	4
3	3	0	/
1	3	-2	4

- Total of ranks for differences with a plus (+) sign = 0
- Total of ranks for differences with a minus (–) sign = 21
- The smaller of these is the T statistic, so T = 0.
- Just one more figure is required – *N* (*n*), which is the number of participants. However, this is not ten, even though there were ten participants. Results for only six participants are used because, for the other four participants, their scores were the same in the two conditions. So here *N* = 6.

Progress check 7.15

For the following hypothesis, would you need to look at the 'one-tailed' or 'two-tailed' values in the critical values table?

'There will be more letters recalled in the same order as they are presented if the letters are chunked into three letters with meaning (such as "CIA") than if the same letters are presented in lots of three letters but without meaning (such as "IAC").'

You can use Chapter 5 (pp. 316–318) to help in understanding this hypothesis and to look more at hypotheses and 'one-tailed/two-tailed'.

STUDY HINT

You should be able to see from these calculations that this test is not too difficult and does not take long. Make up some data and, using a step-by-step procedure, carry out the Wilcoxon test a few times and you will soon see that it is very straightforward.

Interpreting the T statistic from your test

- To interpret the T statistic, which is 0, you will need to use critical values tables. You also need to know that $N = 6$, $p \leq 0.025$ and this is one-tailed.
- If you study the critical values table carefully (e.g. see link provided above or p. 404), you will see, using the columns and rows, that the critical value for $N = 6$, $p \leq 0.025$ and one-tailed is 0.
- In the Wilcoxon signed-rank test, if the observed value/calculated value is equal to or lower than the critical value then the result is significant – the null hypothesis can be rejected and the experimental hypothesis accepted.
- T = 0, which is equal to the critical value (0) and so the null hypothesis is rejected. The study 'worked' and it was found that the more rehearsal, the better recall (in short-term memory).

Consider your findings

Decide how far your findings support the idea that the more we rehearse, the better we recall. Some ideas from the suggested data are as follows:

- The mean, median and mode all show that repeating three times gives better recall than repeating once.
- The ranges are similar. This shows that the scores are similarly distributed. However, with only four possible scores, this is not a useful measure. The mean, median and mode for each of the two sets of scores (scores for the two conditions) are similar, which suggests normal distribution, but with a limited number of scores, it is hard to consider normal distribution.
- Some nonsense syllables are recalled better than others. For example, FOM is always recalled correctly. It may be that the ones better remembered were remembered as words. One participant remembered VW, which suggests that people may search for meaning when trying to learn.
- Some of the mistakes show that short-term memory uses sound because the mistakes show letters replaced with similar sounding letters, such as REM for REL.
- Three participants remembered all six syllables.
- In general, rehearsal for three seconds gives better recall than rehearsal for one second, which was predicted, given the findings of Peterson and Peterson (1959).
- A Wilcoxon signed-rank test shows the results are significant at $p \leq 0.025$ and the experimental hypothesis is accepted.
- There is a possibility of making a Type I error – the test means the results are said to be significant, but with just six participants, and the range of scores so narrow, it is possible that this rejection of the null is not justified.

Record your study

The notes in your practical notebook should provide you with enough material for exam revision. When you have carried out a practical, you should have a better understanding of the methodological terms.

Strengths and weaknesses of the study

Strengths

- The study has a lot of careful controls. When extraneous variables, such as situational variables and experimenter variables, are controlled, it is likely that there are no confounding variables and it is the change in the independent variable that causes the change in the dependent variable. In this study, controls included standardised instructions and careful planning of the procedure so that the participants all did the same thing. Order effects were controlled using counterbalancing too. This study reflects scientific methods and so has scientific credibility, which is a strength.
- Another strength is that the findings in this study (here refer to your own findings and your own practical investigation) reflect the findings in the Peterson and Peterson (1959) study and show that the more rehearsal, the better the recall. This conclusion reflects the multi-store model of memory and the working memory model and the results can be used as evidence for those models, as can results from other studies. It is a strength of the study that there is other evidence to support the results.

- Another strength is that this is a repeated measures design so the memory abilities of the participant are the same for each condition. There could have been order effects because the participant might have got tired after the first condition or got better with practice after the first condition. However, counterbalancing was used, so having the same people do both conditions is a strength.

Weaknesses

- A weakness is that participant variables are extraneous variables that are not controlled for, so differences between the participants might affect results. Having said that, it is a repeated measures design, so any differences should cancel out, but with just ten participants that is not certain.
- Another weakness relates to the apparatus. It can't be certain that the nonsense syllables used did not have meaning for individuals, such as being the initials of their name, or having meaning in some other way. Also with use of vowels, 'words' could be made such as DUS being remembered as DUST, and indeed DUS was well remembered. An idea for doing a better study might be to use just consonants (e.g. DST).
- Another weakness is that perhaps there was not enough of a difference between the two conditions, having just one repeat (one second's worth of rehearsal) and three repeats (three seconds' worth of rehearsal). Having three repeats in one condition and nine repeats in another condition might make a larger difference in the results. It is possible that improvement is not linear (so that the more repeats, the better the recall) but has a different pattern (such as up to a threshold of repetition recall is the same, but crossing that threshold means more recall). The question is whether the operationalisation of one-second rehearsal being one repeat and three-second rehearsal being three repeats works.

Progress check 7.16

In general, experiments tend to be reliable but not valid. Explain how the practical investigation explained here can be said to have reliability but lack validity.

Possible improvements

- Using nonsense syllables of three items might be better if vowels were not used. Vowels in the English language tend to make words, or at least three letters that can be seen as a word and pronounced. This might bring in elements of semantic learning (meaning) that were not required in this experiment. Taking out vowels means it is much less likely that participants will use meaning to help recall.
- Timing rehearsal/repetition might be more accurate than using the numbers of repetitions. Timing is a better control as it would be exactly the same for everyone, whereas using the number of repetitions might have meant differences between participants as some might have repeated the nonsense syllables at a different speed.
- Using some qualitative data might add to the validity of the findings. After the data were gathered, each participant could have been asked about the experience. For example, they might say that one nonsense syllable spelled out their initials or they might say they did make up words to help their recall (such as DUS reminding them of DUST).
- There could have been individual differences between some or all of the ten participants such that the results were because of those differences, not because of the manipulation of the independent variable. For example, some might have been better at recall than others. If there were perhaps more participants, this should not matter as, no matter what the individual differences, each person does both conditions so if there is a difference between the conditions for each individual that should give credible results.

STUDY HINT

The cycle of enquiry is taking a theory, developing a hypothesis from it, testing empirically (using sense data) and then accepting, amending or rejecting the theory in light of the results of the study. One important feature of this cycle of enquiry is that there is a need to consider ideas to improve the study. That is an important feature of your course so be ready to give ideas for possible improvements to any study you are asked about.

Writing up the practical investigation

A report has the following sections: abstract, background/introduction, method, results, discussion/conclusion.

For the practical investigation in cognitive psychology, you have to know how to write up the procedure, results and discussion sections of a report. The studies explained in the relevant chapters will give you guidance on how to do that. For example, Baddeley's (1966b) study is set out in a relevant format for a report, as are other studies. Use what you have learned about the procedure, results and discussion sections of a report to write up those parts of the report of your practical investigation. If you have time, write up the abstract as that would be a useful summary for your revision.

If you have not already looked at a report of a study, then use this link: www-personal.umich.edu/~rickl/pubs/berman-jonides-lewis-2009-jeplmc.pdf. This is a study about short-term memory that links to some of the ideas about memory in your course and will show you how to write up the different sections.

Test yourself

1. What is the hypothesis of your own practical investigation in cognitive psychology? **(2 marks)**
2. Explain controls that you used in your practical investigation in cognitive psychology. **(4 marks)**
3. Explain whether your T statistic (from carrying out a Wilcoxon signed-rank test) was significant or not, which level of significance you used and what this meant for your hypothesis. **(6 marks)**

Biological psychology – a correlation

Course requirements for this practical investigation

This practical investigation involves doing a study that yields data that can be analysed using a correlation. As in social and cognitive psychology, this practical investigation must relate to a topic that is in the material in biological psychology for your course.

Check that the focus suits the course material

The topic chosen for the example practical investigation in this chapter is aggression, as that is a main focus in biological psychology in your course. This practical investigation looks at stress and aggression, which links to the material in biological psychology.

What must be done

The instructions are to design and conduct a correlation study that links to aggression or to attitudes to drug use. This correlation relates to aggression. You have to make appropriate design decisions to plan and gather data to suit correlation analysis. Decisions must include a hypothesis and/or research question, the research method, sampling decisions, ethical considerations, data collection tools, data analysis, results and discussion.

The data must be collected and commented upon, including using appropriate descriptive statistics (measures of central tendency, measures of dispersion, graphs and tables) and also Spearman's rank correlation coefficient as an inferential test to look for a significant relationship. The significance of the results must be explained, including level of significance. The strength and direction of the correlation must also be commented upon. Commenting on the study includes considering strengths and weaknesses as well as possible improvements. There is also a requirement to write up the abstract and the discussion sections of a report, with the discussion including a conclusion.

Progress check 7.17

What form must the analysis of the correlation take?

Aims

Research question or hypothesis?

With a correlation design, you can sometimes develop an idea that comes only briefly from existing studies, if anything in the area has been studied at all. This is because a correlation is testing for a relationship and not a difference between conditions. If a researcher is not sure whether two variables, for example, are related or not, then an exploratory study collecting scores for the two variables and then testing to see if there is a correlation can be useful. There may not be as much background information as if the study is an experiment, testing an established theory. When looking for a difference, previous results are often there to draw on, as was shown in the two practical investigations in social and cognitive psychology.

An exploratory study might have a research question more than a hypothesis and aims may not be so clearly set out. A hypothesis is a statement of what is expected when a study is carried out, with the variables operationalised. A research question is more general and allows for exploration of ideas. A study gathering qualitative data is likely to have a research question and not a hypothesis, as it is more likely to be exploratory and looking in depth at an issue rather than having an operationalised hypothesis that is derived from theory.

The study proposed here does have evidence for what is suggested and so there is a hypothesis. The research question is: 'Do people who report more stressful life events in the last 12 months report themselves as responding more aggressively in situations?'.

The hypothesis in this practical investigation is that the more stress/stressful events someone reports in their life, the more they report feelings of aggression. It is OK to have a hypothesis as there is relevant background to show that stress links to aggression. In fact, there is quite a bit of evidence for that being the case, including biological evidence.

Progress check 7.18

Decide whether the following studies would have a hypothesis or just a research question.

Proposed study	Research question or hypothesis?
A pilot study to listen to children while they are drawing, to find out about their ideas and concepts	
An experiment to see whether recall of a story reduces over time	
A case study to look at one person with brain damage and how their memory is affected	
A questionnaire to find out about young people's use of social media sites	
A correlation design to see if the older people are, the more they are willing to help people, as measured by self-report data	

Brief background

In March 2014, a study using mice showed biological effects of early stress (e.g. in the HPA axis). When some mice were then given a rest period, the biological effects of stress reduced, as did levels of aggression. What was observed in some mice, however, was that the emotional effects of early stress did seem to have led to more aggression later in their life cycle. Another study, using rats this time, in 2004, detected what was called a 'fast positive feedback loop' between a 'hormonal stress response' and aggression. Experiments gave electric stimulation to the brain area for aggression and found a stress response in the form of blood levels of a hormone.

Some studies measure aggressive behaviour and some measure brain areas for aggression. Some studies measure environmental stress and some measure stress hormones. There is a lot more that has been done looking at the link between stress and aggression, whether measured 'biologically' or 'environmentally'. However, for this practical investigation, there is just a small amount of information given here to link the correlation study with past evidence.

Choosing the level of significance

The level of significance is chosen early in a study, as it should rest on what can be expected from what is already known. As the background to this study suggests that people who report stress events more over the last 12 months also report more aggression, this means that the level of significance chosen could be $p \leq 0.01$. However, as some of the studies reported here are animal studies and perhaps findings might not be true of humans, and also because the studies are not replicated exactly here, the level of significance chosen is $p \leq 0.05$.

Explore

You can see the article that discusses how early stress can affect later aggression by using the following link: www.sciencedaily.com/releases/2014/03/140327123654.htm.

Progress check 7.19

1 For the following levels of significance, show what they mean in terms of X out of 100 or X out of 1,000:
   a $p \leq 0.03$
   b $p \leq 0.002$.
2 Give the levels of significance ($p \leq$) for the following:
   a 1 in 1,000
   b 5 in 100.

STUDY HINT

In the examination, you will be asked questions about your practical investigations. Keep a notebook, so that you have information that you can revise for each examination.

Research method

The research design suggested is a correlation. A correlation can come from various research methods, including questionnaire and interview (which is why it is called a 'design' here rather than a 'research method'). The research method used here is a questionnaire, but other research methods can generate correlation data.

Data collected for correlation analysis

Often data used for correlation analysis are self-report data. However, a correlation can have other measures, such as measuring stress hormone levels and aggression in rats to see if there is a correlation. Studies have also found a correlation between temperature and aggression, with the hotter the temperature, the more aggression shown, as measured by level of car horn hooting, among other measures (see Baron, 1979). More recent studies have looked at aggression and driving in India and found that the higher someone's level of aggression, the more aggressive they will be when reacting to other drivers (Sagar *et al.*, 2013). So correlation measures do not have to be self-report. For your practical investigation, however, self-report data are probably easier to access than temperature, or car horn hooting, or measures of hormonal stress. Here self-report data are gathered. To do that, a questionnaire is a suitable research method.

You could carry out your practical alone or work in a small group so that you can pool data. The self-report data are collected by questionnaire and there are rating scales to provide scores that can be correlated. Note that yes/no answers are not scores and so cannot lead to a correlation test. However, they can be useful to check for reliability in the answers and they can help to test for bias, such as social desirability (this is explained later in this section).

Progress check 7.20

List three ideas for correlations given in this 'Research method' section.

Hypotheses

The alternative hypothesis for this study is: 'There is a positive relationship between self-reported amount of stress events (over the last 12 months) and self-reported aggressive tendencies'. The null hypothesis is: 'There is no relationship between self-reported amount of stress events (over the last 12 months) and self-reported aggression and any difference is due to chance or some other variable'.

Directional or non-directional hypothesis

The above hypothesis is directional because the relationship expected is positive. This means that, as self-reported stress events get a *higher* score, then self-reported aggressive tendencies *rise*. This means that, when you use critical values tables after carrying out the statistical test, you will use the one-tailed column. The level of significance has already been set at $p \leq 0.05$.

Progress check 7.21

For the following hypotheses, note whether they are one-tailed or two-tailed and whether they are correlations or looking for difference.

Hypothesis	One- or two-tailed?	Correlation or difference?
The temperature of the day relates to the amount of car hooting on that day.		
The more times someone hears a story, the less they will recall about it.		
People will recall more words if the words are sorted into categories than if presented randomly.		

Design

This is a correlation design. Although it has features of a repeated measures design (the same people do both parts of the study, reporting their stress events and their aggression), a correlation is in itself a design.

A correlation has two variables that are of equal status so there is no independent or dependent variable. In this study, one variable is what the participant reports about stress events in their lives in the last 12 months and the other variable is their report about their aggression.

Drawing up the questionnaires

The data are collected by means of two questionnaires, or one questionnaire with two sections, one for each variable:

- One questionnaire or section will ask about an individual's stress events over the last year.
- The other will ask about an individual's rating of their own aggression at the time of asking.

The scores from the questionnaires, if you are using two, have to be correlated. It is, therefore, a good idea to write them on either side of the same sheet of paper, so that you are certain to match the correct scores for each participant. Another way to collect the data is to use one questionnaire incorporating both variables. You do not want the participants to guess exactly what the study is asking, because you might then have bias in the form of social desirability or demand characteristics, but you do want to be relatively honest, because of ethical issues, such as getting informed consent. Incorporating both variables can help to mask, to an extent, the actual focus of the study. This requires some deceit, so a debrief would be needed.

Just asking for a rating of stress and then a rating of aggression would be one way of gathering data. However, it is better to devise more than one way of measuring stress and more than one way of measuring aggression. In this study, instead of asking someone about their aggression, they are asked about their emotional reactions, as that is not so 'leading'. Asking about specific emotional reactions (such as angry outbursts or practical responses to a situation) can yield an 'aggression' score without leading the participant. Also asking about their stress events can be distressing, so the questions are not too direct.

For this practical investigation, there is no need to gather personal data such as age, gender or other information. It might be of interest, but this practical investigation is about the correlation itself. It might be interesting to see if the results are affected by age, or by gender, but that is not the main focus. Ethically, you should only ask for personal data that are required.

With regard to specific items on the questionnaire, there are some issues to note. The questions about life events ask about 'the last 12 months' rather than 'the last year', as 'the last year' might cause confusion. The questions are asked rather informally so that a respondent can avoid going into things too deeply if they wish to. It would be rather leading and perhaps distressing to ask directly about 'stress events'. Also this has the benefit of letting the respondent decide what 'events' mean to them. The disadvantage is that 'events' can mean different things to different people. In a way, there is no need to ask about 'bad' events as it has been shown that even 'good' events lead to stress (e.g. Holmes and Rahe, 1967).

Explore

You might like to investigate further the idea that life events lead to stressful reactions. Stress is defined as not having the resources to cope with a situation, so what is stressful for one person might not be for another. Here is a link to consider such issues. www.mindtools.com/pages/article/newTCS_82.htm.

Progress check 7.22

For the study given here, list three issues that arose in designing the questionnaires and explain how they were dealt with.

Data collection tools

Data collection tools refer to the way the data are gathered. For this practical investigation, that is by means of one questionnaire, with items gathering data for both variables.

Examples of possible questions are given, but it would be more interesting and useful for you to design your own.

Suggested standardised instructions are:

Thank you for taking part in this study. Although the questions are about you, please note that your name will not be recorded. I am interested in how events over the last 12 months predict emotional responses, rather than in analysing your particular situation. Are you happy to continue? Please remember that you can stop taking part at any time. There is one questionnaire asking questions about events in your life over the last 12 months and one about your emotional reactions to certain situations. I will explain fully after you have completed both questionnaires. The questionnaire will take about 20 minutes. I hope that is all right.

The questionnaire

Suggested debriefing instructions are:

Thank you for taking part in this study, which is for my A level (AS level) practical investigation. My idea is that the more stressful life events someone has had over the past 12 months, the more their reactions are likely to be aggressive or angry. Our biology is such that stress hormones and aggression are linked and that is what I am investigating. This is not about you personally; this is studying people in general. I am not using the data for any purpose other than gathering data for me, for my course, and I am not recording your name at all. Is it OK for me to use your data? I am happy if you feel you would not like me to do that. Is there anything you would like to ask?

STUDY HINT

A note on ethics: the questions on aggression and those about stress events are not direct. Hopefully, they are not distressing. Thinking about stressful life events is upsetting and the aim is not to upset participants. That is why questions are rather general but they should still yield a 'stress events' and an 'aggression' score.

Events in your life

(1) In general, would you say that you are a stressed or relaxed person? Please tick the appropriate box.

Stressed ☐ Relaxed ☐

(2) Please rate each statement, as it applies to you, by ticking the appropriate box:

SA = strongly agree; A = agree; DK = unsure (don't know); D = disagree; SD = strongly disagree

Statement	SA	A	DK	D	SD
I have had a fairly relaxed 12 months.	☐	☐	☐	☐	☐
There is a lot going on in my life.	☐	☐	☐	☐	☐
My friends would say that I have a good life.	☐	☐	☐	☐	☐
I feel rushed to get things done that I have to do.	☐	☐	☐	☐	☐

(3) If you would like to add more please do so here, but you do not have to. These answers are confidential.

Your emotional reactions recently

(4) In general, would you say you react to events using anger or withdrawal? Please tick the appropriate box.

Anger ☐ Withdrawal ☐ Not emotional ☐

(5) Please rate each statement, as it applies to you, by ticking the appropriate box:

SA = strongly agree; A = agree; DK = unsure (don't know); D = disagree; SD = strongly disagree

Statement	SA	A	DK	D	SD
When things get tough, I get angry.	☐	☐	☐	☐	☐
I tackle things in a practical, measured way.	☐	☐	☐	☐	☐
I would rate myself as quick to turn on someone.	☐	☐	☐	☐	☐
I feel I mostly control my emotions successfully.	☐	☐	☐	☐	☐

(6) If you would like to add more please do so here, but you do not have to. These answers are confidential.

Ethical issues

The subject matter of this study might cause anxiety for some participants. It is important to allow people not to take part if they do not wish to. If people have had stressful life events over the last 12 months, remembering details may distress them.

If this is a class practical, it might be difficult to allow some class members not to take part. One way round this is to work on the questionnaires as a group and to make sure that everyone understands the practical. Then, ask the members of the group to take the questionnaires away with them and return them next lesson. If the questionnaires are on either side of a sheet of paper (i.e. they are linked), there is no need for names to be on them. It would, therefore, not be known which class members did not complete the task. Ethical issues should take precedence over other issues and all class members should be allowed to share the data. Remember to:

- give the right to withdraw
- get informed consent
- maintain confidentiality
- debrief afterwards
- ensure competence.

Risk management

Risk management must be considered for each of your practical investigations. Risk management is about protecting participants, others and yourself as researcher. Different studies carry different risks as they use different research methods and data collection tools. This practical investigation is considered here, with regard to managing risk.

Risk to participants

This is just a questionnaire so there is no apparatus that causes risk and the setting can be chosen by the researcher. The participant can say they do not want to take part, thus avoiding risk. However, the study does ask about stress, in the form of 'things going on' and that might bring up feelings and thoughts that a participant does not want brought up. It also asks about anger, which can be threatening for an individual to answer. The standardised instructions go some way to saying that the focus is on emotional reactions and issues that have happened, so a participant should refuse to take part if they feel taking part is a risk for them. However, they might take part anyway so the debrief does cover the issue of their being distressed. To manage the risk as far as possible, statements were kept very general.

Risk to researchers

The same risk applies as in other studies, and that is the unlikely event of a participant posing a risk to a researcher. The researcher should make sure someone else is near, such as using the questionnaire in a public place and not alone. Having someone else there can protect the participant as well, which is good risk management.

Risk to others

There is no need to involve others and the questionnaire can be administered individually, when nobody is around – other than someone nearby as support, as outlined above.

Carrying out the practical

You need to gather at least ten sets of data. If you are working on a class practical, you can complete the questionnaires yourselves and pool the data, and you could get more data. If you are working alone or in a small group, you will need to ask other participants to help you.

Sampling

You need to understand sampling decisions and design decisions. For your practical investigation, it is likely that an opportunity sample will be used. However, you could put up posters asking for volunteers if you are carrying out your practical in a specific place, such as a school or college. That would yield a volunteer sample. Random sampling is possible if you have access to a list of participants who would like to take part – that would involve volunteer sampling at first and then random sampling to get the final group of participants. However, if people do volunteer, it might be more ethical to engage them in the study rather than to 'reject' them.

Progress check 7.23

How would you generate a random sample for this study?

Gathering the data

Print off sufficient copies of your questionnaire, depending on how you are going to gather the data. You could do this online if you want to set that up. If you are going to ask people as you come across them (an opportunity sample), then make sure you have something to write with and also perhaps take a card to hand to them with some information in case they want to contact you, such as to withdraw their data.

Make sure you take some care in gathering the data, such as giving each participant privacy. The questions here are not asking in detail about someone's problems, but they are close to that so there needs to be competence and sensitivity on your part. Ethical issues are of the utmost importance. If at any time you feel your participant is uncomfortable, then do not continue, though thank them of course.

Analysing the data

The questionnaires have to be analysed to obtain a score for each participant. One score is a 'stress events' score and one score is an 'aggressive reaction' score. It is best to give high scores to 'high stress' and 'aggressive' and low scores to 'low stress' and 'relaxed'. That suits the hypothesis, which is that there will be more aggression the more stress events experienced.

The first and last questions on each questionnaire are checks to make sure that the data seem appropriate. For example, if someone gets a high 'stress events' score but says they are not stressed, then the data might not be valid. Similarly, answers given to the open question should help to see if the data are valid. These two additional questions (the one that asks directly about a) stressed/not stressed and b) anger, distress or not emotional, and the open question) also check for reliability because, in a way, they are asking the question again to see if the same results are found.

Remember to check the questionnaires for validity and reliability. If the answers do not match up for the same person, you might consider not using that set of data.

The middle questions for the two questionnaires, where ratings are given to statements, are the scores used for the correlation.

Scoring for the questionnaire about stress events

Statement	SA	A	DK	D	SD
I have had a fairly relaxed 12 months.	1	2	3	4	5
There is a lot going on in my life.	5	4	3	2	1
My friends would say that I have a good life.	1	2	3	4	5
I feel rushed to get things done that I have to do.	5	4	3	2	1

Scoring for the questionnaire about aggression

Statement	SA	A	DK	D	SD
When things get tough, I get angry.	5	4	3	2	1
I tackle things in a practical, measured way.	1	2	3	4	5
I would rate myself as quick to turn on someone.	5	4	3	2	1
I feel I mostly control my emotions successfully.	1	2	3	4	5

The data

- Both questionnaires have two statements where strongly agree gets 5 points and two questions where strongly agree gets 1 point.
- Calculate two scores for each participant, one for their 'stress score' and one for 'aggression'.
- A person whose perception was 'stressed' could score a maximum of 20 points. A person with a perception of themselves as 'aggressive' could score a maximum of 20 points. The lowest possible score is 4 (either 'no stress' or 'no aggression').

STUDY HINT

Remember, the scores from self-report data are only perceived.

Progress check 7.24

Why are the scores reversed in both sets of statements (Q2 and Q5)?

Writing up the results

- For a correlation, you need to show the actual scores, so that the rankings are clear and can be judged, before the scatter diagram and statistical test.
- The results section of a report should include a results table. The raw scores usually go in an appendix, but for this correlation, as there are few data, they are all displayed in Table 7.15. In a report, the table should be followed by a commentary, explaining what it represents.
- The graph for a correlation is always a scatter diagram. The graph should be followed by a commentary.
- A statistical test is carried out. The actual calculations go in an appendix. The result of the test is given in the results section, with a commentary explaining what it means, such as whether it is significant or not.

A table of possible results

Some possible results (made-up data) are given in Table 7.15, but you should draw up your own table with your own results. The scores come from self-rating, so are ordinal data and the mean is, therefore, not calculated. Ordinal data are ranked data, not necessarily with real mathematical scores.

STUDY HINT

Review Chapter 6, where descriptive statistics are discussed, if you are not sure about mathematical elements. Check that you understand about measures of central tendency, measures of dispersion and levels of measurement. Write out your own definitions of these terms, including mode, median, mean, range, standard deviation, nominal data, ordinal data and interval/ratio data.

Table 7.15 The relationship between reported stress events over the last 12 months and reported aggression

Participant	'Stress events' score (self-report data on rating scale) (Q2)	'Aggression' score (self-report data on rating scale) (Q5)	Ranking for 'stress events' score	Ranking for 'aggression' score
1	15	12	8	4.5
2	9	7	3.5	1
3	18	16	10	9.5
4	10	15	5	8
5	6	8	1	2.5
6	14	13	7	6
7	11	16	6	9.5
8	8	8	2	2.5
9	9	12	3.5	4.5
10	17	14	9	7
	Mode = 9	Mode = 8/12/16		
	Median = 10.5	Median = 12.5		
	Range = 12	Range = 9		

Sense checking

Now carry out a sense check to see if there seems to be a relationship between the two sets of scores for each participant. If there is a relationship, then a high rank for one score will go with a high rank for the other score; low ranks will also go together.

Participants 3, 6, 8, and 9 have rankings that are within one unit of each other, which is a good match and shows a relationship. Participants 5 and 10 have ranks up to two apart, which is a fair relationship. Participant 2 has two reasonably close ranks. However, participants 1, 4 and 7 have ranks further apart, which suggests no relationship.

This seems close to a correlation but by no means certain. A scatter diagram will help to see the correlation, if there is one, more easily. Of course doing a statistical test will tell us whether there is a correlation or not and at what strength.

A scatter diagram

A scatter diagram can help to show whether there is a relationship present.

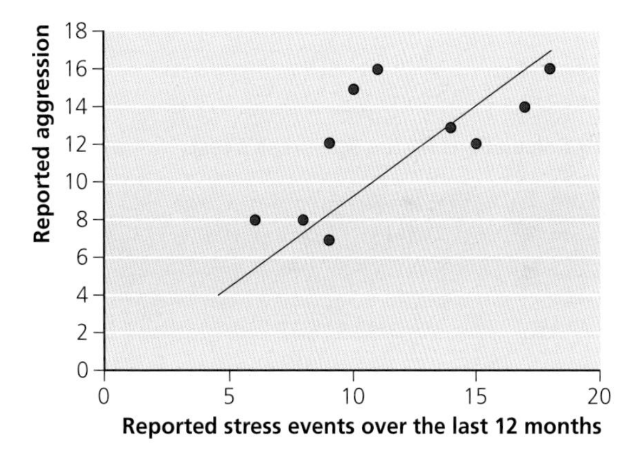

A scatter diagram to show the relationship between reported stress events over the last 12 months and reported aggression

The line of best fit, with five scores on each side, is in a positive direction, although some scores are quite a distance from the line. The graph, together with the sense check, seem to suggest that there is a positive correlation between stress and aggression. A statistical test will show whether this is the case.

Progress check 7.25

What is the line of best fit on a scatter diagram?

Spearman's rank correlation coefficient test

A Spearman's test is carried out on the data because it is the correct test for a correlation with ordinal data.

Explanation

Levels of measurement are nominal (categories), ordinal (ranks) and interval/ratio (real measurements, such as time).

STUDY HINT

All four tests for your Year 1 course have been explained in Chapter 6. For more about how to do a Spearman's rank correlation coefficient test, refer to pp. 409–411. All the information you need for your practical investigations is in Chapter 5 (method) and Chapter 6 (maths).

Progress check 7.26

Why is the Spearman's rank correlation coefficient the right test?

How to calculate the Spearman coefficient

$$1-\frac{6\,\Sigma d^2}{n(n^2-1)}$$

You can use the formula to calculate the result of the Spearman's test for the data given in this practical investigation. A step-by-step approach is given below to help.

Refer to Table 7.16.

Step 1: Rank both sets of data.

Step 2: Work out the difference between the ranks for each participant.

Step 3: Square (multiply by itself) the difference found in Step 2 for each participant. This gets rid of the minus signs.

Step 4: Add up the squared differences (the numbers worked out in Step 3). For the data given in Table 7.16, the total is **48.5**.

Step 5: Find N, which is the number of scores. (Here, N = **10**)

Step 6: Multiply the sum of the squared differences (from Step 4) by 6. (Here, 48.5 × 6 = **291**)

Step 7: Square N and subtract 1. (Here, 10 × 10 – 1 = **99**)

Table 7.16 Calculations for the Spearman's test

Participant	'Stress events' score (self-report data on rating scale)	'Aggression' score (self-report data on rating scale)	Ranking for 'stress events' score (Step 1)	Ranking for 'aggression' score (Step 1)	Difference between ranks (Step 2)	Differences squared (Step 3)
1	15	12	8	4.5	+3.5	12.25
2	9	7	3.5	1	+2.5	6.25
3	18	16	10	9.5	+0.5	0.25
4	10	15	5	8	-3	9
5	6	8	1	2.5	-1.5	2.25
6	14	13	7	6	+1	1
7	11	16	6	9.5	-3.5	12.25
8	8	8	2	2.5	-0.5	0.25
9	9	12	3.5	4.5	-1	1
10	17	14	9	7	+2	4
	Mode = 9	Mode = 8/12/16				Total (Σ) = 48.5 (Step 4)
	Median = 10.5	Median = 12.5				

Step 8: Multiply the answer found in Step 7 by N. (Here, $99 \times 10 =$ **990**)

Step 9: Divide the answer to Step 6 by the answer to Step 8. (Here, 291/990 = **+ 0.29**)

Step 10: Subtract the answer to Step 9 from 1. (Here, 1 – 0.29 = **+0.71**) This is the result of the test. It is in Step 10 that a minus or plus sign is allocated. If the answer to Step 6 is larger than the answer to Step 8, the result of Step 10 will be negative and any correlation will be negative. If the answer to Step 6 is smaller than the answer to Step 8, the result of Step 10 will be positive and any correlation will be positive.

Step 11: Look up the result of the test in statistical tables to see if it is significant. Statistical tables show that for $N = 10$ and a significance level of 0.05, the critical result is 0.56. As +0.71 is greater than 0.56, the result is significant. Therefore, there is a positive correlation between reported stress events in the last 12 months and reported aggression.

STUDY HINT

Level of significance and how to look up the result of a statistical test is explained in Chapter 5 (pp. 331–335). Another Spearman's test is worked through in Chapter 6 (pp. 409–411).

Using critical value tables to check significance

Table 7.17 Critical values for Spearman's rank, one-tailed

n	0.05	0.025	0.01	0.005
5	0.900	1.000	1.000	–
6	0.829	0.886	0.943	1.000
7	0.714	0.786	0.893	0.929
8	0.643	0.738	0.833	0.881
9	0.600	0.683	0.783	0.833
10	0.564	0.648	0.746	0.794
12	0.506	0.591	0.712	0.777

Step 11 outlines how to use the critical values table. There are ten participants so $N = 10$. The columns needed from the critical values table are the one-tailed ones, so they are given here (Table 7.17). The chosen level of significance was $p \leq 0.05$. The observed value is +0.71. The relevant critical value is 0.564. As +0.71 is larger than this value, it is significant at $p \leq 0.05$. If the level of significance chosen had been $p \leq 0.025$, which is a stricter level than $p \leq 0.05$, then the critical value would be 0.648, so the result is in fact still significant at $p \leq 0.025$. The null hypothesis is rejected and the alternative hypothesis is accepted.

It was interesting that both the sense check and a study of the scatter diagram suggested that the results might be significant, but it was not obvious. And yet the result is clearly significant. This helps to show the value of using statistical testing.

Progress check 7.27

1. If the result of the test was +0.45 and the chosen level of significance was $p \leq 0.01$, with $N = 9$, would the null hypothesis be accepted or rejected?
2. If the result of the test was +0.683 and the chosen level of significance was $p \leq 0.025$, with $N = 9$, would the null hypothesis be accepted or rejected?

Type I or Type II error

If an error was made and the null hypothesis was rejected wrongly, with other studies or a re-analysis showing that in fact the results were not significant, then that is a Type I error. This would not come to light immediately but is worth noting.

STUDY HINT

Chapter 5 (page 336) explained Type I and Type II errors. Type I was thought of as being optimistic in accepting that the study 'worked', when it was found later that the hypothesis should not have been accepted. 'Type One' and 'Optimistic' might help you to remember what Type I and Type II means (Type II is accepting the null wrongly, being pessimistic).

Consider the findings

- The result has shown that the correlation was significant at quite a good level of significance so it is a strong correlation, as 0.71 would predict.
- The result is +0.71 so a positive correlation: as someone rates highly having 'things going on' over the last year or feeling rushed, they have also rated highly 'getting angry' and 'turning on someone'. The more they feel they have a lot on, the more they feel they get angry (and the less they feel in control of their emotions).
- Of course this is self-report data and just four items were given to rate each variable. There would be cross-checking to see whether those who rate themselves 'high' on stress events and 'high' on anger should have ticked 'stressed' and 'anger' for Q1 and Q4. If the claims regarding stress events match the 'stressed' tick and the claims about aggression match the 'anger' tick, then that can help to claim reliability.

Table 7.18 Answers to Q1 and Q4 alongside answers to Q2 and Q5

Participant	'Stress events' score (self-report data on rating scale) (Q2)	'Aggression' score (self-report data on rating scale) (Q5)	Stressed or relaxed (Q1)	Anger (A), withdrawal (W) or not emotional (NE) (Q4)
1	15	12	Stressed	A
2	9	7	Relaxed	W
3	18	16	Stressed	A
4	10	15	Relaxed	NE
5	6	8	Relaxed	NE
6	14	13	Stressed	A
7	11	16	Stressed	W
8	8	8	Relaxed	NE
9	9	12	Relaxed	A
10	17	14	Stressed	A

Table 7.18 shows that four out of five of those with more than 12 on the 'aggression' score (Q5) also said they were stressed (Q1). Of those with 12 or under on the 'aggression' score, one said they were stressed (and they had a score of 12), with the other four saying they were relaxed. This supports the validity of the data, in showing a correlation.

Table 7.18 also shows that the four participants with more than 12 on the 'stress events' score said they react with anger. One participant with a score of 9 said they react with anger. The other, lower scores for 'stress events' either say they withdraw or they are not emotional. This too gives weight to the conclusions.

- No qualitative data are given here but the questionnaire does gather qualitative data to give the participants chance to make further comment. They can then talk about the life events if they wish to, which might help any ethical issues, such as their feeling distressed and not able to talk about it. Qualitative data would be used to check the findings and can help to add validity to the results.
- With just ten scores and an opportunity sample, there is not likely to be generalisability in this study. The sampling could easily show bias, such as asking just people of one age group or gender. It was decided for this study, which is for an A level or AS course, that asking for personal data was not justified. However, personal data can help to see characteristics of the sample to see if generalising is justified.
- Ethics in this study are dealt with reasonably well, but there is still the worry that asking about stressful events and asking about aggressive reactions will trigger distress. Items were kept very general but the word 'stressed' was used and the word 'anger' was used. It would be very important to debrief carefully. The right to withdraw is given carefully, including in the questionnaire itself.
- There is some deceit in order to avoid social desirability and demand characteristics but those features may be present. Perhaps a question about 'things going on' will give an answer of 'strongly agree' because someone does not want to be seen as someone with not a lot 'going on'. Similarly, by including headings on the two sections of the questionnaire, enough might be understood about the aims for the participant to give certain responses through demand characteristics.

Record your study

You need to record all the information you might need about your practical investigation so that you can answer questions about it in an examination. The more you have worked on your practical investigation yourself and the more you analyse the data and consider the findings, the better you will remember the issues and be able to write about them.

Strengths and weaknesses of the study

Strengths

- One strength of this study is having Q1 and Q4 as checks for reliability and Q3 and Q6 as well, so that the participant can add qualitative data in the form of comment. There can be a test for reliability, which is a strength, and indeed in the example study given here it is claimed that there is reliability.

- Another strength is having qualitative data as well. These were not given or analysed in this practical investigation but having the possibility of analysing rich and detailed comments means validity can be assessed.
- Another strength is the controls that were put in place, such as standardised instructions and having the statements scored to avoid a response bias (so that not all statements that would give 'aggression' were 'strongly agree' and not all statements that would give 'stress from life events' were 'strongly agree'). There was an attempt to avoid bias from social desirability.

Weaknesses

- One weakness is having the check questions (Q1 and Q4) in the sense that they might lead to demand characteristics as they are rather specific and leading (Q1 mentions 'stressed' and Q4 mentions 'anger'). Participants might want to reply according to what they think the purpose is, which is what is meant by demand characteristics.
- Another weakness is that, although the alternative hypothesis was accepted, this is only a correlation. It cannot be concluded that stress in the form of life events causes aggressive reactions. A correlation just shows a relationship between two variables. Stress and aggression vary together and a positive relationship was shown; however, there might be some other variable involved – for example, personality. The individual asked might have had individual differences that linked to stress and aggression.
- A third weakness is the lack of generalisability as a random sample was not used, but an opportunity sample. With just ten people, and chosen for convenience, it is not likely that an unbiased sample was picked.
- A fourth weakness is that self-report data were gathered, which is a useful measure but perhaps not an objective one. The data were not measuring someone's stress, which might be measured by seeing how much stress hormone was in the blood. The data were not about actual aggression either, but about what someone says about themselves in terms of being aggressive. It is important to note these differences, although there is validity in gathering self-report data because it is 'real' in the sense of being what someone says about themselves.

Progress check 7.28

Write out definitions for the terms a) reliability, b) validity, and c) generalisability. (Turn to Chapter 5, pp. 324–325 if you need to.)

Possible improvements

- Self-report data can be checked by using peer-report data alongside it. This was done by Cohrs *et al.* (2012), one of the contemporary studies in social psychology. Another questionnaire could be given to each participant for them to ask someone who knows them to complete and return it. Similar items could be used, phrased accordingly, and a test done to see if self-report data match peer-report data.
- An interview could be used to follow up on the questionnaire. This would help regarding ethics as then any distress from being asked about stress and anger could be checked. Though if it was thought that that was the case, then the study would not have been done, of course. An interview could gather qualitative data in more detail than was offered by the questionnaire and more depth could be uncovered about stress, life events and aggressive responses. It is only suggested that the interview backs the questionnaire because a correlation is required and an interview gathering just qualitative data would not suit that design.
- There could be other measures of stress, such as modelling on Holmes and Rahe's (1967) list of life events and how they relate to stress. They had a longer, more comprehensive list to measure both life events and stress levels. This was not chosen as an option because of possible ethical issues but it might be a better measure of life events. They did not measure aggression but a similar, longer set of items for aggression could be generated. This might yield more credible measures.

Writing up a psychology study

Studies in psychology are written up using the following sections: abstract, introduction, procedure/method, results, discussion, references and appendices. For your course, you do not have to write up a full report. However, you are asked to write up sections of a report, so that you know how this is done. For this practical, you are asked to write up the abstract of a report, the method section and a discussion section, including conclusions.

Abstract/summary

This study looked at whether there is a relationship in that the more stress in the form of life events that are experienced, the more they report feelings of aggression. Studies have shown links between stress and aggression. When animals have areas for aggression in the brain stimulated, stress hormones arise, for example. It seemed reasonable to suggest that if someone reports a 'lot going on' in the last 12 months they might be more likely to say they have feelings of anger than someone feeling relaxed about the last 12 months. A questionnaire gathered self-report data about life events and emotional reactions. It was found that there was a positive correlation (+0.71, $p \leq 0.025$) and this meant that the alternative hypothesis was accepted. The higher the score on life events and things 'going on' in the last 12 months, the higher the score on emotional responses in the form of being 'quick to turn on someone'. It was concluded that there is a relationship between being stressed and being aggressive.

Method

The box below details a possible procedure, sampling and apparatus for this study, as these are important elements of the method part of a report. The design is a correlation.

Test yourself

1 You will have carried out a study using a correlation design. Describe how you gathered the data for your correlation. **(4 marks)**

2 Outline the aim of a study you carried out yourself as part of your course using a correlation design. **(2 marks)**

3 When you carried out your correlation design study, outline two controls that you used to make sure the data were either reliable or valid. **(4 marks)**

4 Explain the aim(s), procedure, results and conclusions of the practical investigation you carried out within biological psychology. Give two criticisms of your study. **(16 marks)**

Learning theories – an observation

Course requirements for this practical investigation

For the learning approach, you have to carry out an observation. The one suggested here is an observation of people in the street, their age, gender and their mobile phone use, including noting issues about it, so it is non-participant. You are free to choose a different observation.

You need to do two observations if one does not cover both qualitative and quantitative data. Here one observation has been chosen to gather both types of data at the same time, but you do not need to take that course of action.

Check that the focus suits the course material

Your observation must relate to behaviour that can link to learning. Here the idea is that linking age and gender to mobile phone use might pick up peer-related behaviour that could show social learning in action. If one gender or one age group shows different mobile phone use, this suggests that such use is learned by observing role models or though reinforcement and rewards.

Suggested procedure, sampling and apparatus sections for the study

Apparatus: copies of the questionnaire and pens or pencils to complete it.

Sample: opportunity sampling of ten participants was carried out by asking the first person available in the student common room of a sixth form college. When one person had completed the questionnaire, the next was approached. There were six males and four females in the sample, all aged 16 years. They were all students in the sixth form and none was studying psychology.

Opportunity sampling was chosen because it was convenient and quick, while still being ethical. There was no need to access registers, as for a random sample, and no need to select certain sorts of people as for a stratified sample. The students were asked clearly if they would like to participate or not, so were able to volunteer. They were told it would take around 20 minutes.

Procedure: the questionnaire was drawn up making sure that there were two rating scales (one about stress events, Q2, and one about aggression, Q5) and that the scores were sufficient to see if there were a correlation. There were also some checking questions to see if the ratings matched the other data (Q1 and Q4). Qualitative data were requested (Q3 and Q6), so that information could be found to see if the ratings were valid and reliable. The questionnaires were short, so that participants were not inconvenienced for a long time. It was decided that opportunity sampling would be used and that questionnaires would be completed with the researcher present. A pen was taken for the participant to use. It was decided to have the questionnaires completed individually, rather than in a group, to make sure that each participant was not affected by the others. This was in order to get data that were more valid. One researcher collected the data. The participants were asked if they had 20 minutes to help with a psychology study. Standardised instructions were read out (these could be in an appendix to the report). When the participant was happy to start, the questionnaire was handed out, with the pen. At the end, the participant was thanked and debriefed by telling him or her the aim of the study and that the data would be kept confidential.

What must be done

In the observation, there must be note-taking and tallying. To analyse the qualitative data, there must be thematic analysis. A chi-squared test must be carried out to analyse the quantitative data, which will be in the form of nominal data (categories obtained from the tallying). The practical investigation must be evaluated in terms of validity, reliability, generalisability and credibility. There must also be a write up of the results part of the practical investigation, including any graphs and tables, as well as writing up the results of thematic analysis.

Aim(s)

The aim of this observation is to look at mobile phone use in the street and factors such as age, gender and issues like having a pushchair or being in a family group. The study arose after a pilot observation, which suggested that older people use mobile phones less in public places than younger people do. Also the observation suggested that people with a child in a pushchair were often using their mobile phone. It seemed from the pilot that younger females used the phone more in the street than younger males. The aim of this practical investigation is to carry out a more detailed and 'scientific' observation, including some qualitative data in the form of notes, to look at age, gender and other issues. To an extent, themes arose from the pilot observation (such as whether the mobile phone user was in a group or not). This observation has general aims and a research question rather than specific hypotheses, though hypotheses can be generated.

Brief background

A study is currently taking place (in 2015) to look at the effect of mobile phone use on cognitive development. The focus of the study stems from claims that using a mobile phone could damage the brain in some way, a finding that has not been backed by evidence. Since scientific studies can produce findings that have credibility, the study is being done to see if cognitive development is affected by mobile phone use. Reading that such a study is being done is evidence that the issues are of interest currently. Statistics reported in *The Independent* in May 2014 suggest that about 90 per cent of children aged 14 use a mobile phone. This high usage backs the idea that studies into mobile phone use are relevant. The current study outlined here is called the Study of Cognition, Adolescents and Mobile Phones (SCAMP).

The present study, suggested for learning theories in your course, does not look at the biology of the brain, as the SCAMP study does, but looks at how people use mobile phones. It is suggested for the present study that mobile phone use comes from learning from others, such as social learning and reinforcement from peers. There are many reasons for using a mobile phone – from need (such as to get a lift home) to social networking (such as getting a group of friends together for a night out) and chatting. Some reasons might not be about learning – they might be purely practical. However, other reasons might be about learning, such as feeling that we ought to have a smart phone, as 'everyone else has one'. It is hard to believe that 90 per cent of 14 year olds need one; it is more likely that they are following the patterns of their generation. TV adverts and programmes show people using mobile phones and mobile phone manufacturers promote their products using role models. There are issues of learning in mobile phone use. These are looked at in this practical investigation.

Ahmed *et al.* (2014), a study of age differences in mobile phone usage

Ahmed *et al.* (2014) used questionnaires to look at students and professionals and their mobile phone use to look for differences. They found no differences between the two groups, when looking at the manufacturer of their phones, how often they charged them, the tariff they were on and such issues. They concluded that mobile phone use was similar and they did not find age differences. One aim of the present study, however, is to look for age differences.

Chung-Chu (2010), a study of gender differences in mobile phone usage

Chung-Chu (2010) in Taiwan looked at gender and mobile phone use. This study looked at situational factors in mobile phone use, such as time pressures and convenience. This study also looked at individual issues in mobile phone use, such as personality and verbal ability. No gender differences were found. One aim of the present study, however, is to look for gender differences.

Chung-Chu (2010) found no difference in mobile phone use between males and females in certain categories, such as convenience and personality

Mak *et al.* (2009), a study looking at culture and age differences in mobile phone usage

Mak *et al.* (2009) used questionnaires to look at attitudes to mobile phone use in public places and to see if this is affected by characteristics such as age and culture. The study was carried out in the US, France, Turkey, Finland and Italy. They found that the attitude towards mobile phone use did affect usage and attitudes differed between cultures and between ages. One aim of the present study is to look at age differences in mobile phone usage.

From the three studies briefly explained here, it can be seen that perhaps gender differences in mobile phone usage won't be found, but there might be age differences, and there might be other issues that affect mobile phone usage, possibly reflecting attitudes to using mobile phones in a public place.

> **Progress check 7.29**
>
> Why is it important to give some background information when carrying out a study?

Research question, hypotheses and variables

- The research question is 'what factors are noted when someone is observed using their mobile phone in a public place?'.
- One alternative hypothesis is: 'It is less likely when in a public place to see an older person use their mobile phone than a younger person'. The exact operationalisation of 'older' and 'younger' was left until the observation took place, but it was thought that '18–35' and 'over 50' would be two categories that could be observable.
- Variables were thought to be age, gender, whether someone was pushing a pushchair and whether someone was in a family group. These variables came from the pilot study.
- Notes would be made to gather some qualitative data in the form of a story about the individuals using their phones, to see if other variables would arise, as this is an exploratory study to see what variables were observed.

> **Progress check 7.30**
>
> How is age operationalised in this observation?

Design

The present study is an observation in a public place (in the street) and is covert – participants are not told they are part of a study. It is a non-participant observation – the observer is not part of the group or part of the individual's choice to use their phone or not. This is not a structured observation and there is no interference in the setting, so this is a naturalistic observation.

Ethical issues with observation

The suggested practical investigation is an observation in the street, which is a public area and so an observation is ethically acceptable as people would expect to be observed in the street. Usually, of course, an observation must only be done with informed consent.

Some ethical issues include:

- Individuals must not be identified or discussed.
- The researcher must be competent to carry out the observation, so make sure you have that competence before doing your own observation.
- There will not be a debrief as the observation is of people passing by, involved in their own lives and business, so a debrief is likely to be more upsetting than not debriefing.
- The participants must not be named in any way (their names are not known) or photographed or identified at all, which can help ethically. There is confidentiality and privacy, and that is maintained by not revealing the street or area at all.

> **Progress check 7.31**
>
> Some ethical issues were not put into place, such as getting informed consent and debriefing. This is a concern, but explain why it was thought acceptable to do this and still carry out the study.

> **STUDY HINT**
>
> Use the Progress check answers, as well as carrying out the Progress check tasks. The answers are informative and can help with understanding.

Risk management

As part of the study, risk must be managed. This can involve risk to participants, risk to researchers and risk to others around.

Risk to participants

The main risk is that participants might be upset if they feel 'spied' upon and, as they are not giving informed consent, they must be treated with the utmost respect. They must not feel spied upon and the only information taken down must be related to the study, and not discussed with others.

Risk to the researcher(s)

Researchers can be at risk. If they are taking notes and tallying in a public place, that can put them at risk, and it can put others at risk if they feel they are being watched. This is solved by the researcher sitting outside a café with tea/coffee so that they have a table to make notes on and a role in the setting (though not enough of a role to make this a participant observation, as they are not taking part in the situation of the participants themselves).

Risk to others

There is little risk to others. No children were used in the study, as that would have needed special ethics, was considered unnecessary and would have carried more risk. Children were likely to be with 'others' but not recorded or counted in the study.

Progress check 7.32

What is the value of risk management in a psychology study?

Carrying out the study

The study is an observation and, although there are no data collection tools as such, there are a lot of issues to deal with. A useful way to set the study up is to carry out a quick pilot study, so that you can note down issues and find ways to deal with them. A pilot study was done before the one written up here. The issue of preparing to make notes and do the tallying is covered next.

Getting ready to make notes and do tallying

Some paper and a pen were needed for taking notes to get some qualitative data in the form of a story about the participants. Tallying was required to get quantitative data, so a table was drawn up beforehand with plenty of room. The pilot observation had shown that age was to be recorded (18–35 and 50+ to make assessment of age easier). Gender was needed. Other factors that were tallied can be seen in Table 7.19.

Table 7.19 Format of table used to collect tallied data

Participant	18–35	50+	M/F	Pushchair (Y/N)	Family group (Y/N)
1					
2					
3					
4					
5					
6					
7...					

Notes were made after the tallying. There was just one researcher. It would be useful to have two people, one to tally and one to make the notes. Inevitably, people passing while brief notes were made were missed. This means that time sampling was not used and, although event sampling was used, in that everyone seen using a mobile phone was part of the study, it was not a strict example of event sampling as some were missed. The issue of where to 'be' as researcher is covered next. Some consideration was given to the idea that everyone passing should be noted, including the variables such as age and gender, so that there could be stronger conclusions, such as percentages of gender and age using a phone. However, this was not practicable. It is a suggestion for further research. All this study could aim for was notes about those actually using a mobile phone.

Where to sit/stand as researcher?

The pilot study quickly showed that walking along the street to watch who used a mobile phone meant that tallying was difficult and note-taking even more so. For the actual observation, a café in the main street in a town was chosen. The researcher chose a day with good weather and sat with coffee/tea in the outside seating area of a café. Sitting at a table meant that there was space to make notes and tally marks. Others around would assume that the researcher was simply taking notes from a book that was on the table. This was also an ethical place to observe from as participants would not be disturbed and others would not be curious about the study.

How and who to observe

Having decided where to sit and what materials were needed to do the observation, the next decision was how to do the observation in terms of when to record data and what to watch. The café idea seemed to be a good one and the café itself was picked out. The café was positioned where the street narrowed enough to see everyone using a mobile phone, but the street was still sufficiently busy. The materials were drawn up and ready. Some decisions taken following findings from the pilot were important.

Decisions

- One decision was to exclude anyone using their mobile phone with earphones, presumably listening to music, as that was not the original intention of the observation. The aim was to see who was 'on the phone' rather than using it to listen to music. If it was clear someone was playing a game on their phone, they were excluded too.
- Another decision was to exclude anyone if it was too hard to fit them into the two age categories, though this was not expected as the age ranges were far apart.
- The next decision was to watch everyone using a mobile phone that was seen, excluding just those who 'slipped through' while notes were being made.
- Another decision was not to try to record everyone so that percentages of those using a mobile phone could be calculated. It was decided that knowing how many of that age or gender were not using the mobile phone would not be easy data to gather, and this was not, in any case, the focus of the study. For this observation, people not using mobile phones would be missed. This would limit the data though.
- It was important which day was chosen and which time of day, as different people would be in the street depending on these factors. It was thought that the weekend would be too busy. The aim was to capture everyone using a mobile phone during the observation, even though it was admitted that some would be missed. The aim was to miss as few as possible, so although the street had to be reasonably busy, it should not be too busy. Mondays were rather quiet, so a Tuesday was chosen. The time frame chosen was 3.00 p.m. to 5.30 p.m. Schools finished at 3.00 p.m. so parents would be around collecting their children and, by 5.30 p.m., workers would start to move up and down the street. It was thought that would get a reasonable cross-section of ages and people. Older people would be in the street too during those times.
- With regard to the qualitative data, it was thought that as many notes about the participants would be made as possible. This would include who they were with, what they were doing and whether they seemed in a hurry. It was decided not to record what was said on the phone, if that could be heard, as that was not part of the study and would be an unnecessary intrusion. The notes had a number that matched the participant number so the two could be matched up as necessary.
- It was decided that 'group' would mean more than two people.

Collecting the data

One Tuesday at the end of summer (2014) at 2.45 p.m. the researcher sat at the outside café table ready to start the observation, with the table for recording the tallying as well as a notepad. There were a reasonable number of people about, some with pushchairs, some on their own and some in groups. It was not hard to tally those on the phone as there were, on balance, not that many. Notes could be taken mostly, though they were done with 'half an eye' on those passing in order to catch everyone and it was possible to stop and tally another instance of someone on the phone and go back to the notes, as there were not that many.

Any people who went into the café using their phone were counted, as they came in off the street. No children were seen using a mobile phone so that was not an issue (though they would not have been counted). Issues such as this were noted down as qualitative data.

Analysing the results

Raw data – quantitative

Some of the raw data are given here as an indication (Table 7.20).

Table 7.20 Raw data from the observation

Participant	18–35	50+	M/F	Pushchair (Y/N)	Family group (Y/N)
1	✓		M	Y	N
2	✓		M	Y	N
3		✓	F	Y	N
4	✓		F	N	N
5	✓		F	Y	Y
6	✓		F	Y	N
7		✓	M	N	Y
8	✓		F	N	N
9	✓		F	N	N
10	✓		F	Y	N
11	✓		M	N	N
12	✓		F	N	Y
13	✓		M	N	Y
14		✓	M	N	Y
15		✓	M	N	N
16		✓	M	Y	Y
TOTALS	**11**	**5**	**M=8, F=8**	**Y=7, N=9**	**Y=6, N=10**

Qualitative data

Some of the qualitative data are given here as an indication (Table 7.21).

Table 7.21 Qualitative data from the observation

Participant	Notes
1	Male pushing a child in a pushchair at school leaving time. Smoking as well as on the phone. Talking rather animatedly and seemingly argumentative. Walking rather fast. (18–35 years old, not in a group)
2	Similar to Participant 1, a male with a child in a pushchair and again just after 3.00 p.m. on a Tuesday afternoon. Smiling and more calm, and seemingly listening as had the phone to his ear but was not talking. (18–35 years old, not in a group)
3	Older woman pushing a pushchair talking quickly on the phone. Not talking to the child in the pushchair or to another child walking with her. They are walking quite slowly. (50+, not in a group)
4	Younger woman talking on the phone quite animatedly and gesturing too. Nobody with her, walking quite fast. She was dressed in office clothes. It was about 3.30 p.m. (18–35 years, not in a group)
5	Younger woman talking on the phone quite animatedly and gesturing too. No other adult with her, walking quite fast, pushing a pushchair, with two other children with her. (18–35 years, in a group of three)
6	Younger woman listening on the phone but not talking while I am watching. No other adult with her, walking slowly, pushing a pushchair. (18–35 years, not in a group)
7	Older male in a group that looked like a family with a woman his age, two younger women and quite a few children. He was talking slowly and a little behind the group, glancing at them as they walked on. (50+)
8	Younger woman talking on the phone at first and then she stopped to listen. Nobody with her, walking at an average speed. She was dressed in office clothes. (18–35 years, not in a group)
9	Younger woman holding a phone to her ear but I did not see her talk into it so I assume she was listening. Nobody with her, walking slowly. She was not dressed in office clothes. (18–35 years, not in a group)
10	Younger woman talking on the phone quite animatedly. No other adults with her, walking quite fast, pushing a pushchair, with one other child. (18–35 years, not in a group)
11	Younger male on his own, talking on the phone as if it was a business call. It seemed that way because his demeanour was formal and he was dressed in a suit. He seemed to be concentrating and neither smiling nor animated. (18–35, not in a group)
12	Younger female in a group on the phone, with nobody else in the group on the phone. She was talking quietly and slightly away from the group. (18–35)
13	Younger male in a group of males of a similar age, all talking and laughing, with this younger male laughing on the phone as if someone at the other end was sharing their outing. (18–35)
14	Older male in a group, two older females and one other older male so I suppose two couples. Nobody else in the group was on the phone. They were walking slowly for him to finish the phone call, or it seemed that way. He was neither laughing nor frowning. A business call maybe. (50+)
15	Older male on his own walking purposefully with the phone in his hand seemingly listening. Dressed casually. (50+, not in a group)
16	Older male with a pushchair in a group with some other women and children. He was the only one on the phone and was talking rather sharply, it seemed. (50+, in a group)

Progress check 7.33

Why does this observation include both qualitative and quantitative data?

Carrying out a chi-squared test

From the raw tally/tick data, draw up a two-by-two table so that you can carry out a chi-squared test. This is the correct test because you have nominal data, as you made tally marks according to the categories. The data include age (two groups), gender, pushing a pushchair (or not), being in a group (or not). The test can cover two of those variables or you can do more than one test. In this study, the variables chosen were age and gender, as it was thought that older men and younger women used the phone most (from the pilot study). The background studies chosen did suggest no difference regarding gender, but here gender is put with age and that might show a difference. The data about pushing a pushchair and being in a group are additional and not included in the inferential testing. In fact, other data were gathered in the notes, such as how fast they were walking and how animated they were when talking, so you could use that information when testing for difference.

This is an independent groups design because the people are in different age groups and of different gender. It is a test of difference because the alternative hypothesis to be tested is that age and gender affect mobile phone use in the street. Anyone outside the chosen age groups (which were estimated) was not used in the study. There are other alternative hypotheses you could test, such as that there is a gender difference in mobile phone use when considered alongside pushing a pushchair.

It would be interesting to test 'using the phone or not', but those data were not gathered in this observation.

For the practical outlined here, data are given in Table 7.22. Refer to Chapter 6 (pp. 412–416) for details of the chi-squared test, which is also carried out here to demonstrate.

Table 7.22 A two-by-two table for a chi-squared test: use of mobile phone using the variables age and gender

Age	Men	Women	Total
18-35	IIII (4) (A)	~~IIII~~ II (7) (B)	11
50+	IIII (4) (C)	I (1) (D)	5
Total	**8**	**8**	**16**

Progress check 7.34

Why is the test for this study (the quantitative data) a chi-squared test?

Finding the expected values

The formula for the expected value for each cell is:

$$\frac{\text{total of the row of cells} \times \text{total of the column of cells}}{\text{total of all cells}}.$$

where

total of the row of cells = total of the row of cells containing the required cell

total of the column of cells = total of the column of cells containing the required cell.

Data found from Table 7.22 are:

- observed frequency for cell A = 4
- observed frequency for cell B = 7
- observed frequency for cell C = 4
- observed frequency for cell D = 1
- row total for C and D = 5
- column total for A and C = 8
- column total for B and D = 8
- row total for A and B = 11
- total observations = 16

Using Cell A as an example:

Step 1: Find the total of the row containing the cell. (Here, row total = **11**)

Step 2: Find the total of the column containing the cell. (Here, column total = **8**)

Step 3: Multiply the answer to Step 1 by the answer to Step 2. (Here, 11 × 8 = **88**)

Step 4: Find the overall total of observations. (Here, overall total = **16**)

Step 5: Divide the answer to Step 3 by the answer to Step 4. (Here, 88/16 = **5.5**)

This is the expected value for the cell. (Here, the cell is A.)

Repeat Steps 1 to 5 for each cell. The results are shown in Table 7.23.

Table 7.23 Expected values for Cells A, B, C and D

Step	Cell A	Cell B	Cell C	Cell D
Step 1: Find the total of the row containing the cell	11	11	5	5
Step 2: Find the total of the column containing the cell	8	8	8	8
Step 3: Multiply the answer to Step 1 by the answer to Step 2	11 × 8 = 88	11 × 8 = 88	5 × 8 = 40	5 × 8 = 40
Step 4: Find the overall total of observations	16	16	16	16
Step 5: Divide the answer to Step 3 by the answer to Step 4	88/16 = 5.5	88/16 = 5.5	40/16 = 2.5	40/16 = 2.5
Expected value for cell	5.5	5.5	2.5	2.5

Redraw the two-by-two table, giving both the observed (*O*) and the expected (*E*) frequencies (Table 7.24).

Table 7.24 Observed (*O*) and expected (*E*) frequencies

Age	Men	Women	Total
18-35	4 (O) and 5.5 (E)	7 (O) and 5.5 (E)	11
50+	4 (O) and 2.5 (E)	1 (O) and 2.5 (E)	5
Total	**8**	**8**	**16**

Carrying out a sense check

A sense check can tell you whether you think the test will show a significant difference or not. There were the same number of men and women, and the number of young and older people was rather different. The differences between the expected and observed frequencies are reasonably high, but possibly not quite high enough. There seems to be something here in that age and gender affect mobile phone use but perhaps not enough for significant results. The expected frequencies are within 1.5 of the observed values, which seems borderline with regard to showing a significant difference.

Progress check 7.35

Why is a sense check carried out?

Doing the test

The formula to find the chi-squared result is:

$$\chi = \Sigma \frac{(O-E)^2}{E}$$

where

χ^2 = chi-squared (the result of the test)

Σ = the sum of (note: calculate the sum after doing the rest of the calculation as the symbol is alongside the rest)

O = the observed result

E = the expected result

( ) = do this bit separately

$( )^2$ = square the answer that is found after doing the task in the brackets.

Referring to Table 7.24 and using Cell A (younger men) as an example:

Step 1: Subtract *E* from *O*. (Here, 4 – 5.5= **–1.5**.)

Step 2: Square the answer from Step 1 (multiply the answer to Step 1 by itself). (Here, 1.5 × 1.5 = **2.25**.)

Step 3: Divide the answer to Step 2 by *E*. (Here, 2.25/5.5 = **0.41**.)

The results for all four cells are shown in Table 7.25.

Table 7.25 Calculating χ^2 for the study of age and gender, and mobile phone use

	Cell A	Cell B	Cell C	Cell D
Step 1: Subtract E from O	4 - 5.5 = -1.5	7 - 5.5 = 1.5	4 - 2.5 = 1.5	1 - 2.5 = -1.5
Step 2: Square the answer from Step 1	-1.5 × -1.5 = 2.25*	1.5 × 1.5 = 2.25	1.5 × 1.5 = 2.25	-1.5 × -1.5 = 2.25*
Step 3: Divide the answer to Step 2 by E.	2.25/5.5 = 0.41	2.25/5.5 = 0.41	2.25/2.5 = 0.9	2.25/2.5 = 0.9

*Squaring numbers removes the minus sign

The final step is the calculation of the value of chi-squared (χ^2). This is obtained by adding together all answers (in this case, four) for Step 3. In this example:

$\chi^2 = 0.41 + 0.41 + 0.9 + 0.9 = \mathbf{2.62}$.

This is the value of chi-squared.

Checking for significance

The example given here tested the hypothesis that age and gender are variables that show a difference in those using a mobile phone in the street. This is a non-directional hypothesis, so the test required is a two-tailed test. If the level of significance chosen is $p \leq 0.05$, it will be accepted that the probability of the results being due to chance is 1 in 20 (5 per cent) and the null hypothesis will be rejected. At this level of significance when *df* is 1, the critical value that has to be equalled or exceeded is 3.84. (see p. 415). In this example, the value of chi-squared is 2.62. This is less than 3.84, so the null hypothesis is accepted and the alternative hypothesis is rejected. Note that, before the chi-squared test was carried out, it was possible to see the perceived difference by looking at the two-by-two table. It is concluded that there was no difference in use of mobile phone on the street depending on age or gender. None of the variables – younger males, older males, younger females, older females – showed differences when they were tested together. Although the overall number of males and females were the same (eight of each), and the males split equally between the age groups, there was a difference in mobile phone use among the females, with most being in the younger age group. There does seem to be something worth looking at more here, even though the chi-squared result is not significant. It was 2.62, which is getting towards significance.

Analysing the qualitative data

Some of the qualitative data are given in Table 7.21.

Thematic analysis

The data are considered carefully and each piece of data coded as a theme, grouping data accordingly. The first piece of data is coded, then the next and so on, until a set of themes is formed. Even if there is one piece of data with one theme, that is counted as a theme at first (Tables 7.26 and 7.27).

Table 7.26 Qualitative data, groups of ideas, suggested themes

Participant	Notes	Ideas (themes in brackets)
1	Male pushing a child in a pushchair at school leaving time. Smoking as well as on the phone. Talking rather animatedly and seemingly argumentative. Walking rather fast. (18–35 years old, not in a group)	Men and children (company) Smoking (other activity) Animated talk (type of talk) Argumentative (type of talk) Fast walking (type of walk)
2	Similar to Participant 1, a male with a child in a pushchair and again just after 3.00 p.m. on a Tuesday afternoon. Smiling and more calm, and seemingly listening as had the phone to his ear but was not talking. (18–35 years old, not in a group)	Men and children (company) Smiling (emotion) Calm talking (type of talk) Listening, not talking (focus of attention)
3	Older woman pushing a pushchair talking quickly on the phone. Not talking to the child in the pushchair or to another child walking with her. They are walking quite slowly. (50+, not in a group)	Woman and children (company) Slow walking (type of walk) Quick talking (type of talk)
4	Younger woman talking on the phone quite animatedly and gesturing too. Nobody with her, walking quite fast. She was dressed in office clothes. It was about 3.30 p.m. (18–35 years, not in a group)	Animated talk (type of talk) Gesturing (body language) Fast walking (type of walk) Office clothes (dress)
5	Younger woman talking on the phone quite animatedly and gesturing too. No other adult with her, walking quite fast, pushing a pushchair, with two other children with her. (18–35 years, in a group of three)	Animated talk (type of talk) Gesturing (body language) Woman and children (company) Fast walking (type of walk)
6	Younger woman listening on the phone but not talking while I am watching. No other adult with her, walking slowly, pushing a pushchair. (18–35 years, not in a group)	Listening not talking (focus of attention) Woman with children (company)
7	Older male in a group that looked like a family with a woman his age, two younger women and quite a few children. He was talking slowly and a little behind the group, glancing at them as they walked on. (50+)	Man with family (company) Talking slowly (type of talk) Lagging behind (physical position) Looking at family (focus of attention)

Participant	Notes	Ideas (themes in brackets)
8	Younger woman talking on the phone at first and then she stopped to listen. Nobody with her, walking at an average speed. She was dressed in office clothes. (18–35 years, not in a group)	Talking and listening (focus of attention) Average speed walking (type of walk) Office clothes (dress)
9	Younger woman holding a phone to her ear but I did not see her talk into it so I assume she was listening. Nobody with her, walking slowly. She was not dressed in office clothes. (18–35 years, not in a group)	Not talking, listening (focus of attention) Slow walk (type of walk) Not in office clothes (dress)
10	Younger woman talking on the phone quite animatedly. No other adults with her, walking quite fast, pushing a pushchair, with one other child. (18–35 years, not in a group)	Animated talk (type of talk) Fast walk (type of walk) Woman with children (company)
11	Younger male on his own, talking on the phone as if it was a business call. It seemed that way because his demeanour was formal and he was dressed in a suit. He seemed to be concentrating and neither smiling nor animated. (18–35, not in a group)	Business call (reason for call) Formal demeanour (body language) Suit clothing (dress) Concentrating (focus of attention) Not smiling (emotion) Not animated (type of talk)
12	Younger female in a group on the phone, with nobody else in the group on the phone. She was talking quietly and slightly away from the group. (18–35)	Quiet talking (type of talk) Away from group (physical position)
13	Younger male in a group of males of a similar age, all talking and laughing, with this younger male laughing on the phone as if someone at the other end was sharing their outing. (18–35)	Talking and laughing (type of talk) Laughing on phone (emotion)
14	Older male in a group, two older females and one other older male so I suppose two couples. Nobody else in the group was on the phone. They were walking slowly for him to finish the phone call, or it seemed that way. He was neither laughing nor frowning. A business call maybe. (50+)	Man with family (company) Slow walking (type of walk) Not laughing or frowning (emotion) Business call perhaps (reason for call)
15	Older male on his own walking purposefully with the phone in his hand seemingly listening. Dressed casually. (50+, not in a group)	Purposeful walking (type of walk) Casual dress (dress) Listening (focus of attention)
16	Older male with a pushchair in a group with some other women and children. He was the only one on the phone and was talking rather sharply, it seemed. (50+, in a group)	Man with family (company) Sharply talking (type of talk)

Dress, age, gender, type of walk, whether someone is alone or not and body language are features that might be noted when observing mobile phone use on the street

Table 7.27 Ten themes from the qualitative data

Theme	Comment
Company	Whether alone or with company may affect whether on the phone or not
Type of talk	The type of talk (sharp, average, fast, slow, argumentative, animated...) may link with age, gender or another factor
Type of walk	The type of walk (purposeful, slow, fast...) may link to type of talk or other factor
Focus of attention	Where attention is focused might be of interest if it links with company
Dress	There was information about business dress and casual dress – this may show the constructs of the observer or the culture, which could be of interest and might go with type of talk
Reason for call	Reason for call may link to dress
Emotion	Emotion (laughing, smiling, not smiling) may link with type of talk
Body language	Gesturing and formal demeanour might be of interest culturally or by gender
Other activity	There was just one person smoking in the street, which might show cultural attitudes; with just one person, could not link with age or gender, but could be possible links
Physical position	Lagging behind or away from the group might show some link to company (both notes went with someone in company)

Discussion of themes

The ten themes can be reduced further to show some of the features noted down. Table 7.28 makes some suggestions for linking to broader themes of physical, social, emotional and cultural features. This might be useful when writing up the findings from the qualitative data. However, by reducing this much, a lot of the detail and meaning is lost. There could, however, be counting of such overarching themes (or the basic themes) and, in this way, qualitative data can become quantitative data for analysis. Table 7.29 illustrates how this might look, using Table 7.27 for the data.

Table 7.28 Reduction of ten themes

Overarching theme	Themes made up of:
Physical features	Body language, physical position
Emotional features	Type of talk, type of walk, emotion
Cultural features	Dress, other activity, reason for call
Social features	Company, focus of attention

Progress check 7.36

How does reducing the themes into overarching themes both help and not help analysis of the study?

Table 7.29 Overarching themes and numbers in categories

Overarching theme	Tallying
Physical features	𝍸 (5)
Emotional features	𝍸 𝍸 𝍸 𝍸 𝍸 (25)
Cultural features	𝍸 III (8)
Social features	𝍸 𝍸 𝍸 I (16)

Table 7.29 suggests that emotional features and social features were noted most, with cultural features next and not many physical features. This perhaps indicates the **social constructs** of the observer and what they thought was of interest regarding mobile phone use. A study looking at whether different observers note down different features might be interesting, particularly looking at whether observers from different cultures note down different features. Mak *et al.* (2009) showed that cultural attitudes affect mobile phone use so culture seems to be important in this area of study.

Explanation

Social constructionism holds that a lot of what we think is real and fact is actually socially constructed. Gender can be socially constructed, for example, such as what we consider appropriate gender behaviour. Health is a social construct – what is seen as 'health' can vary between cultures.

The social and cultural issues that arose give weight to the idea that what was observed was about learning. This could be from observational learning and copying of role models, or from patterns of reinforcement and what behaviour has been rewarded, such as by peers. Perhaps people use mobile phones on the street under peer pressure and the need to keep in touch, for example.

This study is just for illustration purposes to give ideas for analysis of qualitative data among ideas for carrying out an observation, so just a short discussion is given here. However, there are probably a lot of other issues that could be raised from this example of qualitative data. This shows how valuable rich and detailed data can be and how they can add to research findings and suggest ideas for further research.

Consider the findings

Applying issues of validity, reliability, generalisability and credibility

Validity

Validity refers to the degree to which findings are 'real life'.

- This study used an observation of real behaviour in the street, in a public place, so the results are likely to be valid. It is a naturalistic observation, so there is ecological validity and the task itself is valid because it is natural phone-using behaviour. The observation is non-participant so effects from the researcher would not be involved, and it is covert, so again there would be no effect on behaviour from the study being carried out.
- There is the possibility that participants noticed the researcher and the observation but none of them looked in the researcher's direction at all and there was no suggestion of there being such an effect.
- The themes generated from the qualitative data start to lose validity because they are interpretations of the data. Also the choice of what to record was down to one individual observer and their constructs of what was important, which introduces an element of subjectivity and reduces the validity of the data.

Reliability

Reliability is about whether, if a study was done again, the same results would be found.

- Naturalistic observations may not be reliable because behaviour is often observed at one moment in time. If that is the case, the study cannot be repeated to test for reliability. This was one street in one town, on one day and over just a few hours in the afternoon. Any repetition would be different. As far as was known, there was no special event in that town on that day, but that could be the case, and days are different in so many ways for individuals.
- Another observer would help with the reliability with regard to any interpretation such as of age or of mobile phone use. For example, when someone had the phone in their hand only (Participant 9), perhaps it was wrong to call that 'mobile phone use'. If more than one observer did the same observation at the same time, then the reliability of that data would be checked. However, this was not done. This could be an improvement on the design.

Generalisability

Generalisability is found when a sample represents the target population so results can be said to be true of that target population. Whether the results are generalisable to other situations depends on the sampling.

- A sample wasn't chosen in this study – participants were self-selecting in a way, by using their mobile phone in the street, though they did not choose to take part. The sample was people in that street at that time, in that town. There is bias here as anyone working elsewhere, or anyone who was unwell, or anyone who couldn't get out of the house, would not be in the sample. These issues illustrate that one observation, over a short space of time, in one place, is a limited one. Therefore, there is a lack of generalisability.

Credibility

Scientific credibility is found when a study has the features of science so that knowledge can be accepted by others and a body of knowledge can be built.

- The lack of generalisability affects the credibility of the study. The observer might have chosen the only time during which there was just one older woman who used her mobile phone in the street. Usually, there might be many more. In fact, the first two people to be observed were men with pushchairs, whereas you might expect more women with pushchairs. In fact, that would be an interesting observation – to see if more women meet children at the school gate than men (though of course there would be ethical issues here).
- To claim credibility, you would need to show that your results were valid, reliable and generalisable.

Strengths and weaknesses of the study

Strengths

- There is quantitative data and qualitative data. The statistical testing is useful in showing no difference using the quantitative data, and the qualitative data add depth and detail that help with the conclusions and interpretation of the data gathered.

- Ahmed *et al.* (2014) concluded that mobile phone use was similar and they did not find age differences, which backs the findings of this study, where age differences were not found either, with regard to significance. Chung-Chu (2010) did not find gender differences in mobile phone use, again supporting the findings of this study. Mak *et al.* (2009) did find that a culture's attitudes to mobile phone use affected usage, but such attitudes were not investigated in this study. The background evidence backed up the findings.

Weaknesses

- Just one observer meant that their constructs and features they chose to observe gave an element of subjectivity to the qualitative data and themes arising.
- The limitations of the observation in terms of one day, one time, one place mean that reliability is low. This is a specific observation of one moment in time, which has validity, but this reduces the reliability of the data.

Improving the design

Suggestions for improving the design include the following:

- Using a narrower street and perhaps fewer people so that those not using a mobile phone could be tallied. Then conclusions might be drawn about percentages of those using a phone according to age group and gender, which would be of interest.
- Having more than one observer so that reliability could be checked.
- Repeating the study on a different day, at a different time, in a different town and so on, to test for reliability of the findings.
- Repeating the study using a different sample to improve generalisability as the sample in the current study would be biased.
- Repeating the study using different observers to show if the themes that were generated from the qualitative data were reliable, had cultural bias or showed bias from individual perceptions.
- Interviewing the participants to ask them about the phone call that was observed – this would be interesting, but not easy to do in practical terms.

Ideas for further research

- An interesting observation that could be explored is whether more women meet children at the school gate after school than men.
- Carrying out an observation of mobile phone use but doing it in different cultures might help to see whether cultural attitudes feature in mobile phone use in the street.

Writing up a psychology study

Studies in psychology are written up using the following sections: abstract, introduction, procedure/method, results, discussion, references and appendices. For your course, you do not have to write up a full report. However, you are asked to write up some of the sections, so that you know how this is done. For this practical, you are asked to write up the results.

Results are given in good detail for this study. Be sure to do the same for you own results so you can write up the results section of a report. You can use one of the studies you have covered in your course to see how results are presented.

Explore

You can find observation studies on the internet as well as studies using qualitative data, to see how they are presented in a report. One example is found using the link: http://mcs.open.ac.uk/pervasive/pdfs/duenserEdutainment07.pdf.

Test yourself

1. You will have carried out a study using one or more observations. Describe how you gathered both quantitative and qualitative data in your observation(s). **(4 marks)**
2. Explain one strength and one weakness of your observation, apart from ethical issues. **(6 marks)**
3. Explain two ethical issues with your observation and how you addressed them. **(6 marks)**
4. Explain the aim(s), procedure, results and conclusions of the practical you carried out within learning theories. Give two criticisms of your study. **(16 marks)**

Chapter summary

Social psychology

For the practical investigation in social psychology, you need to carry out a questionnaire focusing on material you cover in social psychology for your course. In this textbook, a questionnaire about obedience is worked through.

- You need to consider questionnaire construction, sampling, design and ethical issues. You also need to consider strengths and weaknesses of your questionnaire, as well as writing up the procedure, results and a discussion of the findings.
- Data analysis must cover analysis of quantitative data using measures of central tendency and measure of dispersion, including bar charts and a frequency table. Analysis of qualitative data must use thematic analysis.

Cognitive psychology

For the practical investigation in cognitive psychology, you need to carry out a laboratory experiment gathering quantitative data and focusing on material you cover in cognitive psychology for your course. In this textbook, an experiment on rehearsal is worked through.

- For the analysis, you need to include descriptive statistics and a test of difference. You have to choose between a Mann-Whitney U test and a Wilcoxon test, depending on your experimental/research design. You need to consider levels of significance and using critical and observed values.
- You have to make appropriate design decisions to plan and conduct the experiment, including experimental/research design (independent groups, repeated measures or matched pairs), sampling decisions, operationalisation of the independent and dependent variables, use of appropriate controls, ethical considerations and hypotheses. The design decisions should also consider the avoidance of demand characteristics and experimenter effects.
- The data must be collected and commented upon, including using measures of central tendency, measures of dispersion, bar graph, histogram/frequency graph and issues of normal distribution, as appropriate. Commenting on the study includes considering strengths and weaknesses as well as possible improvements.
- A write up of the procedure, results and discussion sections of a report is also required.

Biological psychology

For the practical investigation in biological psychology, you need to carry out a correlation focusing on aggression or drug abuse. In this textbook, a correlation about life events relating to emotional response is worked through.

- You have to make appropriate design decisions, including a hypothesis and/or research question, the research method, sampling decisions, ethical considerations, data collection tools, data analysis, results and discussion.
- The data must be collected and commented upon, including using appropriate descriptive statistics (measures of central tendency, measures of dispersion, graphs and tables) and also Spearman's rank correlation coefficient as an inferential test to look for a significant relationship. The significance of the results must be explained, including level of significance. The strength and direction of the correlation must also be commented on. Commenting on the study includes considering strengths and weaknesses as well as possible improvements.
- There is also a requirement to write up the abstract and the discussion sections of a report, with the discussion including a conclusion.

Learning theories

For the practical investigation within learning theories, you need to carry out an observation gathering both quantitative and qualitative data and focusing on an area that can involve learning. In this textbook, an observation of mobile phone use is worked through. Here one observation has been chosen to gather both qualitative and quantitative data.

- In the observation, there must be note-taking and tallying and, to analyse the qualitative data, there must be thematic analysis. A chi-squared test must be carried out to analyse the quantitative data, which will be in the form of nominal data.
- The practical investigation must be evaluated in terms of validity, reliability, generalisability and credibility. There must also be a write up of the results part of the practical investigation, including any graphs and tables, as well as writing up the results of thematic analysis.

Chapter Eight: Issues and Debates

Introduction

Studying important issues and debates in psychology helps to develop an overview of what psychology is and to consider wider issues around studying mind and behaviour. Your A level course includes 11 issues and debates. These are examined in detail in Book 2. They are summarised in this section, including a brief outline of what each issue/debate is about, followed by examples of how each topic area can illustrate each issue/debate. You will need to be able to discuss these issues and debates in your examination papers, including the paper assessing your Year 1 material (Paper 1).

The 11 issues and debates for your A level course are:

- Ethical issues in research
- Practical issues in the design and implementation of research
- Reductionism in the explanation of behaviour
- Comparisons between ways of explaining behaviour using different themes
- Psychology as a science
- Cultural and gender issues within psychological research
- The role of both nature and nurture within psychology
- An understanding of how psychological understanding has developed over time
- The use of psychology in social control
- The use of psychological knowledge within society
- Issues related to socially sensitive research.

You will find that the issues and debates are not new to you as you work through the course. For example, there is a section in the content for social psychology that considers the ethics of Milgram's work (pp. 30–31) and, when discussing Milgram's agency theory of obedience, the nature–nurture debate is mentioned as well as looking at culture (pp. 19–21 and pp. 25–26).

Each issue/debate is covered below, showing what the issue or debate is and followed by a table with examples related to the issue/debate in each topic area.

STUDY HINT

You can choose to review issues and debates at the end of your course. It is a section that is found in each topic area, with the same issues and debates considered, giving relevant examples for that topic area each time. Or you can review the issues and debates as you study your course. Making notes against each of the issues as you move through your course will remind you of different examples where an issue/debate arises, which can be helpful for Topic Area 9 (Topic Area 9 covers Paper 3, and you reach that near the end of your course). Questions relating to issues and debates in psychology can be found in any of the three exam papers for your course, so it is worth reviewing at the end of each topic area.

Ethical issues in research

Ethics is about good practice, and covers moral issues too, which can be socially given or universal. Chapter 5 looks at ethics in more detail (pp. 304–314).

In social psychology, ethical issues in studies of obedience are considered in the content section (pp. 30–31), as well as the British Psychological Society's (BPS) Code of Ethics and Conduct (2009), which is found in the method section for social psychology (pp. 304–314), and in more detail in Chapter 5. So this 'issue and debate' in psychology is covered in some depth throughout this book.

In psychology, it can be said that there are three different ways of looking at ethical issues:

- The first involves ethical issues as a practising psychologist, such as how to rebalance any power that a therapist has so that treatment is fair and focused on the client. In a discussion about treatments and therapies, ethics are about how treatment is carried out and the decisions and behaviour of the therapist/psychologist.

- The second issue involves the ethics of doing psychology, such as in research when participants must be protected and respected. In a method discussion, ethics can either be about how participants are treated and a study is run, or they can be about the implications of the findings of a study.
- The third issue is the ethics of the use of findings of research or the application of a theory, such as whether findings are used 'for good' or 'for evil'. In a discussion about key questions in psychology, ethics are about how psychological knowledge and understanding is used by others, such as in a society. This third interpretation of ethics can link with the 'issue and debate' of social control and with the 'issue and debate' related to socially sensitive research.

The BPS Code of Ethics and Conduct (2009) has four main ethical principles, which are respect, competence, responsibility and integrity. An example of respect is giving the right to withdraw, which means someone can leave the study or therapy at any time. Competence is about keeping up to date in a field and making sure that anything necessary is known about. Responsibility includes debriefing, so that someone understands exactly what has occurred and their role in that. Integrity includes not deceiving someone and being open and honest about any dealings with them.

Progress check 8.1

List the four principles in the BPS Code of Ethics and Conduct (2009) and give one ethical aspect/guideline in each of the four principles.

Practical issues in the design and implementation of research

Practical issues in research tend to be called 'practical' to separate them from ethical or theoretical issues.

- Practical issues include ethical issues, in that they have to be taken into account when designing a study and when implementing the design. This is because animals or humans are going to be the participants, and participants must be treated ethically, which may limit what can be done in terms of design of a study. However, it is usual not to include ethical issues when talking about 'practical' issues as they have separate features in a study.
- Theoretical issues would arise when setting out a research question for a study, which would be putting forward an idea for a study, usually based on theory and the work of others. These are not practical issues.
- Practical issues in the design and implementation of research are what a researcher has to think about in

Table 8.1 Examples of ethical issues in research from the four Year 1 topic areas

Social	Cognitive	Biological	Learning
• The implications of findings in prejudice and obedience involve ethics, including thinking of how psychology is used in society and by others. • The 'ethics of doing research', such as ethical issues for participants, is explored when considering work on obedience, such as Milgram's work, which was widely criticised but had ethical strengths. • The BPS Code of Ethics and Conduct (2009) lays down four ethical principles and the BPS also consider issues around risk management.	• Field experiments – 'people on the street' can become participants, with specific ethical issues around 'using' them (e.g. difficulty of debrief, difficulty of informed consent). • Laboratory experiments – for example, people are being taken out of their environment and put into a strange situation, which can be stressful. • Case studies of people with damage to their brains – for example, the obvious stress involved for the participants and because of issues such as confidentiality and privacy. • Consequences of findings of studies – such as knowing more about working memory helping those with dementia, working with vulnerable people – carry ethical implications.	• When animal studies are explained in this chapter, there are special ethics required such as the Animals (Scientific Procedures) Act (1986) (e.g. van den Oever, 2008). • Studying aggression and how findings are used involves moral issues, to do with blame and punishment. • Raine *et al.* (1997) used PET scans that showed brain differences in murderers compared with non-murderers, used as controls, which has ethical implications. • Participants in studies also must be treated ethically.	• Using animals in laboratory experiments – there are special ethical principles with regard to using animals. • Ethical issues were considered in the Watson and Rayner (1920) Little Albert study where a young child was conditioned to fear his pet rat and other similar things, and the conditioning was done by scaring him. • There are ethical issues in research such as classical conditioning experiments that involve phobias, and might be stressful. • Operant conditioning studies can lead to a learned behaviour that changes someone or an animal, bringing ethical issues around responsibility.

order to run a credible and acceptable study, which has few issues that can lead to criticisms or lack of acceptance of the findings.

This issue is about 'design' and 'implementation' of research. There are three research designs in a study, which you will learn about in cognitive psychology (pp. 321–323), but here 'design' is a broader term covering how a study is set up. 'Implementation' means how a study is put into practice.

> **STUDY HINT**
> Terms in psychology are used in examinations, so it is important to understand what they mean so you know what the question is asking. When you have a term like 'practical issues', or 'design' and 'implementation', be sure to make a note of what they mean, to help your learning. You could have a separate section of notes around 'examination issues', for this purpose.

> **Explore**
> Choose two studies that you have looked at in reasonable depth and make a list of any practical issues in the design and implementation. In the examination, you are likely to be given a short account of a study and to be asked to consider 'problems' in design and implementation, so it is good practice to look at such issues, to develop your skills of evaluation.

This 'issue and debate' is here to help you to draw together all the practical issues in the design of studies in psychology and how they are put into practice. You will have a lot of issues covered by the time you get to the end of your course.

When designing and carrying out (implementing) an interview, practical issues such as sitting arrangements and sharing the interview schedule with a respondent must be considered

Table 8.2 Examples of practical issues in the design and implementation of research from the four Year 1 topic areas

Social	Cognitive	Biological	Learning
• Issues of social desirability and researcher bias when designing a questionnaire are practical ones (to solve). • In your practical investigation, you will come across practical issues, such as how to choose a sampling technique that allows for generalisability of findings. • Writing questionnaire items that are clear and unambiguous and gathering the required data in a reliable and valid way are practical issues. • Recruiting participants for research is a practical issue, such as interviewees, if the area of research is a sensitive one (e.g. prejudice).	• Trying to control for all variables other than the independent variable, to see the effect on the dependent variable. • How to achieve validity when there is so much control, and control is going to make the experience unnatural for the participants. • How to measure memory: memory is about encoding, storage and retrieval, which all appear to be different processes. There are also many different types of memory, such as episodic, semantic, acoustic, short-term and long-term. Memory is not one 'thing' but a process and it is hard to measure.	• How to measure the variables so that there is validity. For example, measuring car hooting might not be measuring aggression – hooting may be a normal feature of driving. • How to find the sample, e.g. finding people exhibiting aggression in order to test saliva (e.g. Barzman *et al.*, 2013). Testing their saliva would not be difficult with the right equipment, but finding people who are aggressive might not be so easy. • Raine *et al.* (1997) chose to look at areas that are already known to relate to aggression. Because the brain is so complex, studies have to choose where to look (and what to look for).	• Doing research in psychology involves the use of animals, and in practical terms it might not be possible to generalise from findings with animals to say they are true of human behaviour. • Studying behaviour came about as a preference of behaviourists because of the difficulty of studying internal processing – behaviour is measurable in a practical way. • Isolating behaviour to measure it (such as separating out a reward) is not easy given that behaviour is complex.

Reductionism in the explanation of behaviour

Reductionism is not really a difficult concept, though the term might be new to you. Studies in psychology tend to break human behaviour, or what is to be studied, into parts so that it can be studied. For example, Milgram used a controlled environment, scripted verbal prods and a measurable way of studying obedience, where participants either agreed to 'give' an electric shock to someone or they did not, and the voltage could be measured. This is 'reducing' obedience to this specific behaviour. Reductionism means breaking something down into parts to study it. Then the findings from studying the 'parts' are put together to try to make sense of the 'whole'. For example, you will see in biological psychology how different parts of the brain are linked to certain aspects of behaviour; this is an example of reductionism. Cognitive psychology gives you the example of HM, a person whose memory was badly affected. In the case study of HM, the whole person is not studied so much as the parts of the brain that were damaged, to see if those parts could be linked to memory deficits. Looking at parts of the brain is a reductionist approach.

Science is reductionist in that experiments take one aspect of something and then study it using careful controls so that a study can be repeated. Psychology draws on scientific methodology a lot, and as such can be said to be reductionist. **Holism** is when something is studied as a whole – for example, in considering a treatment for someone, there might be a holistic approach, which means considering everything about that individual. Holism is, therefore, the opposite of reductionism.

When trying to understand ideas, such as reductionism and holism, it can be useful to relate the ideas to something you know about. For example, if I have every single part of an old 1970s sports car in my garage, but all in pieces, I do not have a 'car'. The 'car' involves the parts in relation to one another and the relationship between the parts is very important (e.g. they have to be bolted together). A reductionist approach might, like the example of the 'car', miss the important relationship between the parts. This is why 'taking a reductionist view' tends to be a criticism. However, note that 'taking a reductionist view' can have advantages in terms of controls over a study, giving more reliable results, for example. Also, you might not be able to study something at all if it is not somehow broken up into manageable and measurable parts. If evidence is required to be valid, perhaps reductionism is not useful, but if evidence is required to be reliable, objective, credible and scientific, perhaps reductionism is a good thing. The 'issue and debate' about whether psychology is a science picks up on some of these ideas.

You can break human behaviour into parts such as neurotransmitter functioning, movement of the limbs, motivation and emotions; however, reducing behaviour to parts, just like reducing a car to its parts, loses something that is the whole

Table 8.3 Examples of reductionism from the four Year 1 topic areas

Social	Cognitive	Biological	Learning
• Milgram's work reduced obedience to authority to a lab experimental task, not taking into account other factors that relate to obedience. • Though Milgram used a lot of variations to test different factors, they were still tested individually, which is 'reductionist'. • Being 'social' is a 'whole' thing and looking at parts (such as in-group/out-group behaviour) can lose the 'whole'. • Social impact theory looks at the parts of social behaviour. This is reductionist and can help to study an area that is complex and hard to study otherwise.	• Memory is reduced into two main parts, short-term and long-term, or into different types, such as semantic and acoustic. • 'Memory' as a whole is hard to study, though life histories perhaps could be carried out using someone older and noting what they say about where their memory is reliable and where it is not. • Using experiments to try to find specific cause-and-effect conclusions about 'memory' so that a firm body of knowledge can be built does tend to require a narrower (or more 'reduced') way of looking at memory than a life history might uncover. • Neurophysiology looks at how different parts of the brain relate to memory in real life, which overlooks the brain as an holistic processor.	• The biological approach breaks behaviour (and emotions such as anger) into parts, e.g. separating anger, impulsive aggression, instrumental aggression, frustration. • It studies the limbic system and prefrontal cortex relating to aggression, not the whole brain. • Connectivity is studied (e.g. Li *et al.*, 2012), which begins to join parts of the brain; however, specific connectivity (e.g. between the prefrontal cortex and amygdala) has to be looked at, as overall brain functioning is so complex. • Single genes are tracked to see their function. • Studies have begun to look at the testosterone/cortisol ratio as they found the two linked and also they draw on the role of serotonin, a neurotransmitter, when drawing conclusions (e.g. Montoya *et al.*'s 2011 review), showing the value of a more holistic approach (though still reductionist).	• Looking at a stimulus and seeing the effect on the response, which is not focusing on the cognitive processes between the stimulus and the response, is a reductionist approach. • Learning theories use experiments and fit this idea of science very well, so they also fit in with the idea of being reductionist. In considering a treatment for someone, there might be a holistic approach, which means considering everything about that individual. • It could be said that systematic desensitisation treats the whole person as the individual can build their own hierarchy and can use various means to relax. In fact, there are cognitive elements of systematic desensitisation. • Therefore, although behaviourism seems to take a reductionist view, when being used in therapy, there is a more holistic focus.

Comparisons between ways of explaining behaviour using different themes

In psychology, it is rare that there is one single accepted theory that explains a certain sort of behaviour because there are many theories and many different areas studied. Even in one specific area, such as theories of prejudice, there are a number of theories. In social psychology, you will have covered social identity theory and realistic group conflict theory. Comparisons between ways of explaining behaviour using different themes in psychology is a main 'issue and debate', partly because of this lack of a single **paradigm**. A paradigm is a world view of something, where there is agreement with one overall theory and research is all within that theory.

Aggression comes in many forms, including aggression in personal situations, aggression in sport, aggression in war and animal aggression; all these might have different causes and might be explained using different themes

Explore

Look up 'paradigm' and explore the idea some more. One way of exploring this term briefly is to use a dictionary, such as www.thefreedictionary.com/paradigm.

Table 8.4 Examples of comparisons between ways of explaining behaviour using different themes from the four Year 1 topic areas

Social	Cognitive	Biological	Learning
• Two different theories of prejudice, social identity and realistic group conflict theories, are used to explain prejudice. • Issues of personality, situation, culture and gender, and their possible effects on obedience are different themes that can be compared. • Issues of personality, culture and situation, and their possible effects on prejudice are different themes.	• Four models or ideas about memory show different ways of explaining memory. • This might not be behaviour as such, more processing, though it can be said that recalling something is a 'behaviour'. • There are themes in memory, such as how it is represented (acoustic, semantic, visual, episodic or reproductive, for example) and which parts of the brain are responsible for which function.	• Aggression has been explained by looking at our inherited characteristics (genes), hormones, neurotransmitters, brain structures and, as a contrast, Freud's ideas about aggression. • However, genes, hormones, neurotransmitters and brain structures all have the main theme of being about our biology and our nature. • Freud's ideas and concepts are separate. • A contrasting way of explaining aggression might be the frustration-aggression hypothesis, (Dollard *et al.*, 1939). Aggression can come from our environment, and is perhaps more 'nurture' led.	• There are three learning theories covered in this chapter and they have been compared. • They have a similar theme, such as the importance of behaviour being learned (rather than innate) but they also have different themes, such as the response following the stimulus (classical conditioning) and the response coming before the consequence (operant conditioning). • Social learning theory suggests that not all behaviour comes from association or pattern of reinforcement; some behaviour comes from imitating a role model, which is a different theme.

Psychology as a science

The discussion about reductionism raises some issues about psychology as a science. If studies in psychology favour controlled conditions and controlled procedures so that cause-and-effect conclusions can be drawn, then that is doing science, whereas, if psychology focuses on the person as a whole, then perhaps that is less scientific. Questions are raised about how far psychology is a science, and how far it is not scientific.

In psychology, you will have looked at experiments like Sherif *et al.*'s field experiment, which takes a scientific approach to studying how prejudice arises and how it might be reduced. Baddeley (1966b) used experiments to look at memory, and the experimental method is a scientific approach to research. Other studies in psychology, however, use questionnaires or interviews or other research methods, and you will have carried out a questionnaire in social psychology – open questions, gathering qualitative data, and asking people about their opinions or attitudes are less scientific and more about the individual as a person.

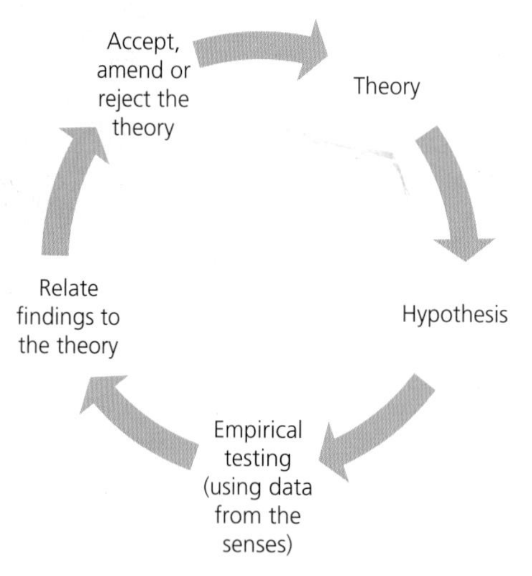

A model of psychology 'doing science'

Table 8.5 Examples of psychology as a science from the four Year 1 topic areas

Social	Cognitive	Biological	Learning
• Issues about methodology, such as social desirability in a questionnaire and related issues of validity. For example, if someone's responses are guided by what they think they should say (social desirability), then that is not valid data because it is not about their 'real' feelings or attitudes (not valid). • Lack of validity might mean data that are not useful, and scientific method is all about getting usable and useful data. • Milgram used careful controls and aimed for cause-and-effect conclusions, making his work scientific in terms of reliability, objectivity and credibility. • Sherif *et al.* aimed for controls such as in their sampling, which is scientific, though a field study tends to be less scientific as environment is hard to control. • In Sherif *et al.*, there were efforts to control issues, such as the boys not meeting, which is scientific.	• The experimental method takes its methodology from science. Science takes a theory, puts forward a hypothesis, tests the hypothesis using empirical data (data from our senses, such as sight, sound and so on) and then amends the theory, accepts it or rejects it. This is what is done in experiments in psychology. • Reductionism relates to psychology as a science, as to study issues in a controlled and scientific way, the whole is often reduced to parts. • Psychology is complex, involving people or animals in all their complexity, so taking an holistic view is not likely to lead to cause-and-effect conclusions (though results might have more validity). • Case studies of brain-damaged patients allow a systematic approach to matching damage to function, which has elements of science.	• The study of genes and their role in our behaviour and characteristics is an example of scientific methods at work. There is isolating of variables for testing, and the actual testing. • Experiments using animals are scientific, such as van den Oever *et al.* (2008), who focus on changes in a rat's brain when they re-encounter cues they have associated with heroin addiction. • Scanning takes a scientific approach, such as scanning a particular area with an idea in mind, measuring and then amending the theory. • Neurotransmitter functioning uses biological understanding.	• If studies in psychology favour controlled conditions and controlled procedures so that cause-and-effect conclusions can be drawn, then that is doing science, whereas, if psychology focuses on the person as a whole, then perhaps that is less scientific. • When looking at learning theories you have looked at many experiments, using scientific methods and careful controls. • Pavlov, Skinner and Bandura wanted to study measurable behaviour to draw cause-and-effect conclusions about behaviour.

Cultural and gender issues within psychological research

Research in psychology is not easy, because people are not 'easy' and straightforward. People are complex beings and any results from studies have to take that complexity into account. In looking at obedience, you will have considered the issues of culture and gender and how they might impact on whether someone obeys an authority figure or not. Culture and gender are just some factors that affect behaviour and are seen as issues in psychology. That is because culture and gender are two ways in which we are socialised in a society, and there are norms and rules associated with being in a particular culture or being a particular gender. Within culture and gender are ideas about nature–nurture as well, because our sex is determined by our biology and historically there has been discussion about genes and cultural differences.

Progress check 8.2

Looking back at the content on obedience in social psychology, were gender and culture seen to be factors in obedience?

Table 8.6 Examples of cultural and gender issues within psychological research from the four Year 1 topic areas

Social	Cognitive	Biological	Learning
• Culture and gender are both referred to in obedience research and in prejudice research. • With regard to obedience, culture is not considered to be a factor as similar levels of obedience to authority, for example, are found across cultures. • With regard to gender, there are few gender differences in obedience to authority; however, there are gender differences in response to such obedience, such as females showing more anxiety and distress. • With regard to prejudice, cultural differences are found, such as how a multicultural policy in a society leads to less prejudice than a policy of assimilation (Guimond *et al.*, 2013).	• Memory as a process does not seem to be different according to gender or culture as it is a process - processing seems to be similar across cultures and gender. • Age might affect memory - damage to the brain that might come with age, such as the development of Alzheimer's disease. However, gender and culture have not been covered in this topic area. • There may be some differences in memory according to gender, such as memory for facial expressions and when emotions are involved in memory, as well as some differences related to areas like this in brain functioning and memory, but overall the processing is not thought to be different. • Given the role of episodic memory, it seems clear that there will be cultural differences in perceptions around what is encoded. • Semantic memory might be different according to the way a language is structured. Sebastián and Hernández-Gil (2012) discussed how digit span might be affected by the words for numbers and how they are 'said' (Spanish v. English).	• There are gender differences in hormones, such as testosterone (male) and oestrogen (female). • There are gender differences in genes - XX and XY. • An evolutionary link is suggested regarding male aggression, which may have the purpose of gene protection, such as defending offspring or a mate. • Dabbs *et al.* (1987) used just male prisoners to look at a link between testosterone and violent crime (and found that link), which emphasises gender differences in genes and hormones. • There is mention of culture when discussing a link between temperature and aggression, measured by car hooting, just as a reminder that studies are set within cultures and cultural differences can be the cause of behaviour.	• Learning theories consider effects on behaviour such as rewards or punishments (operant conditioning) or making associations (classical conditioning), as well as the effect of role models on behaviour (social learning theory). Such effects can be cultural. • What is rewarded in one culture might not be rewarded in another culture. For example, aggression in children is frowned upon in UK culture (and indeed in many cultures); however, there might be a culture that praises boys for showing aggression (showing leadership perhaps). • Gender too affects behaviour, as Bandura showed in his studies (1961, 1963 and 1965): boys imitated aggression more than girls and both boys and girls in general tended to imitate their same-sex role model. • Learning theories emphasise the role of the environment, and culture and gender are important features of many environments.

The role of both nature and nurture within psychology

There is a nature–nurture debate in psychology; indeed, you have probably come across this debate in other areas of study. This is about people being complex beings, being both 'nature', which is given through genes, and 'nurture', which is the sum total of all environmental influences on a person.

Genes come from both mother and father, and although identical twins share their genetic make-up, nobody else does, although you do share 50 per cent of your genes with your siblings.

> **STUDY HINT**
> You can find out more about genes, including looking at identical twins, in the biological approach (pp. 353–359).

Genes do not just act once on the foetus; they continue to act, through life, such as during puberty or when someone gets older. Genes might affect our personality or, perhaps more accurately, our temperament. Genes affect our gender behaviour. Some issues are genetic or have a genetic element, not only our eye colour but also issues such as schizophrenia, which you will study in Year 2 if you are doing the A level course.

What we are through our nurture comes from many sources, including our parents. Environmental influences start from the moment of conception, not from the moment of birth. The womb is an influential environment. Other environmental influences include family, school, where we live and what we watch on TV.

The nature–nurture debate is the debate about what in our behaviour and what in our 'selves' comes from our biology, and what comes from environmental influences. In practice, it is hard to separate our nature from our nurture as we are a product of the two from the start.

An interactional approach: nature and nurture

Psychology has no single paradigm (conceptual framework). This is shown in your course as you look at the different topic areas in psychology. These are social, cognitive and biological psychology, as well as learning theories, and you have also studied the psychodynamic approach (Freud's work), as well as issues around individual differences and developmental psychology. Biological psychology and cognitive psychology focus quite a lot on biological factors, such as brain structure and functioning, as well as the role of hormones on behaviour. You have also looked at how social factors, environment and experiences affect people; particularly in learning theories, you can see the role of experiences.

In some areas in psychology, the focus is on nature and inherited characteristics; in others, it is on nurture and experiences. However, it is more likely that what people become is due to a combination of nature and nurture, not working separately, but interacting even from before birth.

Learning theorists suggest that parents reinforce what is seen in their society to be appropriate behaviour. For example, it could be that girls are better communicators because they are born with a focus on communication, or they might be better at language because their parents expect that and reward them for linguistic skills and focus more on language in the toys that they buy. It seems likely that there is a continuum from having good language skills to having poor language skills, with more girls at the 'good' end and more boys at the 'poor' end. (Of course, there are boys who have good language skills and girls who have poor language skills.) It is probably not even useful to ask whether biological preferences and tendencies guide how babies are responded to, or whether learning guides their biological development. The conclusion is usually that it is neither possible nor desirable to separate biology from learning.

Explore

Consider the idea of dichotomies, which is a term for two opposites, such as 'prejudiced–non-prejudiced' or 'agentic–autonomous'. In language, using such terms is easy and language can guide our thinking. Words can lead us to think of 'X or Y', whereas that split might be artificial. It might not be that there are two opposites, but there might be a continuum. A continuum is where there are two ends of a scale (e.g. prejudiced and non-prejudiced) and someone may be placed anywhere along that scale – for example, in terms of their prejudice (e.g. sometimes prejudiced). Nature–nurture might be a continuum despite sounding like a dichotomy. If you are interested in this sort of thinking, explore the terms further.

Table 8.7 Using twin and adoption studies in the nature–nurture debate in psychology

Argument	Nature	Nurture	Interaction (both)
Definition	Characteristic given by genes	Characteristic given by environment	Genes need environmental trigger
Schizophrenia	Around 50 per cent genetic (from twin studies)	Some instances caused by environment	If 50/50, then might be different causes or different types
Twin studies	MZ twins have identical DNA, so when a characteristic is the same, it is probably genetic	MZ twins share their environment	MZ twins become more different over time – epigenetic modification
Twins reared apart	MZ twins have identical DNA, so when a characteristic is the same, it is probably genetic	Environment is controlled (different), so if a characteristic is the same, it is probably genetic	Environment might be more similar than thought – it might be within the same family
Adoption studies	Compare adopted children with biological parents to see similarities – said to be genetic	Environment is controlled (different from biological family) so if a characteristic is the same, it is probably genetic	Environment might be more similar than thought because they might be matched when adopted
Environment	People are responded to according to the type of person they are (genetic)	Genes (personality) shape the environment, rather than the other way around	If personality (temperament) is genetic and environment responds, there is interaction
Genes	Each person is unique, with 50 per cent of genes from each parent	Each person has a particular environment from conception	From the start, there is interaction; nature and nurture are never separate

Babies imitate their parents and learn to babble and talk that way too, though there is innate babbling to be built on by the environment

An understanding of how psychological understanding has developed over time

One important issue in psychology is that research takes time to develop and understanding of issues changes as studies are carried out and findings tested and disseminated. Psychology is a relatively new subject – it is said that the first laboratory was used in the late nineteenth century, and much of the research you look at in your course is from the twentieth and twenty-first centuries. It is important that you get a sense of how psychology has developed over time. This is one reason for your course asking you to study one classic study and one contemporary study, to make sure you cover some 'history' in psychology as well as current research and focus.

Table 8.8 Examples of the role of both nature and nurture within psychology from the four Year 1 topic areas

Social	Cognitive	Biological	Learning
• Considering whether obedience to authority is from personality or the situation can be seen as a nature-nurture issue. • When we are agents to those in authority, this might be something that evolved in humans because being in a society protects us and is a survival trait. This is 'nature'. • The authoritarian personality (studied in prejudice) is found in different cultures and suggests personality is innate (nature). However, it might just be that all societies generate this sort of personality among others, which would point to nurture.	• Episodic memory and semantic memory both use experiences (nurture), as does the idea of reconstructive memory. • Episodes are events in our lives and semantic memory involves the language we use and objects we encounter. • Reconstructive memory is about the use of schemas, built from past experiences. • There is focus on brain functioning and brain structure (nature), such as suggesting that the medial temporal lobe and the hippocampus are connected to short-term memory processing. • It would not be expected that there are cultural differences in structure and brain functioning, which is nature, but there might be cultural differences in what is encoded and recalled and how that affects memory, which is nurture.	• Heinz *et al.* (2011) carried out a review looking at alcohol and aggression and used both nature and nurture explanations. • There is evidence for addiction linking to brain changes, such as cues related to heroin addiction triggering changes at the synapses (van den Oever *et al.*, 2008). This means that cues in the environment are involved, as are changes in biology. • The nature-nurture debate was discussed when the idea of evolution and genes was introduced. • The research methods using twins and adopted children present arguments for and against claims about whether characteristics arise from nature or nurture, or both.	• Learning theories are all about nurture, such as how environmental stimuli are those that condition us to certain responses (classical conditioning). • Operant conditioning is about rewards and punishments and their effects on behaviour, and rewards and punishments are environmental (such as money to buy things being a reward), not nature. • Social learning theory suggests we copy behaviour from others (e.g. if it is rewarded) – again, our environment and not our nature. • Phobias might come from evolved survival traits (nature) and might be learned from environmental influences (e.g. a bad experience).

Wilhelm Wundt opened the first psychology laboratory in 1879 in Leipzig, Germany

The use of psychology in social control

Psychology is studied for a reason, and that reason is often to help society or people in a society. Psychology contributes treatments and therapies, for example. Psychology, however, can also help to control people – such as, if someone is 'reducing prejudice' in a society, that might help one group (the victims of prejudice) but not another group (those gaining by discrimination), and we might say that helping some is disadvantaging others. Therapies can act as a form of control, such as drug therapy in the case of depression. Biological psychology and learning theories look more at therapies (such as for phobias).

Table 8.9 Examples of how psychological understanding has developed over time from the four Year 1 topic areas

Social	Cognitive	Biological	Learning
• Milgram's important work on obedience was done in the 1960s and you might have looked at Burger's work in 2009, where he replicated Milgram's basic study. Burger found similar levels of obedience, despite the difference in dates, showing similarity in behaviour over time and similarity too in how research is undertaken. • You might have considered Milgram's work and then Slater *et al.*'s (2006) obedience study, to see that Slater *et al.* used a 'virtual' set-up, which would not have been possible in Milgram's time. • Cohrs *et al.* (2012) looked at issues like an authoritarian personality predicting prejudice, as did Adorno *et al.* in 1950. This shows similar issues found over time. Although Cohrs *et al.* used different methods, questionnaires were still important. • Sherif *et al.* and Tajfel, looking at realistic conflict theory and social identity theory at around the same time, show similarities in their focus on prejudice. This suggests at one time in one area (social psychology) similar ideas are being researched (the effects of groups on prejudice).	• Baddeley did a lot of memory experiments in the 1960s to test his ideas about long-term and short-term memory. Then, in 1974, Baddeley and Hitch proposed the working memory model, showing development. • Baddeley used evidence from brain scanning to fit what was being uncovered about how memory took place in the brain into his model, and the model was adapted accordingly. He also used evidence from people with brain damage. • As Baddeley (and others) did more experiments and found out more, he added to the model. • In 2003, Baddeley wrote a review about working memory, helping to show these changes over time. • The working memory model extended understanding of short-term memory, just as Tulving examined long-term memory and split memory into episodic and semantic, with the reconstructive theory of memory linking to episodic and semantic memory too. This shows how knowledge is built. • Sebastián and Hernández-Gil (2012) looked at memory span in 2012, referring to both Atkinson and Shiffrin's (1968) multi-store model and Baddeley and Hitch's (1974) working memory model.	• Brain structures can be measured, for example, using pictures from scans, which, before scanning was introduced, was not possible until an autopsy. Scanning can look at brain functioning. • Brain scanning has changed over time, with fMRI scans offering very useful views of the brain that MRI scanning could not achieve, for example. • Van den Oever *et al.* (2008), in their study of animals, looked at the way cues related to heroin can bring relapse and how brain changes occur. They mention how new ways of studying the brain slices meant more precision and ability to look at those brain changes.	• In learning theories, for example, you studied Pavlov's work on classical conditioning (around 1927) and Skinner's focus on operant conditioning (such as in the 1950s). • Then there was a study by Olsson *et al.* (2007) that used both classical and operant conditioning principles when applying the ideas to calves. • These examples show that psychological knowledge can stand the test of time.

Table 8.10 Examples of the use of psychology in social control from the four Year 1 topic areas

Social	Cognitive	Biological	Learning
• Using psychology, obedience can be obtained, such as using uniforms and authority figures (Milgram). • Prejudice, such as the idea from Sherif *et al.*'s study that co-operating towards joint goals can help to reduce prejudice, can control people so that a society is more peaceful, which can be seen as manipulative.	• The study of memory is removed, in a way, from using psychology to control social situation, as it is about information processing in the brain, so perhaps not involved with how people behave in society. • However, memory studies have been used to inform social issues. One such issue is the use of eyewitness memory in courtroom situations to convict defendants. If eyewitness testimony is discounted in a trial because of psychological understanding of it, then perhaps someone is acquitted rather than found guilty (though generally focus is on how someone not guilty is found guilty because of unreliability of eyewitness testimony). • Generally in cognitive psychology, it is less about trying to control someone and more about helping to 'free' them, such as helping with strategies to overcome any deficit.	• Van den Oever *et al.* (2008) suggested that an injection that stopped the brain changes that go with relapse in the face of cues that were associated with heroin taking could be a useful treatment – which can be seen as social control. • Similarly, drug therapy to treat heroin that is currently in use, such as buprenorphine or methadone, can be seen as social control. • Understanding genes has led to gene therapy, and that too can be seen as social control. • Understanding aggression, such as it coming from jealousy and being an evolved response, could be used as a form of social control if, for example, someone had to undergo anger management as a punishment for a crime committed for such reasons. • Studies have found that stimulating parts of the brain, such as the hypothalamus, can lead to a fight response, and to aggression (Hermans *et al.*, 1993). Studies have found that low levels of serotonin can link in with aggression (van Honk *et al.*, 2010, cited in Montoya *et al.*, 2011). These sorts of findings can be used as a form of social control. Serotonin levels could be boosted in someone to help to control their aggression, for example.	• In learning theories, there are five therapies explained (systematic desensitisation, flooding, CBT, aversion therapy and token economy). When looking at these therapies, you will have seen issues around social control, such as how in flooding the therapist has control over the client, whereas in systematic desensitisation the client can choose their own hierarchy and has to do the relaxation, so they have power in the situation. • In CBT, the client has a fair amount of power as they decide what actions to take and how far to stick with anxiety (in this case, thinking about CBT to treat phobias). • Aversion therapy can give control to the therapist and token economy gives control to the person giving out the tokens, at least to some extent.

The use of psychological knowledge within society

When discussing how psychology can be used in social control, there was explanation about how psychological knowledge can be used within a society. You will have covered a key question in social psychology (pp. 66–69), and that will be an example of the use of psychological knowledge within society too. In social psychology in your course, the example of the use of psychological knowledge within society is reducing conflict in society.

Table 8.11 Examples of the use of psychological knowledge within society from the four Year 1 topic areas

Social	Cognitive	Biological	Learning
• Reducing prejudice in society is informed by ideas such as working towards superordinate goals (Sherif *et al.*). • Obtaining obedience can be helped by giving face-to-face orders, wearing uniforms, ensuring all obey so nobody models disobedience and using places of authority. • Understanding that some policies reduce prejudice more than others, such as multiculturalism, can help society. • Understanding personality that can link to discrimination, such as right-wing authoritarianism and social dominance, can help to see what to reduce (if that is desired).	• Issues around reliability of eyewitness memory can be used to challenge eyewitness testimony and to avoid miscarriages of justice. • Memory findings can help society to understand memory difficulties; that in itself can help someone to cope. • Strategies can be developed, such as writing things down if short-term memory is faulty, or using mnemonics (memory aids) to help a poor short-term memory so that meaning is added.	• If causes of aggression are understood, then that gives guidance about how to deal with them, as shown in the section above looking at social control issues. • Biological understanding, such as about heroin addiction and relapse (van den Oever *et al.*, 2008), can help in developing treatment for heroin addiction. • Gene therapy can help families.	• One example of using learning theory in society is how rewards are given in schools (such as using gold stars) to shape required behaviour. • Token economy programmes can be used in prisons, also to shape required behaviour. • Principles of classical conditioning can be used to help with phobias and anxiety. • Social learning theory has helped to show that watching TV violence can be harmful for children and can lead to aggressive behaviour. Therefore, the 9 o'clock watershed was brought in and films are categorised.

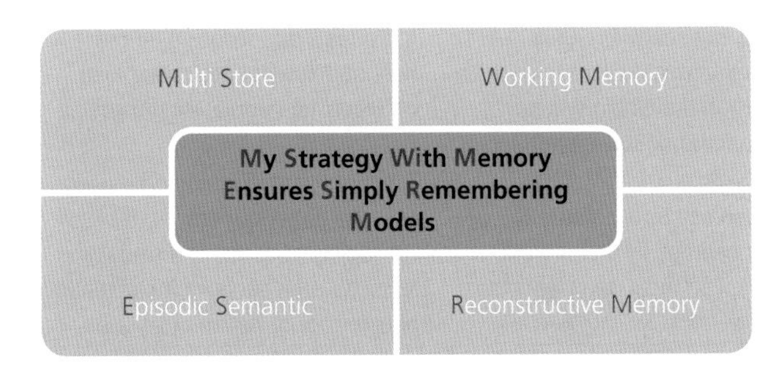

Mnemonics aid memory: a mnemonic for remembering the four memory models

> **STUDY HINT**
> Research into memory has shown that adding meaning can aid short-term memory, such as using mnemonics. You can use these in your revision. For example, you could make up something that has meaning for you to help you remember the four memory models in cognitive psychology. One suggestion is given in the diagram here.

Issues related to socially sensitive research

Some research in psychology is sensitive in a society as it is about individuals and their well-being, or it can be sensitive regarding other societies and cultures. How socially sensitive research is carried out, and how findings are used, are important issues in psychology that link to ethics. Some research is harder to carry out than others, if focused on issues about people that are vulnerable, for example. In some areas in a society, feelings will run high.

Children behave according to social norms; research can be socially sensitive if it is about fitting or not fitting in with social norms

Table 8.12 Examples of issues related to socially sensitive research from the four Year 1 topic areas

Social	Cognitive	Biological	Learning
• Cultural issues in social psychology can lead to racist comments and racism. • If one type of culture is seen as leading to more prejudice than another (such as multiculturalism as opposed to assimilation as a policy; Guimond *et al.*, 2013), that can be a sensitive finding, as it may be seen as criticising a particular country. • Issues about gender can be socially sensitive and findings have to be dealt with sensitively if they might upset individuals or groups.	• Alzheimer's and other forms of dementia are very debilitating for someone, and being diagnosed with memory problems at any age is distressing. • For example, Sebastián and Hernández-Gil (2012) discuss the poor digit span (memory span) for people with Alzheimer's and another form of dementia, and indeed for older people in general. This can be a socially sensitive finding. • People with brain damage might benefit from knowing what the damage means but this needs to be dealt with sensitively. The findings of research do impact on others, which means care needs to be taken in how society uses such findings.	• Case studies of brain-damaged patients, such as HM, look at brain structure and functioning and so relate to biological psychology. When studying someone in depth, especially perhaps when looking at something that has gone wrong for them, issues of sensitivity are likely to apply. • Similar issues apply when looking at people with heroin addiction. They can come to realise that they have what is called here 'brain damage', caused by re-exposure to heroin cues in their environment, even after getting over their heroin addiction (van den Oever *et al.*, 2008). • People can see where their aggression might come from (activity in the limbic system, for example), which might affect them. • Men can see how jealousy is driven perhaps by their nature, which might mean they feel out of control.	• A society might want children to develop in a more open and individual way, whereas schools can be seen as producing behaviour that suits social norms and shapes citizens to adhere to those specific norms. • Learning theories are used in therapies, which again is around shaping required behaviour. Szasz (1961) preferred the idea of people with schizophrenia being themselves and wrote a book called *The Myth of Mental Illness*, criticising social control in the areas of diagnosis and treatment of those labelled mentally ill. • R.D. Laing (e.g. 1965) also had existential ideas, meaning he thought that people were all individuals and focusing on the here and now is best, rather than on labels for people, such as being 'mentally ill'. • Token economy ideas can be used to make behaviour acceptable (to society), but this is a socially sensitive area because it can mean people cannot be 'who they are'.

ANSWERS TO PROGRESS CHECKS

Chapter 1

1.1 a) In school, children interact with one another. They might help one another or they might bully one another, but their behaviour will be influenced by others; b) People have roles within a society and act according to how that society sees that role. For example, guards have to control prisoners and prisoners have to obey guards. Or maybe prisoners have to stick together against the guards; c) People can be in groups and the norms of the group can guide their behaviour, even going against what they might do as an individual. For example, people can be hostile to someone in another group, even if they do not really know them.

1.2

Obedience is obeying the orders of someone in authority, even if against your own moral code.	Conformity is going along with others against your own inclinations with the intention of matching your behaviour with the majority's behaviour.
Compliance is going along with what someone says, though not necessarily agreeing with it.	Internalisation is obeying but with agreement, so there is no conflict with a moral code.

1.3

Statement	True	False
The participants knew that the 'learner' was a confederate.		✗
People Milgram asked beforehand thought that there would be a lot of obedience.		✗
The verbal prods were pre-set and remained the same for every participant.	✓	
Milgram's participants volunteered to take part by responding to an advert.	✓	
There was just one actual shock, received by the participant.	✓	

1.4 Aim: Milgram wanted to see how far someone would go to obey an authority figure. This was in order to test whether 'Germans are different'. Procedure: He used 40 male participants and individually they had to give what they thought were electric shocks to a 'victim', who was in fact a confederate of the experimenter. The participants faced a generator that had switches purporting to go from 15V, in 15V increments, up to 450V and the participant had to press the switch to deliver the (fake) shock to the victim who was in another room, and could be heard but not seen. The learner/victim gave answers to test questions. The answers were pre-set to be wrong sometimes, and so the shocks were delivered. How far would the participant go? If the participant hesitated, the experimenter 'prodded' them to continue, using a pre-set list of prods. Results: 100 per cent went to 300V before stopping and 65 per cent went all the way to 450V. The participants were very distressed, but still obeyed. Conclusion: People obey others even when to obey means going against their own moral code.

1.5 If there is less obedience in a rundown office block than in the Yale University setting, then this suggests that there is power in the setting and the participants felt more obliged to obey there. The authority of the figure is one feature, but the authority of the setting in the basic study seems to be another feature of obedience. This can be seen as a strong conclusion particularly because the variations used the same basic procedure and the controls were all there except for the change in the setting. A difficulty is that Milgram felt that 47.5 per cent compared with 65 per cent was not a sufficient difference to draw a conclusion that obedience had fallen, whereas others might see this as quite a bit less obedience. If it is accepted that there is some reduction, even if not much reduction, when the study is outside Yale, then this is about obedience falling as the power of authority falls. If there is even less obedience when an ordinary man gives the orders (20 per cent), then that emphasises the power of the authority figure in the basic study. And if when the experimenter gives orders over the phone there is less obedience (22.5 per cent), this also serves to underline the power of the authority figure. When that authority figure is 'further away', such as not in the room, then obedience is less. So it is the situation – the setting, the authority of the experimenter and the presence of the experimenter – that gives the obedience rather than the personality of the experimenter or of the participant.

1.6 Milgram found that the situation had led to obedience, such as the person giving the orders being seen as an authority figure. In order to vary the situation and the conditions, Milgram furthered his work using his variations. He varied the setting itself, from the university to a downtown office block. He varied where the victim was situated, from being in a separate room, heard but not seen, to being in the same room. In fact, the participant in one condition had to hold the victim's hand on the plate to receive the shock. He varied how many experimenters there were, and he varied how many teachers (the participant was a 'teacher' in the study). He varied how near or far the experimenter was. By doing all these variations, so much more was concluded about obedience and how the situation would be likely to affect the level of obedience. This was found to be very useful in society, such as in giving advice to those needing to give orders (for society) and also to those needing to understand how to resist obedience.

1.7 Meeus and Raaijmakers (1986) deliberately had the 15 stress remarks to match 15 verbal prods that Milgram used. They also gave orders and their aim was to see if participants would obey them. Their orders would put the participant under pressure, as Milgram's orders did, as both studies involved a high level of punishment (fake) that the participant would be administering. However, there were differences: a) Meeus and Raaijmakers used psychological punishment rather than physical punishment (both fake); b) Their participants were more involved in the punishment as they knew the 'victim' had to carry on with the test if the job was wanted (the victim could not just leave), whereas Milgram's 'victim', who the participants thought was also a participant, could leave.

1.8 In the Slater *et al.* (2006) study, the participants knew for sure that the learner was not being hurt and so, when ordered to give electric shocks, they knew that there were no shocks and no harm was being done. The problem, therefore, is that this might not be measuring obedience so much as measuring politeness or the participants being willing to help scientific growth and knowledge. This is about validity and using a virtual environment means lack of ecological validity as well as lack of construct validity perhaps. It can be said that a lab study lacks validity too, in that it is in an artificial environment. Though in Milgram's study, using a laboratory setting is a formal setting and obedience can take place in settings like that, so Milgram's findings are more likely to be valid. Using a virtual environment was better in ethical terms, but with regard to measuring obedience, perhaps it was not better.

1.9 If obedience to authority is explained by saying that people are agents to those in authority and so they obey, then this is a circular argument. The explanation is that obeying authority is explained because people obey authority, which is not useful. A theory usually predicts behaviour and agency theory can predict that people will obey authority figures, so that is useful. However, this is just saying really that either we have an innate tendency to obey authority or we learn to obey authority (to keep society functioning), and so we will obey authority. There is perhaps some element of explanation here for obedience to authority (such as it being an innate tendency and/or we learn it from interactions with those in authority, such as parents and schooling), so perhaps it is not fair to say agency theory just restates that we obey authority figures.

1.10 The first individual has the attitude that they do not rate football as a game but they are influenced by their friends, who are in quite a large group, whereas they are alone – this is the number of sources. They see their friends as experts in football and, from the discussion, they hear a lot of persuasive argument that the one team is better than the other – this is the strength of the sources. The fact that members of the group are the individual's friends means that the message is different from if it were from a group of strangers – this is the immediacy of the sources. So this individual has lots of factors that mean there is a strong impact on them and they change their attitude, agreeing to go to a game. The second individual experiences less impact. The people they listen to are strangers so there is less immediacy, and the request to change their attitude and behaviour towards team work is a week after the training – again less immediacy. The people doing the training may be experts but are not seen as such; they are seen as people from a different place of work, that is all, so there is less strength in the message. There may be a group of people doing the training but presumably this is not a large group, so the influence is not increased because of a large number of sources. So this individual does not change their attitude to team work or their behaviour.

1.11 When the only change in a study by Milgram was the setting – Yale University or the rundown office block, obedience dropped in the less prestigious setting. When there is more than one experimenter, obedience changes too, suggesting that the situation (the people present) changes obedience. In Slater *et al.*'s (2006) study, when a virtual 'victim' was heard and seen, there was much less obedience than when they were hidden, which suggests that the situation (the feedback from the 'victim') affects obedience.

1.12

Evidence for cultural differences in obedience	Evidence against cultural differences in obedience
There are different levels of obedience in different cultures: • Kilham and Mann (1974) in Australia found obedience in 68 per cent of males and 40 per cent of females when they had to order someone else to administer punishment, which is different from Milgram's findings (but see arguments against this being because of cultural differences). • Meeus and Raaijmakers (1986) in the Netherlands found 91.7 per cent obedience, which was much higher (but see arguments against this being because of cultural differences) • Mantell and Panzarella (1976) in Germany found 85 per cent obedience (but see arguments against this being because of cultural differences; they too used different procedures).	• There are differences in how the studies are carried out in the different cultures. Therefore, even if there is still obedience, it is not clear whether this is showing something about nature (similar in finding obedience even though different levels) or nurture (different levels of obedience across cultures so cultural differences are involved). The differences in findings can be a result of the differences in the procedure rather than the differences in culture. • Meeus and Raaijmakers (1986) found much more obedience than Milgram and were in a different culture, but the punishment was quite different. • Kilham and Mann (1974) asked participants to order someone else to give the punishment. In the part where the participant administered the punishment, there was much less obedience. So it is not likely to be down to culture.

1.13 a) The interviews of Milgram's participants suggested some ideas about authoritarian personality linking to the obedience shown. There was some link to issues with parenting in those who obeyed more than in the 'defiants'. There was some link in that those with high authoritarianism blamed those punishing the learner less than those without that authoritarianism. Evidence suggested that the obedient group saw the experimenter as more admirable; perhaps seeing the person in authority as 'admirable' is a trait that goes with authoritarianism; b) There is evidence for an internal locus of control linking with resistance to obedience. Schurz (1985) found some evidence for an internal locus of control linking to not obeying. Blass (1991) reviewed evidence that Holland had looked at – while Holland found no link between resisting orders and having an internal locus of control, Blass did find such a link in his review. There is some evidence that people in an agentic state (obeying orders) give the responsibility to the person in authority and perhaps those with an internal locus of control would 'give away' responsibility less, so would be more resistant to obedience.

1.14 A police officer will be taking and giving orders. If he or she wants to get people to obey quickly, perhaps to clear an area in an emergency, they need to be visible rather than giving orders more indirectly (when Milgram's participants were ordered over the phone, they obeyed less). They need to wear uniform, to get more obedience (Milgram's participants obeyed the experimenter in the grey coat more than the 'ordinary man'). They need to persuade someone to obey because others are then likely to follow the order too (with others around, obedience changed), or perhaps stop someone else from dissenting as others will follow (when peers rebelled, obedience dropped). They need to be sure that any other police officers are giving the same orders and not different ones (with more than one experimenter, when one said 'stop', participants stopped, even if another experimenter told them to continue).

1.15 For someone to remain autonomous, it is better if they have an internal locus of control, though this might be in-built personality rather than something they can change. But perhaps they can think of themselves as being responsible and not give the responsibility to the person giving the orders (which is about not going into an agentic state). Those without an authoritarian personality might also be more autonomous, but that type of personality comes with upbringing and experiences, so perhaps not easily overcome. If the individual pays attention to their own moral code, rather than going into an agentic state, that would help to remain autonomous. Knowing the situational reasons for being in an agentic state can help, such as watching if someone else dissents, and considering whether it is a uniform or an official situation as that might lead to more obedience.

1.16 Milgram's work is not ethical in that the right to withdraw, though given at the start, was not reinforced and not only were participants not reminded that they had that right but they were pushed into continuing when they wanted to use that right. The experiment was also not ethical because there was deception, in that the study was not fully explained at the start. This meant another unethical feature, in that there was consent, but not informed consent, as there were parts of the study where there was deception. A fourth ethical criticism of Milgram's work is that the participants were clearly distressed, whereas there should be little harm done. Milgram's work was not carried out without regard to ethics though. He debriefed the participants thoroughly at the end. He worked to reduce distress by having them meet the 'learner' at the end, to see he was OK. Milgram also showed competence in that he checked beforehand whether other colleagues (and others) thought that the participants would go so far to obey that they became distressed, and nobody thought even one participant would go to the maximum voltage. A fourth way in which ethics were adhered to is that Milgram did give the right to withdraw, and some did – they were free to leave at any time.

1.17 The three stages are social categorisation, social identification and social comparison. Social categorisation is about simply categorising oneself as in an in-group, such as being a rock music lover. Social identification is going further to identify with the group, such as wearing 'rock' clothes or having a tattoo appropriate to the group (apologies for the stereotyping here!). Social comparison then goes further and involves comparing one's group with an out-group, in ways that make the in-group seem favourable, and there will be hostility to the out-group. This means, for the rock music fan, taking the attitude that rap is rubbish and rock musicians are 'real' musicians.

1.18 Realistic group conflict theory holds that prejudice arises when two equal groups are in conflict over scarce resources. Conflict is relatively fierce if the resources are such that when one group wins them, the other loses, rather than resources that can be more effectively shared. Scarce resources can be water and food, or jobs as a resource in a society, or power. They can be territory, in fact, which is likely to be zero-sum, which means you either have it or you do not.

1.19 Superordinate goals are where two or more groups have to work together to achieve the goal, which cannot be achieved by one group alone. For example, a national football team might need players from more than one football side and so the players have to work together for the superordinate goal – to compete as the national team in a competition. If groups have to work together to achieve a goal they need or want, then that will reduce the prejudice because it is no longer the case that the smaller groups are competing for resources. They are, instead, working together for resources and conflict is reduced.

1.20 Personality characteristics like the Big Five are seen to be stable in someone, such as someone being always open to experience or an extravert. Ideological attitudes are not characteristics of someone but ways of behaving – they show how someone is likely to behave in a social way, such as a right-wing authoritarian, who has rigid thinking and wants to obey and follow social rules. Prejudice is an attitude towards others that is not based on facts and knowledge, more based on stereotypes and ideas. The idea is that perhaps personality characteristics do not themselves predict prejudiced attitudes but that personality characteristics predict the ideological attitude, which then in turn predicts prejudice. (Though having said that, Cohrs *et al.* (2012) did find, to an extent, that personality characteristics did predict prejudice directly.)

1.21 a) Guimond *et al.* (2013) showed that countries with stronger multiculturalism as a pro-diversity policy (and cultural norm) showed less prejudice than countries with a lower pro-diversity policy; b) Becker *et al.* (2012) looked at 21 cultural groups and found that cultural norms affected prejudice as well as personal beliefs and attitudes; c) Verkuyten (2005) showed that multicultural attitudes mean lower levels of prejudice.

1.22 An interview can be structured, unstructured, or semi-structured. The sampling techniques are random, stratified, volunteer and opportunity. The four main ethical principles are respect, competence, integrity and responsibility.

1.23 There were 11 boys in each group though in one group two went home. The percentage of friendship choices at the end of Stage 3 in the in-group for the Rattlers was 63.6 per cent and for the out-group was 36.4 per cent. The percentage of friendship choices at the end of Stage 3 in the in-group for the Eagles was 76.8 per cent and for the out-group was 23.2 per cent. The percentage difference between the friendship choices before and after the introduction of the superordinate goals for the Rattlers was 30 per cent (more) and for the Eagles was 15.7 per cent (more).

1.24 a) The pair words were the same as Milgram used; b) The shock generator had the same number of switches and went up in 15-volt steps; c) There were verbal prods to get the obedience that was being measured and similarity in what the experimenter said (such as 'There is no permanent tissue damage'); d) The participant heard the 'learner' cry out a little from 75 volts but it was at 150 volts that the learner first demanded to be let out.

1.25 Baseline condition: a) stopped = 12; b) not stopped = 28. Modelled refusal condition: a) stopped = 11; b) not stopped = 19. Milgram's Experiment 5: a) stopped = 7; b) not stopped = 33.

1.26 When a study has more than one means of collecting the data, there will be a lot more data gathered, from different viewpoints perhaps, and gathered in different ways. There might be participant observers who gather qualitative data in the form of written notes or quantitative measures (such as measuring cortisol). Tape recordings can be analysed carefully from complete transcripts. If the data come from the same study, then it is likely that the same questions will be answered in different ways and, if the same data are gathered using these different ways, then this suggests that the data are both valid (they measure 'real-life' events and attitudes) and reliable (they have been gathered in more than one way and yet are the same, which shows consistency). Triangulation means looking at all the different data, gathered by different means, and comparing them, to see if the findings match. Triangulation is the process of putting together data gathered using different data collection methods. The reason for putting the data together to see if they 'match' is to test for validity and reliability.

1.27 Cohrs *et al.* thought that self-report data was used so much when testing ideological attitudes, personality dimensions and prejudice that perhaps findings of studies were affected by the method and similar results were found in studies because of similar flaws in the methodology. Peer-report data were found to be valid and useful in the areas to be studied. They thought that using both self-report and peer-report would enable triangulation and a check on validity and reliability of the data. Also by using both, they could see if self-report data did have validity (by checking against peer-report data), which was one of their aims.

1.28 a) Openness to experience relates to generalised prejudice (–0.40), which means the more someone is open to experience the less they show generalised prejudice (or this is what they say – this is self-report data). This is a negative correlation. b) Openness to experience relates to extraversion (0.41), which means that the more someone is extravert the more they are open to experience (or say they are). This is a positive correlation. c) Extraversion relates to agreeableness (0.31). This means the more someone says they are extravert the more they say they are agreeable. This is a positive correlation. d) RWA and conscientiousness show a positive correlation (0.20). This is a positive correlation. The more someone says they are conscientious, the more they say they have other characteristics that fit being right-wing authoritarian in ideology.

Chapter 2

2.1 Cognitive psychology is about the processing of information in the brain, not only the processing but also the inputting of that information and how the processing leads to an output. There can be a computer analogy where human information processing is likened to how a computer works, with input, processing and output. Cognitive psychology covers issues like talking, thinking, perceiving, remembering, problem-solving and paying attention. All are examples of information processing. Issues of interest include not only how such input, processing and output takes place but also where in the brain such working happens.

2.2 Information is **encoded**, which is the early part of the process, and then it is **stored**, such as in short-term and long-term memory. When a memory is needed, there is **retrieval** and without that there would be forgetting. The **capacity** of a store is its size and the **duration** is how long information lasts in that store. Finally, there is focus on the **mode of representation**, which is the form in which the information is encoded and stored.

2.3 1) LTM; 2) sensory memory; 3) STM; 4) LTM.

2.4 1) The task took a minute, which is longer than short-term memory lasts, so the first words at least should be in LTM. 2) One minute is not long enough for all the words to be rehearsed into long-term memory as STM can last up to 30 seconds, so the last words should still be being rehearsed in STM. 3) There might be participant variables – features of the participants that affect the results, such as eyesight or if they were not concentrating on the task. 4) STM has the capacity of 5–9 words so there has to be more than that, and enough so that the participant cannot learn them all in the one minute, so 25 seems about right (leaves some to be rehearsed into LTM, some to be in STM and others in the middle).

2.5 A model is a suggestion of how something might work and it can be tested using experimental evidence, and found to work as a model, but it does not link to 'reality' in that it remains an idea that is not rooted in our biology. Biological evidence from neuroimaging (scanning) and lesions (brain damage) can help to root the model in reality and also can be useful in using the model in a practical sense. For example, if it is thought that the phonological loop is in a specific brain area, because those with damage to that area have problems with the loop, then in future people with such damage can a) have their issues explained, which is empowering, and b) be helped to see how to use other strategies to combat the damage and their memory issues.

2.6 1) The experiment was in STM because the reading of the list lasted ten seconds, then a few seconds before recall was allowed, then recall, so all within around 30 seconds. 2) The words that sound alike would be harder to recall as the 'sound alike' words would affect the use of the phonological loop more than those that did not sound alike.

2.7 The temporary stores served the purpose of enabling visual and auditory information to be processed and indeed the visuospatial sketchpad explains both visual and spatial information. However, there are issues that the two stores do not explain. One issue is that there has to be decision-making when it comes to allocating to a store. Another issue is that it is clear that meaning can form part of STM processing, whereas meaning is in LTM, according to the multi-store model and studies. For example, if chunks can be rehearsed as well as individual letters (such as FBI, PHD as two items whereas 'F' and 'B' are two items) then the meaning (e.g. FBI) has to come from somewhere and that seems to be the LTM. A central executive is required as a control/organiser and indeed another store, the episodic buffer, was suggested to help to explain how meaning can be brought to STM.

2.8 1) episodic; 2) semantic; 3) semantic; 4) episodic; 5) semantic.

2.9 Recall of episodic memories is only possible if they have been encoded and stored – they are not otherwise available. Recall of something that is semantic in nature, however, is possible because it can be worked out using other semantic memories, such as rules. We can work out a King of England on a particular date if we know the list of Kings and their dates. Even if we are not sure of one of the dates, we can work it out from knowing the ones either side. Retrieving a memory from the semantic store does not change the store for a future retrieval, whereas retrieving from the episodic store does change the store because that retrieval is an event itself.

2.10 In the first part of their study, Baddeley and Dale (1966) showed that in LTM there was more forgetting if learning had involved two lists of similar meaning than if learning had involved two lists where meaning was different. This suggests that encoding in LTM involves meaning, so coding is semantic. In the second part, Baddeley and Dale (1966) repeated their study but this time keeping learning and recall in STM and found that pairs of adjectives with similar meaning (they used the same materials as when they studied LTM) did not affect recall in STM. This enhances the findings that semantic memory (meaning) is involved in LTM. Baddeley (1966) studied STM and found that acoustic similarity affected recall in STM (it was 72.5 per cent lower than no similarity) but semantic similarity did not (it was just 6.3 per cent lower than no similarity). This suggests that STM uses acoustic coding and not semantic coding.

2.11 When there was acoustic similarity, there was a lot more recall in the control condition than in the condition where there was acoustic similarity. When there was semantic similarity, the control condition was not different to the semantic similarity condition in recall. So with regard to similarity, in Experiment I in the first part acoustic similarity affected recall, semantic similarity did not. As for forgetting (part 2), acoustic similarity meant that there was not much difference in score from trial 4 to the re-test – there was little or no forgetting. Whereas for the two control conditions and the semantic similarity condition, there was indeed forgetting and the score in trial 4 was significantly higher than the score at re-test (after 20 minutes) for all three of these conditions. So acoustic similarity affects recall at first, but going into LTM does not affect recall (it stayed the same as in STM).

2.12

Statement about Baddeley's (1966b) results	Tick or cross
The semantic similarity condition when use of STM was blocked (Condition Y) had similar recall as in the acoustic condition in Experiment I.	✓
The semantic similarity condition when use of STM was blocked (Condition Y) had different recall to the acoustic condition in Experiment I.	✗
The semantic similarity condition when use of STM was blocked (Condition Y) shows little forgetting (recall at re-test 20 minutes later is not different).	✓
The semantic similarity condition without STM blocked showed significant forgetting (recall at re-test 20 minutes later is different).	✗
The acoustic similarity condition without interference (same in Experiment I and Experiment II) shows slower learning and recall when recall is immediate, but no forgetting (recall at re-test 20 minutes later is not different).	✓

2.13 1) Acoustically similar words were learned best; 2) There was little forgetting.

2.14 570 Spanish children and young people aged from 5 years to 17 years old took part in the main study. They were Spanish speaking and in Spanish schools in Madrid. They volunteered to take part in the study in their break time. They had no hearing problems and no reading or writing difficulties either. Alongside these participants, participants' data from another study were used too. These participants were 25 healthy elderly people, 25 people with Alzheimer's dementia and 9 people with fronto-temporal dementia.

2.15 It was clear that the older the child or young person, the higher their digit span. The 5 year olds had a much lower digit span. The 6–8 year olds clustered around a digit span of 4, with 0.5 digit span between the 6 year olds and 8 year olds. From 9 to 12 years old, there was a similar digit span of around 5.20 digits. With a dip at 14 years old, there is a similar digit span again from 13 to 17 years old, with 13 year olds having an average digit span of 5.89 and 17 year olds having 5.91. Using the age periods rather than school years, this shows a steady rise in digit span from 5 years to 17 years.

2.16 One conclusion, drawn from the 2010 study but reported in the 2012 study, is that, although digit span reduced with age, as shown by the healthy elderly adults having a digit span to match 7 year olds and those with dementia (both types) having a digit span to match 6 year olds, dementia did not have an effect on digit span. This conclusion comes from the fact that the digit span between the healthy elderly control group and the two groups with dementia does not differ significantly. Another conclusion is that word length affects digit span. This is concluded because English studies show a one digit higher digit span across the ages, even though age is still seen to affect digit span. It was thought that, as Spanish digit words are longer than English digit words, it would affect subvocal rehearsal and account for the one digit lower in average digit span.

2.17 The three MTL+ patients had damage to all of the amygdala, all of the hippocampal formation, all of the entorhinal cortex and perirhinal cortex, and much of the parahippocampal cortex. They also had damage to the medial temporal lobe of course.

2.18 The control group got more or less 100 per cent of the answers right in the tests and the patients with hippocampal formation damage did too. In fact, when answering yes/no to questions about semantic knowledge, the two HF patients did better than the controls. As the MTL+ patients did less well throughout, it seems that it is MTL+ damage that causes difficulties with semantic knowledge. For example, in the test where definitions of objects are given and participants are asked to name the object, the MTL+ patients achieved around 50 per cent for the living objects and 62 per cent for the non-living objects compared to 100 per cent for the HF patients in both the 'living' and 'non-living' conditions.

2.19 One conclusion was that HM had unique differences in his difficulties, such as grammar difficulties, and it was thought this might be due to something other than his brain damage. Other studies backed up the idea that his difficulties were different from others with similar damage to the brain (such as Milner *et al.*, 1968). He had problems with fluency and the way he talked too, which suggests something different from issues with semantic knowledge. He had seizures when he was young, which might account for difficulties. This suggests that having a cause (damage to the brain) and an effect (language problems) seems to mean the two are connected but there can be another cause at work. Another conclusion is that the scale of damage matched the amount of difficulty with semantic knowledge – the more damage to the anterolateral temporal cortex, the more the difficulty. This was shown by performance on the semantic tests. The damage was carefully measured so that the scale of damage could be ascertained. There was a relationship between the amount of damage and the performance on the tests, with more difficulty on the tests related to more damage. However, it is hard to be exact about damage, using scanning, and there were only three MTL+ patients so there might be unique issues that led to the conclusions rather than the amount of anterolateral temporal cortex.

2.20 Generalisability is OK when sampling is done carefully and the sample represents the target population. It is not just about sample size. However, a small sample might be less representative because it might not have all the characteristics of the target population, so having a small sample tends to challenge the generalisability of the findings. Schmolck *et al.* (2002) used unique people, such as three patients with damage to the medial temporal lobe and some damage to the lateral temporal cortex too, as well as two patients with hippocampal formation damage, and the well-known case of Henry Molaison. They also used eight healthy controls. Their patients did represent the population of those with such damage, so generalising has some value. Also they did choose patients with specifically different damage. However, their damage will be unique to them, and so it is hard to generalise the ideas to everyone.

2.21 Memory in particular seems to rely on prior knowledge and so any studies of recall of nonsense syllables or material and situations that lack validity are not going to have results that apply to real-life memory. Stimulus material used in memory studies, even if they are carried out in a lab setting, should represent real life to the extent that participants have prior knowledge (semantic/meaning) to draw on as well as episodic memories. This is so results can be found that are relevant to real life.

2.22 Steyvers and Hemmer (2012) reported that thinking about an object that might be expected in a scene and having it not in the scene might affect recall. They found that one of the dining scenes had no tablecloth and that helped to uncover a 19 per cent error rate in the reporting of objects (participants said they saw a tablecloth when one was not present, so that was an error). Even so, Brewer and Treyens (1981) found a 30 per cent rate of false recall, which is much higher. Steyvers and Hemmer (2012) used their finding to show that, if real-life scenes are used in a study, the error rate is not so high, because the task has ecological validity and usually what is in the scene is what is expected in the scene.

2.23 The first weakness is about the setting and talks about the ecology being where someone is in time and place. If a study is in a laboratory setting, which by definition is artificial, then findings are not going to represent the natural setting for the participants so there is a lack of validity. The second weakness is also about the ecology of the participants, but this time not the setting but the task. The task is not valid in that it uses real-life scenes, which goes some way towards ecological validity, but does not make the task valid. Real-life scenes would have more information as they would be three-dimensional, for example.

2.24 Numbers of people with dementia are substantial – 800,000, it is suggested at the time of writing this textbook – so they are a large part of society in the UK and, for that reason alone, having ways to help is of benefit to society. Also numbers are set to rise and the cost of treating those with dementia is set to rise, from £23 billion to £27 billion in 2018. These costs show what an important area it is for society. It helps a society to have individuals that are as fully functioning as possible, and the government has been focusing on setting up dementia hubs where anyone can go to get checked out and helped and to where GPs can refer people. The government has also focused on an awareness campaign to show how those with dementia can function well quite often; they just need help, support and understanding. This government interest and intervention underlines the fact that helping with dementia is important for society, partly because of a focus on getting all society's citizens to be as self-reliant as possible. This can be for cost reasons and for personnel reasons, as having to provide care takes up valuable resources.

2.25 One way in which knowledge of working memory has helped to inform the treatment of dyslexia is to take what is known about the possible limitations in working memory for children with dyslexia and ask teachers to amend their tasks in class to take such limitations into account. For example, instructions can be simple and one step at a time, so that the child does not struggle trying to follow complex instructions. If working memory is limited in capacity, a child is likely to have difficulties with retaining instructions while working on a task. Another way is to generate working memory tasks and to set them up on a computer for a child with working memory deficit (manifesting as dyslexia) to practise using working memory. This can help them to extend its capacity or at least to use it more effectively.

Chapter 3

3.1 Identical twins share 100 per cent of their genes and they share their environment. Non-identical twins share 50 per cent of their genes and they share their environment. Differences between non-identical and identical twins (e.g. if identical twins share depression more than non-identical twins) are likely to be due, at least to some extent, to genes.

3.2 The hippocampus has the role of enabling short-term memories to go into long-term memory. The cerebellum stores well-learned processing and also skills. The amygdala has a role in aggression and emotions.

3.3 Norepinephrine is involved in the fight-or-flight response and affects our attention. Dopamine is associated with feelings of pleasure and is involved in addiction. Serotonin is related to happiness and being in a good mood. Low levels are associated with depression and anxiety.

3.4 a) To support the neurons and protect them; b) To have a role in building myelin to protect the axon and enable the action potential to travel more quickly down the axon.

3.5 The synaptic gap is a real gap that is found between the terminal buttons and the end of one neuron and the dendrites of another neuron. Neurotransmitters are in the terminal buttons of a neuron sending a message and are released by an electrical impulse down the axon of the sending neuron (the presynaptic neuron) into the synaptic gap. Neurotransmitters are chemicals that affect brain functioning, such as serotonin. Receptors are found at the dendrites of the receiving neuron (the postsynaptic neuron) and the receptors are suitable for certain neurotransmitters but not others. If the neurotransmitter in the gap suits the receptor, then it is 'received' and starts a message off in the receiving neuron.

3.6 Reuptake is done by transporter proteins and these take any excess neurotransmitter that is in the synaptic gap, which then gets absorbed into the presynaptic neuron. This has the function of clearing out the neurotransmitter in the gap and enabling its reuse. Also it means the message stops more quickly as there is no neurotransmitter in the gap to keep filling the receptors.

3.7 There are cannabinoid receptors in the brain called CB1 receptors. The dopaminergic neurons in the reward system in the brain do not have CB1 receptors so you would think cannabis would not work there. However, there are in the GABAergic neurons, which act to inhibit the release of dopamine by the dopaminergic neurons. Cannabis blocks the GABAergic neuron's inhibiting of the dopaminergic neuron and so dopamine is released when cannabis is in the system. This is a three-step procedure: a) GABAergic neurons inhibit dopaminergic neurons; b) Cannabis prevents GABAergic neurons from inhibiting dopaminergic neurons, so there is no inhibiting of the dopamine; c) Dopamine is released.

3.8 The corpus callosum bridges the two hemispheres of the brain. Without it, communication between the two halves more or less stops.

3.9 If someone has specific brain damage that can be seen and measured (such as using scanning) and they also have deficits in functioning, then it is seen as logical to assume that it is because the area is missing or damaged that the functioning is limited. It is then assumed that that area of the brain is 'for' that specific functioning. There is some logic in this, especially if the person had no functional deficit before the damage. Also if more than one person with damage to that area has the same or similar deficits in functioning, that adds to the evidence for drawing such conclusions. Schmolck *et al.* (2002), one of the contemporary studies in cognitive psychology in your course, did a study based on the assumption explained here.

3.10 a) Bechara and van der Linden (2005) found that the prefrontal cortex is about planning, deferring rewards and taking account of information for long-term planning. If there is damage or low functioning in the prefrontal cortex, this can show up as aggression as the regulating mechanisms are not fully functioning; b) Perach-Barzilay *et al.* (2012) found that the dorsolateral region of the prefrontal cortex links to controlling impulses and putting inhibitors in place so low functioning there could mean less inhibition and more behaviour such as aggression.

3.11 The hypothalamus is in the limbic system in the brain and has a balancing role. The hypothalamus checks our overeating, regulates temperature and also blood pressure and pulse rate. It links to emotions, in controlling the fight-or-flight response too. It is about keeping our bodies in balance.

3.12 Swantje *et al.* (2012).

3.13 a) Delville *et al.* (1997) showed that the hypothalamus has receptors relating to the neurotransmitter serotonin and the hormone vasopressin and these (e.g. low levels) can determine aggression and mood; b) Andy and Velamati (1978) showed that cats became aggressive if certain neurotransmitters were blocked and they showed aggression if there was electrical stimulation to the hypothalamus and basal ganglia. This is evidence that structures in the brain do relate directly with aggressive behaviour.

3.14 Each person inherits 50 per cent of their genes from their father and 50 per cent from their mother, and that is their genotype. That is what 'nature' refers to. We have characteristics such as eye colour and temperament, and a great deal more, that we have inherited from our parents. There is also the phenotype, which is what we 'are', taking our genotype and interacting with our environment. What we encounter in our environment is what is called 'nurture'. People interact with the environment from conception. For example, foetal alcohol syndrome can come from alcohol from the mother while the baby is in the womb. Our genotype is given at conception and our nurture works with that genotype to make us what we are. The nature–nurture debate refers to difficulties in knowing which characteristics are genetic and inherited, and which come from our environment. Of course this assumes it is one or the other, but it is likely that many characteristics are formed by both interacting on one another.

3.15 a) natural selection; b) genetic mutation; c) genetic drift.

3.16 Variation means different genes in a species. Species do share a lot of their genes of course – that is what makes the species; however, within a species there is going to be variation. If there is variation, then the genes that give characteristics that suit survival to reproduce are the ones passed on. If there is very little variation, then all would have the same or very similar characteristics and those may not suit the environment so the genes (and species) would die out, though a small difference in the overall genotype can be enough variation for natural selection to occur. It is just that there must be variation.

3.17 Genetic mutation means some change in genes from something like cancer, radiation, a virus or some other cause. The gene changes and the changed genes can be passed on through reproduction. Genetic drift does not refer to a change in genes but to the genes not being passed on through reproduction. Genes may not be inherited and this can be by chance as just 50 per cent of a male's genes are inherited by an offspring – for example, the same for the female. It might be that some gene is by chance not inherited by any of the offspring, and it might die out. This is genetic drift. Genetic mutation is when genes change and that change is inherited. If the change is advantageous for survival and reproduction, then it can be passed on and can 'save' the organism if the other genes are not suitable. Genetic drift is the opposite really – genes are not passed on and this is by chance; the genes in that organism die out.

3.18 a) One strength is that he gathered evidence carefully and painstakingly and others since have also found evidence for his ideas. Kettlewell found more darker moths in an area where 'dark' would be good camouflage and would mean a better chance of survival, and he found more light moths in an area where 'light' would be better camouflage because the trees, for example, were light coloured. b) One weakness is that other theories had to be produced because his theory did not account for all behaviour. Animals that give warning cries draw attention to themselves and their genes are then under threat, which seems to go against the idea of natural selection. Kin selection theory is required to explain that one animal's non-survival can mean their genes are passed on through relatives that are saved by the warning cry.

3.19 Jealousy can be about holding on to a mate and, by doing that, reproducing so one's genes are carried on. Jealousy that leads to aggression might be successful because it might frighten off others that might 'take' one's mate or might prevent the mate from turning to others, out of fear. Thus jealousy can act as a survival instinct in the sense of allowing genes to be passed on.

3.20 a) tissue function; b) growth and development; c) regulating the sleep–wake cycle; d) regulating breathing; e) reproduction.

3.21 Hormones work by binding to receptors in cells that have the relevant receptor proteins. The binding of the hormone to the receptor proteins changes the cell function. The effects of hormones can depend on how concentrated they are – it is not an 'off/on' process, unlike neurotransmitter functioning.

3.22 a) Dabbs *et al.* (1997) found that there were high levels of testosterone in criminals that had been violent in their crimes and they also found those with low levels of testosterone were those not involved in violent crime, so the conclusion is that testosterone does relate to aggression. b) Barzman *et al.* (2013) found that cortisol, testosterone and DHEA are related to aggression in children aged 7–9 years old. They found that levels of cortisol on waking related to aggressive incidents during the day and that a rating scale (the BRACHA) predicted aggression, in that an 'aggression' score on the BRACHA related to aggression shown by number of incidents recorded.

3.23 a) Adelson (2004) reports studies using animals showing links between aggression and hormones. It was found that there is a link between the aggression centre in the brain of animals (e.g. the hypothalamus) and stress hormone release. Stress hormone release leads to activity in the aggression centre and stimulating the aggression centre links to stress hormone release, so there is a feedback loop. b) Chang *et al.* (2012) found that aggression, boldness and exploring behaviour in fish related to the amount of testosterone before the behaviour. Aggression and boldness also related to the amount of cortisol (exploring behaviour did not have this link). Aggression and boldness correlated strongly with one another too. The conclusion was that testosterone and cortisol (cortisol is the hormone linked with stress) relate to aggression, boldness and exploring in some way.

3.24 The argument for using animal studies is that they are easier to handle and things can be done that ethically cannot be done to humans, such as stimulation of the hypothalamus (reported in Adelson, 2004). Also, there can be generalisation from animal studies to humans because the brain structures and functioning of animals and humans have a lot of similarities, as Trainor (2009) explains. The hypothalamus and limbic system are similar enough, for example, so findings about aggression can be usefully linked to human aggression. The argument against using findings from animal studies and relating them to humans is that there are brain differences that are different enough to question any generalisation of findings. Also when mice are used, for example (as reported in Trainor, 2009), they are not in their natural environment and findings of the workings of the brain might not be valid for the mice, so it is unlikely that they would be valid for humans.

3.25 a) Freud thought that development in the first five years of life sets the scene for how someone develops later. He put forward the idea of a child passing through set stages in the first five years, where they worked through different issues, and how they did this affected the person they became. b) Freud laid a great deal of emphasis on the unconscious part of the mind, which he thought held wishes and desires that the conscious part of the mind cannot access. Those wishes and desires underpin a person's behaviour even though they are not known.

3.26 The conscious mind is the only one of the three that has awareness of thoughts, memories and emotions, whereas the preconscious mind, though also storing memories and thoughts, has them just under the surface of consciousness. However, they can, in the preconscious mind, be accessed, which is not true of thought, desires and emotions in the unconscious. In the unconscious, they are buried and can only be uncovered by watching/listening carefully for 'leaks' and clues.

3.27

Situation	Part of the personality according to Freud
We want to move to a bigger house to show off to friends.	Id
We always stop at traffic lights when they are red and even when just turning red.	Superego
We want to go to a party that will go on into the early hours but our parents are worried and don't want us to go. We decide to go but to leave to go home at eleven o'clock.	Ego

3.28 a) Aggression comes from the death instinct. Aggression is the outlet for that instinct which keeps it from interfering with the life instinct, so aggression in that mental sense is healthy and necessary. b) Aggression is linked to the superego as the child unconsciously feels aggression towards parents who thwart the demand of the id by putting up rules and, not being able to feel aggression towards them directly, has that aggression in with the superego. The more the aggression and frustration towards the parents, the stronger the conscience and greater the guilt (which means having a strong superego).

3.29 a) Hokansen (1974) found evidence that behaving in an aggressive way is cathartic in that physiological measures show calming of tension. b) Verona and Sullivan (2008) found that heart rate was reduced if someone responded aggressively to something that was frustrating. Though they also found, as did Hokansen, that alleviating tension by using aggression did seem to lower heart rate and reduce tension, but it did not mean that later aggression was reduced, so the aggressive drive itself was not reduced. c) Bushman *et al.* (1999) found that someone reading about catharsis did not then reduce aggressive behaviour in response to being frustrated (negative mark on an essay). In fact, they carried out more aggression than someone who had not read the article. So reading about aggression and catharsis does not reduce aggression.

3.30 a) The limbic system is the place for emotions such as aggression (the limbic system includes the amygdala) and, although there are links to the prefrontal cortex, where planning takes place, the limbic system does seem to be about emotions and not logical thinking. This links with the idea that this area of the brain is inaccessible regarding conscious thought so we can say that emotions including aggression are 'in the unconscious'. b) A very young child is using the right hemisphere, which in general is non-verbal and in that sense non-conscious, which matches with the idea of the id in the early child being demanding, with rational thinking about those demands only developing later.

3.31 a) prefrontal cortex; b) corpus callosum; c) amygdala (there are others).

3.32 The participants all carried out the same continuous performance task, which was chosen to activate certain areas of the brain. They carried out a practice task before the scanning started. Ten minutes after the practice task, they started the task and 30 seconds afterwards the glucose tracer was injected. They continued with the task for 32 minutes, for the tracer to be taken up into the brain. After that the PET scan was undertaken and images of the brain were produced.

3.33 a) The corpus callosum showed differences between the controls and the murderers. The murderers had lower glucose metabolism in the corpus callosum than the controls. b) The amygdala showed differences between left and right hemispheres. The murderers showed lower glucose activity in the left amygdala than the controls and higher glucose metabolism in the right amygdala than the controls. c) In some areas of the prefrontal cortex, the murderers had lower glucose metabolism than the controls, including left and right medial superior frontal cortex, the left anterior medial cortex, the right orbitofrontal cortex and the lateral middle frontal gyri of both the left and the right hemispheres.

3.34 a) The right hemisphere in humans might generate negative effects and, if the corpus callosum shows dysfunction, then the control of the left hemisphere might not be there in violent offenders. This conclusion comes from the finding that there is reduced functioning in murderers compared with controls in the corpus callosum. b) The posterior parietal cortex seems to be about cognitive functioning and in particular forming abstract concepts, so any dysfunction in that region might lead to issues such as reduced verbal ability. This might affect education and job success and might lead to violent behaviour.

3.35 a) Volkow *et al.* (1995) showed that prefrontal, frontal and temporal medial cortex functioning was reduced in violent patients compared with non-violent patients. b) Tonkonogy (1991) did not find orbitofrontal cortex reduced functioning in violent patients with organic mental issues, contrary to some studies; however, they did find damage to the hippocampus/amygdala regions, which matches other studies such as Raine *et al.* (1997). c) Goyer *et al.* (1994) looked at patients with personality disorder and a control group and used brain scanning as well as self-report aggression scores. They found reduced functioning in orbitofrontal and anterior-medial frontal cortices related to self-reported aggression scores. (There are other answers.)

3.36 The main aim of the study involved getting four measures using fMRI scanning and focusing on connections between brain areas. The four measures were; a) the brain in resting state; b) the brain looking at cue-related pictures for the heroin-user group; c) the brain in resting state; and d) the brain looking at cue-related pictures for the controls. Using those measures, the aim was to look for differences (brain damage) in the heroin users compared with the controls and also to see if connectivity in the brain correlated with length of heroin use.

3.37 a) Li *et al.* (2013) concluded that there is a difference in links between different brain regions in heroin users compared with healthy controls. They found links (functional connectivity) between certain structures and the posterior cingulate cortex in the heroin users that they did not find in the controls. b) They found correlations (significant at $p \leq 0.05$) between the length of time of heroin usage and the link between the posterior cingulate cortex connecting with the bilateral insula and also between the posterior cingulate cortex connecting with the bilateral dorsal striatum. It seems that the longer the heroin usage, the more the difference in functional connectivity and, as this was different from the controls, it could be said that the longer the heroin usage, the greater the damage to the brain. The areas they found differences in were areas already linked to reward and dopamine pathways, and addiction, so they concluded that taking heroin and becoming reliant on it does affect brain connectivity between structures.

3.38 a) How far is social aggression caused by genes, shared environment or non-shared environment compared with physical aggression? b) How far is physical aggression taken over by social aggression in an individual from early to middle childhood?

3.39 The teachers used standardised questionnaires to rate each child for social aggression (e.g. 'tries to make others dislike a child') and for physical aggression (e.g. 'gets into fights'). Peers had to choose three children from photos of all the children in the class, choosing who fitted a behaviour that was read to them, such as, for social aggression, 'tells others not to play with a child', and for physical aggression, 'hits, bites or kicks others'. In each case, each child was given a total social aggression score and a total physical aggression score.

3.40

Statement	Correct
Children who show physical aggression rarely show social aggression.	No. The link is the other way - the two are linked together
A child who shows physical aggression when young is likely to move to social aggression as they mature.	Yes
Social aggression can replace physical aggression because it is more subtle and less likely to be punished as less overtly disapproved of by society and parents.	Yes
Physical aggression is mostly down to environmental factors.	No. It is the opposite - quite a lot is down to genes.
About 50 to 60 per cent of physical aggression in children is genetic.	Yes
Physical aggression in a child predicts social aggression, so is best reduced as much as possible.	Yes

3.41 a) The researchers wanted to set up a study where rats who had had a heroin 'habit' and then had that habit extinguished were then exposed to cues in their environment that had been there when they were taking heroin. This is re-exposure to drug-related cues. They wanted to study what happened when these rats were re-exposed and, in particular, what changes were found at the synapse because of re-encountering these cues. They wanted to see what changes at the synapse were found in this situation – when commonly in people, when they re-encounter cues they associate with heroin-taking, there is relapse. This was to see if they could suggest a treatment for heroin users based on biological understanding of synaptic transmission. If they could block the changes that happened when the cues were re-encountered, they might be able to forestall a relapse.

3.42 a) Van den Oever *et al.* found synaptic changes in rats when cues that were previously associated with heroin-taking were reintroduced and so there was relapse to heroin-taking even after extinction of the habit. The synaptic changes were around depression (less activity) and the AMPA receptors in the medial prefrontal cortex. b) They found that injecting rats before the cues were re-introduced so that there was relapse meant that the changes were no longer observed. TAT-GluR2_{3Y} prevents GluR2 endocytosis, which is what alters the synaptic AMPA currents in the medial prefrontal cortex after the re-exposure to cues.

3.43 a) They found that injecting a substance that seems to prevent the synaptic depression that comes from cue-related heroin relapse is successful and they suggested that this might be a way of treating human heroin relapse in the face of cues. b) They found that acute synaptic depression of the ventral medial prefrontal cortex when there is re-exposure to heroin-seeking cues leads to a 'loss of inhibitory control over heroin-seeking'.

3.44 Addiction affects a lot of people in the country, such as 293,879 taking opiates in England, according to 2013/2014 figures. Addiction costs money in terms of treatments and therapies, clinics and support services. There are people who want to be free of their drug habit, and society needs to recognise that help is needed. Addiction is seen as an illness so drug therapy will be part of what the NHS provides, and the NHS is a social provision. If treatment is effective, then it is better for society in terms of financial cost and also in terms of human cost.

3.45 a) synaptic transmission; b) limbic system; c) prefrontal cortex; d) vicarious reinforcement (also: synaptic depression, euphoria, brain functioning and opioid).

3.46 a) testosterone; b) limbic system; c) PET scanning; d) cortisol (also: hypothalamus, aggression centre, natural selection, punishment).

Chapter 4

4.1 a) Learning theories focus on a stimulus and a response without looking at mental processes in detail. This means that behaviour is what is observed, and the stimulus or stimuli leading to the behaviour are studied. This is a simplistic view of human behaviour perhaps, as it does not look at why someone performs the behaviour in terms of their personality, for example. b) Learning theories take a scientific viewpoint as they want to build a body of knowledge. Science means setting up an independent variable, for example (such as a red light giving food and a green light not giving food), and then observing behaviour (such as the rat learning to press the lever only when the red light is on). Controls are used to make sure that only one variable is changing and the dependent variable is changing because of that one variable. c) Learning theories focus on nurture and not nature. Genes are not studied, or any inherited characteristics – the focus is on learning our behaviour through interaction with our environment.

4.2 Unconditioned stimulus (UCS) – flowers → Unconditioned response (UCR) – sneezing

UCS + Neutral stimulus (NS) → Unconditioned response (UCR) – sneezing

Flowers (UCS) + Aunt (NS)

Aunt (CS when conditioned, no longer NS) → Conditioned response (CR) – sneezing

4.3 Forward conditioning is when the conditioned stimulus is presented before the unconditioned stimulus. The conditioned stimulus can be presented and then remain while the unconditioned stimulus is presented, so there is overlap – this is delay conditioning. Alternatively, the conditioned stimulus can be presented, end and then the unconditioned stimulus is presented so they do not overlap – this is trace conditioning. They are both types of forward conditioning.

4.4 Beautiful woman (UCS) → arousal/desire (UCR)

Beautiful woman (UCS) + car being advertised (CS/NS) → arousal/desire (UCR)

Car being advertised (CS) → arousal/desire (CR)

4.5 It is important that people drink water and soft drinks, so if conditioning to stop alcoholism generalises to all drinks that would be dangerous. The emetic drug is paired with alcohol to associate the feelings of sickness with the alcohol to stop drinking but to make sure that, when the person is not suffering from the effects of the drug, they drink water or other drinks without the unpleasant association.

4.6 a) Dogs have a salivation reflex in response to, for example, food in the mouth, and this is there even when there is no use of the cerebral cortex. Pavlov concludes that the cerebral cortex is not involved in such reflexes. b) Experiments are needed and careful controls because observing subjectively cannot pick out the details involved to study higher-order thinking in dogs. There are so many stimuli affecting an animal that separating out stimulus from response can only be done in controlled experimental conditions. c) Evolution ideas show that animals and humans have developed using the same processes and so it is in order to study animals like dogs and how their cerebral cortex works and say that is the case for humans as well. It is reasonable to assume that the brain works in a similar way and that survival instincts apply.

4.7 a) Pavlov gave meat to the dog and paired the meat with the sound of a metronome a few times. The metronome sound came before the meat rather than afterwards. Salivation took nine seconds to get going and, by 45 seconds, there were 11 drops of salivation. The metronome became a conditioned stimulus and the salivation in response to the metronome (no meat needed) became a conditioned response. b) Pavlov sounded a buzzer and paired it with meat to get salivation, aiming to get the buzzer to be a conditioned stimulus and the salivation to the buzzer would be a conditioned response. In one part of this study, he sounded the buzzer after the meat gave salivation and, in another part, he sounded the buzzer before the meat. The buzzer before the meat did become a conditioned stimulus and gave the conditioned response of salivation. The buzzer after the meat did not become a conditioned stimulus and did not give salivation.

4.8 1a) Positive reinforcement; b) Negative reinforcement; c) Positive punishment; d) Negative punishment.
2a) The child stops the bad behaviour to avoid something unpleasant happening so this is punishment and it is positive punishment because being made to stay in her room is 'something unpleasant given'; b) The family carry out the behaviour of going to the second bench to avoid something unpleasant, so that is negative reinforcement.

4.9 1) primary; 2) secondary; 3) primary; 4) secondary.

4.10 1) fixed ratio; 2) variable interval; 3) fixed interval; 4) variable ratio.

4.11 When something is said to be 'superstitious', it means that behaviour occurs for no reason other than that it is thought to relate to emotions or ideas, such as being 'lucky' or 'unlucky'. For example, if someone passes an exam while wearing a favourite scarf, they may come to see the scarf as lucky for them. Then they wear the scarf to their next exam and this is superstitious behaviour. The link to operant conditioning is that that person has linked 'wearing the scarf' to the reward of passing the exam and, though there is no such link (we assume!), they wear the scarf again in order to pass an exam. This is like the pigeons in Skinner's study. They were doing some movement, like turning, and the food appeared. They linked 'turning' with the reward of food (wrongly) and then kept turning, in order to get the reward of food.

4.12 The UCS is the diuretic, which automatically leads to the UCR, urination. The NS is the stall. The UCS and the NS (which is then the CS) together will give the UCR for a few pairings. Until, hopefully, the CS (the stall) will give the UCR (which is then conditioned so is the CR), urination. Though in fact this did not happen in their study, this is what they studied.

4.13 The bell is a secondary reinforcer because it does not fulfil a primary need as food would. The milk is a primary reinforcer. The calf is rewarded by milk for the behaviour of urinating in the stall. This is positive reinforcement – the consequence of doing the required behaviour is that a reward is given.

4.14 Two reasons for: a) Animals are easier to handle and study in practical terms, because of their size and their needs. b) Animals can learn something new that it can be fairly sure has not been observed or learned before. Two reasons against: a) Animals are not like humans in that they do not have the same problem-solving abilities and brain functioning (even though there are similarities). b) Animals are not the same as one another, as Vaughan *et al.* (2014) mention in their study of dairy cows.

4.15 Attention, retention, reproduction and motivation.

4.16

Situation	Number	Person observing	Number
A father holding his hand up to be heard when at a family meal	1	A teenage boy who likes technology	2
A teenage boy playing a video game in a shop	2	Formula One fan	3
A bank advert using a racing driver	3	A young mother	4
A mother taking cupcakes to a school function	4	The father's young son	1

4.17

Group	Aggression score	Group	Aggression score
Aggression condition, physical aggression, boys, male model	25.8	Aggression condition, mallet aggression, girls, female model	17.2
Aggression condition, physical aggression, girls, male model	7.2	Aggression condition, physical aggression, girls, female model	5.5
Non-aggression condition, non-imitative aggression, boys, male model	22.3	Non-aggression condition, non-imitative aggression, girls, male model	1.4
Control condition, gun play, boys	14.3	Control condition, gun play, girls	3.7

4.18 a) Children imitate behaviour without reinforcement so there is more to learning then operant conditioning suggests. b) Children tend to identify with significant people in their lives, such as the same-sex parent, and this agrees with Freud's views. However, this study found imitation of 'neutral' people and so there is more to imitation than identification. c) Children may use cultural norms in their imitation because both boys and girls imitated the male model who showed physical aggression more than the female one, though with regard to verbal aggression there were no such differences.

4.19 a) mallet aggression, which is hitting something with the mallet aggressively but not the Bobo doll as that is imitative aggression; b) imitative aggression, which is doing the exact aggressive acts that the observed model had displayed; c) aggressive gun play, which was using a gun in an aggressive manner, such as pretend shooting; d) partially imitative acts, which were when the essence of what the model had done was displayed but not exactly what had been observed.

4.20 $p \leq 0.001$ is: p (the probability of the results being due to chance) is equal to or less than (≤) 0.001 (1 in 1,000). This means that 999 out of 1,000 of the participants would go with the hypothesis (that male models mean more aggressive gun play shown, as in the example given on this page). This is a strong level of significance.

4.21 So that a study has reliability, there are likely to be careful controls and then a study can be repeated to see if the same results are found. If the results are the same, then there is consistency, which is reliability. However, one issue about having careful controls is that there is likely to be a lack of naturalness to the situation and the task. A controlled environment is not natural and controlled tasks are not natural either. Validity refers to getting real-life data. The more controls, the less validity. The more controls, the more reliability. This tends to mean that the more a study can be shown to have reliable findings, the less they are shown to be valid.

4.22 UCS = unconditioned stimulus; UCR = unconditioned response; NS = neutral stimulus; CS = conditioned stimulus; CR = conditioned response.

4.23 a) operant conditioning; b) social learning/observational learning; c) cognition.

4.24

Statement about a treatment for phobia	Flooding	SD
The individual is immersed into their feared situation or object.	✓	
The individual learns muscle relaxation.		✓
It is about not being able to maintain the fear over the short period.	✓	

4.25

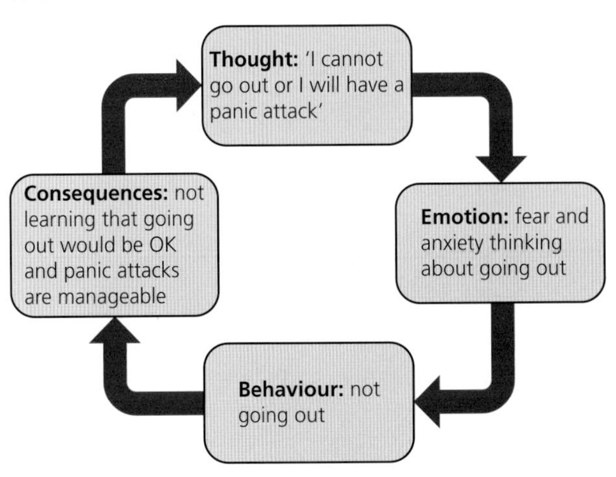

4.26

Statement	Therapy
Rewarding required behaviour with something that can be exchanged for something desired	Token economy
Exchanging an unpleasant feeling for the pleasant feeling that a drug gives, to help to prevent use of the drug	Aversion therapy
Immersing someone 'in' their fear so that their reaction, which cannot last, recedes and they think they have overcome the fear	Flooding
Gradually facing a fear bit-by-bit while remaining relaxed, to replace the fear response with a relaxation response	Systematic desensitisation

4.27 a) Validity means measuring what you claim to be measuring, such as if measuring helpfulness, being sure that what is measured is indeed 'helpful' and not just 'smiling', for example. b) Reliability means that if a study is repeated the same results are found, so if someone tries classical conditioning principles such as blowing on eyes to yield a blink response and at the same time ringing a bell so that soon the bell gives the blink, then that is what should happen if findings about classical conditioning are reliable. c) Reductionism means looking at parts of something, not the whole thing – particularly where people are concerned as they are complex so behaviour is going to use a lot of variables (such as thinking and emotions). Looking at helpfulness as smiling or pointing might seem reasonable, but it is just part of human behaviour, the observable part. What if the person is smiling and pointing but sending someone in the wrong direction? Gathering qualitative data about the whole idea of helping might be less reductionist, give less reliable data and yet be more valid and holistic. d) Controls are part of doing a scientific study as they keep all variables the same except what is measured (such as participant variables, whether participants are tired or hungry, and situational variables, whether there is noise or it is cold).

4.28 a) Little Albert was startled by the loud noise, such that he burst into tears, and this is causing distress so against the BPS guidelines (Code of Ethics and Conduct, 2009) of responsibility and causing no harm. b) His mother seems to have been asked to consent to the study, though the child was not asked. It could be said that he was too young to give consent, but it can be assumed that he wanted to withdraw, in that he was crying and afraid – this was not paid attention to, and should have been. c) There may have been an issue with competence in that, although the researchers had an element of general competence, they did not know what course the study would take. This was evidenced by the way they found that more conditioning was needed as the association began to wear off, and this did not seem to be expected. The researchers seemed to be learning as they went, which does not match up perhaps with the competence that was needed.

4.29 a) 74 per cent in 1998 felt too big or too fat. b) 12.7 per cent had a score on the EAT-26 questionnaire of over 20 in 1995, compared with 29.2 per cent in 1998. This is more than double. c) There was no (0 per cent) self-induced vomiting to control weight in 1995, but 11.3 per cent said they had done this in 1998. d) Girls from households with a television were three times more likely to have an EAT-26 score of over 20.

4.30 The independent variable is whether the person plays the violent or the non-violent video game and the dependent variable is the rating of how 'human' they see themselves as measured using questionnaire and scale items.

4.31 In Study 1, the 'other' is the person being played against in either the violent or the non-violent video game. In Study 2, the 'other' is the co-player who is playing with the main player against a computer-generated avatar.

4.32 If the therapy group is different in characteristics from the waiting control group then that difference might be what gives any differences in results from the therapy. In order to make sure that one group is not different from the other group in terms of participant variables, each person is chosen at random to be in either the control or the treatment group. Random sampling means each person has an equal chance of being in either group and it can take place by putting names into a container (for Capafóns *et al.*, 1998, 41 names into a hat) and pulling out a name at a time for either of the groups. In fact for this study, age, gender, how strong their fear was and some physical measures were balanced between the two groups even though, within those 'rules', the choice was random. This was not, therefore, true random assignment and that often happens in a study as, even using random sampling, a group can end up with different characteristics from another group (such as an imbalance regarding gender).

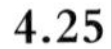

4.33 a) 'Stop-think' and brief relaxation training gave people help after the treatment. b) Imagined situations were used first for a while so that 'real' situations came at the right time. c) Training in relaxation and breathing was thorough and practice was encouraged. d) The hierarchy was very gradual, with between 25 and 33 steps, and a smooth small change each time, no large steps.

4.34 a) With regard to validity, the many measures, which include self-report data and interview data, seem to confirm that the patients had a phobia of flying and they then found that fear was reduced after systematic desensitisation (90 per cent of them). This seems to suggest that the results are valid. b) With regard to generalisability, as the researchers themselves say, the results are only generalisable to a fear of flying. The sampling was self-selected, which may have affected generalisability. However, the control sample and treatment sample did differ so it seems that the sampling did not affect the conclusions. c) With regard to scientific credibility, the before and after treatment measures and the treatment and waiting control conditions showed careful methodology and so the conclusions can claim scientific credibility.

4.35 a) Capafóns *et al.* (1998) show that systematic desensitisation did work to reduce fear and anxiety in those with fear of flying. They used a control group, where there was not the same reduction in fear, so their conclusions were strong. b) Meiliyana and Fauzia (2014 used systematic desensitisation to help with one man's aerophobia. There was reduction in anxiety levels after the treatment, though this was a single-case study so it is hard to show generalisability of the findings. Taken with Capafóns *et al.* (1998), though, it does appear that fear of flying can be successfully treated.

4.36

Statement	%
Percentage of people getting treatment for anorexia who receive it in a specialist facility	35
Percentage of those with an eating disorder aged between 12 and 29 years old	95
Percentage of those waiting for treatment for anorexia or bulimia that are male	10 to 15

Chapter 5

5.1 Methodology studies how data are gathered and how a study is carried out. Without knowing that, it would be hard to know how far findings can be generalised, for example. Findings from studies are the way knowledge is built and, if the findings can be criticised, then the knowledge can be criticised too. The study of method helps to criticise findings (and to support them if appropriate). If knowledge is not secure then policy and practice might not be fair or justified. Methodology is about learning how a study is done, and then there can be replication of the study. Replication can show whether findings are repeated, and if they are, then the findings are said to be reliable. Knowledge built on unreliable findings would not be knowledge a society would want to use.

5.2 Study findings are **valid** if they represent real life in some way and the data are not artificial. Study findings are **reliable** if they are such that, when a study is done again, the same results are found. Study findings are **generalisable** if the sample is representative enough of the population of interest so that findings can be said to apply to that whole population.

5.3 A matches 2; B matches 4; C matches 1; D matches 3.

5.4 The right answer is 2: Peer reviewing involves a publisher sending out a study report to check for scientific credibility before publishing the study.

5.5 Statement 1 is the aim and Statement 2 is the hypothesis. An aim is a general statement of what a researcher wants to find out, and a hypothesis is a statement of what they think they will find out, looking at something specific that will measure the variables of interest in the aim. In a hypothesis, the variables are operationalised, which means they are made measurable.

5.6

1. You eat snacks at school SA A DK D SD
2. Enjoy fruit (10)________________Hate fruit (0)
3. Circle food you eat each day:

Crisps	Egg	Chocolate	
Apple	Cereal	Bread	Orange
Sweets	Meat	Potatoes	Fish
Burger	Pasta	Cheese	Pasty

4. How would you say you eat in terms of being healthy?

5.7 1) quantitative; 2) quantitative; 3) qualitative.

5.8 A problem with a questionnaire is that the **respondent** might not tell the truth. They may say what they think society wants them to say, which is called **social desirability**. They may respond to try and help the researcher by guessing the aim of the study and replying accordingly. This is called **demand characteristics**. If data are affected by these sorts of issues, then they are probably not **valid** data. A researcher uses **standardised instructions** as a control, to be sure all the respondents receive the same information about the study. Often a questionnaire involves gathering both in-depth, detailed **qualitative** data as well as using closed questions, which yield **quantitative** data.

5.9 First, data are gathered and then they are transcribed or set out so that they can be analysed. These are the first two steps. A reflexive journal is begun and kept up throughout the analysis. Coders are identified, possibly more than one so that tests for validity and reliability can be carried out – and possibly not the researcher so there is more objectivity in the coding. These are two more steps. The coder then goes through all the data carefully, noting down the ideas offered in the data. Then the ideas are considered and themes generated from them. The themes are named. These are three more steps – eight steps so far. If there is more than one coder, the themes are then compared to look for validity and reliability. Finally, a report giving the results is written. There are, therefore, ten steps.

5.10 Issues that might affect the results include: gender of the researcher; age of the researcher; day of the week; questions asked personally or not; shoppers or golfers.

5.11 1) structured; 2) semi-structured; 3) unstructured.

5.12 Unstructured interviews are useful when a research question is exploratory, such as when not much is known about an area. They gather in-depth and detailed data and do so from the viewpoint of the interviewee not the interviewer. Data are, therefore, more likely to be valid and 'real life'. Valid data have more value, and if policy and practice are to be changed because of what comes from interview data, then they need to be valid. Structured interviews have set questions and so cannot get the depth and detail of an unstructured interview. They can gather quantitative data and can be more reliable because they are replicable. However, the perspective of the interviewee can be missed if the set questions do not tap into issues of relevance to the interviewee.

5.13 It is important for a study's findings to be useful. A study tends to only be able to use a small number of participants, for practical reasons and also for reasons of access (getting hold of participants), as well as ethics. Results from a small number of people, therefore, might have to be used to say they are true of a much larger population. This is about generalising findings, and if findings are generalisable, then they are more useful and can, for example, drive policy and practice. Sampling is the way of ensuring as far as possible that the participants used represent the target population and so knowing how the sampling is done helps when judging the value of findings of a study.

5.14 Respect involves privacy, confidentiality, right to withdraw and informed consent. Competence involves keeping up to date in the relevant area of work/research and asking others if there is doubt. Responsibility involves monitoring physical and mental health of a client or participant, and being aware of individual differences in clients or participants. Integrity involves being aware of issues another psychologist or researcher may have and, if aware, acting on such information. Integrity also involves honesty at all times.

5.15 a) Where children are participants; b) Whenever an experience is involved that is over and above someone's normal lifestyle, such as doing rigorous physical exercise; c) When, as a result of a study, someone labels themselves as 'stupid', or something similar; d) In a study where there is a large element of deception; e) When researching in a sensitive area, such as sexuality or race.

5.16 1) Experimental hypothesis: there is a difference in recall of a list of letters, and counting backwards for 15 seconds after seeing the letters will lead to poorer recall than if there was no counting backwards. Null hypothesis: there is no difference in recall of a list of letters, and counting backwards for 15 seconds after seeing the letters will not lead to poorer recall than if there was no counting backwards. 2) Experimental hypothesis: there is a difference in recall of a story depending on the length of time after hearing the story the recall takes place, and the longer the time (over weeks) after the story is heard the less well the story is recalled. Null hypothesis: there is no difference in recall of a story depending on the length of time after hearing the story the recall takes place, and the longer the time after the story is heard (over weeks) it is not the case that less of the story is recalled. 3) Experimental hypothesis: there is a difference in words recalled from a list depending on whether the list is presented in categories or the same words are randomly presented. Null hypothesis: there is no difference in the number of words recalled from a list depending on whether the list is presented in categories or the same words are randomly presented, and if there is a difference, it is due to chance or some other factor.

5.17 1) directional (one-tailed); 2) non-directional (two-tailed); 3) non-directional (two tailed).

5.18 The independent variable is what is being varied by the experimenter and in the memory span study it is whether the letters are chunked or not. The dependent variable is how many letters are recalled in order from the 15 letters presented. Both the IV and the DV have to be fully operationalised, which means fully measurable, and so a hypothesis will have a lot of detail. Just writing 'recall' for the DV does not explain fully. Just writing 'of 15 letters' is not explaining fully either.

5.19 1) The independent variable is whether the diver is recalling underwater or on the surface. The dependent variable is the number of words recalled from the list. 2) The independent variable is whether the examination is taken in the same room or a different room from that in which learning took place. The dependent variable is the marks scored. 3) The independent variable is whether the letters are grouped (chunked) into recognisable sets of three letters or presented randomly. The dependent variable is the number of letters recalled from the 21.

5.20 The number of letters was the same in both conditions. There were the same letters in each condition and in each condition the letters were grouped into threes.

5.21 1) Independent groups – the independent variable is gender and people can only be male or female. 2) Repeated measures – the same person has to keep recalling the story. (You could possibly use different people and an independent groups design. However, the thoroughness of reading the story and the memories could be different.) 3) Independent groups would mean the study can be done in one go with one group using the 'sound alike' words and the other using a matched list of words, not sounding alike. (A repeated measures design can work if there is a delay between doing the two conditions.)

5.22 Counterbalancing means that half the participants do condition 1 in a study first and half do condition 2. If there is a practice effect, those doing condition 1 first will do better on condition 2, but this is not as biased as it might be because those doing condition 2 first, with a practice effect, would do better on condition 1. There would be some cancelling out.

5.23 Both are experiments with controls over extraneous variables to make sure that only the independent variable changes cause any change in the measured dependent variable. However, the difference is that field experiments are carried out 'in the field', which means in the participants' natural environment. Although a laboratory experiment with its controlled environment has more scientific credibility perhaps, as there can be a stronger claim about cause-and-effect conclusions, a field experiment can often claim more validity. This is because a field experiment is more likely to be getting close to natural behaviour than a laboratory experiment.

5.24 In order to analyse data, they are described, which means displaying them in useful and meaningful ways. When all the data are displayed in a table, these are the **raw data**. Using these data, graphs can be created, which help to display data more clearly. If two simple bars are presented, to show different scores of two groups, this is a **bar chart**. Another graph that can be used to show scores of individuals on two different conditions is a **line graph**. If the design is a correlation, then a **scatter diagram** is used to show all the individual scores using both measures so that a line of best fit can be created. Graphs help to compare data and they are visual. Graphs can display percentages too, which are another way of making data comparable. When it comes to seeing the distribution of scores of sets of data, measures of central tendency are required. These are the **mean**, median and **mode**. If they are more or less the same, it is said that the scores are normally distributed. Another useful statistic, to show the distribution of data, is the **range**, which is the span between the highest and lowest score. A similar statistic is the **standard** deviation, which shows how the scores differ from the mean average.

5.25 1) This is looking for a relationship between the number of words generated and the length of time in education. Whenever there are two scores (here they are number of words and time in education) for each participant a correlation test is carried out. This study is not investigating whether the number of words is caused by the length of time in education, only to see if the two are related. 2) This is looking for a difference between men and women. Gender is the independent variable and the amount of brain activity is the dependent variable. This cannot be a correlation because gender does not give a score or a rating – there are only male and female. This would be an independent groups design as the two groups are naturally defined as either male or female. 3) This is looking for a difference between men and women. Gender is the independent variable; the number of obstacles hit on the driving course is the dependent variable. This is an independent groups design, not a correlation.

5.26 1) The null hypothesis is 'any relationship found between the number of words generated and length of time in education is due to chance or some other variable'. 2) The null hypothesis is 'any difference found between men and women in brain activity when doing a language task is due to chance or some other variable'. 3) The null hypothesis is 'any difference found between men and women and their driving ability is due to chance or some other variable'.

5.27 1) This is directional (one-tailed) because a positive relationship is predicted – the number of words is expected to increase with length of time in education. 2) This is directional (one-tailed) because women are predicted to have more brain activity in a certain brain area when doing a language task than men. 3) This is non-directional (two-tailed) because the hypothesis does not say whether men or women will perform better.

5.28 1) Nominal – people would be allocated as 'aggressive' or 'not aggressive'. 2) Interval/ratio – reaction time is a real measure. Reaction time is likely to be measured in seconds and seconds are equal intervals. 3) Ordinal – people would have to be ranked in order of attractiveness. You could argue this is nominal because people could be allocated as 'attractive' or 'not attractive', although having to say *how* attractive they are does suggest ratings.

5.29 1) This is about difference so not a correlation. This must be an independent groups design because 40 year olds and 80 year olds must be different people and it can be assumed that the researchers will not wait until the participants are 80 (though they could). The data are number of events so that is interval data. The test for difference, independent groups, interval data in your course is the Mann-Whitney U test. 2) It cannot be known that it is the number of days passed that will cause the reduction in words used to explain the story, and both number of days and number of words used are scales of data. A correlation can be carried out to see if the higher the number of days the lower the word count (a negative correlation). A correlation is a design – both scores (days and words) come from the same participant). For your course, only one test for a correlation is given, Spearman's rank correlation coefficient, and that is the right choice here. The data are interval. For interval data, you could choose a test called Pearson's, but you are not asked to learn about that.

5.30 1) 1 in 200 is 5 in 1,000; decimal form is 0.005. 2) 1 in 50 is 2 in 100; decimal form is 0.02. 3) Decimal form of 1 in 10,000 is 0.0001. 4) 1 in 2,000 is 5 in 10,000; decimal form is 0.0005.

5.31 One factor to take into account is whether there are a lot of studies to back the hypothesis and give a direction for the results. If quite a few have found something similar, or if the study is a replication, then a stricter level of significance might be chosen, such as $p \leq 0.01$. If a study is an exploratory study in a new area, then a lenient level of significance might be acceptable, such as $p \leq 0.05$. Another factor is the consequences of the study and whether policy and practice, for example, are to be changed as a result. If there are important consequences, then a strict level of significance might be chosen, such as $p \leq 0.01$ or even $p \leq 0.001$.

5.32 Mann-Whitney U and Wilcoxon.

5.33 1) Type I error; 2) Type II error.

5.34 Schmolck *et al.* (2002) used six patients with brain damage. They looked carefully at the damage each had to the brain and then at the difficulties they had with processing semantic information. They found matches between the patients, in their damage and in their problems in functioning, and used these matches as evidence for certain brain areas being for certain functions.

5.35 HM had his medial temporal lobe removed to help him with his debilitating epilepsy. After the surgery, he had developed amnesia. This was selective amnesia, in that he could remember some long-term events, such as a stock market crash, but he could not remember anything after his surgery, and indeed for about 11 years before that. He could remember skills and could learn new skills, so his procedural memory was intact. He could function in the short term and could remember things for a very short time, so his short-term memory did function. However, he did not have new long-term memories so his short-term memory did not work to move material into his long-term memory. As he had such specific damage to his brain, it was assumed that his deficits in cognitive functioning came from his missing the MTL. So it was concluded that it is the MTL where short-term memory works to pass information into long-term memory.

5.36 Quantitative data, such as a measure of the damage in the brain from scans and scores in semantic tests, are reliable in that they can be gathered again and measures confirmed. Graphs can be produced, statistical testing can take place and results can be seen to be reliable. This gives scientific credibility. However, tests might not be valid ones as they represent processing but might not reflect such processing in 'real life'. Qualitative data can fill in gaps left by quantitative data, such as talking with patients about their skills (procedural memory) and their long-term memories. Qualitative data give depth and detail that are not found in quantitative data.

5.37 1) Negative correlation – as age rises, driving speed falls. 2) Positive correlation – as the size of that part of the brain rises, so the aggression score rises. 3) Direction not stated – it could be the taller someone is, the smaller the brain, or vice versa.

5.38 Brain structure refers to the physiological parts of the brain, such as the prefrontal lobe or the medial temporal lobe (MTL). The brain is made up of many different structures which are thought to have different functions. This leads on to what 'functions' are. They are what each part of the brain, each 'structure', does – what its function is. Brain functioning, though, is not just what the function is of each structure, it is the functioning – the brain working, using the different structures. Brain functioning occurs using synaptic transmission and neurotransmitters. Some scans look at physiological structures of the brain, which can be measured for things like size and shape. Other scans look at brain functioning, the activity in the brain, measured by blood flow to show activity.

5.39 1) CT; 2) CT; 3) MRI.

5.40 PET scanning claims to show the brain in action and to use images so that such activity is visible and can be tracked. There is little doubt that PET scans are showing the active brain with hot spots showing where there is the most activity. These are valid data because they measure 'real life'. Also other methods back up PET scan data, such as showing that Broca's area is for speech, and that adds weight to the claim that PET scan data are valid.

5.41

Statement	Tick if the statement is true
fMRI scanning uses magnetic imaging and is useful for looking at brain structure only.	Used to see brain functioning
PET scanning is less expensive than CT scanning.	More expensive
MRI scans are useful for looking at brain structure more than brain functioning.	✓
CT scans can be used with PET scans to help to show a 3D image as well as brain activity.	✓
To an extent, fMRI scans are starting to take the place of PET scans.	✓
CAT stands for computed axial tomography.	✓
Tomography means the study of images of sections (e.g. of the body).	✓

5.42 MRI: Matthies *et al.* (2012) found that a smaller volume amygdala is found in females with higher aggression scores. PET: Raine *et al.* (1997) showed that there are brain differences in those pleading not guilty to murder by reason of insanity compared with a control group. fMRI: Brunnlieb *et al.* (2013) found no difference in those that took vasopressin and those that did not with regard to aggressive behaviour, but some differences in brain functioning.

5.43 The concordance rate for a behaviour or characteristic in twins is how far if one twin shows that behaviour or has that characteristic, the other twin does too. If MZ twins share the behaviour or characteristic more than DZ twins, that is evidence for genes being involved in that behaviour or characteristic. This is because MZ twins share 100 per cent of their DNA and DZ twins share just 50 per cent, as do all siblings. They are twins, so they share their environment in a similar way. However, the MZ twins share more genes. So if MZ twins each have X per cent of a characteristic and DZ twins have Y per cent and X is significantly greater than Y, then that characteristic has a genetic element. That is the basic idea of using twin studies.

5.44 Lacourse *et al.* (2014) found a lot of evidence that showed there are environmental and genetic factors regarding aggression and how it develops from infancy through early childhood (e.g. NICHD Early Child Care Research Network, 2004). They noted that aggression tended to be measured as being disruptive and similar behaviour, rather than as physical aggression, so they chose to look at physical aggression. Studies showed a clear effect that aggression grows quickly in infants and then steadies to a slow increase from 20 months to 50 months. Lacourse *et al.* (2014) wanted to test the development of physical aggression over this time period to see if they could find this gradual slope and also to see what they could discover about genetic influences on this developmental pattern. They had data from an existing longitudinal study, which included mothers' ratings of physical aggression in MZ and DZ twins at 20, 32 and 50 months, so their data were already available.

5.45 Adoption studies can look at a child's behaviour or characteristics when the child has been brought up in one environment without influence from their parents' genes. This can split environmental influences from genetic influences and this is hard to do any other way. If the parent has a characteristic thought to be inherited, like schizophrenia, then you would expect to find it in the child more than if a family does not have such a history. If adopted children show a characteristic from their biological family, then that might show such a characteristic is genetic.

5.46 Children adopted, especially within three months of their birth, as in Leve *et al.*, (2010), are not influenced by their birth parents' environment. They take with them their genetic inheritance but then it is a different environment that affects them – their adoptive environment. Adoption studies are a useful way to separate nature (genetic inheritance) from nurture (environment), which cannot easily be done any other way. Children are brought up by their birth parents (if not adopted) and what they inherit genetically cannot be separated from the environment.

5.47 They checked the demographics of the participants, looking at birth mothers, birth fathers that were recruited, birth fathers that were not recruited, adoptive mothers and adoptive fathers and examined their age, race, education level and household income. Then they compared the groups using statistical testing to look for differences in these sorts of areas, including regional differences. They found a few differences but with small effect sizes and concluded that there was generalisability – though this is for adoption placements throughout the US, not necessarily beyond.

5.48 Structured observation involves an element of setting up a situation but not to the extent that it is manipulated as much as having a fixed independent variable. The structured observation can be in an artificial laboratory style setting, which could help the structuring. However, it can also be in a natural setting, as long as there is an element of setting up a situation which then leads to data being gathered by observation. A naturalistic observation does not involve structuring at all by researchers. The setting and the situation is natural to the participants and someone observes the behaviour of interest. So a structured observation uses a set-up situation so that the behaviour can be observed; a naturalistic observation does not.

5.49 1) Non-participant – the two observers did not have a role in the situation. 2) Hugging and walking away were two categories that were observed. 3) The observers recorded a behaviour every ten seconds and each observation lasted three minutes, which is the time behaviour was recorded for. 4) They used two coders and then checked their results to see if they were similar. If the results are the same from both coders, then data are reliable.

5.50 One strength is that this is a valid study in that the behaviour is natural, in a natural setting, with no interference from the researcher. The observation is non-participant and covert so behaviour should not be affected. Another strength is that there is some control over what is seen as helping behaviour – if event sampling is used, that behaviour was decided beforehand, so there is some operationalisation of variables. That means that the study can be repeated and there is an understanding of what was observed. One weakness is that you might need two coders in the practical as that would help to show reliability. As the practical stands, there is just one researcher. If more than one person watches the same situation using the same criteria, then the two lots of results can be compared and should match. Another weakness is that helping behaviour is operationalised and that limits what is being observed with regard to validity. It is one person's and one culture's view of helping behaviour (e.g. holding doors open), and that should be acknowledged.

5.51 The study was a naturalistic observation because it took place in the children's nursery, which was their natural setting. It was an overt observation because the children and staff knew that it was taking place. There was nothing covert about it; the study did not take place in secret, which would have been difficult because the presence of the observers would have had to be explained. The observation was non-participant because the researchers were not nursery staff. They could not be participants, because the participants were children and the observers were adults. There were two observers, so there was the potential for inter-observer reliability.

5.52 Two suggestions: 1) A hypothesis to look at references to aggression in the music 'Top 20', looking at whether there are more references when singers are male than female. 2) A hypothesis to see if experiences of friendship in eight year olds differ between boys and girls, using stories they have written.

5.53 Arguments for: 1) We owe it to our own species and have a moral obligation (Gray, 1991). 2) Darwin showed through evolution theory that we have similarities with animals so there is no reason not to use them – findings will have relevance. 3) We can find out useful information more effectively (and ethically) because of features such as a shorter breeding cycle. Arguments against: 1) We should not do to animals what we would not do to ourselves, which is a different argument in the 'moral obligation' discussion. 2) If findings lack validity and generalisability, then we should not cause suffering on the basis of findings that are not applicable. 3) Cost–benefit analysis does not work as we often do not know the costs in terms of distress for the animal or the benefits perhaps, as results would not be known.

5.54 1) Meisch (2001) used rhesus monkeys to show that they chose to take drugs by mouth as a reward as drugs become a reinforcer. Other studies have shown that animals prefer drugs to water if they have the choice. 2) Mice have been given heroin or cocaine and afterwards their renal function has been tested to see if there has been an effect. Cocaine gave the effect; heroin did not.

5.55 The issue is that animals are not the same as humans, either in their biological makeup or in their way of living. The argument against using findings from animal studies is that humans are different enough so that the results might not be sufficiently applicable. However, there is some argument for generalising from animal studies to humans. There are similarities in their biology, at least with some animals. The rhesus monkey shares about 93 per cent of its genes with both chimpanzees and humans, so there is quite a large similarity. There is a 90 per cent similarity in the genes that govern brain structure in mice and in humans. There are similar structures in the brains of mice as in humans. Humans are animals. In summary, there are difficulties in generalising findings from animals to humans because of differences, but there are ways in which such generalising is useful.

5.56 1) An issue is whether a study takes a reductionist view and, if it does, then that relates to science. For example, when Baddeley (1966b) studied short-term and long-term memory and used words that sound alike as representing auditory stimulus, that is reductionism. A more holistic view about using sound in memory would be to ask people how they recall phone numbers. By breaking something into parts that can be studied, a scientific approach can be taken, isolating a variable to study and putting in controls. 2) Another issue is using the hypothetico-deductive model and empiricism. If a theory is looked at carefully, a hypothesis generated and then that hypothesis carefully tested using empirical (sense) data, then that is 'doing science'. For example, realistic conflict theory is a theory from which we can hypothesise that someone will reward their in-group more than they will reward an out-group. We can test that empirically and then accept, reject or amend the theory. That is doing science.

Chapter 6

6.1 The scores in order are: 2, 2, 2, 3, 4, 5, 6, 7, 8, 8, 9, 9. The mode is 2 as there are three scores of 2. The median is 5.5, in between 5 and 6. The mean is 5.42 (5.4166666 rounded up to 5.42).

6.2 1) 0.36; 2) 0.27; 3) 0.90.

6.3 1) negatively skewed; 2) positively skewed; 3) normal distribution.

6.4 1) The table needs a title; 2) The third column needs a heading ('Frequency'); 3) Score not entered (4) on third row of the third column; 4) A final row should be inserted giving the totals; 5) The heading 'Scores' in the first column should be more informative (what are the scores?); 6) The final row '20–27' should be '21–27', so the number spans are even and '20' is used only once.

6.5

Participant	Score (x)	Difference from the mean for each score	Squared difference for each score
1	10	10 - 11 = -1	1 × 1 = 1
2	6	6 - 11 = -5	5 × 5 = 25
3	15	15 - 11 = +4	4 × 4 = 16
4	3	3 - 11 = -8	8 × 8 = 64
5	20	20 - 11 = +9	9 × 9 = 81
6	12	12 - 11 = +1	1 × 1 = 1
N=6	Mean $\bar{x}$ = 11		
			Total of the squared differences (Σ) = 188
Standard deviation for this set of scores: Take the sum of the squared differences (188) and divide by the number of scores minus 1 (N-1, which is 5 in this example). 188/5 = 37.6. This is the variance. The square root of 37.6 is the standard deviation, which is $\sqrt{37.6}$ = 6.13.			

6.6 1) square root; 2) sum of; 3) number of scores minus 1; 4) mean of a set of numbers where each number is x.

6.7 A score of 60 males and 150 females, even though there were more females, does suggest that more females showed hostility. Sixty per cent of the males (60 out of 100) and 75 per cent of the females (150 out of 200) showed hostility. It is more comfortable to judge the findings having worked out the percentage, rather than just looking at the findings themselves – 60 per cent and 75 per cent are figures that are easier to compare. The 60 and 150 looked so different but 60 per cent and 75 per cent do not seem so different.

6.8

Statistical test	Does the observed value have to be equal to, greater than or less than the critical value in the table (in order to be significant)?
Mann-Whitney U (U)	Equal to or less than the critical value
Wilcoxon signed-rank (T)	Equal to or less than the critical value
Spearman's rank correlation coefficient (rho)	Equal to or more than the critical value
Chi-squared (χ^2)	Equal to or more than the critical value

6.9 1) Yes, 13 is less than the critical value of 17; 2) Yes, 8 is equal to the critical value; 3) No, 4 is more than the critical value of 3.

6.10 1) Yes, 20 is less than the critical value of 27 so the result is significant and the null hypothesis is rejected; 2) No, 39 is larger than the critical value of 38 so the null hypothesis is accepted.

6.11 1) No, 0.456 is the critical value and 0.40 is less than that; 2). Yes, 0.746 is the critical value and 0.85 is more than that; 3) No, 0.618 is the critical value and 0.23 is much less than that.

6.12 1) 0.648 is the critical value. The observed value is more than that so there is a significance and it is a positive correlation, as seen by the + sign. The more one score rises, the more the other rises. This is a strong correlation as it is quite a bit more than the critical value and 0.74 is near to 1, a perfect correlation. 2) 0.456 is the critical value. The observed value is more at 0.48, so there is a significance, and it is a negative correlation, as seen by the – sign. The more one score rises, the more the other falls. 0.48 is not that strong in the sense of being between 0 (no correlation) and 1 (a perfect correlation) – it is medium rather than weak though. 3) 0.833 is the critical value and 0.24 is much lower than that so there is no significance. If there were a significance, it would be a positive correlation, but there is not. 0.24 is not enough to show a significant correlation and is close to 0 so would be a weak correlation anyway.

6.13 A two-by-two table means there are two columns and two rows containing data. This means that there are two pairs of variables. In the example, one variable pair is boy or girl and the other variable pair is climbing frame choice or book corner choice.

6.14

Information available regarding four studies	Appropriate statistical test out of Mann-Whitney U, Wilcoxon, Spearman's, chi-squared
Study 1: An experiment using a repeated measures design, giving interval data	Wilcoxon signed-rank test (experiments look for differences in conditions of the IV)
Study 2: A study looking for a relationship between two variables measured using at least ordinal data	Spearman's rank correlation coefficient (when looking for a relationship, a correlation is the design)
Study 3: An experiment using an independent groups design, giving at least ordinal data	Mann-Whitney U test (experiments look for differences in conditions of the IV)
Study 4: An observation gathering nominal data looking for a difference using an independent groups design	Chi-squared test

6.15 1) 6 times out of 30 is 20 per cent (6/30 x 100); 2) 24 times out of 30 is 80 per cent (24/30 x 100); 3) 15 times out of 22 is 68 per cent (15/22 x 100 = 68); 4) 7 times out of 22 is 32 per cent (7/22 x 100). Note that it is not that 20 per cent of older people open doors for younger people but that the observations of older people holding doors showed that 20 per cent of the time this was done for younger people and 80 per cent of the time it was done for older people. The same with younger people – when they held doors open, 68 per cent of the time it was for younger people and 32 per cent of the time it was for older people. You need to think about percentages when using them to make statements. Although this was not asked, note that 21 times doors were held open for younger people in total and 31 times doors were held open for older people. So 59.6 per cent of the time doors were held open for older people (31/52 x 100) and 40.4 per cent of the time doors were held open for younger people, using the 52 observations made.

6.16

	Younger people	Older people	Total
Holding doors for younger people	15	6	21
Holding doors for older people	7	24	31
Total	22	30	52

6.17 a) No, because 2.71 is the critical value and 2.5 is lower than that so the result is not significant; b) Yes, because 5.41 is the critical value and 6.1 is greater than the critical value so the null hypothesis is rejected; c) No, because 5.99 is the critical value and 4.51 is less than that so the null hypothesis is not rejected, the results are not significantly different.

Chapter 7

7.1 The questionnaire looks at obedience to authority and agency theory. Milgram suggested that for society to function people act as agents to authority, so when someone in authority gives orders people obey because they are in an agentic state. This explains why they obey even if doing so goes against their own moral code. When not in an agentic state, people are autonomous and make their own decisions using their own moral code. A linked concept, looking at personality, is that there is an authoritarian personality. People with this personality tend to be prejudiced and also obedient to social norms. The questionnaire considers how people categorise themselves, such as 'agentic', 'autonomous' or 'authoritarian', and how such self-categorisation might link to other aspects about them, such as age, gender, education level or whether they see themselves as leaders or followers.

7.2 The other two are stratified and volunteer sampling. Random sampling is best because each person in the target population (or selected part of the target population) has an equal chance of being chosen so there is no bias in who is chosen. As there is no bias, this type of sampling will be more representative of the chosen population.

7.3 Closed-ended questions have a forced and limited choice of answers, such as 'yes/no' questions or questions where statements have a choice of 'strongly agree', 'agree', 'don't know', 'disagree' or 'strongly disagree'. For closed-ended questions, there is no room for a respondent to use another category or make a comment such as 'unsure' or 'not applicable'. They are forced in their choice of answers. Open-ended questions leave the respondent able to give their own views about a topic, and there can be depth and detail. In questionnaires, the detail can be limited due to the space allowed (though the respondent could find a blank space and continue with their answer if that were an option).

7.4 Q14, Q15, Q16 and Q17 are open questions.

7.5 Personal data are there as variables to test answers against. For example, if the researchers want to see if there are gender differences in answers about obedience, then they need to know the gender of respondents. Sometimes personal data are requested to look for links, rather than in anticipation of a link.

7.6 A frequency table and graph will show the number of times a particular response is given and can show the curve of information. In a set of data, you would expect a reasonable spread of answers. A frequency graph can show whether there is a reasonable spread. For example, for Q9 a respondent might read 'I like to make my own decisions' and it might be that everyone answers 'agree' or 'strongly agree' to this, as people are not likely to want to say they don't make their own decisions. A frequency graph would show that there were no scores of 1, 2 or 3 against that question and would highlight this question as not perhaps being a useful discriminator. In fact, this question did read 'I like to make my own decisions' but the other part was added when it was seen, using a pilot study, that this question would not yield a spread of data.

7.7 Thematic analysis refers to finding themes in qualitative data, which on a questionnaire will come from open questions. Themes should not be thought up before the analysis. Each piece of data (each comment) must be studied carefully to identify the thoughts therein, and those thoughts are then categorised. Categories are carefully studied to identify themes, which can be emerging and can be changed as the analysis continues. The aim is to arrive at a number of themes within which the data fit.

7.8 One strength is that by gathering both qualitative and quantitative data there is a check on reliability as answers can be compared to look for consistency. A weakness is that questions are limited. Closed-ended questions are limited in the choice of response so the respondent cannot extend their answer, and open questions, despite offering room for detail to an extent, do not offer much space on this questionnaire, so again will be limited. The limitations affect validity.

7.9

Statement about the cognitive psychology practical investigation	Tick if true	Cross if not
Write out the experimental and null hypothesis	✓	
Give the relevant experimental design	✓	
Give the standardised instructions **(not necessary, but can do this)**		✗
Use a Spearman's rank correlation coefficient **(either Mann-Whitney U or Wilcoxon)**		✗
Use relevant measures of central tendency and dispersion	✓	
Write up the background, procedure, results, discussion sections **(all but the background)**		✗
Consider experimenter effects and demand characteristics	✓	
Discuss sampling decisions	✓	

7.10 Short-term memory involves rehearsal because it has a limited capacity, limited to 5–9 items, and without rehearsal not enough would be held in short-term memory for much information to go into long-term memory to be remembered for the future. The working memory model examines short-term memory in more depth, including rehearsal. As short-term memory has been found to use acoustic (sound) coding, the working memory also examined acoustic coding (as well as visual and spatial coding). The working memory model proposes the phonological loop as where rehearsal takes place using acoustic coding, and within the phonological loop proposes subvocal rehearsal (rehearsing information by repeating it silently to oneself).

7.11 The independent variable is whether the letters to be recalled are chunked or not and the dependent variable is the number of letters recalled in order.

7.12 A repeated measures design is when a participant does both or all of the conditions in a study. This is the opposite of an independent groups design, where there are different participants in the different conditions.

7.13 There is the practice effect, which is when a second condition is done better because the participant has 'practised' on the first condition. There is the fatigue effect, which is when a second condition is done less well because the participant has become tired after the first condition. Counterbalancing alternates the order the conditions are done by each participant, which may not iron out order effects but will mean they are balanced out.

7.14 The mean average because it only works if scores have equal intervals between them. For example, the number of words recalled can be manipulated mathematically. If you remember half the words, you remember 50 per cent; if you remember a quarter of them, that is 25 per cent. Ratings such as 'strongly agreeing' to a statement and so scoring 5, or rating attractiveness on a scale of 0 to 10 and giving 5, are not mathematical scores. Your '5' rating of attractiveness might not be the same as my '5' rating and we cannot use percentages (or the mean average, or standard deviation).

7.15 This is directional – there are 'more letters recalled'. So in the critical values tables, use one-tailed.

7.16 The careful controls, use of standardised instructions and carefully written down procedure mean that the study can be repeated fairly easily by others. If when a study is repeated the same results are found, the findings are said to have reliability. A study that is replicable, as experiments are, is said to be reliable, especially if it fits with previous research, as the results of this one fit with Peterson and Peterson (1959). Having such careful controls and operationalising rehearsal time as number of repetitions, for example, means the task it not very natural. We do not repeat nonsense syllables and then recall them. We do not interact with people and use our memory in artificial, set-up environments like laboratories. The setting is not natural and the task is not natural, so this means the study suffers from low validity. However, rehearsal in memory was checked by asking the participant to repeat the nonsense syllables aloud, so to that extent the task had validity.

7.17 Descriptive statistics must be used, including measures of central tendency, measures of dispersion, graphs and tables. Inferential testing must take place and, as this is a correlation, the test is Spearman's rank correlation coefficient. As part of the inferential testing, a level of significance must be chosen as well as the use of critical values tables to find the significance of the result.

7.18

Proposed study	Research question or hypothesis?
A pilot study to listen to children while they are drawing, to find out about their ideas and concepts	Research question
An experiment to see whether recall of a story reduces over time	Hypothesis
A case study to look at one person with brain damage and how their memory is affected	Research question
A questionnaire to find out about young people's use of social media sites	Research question
A correlation design to see if the older people are, the more they are willing to help people, as measured by self-report data	Hypothesis

7.19 1a) 3 in 100, b) 2 in 1,000; 2a) $p \leq 0.001$, b) $p \leq 0.05$.

7.20 1) The more aggressive someone is, the more they react aggressively to people's driving (in India). 2) The hotter the weather, the more car horn hooting there is. 3) The more stress hormone in the blood, the more aggressive behaviour is observed. 4) The more stress events someone reports, the more they report aggression in response to others.

7.21

Hypothesis	One- or two-tailed?	Correlation or difference?
The temperature of the day relates to the amount of car hooting on that day.	Two-tailed	Correlation
The more times someone hears a story, the less they will recall about it.	One-tailed	Correlation
People recall more words if the words are sorted into categories than if presented randomly.	One-tailed	Difference

7.22 1) One issue is about ethics and causing distress, which was dealt with by giving rather vague statements, such as 'a lot going on' so that statements were not too direct. 2) Another issue is that life events might mean different things to different people and this was dealt with by giving some space for a participant to enlarge on their answers. Also this was self-report data, so having some subjectivity in interpreting the statements suits this type of data. 3) A third issue is having to deceive the participants to avoid social desirability and demand characteristics. This was dealt with by giving a debrief at the end and writing that out so that it was not forgotten and was the same for all participants.

7.23 If the study is done in a sixth form centre, then registers can give all the names. Then all the names can be printed off, cut up and put into a box, or something similar, with ten names being drawn out. Though there are data protection issues with doing this. A study could be done in a sports club, where all members there on one evening agreed to be in the sample, then all their names can go into a box.

7.24 If the scores for 'being aggressive' or 'having stressful life events in the last 12 months' are all scored as 5 for 'strongly agree', and so on, then there might be a response bias. By changing the focus of the statements, this can help with such bias and can also help to avoid demand characteristics.

7.25 A scatter diagram is a graph showing all the plots, one for each participant on a graph, giving the two variables, one on the x axis and one on the y axis. The line of best fit is the straight line that can be drawn with an even number of plots on each side of it. This can highlight how near to such a straight line the plots are. The closer they are, the more likely there is to be a strong correlation. A strong correlation is near 1, whether positive (+) or negative (–).

7.26 This is because the data are ordinal, being rankings, and this is a correlation, so a relationship is being tested. The right test for ordinal data and a correlation is Spearman's.

7.27 1) Accepted (the critical value is 0.783 and 0.45 is lower than that so not significant); 2) Rejected (the critical value is 0.683 and so the observed value is equal to that, which means the null is rejected – the result is significant).

7.28 a) Reliability is when a study is repeated and the same results are found. b) Validity is found in a study if the findings relate to real life, if what is being measured is what is claimed. c) Generalisability is found if a sample is not biased and is representative of the target population.

7.29 Knowing something about what others have found can help situate research within a body of knowledge and, in that way, knowledge can be built. A study on its own might be interesting but, if linked to what others have done, there is more value to the findings – they can be supported by, or can support, research of others. That is why research must be valid, reliable and credible, so that when others build on a piece of research, the building is steady.

7.30 Age is in two groups: 'younger' and 'older'. 'Younger' is measured as 18–35 years old. 'Older' is measured as 50 and over.

7.31 Observation in a public place is considered acceptable because people are in a place where they would expect to be seen and observed and would behave accordingly. So they would not exhibit behaviour they did not want seen. Getting informed consent would affect their natural behaviour so in practical terms it is avoided. From an ethical point of view, this is considered acceptable as the study is pure observation with no manipulation. If there is no informed consent (no consent at all in fact), there should be a debrief. Possibly this is an ethical issue with this study. However, debriefing would take up a participant's time and would not lead to them feeling better about being a participant, so it was decided that there was less distress in not debriefing, though this is a questionable decision. From a practical point of view, a debrief would affect observing the next person on the phone. This study does not have great value, and will not be of any cost really to a participant. On a cost–benefit decision, it was thought that the ethics of the study were acceptable.

7.32 Risk management is about safety and, as people are involved in a psychology study, including the researcher, participants and others around, risk management is important ethically. When animals are used, risk management is also important. It is tempting to focus ethically on participants and others, but the researcher can also be at risk so there needs to be risk management there too.

7.33 Quantitative data are good for analysis purposes and having data that can be clearly displayed. Results are often easy to read and understand using quantitative data. Also, a statistical test can be carried out to look for significance. Findings are more scientifically credible. Qualitative data are good for depth and detail, though harder to analyse without subjectivity. There can be triangulation using both qualitative and quantitative data, which means findings from different sources on the same topic can back one another up to show reliability. Quantitative data are better when it comes to replicating a study and so can show reliability more easily. Qualitative data are better when it comes to getting real-life data and can show validity more easily. Having both gives strengths that one would not achieve alone.

7.34 An independent groups design, with nominal data and looking for a difference not a relationship requires a chi-squared test.

7.35 A sense check is useful to show what would be expected if a statistical test were to be carried out. Someone can see whether the results look significant or not and this can help to understand the results of the test. If data look significantly different and the test does not reach significance, this alerts the researcher to look for mistakes or explanations.

7.36 Having a smaller number of themes can give the numbers in categories more meaning and a table of the data can show the findings at a glance and in a more digestible form. Having fewer themes gives the advantages of quantitative data in that they are more easily displayed and understood. However, reducing to overarching themes loses the depth and detail that qualitative data add to research findings. Validity is compromised by reducing data to artificial themes.

Chapter 8

8.1 The four principles are respect, competence, responsibility and integrity. In respect, there is mention of confidentiality and the right to withdraw, as well as getting informed consent. Informed consent means getting permission from the participant and, importantly, the participant is as fully informed as possible about what they are agreeing to. In competence, there is the need to keep fully up to date in the field the researcher or practitioner is in, and to maintain competence in what they are doing. In responsibility, there is debriefing, which means at the end of a study letting the participant know all that has taken place and making sure the participant is not in a distressed state. Integrity means not deceiving anyone, including in research. There should be honesty and the participant must be put first.

8.2 Neither gender nor culture was seen to be an important factor in obedience. There were two studies that suggested gender differences in actual obedience, but many others that did not, although there appeared to be gender differences in response to obedient behaviour and someone going against their moral code. Culture was not thought to be a factor in obedience. Indeed, when studies looking at obedience were compared, it was found that the average percentage of obedience was similar across cultures.

GLOSSARY

ablation: removal of a brain structure.

abstract: short summary of the aim(s), procedure, results and conclusion(s) of a study.

access: finding the participants and getting permission from them and/or for them to take part in a study.

accomplice: someone 'in on' a study, part of the study team, but who the participant thinks is also a participant.

acoustic: sound.

across-culture: something that is found in all cultures (or many cultures).

action potential: electrical impulse in a neuron.

addiction: the reward system in the brain giving such good feelings that the individual 'must' have that reward and so continues with the drug; an addictive drug is rewarding or the drug is needed for normal functioning.

agency theory: people are agents for society and behave in such a way as to benefit society.

agentic state: being the agent of another individual and therefore obeying their orders.

aim (of a study): what the researcher wants to find out in a study – the research question.

allele: variant of a gene.

alternative hypothesis: the hypothesis that states what will happen in a given situation.

altruism: acts that involve risk to an individual and good to someone else, with no gain for the individual.

anti-social behaviour: acting in a way that is against society.

apparatus: the materials used in a study.

assumptions: the underpinning beliefs and ideas that support an area of psychology, such as social psychology focusing on the 'social' aspect of humans.

authoritarian personality: those who are likely to admire rules, to be distant from their fathers, to be in a military role and to obey orders, according to Milgram.

autobiographical: memories about the individual; episodes in an individual's life.

autonomy: being under one's own control and having the power to make one's own decisions.

axon: long extension from the cell body of a neuron.

axon hillock: a specialised part of the cell body of a neuron that connects to the axon.

axon terminal: where an axon ends.

backward conditioning: when the unconditioned stimulus is presented and ends and then the conditioned stimulus is presented; not as effective as forward conditioning.

baseline measure: what the dependent variable would be like without manipulation.

before and after studies: those that take a measure before an intervention, then a measure afterwards, to see if the intervention has made a difference and, if so, how much of a difference.

between-culture: differences between cultures.

bilateral: affecting both sides, e.g. of the brain.

BPS Code of Ethics and Conduct (2009): ethical issues to follow in psychology research; emphasises the importance of 'respect', 'responsibility', 'competence' and 'integrity'.

brief: occurs before a study and tells the participant about the study.

capacity (memory): the size of the memory store.

case study: research method involving in-depth, detailed examination of a subject of study.

cause-and-effect relationship: when changes in the independent variable cause changes in the dependent variable.

cell body: the end of a neuron, containing the cell nucleus.

central nervous system: consists of the brain and the spinal cord.

closed-ended (closed) questions: where there is a specific answer and no possibility of extending the answer.

coding: interpreting data/grouping data.

cognitive alternative: when someone sees that there is a different way of thinking about something.

competence: all research or practice must be within a person's ability.

compliance: going along with what someone says, while not necessarily agreeing with it.

computer analogy: the idea that human brains work like computers.

concordance rate: agreement rate.

condition: part of the independent variable, which has been set up by the experimenter; for example, if half the participants have a categorised list to recall and half have the same list but randomly presented, one condition is 'categorised' and one condition is 'randomised'.

conditioned response: the result of a conditioned stimulus.

conditioned stimulus: the result of pairing a neutral stimulus with an unconditioned stimulus.

confabulation: in reconstructive memory confabulation is adding to a story/memory to make sense of it.

confederate: someone 'in on' a study, part of the study team, but who the participant thinks is also a participant.

confidentiality: keeping someone's identity secret, so that they are not identifiable from information given in a study (or given about a client by a practitioner).

conforming: doing something that is against the individual's own inclinations, but doing it with the intention of matching the behaviour of the majority.

confounding variables: extraneous variables that are not controlled in a study and therefore affect the results.

conscious mind: contains the thoughts and ideas that we are aware of; we can manipulate those thoughts and make decisions using them.

contiguity: the idea that the timing between the behaviour and the consequences must not be too long, so that they relate to one another.

contingency: the idea that behaviour and the consequences (reward or punishment) must be dependent on one another – the link must be clear.

control group: used as a baseline measure, so that it is clear what would have happened without experimental intervention.

controls: tools put in place in a study to make sure that only what is of interest is affecting the findings of a study, not other issues or variables.

correlation design: one that compares data from the same participants or two sets of data.

cortex: outer layer of the brain.

counterbalancing: alternating the order of the conditions that each participant does.

covert observation: one in which the participants do not know they are being observed; it is being done secretly.

credibility (scientific): when findings are seen to use the scientific method, such as careful controls and careful drawing of conclusions from data that have come from well-explained methods of measurement.

critical value: the number on the critical value tables.

data: the numbers, or writing, photos or conversations, gathered or recorded in a study.

debrief: an ethical guideline; occurs after a study and is the opportunity to put right any misunderstandings, distress or other issues arising from the study.

deception: being dishonest in dealings with others.

defiance: disobedience.

deindividuation: when individual people do not feel recognised as individuals, which means they no longer feel responsible for their own actions.

delayed conditioning: a type of forward conditioning, when the conditioned stimulus appears and continues as the unconditioned stimulus is introduced, so there is overlap.

demand characteristics: when a participant can guess the aim(s) of a study and so works to 'help' the researcher (or works against the researcher), which means data are not valid.

dendrites: finger-like structures surrounding a cell body.

dependent variable: what is measured in a study and, in a table of results, represented by the numbers.

desensitisation: when more of a substance is needed to get the same feeling; this is because of changes at the synapse.

design: a) can have a specific meaning. See 'experimental design'. b) But can be the features of a study.

dichotomy: division into two parts.

digit span: refers to memory span and capacity of short-term memory without rehearsal.

direct fitness: when a gene gives a characteristic that benefits survival of the individual so they live to reproduce and pass on that gene.

directional (or one-tailed) hypothesis: states the direction that is expected.

discipline: field of study.

discrimination (classical conditioning): when the conditioning is focused in on a specific stimulus.

discrimination (social psychology): an action that occurs because of prejudice.

disinhibiting effect: when someone who would not normally carry out a particular action does so after seeing someone else do it with no negative consequences.

dissent: not obeying an order.

dizygotic (DZ) twins: non-identical twins, coming from two fertilised eggs and sharing 50 per cent of their genes, like other siblings.

dominant genes: genes that will always lead to their characteristic(s).

double-blind technique: when neither the participant nor the experimenter knows which group a participant is in.

dual-task paradigm: different parts of the cognitive system are involved if a task seems to interfere with one type of processing (such as processing using sound) but not with another type of processing (such as using vision).

duration (memory): how long information remains in the store.

ecological validity: connected with the setting (ecology) of the participant/experiment.

ego: balances the demands of the id with the demands of the superego, to make rational decisions.

ego ideal: the idea people have of what they should be like, given by parents and society.

emic: focusing on similarities across cultures.

empirical data: those gathered from the senses through seeing, touching, tasting, hearing or smelling.

empiricism: the use of sense data to test an idea and get evidence for it.

encoding (memory): how memories are encoded, which means how they are registered as memories

engrams: memory traces stored as structural changes in the brain.

epigenetic modification: how, over time, different environmental influences affect which genes are switched on and off.

episodic memory: memory for episodes/events that have happened to us

eros: our instinct for life and self-preservation.

ethical issues: issues that arise from values and beliefs, such as giving participants in research the right to withdraw from a study at any time.

ethics: values and beliefs, what is right and wrong when working with people in society; how psychology is done in practice, both as a practitioner and as a researcher.

ethnocentrism: focus on own in-group and hostility towards any out-group.

etic: focusing on individual characteristics of cultures.

eusocial: groups that function as a whole, with different roles and abilities, such that the individuals could not perform all the required roles alone.

evaluation: weighing up different points of view and coming to a conclusion.

event sampling: during observation, focusing on a predetermined event, such as aggressive interactions.

evolution: how inherited characteristics in organisms (including humans) change from generation to generation.

evolution theory: the idea of natural selection – any tendency that aids survival would lead to the gene or gene combination for that tendency being passed on.

experimental design: repeated measures; independent groups; or matched pairs. How the participants are 'used'.

experimental group: the group that 'does something' in an experiment (as opposed to the control group, which provides the baseline measure).

experimental hypothesis: the name of the alternative hypothesis in an experiment.

experimenter bias: when an experimenter affects the data that are gathered.

experimenter effects: things about the experimenter that affect the results, rather than the change in the independent variable, such as gender, age, tone of voice and what the experimenter is wearing.

exploratory research: when not much is already known about an area of study and where a researcher wants to start off a research process, finding qualitative, in-depth, valid data, before perhaps choosing a more focused research question.

external locus of control: when someone believes that what happens to them comes from outside their control and so if they were in a stressful situation they would feel helpless to do anything about it.

external validity: true findings with regard to the outside world, in that results are generalisable beyond the sample.

extinction (classical conditioning): when an association using classical conditioning has been extinguished (it is no longer there).

extraneous variables: those that can affect the findings of a study; situational and participant variables are extraneous variables.

falsifiability: the idea that, in science, the search should be for falsification of a theory not focusing on finding data that fit the theory.

falsification: the process of disproving (falsifying), rather than verifying, a hypothesis.

fatigue effect: when participants do worse in the second condition, having become tired doing the first condition, resulting in bias in the data.

field experiment: carried out 'in the field', i.e. the participants' natural environment.

forward conditioning: when the conditioned stimulus is presented before the unconditioned stimulus when pairing them.

free recall: recalling of information, e.g. a list of words, in any order.

function: what something is for; for example, 'function' of neurotransmitters refers to what they do and the role they play.

gene: a set of instructions and a carrier of information.

generalisability: when a sample in a study represents the chosen population, so that any findings can be said to be true of that population and not just true of that sample.

genetic drift: random chance in genes that are passed on.

genetic mutation: a permanent change in the gene sequence, which can come, for example, from a virus or damage due to radiation.

genome: all the genes in a cell, all the genetic material in an organism.

genotype: genetic constitution; what our genes will dictate in us.

glial cells: cells that surround neurons, protect them and have some other functions, such as being involved in giving a myelin sheath to protect the axon.

group: a social unit with a number of individuals who are interdependent and have a set of norms and values for self-regulation; individuals have roles within the unit.

group polarisation: the idea that a group tends to have more extreme ideas and attitudes than the individuals in the group.

group selection: how social beings are benefitted in that they are more protected in terms of safety, food and shelter, and so individuals that are predisposed by their genes to live in groups are likely to survive and pass on their genes.

holism: looking at something in its entirety.

Holocaust: the slaughter of millions of Jews, gypsies, homosexuals and others by the Nazis during the Second World War.

hypothesis: a statement set out in such a way that it is testable; what is to be measured and how it is to be measured are operationalised.

hypothetico-deductive model: the cycle of testing a theory and amending it, building on scientific knowledge.

id: what an individual wants, their desires and needs.

identification: in social learning, means connecting with a role model in some way.

ideological attitudes: those that focus on social needs and wishes of a group or a society, or indeed an individual; they link to political ideas and refer to someone's outlook on how a society should be and can function.

idiographic: studying individuals in details.

imitation: copying the behaviour of others.

immersive virtual environment: the setting for Slater et al.'s (2006) study – a computer-generated display of 'virtual sensory data' with a life-sized virtual reality for the participant.

in the field: in the participant's natural setting.

inclusive fitness: involves direct fitness and also how a gene, with a characteristic that seems to be disadvantageous to the individual but can help relatives of that individual, will survive to be passed on.

independent groups design: participants do only one condition of an experiment and data from different participants are compared.

independent variable: the variable set up by the experimenter, such as whether there is an interference task or not.

individual differences: how people have different identities, such as cultural, age and gender identity; individual differences can be about language, economic status, marital status, disability, education, religion and other differences too.

information processing: can be likened to how a computer works, with input, processing and output; cognitive psychology covers issues like talking, thinking, perceiving, remembering, problem-solving and paying attention.

informed consent: getting permission from participants when 'using' them in a study; permission must come after all possible information has been given to the participants.

integrity: being honest and accurate in dealings with others.

inter-group: between two (or more) groups.

inter-rater reliability, or inter-observer reliability: when more than one person rates the behaviour (what is of interest) and their ratings are compared; if there is agreement between the ratings, then there is said to be reliability.

internal locus of control: when someone thinks that they are in control of their own actions and believes that what happens is something they have caused.

internalising: obeying with agreement.

internal validity: found when cause and effect conclusions are justified because of no confounding variables.

interval data: data where real measurements are involved, such as time or height.

interviewee: the person being interviewed.

interviewer: the person carrying out the interview.

interviews: when a researcher asks a participant questions; usually questions can be varied according to responses.

intra-group: relations within a single group.

introspection: involves individuals thinking about their thinking or how they process information and explaining those processes.

item (on a questionnaire): a question or a statement asking for a response.

kin selection: the idea that it is not necessarily that the individual organism most suited to the environment survives to reproduce its genes, just as long as the genes survive (e.g. in relatives).

laboratory experiment: takes place in an artificial controlled environment that is not natural for the participants.

lateralisation: the idea that the brain is split into two halves, or hemispheres.

law of effect: if the effect of the learning is good, then the behaviour is learned and repeated.

lesion: damage to the brain.

level of significance: the probability that the results are due to chance.

libido: sexual energy.

line of best fit (scatter diagram): the line that takes in most of the plots on the graph; the line can be drawn by eye so that the points are as evenly distributed each side of the line as possible.

linear: occurring in a way that is logical; 'linear' refers to a single straight line.

longitudinal studies: when the same people are studied over time to look for developmental issues and patterns.

long-term store, or long-term memory: store where information can stay (potentially) for ever; information is held largely in semantic form and can also be visually or acoustically stored; an infinite amount of information can be stored in long-term memory.

matched pairs design: uses different participants, as in an independent groups design, but the participants are paired up, one from each group, according to what the researcher thinks are important factors, e.g. age, gender, social class or ethnicity.

mean: measure of central tendency, found by adding up the scores and dividing by number of scores/participants.

measures of central tendency: mean, median and mode.

measures of dispersion: range and standard deviation.

median: measure of central tendency; the middle score.

meta-analysis: study that uses results from a number of other studies that have used a methodology and focus that are similar enough so that results can be compared to come to an overall conclusion about an area of study.

methodology: the study of how research is carried out and about how science works.

mixed methods: where both qualitative and quantitative data are involved, though can mean using different methods even if gathering only one of these types of data.
modality specific: when information is in the same form as it is received.
mode: measure of central tendency; the most usual in the set of scores, the score that appears most often.
mode of representation (mode of storage): the form in which information is stored.
modelling: displaying behaviour and the process of being the model.
monozygotic (MZ) twins: identical twins, coming from one fertilised egg and sharing 100 per cent of their genes.
moral strain: when people become uncomfortable with their behaviour because they feel that it is wrong and goes against their values.
multi-store model: the idea that there is a sensory store, as well as short-term and long-term memory.
myelin sheath: cells that surround and protect axons, forming an insulation layer.
N/n: the number of scores (number of participants often, in psychology).
natural selection: the idea that some characteristics are inherited because they aid survival of an organism so that there can be reproduction and passing on of genes, whereas some characteristics do not aid survival in the environment so there is no reproduction of those genes.
naturalistic observations: capture real-life data in a real situation and real behaviour by watching.
negative correlation: one score rises as the other falls – for example, as age rises, average driving speed falls.
negative punishment: when something pleasant is taken away to stop or reduce the unwanted behaviour.
negative reinforcement: when a reward is removal of something unpleasant.
negatively skewed distribution: when the scores are clustered below the mean, and the mode shows that.
neuroimaging: using scans to generate images either of brain functioning and the brain at work or of brain structure, such as where there is damage.
neurons: cells that receive and transmit messages, passing messages from cell to cell.
neuroscience: scientific study of the nervous system; draws together not only biology and psychology, but also chemistry, computer science, engineering and other disciplines, such as physics, philosophy and genetics.
neuroses: mental health problems in individuals who are aware that they have difficulties and are capable of having insight into these problems to help themselves get better.
neurotransmitters: chemical messengers that act between the neurons in the brain; this allows the brain to process thoughts and memories.
neutral stimulus: what is paired with the unconditioned stimulus to eventually give the same response (which is then called a 'conditioned' response).
nodes of Ranvier: areas where the myelin sheath around an axon thins.
nominal data: in the form of categories, simply putting data into sets.
nomothetic: looking for general laws.
non-directional (or two-tailed) hypothesis: direction is not stated; results can go either way.
non-parametric tests: those that are used when the criteria for parametric tests are not met.
non-participant observation: when the person getting the data by observing is not part of what is happening; they are apart from the situation.
norm: a product of group interaction that regulates the behaviour of members in terms of the expected or ideal behaviour.
normal distribution: when results cluster nicely around the mean and around the centre point of a spread of scores; there is normal distribution when the mean, median and mode more or less match.
null hypothesis: the hypothesis that states that something that is predicted in an alternative hypothesis will not happen, and changes that are found as a result of a study are down to chance and not to the prediction.
obedience: obeying direct orders from someone in authority.
objectivity: when results are not affected by the researcher or by preconceived ideas; opposite to subjectivity.
observational learning: watching what others do and copying their actions, thus learning new behaviours.
observed value: the result of the test, the answer to your calculations.
one-tailed: see *directional hypothesis*.
open-ended (open) questions: where the respondent can answer freely, without the responses being constrained.
operationalisation: making a variable measurable in practice.
opportunity sampling: using whoever is available; sometimes called grab sampling or convenience sampling.
order effects: occur when participants do more than one condition in a study and they all do the conditions in the same order; order effects include the practice effect and the fatigue effect.
ordinal data: ranked data, such as ratings.
overt observation: the participants know that the observation is taking place and they are aware of all aspects of the study.
paradigm: an accepted theory of how things work.
parametric tests: those that can be used when data a) have normal distribution, b) are interval/ratio (which means the mean average is used), and c) have similarity of variance.

participant design: see 'experimental design'.

participant observation: the person getting the data by observing has a role in what is happening; they are part of the situation.

participant variables: those that are connected with the participant, such as their mood, or whether they are hungry, or male or female.

peer-report data: when someone who knows the participant (a peer) answers questions about the participant.

peer reviewing: the process whereby peers of researchers, people who know the area of study, check a study before it is published, to make sure there is scientific credibility.

peripheral nervous system: consists of the nerves and ganglia outside of the brain and spinal cord.

personal data: information about someone that is personal to them, such as their age, occupation, gender, characteristics.

personality: someone's unique and stable responses to specific situations.

phenotype: what we become when our genes interact, both with one another and with our environment and experiences.

phobia: an irrational, life-limiting fear.

pilot: practice run, e.g. to test the clarity of wording of a questionnaire.

placebo: something that does not contain the substance of interest; it is not possible for the participant to tell whether it is a placebo or the real thing.

positive correlation: one score rises as the other rises – for example, as age increases so does the time it takes to react to a stimulus.

positive punishment: when something unpleasant is given to stop or reduce the unwanted behaviour.

positive reinforcement: when a reward is given.

positively skewed distribution: when the scores are clustered above the mean, and the mode shows that.

postsynaptic neuron: the neuron receiving the neurotransmitter at the receptors of the dendrites.

practice effect: when a participant does the second condition better, having practised with the first, resulting in bias in the data.

preconscious mind: contains the thoughts that we can be aware of and we can access, but currently are not being accessed so not in the conscious mind.

predictive validity: when a later measure confirms an earlier measure of a characteristic, such as someone getting an 'aggression' score on a rating scale and the score matching 'real life' aggression later.

prejudice: an attitude (usually negative).

presumptive consent: other people are asked whether they would take part in the study, if they were the participants; they are not the participants but can show whether people would be OK with doing what was going to be asked.

presynaptic neuron: the neuron sending the message and releasing the neurotransmitters.

primacy effect: the idea that information learned first is well remembered, probably because it has gone to the long-term store through the rehearsal loop.

primary data: data gathered by the researchers in an actual study at the time and for the purpose of testing one or more hypotheses.

primary reinforcement: when the reward is a basic need like food and water.

principle of competence: holds that someone will not claim to be competent when they are not, as a researcher or as a psychologist; all research and practice in psychology should be carried out within the researcher's or the psychologist's competence.

principle of integrity: maintaining professional boundaries and looking for, and acting on, misconduct in others.

principle of respect: ethical issues around treating a person as an individual and in a fair and unprejudiced way.

principle of responsibility: holds a researcher or psychologist responsible for their work; they must be sure that they do no harm and they must assess harm in a debrief after a study (or after therapy).

prior consent: before a study takes part, participants agree to whatever is going to take place, even though they are not able to give informed consent for the study itself.

privacy: avoiding publicising something that someone would prefer not to be known to others.

proactive interference: when something learned earlier interferes with current learning.

pro-social behaviour: acting for members of society or for other individuals; the opposite of anti-social behaviour.

psychoanalysis: Freud's therapy; involves uncovering unconscious thoughts and desires, including repressed material, bringing them into the conscious so that they can be dealt with.

psychoses: mental health problems in individuals where they are not aware of their problems and do not have the insight to help themselves to get better because of the nature of the problems.

punishment: when a behaviour has unpleasant consequences and so is likely to stop; punishment is in response to unwanted behaviour.

qualitative data: results in words, from open questioning, where ideas, opinions or narratives are recorded as data.

quantitative data: results from studies that are in numbers, such as the number of words recalled in a memory test.

random sampling: when everyone in the sampling frame has the chance of being picked each time a participant is chosen; it is the most representative as nobody is excluded from being chosen.

randomisation: when the order in which the participants do the conditions is randomised.

rationalisation: in reconstructive memory theory, rationalisation is the idea that memory is changed to make more sense to the individual doing the recall.

raw scores: the actual scores of the participants.

realistic group conflict theory: the idea that, if there is competition for scarce resources, prejudice can arise.

recency effect: the idea that information that is learned last is well remembered, probably because it is still in the rehearsal loop and so is available for immediate recall.

receptor: receives neurotransmitters from other neurons.

recessive genes: genes that need more than one copy so will not always lead to their characteristic(s) (they have to be on both chromosomes for the characteristic to occur).

reciprocal determinism: the idea that not only does the environment act on the individual to 'cause' learning but also the individual acts on their environment, such as by attending to a modelled behaviour, retaining it, reproducing it and being motivated to reproduce it.

reconstructive memory: the theory that memories are not exact copies of what is encoded and stored, but are affected by prior experience and prior knowledge in the form of schemas.

reductionism: the study of something by breaking it down into parts.

reflexive journal (in thematic analysis): record of the whole process of analysis, including coding, thoughts when coding and ideas that relate to the research question.

reinforcement: when a behaviour has pleasant consequences of reward and so is likely to be done again; reinforcement is in response to wanted behaviour.

reliability: when the same results are found when the study is repeated – the results are consistent.

repeated measures design: the same person is involved in all the conditions (in an experiment).

replicability: a study can be done again; there is enough information to repeat it fully, so that findings from a replication can be compared with the original findings to help to build a body of knowledge; replicability is required to test reliability.

report: the way studies in psychology are written up, including a set structure.

representative: having the characteristics of the target population.

repression: a defence mechanism whereby material is in the unconscious and not accessible to conscious thought.

research design: the overall strategy for a study, involving collection, measurement and analysis of data.

research method: a main method used in a study, such as questionnaire, interview, experiment, case study; 'method' can be used for different parts of methodology, so in this book 'research method' is used for the overall method used.

researcher bias: when a researcher affects the responses/data that are gathered.

respect: treating a person as an individual and in a fair and unprejudiced way.

respondent: the person responding, e.g. the person answering items on a questionnaire.

response bias: the tendency to stick to one response throughout, e.g. in a questionnaire.

response cost: rewards are either withheld or taken away for undesirable behaviour or when a goal has not been met.

responsibility: an ethical principle around doing no harm.

retrieval (memory): how we retrieve memories when the output is needed (find them/access them).

retroactive interference: when something learned later gets in the way of something learned previously.

reuptake: when the neurotransmitter is absorbed back into the presynaptic neuron.

reward pathway (or pleasure centre): where pleasure seems to be so desired that someone or an animal will continue to behave in such a manner that the pleasure is received, even when starving or thirsty; the desire for the pleasure overrides other drives; the reward pathway involves parts of the brain, including the prefrontal cortex.

right to withdraw: allowing someone to withdraw from a study or from therapy and making sure they understand this right, at the start and throughout the process.

right-wing authoritarianism (RWA): refers to someone who has rigid thinking and likes society to have rules, which people must stick to, so that society can function; someone with such an ideological attitude will obey the rules and obey those in authority – they will also want to punish anyone who does not obey the rules; they prefer it that everyone agrees to submit to authority rather than having to force people.

role model: someone significant/important to an individual, such as a friend, a parent or someone they look up to, perhaps an athlete.

sampling: involves choosing participants from the target population; used when not all members of a target population can be involved in a study.

sampling frame: the people available to choose a sample from, such as all sixth-formers in a school.

scatter diagram: a means of displaying correlational data; also called scattergrams, scatterplots and scattergraphs.

schedule: a list of questions or an idea of what is to be asked in an interview.

schema theory: the idea that all knowledge is organised into units – schemata.

schemas (schemata): (cognitive) plans/scripts that are built up using experiences about everyday life and that affect the processing of information.

secondary data: data gathered for a previous study, possibly for a different purpose and already existing when used in a new study.

secondary reinforcement: when the reward is something that is not a basic need but leads to a basic need, such as money (to buy food).

self-report data: data that someone has given about themselves.

semantic: meaning.

semantic memory, or declarative memory: memory for meanings, such as meanings of words and symbols.

semi-structured interview: includes some fixed questions and some structure regarding what will be asked – there is room for the respondent to lead the direction of the questions.

sense check: looking carefully at data in a table or a graph to see if it looks as if the appropriate statistical test would show a significant difference or relationship or not; can be called an eye-ball test.

sensory register, or sensory memory: where the information comes into the brain from the senses and is held for a short time.

shaping (operant conditioning): using operant conditioning in the form of rewards and punishments to form a complex behaviour that would not occur as a whole naturally so could not be reinforced itself.

short-term store, or short-term memory: stores information in auditory form; information is retained for up to 30 seconds; capacity is limited to 5–9 chunks.

single-blind technique: when a participant does not know what group they are in, but the experimenter does.

situational variables: those that are connected with the situation that the study takes place in, such as a noisy environment or it being morning.

skewed distribution: when the mean, median and mode do not match.

small group: individuals share a common goal that fosters interaction; individuals are affected differently by being in a group; an in-group develops with its own hierarchy and a set of norms is standardised.

social categorisation: seeing oneself as part of a group.

social comparison: when the individual's self-concept becomes wrapped up with the in-group.

social constructionism: the theory that 'things' are not 'what we think they are' – they are constructed by a society.

social desirability: in results of a study, this means that someone has given data that make them look good from society's point of view so this data might not be 'valid' because it might not 'really' be what they think.

social dominance orientation (SDO): an ideological attitude and someone who sees society as hierarchical with themselves in a position of dominance over those of lower status; people with this ideological attitude are not egalitarian – they do not believe in equality in a society.

social identification: the process of moving from categorising oneself as part of the in-group to identifying with the group more overtly.

social identity: an individual's self-concept; comes about from how an individual sees themselves in relation to membership of their social groups.

social identity theory: the idea that by identifying oneself as being a member of a group, a person can become prejudiced against members of a rival group.

social impact theory: the idea that strength of the impact of something on someone, the number of forces involved and whether the impact is near (immediate) or further away all affect how people behave.

social loafing: a term for people who are in a group but do not contribute to the group's decisions or actions.

spatial information: where things are situated in physical space.

spontaneous conditioning: when the conditioned stimulus and unconditioned stimulus are presented together.

spontaneous recovery: when, after extinction, suddenly and without re-conditioning, an association reappears.

standardised instructions: a control whereby what is said to the participant about a study is the same for all participants so that the findings are not different because of different instructions.

stereotyping: developing an idea about someone and carrying that idea forward to apply it to other similar people.

stimulus: something that produces a response.

stimulus generalisation: when a stimulus similar to the specific (conditioned) one elicits the conditioned response.

stimulus-substitution theory: a theory of how classical conditioning works, which says that the conditioned stimulus simply replaces the unconditioned stimulus as something that elicits the reflexive response.

storage (memory): how memories are stored, which means how they remain as memories after they have been registered.

stratified sampling: when certain groups need to be represented in a study and so sampling is done to ensure those groups are found in the sample; the proportion of the sample should match the proportions in the groups themselves.

structure: how something is set up; for example, 'structure' of a neuron is what forms the neuron.

structured interview: closed and predetermined so that a respondent has no options and does not lead the direction of the interview.

structured observation: one that aims to capture real-life data but in a structured ('set up') situation/setting.

sub-cortex: structures below the cortex.

subjectivity: when data are affected by individuals; opposite to objectivity.

superego: holds our 'shoulds' and 'oughts' and is what we should be like, as well as holding our conscience, given by society and others.

superordinate goals: goals in which the resources and energies of either single group are not adequate for the attainment of the goal; to achieve the goal, two groups have to work together.

survival of the fittest: how organisms that suit their environment will survive long enough to reproduce so their genes will continue, whereas organisms not suited to their environment will not survive so their genes will not continue.

synapse: gap between the axon terminal and the dendrites.

synaptic gap: separates the terminal buttons of one neuron from the dendrites of another neuron.

systematic desensitisation: a step-by-step treatment to get a person used to a phobic object or situation; also called graduated exposure therapy or counter conditioning.

tallying: making a mark when observing a behaviour.

target population: the people the researchers want the findings to represent; the population of interest to the researcher.

terminal button: small structures at the end of an axon that contain neurotransmitters that carry the neuron's message into the synapse.

thanatos: our drive to reduce arousal, to reduce 'life'; a death instinct.

thematic analysis: a researcher identifies a limited number of themes that reflect their data, by going into great detail in studying their data to develop the themes.

time sampling: when observing, making a note of behaviour or what is being observed every so often, measured by time and over a specified period of time.

tools: means of collecting data.

trace conditioning: a type of forward conditioning, when the conditioned stimulus appears, stops and then the unconditioned stimulus is introduced – there is no overlap.

transcribing: preparing data in written form, whether from a video, a discussion or something similar; all qualitative data must be transcribed ready for analysis.

transcript: a full account of the data, including, with regard to qualitative data, all the words from each respondent, so that a full analysis can take place.

trials: individual tests in a study.

triangulation: taking data from different sources and comparing them.

twin studies: studies that compare MZ and DZ twins on certain characteristics to see if there are differences between the MZ twins and the characteristic and between DZ twins and the characteristic.

two-by-two table: consists of two rows and two columns.

two-tailed: see *non-directional hypothesis*.

Type I error: when someone optimistically accepts their alternative/experimental hypothesis and rejects the null hypothesis (wrongly).

Type II error: when someone accepts the null hypothesis pessimistically (wrongly).

unconditioned response: reflex response, which results from an unconditioned stimulus.

unconditioned stimulus: a stimulus that gives a reflex response; it gives the unconditioned response naturally.

unconscious mind: not knowable in any easy way – it holds many thoughts, emotions and desires that we do not know about; it can guide our thinking and emotions nonetheless and the 'cure' is to get those thoughts into our conscious mind.

unstructured interview: open for the respondent to lead the questions and the course of the interview.

validity: the 'reality' of results, and whether what is claimed to be measured has actually been measured.

variable: whatever is likely to affect the experiment.

variation (natural selection): differences between the genes of organisms in a species.

vicarious reinforcement: copying the behaviour of others because of seeing them rewarded for it.

volunteer sampling: when the participants select themselves by putting themselves forward as volunteers.

working memory: a system between perception and long-term memory.

working memory model: the idea that there is a system in the short term that is there to maintain and store information and this system underlies all thinking, not just focusing on memory; the idea is a system that has limited capacity to bridge between perception, long-term memory and action.

Yale: a prestigious university in the USA.

INDEX

C

F

G

H

I

S

T

U

V

W

Z